SOLIDWORKS®
and Engineering Graphics

Randy H. Shih
Oregon Institute of Technology

SDC Publications
P.O. Box 1334
Mission, KS 66222
913-262-2664
www.SDCpublications.com
Publisher: Stephen Schroff

ISBN-13: 978-1-58503-932-6
ISBN-10: 1-58503-932-2

Printed and bound in the United States of America.

Preface

The primary goal of **SolidWorks 2015 and Engineering Graphics**: *An Integrated Approach* is to introduce Engineering Graphics with the use of modern Computer Aided Design package – SolidWorks® 2015. This text is intended to be used as a training guide for students and professionals. The chapters in this text proceed in a pedagogical fashion to guide you from constructing basic shapes to making complete sets of engineering drawings. This text takes a hands-on, exercise-intensive approach to all the important concepts of Engineering Graphics, as well as in-depth discussions of parametric feature-based CAD techniques. This textbook contains a series of fifteen chapters, with detailed step-by-step tutorial style lessons, designed to introduce beginning CAD users to the graphic language used in all branches of technical industry. This book does not attempt to cover all of SolidWorks 2015's features, only to provide an introduction to the software. It is intended to help you establish a good basis for exploring and growing in the exciting field of Computer Aided Engineering.

Acknowledgments

This book would not have been possible without a great deal of support. First, special thanks to two great teachers, Prof. George R. Schade of University of Nebraska-Lincoln and Mr. Denwu Lee, who taught me the fundamentals, the intrigue and the sheer fun of Computer Aided Engineering.

The effort and support of the editorial and production staff of SDC Publications is gratefully acknowledged. I would especially like to thank Stephen Schroff for the support and helpful suggestions during this project.

I am grateful that the Mechanical and Manufacturing Engineering Technology Department of Oregon Institute of Technology has provided me with an excellent environment in which to pursue my interests in teaching and research. I would especially like to thank Emeritus Professor Charles Hermach and Professor Brian Moravec for helpful comments and encouragement.

Finally, truly unbounded thanks are due to my wife Hsiu-Ling and our daughter Casandra for their understanding and encouragement throughout this project.

Randy H. Shih
Klamath Falls, Oregon
Fall, 2014

Table of Contents

Chapter 1
Introduction

Chapter 2
Parametric Modeling Fundamentals

Chapter 3
Constructive Solid Geometry Concepts

Chapter 6
Geometric Construction Tools

Chapter 7
Orthographic Projections and Multiview Constructions

Chapter 10
Pictorials and Sketching

Chapter 11
Section Views & Symmetrical Features in Designs

Chapter 12
Auxiliary Views and Reference Geometry

Chapter 13
Threads and Fasteners

Chapter 14
Working Drawings

Chapter 15
CSWA Exam Preparation

Appendix

Index

Certified SolidWorks Associate (CSWA) Exam Overview

The Certified SolidWorks Associate (CSWA) Exam is a performance-based exam. The examination is comprised of 10 – 20 questions to be completed in three hours. The test items will require you to use the SolidWorks software to perform specific tasks and then answer questions about the tasks.

Performance-based testing is defined as *Testing by Doing*. This means you actually perform the given task then answer the questions regarding the task. Performance-based testing is widely accepted as a better way of insuring the user has the skills needed, rather than just recalling information.

The CSWA examination is designed to test specific performance tasks in the following areas:

Sketch Entities – Lines, Rectangles, Circles, Arcs, Ellipses, Centerlines
Objectives: Creating Sketch Entities.

Sketch Tools – Offset, Convert, Trim
Objectives: Using Sketch Tools.

Sketch Relations

Objectives: Using Geometric Relations.

Boss and Cut Features – Extrudes, Revolves, Sweeps, Lofts

Objectives: Creating Basic Swept Shapes.

Fillets and Chamfers

Objectives: Creating Fillets and Chamfers.

Linear, Circular, and Fill Patterns

Objectives: Creating Patterned Features.

Dimensions

Objectives: Applying and Editing Smart Dimensions.

Certified Associate Reference Guide

Feature Conditions – Start and End
Objectives: Controlling Feature Start and End Conditions.

Mass Properties
Objectives: Obtaining Mass Properties for Parts and Assemblies.

Materials
Objectives: Applying Material Selection to Parts.

Inserting Components
Objectives: Inserting Components into an Assembly.

Certified Associate Reference Guide

Standard Mates – Coincident, Parallel, Perpendicular, Tangent, Concentric, Distance, Angle

Objectives: Applying Standard Mates to Constrain Assemblies.

Reference Geometry – Planes, Axis, Mate References

Objectives: Creating Reference Planes, Axes, and Mate References.

Drawing Sheets and Views

Objectives: Creating and Setting Properties for Drawing Sheets; Inserting and Editing Standard Views.

Annotations

Objectives: Creating Annotations.

Certified Associate Reference Guide

Tips about Taking the Certified SolidWorks Associate (CSWA) Examination

1. **Study**: The first step to maximize your potential on an exam is to sufficiently prepare for it. You need to be familiar with the SolidWorks package, and this can only be achieved by doing designs and exploring the different commands available. The Certified SolidWorks Associate (CSWA) exam is designed to measure your familiarity with the SolidWorks software. You must be able to perform the given task and answer the exam questions correctly and quickly.

2. **Make Notes**: Take notes of what you learn either while attending classroom sessions or going through study material. Use these notes as a review guide before taking the actual test.

3. **Time Management**: The examination has a time limit. Manage the time you spend on each question. Always remember you do not need to score 100% to pass the exam. Also, keep in mind that some questions are weighed more heavily and may take more time to answer. You can flip back and forth to view different problems during the test time by using the arrow buttons. If you encounter a question you cannot answer in a reasonable amount of time, use the *Save As* feature in SolidWorks to save a copy of the file, and move on to the next question. You can return to any question and enter or change the answer as long as you do not hit the [**End Examination**] button.

4. **Use the *SolidWorks Help System***: If you get confused and can't think of the answer, remember the *SolidWorks Help System* is a great tool to confirm your considerations. In preparing for the exam, familiarize yourself with the help utility organization (e.g., Contents, Index, Search options).

5. **Use Internet Search**: Use of an internet search utility is allowed during the test. If a test question requires general knowledge, for example definitions of engineering or drafting concepts (stress, yield strength, auxiliary view, etc.), remember the internet is available as a tool to assist in your considerations.

6. **Use Common Sense**: If you are unable to get the correct answer and unable to eliminate all distracters, then you need to select the best answer from the remaining selections. This may be a task of selecting the best answer from amongst several correct answers, or it may be selecting the least incorrect answer from amongst several poor answers.

7. **Be Cautious and Don't Act in Haste**: Devote some time to ponder and think of the correct answer. Ensure that you interpret all the options correctly before selecting from available choices. Don't go into panic mode while taking a test. Use the ***Arrow Buttons*** to review each question. When you are confident that you have answered all questions, end the examination using the [**End Examination**] button to submit your answers for scoring. You will receive a score report once you have submitted your answers.

8. **Relax before Exam**: In order to avoid last minute stress, make sure that you arrive 10 to 15 minutes early and relax before taking the exam.

Chapter 1
Introduction

Learning Objectives

- ♦ **Introduction to Engineering Graphics**
- ♦ **Development of Computer Geometric Modeling**
- ♦ **Feature-Based Parametric Modeling**
- ♦ **Startup Options and Units Setup**
- ♦ **SolidWorks Screen Layout**
- ♦ **User Interface & Mouse Buttons**
- ♦ **SolidWorks Online Help**

Introduction

Engineering Graphics, also known as **Technical Drawing**, is the technique of creating accurate representations of designs, an *engineering drawing*, for construction and manufacturing. An **engineering drawing** is a type of drawing that is technical in nature, used to fully and clearly define requirements for engineered items, and is usually created in accordance with standardized conventions for layout, nomenclature, interpretation, appearance, size, etc. A skilled practitioner of the art of engineering drawing is known as a *draftsman* or *draftsperson*.

The basic mechanics of drafting is to use a pencil and draw on a piece of paper. For engineering drawings, papers are generally placed on a drafting table and additional tools are used. A T-square is one of the standard tools commonly used with a drafting table.

A T-square is also known as a *sliding straightedge*; parallel lines can be drawn simply by moving the T-square and running a pencil along the T-square's straightedge. The T-square is more typically used as a tool to hold other tools such as triangles. For example, one or more triangles can be placed on the T-square and lines can be drawn at chosen angles on the paper.

In addition to the triangles, other tools are used to draw curves and circles. The most common among these are the compass, used for drawing simple arcs and circles, and the French curve, typically a piece of plastic with a complex curve on it. A spline is a rubber coated articulated metal that can be manually bent to almost any curve.

This basic drafting system requires an accurate table and constant attention to the positioning of the tools. A common error draftspersons faced was allowing the triangles to push the top of the T-square down slightly, thereby throwing off all angles. Drafting in general was already a time consuming process.

A solution to these problems was the introduction of the **"drafting machine,"** a device that allowed the draftsperson to have an accurate right angle at any point on the page quite quickly. These machines often included the ability to change the angle, thereby removing the need for the triangles as well.

In addition to the mechanics of drawing the lines onto a piece of paper, drafting requires an understanding of geometry and the professional skills of the specific designer. At one time, drafting was a sought-after job; considered one of the more demanding and highly-skilled positions of the trade. Today, the mechanics of the drafting task have been largely automated and greatly accelerated through the use of **computer aided design** (CAD) systems. Proficiency in using CAD systems have also become one of the more important requirements for engineers and designers.

Drawing in CAD Systems

Computer Aided Design (CAD) is the process of creating designs with the aid of computers. This includes the generation of computer models, analysis of design data and the creation of necessary drawings. SolidWorks is a CAD software package developed by *Dassault Systèmes*. The SolidWorks software is a tool that can be used for design and drafting activities. Two-dimensional and three-dimensional models created in SolidWorks can be transferred to other computer programs for further analysis and testing. The computer models can also be used in manufacturing equipment such as machining centers, lathes, mills or rapid prototyping machines to manufacture the product.

Rapid changes in the field of **computer aided engineering** (CAE) have brought exciting advances to the industry. Recent advances have made the long-sought goal of reducing design time, producing prototypes faster, and achieving higher product quality closer to a reality.

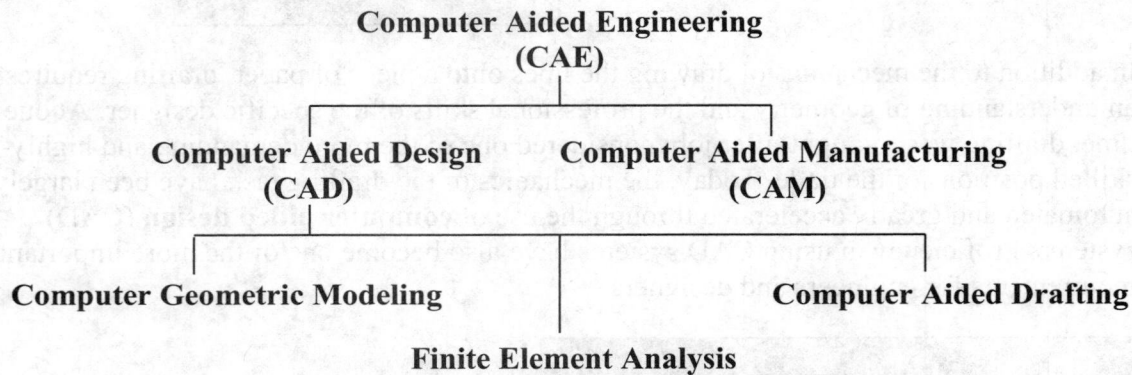

Development of Computer Geometric Modeling

Computer geometric modeling is a relatively new technology, and its rapid expansion in the last fifty years is truly amazing. Computer-modeling technology has advanced along with the development of computer hardware. The first generation CAD programs, developed in the 1950s, were mostly non-interactive; CAD users were required to create program-codes to generate the desired two-dimensional (2D) geometric shapes. Initially, the development of CAD technology occurred mostly in academic research facilities. The Massachusetts Institute of Technology, Carnegie-Mellon University, and Cambridge University were the leading pioneers at that time. The interest in CAD technology spread quickly and several major industry companies, such as General Motors, Lockheed, McDonnell, IBM, and Ford Motor Co., participated in the development of interactive CAD programs in the 1960s. Usage of CAD systems was primarily in the automotive industry, aerospace industry, and government agencies that developed their own programs for their specific needs. The 1960s also marked the beginning of the development of finite element analysis methods for computer stress analysis and computer aided manufacturing for generating machine tool paths.

The 1970s are generally viewed as the years of the most significant progress in the development of computer hardware; namely with the invention and development of **microprocessors**. With the improvement in computing power, new types of 3D CAD programs that were user-friendly and interactive became reality. CAD technology quickly expanded from very simple **computer aided drafting** to very complex **computer aided design**. The use of 2D and 3D wireframe modelers was accepted as the leading edge technology that could increase productivity in industry. The development of surface modeling and solid modeling technologies was taking shape by the late 1970s, but the high cost of computer hardware and programming slowed the development of such technology. During this period, the available CAD systems all required room-sized mainframe computers that were extremely expensive.

In the 1980s, improvements in computer hardware brought the power of mainframes to the desktop at less cost and with more accessibility to the general public. By the mid-1980s, CAD technology had become the main focus of a variety of manufacturing industries and was very competitive with traditional design/drafting methods. It was during this period of time that 3D solid modeling technology had major advancements, which boosted the usage of CAE technology in industry.

The introduction of the *feature-based parametric solid modeling* approach, at the end of the 1980s, elevated CAD/CAM/CAE technology to a new level. In the 1990s, CAD programs evolved into powerful design/manufacturing/management tools. CAD technology has come a long way, and during these years of development, modeling schemes progressed from two-dimensional (2D) wireframe to three-dimensional (3D) wireframe, to surface modeling, to solid modeling and, finally, to feature-based parametric solid modeling.

The first generation CAD packages were simply 2D **computer aided drafting** programs, basically the electronic equivalents of the drafting board. For typical models, the use of this type of program would require that several views of the objects be created individually as they would be on the drafting board. The 3D designs remained in the designer's mind, not in the computer database. Mental translations of 3D objects to 2D views were required throughout the use of these packages. Although such systems have some advantages over traditional board drafting, they are still tedious and labor intensive. The need for the development of 3D modelers came quite naturally, given the limitations of the 2D drafting packages.

The development of three-dimensional modeling schemes started with three-dimensional (3D) wireframes. Wireframe models are models consisting of points and edges, which are straight lines connecting between appropriate points. The edges of wireframe models are used, similar to lines in 2D drawings, to represent transitions of surfaces and features. The use of lines and points is also a very economical way to represent 3D designs.

The development of the 3D wireframe modeler was a major leap in the area of computer geometric modeling. The computer database in the 3D wireframe modeler contains the locations of all the points in space coordinates, and it is typically sufficient to create just one model rather than multiple views of the same model. This single 3D model can then be viewed from any direction as needed. Most 3D wireframe modelers allow the user to create projected lines/edges of 3D wireframe models. In comparison to other types of 3D modelers, the 3D wireframe modelers require very little computing power and generally can be used to achieve reasonably good representations of 3D models. However, because surface definition is not part of a wireframe model, all wireframe images have the inherent problem of ambiguity. Two examples of such ambiguity are illustrated.

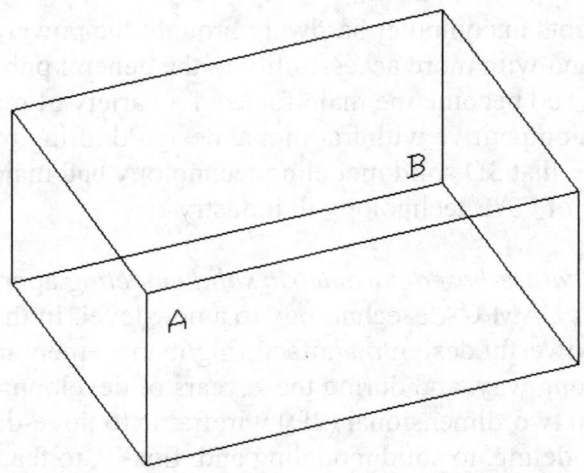

Wireframe Ambiguity: Which corner is in front, A or B?

A non-realizable object: Wireframe models contain no surface definitions.

Surface modeling is the logical development in computer geometry modeling to follow the 3D wireframe modeling scheme by organizing and grouping edges that define polygonal surfaces. Surface modeling describes the part's surfaces but not its interiors. Designers are still required to interactively examine surface models to insure that the various surfaces on a model are contiguous throughout. Many of the concepts used in 3D wireframe and surface modelers are incorporated in the solid modeling scheme, but it is solid modeling that offers the most advantages as a design tool.

In the solid modeling presentation scheme, the solid definition includes nodes, edges, and surfaces, and it is a complete and unambiguous mathematical representation of a precisely enclosed and filled volume. Unlike the surface modeling method, solid modelers start with a solid or use topology rules to guarantee that all of the surfaces are stitched together properly. Two predominant methods for representing solid models are **constructive solid geometry** (CSG) representation and **boundary representation** (B-rep).

The CSG representation method can be defined as the combination of 3D solid primitives. What constitutes a "primitive" varies somewhat with the software but typically includes a rectangular prism, a cylinder, a cone, a wedge, and a sphere. Most solid modelers also allow the user to define additional primitives, which are shapes typically formed by the basic shapes. The underlying concept of the CSG representation method is very straightforward; we simply **add** or **subtract** one primitive from another. The CSG approach is also known as the machinist's approach, as it can be used to simulate the manufacturing procedures for creating the 3D object.

In the B-rep representation method, objects are represented in terms of their spatial boundaries. This method defines the points, edges, and surfaces of a volume, and/or issues commands that sweep or rotate a defined face into a third dimension to form a solid. The object is then made up of the unions of these surfaces that completely and precisely enclose a volume.

By the 1980s, a new paradigm called *concurrent engineering* had emerged. With concurrent engineering, designers, design engineers, analysts, manufacturing engineers, and management engineers all work together closely right from the initial stages of the design. In this way, all aspects of the design can be evaluated and any potential problems can be identified right from the start and throughout the design process. Using the principles of concurrent engineering, a new type of computer modeling technique appeared. The technique is known as the *feature-based parametric modeling technique*. The key advantage of the *feature-based parametric modeling technique* is its capability to produce very flexible designs. Changes can be made easily and design alternatives can be evaluated with minimal effort. Various software packages offer different approaches to feature-based parametric modeling, yet the end result is a flexible design defined by its design variables and parametric features.

Feature-Based Parametric Modeling

One of the key elements in the SolidWorks solid modeling software is its use of the **feature-based parametric modeling technique**. The feature-based parametric modeling approach has elevated solid modeling technology to the level of a very powerful design tool. Parametric modeling automates the design and revision procedures by the use of parametric features. Parametric features control the model geometry by the use of design variables. The word *parametric* means that the geometric definitions of the design, such as dimensions, can be varied at any time during the design process. Features are predefined parts or construction tools for which users define the key parameters. A part is described as a sequence of engineering features, which can be modified and/or changed at any time. The concept of parametric features makes modeling more closely match the actual design-manufacturing process than the mathematics of a solid modeling program. In parametric modeling, models and drawings are updated automatically when the design is refined.

Parametric modeling offers many benefits:

- **We begin with simple, conceptual models with minimal detail; this approach conforms to the design philosophy of "shape before size."**

- **Geometric constraints, dimensional constraints, and relational parametric equations can be used to capture design intent.**

- **The ability to update an entire system, including parts, assemblies and drawings after changing one parameter of complex designs.**

- **We can quickly explore and evaluate different design variations and alternatives to determine the best design.**

- **Existing design data can be reused to create new designs.**

- **Quick design turn-around.**

With parametric modeling, designers and engineers can maximize the productivity of the design and engineering resources to create products better, faster, and more cost-effectively. The tools available in parametric modeling are designed to cover the entire design process; from design and validation to technical communications and data management. The intuitive design interface and integrated software work together and provide designers and engineers the freedom to focus on innovation.

Getting Started with SolidWorks

- SolidWorks is composed of several application software modules (these modules are called *applications*), all sharing a common database. In this text, the main concentration is placed on the solid modeling modules used for part design. The general procedures required in creating solid models, engineering drawings, and assemblies are illustrated.

Starting SolidWorks

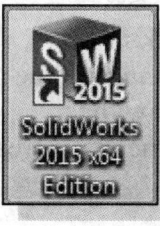

- How to start SolidWorks depends on the type of workstation and the particular software configuration you are using. With most *Windows* systems, you may select **SolidWorks** on the *Start* menu or select the **SolidWorks** icon on the desktop. Consult your instructor or technical support personnel if you have difficulty starting the software.

❖ The program takes a while to load, so be patient. The tutorials in this text are based on the assumption that you are using SolidWorks' default settings. If your system has been customized for other uses, some of the settings may appear differently and not work with the step-by-step instructions in the tutorials. Contact your instructor and/or technical support personnel to restore the default software configuration.

Once the program is loaded into memory, the SolidWorks program window appears. This screen contains the *Menu Bar* and the *Task Pane*. The *Menu Bar* contains a subset of commonly used tools from the *Menu Bar* toolbar (New, Open, Save, etc.), the SolidWorks menus, the SolidWorks *Search* oval, and a flyout menu of *Help* options. By default, the *Menu Bar* menus are hidden. To display them, move the cursor over or click the SolidWorks logo.

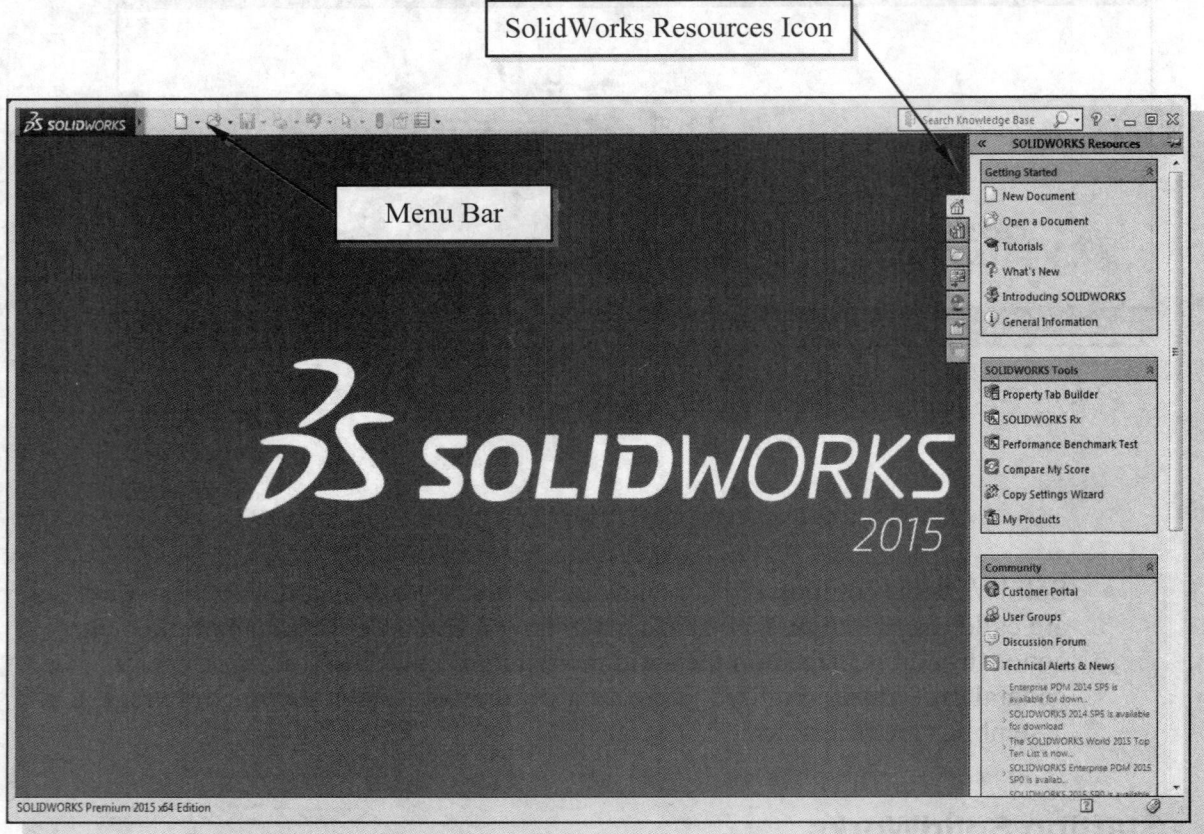

If the *task pane* does not appear to the right of the screen, click the SolidWorks Resources icon on the right side of the window. Other options for the *task pane* are the *Design Library* and the *File Explorer*. The icons for these options appear below the SolidWorks Resources icon. To collapse the *task pane*, click anywhere in the main area of the SolidWorks window.

The following two startup options are available: New and Open. The New option allows us to start a new modeling task. The Open option allows us to open an existing model file. These two commands can be executed in the *Getting Started* dialog box in the *SolidWorks Resources task pane* or on the *Menu Bar*. The *Getting Started* dialog box also contains a Tutorials option which provides some quick helps that illustrate the features and general procedures of using SolidWorks.

> Select the **New** icon on the *Menu Bar* with a single click of the left-mouse-button. The *New SolidWorks Document* dialog box appears.

Three icons appear in the *New SolidWorks Document* dialog box. Selecting the appropriate icon will allow creation of a new **Part**, **Assembly** or **Drawing** file. A part is a single three-dimensional (3D) solid model. Parts are the basic building blocks in modeling with SolidWorks. An assembly is a 3D arrangement of parts (components) and/or other assemblies (subassemblies). A drawing is a 2D representation of a part or assembly.

> Select the **Part** icon as shown. Click **OK** in the *New SolidWorks Document* dialog box to open a new part file.

Units Setup

When starting a new CAD file, the first thing we should do is to choose the units we would like to use. We will use the English (feet and inches) setting for this example.

> Select the **Options** icon from the *Menu Bar* as shown to open the *Options* dialog box. (The *Options* dialog box can also be opened from the *Tools* pull-down menu.)

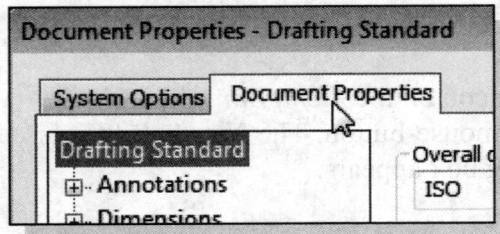

> ➢ When the *Options* dialog box opens, the **System Options** tab is active. The units setup is located under the Document Properties tab. Select the **Document Properties** tab as shown.

➢ Select **Units** on the left menu as highlighted below. Select **IPS (inch, pound, second)** under the *Unit system* options. Select **.123** in the *Decimals* spin box for the *Length* units as shown to define the degree of accuracy with which the units will be displayed.

Document Properties - Units

System Options | Document Properties

Drafting Standard
  Annotations
  Dimensions
  Virtual Sharps
  Tables
Detailing
Grid/Snap
Units
Model Display
Material Properties
Image Quality
Sheet Metal
Plane Display
DimXpert
  Size Dimension
  Location Dimension
  Chain Dimension
  Geometric Tolerance
  Chamfer Controls
  Display Options

Unit system
- ○ MKS (meter, kilogram, second)
- ○ CGS (centimeter, gram, second)
- ○ MMGS (millimeter, gram, second)
- ● IPS (inch, pound, second)
- ○ Custom

Type	Unit	Decimals	Fractions	More
Basic Units				
Length	inches	.123		...
Dual Dimension Length	inches	.12		...
Angle	degrees	.123		
		.1234		
		.12345		
		.123456		
Mass/Section Properties		.1234567		
Length	inches	.12345678		
Mass	pounds			
Per Unit Volume	inches^3			
Motion Units				
Time	second	.12		
Force	pound-force	.12		
Power	watt	.12		
Energy	BTU	.12		

➢ Click **OK** at the bottom of the *Document Properties - Units* window to set the units.

SolidWorks Screen Layout

The default SolidWorks drawing screen contains the *Menu Bar*, the *Heads-up View* toolbar, the *Feature Manager Design Tree*, the *Features* toolbar (at the left of the window by default), the *Sketch* toolbar (at the right of the window by default), the graphics area, the *task pane* (collapsed to the right of the graphics area in the figure below), and the *Status Bar*. A line of quick text appears next to the icon as you move the *mouse cursor* over different icons. You may resize the SolidWorks drawing window by clicking and dragging on the edge of the window, or relocate the window by clicking and dragging on the *window title* area.

- **Menu Bar**

In the default view of the *Menu Bar*, only the toolbar options are visible. The default *Menu Bar* consists of a subset of frequently used commands from the *Menu Bar* toolbar as shown above.

- **Menu Bar Pull-down Menus**

To display the *pull-down* menus, move the cursor over or click the SolidWorks logo. The pull-down menus contain operations that you can use for all modes of the system.

- **Heads-up View Toolbar**

The *Heads-up View* toolbar allows us quick access to frequently used view-related commands, such as Zoom, Pan and Rotate. Note: You cannot hide or customize the *Heads-up View* toolbar.

- **Features Toolbar**

By default, the *Features* toolbar is displayed at the top of the SolidWorks window. The *Features* toolbar allows us quick access to frequently used feature-related commands, such as Extruded Boss/Base, Extruded Cut, and Revolved Boss/Base.

- **Sketch Toolbar**

By default, the *Sketch* toolbar can be accessed by clicking on the **Sketch** tab in the *Ribbon* toolbar area. The *Sketch* toolbar provides tools for creating the basic geometry that can be used to create features and parts.

• **Feature Manager-Design Tree/Property Manager/Configuration Manager/ DimXpert Manager/Display Manager**

The left panel of the SolidWorks window is used to display the *Feature Manager-Design Tree*, the *Property Manager*, the *Configuration Manager*, and the *DimXpert Manager*. These options can be chosen by selecting the appropriate tab at the top of the panel. The *Feature Manager Design Tree* provides an overview of the active part, drawing, or assembly in outline form. It can be used to show and hide selected features, filter contents, and manage access to features and editing. The *Property Manager* opens automatically when commands are executed or entities are selected in the graphics window, and is used to make selections, enter values, and accept commands. The *Configuration Manager* is used to create, select and view multiple configurations of parts and assemblies. The *DimXpert Manager* lists the tolerance features defined using the SolidWorks '*DimXpert for parts*' tools. The *Display Manager* lists the appearance, decals, lights, scene, and cameras applied to the current model. From the *Display Manager*, we can view applied content, and add, edit, or delete items. The *Display Manager* also provides access to *Photo View* options if the module is available.

- **Graphics Area**

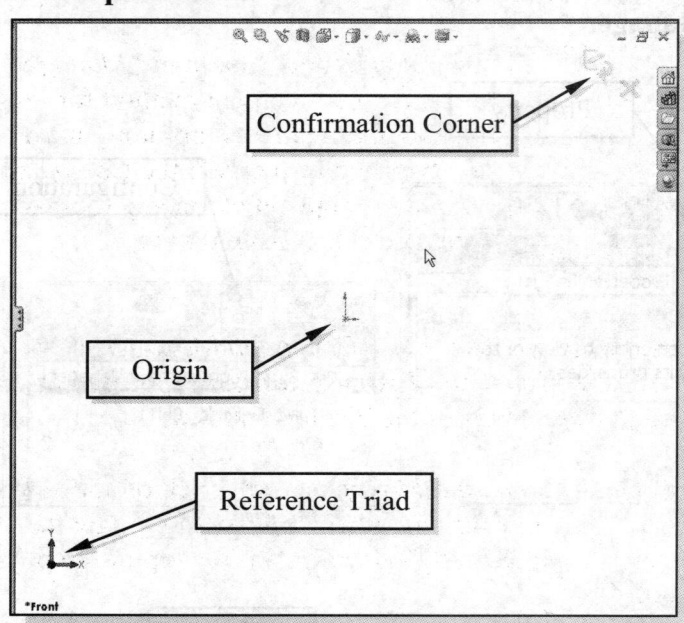

The graphics area is the area where models and drawings are displayed.

- **Reference Triad**

The *Reference Triad* appears in the graphics area of part and assembly documents. The triad is shown to help orient the user when viewing models and is for reference only.

- **Origin**

The *Origin* represents the (0,0,0) coordinate in a model or sketch. A model origin appears blue, and a sketch origin appears red.

- **Confirmation Corner**

The *Confirmation Corner* offers an alternate way to accept features.

- **Graphics Cursor or Crosshairs**

The *graphics cursor* shows the location of the pointing device in the graphics window. During geometric construction, the coordinate of the cursor is displayed in the *Status Bar* area, located at the bottom of the screen. The cursor's appearance depends on the selected command or option.

- **Message and Status Bar**

The *Message and Status Bar* area displays a single-line description of a command when the cursor is on top of a command icon. This area also displays information pertinent to the active operation. In the figure above, the cursor coordinates are displayed while in the *Sketch* mode.

Using the SolidWorks Command Manager

The SolidWorks *Command Manager* provides a convenient method for displaying the most commonly used toolbars. To turn on/off the *Command Manager*, **right click** on any toolbar icon and select from the list.

You will notice that, when the *Command Manager* is turned off, the *Sketch* and *Features* toolbars appeared on the left and right edges of the display window.

To turn on the *Command Manager*, right click on the *Command Manager* (or any other) toolbar and toggle the *Command Manager* on by selecting it at the top of the pop-up menu.

The *Command Manager* is a context-sensitive toolbar that dynamically updates based on the user's selection. When you click a tab below the *Command Manager*, it updates to display the corresponding toolbar. For example, if you click the Sketches tab, the *Sketch* toolbar appears. By default, the *Command Manager* has toolbars embedded in it based on the document type.

The default display of the *Command Manager* is shown below. You will notice that, when the *Command Manager* is used, the *Sketch* and *Features* toolbars no longer appear on the left and right edges of the display window.

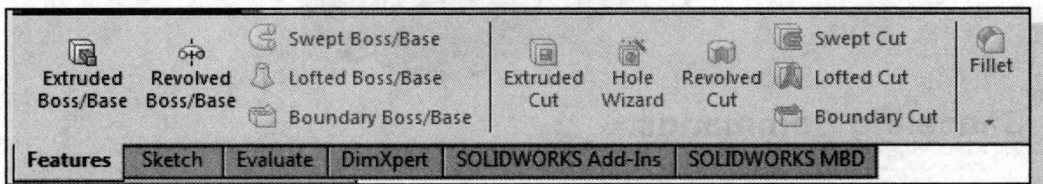

Important Note: The illustrations in this text use the *Command Manager*. If a user prefers to use the standard display of toolbars, the only change is that it may be necessary to activate the appropriate toolbar prior to selecting a command. For example, if the instruction is to "select *Extruded Boss* on the *Command Manager*" it may be necessary to first display the *Features* toolbar through the Customize Toolbar command.

Mouse Buttons

SolidWorks utilizes the mouse buttons extensively. In learning SolidWorks' interactive environment, it is important to understand the basic functions of the mouse buttons.

- **Left mouse button**
  The **left mouse button** is used for most operations, such as selecting menus and icons, or picking graphic entities. One click of the button is used to select icons, menus and form entries, and to pick graphic items.

- **Right mouse button**
  The **right mouse button** is used to bring up additional available options in a context-sensitive pop-up menu. These menus provide shortcuts to frequently used commands.

- **Middle mouse button/wheel**
  The middle mouse button/wheel can be used to Rotate (hold down the wheel button and drag the mouse), Pan (hold down the wheel button and drag the mouse while holding down the [**Ctrl**] key), or Zoom (hold down the wheel button and drag the mouse while holding down the [**Shift**] key) realtime. Spinning the wheel allows zooming to the position of the cursor.

Brings up additional available options.

Allows quick Pan, Zoom, and Rotate.

Picks icons, menus, and graphic entities.

[Esc] – Canceling Commands

The [**Esc**] key is used to cancel a command in SolidWorks. The [**Esc**] key is located near the top left corner of the keyboard. Sometimes, it may be necessary to press the [**Esc**] key twice to cancel a command; it depends on where we are in the command sequence. For some commands, the [**Esc**] key is used to exit the command.

SolidWorks Help System

❖ Several types of online help are available at any time during a SolidWorks session. SolidWorks provides many online help functions, such as:

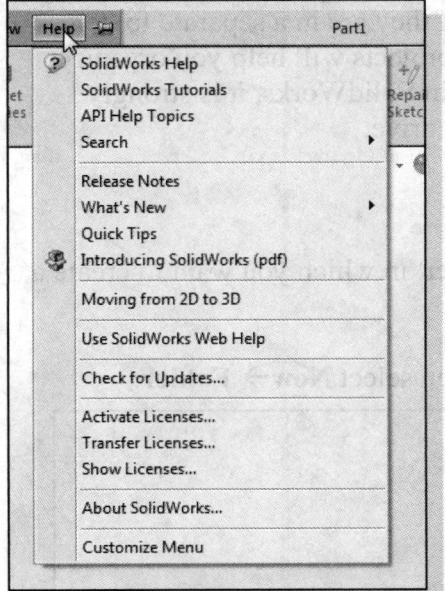

- The **Help** menu: Click on the **Help** option in the *Menu Bar* to access the *SolidWorks Help* menu system. (Note: Move the cursor over the SolidWorks logo in the *Menu Bar* to display the pull-down menu options.) The **SolidWorks Help** option provides general help information, such as command options and command references. The **SolidWorks Tutorials** option provides a collection of tutorials illustrating different SolidWorks operations.

- The SolidWorks Tutorials can also be accessed from the *SolidWorks Resources task pane* on the right side of the screen by selecting **Tutorials**.

- The **SolidWorks Help** option can also be accessed by clicking on the **Help** icon at the right end of the *Menu Bar*.

Leaving SolidWorks

➢ To leave SolidWorks, left-click on **File** at the top of the SolidWorks screen window, then choose **Exit** from the pull-down menu. (Note: Move the cursor over the SolidWorks logo in the *Menu Bar* to display the pull-down menu options.)

Creating a CAD File Folder

It is a good practice to create a separate folder to store your CAD files. You should not save your CAD files in the same folder where the SolidWorks application is located. It is much easier to organize and back up your project files if they are in a separate folder. Making folders within this folder for different types of projects will help you organize your CAD files even further. When creating CAD files in SolidWorks, it is strongly recommended that you *save* your CAD files on the hard drive.

➢ To create a new folder in the *Windows* environment:

1. On the *desktop* or under the *My Documents* folder, in which you want to create a new folder.

2. *Right-click* once to bring up the option menu, then select **New→ Folder**.

3. Type a name, such as ***Engr-Graphics***, for the new folder, and then press **[ENTER]**.

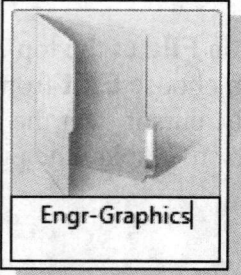

Chapter 2
Parametric Modeling Fundamentals

Learning Objectives

- ♦ **Create Simple Extruded Solid Models**
- ♦ **Understand the Basic Parametric Modeling Procedure**
- ♦ **Create 2D Sketches**
- ♦ **Understand the "Shape before Size" Design Approach**
- ♦ **Use the Dynamic Viewing Commands**
- ♦ **Create and Edit Parametric Dimensions**

Certified SolidWorks Associate Exam Objectives Coverage

Certified Associate Reference Guide

Sketch Entities – Lines, Rectangles, Circles, Arcs, Ellipses, Centerlines

Objectives: Creating Sketch Entities.

Sketch Relations

Objectives: Using Geometric Relations.

Boss and Cut Features – Extrudes, Revolves, Sweeps, Lofts

Objectives: Creating Basic Swept Features.

Dimensions

Objectives: Applying and Editing Smart Dimensions.

Feature Conditions – Start and End

Objectives: Controlling Feature Start and End Conditions.

Introduction

The **feature-based parametric modeling** technique enables the designer to incorporate the original **design intent** into the construction of the model. The word *parametric* means the geometric definitions of a design, such as dimensions, can be varied at any time in the design process. Parametric modeling is accomplished by identifying and creating the key features of the design with the aid of computer software. The design variables, described in the sketches and described as parametric relations, can then be used to quickly modify/update the design.

In SolidWorks, the parametric part modeling process involves the following steps:

1. **Determine the type of the base feature, the first solid feature, of the design. Note that *Extrude*, *Revolve*, or *Sweep* operations are the most common types of base features.**

2. **Create a rough two-dimensional sketch of the basic shape of the base feature of the design.**

3. **Apply/modify constraints and dimensions to the two-dimensional sketch.**

4. **Transform the two-dimensional parametric sketch into a 3D feature.**

5. **Add additional parametric features by identifying feature relations and complete the design.**

6. **Perform analyses/simulations, such as finite element analysis (FEA) or cutter path generation (CNC), on the computer model and refine the design as needed.**

7. **Document the design by creating the desired 2D/3D drawings.**

The approach of creating two-dimensional sketches of the three-dimensional features is an effective way to construct solid models. Many designs are in fact the same shape in one direction. Computer input and output devices we use today are largely two-dimensional in nature, which makes this modeling technique quite practical. This method also conforms to the design process that helps the designer with conceptual design along with the capability to capture the *design intent*. Most engineers and designers can relate to the experience of making rough sketches on restaurant napkins to convey conceptual design ideas. SolidWorks provides many powerful modeling and design-tools, and there are many different approaches to accomplishing modeling tasks. The basic principle of **feature-based modeling** is to build models by adding simple features one at a time. In this chapter, the general parametric part modeling procedure is illustrated; a very simple solid model with extruded features is used to introduce the SolidWorks user interface. The display viewing functions and the basic two-dimensional sketching tools are also demonstrated.

The *Adjuster* Design

Starting SolidWorks

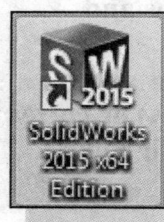

1. Select the **SolidWorks** option on the *Start* menu or select the **SolidWorks** icon on the desktop to start SolidWorks. The SolidWorks main window will appear on the screen.

2. Select the **New** icon on the *Menu Bar* with a single click of the left-mouse-button. The *New SolidWorks Document* dialog box appears.

3. Select **Part** by clicking on the first icon in the *New SolidWorks Document* dialog box as shown.

4. Click on the **OK** button to accept the settings.

SolidWorks Screen Layout & Units Setup

The default SolidWorks drawing screen contains the *Menu Bar*, the *Heads-up View* toolbar, the *Feature Manager Design Tree*, the *Command Manager* toolbar the graphics area, the *task pane* (collapsed to the right of the graphics area in the figure below), and the *Status Bar*. A line of quick text appears next to the icon as you move the *mouse cursor* over different icons. You may resize the SolidWorks drawing window by clicking and dragging on the edge of the window, or relocate the window by clicking and dragging on the *window title* area.

5. In the *Standard* toolbar area, **right-click** on any icon and activate **Command Manager** in the option list if it is not activated.

6. Select the **Options** icon from the *Menu* toolbar to open the *Options* dialog box.

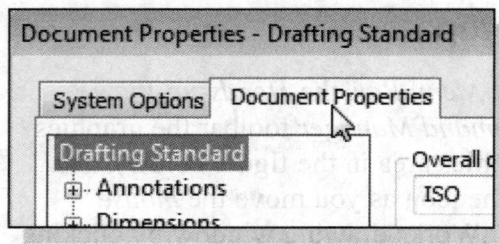

7. Select the **Document Properties** tab as shown in the figure.

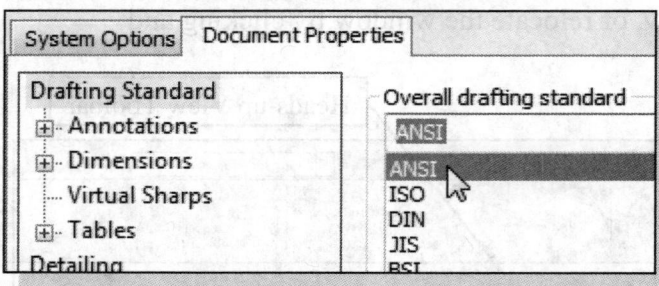

8. On your own, select two of the drafting standards and compare some of the related settings.

9. Set the *Overall drafting standard* to **ANSI** as shown.

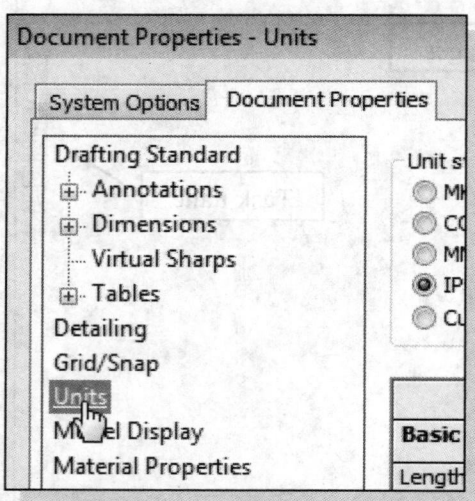

10. Click **Units** as shown in the figure.

11. Select **IPS (inch, pound, second)** under the *Unit system* options.

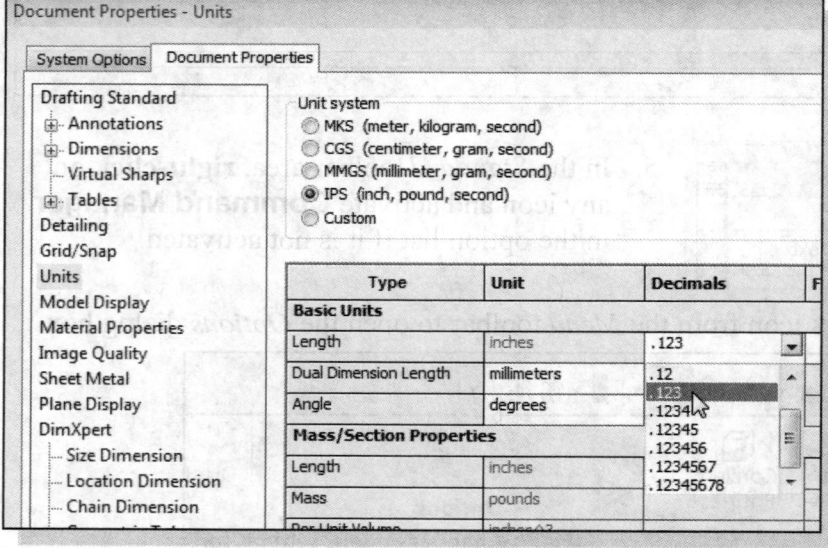

- Note the different options available to set/adjust the display of the selected units set.

12. Click **OK** in the *Options* dialog box to accept the selected settings.

Step 1: Determine/Setup the Base Solid Feature

1. In the *Features* toolbar select the **Extruded Boss/Base** command by clicking once with the left-mouse-button on the icon.

• Note the *Extrude Property Manager* is displayed in the left panel. We have activated the extrude feature; SolidWorks requires the use of an existing 2D sketch or the creation of a new 2D sketch.

Sketching Plane – It is an XY CRT, but an XYZ World

Design modeling software is becoming more powerful and user friendly, yet the system still does only what the user tells it to do. When using a geometric modeler, we therefore need to have a good understanding of what its inherent limitations are.

In most 3D geometric modelers, 3D objects are located and defined in what is usually called **world space** or **global space**. Although a number of different coordinate systems can be used to create and manipulate objects in a 3D modeling system, the objects are typically defined and stored using the world space. The world space is usually a **3D Cartesian**

coordinate system that the user cannot change or manipulate.

In engineering designs, models can be very complex, and it would be tedious and confusing if only the world coordinate system were available. Practical 3D modeling systems allow the user to define **Local Coordinate Systems (LCS)** or **User Coordinate Systems (UCS)** relative to the world coordinate system. Once a local coordinate system is defined, we can then create geometry in terms of this more convenient system.

Although objects are created and stored in 3D space coordinates, most of the geometric entities can be referenced using 2D Cartesian coordinate systems. Typical input devices such as a mouse or digitizer are two-dimensional by nature; the movement of the input device is interpreted by the system in a planar sense. The same limitation is true of common output devices, such as CRT displays and plotters. The modeling software performs a series of three-dimensional to two-dimensional transformations to correctly project 3D objects onto the 2D display plane.

The SolidWorks **sketching plane** is a special construction approach that enables the planar nature of the 2D input devices to be directly mapped onto the 3D coordinate system. The *sketching plane* is a local coordinate system that can be aligned to an existing face of a part, or a reference plane.

Think of the sketching plane as the surface on which we can sketch the 2D sections of the parts. It is similar to a piece of paper, a white board, or a chalkboard that can be attached to any planar surface. The first sketch we create is usually drawn on one of the established datum planes. Subsequent sketches/features can then be created on sketching planes that are aligned to existing **planar faces of the solid part** or **datum planes**.

1. Move the cursor over the edge of the Front Plane in the graphics area. When the Front Plane is highlighted, click once with the **left-mouse-button** to select the Front Plane as the sketch plane for the new sketch. The *sketching plane* is a reference location where two-dimensional sketches are created. The *sketching plane* can be any planar part surface or datum plane.

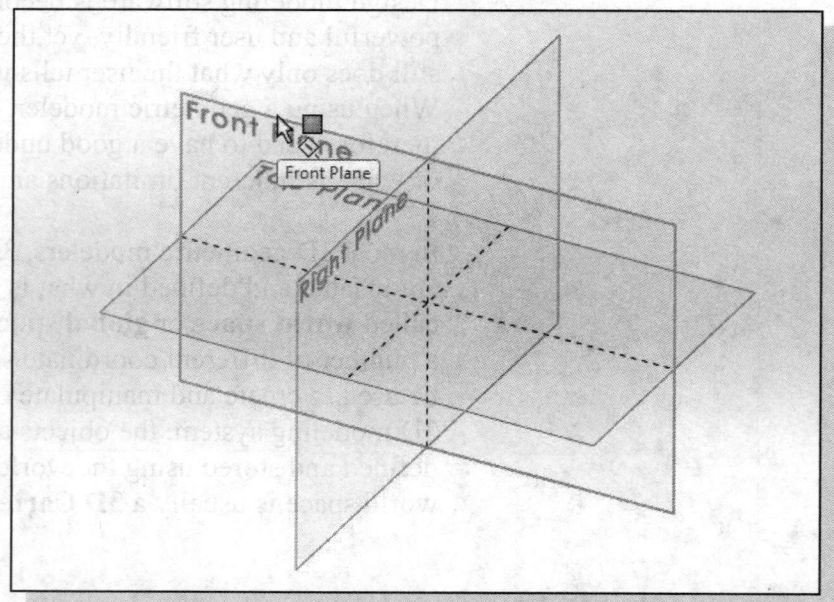

Creating Rough Sketches

Quite often during the early design stage, the shape of a design may not have any precise dimensions. Most conventional CAD systems require the user to input the precise lengths and locations of all geometric entities defining the design, which are not available during the early design stage. With *parametric modeling*, we can use the computer to elaborate and formulate the design idea further during the initial design stage. With SolidWorks, we can use the computer as an electronic sketchpad to help us concentrate on the formulation of forms and shapes for the design. This approach is the main advantage of *parametric modeling* over conventional solid-modeling techniques.

As the name implies, a ***rough sketch*** is not precise at all. When sketching, we simply sketch the geometry so that it closely resembles the desired shape. Precise scale or lengths are not needed. SolidWorks provides us with many tools to assist us in finalizing sketches. For example, geometric entities such as horizontal and vertical lines are set automatically. However, if the rough sketches are poor, it will require much more work to generate the desired parametric sketches. Here are some general guidelines for creating sketches in SolidWorks:

- **Create a sketch that is proportional to the desired shape.** Concentrate on the shapes and forms of the design.

- **Keep the sketches simple.** Leave out small geometric features such as fillets, rounds and chamfers. They can easily be placed using the Fillet and Chamfer commands after the parametric sketches have been established.

- **Exaggerate the geometric features of the desired shape.** For example, if the desired angle is 85 degrees, create an angle that is 50 or 60 degrees. Otherwise, SolidWorks might assume the intended angle to be a 90-degree angle.

- **Draw the geometry so that it does not overlap.** The geometry should eventually form a closed region. *Self-intersecting* geometry shapes are not allowed.

- **The sketched geometric entities should form a closed region.** To create a solid feature, such as an extruded solid, a closed region is required so that the extruded solid forms a 3D volume.

- ➤ **Note:** The concepts and principles involved in *parametric modeling* are very different, and sometimes they are totally opposite, to those of conventional computer aided drafting. In order to understand and fully utilize the functionality of SolidWorks, it will be helpful to take a *Zen* approach to learning the topics presented in this text: **Have an open mind and temporarily forget your experiences using conventional Computer Aided Drafting systems.**

Step 2: Creating a Rough Sketch

➢ The *Sketch* toolbar provides tools for creating the basic geometry that can be used to create features and parts.

1. Move the graphics cursor to the **Line** icon in the *Sketch* toolbar. A *Help tip* box appears next to the cursor and a brief description of the command is displayed at the bottom of the drawing screen: "*Sketches a line.*" Select the icon by clicking once with the **left-mouse-button**.

• Note the *Insert Line Feature Manager* is displayed in the left panel with different options related to the active command.

Graphics Cursors

➢ Notice the cursor changes from an arrow to a pencil when graphical input is expected.

1. Left-click a starting point for the shape, roughly near the lower center of the graphics window.

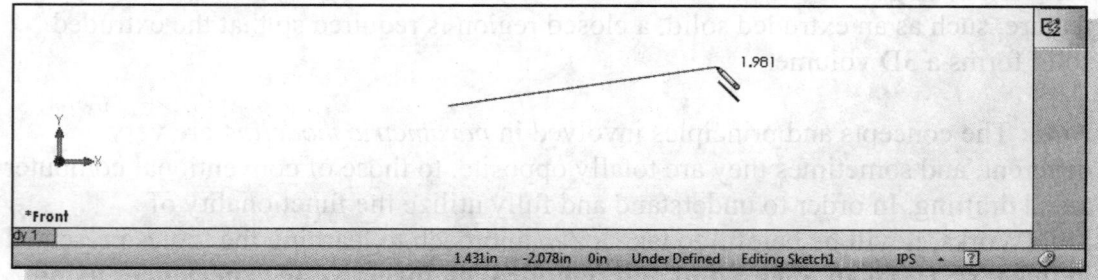

2. As you move the graphics cursor, you will see a digital readout next to the cursor. This readout gives you the line length. In the *Status Bar* area at the bottom of the window, the readout gives you the cursor location. Move the cursor around and you will notice different symbols appear at different locations.

3. Move the graphics cursor toward the right side of the graphics window to create a horizontal line as shown below. Notice the geometric relation symbol displayed. When the **Horizontal** relation symbol is displayed, left-click to select **Point 2**.

4. Complete the sketch as shown below, creating a closed region **ending at the starting point** (Point 1). Do not be overly concerned with the actual size of the sketch. Note that all line segments are sketched horizontally or vertically.

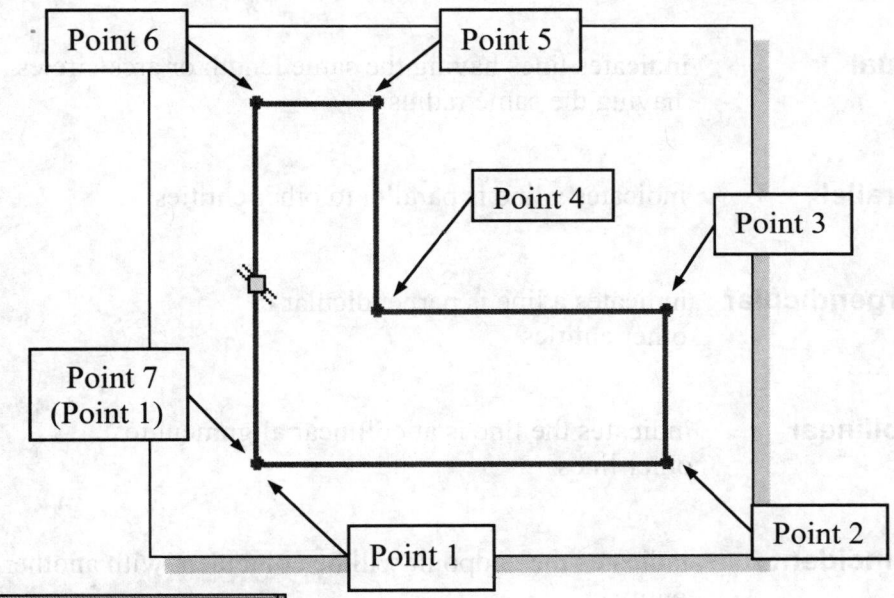

5. Click the **OK** icon (green check mark) in the *Property Manager* to end editing of the current line, then click the **OK** icon again to end the Sketch Line command, or hit the **[Esc]** key once to end the Sketch Line command.

6. Switch on the **View Sketch Relations** option as shown.

Geometric Relation Symbols

SolidWorks displays different visual clues, or symbols, to show you alignments, perpendicularities, tangencies, etc. These relations are used to capture the *design intent* by creating relations where they are recognized. SolidWorks displays the governing geometric rules as models are built. To prevent relations from forming, hold down the [**Ctrl**] key while creating an individual sketch curve. For example, while sketching line segments with the Line command, endpoints are joined with a Coincident relation, but when the [**Ctrl**] key is pressed and held, the inferred relation will not be created.

Vertical   indicates a line is vertical

Horizontal   indicates a line is horizontal

Equal   indicates lines having the same length or arcs/circles having the same radius

Parallel   indicates a line is parallel to other entities

Perpendicular   indicates a line is perpendicular to other entities

Collinear   indicates the line is at collinear alignment to other lines

Coincident   indicates the endpoint will be coincident with another entity

Concentric   indicates the cursor is at the center of an entity

Tangent   indicates the cursor is at tangency points to curves

Intersect   indicates the cursor is at intersection points to curves

Midpoint   indicates the cursor is at midpoint locations to curves

Step 3: Apply/Modify Relations and Dimensions

➢ As the sketch is made, SolidWorks automatically applies some of the geometric constraints (such as horizontal, parallel, and perpendicular) to the sketched geometry. We can continue to modify the geometry, apply additional constraints, and/or define the size of the existing geometry. In this example, we will illustrate adding dimensions to describe the sketched entities.

1. Move the cursor to the second icon of the *Sketch* toolbar; it is the **Smart Dimension** icon. Activate the command by left-clicking once on the icon.

2. Select the bottom horizontal line by left-clicking once on the line.

2. Pick the bottom horizontal line as the geometry to dimension.

2.360

3. Pick a location toward the left to place the dimension.

3. Enter **2.0** in the *Modify* dialog box.

4. Left-click **OK** (green check mark) in the *Modify* dialog box to save the current value and exit the dialog. Notice the associated geometry is adjusted.

5. Select the lower right-vertical line.

6. Pick a location toward the right of the sketch to place the dimension.

7. Enter **0.75** in the *Modify* dialog box.

8. Click **OK** in the *Modify* dialog box.

❖ The Smart Dimension command will create a length dimension if a single line is selected.

9. Select the top-horizontal line as shown below.

10. Select the bottom-horizontal line as shown below.

9. Pick the top line as the 1st geometry to dimension.

10. Pick the bottom line as the 2nd geometry to dimension.

11. Place the dimension next to the sketch.

11. Pick a location to the left of the sketch to place the dimension.

12. Enter **2.0** in the *Modify* dialog box.

13. Click **OK** in the *Modify* dialog box.

❖ When two parallel lines are selected, the Smart Dimension command will create a dimension measuring the distance between them.

14. On your own, repeat the above steps and create an additional dimension for the top line. Make the dimension **0.75**.

15. Click the **OK** icon in the *PropertyManager* as shown, or hit the [**Esc**] key once, to end the Smart Dimension command.

Viewing Functions – Zoom and Pan

- SolidWorks provides a special user interface that enables convenient viewing of the entities in the graphics window. There are many ways to perform the **Zoom** and **Pan** operations.

1. Hold the [**Ctrl**] function key down. While holding the [**Ctrl**] function key down, press the mouse wheel down and drag the mouse to **Pan** the display. This allows you to reposition the display while maintaining the same scale factor of the display.

2. Hold the [**Shift**] function key down. While holding the [**Shift**] function key down, press the mouse wheel down and drag the mouse to **Zoom** the display. Moving downward will reduce the scale of the display, making the entities display smaller on the screen. Moving upward will magnify the scale of the display.

3. Turning the mouse wheel can also adjust the scale of the display. Turn the mouse wheel forward. Notice the scale of the display is reduced, making the entities display smaller on the screen.

4. Turn the mouse wheel backward. Notice the scale of the display is magnified. (**NOTE:** Turning the mouse wheel allows zooming to the position of the cursor.)

5. On your own, use the options above to change the scale and position of the display.

6. Press the **F** key on the keyboard to automatically fit the model to the screen.

Delete an Existing Geometry of the Sketch

1. Select the top horizontal line by **left-clicking** once on the line.

2. Click once with the **right-mouse-button** to bring up the *option menu*.

3. Select **Delete** from the option list as shown.

4. Click **Yes** to proceed with deleting the selected line.

    ❖ Note that the height dimensions and the horizontal constraint attached to the geometry are also deleted.

5. Activate the **Undo** command by left-clicking once on the icon in the standard toolbar as shown.

Modifying the Dimensions of the Sketch

1. Select this dimension to modify.

1. Select the dimension that is to the bottom of the sketch by **double-clicking** with the **left-mouse-button** on the dimension text.

2. In the *Modify* window, the current length of the line is displayed. Enter **2.5** to reset the length of the line.

3. Click on the **OK** icon to accept the entered value.

➢ SolidWorks will now update the profile with the new dimension value.

4. Select this dimension to modify.

4. On your own, repeat the above steps and adjust the left vertical dimension to **2.5** so that the sketch appears as shown.

5. Press the [**Esc**] key once to exit the Dimension command.

6. Click once with the **left-mouse-button** on the **Exit Sketch** icon on the *Sketch* toolbar to exit the sketch

Step 4: Completing the Base Solid Feature

Now that the 2D sketch is completed, we will proceed to the next step: creating a 3D part from the 2D profile. Extruding a 2D profile is one of the common methods that can be used to create 3D parts. We can extrude planar faces along a path. We can also specify a height value and a tapered angle. In SolidWorks, each face has a positive side and a negative side; the current face we're working on is set as the default positive side. This positive side identifies the positive extrusion direction and it is referred to as the face's ***normal***.

1. In the *Extrude Property Manager*, enter **2.5** as the extrusion distance. Notice that the completed sketch region is automatically selected as the extrusion profile.

2. Click on the **OK** button to proceed with creating the 3D part.

➢ Note that all dimensions disappeared from the screen. All parametric definitions are stored in the **SolidWorks database** and any of the parametric definitions can be re-displayed and edited at any time.

Isometric View

❖ SolidWorks provides many ways to display views of the three-dimensional design. We will first orient the model to display in the *isometric view,* by using the *View Orientation* pull-down menu on the *Heads-up View* toolbar.

1. Select the **View Orientation** button on the *Heads-up View* toolbar by clicking once with the left-mouse-button.

2. Select the **Isometric** icon in the *View Orientation* pull-down menu.

❖ Note that many other view-related commands are also available under the **View** *pull-down menu.*

Rotation of the 3D Model – Rotate View

The Rotate View command allows us to rotate a part or assembly in the graphics window. Rotation can be around the center mark, free in all directions, or around a selected entity (vertex, edge, or face) on the model.

1. Move the cursor over the **SolidWorks** logo to display the pull-down menus. Select **View → Modify → Rotate** from the pull-down menu as shown.

2. Move the cursor inside the graphics area. Press down the left-mouse-button and drag in an arbitrary direction; the Rotate View command allows us to freely rotate the solid model.

- The model will rotate about an axis normal to the direction of cursor movement. For example, drag the cursor horizontally across the screen and the model will rotate about a vertical axis.

3. Click on this edge.

3. Move the cursor over one of the vertical edges of the solid model as shown. When the edge is highlighted, click the **left-mouse-button** once to select the edge.

4. Press down the left-mouse-button and drag. The model will rotate about this edge.

5. Left-click in the graphics area, outside the model, to unselect the edge.

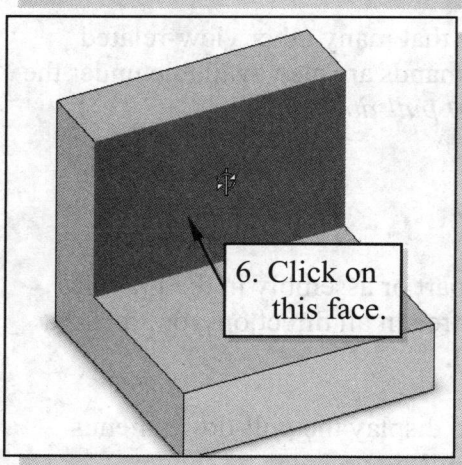

6. Click on this face.

6. Move the cursor over the front face of the solid model as shown. When the face is highlighted, click the **left-mouse-button** once to select the face.

7. Press down the left-mouse-button and drag. The model will rotate about the direction normal to this face.

8. Left-click in the graphics area, outside the model, to unselect the face.

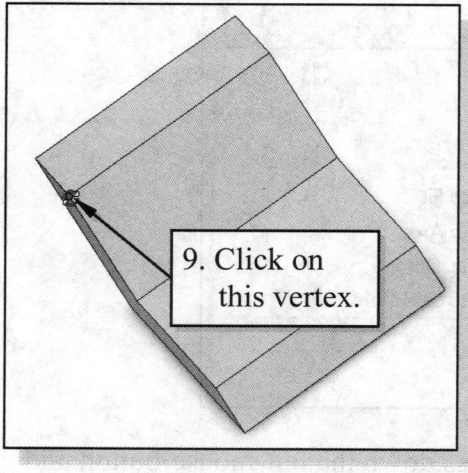

9. Click on this vertex.

9. Move the cursor over one of the vertices as shown. When the vertex is highlighted, click the left-mouse-button once to select the vertex.

10. Press down the left-mouse-button and drag. The model will rotate about the vertex.

11. Left-click in the graphics area, outside the model, to unselect the vertex.

12. Press the [**Esc**] key once to exit the **Rotate View** command.

13. On your own, reset the display to the *isometric* view.

Rotation and Panning – *Arrow Keys*

➢ SolidWorks allows us to easily rotate a part or assembly in the graphics window using the **arrow** keys on the keyboard.

• Use the **arrow** keys to rotate the view horizontally or vertically. The **left-right** keys rotate the model about a vertical axis. The **up-down** keys rotate the model about a horizontal axis.

• Hold down the [**Alt**] key and use the **left-right arrow** keys to rotate the model about an axis normal to the screen, i.e., to rotate clockwise and counter-clockwise.

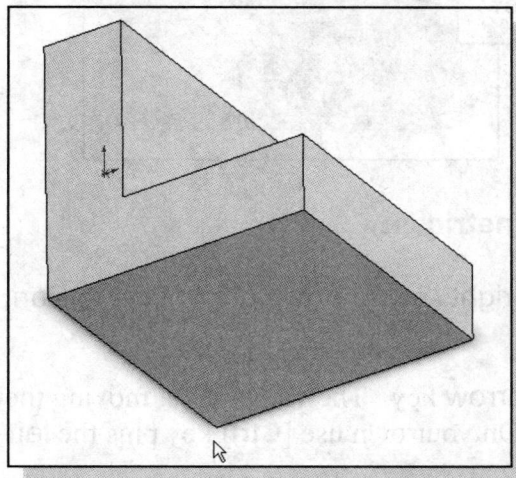

1. Hit the **left arrow** key. The model view rotates by a pre-determined increment. The default increment is 15°. (This increment can be set in the *Options* dialog box.) On your own, use the **left-right** and **up-down arrow** keys to rotate the view.

2. Hold down the [**Alt**] key and hit the **left arrow** key. The model view rotates in the clockwise direction. On your own use the **left-right** and **up-down arrow** keys, and the [**Alt**] key plus the **left-right arrow** keys, to rotate the view.

3. On your own, reset the display to the *isometric* view.

• Hold down the [**Shift**] key and use the **left-right** and **up-down arrow** keys to rotate the model in 90° increments.

4. Hold down the [**Shift**] key and hit the **right arrow** key. The view will rotate by 90°. On your own use the [**Shift**] key plus the **left-right arrow** keys to rotate the view.

5. Select the **Front** icon in the *View Orientation* pull-down menu as shown to display the Front view of the model.

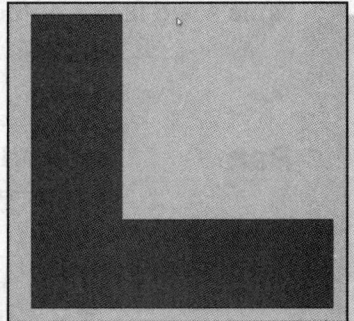

6. Hold down the [**Shift**] key and hit the left arrow key. The view rotates to the Right side view.

7. Hold down the [**Shift**] key and hit the down arrow key. The view rotates to the Top view.

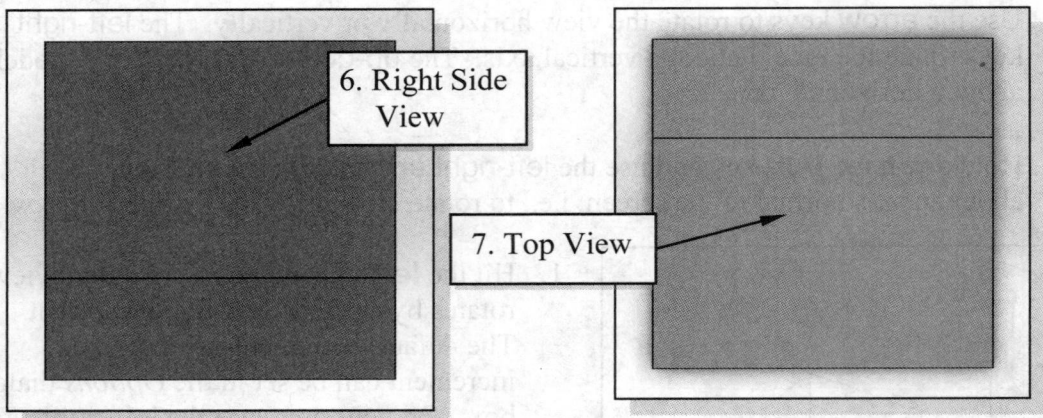

8. On your own, reset the display to the **Isometric** view.

- Hold down the [**Ctrl**] key and use the left-right and up-down arrow keys to Pan the model in increments.

9. Hold down the [**Ctrl**] key and hit the left arrow key. The view Pans, moving the model toward the left side of the screen. On your own use [**Ctrl**] key plus the left-right and up-down arrow keys to Pan the view.

Dynamic Viewing – Quick Keys

We can also use the function keys on the keyboard and the mouse to access the *Dynamic Viewing* functions.

❖ **Panning**

(1) Hold the Ctrl key; press and drag the mouse wheel

Hold the [**Ctrl**] function key down, and press and drag with the mouse wheel to **Pan** the display. This allows you to reposition the display while maintaining the same scale factor of the display.

Pan   Ctrl   +

(2) Hold the Ctrl key; use arrow keys

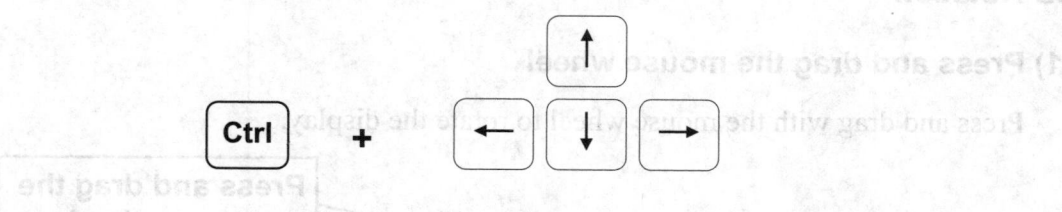

❖ **Zooming**

(1) Hold the Shift key; press and drag the mouse wheel

Hold the [**Shift**] function key down, and press and drag with the mouse wheel to **Zoom** the display. Moving downward will reduce the scale of the display, making the entities display smaller on the screen. Moving upward will magnify the scale of the display.

(2) Turning the mouse wheel

Turning the mouse wheel can also adjust the scale of the display. Turning forward will reduce the scale of the display, making the entities display smaller on the screen. Turning backward will magnify the scale of the display.

- Turning the mouse wheel allows zooming to the position of the cursor.

- The cursor position, inside the graphics area, is used to determine the center of the scale of the adjustment.

(3) Z key or Shift + Z key

Pressing the [**Z**] key on the keyboard will zoom out. Holding the [**Shift**] function key and pressing the [**Z**] key will zoom in.

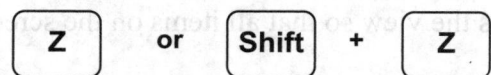

❖ 3D Rotation

(1) Press and drag the mouse wheel

Press and drag with the mouse wheel to rotate the display.

Rotation

Press and drag the mouse wheel

(2) Use arrow keys

| Rotate left, right, up, down | Rotate left, right, up, down -90° | Rotate clockwise, counter-clockwise |

Viewing Tools – Heads-up View Toolbar

The *Heads-up View* toolbar is a transparent toolbar that appears in each viewport and provides easy access to commonly used tools for manipulating the view. The default toolbar is described below.

Zoom to Fit – Adjusts the view so that all items on the screen fit inside the graphics window.

Zoom to Area – Use the cursor to define a region for the view; the defined region is zoomed to fill the graphics window.

Previous View – Returns to the previous view.

Section View – Displays a cutaway of a part or assembly using one or more section planes.

View Orientation – This allows you to change the current view orientation or number of viewports.

Display Style – This can be used to change the display style (shaded, wireframe, etc.) for the active view.

Hide/Show Items – This pull-down menu is used to control the visibility of items (axes, sketches, relations, etc.) in the graphics area.

Edit Appearance – Modifies the appearance of entities in the model.

Apply Scene – Cycles through or applies a specific scene.

View Settings – Allows you to toggle various view settings (e.g., shadows, perspective).

View Orientation

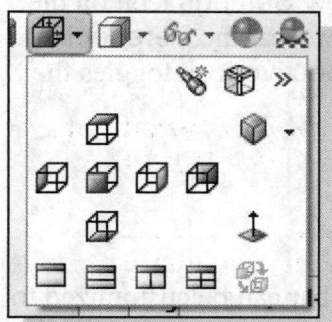

1. Click on the **View Orientation** icon on the *Heads-up View* toolbar to reveal the view orientation and number of viewports options.

   ❖ Standard view orientation options: **Front**, **Back**, **Left**, **Right**, **Top**, **Bottom**, **Isometric**, **Trimetric** or **Dimetric** icons can be selected to display the corresponding standard view.

 Normal to – In a part or assembly, zooms and rotates the model to display the selected plane or face. You can select the element either before or after clicking the Normal to icon.

❖ The icons across the bottom of the pull-down menu allow you to display a single viewport (the default) or multiple viewports.

Display Style

1. Click on the **Display Style** icon on the *Heads-up View* toolbar to reveal the display style options.

Shaded with Edges – Allows the display of a shaded view of a 3D model with its edges.

Shaded – Allows the display of a shaded view of a 3D model.

Hidden Lines Removed – Allows the display of the 3D objects using the basic wireframe representation scheme. Only those edges which are visible in the current view are displayed.

Hidden Lines Visible – Allows the display of the 3D objects using the basic wireframe representation scheme in which all the edges of the model are displayed, but edges that are hidden in the current view are displayed as dashed lines (or in a different color).

Wireframe – Allows the display of 3D objects using the basic wireframe representation scheme in which all the edges of the model are displayed.

Orthographic vs. Perspective

1. Besides the basic display modes, we can also choose an orthographic view or perspective view of the display. Clicking on the View Settings icon on the *Heads-up View* toolbar will reveal the **Perspective** icon. Clicking on the **Perspective** icon toggles the perspective view *ON* and *OFF*.

Customizing the Heads-up View Toolbar

1. The *Heads-up View* toolbar can be customized to contain icons for user-preferred view options. **Right-click** anywhere on the *Heads-up View* toolbar to reveal the display menu option list. Click on the **View (Heads-up)** icon to turn *OFF* the display of the toolbar. Notice the **Customize** option is also available to add/remove different icons.

➢ On your own, use the different options described in the above sections to familiarize yourself with the 3D viewing/display commands. Reset the display to the standard **Isometric view** before continuing to the next section.

Step 5-1: Adding an Extruded Feature

1. In the *Features* toolbar select the **Extruded Boss/ Base** command by clicking once with the left-mouse-button on the icon.

- In the *Extrude Manager* area, SolidWorks indicates the two options to create the new extrusion feature. We will select the back surface of the base feature to align the sketching plane.

3. Pick the top face of the solid model.

2. On your own, use one of the rotation quick keys/mouse-button and view the back face of the model as shown.

3. Pick the top face of the 3D solid object.

- Note that SolidWorks automatically establishes a *User Coordinate System* (UCS), and records its location with respect to the part on which it was created.

4. Select the **Line** command by clicking once with the **left-mouse-button** on the icon in the *Sketch* toolbar.

➤ To illustrate the usage of dimensions in parametric sketches, we will intentionally create a sketch away from the desired location.

5. Create a sketch with segments perpendicular/parallel to the existing edges of the solid model as shown below. (Hint: Use the **Normal To** command to adjust the display normal to the sketching plane direction.)

6. Select the **Smart Dimension** command in the *Sketch* toolbar. The Smart Dimension command allows us to quickly create and modify dimensions.

7. On your own, create and modify the size dimensions to describe the size of the sketch as shown in the figure.

8. Create the two location dimensions, accepting the default values, to describe the position of the sketch relative to the top corner of the solid model as shown.

9. On your own, modify the two location dimensions to **0.0** and **0.0** as shown in the figure.

➤ In parametric modeling, the dimensions can be used to quickly control the size and location of the defined geometry.

10. Select **Close Dialog** in the *Dimension Property Manager* to end the Smart Dimension command.

11. Click **Exit Sketch** in the *Sketch* toolbar to end the Sketch mode.

12. In the *Boss-Extrude Property Manager*, enter **2.5** as the extrude *Distance* as shown.

13. Click the **Reverse Direction** button in the *Property Manager* as shown. The extrude preview should appear as shown.

14. Confirm the **Merge result** option is activated as shown.

15. Click on the **OK** button to proceed with creating the extruded feature.

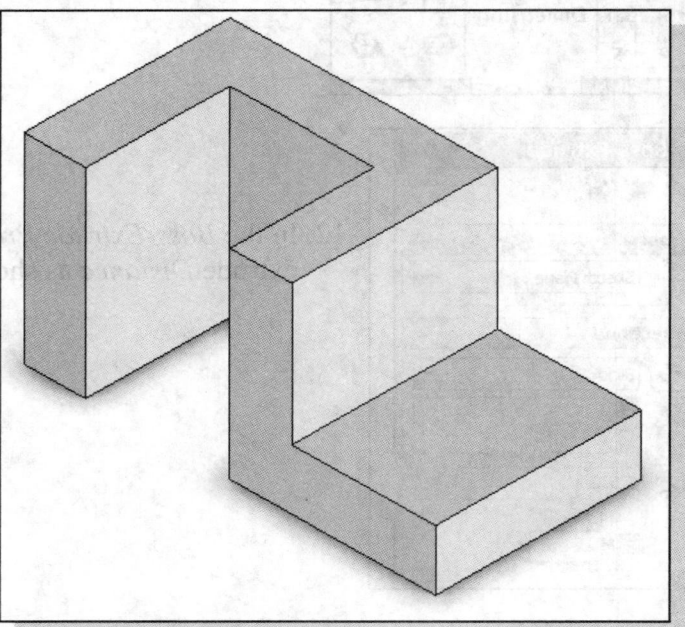

Step 5-2: Adding a Cut Feature

- Next, we will create a **cut** feature that will be added to the existing solid object.

1. In the *Features* toolbar select the **Extruded Cut** command by clicking once with the left-mouse-button on the icon.

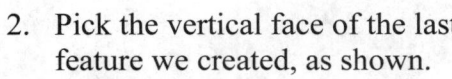

2. Pick the vertical face of the last feature we created, as shown.

3. Select the **Circle** command by clicking once with the **left-mouse-button** on the icon in the *Sketch* toolbar.

4. Create a circle roughly at the center of the surface as shown.

5. On your own, create and modify the dimensions of the sketch as shown in the figure.

6. Click **Exit Sketch** in the *Sketch* toolbar to end the Sketch mode.

7. Adjust the display by using the **Isometric** option in the *View Orientation* panel as shown. (Quick Key: **Ctrl + 7**)

• Next, we will create and profile another sketch, a rectangle, which will be used to create another extrusion feature that will be added to the existing solid object.

8. Set the *Extents* option to **Through All** as shown. The *Through All* option instructs the software to calculate the extrusion distance and assures the created feature will always cut through the full length of the model.

9. Click on the **OK** button to proceed with creating the extruded feature.

Step 5-3: Adding another Cut Feature

- Next, we will create and profile a triangle, which will be used to create a **cut** feature that will be added to the existing solid object.

1. In the *Features* toolbar select the **Extruded Cut** command by clicking once with the left-mouse-button on the icon.

2. Pick the vertical face of the first feature we created, as shown.

3. Select the **Line** command by clicking once with the **left-mouse-button** on the icon in the *Sketch* toolbar.

4. Start at the upper left corner and create three line segments to form a small triangle as shown.

5. On your own, create and modify the two dimensions of the sketch as shown in the figure. (Hint: create the angle dimension by selecting the two adjacent lines as shown and place the angular dimension inside the desired quadrant.)

6. In the *Dimension manager window*, click once with the left-mouse-button on **Close Dialog** to end the Smart Dimension command.

7. In the *Features* toolbar, select **Exit Sketch** in the popup menu to end the Sketch mode.

8. Set the *Extents* option to **Up To Next face/body** as shown. The *Up To Next* option instructs the software to calculate the extrusion distance and assures the created feature will always cut through the proper length of the model.

9. Click on the **OK** button to proceed with creating the extruded feature.

Save the Model

1. Select **Save** in the *Quick Access* toolbar, or you can also use the "**Ctrl+S**" combination (hold down the "Ctrl" key and hit the "S" key once) to save the part.

2. In the popup window, select the directory to store the model in and enter ***Adjuster*** as the name of the file.

3. Click on the **Save** button to save the file.

❖ You should form a habit of saving your work periodically, just in case something might go wrong while you are working on it. In general, one should save one's work at an interval of every 15 to 20 minutes. One should also save before making any major modifications to the model.

Questions:

1. What is the first thing we should set up in SolidWorks when creating a new model?

2. Describe the general *parametric modeling* procedure.

3. Describe the general guidelines in creating *rough sketches*.

4. List two of the geometric constraint symbols used by SolidWorks.

5. What was the first feature we created in this lesson?

6. How many solid features were created in the tutorial?

7. How do we control the size of a feature in parametric modeling?

8. Which command was used to create the last cut feature in the tutorial? How many dimensions do we need to fully describe the cut feature?

9. List and describe three differences between *parametric modeling* and traditional 2D *computer aided drafting* techniques.

Exercises:

1. **Inclined Support** (Thickness: **.5**)

2. **Spacer Plate** (Thickness: **.125**)

3. **Positioning Stop**

4. **Guide Block**

5. Slider Block

Notes:

Chapter 3
Constructive Solid Geometry Concepts

Learning Objectives

- **Understand Constructive Solid Geometry Concepts**
- **Create a Binary Tree**
- **Understand the Basic Boolean Operations**
- **Use the SolidWorks CommandManager User Interface**
- **Setup GRID and SNAP Intervals**
- **Understand the Importance of Order of Features**
- **Use the Different Extrusion Options**

Certified SolidWorks Associate Exam Objectives Coverage

Sketch Entities – Lines, Rectangles, Circles, Arcs, Ellipses, Centerlines
Objectives: Creating Sketch Entities.

Boss and Cut Features – Extrudes, Revolves, Sweeps, Lofts
Objectives: Creating Basic Swept Features.

Dimensions
Objectives: Applying and Editing Smart Dimensions.

Feature Conditions – Start and End
Objectives: Controlling Feature Start and End Conditions.

Introduction

In the 1980s, one of the main advancements in **solid modeling** was the development of the **Constructive Solid Geometry** (CSG) method. CSG describes the solid model as combinations of basic three-dimensional shapes (**primitive solids**). The basic primitive solid set typically includes: Rectangular-prism (Block), Cylinder, Cone, Sphere, and Torus (Tube). Two solid objects can be combined into one object in various ways using operations known as **Boolean operations**. There are three basic Boolean operations: **JOIN (Union)**, **CUT (Difference)**, and **INTERSECT**. The *JOIN* operation combines the two volumes included in the different solids into a single solid. The *CUT* operation subtracts the volume of one solid object from the other solid object. The *INTERSECT* operation keeps only the volume common to both solid objects. The CSG method is also known as the **Machinist's Approach**, as the method is parallel to machine shop practices.

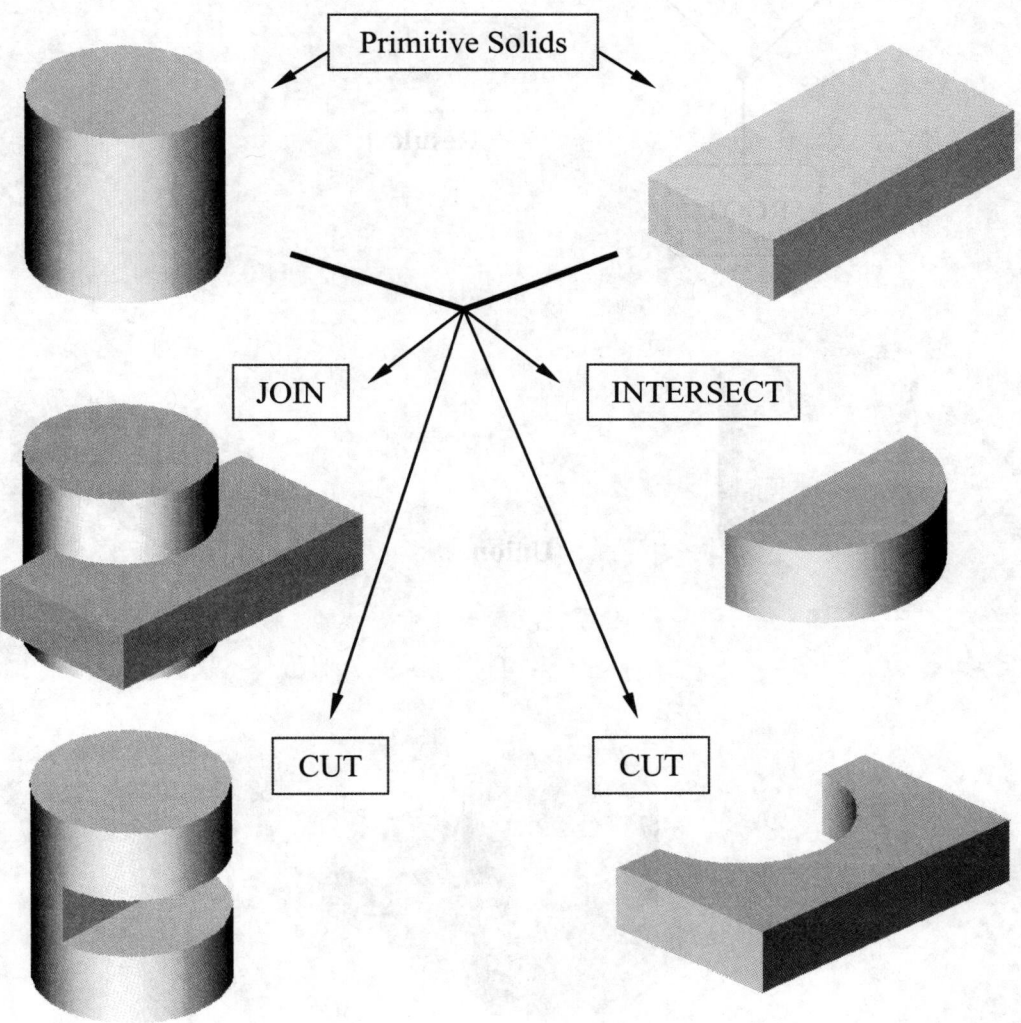

Binary Tree

The CSG is also referred to as the method used to store a solid model in the database. The resulting solid can be easily represented by what is called a **binary tree**. In a binary tree, the terminal branches (leaves) are the various primitives that are linked together to make the final solid object (the root). The binary tree is an effective way to keep track of the *history* of the resulting solid. By keeping track of the history, the solid model can be re-built by re-linking through the binary tree. This provides a convenient way to modify the model. We can make modifications at the appropriate links in the binary tree and re-link the rest of the history tree without building a new model.

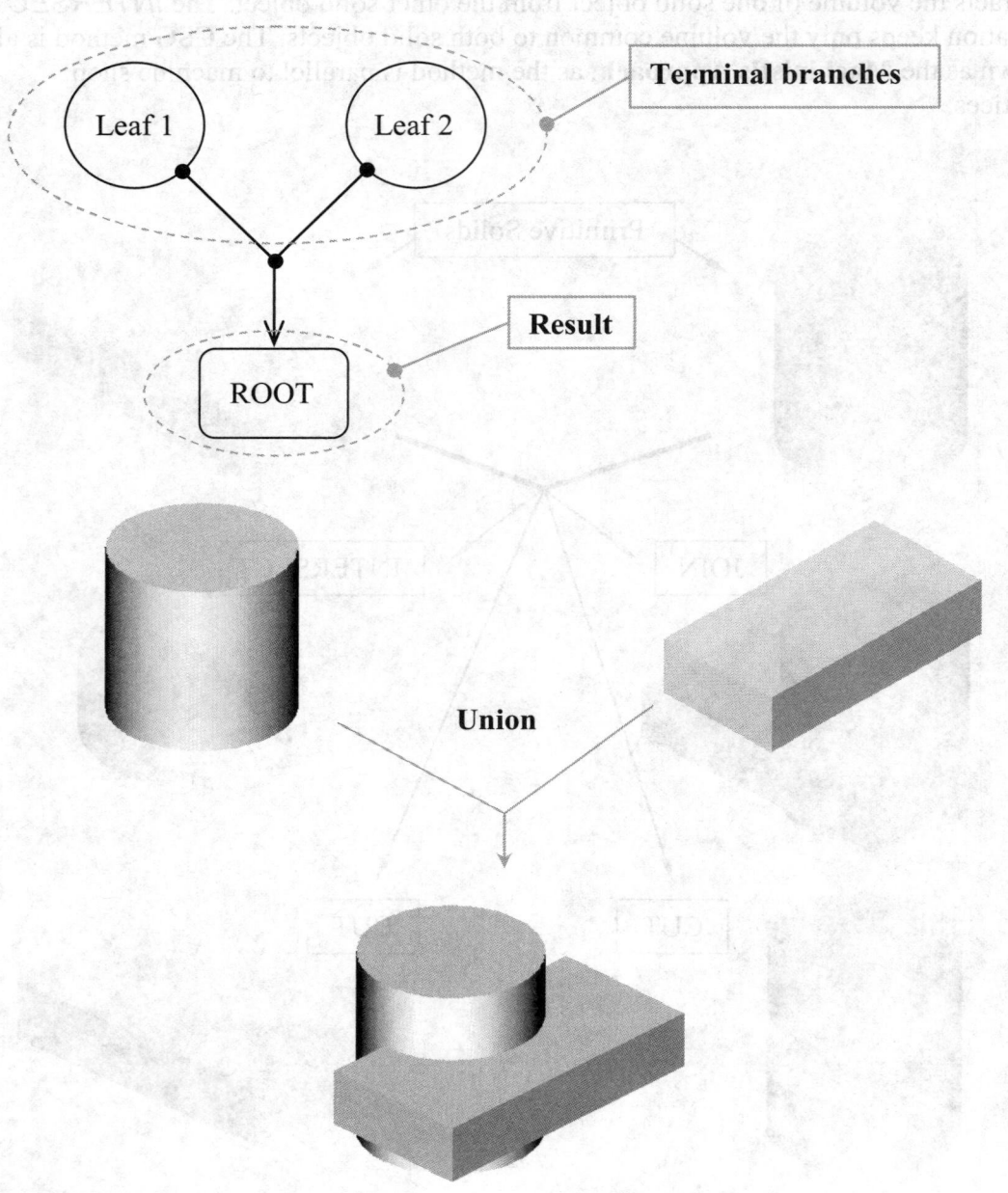

The *Locator* Design

The CSG concept is one of the important building blocks for feature-based modeling. In SolidWorks, the CSG concept can be used as a planning tool to determine the number of features that are needed to construct the model. It is also a good practice to create features that are parallel to the manufacturing process required for the design. With parametric modeling, we are no longer limited to using only the predefined basic solid shapes. In fact, any solid features we create in SolidWorks are used as primitive solids; parametric modeling allows us to maintain full control of the design variables that are used to describe the features. In this lesson, a more in-depth look at the parametric modeling procedure is presented. The equivalent CSG operation for each feature is also illustrated.

➢ Before going through the tutorial, on your own, make a sketch of a CSG binary tree of the ***Locator*** design using only two basic types of primitive solids: cylinder and rectangular prism. In your sketch, how many *Boolean operations* will be required to create the model? What is your choice of the first primitive solid to use, and why? Take a few minutes to consider these questions and do the preliminary planning by sketching on a piece of paper. Compare the sketch you make to the CSG binary tree steps shown on page 3-6. Note that there are many different possibilities in combining the basic primitive solids to form the solid model. Even for the simplest design, it is possible to take several different approaches to creating the same solid model.

Modeling Strategy – CSG Binary Tree

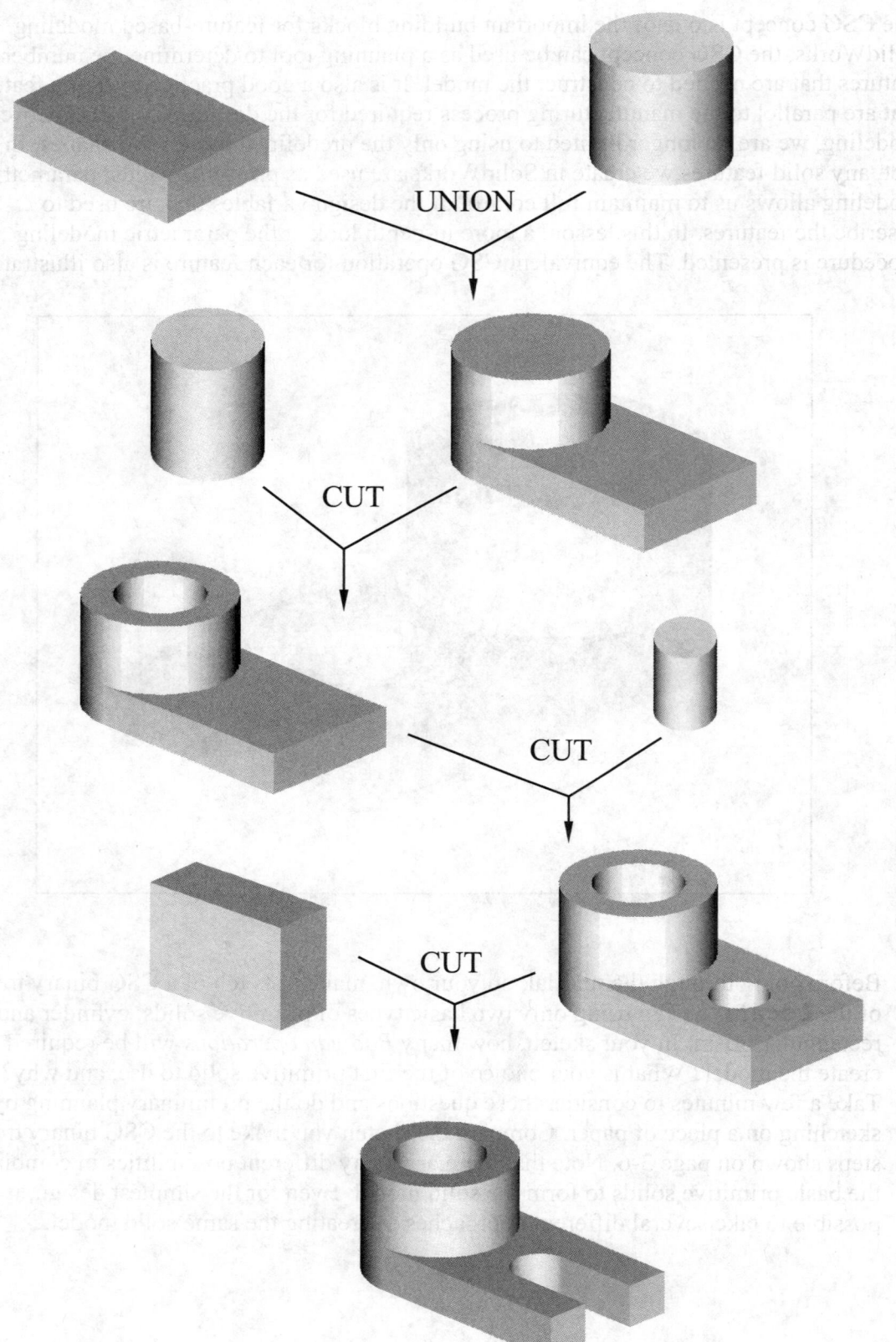

Starting SolidWorks and Activating the Command Manager

1. Select the **SolidWorks** option on the *Start* menu or select the **SolidWorks** icon on the desktop to start SolidWorks. The SolidWorks main window will appear.

2. Select the **New** icon with a single click of the left-mouse-button on the *Menu Bar* toolbar.

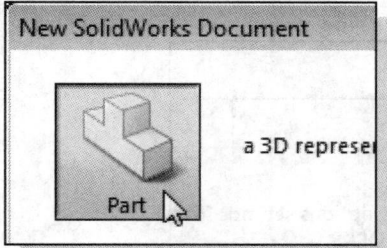

3. Select the **Part** icon with a single click of the left-mouse-button in the *New SolidWorks Document* dialog box.

4. Select **OK** in the *New SolidWorks Document* dialog box to open a new part document.

5. To turn **ON** the *Command Manager*, right click on any toolbar and toggle the *Command Manager ON* by selecting it at the top of the pop-up menu.

❖ Notice the *Features* and *Sketch* toolbars no longer appear at the edge of the window. These toolbars appear on the *Ribbon* display of the *Command Manager*.

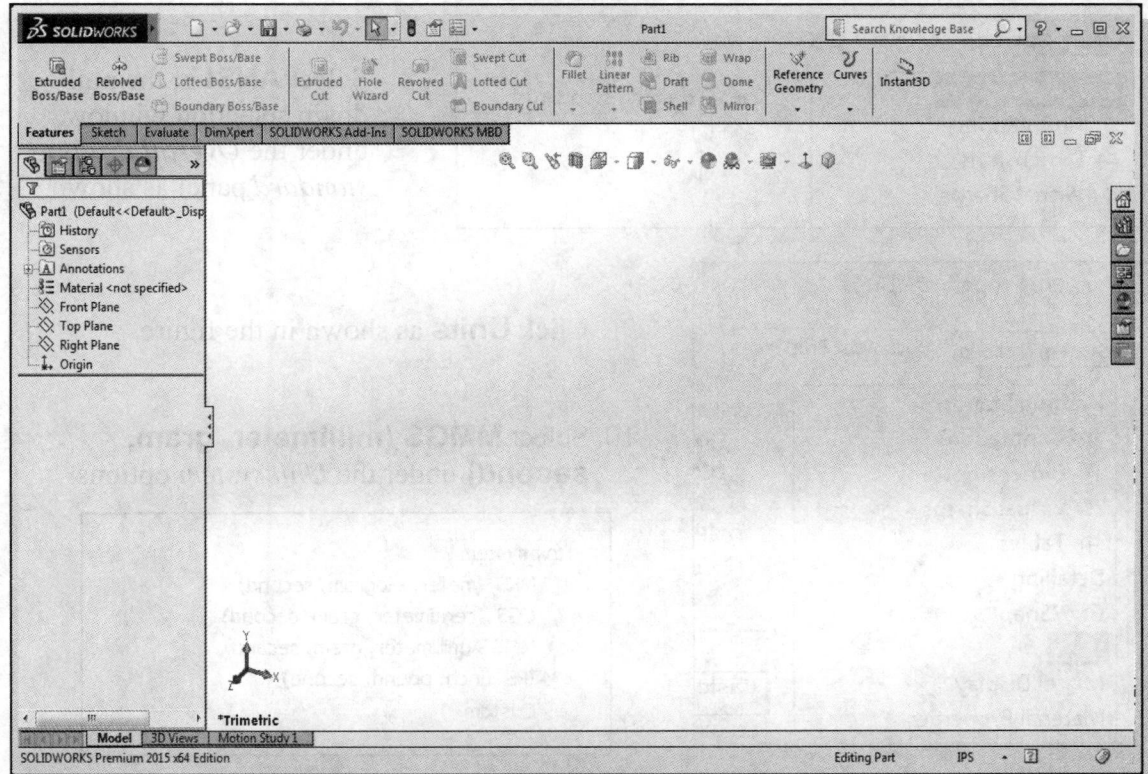

- Every object we construct in a CAD system is measured in units. We should determine the value of the units within the CAD system before creating the first geometric entities. For example, in one model, a unit might equal one millimeter of the real-world object; in another model, a unit might equal an inch. In most CAD systems, setting the model units does not always set units for dimensions. We generally set model units and dimension units to the same type and precision.

6. Select the **Options** icon from the *Menu Bar* toolbar to open the *Options* dialog box.

7. Select the **Document Properties** tab and the **Drafting Standard** option at the left of the *Document Properties* panel.

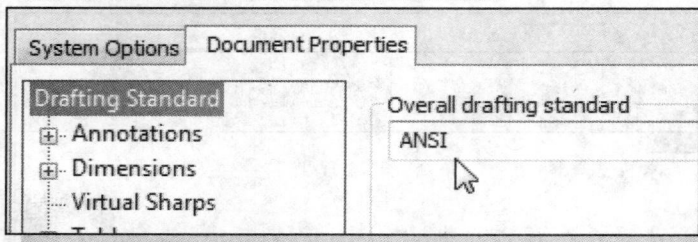

8. Select **ANSI** in the pull-down selection window under the *Overall drafting standard* panel as shown.

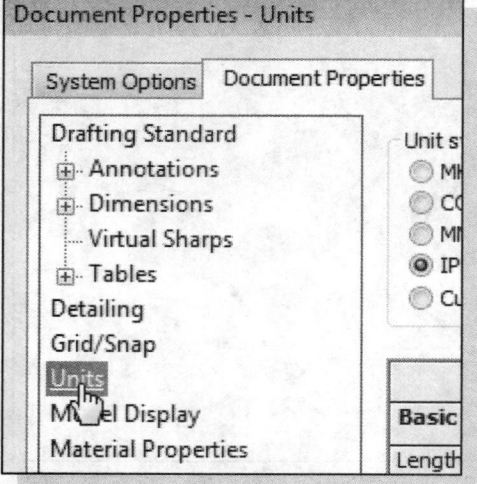

9. Click **Units** as shown in the figure.

10. Select **MMGS (millimeter, gram, second)** under the *Unit system* options.

Unit system
- MKS (meter, kilogram, second)
- CGS (centimeter, gram, second)
- MMGS (millimeter, gram, second)
- IPS (inch, pound, second)
- Custom

11. Select **None** in the *Decimals* spin box for the *Length units* as shown to set the display to no decimal places. (Note the *Overall Drafting Standard* is automatically adjusted with our setting as shown.)

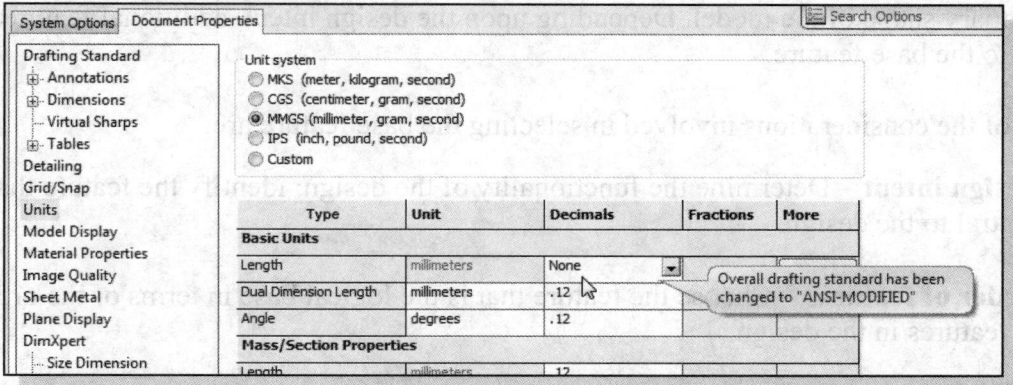

GRID and *SNAP* Intervals Setup

1. Click **Grid/Snap** as shown below.

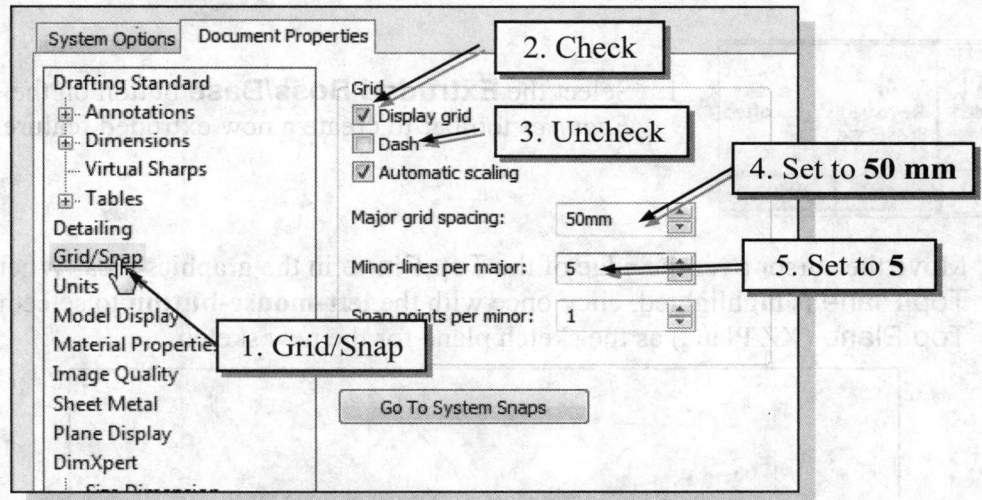

2. Check the Display grid checkbox under the *Grid* options.

3. Uncheck the Dash checkbox under the *Grid* options.

4. Set the Major grid spacing to **50 mm** under the *Grid* options.

5. Set the Minor-lines per major to **5** under the *Grid* options.

6. Click **OK** in the *Options* dialog box to accept the selected settings.

➢ Note that the above settings set the grid displaying in SolidWorks. Although the **Snap to grid** option is available in SolidWorks, its usage in parametric modeling is not recommended.

Base Feature

In *parametric modeling*, the first solid feature is called the **base feature**, which usually is the primary shape of the model. Depending upon the design intent, additional features are added to the base feature.

Some of the considerations involved in selecting the base feature are:

- **Design intent** – Determine the functionality of the design; identify the feature that is central to the design.

- **Order of features** – Choose the feature that is the logical base in terms of the order of features in the design.

- **Ease of making modifications** – Select a base feature that is more stable and is less likely to be changed.

➢ A rectangular block will be created first as the base feature of the *Locator* design.

1. Select the **Extruded Boss/Base** button on the *Features* toolbar to create a new extruded feature.

2. Move the cursor over the edge of the Top Plane in the graphics area. When the Top Plane is highlighted, click once with the **left-mouse-button** to select the Top Plane (XZ Plane) as the sketch plane for the new sketch.

3. Select the **Corner Rectangle** command by clicking once with the **left-mouse-button** on the icon in the *Sketch* toolbar.

4. Create a rectangle of arbitrary size by selecting two locations on the screen as shown below.

5. Inside the graphics window, click once with the right-mouse-button to bring up the option menu.

6. Choose **Select** to end the Rectangle command.

7. Select the **Smart Dimension** command by clicking once with the **left-mouse-button** on the icon in the *Sketch* toolbar.

8. The message "*Select one or two edges/vertices and then a text location*" is displayed in the *Status Bar* area at the bottom of the SolidWorks window. Select the bottom horizontal line by left-clicking once on the line.

8. Select the bottom horizontal line as the geometry to dimension.

10. Enter **75**.

9. Pick a location below the line to place the dimension.

9. Move the graphics cursor below the selected line and left-click to place the dimension. (Note that the value displayed on your screen might be different than what is shown in the figure above.)

10. Enter **75** in the *Modify* dialog box.

11. Click **OK** in the *Modify* dialog box.

12. On your own, create the vertical size dimension of the sketched rectangle as shown. Enter **50** to set the length of the line.

13. Click on the **OK** icon to accept the entered value.

14. Hit the [**Esc**] key once to end the Dimension command.

Repositioning Dimensions

1. Move the cursor near the vertical dimension; note that the dimension is highlighted. Move the cursor slowly until a small marker appears next to the cursor, as shown in the figure.

2. Drag with the left-mouse-button to reposition the selected dimension.

3. Repeat the above steps to reposition the horizontal dimension.

4. Click once with the **left-mouse-button** on the **Exit Sketch** icon on the *Sketch* toolbar to end the **Sketch** option.

Completing the Base Solid Feature

- In the *Extrude PropertyManager* panel, enter **15** as the extrusion distance. Notice that the sketch region is automatically selected as the extrusion profile.

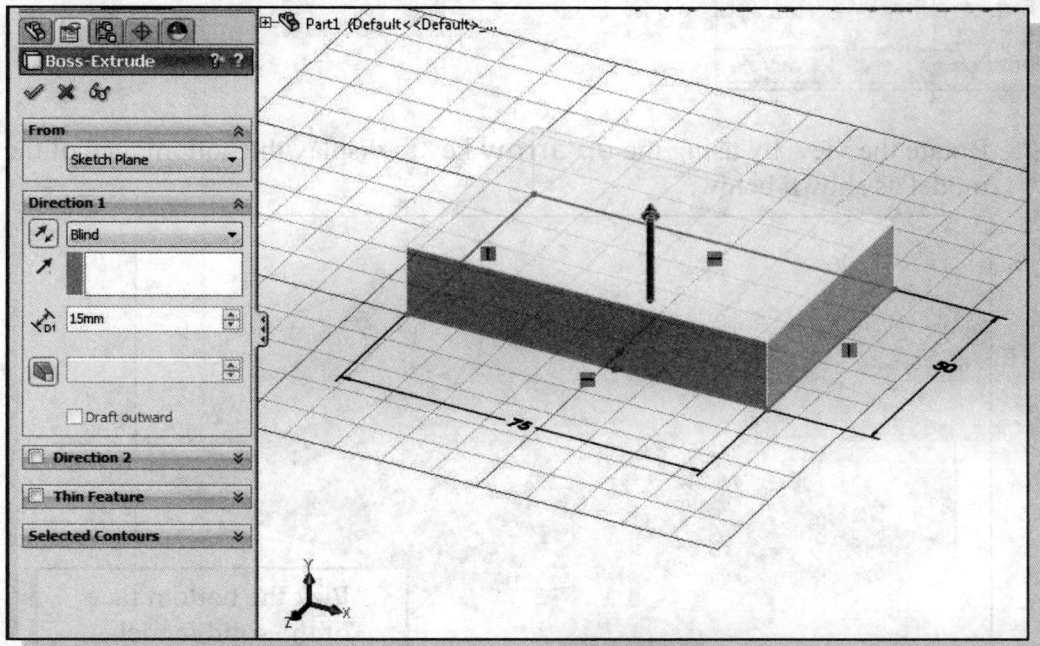

- Click on the **OK** button to proceed with creating the 3D part.

- Use the *Viewing* options to view the created part. On the *Heads-up View* toolbar, select **View Orientation** (to open the *View Orientation* pull-down menu) and select the **Isometric** icon to reset the display to the **Isometric** view before going to the next section.

- Note the Extruded feature you created is listed in the *Feature Manager Design Tree* as shown. Note the Design Tree can be used to identify all features used to create the design.

Creating the Next Solid Feature

1. Select the **Extruded Boss/Base** button on the *Features* toolbar to create a new extruded feature.

2. Rotate the view by using the **up arrow** key to display the bottom face of the solid model as shown below.

> 3. Pick the bottom face of the solid model.

3. Pick the bottom face of the 3D model as the sketching plane.

> Note that the sketching plane is aligned to the selected face.

4. Select the **Circle** command by clicking once with the left-mouse-button on the icon in the *Sketch* toolbar.

> We will align the center of the circle to the midpoint of the base feature.

5. Move the cursor along the shorter edge of the base feature; when the **midpoint** is highlighted and the Midpoint sketch relation icon appears, click once with the left-mouse-button to select the midpoint.

6. Move the cursor over the corner of the base feature; when the corner is highlighted, click once with the left-mouse-button to create a circle, as shown.

7. Press the [**Esc**] key once to end the **Circle** command.

8. Click once with the **left-mouse-button** on the **Exit Sketch** icon on the *Sketch* toolbar to exit the **Sketch** option.

➤ Notice that the sketch region is automatically selected as the extrusion profile.

9. Select the **Isometric** icon in the *View Orientation* pull-down menu.

❖ Note that many other view-related commands are also available under the **View** *pull-down menu*.

10. In the *Extrude Property Manager* panel, click the **Reverse Direction** icon to set the extrusion direction as shown below.

11. In the *Extrude PropertyManager* panel, enter **40** as the extrusion distance.

12. Confirm the **Merge result** checkbox is checked as shown.

13. Click on the **OK** button to proceed with creating the extruded feature.

- The two features are joined together into one solid part; the *CSG-Union* operation was performed. This is the effect of the *Merge result* option.

Creating an Extruded Cut Feature

- We will create a circular cut as the next solid feature of the design. We will align the sketch plane to the top of the last cylinder feature.

1. In the *Features* toolbar select the **Extruded Cut** command by clicking once with the left-mouse-button on the icon.

2. Pick the top face to align the sketch.

2. Pick the top face of the cylinder as shown.

3. Select the **Circle** command by clicking once with the left-mouse-button on the icon in the *Sketch* toolbar.

4. Move the cursor over the circular edge of the top face as shown. (Do not click.) Notice the center and quadrant marks appear on the circle.

5. Select Center

6. Draw Circle

5. Select the **Center** point of the top face of the 3D model by left-clicking once on the icon as shown.

6. Sketch a circle of arbitrary size inside the top face of the cylinder by left-clicking as shown.

7. Use the right-mouse-button to display the option menu and choose **Select** in the popup menu to end the Circle command.

8. Inside the graphics window, click once with the right-mouse-button to display the option menu. Select the **Smart Dimension** option in the popup menu.

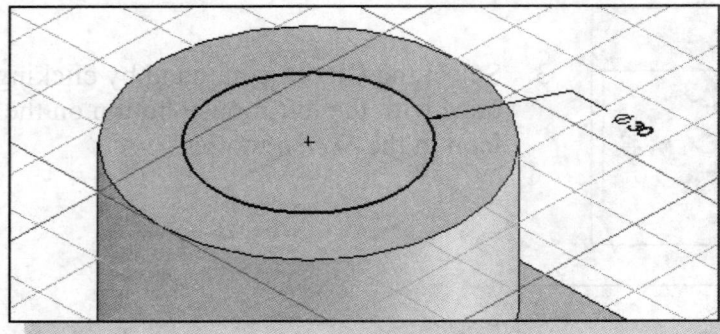

9. Create a dimension to describe the size of the circle and set it to **30mm**.

10. Inside the graphics window, click once with the right-mouse-button to display the option menu. Choose **Select** in the popup menu to end the Smart Dimension command.

11. Click once with the **left-mouse-button** on the **Exit Sketch** icon on the *Sketch* toolbar to exit the Sketch mode.

➢ The *Cut-Extrude PropertyManager* is displayed in the left panel. Notice that the sketch region (the circle) is automatically selected as the extrusion profile.

12. In the *Cut-Extrude PropertyManager* panel, click the arrow to reveal the pull-down options for the *End Condition* (the default end condition is 'Blind') and select **Through All** as shown.

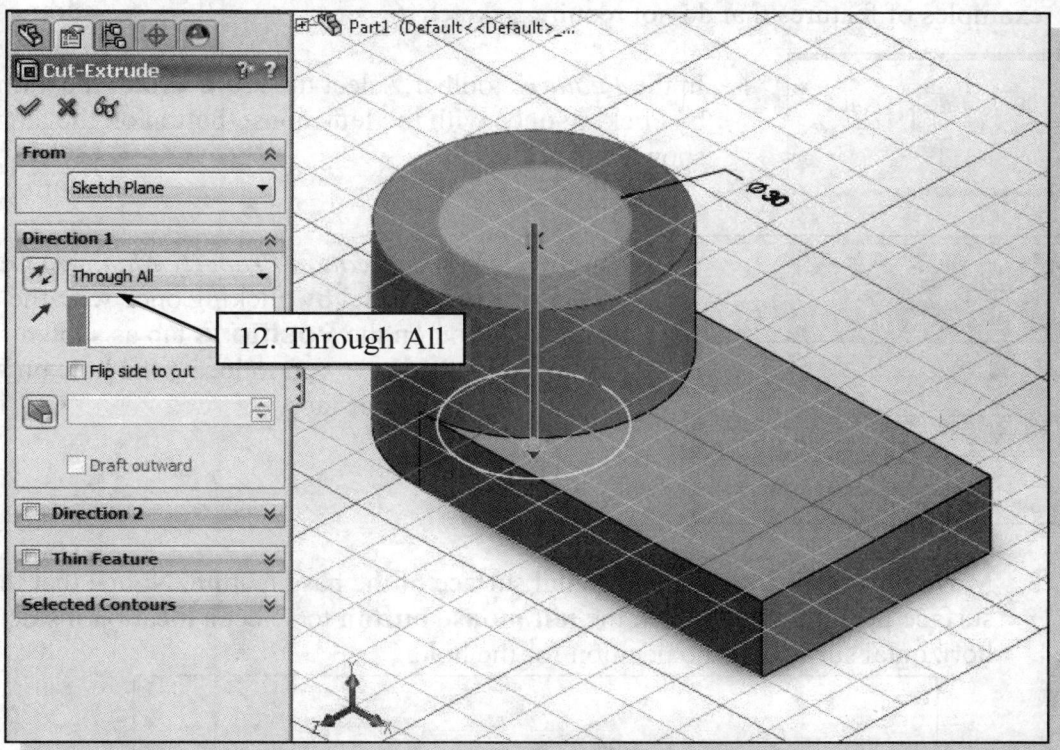

13. Click the **OK** button (green check mark) in the *Cut-Extrude PropertyManager* panel.

CSG Cut

- The circular volume is removed from the solid model; the *CSG-Cut* operation resulted in a single solid.

Creating a Hole with the *Hole Wizard*

- The last cut feature we created is a *sketched feature*, where we created a rough sketch and performed an extrusion operation. We can also create a hole using the SolidWorks Hole Wizard. With the Hole Wizard, the hole feature does not need a sketch and can be created automatically. Holes, fillets, chamfers, and shells are all examples of features that do not require a sketch.

1. In the *Features* toolbar, select the **Hole Wizard** command by clicking once with the left-mouse-button on the icon as shown.

2. In the *Hole Specification Property Manager*, select the **Positions** panel by clicking once with the left-mouse-button on the **Positions** tab as shown. The Positions tab allows you to locate the hole on a planar or non-planar face.

3. Move the cursor over the horizontal surface of the base feature. Notice that the surface is highlighted. Click the **left mouse button** to select a location inside the horizontal surface as the position for the hole.

➢ Notice the *Sketch* toolbar is active and the **Point** button is now selected. The Point command has been automatically executed to allow the insert of a point to serve as the center for the hole. We will insert the point and use dimensions to locate it.

4. Move the cursor to a location on the horizontal surface of the base feature to move the center location and click the **left mouse button** to insert the point near the center of the surface.

5. Select the **Smart Dimension** command by clicking once with the **left-mouse-button** on the icon in the *Sketch* toolbar.

6. Pick the center point by clicking once with the left-mouse-button as shown.

7. Pick the right-edge of the top face of the base feature by clicking once with the left-mouse-button as shown.

8. Select a location for the dimension by clicking once with the left-mouse-button as shown.

9. Enter **30** in the *Modify* dialog box, and select **OK**.

10. On your own, enter the additional dimension as shown (the dimension is **25** mm).

11. Press the [**Esc**] key once to end the **Smart Dimension** command.

12. In *Hole Property Manager*, select the **Type** panel by clicking once with the left-mouse-button on the **Type** tab as shown.

13. Select the **Hole** icon under the *Hole Specification* option. (This is the default setting and is probably already selected.)

14. Select **ANSI Metric** and **Drill Sizes** in the *Standard* option window.

15. Set the *Size* option to a diameter of **20** mm.

16. Set the *End Condition* option to **Through All**.

17. Click the **OK** button (green check mark) in the *Hole Property Manager* to proceed with the *Hole* feature.

- The circular volume is removed from the solid model; the *CSG-Cut* operation resulted in a single solid.

CSG Cut

Creating a Rectangular Extruded Cut Feature

* Next create a rectangular cut as the last solid feature of the *Locator*.

1. In the *Features* toolbar select the **Extruded Cut** command by clicking once with the left-mouse-button on the icon.

2. Pick the right face of the base feature as shown.

3. Select the **Corner Rectangle** command by clicking once with the left-mouse-button on the icon in the *Sketch* toolbar.

4. Create a rectangle that is aligned to the top and bottom edges of the base feature as shown.

5. On your own, create and modify the two dimensions as shown. The dimensions are **15** mm and **20** mm.

6. Click once with the **left-mouse-button** on the **Exit Sketch** icon on the *Sketch* toolbar to exit Sketch option.

7. Select the **Isometric** icon in the *View Orientation* pull-down menu.

❖ Note that many other view-related commands are also available under the **View** *pull-down menu.*

8. In the *Extrude Property Manager* panel, click the arrow to reveal the pull-down options for the *End Condition* (the default end condition is Blind) and select **Up To Next** as shown.

9. Click the **OK** button (green check mark) in the *Cut-Extrude Property Manager* panel.

Using the View Selector

The **View Selector** provides an in-context method to select standard and non-standard views.

1. Click on the **View Orientation** icon on the *Heads-Up View Toolbar* to reveal the view orientation options.

1. Select the **View Orientation** icon.

2. Toggle **View Selector ON**.

2. **Toggle** the View Selector **ON** by left-clicking on the **View Selector** icon in the *Orientation dialog box*.

➤ The View Selector appears in the graphics area. The View Selector provides an in-context method to select right, left, front, back, top, and isometric views of your model, as well as additional standard and isometric views.

3. Select the **bottom isometric view** on the *View Selector* as shown below. Note the corresponding view appears.

4. On your own, experiment with selecting other views using the *View Selector*. Notice that with the *View Selector* toggled **ON**, it automatically appears when the *View Orientation* option is selected on the *Heads-Up View* toolbar.

5. **Toggle** the View Selector **OFF** by left-clicking on the **View Selector** icon in the *Orientation dialog box*.

6. Hold down the **[Ctrl]** button and press the **[Spacebar]**. Notice the *View Selector* appears. This is an alternate method to activate the *View Selector*.

7. Select the isometric view as shown.

8. Save the model with the name *Locator*.

Questions:

1. List and describe three basic *Boolean operations* commonly used in computer geometric modeling software?

2. What is a *primitive solid*?

3. What does *CSG* stand for?

4. Which *Boolean operation* keeps only the volume common to the two solid objects?

5. What is the main difference between an *EXTRUDED CUT feature* and a *HOLE feature* in SolidWorks?

6. Using the CSG concepts, create *Binary Tree* sketches showing the steps you plan to use to create the two models shown on the next page:

Ex.1)

Ex.2)

Exercises: (All dimensions are in inches)

1.

2.

3.

4.

5.

Chapter 4
Geometric Constructions

- 30°
- 45°
- 2X∅1.0
- R6.0
- R1.25 TYP.
- .75 TYP.
- R2.5
- Rounds & fillets: R.5
- ∅1.25

Learning Objectives

- ♦ **Understand the Classic Geometric Construction Tools and Methods**
- ♦ **Create Geometric Relations**
- ♦ **Use Dimensional Variables**
- ♦ **Display, Add, and Delete Geometric Relations**
- ♦ **Understand and Apply Different Geometric Relations**
- ♦ **Display and Modify Parametric Relations**
- ♦ **Create Fully Defined Sketches**

Certified SolidWorks Associate Examination Objectives Coverage

Sketch Relations

Objectives: Using Geometric Relations.

Dimensions

Objectives: Applying and Editing Smart Dimensions.

Geometric Constructions

The creation of designs usually involves the manipulations of geometric shapes. Traditionally, manual graphical construction uses simple hand tools like the T-square, straightedge, scales, triangles, compass, dividers, pencils, and paper. The manual drafting tools are designed specifically to assist the construction of geometric shapes. For example, a T-square and drafting machine can be used to construct parallel and perpendicular lines very easily and quickly. Today, modern CAD systems provide designers much better control and accuracy in the construction of geometric shapes.

In technical drawings, many of the geometric shapes are constructed with specific geometric properties, such as perpendicularity, parallelism and tangency. For example, in the below drawing, quite a few **implied** geometric properties are present.

Geometric Constructions – Classical Methods

Geometric constructions are done by applying geometric rules to graphics entities. Knowledge of the principles of geometric construction and its applications are essential to Designers, Engineers and CAD users.

For 2D drawings, it is crucial to be able to construct geometric entities at specified angles to each other, various plane figures, and other graphic representations. In this section, we will examine both the traditional graphical methods and the CAD methods of the basic geometric constructions commonly used in engineering graphics. This chapter provides information that will aid you in drawing different types of geometric constructions.

- ## Bisection of a Line or Arc

    1. Given a line or an arc AB.

    2. From A and B draw two equal arcs with a radius that is greater than one half of line AB.

    3. Construct a line by connecting the intersection points, D and E, with a straight line to locate the midpoint of line AB.

  ❖ Note that the constructed bisecting line DE is also perpendicular to the given line AB at the midpoint C.

- **Bisection of an Angle**

    1. Given an angle ABC.

    2. From A draw an arc with an arbitrary radius.

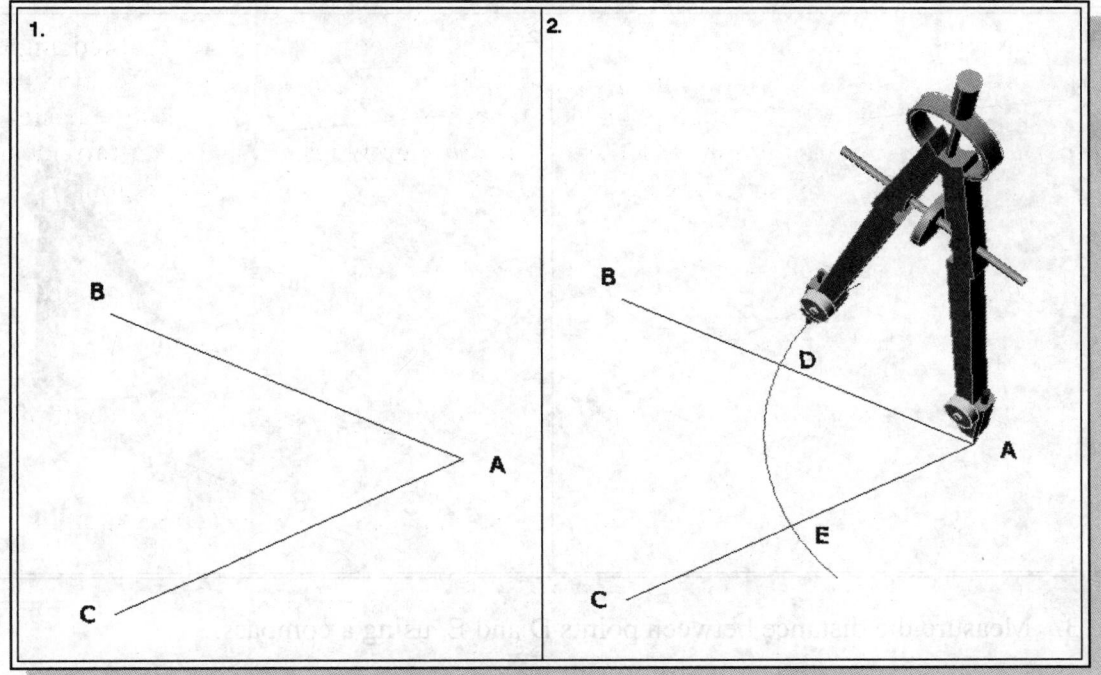

    3. Construct two equal radius arcs at D and E.

    4. Construct a straight line by connecting point A to the intersection of the two arcs.

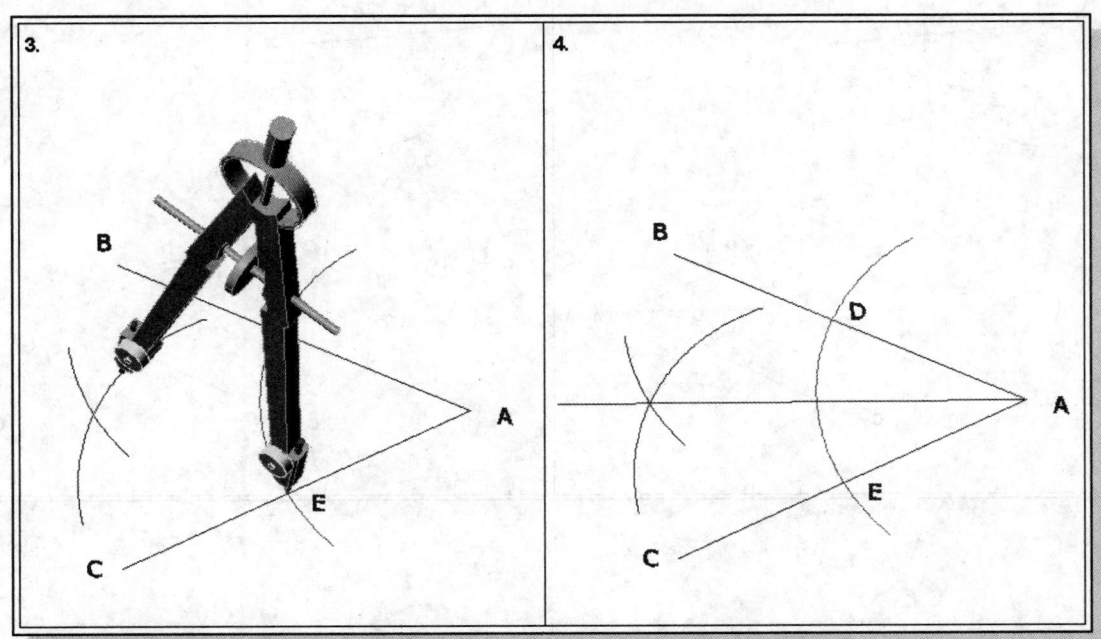

- **Transfer of an Angle**

  1. Given an angle ABC, transfer the angle to line XY.

  2. Create two arcs, at A and X, with an arbitrary radius R.

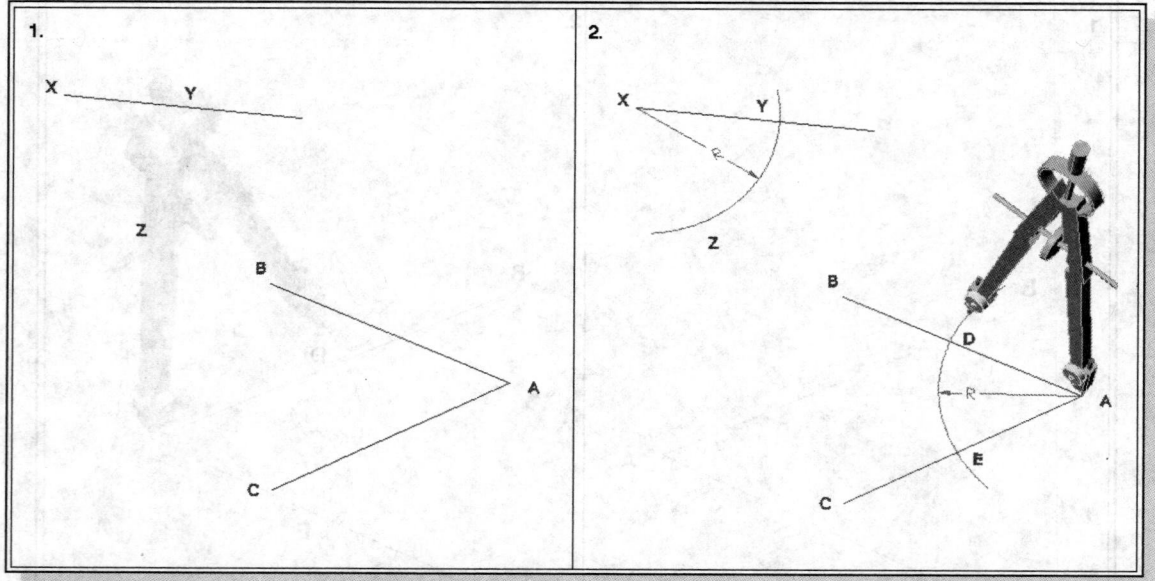

  3. Measure the distance between points D and E, using a compass.

  4. Construct an arc at Y, using the distance measured in the previous step.

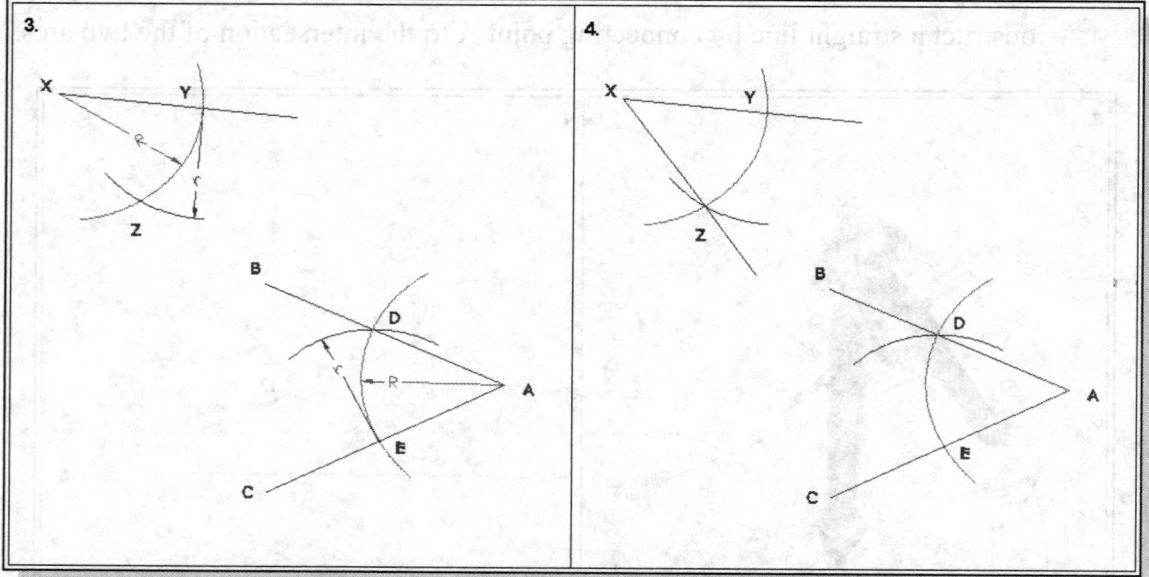

- **Dividing a Given Line into a Number of Equal Parts**

   1. Given a line AB; the line is to be divided into five equal parts.

   2. Construct another line at an arbitrary angle. Measure and mark five units along the line.

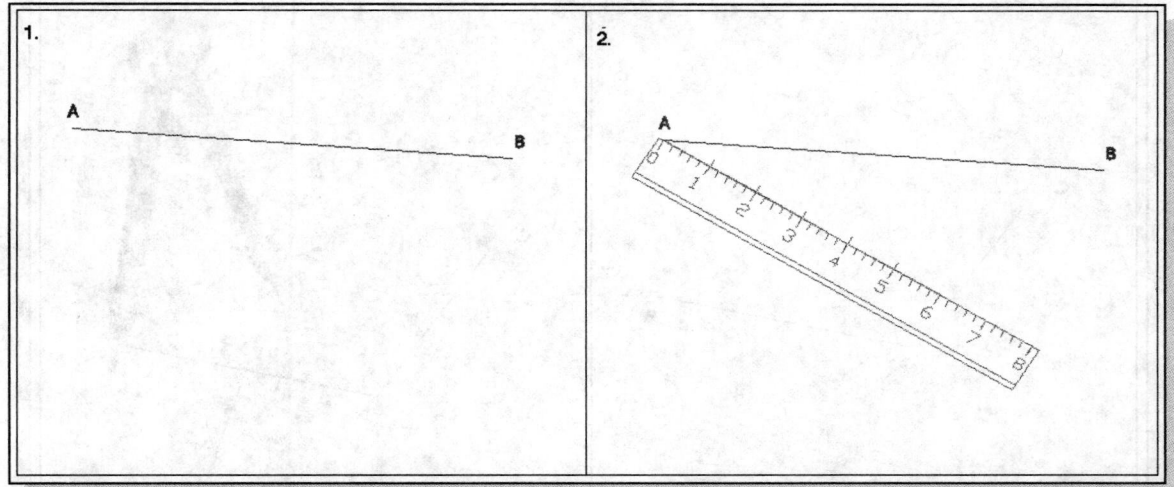

   3. Construct a line connecting the fifth mark to point B.

   4. Create four lines parallel to the constructed line through the marks.

- ## Circle through Three Points

  1. Given three points A, B and C.

  2. Construct a bisecting line through line AB.

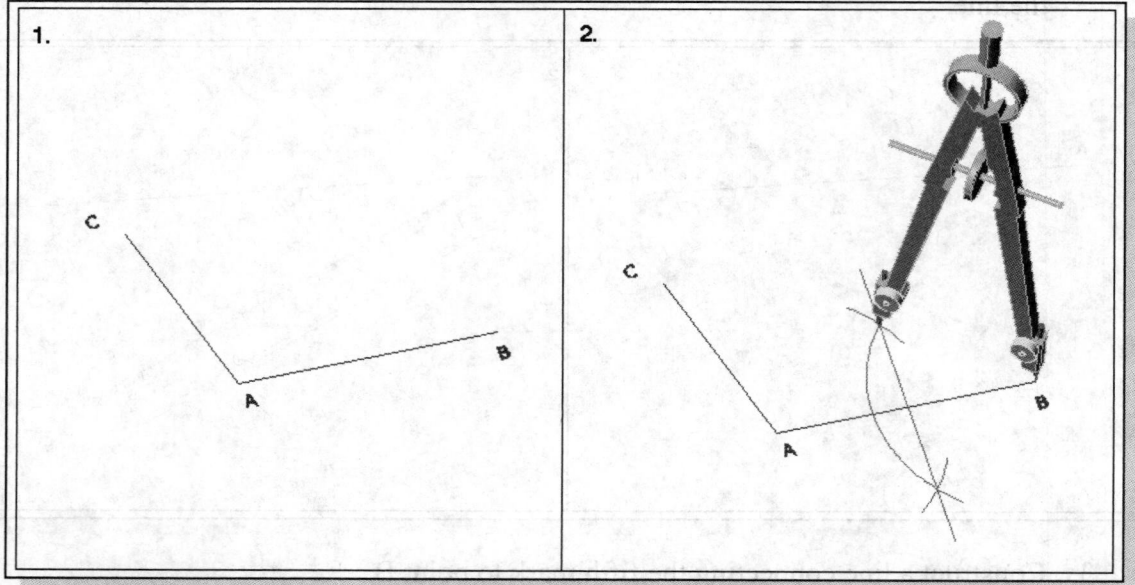

  3. Construct a second bisecting line through line AC. The two bisecting lines intersect at point D.

  4. Create the circle at point D, using DA, DB or DC as the radius.

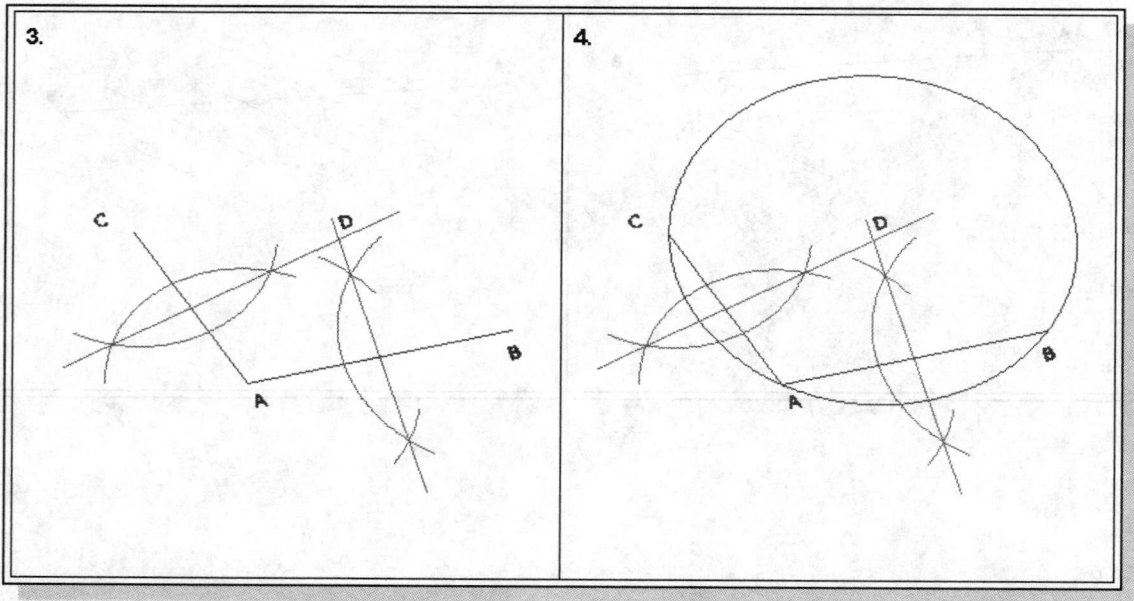

- **A Line Tangent to a Circle**

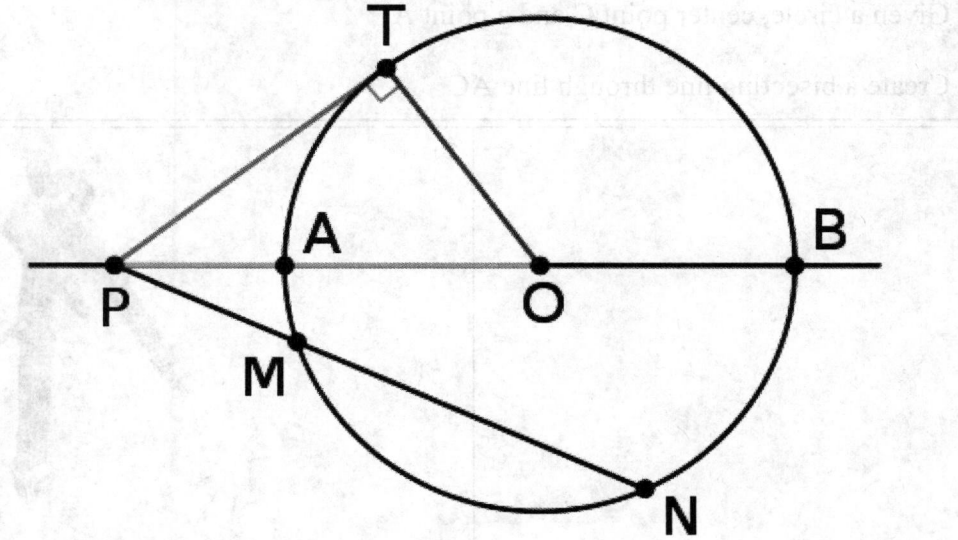

A line tangent to a circle intersects the circle at a single point. For comparison, secant lines intersect a circle at two points, whereas another line may not intersect a circle at all. In machine design, a smooth transition from surface to surface is typically desired, both for esthetic and functionality considerations. Tangency is therefore a common implied geometric property in Mechanical and Manufacturing Engineering practices.

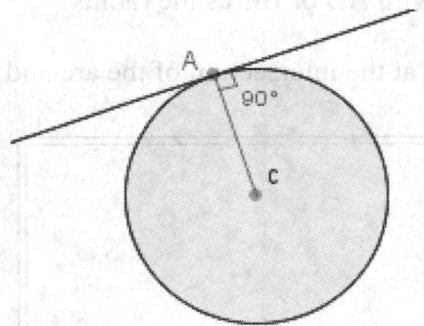

One unique property exists for the tangency between a line and a circle: *The radius of a circle is perpendicular to the tangent line through its endpoint on the circle's circumference.* Conversely, the perpendicular to a radius through the same endpoint is a tangent line.

Note that tangency can also be established in between curves.

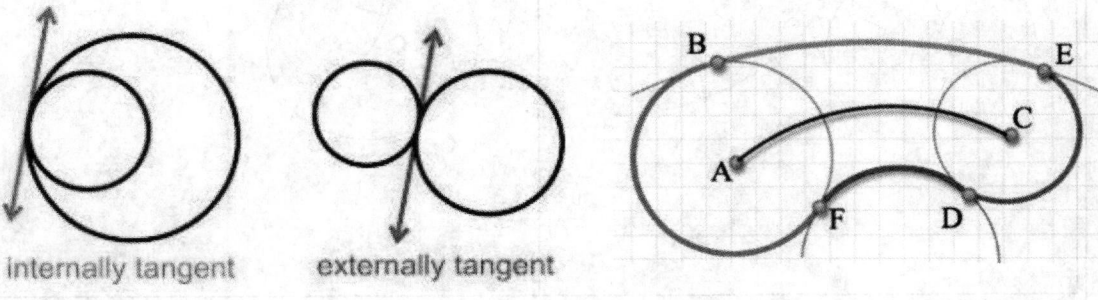

internally tangent   externally tangent

- ## Line Tangent to a Circle from a Given Point

  1. Given a circle, center point C and a point A.

  2. Create a bisecting line through line AC.

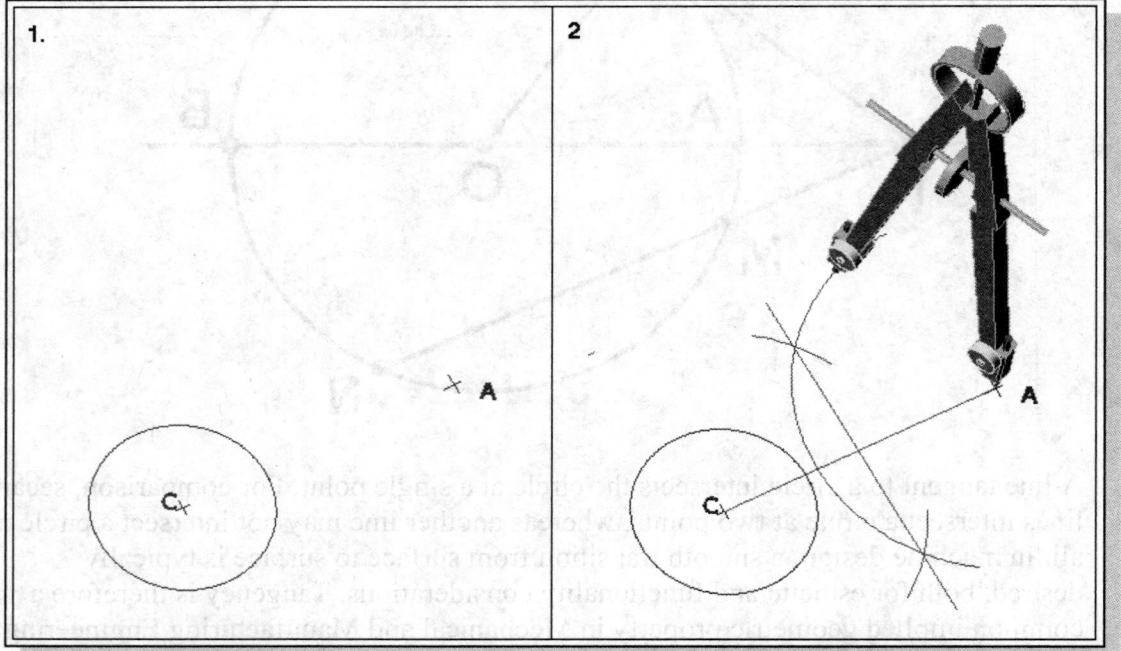

  3. Create an arc at point B (midpoint on line AC), with AB or BC as the radius.

  4. Construct the tangent line by connecting point A at the intersection of the arc and the circle.

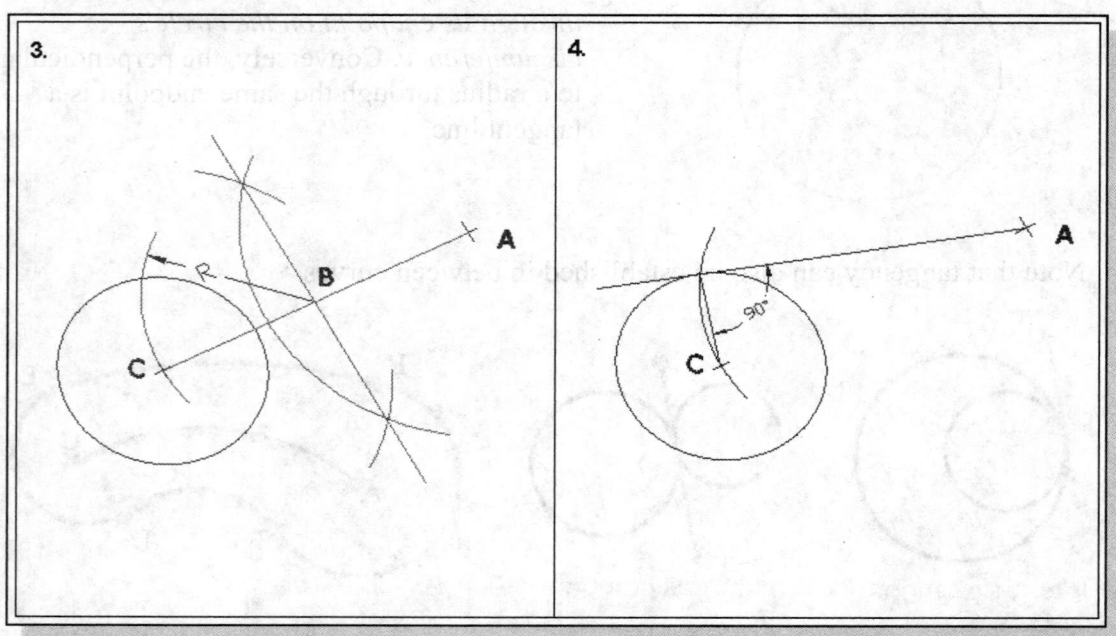

- ## Circle of a Given Radius Tangent to Two Given Lines

    1. Given two lines and a given radius R.

    2. Create a parallel line by creating two arcs of radius R, and draw a line tangent to the two arcs.

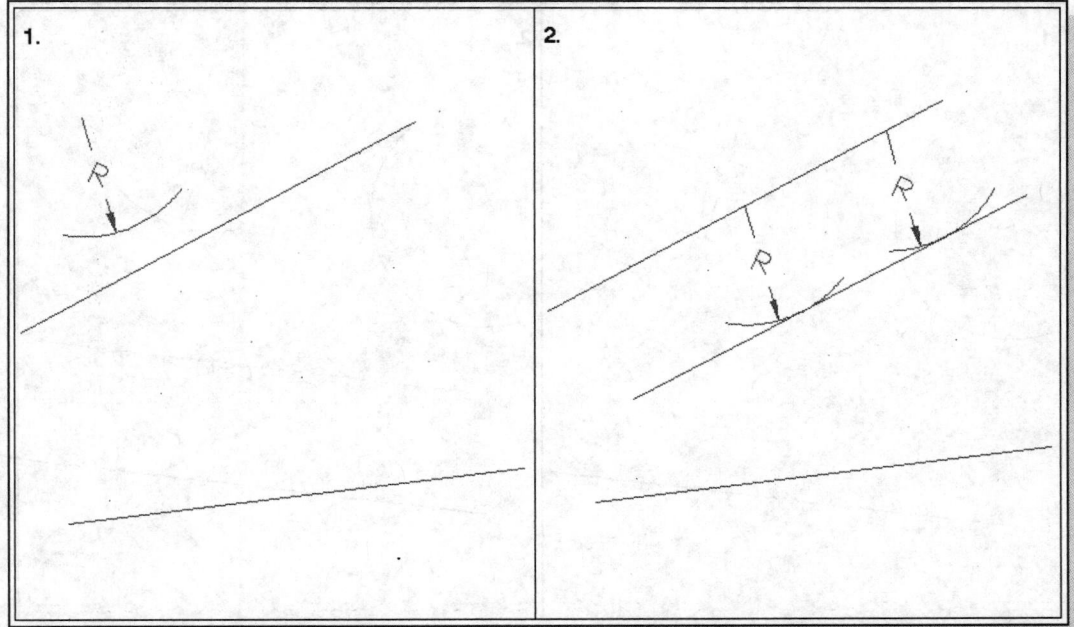

    3. Create another line parallel to the bottom edge by first drawing two arcs.

    4. Construct the required circle at the intersection of the two lines using the given radius R.

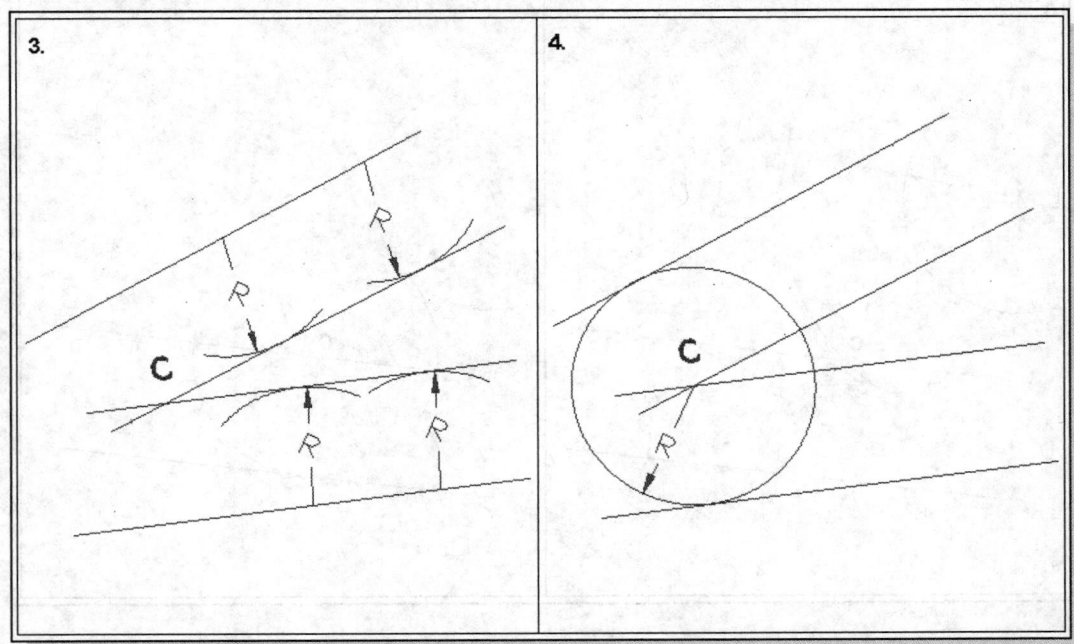

- ## Circle of a Given Radius Tangent to an Arc and a Line

    1. Given a radius R, a line and an arc.

    2. Create a parallel line by creating two arcs of radius R, and draw a line tangent to the two arcs.

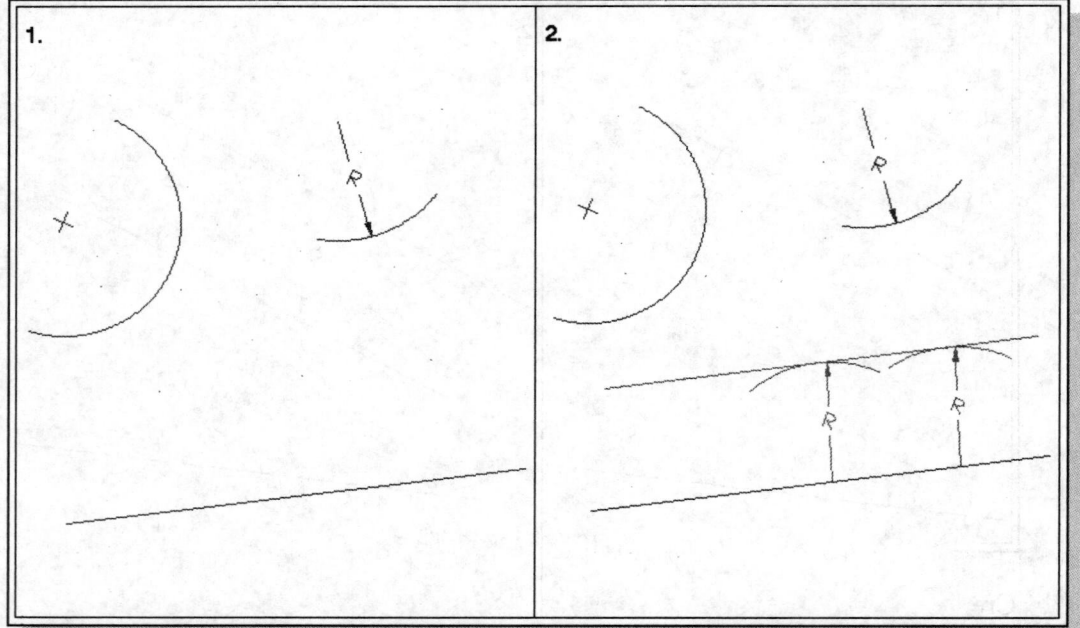

    3. Create a concentric arc at the center of the given arc, using a radius that is r+R.

    4. Create the desired circle at the intersection using the given radius R.

• Circle of a Given Radius Tangent to Two Arcs

1. Given a radius R and two arcs.

2. Create a concentric arc at the center of the small arc, using a radius that is R distance more than the original radius.

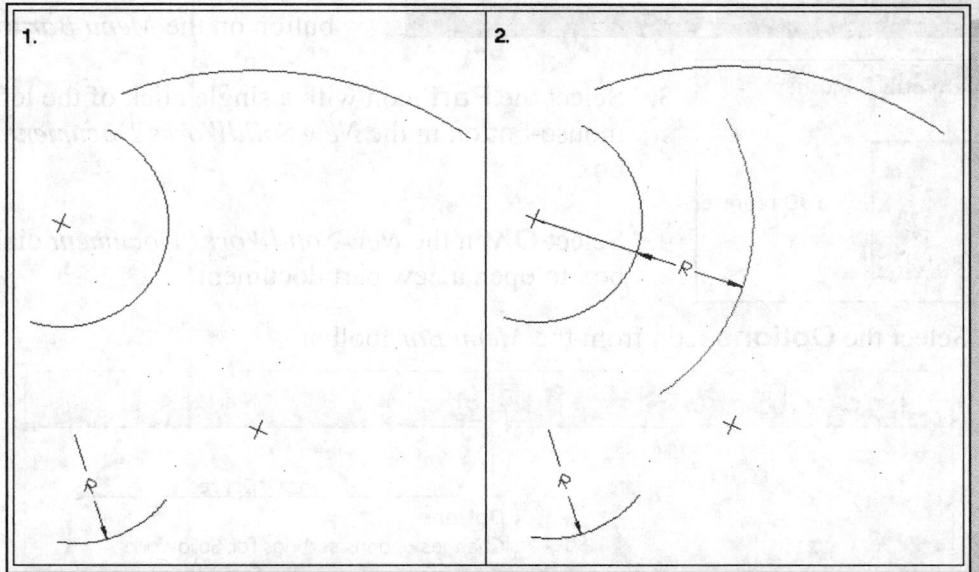

3. Create another concentric arc at the center of the large arc, using a radius that is R distance smaller than the original radius.

4. Create the desired circle at the intersection using the given radius R.

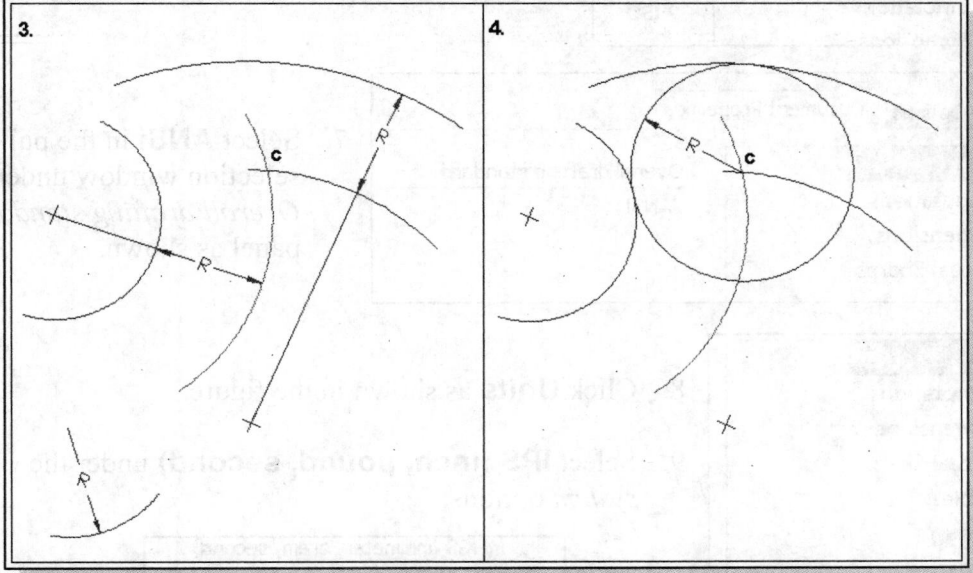

Starting SolidWorks

1. Select the **SolidWorks** option on the *Start* menu, or select the **SolidWorks** icon on the desktop to start SolidWorks. The SolidWorks main window will appear.

2. Select the **New** icon with a single click of the left-mouse-button on the *Menu Bar* toolbar.

3. Select the **Part** icon with a single click of the left-mouse-button in the *New SolidWorks Document* dialog box.

4. Select **OK** in the *New SolidWorks Document* dialog box to open a new part document.

5. Select the **Options** icon from the *Menu Bar* toolbar.

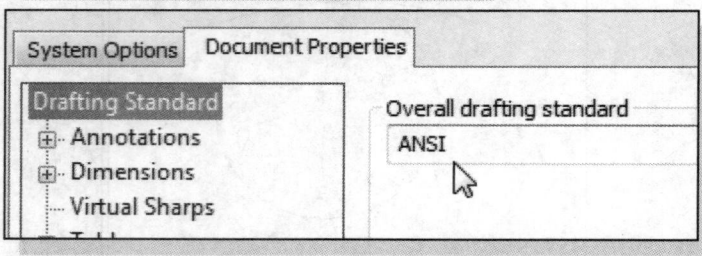

6. Select the **Document Properties** tab and the **Drafting Standard** option at the left of the *Document Properties* panel.

7. Select **ANSI** in the pull-down selection window under the *Overall drafting standard* panel as shown.

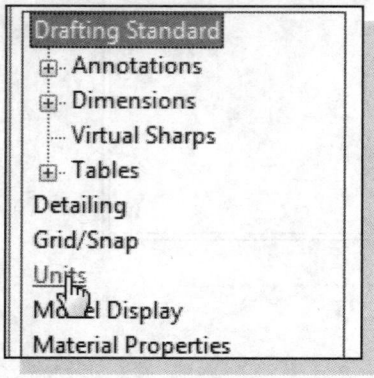

8. Click **Units** as shown in the figure.

9. Select **IPS (inch, pound, second)** under the *Unit system* options.

10. Click OK to accept the settings and exit the options dialog box.

11. Select the **Sketch** tab on the *CommandManager* to display the *Sketch* toolbar.

12. Select the **Sketch** button on the *Sketch* toolbar to create a new sketch.

13. Move the cursor over the edge of the **Front Plane** in the graphics area. When the **Top Plane** is highlighted, click once with the **left-mouse-button** to select the plane as the sketch plane for the new sketch.

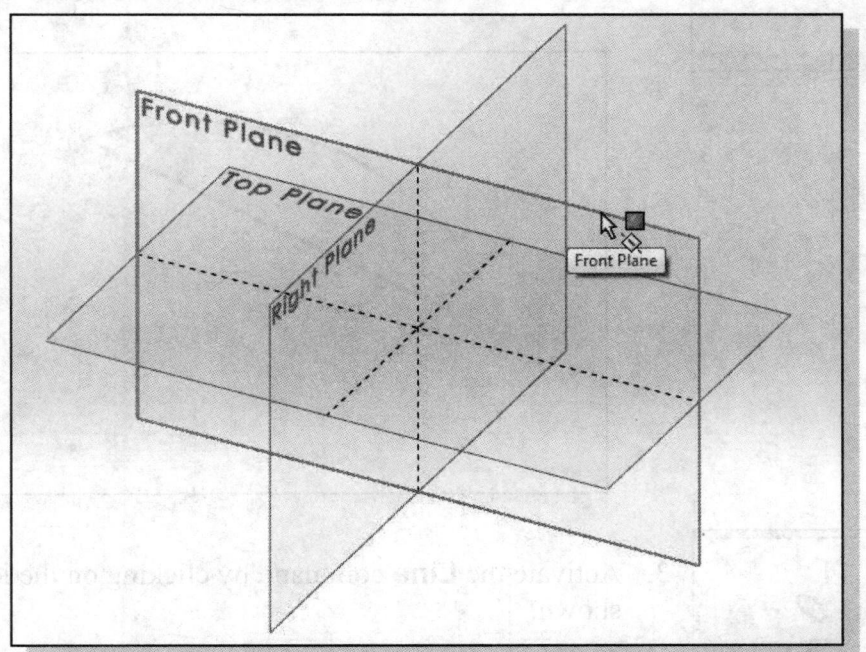

Geometric Construction – CAD Method

The main characteristic of any CAD system is its ability to create and modify 2D/3D geometric entities quickly and accurately. Most CAD systems provide a variety of object construction and editing tools to relieve the designer of the tedious drudgery of this task, so that the designer can concentrate more on design content. A good understanding of the computer geometric construction techniques will enable the CAD users to fully utilize the capability of the CAD systems.

➢ Note that with CAD systems, besides following the classic geometric construction methods; quite a few options are also feasible. In the following sections, additional SolidWorks' sketching/editing tools will be used to illustrate some of the classical geometric construction methods.

• Bisection of a Line or Arc

1. Use the **3 Point Arc** command and create an arbitrary arc at any angle on the screen.

2. Using the **Line** command, create a line connecting the two endpoints of the arc.

3. Activate the **Line** command by clicking on the icon as shown.

4. Move the cursor along the arc and notice a red maker appeared on the arc indicating the midpoint. Click once with the **left mouse button** to attach the first endpoint of the line at this location.

5. Move the cursor along the line and notice a red maker appeared on the arc indicating the midpoint. Click once with the **left mouse button** to attach the first endpoint of the line at this location

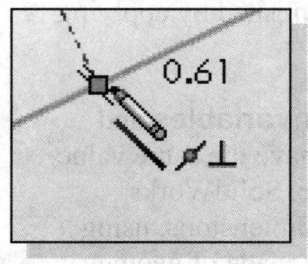

> Note the two small symbols next to the cursor show the geometric properties at the current location. In this case, the new line will be **perpendicular** to the existing line and the endpoint is also aligned to the **midpoint** of the existing line.

> The constructed bisecting line is perpendicular to the line and passes through the midpoints of both the line and arc.

DIMENSIONS and RELATIONS

A primary and essential difference between parametric modeling and previous generation computer modeling is that parametric modeling captures the *design intent*. In the previous lessons, we have seen that the design philosophy of *"shape before size"* is implemented through the use of SolidWorks' **Smart Dimension** commands. In performing geometric constructions, dimensional values are necessary to describe the **SIZE** and **LOCATION** of constructed geometric entities. Besides using dimensions to define the geometry, we can also apply geometric rules to control geometric entities. More importantly, SolidWorks can capture design intent through the use of **geometric relations**, **dimensional constraints** and **parametric relations**.

Geometric relations are geometric restrictions that can be applied to geometric entities; for example, *horizontal*, *parallel*, *perpendicular*, and *tangent* are commonly used *geometric relations* in parametric modeling. For part modeling in SolidWorks, relations are applied to *2D sketches*. They can be added automatically as the sketch is created or by using the **Add Relation** command.

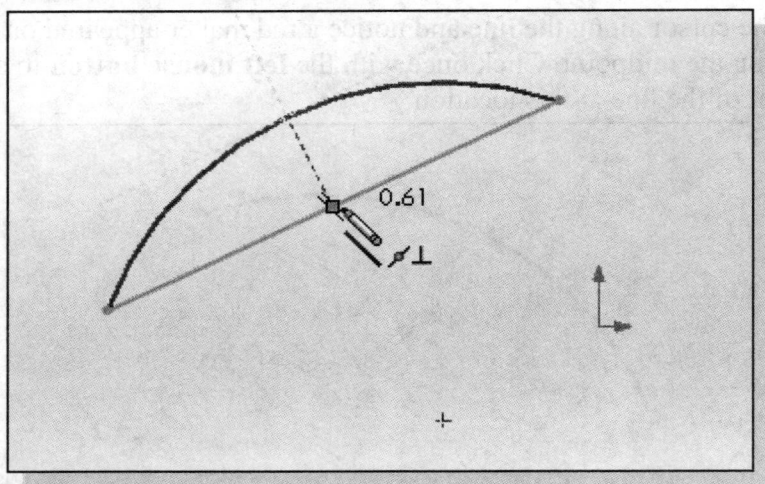

Dimensional constraints are used to describe the SIZE and LOCATION of individual geometric shapes. They are added using the SolidWorks **Smart Dimension** command. One should also realize that depending upon the way the geometric relations and dimensional constraints are applied, the same results can be accomplished by applying different constraints to the geometric entities.

In SolidWorks, **parametric relations** can be applied using **Global Variables** and **Equations**. Global variables are used when multiple dimensions have the same value. The dimension value is applied through the use of a named variable. SolidWorks Equations are user-defined mathematical relations between model dimensions, using dimension names as variables. In parametric modeling, features are made of geometric entities with dimensional, geometric, and parametric constraints describing individual design intent. In this lesson, we will discuss the fundamentals of geometric relations and equations.

Geometric Symbols available in parametric sketching

- SolidWorks geometric relations for 2D sketches are summarized below.

Icon	Relation	Entities Selected	Effect
⊥	Perpendicular	Two lines	Causes selected lines to lie at right angles to one another.
∖∖	Parallel	Two or more lines	Causes selected lines to lie parallel to one another.
∂	Tangent	An arc, spline, or ellipse and a line or arc	Constrains two curves to be tangent to one another.
⦦	Coincident	A point and a line, arc, or ellipse	Constrains a point to a curve.
╱	Midpoint	Two lines or a point and a line	Causes a point to remain at the midpoint of a line or an arc.
◎	Concentric	Two or more arcs, or a point and an arc	Constrains selected items to the same center point.
╱	Colinear	Two or more lines	Causes selected lines to lie along the same line.
—	Horizontal	One or more lines or two or more points	Causes selected items to lie parallel to the X-axis of the sketch coordinate system.
│	Vertical	One or more lines or two or more points	Causes selected items to lie parallel to the Y-axis of the sketch coordinate system.
=	Equal	Two or more lines or two or more arcs	Constrains selected arcs/circles to the same radius or selected lines to the same length.
⊠	Fix	Any entity	Constrains selected entities to a fixed location relative to the sketch coordinate system. However, endpoints of a fixed line, arc, or elliptical segment are free to move along the underlying fixed curve.
⊡	Symmetric	A centerline and two points, lines, arcs or ellipses	Causes items to remain equidistant from the centerline, on a line perpendicular to the centerline.
◌	Coradial	Two or more arcs	Causes the selected arcs to share the same centerpoint and radius.
⊠	Intersection	Two lines and one point	Causes the point to remain at the intersection of the two lines.
◿	Merge Points	Two points (sketchpoints or endpoints)	Causes the two points to be merged into a single point.

- ## Bisection of an Angle

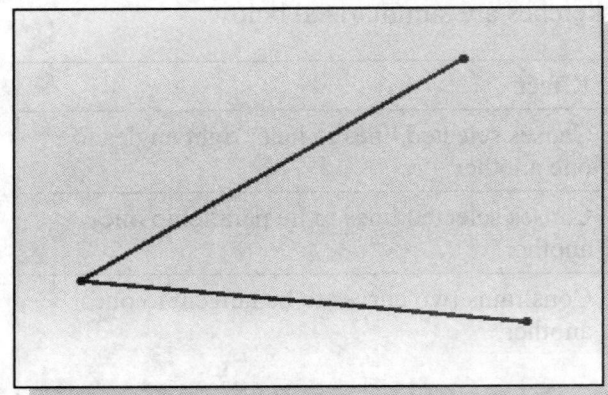

1. Using the **Line** command, create an arbitrary angle as shown in the figure.

2. Activate the **Centerpoint Arc** command by clicking on the icon as shown.

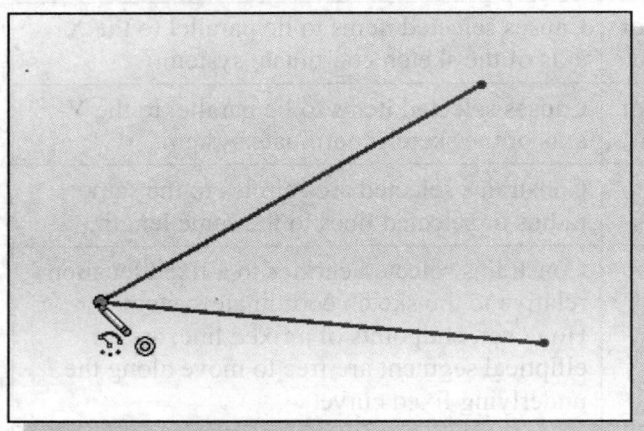

3. Create the arc by first selecting the vertex point of the angle as the center of the new arc.

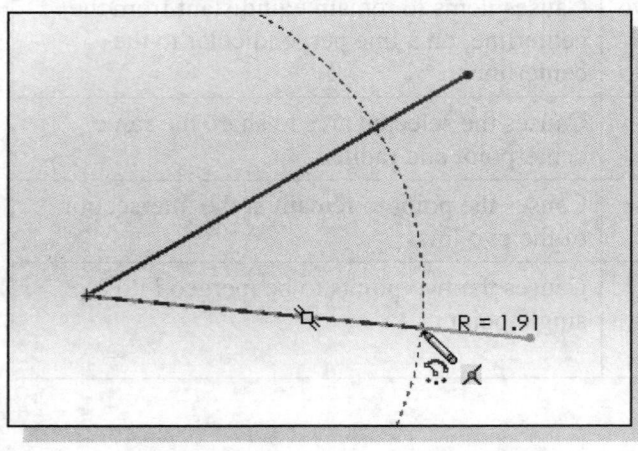

4. Move the cursor along the bottom leg of the angle and place the first endpoint on the line as shown. Confirm the other end of the arc intersects with the other leg as shown.

   ➢ Which geometric property is identified by SolidWorks?

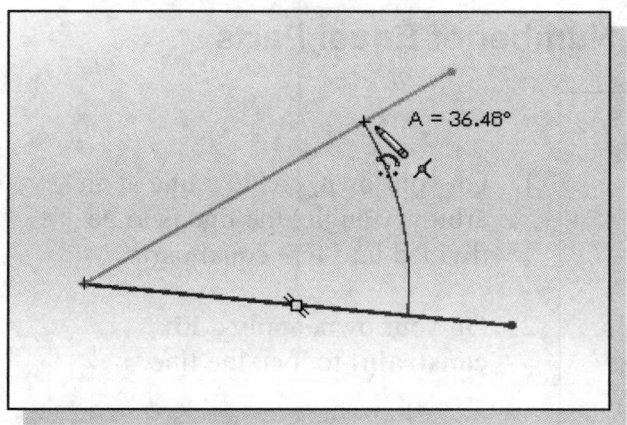

5. Place the other endpoints of the arc on the other leg as shown.

6. Activate the **Line** command by clicking on the icon as shown.

7. Create a bisecting line of the angle as shown.

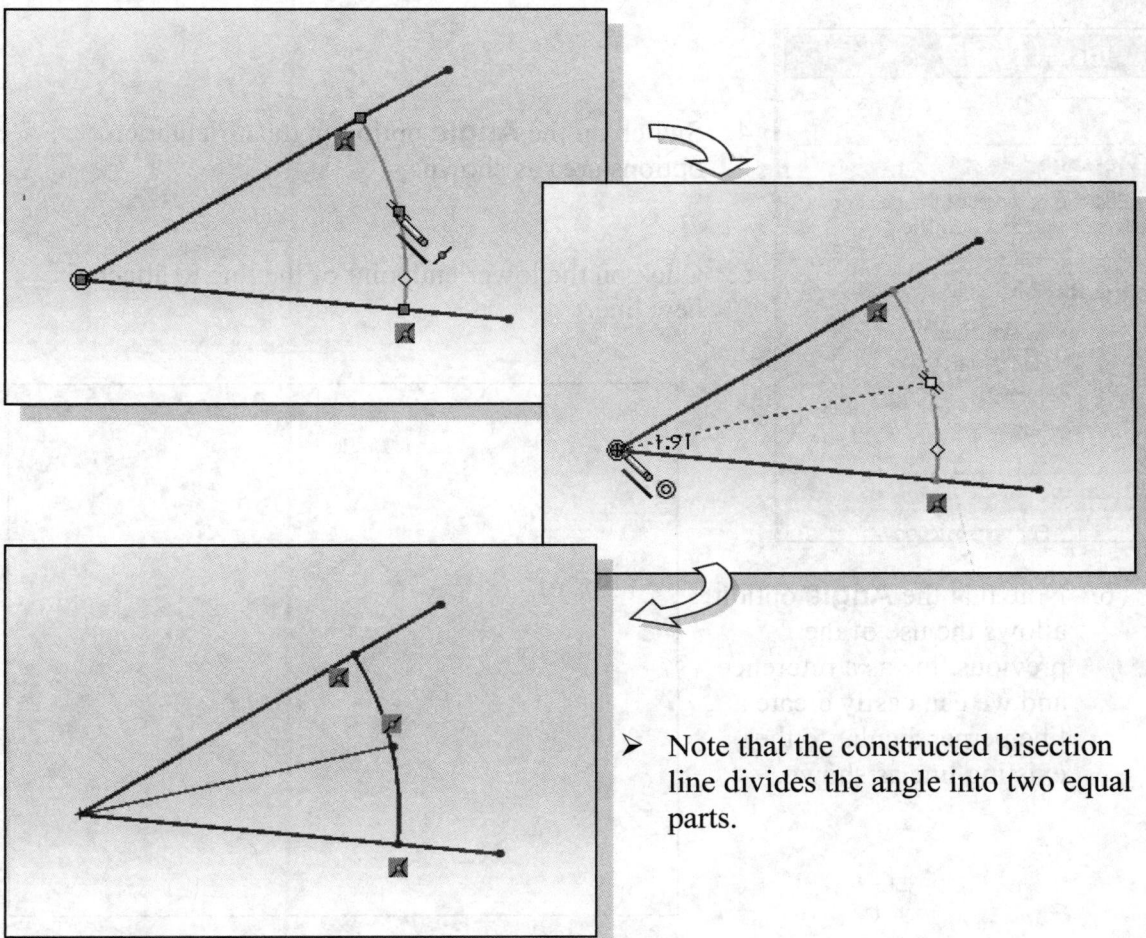

➤ Note that the constructed bisection line divides the angle into two equal parts.

• Dividing a Given Line into a Number of Equal Parts

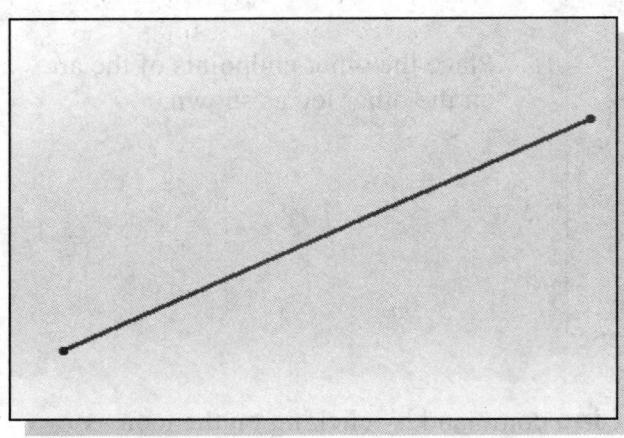

1. On your own, create a line at an arbitrary angle; the line is to be divided into five equal parts.

2. On your own, apply a **Fix constraint** to lock the line.

3. Activate the **Line** command by clicking on the icon as shown.

4. Switch on the **Angle** option in the Orientation options area as shown.

5. Click on the lower endpoint of the line to attach the new line.

6. Note that the **Angle** option allows the use of the previous line as a reference and we can easily create a line perpendicular to the existing line as shown.

7. On your own, create four additional short line segments at arbitrary angles toward the right side of the previous line as shown. Note the first line segment on the right is a vertical line as the *vertical symbol* is displayed next to the line.

8. Select **View Sketch Relations** in the *View* toolbar as shown.

    ➤ Note the icon acts as a toggle switch, each click turns on or off the selected option.

9. On your own, experiment with the available visibility controls. Turn **On** the *View Sketch Relations* before proceeding to the next step.

10. **Right-mouse-click** once to bring up the option list. Scroll down in the list and select **Delete** as shown.

    ➤ Note that any of the applied geometric relations can be deleted.

11. Select **Add Relation** in the *Sketch* toolbar as shown.

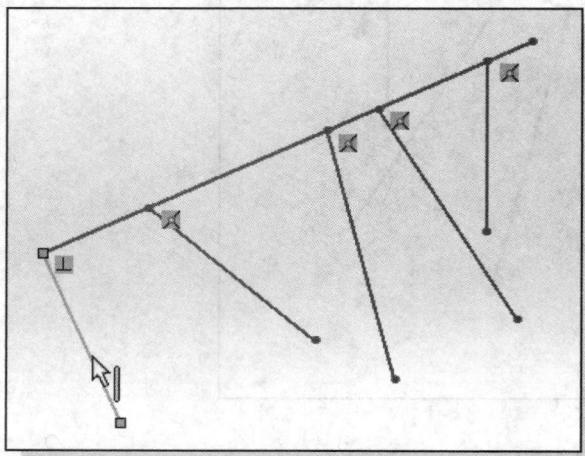

12. Select the first short line segment, the one with the perpendicular constraint, as shown.

- In the *Add Relations Manager*, three panels are available: **Selected Entities**, **Existing Relations** and **Add Relations**. For the selected line, one perpendicular relation is applied, and we can also add *Horizontal*, *Vertical* and *Fix* relation to it.

13. Select the line next to the previously selected line.

➤ The selected entities are identified in the Add Relations panel as shown.

14. In the *Add Relations* panel, additional relations can be applied to the two selected lines. Click on the **Parallel** icon to add the relation to the selected lines as shown.

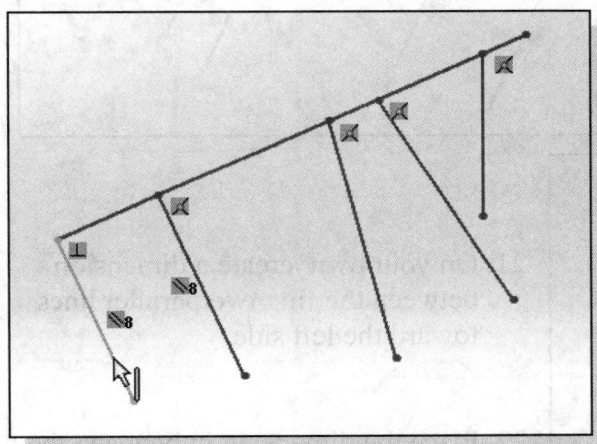

15. On your own, select the first short line segment and the other three non-parallel segments.

16. In the *Add Relations* panel, click on the **Parallel** icon to add the relation to the selected lines as shown.

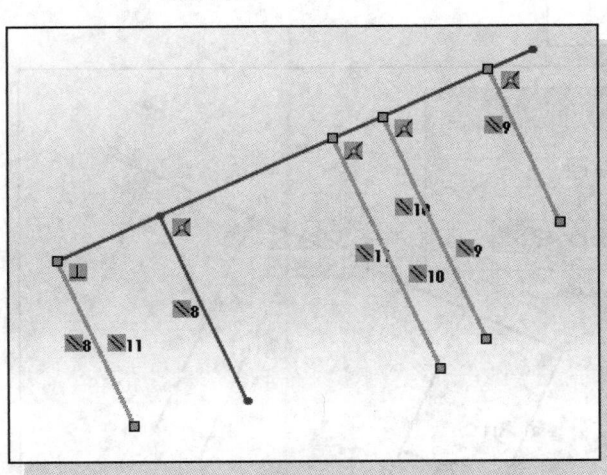

• In SolidWorks, geometric relations can be applied to multiple selected entities.

17. Select the **Smart Dimension** command by clicking once with the **left-mouse-button** on the icon in the *Sketch* toolbar.

18. Select the top line, the line to be divided, by left-clicking once on the line

19. Place the dimension above the line as shown.

20. Click **OK** in the *Modify* dialog box to accept the default dimension. Note that the dimension on your screen may look different than what is shown in the figure.

21. On your own, create a dimension between the first two parallel lines toward the left side.

22. Place the dimension in between the two lines as shown.

23. In the modify dialog box, enter the equal sign (**=**), and click on the top dimension as shown.

24. Enter **/5** (divided by 5) to create a parametric equation as shown.

25. Click **OK** to accept the entered equation as shown.

- Notice, the derived dimension value is displayed with **Σ** in front of the numbers.

26. On your own, repeat the above steps and create the other three parametric relations as shown.

27. Move the cursor over the *SolidWorks* icon on the *Menu Bar* to reveal the pull-down menus, click once with the left-mouse-button on the **Tools** icon and select **Equations** in the pull-down menu as shown.

- The *Equations, Global Variables, and Dimensions* dialog box is displayed. Notice the equation we created appears in the table under '**Equations**'.

- The *Equations, Global Variables, and Dimensions* dialog box can be used to perform all tasks related to equations, including editing existing equations, and creating additional design variables and equations. We will use it here to show an alternate method to add/edit an equation.

28. Click inside the last equation block and change the last equation to **/4** as shown.

29. Click **OK** to accept the settings and close the *Equations* dialog box.

- Notice the dimension has not been updated yet.

30. Double-click on the last dimension, and click on the **Regenerate** button to update the equation.

31. On your own, change the equation back to **/5** and also adjust the top dimension to **3.5** to see the effect.

• Circle through Three Points

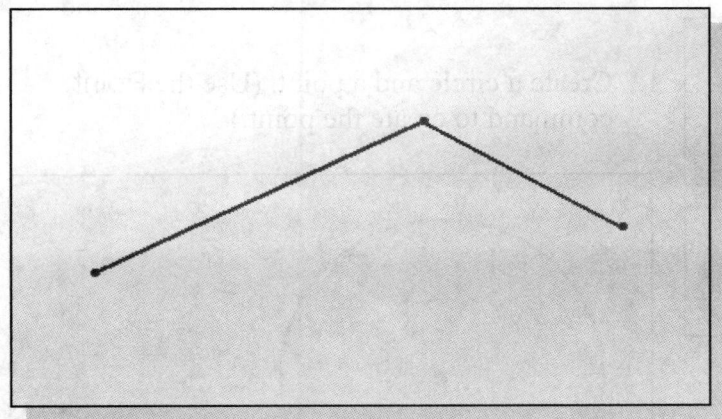

1. Create two arbitrary connected line segments as shown.

2. Select the **Perimeter Circle** command in the *Sketch* toolbar as shown. Note that the order of selecting the three points does not matter for this Circle command.

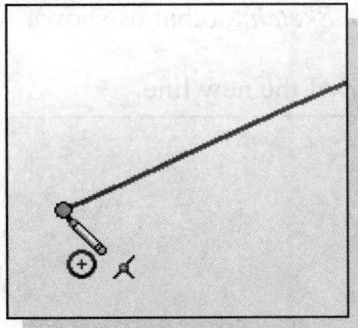

3. Select the **left endpoint** of the left line segment as shown.

4. Select the **right endpoint** of the right line segment as shown.

5. Select the point on top to create the circle that passes through all three points.

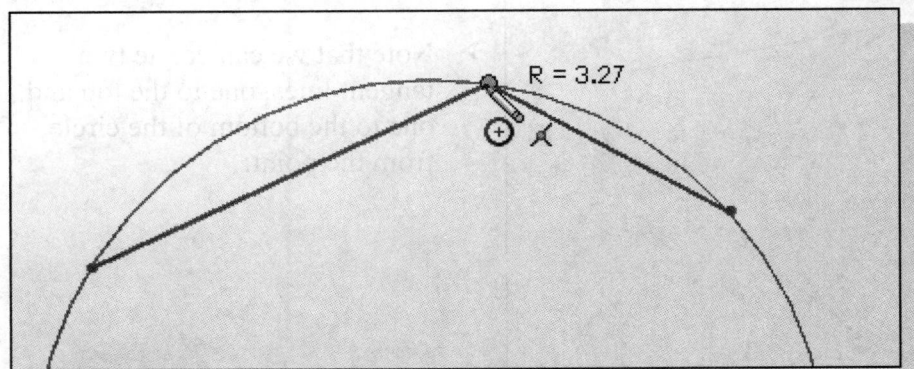

- ## Line Tangent to a Circle from a Given Point

1. Create a circle and a point. (Use the Point command to create the point.)

2. Activate the **Line** command in the *Sketch* toolbar as shown.

3. Select point **A** as the starting point of the new line.

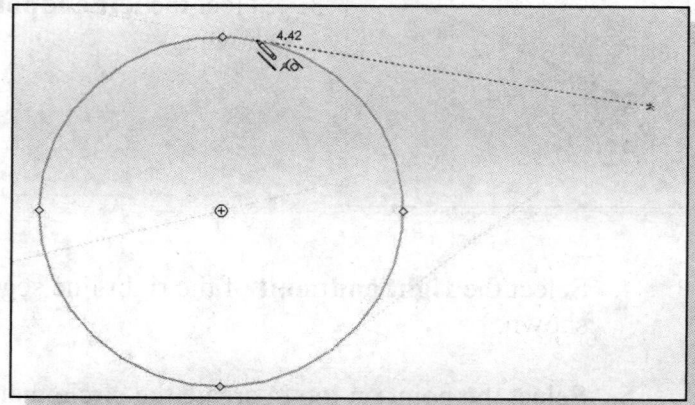

4. Move the cursor on top of the circle and notice the Tangent symbol is displayed.

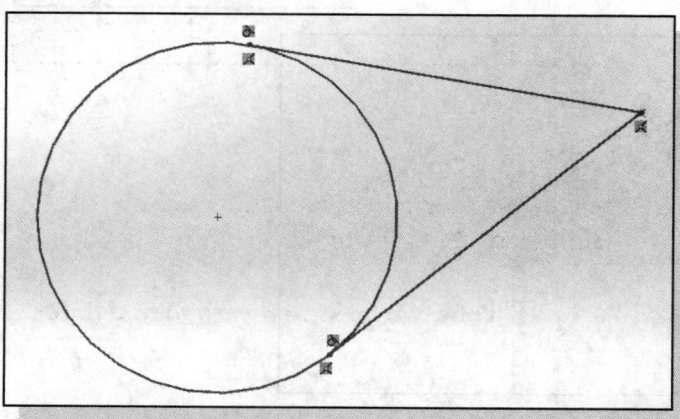

➢ Note that we can create two tangent lines, one to the top and one to the bottom of the circle, from the point.

• Circle of a Given Radius Tangent to two Given Lines

Option I: Using the Add Relations option

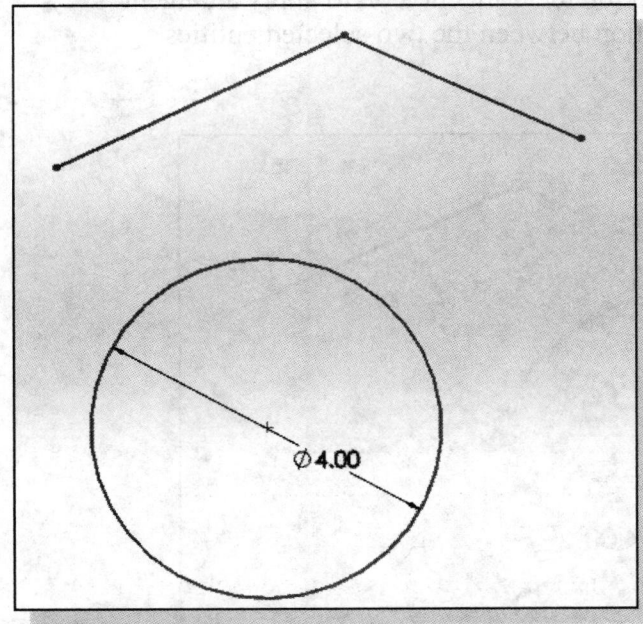

1. Create **two arbitrary line segments** as shown.

2. Create a **circle** below the two line segments as shown.

3. Use the **Smart Dimension** command and adjust the size of the circle to **4.00**.

4. Select **Add Relation** in the *Sketch* toolbar as shown.

5. Select the two line segments and apply a **Fix** relation.

6. Right-mouse-click once inside the Selected Entities panel to bring up the option list.

7. Select Clear Selections to deselect all entities.

8. Select one of the line segments and the circle.

9. Click on the Tangent icon to apply a tangent relation between the two selected entities.

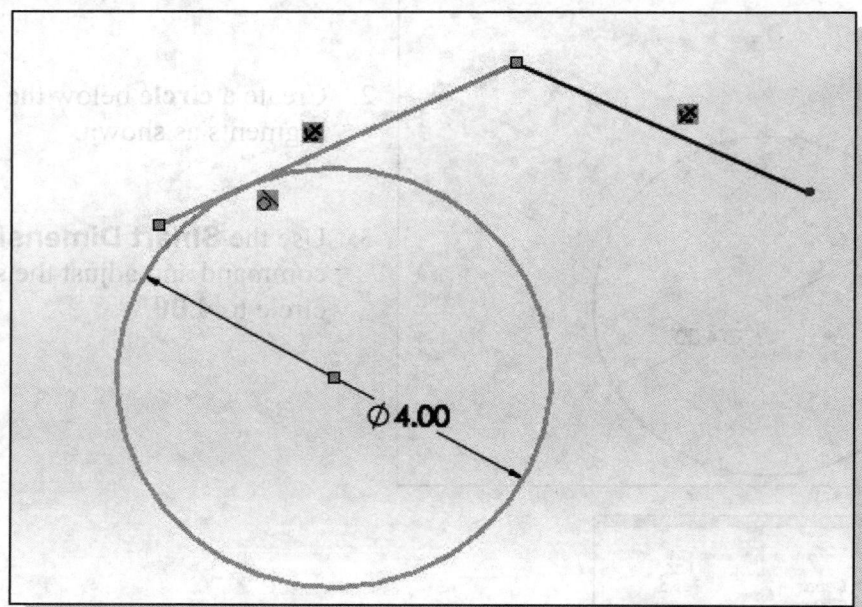

10. On your own, repeat the above steps and add another Tangent relation to complete the construction.

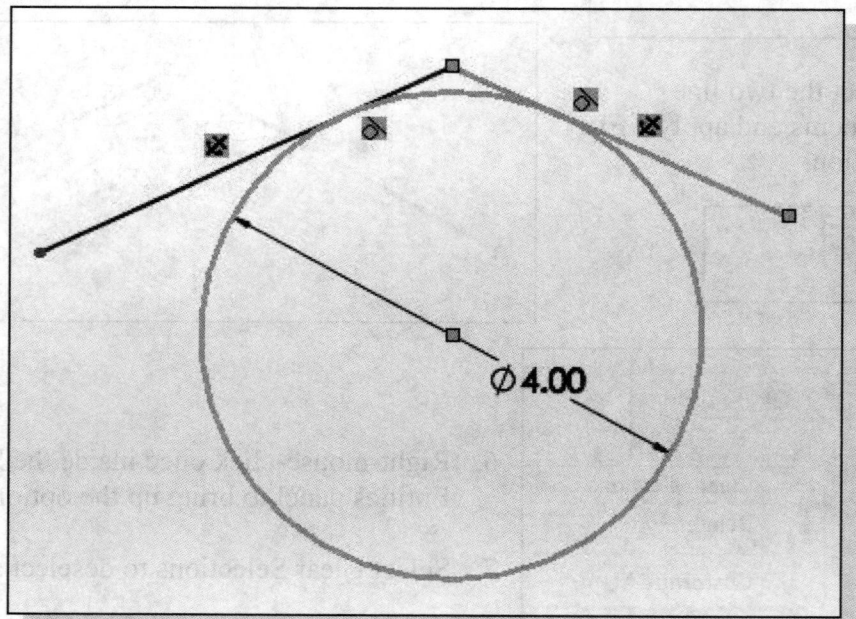

Option II: Fillet command

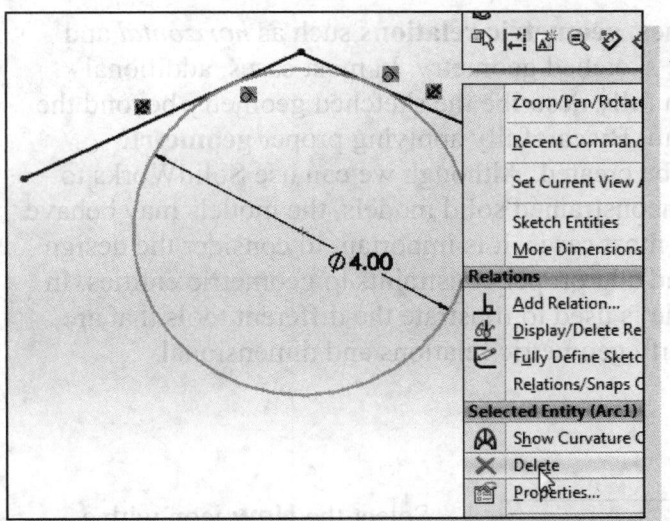

1. On your own, delete the circle by using the **Delete** option with the right-mouse-click option list as shown.

2. Select **Sketch Fillet** in the *Sketch* toolbar as shown.

3. Enter **2** as the new radius of the Fillet command.

4. Select one of the lines as the first object.

5. Select the other line as the second object.

➢ Note that the Fillet command automatically trims the edges as shown in the figure.

Adding Geometric Relations and Fully Defined Geometry

In SolidWorks, as we create 2D sketches, **geometric relations** such as *horizontal* and *parallel* are automatically added to the sketched geometry. In most cases, additional relations and dimensions are needed to fully describe the sketched geometry beyond the geometric relations added by the system. By carefully applying proper **geometric relations**, very intelligent models can be created. Although we can use SolidWorks to build partially constrained or totally unconstrained solid models, the models may behave unpredictably as changes are made. In most cases, it is important to consider the design intent, develop a modeling strategy, and add proper constraints to geometric entities. In the following sections, a simple triangle is used to illustrate the different tools that are available in SolidWorks to create/modify geometric relations and dimensional constraints.

Starting SolidWorks

1. Select the **New** icon with a single click of the left-mouse-button on the *Menu Bar* toolbar.

2. Select the **Part** icon with a single click of the left-mouse-button in the *New SolidWorks Document* dialog box.

3. Select **OK** in the *New SolidWorks Document* dialog box to open a new part document.

4. Select the **Extruded Boss/Base** button on the *Features* toolbar to create a new extruded feature.

5. Click once with the **left-mouse-button** on the Front Plane to use as the sketch plane for the new sketch.

6. Select the **Line** command by clicking once with the **left-mouse-button**.

7. Create a triangle of arbitrary size positioned near the center of the screen as shown below. (Note that the base of the triangle is horizontal.)

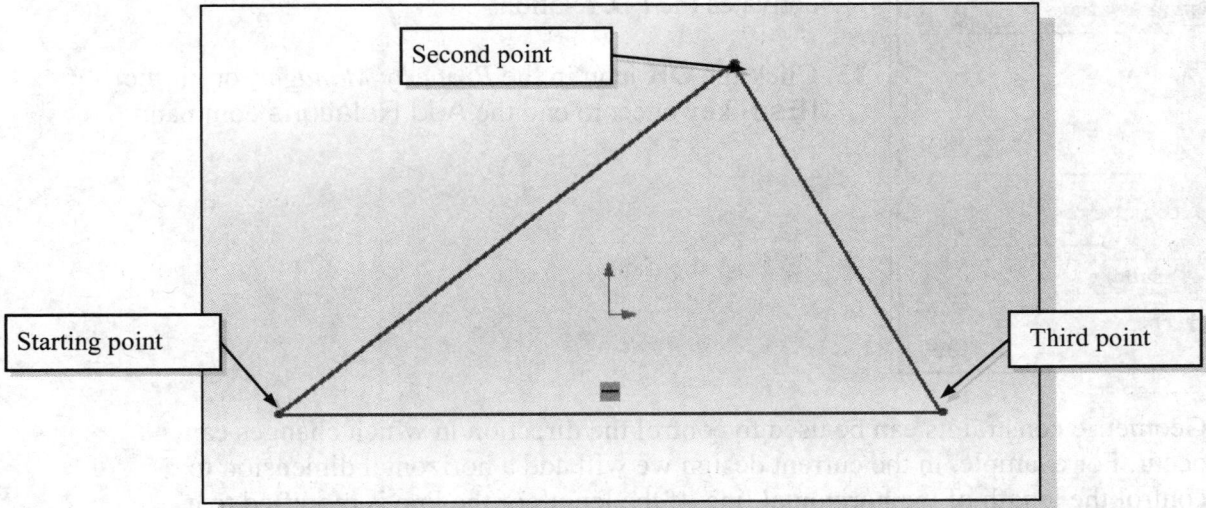

8. Press the **[Esc]** key to exit the Line command.

9. **Left click** on the arrow below the **Display/Delete Relations** button on the *Sketch* toolbar to reveal additional sketch relation commands.

10. Select the **Add Relation** command from the pop-up menu.

11. Select the lower right corner of the triangle by clicking once with the **left-mouse-button**.

➤ Look at the *Add Relations Property Manager*. In the *Selected Entities* window '**Point3**' is now displayed. No entries appear in the *Existing Relations* window. In the *Add Relations* menu, the **Fix** relation is displayed. This represents the only relation which can be added for the selected entity.

12. Click once with the left-mouse-button on the **Fix** icon in the *Add Relations Property Manager* as shown. This activates the **Fix** relation.

13. Click the **OK** icon in the *Property Manager*, or hit the [**Esc**] key once, to end the Add Relations command.

➤ Geometric constraints can be used to control the direction in which changes can occur. For example, in the current design we will add a horizontal dimension to control the length of the horizontal line. If the length of the line is modified to a greater value, SolidWorks will lengthen the line toward the left side. This is due to the fact that the Fix constraint will restrict any horizontal movement of the horizontal line toward the right side.

14. Select the horizontal line by clicking once with the **left-mouse-button**.

➤ Look at the *Line Properties Property Manager*. The **Horizontal** relation appears in the *Existing Relations* window. In the *Parameters* window, a value is displayed for the length. This is the current (as drawn) length of the line.

15. Enter **6.5** for the Length in the *Parameters* window as shown.

➢ Entering values in the *Parameters* panel of the *Property Manager* will set the length of the line to the entered value. However, it **will not define or constrain the length** to remain that value. We will demonstrate this next.

16. Move the cursor on top of the **lower left corner** of the triangle.

17. **Click and drag** the left corner of the triangle and note that the corner can be moved to a new location. Release the mouse button at a new location and notice the corner is adjusted only in the left or right direction.

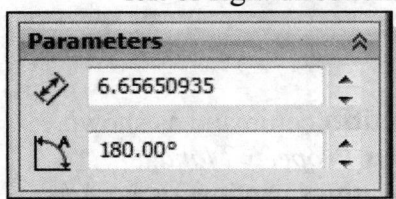

➢ Note that the two adjacent lines are automatically adjusted. On your own, confirm the Length entry in the *Parameter* window on the *Property Manager* has changed to reflect the new length.

➢ It is important to note the difference between entering a value in the *Parameters* window and the application of a constraining **Smart Dimension**. We will now add a Smart Dimension to define the length of the horizontal line.

18. Select the **Smart Dimension** command by clicking once with the **left-mouse-button** on the icon.

19. On your own, create the dimension as shown in the figure below.

20. Press the [**Esc**] key once to exit the Smart Dimension command.

21. On your own, try to drag the lower left corner of the triangle to a new location.

➢ Notice that you cannot drag the lower left corner to a new location. Its position is fully defined by the Fix relation, the Horizontal relation, and the Smart Dimension.

22. Double-click with the left-mouse-button on the dimension text in the graphics area to open the *Modify* dialog box.

23. Enter a value that is greater than the displayed value to observe the effects of the modification. (For example, the dimension value is 6.5; so enter **7** in the text box area.) Click the **OK** button in the *Modify* dialog box.

24. On your own, use the **Undo** command to reset the dimension value to the previous value.

25. Activate the **Add Relation** command as shown. Notice the *Add Relations Property Manager* appears. The *Selected Entities* window in the *Add Relations PropertyManager* is blank because no entities are selected.

26. Select the inclined line on the right by clicking once with the **left-mouse-button** as shown in the figure below.

➢ Look at the *Add Relations PropertyManager*. In the *Selected Entities* text box '**Line2**' is now displayed. There are no relations in the *Existing Relations* text box. In the *Add Relations* panel, the **Horizontal**, **Vertical**, and **Fix** relations are displayed. These are the relations which can be added for the selected entity.

27. Click once with the left-mouse-button on the **Vertical** icon in the *Add Relations Property Manager* as shown. This activates the **Vertical** relation.

28. Click the **OK** icon in the *Property Manager*, or hit the [**Esc**] key once, to end the Add Relations command.

➤ One should think of the relations and dimensions as defining elements of the geometric entities. How many more relations or dimensions will be necessary to fully constrain the sketched geometry? Which relations or dimensions would you use to fully define the sketched geometry?

29. Move the cursor on top of the top corner of the triangle.

30. Click and drag the top corner of the triangle and note that the corner can be moved to a new location. Release the mouse button at a new location and notice the corner is adjusted only in an upward or downward direction. Note that the two adjacent lines are automatically adjusted to the new location.

31. On your own, experiment with dragging the other corners to new locations.

- The relations and dimensions that are applied to the geometry provide a full description for the location of the two lower corners of the triangle. The Vertical relation, along with the Fix relation at the lower right corner, does not fully describe the location of the top corner of the triangle. We will need to add additional information, such as the length of the vertical line or an angle dimension.

32. Select the **Smart Dimension** command by clicking once with the **left-mouse-button** on the icon in the *Sketch* toolbar.

33. Select the *inclined line*.

34. Select the *horizontal line*. Selecting the two lines automatically executes an angle dimension.

35. Select a location for the dimension as shown

36. Enter **45°** in the *Modify* dialog box and select **OK**.

37. Press the [**Esc**] key once to exit the Smart Dimension command.

38. On your own, experiment with dragging the three corners of the triangle.

- The geometry is fully defined with the added dimension and none of the geometry can be adjusted through the dragging with the cursor anymore.

Over-Defining and Driven Dimensions

- We can use SolidWorks to build partially defined solid models. In most cases, these types of models may behave unpredictably as changes are made. However, SolidWorks will not let us over-define a sketch; additional dimensions can still be added to the sketch, but they are used as references only. These additional dimensions are called **driven dimensions**. *Driven dimensions* do not constrain the sketch; they only reflect the values of the dimensioned geometry. They are shaded differently (grey by default) to distinguish them from normal (parametric) dimensions. A *driven dimension* can be converted to a normal dimension only if another dimension or geometric relation is removed.

1. Select the **Smart Dimension** command in the *Sketch* toolbar.

2. Select the *vertical line*.

3. Pick a location that is to the right side of the triangle to place the dimension text.

4. A *warning* dialog box appears on the screen stating that the dimension we are trying to create will over-define the sketch. Click on the **OK** button to proceed with the creation of a driven dimension.

5. Press the [**Esc**] key once to exit the **Smart Dimension** command.

6. On your own, modify the angle dimension to **35°** and observe the changes of the 2D sketch and the driven dimension.

7. Press the [**Esc**] key to ensure that no objects are selected.

Deleting Existing Relations

1. Move the cursor on top of the **Fixed** relation icon and **right-mouse-click** once to bring up the *option menu*.

2. Select **Delete** to remove the Fixed relation that is applied to the lower right corner of the triangle.

3. Move the cursor on top of the top corner of the triangle.

4. Drag the top corner of the triangle and note that the entire triangle is free to move in all directions. Drag the corner toward the top right corner of the graphics window as shown in the figure. Release the mouse button to move the triangle to the new location.

5. On your own, experiment with dragging the other corners and/or the three line segments to new locations on the screen.

❖ **Dimensional constraints** are used to describe the SIZE and LOCATION of individual geometric shapes. **Geometric relations** are **geometric restrictions** that can be applied to geometric entities. The constraints applied to the triangle are sufficient to maintain its size and shape, but the geometry can be moved around; its location definition isn't complete.

6. On your own, reapply the **Fixed** relation to the lower right corner of the triangle.

7. On your own, **delete** the reference dimension on the vertical line.

8. Confirm the same relations and dimensions are applied on your sketch as shown.

❖ Note that the sketch is fully defined and **Fully Defined** is displayed in the *Status Bar* at the bottom of the screen.

Using the Fully Define Sketch Tool

> ➤ In SolidWorks, the **Fully Define Sketch** tool can be used to calculate which dimensions and relations are required to fully define an under defined sketch. Fully defined sketches can be updated more predictably as design changes are implemented. One general procedure for applying dimensions to sketches is to use the **Smart Dimension** command to add the desired dimensions, and then use the **Fully Define Sketch** tool to fully constrain the sketch. It is also important to realize that different dimensions and geometric relations can be applied to the same sketch to accomplish a fully defined geometry.

1. **Right click** once on the **6.5** linear dimension and select **Delete** in the option menu. Notice Under Defined is now displayed in the *Status Bar*.

2. **Left click** on the arrow below the **Display/Delete Relations** button on the *Sketch* toolbar to reveal additional sketch relation commands.

3. Activate the **Fully Define Sketch** command from the pop-up menu.

4. The *Fully Define Sketch Property Manager* appears. **If necessary**, click once with the **left-mouse-button** on the arrows to reveal the Dimensions option panel as shown.

5. Notice that under the *Horizontal Dimensions Scheme* option, Baseline is selected. The origin is selected as the default baseline datum and appears in the datum selection window as Point1@Origin.

6. Switch **On** the *Relations* and *Dimensions* options as shown.

7. Click once with the **left-mouse-button** in the *Datum* selection text box to select a different datum to serve as the baseline.

8. In the graphics window select the vertical line. Notice **Line2** is now displayed in the *Datum* selection window as the *Horizontal Dimensions* baseline.

9. On your own, select the horizontal line as the appropriate baseline datum for the vertical dimensions.

10. Select **Calculate** in the *Property Manager* to continue with the **Fully Define Sketch** command.

❖ Note that SolidWorks automatically applies the horizontal dimension, using the vertical line as the baseline. Since this is the only dimension necessary to fully define the sketch, it is the only dimension added. Notice that **Fully Defined** is now displayed in the *Status Bar*.

11. Click the **OK** button to accept the results and exit the **Fully Define Sketch** tool.

Adding Additional Geometry

1. Select the **Circle** command by clicking once with the left-mouse-button on the icon in the *Sketch* toolbar.

2. On your own, create a circle of arbitrary size inside the triangle as shown below.

3. Press the [**Esc**] key to ensure that no objects are selected.

❖ Notice that **Under Defined** is now displayed in the *Status Bar*.

4. Select **Add Relation** from the *Sketch* toolbar.

5. Pick the circle by left-mouse-clicking once on the geometry.

6. Pick the inclined line.

➤ Look at the *Add Relations Property Manager*. In the *Selected Entities* text box **Arc1** and **Line1** are now displayed. There are no relations in the *Existing Relations* window. In the *Add Relations* menu, the **Tangent** and **Fix** relations are displayed. These are the relations which can be added for the selected entities.

7. Click once with the left-mouse-button on the **Tangent** icon in the *Add Relations Property Manager* as shown. This activates the Tangent relation.

8. Click the **OK** icon in the *Property Manager*, or hit the [**Esc**] key once, to end the Add Relations command.

➤ How many more relations or dimensions do you think will be necessary to fully define the circle? Which relations or dimensions would you use to fully define the geometry?

9. Move the cursor on top of the right side of the circle, and then drag the circle toward the right edge of the graphics window. Notice the size of the circle is adjusted while the system maintains the **Tangent** relation.

10. Drag the center of the circle toward the upper right direction. Notice the **Tangent** relation is always maintained by the system.

➢ On your own, experiment with adding additional relations and/or dimensions to fully define the sketched geometry. Use the **Undo** command to undo any changes before proceeding to the next section.

11. Press the [**Esc**] key to ensure that no objects are selected.

12. Inside the graphics window, click once with the **left-mouse-button** and select the **center of the circle**.

13. Hold down the **[Ctrl]** key and click once with the **left-mouse-button** on the **vertical line**. Holding the [Ctrl] key allows selecting the vertical line while maintaining selection of the circle centerpoint. This is a method to select multiple entities.

• Notice the *Properties Property Manager* for the selected entities is displayed. This provides an alternate way to control the relations for selected properties.

14. Click once with the left-mouse-button on the **Coincident** icon in the *Add Relations* panel in the *Property Manager* as shown. This activates the Coincident relation.

15. Click the **OK** icon in the *Property Manager*.

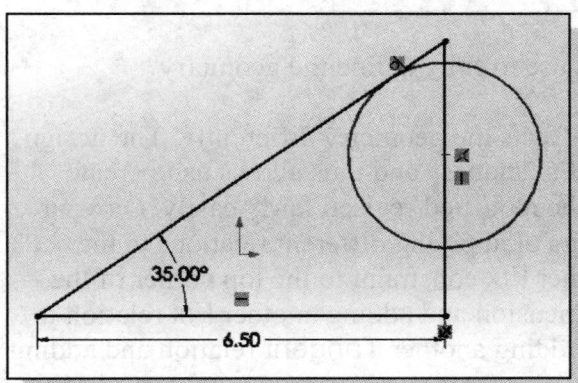

• Is the circle fully defined? (**HINT:** Drag the circle to see whether it is fully defined.)

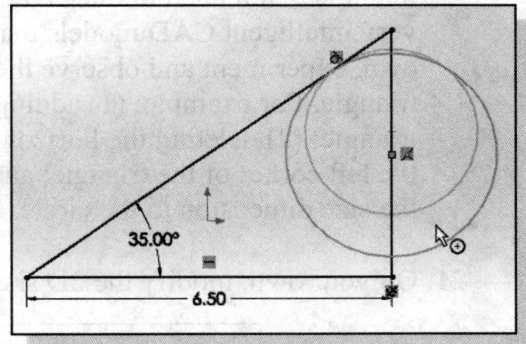

16. On your own, select the circle centerpoint <u>and</u> the vertical line in the graphics area. Notice the *Property Manager* appears.

17. In the *Property Manager*, Coincident1 is listed under *Existing Relations*. Move the cursor over **Coincident1** and click once with the **right-mouse-button**.

18. Select **Delete** in the pop-up menu by clicking once with the **left-mouse-button**.

19. Click the **OK** icon in the *Property Manager*.

20. On your own, add a **Coincident** relation between the center of the circle and the horizontal line.

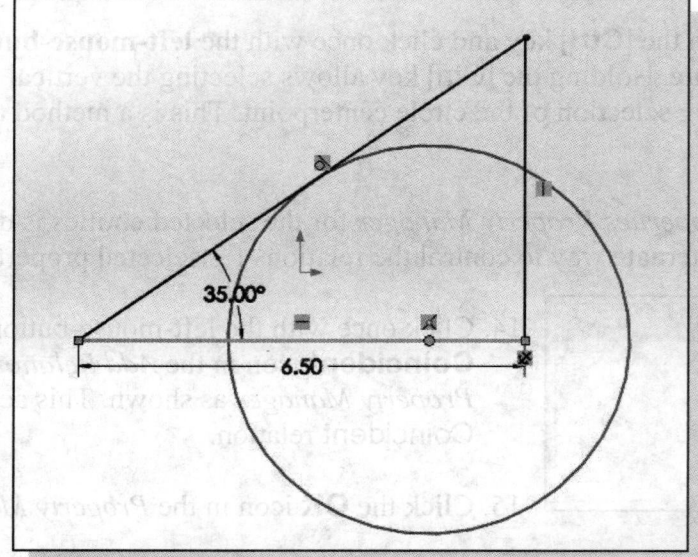

- Which relations or dimensions would you use to fully define the geometry?

❖ The application of different relations affects the geometry differently. The design intent is maintained in the CAD model's database and thus allows us to create very intelligent CAD models that can be modified/revised fairly easily. On your own, experiment and observe the results of applying different relations to the triangle. For example: (1) adding another **Fix** constraint to the top corner of the triangle; (2) deleting the horizontal dimension and adding another **Fix** relation to the left corner of the triangle; and (3) adding another **Tangent** relation and adding the size dimension to the circle.

21. On your own, modify the 2D sketch as shown below.

Adding New Equations

1. Move the cursor over the *SolidWorks* icon on the *Menu Bar* to reveal the pull-down menus, click once with the left-mouse-button on the **Tools** icon and select **Equations** in the pull-down menu as shown.

2. The *Equations, Global Variables, and Dimensions* dialog box is displayed. Notice the equation we created appears in the table under '**Equations**'.

3. Switch to the **Equation View** and click the **Add equation** cell in the *Equations, Global Variables, and Dimensions* dialog box as shown. The cell becomes active, awaiting the start of a new equation.

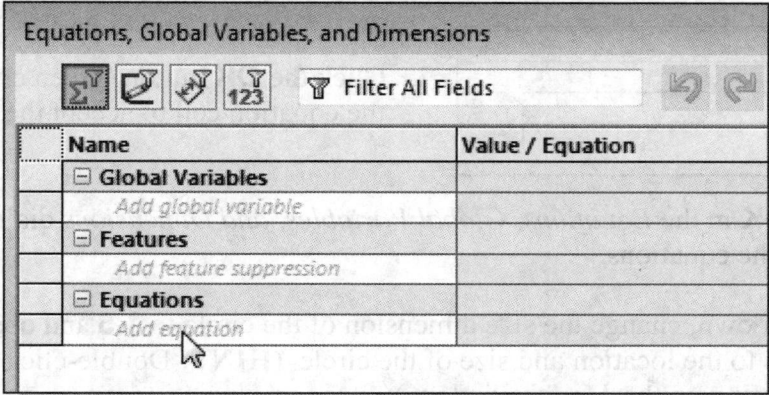

4. We will enter an equation to constrain the vertical location dimension for the circle equal to the size of the circle.

5. Move the cursor to the graphics area and click once with the **left-mouse-button** on the vertical (1.75″) location dimension. (**NOTE:** You may have to reposition the *Add Equation* window to uncover the dimension in the graphics area.) Notice the dimension name automatically appears in the new equation line of the *Equations, Global Variables, and Dimensions* dialog box.

6. Click once with the **left-mouse-button** on the Size (1.75″) dimension of the circle. Notice the dimension name appears in the equation line as shown.

7. Click the **OK** button (green check mark) in the equation cell to accept the new equation.

8. Click **OK** in the *Equations, Global Variables, and Dimensions* dialog box to accept the equations.

9. On your own, change the size dimension of the circle to **1.5** and observe the changes to the location and size of the circle. (**HINT:** Double-click the dimension text to bring up the *Modify* window.)

❖ SolidWorks automatically adjusts the dimensions of the design, and the parametric relations we entered are also applied and maintained. The dimensional constraints are used to control the size and location of the hole.

Questions:

1. What is the difference between *dimensional* constraints and *geometric* relations?

2. How can we confirm that a sketch is fully defined?

3. How do we distinguish between derived dimensions and parametric dimensions on the screen?

4. Describe the procedure to Display/Edit user-defined equations.

5. List and describe three different geometric relations available in SolidWorks.

6. Does SolidWorks allow us to build partially defined solid models? What are the advantages and disadvantages of building these types of models?

7. Identify and describe the following constraints.

    (a)

    (b)

    (c)

    (d)

Exercises: (Unless otherwise specified, dimensions are in inches.)

1. **Adjustable Support**

2. **V-Slide Plate** (The design has two sets of parallel lines with implied tangency.)

3. **Swivel Base** (Dimensions are in **Millimeters**.)

4. **Sensor Mount**

5. **Flat Hook** (Dimensions are in **Millimeters**. Thickness: **25 mm**.)

Chapter 5
Feature Design Tree

Learning Objectives

- ◆ **Understand Feature Interactions**
- ◆ **Use the Feature Manager Design Tree**
- ◆ **Modify and Update Feature Dimensions**
- ◆ **Perform History-Based Part Modifications**
- ◆ **Change the Names of Created Features**
- ◆ **Implement Basic Design Changes**

Certified SolidWorks Associate Exam Objectives Coverage

Sketch Entities – Lines, Rectangles, Circles, Arcs, Ellipses, Centerlines
Objectives: Creating Sketch Entities.

Boss and Cut Features – Extrudes, Revolves, Sweeps, Lofts
Objectives: Creating Basic Swept Features.

Dimensions
Objectives: Applying and Editing Smart Dimensions.

Feature Conditions – Start and End
Objectives: Controlling Feature Start and End Conditions.

Introduction

In SolidWorks, the **design intents** are embedded into features in the **Feature Manager Design Tree**. The structure of the design tree resembles that of a **CSG binary tree**. A CSG binary tree contains only *Boolean relations*, while the **SolidWorks design tree** contains all features, including *Boolean relations*. A design tree is a sequential record of the features used to create the part. This design tree contains the construction steps, plus the rules defining the design intent of each construction operation. In a design tree, each time a new modeling event is created, previously defined features can be used to define information such as size, location, and orientation. It is therefore important to think about your modeling strategy before you start creating anything. It is important, but also difficult, to plan ahead for all possible design changes that might occur. This approach in modeling is a major difference of **FEATURE-BASED CAD SOFTWARE**, such as SolidWorks, from previous generation CAD systems.

Sequential record of the construction steps

Feature-based parametric modeling is a cumulative process. Every time a new feature is added, a new result is created and the feature is also added to the design tree. The database also includes parameters of features that were used to define them. All of this happens automatically as features are created and manipulated. At this point, it is important to understand that all of this information is retained, and modifications are done based on the same input information.

In SolidWorks, the design tree gives information about modeling order and other information about the feature. Part modifications can be accomplished by accessing the features in the design tree. It is therefore important to understand and utilize the feature design tree to modify designs. SolidWorks remembers the history of a part, including all the rules that were used to create it, so that changes can be made to any operation that was performed to create the part. In SolidWorks, to modify a feature, we access the feature by selecting the feature in the *Feature Manager Design Tree* window.

Starting SolidWorks

1. Select the **SolidWorks** option on the *Start* menu or select the **SolidWorks** icon on the desktop to start SolidWorks. The SolidWorks main window will appear.

2. Select the **New** icon with a single click of the left-mouse-button on the *Menu Bar*.

3. The *New SolidWorks Document* dialog window appears in Novice mode. Click once with the left-mouse-button on the **Advanced** button to switch to Advanced mode.

❖   In Advanced mode, the *New SolidWorks Document* dialog box offers the same basic options as in Novice mode. These basic options allow starting a new document using the default templates for a Part, Assembly, or Drawing. However, the Advanced mode also allows us to start new documents with user-defined templates.

4. Select the **Part** icon with a single click of the left-mouse-button in the *New SolidWorks Document* dialog box.

5. Select **OK** in the *New SolidWorks Document* dialog box to open a new part document.

Creating a User-Defined Part Template

❖ We will create a part template which includes settings Following the ANSI standards for dimensions in English (inch, pound, second) units. In the future, using this template will eliminate the need to adjust these document settings each time a new part is started.

1. Select the **Options** icon from the *Menu Bar* to open the *Options* dialog box.

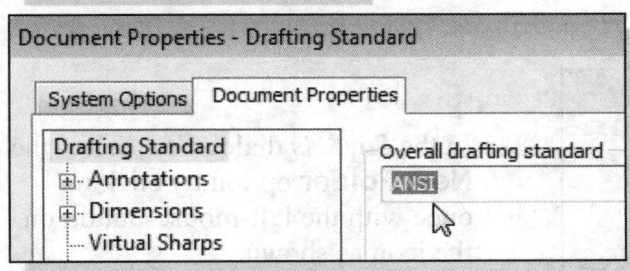

2. Select the **Document Properties** tab.

3. Select **ANSI** in the *Overall drafting standard* panel as shown.

4. On your own, confirm the ANSI standard is set for the different options under **Annotations** and **Dimensions**.

5. Select **IPS (inch, pound, second)** under the *Unit system* options.

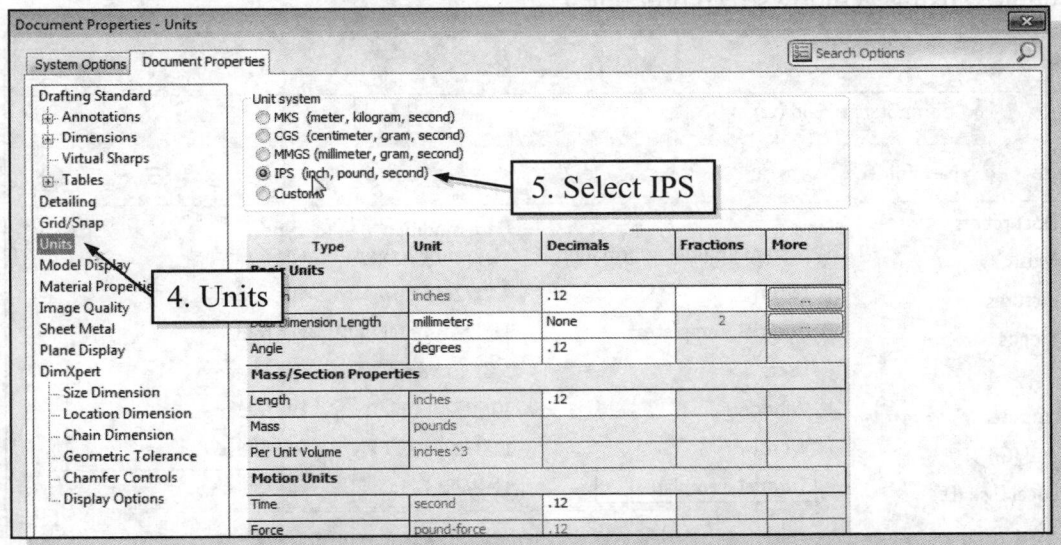

6. Click **OK** in the *Options* dialog box to accept the selected settings.

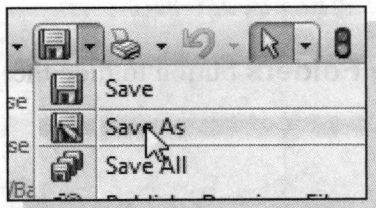

7. Click the arrow next to the **Save** icon in the *Menu Bar* to reveal the save options and select **Save As**.

8. We will create a new folder for the user-defined templates. Decide where you want to locate this new folder and use the browser in the *Save As* dialog box to select the location. It may be necessary to expand the browser by clicking the **Browse Folders** button as shown. (**NOTE:** In the figure below, the **C:** folder is chosen.)

9. In the *Save As* dialog box, select the **New Folder** option by clicking once with the left-mouse-button on the icon as shown.

10. The new folder appears with the default name *New Folder*. Type the folder name **Tutorial_Templates** for the new folder. (**NOTE:** This folder could also be created using Windows Explorer, etc.)

11. Left click on the **Hide Folders** button to hide the browser.

12. Under *Save as type*, select **Part Templates (*.prtdot)**. Notice the browser automatically goes to the default *templates* folder.

13. Use the *Save As* browser to select the **Tutorial_Templates** folder you created.

14. Enter the *File name* **Part_IPS_ANSI**.

15. Click **Save** to save the new part template file.

16. Select **Close** in the *File* pull-down menu, or use the key combination **Ctrl+W**, to close the document.

➢ We will now open a new part document using the template we just saved.

17. Select the **New** icon with a single click of the left-mouse-button on the *Menu Bar*.

18. Notice that the new template does not appear as an option. Click **Cancel** in the *New SolidWorks Document* dialog box.

19. Select the **Options** icon from the *Menu Bar* to open the *Options* dialog box.

20. Select **File Locations** under the *System Options* tab as shown.

21. Make sure **Document Templates** is selected as the *Show folders for:* option.

22. Click the **Add** button to add the directory with the user-defined templates to the list of folders containing document templates.

23. Locate and select the **Tutorial_Templates** folder using the browser, and click **OK** in the *Browse For Folder* dialog box.

24. Select **OK** in the *System Options* dialog box.

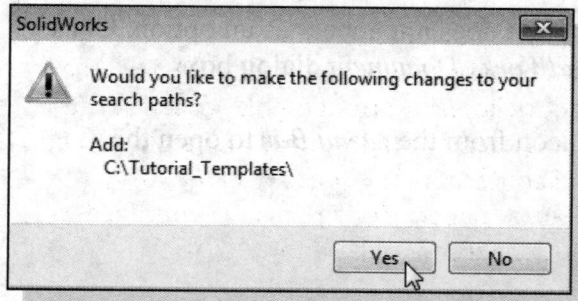

25. If a pop-up window appears with the question "*Would you like to make the following changes to your search paths?*" click **Yes**.

26. Select the **New** icon with a single click of the left-mouse-button on the *Menu Bar*. Notice the Tutorial_Templates folder now appears as a tab in the *New SolidWorks Document* dialog box.

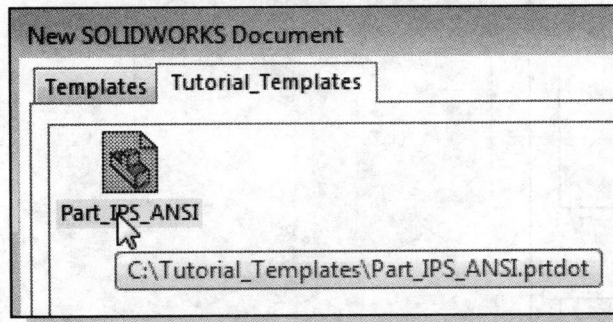

27. Select the **Tutorial_Templates** tab.

28. Notice the Part_IPS_ANSI template appears. Select the **Part_IPS_ANSI** template as shown.

29. Click on the **OK** button to open a new document.

The *Saddle Bracket* Design

❖ Based on your knowledge of SolidWorks so far, how many features would you use to create the design? Which feature would you choose as the **BASE FEATURE**, the first solid feature, of the model? What is your choice in arranging the order of the features? Would you organize the features differently if additional fillets were to be added in the design? Take a few minutes to consider these questions and do preliminary planning by sketching on a piece of paper. You are also encouraged to create the model on your own prior to following through the tutorial.

Modeling Strategy

The SolidWorks *Feature Manager Design Tree*

- In the SolidWorks screen layout, the **Feature Manager Design Tree** is located to the left of the graphics window. SolidWorks can be used for part modeling, assembly modeling, part drawings, and assembly presentation. The *Feature Manager Design Tree* window provides a visual structure of the features, relations, and attributes that are used to create the part, assembly, or scene. The *Feature Manager Design Tree* also provides right-click menu access for tasks associated specifically with the part or feature, and it is the primary focus for executing many of the SolidWorks commands.

➢ The first item displayed in the *Feature Manager Design Tree* is the name of the part, which is also the filename. By default, the name "*Part1*" is used when we first start SolidWorks. The parts are then numbered sequentially as new parts are created. If the part is saved with a new filename, this name will replace "*Part1*." Do not be concerned if your part is numbered differently than the labels in the figures, e.g. "*Part3*."

➢ The *Feature Manager Design Tree* can also be used to modify parts and assemblies by moving, deleting, or renaming items within the hierarchy. Any changes made in the *Feature Manager Design Tree* directly affect the part or assembly and the results of the modifications are displayed on screen instantly. The *Feature Manager Design Tree* also reports any problems and conflicts during the modification and updating procedure.

Creating the Base Feature

1. Move the graphics cursor to the **Front Plane** icon in the *Feature Manager Design Tree*. Notice the *Front Plane* icon is highlighted in the design tree and the *Front Plane* outline appears in the graphics area. Click once with the **left-mouse-button** to select the Front Plane.

- Note that with SolidWorks, we can also create the sketch of a feature first then use the feature command to select the sketch and create the solid feature.

2. In the *Sketch* toolbar, select the **Sketch** command by left-clicking once on the icon. Notice the Front Plane automatically becomes the sketch plane because it was pre-selected.

3. Select the **Line** icon on the *Sketch* toolbar by clicking once with the **left-mouse-button**; this will activate the Line command.

4. On your own, create and adjust the geometry by adding and modifying dimensions as shown below. (Note the lower left corner of the sketch is aligned to the origin.)

5. Click once with the **left-mouse-button** on the **Exit Sketch** icon on the *Sketch* toolbar to exit the Sketch option.

6. Select the **Isometric** option in the *Heads-up View* toolbar as shown.

➤ NOTE: If the *View Selector* is toggled ON, either toggle it off or use it to select the *Isometric* view.

7. Make sure the sketch – Sketch1 – is selected in the *Feature Manager Design Tree*.

8. In the *Features* toolbar, select the **Extruded Boss/Base** command by clicking once with the left-mouse-button on the icon.

9. In the *Extrude Property Manager* panel, click the drop down arrow to reveal the options for the *End Condition* (the default end condition is Blind) and select **Mid Plane** as shown.

10. In the *Extrude Property Manager* panel, enter **2.5** as the extrusion distance. Notice that the sketch region is automatically selected as the extrusion profile.

11. Click

9. Select **Mid Plane**.

10. Enter **2.5**

11. Click on the **OK** button to accept the settings and create the base feature.

➤ On your own, use the *Viewing* functions to view the 3D model. Also notice the **Boss-Extrude** feature is added to the *Model Tree* in the *Feature Manager Design Tree* area.

Adding the Second Solid Feature

1. In the *Sketch* toolbar, select the **Sketch** command by left-clicking once on the icon.

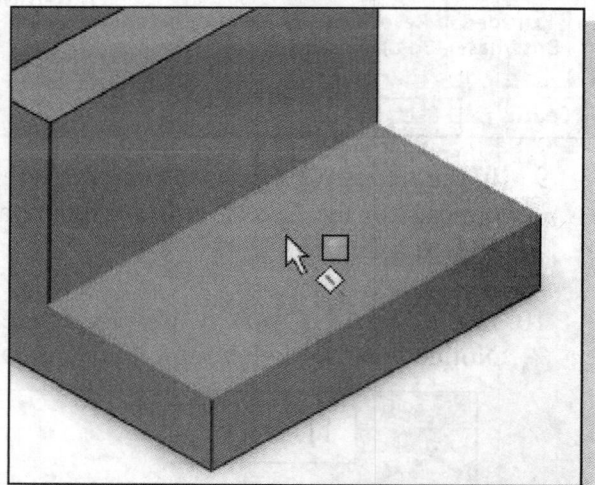

2. Notice the left panel displays the *Edit Sketch Property Manager* with the instruction "*Select a plane on which to create a sketch for the entity.*" Move the graphics cursor on the 3D part and notice that SolidWorks will automatically highlight feasible planes and surfaces as the cursor is on top of the different surfaces. Move the cursor inside the upper horizontal face of the 3D object as shown.

3. Click once with the **right-mouse-button** to bring up the option menu and choose **Select Other** to switch to the next feasible choice.

4. The *Select Other* pop-up dialog box appears. On your own, move the cursor over the options (e.g., Face) in the box to examine all possible surface selections.

5. Click on the **Face** selection in the *Select Other* dialog box to select the **bottom horizontal face** of the solid model when it is highlighted as shown in the figure.

Accept the bottom surface to align the sketching plane.

Creating a 2D Sketch

1. Select the **Circle** command by clicking once with the left-mouse-button on the icon in the *Sketch* toolbar.

➢ We will align the center of the circle to the midpoint of the base feature.

2. Move the cursor along the shorter edge of the base feature; when the **Midpoint** is highlighted as shown in the figure, left-click to select this point.

3. Select the front corner of the base feature to create a circle as shown below.

R = 1.25

4. Inside the graphics window, click once with the right-mouse-button to display the option menu. Choose **Select** in the popup menu to end the Circle option.

5. Click once with the **left-mouse-button** on the **Exit Sketch** icon on the *Sketch* toolbar to exit the Sketch option.

6. Make sure the sketch – Sketch2 – is selected in the *Feature Manager Design Tree*.

7. In the *Features* toolbar, select the **Extruded Boss/Base** command by clicking once with the left-mouse-button on the icon.

8. Click the **Reverse Direction** button in the *Property Manager* as shown. The extrude preview should appear as shown below.

9. In the *Extrude Property Manager* panel, click the drop down arrow to reveal the pull options for the *End Condition* (the default end condition is Blind) and select **Up To Surface**.

10. Select the top face of the base feature as the termination surface for the extrusion. Notice Face<1> appears in the surface selection window in the *Extrude Property Manager*.

11. Confirm the **Merge result** checkbox is checked.

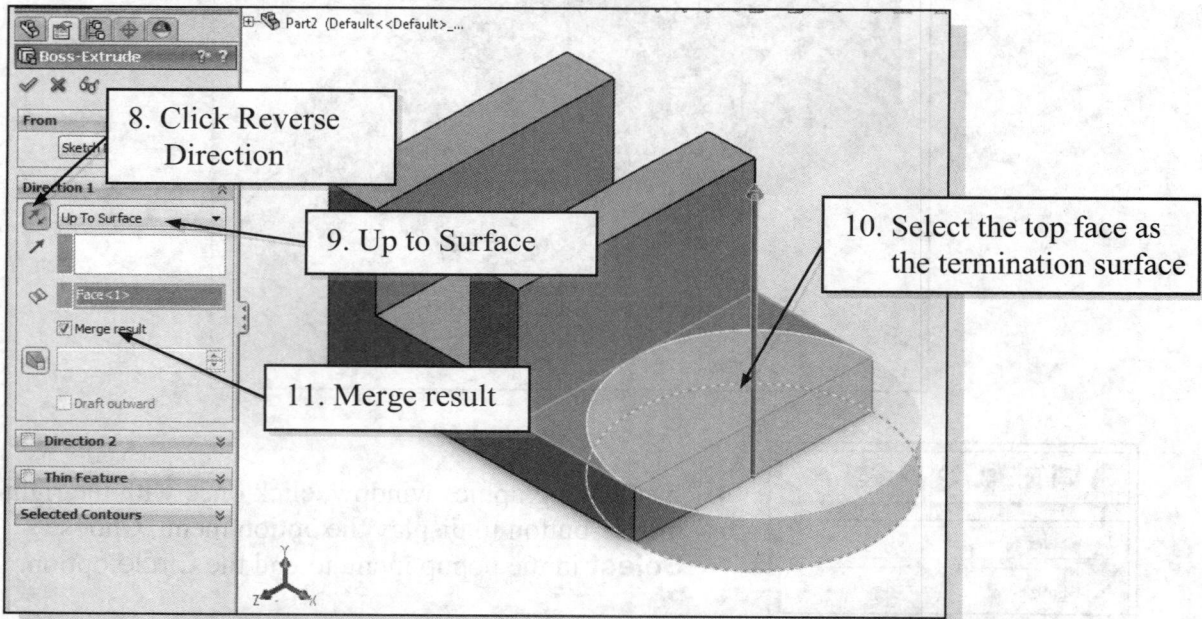

12. Click on the **OK** button to proceed with the Boss-Extrude operation.

Renaming the Part Features

♦ Currently, our model contains two extruded features. The feature is highlighted in the display area when we select the feature in the *Feature Manager Design Tree* window. Each time a new feature is created, the feature is also displayed in the *Design Tree* window. By default, SolidWorks will use generic names for part features. However, when we begin to deal with parts with a large number of features, it will be much easier to identify the features using more meaningful names. Two methods can be used to rename the features: 1. **clicking** twice on the name of the feature; and 2. using the **Properties** option. In this example, the use of the first method is illustrated.

1. Select the first extruded feature in the *Model Browser* area by left-clicking once on the name of the feature, **Extrude1**. Notice the selected feature is highlighted in the graphics window.

2. Left-mouse-click on the feature name again to enter the Edit mode as shown.

3. Type **Base** as the new name for the first extruded feature and press the **[Enter]** key.

4. On your own, rename the second extruded feature to **Circular_End**.

Adjusting the Width of the Base Feature

❖ One of the main advantages of parametric modeling is the ease of performing part modifications at any time in the design process. Part modifications can be done through accessing the features in the design tree. SolidWorks remembers the history of a part, including all the rules that were used to create it, so changes can be made to any operation that was performed to create the part. For our *Saddle Bracket* design, we will reduce the size of the base feature from 3.25 inches to 3.0 inches, and the extrusion distance to 2.0 inches.

1. Inside the *Feature Manager Design Tree* area, **right-mouse-click** on **Annotations** to bring up the *option menu* and select the **Show Feature Dimensions** option in the pop-up menu. This option will allow us to view and edit dimensions by moving the cursor over the corresponding feature on the model.

2. Move the cursor over the model to reveal the dimension indicating the **3.25** overall width of the **Base** feature.

3. Select the overall width of the **Base** feature, the **3.25** dimension value, by double-clicking on the dimension text, as shown.

4. Enter **3.0** in the *Modify* window and click the **OK** button.

5. Hit the [**Esc**] key to exit the Dimension command.

6. On your own, repeat the above steps and modify the extruded distance from **2.5** to **2.0**.

    7. Click **Rebuild** in the *Menu Bar*.

➢ Note that SolidWorks updates the model by relinking all elements used to create the model. Any problems or conflicts that occur will also be displayed during the updating process.

8. **Right-mouse-click** on **Annotations** to bring up the option menu and de-select the **Show Feature Dimensions** option in the pop-up menu.

Adding a Cut Feature

1. Select the **Sketch** button on the *Sketch* toolbar to create a new sketch.

2. Pick the upper horizontal face as shown.

3. Select the **Circle** command by clicking once with the left-mouse-button on the icon in the *Sketch* toolbar.

4. Move the cursor over the circular edge of the face as shown. (Do not click.) Notice the center and quadrant marks appear on the circle.

5. Select the **Center** point of the top face of the 3D model by left-clicking once on the icon as shown.

6. Sketch a circle of arbitrary size inside the top face of the cylinder as shown.

7. Use the right-mouse-button to display the option menu and choose **Select** in the popup menu to end the Circle command.

8. Inside the graphics window, click once with the right-mouse-button to display the option menu. Select the **Smart Dimension** option in the popup menu.

9. Create a dimension to describe the size of the circle and set it to **0.75 in**.

10. Inside the graphics window, click once with the right-mouse-button to display the option menu. Choose **Select** in the popup menu to end the Smart Dimension command.

11. Click once with the **left-mouse-button** on the **Exit Sketch** icon on the *Sketch* toolbar to exit the Sketch option.

12. In the *Features* toolbar, select the **Extruded Cut** command by clicking once with the left-mouse-button on the icon.

➢ The *Cut-Extrude Property Manager* is displayed in the left panel. Notice that the sketch region (the circle) is automatically selected as the extrusion profile.

13. In the *Cut-Extrude Property Manager* panel, click the arrow to reveal the pull-down options for the *end condition* (the default end condition is Blind) and select **Through All** as shown.

14. Click the **OK** button (green check mark) in the *Cut-Extrude Property Manager* panel.

15. On your own, rename the feature as **3/4″ Hole** in the *Feature Manager Design Tree*.

Creating a Rectangular Extruded Cut Feature

1. Move the cursor into the graphics area, away from the model, and click once with the left-mouse-button to ensure that no features are selected.

2. Select the **Sketch** button on the *Sketch* toolbar to create a new sketch.

3. Pick the **vertical face** of the solid as shown. (Note the alignment of the origin of the sketch plane.)

3. Pick this face as the sketch plane.

4. On your own, sketch a rectangle (**1.0″ W × 0.75″ H** offset **0.5″** from the edge) as shown. Exit the sketch and create an **Extruded Cut** feature using the **Up To Next** option for the *End Condition* as shown. In the *Feature Manager Design Tree*, change the name of the new feature to ***Rect_Cut***.

History-Based Part Modifications

• SolidWorks uses the *history-based part modification* approach, which enables us to make modifications to the appropriate features and relink the rest of the history tree without having to reconstruct the model from scratch. We can think of it as going back in time and modifying some aspects of the modeling steps used to create the part. We can modify any feature that we have created. As an example, we will adjust the depth of the rectangular cutout.

1. In the *Feature Manager Design Tree* window, select the last cut feature, **Rect_Cut**, by left-clicking once on the name of the feature.

2. In the *Feature Manager Design Tree* window, right-mouse-click once on the **Rect_Cut** feature.

3. Select the **Edit Feature** button in the pop-up menu. Notice the *Extrude Property Manager* appears on the screen.

4. In the *Extrude Property Manager*, set the termination *End Condition* to the **Through All** option.

5. Click on the **OK** button to accept the settings.

• As can been seen, the history-based modification approach is very straightforward and it only took a few seconds to adjust the cut feature to the **Through All** option.

A Design Change

❖ Engineering designs usually go through many revisions and changes. SolidWorks provides an assortment of tools to handle design changes quickly and effectively. We will demonstrate some of the tools available by changing the **Base** feature of the design.

1. In the *Feature Manager Design Tree* window, select the **Base** feature by left-clicking once on the name of the feature.

2. Pick the **Edit Sketch** button in the pop-up menu.

❖ SolidWorks will now display the original 2D sketch of the selected feature in the graphics window. We have literally gone back in time to the point where we first created the 2D sketch. Notice the feature being modified is also highlighted in the desktop *Feature Manager Design Tree*.

3. Click on the **Normal To** icon in the *View Orientation* pull-down menu on the *Heads-up View* toolbar.

• The **Normal To** command automatically aligns the *sketch plane* of a selected entity to the screen. We have literally gone back in time to the point where we first created the 2D sketch.

4. Select the **Sketch Fillet** command in the *Sketch* toolbar.

5. In the *Sketch Fillet Property Manager*, enter **0.25** as the new radius of the fillet. (**NOTE:** If the *Fillet Parameters* panel is minimized, click on the double arrows to expand the panel.)

6. Select the two edges as shown.

7. Click the **OK** icon (green check mark) in the *Property Manager* to create the fillet.

- Note that the fillet is created automatically with the dimension attached. The attached dimension can also be modified through the history tree.

8. Click the **OK** icon (green check mark) in the *Property Manager*, or hit the [**Esc**] key once, to end the Sketch Fillet command.

9. Click on the **Exit Sketch** icon to exit the *Sketch* command.

- Note that SolidWorks will **Rebuild** the model by relinking all steps in the design tree.

Feature Manager Design Tree Views

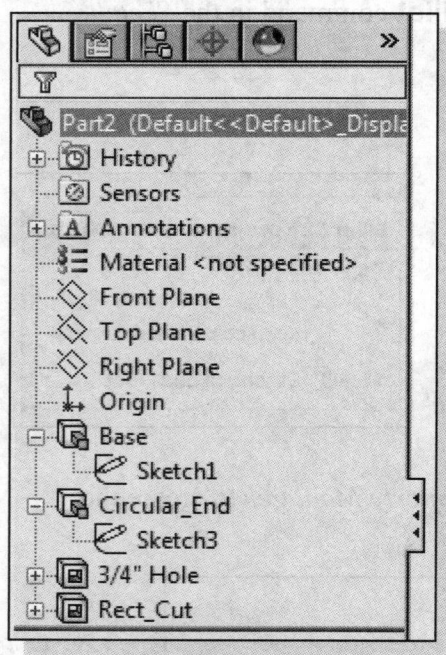

> ➤ The **Normal View** for the Feature Manager Design Tree is **hierarchical**, with sketches absorbed into features.

1. Expand the *Feature Manager Design Tree* to display the absorbed sketches as shown.

> ➤ The Flat Tree View for the Feature Manager Design Tree displays the features in the **order they were created**, instead of hierarchically.

2. Right-click on the **Part** icon in the *Feature Manager Design Tree* and select **Tree Display**, then select **Show Flat Tree View** as shown.

➤ Note the changes in the display of the *Feature Manager Design Tree*. Items are now shown in the order of creation.

3. Right-click on the **Part** icon in the *Feature Manager Design Tree* and select **Tree Display**, then **unselect** the **Show Flat Tree View** to return to the hierarchical display.

❖ In a typical design process, the initial design will undergo many analyses, testing, and reviews. The *history-based part modification* approach is an extremely powerful tool that enables us to quickly update the design. At the same time, it is quite clear that PLANNING AHEAD is also important in doing feature-based modeling.

4. Save the part with the filename **Saddle_Bracket**. (**NOTE:** Do **not** save the part file in the Tutorial_Templates folder.)

Questions:

1. What are stored in the *SolidWorks Feature Manager Design Tree*?

2. When extruding, what is the difference between Blind and Through All?

3. Describe the *history-based part modification* approach.

4. What determines how a model reacts when other features in the model change?

5. Describe the steps to rename existing features.

6. Describe two methods available in SolidWorks to *modify the dimension values* of parametric sketches.

7. Create *Design Tree sketches* showing the steps you plan to use to create the two models shown on the next page:

Ex.1)

Ex.2)

Exercises: (Dimensions are in inches.)

1. **Base plate**: Thickness: **0.25** inches; Boss height **0.5** inches.

2.

3.

4.

5.

Notes:

Chapter 6
Geometric Construction Tools

Learning Objectives

♦ **Apply Geometry Relations**
♦ **Use the Trim/Extend Command**
♦ **Use the Offset Command**
♦ **Understand the Profile Sketch Approach**
♦ **Use the Convert Entities Command**
♦ **Understand and Use Reference Geometry**
♦ **Edit with Click and Drag**
♦ **Use the Fully Define Sketch Tool**
♦ **Use the Selected Contours Option**

Certified SolidWorks Associate Exam Objectives Coverage

Certified Associate Reference Guide

Introduction

The main characteristics of solid modeling are the accuracy and completeness of the geometric database of the three-dimensional objects. However, working in three-dimensional space using input and output devices that are largely two-dimensional in nature is potentially tedious and confusing. SolidWorks provides an assortment of two-dimensional construction tools to make the creation of wireframe geometry easier and more efficient. SolidWorks includes sketch tools to create basic geometric entities such as lines, arcs, etc. These entities are grouped to define a boundary or profile. A *profile* is a closed region and can contain other closed regions. Profiles are commonly used to create extruded and revolved features. An *invalid profile* consists of self-intersecting curves or open regions. In this lesson, the basic geometric construction tools, such as Trim and Extend, are used to create profiles. Mastering the geometric construction tools along with the application of proper geometric and parametric relations is the true essence of *parametric modeling*.

The *Gasket* Design

❖ Based on your knowledge of SolidWorks so far, how would you create this design? What are the more difficult geometry involved in the design? Take a few minutes to consider a modeling strategy and do preliminary planning by sketching on a piece of paper. You are also encouraged to create the design on your own prior to following through the tutorial.

Modeling Strategy

Starting SolidWorks

1. Select the **SolidWorks** option on the *Start* menu or select the **SolidWorks** icon on the desktop to start SolidWorks. The SolidWorks main window will appear on the screen.

2. Select the **New** icon with a single click of the left-mouse-button on the *Menu Bar*.

3. Under the *Templates* tab of the *New SolidWorks Document* dialog box, select the **Part** icon with a single click of the left-mouse-button.

4. Select **OK** in the *New SolidWorks Document* dialog box to open a new part document.

5. Select the **Options** icon from the *Menu Bar* to open the *Options* dialog box.

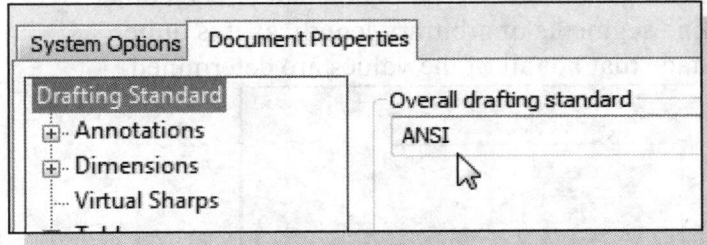

6. Select the **Document Properties** tab.

7. Select **ANSI** in the pull-down selection window under the *Overall drafting standard* panel as shown.

8. Click **Units** as shown in the figure.

9. Select **MMGS (millimeter, gram, second)** under the *Unit system* options.

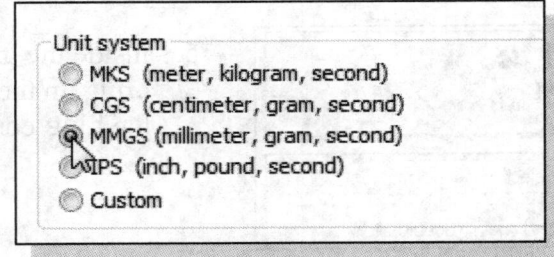

Creating a 2D Sketch

1. Click once with the **left-mouse-button** to select the **Front Plane** icon in the *Feature Manager Design Tree*. Notice the **Front Plane** icon is highlighted in the design tree and the *Front Plane* outline appears in the graphics area.

2. Select the **Extruded Boss/Base** button on the *Features* toolbar to create a new extruded feature. Notice the **Front Plane** automatically becomes the sketch plane because it was pre-selected.

3. Click on the **Line** icon in the *Sketch* toolbar.

4. Create a sketch as shown in the figure below. Start the sketch from the top right corner. The line segments are all parallel and/or perpendicular to each other. We will intentionally make the line segments of arbitrary length, as it is quite common during the design stage that not all of the values are determined.

5. Inside the graphics window, right-mouse-click to bring up the option menu and choose **Select** to end the Line command.

6. Select the **Circle** command by clicking once with the left-mouse-button on the icon in the *2D Sketch Panel*.

7. Pick a location that is above the bottom horizontal line as the center location of the circle.

8. Move the cursor toward the right and create a circle of arbitrary size, by clicking once with the left-mouse-button.

9. Click on the **Line** icon in the *Sketch* toolbar.

10. Move the cursor near the upper portion of the circle and, when the **Coincident** constraint symbol is displayed, click once with the **left-mouse-button** to select the starting point for the line.

Coincident Symbol

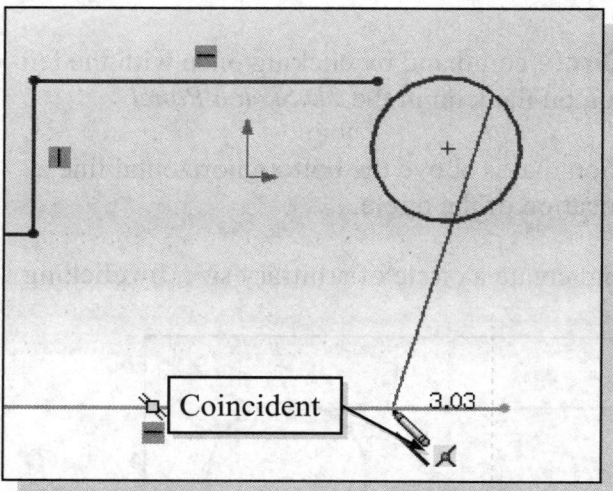

11. For the other end of the line, select a location that is on the lower horizontal line and about one-third from the right endpoint. Notice the **Coincident** constraint symbol is displayed when the cursor is on the horizontal line.

12. Inside the graphics window, right-mouse-click to bring up the option menu.

13. In the option menu, choose **Select** to end the Line command.

Editing the Sketch by Dragging the Entities

❖ In SolidWorks, we can click and drag any under-defined curve or point in the sketch to change the size or shape of the sketched profile. As illustrated in the previous chapter, this option can be used to identify under-defined entities. This *editing by dragging* method is also an effective visual approach that allows designers to quickly make changes.

1. Move the cursor on the lower left vertical edge of the sketch. Click and drag the edge to a new location that is toward the right side of the sketch.

Click and drag

❖ Note that we can only drag the vertical edge horizontally; the connections to the two horizontal lines are maintained while we are moving the geometry.

2. Click and drag the center point of the circle to a new location.

❖ Note that as we adjust the size and the location of the circle, the connection to the inclined line is maintained.

3. Click and drag the lower endpoint of the inclined line to a new location.

❖ Note that as we adjust the size and the location of the inclined line, the location of the bottom horizontal edge is also adjusted.

➢ Note that several changes occur as we adjust the size and the location of the inclined line. The location of the bottom horizontal line and the length of the vertical line are adjusted accordingly.

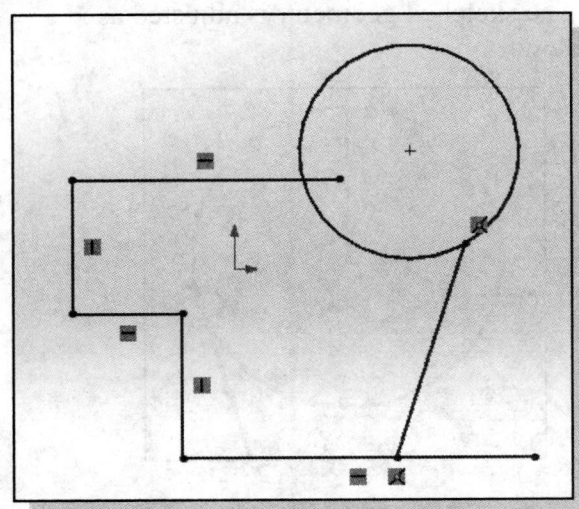

4. On your own, adjust the sketch so that the shape of the sketch appears roughly as shown.

❖ The *editing by dragging* method is an effective approach that allows designers to explore and experiment with different design concepts.

Adding Additional Relations

1. Choose **Smart Dimension** in the *Sketch* toolbar.

2. Add the horizontal location dimension, from the top left vertical edge to the center of the circle as shown. (Do not be overly concerned with the dimensional value; we are still working on creating a *rough sketch*.)

3. Click the **OK** icon in the *Property Manager*, or hit the [**Esc**] key once, to end the Smart Dimension command.

4. Select the **Add Relation** command in the *Sketch* toolbar. Notice the *Selected Entities* window in the *Add Relations Property Manager* is blank because no entities are selected.

5. Pick the **inclined line** and the **circle** by left-mouse-clicking once on the geometry.

6. Click once with the left-mouse-button on the **Tangent** icon in the *Add Relations Property Manager* as shown. This activates the Tangent relation. The sketched geometry is adjusted as shown below.

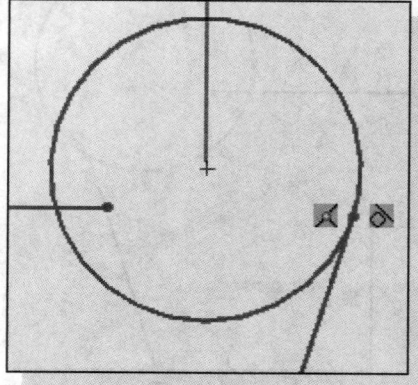

7. Click the **OK** icon in the *Property Manager*, or hit the [**Esc**] key once, to end the Add Relations command.

8. Click and drag the circle upward so that there is a gap between the circle and the top horizontal line as shown.

❖ Note that the dimension we added now restricts the horizontal movement of the center of the circle. The Tangent relation to the inclined line is maintained.

Using the *Trim* and *Extend* Commands

➤ In the following sections, we will illustrate using the Trim and Extend commands to complete the desired 2D profile.

❖ The **Trim** and **Extend** commands can be used to shorten/lengthen an object so that it ends precisely at a boundary. As a general rule, SolidWorks will try to clean up sketches by forming a closed region sketch.

1. **Left-click** on the **arrow** below the **Trim Entities** button on the *Sketch* toolbar to reveal additional commands.

2. Select the **Extend Entities** command from the pop-up menu.

3. We will first extend the top horizontal line to the circle. Move the cursor near the right hand endpoint of the top horizontal line. SolidWorks will automatically display the possible result of the selection. When the extended line appears, click once with the left-mouse-button.

4. Press the [**Esc**] key once to end the Extend command.

5. We will next trim the bottom horizontal line to the inclined line. Select the **Trim Entities** icon on the *Sketch* toolbar.

6. Select the **Trim to closest** option in the *Trim Property Manager*.

7. Move the cursor near the right hand endpoint of the bottom horizontal line. The portion of the line that will be trimmed is highlighted. Click once with the **left-mouse-button** to trim the line.

8. Click the **OK** icon in the *Property Manager*, or hit the [**Esc**] key once, to end the Trim command.

9. Activate the **Add Relation** command in the *Sketch* toolbar.

10. In the graphics area, select the **center point of the circle** and the **top horizontal line** as shown.

11. Click once with the left-mouse-button on the **Coincident** icon in the *Add Relations Property Manager* as shown. This activates the **Coincident** relation.

12. Click the **OK** icon in the *Property Manager*, or hit the [**Esc**] key once, to end the **Add Relations** command.

13. On your own, create the **height dimension** to the left of the sketch as shown.

14. On your own, **Trim** the circle as shown.

15. Hit the [**Esc**] key to end the **Trim** command.

Adding Dimensions with the Fully Define Sketch Tool

➢ In SolidWorks, the **Fully Define Sketch** tool can be used to calculate which dimensions and relations are required to fully define an under defined sketch. Fully defined sketches can be updated more predictably as design changes are implemented. The general procedure for applying dimensions to sketches is to use the **Smart Dimension** command to add the desired key dimensions, and then use the **Fully Define Sketch** tool as a quick way to calculate all other sketch dimensions necessary. SolidWorks remembers which dimensions were added by the user and which were calculated by the system, so that automatic dimensions do not replace the desired dimensions. In the following steps we will use the Fully Define Sketch tool to apply the dimensions necessary, but will disable the automatic application of sketch relations.

1. Select the **Fully Define Sketch** command in the *Sketch* toolbar.

2. The *Fully Define Sketch Property Manager* appears. **Uncheck** the Relations box to disable the calculation of geometric relations.

3. Click once with the **left-mouse-button** on the arrows to reveal the Dimensions option panel, **if necessary**.

4. Notice that under the *Horizontal Dimensions Scheme* option, Baseline is selected. The origin is selected as the default baseline datum and appears in the datum selection window as Point1@Origin. Click once with the **left-mouse-button** in the *Datum* selection text box to select a different datum to serve as the baseline.

5. In the graphics window, select the left **vertical line** as shown. Notice Line2 is now displayed in the *Datum* selection text box as the *Horizontal Dimensions* baseline.

6. In the *Property Manager*, under the *Vertical Dimensions Scheme* option panel, click once with the **left-mouse-button** in the *Datum* selection text box.

7. In the graphics window, select the top horizontal line as shown. Notice Line1 is now displayed in the *Datum* selection text box as the *Vertical Dimensions* baseline.

8. Select **Calculate** in the *Property Manager* to continue with the Fully Define Sketch command.

9. A dialog box appears with the statement "*Fully Define Sketch is complete but the sketch is still under defined.*" This is because the sketch is not fixed to a location in the coordinate system. Select **OK** to close the dialog box.

10. Click **OK** in the *Property Manager* to accept the results and exit the Fully Define Sketch command.

➤ The *Auto-dimension* results should appear as shown. (**NOTE:** Dimensional values will be different; this is only a rough sketch.)

11. On your own, change the dimensions to the desired values as shown. (**HINT:** Change the larger values first.)

Fully Defined Geometry

The sketch is under defined. The shape is now fully constrained, but the position is not fixed. On your own, left-click on any sketch feature and drag the mouse. Notice the sketch shape does not change, but the entire sketch is free to move.

1.   Press the [**Esc**] key to ensure no items are selected.

2.   Select the **Add Relation** command from the pop-up menu on the *Sketch* toolbar.

3.   Pick the **centerpoint** of the arc by left-mouse-clicking once on the geometry.

4.   Pick the sketch plane coordinate **origin**. (**NOTE:** If the origin symbol is not visible in the graphics area, turn *ON* the visibility by selecting Origins under the *View* toolbar.)

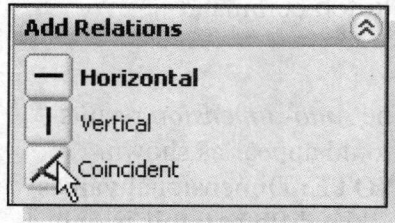

5.   Click once with the left-mouse-button on the **Coincident** icon in the *Add Relations Property Manager* as shown.

6.   Click the **OK** icon in the *Property Manager* to end the Add Relations command.

7.   Press the [**F**] key to zoom the sketch to fit the graphics area. Note that the sketch is fully defined with the added relation. **Fully Defined** is displayed in the *Status Bar* at the bottom of the screen, and the color of the sketch features changes to **black**.

Creating Fillets and Completing the Sketch

1. Click on the **Sketch Fillet** icon in the *Sketch* toolbar.

2. The *Sketch Fillet Property Manager* appears. Enter **20 mm** for the fillet radius as shown.

3. Notice *"Select a sketch vertex or entities to fillet"* is displayed in the *Message* panel of the *Property Manager*. Select the corner where the horizontal line meets the arc, as shown.

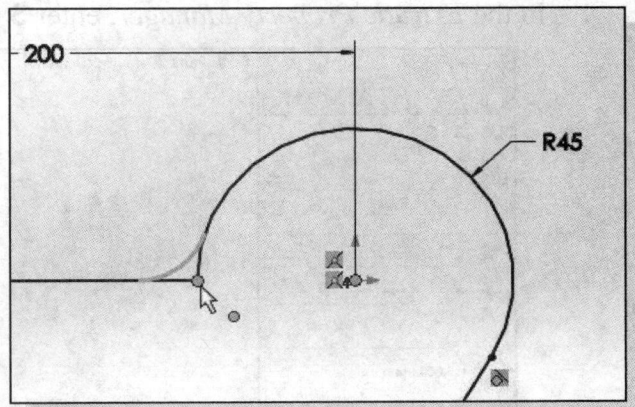

4. On your own, create the three additional fillets as shown in the figure below. Note that all the rounds and fillets are created with the same radius.

5. Click on the **OK** icon in the *Property Manager* to end the Sketch Fillet command.

6. Click once with the **left-mouse-button** on the **Exit Sketch** icon on the *Sketch* toolbar to exit the Sketch option.

Profile Sketch

❖ In SolidWorks, *profiles* are closed regions that are defined from sketches. Profiles are used as cross sections to create solid features. For example, **Extrude**, **Revolve**, **Sweep**, **Loft**, and **Coil** operations all require the definition of at least a single profile. The sketches used to define a profile can contain additional geometry since the additional geometric entities are consumed when the feature is created. To create a profile we can create single or multiple closed regions, or we can select existing solid edges to form closed regions. A profile cannot contain self-intersecting geometry; regions selected in a single operation form a single profile. As a general rule, we should dimension and constrain profiles to prevent them from unpredictable size and shape changes. SolidWorks does allow us to create under-defined profiles; the dimensions and/or geometric relations can be added/edited later.

❖ SolidWorks automatically highlights the closed region in the sketch and the defining geometry, which forms the profile required for the Extrude operation.

1. In the *Extrude Property Manager*, enter **5 mm** as the extrusion distance.

2. Click on the **OK** button to accept the settings and create the base feature.

❖ Note that all the sketched geometric entities and dimensions are consumed and have disappeared from the screen when the feature is created.

Redefining the Sketch and Profile using Contour Selection

• Engineering designs usually go through many revisions and changes. SolidWorks provides an assortment of tools to handle design changes quickly and effectively. We will demonstrate some of the tools available by changing the base feature of the design. The profile used to create the extrusion is selected from the sketched geometry entities. In SolidWorks, any profile can be edited and/or redefined at any time. It is this type of functionality in parametric modeling software that provides designers with greater flexibility and the ease to experiment with different design considerations.

• In the *SolidWorks Property Manager* for features requiring definition of a profile, the **Selected Contours** selection window can be used to select sketch contours and model edges, and apply features to them. **Contour Selection** is a grouping mechanism that allows us to use a partial sketch to create features. It is a tool that helps maintain design intent by reducing the amount of trimming necessary to build the contour. In the previous section, the **Boss-Extrude** feature was created using a single continuous sketch contour to define the profile. In this section we will demonstrate the utility of the **Contour Selection** tool to generate a similar profile from a sketch containing self-intersecting geometry and multiple closed regions.

1. In the *Feature Manager Design Tree*, **right-mouse-click** once on the **Boss-Extrude1** feature to bring up the option menu; then pick the **Edit Sketch** icon in the pop-up menu as shown.

2. Select the **View Orientation** button on the *Heads-up View* toolbar to show the available pre-defined view orientations.

3. Select the **Normal to** icon to obtain a view normal to the sketch.

4. On your own, create the very rough sketch as shown in the figure below. We will intentionally under-define the new sketch to illustrate the flexibility of the system. The dimensions of the new sketch elements are not important. It is important that **tangent relations** are added where the circles meet tangent to lines or other circles. (Hint: Use the **Perimeter Circle** option for the *Circle* command.)

5. Select the **Exit Sketch** icon on the *Sketch* toolbar to exit the Sketch option.

➤ The SolidWorks pop-up window may appear indicating an error will occur when SolidWorks attempts to rebuild the model. This is due to the multiple possible contours for extrusion now present in the sketch. We will next redefine the profile for the base feature using the **Selected Contours** tool.

6. If the SolidWorks pop-up window appears select the option '**Exit the sketch and rebuild anyway**.'

7. The red **x** next to the icon indicating the error in the feature.

8. In the *Feature Manager Design Tree*, **right-mouse-click** once on the **Boss-Extrude1** feature to bring up the option menu; then pick the **Edit Feature** icon in the pop-up menu.

❖ SolidWorks will now display the 2D sketch of the selected feature in the graphics window. We have literally gone back in time to the point where we define the extrusion feature. The original sketch and the new sketch we just created are wireframe entities recorded by the system as belonging to the same **SKETCH**; but only the **selected profile** entities are used to create the feature. We will now change the selected profile entities.

9. In the *Boss-Extrude1 Property Manager*, click on the arrow to reveal the *Selected Contours* option panel as shown (if necessary).

10. If the *Selected Contours* panel is not blank, move the cursor over the panel and click once with the **right mouse button**. In the pop-up option menu, select **Clear Selections**.

➢ **Sketch1** is displayed in the graphics area with no entities selected to define the profile for extrusion. The instruction *"Pick a sketch entity to define an open or closed contour. To define a region, pick inside an area bounded by sketch geometry"* appears in the *Status Bar*. The profile can be defined by either selecting sketch entities (lines, circles, etc.) to define a boundary, or by selecting bound areas for inclusion. We will use the latter option here.

11. Move the cursor inside the bound area shown in the figure. When the area is highlighted, click once with the **left-mouse-button** to select the area for inclusion in the profile. Notice **Sketch1-Region<1>** now appears in the *Selected Contours* panel on the *Property Manager*.

12. On your own, select additional areas for inclusion as shown. (If an incorrect area is selected, simply click on it again to unselect it. Be careful to click inside bound areas and not on the sketch entities. If difficulty is encountered, clear the selections and start over.)

13. In the *Boss-Extrude1 Property Manager*, click on the **OK** button to accept the settings and update the solid feature. The feature is recreated using the newly sketched geometric entities.

- The *Selected Contours* approach eliminates the need to trim the geometry manually. This approach encourages engineering content over drafting technique.

14. On your own, repeat the above steps and set the profile back to the **original profile**. The model should again look like the one shown at the top of page 6-18.

Create an OFFSET Extruded Cut Feature

➢ To complete the design, we will create a cutout feature by using the **Offset** command. First, we will set up the sketching plane to align with the front face of the 3D model.

1. In the *Features* toolbar, select the **Extruded Cut** command by left-clicking once on the icon.

2. Notice the left panel displays the *Edit Sketch Property Manager* with the instruction "*Select: a plane, planar face...*" **Select the front face** of the 3D model in the graphics window.

3. We will now convert the edge of the front face of the model into segments in the new sketch. **Select the front face again** as shown.

4. Select the **Convert Entities** icon in the *Sketch* toolbar.

➢ The Convert Entities command converts selected model features into sketch segments. Notice the edges of the selected surface have been converted to line and arc segments in the current sketch.

5. Select the **Offset Entities** icon in the *Sketch* toolbar.

6. In the *Offset Property Manager*, enter **5 mm** for the offset distance.

7. In the *Offset Property Manager*, select the options for *Add dimensions*, *Reverse*, and *Select chain* as shown.

8. In the graphics area, select any segment of the face outline which was just converted. Because the *Select chain* option is active, SolidWorks will automatically select all of the connecting geometry to form a closed region.

9. Click on the **OK** button to accept the settings and create the offset feature.

10. On your own, modify the offset dimension to **15 mm** as shown in the figure.

11. Click once with the **left-mouse-button** on the **Exit Sketch** icon on the *Sketch* toolbar to exit the Sketch option.

12. In the *Cut-Extrude Property Manager* panel, click the arrow to reveal the pull-down options for the *End Condition* (the default end condition is Blind) and select **Through All** as shown.

13. In the *Cut-Extrude Property Manager* panel, click on the arrow to reveal the *Selected Contours* option text box as shown. On your own, clear the selection in the box.

14. In the graphics area, move the cursor over the interior of the offset contour as shown in the figure below. Click once with the **left-mouse-button** to select the profile. Notice Sketch2-Region<1> now appears in the *Selected Contours* box on the *Property Manager*.

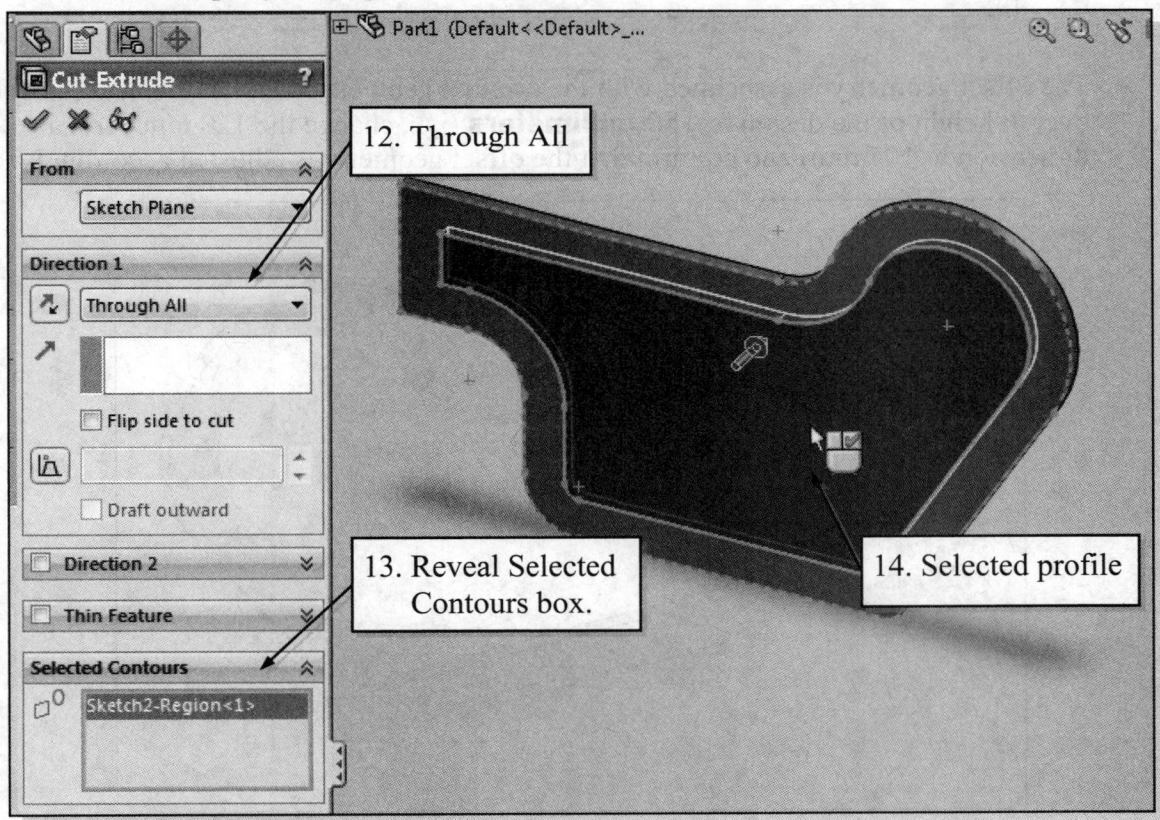

15. Click on the **OK** button to accept the settings and create the cut-extrude feature.

➤ The offset geometry is associated with the original geometry. On your own, adjust the overall height of the design to **150 millimeters** (i.e., change the 120 mm vertical dimension to 105 mm) and confirm that the offset geometry is adjusted accordingly.

16. Save the part with the filename *Gasket*.

Questions:

1. Can we create a profile with extra 2D geometry entities?

2. How do we access the SolidWorks **Edit Sketch** option?

3. How do we create a *profile* in SolidWorks?

4. Can we build a profile that consists of self-intersecting curves?

5. Describe the procedure to create an offset copy of a sketched 2D geometry.

6. Describe the **Selected Contours** option in SolidWorks.

7. Identify and briefly describe the following commands:

    (a)

    (b)

    (c)

    (d)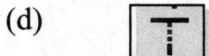

Exercises:

1. Dimensions are in inches. Plate Thickness: **0.25**

2. Dimensions are in inches. Plate thickness: **0.25**

3. Dimensions are in millimeters. Note the two R40 arcs at the base share the same center.

4. Dimensions are in inches.

5.   Dimensions are in inches.

Chapter 7
Orthographic Projection and Multiview Constructions

Learning Objectives

- ♦ **Understand the Basic Orthographic Projection Principles**
- ♦ **Be able to Perform 1st and 3rd Angle Projections**
- ♦ **Understand the Concept and Usage of the BORN Technique**
- ♦ **Understand the Importance of Parent/Child Relations in Features**
- ♦ **Use the *Suppress Feature* Option**
- ♦ **Resolve Undesired Feature Interactions**

Certified SolidWorks Associate Examination Objectives Coverage

Introduction

Most drawings produced and used in industry are *multiview drawings*. Multiview drawings are used to provide accurate three-dimensional object information on two-dimensional media, a means of communicating all of the information necessary to transform an idea or concept into reality. The standards and conventions of multiview drawings have been developed over many years, which equip us with a universally understood method of communication.

Multiview drawings usually require several orthographic projections to define the shape of a three-dimensional object. Each orthographic view is a two-dimensional drawing showing only two of the three dimensions of the three-dimensional object. Consequently, no individual view contains sufficient information to completely define the shape of the three-dimensional object. All orthographic views must be looked at together to comprehend the shape of the three-dimensional object. The arrangement and relationship between the views are therefore very important in multiview drawings. Before taking a more in-depth look into the multiview drawings, we will first look at the concepts and principles of projections.

Basic Principles of Projection

To better understand the theory of projection, one must become familiar with the elements that are common to the principles of **projection**. First of all, the **POINT OF SIGHT** (aka **STATION POINT**) is the position of the observer in relation to the object and the plane of projection. It is from this point that the view of the object is taken. Secondly, the observer views the features of the object through an imaginary PLANE OF PROJECTION (or IMAGE PLANE). Imagine yourself standing in front of a glass window, IMAGE PLANE, looking outward, the image of a house at a distance is sketched on to the glass which is a 2D view of a 3D house.

Orthographic Projection

The lines connecting from the *Point of Sight* to the 3D object are called the **Projection Lines** or **Lines of Sight**. Note that in the above figure, the projection lines are connected at the point of sight, and the projected 2D image is smaller than the actual size of the 3D object.

Now, if the *projection lines* are **parallel** to each other and the image plane is also **perpendicular** (*normal*) to the projection lines, the result is what is known as an **orthographic projection**. When the projection lines are parallel to each other, an accurate outline of the visible face of the object is obtained.

The term **orthographic** is derived from the word *orthos* meaning **perpendicular** or **90°**.

In *Engineering Graphics*, the projection of one face of an object usually will not provide an overall description of the object; other planes of projection must be used. To create the necessary 2D views, the *point of sight* is changed to project different views of the same object; hence, each view is from a different point of sight. If the point of sight is moved to the front of the object, this will result in the front view of the object. And then move the point of sight to the top of the object and looking down at the top, and then move to the right side of the object, as the case may be. Each additional view requires a new point of sight.

Principal Views
(Each with its point of sight)

Multiview Orthographic Projection

In creating multiview orthographic projection, different systems of projection can be used to create the necessary views to fully describe the 3D object. In the figure below, two perpendicular planes are established to form the image planes for a multiview orthographic projection.

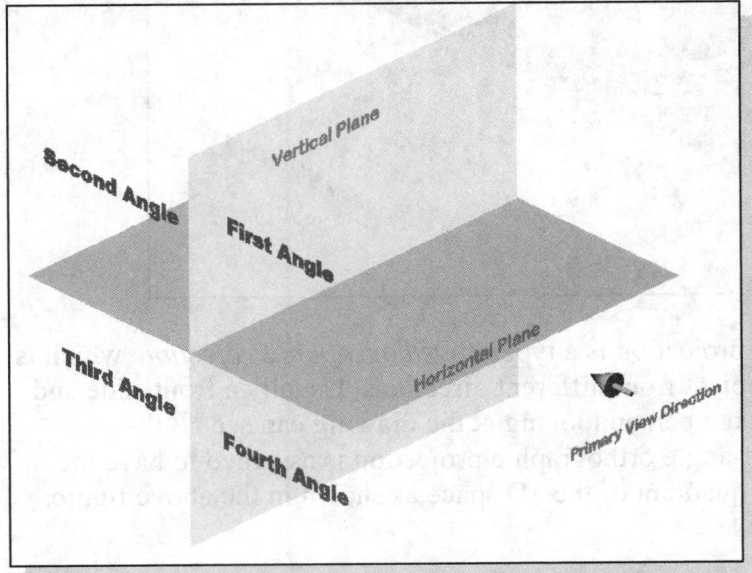

The angles formed between the horizontal and the vertical planes are called the **first**, **second**, **third** and **fourth angles**, as indicated in the figure. For engineering drawings, both **first angle projection** and **third angle projection** are commonly used.

FIRST-ANGLE PROJECTION

❖ First-angle orthographic projection is commonly used in countries that use the metric (International System of Units: SI) system as the primary units of measurement. The metric system was first developed in 17ᵗʰ century France, most European countries adopted the metric system by the end of the 18th century. Today, most countries in the world have adopted and are using the metric SI system as the primary units of measurement. In 1875, the United States solidified its commitment to the development of the internationally recognized metric system by becoming one of the original seventeen signatory nations to the Metre Convention or the Treaty of the Metre. Over the last 50 years, there has been a quiet ongoing debate in Washington over metric conversion. Many people have said that the United States must adopt the Metric System or face irreparable economic harm. And, several efforts have been made to start conversion. Back in 1975, Congress passed the *Metric Conversion Act*. The act mandated a ten year voluntary conversion period starting in 1975. The full conversion to the metric system was expected to occur in 1985. Yet, today, in spite of years of arguments and Federal efforts, very little has happened. The US is one of a handful of countries that still use the *Imperial Units* of Measurement.

- First-angle orthographic projection is a type of *Orthographic Projection*, which is a way of drawing a 3D object from different directions. Usually a front, side and top view are drawn so that a person looking at the drawing can see all the important sides. The first-angle orthographic projection is assumed to have the object placed in the first quadrant of the 3D space as shown in the above figure.

❖ In first-angle projection, the object is placed in **front** of the image planes. And the views are formed by projecting to the image plane located at the back.

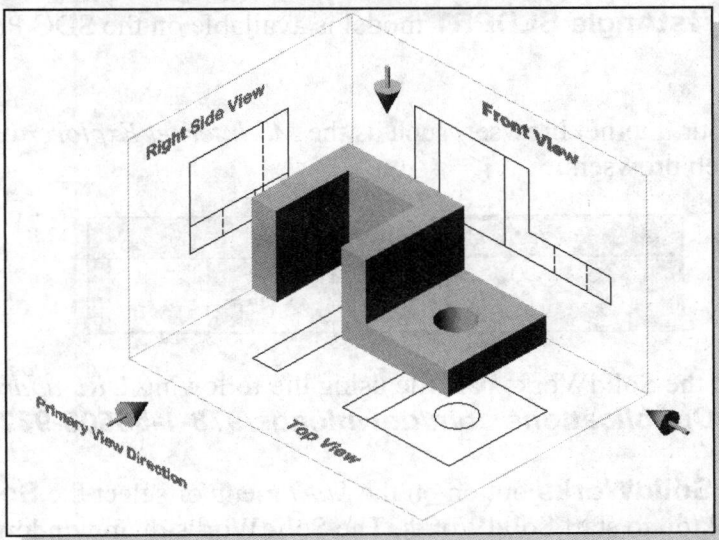

Rotation of the Horizontal and Profile Planes

In order to draw all three views of the object on the same plane, the horizontal (*Top View*) and profile (*Right Side view*) are rotated into the same plane as the primary image plane (*Front View*). Dashed lines are used to indicate edges of the design that are not visible.

The 3D Adjuster Model and 1ˢᵗ angle projection

❖ The **Adjuster1stAngle.SLDPRT** model is available on the SDC Publications website.

1. Launch your internet browser, such as the *MS Internet Explorer* or *Mozilla Firefox* web browsers.

2. Download the SolidWorks part file using the following *URL address*:
   www.SDCpublications.com/downloads/978-1-58503-932-6

3. Select the **SolidWorks** option on the *Start* menu or select the **SolidWorks** icon on the desktop to start SolidWorks. The SolidWorks main window will appear.

4. Select the **Open** icon with a single click of the left-mouse-button on the *Menu Bar* toolbar.

5. Select the downloaded file and click **Open** as shown.

- On your own, use the real-time dynamic rotation feature and examine the relations of the 2D views, projection planes and the 3D object.

General Procedure: 1st Angle Orthographic Projection

Choose the Primary View direction

Create the Front View (Primary View)

Create the Top View

Create the Right View

Example 2: 1st Angle Orthographic Projection

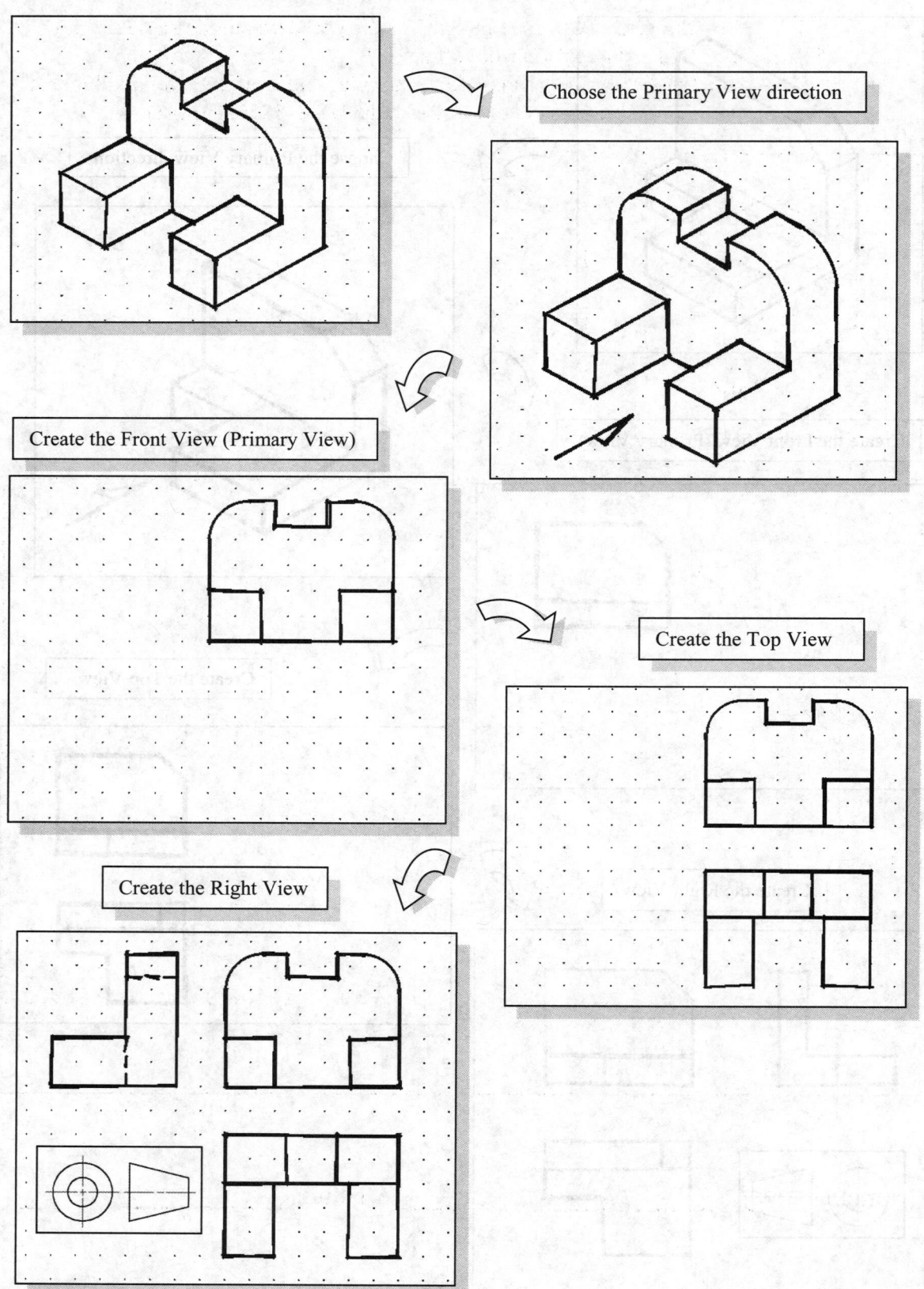

Choose the Primary View direction

Create the Front View (Primary View)

Create the Top View

Create the Right View

Chapter 7 - 1ˢᵗ Angle Orthographic Sketching Exercise 1:

Using the grid to estimate the size of the parts, create the standard three views by freehand rough sketching.

(Note that 3D Models of chapter examples and exercises are available at: www.SDCpublications.com/downloads/978-1-58503-932-6)

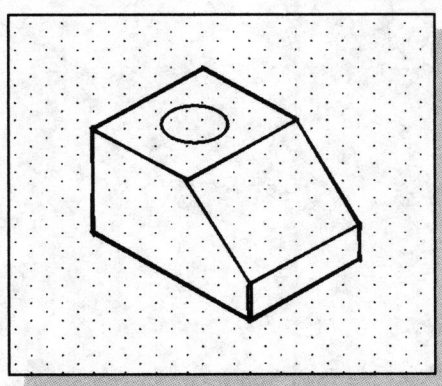

Name: _____   Date: _____

Notes:

Chapter 7 - 1st Angle Orthographic Sketching Exercise 2:

Using the grid to estimate the size of the parts, create the standard three views by freehand rough sketching.
(Note that 3D Models of chapter examples and exercises are available at: www.SDCpublications.com/downloads/978-1-58503-932-6)

Name: _____   Date: _____

Notes:

Chapter 7 - 1st Angle Orthographic Sketching Exercise 3:

Using the grid to estimate the size of the parts, create the standard three views by freehand rough sketching.
(Note that 3D Models of chapter examples and exercises are available at: www.SDCpublications.com/downloads/978-1-58503-932-6)

Name: _____   Date: _____

Notes:

Chapter 7 - 1st Angle Orthographic Sketching Exercise 4:

Using the grid to estimate the size of the parts, create the standard three views by freehand rough sketching.
(Note that 3D Models of chapter examples and exercises are available at: www.SDCpublications.com/downloads/978-1-58503-932-6)

Name: _____   Date: _____

Notes:

Chapter 7 - 1ˢᵗ Angle Orthographic Sketching Exercise 5:

Using the grid to estimate the size of the parts, create the standard three views by freehand rough sketching.
(Note that 3D Models of chapter examples and exercises are available at: www.SDCpublications.com/downloads/978-1-58503-932-6)

Name: _____   Date: _____

Notes:

Chapter 7 - 1st Angle Orthographic Sketching Exercise 6:

Using the grid to estimate the size of the parts, create the standard three views by freehand rough sketching.
(Note that 3D Models of chapter examples and exercises are available at: www.SDCpublications.com/downloads/978-1-58503-932-6)

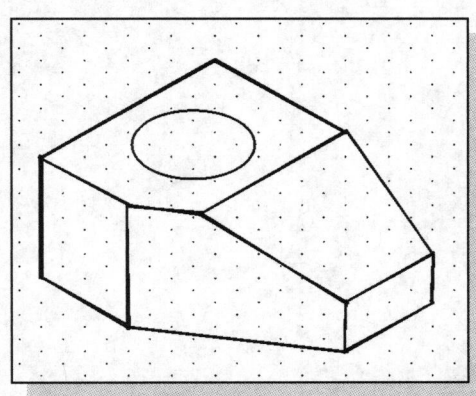

Name: _____   Date: _____

Notes:

Third-Angle Projection

❖ In United States, the *third-angle projection* is commonly used in Engineering Drawings.

❖ In *third-angle projection*, the image planes are placed in between the object and the observer. And the views are formed by projecting to the image plane located in front of the object.

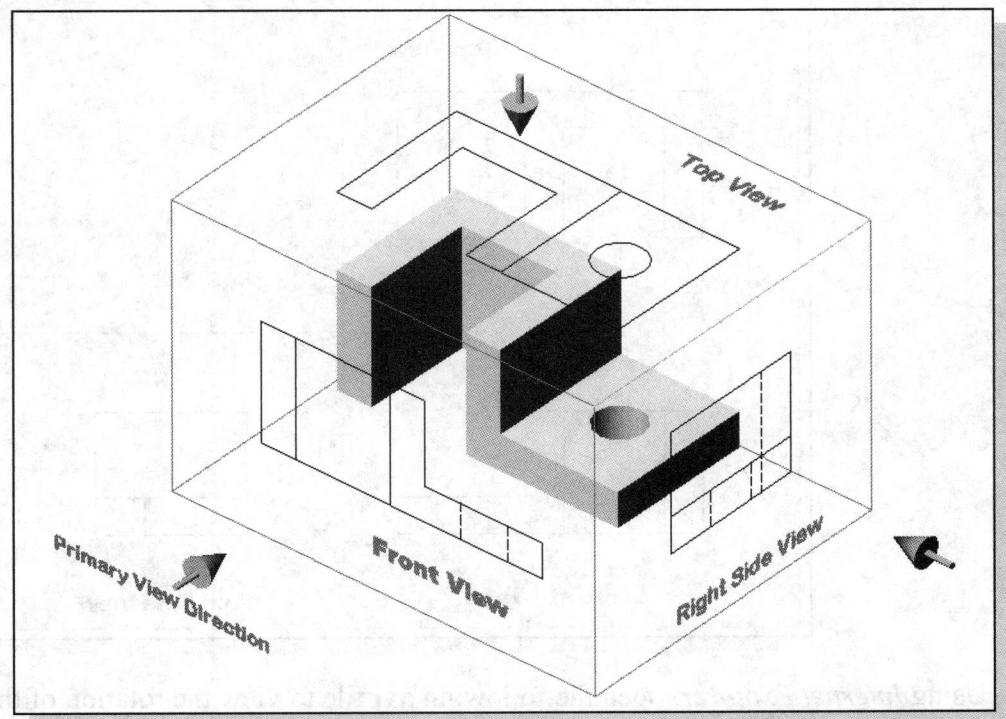

Rotation of the Horizontal and Profile Planes

In order to draw all three views of the object on the same plane, the horizontal (Top View) and profile (Right Side view) are rotated into the same plane as the primary image plane (Front View). Notice the use of dashed lines to indicate edges of the design that are not visible in the specific view direction.

> Using *Internet Explorer*, open the following **avi** file to view the rotation of the projection planes:
> ***www.SDCpublications.com/downloads/978-1-58503-932-6***

The 3D Adjuster Model and 3rd Angle Projection

❖ The **Adjuster3rdAngle.SLDPRT** model file is available on the SDC Publications website.

1. Launch your internet browser, such as the *MS Internet Explorer* or *Mozilla Firefox* web browsers.

2. Download the SolidWorks part file using the following *URL address*:
   www.SDCpublications.com/downloads/978-1-58503-932-6

3. Select the **SolidWorks** option on the *Start* menu or select the **SolidWorks** icon on the desktop to start SolidWorks. The SolidWorks main window will appear.

4. Select the **Open** icon with a single click of the left-mouse-button on the *Menu Bar* toolbar.

5. Select the downloaded file and click **Open** as shown.

- On your own, use the real-time dynamic rotation feature and examine the relations of the 2D views, projection planes and the 3D object.

The Glass Box and the Six Principal Views

Considering the third angle projection described in the previous section further, we find that the object can be entirely surrounded by a set of six planes, a Glass box. On these planes, views can be obtained of the object as it is seen from the top, front, right side, left side, bottom, and rear.

❖ Consider how the six sides of the glass box are being opened up into one plane. The front is the primary plane, and the other sides are hinged and rotated into position.

❖ In actual work, there is rarely an occasion when all six principal views are needed on one drawing, but no matter how many are required, their relative positions need to be maintained. These six views are known as the **six principal views**. In performing orthographic projection, each of 2D views shows only two of the three dimensions (**height**, **width**, and **depth**) of the 3D object.

❖ The most common combination selected from the six possible views consists of the *top*, *front* and *right-side* views. The selection of the *Primary View* is the first step in creating a *multi-view drawing*. The Primary View should typically be (1) the view which describes the main features of the design and (2) considerations of the layout of the other 2D views to properly describe the design.

General Procedure: 3rd Angle Orthographic Projection

Choose the Primary View direction

Create the Front View (Primary View)

Create the Top View

Create the Right View

Example 2: 3ʳᵈ Angle Orthographic Projection

Choose the Primary View direction

Create the Front View (Primary View)

Create the Top View

Create the Right View

Example 3: 3rd Angle Orthographic Projection

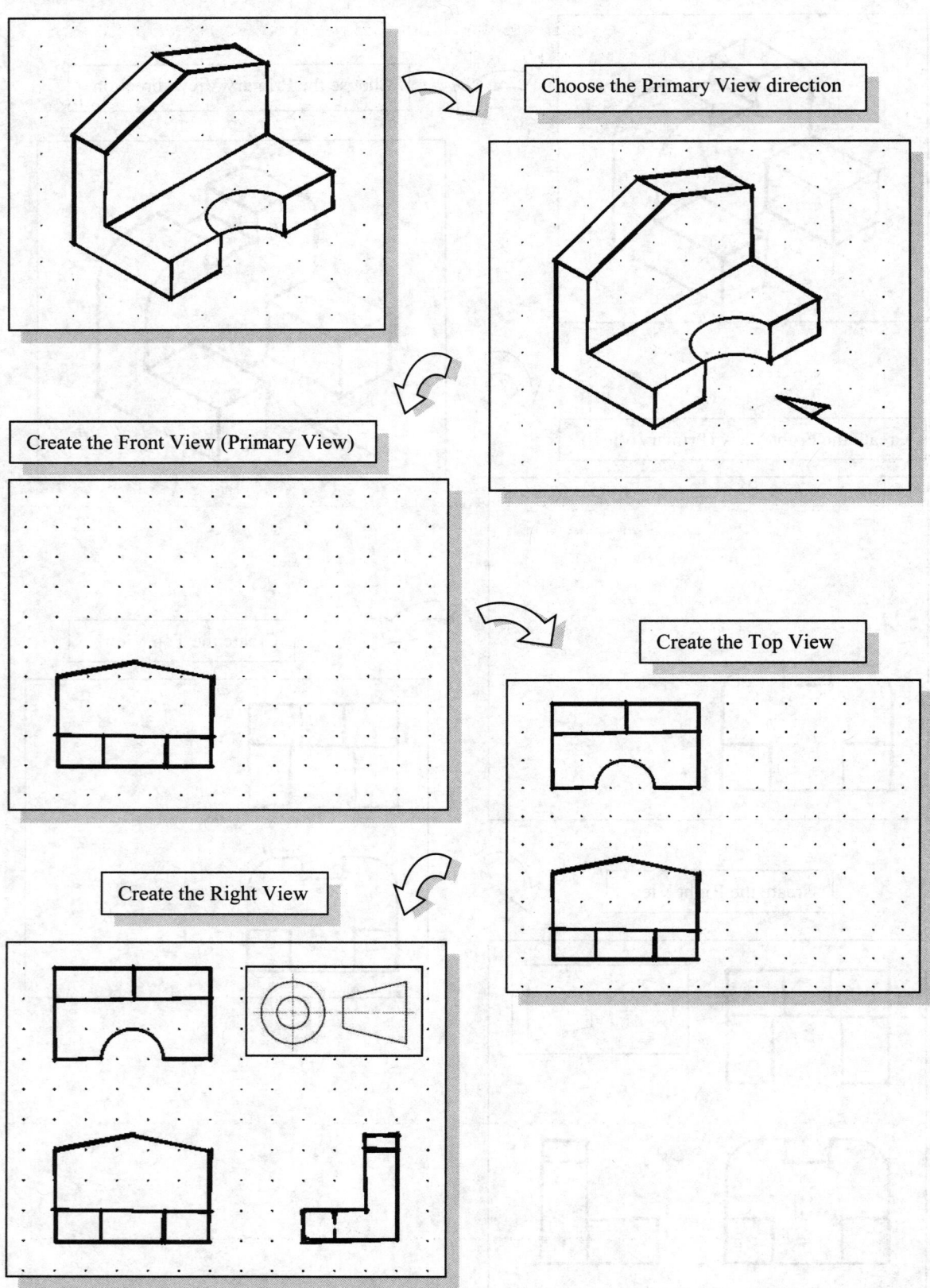

Choose the Primary View direction

Create the Front View (Primary View)

Create the Top View

Create the Right View

Chapter 7 - 3rd Angle Orthographic Sketching Exercise 1:

Using the grid to estimate the size of the parts, create the standard three views by freehand rough sketching.
(Note that 3D Models of chapter examples and exercises are available at: www.SDCpublications.com/downloads/978-1-58503-932-6)

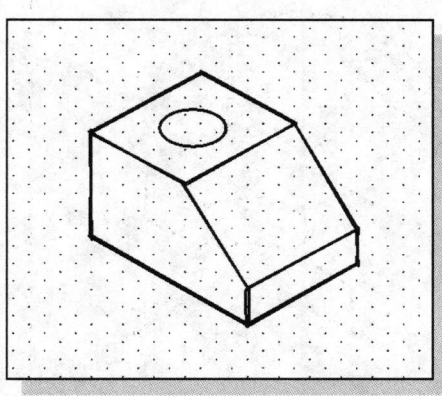

Name: _____   Date: _____

Notes:

Chapter 7 - 3rd Angle Orthographic Sketching Exercise 2:

Using the grid to estimate the size of the parts, create the standard three views by freehand rough sketching.

(Note that 3D Models of chapter examples and exercises are available at: www.SDCpublications.com/downloads/978-1-58503-932-6)

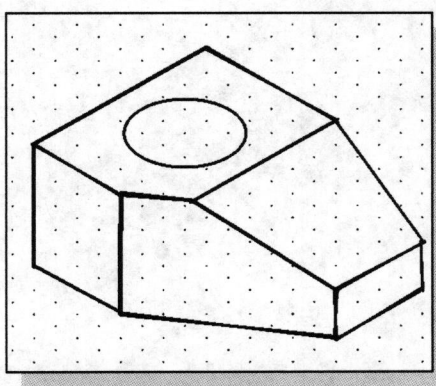

Name: _____   Date: _____

Notes:

Chapter 7 - 3rd Angle Orthographic Sketching Exercise 3:

Using the grid to estimate the size of the parts, create the standard three views by freehand rough sketching.
(Note that 3D Models of chapter examples and exercises are available at: www.SDCpublications.com/downloads/978-1-58503-932-6)

Name: _____   Date: _____

Notes:

Chapter 7 - 3rd Angle Orthographic Sketching Exercise 4:

Using the grid to estimate the size of the parts, create the standard three views by freehand rough sketching.
(Note that 3D Models of chapter examples and exercises are available at: www.SDCpublications.com/downloads/978-1-58503-932-6)

Name: _____   Date: _____

Notes:

Chapter 7 - 3ʳᵈ Angle Orthographic Sketching Exercise 5:

Using the grid to estimate the size of the parts, create the standard three views by freehand rough sketching.
(Note that 3D Models of chapter examples and exercises are available at: www.SDCpublications.com/downloads/978-1-58503-932-6)

Name: _____   Date: _____

Notes:

Chapter 7 - 3rd Angle Orthographic Sketching Exercise 6:

Using the grid to estimate the size of the parts, create the standard three views by freehand rough sketching.

(Note that 3D Models of chapter examples and exercises are available at: www.SDCpublications.com/downloads/978-1-58503-932-6)

Name: _____   Date: _____

Notes:

Alphabet of Lines

In *Technical Engineering Drawings*, each line has a definite meaning and is drawn in accordance to the line conventions as illustrated in the figure below. Two widths of lines are typically used on drawings, the thick line width should be 0.6 mm and the thin line width should be 0.3 mm.

Visible Line Visible lines are used to represent visible edges and boundaries. The line weight is thick, 0.6mm/0.024".

Hidden Line Hidden lines are used to represent edges and boundaries that are not visible from the viewing direction. The line weight is thin, 0.3mm/0.012".

Center Line Center lines are used to represent axes of symmetry. The line weight is thin, 0.3mm/0.012".

Dimension Line, Extension Line and Leader Dimension lines are used to show the sizes and locations of objects. The line weight is thin, 0.3mm/0.012".

Cutting Plane Lines Cutting Plane lines are used to represent the location of where an imaginary cut has been made, so that the interior of the object can be viewed. The line weight is thick, 0.6mm/0.024". (Note that two forms of line types can be used.)

Phantom Line Phantom lines are used to represent imaginary features or objects, such as a rotated position of a part. The line weight is thin, 0.3mm/0.012".

Break Line Break lines are used to represent imaginary cuts, so that the interior of the object can be viewed. The line weight is thick, 0.6mm/0.024".

Section Line Section lines are used to represent the regions that have been cut with the *break lines* or *cutting plane lines*. The line weight is thin, 0.3mm/0.012".

Precedence of Lines

In multiview drawings, coincidence lines may exist within the same view. For example, hidden features may project lines to coincide with the visible object lines. And center lines may occur where there is a visible or hidden outline.

In creating a multiview drawing, the features of the design are to be represented, therefore object and hidden lines take precedence over all other lines. And since the visible outline is more important than hidden features, the visible object lines take precedence over hidden lines. As shown in the below figure.

The following list gives the order of precedence of lines:
1. **Visible object lines**
2. **Hidden lines**
3. **Center line or cutting-plane line**
4. **Break lines**
5. **Dimension and extension lines**
6. **Crosshatch/section lines**

In the following sections, the general procedure of creating a 3rd angle three-view orthographic projection from a solid model using SolidWorks is presented.

The *U-Bracket* Design

> Based on your knowledge of SolidWorks so far, how many features would you use to create the model? What is your choice for arranging the order of the features? Would you organize the features differently if the rectangular cut at the center is changed to a circular shape (Radius: 80mm)?

Starting SolidWorks

1. Select the **SolidWorks** option on the *Start* menu or select the **SolidWorks** icon on the desktop to start SolidWorks. The SolidWorks main window will appear on the screen.

2. Select the **New** icon with a single click of the left-mouse-button on the *Menu Bar*. The *New SolidWorks Document* dialog box should appear in Advanced mode. If it appears in Novice mode, click once with the left-mouse-button on the **Advanced** icon.

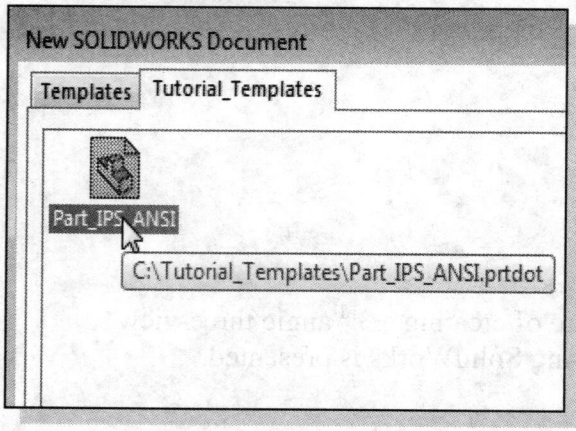

3. Select the **Tutorial_Templates** tab. (**NOTE:** You added this tab in Chapter 5. If your template is not available, open the standard Part template, then set the *Drafting Standard* to ANSI and the *Units* to IPS.)

4. Select the **Part_IPS_ANSI** template as shown.

5. Click on the **OK** button to open a new document using the template.

Applying the BORN Technique

In the previous chapters, we have used a technique of creating solid models known as the **"Base Orphan Reference Node"** (**BORN**) technique. The basic concept of the BORN technique is to use a *Cartesian coordinate system* as the first feature prior to creating any solid features. With the *Cartesian coordinate system* established, we then have three mutually perpendicular datum planes (namely the *XY or 'front'*, *YZ or 'right'*, and *ZX or 'top' planes*) available to use as sketching planes. The three datum planes can also be used as references for dimensions and geometric constructions. Using this technique, the first node in the design tree is called an "orphan," meaning that it has no history to be replayed. The technique of creating the reference geometry in this "base node" is therefore called the "Base Orphan Reference Node" (BORN) technique.

SolidWorks automatically establishes a set of reference geometry when we start a new part, namely a *Cartesian coordinate system* with three work planes, three work axes, and an origin. All subsequent solid features can then use the coordinate system and/or reference geometry as sketching planes.

❖ In the *Feature Manager Design Tree* panel, notice a new part name (Part1) appears with four work features established. The four work features include three *workplanes*, and the *origin*. By default, the three workplanes are aligned to the **world coordinate system** and the origin is aligned to the *origin* of the **world coordinate system**.

1. Inside the *Feature Manager Design Tree* panel, move the cursor on top of the first work plane, the **Front (XY) Plane**. Notice a rectangle, representing the workplane, appears in the graphics window.

2. Inside the *Feature Manager Design Tree* panel, click once with the right-mouse-button on Front (XY) Plane to display the option menu. Click on the **Show** icon to toggle *ON* the display of the plane.

3. On your own, repeat the above steps and toggle *ON* the display of all of the *workplanes* on the screen.

4. On your own, use the *Dynamic Viewing* options (Rotate, Zoom and Pan) to view the planes.

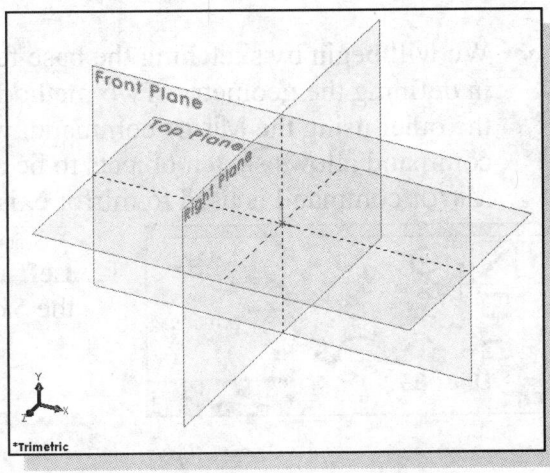

❖ By default, the basic set of planes is aligned to the world coordinate system; the workplanes are the first features of the part. We can now proceed to create solid features referencing the three mutually perpendicular datum planes. We will sketch the first feature, the base feature, in the top (XZ) plane. We will sketch the second feature in the front (XY) plane. Due to the symmetry in the shape of the part, we will use the right (YZ) plane and the front (XY) planes as planes of symmetry for the part. Thus before starting, we have decided on the orientation and the location of the part in relation to the basic workplanes.

5. Move the cursor inside the graphics area, but away from the planes, and click once with the **left-mouse-button** to make sure no plane is selected.

6. Select the **Extruded Boss/Base** button on the *Features* toolbar to create a new extruded feature.

7. In the *Edit Sketch Property-Manager*, the message "*Select a plane on which to create a sketch for the entity*" is displayed. Move the cursor over the edge of the Top Plane in the graphics area. When the Top Plane is highlighted, click once with the **left-mouse-button** to select the **Top (XZ) Plane** as the sketch plane for the new sketch.

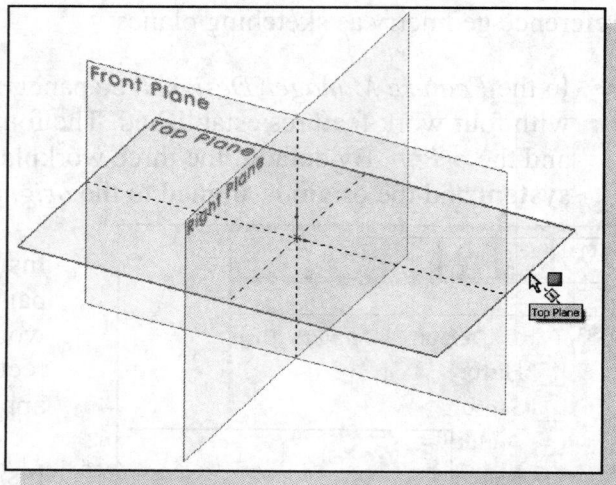

8. On your own, turn *OFF* the visibility of the three planes. (**HINT:** Right-click on each plane in the *Feature Manager Design Tree* and select Hide.)

Creating the 2D Sketch for the Base Feature

❖ We will begin by sketching the base feature. The symmetry of the feature will be used in defining the geometry. Two methods, one using the Dynamic Mirror command, the other using the Mirror command, will be demonstrated. The Dynamic Mirror command allows sketch objects to be automatically mirrored as they are drawn. The Mirror command is used to mirror existing objects.

1. **Left-click** on the arrow next to the **Line** button on the *Sketch* toolbar to reveal additional commands.

2. Select the **Centerline** command from the pop-up menu.

3. Move the cursor to a point directly above the *origin*. The Vertical relation will be automatically highlighted as shown. Click once with the **left-mouse-button** to select the first endpoint of the centerline.

4. Move the cursor to a point directly below the *origin*. The Vertical relation will be highlighted as shown. Click once with the **left-mouse-button** to select the second endpoint of the centerline.

5. Inside the graphics window, right-mouse-click to bring up the **option menu**.

6. In the option menu, choose **Select** to end the Centerline command.

❖ The **Mirror** and **Dynamic Mirror** commands can be used to generate sketch objects with symmetry about a centerline.

7. Select the **Tools** pull-down menu, then click on **Sketch Tools**. A complete list of sketch tools will appear. (Some of these also appear in the *Sketch* toolbar.)

8. Select **Dynamic Mirror** as shown.

9. The message *"Please select a sketch line or linear edge to mirror about"* appears in the *Mirror Property Manager*. Move the cursor over the centerline in the graphics area and click once with the **left-mouse-button** to select it as the line to mirror about.

➢ Notice the *hash marks* which appear on the centerline to indicate that the Dynamic Mirror command is active.

10. Click on the **Line** icon in the *Sketch* toolbar.

11. Move the cursor to a point on the centerline, above the *origin*. The Coincident relation will be highlighted as shown. Click once with the **left-mouse-button** to select the first endpoint of the line.

12. Move the cursor to a point to the right, activating the Horizontal relation, as shown. Click once with the **left-mouse-button** to select the second endpoint of the line.

13. Hit the [**Esc**] key once to end the Line command.

➢ Notice the mirror image of the line appears to the left of the centerline.

14. On your own, repeat the above steps to create a similar horizontal line below the origin. Be sure that the Horizontal and Vertical relations are active for the second endpoint as shown in the image to the right.

15. **Left-click** on the arrow next to the **Arc** button on the *Sketch* toolbar to reveal additional commands.

16. Select the **Tangent Arc** command from the pop-up menu.

17. Select the right endpoint of the top horizontal line, as shown below.

18. Select the right endpoint of the bottom horizontal line, as shown below.

19. Inside the graphics window, right-click to bring up the option menu. In the option menu, select **Select** to end the Tangent Arc command.

❖ SolidWorks offers the option to *autotransition* from the Line to the Tangent Arc command (and vice versa) without selecting the Arc command. We will redraw the second line and the arc to demonstrate this utility.

20. Click once with the left mouse button on the **Undo** command on the *Menu Bar* to reverse the last action – the creation of the arc.

21. Click a second time on the **Undo** command to reverse the creation of the line.

   ❖ Notice that the Dynamic Mirror tool has been disabled by the Undo command.

22. On your own, **turn ON** the Dynamic Mirror tool.

23. Execute the **Line** command and select a point on the centerline to restart the second horizontal line. Be sure that the **Horizontal** and **Vertical** relations are active for the endpoint as shown in the image to the right, then click once to select the endpoint.

24. Move the cursor away from the endpoint of the horizontal line. **Do not click**. Notice the preview shows another line.

25. Move the cursor back to the endpoint. **Do not click**.

26. Move the cursor away again. Notice the preview now shows a tangent arc.

27. Select the right endpoint of the top horizontal line to end the arc.

28. Inside the graphics window, right-mouse-click to bring up the option menu. In the option menu, choose **Select** to end the Line/Tangent Arc command.

29. On your own, **turn OFF** the Dynamic Mirror command.

❖ We will now constrain the center of the arc to be on a horizontal line with the origin.

30. **Left-click** on the arrow next to the **Display/Delete Relations** button on the *Sketch* toolbar to reveal additional sketch relation commands.

31. Select the **Add Relation** command from the pop-up menu. Notice the *Add Relations Property Manager* appears.

32. Pick the **centerpoint** of the tangent arc to the right side by left-clicking once on the geometry.

33. Pick the **origin**.

34. Click once with the left-mouse-button on the **Horizontal** icon in the *Add Relations Property Manager* as shown. This activates the Horizontal relation.

35. Click the **OK** icon in the *Property Manager*, or hit the [**Esc**] key once, to end the Add Relations command.

36. On your own, draw a **circle** as shown in the figure. Make sure the centerpoint for the circle is selected at the center of the tangent arc.

37. Press the [**Esc**] key to ensure no sketch features are selected.

38. Select the **Mirror Entities** command on the *Sketch* toolbar.

39. In the *Options* panel of the *Mirror Property Manager*, the *Entities to mirror:* text box is highlighted. Move the cursor over the **new circle** in the graphics area and click once with the **left-mouse-button** to select it as the object to mirror.

40. Move the cursor into the *Mirror about:* text box in the *Mirror Property Manager* and click once with the **left-mouse-button**.

41. Move the cursor over the **centerline** in the graphics area and click once with the **left-mouse-button** to select it as the object to mirror about.

42. Select **OK** in the *Mirror Property Manager*.

❖ We have now completed the rough sketch, and applied the appropriate geometric relations. Remember the concept is 'shape before size'.

43. On your own, apply the *Smart Dimensions* as shown below. Notice the sketch is now Fully Defined.

44. Select the **Exit Sketch** icon on the *Sketch* toolbar to exit the **Sketch** option.

Creating the First Extrude Feature

1. On your own, proceed with the **Boss Extrude** command and create a base with a height of **0.5** inches.

2. On your own, turn the visibility of the three major planes back *ON*. (**HINT:** Right-click on each plane in the *Feature Manager Design Tree* and select Show.)

➢   Notice the orientation of the base in relation to the major workplanes of the world coordinate system.

The Implied Parent/Child Relationships

•   The *Feature Manager Design Tree* display includes the **Front**, **Top**, and **Right Planes**, the **Origin** (default work features) and the base feature (**Boss-Extrude1** shown in the figure) we just created. The parent/child relationships were established implicitly when we created the base feature: (1) Top (*XZ) workplane* was selected as the sketch plane; (2) Origin was used as the reference point to align the 2D sketch of the base feature.

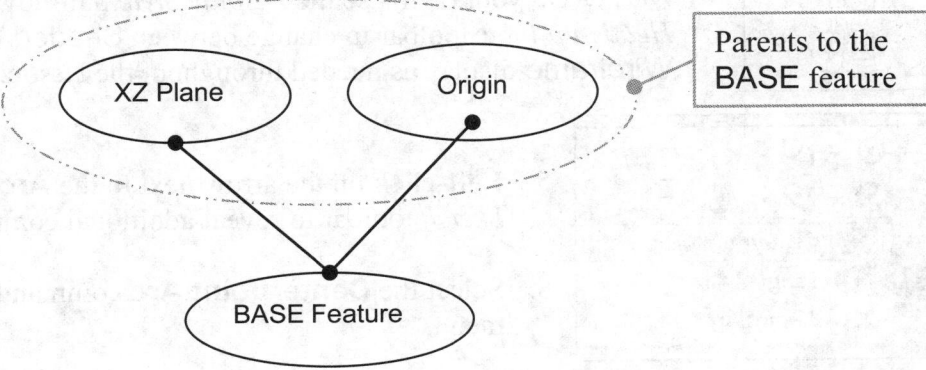

Creating the Second Solid Feature

- For the next solid feature, we will create the top section of the design. Note that the center of the base feature is aligned to the **Origin** of the default work features. This was done intentionally so that additional solid features can be created referencing the default work features. For the second solid feature, the **Front** *(XY) workplane* will be used as the sketch plane.

1. Move the cursor inside the graphics area, but away from the planes and click once with the **left-mouse-button** to make sure no plane is selected.

2. In the *Sketch* toolbar select the **Sketch** command by left-clicking once on the icon.

3. In the *Edit Sketch Property Manager*, the message "*Select a plane on which to create a sketch for the entity*" is displayed. Move the cursor over the edge of the Front Plane in the graphics area. When the **Front Plane** is highlighted, click once with the **left-mouse-button** to select the **Front (XY) Plane** as the sketch plane for the new sketch.

4. Change the display to wireframe by clicking once with the **left-mouse-button** on the **Wireframe** icon on the *Display Style* pull-down menu on the *Heads-up View* toolbar.

➢ NOTE: On your own, use the *Display Style* pull-down menu on the *Heads-up View* toolbar to change between **Shaded With Edges** and **Wireframe** display as needed throughout the lesson.

5. **Left-click** on the arrow next to the **Arc** button on the *Sketch* toolbar to reveal additional commands.

6. Select the **Centerpoint Arc** command from the pop-up menu.

7. Pick the **Origin** as the center location of the new arc.

8. On your own, create a semi-circle of arbitrary size, with both endpoints aligned to the X-axis, as shown below.

9. Move the cursor on top of the **Smart Dimension** icon. Left-click once on the icon to activate the Smart Dimension command.

10. On your own, create and adjust the radius dimension of the arc to **1.75**.

11. Select the **Line** command in the *Sketch* toolbar.

12. Create a line connecting the two endpoints of the arc as shown in the figure below.

13. On your own, add a **Coincident** relation between the **origin** and the **horizontal line**. The sketch should now be Fully Defined.

14. On your own, turn *OFF* the visibility of the workplanes.

15. Select the **Exit Sketch** icon on the *Sketch* toolbar to exit the Sketch option.

16. On your own, change the display style back to '*Shaded with edges*'.

17. In the *Extrude Property Manager* panel, click the drop down arrow to reveal the options for the *End Condition* (the default end condition is Blind) and select **Mid Plane** as shown.

18. In the *Extrude Property Manager* panel, enter **2.5** as the extrusion distance. Notice that the sketch region is automatically selected as the extrusion profile.

19. Make sure the **Merge result** box is checked.

20. Click on the **OK** button to proceed with the Extrude operation.

Creating the First Extruded Cut Feature

- A rectangular cut will be created as the next solid feature.

1. In the *Sketch* toolbar select the **Sketch** command by left-clicking once on the icon.

2. In the *Edit Sketch Property Manager*, the message *"Select a plane on which to create a sketch for the entity"* is displayed. Pick the front vertical face of the solid model shown.

3. We will use the origin as an endpoint for one of the dimensions. Make sure the **View Origins** option is toggled *ON* using the *Hide/Show Items* pull-down menu on the *Heads-up View* toolbar.

4. On your own, create a rectangle and apply the dimensions as shown. (**HINT:** To apply the horizontal dimension from the midpoint of the lower edge, select the **origin** of the world coordinate system as an endpoint. SolidWorks will automatically project the origin onto the workplane.)

5. On your own, exit the sketch and use the **Extruded Cut** command with the **Through All** end condition option to create a cutout that cuts through the entire 3D solid model as shown.

Creating the Second Extruded Cut Feature

1. In the *Features* toolbar select the **Extruded Cut** command by left-clicking once on the icon.

2. In the *Edit Sketch Property Manager*, the message "*Select a plane on which to create a sketch for the entity*" is displayed. Select the horizontal face of the last cut feature as the *sketching plane.*

3. Left-click on the **View Orientation** icon on the *Heads-up View* toolbar to reveal the *View Orientation* pull-down menu. Select the **Normal To** command.

❖ The *Normal To* command can be used to switch to a 2D view of a selected surface. Since the surface defining the current sketch plane was pre-selected, this surface is automatically used for the 2D view.

4. Select the **Circle** command by clicking once with the left-mouse-button on the icon in the *Sketch* toolbar.

5. Pick the projected origin to align the center of the new circle.

6. Create a circle of arbitrary size.

Ø.250

7. On your own, add the size dimension of the circle and set the dimension to **0.25**.

8. Select the **Sketch** icon on the *Sketch* toolbar to exit the Sketch option.

9. In the *Cut-Extrude Property Manager* panel, click the arrow to reveal the pull-down options for the *end condition* (the default end condition is Blind) and select **Through All**.

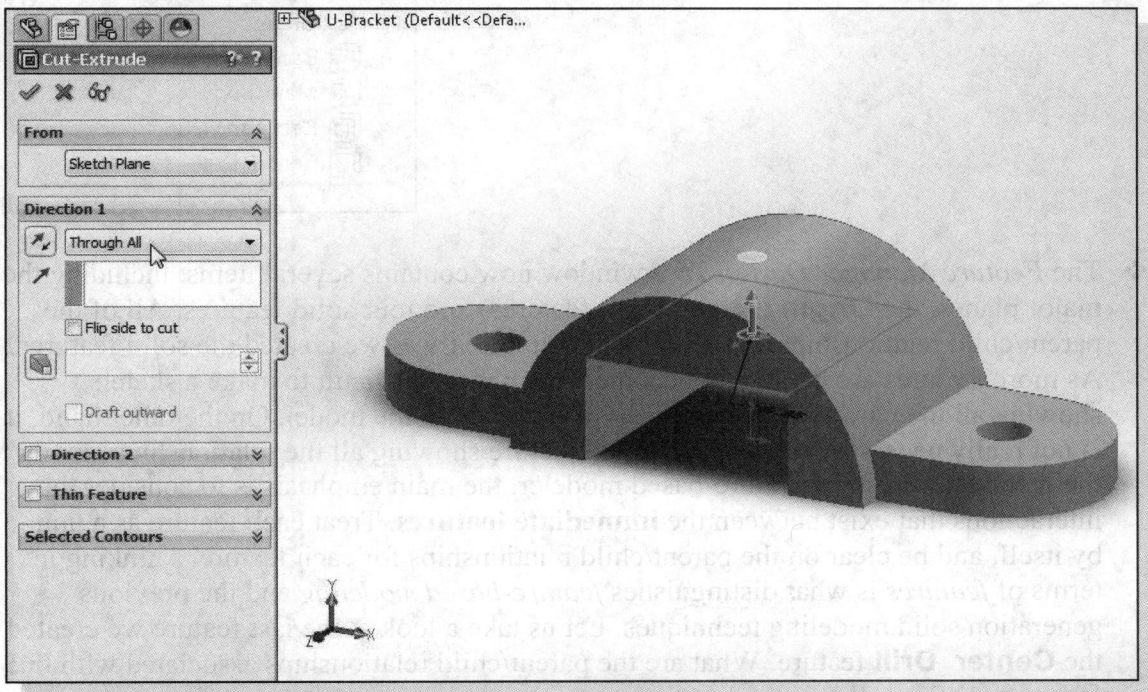

10. Click the **OK** button (green check mark) in the *Cut-Extrude Property Manager* panel.

Examining the Parent/Child Relationships

1. On your own, rename the feature names to: **Base**, **Main_Body**, **Rect_Cut** and **Center_Drill** as shown in the figure.

2. On your own, save the model using **U-Bracket** as the filename.

❖ The *Feature Manager Design Tree* window now contains several items, including the major planes, the **Origin** (default work features) and four solid features. All of the parent/child relationships were established implicitly as we created the solid features. As more features are created, it becomes much more difficult to make a sketch showing all the parent/child relationships involved in the model. On the other hand, it is not really necessary to have a detailed picture showing all the relationships among the features. In using a feature-based modeler, the main emphasis is to consider the interactions that exist between the **immediate features**. Treat each feature as a unit by itself, and be clear on the parent/child relationships for each feature. Thinking in terms of *features* is what distinguishes *feature-based modeling* and the previous generation solid modeling techniques. Let us take a look at the last feature we created, the **Center_Drill** feature. What are the parent/child relationships associated with this feature? (1) Since this is the last feature we created, it is not a parent feature to any other features. (2) Since we used one of the surfaces of the rectangular cutout as the sketching plane, the **Rect_Cut** feature is a parent feature to the **Center_Drill** feature. (3) We also used the projected Origin as a reference point to align the center; therefore, the **Origin** is also a parent to the **Center_Drill** feature.

Modify a Parent Dimension

❖ Any changes to the parent features will affect the child feature. For example, if we modify the height of the **Rect_Cut** feature from 1.0 to 0.75, the depth of the child feature (**Center_Drill** feature) will be affected.

1. In the *Feature Manager Design Tree* window, move the cursor on top of **Annotations** and click once with the **right-mouse-button** to bring up the option menu.

2. In the option menu, select **Show Feature Dimensions**.

3. Select the height dimension (1.0) by double-clicking on the dimension.

4. Enter **0.75** as the new height dimension as shown.

5. Select **OK** in the *Modify* window.

6. Click on the **Rebuild** button in the *Menu Bar* to proceed with updating the solid model.

➤ Note that the position of the **Center_Drill** feature is also adjusted as the placement plane is lowered. The drill-hole still goes through the main body of the *U-Bracket* design. The parent/child relationship assures the intent of the design is maintained.

7. On your own, adjust the height of the **Rect_Cut** feature back to **1.0 inch** before proceeding to the next section.

8. Repeat steps 1 and 2 to turn off the **Show Feature Dimensions** option.

A Design Change

➢ Engineering designs usually go through many revisions and changes. For example, a design change may call for a circular cutout instead of the current rectangular cutout feature in our model. SolidWorks provides an assortment of tools to handle design changes quickly and effectively. In the following sections, we will demonstrate some of the more advanced tools available in SolidWorks, which allow us to perform the modification of changing the rectangular cutout (2.0 × 1.0 inch) to a circular cutout (radius: 1.25 inch).

❖ Based on your knowledge of SolidWorks so far, how would you accomplish this modification? What other approaches can you think of that are also feasible? Of the approaches you came up with, which one is the easiest to do and which is the most flexible? If this design change were anticipated right at the beginning of the design process, what would be your choice in arranging the order of the features? You are encouraged to perform the modifications prior to following through the rest of the tutorial.

Feature Suppression

❖ With SolidWorks, we can take several different approaches to accomplish this modification. We could (1) create a new model, or (2) change the shape of the existing cut feature, or (3) perform **feature suppression** on the rectangular cut feature and add a circular cut feature. The third approach offers the most flexibility and requires the least amount of editing to the existing geometry. **Feature suppression** is a method that enables us to disable a feature while retaining the complete feature information; the feature can be reactivated at any time. Prior to adding the new cut feature, we will first suppress the rectangular cut feature.

1. Move the cursor inside the *Feature Manager Design Tree* window. Click once with the **right-mouse-button** on top of **Rect_Cut** to bring up the option menu.

2. Pick **Suppress** in the pop-up menu.

❖ We have literally *gone back in time*. The Rect_Cut and Center_Drill features have disappeared in the graphics area and both are shaded grey (meaning they are suppressed) in the *Feature Manager Design Tree*. The child feature cannot exist without its parent(s), and any modification to the parent (Rect_Cut) influences the child (Center_Drill).

3. Move the cursor inside the *Feature Manager Design Tree* window. Click once with the **right-mouse-button** on top of **Center_Drill** to bring up the option menu.

4. Pick **Unsuppress** in the pop-up menu.

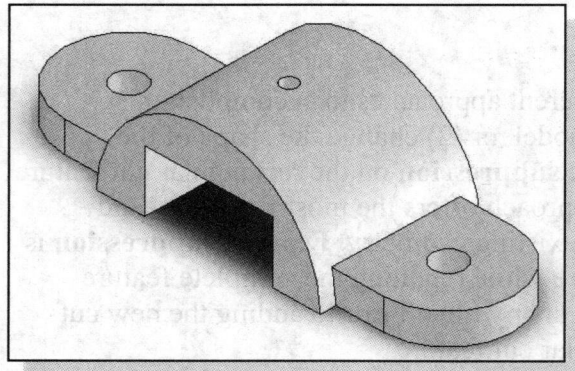

> In the display area and the *Model Tree* window, both the **Rect_Cut** feature and the **Center_Drill** feature are re-activated. The child feature cannot exist without its parent(s); the parent (Rect_Cut) must be activated to enable the child (Center_Drill).

A Different Approach to the CENTER_DRILL Feature

❖ The main advantage of using the BORN technique is to provide greater flexibility for part modifications and design changes. In this case, the Center_Drill feature can be placed on the Top (XZ) Workplane and therefore not be linked to the Rect_Cut feature. Again, we can take several different approaches to accomplish this modification. We could (1) delete the Center_Drill feature and the corresponding sketch, create a new sketch on the Top (XZ) Workplane, and recreate the Center_Drill feature, or (2) redefine the sketch plane for the existing sketch associated with the Center_Drill feature. We will perform the second option.

1. Move the cursor inside the *Feature Manager Design Tree* window. Click once with the **left-mouse-button** on the tree to reveal the Sketch defining the Center_Drill feature as shown.

2. Move the cursor inside the *Feature Manager Design Tree* window. Click once with the **right-mouse-button** on top of **Sketch4** to bring up the option menu.

3. Pick **Edit Sketch Plane** in the pop-up menu. This will allow us to redefine the workplane for Sketch4.

❖ The *Sketch Plane Property Manager* appears, with the *Sketch Plane/Face* text box highlighted. The original sketch plane for Sketch4 (Face<1>) appears in the field.

4. Notice the Part icon of the design tree now appears at the upper left corner of the graphics area. **Left-click** on the box next to the Part icon to reveal the design tree as shown.

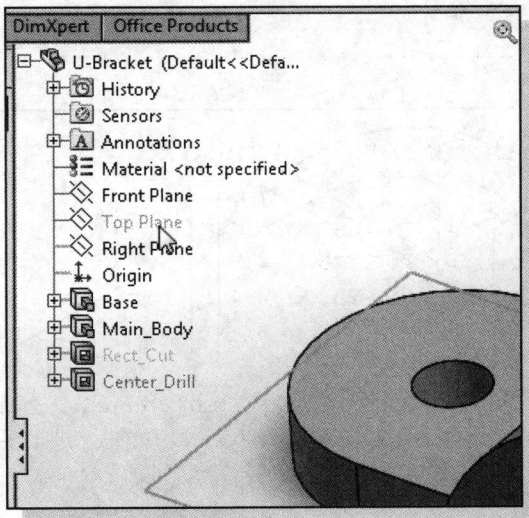

5. Move the cursor over the **Top Plane** icon. When the Top Plane is highlighted, click once with the **left-mouse-button** to select the Top (XZ) Plane as the sketch plane for Sketch4.

6. Top Plane now appears in the *Sketch Plane/Face* field of the *Sketch Plane Property Manager*. Click once with the **left-mouse-button** on the **OK** icon to accept the new definition of the sketch plane.

Suppress the Rect_Cut Feature

❖ Now the **Center_Drill** feature is no longer a child of the **Rect_Cut** feature, any change to the **Rect_Cut** feature does not affect the **Center_Drill** feature.

1. Move the cursor inside the *Model Tree* window. Click once with the right-mouse-button on top of **Rect_Cut** to bring up the option menu.

2. Pick **Suppress** in the pop-up menu.

❖ The **Rect_Cut** feature is now disabled without affecting the **new Center_Drill** feature.

Creating a Circular Extruded Cut Feature

1. In the *Features* toolbar select the **Extruded Cut** command by left-clicking once on the icon.

2. In the *Edit Sketch Property Manager*, the message "*Select a plane on which to create a sketch for the entity*" is displayed. **Left-click** on the Feature Manager Design Tree tab to reveal the design tree as shown.

3. Move the cursor over the edge of the **Front Plane** icon in the *Feature Manager Design Tree*. When the Front Plane is highlighted, click once with the **left-mouse-button** to select the Front (XY) Plane as the sketch plane for the new sketch.

4. Select the **Circle** command by clicking once with the left-mouse-button on the icon in the *Sketch* toolbar.

5. Pick the **Origin** to align the center of the new circle.

6. Create a circle of arbitrary size.

7. On your own, create the size dimension of the circle and set the dimension to **2.5**, as shown in the figure.

8. On your own, complete the cut feature using the **Extruded Cut** command. Use the **Mid Plane** *end condition* option and **Through All-Both** for the *depth*.

9. Rename the feature **Circular_Cut**.

❖ Note that the parents of the Circular_Cut feature are the Front (XY) Plane and the Origin.

A Flexible Design Approach

In a typical design process, the initial design will undergo many analyses, testing, reviews and revisions. SolidWorks allows the users to quickly make changes and explore different options of the initial design throughout the design process.

The model we constructed in this chapter contains two distinct design options. The *feature-based parametric modeling* approach enables us to quickly explore design alternatives and we can include different design ideas into the same model. With parametric modeling, designers can concentrate on improving both the design and the design process. The key to successfully using parametric modeling as a design tool lies in understanding and properly controlling the interactions of features, especially the parent/child relations.

1. Select **Save** in the *standard toolbar* to save the model using **U-Bracket** as the filename.

Drawings from Parts and Associative Functionality

With the software/hardware improvements in solid modeling, the importance of two-dimensional drawings is decreasing. Drafting is considered one of the downstream applications of using solid models. In many production facilities, solid models are used to generate machine tool paths for *computer numerical control* (CNC) machines. Solid models are also used in *rapid prototyping* to create 3D physical models out of plastic resins, powdered metal, etc. Ideally, the solid model database should be used directly to generate the final product. However, the majority of applications in most production facilities still require the use of two-dimensional drawings. Using the solid model as the starting point for a design, solid modeling tools can easily create all the necessary two-dimensional views. In this sense, solid modeling tools are making the process of creating two-dimensional drawings more efficient and effective.

SolidWorks provides associative functionality in the different SolidWorks modes. This functionality allows us to change the design at any level, and the system reflects it at all levels automatically. For example, a solid model can be modified in the *Part Modeling* mode and the system automatically reflects that change in the *Drawing* mode. And we can also modify a feature dimension in the *Drawing* mode, and the system automatically updates the solid model in all modes.

In this lesson, the general procedure of creating multi-view drawings is illustrated. The *U_Bracket* design from last chapter is used to demonstrate the associative functionality between the model and drawing views.

Drawing Mode

➤ SolidWorks allows us to generate 2D engineering drawings from solid models so that we can plot the drawings to any exact scale on paper. An engineering drawing is a tool that can be used to communicate engineering ideas/designs to manufacturing, purchasing, service, and other departments. Until now we have been working in *Model* mode to create our design in *__full size__*. We can arrange our design on a two-dimensional sheet of paper so that the plotted hardcopy is exactly what we want. This two-dimensional sheet of paper is saved in a *drawing* file in SolidWorks. We can place borders and title blocks, objects that are less critical to our design, in the *drawing*. In general, each company uses a set of standards for drawing content, based on the type of product and also on established internal processes. The appearance of an engineering drawing varies depending on when, where, and for what purpose it is produced. However, the general procedure for creating an engineering drawing from a solid model is fairly well defined. In SolidWorks, creation of 2D engineering drawings from solid models consists of four basic steps: drawing sheet formatting, creating/positioning views, annotations, and printing/plotting.

1. Click on the arrow next to the **New** icon on the *Menu Bar* and select **Make Drawing from Part/Assembly** in the pull-down menu.

➤ We must now select a drawing template. A drawing template is the foundation for drawing information in SolidWorks. The template contains specifications including sheet size and orientation, and the SolidWorks sheet format. The sheet format includes borders, title blocks, bill of materials table format, etc. The user can select from the SolidWorks 'Standard' drawing template, the SolidWorks 'Tutorial' drawing template, user-defined custom templates, or use no template. We will use the SolidWorks 'Tutorial' drawing template.

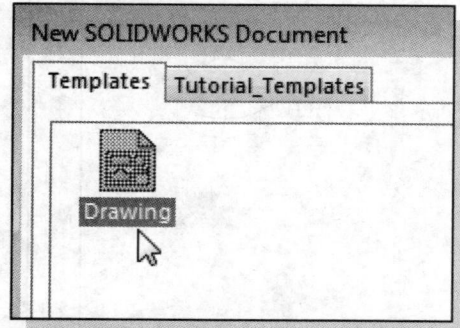

2. In the *New SolidWorks Document* window, select the **Templates** tab.

3. Select the **Drawing** template file icon.

4. Select **OK** to open a drawing using the *draw* template.

5. In the *Sheet Format/Size* window, accept the default settings and click **OK**. (We will reset the paper size and formatting in subsequent steps.)

➤ Note that a new graphics window appears on the screen. We can switch between the solid model and the drawing by clicking the corresponding file from the *Window* pull-down menu.

➢ In the graphics window, SolidWorks displays a default drawing sheet that includes a title block. The title block also indicates the paper size being used.

➢ The **View Palette** appears in the task pane. This can be used to insert drawing views. We will first set the document properties and sheet properties for the drawing.

➢ In the *Feature Manager Design Tree* area, the **Drawing** icon is displayed at the top, which indicates that we have switched to *Drawing* mode. The default filename is the filename of the solid part file from which we created the drawing – U-Bracket. *Sheet1* is the current drawing sheet that is displayed in the graphics window.

Setting Document Properties

➤ The document properties, such as dimensioning standard, units, text fonts, etc., must be set for the new drawing file. If a set of document properties will be used regularly, a new drawing file template can be saved which contains these settings.

1. Select the **Options** icon from the *Menu Bar* to open the options dialog box.

2. Under the **System Options** tab, select **Display Style** as shown.

3. Under '*Display style for new views*', select **Hidden lines visible**. This will be the default display style for orthographic views (e.g., front view) added to the drawing.

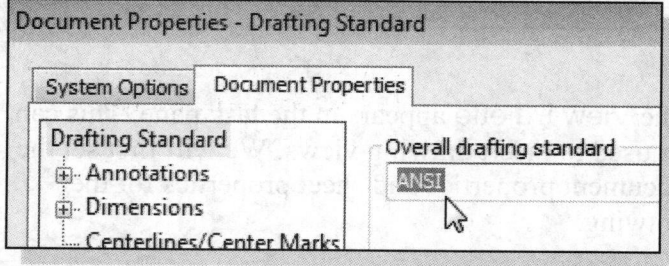

4. Select the **Document Properties** tab.

5. Select **ANSI** in the drop-down selection window under the *Dimensioning standard* panel as shown.

6. On your own, confirm the ANSI standard is set for the different options under **Annotations** and **Dimensions**.

7. Select **IPS (inch, pound, second)** under the *Unit system* options.

8. Select **.12** in the *Decimals* spin boxes for the *Length* and *Dual Dimension Length* units as shown to define the degree of accuracy with which the units will be displayed to 2 decimal places.

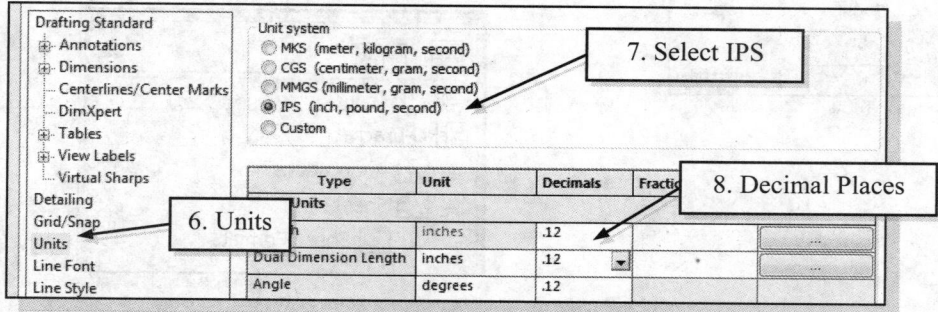

9. Click **OK** in the options dialog box to accept the selected settings.

Setting Sheet Properties using the Pre-Defined Sheet Formats

➢ Another set of properties are set for each sheet in the drawing file. These settings include sheet size, sheet orientation, scale, and projection type.

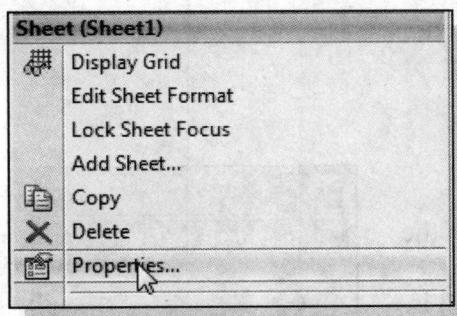

1. Move the cursor onto the graphics area and click once with the **right-mouse-button** to open the pop-up menu.

2. Expand the pop-up menu, select **Properties** from as shown to edit the properties for Sheet1.

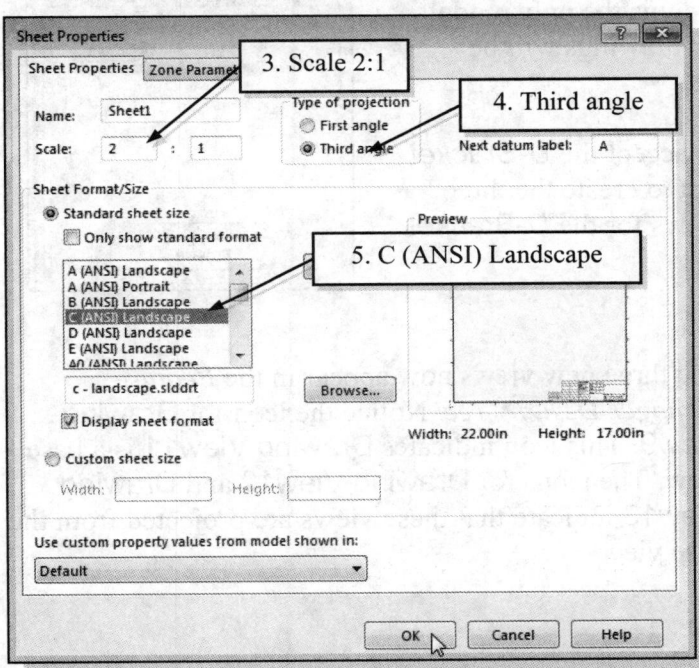

3. In the *Sheet Properties* window, set the scale to **2:1** as shown.

4. Set the *Type of projection* to **Third angle**.

5. Set the *Standard sheet size* to **C (ANSI) Landscape**.

6. Click **OK** in the *Sheet Properties* window to accept the selected settings.

7. Press the **[F]** key to scale the new sheet to fit the display area.

8. Click on the **View Layout tab** to display the Layout related commands as shown.

Creating Three Standard Views

1. Select the **Standard 3 View** button on the *Drawing* toolbar.

➤ The *Standard 3 View Property Manager* appears. In the *Open documents* field of the *Part/Assembly to Insert* option window, the **U-Bracket** part file appears and is highlighted. The *U-Bracket* model is the only model opened. By default, all of the 2D drawings will be generated from this model file.

2. Left-click on the **OK** icon to accept the *U-Bracket* part file as the document used to create the three views. The three standard views for the *U-Bracket* appear on the active sheet.

➤ The three new views now appear in the *Feature Manager Design Tree*. Notice the icon for Drawing View9. This icon indicates Drawing View11 is a base view. The icons for Drawing View12 and Drawing View13 indicate that these views are projected from the base view.

Repositioning Views

1. Move the cursor on top of the front view and watch for the **four-arrow Move symbol** as the cursor is near the border indicating the view can be dragged to a new location as shown in the figure.

2. Press and hold down the left-mouse-button and reposition the view to a new location.

3. On your own, reposition the views we have created so far. Note that the top view can be repositioned only in the vertical direction. The top view remains aligned to the base view, the front view. Similarly, the right side view can be repositioned only in the horizontal direction.

Adding a New Sheet

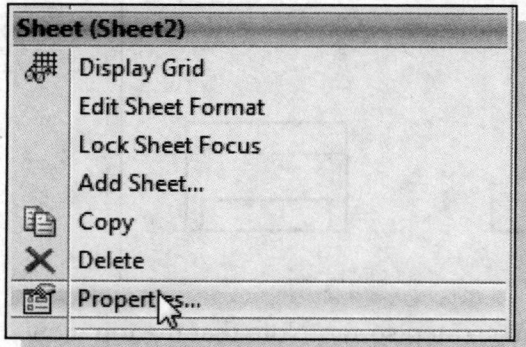

1. Move the cursor into the graphics area and click once with the **right-mouse-button** to reveal the pop-up menu.

2. Select **Add Sheet** from the pop-up menu as shown.

➤ The new sheet appears in the graphics area as the active sheet.

3. Move the cursor onto the graphics area and click once with the **right-mouse-button** to open the pop-up menu.

4. Select **Properties** from the pop-up menu as shown to edit the properties for Sheet2.

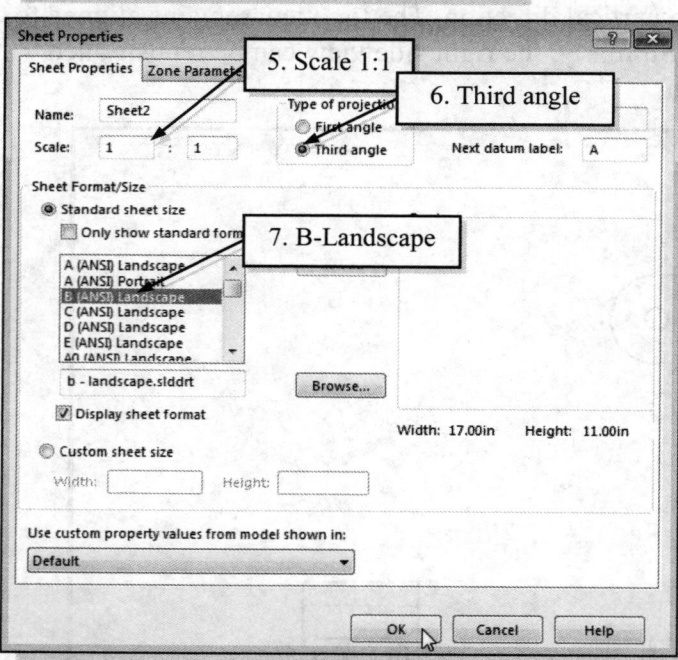

5. In the *Sheet Properties* window, set the scale to **1:1** as shown.

6. Set the *Type of projection* to **Third angle**.

7. Set the *Standard sheet size* to **B-Landscape**.

8. Click **OK** in the *Sheet Properties* window to accept the selected settings.

9. Press the **[F]** key to scale the new sheet to fit the display area.

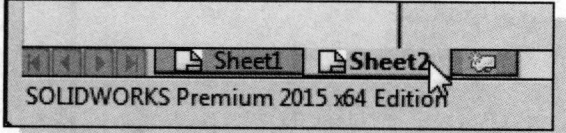

➤ The active sheet can be changed by left-clicking on the sheet tabs at the bottom of the graphics area.

Adding a Base View

❖ In *SolidWorks Drawing* mode, the first drawing view we create is called a *base view*. A *base view* is the primary view in the drawing; other views can be derived from this view. When creating a *base view*, SolidWorks allows us to specify the view to be shown. By default, SolidWorks will treat the *world XY plane* as the front view of the solid model. Note that there can be more than one *base view* in a drawing.

1. Make sure Sheet2 is the active drawing sheet.

2. Click on the **View Layout tab** to display the Layout related commands as shown.

3. Click on the **Model View** icon on the *Drawing* toolbar.

4. The *Model View Property Manager* appears with the U-Bracket part file selected as the part from which to create the base view. Click the **Next** arrow as shown to proceed with defining the base view.

5. In the *Orientation* panel of the *Model View Property Manager*, select the **Front View** for the *Orientation*, as shown. (Make sure the *Create multiple views* box is **unchecked**.)

6. **Scroll down** in the *Property Manager* to the *Display Style* panel. Notice the default display style is *Hidden Lines Visible*. This was defined in the *Document Settings*.

7. Under the *Scale* option, select **Use custom scale**.

8. Select **1:1** from the pull-down window, as shown.

9. Move the cursor inside the graphics area and left-click to place the base view near the lower left corner of the drawing sheet as shown below.

10. Upon placement of the base view, SolidWorks automatically enters the **Projected View** command. Move the cursor above the base view and select a location to position the projected top view of the model.

11. Click **OK** in the *Property Manager* to exit the Projected View command.

❖ In *SolidWorks Drawing* mode, **projected views** can be created with a first-angle or third-angle projection, depending on the drafting standard used for the drawing. We must have a base view before a projected view can be created. Projected views can be orthographic projections or isometric projections. Orthographic projections are aligned to the base view and inherit the base view's scale and display settings.

> **NOTE:** In your drawing, the inserted views may include *center marks*, *centerlines*, and/or *dimensions*. If so, these were added with the **auto-insert** option. To access these options, click **Options** (*Standard* toolbar), select the **Document Properties** tab, and then select **Detailing**. This lesson was done with only the **Center marks-holes-part** auto-insert option selected. Other center marks, centerlines, and dimensions will be added individually.

> Notice the hidden lines are visible. The dash lengths and spaces can be adjusted in the document properties.

12. Select the **Options** icon from the *Menu Bar* to open the options window.

13. Select the **Document Properties** tab.

14. Select **Line Style**.

15. Select the **Dashed** line style.

16. Adjust the *Line length and spacing values* to, for example, **A,0.75,-0.25**. (This will scale the dash length by 0.75 and the space by 0.25.)

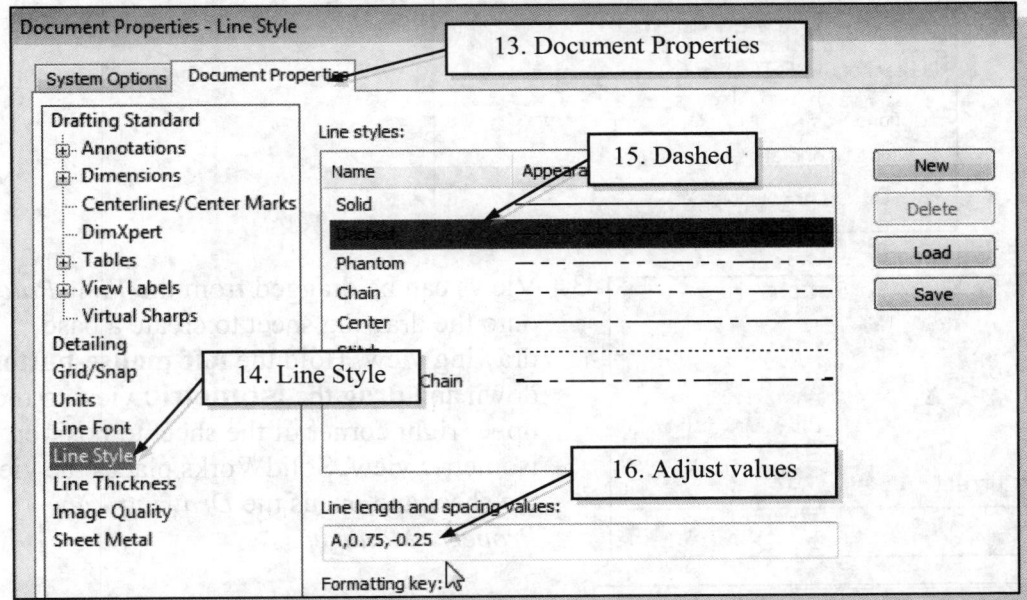

17. Left-click on the **OK** button to accept the settings.

18. Press the **[F]** key to fit the drawing to the graphics viewing area.

Adding an Isometric View using the View Palette

❖ We will add an isometric view. The isometric view could be added as a *Projected View* based on the existing *Front View*. We will add the isometric view as a second base view. It can be added using the Model View command as was used for the *Front View*. An alternate method to add a base view is to use the **View Palette**. We will use this option.

1. Click on the **View Palette** icon to the right of the graphics area.

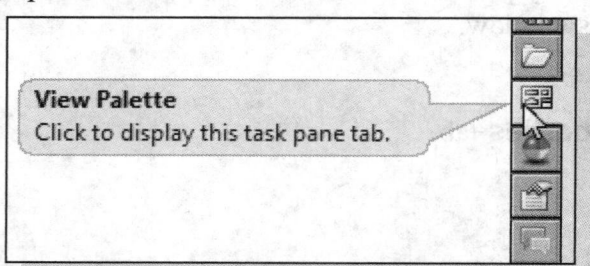

2. The *View Palette* appears in the task pane. Confirm the **U-Bracket** part is identified as shown.

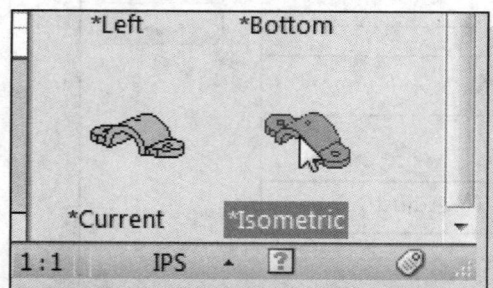

3. Views can be dragged from the *View Palette* onto the drawing sheet to create a base drawing view. Hold the **left-mouse-button** down and **drag** the **Isometric** view to the upper right corner of the sheet to position the isometric view. SolidWorks places the view on the sheet and opens the *Drawing View Property Manager*.

➢ Note that as a general rule, hidden lines are not shown in isometric views.

4. In the *Drawing View Property Manager*, select the **Hidden Lines Removed** option for the *Display Style*.

5. Left-click on the **OK** icon in the *Drawing View Property Manager* to accept the view.

Adjusting the View Scale

❖ SolidWorks allows us to easily adjust the drawing view settings. Simply selecting a drawing view will open the corresponding *Property Manager*.

1. Move the cursor on top of the isometric view and watch for the box around the entire view indicating the view is selectable as shown in the figure. **Left-mouse-click** once to bring up the *Property Manager*.

2. Under the *Scale* options in the *Drawing View Property Manager*, select **Use custom scale**.

3. Select **User Defined** from the pull-down options (scroll to the top of the list), as shown.

4. Enter **3:4** as the user defined scale.

5. Left-click on the **OK** icon in the *Drawing View Property Manager* to accept the new settings.

6. If necessary, reposition the views to appear as shown below.

7. Click Save to save the drawing file

➢ Note that we have completed the creation of the necessary 2D orthographic views of the U-Bracket design for a multiview engineering drawing. In the next chapter, we will look into the general procedure in providing detailed descriptions of the created 2D views to document the design.

Questions:

1. Explain what an orthographic view is and why it is important to engineering graphics.

2. What is the purpose of creating 2D orthographic views?

3. What information is missing in the front view? Top view? Right view?

4. Which dimension stays the same in between the Top view and the front view?

5. How do you decide which views are necessary for a multi-view drawing?

6. Explain the creation of 2D views using the 1st Angle Projection method.

7. Explain the creation of 2D views using the 3rd Angle Projection method.

8. How do you modify the sheet size in SolidWorks?

Exercises: (Unless otherwise specified, dimensions are in inches.)

1. Tube Hanger

2. Anchor Base

3. **Bearing Base**

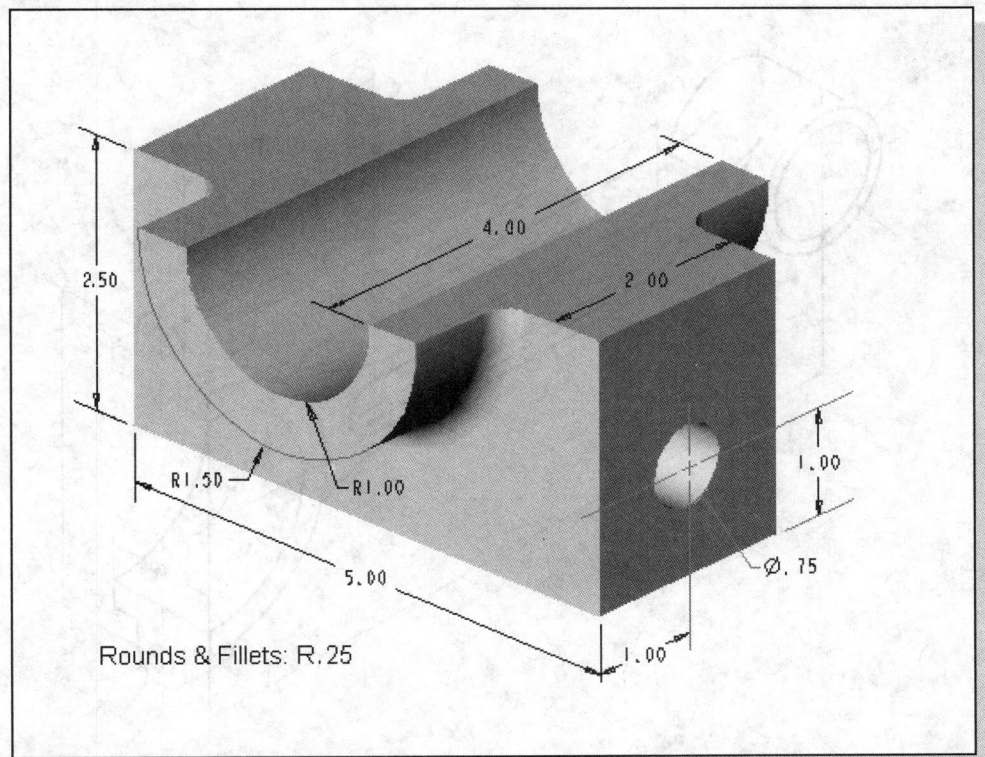

4. **Shaft Support** (Dimensions are in Millimeters.)

5. Connecting Rod

Chapter 8
Dimensioning and Notes

Learning Objectives

♦ **Understand Dimensioning Nomenclature and Basics**
♦ **Create Drawing Layouts from Solid Models**
♦ **Understand Associative Functionality**
♦ **Using the default Sheet Formats**
♦ **Arrange and Manage 2D Views in Drawing Mode**
♦ **Display and Hide Feature Dimensions**
♦ **Create Reference Dimensions**
♦ **Understand *Edit Sheet* and *Edit Sheet Format* Modes**

Certified SolidWorks User Examination Objectives Coverage

Certified Associate Reference Guide

Annotations
Objectives: Creating Annotations.

Introduction

In engineering graphics, a detailed drawing is a drawing consisting of the necessary orthographic projections, complete with all the necessary dimensions, notes, and specifications needed to manufacture the design. The dimensions put on the drawing are not necessarily the same ones used to create the drawing but are those required for the proper functioning of the part, as well as those needed to manufacture the design. It is therefore important, prior to dimensioning the drawing, to study and understand the design's functional requirements; then consider the manufacturing processes that are to be performed by the pattern-maker, die-maker, machinist, etc., in determining the dimensions that best give the information. In engineering graphics, a **detailed drawing** is a drawing consisting of the necessary orthographic projections, complete with all the necessary dimensions, notes, and specifications needed to manufacture the design.

Considerable experience and judgment is required for accurate size and shape description. Dimensioning a design correctly requires conformance to many rules. For example, detail drawings should contain only those dimensions that are necessary to make the design. Dimensions for the same feature of the design should be given only once in the same drawing. Nothing should be left to chance or guesswork on a drawing. Drawings should be dimensioned to avoid any possibility of questions. Dimensions should be carefully positioned; preferably near the profile of the feature being dimensioned. The designer and the CAD operator should also be as familiar as possible with materials, methods of manufacturing and shop processes.

Dimensioning Standards and Basic Terminology

The first step to learning to dimension is a thorough knowledge of the terminology and elements required for dimensions and notes on engineering drawings. Various industrial standards exist for the different industrial sectors and countries; the appropriate standards must be used for the particular type of drawing that is being produced. Some commonly used standards include: **ANSI** (American National Standard Institute), **BSI** (British Standards Association), **DIN** (Deutsches Institut fur Normüng), **ISO** (International Standardization Organization), and **JIS** (Japanese Industry Standards). In this text, the discussions of dimensioning techniques are based primarily on the standards of the *American National Standard Institute* (ANSI/ASME Y14.5); other common sense practices are also illustrated.

In engineering graphics, two basic methods are used to give a description of a measurement on a drawing: **Dimensions** and **Notes**.

A dimension is used to give the measurement of an object or between two locations on a drawing. The **numerical value** gives the actual measurement, the **dimension lines** and the **arrowheads** indicate the direction in which the measurement applies. **Extension lines** are used to indicate the locations where the dimension is associated.

Two types of notes are generally used in engineering drawings: **Local Notes** and **General Notes**. A *Local Note* is done with a leader and an arrowhead referring the statement of the note to the proper place on the drawing. A *General Note* refers to descriptions applying to the design as a whole and it is given without a leader.

Selection and Placement of Dimensions and Notes

One of the most important considerations to assure proper manufacturing and functionality of a design is the selection of dimensions to be given in the drawing. The selection should always be based on the **functionality of the part**, as well as the **production requirements in the shop**. The method of manufacturing can affect the type of detailed dimensions and notes given in the drawing. It would be very beneficial to have a good knowledge of the different shop practices to give concise information on an engineering drawing.

After the dimensions and notes to be given have been selected, the next step is the actual placement of the dimensions and notes on the drawing. In reading a drawing, it is natural to look for the dimensions of a given feature wherever that feature appears most characteristic. One of the views of an object will usually describe the shape of some detailed feature better than with other views. Placing the dimensions in those views will promote clarity and ease of reading. This practice is known as the **Contour Rule**.

The two methods of positioning dimension texts on a dimension line are the **aligned** system and the **unidirectional** system. The *unidirectional* system is more widely used as it is easier to apply, and easier to read, the text horizontally. The texts are oriented to be read from the **bottom** of the drawing with the *unidirectional* system. The *unidirectional* system originated in the automotive and aircraft industries, and is also referred to as the "horizontal system."

For the *aligned* system, the texts are oriented to be aligned to the dimension line. The texts are oriented to be read from the **bottom or right side** of the drawing with the *aligned* system.

General Notes must be oriented horizontally and be read from the bottom of the drawing in both systems.

(a) **Unidirectional System**   (b) **Aligned System**

The following rules need to be followed for clearness and legibility when applying dimensions and/or notes to a design:

1. Always dimension **features**, not individual geometric entities. Consider the dimensions related to the **sizes** and **locations** of each feature.

Three dimensions are used to show the Size and Location of the Hole feature.

2. Choose the view that best describes the feature to place the associated dimensions; this is known as the **Contour Rule**.

3. Place the dimensions next to the features being described; this is known as the **Proximity Rule**.

4. Dimensions should be placed outside the view if possible; only place dimensions on the inside if they add clarity, simplicity, and ease of reading.

5. Dimensions common to two views are generally placed in between the views.

6. Center lines may also be used as extension lines; therefore there should be **no gap** in between an extension line and a center line.

Center lines may also be used as extension lines.

7. Dimensions should be applied to one view only. When dimensions are placed between views, the extension lines should be **drawn from one view**, not from both views.

8. Center lines are also used to indicate the **symmetry** of shapes, and frequently eliminate the need for a positioning dimension. They should extend about 6 mm (0.25 in.) beyond the shape for which they indicate symmetry, unless they are carried further to serve as extension lines. Center lines should not be continued between views.

9. Dimensions should be placed only on the view that shows the measurement in its **true length**.

10. Always place a shorter dimension line inside a longer one to avoid crossing dimension lines with the extension lines of other dimensions. Thus an overall dimension, the maximum size of part in a given direction, will be placed outside all other dimensions.

11. As a general rule, local notes (leaders) and general notes are created and placed after the regular dimensions.

12. Dimensions should never be crowded. If the space is small and crowded, an enlarged view or a partial view may be used.

13. Do not dimension to hidden lines, if necessary create sectional views to convert the hidden features into visible features.

14. The spacing of dimension lines should be uniform throughout the drawing. Dimension lines should be spaced, in general, **10 mm** (0.4 inches) away from the outlines of the view. This applies to a single dimension or to the first dimension of several in a series. The space between subsequent dimension lines should be at least **6 mm** (0.25 inches) and uniformly spaced.

15. The **Overall Width**, **Height**, and **Depth** of the part should generally be shown in a drawing unless curved contours are present.

16. Never allow the crossing of dimension lines.

17. Dimension texts should be placed midway between the arrowheads, except when several parallel dimensions are present, where the texts should be staggered.

18. A leader should always be placed to allow its extension to pass through the **center** of all round features.

19. **Symbols** are preferred for features such as counter-bores, countersinks and spot faces; they should also be dimensioned using a leader. Each of these features has a special dimensioning symbol that can be used to show (a) Shape (b) Diameter and (c) Depth.

20. For leaders: avoid crossing leaders, avoid long leaders, avoid leaders in a horizontal or vertical direction, and avoid leaders parallel to adjacent dimension lines, extension lines, or section lines.

21. When dimensioning a circular feature, full cylinders (holes and bosses) must always be measured by their diameters. Arcs should always be shown by specifying a radius value. If a leader is used, the leader should meet the surface at an angle between 30° to 60° if possible.

22. Dual dimensions may be used, but they must be consistent and clearly noted. The dual-dimensioning can be shown by placing the alternate-units values below or next to the primary-units dimension, as shown in the figure.

23. Never pass through a dimension text with any kind of line.

24. In general, *Metric* system is given in millimeters and they are generally rounded to the nearest whole number. English system is given in inches and they are typically shown with two decimal places. When a metric dimension is less than a millimeter, a zero is placed before the decimal point, but no zero is placed before a decimal point when inches are used.

Machined Holes

In machining, a hole is a cylindrical feature that is cut from the work piece by a rotating cutting tool. The diameter of the machined hole will be the same as the cutting tool with matching the geometry. Non-cylindrical features, or pockets, can also be machined, but these features require end milling operations, not the typical hole-making operations. While all machined holes have the same basic form they can still differ in many ways to best suit a given application.

A machined hole can be characterized by several different parameters or features which will determine the hole machining operation and tool that is required.

Diameter - Holes can be machined in a wide variety of diameters, determined by the selected tool. The cutting tools used for hole-making are available in standard sizes that can be as small as 0.0019 inches and as large as 3 inches. Several standards exist, including fractional sizes, letter sizes, number sizes, and metric sizes. A custom tool can be created to machine a non-standard diameter, but it is generally more cost effective to use the standard sized tool.

Tolerance - In any machining operation, the precision of a cut can be affected by several factors, including the sharpness of the tool, any vibration of the tool, or the buildup of chips of material. The specified tolerance of a hole will determine the method of hole-making used, as some methods are suited for tight-tolerance holes. Refer to the next section and Chapter 9 for more details on tolerances.

Depth - A machined hole may extend to a point within the work piece, known as a blind hole, or it may extend completely through the work piece, known as a through hole. A blind hole may have a flat bottom, but typically ends in a point due to the pointed end of the tool. When specifying the depth of a hole, one may reference the depth to the point or the depth to the end of the full diameter portion of the hole. The total depth of the hole is limited by the length of the cutting tool. For a through hole, the depth information is typically omitted in a drawing.

Recessed top - A common feature of machined holes is to recess the top of the hole into the work piece. This is typically done to accommodate the head of a fastener and allow it to sit flush with the work piece surface. Two types of recessed holes are typically used: a counterbore, which has a cylindrical recess, and a countersink, which has a cone-shaped recess.

Threads - Threaded holes are machined to accommodate a threaded fastener and are typically specified by their outer diameter and pitch. The pitch is a measure of the spacing between threads and may be expressed in the English standard, as the number of threads per inch (TPI), or in the metric standard, as the distance in between threads. For more details on threads, refer to Chapter 13 of this text.

Drilling   Reaming   Counterbore   Spotface   Countersink   Tapping

Drilling - A drill bit enters the work piece in the axial direction and cuts a blind hole or a through hole with a diameter equal to that of the tool. A drill bit is a multi-point tool and typically has a pointed end. A twist drill is the most commonly used, but other types of drill bits, such as center drill, spot drill, or tap drill can also be used to start a hole that will be completed by additional operation.

Reaming - A reamer enters the work piece in the axial direction and enlarges an existing hole to the diameter of the tool. A reamer is a multi-point tool that has many flutes, which may be straight or in a helix. Reaming removes a minimal amount of material and is often performed after drilling to obtain both a more accurate diameter and a smoother internal finish.

Counterbore - A counterbore tool enters the work piece axially and enlarges the top portion of an existing hole to the diameter of the tool. Counterboring is often performed after drilling to provide space for the head of a fastener, such as a bolt, to sit flush with the work piece surface. The counterboring tool has a pilot on the end to guide it straight into the existing hole. The depth of the counterbored portion is typically identified and dimensioned as a second operation on a drawing.

Spotface - A spotfaced hole is similar to a counterbored hole, but a spotfaced hole has a relatively shallow counterbored depth. The depth of the counterbored portion is left to the judgment of the machinist and thus, not dimensioned in the drawing. The smoothing is necessary in cast or forged surfaces to provide better contact between assembled pieces. For drawing purposes, the depth of the counterbored portion is typical 1/16″ or 2 mm.

Countersink - A countersink tool enters the work piece axially and enlarges the top portion of an existing hole to a cone-shaped opening. Countersinking is often performed after drilling to provide space for the head of a fastener, such as a screw, to sit flush with the work piece surface. Common included angles for a countersink include 60, 82, 90, 100, 118, and 120 degrees.

Tapping - A tap enters the work piece in the axial direction and cuts internal threads inside an existing hole. The existing hole is typically drilled with a drill size that will accommodate the desired tap. The tap is selected based on the major diameter and pitch of the threaded hole. Threads may be cut to a specified depth inside the hole (bottom tap) or the complete depth of a through hole (through tap).

Baseline and Chain Dimensioning

Frequently the need arises to dimension a feature which involves a series of dimensions. Two methods should be considered for this type of situation: **Baseline dimensioning** and **Chain dimensioning**. The baseline dimensioning method creates dimensions by measuring from a common baseline. The chain dimensioning method creates a series or a chain of dimensions that are placed one after another. It is important to always consider the functionality and the manufacturing process of the specific features to be dimensioned. Note that both methods can be used to different features within the same drawing as shown in the below figure.

- **Baseline dimensioning:** Used when the **location** of features must be controlled from a common reference point or plane.

- **Chain dimensioning:** Used when **tolerances** between adjacent features is more important than the overall tolerance of the feature. For example, dimensioning mating parts, hole patterns, slots, etc. Note that more in-depth discussions on tolerances are presented in the next section and also in the next chapter.

Dimensioning and Tolerance Accumulation

Drawings with dimensions and notes often serve as construction documents to ensure the proper functioning of a design. When dimensioning a drawing, it is therefore critical to consider the *precision* required for the part. *Precision* is the degree of accuracy required during manufacturing. Different machining methods will produce different degrees of precisions. However, one should realize it is nearly impossible to produce any dimension to an absolute, accurate measurement; some variation must be allowed in manufacturing. **Tolerance** is the allowable variation for any given size and provides a practical means to achieve the precision necessary in a design. With **tolerancing**, each dimension is allowed to vary within a specified zone. The general machining tolerances of some of the more commonly used manufacturing processes are listed in the figure below.

International Tolerance Grade (IT)							
4	5	6	7	8	9	10	11
Lapping or Honing							
	Cylindrical Grinding						
	Surface Grinding						
	Diamond Turning or Boring						
	Broaching						
	Powder Metal-sizes						
		Reaming					
			Turning				
			Powder Metal-sintered				
			Boring				
						Milling, Drilling	
						Planing & Shaping	
						Punching	
							Die Casting

As it was discussed in the previous sections, the selections and placements of dimensions and notes can have a drastic effect on the manufacturing of the designs. Further more, a poorly dimensioned drawing can create problems that may invalidate the design intent and/or become very costly to the company. One of the undesirable results in poorly dimensioned drawings is **Tolerance Accumulation**. *Tolerance Accumulation* is the effect of cumulative tolerances caused by the relationship of tolerances associated with relating dimensions. As an example, let's examine the *tolerance accumulation* that can occur with two mating parts, as shown in the below figure, using a standard tolerance of ± 0.01 for all dimensions.

(1) Tolerance Accumulation - Baseline Dimensioning

Consider the use of the *Baseline dimensioning* approach, as described in the previous sections, to dimension the parts. At first glance, it may appear that the tolerance of the overall size is maintained and thus this approach is a better approach in dimensioning the parts!?

Now let's examine the size of the center slot, which is intended to fit the other part:

Upper limit of the slot size: 3.26-1.49= 1.77
Lower limit of the slot size: 3.24-1.51= 1.73

The tolerance of the center slot has a different range of tolerance than the standard ± 0.01. With this result, the two parts will not fit as good as the tolerance has been loosened.

(2) Tolerance Accumulation - Chain Dimensioning

Now consider the use of the *chain dimensioning* approach, as described in the previous sections, to dimension the parts.

The *tolerance accumulation* occurred since the overall size is determined with the three dimensions that are chained together. Considering the upper and lower limits of the overall size of the bottom part:

> **Upper limit** of the overall size: 1.51+1.76+1.51= 4.78
> **Lower limit** of the overall size: 1.49+1.74+1.49= 4.72

With the chaining of the dimensions, the tolerance of the overall size has been changed, perhaps unintentionally, to a wider range.

(3) Avoid Tolerance Accumulation – Dimensioning Features

The effect of the *tolerance accumulation* is usually undesirable. We could be using fairly precise and expensive manufacturing processes, but resulting in lower quality products simply due to the poor selections and placements of dimensions.

To avoid *tolerance accumulation,* properly dimensioning a drawing is critical. The first rule of dimensioning states that one should always dimension **features**, not individual geometric entities. Always consider the dimensions related to the **sizes** and **locations** of each feature. One should also consider the associated **design intent** of the **feature**, the **functionality** of the design and the related **manufacturing processes**.

For our example, one should consider the center slot as a feature, where the other part will be fit into, and therefore the **size** and **location** of the feature should be placed as shown in the figure below.

> More detailed discussions on tolerances are covered in the next chapter; however, the effects of *tolerance accumulation* should be avoided even during the initial selection and placement of dimensions. Note that there are also other options, generally covered under the topics of **Geometric Dimensioning and Tolerancing (GD&T)**, to assure the accuracy of designs through productions.

Dimensioning Tools in SolidWorks

Thus far, the use of SolidWorks to define the **shape** of designs has been illustrated. In this chapter, the general procedures to convey the **size** definitions of designs using SolidWorks are discussed. The *tools of size description* are known as *dimensions* and *notes*.

Considerable experience and judgment is required for accurate size description. As it was outlined in the previous sections, detail drawings should contain only those dimensions that are necessary to make the design. Dimensions for the same feature of the design should be given only once in the same drawing. Nothing should be left to chance or guesswork on a drawing. Drawings should be dimensioned to avoid any possibility of questions. Dimensions should be carefully positioned; preferably near the profile of the feature being dimensioned. The designer and the CAD operator should be as familiar as possible with materials, methods of manufacturing, and shop processes.

Traditionally, detailing a drawing is the biggest bottleneck of the design process; and when doing board drafting, dimensioning is one of the most time consuming and tedious tasks. Today, most CAD systems provide what is known as an **auto-dimensioning feature**, where the CAD system automatically creates the extension lines, dimensional lines, arrowheads, and dimension values. Most CAD systems also provide an **associative dimensioning feature** so that the system automatically updates the dimensions when the drawing is modified.

The *U-Bracket* Design

Starting SolidWorks

1. Select the **SolidWorks** option on the *Start* menu or select the **SolidWorks** icon on the desktop to start SolidWorks. The SolidWorks main window will appear on the screen.

2. Select the **Open** icon on the *Menu Bar* with a single click of the left-mouse-button.

3. In the *Open* window, select the **U-Bracket.SLDDRW** file. Use the *browser* to locate the file if it is not displayed in the *File name* list box.

4. Click on the **Open** button in the *Startup* dialog box to accept the selected settings.

Displaying Feature Dimensions

- By default, feature dimensions are not displayed in 2D views in SolidWorks. The dimensions used to create the part can be imported into the drawing using the **Model Items** command. We can also add dimensions to the drawing manually using the **Smart Dimension** command. The **Model Items** command appears on the *Annotation* toolbar.

1. By default the *Annotation* toolbar appears at the left of the SolidWorks window (below or next to the *Drawing* toolbar). If it is not displayed, right-click on the *Menu Bar* and select the **Annotation** icon to display the *Annotation* toolbar.

2. Left-mouse-click on the **Model Items** icon on the *Annotation* toolbar. This command allows us to import dimensions from the referenced model into selected drawing views.

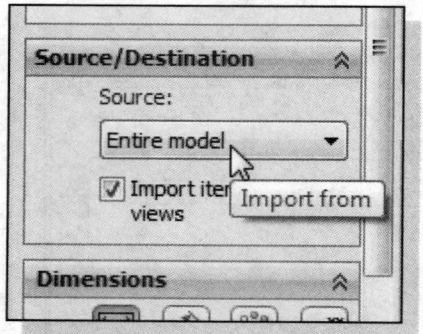

3. In the *Source/Destination* options panel of the *Model Items Property Manager*, select the **Entire model** option from the *Import from* pull-down menu and check **Import items into all views** as shown.

4. Under the *Dimensions* options panel, select the **Marked for drawing** icon and check **Eliminate duplicates** as shown.

5. Click the **OK** icon in the *Model Items Property Manager*. Notice dimensions are automatically placed on the front and top drawing views.

Repositioning, Appearance, and Hiding of Feature Dimensions

1. Move the cursor on top of the width dimension text **5.00** and watch for when the dimension text becomes highlighted as shown in the figure, indicating the dimension is selectable.

2. Reposition the dimension by using the left-mouse-button to drag the dimension text to a new location. (**NOTE:** SolidWorks may execute snaps to align the text automatically. To negate these, hold down the **[Alt]** key while dragging the text and it will move freely.)

3. Move the cursor on top of the diameter dimension **0.50** and click once with the left-mouse-button to select the dimension.

4. Left-click on the arrow at the end of the leader line and drag to lengthen the bent leader line as shown.

❖ The default bent leader length can be adjusted to improve the appearance of the current view. This is done using the **Document Settings**. There are many document settings, including dimension settings, line style, etc., which can be adjusted to achieve the desired drawing display.

5. On your own, change the **Bent leader length** to **0.2 in**. (Select the **Options** icon from the *Menu Bar* to open the *Options* window. Select the **Document Properties** tab. Select **Dimensions**. In the **Leader length:** field, enter **0.2 in**. Click **OK**.)

6. Move the cursor on top of the diameter dimension **0.50**, and click once with the left-mouse-button to select the dimension.

7. Select the **Leaders** tab in the *Dimension Property Manager*.

8. Select the **Smart** display button.

9. Check the **Use document bend length** box.

10. Click **OK** in the *Property Manager*.

➢ Notice the bent leader length (that we lengthened in step 4) now reverts to the length we set in the *Document Settings*.

11. On your own, reposition the dimensions displayed in the *top* view as shown. (Note the 2.5 vertical dimension is intentionally placed to the right with the extension lines crossing the other dimensions.)

➢ Any feature dimensions can be removed from the display just as they are displayed.

12. Move the cursor on top of the vertical **2.50** dimension and **right-mouse-click** once to bring up the option menu.

13. Select **Hide** from the pop-up option menu and remove the selected dimension.

Adding Additional Dimensions – Reference Dimensions

- Besides displaying the **feature dimensions**, dimensions used to create the features, we can also add additional **reference dimensions** in the drawing. *Feature dimensions are used to control the geometry, whereas reference dimensions are controlled by the existing geometry.* In the drawing layout, therefore, we can **add** or **delete** *reference dimensions* but we can only **hide** the *feature dimensions.* One should try to use as many *feature dimensions* as possible and add *reference dimensions* only if necessary. It is also more effective to use *feature dimensions* in the drawing layout since they are created when the model was built. Note that additional *Drawing* mode entities, such as lines and arcs, can be added to drawing views. Before *Drawing* mode entities can be used in a reference dimension, they must be associated to a *drawing view*.

1. Left-mouse-click on the **Smart Dimension** icon on the *Annotation* toolbar.

2. In the top view, select the top horizontal line as the first entity to dimension.

3. In the top view, select the bottom horizontal line as the second entity to dimension.

4. Place the **2.50** vertical dimension to the left side of the top view as shown.

5. On your own, add the **2.50** horizontal dimension and arrange the display of the top view to look like the figure below.

6. In the front view, left click on the **R1.75** dimension to select the radius dimension.

7. In the *Dimension Property Manager*, select the **Leaders** tab.

8. In the *Witness/Leader Display* panel, select the **Inside** option as shown.

9. On your own, select the Ø**2.50** dimension and select the **Smart** display option.

10. On your own, adjust the front view dimension display to appear as in the figure below.

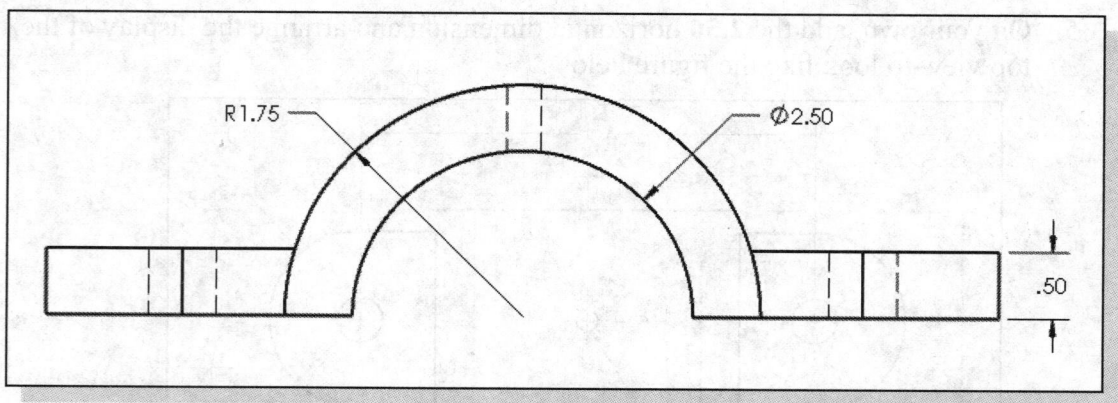

Tangent Edge Display

❖ Another important setting for drawing views is the way tangent edges – where a curved surface meets tangent to a flat surface – are represented. In the figure above, the tangent edges (the vertical lines coincident with the centerlines of the two hidden holes) are visible.

1. Press the **[Esc]** key to ensure no objects are selected.

2. Move the cursor over the *front view* in the graphics area and **right-click** to open the pop-up option menu.

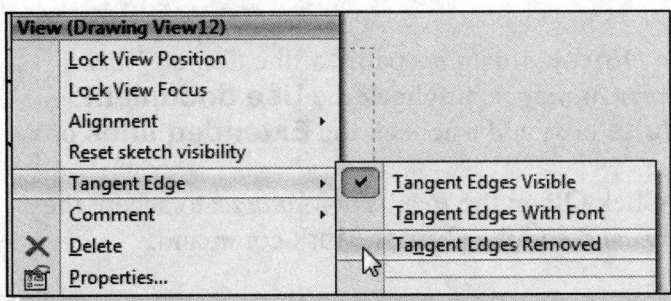

3. Select **Tangent Edge**, then **Tangent Edges Removed** from the pop-up menu, as shown.

4. Click **OK** in the *Property-Manager* or press the **[Esc]** key to accept the setting.

❖ Notice the tangent edges are no longer visible.

5. On your own, remove the tangent edges from the isometric view.

Adding Center Marks, Center Lines, and Sketch Objects

1. Click on the **Center Mark** button in the *Annotation* toolbar.

2. Click on the larger arc in the front view to add the center mark.

3. A preview of the center mark appears in the graphics area and the *Center Mark Property Manager* is opened.

❖ The default center mark included extended lines in all four directions. Since the feature is semicircular, we will turn *OFF* the default extended lines and sketch them where desired.

4. In the *Display Attributes* panel of the *Center Mark Property Manager*, **uncheck** the **Use document defaults** box, and **uncheck** the **Extended lines** box.

5. Left-Click **OK** in the *Property Manager* to accept the settings and end the **Center Mark** command.

6. Switch to the *Sketch* toolbar as shown.

7. Left-click on the **Line** button on the *Sketch* toolbar.

8. Move the cursor over the center mark, then move the cursor above the center to engage the **Vertical** relation. Click once with the **left-mouse-button** to locate the first point for the line.

9. Move the cursor vertically to locate the endpoint for the line. Click once with the **left-mouse-button** to locate the endpoint.

10. Click once with the **right-mouse-button** to open the pop-up menu.

11. Left-click on the **Select** option on the pop-up menu to end the **Line** command.

12. On your own, sketch the two horizontal lines as shown in the figure below.

13. Click on the **Centerline** button in the *Annotation* toolbar. (**NOTE:** This is different from the Centerline command on the *Sketch* toolbar.)

14. Inside the graphics window, click on the two hidden edges of the **Hole** on the left as shown in the figure.

• Note the centerline on the right side of the front view is created automatically as shown below.

15. Left-click the **OK** icon in the *Centerline Property Manager* or press the **[Esc]** key to end the Centerline command.

16. Add the three center marks if they were not added automatically. Drag the endpoint of the *Extended Lines* to desired locations.

17. On your own, adjust your settings and endpoint locations until the top view appears as in the figure below.

18. Click on the **Save** icon in the *Menu Bar* as shown.

19. If the SolidWorks window appears asking to *'Update the drawing?'* select **Yes**.

Edit Sheet vs. Edit Sheet Format

❖ There are two modes in a SolidWorks drawing: *Edit Sheet* and *Edit Sheet Format*. To this point we have been operating in the *Edit Sheet* mode. The *Edit Sheet* mode is used to make detail drawings, including adding and modifying views, adding and modifying dimensions, and adding and modifying drawing notes. The *Edit Sheet Format* mode is used to add and edit title blocks, borders, and standard text that appear in every drawing. The correct mode must be selected in order to execute the corresponding commands.

1. Move the cursor into the graphics area and **right-click** to open the pop-up option menu.

2. Select **Edit Sheet Format** from the pop-up option menu to change to *Edit Sheet Format* mode.

❖ Notice the title block is highlighted.

Completing the Drawing Sheet

1. On your own, use the **Zoom** and **Pan** commands to adjust the display as shown, this is so that we can complete the title block.

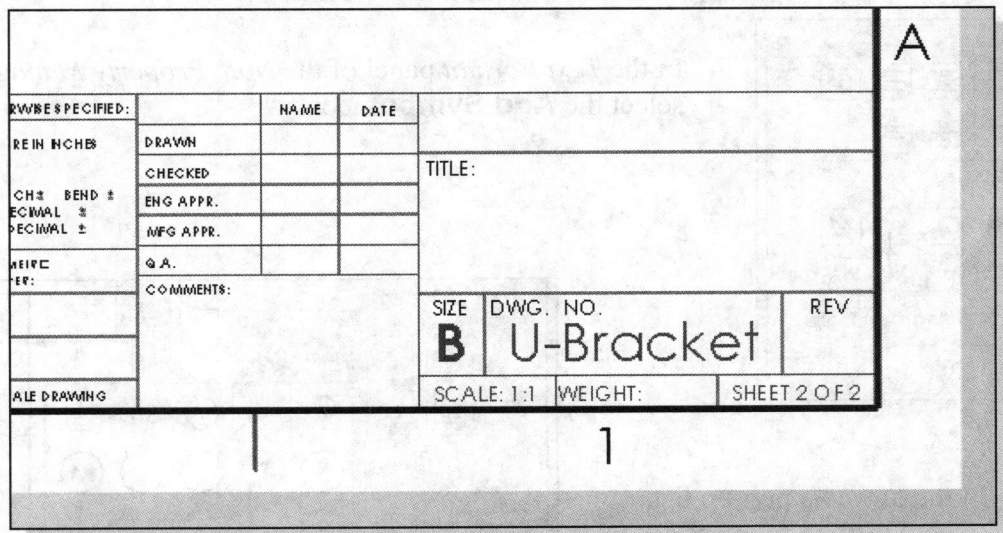

❖ There are many notes added as entries in the default title block. Some are simple **Text** notes; some include **Property Links** to automatically display document properties. In the following steps, we will learn to (1) edit existing notes, (2) insert new notes, and (3) control **Property Links**. We will first edit a simple text note.

2. Zoom in on the tolerance specification box. This note contains only simple text entries. **Double-click** with the **left-mouse-button** on the text to enter the text editor.

3. Highlight the FRACTIOANAL ± line as shown by clicking and dragging with the left-mouse-button.

4. Press the [**Delete**] key twice to delete the line.

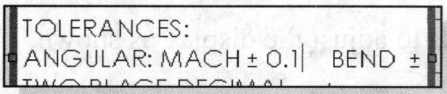

5. Move the cursor to a location to the right of the MACH ± text, and click once with the **left-mouse-button** to select a location to enter text.

6. Enter **0.1**.

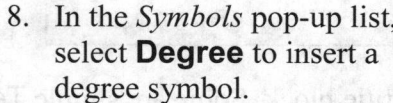

7. In the *Text Format* panel of the *Note Property Manager*, select the **Add Symbol** icon.

8. In the *Symbols* pop-up list, select **Degree** to insert a degree symbol.

9. On your own, continue editing the text in the tolerance box until it appears as shown.

10. Select the **OK** icon in the *Note Property Manager* or press the **[Esc]** key to accept the change to the note.

11. We will now insert a new note. Left-click on the **Note** icon on the *Annotation* toolbar.

12. Select the **No Leader** option in the *Leader* panel of the *Note Property Manager*.

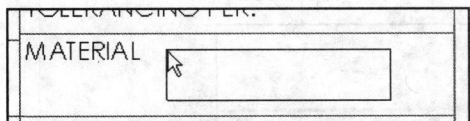

13. Move the cursor into the MATERIAL box and click once with the **left-mouse-button** to select the location for the new note.

14. Enter the text **1060 ALLOY**.

15. **Highlight** the text **1060 ALLOY**.

16. Change the font size to **6** in the *Formatting* window as shown and press the **[Enter]** key to reset the font size.

17. Select the **OK** icon in the *Note Property Manager* or press the **[Esc]** key to accept the note.

18. Click and drag on the new note to locate it as shown. (**NOTE:** SolidWorks may execute snaps to align the text automatically. To negate these, hold down the **[Alt]** key while dragging the text and it will move freely.)

Property Links

➢ SolidWorks allows notes to be linked to properties for automatic display. In SolidWorks, these properties are classified as system-defined *System Properties* and user-defined *Custom Properties*. Each system or custom property has a property name. There are system and custom properties associated with each SolidWorks **Part**, **Assembly**, or **Drawing** file. Each **Property Link** contains (1) the definition of the source and (2) the property name. The source can be (1) the current document, (2) a model specified in a sheet, (3) a model in a specified drawing view, or (4) a component to which the annotation is attached. Several linked properties are automatically included in the default SolidWorks sheet formats.

1. Move the cursor over the note in the center of the DWG. NO. box, as shown. A letter **A** appears indicating a note. A pop-up dialog box appears which reads *$PRP:* "*SW-File Name*". This is the definition of a **Property Link**. The prefix *$PRP:* defines the source as the current document. The Property Name is *SW-File Name*. This is an example of a **System Property**. Based on this Property Link, the filename – **U-Bracket** – of the current file is displayed.

2. We will change the file name. Select **Save As** from the *Menu Bar* pull-down menu.

3. Enter **MECH 475** for the *File name*.

4. Enter **U-Bracket Detail** for the *Description* and click **Save**.

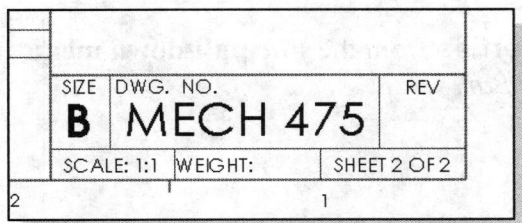

5. Notice the new file name is now displayed in the **DWG. NO.** box. Click once with the left-mouse-button on the **MECH 475** note to open the *Note Property Manager*.

6. Click the **Font** button in the *Text Format* panel of the *Note Property Manager*.

7. In the *Choose Font* pop-up window, select **Points** under the *Height* option.

8. Select **16** as the font size.

9. Click **OK** in the *Choose Font* pop-up window.

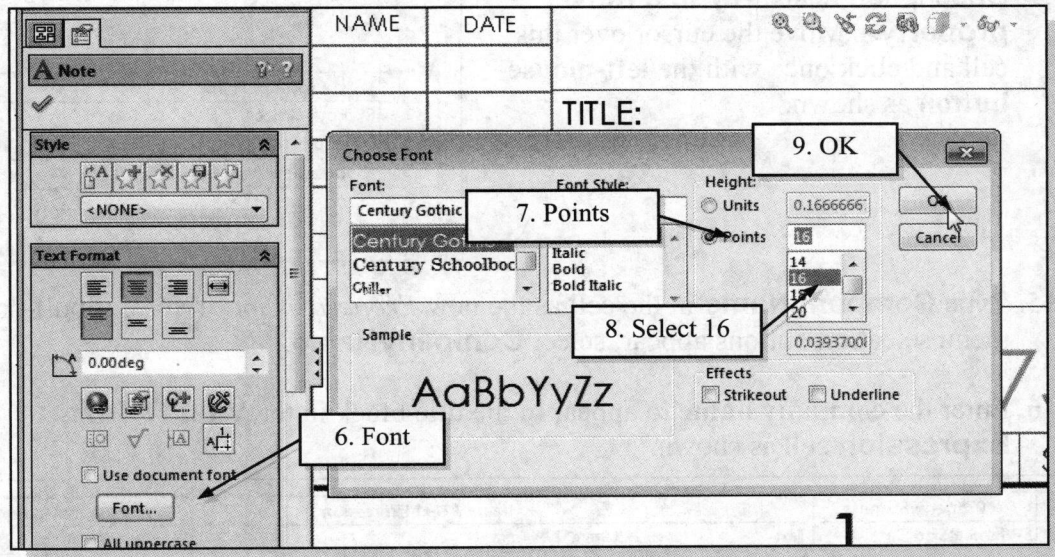

10. Press the **[Esc]** key to accept the change and unselect the note.

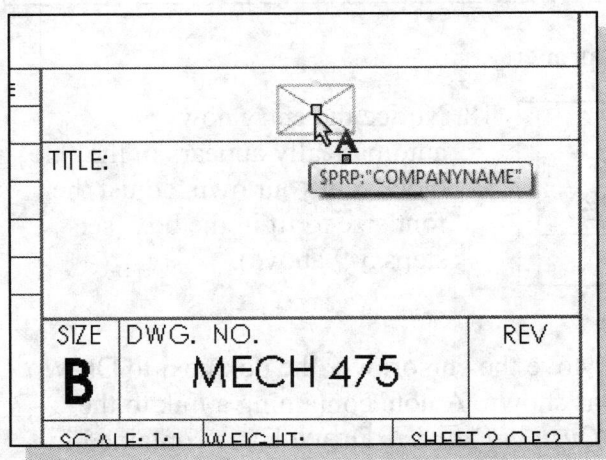

11. Left-click near the center of the box above the **Title:** box. A letter **A** appears indicating a note. A pop-up dialog box appears identifying a **Property Link** which reads *$PRP: "CompanyName"*. The prefix *$PRP:* defines the source as the current document. The **Property Name** is **CompanyName**. This is an example of a **Custom Property**. The note is currently blank because the *CompanyName Custom Property* has not been defined.

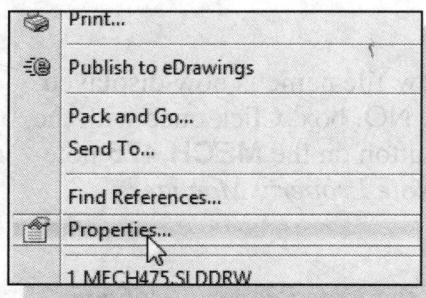

12. Select **Properties** from the *File* **pull-down menu** on the *Menu Bar*.

13. In the *Summary Information* window select the **Custom** tab. Notice the *Custom Property* **Description** appears in the table. We defined this property when we saved the drawing file.

14. The cell below the cell containing Description reads **<Type a new property>**. Move the cursor over this cell and click once with the **left-mouse-button** as shown.

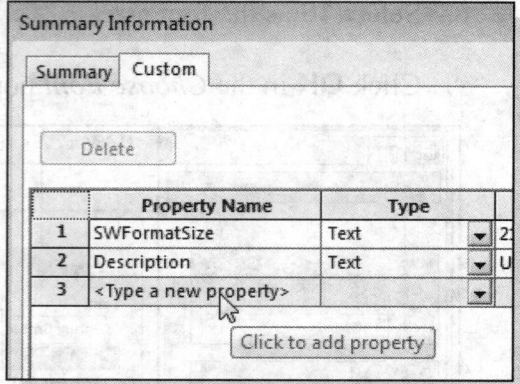

15. Type **CompanyName** in the cell as the new *Property Name*. (Note: If pull-down menu selection options appear, select **CompanyName**.)

16. Enter the **company name** to appear in the title block in the **Value / Text Expression** cell as shown.

	Property Name	Type	Value / Text Expression	Evaluated Value
1	SWFormatSize	Text	215.9mm*279.4mm	215.9mm*279.4mm
2	Description	Text	U-Bracket Detail	U-Bracket Detail
3	CompanyName	Text	Oregon Institute of Technology	OREGON INSTITUTE OF TE
4	<Type a new property>			

17. Click **OK** to accept the user-defined property.

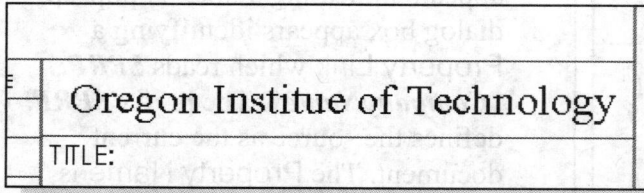

18. Notice the entry now automatically appears in the title block. On your own, adjust the font size to fit in the box (see steps 5-9 above).

19. Move the cursor over the box next to **Drawn** as shown. A note containing a link to the *Custom Property* **DrawnBy** is contained in this box.

20. On your own, go to the *File Properties* window and enter your name or initials as the entry for the **DrawnBy** *Custom Property*.

21. On your own, determine the *Property Link* in the **DrawnDate** box. Enter the date for the *Custom Property*.

	NAME	DATE
DRAWN	A. Smith	1/7/2015
CHECKED		

22. Left-click near the center of the **Title** box. A letter **A** appears indicating a note. A pop-up dialog box appears identifying a *Property Link* which reads *$PRPSHEET: "Description"*. The prefix *$PRPSHEET:* defines the source as the model (part file) appearing in the sheet. The *Property Name* is **Description**. This is a **Custom Property**. We can define this description when we save the U-Bracket part file or add this as a custom property.

23. Open the part file (**U-Bracket.SLDPRT**). Follow the same procedure as we did in the drawing file to change the **Description** property (P. 8-34). Then return to the drawing window, and hit the **Rebuild** button to update the drawing.

TITLE:

2-1/2" U-Bracket

$PRPSHEET:"Description"

24. On your own investigate the rest of the title block to determine where other *Property Links* appear.

25. Press the [**F**] key to scale the view to fit the graphics area.

		UNLESS OTHERWISE SPECIFIED:		NAME	DATE	Oregon Institue of Technology		
		DIMENSIONS ARE IN INCHES TOLERANCES: ANGULAR: MACH ±0.1° TWO PLACE DECIMAL ±0.01 THREE PLACE DECIMAL ±0.003	DRAWN	A. smith	00/23/13			
			CHECKED			TITLE:		
			ENG APPR.					
			MFG APPR.			2-1/2" U-Bracket		
		INTERPRET GEOMETRIC TOLERANCING PER:	Q.A.					
			COMMENTS:					
		MATERIAL 1060 ALLOY				SIZE	DWG. NO.	REV
		FINISH				B	MECH 475	
NEXT ASSY	USED ON							
APPLICATION		DO NOT SCALE DRAWING				SCALE: 1:1	WEIGHT:	SHEET 2 OF 2
4		3		2			1	

26. Move the cursor into the graphics area and **right-click** to open the pop-up option menu.

Sheet (Sheet Format2)
Display Grid
Define Title Block
Zone Tag Editor
Edit Sheet
Add Sheet...

27. Select **Edit Sheet** from the pop-up option menu to change to *Edit Sheet* mode.

Associative Functionality – Modifying Feature Dimensions

- *SolidWorks' associative functionality* allows us to change the design at any level, and the system reflects the changes at all levels automatically.

1. Select the **U-Bracket** part window from the *Window* pull-down menu to switch to *Part Modeling* mode.

2. In the *Feature Manager Design Tree*, **right-click** on **Annotations** to open the option menu.

3. Select **Show Feature Dimensions** in the popup option menu.

4. Double-click on the diameter dimensions (**0. 50**) of the hole on the base feature as shown in figure. (Change the display to *Wireframe* mode if necessary.)

5. In the *Modify* dialog box, enter **0.625** as the new diameter dimension.

6. Click on the **OK** button to accept the new setting.

7. Select the **Rebuild** icon on the *Menu Bar*. Notice both holes are increased to 0.625 due to the **Mirror** relation.

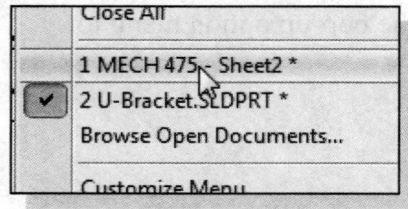

8. Select the **MECH 475- Sheet2** drawing window from the *Window* pull-down menu to switch to *Drawing* mode.

➤ Notice the change made to the model – the changed hole diameter – is reflected in the drawing.

9. Inside the graphics window, left-click on the **0.63** dimension in the *top* view to bring up the *Dimension Property Manager*.

10. In the *Tolerance/Precision* panel of the *Dimension Property Manager*, set the **Unit Precision** option to **3 digits after the decimal point** as shown.

11. Click **OK** in the *Property Manager* to accept the new setting. Notice the accurate dimension of **.625** is now displayed.

12. Inside the graphics window, **double-click** with the **left-mouse-button** on the **R 1.75** dimension in the *front* view to bring up the *Modify* pop-up option window.

13. Change the dimension to **1.625**.

14. Click on the **check mark** button in the *Modify* window to accept the setting.

15. In the *Dimension Property Manager*, set the **Unit Precision** option to **3 digits after the decimal point**.

16. Click **OK** in the *Property Manager* to accept the new setting.

➤ Notice the views become shaded with cross-hatching. This is an indication by SolidWorks that changes have been made and a rebuild is needed to update the drawing and model.

17. Select the **Rebuild** icon on the *Menu Bar*.

❖ Note the geometry of the cut feature is updated in all views automatically. On your own, switch to the *Part Modeling* mode and confirm the design is updated as well.

Saving the Drawing File

1. Go to *Drawing* mode with **MECH 475.SLDDRW** as the active document.

2. Select the **Save** icon on the *Menu Bar*. This command will save the **MECH 475.SLDDRW** file. This file includes the document properties, the sheet format, and the drawing views.

3. In the *Save Modified Documents* window, select **Save All**.

4. If the SolidWorks window appears asking to *'Update the drawing?'*, select **Yes**.

Saving a Drawing Template

❖ In SolidWorks, each new drawing is created from a template. During the installation of SolidWorks, a default drafting standard was selected which sets the default template used to create drawings. We can use this template or another predefined template, modify one of the predefined templates, or create our own templates to enforce drafting standards and other conventions. Any drawing file can be used as a template; a drawing file becomes a template when it is saved as a template (*.drwdot) file. Once the template is saved, we can create a new drawing file using the new template.

❖ We will create a custom SolidWorks drawing template file with the document properties (e.g., ANSI dimension standard, English units, etc.) and sheet format (size B paper size, etc.) we have created. The template can include the layout of the drawing views, but we will want to choose different views in future drawings. We will therefore delete the views. **NOTE:** Do not save MECH 475.SLDDRW after these changes.

1. We will want only the sheet format in *Sheet2* in the template. Move the cursor over **Sheet1** in the *FeatureManager Design Tree* and click once with the **right-mouse-button**.

2. Select **Delete** from the pop-up option menu.

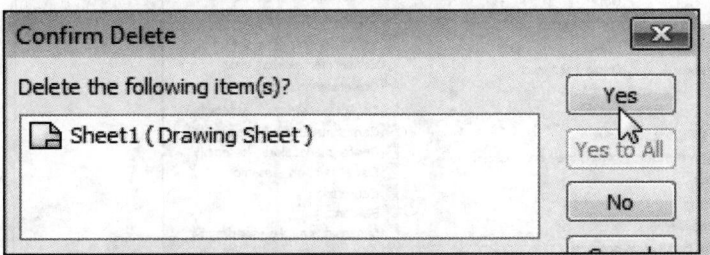

3. Select **Yes** in the *Confirm Delete* window.

4. On your own, delete the three drawing views (the front view, top view, and isometric view). **Right-click** on the view in the graphics area or the corresponding icon in the *Feature Manager Design Tree*; then select **Delete** from the pop-up option menu; then select **Yes** in the *Confirm Delete* window.

5. Select the **Options** icon, then select the **Document Properties** tab.

6. Click **Units** as shown.

7. Verify that **IPS (inch, pound, second)** is selected under the *Unit system* options.

8. Verify that **.12** is selected in the *Decimals* spin boxes.

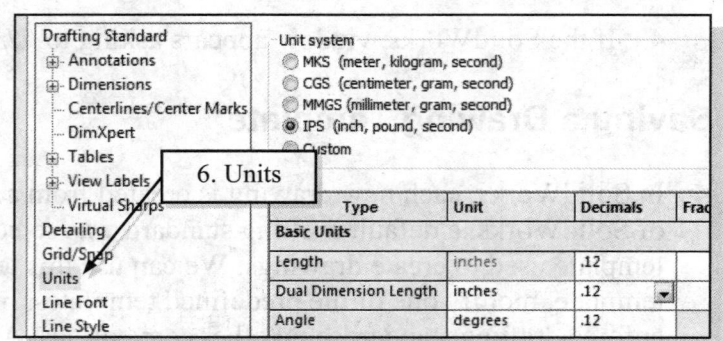

9. Click **Dimensions** as shown.

10. Verify that **.12** is selected in the *Primary precision* spin box.

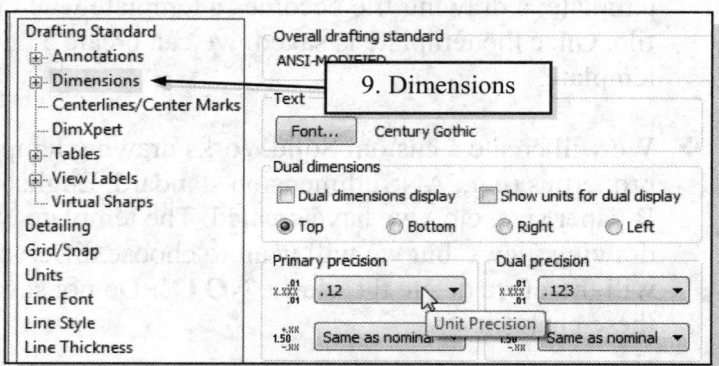

11. Click **Detailing** as shown below.

12. **Uncheck** all of the *Auto insert on view creation* options at the right of the window as shown.

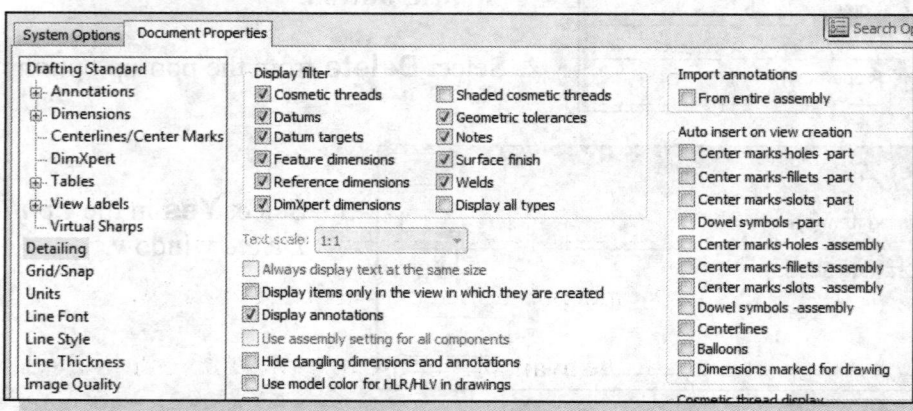

13. Click **OK** in the options dialog box to accept the selected settings.

14. Select **Save As** from the *File* pull-down menu as shown. (**NOTE:** Use the *File* pull-down menu instead of the *Menu Bar* to ensure you do not accidentally click **Save**. This would write over the MECH 475.SLDDRW file.)

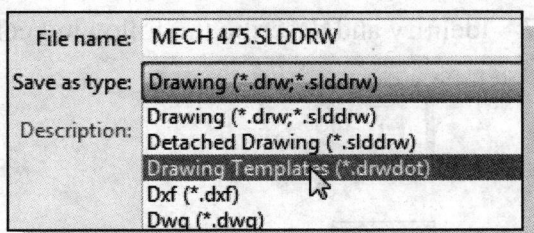

15. Click in the *Save as type:* entry box and select **Drawing Templates** from the pull-down options.

16. The folder selection will automatically change to the default Templates folder. Use the browser to change the folder selection to the **Tutorial Templates** folder you created in Chapter 5.

17. Enter ***ANSI-B-Inch*** for the *File name* and enter ***ANSI B Inch*** for the *Description.*

18. Select **Save**. If the SolidWorks pop-up window appears, click **OK**.

❖ This drawing template will now be available for use to create future drawings.

Questions:

1. What does *SolidWorks*' *associative functionality* allow us to do?

2. How do we move a view on the *Drawing Sheet*?

3. How do we display feature/model dimensions in the *Drawing* mode?

4. What is the difference between a *feature dimension* and a *reference dimension*?

5. How do we reposition dimensions?

6. What is a *base view*?

7. Identify and describe the following commands:

    (a)

    (b)

    (c)

    (d)

Exercises:

1. **Shaft Guide** (Design is symmetrical and dimensions are in inches.)

2. **Support Fixture** (Dimensions are in inches.)

3. **Cylinder Support** (Dimensions are in inches.)

4. **Swivel Base** (Dimensions are in inches.)

Chapter 9
Tolerancing and Fits

Basic Hole System: RC1, nominal size 1.25

RC1 Close Sliding Fits

Basic Hole System: RC9, nominal size 1.25

RC9 Loose Running Fits

Learning Objectives

♦ **Understand Tolerancing Nomenclature**
♦ **The Tolerancing Designation Method**
♦ **Understand the Basics of ANSI Standard Fits**
♦ **Use of the ISO Metric Standard Fits**
♦ **Use the Open Files SolidWorks Option**
♦ **Setup the Tolerancing Option in SolidWorks**

Precision and Tolerance

In the manufacturing of any product, quality and cost are always the two primary considerations. Drawings with dimensions and notes often serve as construction documents and legal contracts to ensure the proper functioning of a design. When dimensioning a drawing, it is therefore critical to consider the *precision* required for the part. *Precision* is the degree of accuracy required during manufacturing. However, it is impossible to produce any dimension to an absolute, accurate measurement; some variation must be allowed in manufacturing. Specifying higher precision on a drawing may ensure better quality of a product, but doing so may also raise the costs of the product. And requiring unnecessary high precision of a design, resulting in high production costs, may cause the inability of the design to compete with similar products in the market. As an example, consider a design that contains cast parts. A cast part usually has two types of surfaces: mating surfaces and non-mating surfaces. The mating surfaces, as they will interact with other parts, are typically machined to a proper smoothness and require higher precision on all corresponding dimensions. The non-mating surfaces are usually left in the original rough-cast form as they have no important relationship with the other parts. The dimensions on a drawing must clearly indicate which surfaces are to be finished and provide the degree of precision needed for the finishing.

The method of specifying the degree of precision is called **Tolerancing**. **Tolerance** is the allowable variation for any given size and provides a practical means to achieve the precision necessary in a design. Tolerancing also ensure interchangeability in manufacturing, parts can be made by different companies in different locations and still maintain the proper functioning of the design. With tolerancing, each dimension is allowed to vary within a specified zone. By assigning as large a tolerance as possible, without interfering with the functionality of a design, the production costs can be reduced. The smaller the tolerance zone specified, the more expensive it is to manufacture.

Methods of Specifying Tolerances – English System

Three methods are commonly used in specifying tolerances: **Limits**, **Unilateral tolerances** and **Bilateral tolerances**. Note that the unilateral and bilateral methods employ the use of a **Base Dimension** in specifying the variation range.

- **Limits** – Specifies the range of size that a part may be.
  This is the preferred method as approved by ANSI/ASME Y14.5M; the maximum and minimum limits of size and locations are specified. The maximum value is placed above the minimum value. In single-line form, a dash is used to separate the two values.

    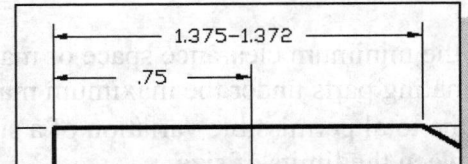

- **Bilateral** – Variation of size is in both directions.
  This method uses a basic size and is followed by a plus-and-minus expression of tolerance. The bilateral tolerances method allows variations in both directions from the basic size. If an equal variation in both directions is desired, the combined plus-and minus symbol is used with a single value.

- **Unilateral** – Variation of size is in only one direction.
  This method uses a basic size and is followed by a plus-or-minus expression of tolerance. The unilateral tolerances method allows variations only in one direction from the basic size.

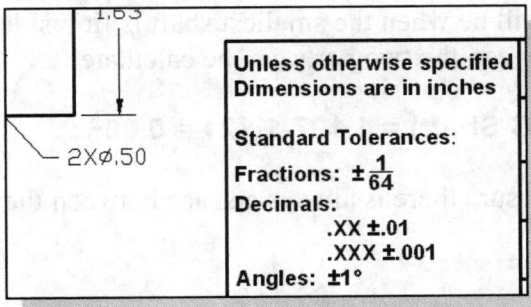

- **General tolerances** – General tolerances are typically covered in the title block; the general tolerances are applied to the dimensions in which tolerances are not given.

Nomenclature

The following are terms used in Tolerancing and Dimensioning as defined in the ANSI/ASME Y 14.5M standard.

- **Nominal size** is the designation used for the purpose of general identification.
- **Basic size, or basic dimension,** is the theoretical size from which limits of size are derived. It is the size from which limits are determined for the size or location of a feature in a design.
- **Actual size** is the measured size of the manufactured part.
- **Fit** is the general term used to signify the range of tightness in the design of mating parts.
- **Allowance** is the minimum clearance space or maximum interference intended between two mating parts under the maximum material condition.
- **Tolerance** is the total permissible variation of a size. The tolerance is the difference between the limits of size.
- **Maximum Material Condition** (MMC) is the size of the part when it consists of the most material.
- **Least Material Condition** (LMC) is the size of the part when it consists of the least material.

In the figure above, the tightest fit between the two parts will be when the largest shaft is fit inside the smallest hole. The allowance between the two parts can be calculated as:

Allowance = (MMC Hole)-(MMC Shaft) = 1.125-1.124 = 0.001

The loosest fit between the above two parts will be when the smallest shaft is fit inside the largest hole. The maximum clearance between the two parts can be calculated as:

Max. Clearance = (LMC Hole)-(LMC Shaft) = 1.127-1.121 = 0.006

➤ Note that the above dimensions will assure there is always a space between the two mating parts.

Example 9.1

The size limits of two mating parts are as shown in the below figure. Determine the following items, as described in the previous page: nominal size, tolerance of the shaft, tolerance of the hole, allowance and maximum clearance between the parts.

Solution:

  Nominal size = 1.25

  Tolerance of the shaft = Max. Shaft - Min. Shaft
    = 1.2496-1.2493 = 0.0003

  Tolerance of the hole = Max. Hole - Min. Hole
    = 1.2504-1.2500 = 0.0004

  Allowance = Min. Hole (MMC Hole) - Max. Shaft (MMC Shaft)
    = 1.2500-1.2496 = 0.0004

  Max. Clearance = Max. Hole (LMC Hole) - Min. Shaft (LMC Shaft)
    =1.2504-1.2493 = 0.0011

Exercise: Given the size limits of two mating parts, determine the following items: nominal size, tolerance of the shaft, tolerance of the hole, allowance and maximum clearance between the parts.

Fits between Mating Parts

Fit is the general term used to signify the range of tightness in the design of mating parts. In ANSI/ASME Y 14.5M, four general types of fits are designated for mating parts.

- **Clearance Fit:** A clearance fit is the condition in which the internal part is smaller than the external part; and always leaves a space or clearance between the parts.

- **Interference Fit:** An interference fit is the condition in which the internal part is larger than the external part; and there is always an interference between the parts.

- **Transition Fit:** A transition fit is the condition in which there is either a *clearance* or *interference* between the parts.

- **Line Fit:** A line fit is the condition in which the limits of size are such that a clearance or surface contact may result between the mating parts.

Selective Assembly

By specifying the proper allowances and tolerances, mating parts can be completely interchangeable. But sometimes the fit desired may require very small allowances and tolerances, and the production cost may become very high. In such cases, either manual or computer-controlled selective assembly is often used. The manufactured parts are then graded as small, medium and large based on the actual sizes. In this way, very satisfactory fits may be achieved at a much lower cost compared to manufacturing all parts to very accurate dimensions. Interference and transition fits often require the use of selective assembly to get the desirable interference or clearance.

Basic Hole and Basic Shaft Systems

In manufacturing, standard tools (such as reamers, drills) are often used to produce holes. In the **basic hole system**, the **minimum size of the hole** is taken as a base, and an allowance is assigned to derive the necessary size limits for both parts. The hole can often be made with a standard size tool and the shaft can easily be machined to any size desired.

Basic Hole System: The nominal size (1.125) is assigned as the Minimum hole size.

On the other hand, in some branches of manufacturing industry, where it is necessary to manufacture the shafts using standard sizes, the **basic shaft system** is often used. This system should only be used when there is a special need for it. For example, if a shaft is to be assembled with several other parts using different fits. In the **basic shaft system**, the **maximum shaft** is taken as the basic size, and all size limits are derived from this basic size.

Basic Shaft System: The nominal size (1.125) is assigned as the Maximum Shaft size.

American National Standard Limits and Fits – Inches

The standard fits designated by the American National Standards Institute are as follows:

- **RC**   Running or Sliding Clearance Fits (See appendix A for the complete table.)
- **LC**   Locational Clearance Fits
- **LT**   Transition Clearance or Interference Fits
- **LN**   Locational Interference Fits
- **FN**   Force or Shrink Fits

These letter symbols are used in conjunction with numbers for the class of fit. For example, **RC5** represents a class 5 Running or Sliding Clearance Fits. The limits of size for both of the mating parts are given in the standard.

1. **Running or Sliding Clearance Fits :** RC1 through RC9
    These fits provide limits of size for mating parts that require sliding and running performance, with suitable lubrication allowance.
    RC1, **close sliding fits,** are for mating parts to be assembled without much play in between.
    RC2, **sliding fits,** are for mating parts that need to move and turn easily but not run freely.
    RC3, **precision running fits,** are for precision work running at low speed and light journal pressure. This class provides the closest running fits.
    RC4, **close running fits,** are for moderate running speed and journal pressure in accurate machinery.
    RC5, RC6 and RC7, **medium running fits,** are for running at higher speed and/or higher journal pressure.
    RC8 and RC9, **loose running fits,** are for general purpose running condition where wide commercial tolerances are sufficient; typically used for standard stock parts.

2. **Locational Clearance Fits :** LC1 through LC11
These fits provide limits of size for mating parts that are normally stationary
and can be freely assembled and disassembled. They run from snug fits for parts
requiring accuracy location, through the medium clearance fits for parts (such as
spigots), to the looser fastener fits where freedom of assembly is of prime
importance.

3. Transition Clearance or Interference Fits : LT1 through LT6

These fits provide limits of size for mating parts requiring accuracy location, but either a small amount of clearance or interference is permissible.

Basic Hole System LT1, nominal size 1.25

ϕ1.2500
1.2510

ϕ1.2503
1.2497

Basic Hole System LT6, nominal size 1.25

ϕ1.2500
1.2510

ϕ1.2517
1.2507

Basic Hole System - LT1 Nominal Size 1.25
Loosest Fit : Smallest shaft in Largest Hole

Ø1.2510

Ø1.2497

Max Clearance = 1.2510-1.2497 =.0013

Basic Hole System - LT1 Nominal Size 1.25
Tightest Fit : Largest shaft in Smallest Hole

Ø1.2500

Ø1.2503

Allowance = MMC Hole - MMC Shaft
=1.2500 - 1.2503 = -.0003
(Interference)

4. Locational Interference Fits : LN1 through LN3

These fits provide limits of size for mating parts requiring accuracy location, and for parts needing rigidity and alignment. Such fits are not for parts that transmit frictional loads from one part to another by the tightness of the fit.

Basic Hole System LN1, nominal size 1.25

$\phi \begin{array}{c} 1.2500 \\ 1.2506 \end{array}$ $\phi \begin{array}{c} 1.2511 \\ 1.2506 \end{array}$

Basic Hole System LN3, nominal size 1.25

$\phi \begin{array}{c} 1.2500 \\ 1.2510 \end{array}$ $\phi \begin{array}{c} 1.2520 \\ 1.2514 \end{array}$

Basic Hole System - LN1 Nominal Size 1.25
Loosest Fit : Smallest shaft in Largest Hole

ϕ1.2506 ϕ1.2506

Max Clearance = 1.2506-1.2506 = 0

Basic Hole System - LN1 Nominal Size 1.25
Tightest Fit : Largest shaft in Smallest Hole

ϕ1.2500 ϕ1.2511

Allowance = MMC Hole - MMC Shaft
=1.2500 - 1.2511 = -.0011
(Interference)

5. Force or Shrink Fits : FN1 through FN5
These fits provide limits of size for mating parts requiring constant bore pressure
in between the parts. The interference amount varies almost directly with the size
of parts.
FN1, **light drive fits,** are for mating parts that requiring light assembly pressures,
and produce more or less permanent assemblies. They are suitable for thin sections
or long fits, or in cast-iron external members.
FN2, **medium drive fits,** are suitable for ordinary steel parts or for shrink fits in
light sections.
FN3, **heavy drive fits,** are suitable for ordinary steel parts or for shrink fits in
medium sections.
FN4, **force fits,** are for parts that can be highly stressed or for shrink fits where
heavy pressing forces are impractical.

Example 9.2 Basic Hole System

A design requires the use of two mating parts with a nominal size of **0.75** inches. The shaft is to run with moderate speed but with a fairly heavy journal pressure. The fit class chosen is **Basic Hole System RC6**. Determine the size limits of the two mating parts.

From Appendix A, the RC6 fit for 0.75 inch nominal size:

Nominal size Range	Limits of Clearance	RC6 Standard Limits – Basic Hole	
		Hole	Shaft
0.71 - 1.19	1.6	+2.0	-1.6
	4.8	-0.0	-2.8

Using the *Basic Hole System*, the *BASIC* size 0.75 is designated as the minimum hole size. And the maximum hole size is 0.75+0.002 = 0.752 inches.

The maximum shaft size is 0.75-0.0016 = 0.7484 inches
The minimum shaft size is 0.75-0.0028 = 0.7472 inches

➤ Note the important tolerances and allowance can also be obtained from the table:

Tolerance of the shaft = Max. Shaft – Min. Shaft = 0.7484 – 0.7472 = 0.0012
This can also be calculated from the table above = 2.8 – 2.6 = **1.2 (thousandths)**

Tolerance of the hole = Max. Hole – Min. Hole = 1.2520 – 1.2500 = 0.002
This can also be calculated from the table above = 2.0 – 0.0 = **2.0 (thousandths)**

Allowance = Min. Hole (MMC Hole) – Max. Shaft (MMC Shaft)
= 0.7500 – 0.7484 = 0.0016
This is listed as the minimum clearance in the table above: **+1.6 (thousandths)**

Max. Clearance = Max. Hole (LMC Hole) – Min. Shaft (LMC Shaft)
= 0.7520 – 0.7472 = 0.0048
This is listed as the maximum clearance in the table above: **+4.8 (thousandths)**

Example 9.3 Basic Hole System

A design requires the use of two mating parts with a nominal size of **1.25** inches. The shaft and hub is to be fastened permanently using a drive fit. The fit class chosen is **Basic Hole System FN4**. Determine the size limits of the two mating parts.

From ANSI/ASME B4.1 Standard, the FN4 fit for 1.25 inches nominal size:

Nominal size Range	Limits of Interference	FN4 Standard Limits – Basic Hole	
		Hole	Shaft
1.19 - 1.97	1.5	+1.0	+3.1
	3.1	-0.0	+2.5

Using the *Basic Hole System*, the *BASIC* size 1.25 is designated as the minimum hole size. And the maximum hole size is 1.25+0.001 = 1.251 inches.

The maximum shaft size is 1.25+0.0031 = 1.2531 inches
The minimum shaft size is 1.25+0.0025 = 1.2525 inches

Basic Hole System: FN4, nominal size 1.25

➢ Note the important tolerances and allowance can also be obtained from the table:

Tolerance of the shaft = Max. Shaft – Min. Shaft = 1.2531 – 1.2525 = 0.0006
This can also be calculated from the table above = 3.1 – 2.5 = 0.6 (thousandths)

Tolerance of the hole = Max. Hole – Min. Hole = 1.2510 – 1.2500 = 0.001
This can also be calculated from the table above = 1.0 – 0.0 = 1.0 (thousandths)

Allowance = Min. Hole (MMC Hole) – Max. Shaft (MMC Shaft)
               = 1.2500 – 1.2531 = -0.0031
This is listed as the maximum interference in the table above: 3.1 (thousandths)

Min. interference = Max. Hole (LMC Hole) – Min. Shaft (LMC Shaft)
                        = 1.2510 – 1.2525 = -0.0015
This is listed as the minimum interference in the table above: 1.5 (thousandths)

Example 9.4 Basic Shaft System

Use the **Basic Shaft System** from example 9.2. A design requires the use of two mating parts with a nominal size of **0.75** inches. The shaft is to run with moderate speed but with a fairly heavy journal pressure. The fit class chosen is **Basic Shaft System RC6**. Determine the size limits of the two mating parts.

From Appendix A, the Basic Hole System RC6 fit for 0.75 inch nominal size:

Nominal size Range	Limits of Clearance	RC6 Standard Limits – Basic Hole	
		Hole	Shaft
0.71 - 1.19	1.6	+2.0	-1.6
	4.8	-0.0	-2.8

Using the Basic Shaft System, the BASIC size 0.75 is designated as the MMC of the shaft, the maximum shaft size. The conversion of limits to the Basic shaft System is performed by adding 1.6 (thousandths) to the four size limits as shown:

Nominal size Range	Limits of Clearance	RC6 Standard Limits – Basic Shaft	
		Hole	Shaft
0.71 - 1.19	1.6	+3.6	-0.0
	4.8	+1.6	-1.2

Therefore, the maximum shaft size is 0.75
The minimum shaft size is 0.75-0.0012 = 0.7488 inches.
The maximum hole size is 0.75+0.0036 = 0.7536 inches
The minimum hole size is 0.75+0.0016 = 0.7516 inches

Basic Shaft System RC6, nominal size 0.75

> ➤ Note that all the tolerances and allowance are maintained in the conversion.

Allowance = Min. Hole – Max. Shaft = 0.7517 – 0.7500 = 0.0016
This is listed as the minimum clearance in the table above: **1.6 (thousandths)**

Max. Clearance = Max. Hole – Min. Shaft = 0.7537 – 0.7488 = 0.0048
This is listed as the maximum clearance in the table above: **4.8 (thousandths)**

Example 9.5 Basic Shaft System

Use the **Basic Shaft System** from example 9.3. A design requires the use of two mating parts with a nominal size of **1.25** inches. The shaft and hub is to be fastened permanently using a drive fit. The fit class chosen is **Basic Shaft System FN4**. Determine the size limits of the two mating parts.

From ANSI/ASME B4.1 Standard, the FN4 fit for 1.25 inches nominal size:

Nominal size Range	Limits of Interference	FN4 Standard Limits – Basic Hole	
		Hole	Shaft
1.19 - 1.97	1.5	+1.0	+3.1
	3.1	-0.0	+2.5

With the *Basic Shaft System*, the *BASIC* size 1.25 is designated as the MMC of the shaft, the maximum shaft size. The conversion of limits to the Basic shaft System is performed by subtracting 3.1 (thousandths) to the four size limits as shown:

Nominal size Range	Limits of Interference	FN4 Standard Limits – Basic Shaft	
		Hole	Shaft
1.19 - 1.97	1.5	-2.1	-0.0
	3.1	-3.1	-0.6

Therefore, the maximum shaft size is 1.25
The minimum shaft size is 1.25-0.0006 = 1.2494 inches.
The maximum hole size is 1.25-0.0021 = 1.2479 inches
The minimum hole size is 1.25-0.0031 = 1.2469 inches

Basic Hole System: FN4, nominal size 1.25

➢ Note that all the tolerances and allowance are maintained in the conversion.

Allowance = Min. Hole – Max. Shaft = 1.2469 – 1.2500 = -0.0031
This is listed as the maximum interference in the table above: **3.1 (thousandths)**

Min. Interference = Max. Hole – Min. Shaft = 1.2479 – 1.2494 = -0.0015
This is listed as the minimum interference in the table above: **1.5 (thousandths)**

Tolerancing – Metric System

The concepts described in previous sections on the English tolerancing system are also applicable to the Metric System. The commonly used system of preferred metric tolerancing and fits are outlined by the International Organization for Standardization (ISO). The system is specified for holes and shafts, but it is also adaptable to fits between features of parallel surfaces.

- **Basic size** is the theoretical size from which limits or deviations of size are derived.

- **Deviation** is the difference between the basic size and the hole or shaft size. This is equivalent to the word "Tolerance" in the English system.

- **Upper Deviation** is the difference between the basic size and the permitted maximum size. This is equivalent to "Maximum Tolerance" in the English system.

- **Lower Deviation** is the difference between the basic size and the permitted minimum size. This is equivalent to "Minimum Tolerance" in the English system.

- **Fundamental Deviation** is the deviation closest to the basic size. This is equivalent to "Minimum Allowance" in the English system.

- **Tolerance** is the difference between the permissible variations of a size. The tolerance is the difference between the limits of size.

- **International tolerance grade (IT)** is a set of tolerances that varies according to the basic size and provides a uniform level of accuracy within the grade. There are 18 IT grades- IT01, IT0, and IT1 through IT16.

  ❖ IT01 through IT7 is typically used for measuring tools; IT5 through IT11 are used for Fits and IT12 through IT16 for large manufacturing tolerances.

  ❖ The following is a list of IT grade related to machining processes:

International Tolerance Grade (IT)							
4	5	6	7	8	9	10	11
Lapping or Honing							
	Cylindrical Grinding						
	Surface Grinding						
	Diamond Turning or Boring						
	Broaching						
	Powder Metal-sizes						
		Reaming					
			Turning				
			Powder Metal-sintered				
			Boring				
						Milling, Drilling	
						Planing & Shaping	
						Punching	
							Die Casting

Metric Tolerances and Fits Designation

Metric tolerances and fits are specified by using the fundamental deviation symbol along with the IT grade number. An upper case **H** is used for the fundamental deviation for the hole tolerance using the **Hole Basis system**, where a lower case **h** is used to specify the use of the **Shaft Basis System**.

1. **Hole: 30H8**

    Basic size = 30 mm
    Hole size is based on hole basis system using IT8 for tolerance.

2. **Shaft: 30f7**

    Basic size = 30 mm
    Shaft size is based on hole basis system using IT7 for tolerance.

3. **Fit: 30H8/f7**

    Basic size = 30 mm
    Hole basis system with IT8 hole tolerance and IT7 for shaft tolerance.

Preferred ISO Metric Fits

The symbols for either the hole-basis or shaft-basis preferred fits are given in the table below. These are the preferred fits; select the fits from the table whenever possible. See **Appendix B** for the complete *ISO Metric Fits* tables.

- The **Hole-Basis** system is a system in which the basic size is the minimum size of the hole. The *hole-basis* system is the preferred method; the fundamental deviation is specified by the uppercase **H**.

- The **Shaft-Basis** system is a system in which the basic size is the maximum size of the shaft. The fundamental deviation of the *shaft-basis* system is specified by the lowercase **h**.

	Hole Basis	Shaft Basis	Description
ISO Preferred Metric Fits			
Clearance Fits	H11/c11	C11/h11	*Loose running* fit for wide commercial tolerance or allowances.
	H9/d9	D9/h9	*Free running* fit not for use when accuracy is essential, but good for large temperature variation, high running speed, or heavy journal pressure.
	H8/f7	F8/h7	*Close running* fit for running on accurate machines running at moderate speeds and journal pressure.
	H7/g6	G7/h6	*Sliding* fit not intended to run freely, but to move and turn freely and locate accurately.
Transition Fits	H7/h6	H7/h6	*Locational clearance* fit provides snug fit for locating stationary parts; but can be freely assembled and disassembled.
	H7/k6	K7/h6	*Locational transition* fit for accurate location, a compromise between clearance and interference.
	H7/n6	N7/h6	*Locational transition* fit for accurate location where interference is permissible.
	H7/p6	P7/h6	*Locational interference* fit for parts requiring rigidity and alignment with prime accuracy but without special bore pressure.
Interference	H7/s6	S7/h6	*Medium drive* fit for ordinary steel parts or shrink fits on light sections, the tightest fit usable with cast iron.
	H7/u6	U7/h6	*Force* fit suitable for parts which can be highly stressed or for shrink fits where the heavy pressing forces required are impractical.

Example 9.6 Metric Hole Basis System

A design requires the use of two mating parts with a nominal size of **25** millimeters. The shaft and hub is to be fastened permanently using a drive fit. The fit class chosen is **Hole-Basis System H7/s6**. Determine the size limits of the two mating parts.

From Appendix B, the H7/s6 fit for 25 millimeters size:

Basic size	H7/s6 Medium Drive –Hole Basis		
	Hole H7	Shaft s6	Fit
25	25.021	25.048	-0.014
	25.000	25.035	-0.048

Using the *Hole Basis System*, the *BASIC* size 25 is designated as the minimum hole size. And the maximum hole size is 25.021 millimeters
The maximum shaft size is 25.048 millimeters
The minimum shaft size is 25.035 millimeters

**Acceptable Tolerances Designation
Hole Basis H7/s6 Medium drive**

Tolerance of the shaft = Max. Shaft – Min. Shaft = 25.048 – 25.035 = 0.013

Tolerance of the hole = Max. Hole – Min. Hole = 25.021 – 25.000 = 0.021

**Allowance = Min. Hole (MMC Hole) – Max. Shaft (MMC Shaft)
      = 25.000 – 25.048 = -0.0048**
This is listed as the maximum interference in the table above: **-0.048**

**Min. interference = Max. Hole (LMC Hole) – Min. Shaft (LMC Shaft)
      = 25.021 – 25.035 = -0.0014**
This is listed as the minimum interference in the table above: **-0.0014**

Example 9.7 Shaft Basis System

A design requires the use of two mating parts with a nominal size of **25** millimeters. The shaft is to run with moderate speed but with a fairly heavy journal pressure. The fit class chosen is **Shaft Basis System F8/h7**. Determine the size limits of the two mating parts.

From Appendix B, the Shaft Basis System F8/h7 fit for 25 millimeters size:

Basic size	F8/h7 Medium Drive –Shaft Basis		
	Hole F8	Shaft h7	Fit
25	25.053	25.000	0.074
	25.020	24.979	0.020

Therefore, the maximum shaft size is 25
The minimum shaft size is 24.979
The maximum hole size is 25.053
The minimum hole size is 25.020

Shaft Basis F8/h7 Close running fit

$\varnothing$ 25.000
24.979

$\varnothing$ 25.053
25.020

Tolerance of the shaft = Max. Shaft – Min. Shaft = 25.000 – 24.979 = 0.021

Tolerance of the hole = Max. Hole – Min. Hole = 25.053 – 25.020 = 0.023

Allowance = Min. Hole – Max. Shaft = 25.020 – 25.000 = 0.020
This is listed as the minimum clearance in the table above: **0.020**

Max. Clearance = Max. Hole – Min. Shaft = 25.053 – 24.979 = 0.074
This is listed as the maximum clearance in the table above: **0.074**

Updating the U-Bracket Drawing

1. Select the **SolidWorks 2015** option on the *Program* menu or select the **SolidWorks 2015** icon on the *Desktop*.

2. In the SolidWorks *Startup* dialog box, select **Open a Drawing** with a single click of the left-mouse-button.

3. In the *Open* window, select the **MECH475.SLDDRW** file. Use the *browser* to locate the file if it is not displayed in the *File name* list box.

4. Click on the **Open** button in the *Startup* dialog box to accept the selected settings.

Determining the Tolerances Required

The *Bracket* design requires one set of tolerances: the nominal size of the **0.625** inch holes.

RC2 - Nominal size of 0.625

A pin is to be placed through the diameter 0.625 hole. The fit class chosen is **Basic Hole System RC2**. We will first determine the size limits of the two mating parts.

From Appendix A, the RC2 fit for 0.625 inch nominal size:

Nominal size Range	Limits of Clearance	RC2 Standard Limits – Basic Hole	
		Hole	Shaft
0.40 - 0.71	0.25	+0.4	-0.25
	0.95	-0.0	-0.55

Using the *Basic Hole System*, the *BASIC* size 0.625 is designated as the minimum hole size.

The maximum hole size is 0.625+0.0004 = 0.6254 inches
The minimum hole size is 0.625-0.00 = 0.62500 inches

1. Select the diameter **0.625** dimension as shown.

2. In the Property Manager, select Limit as the style of Tolerance as shown.

   • Note that the other styles are also available.

3. Enter +0.0004 in the lower bound box and set to display 4 digits after the decimal point as shown. Note that we are setting the limits using the MMC (Maximum material condition) approach.

➢ The tolerances for the hole are set as shown.

Questions:

1. Why are **Tolerances** important to a technical drawing?

2. Using the **Basic Shaft system**, calculate the size limits of a nominal size of 1.5 inches.

    Use the following FN4 fit table for 1.5 inches nominal size: (numbers are in thousandth of an inch.)

Nominal size Range	Limits of Interference	FN4 Standard Limits – Basic Hole	
		Hole	Shaft
1.19 - 1.97	1.5	+1.0	+3.1
	3.1	-0.0	+2.5

3. Using the **Shaft Basis D9/h9** fits, calculate the size limits of a nominal size of 30 mm.

4. What is the procedure to set tolerances in SolidWorks?

5. Explain the following terms:

    (a) Limits

    (b) MMC

    (c) Tolerances

    (d) Basic Hole System

    (e) Basic Shaft System

6. Given the dimensions as shown in the below figure, determine the tolerances of the two parts, and the allowance between the parts.

Basic Shaft System   RC6, nominal size 0.75

ø.7516
.7536

ø.7500
.7488

Exercises: (Create the drawings with the following Tolerances.)

1. **Shaft Guide** (Dimensions are in inches.)
    Fits: Diameter 0.25, Basic Hole system RC1, Diameter 1.00, Basic Hole system RC6

2. **Pivot Lock** (Dimensions are in inches.)
    Fits: Diameter 0.5, Basic Hole system RC2, Diameter 1.00, Basic Hole system RC5

3. **U-Bracket** (Dimensions are in millimeters.) Fits: Diameter 40, H7/g6.

4. **Cylinder Support** (Inches.) Fits: Diameter 1.50, Basic Hole system RC8.

Notes:

Chapter 10
Pictorials and Sketching

Learning Objectives

- ◆ **Understand the Importance of Freehand Sketching**
- ◆ **Understand the Terminology Used in Pictorial Drawings**
- ◆ **Understand the Basics of the Following Projection Methods: Axonometric, Oblique and Perspective**
- ◆ **Be Able to Create Freehand 3D Pictorials**

Engineering Drawings, Pictorials and Sketching

One of the best ways to communicate your ideas is through the use of a picture or a drawing. This is especially true for engineers and designers. Without the ability to communicate well, engineers and designers will not be able to function in a team environment and therefore will have only limited value in the profession.

For many centuries, artists and engineers used drawings to express their ideas and inventions. The two figures below are drawings by Leonardo da Vinci (1452-1519) illustrating some of his engineering inventions.

Engineering design is a process to create and transform ideas and concepts into a product definition that meet the desired objective. The engineering design process typically involves three stages: (1) Ideation/conceptual design stage: this is the beginning of an engineering design process, where basic ideas and concepts take shapes. (2) Design development stage: the basic ideas are elaborated and further developed. During this stage, prototypes and testing are commonly used to ensure the developed design meets the desired objective. (3) Refine and finalize design stage: This stage of the design process is the last stage of the design process, where the finer details of the design are further refined. Detailed information of the finalized design is documented to assure the design is ready for production.

Two types of drawings are generally associated with the three stages of the engineering process: (1) Freehand Sketches and (2) Detailed Engineering Drawings.

Freehand sketches are generally used in the beginning stages of a design process: (1) to quickly record designer's ideas and help formulating different possibilities, (2) to communicate the designer's basic ideas with others and (3) to develop and elaborate further the designer's ideas/concepts.

During the initial design stage, an engineer will generally picture the ideas in his/her head as three-dimensional images. The ability to think visually, specifically three-dimensional visualization, is one of the most essential skills for an engineer/designer. And freehand sketching is considered as one of the most powerful methods to help develop visualization skills.

Detailed engineering drawings are generally created during the second and third stages of a design process. The detailed engineering drawings are used to help refine and finalize the design and also to document the finalized design for production. Engineering drawings typically require the use of drawing instruments, from compasses to computers, to bring precision to the drawings.

Freehand Sketches and Detailed Engineering Drawings are essential communication tools for engineers. By using the established conventions, such as perspective and isometric drawings, engineers/designers are able to quickly convey their design ideas to others.

The ability to sketch ideas is absolutely essential to engineers. The ability to sketch is helpful, not just to communicate with others, but also to work out details in ideas and to identify any potential problems. Freehand sketching requires only simple tools, a pencil and a piece of paper, and can be accomplished almost anywhere and anytime. Creating freehand sketches does not require any artistic ability. Detailed engineering drawing is employed only for those ideas deserving a permanent record.

Freehand sketches and engineering drawings are generally composed of similar information, but there is a tradeoff between time required to generate a sketch/drawing verses the level of design detail and accuracy. In industry, freehand sketching is used to quickly document rough ideas and identify general needs for improvement in a team environment.

Besides the 2D views, described in the previous chapter, there are three main divisions commonly used in freehand engineering sketches and detailed engineering drawings: (1) **Axonometric**, with its divisions into **isometric**, **dimetric** and **trimetric**; (2) **Oblique**; and (3) **Perspective**.

1. **Axonometric projection**: The word *Axonometric* means "to measure along axes." Axonometric projection is a special *orthographic projection* technique used to generate *pictorials*. **Pictorials** show a 2D image of an object as viewed from a direction that reveals three directions of space. In the figure below, the adjuster model is rotated so that a *pictorial* is generated using *orthographic projection* (projection lines perpendicular to the projection plane) as described in Chapter 4. There are three types of axonometric projections: isometric projection, dimetric projection, and trimetric projection. Typically in an axonometric drawing, one axis is drawn vertically.

In **isometric projections**, the direction of viewing is such that the three axes of space appear equally foreshortened, and therefore the angles between the axes are equal. In **dimetric projections**, the directions of viewing are such that two of the three axes of space appear equally foreshortened. In **trimetric projections**, the direction of viewing is such that the three axes of space appear unequally foreshortened.

Isometric   Dimetric   Trimetric

Isometric projection is perhaps the most widely used for pictorials in engineering graphics, mainly because isometric views are the most convenient to draw. Note that the different projection options described here are not particularly critical in freehand sketching as the emphasis is generally placed on the proportions of the design, not the precision measurements. The general procedure to constructing isometric views is illustrated in the following sections.

2. **Oblique Projection** represents a simple technique of keeping the front face of an object parallel to the projection plane and still reveals three directions of space. An **orthographic projection** is a parallel projection in which the projection lines are perpendicular to the plane of projection. An **oblique projection** is one in which the projection lines are other than perpendicular to the plane of projection.

Orthographic Projection

Oblique Projection

In an oblique drawing, geometry that are parallel to the frontal plane of projection are drawn true size and shape. This is the main advantage of the oblique drawing over the axonometric drawings. The three axes of the oblique sketch are drawn horizontal, vertical, and the third axis can be at any convenient angle (typically between 30 and 60 degrees). The proportional scale along the 3rd axis is typically a scale anywhere between ½ and 1. If the scale is ½, then it is a **Cabinet** oblique. If the scale is 1, then it is a **Cavalier** oblique.

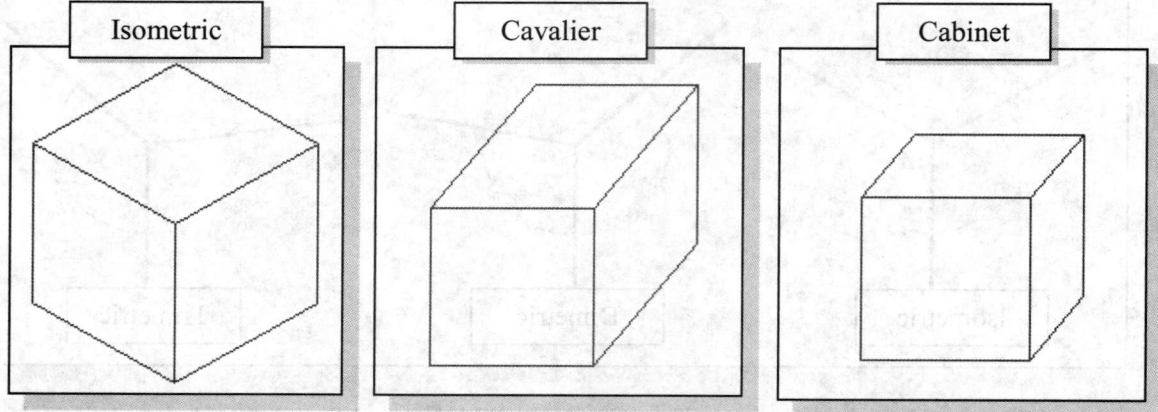

3. **Perspective Projection** adds realism to the three-dimensional pictorial representation; a perspective drawing represents an object as it appears to an observer; objects that are closer to the observer will appear larger to the observer. The key to the perspective projection is that parallel edges converge to a single point, known as the **vanishing point**. If there is just one vanishing point, then it is called a one-point perspective. If two sets of parallel edge lines converge to their respective vanishing points, then it is called a two-point perspective. There is also the case of a three-point perspective in which all three sets of parallel lines converge to their respective vanishing points.

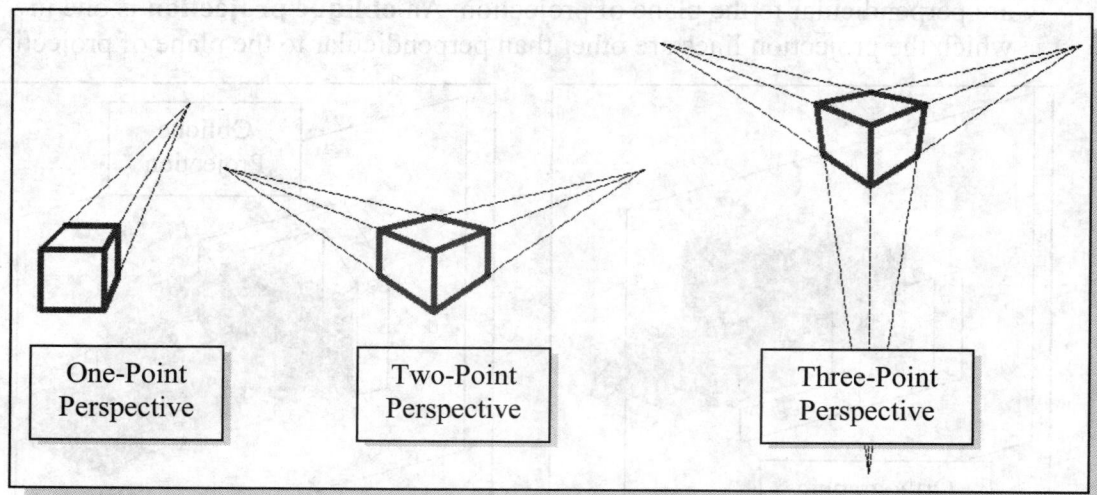

* Although there are specific techniques available to create precise pictorials with known dimensions, in the following sections, the basic concepts and procedures relating to freehand sketching are illustrated.

Isometric Sketching

Isometric drawings are generally done with one axis aligned to the vertical direction. A **regular isometric** is when the viewpoint is looking down on the top of the object, and a **reversed isometric** is when the viewpoint is looking up on the bottom of the object.

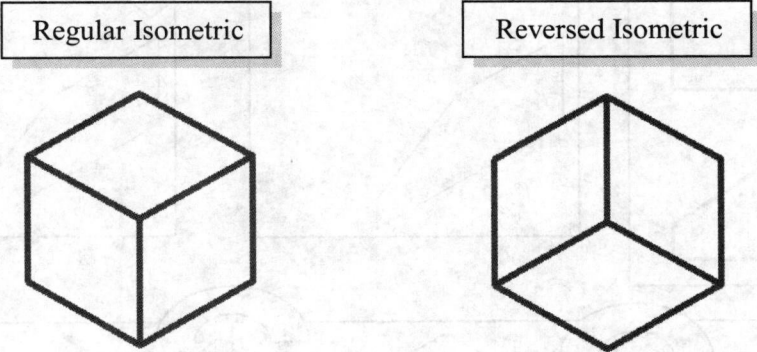

Regular Isometric   Reversed Isometric

Two commonly used approaches in creating isometric sketches are: (1) the **enclosing box** method and (2) the **adjacent surface** method. The enclosing box method begins with the construction of an isometric box showing the overall size of the object. The visible portions of the individual 2D-views are then constructed on the corresponding sides of the box. Adjustments of the locations of surfaces are then made, by moving the edges, to complete the isometric sketch.

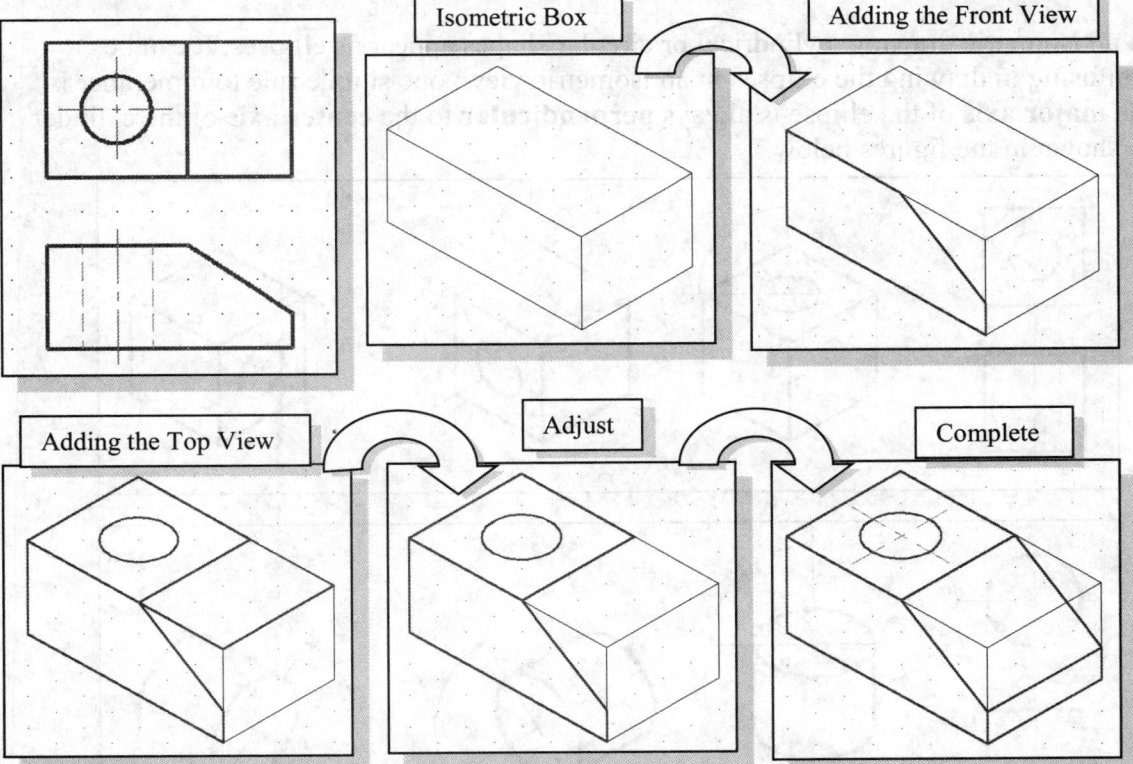

Isometric Box   Adding the Front View   Adding the Top View   Adjust   Complete

The adjacent surface method begins with one side of the isometric drawing, again with the visible portion of the corresponding 2D-view. The isometric sketch is completed by identifying and adding the adjacent surfaces.

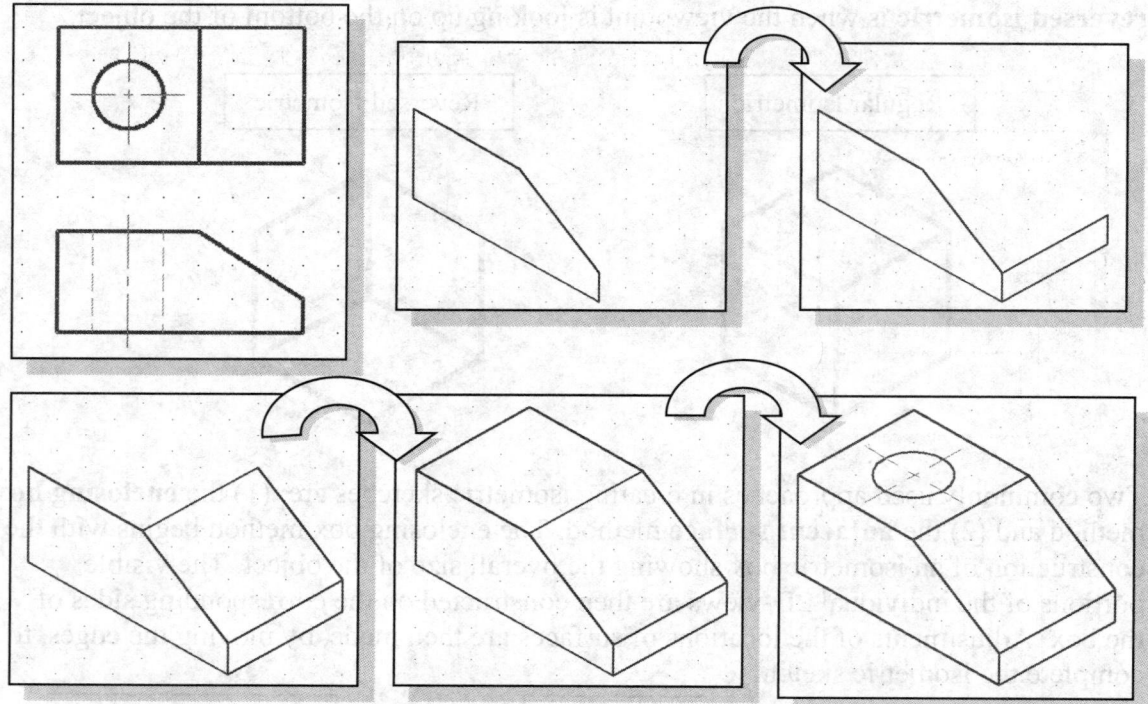

In an isometric drawing, cylindrical or circular shapes appear as ellipses. It can be confusing in drawing the ellipses in an isometric view; one simple rule to remember is the **major axis** of the ellipse is always **perpendicular** to the **center axis** of the cylinder as shown in the figures below.

Chapter 10 - Isometric Sketching Exercise 1:

Given the Orthographic Top view and Front view, create the isometric view.
   (Note that 3D Models of chapter examples and exercises are available at: www.SDCpublications.com/downloads/978-1-58503-932-6)

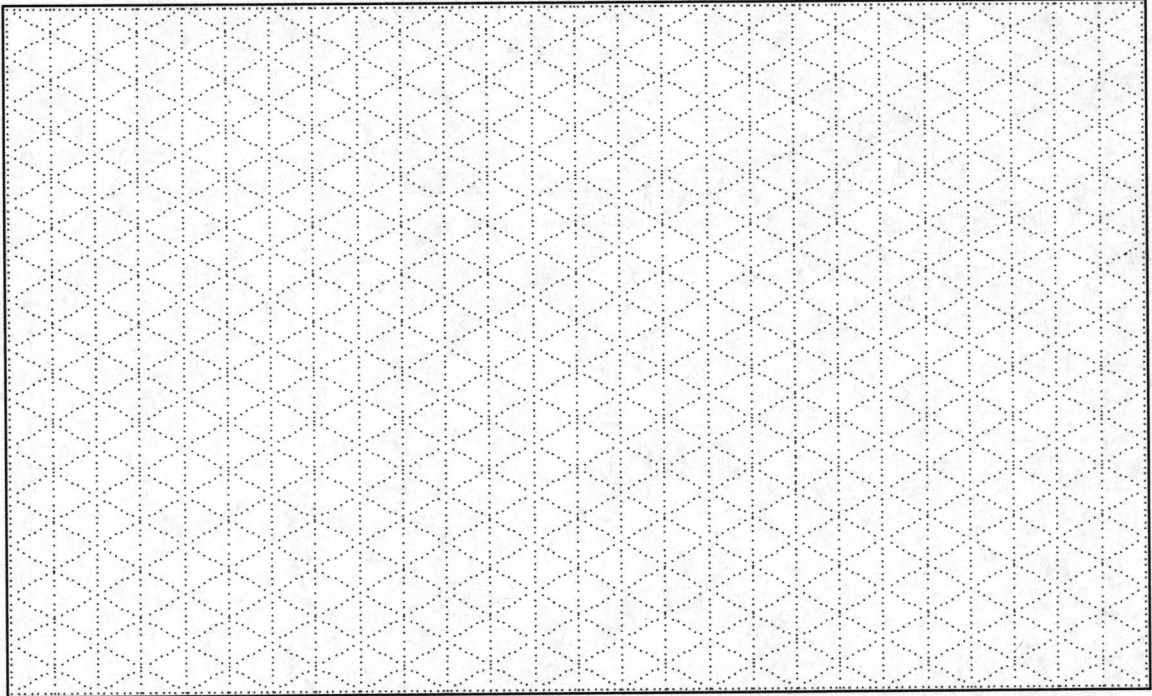

Name: _____   Date: _____

Notes:

Chapter 10 - Isometric Sketching Exercise 2:

Given the Orthographic Top view and Front view, create the isometric view.

(Note that 3D Models of chapter examples and exercises are available at: www.SDCpublications.com/downloads/978-1-58503-932-6)

Name: _____   Date: _____

Notes:

Chapter 10 - Isometric Sketching Exercise 3:

Given the Orthographic Top view and Front view, create the isometric view.

    (Note that 3D Models of chapter examples and exercises are available at: www.SDCpublications.com/downloads/978-1-58503-932-6)

Name: _____   Date: _____

Notes:

Chapter 10 - Isometric Sketching Exercise 4:

Given the Orthographic Top view and Front view, create the isometric view.

(Note that 3D Models of chapter examples and exercises are available at: www.SDCpublications.com/downloads/978-1-58503-932-6)

Name: _____   Date: _____

Notes:

Chapter 10 - Isometric Sketching Exercise 5:

Given the Orthographic Top view, Front view, and Side view create the isometric view.

(Note that 3D Models of chapter examples and exercises are available at: www.SDCpublications.com/downloads/978-1-58503-932-6)

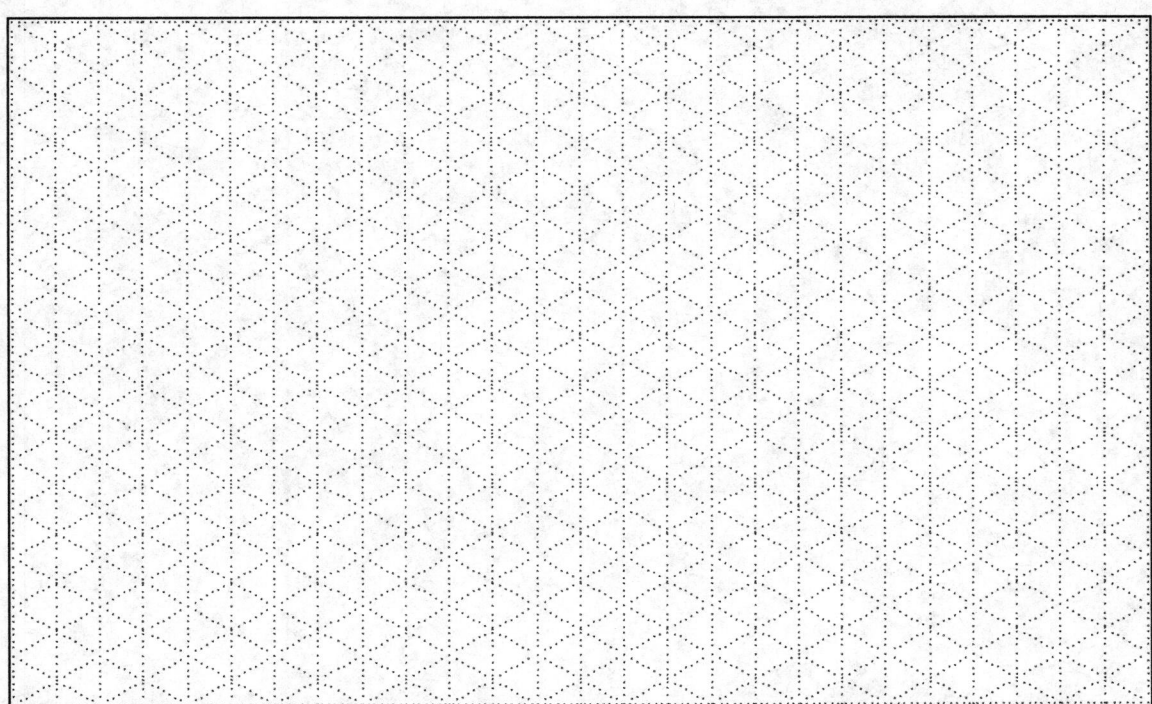

Name: _____   Date: _____

Notes:

Chapter 10 - Isometric Sketching Exercise 6:

Given the Orthographic Top view, Front view, and Side view create the isometric view.

(Note that 3D Models of chapter examples and exercises are available at: www.SDCpublications.com/downloads/978-1-58503-932-6)

Name: _____   Date: _____

Notes:

Chapter 10 - Isometric Sketching Exercise 7:

Given the Orthographic Top view, Front view, and Side view create the isometric view.

(Note that 3D Models of chapter examples and exercises are available at: www.SDCpublications.com/downloads/978-1-58503-932-6)

Name: _____   Date: _____

Notes:

Chapter 10 - Isometric Sketching Exercise 8:

Given the Orthographic Top view, Front view, and Side view create the isometric view.

(Note that 3D Models of chapter examples and exercises are available at: www.SDCpublications.com/downloads/978-1-58503-932-6)

Name: _____   Date: _____

Notes:

Chapter 10 - Isometric Sketching Exercise 9:

Given the Orthographic Top view, Front view, and Side view create the isometric view.

(Note that 3D Models of chapter examples and exercises are available at: www.SDCpublications.com/downloads/978-1-58503-932-6)

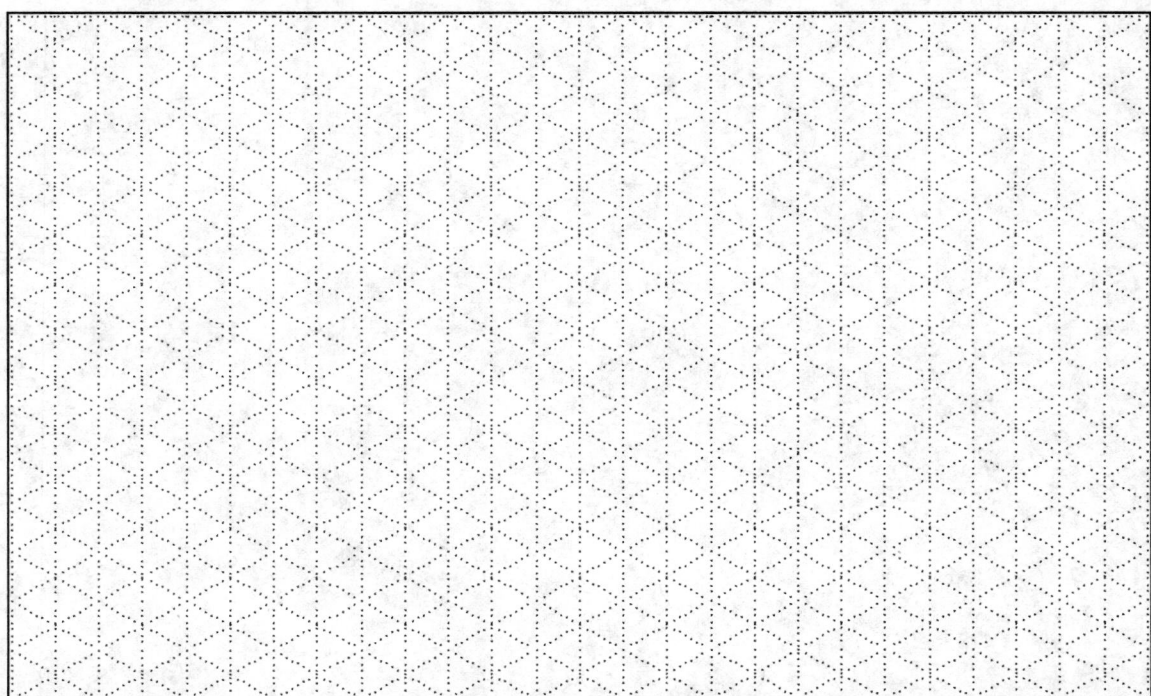

Name: _____   Date: _____

Notes:

Chapter 10 - Isometric Sketching Exercise 10:

Given the Orthographic Top view, Front view, and Side view create the isometric view.

(Note that 3D Models of chapter examples and exercises are available at: www.SDCpublications.com/downloads/978-1-58503-932-6)

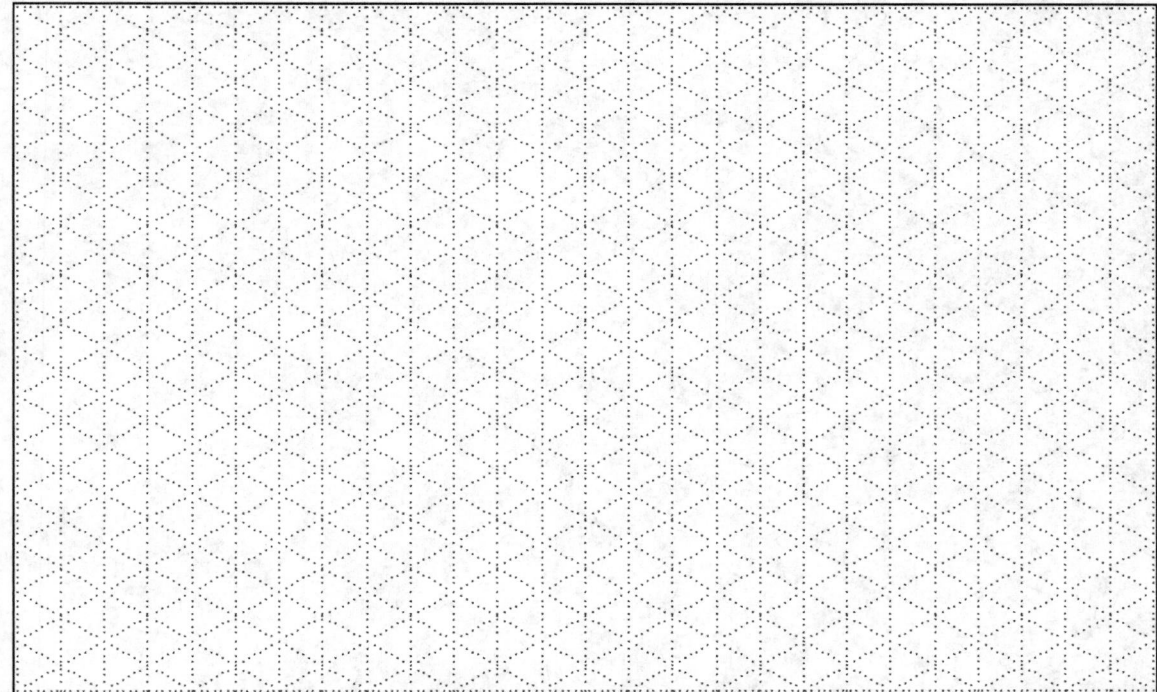

Name: _____   Date: _____

Notes:

Oblique Sketching

Keeping the geometry that is parallel to the frontal plane true to size and shape is the main advantage of the oblique drawing over the axonometric drawings. Unlike isometric drawings, circular shapes that are paralleled to the frontal view will remain as circles in oblique drawings. Generally speaking, an oblique drawing can be created very quickly by using a 2D view as the starting point. For designs with most of the circular shapes in one direction, an oblique sketch is the ideal choice over the other pictorial methods.

Notes:

Chapter 10 - Oblique Sketching Exercise 1:

Given the Orthographic Top view and Front view, create the oblique view.

(Note that 3D Models of chapter examples and exercises are available at: www.SDCpublications.com/downloads/978-1-58503-932-6)

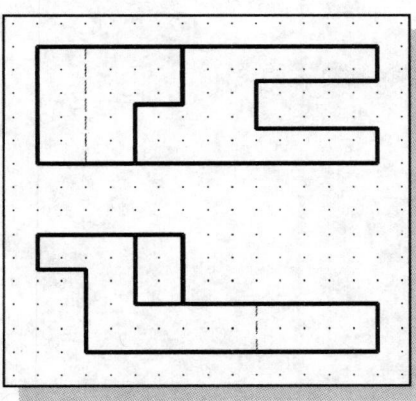

Name: _____   Date: _____

Notes:

Chapter 10 - Oblique Sketching Exercise 2:

Given the Orthographic Top view and Front view, create the oblique view.

(Note that 3D Models of chapter examples and exercises are available at: www.SDCpublications.com/downloads/978-1-58503-932-6)

Name: _____   Date: _____

Notes:

Chapter 10 - Oblique Sketching Exercise 3:

Given the Orthographic Top view and Front view, create the oblique view.

(Note that 3D Models of chapter examples and exercises are available at: www.SDCpublications.com/downloads/978-1-58503-932-6)

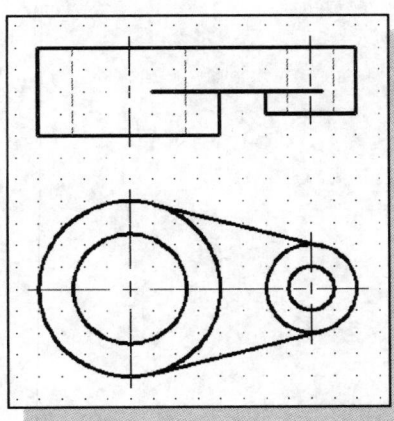

Name: _____   Date: _____

Notes:

Chapter 10 - Oblique Sketching Exercise 4:

Given the Orthographic Top view and Front view, create the oblique view.

(Note that 3D Models of chapter examples and exercises are available at: www.SDCpublications.com/downloads/978-1-58503-932-6)

Name: _____   Date: _____

Notes:

Chapter 10 - Oblique Sketching Exercise 5:

Given the Orthographic Top view and Front view, create the oblique view.

   (Note that 3D Models of chapter examples and exercises are available at: www.SDCpublications.com/downloads/978-1-58503-932-6)

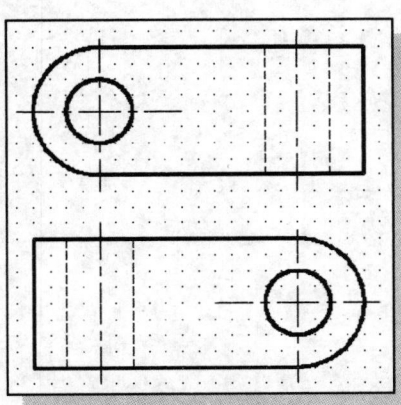

Name: _____   Date: _____

Notes:

Chapter 10 - Oblique Sketching Exercise 6:

Given the Orthographic Top view and Front view, create the oblique view.

(Note that 3D Models of chapter examples and exercises are available at: www.SDCpublications.com/downloads/978-1-58503-932-6)

Name: _____   Date: _____

Notes:

Perspective Sketching

A perspective drawing represents an object as it appears to an observer; objects that are closer to the observer will appear larger to the observer. The key to the perspective projection is that parallel edges converge to a single point, known as the **vanishing point**. The vanishing point represents the position where projection lines converge.

The selection of the locations of the vanishing points, which is the first step in creating a perspective sketch, will affect the looks of the resulting images.

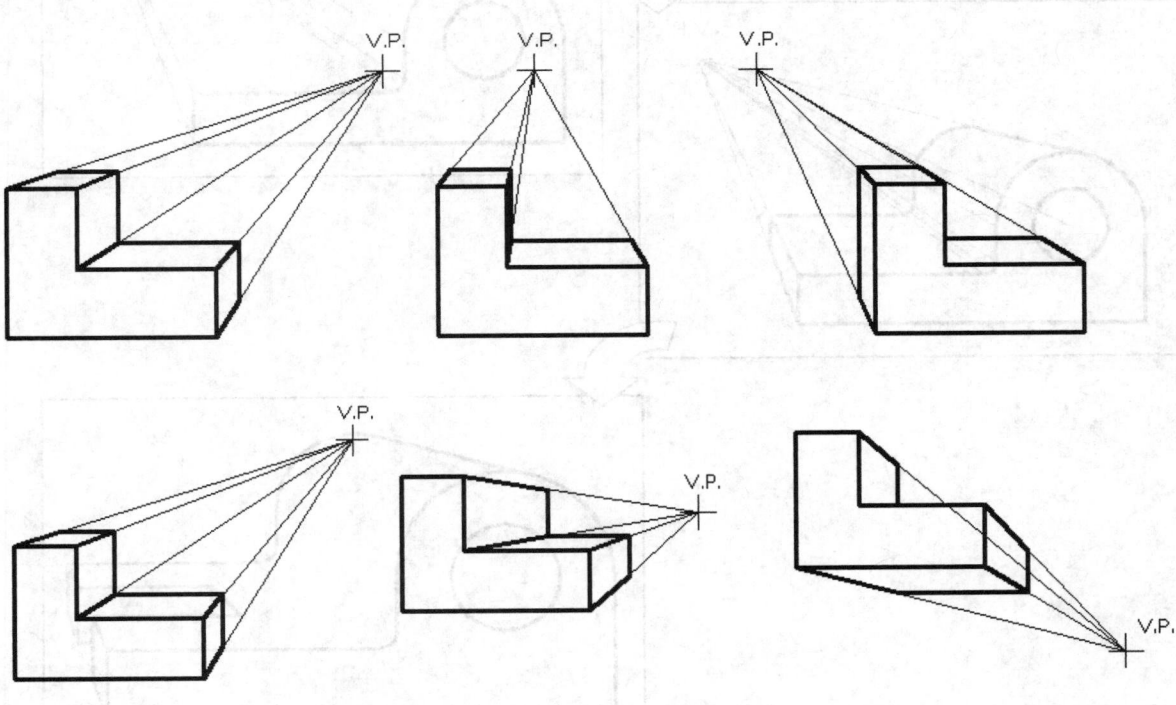

One-Point Perspective

One-point perspective is commonly used because of its simplicity. The first step in creating a one-point perspective is to sketch the front face of the object just as in oblique sketching; followed by selecting the position for the vanishing point. For Mechanical designs, the vanishing point is usually placed above and to the right of the picture. The use of construction lines can be helpful in locating the edges of the object and to complete the sketch.

Two-Point Perspective

Two-point perspective is perhaps the most popular of all perspective methods. The use of the two vanishing points gives very true to life images. The first step in creating a two-point perspective is to select the locations for the two vanishing points; followed by sketching an enclosing box to show the outline of the object. The use of construction lines can be very helpful in locating the edges of the object and to complete the sketch.

Notes:

Chapter 10 - Perspective Sketching Exercise 1:

Given the Orthographic Top view and Front view, create one-point or two-point perspective views.
(Note that 3D Models of chapter examples and exercises are available at: www.SDCpublications.com/downloads/978-1-58503-932-6)

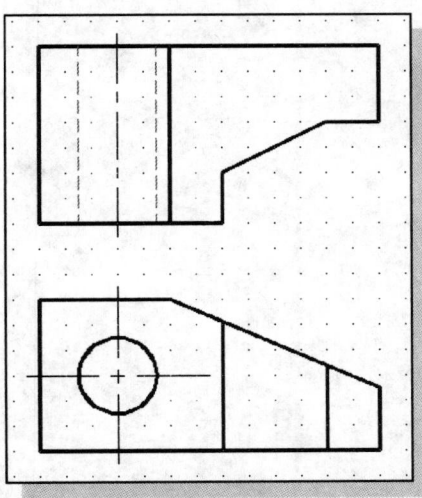

Name: _____   Date: _____

Notes:

Chapter 10 - Perspective Sketching Exercise 2:

Given the Orthographic Top view and Front view, create one-point or two-point perspective views.
(Note that 3D Models of chapter examples and exercises are available at: www.SDCpublications.com/downloads/978-1-58503-932-6)

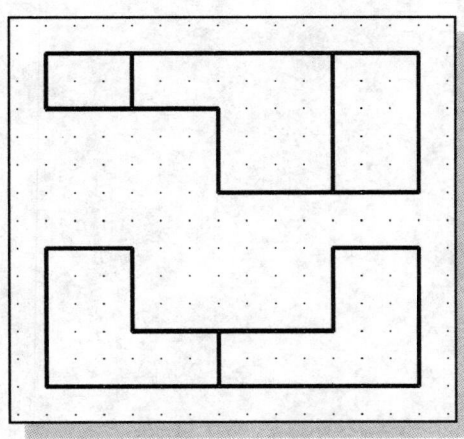

Name: _____   Date: _____

Notes:

Chapter 10 - Perspective Sketching Exercise 3:

Given the Orthographic Top view and Front view, create one-point or two-point perspective views.

(Note that 3D Models of chapter examples and exercises are available at: www.SDCpublications.com/downloads/978-1-58503-932-6)

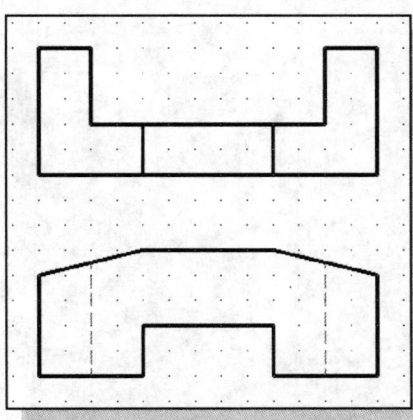

Name: _____   Date: _____

Notes:

Chapter 10 - Perspective Sketching Exercise 4:

Given the Orthographic Top view and Front view, create one-point or two-point perspective views.
(Note that 3D Models of chapter examples and exercises are available at: www.SDCpublications.com/downloads/978-1-58503-932-6)

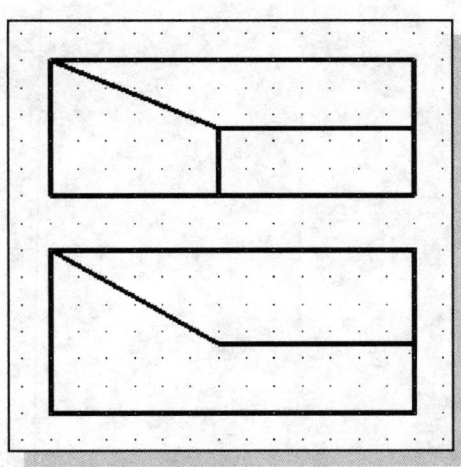

Name: _____   Date: _____

Notes:

Chapter 10 - Perspective Sketching Exercise 5:

Given the Orthographic Top view and Front view, create one-point or two-point perspective views.
(Note that 3D Models of chapter examples and exercises are available at: www.SDCpublications.com/downloads/978-1-58503-932-6)

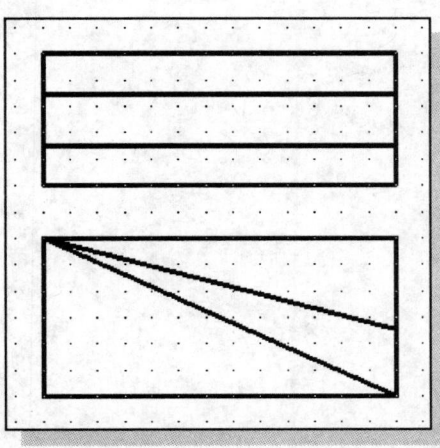

Name: _____   Date: _____

Notes:

Chapter 10 - Perspective Sketching Exercise 6:

Given the Orthographic Top view and Front view, create one-point or two-point perspective views.
(Note that 3D Models of chapter examples and exercises are available at: www.SDCpublications.com/downloads/978-1-58503-932-6)

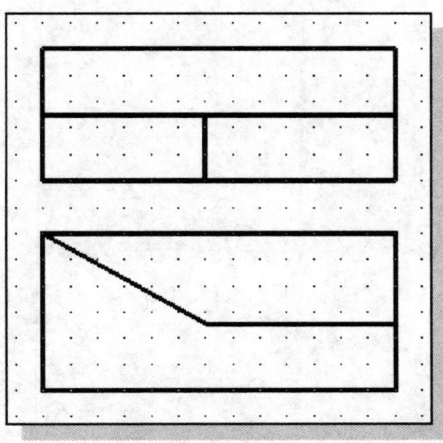

Name: _____   Date: _____

Notes:

Questions:

1. What are the three types of Axonometric projection?

2. Describe the differences between an Isometric drawing and a Trimetric drawing.

3. What is the main advantage of Oblique projection over the isometric projection?

4. Describe the differences between a one-point perspective and a two-point perspective.

5. Which pictorial methods maintain true size and shape of geometry on the frontal plane?

6. What is a vanish point in a perspective drawing?

7. What is a Cabinet Oblique?

8. What is the angle between the three axes in an isometric drawing?

9. In an Axonometric drawing, are the projection lines perpendicular to the projection plane?

10. A cylindrical feature, in a frontal plane, will remain a circle in which pictorial methods?

11. In an Oblique drawing, are the projection lines perpendicular to the projection plane?

12. Create freehand pictorial sketches of:
    *   Your desk
    *   Your computer
    *   One corner of your room
    *   The tallest building in your area

Exercises:

Complete the missing views. (Hint: Create a pictorial sketch as an aid in reading the views.)

Chapter 11
Section Views & Symmetrical Features in Designs

Learning Objectives

- **Create Revolved Features**
- **Use the Mirror Feature Command**
- **Create New Borders and Title Blocks**
- **Create Circular Patterns**
- **Create and Modify Linear Dimensions**
- **Use SolidWorks' Associative Functionality**
- **Identify Symmetrical Features in Designs**
- **Create a Section View in a Drawing**

Certified SolidWorks Associate Exam Objectives Coverage

Sketch Entities – Lines, Rectangles, Circles, Arcs, Ellipses, Centerlines
Objectives: Creating Sketch Entities.

Boss and Cut Features – Extrudes, Revolves, Sweeps, Lofts
Objectives: Creating Basic Swept Shapes.

Linear, Circular, and Fill Patterns
Objectives: Creating Patterned Features.

Drawing Sheets and Views
Objectives: Creating and Setting Properties for Drawing Sheets; Inserting and Editing Standard Views.

Annotations
Objectives: Creating Annotations.

Introduction

In the previous chapters, we have explored the basic CAD methods of creating orthographic views. By carefully selecting a limited number of views, the external features of most complicated designs can be fully described. However, we are frequently confronted with the necessity of showing the interiors of parts, or when parts are assembled, that cannot be shown clearly by means of hidden lines.

Hidden features can be difficult to visualize

In cases of this kind, to aid in describing the object, one or more views are drawn to show the object as if a portion of the object had been cut away to reveal the interior.

This type of convention is called a **section**, which is defined as an imaginary cut made through an object to expose the interior of a part. Such kind of cutaway view is known as a **section view**.

In a *section view*, the place from which the section is taken must be identifiable on the drawing. If the place from which the section is taken is obvious, as it is for the below figure, no further description is needed.

If the place from which the section is taken is not obvious, as it is for the below figure, a **cutting plane** is needed to identify the section. Two arrows are also used to indicate the viewing direction. A *cutting plane line* is drawn with the *phantom* or *hidden* line.

General Rules of Section Views

Section views are used to make a part drawing more understandable, showing the internal details of the part. Since the sectioned drawing is showing the internal features there is generally no need to show hidden lines.

A section view still follows the general rules of any view in a multiview drawing. Cutting planes may be labeled at their endpoints to clarify the association of the cut and the section views, especially when multiple cutting plane lines are used. When using multiple cutting planes, each sectioned drawing is drawn as if the other cutting plane lines do not exist. The cutting plane line takes precedence over center lines and, remember, cutting plane lines may be omitted when their location is obvious.

Section lines or **cross-hatch lines** are drawn where the cutting plane passes through the object. This is done as if a saw was used to cut the part and then section lines are used to represent the cutting marks left by the saw blade. Different materials are represented by the use of different section line types. The line type for iron may be used as the general section line type for any material.

Cast iron, Malleable iron and general use for all materials

Steel

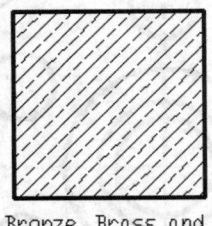
Bronze, Brass and composition Materials

Magnesium, aluminum and aluminum alloys

Section lines should not be parallel or perpendicular to object lines. Section lines are generally drawn at 45°, 30° or 60°, unless there are conflicts with other rules. Section lines should be oriented at different angles for different parts.

Section Drawing Types

- **Full Section:** The cutting plane passes completely through the part as a single flat plane.

- **Half Section:** The cutting plane only passes half way through the part and the other half is drawn as usual. Hidden lines are generally not shown on either half of the part. However, hidden lines may be used in the un-sectioned half if necessary for clarity. Half section is mostly used on cylindrical parts, and a center line is used to separate the two halves.

- **Offset Section:** It is often difficult to interpret a multiview drawing when there are multiple features on the object. An **offset section** allows the cutting plane to pass through several places by **"offsetting"** or **bending** the cutting plane. The offsets or bends in the cutting plane are all 90° and are *not* shown in the section view.

- **Broken-Out Section:** It is quite often that a full section is not necessary, but only a partial section is needed to show the interior details of a part. In a **broken-out section**, only a portion of the view is sectioned and a jagged break-line is used to divide the sectioned and un-sectioned portion of the view.

- **Aligned Section:** To include certain angled features in a section view, the cutting plane may be bent to pass through those features to their true radial position.

- **Half Views:** When space is limited, a symmetrical part can be shown as a half view.

Half View with a Full Section

Half View with a Half Section

- **Thin Sections:** For thin parts, typically parts that are less than 3mm thick such as sheet metal parts and gaskets, section lines are ineffective and therefore should be omitted. Thin sections are generally shown in solid black without section lines.

- **Revolved Section:** A cross section of the part is revolved 90° and superimposed on the drawing.

- The object lines adjacent to a revolved section may be broken out with short break lines. The true shape of a revolved section is retained regardless of the object lines in the view.

- **Removed Section:** Similar to the revolved section, except that the sectioned drawing is not superimposed on the drawing but placed adjacent to it. The removed section may also be drawn at a different scale. Very useful for detailing small parts or features

- **Conventional Breaks:** In making the details of parts that are long and with a uniform cross section, it is rarely necessary to draw its whole length. Using the Conventional Breaks to shorten such an object will allow the part to be drawn with a larger scale. S-Breaks are preferred for cylindrical objects and jagged lines are used to break non-circular objects.

- **Ribs and Webs in Sections:** To avoid a misleading effect of thickness and solidity; ribs, webs, spokes, gear teeth and other similar are drawn without crosshatching when the cutting plane passes through them lengthwise. Ribs are sectioned if the cutting plane passes through them at other orientations.

- **Parts Not Sectioned:** Many machine elements, such as fasteners, pins, bearings and shafts, have no internal features, and are generally more easily recognized by their exterior views. Do not section these parts.

Section Views in SolidWorks

In parametric modeling, it is important to identify and determine the features that exist in the design. *Feature-based parametric modeling* enables us to build complex designs by working on smaller and simpler units. This approach simplifies the modeling process and allows us to concentrate on the characteristics of the design. Symmetry is an important characteristic that is often seen in designs. Symmetrical features can be easily accomplished by the assortments of tools that are available in feature-based modeling systems, such as SolidWorks.

The modeling technique of extruding two-dimensional sketches along a straight line to form three-dimensional features, as illustrated in the previous chapters, is an effective way to construct solid models. For designs that involve cylindrical shapes, shapes that are symmetrical about an axis, revolving two-dimensional sketches about an axis can form the needed three-dimensional features. In solid modeling, this type of feature is called a *revolved feature*.

In SolidWorks, besides using the **Revolved Boss/Base** command to create revolved features, several options are also available to handle symmetrical features. For example, we can create multiple identical copies of symmetrical features with the **Circular Pattern** command, or create mirror images of models using the **Mirror** command. We can also use *construction geometry* to assist the construction of more complex features. In this lesson, the construction and modeling techniques of these more advanced options are illustrated.

A Revolved Design: *PULLEY*

❖ Based on your knowledge of SolidWorks, how many features would you use to create the design? Which feature would you choose as the **base feature** of the model? Identify the symmetrical features in the design and consider other possibilities in creating the design. You are encouraged to create the model on your own prior to following through the tutorial.

Modeling Strategy – A Revolved Design

Starting SolidWorks

1. Select the **SolidWorks** option on the *Start* menu or select the **SolidWorks** icon on the desktop to start SolidWorks. The SolidWorks main window will appear on the screen.

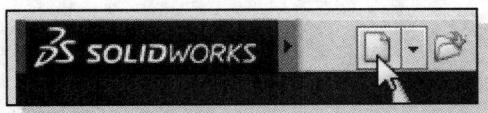

2. Select the **New** icon with a single click of the left-mouse-button on the *Menu Bar*.

3. The *New SolidWorks Document* dialog box should appear in Advanced mode. If it appears in Novice mode, click once with the left-mouse-button on the **Advanced** icon.

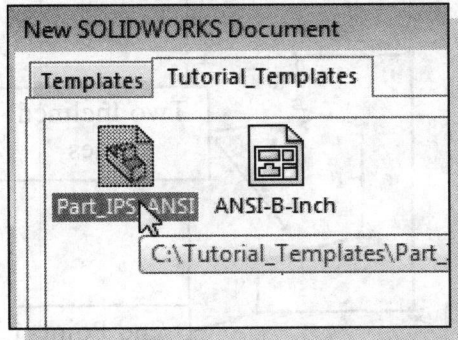

4. Select the **Tutorial_Templates** tab. (**NOTE:** If your templates are not available, open the standard Part template and set the *Drafting Standard* to ANSI and the *Units* to IPS.)

5. Select the **Part_IPS_ANSI** template as shown.

6. Click on the **OK** button to open a new document using the Part_IPS_ANSI template.

Creating the Base Feature

1. Select the **Revolved Boss/Base** button on the *Features* toolbar to create a new feature.

2. Move the cursor over the edge of the Front Plane in the graphics area. When the Front Plane is highlighted, click once with the **left-mouse-button** to select the Front (XY) Plane as the sketch plane for the new sketch.

3. Click on the **Line** icon in the *Sketch* toolbar.

4. Create a closed-region sketch, above the origin, as shown below. (Note that the *Pulley* design is symmetrical about a horizontal axis as well as a vertical axis, which allows us to simplify the 2D sketch as shown below.)

5. We want the left vertical edge to be aligned with the Y-axis. Select the **Add Relation** command from the *Display/Delete Relations* pop-up menu on the *Sketch* toolbar.

6. On your own, select the **left vertical edge** and the **origin** and add a **Coincident** relation.

➤ The X-axis is an axis of symmetry. It will serve as the rotation axis for the revolve feature, and we will use it to apply dimensions. A centerline will be created along the X-axis for these purposes.

7. Select the **Centerline** command from the *Line* pop-up menu on the *Sketch* toolbar.

8. Left-click on the **origin** as the first endpoint of the centerline.

9. Move the cursor to the right and left-click to create a **horizontal centerline** along the X-axis.

10. Press the **[Esc]** key to exit the Centerline command.

11. Select the **Smart Dimension** command in the *Sketch* toolbar.

12. Pick the **centerline** as the first entity to dimension as shown in the figure below.

13. Select the **bottom horizontal line** as the second object to dimension.

14. Locate the dimension **below the centerline**. This will automatically create a diameter dimension bisected by the centerline.

13. Select the bottom horizontal edge

12. Select the centerline

14. Locate dimension below the centerline

15. In the *Modify* pop-up window enter **.75** for the dimension.

16. Select **OK** in the *Modify* pop-up window.

- **To create a dimension that will account for the symmetrical nature of the design: pick the centerline (axis of symmetry), pick the entity, and then place the dimension on the side of the centerline opposite to the entity.**

17. Pick the **centerline** as the first entity to dimension as shown in the figure below.

18. Select the **corner point** as the second object to dimension as shown in the figure below.

19. Locate the dimension **below the centerline**. This will automatically create a diameter dimension bisected by the centerline.

18. Select this corner

19. Locate dimension below centerline

17. Select the centerline

.750

1.483

Modify
D2@Sketch1
1.25in

20. In the *Modify* pop-up window enter **1.25** for the dimension.

21. Select **OK** in the *Modify* pop-up window.

22. On your own, create and adjust the vertical size/location dimensions as shown.

.500

.125

.750

.750   1.500

1.250

3.500   4.000

3.750

Creating the Revolved Feature

1. Select the **Exit Sketch** icon on the *Sketch* toolbar to exit the Sketch option.

2. The *Revolve Property Manager* appears. In the *Revolve Parameters* panel; the centerline is automatically selected as the revolve axis. The default revolution is **360°**. Click the **OK** icon to accept these parameters and create the revolved feature.

Mirroring Features

• In SolidWorks, features can be mirrored to create and maintain complex symmetrical features. We can mirror a feature about a work plane or a specified surface. We can create a mirrored feature while maintaining the original parametric definitions, which can be quite useful in creating symmetrical features. For example, we can create one quadrant of a feature, then mirror it twice to create a solid with four identical quadrants.

1. In the *Features* toolbar, select the **Mirror** command as shown.

2. The *Mirror Property Manager* appears. The *Mirror Face/Plane* panel is highlighted and the message "*Select a plane or planar face about which to mirror ...*" appears in the *Status Bar* area. Use the dynamic viewing options to rotate/position the model so that we are viewing the back surface as shown.

3. Select the surface as shown in the figure as the planar surface about which to mirror. The selection appears in the *Mirror Face/ Plane* panel.

4. The **Features to Mirror** panel in the *Property-Manager* should contain **Revolve1** as the feature to mirror because this was pre-selected when we entered the Mirror command. If it does not, select the Revolve1 feature as the feature to mirror.

5. Click **OK** in the *Property Manager* to accept the settings and create the mirrored feature.

6. On your own, return to an isometric view.

➢ Now is a good time to save the model. It is a good habit to save your model periodically, just in case something might go wrong while you are working on it. You should also save the model after you have completed any major constructions.

7. On your own, save the model as a **.sldprt* file, entering **Pulley** for the filename and **4″ Pulley** for the Description.

Creating an Extruded Cut Feature using Construction Geometry

- In SolidWorks, we can also use **construction geometry** to help define, constrain, and dimension the required geometry. **Construction geometry** can be lines, arcs, and circles that are used to line up or define other geometry, but are not themselves used as the shape geometry of the model. When profiling the rough sketch, SolidWorks will separate the construction geometry from the other entities and treat them as construction entities. Construction geometry can be dimensioned and constrained just like any other profile geometry. When the profile is turned into a 3D feature, the construction geometry remains in the sketch definition but does not show in the 3D model. Using construction geometry in profiles may mean fewer constraints and dimensions are needed to control the size and shape of geometric sketches. In SolidWorks, any sketch entity can be converted to construction geometry. Points and centerlines are always construction entities. We will illustrate the use of the construction geometry to create a cut feature.

- The *Pulley* design requires the placement of five identical holes on the base solid. Instead of creating the five holes one at a time, we can simplify the creation of these holes by using the **Circular Pattern** command, which allows us to create duplicate features. Prior to using the Circular Pattern command, we will first create a *pattern leader*, which is a regular extruded feature.

1. In the *Features* toolbar select the **Extruded Cut** command by left-clicking once on the icon.

2. Use the *Design Tree* in the graphics area to select the **Right** (YZ) **Plane** as shown.

3. Select the **Circle** command by clicking once with the left-mouse-button on the icon in the *Sketch* toolbar.

4. Create a circle of arbitrary size as shown.

5. Select the **Line** command in the *Sketch* toolbar.

6. Create 2 *lines* by left-clicking on (1) the center of the circle we just created, (2) the *origin*, and (3) a point to the right of the origin creating a horizontal line, as shown below.

6-1. First point: the **center** of the small circle

6-2. Second point: the **origin**

6-3. Third point: Creating a horizontal line

2.188

7. Press the [Esc] key to exit the Line command.

8. Select the **Circle** command on the *Sketch* toolbar.

9. Place the center at the ***origin***.

10. Pick the center of the small circle to set the size of the circle as shown.

11. Press the **[Esc]** key to exit the *Circle* command.

12. In the graphics area, left-click on the ***horizontal line*** to select it.

13. Press and hold down the **[Ctrl]** key and left-click on the **angled line** and **the last circle** drawn. The two lines and the circle are all highlighted. All three appear as selected entities (*Arc2, Line1, Line2*) in the *Properties Property Manager*.

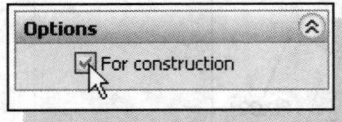

14. **Check** the box next to the **For construction** option in the options panel of the *Properties Property Manager*.

15. Click **OK** in the *Property Manager* to accept the setting. Notice the entities have been converted to construction geometry and appear with the same line style as centerlines.

16. Select the **Smart Dimension** command in the *Sketch* toolbar.

17. Pick the **horizontal construction line** as the first entity to dimension.

18. Select the **angled construction line** as the second entity to dimension.

19. Place the dimension text to the right of the model as shown.

20. Enter **30 deg** for the angle dimension.

21. Click **OK** in the *Modify* window.

➤ Note that the location of the small circle is adjusted as the location of the construction line is adjusted by the *angle dimension* we created.

22. On your own, create the two diameter dimensions, **.5** and **2.5**, as shown below.

23. Select the **Sketch** icon on the *Sketch* toolbar to exit the Sketch option.

24. On your own, complete the **Extruded Cut** feature. Use the **Mid Plane** option and enter **0.25** for the distance.

25. Click **OK** in the *Property Manager* to create the extruded cut feature.

26. On your own, adjust the angle dimension applied to the construction line of the cut feature to **90** and observe the effect of the adjustment.

27. Reset the angle dimension to **30** degrees before continuing to the next section.

Circular Pattern

➤ In SolidWorks, existing features can be easily duplicated. The **Linear Pattern** and **Circular Pattern** commands allow us to create rectangular and polar arrays of features. The patterned features are parametrically linked to the original feature; any modifications to the original feature are also reflected in the arrayed features.

1. Select the **View Temporary Axes** option from the *Hide/Show* pull-down menu on the *Heads-up View* toolbar. Temporary axes are those created implicitly by cones and cylinders in the model. We will use the central axis for our circular pattern.

➤ Alternately, the visibility can be toggled *ON* by selecting Temporary Axes on the *View* pull-down menu.

2. Press the [**Esc**] key once to ensure no feature is selected.

3. In the *Features* toolbar, left-click on the **arrow** below the **Linear Pattern** icon and select the **Circular Pattern** command from pop-up menu.

4. The message "*Select edge or axis for direction reference...*" is displayed in the *Status Bar* area. SolidWorks expects us to select an axis to pattern about. Select the **axis** at the center of the *Pulley* as shown. Notice the axis (Axis<1>) appears in the *Pattern Axis* box in the *Parameters* panel of the *Circular Pattern Property Manager*.

5. In the *Parameters* panel, check the **Equal Spacing** box, enter **5** in the *Number of Instances* box, and enter **360** in the *Angle* box as shown.

6. **Left-click** in the *Features to Pattern* text box as shown to begin selection of features to pattern.

7. Select the **circular cut feature** when it is highlighted as shown.

8. Select **OK** in the *Circular Pattern Property Manager* to accept the settings and create the circular pattern.

9. On your own, turn *OFF* the visibility of the **Temporary Axes** and the **Origins**. (See Step 1 above.)

10. Select **Save** in the *Menu Bar*; we can also use the "**Ctrl+S**" combination (press down the [Ctrl] key and hit the [S] key once) to save the part as *Pulley*.

Drawing Mode – Defining a New Border and Title Block

1. Click on the arrow next to the **New** icon on the *Menu Bar* and select **Make Drawing from Part/Assembly** in the pull-down menu.

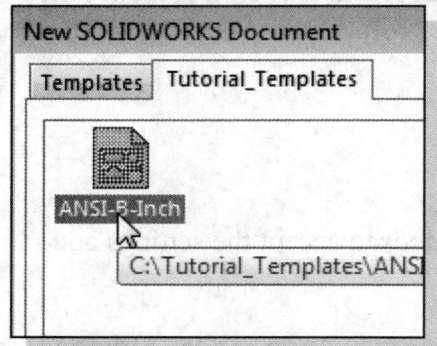

2. In the *New SolidWorks Document* window, select the **Tutorial_Templates** tab.

3. Select the **ANSI-B-Inch** template file icon. This is the custom drawing template you created in Chapter 8. (If your ANSI-B-Inch template is not available, see note below.)

4. Select **OK** in the *New SolidWorks Document* window to open the new drawing file.

❖ **NOTE:** If your ANSI-B-Inch template is not available: (1) open the default **Drawing** template; (2) set document properties following instructions on page 8-37.

➢ We will use the *Document Properties* in this template, but will create a new *Sheet Format*.

5. Right-click on the **Sheet** icon in the *Design Tree* to reveal the pop-up option menu.

6. Select **Properties** from the menu.

7. Set the scale to **1:1** and select **A (ANSI) Landscape** for the *Sheet Format/Size* in the *Sheet Properties* window.

8. Select **OK** in the *Sheet Properties* window.

9. Move the cursor into the graphics area and **right-click** to open the pop-up option menu.

10. Select **Edit Sheet Format** from the pop-up option menu to change to *Edit Sheet Format* mode. (Notice this method could also be used to access the *Sheet Properties*.)

11. Inside the graphics area, click and drag to create a window selecting all the entities in the title block, leaving only the border.

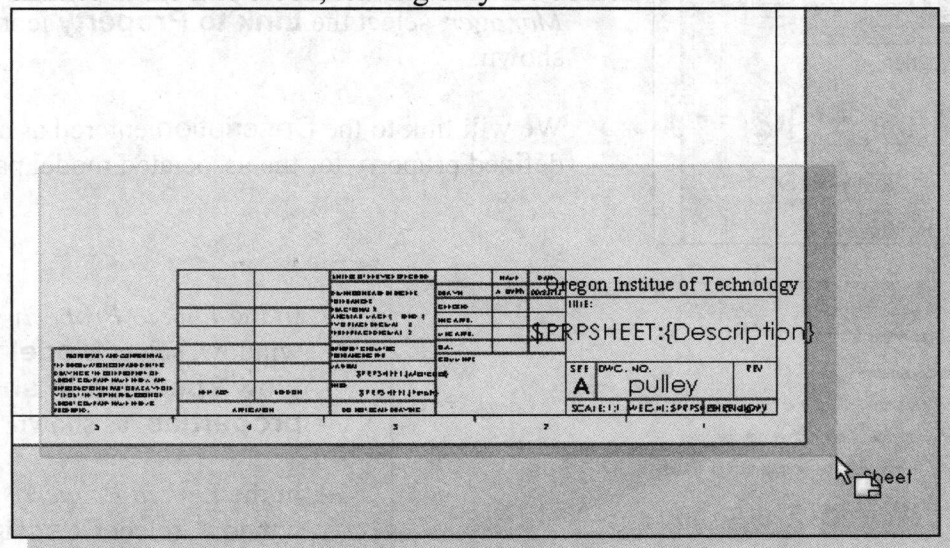

12. Press the [**Delete**] key to delete these entities.

13. On your own, create a title block using the **Line** and **Smart Dimension** commands in the *Sketch* toolbar and the **Note** command in the *Annotation* toolbar.

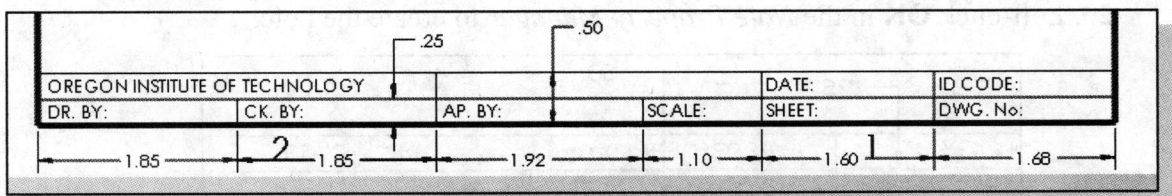

➢ We will now add a **Note** with a **Property Link**.

14. Left-click on the **Note** icon on the *Annotation* toolbar.

15. Select a location inside the central empty box in the new title block as shown.

16. In the *Text Format* panel of the *Note Property Manager*, select the **Link to Property** icon as shown.

➤ We will link to the Description entered as a user-defined property for the associated model part file.

17. In the *Link to Property* window, select **Model in view specified in sheet properties**, as shown.

18. In the *Link to Property* window, select **Description** from the pull-down menu as shown.

19. Left-click **OK** in the *Link to Property* window to accept the selection.

20. Left-click **OK** in the *Note Property Manager* to create the note.

➤ Notice the Property Link appears in the title block as **$PRPSHEET:{Description}**. The prefix **$PRPSHEET:** defines the source as the model (part file) appearing in the sheet. The Property Name is **Description**, which is a *Custom Property*.

21. Move your cursor on top of any icon in the *Command Manager* area.

22. **Right-click** once to open the pop-up option menu and switch on the Line Format toolbar as shown.

• The **Line Format** toolbar appears near the bottom of the SolidWorks main window.

Thick2 line.

23. Select the top horizontal line we just created.

24. Set the line thickness to Thick2 line thickness, which is 0.0197 in.

25. On your own, also adjust the color of the lines.

26. On your own, repeat the above steps and adjust the thickness of the lines we created.

27. On your own, delete the dimensions you created to set up the title block.

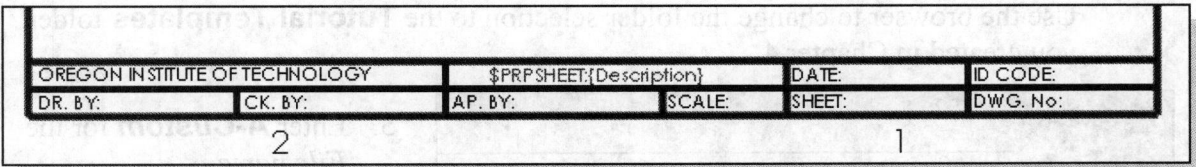

OREGON INSTITUTE OF TECHNOLOGY	$PRP SHEET:{Description}		DATE:	ID CODE:
DR. BY:	CK. BY:	AP. BY:	SCALE:	SHEET:	DWG. No:

2   1

28. Move the cursor into the graphics area and **right-click** to open the pop-up option menu.

29. Select **Edit Sheet** from the pop-up option menu to change to *Edit Sheet* mode.

30. Select the **Rebuild** icon on the *Menu Bar*.

Creating a New Drawing Template

1. On your own, use the **System Options** and choose **Color** and set the color of the **Inactive Entities** to black as shown.

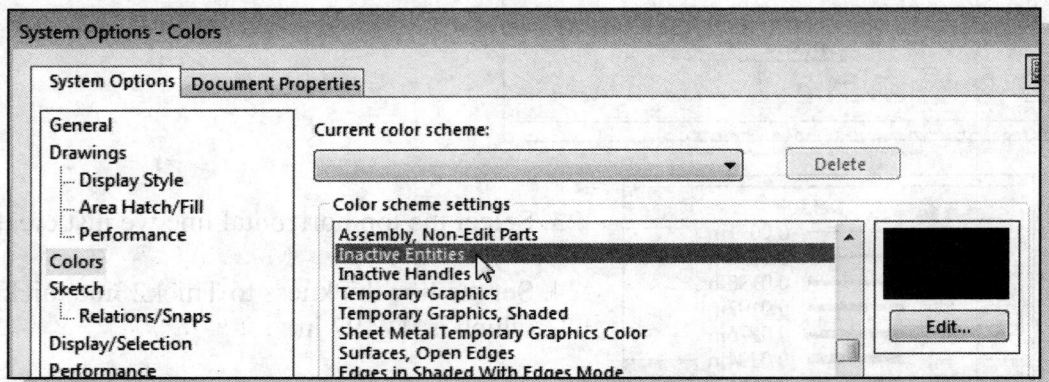

2. Select **Save as** from the *File* pull-down menu.

3. Click in the *Save as type:* entry box and select **Drawing Template** from the pull-down options.

4. The folder selection will automatically change to the default Templates folder. Use the browser to change the folder selection to the **Tutorial Templates** folder you created in Chapter 4.

5. Enter **A-Custom** for the *File name*.

6. Enter **ANSI A Inch Custom** for the *Description*.

7. Click **Save**.

8. If the SolidWorks pop-up window appears, click **OK**.

Creating Views

1. Click on the **Model View** icon in the *View Layout* toolbar.

2. The *Model View Property Manager* appears with the *Pulley* part file selected as the part from which to create the base view. Click the **Next** arrow as shown to proceed with defining the base view.

3. In the *Model View Property Manager*, select the **Left View** for the *Orientation*, as shown. (Make sure the *Create multiple views* box is unchecked.)

4. Under the *Scale* options in the *Drawing View Property Manager*, select **Use custom scale**.

5. Select **User Defined** from the pull-down options, as shown. (You may have to use the scroll bar to locate the User Defined option.)

6. Enter **3:4** as the user defined scale.

7. Move the cursor inside the graphics area and place the **base view** toward the left side of the border as shown.

➢ When the base view is placed, SolidWorks automatically executes the **Projected View** command and the *Projected View Property Manager* appears.

8. Press the **[Esc]** key once to exit the Projected View command.

➢ Notice the Description we entered for the *Pulley* model part file – **4″ Pulley** – appears in the title block due to the Property Link. (Hint: Click **Rebuild** if the text does not appear automatically.)

9. Select the **Section View** icon in the *View Layout* toolbar.

10. Verify that the **Vertical** option is selected in the *Cutting Line* panel of the *Section View* Property Manager.

11. Inside the graphics window, align the cursor to the center of the base view and click the **left mouse button** to create the vertical cutting plane line as shown.

12. Select **OK** to create the vertical section line.

13. In the *Section View Property Manager*, confirm the **Hidden Lines Removed** option is set for the *Display Style*.

14. Next, SolidWorks expects us to place the projected section. Select a location that is toward the right side of the base view as shown in the figure and click once with the **left mouse button**.

15. Select **OK** in the *Property Manager* to create the *Section View*.

16. Press the **[Esc]** key to ensure that no view or objects are selected.

➤ We will add an isometric view using the **Projected View** command.

17. Select the **Projected View** icon from the toolbar.

18. **Left-click** to select the **base view** for the projection as shown.

19. In the *Projected View Property Manager*, select the **Hidden Lines Removed** option for the *Display Style*.

20. Place the projected isometric view by moving the cursor to the left and above the base view as shown and clicking once with the **left-mouse-button**. (**NOTE:** When it is created, the projected isometric view is automatically aligned along a line at a 45° angle from the base view. We can relocate the isometric view after it is created.)

21. Press the [Esc] key to exit the Projected View command.

OREGON INSTITUTE OF TECHNOLOGY | DATE: | ID CODE:
DR. BY: | CK. BY: | A.P. BY: | SCALE: | SHEET: | DWG. No:

➤ On your own, reposition the views so that they appear as shown.

Retrieve Dimensions – Model Items Command

1. Left-click on the **Model Items** icon on the *Annotation* toolbar.

2. In the *Source/Destination* options panel of the *Model Items Property Manager*, select the **Entire model** option from the *Import from* pull-down menu and check **Import items into all views** as shown.

3. Under the *Dimensions* options panel, select the **Marked for drawing** icon and check **Eliminate duplicates** as shown.

4. Click the **OK** icon in the *Model Items Property Manager*. Notice dimensions are automatically placed on the side and section drawing views.

5. On your own, adjust the drawing to appear as shown below. You will have to reposition some dimensions, and hide some dimensions. You may also have to reposition the views.

Save the Drawing File

1. Select **Save as** from the *File* pull-down menu.

2. Select SolidWorks **Drawing** (*.slddrw) as the file type.

3. Use the browser to select the directory. Save the drawing file in the same directory as the part file.

4. Enter **Pulley** for the *File name* and **Pulley Detail** for the *Description*.

5. Click **Save**.

6. If the SolidWorks window appears, enter **Save All**.

Associative Functionality – A Design Change

❖ *Solidworks' associative functionality* allows us to change the design at any level, and the system reflects the changes at all levels automatically. We will illustrate the associative functionality by changing the circular pattern from five holes to six holes.

1. Inside the *Feature Manager Design Tree* window, right-click on the **Drawing View** icon to bring up the option menu.

2. Select **Open Part (pulley.sldprt)** in the popup menu to switch to the associated solid model.

3. Inside the *Feature Manager Design Tree* window, right-click on the CircularPattern1 feature to bring up the option menu.

4. Select **Edit Feature** in the popup menu to bring up the associated feature option.

5. In the *Circular Pattern Property Manager*, change the number to **6** as shown.

6. Click on the **OK** button to accept the setting.

❖ The solid model is updated showing the 6 equally spaced holes as shown.

7. Switch back to the *Pulley* drawing by selecting it in the *Window* pull-down menu. (**NOTE:** The * appearing next to the filename indicates that this file has been modified but not saved. When you save the file, this * will no longer appear.)

8. If the SolidWorks window appears, select **Yes** to update the drawing sheet.

9. When the drawing window opens, some views may be shaded, indicating that they have not been updated to include the changes to the model. Select the **Rebuild** icon on the *Menu Bar* to update the views.

❖ Notice, in the *Pulley* drawing, the circular pattern is also updated automatically in all views.

Adding Centerlines to the Pattern Feature

In your drawing, the inserted views may include *center marks*. If so, these were added with the **auto-insert** option. This lesson was done with no auto-insert options selected. If your drawing already has the center marks, you can delete them and proceed with Step 1, or select them and proceed to Step 6.

1. Click on the **Center Mark** button in the *Annotation* toolbar.

2. In the *Manual Insert Options* panel of the *Center Mark Property Manager*, select the **Circular Center Mark** option, and **check** the **Circular lines**, **Radial lines**, and **Base center mark** option boxes.

➤ The **Centered Pattern** option allows us to add centerlines to a patterned feature.

3. Inside the graphics area, hold down the [**Ctrl**] key and select the **four circular edges** of the pattern feature as shown.

4. Select **OK** in the *Center Mark Property Manager* to create the center marks.

5. Notice the base circle center mark interferes with the cutting plane line. **Select** any of the newly created center marks or the associated centerlines to reopen the *Property Manager*.

6. In the *Manual Insert Options* panel of the *Center Mark Property Manager*, **uncheck** the **Base center mark** option box.

7. Select **OK** in the *Property Manager* to accept the new setting.

8. On your own, extend the segments of the centerlines so that they appear as shown.

Completing the Drawing

1. Right-click on the **30°** angular dimension and select **Hide** from the pop-up option menu.

2. Use the **Smart Dimension** command to create the **60°** dimension as shown.

3. Select the **Ø2.50** dimension to open the *Property Manager*.

4. Select the **Inside** option for the arrow placement under the **Leaders** tab in the *Property Manager* as shown below.

5. Click on the **Centerline** button in the *Annotation* toolbar.

6. Inside the graphics window, click on the two edges of the *Section View* to create a centerline through the view as shown in the figure.

7. Repeat the above step and create the centerlines through the other two holes.

8. On your own, complete the title block and complete the drawing to appear as shown on the next page. Remember to switch to *Edit Sheet Format* mode to modify the title block.

9. Be sure to switch back to ***Edit Sheet*** mode.

10. Select the **Isometric view**.

11. In the *Property Manager*, set the *Scale* of the view to **Use custom scale** and choose **1:2** as shown.

   • Note the default view scale is set to **Use Parent Scale**.

12. Select the **Save** icon on the *Menu Bar*. This command will save the Pulley.SLDDRW file. This file includes the document properties, the sheet format, and the drawing views.

➤ Because the **Pulley** model part file was not saved after the design change, the *Save Modified Documents* window will appear.

13. Select **Save All** to save the Pulley.SLDDRW drawing file and the Pulley.SLDPRT model part file.

OREGON INSTITUTE OF TECHNOLOGY

DR. BY: J. Luigi	CK. BY: S. Mario	AP. BY: M. Peach

4" Pulley

DATE: 01/07/2015	ID CODE: 110309	
SCALE:3 : 4	SHEET:1 of1	DWG. No: ME 475-9

Ø4.00
Ø3.75
Ø3.50
Ø3.50
Ø1.25
1.00
1.50
.25
.75
Ø1.50
Ø2.50
Ø.50
60°

Questions:

1. What is the purpose and use of Section Views?

2. List the different symmetrical features created in the *Pulley* design.

3. What are the advantages of using a *drawing template*?

4. Describe the steps required in using the Mirror command.

5. Why is it important to identify symmetrical features in designs?

6. When and why should we use the Circular Pattern command?

7. What are the required elements in order to generate a sectional view?

8. How do we create a linear *diameter dimension* for a revolved feature?

9. What is the difference of *construction geometry* and *normal geometry*?

10. Identify and describe the following commands:

(a)

(b)

(c)

(d)

Exercises: (Unless otherwise specified, all dimensions are in inches.)

1.

.36 X .20 KEYWAY

60°

R4.5

R1.5

Ø1.5

Ø4.0

.5

.5

R.25

Ø2.5

Ø8.0

1.0

2.

.25

.25

.25

Ø5.75

Ø3.50

Ø.50

R.50

Ø4.25

1.50

3.

4.

5.   Dimensions are in millimeters.

Lesson 12
Auxiliary Views and Reference Geometry

Learning Objectives

- **Understand the Principles of Creating Auxiliary Views**
- **Understand the Concepts and the Use of Reference Geometry**
- **Use the Different Options to Create Reference Geometry**
- **Create Auxiliary Views in 2D Drawing Mode**
- **Create and Adjust Centerlines**
- **Create Shaded Images in the 2D Drawing mode**

Certified SolidWorks Associate Exam Objectives Coverage

Sketch Relations

Objectives: Using Geometric Relations.

Reference Geometry – Planes, Axis, Mate References

Objectives: Creating Reference Planes, Axes, and Mate References.

Drawing Sheets and Views

Objectives: Creating and Setting Properties for Drawing Sheets; Inserting and Editing Standard Views.

Certified Associate Reference Guide

Introduction

An important rule concerning multiview drawings is to draw enough views to accurately describe the design. This usually requires two or three of the regular views, such as a front view, a top view and/or a side view.

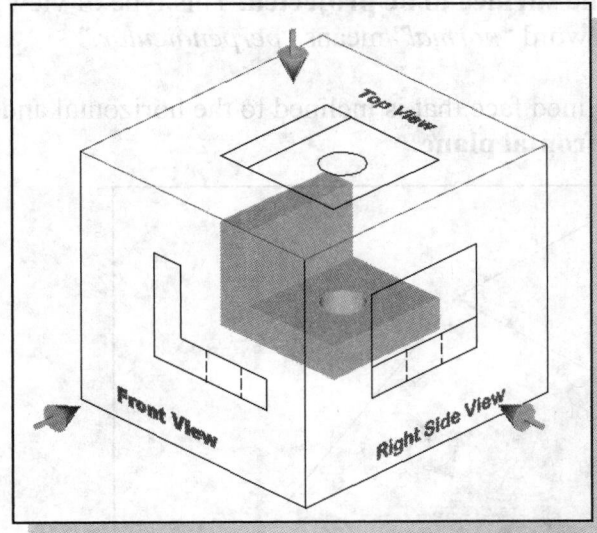

In the left figure, the L-shape object is placed with the surfaces parallel to the principal planes of projection. The top, front and right side views show the true shape of the different surfaces of the object. Note especially that planes of projection are parallel to the top, front and right side of the object.

Based on the principle of orthographic projection, it is clear that a plane surface is shown in true shape when the direction of view is perpendicular to the surface.

Many designs have features located on inclined surfaces that are not parallel to the regular planes of projection. To truly describe the feature, the true shape of the feature must be shown using an **auxiliary view**. An *auxiliary view* has a line of sight that is perpendicular to the inclined surface, as viewed looking directly at the inclined surface. An *auxiliary view* is a supplementary view that can be constructed from any of the regular views. A primary *auxiliary view* is projected onto a plane that is perpendicular to one of the principal planes of projection and is inclined to the other two. A secondary *auxiliary view* is projected onto a plane that is inclined to all three principal planes of projection. In the figures below, the use of the standard views does not show the true shape of the upper feature of the design; the use of an auxiliary view provided the true shape of the feature and also eliminated the need of front and the right side views.

Standard Views

Auxiliary View

Normal View of an Inclined Surface

No matter what the position of a surface may be, the fundamentals of projecting a normal view of the surface remain the same: **The projection plane is placed parallel to the surface to be projected. The line of sight is set to be perpendicular to the projection plane and therefore perpendicular to the surface to be projected.** This type of view is known as **normal view**. In geometry, the word "*normal*" means "*perpendicular*."

In the figure below, the design has an inclined face that is inclined to the horizontal and profile planes and **perpendicular to the frontal plane**.

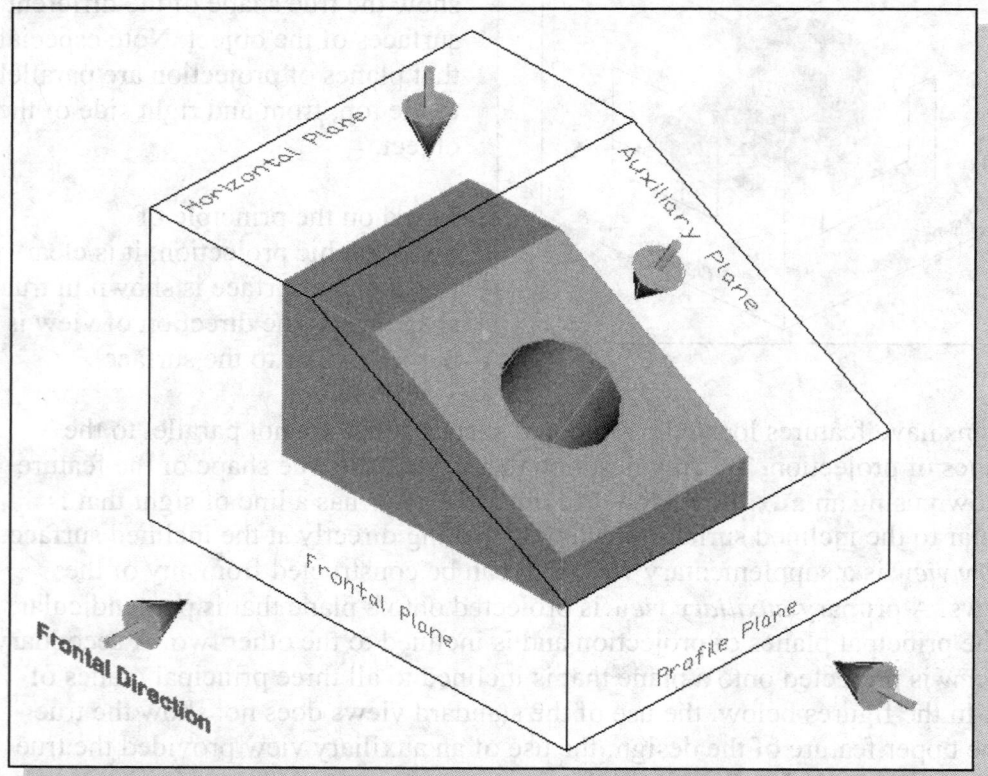

The principal views (Top, Front and Right side views) do not show the **true size and shape** of the inclined surface. Note the inclined surface does appear as an edge in the front view. To show the true size and shape of the inclined surface, a *normal* view is needed.

To get the normal view of the inclined surface, a projection is made perpendicular to the surface. This projection is made from the view where the surface shows as an edge, in this case, the front view. The perpendicularity between the surface and the line of sight is seen in true relationship in the 2D views. These types of extra normal views are known as **auxiliary views** to distinguish them from the principal views. However, since an auxiliary is made for the purpose of showing the true shape of a surface, the terms *normal view* and *edge view* are also used to describe the relations of the views.

An auxiliary is constructed following the rules of orthographic projection. An auxiliary view is aligned to the associated views, in this case, the front view. The line of sight is perpendicular to the edge view of the surface, as shown in the below figures.

The orientation of the inclined surface may be different, but the direction of the normal view remains the same as shown in the below figures.

Construction Method I – Folding Line Method

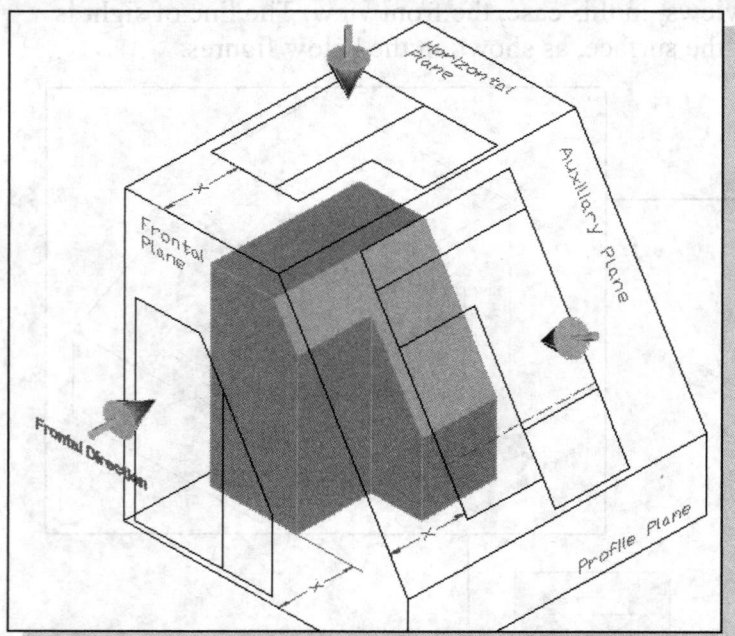

Two methods are commonly used to construct auxiliary views: The **folding-line** method and the **reference plane** method. The folding-line method uses the concept of placing the object inside a glass-box, the distances of the object to the different projection planes are used as measurements to construct the necessary views, including the auxiliary views.

The following steps outline the general procedure to create an auxiliary view:

1. Construct the necessary principal views; in this case, the front and top views.

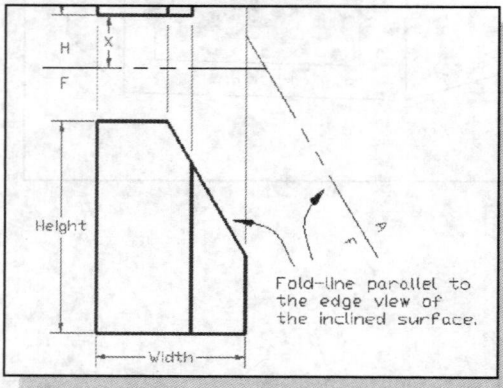

2. Construct a folding line parallel to the edge view of the inclined surface.

3. Construct the projection lines perpendicular to the edge view of the inclined surface, and also perpendicular to the folding line.

4. Use the corresponding distances, X, and the depth of the object from the principal views to construct the inclined surface.

5. Complete the auxiliary view by following the principles of orthographic projection.

Construction Method II – Reference Plane Method

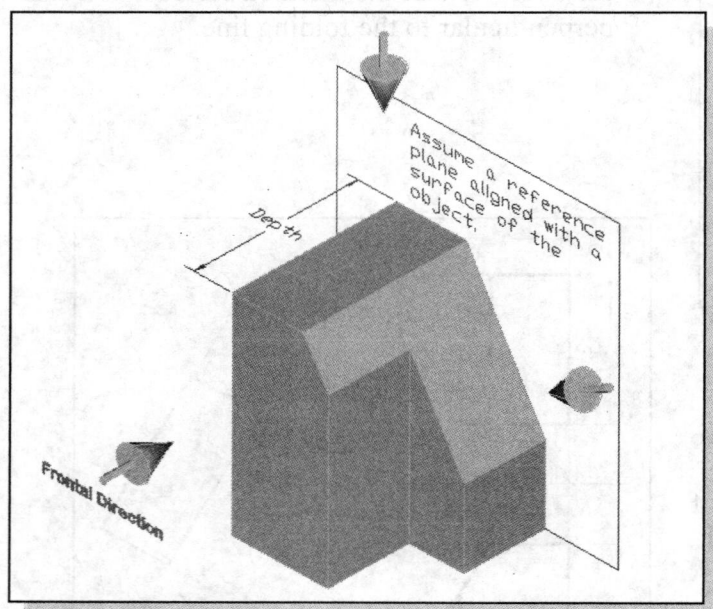

The **Reference plane method** uses the concept of placing a reference plane aligned with a surface of the object that is perpendicular to the inclined surface. The reference plane is typically a flat surface or a plane which runs through the center of the object. The distances of the individual corner to the reference plane is then used as measurements to construct the auxiliary view.

The following steps outline the general procedure to create an auxiliary view:

1. Construct the necessary principal views; in this case, the front and top views.

2. Construct a reference plane line aligned to a flat face and perpendicular to the inclined surface of the object, in this case, the back face of the object.

3. Construct a reference line parallel to the edge view of the inclined surface and construct the projection lines perpendicular to the edge view of the inclined surface.

4. Using the corresponding distances, such as the depth of the object, and construct the inclined surface.

5. Complete the auxiliary view by following the principles of orthographic projection.

Partial Views

The primary purpose of using auxiliary views is to provide detailed descriptions of features that are on inclined surfaces. The use of an auxiliary view often makes it possible to omit one or more standard views. But it may not be necessary to draw complete auxiliary views, as the completeness of detail may be time consuming to construct and add nothing to the clearness of the drawing.

In these cases, partial views are often sufficient, and the resulting drawings are much simpler and easier to read.

Partial Top View

Partial Auxiliary View

- To clarify the relationship of partial auxiliary views and the standard views, a center line or a few projection lines should be used. This is especially important when the partial views are small.

- In practice, hidden lines are generally omitted in auxiliary views, unless they provide clearness to the drawings.

Reference Geometry in SolidWorks

Feature-based parametric modeling is a cumulative process. The relationships that we define between features determine how a feature reacts when other features are changed. Because of this interaction, certain features must, by necessity, precede others. A new feature can use previously defined features to define information such as size, shape, location and orientation. SolidWorks provides several tools to automate this process. *Reference geometry* can be thought of as user-definable datum, which are updated with the part geometry. We can create planes, axes, points, or local coordinate systems that do not already exist. Reference geometry can also be used to align features or to orient parts in an assembly. In this chapter, the use of the **Offset** option and the **Angled** option to create new reference planes, surfaces that do not already exist, are illustrated. By creating parametric reference geometry, the established feature interactions in the CAD database assure the capturing of the design intent. The default planes, which are aligned to the origin of the coordinate system, can be used to assist the construction of the more complex geometric features.

Auxiliary Views in 2D Drawings

An important rule concerning multiview drawings is to draw enough views to accurately describe the design. This usually requires two or three of the regular views, such as a front view, a top view and/or a side view. However, many designs have features located on inclined surfaces that are not parallel to the regular planes of projection. To truly describe the feature, the true shape of the feature must be shown using an **auxiliary view**. An *auxiliary view* has a line of sight that is perpendicular to the inclined surface, as viewed looking directly at the inclined surface. An *auxiliary view* is a supplementary view that can be constructed from any of the regular views. Using the solid model as the starting point for a design, auxiliary views can be easily created in 2D drawings. In this chapter, the general procedure of creating auxiliary views in 2D drawings from solid models is illustrated.

The *Rod-Guide* Design

❖ Based on your knowledge of SolidWorks so far, how would you create this design? What are the more difficult features involved in the design? Take a few minutes to consider a modeling strategy and do preliminary planning by sketching on a piece of paper. You are also encouraged to create the design on your own prior to following through the tutorial.

Modeling Strategy

Starting SolidWorks

1. Select the **SolidWorks** option on the *Start* menu or select the **SolidWorks** icon on the desktop. The SolidWorks main window will appear on the screen.

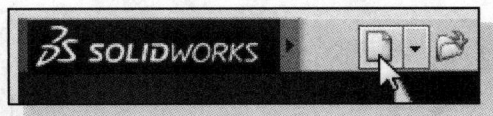

2. Select the **New** icon with a single click of the left-mouse-button on the *Menu Bar*.

3. The *New SolidWorks Document* dialog box should appear in Advanced mode. If it appears in Novice mode, click once with the left-mouse-button on the **Advanced** icon.

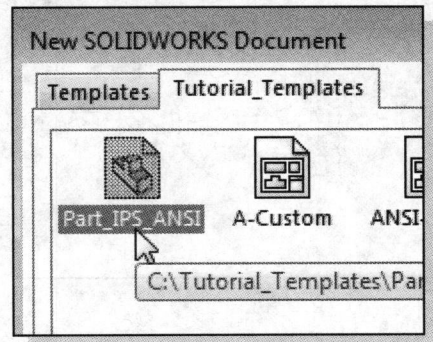

4. Select the **Tutorial_Templates** tab. (**NOTE:** If your templates are not available, open the standard Part template and set the *Drafting Standard* to ANSI and the *Units* to IPS.)

5. Select the **Part_IPS_ANSI** template as shown.

6. Click on the **OK** button to open a new document.

Applying the BORN Technique

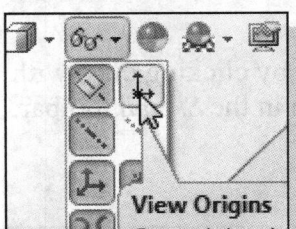

1. Select the **Hide/Show Items** icon on the *Heads-up View* toolbar to reveal the pull-down menu. In the pull-down menu, toggle on the **View Planes** and **View Origins** buttons.

2. In the *Feature Manager Design Tree* window, select the **Front**, **Top**, and **Right Planes** by holding down the **[Ctrl]** key and clicking with the left-mouse-button.

3. Click on any of the planes to display the option menu. Click on **Show** to toggle *ON* the display of the planes.

4. On your own, use the viewing options (**Rotate**, **Zoom** and **Pan**) to view the work features established.

5. Select the **Extruded Boss/Base** button on the *Features* toolbar to create a new extruded feature.

6. In the *Edit Sketch Property-Manager*, the message "*Select a plane on which to create a sketch for the entity*" is displayed. Move the cursor over the edge of the **Top Plane** in the graphics area. When the Top Plane is highlighted, click once with the **left-mouse-button** to select the Top (XZ) Plane as the sketch plane for the new sketch.

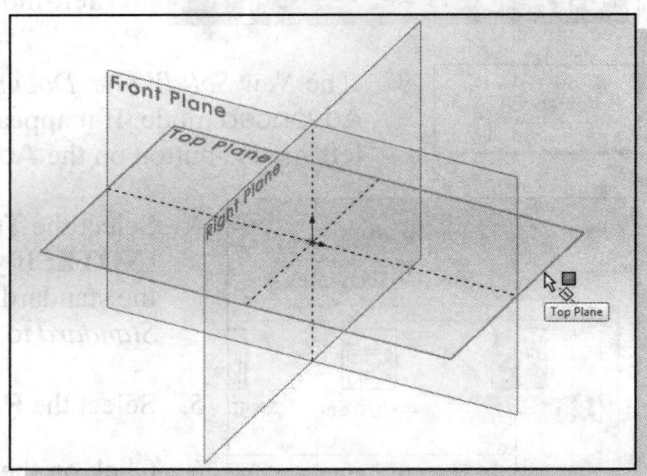

7. On your own, **hide** the three planes.

Creating the Base Feature

1. Select the **Rectangle** command by clicking once with the left-mouse-button on the icon in the *Sketch* toolbar.

2. Create a rectangle of arbitrary size with the origin inside the rectangle as shown.

3. Click on the **Sketch Fillet** icon in the *Sketch* toolbar.

4. Enter **0.25 in** for the fillet radius in the *Fillet Parameters* panel of the *Sketch Fillet Property-Manager*.

5. Create four rounded corners as shown. Each fillet can be created by moving the cursor into the graphics area and (1) clicking on the corner, or (2) clicking on the two lines forming the corner.

6. Select **OK** in the *Property Manager* or press the **[Esc]** key to exit the Sketch Fillet command.

7. On your own, create four circles of the same diameter and with the centers aligned to the centers of arcs. Also create and modify the six dimensions as shown in the figure below. (Hint: Add relations and establish equations.) Note that these dimensions fix the center of the base at the origin.

8. Select the **Exit Sketch** icon on the *Sketch* toolbar to exit the Sketch option.

9. Create a **Blind** extrusion with a distance of **0.75** in.

10. Click **OK** in the *Extrude Property Manager* to accept the settings and create the extrusion.

11. In the *Display Style* pull-down menu on the *Heads-up View* toolbar, select the **Wireframe** option to set the display mode to *Wireframe*

Create an Angled Reference Plane

❖ SolidWorks allows the creation of a plane through an edge, axis, or sketch line at an angle to a face or plane, using the **At Angle** option of the **Plane** command. Using the **At Angle** option requires selection of an existing edge, axis, or sketch line and an existing face or plane. We will create a reference axis along the Y-direction, and create a plane that can be visualized by rotating the Front Plane about the reference (Y) axis.

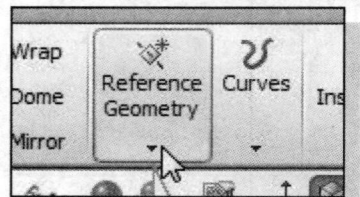

1. In the *Features* toolbar, select the down arrow below the **Reference Geometry** command by left-clicking the icon.

2. In the pull-down option menu of the **Reference Geometry** command, select the **Axis** option.

3. In the *Selections* panel of the *Axis Property Manager*, select the **Two Planes** option. (We will define the Y-axis as the intersection of the Front and Right Planes.)

4. Select the **Front Plane** and **Right Plane** in the *Design Tree* appearing in the graphics area.

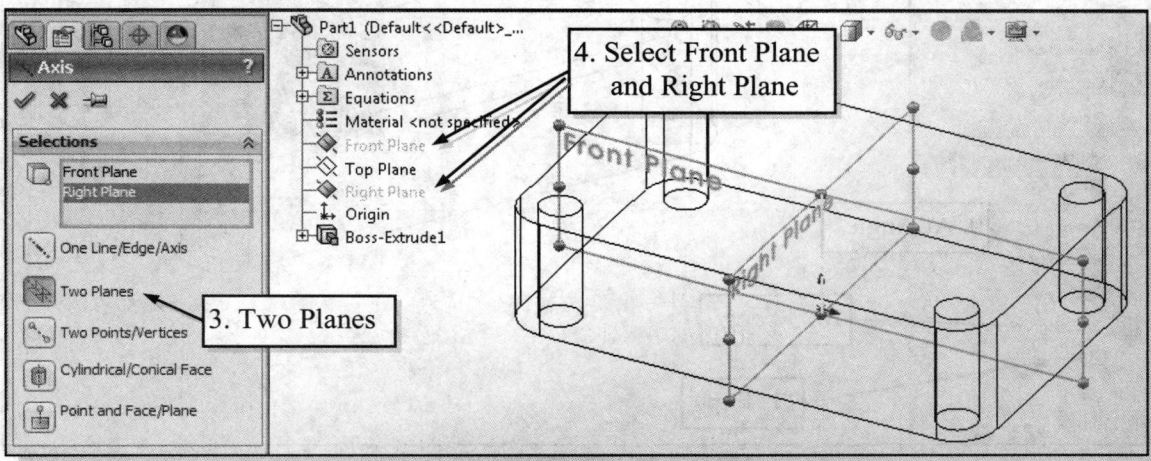

5. Click **OK** in the *Property Manager* to create the new reference axis.

6. Press the **[Esc]** key to make sure no objects are selected.

➢ Notice the reference axis, named **Axis1**, has been created. It is aligned with the Y-axis and passes through the center of the base feature.

7. Select the **Reference Geometry** command from the *Features* toolbar, and select the **Plane** option from the pull-down menu.

➢ Notice the message "*Select references and constraints*" appears and the *First Reference* window is highlighted.

8. In the *Design Tree* appearing in the graphics area, select **Axis1** (the reference axis created above) as the *First Reference* and **Front Plane** as the *Second Reference*.

9. In the *Second Reference* panel of the *Plane Property Manager*, select the **At Angle** option button.

10. Enter **30 deg** as the angle in the *Property Manager*.

11. If necessary, check the **Flip** box.

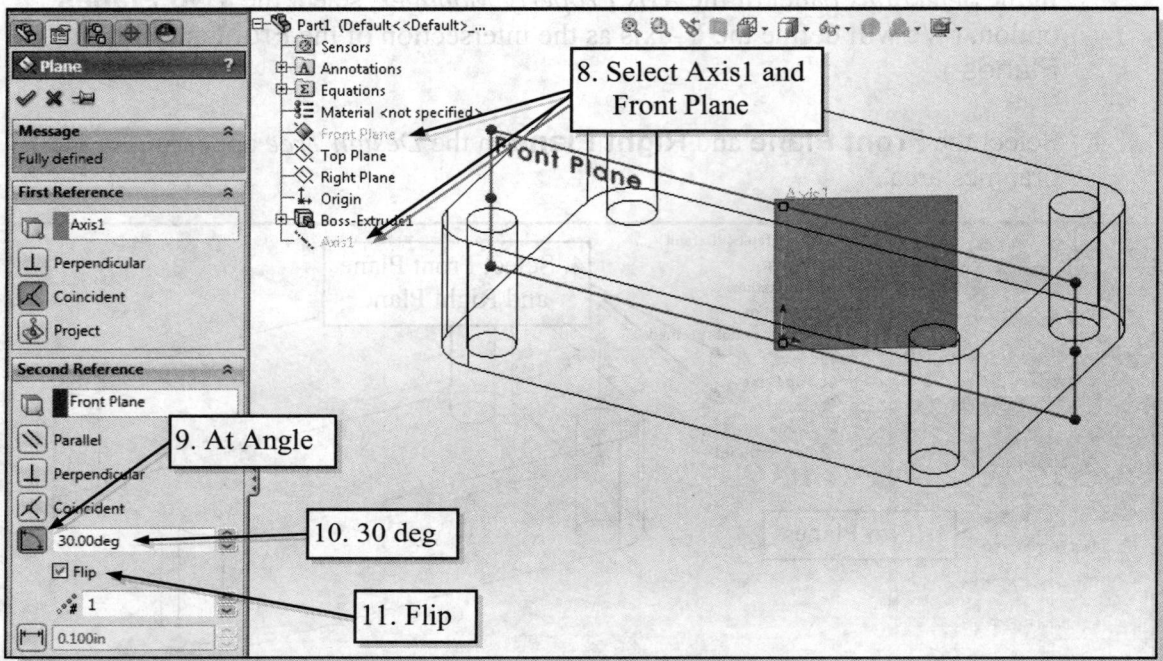

12. Check that the preview of the reference plane appears as shown above.

13. Click **OK** in the *Property Manager* to create the new reference plane.

❖ Note that the *angle* is measured relative to the selected reference plane, the Front (XY) Plane.

Creating an Extruded Feature on the Reference Plane

1. Confirm the reference plane, Plane1, is pre-selected as shown.

2. In the *Features* toolbar, select the **Extruded Boss/Base** command by clicking once with the left-mouse-button on the icon.

- Note the pre-selected angled reference plane, **Plane1**, is automatically used as the sketch plane.

Using the Convert Entities Option

❖ Projected geometry is another type of *reference geometry*. The Convert Entities tool can be used to project entities from previously defined sketches or features onto the sketch plane. The position of the projected geometry is fixed to the feature from which it was projected. We can use the Convert Entities tool to project geometry from a sketch or feature onto the active sketch plane.

Typical uses of the Convert Entities command include:
- Project a silhouette of a 3D feature onto the sketch plane for use in a 2D profile.
- Project a sketch from a feature onto the sketch plane so that the projected sketch can be used to constrain a new sketch.

1. Move the cursor over the top rear edge of the base feature. When the edge is highlighted, click once with the **left-mouse-button** to select the edge.

2. In the *Sketch* toolbar, select the **Convert Entities** command by left-clicking the icon.

❖ Notice the selected edge is projected onto the active sketch plane as shown.

3. Left-click on the **View Orientation** icon on the *Heads-up View* toolbar to reveal the *View Orientation* pull-down menu. Select the **Normal To** command.

4. **Left-click** on the arrow next to the **Line** button on the *Sketch* toolbar to reveal additional commands.

5. Select the **Centerline** command from the pop-up menu.

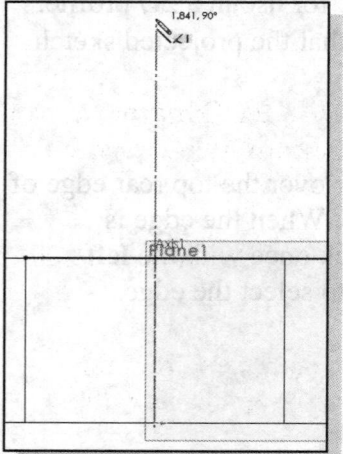

6. Draw a vertical centerline with one end coincident with the **origin** and the other end above the top of the base as shown.

7. Press the **[Esc]** key twice to exit the Centerline command and unselect the centerline you created.

❖ The **Dynamic Mirror** command will be used to generate sketch objects with symmetry about a centerline.

8. Select the **Tools** pull-down menu, then click on **Sketch Tools**. A complete list of sketch tools will appear. (Some of these also appear in the *Sketch* toolbar.)

9. Select **Dynamic Mirror** as shown.

10. The message *"Please select a sketch line or linear edge to mirror about"* appears in the *Mirror Property Manager*. Move the cursor over the **centerline** in the graphics area and click once with the **left-mouse-button** to select it as the line to mirror about.

➤ Notice the hash marks which appear on the centerline to indicate that the Dynamic Mirror command is active.

11. Click on the **Line** icon in the *Sketch* toolbar.

12. On your own, create a rough sketch using the projected edge as the bottom line as shown in the figure. (Note that all edges are either horizontal or vertical.)

13. Press the **[Esc]** key to exit the Line command.

14. On your own, **turn *OFF*** the Dynamic Mirror command. (**HINT:** Perform steps 8 and 9.)

15. Press the **[Esc]** key twice to ensure no entities are selected.

16. Select the **Add Relation** command from the *Display/Delete Relations* pop-up menu on the *Sketch* toolbar.

17. Select the lower and upper vertical lines in the sketch as shown.

Select

Select

18. Select the **Collinear** option in the *Add Relations* panel of the *Add Relations Property Manager*.

19. Repeat the above steps and align the two vertical lines on the left.

20. Press the **[Esc]** key to exit the Add Relations command.

21. **Left-click** on the **arrow** below the **Trim Entities** button on the *Sketch* toolbar to reveal additional commands.

22. Select the **Extend Entities** command from the pop-up menu.

23. Move the cursor near the left endpoint of the horizontal line we created with the Convert Entities command. When the extended line appears, click once with the **left-mouse-button** to extend the horizontal line to meet the bottom of the vertical line as shown.

24. Press the **[Esc]** key once to end the Extend command.

25. We will next trim the bottom horizontal line to the inclined line. Select the **Trim Entities** icon on the *Sketch* toolbar.

26. Select the **Trim to closest** option in the *Trim Property Manager*.

27. Move the cursor near the right endpoint of the horizontal line we created with the **Convert Entities** command. SolidWorks will automatically display the possible result of the selection. When the preview appears, click once with the **left-mouse-button** to trim the horizontal line to meet the bottom of the vertical line as shown.

28. Press the [**Esc**] key once to end the Trim command.

29. **Left-click** on the arrow next to the **Arc** button on the *Sketch* toolbar and select the **Centerpoint Arc** command from the pop-up menu.

30. On your own, create the arc with the centerpoint coincident with the centerline and aligned with the top endpoints of the vertical lines as shown.

31. Use the **Add Relation** command to create a **Tangent** relation between the arc and the upper right vertical line.

32. Inside the graphics window, click once with the right-mouse-button to display the option menu. Select the **Smart Dimension** option in the popup menu.

33. On your own, create the **Dimensions** as shown.

34. Select the **Circle** command by clicking once with the left-mouse-button on the icon in the *Sketch* toolbar.

35. On your own, add a **0.75** inch circle concentric with the arc.

36. On your own, complete the sketch as shown in the figure.

❖ The *Status Bar* should now read *Fully Defined*, because the geometric and dimensional constraints fully define the sketch.

Completing the Solid Feature

1. Select the **Exit Sketch** icon on the *Sketch* toolbar to exit the Sketch option.

2. Select the **Midplane** option.

3. Enter **1 inch** for the extrusion distance.

4. Check the **Merge result** option.

5. Click **OK** in the *Property Manager* to accept the settings and create the extrusion.

6. Using the *Heads-up View* toolbar, set the display style to **Shaded with edges**.

7. On your own, turn **off** the visibility of the angled reference plane.

Create an Offset Reference Plane

1. Select the **Reference Geometry** command from the *Features* toolbar, and select the **Plane** option from the pull-down menu.

❖ In the *Status Bar* area, the message: "*Select valid entities to define a plane (plane, face, edge, line, or point*" is displayed. SolidWorks expects us to select any existing geometry, which will be used as a reference to create the new work plane.

2. Move the cursor over the top face of the base feature. Notice the top face of the base feature is highlighted. Click once with the **left-mouse-button** to select the face.

3. Notice the top face, called **Face<1>**, appears in the *First Reference* panel of the *Plane Property Manager*, and the **Offset Distance** option is automatically selected.

4. Enter **0.75 in** as the offset distance.

5. Click **OK** in the *Property Manager* to accept the settings and create the new reference plane.

Creating another Extruded Feature using the Reference Plane

1. Confirm the reference plane, Plane2, is pre-selected as shown.

2. In the *Features* toolbar, select the **Extruded Cut** command by clicking once with the left-mouse-button on the icon.

*   Note the pre-selected offset reference plane, **Plane2**, is automatically used as the sketch plane

3. In the *Display Style* pull-down menu on the *Heads-up View* toolbar, select the **Wireframe** option to set the display mode to *Wireframe*.

4. In the *View Orientation* pull-down menu on the *Heads-up View* toolbar, select the **Normal To** command.

5. On your own, create a **Ø 0.25** inch circle aligned to the origin as shown in the figure.

6. Select the **Exit Sketch** icon on the *Sketch* toolbar to exit the sketch.

7. On your own, create the **Extruded Cut** feature. Use the **Through All** option and click the Reverse Direction button if necessary.

8. Click **OK** in the *Property Manager* to create the extruded cut feature.

9. On your own, hide all planes, hide Axis1, and set the display to **Shaded With Edges**.

10. Select the **Save As** option from the *File* pull-down menu.

11. Use the *Browser* to select the folder in which you want to save the file.

12. In the *Save As* pop-up window, enter **Rod-Guide** for the *File name*.

13. Enter **3/4" Rod Guide** for the *Description*.

14. Click **Save** to save the file.

Starting a New 2D Drawing and Adding a Base View

1. Click on the arrow next to the **New** icon on the *Menu Bar* and select **Make Drawing from Part/Assembly** in the pull-down menu.

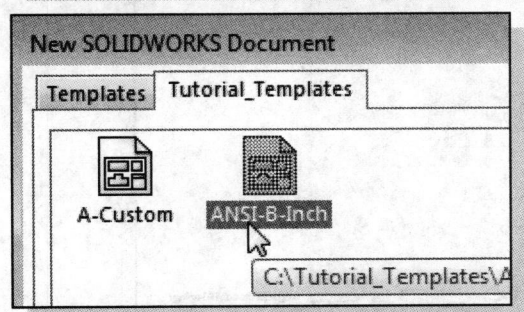

2. In the *New SolidWorks Document* window, select the **Tutorial_Templates** tab.

3. Select the **ANSI-B-Inch** template file icon. This is the custom drawing template you created in Chapter 8. (If your ANSI-B-Inch template is not available, see note below.)

4. Select **OK** in the *New SolidWorks Document* window to open the new drawing file.

➢ The new drawing file opens using the **ANSI-B-Inch.SLDDOT** template. The B-size drawing sheet appears. The *View Palette* appears in the *task pane*.

❖ **NOTE:** If your ANSI-B-Inch template is not available: (1) open the default **Drawing** template; (2) set document properties following instructions on page 8-37.

❖ In SolidWorks, the first drawing view we create is called a **base view**. A *base view* is the primary view in the drawing; other views can be derived from this view. In SolidWorks, a base view can be added using the **Model View** command on the *Drawing* toolbar, or using the **View Palette**. By default, SolidWorks will treat the *world XY plane* as the front view of the solid model. Note that there can be more than one *base view* in a drawing.

5. If the *View Pallette* is collapsed, select the **View Palette** tab at the right of the graphics area.

6. Select the **Top** view in the *View Palette* by clicking on the icon with the **left-mouse-button** as shown.

7. Hold down the **left-mouse-button** and **drag** the top view from the *View Palette* into the graphics window and place the **base view** near the upper left corner of the graphics window as shown below.

➤   When the base view is placed, SolidWorks automatically executes the **Projected View** command and the *Projected View Property Manager* appears.

8. Press the **[Esc]** key to exit the Projected View command.

Creating an Auxiliary View

❖   In *SolidWorks Drawing* mode, the **Projected View** command is used to create standard views such as the *top* view, *front* view or *isometric* view. For non-standard views, the **Auxiliary View** command is used. *Auxiliary views* are created using orthographic projections. Orthographic projections are aligned to the base view and inherit the base view's scale and display settings.

1. Click on the **Auxiliary View** button in the *View Layout* toolbar.

2. The message "*Please select a Reference Edge to continue*" appears in the *Auxiliary View Property Manager*. Pick the front edge of the upper section of the model as shown.

❖ The orthographic projection direction will be perpendicular to the selected edge.

3. Move the cursor below the base view and select a location to position the auxiliary view of the model as shown. Click once with the left-mouse-button to place the view.

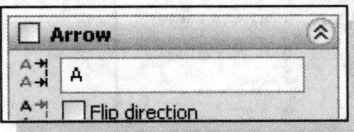

4. In the *Auxiliary View Property Manager* **uncheck** the box next to the **Arrow** option. This will turn *OFF* the display of the direction arrow.

5. Press the **[Esc]** key to accept the settings and exit the Auxiliary View command.

6. Click on the **Model View** icon *Drawing* toolbar.

7. The *Model View Property Manager* appears with the *Rod-Guide* part file selected as the part from which to create the base view. Click the **Next** arrow as shown to proceed with defining the base view.

8. In the *Model View Property Manager*, select the **Isometric** view for the *Orientation*, as shown.

➢ In general, hidden lines are not used in isometric views.

9. In the *Model View Property Manager*, select the **Hidden Lines Removed** option for the *Display Style*.

10. Move the cursor toward the upper right corner of the sheet, and select a location to position the isometric view of the model as shown below.

11. Left-click on the **OK** icon in the *Drawing View Property Manager* to accept the view.

Displaying Feature Dimensions

➢ In your drawing, the inserted views may include *center marks*, *centerlines*, and/or *dimensions*. If so, these were added with the **auto-insert** option. To access these options, click **Options** (*Standard* toolbar), select the **Document Properties** tab, and then select **Detailing**. This lesson was done with no auto-insert options selected. The center marks, centerlines, and dimensions will be added individually. The dimensions used to create the part can be imported into the drawing using the **Model Items** command. We can also add dimensions to the drawing manually using the **Smart Dimension** command.

➢ Before we apply dimensions using the Model Items command we will adjust the size/position of the *Reference Plane 1*. The Model Items command will use the mid-line of the plane to locate the angle dimension.

1. Select the **Rod-Guide.SLDPRT** part window from the *Window* pull-down menu to switch to *Part Modeling* mode.

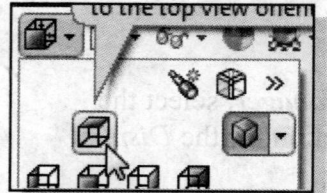

2. In the *View Orientation* pull-down menu on the *Heads-up View* toolbar, select the **Top View** command.

3. On your own, toggle *ON* the visibility of **Plane1**.

4. Using the left-mouse-button, **click and drag** the end of **Plane1** and position it such that the mid-point of the plane coincides with the center of the hole. This point will be used as the reference point for applying the angle dimension when the Model Items command is executed.

5. On your own, switch back to *Drawing* mode.

6. Press the **[Esc]** key to make sure no items are selected.

7. Switch to the *Annotation* toolbar in the *Command Manager*.

8. Left-mouse-click on the **Model Items** icon on the *Annotation* toolbar.

9. In the *Source/ Destination* options panel of the *Model Items Property Manager*, select the **Entire model** option from the *Import from* pull-down menu and check **Import items into all views** as shown.

10. Under the *Dimensions* options panel, select the **Marked for drawing** icon. (**NOTE:** This option may be selected by default.) Check **Eliminate duplicates** as shown.

11. Click the **OK** icon in the *Model Items Property Manager*. Notice dimensions are automatically placed on the top and auxiliary drawing views.

Adjusting the View Scale

1. Move the cursor over the top view and click once with the **left-mouse-button**. The *Drawing View1 Property Manager* appears.

2. Under the *Scale* options in the *Drawing View Property Manager*, select **Use custom scale**.

3. Select **User Defined** from the pull-down options, as shown.

4. Enter **3:2** as the user defined scale.

5. Left-click on the **OK** icon in the *Drawing View Property Manager* to accept the new settings. Notice the auxiliary view is automatically scaled.

6. If necessary, reposition the views so they do not overlap.

Repositioning, Appearance, and Hiding of Feature Dimensions

1. Zoom in on the top view.

2. **Right-click** on the **R.25** *radius* dimension of the round, and select **Hide** from the pop-up option menu.

3. On your own, reposition the dimensions to appear as shown in the figure.

4. **Pan** to the auxiliary view. On your own, hide and reposition dimensions as shown in the figure.

❖ Note the appearance of dimensions can be adjusted independently.

5. Move the cursor over the **0.25** dimension shown in the figure and click once with the **left-mouse-button** to select the dimension. The *Dimension Property Manager* will appear.

6. In the *Dimension Property Manager*, select the **Leaders** tab.

7. In the *Witness/Leader Display* panel, select the **Outside** option as shown. This will result in the arrows being located inside the extension lines.

8. Reposition the dimension as shown.

9. On your own, return to the **Smart** option in the *Witness/Leader Display* panel. Press the **[Esc]** key to exit the Dimension command and unselect the dimension.

10. Move the cursor over the **0.75** height dimension shown in the figure and click once with the **left-mouse-button** to select the dimension.

11. Drag the endpoints of the extension lines to leave a small gap between the object line and extension lines as shown.

12. Adjust the dimensions to appear as shown in the figure. Also notice the note which was automatically added containing the custom scale for the auxiliary view.

Tangent Edge Display

1. Move the cursor over the *auxiliary view* and click once with the **right-mouse-button**.

2. In the pop-up option menu, select **Tangent Edge**, then **Tangent Edges Removed**.

Adding Center Marks and Center Lines

➤ In your drawing, the inserted views may include *center marks*. If so, these were added with the **auto-insert** option. This lesson was done with no auto-insert options selected. The center marks will be added individually. If your drawing already has the center marks, you can delete them and proceed with the lesson, or select them and adjust the *Display Attributes* in the Center *Mark Property Manager* as described below.

1. Click on the **Center Mark** button in the *Annotation* toolbar.

2. In the *Display Attributes* panel of the *Center Mark Property Manager*, **uncheck** the **Use document defaults** box, enter **0.0625** for the Mark size, and **check** the Extended lines box.

3. Click on the four arcs in the top view to add the center marks as shown.

4. Click on the **center circle** in the top view to add the center mark as shown.

5. Click on the **Arc** in the Auxiliary view to add the center mark as shown.

6. Click **OK** in the *Property Manager* to exit the **Center Mark** command.

7. Click on the **Centerline** button in the *Annotation* toolbar.

8. Inside the graphics window, click on the two hidden edges of one of the **Drill** features and create a center line in the auxiliary view as shown in the figure.

9. On your own, repeat the above step and create additional centerlines as shown.

10. Click **OK** in the *Property Manager* to exit the **CenterLine** command.

11. Select the centerline that intercept with the dimension and move the endpoint of the line by **clicking and dragging** as shown.

12. On your own, adjust extension line endpoints, by **clicking and dragging**, to appear approximately as shown in the figure.

Controlling the View and Sheet Scales

➢ The scale for the Sheet is set at 1:1. This setting automatically appears in the title block due to the Property Link described as *$PRP:"SW-Sheet Scale"*. The prefix *$PRP:* defines the source as the current document. The Property Name is *SW-Sheet Scale*. This is a *System Property*. Each view can be set to use the default sheet scale or to use a custom scale defined for the view. When we created the top and auxiliary views, a custom scale of 3:2 was created. For the isometric view the default sheet scale of 1:1 was used. We will change the sheet scale to 3:2.

1. Move the cursor over **Sheet2** in the *Feature Manager Design Tree* and **right-click** to open the option menu.

2. Select **Properties**.

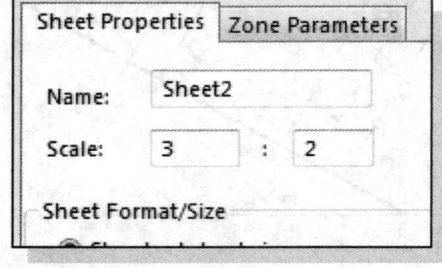

3. Enter **3:2** as the Scale in the *Sheet Properties* window.

4. Click **OK** in the *Sheet Properties* window, and choose Scale the annotations' position.

➢ Notice the scale note in the title block now reads **3:2**. Also notice the scale of the isometric view has changed due to the Use sheet scale option.

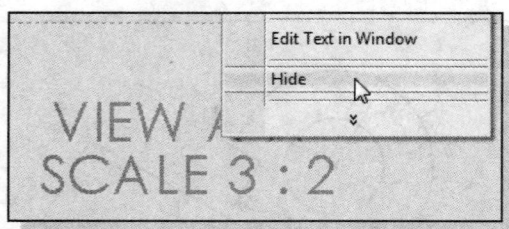

5. Since the sheet scale is labeled as **3:2** in the title block, the view scale note is not necessary. Right click on the note and select **Hide** from the pop-up option menu.

6. On your own, save the drawing file with **MECH 242** as the *File name* and **Rod Guide Detail** as the *Description*.

7. If the SolidWorks pop-up window appears, click **Save All**.

Completing the Drawing Sheet

1. Move the cursor into the graphics area and **right-click** to open the pop-up option menu.

2. Select **Edit Sheet Format** from the pop-up option menu to change to *Edit Sheet Format* mode.

   ❖ Notice the title block is highlighted.

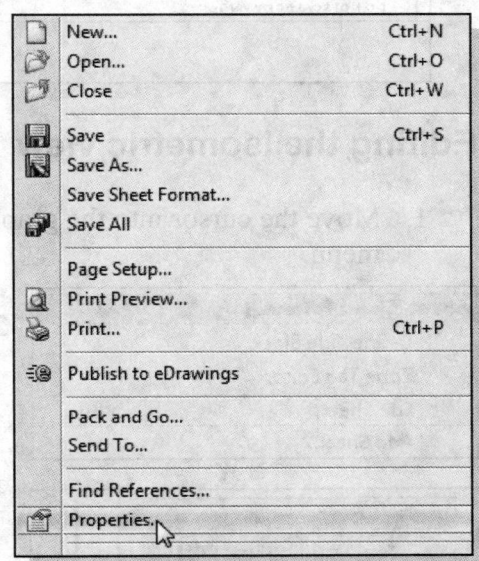

3. On your own, use the **Zoom** and **Pan** commands to adjust the display to work on the title block area. Most of the information is accurate due to **Property Links**.

4. The date probably is inaccurate. Select **Properties** from the *File* pull-down menu on the *Menu Bar*.

5. In the *Summary Information* window select the **Custom** tab. Notice the *Custom Properties* appearing in the list. We defined these properties and saved them in the template file. (Note: If you are not working from the ANSI-B-Inch template, enter the custom properties in the table as shown.)

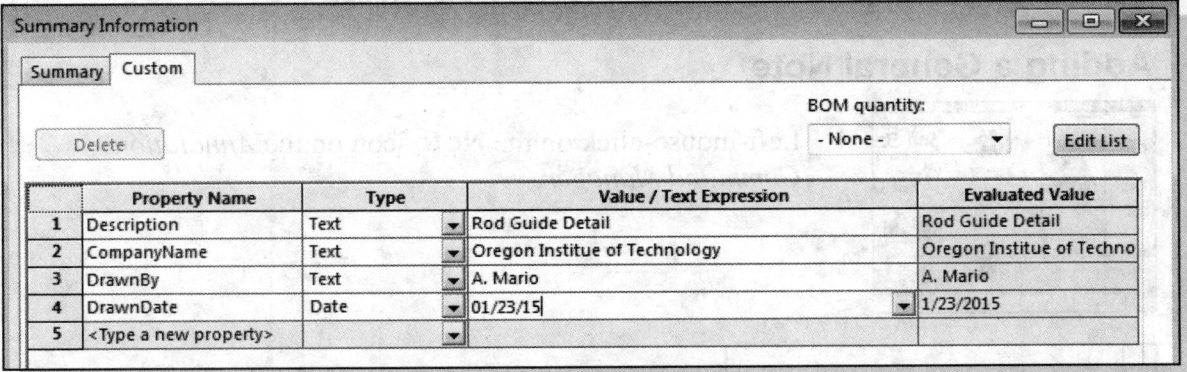

	Property Name	Type	Value / Text Expression	Evaluated Value
1	Description	Text	Rod Guide Detail	Rod Guide Detail
2	CompanyName	Text	Oregon Institue of Technology	Oregon Institue of Techno
3	DrawnBy	Text	A. Mario	A. Mario
4	DrawnDate	Date	01/23/15	1/23/2015
5	<Type a new property>			

6. Change the DrawnDate Value / Text Expression to the current date.

7. Click **OK** in the *Summary Information* window to accept the change.

8. On your own, correct any other entries to the title block if necessary.

UNLESS OTHERWISE SPECIFIED:		NAME	DATE	Oregon Institue of Technology		
DIMENSIONS ARE IN INCHES	DRAWN	A. Mario	1/23/2015			A
TOLERANCES: ANGULAR: MACH ±0.1°	CHECKED			TITLE:		
TWO PLACE DECIMAL ±0.01 THREE PLACE DECIMAL ±0.003	ENG APPR.			3/4" Rod Guide		
	MFG APPR.					
INTERPRET GEOMETRIC TOLERANCING PER:	Q.A.					
	COMMENTS:					
MATERIAL 1060 ALLOY				SIZE **B**	DWG. NO. MECH 242	REV
FINISH						
DO NOT SCALE DRAWING				SCALE: 3:2	WEIGHT:	SHEET 1 OF 1
3			2			1

Editing the Isometric view

1. Move the cursor into the graphics area and **right-click** to open the pop-up option menu.

2. Select **Edit Sheet** from the pop-up option menu to change to *Edit Sheet* mode.

3. Left-click inside the *isometric* view to bring up the *Drawing View Property Manager*.

4. In the *Display Style* panel of the *Drawing View Property Manager*, select **Shaded with Edges**.

5. Click **OK** in the *Property Manager* to accept the setting.

Adding a General Note

1. Left-mouse-click on the **Note** icon on the *Annotations Command Manager*.

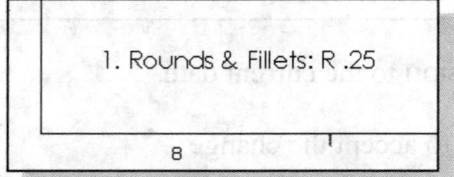

2. On your own, create a general note at the lower left corner of the border as shown.

- On your own, save the final version of the drawing file.

Questions:

1. What are the different types of reference geometry features available in SolidWorks?

2. Why are reference geometry features important in parametric modeling?

3. Describe the purpose of auxiliary views in 2D drawings?

4. What are the required elements in order to generate an auxiliary view?

5. Describe the method used to create centerlines in the chapter.

6. Can we change the View Scale of existing views? How?

7. Identify and describe the following commands:

    (a)

    (b)

    (c)

    (d)

Exercises: (Create the Solid models and the associated 2D drawings.)

1. Dimensions are in inches.

2. Dimensions are in millimeters.

3.   Dimensions are in inches.

4.   Dimensions are in mm.

5.   Dimensions are in inches.

6.   Dimensions are in inches.

7. Dimensions are in inches.

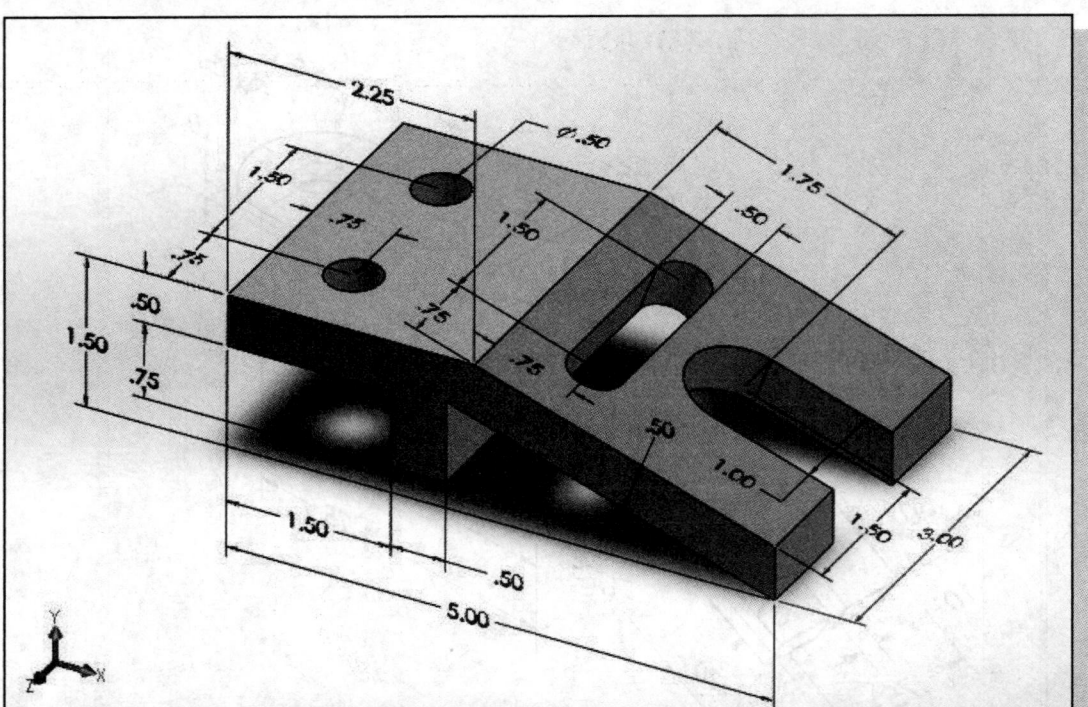

Chapter 13
Threads and Fasteners

Learning Objectives

- ◆ **Understand Screw-Threads Terminology**
- ◆ **Define and Label the Different Parts of a Screw Thread**
- ◆ **Draw Detailed, Schematic and Simplified Threads in Section and Standard Views**
- ◆ **Use the Fastener Clearance Fits**
- ◆ **Identify Various Fasteners and Describe Their Use**
- ◆ **Use SolidWorks' Design Library to create Fasteners**

Introduction

Threads and fasteners are the principal means of assembling parts. Screw threads occur in one form or another on practically all engineering products. Screw threads are designed for many different purposes; the three basic functionalities are to hold parts together, to transmit power, and for use as adjustment of locations of parts.

The earliest records of the screw threads are found in the writings of Archimedes (278 to 212 B.C.), the mathematician who described several designs applying the screw principle. Screw thread was a commonly used element in the first century B.C., but was crudely made during that period of time. Machine production of screws started in England during the Industrial Revolution and the standardization of the screw threads was first proposed by Sir Joseph Whitworth in 1841. His system was generally adopted in England but not in the United States during the 1800s. The initial attempt to standardize screw threads in the United States came in 1864 with the adoption of the thread system designed by William Sellers. The "Sellers thread" fulfilled the need for a general-purpose thread; but it became inadequate with the coming of the modern devices, such as the automobiles and the airplanes. Through the efforts of various engineering societies, the National Screw Thread Commission was authorized in 1918. The Unified Screw Thread, a compromise between the American and British systems, was established on November 18, 1948.

The Metric fastener standard was established in 1946, through the cooperative efforts of several organizations: The International Organization for Standardization (ISO), the Industrial Fasteners Institute (IFI) and the American National Standards Institute.

The following sections describe the general thread definitions, for a more complete description refers to the ANSI/ASME standards: B1.1, B1.7M, B1.13M, Y14.6 and Y14.6aM. (The letter M is for metric system.)

Screw-Thread Terminology

Screw Thread (Thread): A ridge of a uniform section in the form of a helix on the external or internal surface of a cylinder or cone.

External Thread: A thread on the external surface of a cylinder or cone.

Internal Thread: A thread on the internal surface of a cylinder or cone.

Major Diameter: The largest diameter of a screw thread.

Minor Diameter: The smallest diameter of a screw thread.

Pitch Diameter: The diameter of an imaginary cylinder, the surface of which cuts the thread where the width of the thread and groove are equal.

Crest: The outer edge or surface that joins the two sides of a thread.

Root: The bottom edge or surface that joins the sides of two adjacent threads.

Depth of Thread: The distance between crest and root measured normal to the axis.

Angle of Thread: The angle included between the two adjacent sides of the threads.

Pitch: The distance between corresponding points on adjacent thread forms measured parallel to the axis. This distance is a measure of the size of the thread form used, which is equal to 1 divided by the number of threads per inch.

Threads per Inch: The reciprocal of the pitch and the value specified to govern the size of the thread form.

Form of Thread: The profile (cross section) of a thread. The next section shows various forms.

Right-hand Thread (RH): A thread which advances into a nut when turned in a clockwise direction. Threads are always considered to be right-handed unless otherwise specified.

Left-hand Thread (LH): A thread which advances into a nut when turned in a counter-clockwise and receding direction. All left-hand threads are labeled **LH**.

Lead: The distance a threaded part moves axially, with respect to a fixed mating part, in one complete revolution. See the definition and examples of multiple thread in the below figures.

Multiple Threads: A thread having two or more helical curves of the cylinder running side by side. For a single thread, lead and pitch are identical values; for a double thread, lead is twice the pitch; and for a triple thread, lead is three times the pitch. A multiple thread permits a more rapid advance without a larger thread form. The *slope line* can be used to aid the construction of multiple threads; it is the hypotenuse of a right triangle with the short side equals .5P for single threads, P for double threads and so on.

Thread Forms

Screw threads are used on fasteners to fasten parts together, on devices for making adjustments, and for the transmission of power and motion. For these different purposes, a number of thread forms are in use. In practical usage, clearance must be provided between the external and internal threads.

The most common screw thread form is the one with a symmetrical V-Profile. The **Sharp V** is rarely used now, because it is difficult to maintain the sharp roots in production. The form is of interest, however, as the basis of more practical V-type threads; also, because of its simplicity, it is used on drawings as a conventional representation for other (V-profile) threads. The modified V-profile standard thread form in the United States is the **American National**, which is commonly used in fasteners. The V-profile form is prevalent in the **Unified** Screw Thread (UN, UNC, UNF, UNEF) form as well as the ISO/Metric thread. The advantage of symmetrical threads is that they are easier to manufacture and inspect compared to non-symmetrical threads.

The **Unified Screw Thread** is the standard of the United States, Canada, and Great Britain and as such is known as the **Unified** thread. Note that while the crest may be flat or rounded, the root is rounded by design. These are typically used in general purpose fasteners.

The former British standard was the **Whitworth**, which has an angle of 55° with crests and roots rounded. The British Association Standard that uses an angle of 47°, measured in the metric system, is generally used for small threads. The French and the International Metric Standards have a form similar to the American National but are in the metric system.

The V shapes are not desirable for transmitting power since part of the thrust tends to be transmitted to the side direction. **Square thread** is used for this purpose as it transmits all the forces nearly parallel to the axis. The square thread form, while strong, is harder to manufacture. It also cannot be compensated for wear, unlike an **Acme** thread. Because of manufacturing difficulties, the square thread form is generally modified by providing a slight taper (5°) to the sides.

The **Acme** is generally used in place of the square thread. It is stronger, more easily produced, and permits the use of a disengaging or split nut that cannot be used on a square thread.

The **buttress**, for transmitting power in one direction, has the efficiency of the square and the strength of the V thread.

The **knuckle** thread is especially suitable when threads are to be molded or rolled in sheet metal. It is commonly used on glass jars and in a shallow form on bases of ordinary light bulbs.

Internal threads are produced by cutting, while external threads are made by cutting or rolling. For internal threads, a hole is first drilled and then the threads are cut using a tap. The tap drill hole is a little bigger than the minor diameter of the mating external thread. The depth of the tap drill is generally deeper than the length of the threads. There are a few useless threads at the end of a normal tap. For external threads, a shaft that is the same size of the major diameter is cut using a die or on a lathe. Chamfers are generally cut to allow easy assembly.

Thread Representations

The true representation of a screw thread is almost never used in making working drawings. In true representation, the crest and root lines appear as the projections of helical curves, which are extremely tedious to draw.

On practical working drawings, three representation methods are generally used: **detailed**, **schematic** and **simplified**.

True projection of threads

Detailed   Schematic   Simplified

Detailed Representation

The detailed representation simplifies the drawing of the thread principally by constructing the projections of the helical curves into straight lines. And where applicable, further simplifications are made. For example, the 29° angle of the Acme is generally drawn as 30°, and the *American National* and *Unified* threads are represented by the sharp V. In general, true pitch should be shown, although a small increase or decrease in pitch is permissible so as to have even measurements in making the drawing. For example, seven threads per inch may be decreased to six. Remember this is only to simplify the drawing, the actual threads per inch must be specified in the drawing.

External Detailed Threads

Internal Detailed Threads

Schematic Representation

The schematic representation simplifies the drawing of the thread even further. This method omits the true forms and indicates the crests and roots by lines perpendicular to the main axis. And the schematic representation is nearly as effective as the detailed representation, but is much easier to construct. This representation should not be used for section views of external threads or when internal threads are shown as hidden lines; the simplified representation is used instead. Also, to avoid too dense of line pattern, do not use this method when the pitch is less than 1/8 inch or 3 mm.

External Schematic Threads

Section Views

Hidden Threads

Internal Schematic Threads

Simplified Representation

The simplified representation omits both form and crest-lines and indicates the threaded portion by dashed lines parallel to the axis at the approximate depth of thread. The simplified representation is less descriptive than the schematic representation, but they are quicker to draw and for this reason are preferred whenever feasible.

External Simplified Threads

Section Views

Hidden Threads

Internal Simplified Threads

Thread Specification – English Units

The orthographic views of a thread are necessary in order to locate the position of the thread on the part. In addition, the complete thread specification is normally conveyed by means of a local note or dimensions and a local note. The essential information needed for manufacturing are **form**, **nominal (major) diameter**, **threads per inch**, and **thread class** or **toleranced dimensions**. In addition, if the thread is left-hand, the letters **LH** must be included in the specification; also, if the thread is other than single, its multiplicity must be indicated. In general, threads other than the Unified and Metric threads, Acme and buttress require tolerances.

Unified and Metric threads can be specified completely by note. The form of the specification always follows the same order: The first is the nominal size, then the number of threads per inch and the series designation (UNC, NC, etc.), and then the thread fits class. If the thread is left-hand, the letters **LH** are placed after the class. Also, when the Unified-thread classes are used, the letter **A** indicates the thread is external and letter **B** indicates the thread is internal.

For example, a thread specification of **3/4-10UNC-3A**

Major diameter: **3/4** in. diameter
Number of threads per inch: **10** threads per inch
Thread form and Series: **UNC** stands for **Unified National Coarse** series thread
Thread Fits: Class **3** is for high accuracy
External or Internal thread: Letter **A** indicates **external thread**

The descriptions of **thread series** and **thread fits class** are illustrated in the following sections.

Unified Thread Series

Threads are classified in "series" according to the number of threads per inch used with a specific diameter. The above Unified thread example having 20 threads per inch applied to a 1/4-in. diameter results in a thread belonging to the coarse-thread series; note that one with 28 threads per inch on the same diameter describes a thread belonging to the fine-thread series. In the United States, the Unified and Metric threads, the Acme, pipe threads, buttress, and the knuckle thread all have standardized series designations. Note that only the Unified system has more than one series of standardized forms. The Unified and Metric threads standard covers eleven series of screw threads. In the descriptions of the series which follow, the letters "U" and "N" used in the series designations stand for the words "Unified" and "National," respectively. The three standard series include the **coarse-thread series**, the **fine-thread series** and the **extra fine-thread series**.

- The coarse-thread series, designated "**UNC**" or "**NC**," is recommended for general use where conditions do not require a fine thread.

- The fine-thread series, designated "**UNF**" or "**NF**," is recommended for general use in automotive and aircraft work and where special conditions require a fine thread.

- The extra fine-thread series, designated "**UNEF**" or "**NEF**," is used particularly in aircraft and aeronautical equipments, where an extremely shallow thread or a maximum number of threads within a given length is required.

There are also the eight **constant pitch series**: **4, 6, 8, 12, 16, 20, 28** and **32 threads** with constant pitch. The **8, 12** and **16** series are the more commonly used series.

- The 8-thread series, designated **8UN** or **8N**, is a uniform-pitch series using eight threads per inch for any diameter. This series is commonly used for high-pressure conditions. The constant pitch allows excessive torque to be applied and to maintain a proper initial tension during assembly. Accordingly, the 8-thread series has become the general series used in many types of engineering work and as a substitute for the coarse-thread series.

- The 12-thread series, designated **12UN** or **12N**, is a uniform-pitch series using 12 threads per inch for any diameters. Sizes of 12-pitch threads range from 1/2 to 13/4 in. in diameter. This series is commonly used for machine construction, where fine threads are needed for strength. It also provides continuation of the extra fine-thread series for diameters larger than 11/2 in.

- The 16-thread series, designated **16UN** or **16N**, is a uniform-pitch series using 16 threads per inch for any diameters. This series is intended for applications requiring a very fine thread, such as threaded adjusting collars and bearing retaining nuts. It also provides continuation of the extra-fine-thread series for diameters larger than 2 in.

In addition, there are three special thread series, designated **UNS**, **NS** and **UN** as covered in the standards include special combinations of diameter, pitch, and length of engagement.

Thread Fits

The classes provided by the American Standard (ANSI) are classes 1, 2 and 3. These classes are achieved through toleranced thread dimensions given in the standards.

- **Classes 1 fit**: This class of fit is intended for rapid assembly and easy production. Tolerances and allowance are largest with this class.

- **Classes 2 fit**: This class of fit is a quality standard for the bulk of screws, bolts, and nuts produced and is suitable for a wide variety of applications. A moderate allowance provides a minimum clearance between mating threads to minimize galling and seizure. A thread fit class of **2** is used as the normal production fit, this fit is assumed if none is specified.

- **Classes 3 fit**: This class of fit provides a class where accuracy and closeness of fit are important. No allowance is provided. This class of fit is only recommended where precision tools are used.

Thread Specification – Metric

Metric threads, similar to the Unified threads, can also be specified completely by note. The form of the specification always follows the same order: The first is the letter M for metric thread, and then the nominal size, then the pitch and then the tolerance class. If the thread is left-hand, the letters **LH** are placed after the class.

For example, the basic thread note **M15 x 2** is an adequate description for general commercial products.

Letter M: **Metric** thread
Major Diameter: **15** mm.
Pitch: **2** mm.

- **Tolerance Class**: This is used to indicate the tightness or looseness fit between the internal and external threads. In a thread note, the minor or pitch diameter tolerance is stated first followed by the major diameter tolerance if it is different. For general purpose threads, the fit 6H/6g should be used; this fit is assumed if none is specified. For a closer fit, use 6H/5g6g. Note that the number 6 in metric threads is equivalent to the Unified threads class 2 fit. Also, the letter g and G are used for small allowances, where h and H are used for no allowance.

Thread Notes Examples

(a) Metric

External Thread *Metric*

Internal Thread *Metric*

(b) Unified

External Thread *Unified*

Internal Thread *Unified*

Specifying Fasteners

Fastener is a generic term that is used to describe a fairly large class of parts used to connect, fasten, or join parts together. Fasteners are generally identified by the following attributes: **Type**, **Material**, **Size**, and **Thread information**.

- **Type**
  Fasteners are divided into categories based on their function or design; for example, Wood Screw, Sheet Metal Screw, Hex Bolt, Washer, etc. Within the same category, some variations may exist, such as **Drive Type** and **Head Style**.

  (a) Drive Type
  Fasteners in some categories are available with different drive types such as *Philips* or *Slotted*; for example, Philips, Slotted, Allen/Socket, etc.

  (b) Head Style
  Many categories are also available with different head shapes or styles; for example, Flat head, Pan head, Truss head, etc.

  For some types of fasteners, there is either only one drive type or the head style is implied to be of a standard type; for example, Socket screws have the implied Allen drive.

- **Material**
  Fastener material describes the material from which the fastener was made as well as any material grade; for example, Stainless Steel, Bronze, etc

- **Size**
  Descriptions of a fastener's size typically include its **diameter** and **length**. The fastener diameter is measured either as a size number or as a direct measurement. How fastener length is measured varies based on the type of head. As a general rule, the length of fasteners is measured from the surface of the material, to the end of the fastener. For fasteners where the head usually sits above the surface such as hex bolts and pan head screws, the measurement is from directly under the head to the end of the fastener. For fasteners that are designed to be counter sunk such as flat head screws, the fastener is measured from the point on the head where the surface of the material will be, to the end of the fastener.

- **Thread Information**
  Thread pitch or thread count is used only on machine thread fasteners. The thread pitch or count describes how fine the threads are.

Commonly used Fasteners

Hex bolts

A bolt is a fastener having a head on one end and a thread on the other end. A bolt is used to hold two parts together, by means of passing through aligned clearance holes with a nut screwed on the threaded end. (See Appendix E for specs.)

Studs

A stud is a rod with threaded ends.

Cap Screws

A hexagon cap screw is similar to a bolt except it is used without a nut, and generally has a longer thread. Cap screws are available in a variety of head styles and materials. (See Appendix E for specs.)

Machine screws

A machine screw is similar to the slot-head cap screw but smaller, available in many styles and materials. A machine screw is also commonly referred to as a stove bolt. (See Appendix E for specs.)

Wood screws

A tapered shank screw is for use exclusively in wood. Wood screws are available in a variety of head styles and materials.

Sheet metal screws

Highly versatile fasteners designed for thin materials. Sheet metal screws can be used in wood, fiberglass and metal, also called self-tapping screws, available in steel and stainless steel.

Carriage bolts

A carriage bolt is mostly used in wood with a domed shape top and a square under the head, which is pulled into the wood as the nut is tightened.

Socket screws

Socket screws, also known as **Allen head** are fastened with a hexagon Allen wrench, available in several head styles and materials. (See Appendix E for specs.)

Set Screws

Set screws are used to prevent relative motion between two parts. A set screw is screwed into one part so that its point is pushed firmly against the other part, available in a variety of point styles and materials.

Nuts

Nuts are used to attach machine thread fasteners. (See Appendix E for specs.)

Washers

Washers provide a greater contact surface under the fastener. This helps prevent a nut, bolt or screw from breaking through the material. (See Appendix E for specs.)

Keys

Keys are used to prevent relative motion between shafts and wheels, couplings and similar parts attached to shafts.

Rivets

Rivets are generally used to hold sheet metal parts together. Rivets are generally considered as permanent fasteners and are available in a variety of head styles and materials.

Drawing Standard Bolts

As a general rule, standard bolts and nuts are not drawn in the detail drawings unless they are non-standard sizes. The standard bolts and nuts do appear frequently in assembly drawings, and they may be drawn from the exact dimensions from the ANSI/ASME B18.2.1- 1996 standard (see Appendix E) if accuracy is important. Note that for small or unspecified chamfers, fillets, or rounds, the dimension of 1/16 in. (2mm) is generally used in creating the drawing. A simplified version of a bolt is illustrated in the following figure. Note that many companies now offer thousands of standard fasteners and part drawings in AutoCAD DWG or DXF formats for free. You are encouraged to do a search on the internet and compare the downloaded drawings to the specs as listed in the appendix.

Bolt and Screw Clearances

Bolts and screws are generally used to hold parts together; and it is frequently necessary to have a clearance hole for the bolt or screw to pass through. The size of the clearance hole depends on the major diameter of the fastener and the type of fit that is desired. For bolts and screws, three standard fits are available: **normal fit**, **close fit** or **loose fit**. See Appendix for the counter-bore and countersink clearances. (See Appendix G for more details.)

Clearance hole
Example, D= 1 inch

Normal Fit C= $1\frac{3}{32}$
Close Fit C= $1\frac{1}{32}$
Loose Fit C= $1\frac{5}{32}$

Fasteners using SolidWorks' Design Library

In SolidWorks, we also have the option of using the standard parts library through what is known as the *Design Library*. The *Design Library* consists of multiple libraries of reusable elements such as parts, assemblies and sketches. It is accessed through the *Task Pane* at the right of the SolidWorks work area. Significant amounts of time can be saved by using these parts. Note that we can also create and publish our libraries so that others can reuse our parts. The Design Library Task Pane divides the library into four major sections:

- **Design Library** – Contains subfolders populated by SolidWorks with reusable items such as parts, blocks, and annotations. Additional folders and content can be added by the user.

- **Toolbox** – Contains multiple libraries of standard parts that have been created based on industry standards. To access the content, install and add in the *SolidWorks Toolbox* browser.

- **3D Content Central** – Accesses 3D models from component suppliers and individuals via the internet. It includes *Supplier Content* (links to supplier web sites with certified 3D models) and *User Library* (links to models from individuals using 3D PartStream.NET).

- **SolidWorks Content** – Contains additional SolidWorks content for blocks, routing, and weldments in downloadable .zip files.

ANSI Inch - Machine Screw

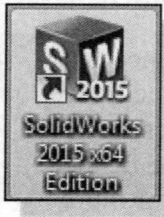

1. Select the **SolidWorks** option on the *Start* menu or select the **SolidWorks** icon on the desktop to start SolidWorks. The SolidWorks main window will appear on the screen.

2. In the *task pane*, select the **Design Library** command by left-mouse-clicking the associated tab.

3. Select the **Toolbox** category and click Add in now to install the SolidWorks Toolbox.

4. Select the **ANSI Inch** folder by double-clicking on the folder as shown.

5. Open the **Bolts and Screws** folder by double-clicking on the folder as shown.

6. Open the **Machine Screws** folder by double-clicking on the folder as shown.

7. *Right-click* once on **Fillister Head Screw** to open the **option menu**.

8. Select **Create Part** in the *option list* as shown.

9. In the *Property Manager* area, set the size to **3/8-16** (Major diameter 3/8 and 16 threads per inch), *Length* to **0.75**, *Drive Type* to **Slotted** and *Thread Display* to **Cosmetic**.

10. Click on the *Thread Display* list and choose **Schematic** to change the threads display as shown.

11. Click **OK** to accept the settings and create the machine screw.

ANSI Metric - Machine Screw

1. In the *Design Library* area, select **ANSI Metric** as shown.

2. Open the **Bolts and Screws** folder by double-clicking on the folder as shown.

3. Open the **Hex Head** folder by double-clicking on the folder as shown.

4. *Right-click* once on **Heavy Hex Bolt** to open the **option menu.**

5. Select **Create Part** in the *option list* as shown.

6. In the *Property Manager* area, set the size to **M12** (Metric Major diameter 12), *Length* to **60**, *Thread Length* to **30** and *Thread Display* to **Schematic**.

7. Click **OK** to accept the configuration and create *Hex Bolt*.

Questions:

1. Describe the thread specification of **3/4-16 UNF -3A**.

2. Describe the thread specification of **M25X3**.

3. List and describe four different types of commonly used fasteners.

4. Determine the sizes of a clearance hole for a **0.75** bolt using the *Close fit* option.

5. Perform an internet search and find information on the different type of **set-screws**, create freehand sketches of four point styles of set screws you have found.

6. Perform an internet search and examine the different types of **machine screws** available, create freehand sketches of four different styles of machine screws you have found.

7. Perform an Internet search and find information on **locknuts**, create freehand sketches of four different styles of locknuts you have found.

Chapter 14
Working Drawings

Learning Objectives

- ♦ **Understand the Terminology Related to Working Drawings**
- ♦ **Understand the Assembly Modeling Methodology**
- ♦ **Understand and Control Degrees of Freedom for Assembly Components**
- ♦ **Understand and Utilize SolidWorks Assembly Mates**
- ♦ **Place parts using SolidWorks SmartMates**
- ♦ **Create Exploded Assemblies**
- ♦ **Create Assembly Drawings**

Certified SolidWorks Associate Exam Objectives Coverage

Fillets and Chamfers
Objectives: Creating Fillets and Chamfer Features.

Materials
Objectives: Applying Material Selection to Parts.

Inserting Components
Objectives: Inserting Components into an Assembly.

Standard Mates – Coincident, Parallel, Perpendicular, Tangent, Concentric, Distance, Angle
Objectives: Applying Standard Mates to Constrain Assemblies.

Drawing Sheets and Views
Objectives: Creating and Setting Properties for Drawing Sheets; Inserting and Editing Standard Views.

Annotations
Objectives: Creating Annotations.

General Engineering Design Process

Engineering design is the ability to create and transform ideas and concepts into a product definition that meets the desired objective.

Conceptual Drawing

Computer Model

Finalized Product

Courtesy of *Wes Fullenwider*, MET Senior Project Oregon Institute of Technology

The general procedure for the design of a new product or improving an existing product involves the following six stages:

1. **Develop and identify the desired objectives.**
2. **Conceptual design stage – concepts and ideas of possible solutions.**
3. **Engineering analysis of components.**
4. **Computer Modeling and/or prototypes.**
5. **Refine and finalize the design.**
6. **Working drawings of the finalized design.**

It is during the **conceptual design** stage, the first drawings, known as **conceptual drawings**, are usually created. The conceptual drawings are typically done in the form of freehand sketches showing the original ideas and concepts of possible solutions to the set objectives. From these conceptual drawings, engineering analyses are performed to improve and confirm the suitability of the proposed design is created. Working from the sketches and the results of the analyses, the design department then creates prototypes or performs computer simulations to further refine the design. Once the design is finalized, a set of detailed drawings of the proposed design is created. It is accurately made and shows the shapes and sizes of the various parts; this is known as the **detail drawing**. On a detail drawing, all the views necessary for complete shape description of a part are provided, and all the necessary dimensions and manufacturing directions are given. The set of drawings is completed with the addition of an **assembly drawing** and a parts list or bill of material. The assembly drawing is necessary as it provides the location and relationship of the parts. The completed drawing set is known as **working drawings**.

Working Drawings

Working drawings are the set of drawings used to give information for the manufacturing of a design.

The description given by a set of working drawings generally includes the followings:

1. The **assembly** description of the design, which provides an overall view of what the design is and also shows the location and relationship of the parts required.
2. A **parts list** or **bill of material** provides a detailed material description of the parts used in the design.
3. The **shape description** of the individual parts, which provides the full graphical representation of the shape of each part.
4. The **size description** of the individual parts, which provides the necessary dimensions of the parts used in the design.
5. **Explanatory notes** are the general and local notes on the individual drawings, giving the specific information, such as material, heat-treatment, finish, etc.

A set of drawings will include, in general, two classes of drawings: **detail drawings** giving details of individual parts; and an **assembly drawing** giving the location and relationship of the parts.

Detail Drawings

A detail drawing is the drawing of the individual parts, giving a complete and exact description of its form, dimensions, and related construction information. A successful detail drawing will provide the manufacturing department all the necessary information to produce the parts. This is done by providing adequate orthographic views together with dimensions, notes, and a descriptive title. Information on a detail drawing usually includes the shape, size, material and finish of a part; specific information of shop operations, such as the limits of accuracy and the number of parts needed are also provided. The detail drawing should be complete and also exact in description, so that a satisfactory part can be produced. The drawings created in the previous chapters are all detail drawings.

Assembly Drawings

An assembly drawing is, as its name implies, a drawing of the design put together, showing the relative positions of the different parts. The assembly drawing of a finalized design is generally done after the detail drawings are completed. The assembly drawing can be made by tracing from the detail drawings. The assembly drawing can also be drawn from the dimensions of the detail drawings; this provides a valuable check on the correctness of the detail drawings.

The assembly drawing sometimes gives the overall dimensions and dimensions that can be used to aid the assembly of the design. However, many assembly drawings need no dimensions. An assembly drawing should not be overloaded with detail, particularly hidden detail. Unnecessary dashed lines (hidden lines) should not be used on any drawing, this is even more critical on assembly drawings.

Assembly drawings usually have reference letters or numbers designating the different parts. These "numbers" are typically enclosed in circles ("balloons") with a leader pointing to the part; these numbers are used in connection with the parts list and bill of material.

For complicated designs, besides the assembly drawing, subassembly drawings are generally used. A subassembly is a drawing showing the details of a related group of parts, as it would not be practical to include all the features on a single assembly drawing. Thus, a subassembly is used to aid in clarifying the relations of a subset of an assembly.

Bill of Materials (BOM) and Parts List

4	Cap screw 3/8	2	STOCK
3	Collar	1	STEEL
2	Bearing	1	STEEL
1	Base Plate	1	C.I.
No	DESCRIPTION	REQ	MATL

A bill of materials (BOM) is a table that contains information about the parts within an assembly. The BOM can include information such as part names, quantities, costs, vendors, and all of the other information related to building the part. The *parts list*, which is used in an assembly drawing, is usually a partial list of the associated BOM.

Drawing Sizes

The standard drawing paper sizes are as shown in the below tables.

American National Standard	International Standard
A – 8.5" X 11.0"	A4 – 210 mm X 297 mm
B – 11.0" X 17.0"	A3 – 297 mm X 420 mm
C – 17.0" X 22.0"	A2 – 420 mm X 594 mm
D – 22.0" X 34.0"	A1 – 594 mm X 841 mm
E – 34.0" X 44.0"	A0 – 841 mm X 1189 mm

Drawing Sheet Borders and Revisions Block

The drawing sheet borders are generally drawn at a distance parallel to the edges of the sheet, typically with distance varying from 0.25" to 0.5" or 5 mm to 10 mm.

Once a drawing has been released to the shop, any alterations or changes should be recorded on the drawing and new prints be issued to the production facilities. In general, the upper right corner of a working drawing sheet is the designated area for such records, this is known as the **revisions** block.

REVISIONS					
ZONE	REV	DESCRIPTION		DATE	APPROVED

Title Blocks

The title of a working drawing is usually placed in the lower right corner of the sheet. The spacing and arrangement of the space depend on the information to be given. In general, the title of a working drawing should contain the following information:

1. **Name of the company and its location.**
2. **Name of the part represented.**
3. **Signature of the person who made the drawing and the date of completion.**
4. **Signature of the checker and the date of completion.**
5. **Signature of the approving personnel and the date of approval.**
6. **Scale of the drawing.**
7. **Drawing number.**

Other information may also be given in the title blocks area, such as material, heat treatment, finish, hardness, general tolerances, depends on the company and the peculiarities of the design.

Working Drawings with SolidWorks

In the previous lessons, we have gone over the fundamentals of creating basic parts and drawings. In this lesson, we will examine the assembly modeling functionality of SolidWorks. We will start with a demonstration on how to create and modify assembly models. The main task in creating an assembly is establishing the assembly relationships between parts. It is a good practice to assemble parts based on the way they would be assembled in the actual manufacturing process. We should also consider breaking down the assembly into smaller subassemblies, which helps the management of parts. In SolidWorks, a subassembly is treated the same way as a single part during assembling. Many parallels exist between assembly modeling and part modeling in parametric modeling software such as SolidWorks.

SolidWorks provides full associative functionality in all design modules, including assemblies. When we change a part model, SolidWorks will automatically reflect the changes in all assemblies that use the part. We can also modify a part in an assembly. Bi-directional full associative functionality is the main feature of parametric solid modeling software that allows us to increase productivity by reducing design cycle time.

Assembly Modeling Methodology

The SolidWorks assembly modeler provides tools and functions that allow us to create 3D parametric assembly models. An assembly model is a 3D model with any combination of multiple part models. SolidWorks Mate Relations can be used to control relationships between parts in an assembly model.

SolidWorks can work with any of the assembly modeling methodologies:

The Bottom Up approach
The first step in the *bottom up* assembly modeling approach is to create the individual parts. The parts are then pulled together into an assembly. This approach is typically used for smaller projects with very few team members.

The Top Down approach
The first step in the *top down* assembly modeling approach is to create the assembly model of the project. Initially, individual parts are represented by names or symbolically. The details of the individual parts are added as the project gets further along. This approach is typically used for larger projects or during the conceptual design stage. Members of the project team can then concentrate on the particular section of the project to which he/she is assigned.

The Middle Out approach
The *middle out* assembly modeling approach is a mixture of the bottom-up and top-down methods. This type of assembly model is usually constructed with most of the parts already created, and additional parts are designed and created using the assembly for construction information. Some requirements are known and some

standard components are used, but new designs must also be produced to meet specific objectives. This combined strategy is a very flexible approach for creating assembly models.

The different assembly modeling approaches described above can be used as guidelines to manage design projects. Keep in mind that we can start modeling our assembly using one approach and then switch to a different approach without any problems.

The Shaft Support Assembly

In this lesson, the *bottom up* assembly modeling approach is illustrated through the creation of the shaft support assembly shown in the figure. All of the parts (components) required to form the assembly are created first. SolidWorks' assembly modeling tools allow us to create complex assemblies by using components that are created in part files or are created in assembly files. A component can be a subassembly or a single part, where features and parts can be modified at any time.

Parts

- Four parts are required for the assembly: (1) **Collar**, (2) **Bearing**, (3) **Base-Plate** and (4) **Cap-Screw**. Create the four parts as shown below, then save the models as separate part files: *Collar, Bearing, Base-Plate*, and *Cap-Screw*. (Close all part files or exit SolidWorks after you have created the parts.)

Creating the Collar with the Chamfer Command

(1) **Collar**

1. On your own, start a new part file using your **Part_IPS_ANSI** template and create the basic *Collar* without the chamfers, as shown below.

2. In the *Features* toolbar, left-click on the **arrow** next to the **Fillet** icon and select the **Chamfer** command from the pop-up menu.

3. In the *Chamfer Parameters* panel of the *Chamfer Property Manager,* select the **Angle distance** option.

4. Set the *Distance* to **1/16 in** (0.0625in).

5. Set the *Angle* to **45°**.

6. Select the two circular edges shown in the figures below.

7. Select **OK** in the *Chamfer Property Manager* to create the chamfers.

8. Save the part with the filename *Collar*.

Creating the Bearing and Base-Plate

➢ On your own, create and save the *Bearing* and *Base-Plate* part files based on the drawings below. Align the base of each part with the **Top Plane**.

(2) ***Bearing*** (Construct the part with the datum origin aligned to the bottom center.)

ALL FILLETS AND ROUNDS R 1/8   SECTION A-A

(3) ***Base-Plate*** (Construct the part with the datum origin aligned to the bottom center.)

Fillets: R 1/8

NOTE: You can ignore the threads and simply create 3/8″ diameter holes.

Creating the Cap-Screw

➢ On your own, create and save the *Cap-Screw* part file based on the drawings below. **NOTE:** Threads are not necessary.

(4) *Cap-Screw*

- SolidWorks provides two options for creating threads: **Cosmetic Thread** and **Helix**. The **Cosmetic Thread** command does not create true 3D threads; a pre-defined thread image is applied on the selected surface, as shown in the figure. The **Helix** command can be used to create true threads, which contain complex three-dimensional curves and surfaces. You are encouraged to experiment with the **Helix** command and/or the **Cosmetic Thread** command to create threads.
  To represent threads on a part using the **Cosmetic Thread** option, first make sure the shading option for Cosmetic Thread is turned on. Open the Options dialog box and on the Document Properties tab, select Detailing. Make sure the Shaded cosmetic threads option is checked. Also (1) check that the All Annotations button is selected under the *View* pull-down menu and (2) right-click on *Annotations* in the *Design Tree* and make sure Display Annotations is activated. To apply a cosmetic thread, click Insert, then Annotations, then Cosmetic Thread. Select the end of the screw shaft and set the threads to **Blind-0.5 in** in the *Property Manager*.

- **HINT:** First create the profile shown here for a revolved feature. Note the centerline is also aligned to the origin.

Starting SolidWorks

1. Close all open SolidWorks part files.

2. Select the **SolidWorks** option on the *Start* menu or select the **SolidWorks** icon on the desktop to start SolidWorks.

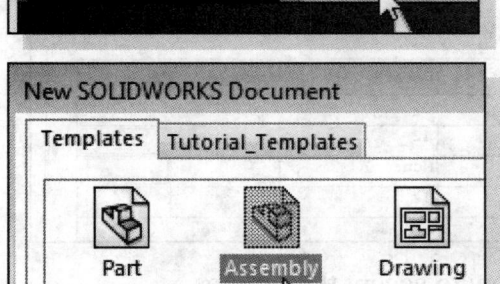

3. Select the **New** icon with a single click of the left-mouse-button on the *Menu Bar*. The *New SolidWorks Document* dialog box appears.

4. Select the **Templates** tab and select the **Assembly** icon as shown.

5. Click **OK** to open the new Assembly file.

❖ SolidWorks opens an assembly file, and automatically opens the *Begin Assembly Property Manager*. SolidWorks expects us to insert the first component. We will first set the document properties to match those of the previously created parts.

6. Cancel the Begin Assembly command by clicking once with the left-mouse-button on the **Cancel** icon in the *Property Manager* as shown.

Document Properties

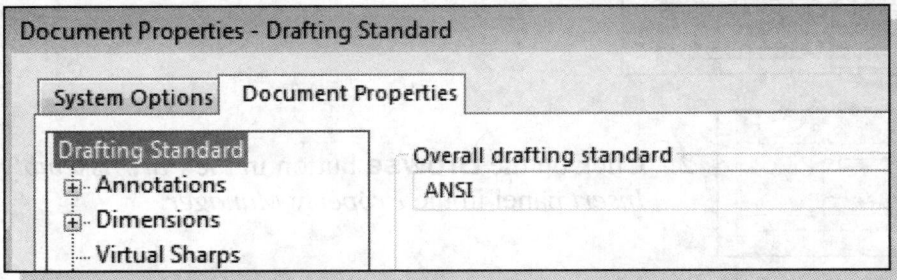

1. Select the **Options** icon from the *Menu Bar* to open the *Options* dialog box.

2. Select the **Document Properties** tab.

3. Select **ANSI** in the pull-down selection window under the *Overall drafting standard* panel as shown.

Document Properties - Drafting Standard

| System Options | Document Properties |

Drafting Standard
  ⊞ Annotations
  ⊞ Dimensions
  — Virtual Sharps

Overall drafting standard

ANSI

4. Click **Units**, select the **IPS (inch, pound, second)** unit system, and select **.12** in the *Decimals* spin box for the *Length units* as shown.

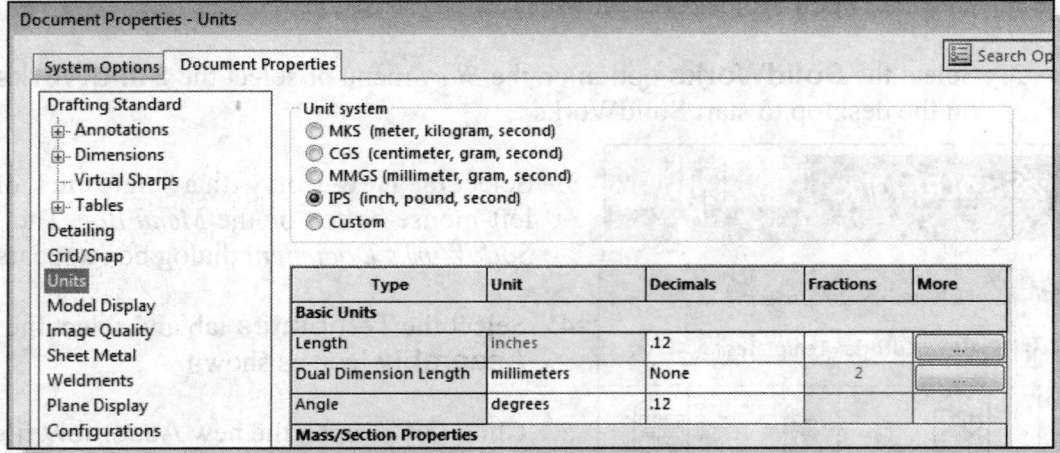

5. Click **OK** in the *Document Properties* window to accept the settings.

Inserting the First Component

*   The first component inserted in an assembly should be a fundamental part or subassembly. The first component in an assembly file sets the orientation of all subsequent parts and subassemblies. The origin of the first component is aligned to the origin of the assembly coordinates and the part is grounded (all degrees of freedom are removed). The rest of the assembly is built on the first component, the ***base component***. In most cases, this *base component* should be one that is **not likely to be removed** and **preferably a non-moving part** in the design. Note that there is no distinction in an assembly between components; the first component we place is usually considered as the *base component* because it is usually a fundamental component to which others are constrained. We can change the base component if desired. For our project, we will use the ***Base-Plate*** as the base component in the assembly.

1. In the *Assembly* toolbar, select the **Insert Component** command by left-clicking the icon.

2. Click on the **Browse** button in the *Part/Assembly to Insert* panel in the *Property Manager*.

3. Use the browser to locate and select the **Base-Plate** part file: **Base-Plate.sldprt.**

4. Click on the **Open** button to retrieve the model.

5. Click **OK** in the *Property Manager* to place the *Base-Plate* at the **origin**.

Inserting the Second Component

➢ We will retrieve the *Bearing* part as the second component of the assembly model.

1. In the *Assembly* toolbar, select the **Insert Component** command by left-clicking the icon.

2. Select the **Bearing** design (part file: **Bearing.sldprt**) in the browser. And click on the **Open** button to retrieve the model.

3. Place the *Bearing* toward the upper right corner of the graphics window, as shown in the figure. Click once with the **left-mouse-button** to place the component. (**NOTE:** Your *Bearing* may initially be oriented differently. We will apply assembly mates to orient the *Bearing*.)

- Inside the *Feature Manager Design Tree*, the retrieved parts are listed in their corresponding order. The **(f)** in front of the *Base-Plate* filename signifies the part is **fixed** and all *six degrees of freedom* are restricted. The number behind the filename is used to identify the number of copies of the same component in the assembly model.

Degrees of Freedom

- Each component in an assembly has six **degrees of freedom** (**DOF**), or ways in which rigid 3D bodies can move: movement along the X, Y, and Z axes (translational freedom), plus rotation around the X, Y, and Z axes (rotational freedom). *Translational DOF*s allow the part to move in the direction of the specified vector. *Rotational DOF*s allow the part to turn about the specified axis.

➢ It is usually a good idea to fully constrain components so that their behavior is predictable as changes are made to the assembly. Leaving some degrees of freedom open can sometimes help retain design flexibility. As a general rule, we should use only enough assembly mate relations to ensure predictable assembly behavior and avoid unnecessary complexity.

Assembly Mates

- We are now ready to assemble the components together. We will start by placing assembly constraints on the ***Bearing*** and the ***Base-Plate*** using SolidWorks assembly **Mates**. Mates create geometric relationships between assembly components. Mates define the allowable directions of linear or rotational motion of the components, limiting the degrees of freedom. A component can be moved within its degrees of freedom, visualizing the assembly's behavior.

To assemble components into an assembly, we need to establish the assembly relationships between components. It is a good practice to assemble components the way they would be assembled in the actual manufacturing process. **Assembly Mates** create a parent/child relationship that allows us to capture the design intent of the assembly. Because the component that we are placing actually becomes a child to the already assembled components, we must use caution when choosing mate types and references to make sure they reflect the intent.

1. In the *Assembly* toolbar, select the **Mate** command by left-clicking once on the icon.

- The *Mate Property Manager* appears on the screen.

- Assembly models are created by applying proper *assembly relations* to the individual components. The **Mate** relations are used to restrict the movement between parts. **Mate** relations eliminate rigid body degrees of freedom (**DOF**). A 3D part has *six degrees of freedom* since the part can rotate and translate relative to the three coordinate axes. Each time we add a **Mate** relation between two parts, one or more DOF is eliminated. The movement of a fully constrained part is restricted in all directions.

- Seven basic types of assembly mates, called **Standard Mates**, are available in SolidWorks: **Coincident, Parallel, Perpendicular, Tangent, Concentric, Distance, and Angle.** Each type of mate removes different combinations of rigid body degrees of freedom. Note that it is possible to apply different constraints and achieve the same results.

- Advanced **Mates** including **Gear** and **Cam Mates** are also available.

The **Standard Mates** are described below:

➢ **Coincident** – positions selected faces, edges, and planes (in combination with each other or combined with a single vertex) so they share the same infinite line. Positions two vertices so they touch.

➢ **Parallel** – places the selected items so they lie in the same direction and remain a constant distance apart from each other.

➢ **Perpendicular** – places the selected items at a 90 degree angle to each other.

➢ **Tangent** – places the selected items in a tangent mate (at least one selection must be a cylindrical, conical, or spherical face).

➢ **Concentric** – places the selections so that they share the same center point.

➢ **Distance** – places the selected items with the specified distance between them.

➢ **Angle** – places the selected items at the specified angle to each other.

Apply the First Assembly Mate

1. Note that the *Mate Selections* panel in the *Mate Property Manager* is highlighted. Select the **top horizontal surface** of the *Base-Plate* part as the first part for the Mate command.

2. On your own, rotate the displayed model to view the bottom of the *Bearing* part, as shown in the figure below. (**HINT:** Use the up arrow [↑] on the keyboard.)

3. Click on the bottom face of the *Bearing* part as the second part selection to apply the relation. The *Bearing* moves to automatically apply the default **Coincident** mate.

> Notice the two faces selected appear in the *Mate Selections* panel of the *Property Manager*.

> Notice the **Tangent** and **Concentric** options are not available. All the mate types are always shown in the *Property Manager*, but only the mates that are applicable to the current selections are available.

> Notice the **Coincident** mate is selected. This is the relation we want to apply.

> For the **Coincident** mate there are two options for *Mate alignment* – **Aligned** and **Anti-Aligned**. These are displayed at the bottom of the *Standard Mates* panel.

4. On your own, select the **Aligned** option at the bottom of the *Standard Mates* panel and observe the effect on the assembly.

5. Select the **Anti-Aligned** option.

6. Select the **Isometric View** to adjust the display of the assembly model.

7. Click the **Accept** button in the *Property Manager* to accept the settings and create the **Anti-Aligned Coincident** mate.

Apply a Second Mate

❖ The Mate command can also be used to align axes of cylindrical features.

1. On your own, turn *ON* the visibility of the **Planes** and the **Temporary Axes**. (**HINT:** Use the *Hide/Show* pull-down menu on the *Heads-up View* toolbar.)

2. Note that the *Mate Selections* panel in the *Mate Property Manager* is highlighted. Select the **axis** of the right counter bore hole of the *Bearing* part.

3. Select the **axis** of the small hole on the *Base-Plate* part, as shown. The *Bearing* moves to automatically apply the default Coincident mate.

4. Click **Add Mate** in the *Option toolbar* to create the Coincident Mate.

5. In the *Property Manager*, click on the **Close** button (the red **X** icon), or press the [Esc] key, to exit the Mate command.

❖ The *Bearing* part appears to be placed in the correct position. But the DOF for the *Bearing* are not fully restricted; the *Bearing* part can still rotate about the displayed vertical axis.

Constrained Move

❖ To see how well a component is constrained, we can perform a constrained move. A constrained move is done by dragging the component in the graphics window with the left-mouse-button. A constrained move will honor previously applied assembly mates. That is, the selected component and parts mated to the component move together in their constrained positions. A fixed component remains fixed during the move.

1. Inside the graphics window, move the cursor on top of the top surface of the *Bearing* part as shown in the figure.

2. Press and hold down the left-mouse-button and drag the *Bearing* part downward.

❖ The *Bearing* part can freely rotate about the mated axis.

3. On your own, use the rotation commands to view the alignment of the *Bearing* part.

4. Rotate the *Bearing* part and adjust the display roughly as shown in the figure.

Apply a Third Mate

- Besides selecting the surfaces of solid models to apply constraints, we can also select the established planes to apply the assembly mates. This is an additional advantage of using the *BORN technique* in creating part models. For the *Bearing* part, we will apply a **Mate** to two of the planes and eliminate the last rotational DOF.

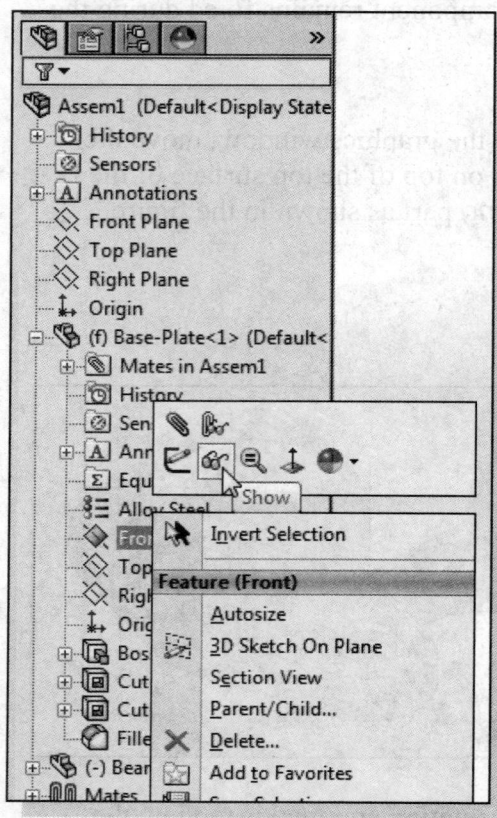

1. On your own, inside the *Feature Manager Design Tree* use the **Show** option to toggle *ON* the visibility for the planes that can be used for alignment of the *Base-Plate* and the *Bearing* parts. (**HINT:** Make sure the visibility of *Planes* is toggled *ON* in the *Hide/Show* pull-down menu.)

2. Press the **[Esc]** key to ensure that no object is selected.

3. In the *Assembly* toolbar, select the **Mate** command by left-clicking once on the icon

4. Select the *plane* of the *Base-Plate* part as the first part for the Mate command.

5. Select the *plane* of the *Bearing* part as the second part for the **Mate** command.

❖ The **Coincident** mate is executed by default and makes two planes coplanar with the **Aligned** option automatically selected. (**NOTE:** If you did not create the base plate with the front plane aligned with the middle of the plate, you will need to select the corresponding plane.)

6. On your own, select the **Anti-aligned** option at the bottom of the *Standard Mates* panel and observe the effect on the assembly.

7. Select the **Aligned** option.

8. Click the **OK** button in the *Property Manager* to accept the settings and create the **Aligned Coincident** mate.

9. In the *Property Manager*, click on the **Close** button (or press the **[Esc]** key) to exit the Mate command.

❖ Note the assembly is *fully defined*.

Inserting the Third Component

➢ We will retrieve the *Collar* part as the third component of the assembly model.

1. In the *Assembly* toolbar, select the **Insert Component** command by left-mouse-clicking the icon.

2. Select the ***Collar*** design (part file: **Collar.sldprt**) in the browser and click on the **Open** button to retrieve the model.

3. Insert the *Collar* part toward the lower left corner of the graphics window, as shown in the figure.

Applying Concentric and Coincident Mates

1. In the *Assembly* toolbar, select the **Mate** command by left-clicking once on the icon.

2. Select the external cylindrical surface of the *Collar* part as shown in the figure as the first part for the **Mate** command. (**HINT:** Use the **arrow** keys on the keyboard to rotate the view.)

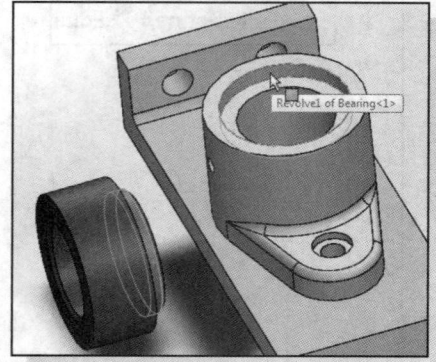

3. Select the internal cylindrical surface of the *Bearing* part as shown in the figure as the second part for the **Mate** command.

4. Notice in the *Mate Property Manager* that the Concentric and Anti-Aligned options are automatically selected. On your own, select the correct alignment (Aligned or Anti-Aligned) for your assembly. Click the **Accept** button in the *Property Manager* to accept the settings and create the **Concentric** mate.

5. On your own, move the ***Collar*** part to a position like that in the figure. Notice that the move is constrained to maintain the concentric relationship.

6. Select the top circular surface of the *Bearing* part as shown in the figure as the first part for a new **Mate** command.

7. Select the circular surface of the *Collar* part as shown in the figure as the second part for a new **Mate** command.

8. Notice in the *Mate Property Manager* that the **Coincident** and **Anti-Aligned** options are automatically selected. Click the **OK** button in the *Property Manager* to accept the settings and create the **Anti-Aligned Coincident** mate.

9. In the *Property Manager*, click on the **Close** button (or press the [**Esc**] key) to exit the **Mate** command.

10. On your own, change the view to **Isometric**.

11. Note that the *Collar* part is not fully constrained. One rotational degree of freedom remains open; the *Collar* part can still freely rotate about the vertical axis. Click on the *Collar* and drag with the **left-mouse-button** to observe this constrained motion.

Assemble the Cap-Screws using SmartMates

❖ We will place two *Cap-Screw* parts to complete the assembly model. We will use SolidWorks **SmartMates** to apply the geometric relations. The SmartMates function allows us to create commonly-used mates without using the *Mate Property Manager*. Application of a SmartMate involves dragging one part to a mating position with another. In most cases, one mate is created. The type of SmartMate created depends on the geometry used to drag the component, and the type of geometry onto which you drop the component.

The SmartMates functionality creates multiple mates under certain conditions. If the application finds circular edges to mate, a **Peg-In-Hole** SmartMate will be applied. Two mates are applied: a Concentric mate between cylindrical or conical faces, and a Coincident mate between the planar faces that are adjacent to the conical faces. This is the type of SmartMate we will apply when inserting the *Cap-Screw* parts.

• **Applying a SmartMate when two components are already in the assembly**

1. On your own, insert a ***Cap-Screw*** part into the assembly as shown.

2. Select the circular edge of the *Cap-Screw* head as shown. Press and hold down the left-mouse-button.

3. Press down and hold the **[Alt]** key. While holding the **[Alt]** key, drag the circular edge of the *Cap-Screw* onto the circular face of the counter sink in the *Bearing* part as shown. Notice the **Peg-In-Hole** mate icon appears.

Revolve1 of Cap-Screw<1>

4. Release **[Alt]** while still holding the mouse key down.

5. If the alignment condition is incorrect (screw is upside down), press the **[Tab]** key while still holding the left mouse button down.

6. When the screw is aligned correctly, release the left-mouse-button to apply the SmartMate.

• **Applying a SmartMate to a new component while adding it to the assembly**

1. Click once with the **left-mouse-button** on the **Open** icon on the *Menu Bar*.

2. Select the *Cap-Screw* design (part file: **Cap-Screw.sldprt**) in the browser, and click on the **Open** button to retrieve the model.

3. Select the **Tile Horizontally** option from the *Window* pull-down menu.

4. In the *Cap-Screw* window, **Rotate** and **Zoom** so that the circular edge of the screw head is visible as shown in the figure.

5. In the *Assembly* window, **Pan, Rotate,** and **Zoom** so that the counter bore of the *Bearing* appears as shown in the figure.

6. Using the left-mouse-button, **click and drag** the **circular edge** of the head of the *Cap-Screw* part into the assembly window.

7. Release the mouse-button when the cursor is over the circular surface of the counter bore, applying the **Peg-In-Hole SmartMate**.

8. Close the *Cap-Screw* window.

9. Maximize the *Assem1* window.

10. On your own, change the view to **Isometric**.

11. Notice isocircles representing the bottom of the Cosmetic Threads on the screws are visible. In the *Feature Manager Design Tree*, **right-click** on the **Cosmetic Thread1** icon under **Cap-Screw(1)** and select **Hide**.

❖ Notice, this setting affects both *Cap-Screws*.

• Inside the *Feature Manager Design Tree*, the retrieved parts are listed in the order they are placed. The number behind the part name is used to identify the number of copies of the same part in the assembly model. Move the cursor to the last part name and notice the corresponding part is highlighted in the graphics window.

• The **(f)** symbol indicates the part is fixed. The **(-)** symbol indicates the part has at least one degree of freedom. The *Collar* and the two *Cap Screws* each have one rotational degree of freedom. Click and drag on each of them to observe the rotational freedom.

Exploded View of the Assembly

- Exploded assemblies are often used in design presentations, catalogs, sales literature, and in the shop to show all of the parts of an assembly and how they fit together. In SolidWorks, exploded views are created by selecting and dragging parts in the graphics area.

1. In the *Assembly* toolbar, select the **Exploded View** command by left-clicking once on the icon.

2. The message *"Select component(s) ..."* appears in the *Explode Property Manager*. Select the *Collar* part by clicking on it with the left-mouse-button.

3. Notice a manipulator appears in the graphics area. Move the pointer over the manipulator handle that points in the upward direction, and drag the manipulator handle to the location shown in the figure.

- ❖ The exploded view component movements can be made along the major axis directions by dragging the manipulator handle that points in the corresponding direction. Dragging the yellow sphere in the center of the manipulator will move the manipulator to a different location. The manipulator can be dropped on an edge or face and an axis of the manipulator will align with the edge or face.

4. On your own, repeat the above steps and create an exploded assembly by repositioning the components as shown in the figure.

5. Click **OK** in the *Property Manager* to close the Exploded View command.

6. Select the **Configuration Manager** tab.

7. In the *Configuration Manager*, expand the tree to reveal the Exploded View icon labeled ExpView1. **Double-click** on the **ExpView1** icon to collapse the exploded view.

❖ Note that the components are reset back to their assembled positions, based on the applied assembly mates.

8. **Double-click** on the **ExpView1** icon again to return to the exploded view.

9. On your own, return to the collapsed view.

10. Select the **Feature Manager Design Tree** tab to return to the *Design Tree*.

Save the Assembly Model

1. Select the **Save As** option from the *File* pull-down menu.

2. In the *Save As* pop-up window, enter **Support_Assembly** for the *File name* and **Shaft-Support Assembly** for the *Description*.

3. Click **Save** to save the file.

4. If the SolidWorks window appears, click **Save All**.

Editing the Components

- The associative functionality of SolidWorks allows us to change the design at any level, and the system reflects the changes at all levels automatically.

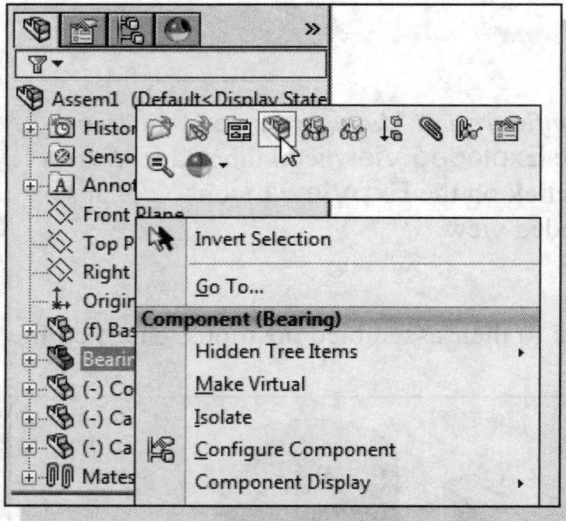

1. Inside the *Feature Manager Design Tree*, move the cursor on top of the **Bearing** part. Right-click once to bring up the option menu and select **Edit Part** in the option list.

❖ Note that we are automatically switched back to *Part Editing* mode. The **Bearing** component portion of the *Feature Manager Design Tree* appears blue to denote that the part model is active.

2. Expand the **Bearing** portion of the *Design Tree*. Move the cursor over the **Annotations** icon **under the Bearing**. Click once with the right-mouse-button to open the pop-up option menu. Select the **Show Feature Dimensions** option.

3. On your own, adjust the diameter of the small *Drill Hole* to **0.25** as shown.

4. Click on the **Rebuild** button in the *Menu Bar* to proceed with updating the model.

5. On your own, turn *OFF* the visibility of the feature dimensions.

6. Inside the graphics window, click once with the **right-mouse-button** to display the *option menu*.

7. Select **Edit Assembly:Support_Assembly** in the popup menu to exit *Part Editing* mode and return to *Assembly* mode.

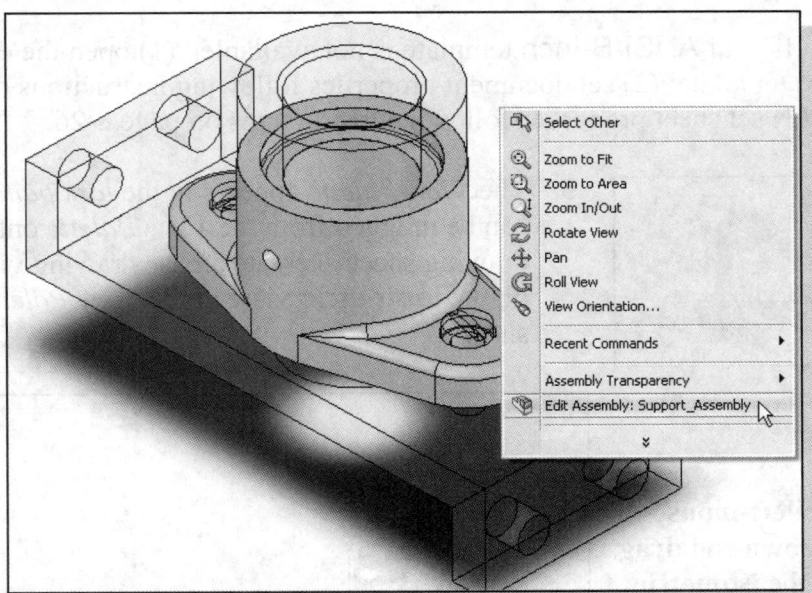

➢ SolidWorks has updated the part in all levels and in the current *Assembly* mode. On your own, open the *Bearing* part to confirm the modification is performed.

8. On your own, save the Support_Assembly file. If the *Save Modified Documents* window appears, select **Save All**.

9. If the SolidWorks window appears, select **Rebuild and save the document**.

Setup a Drawing of the Assembly Model

1. Click on the **arrow** next to the **New** icon on the *Menu Bar* and select **Make Drawing from Part/Assembly** in the pull-down menu.

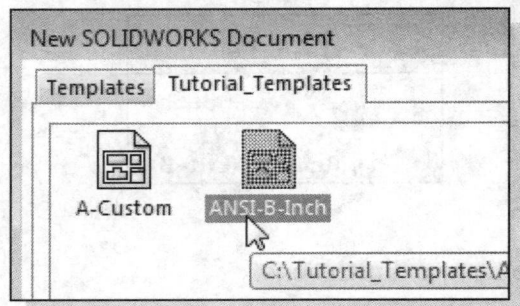

2. In the *New SolidWorks Document* window, select the **Tutorial_Templates** tab.

3. Select the **ANSI-B-Inch** template file icon. This is the custom drawing template you created in Chapter 8. (If your ANSI-B-Inch template is not available, see note below.)

4. Select **OK** in the *New SolidWorks Document* window to open the new drawing file.

➢ The new drawing file opens using the **ANSI-B-Inch.SLDDRW** template. The B-size drawing sheet appears.

❖ **NOTE:** If your ANSI-B-Inch template is not available: (1) open the default Drawing template; (2) set document properties following instructions on page 8-37; and (3) set sheet properties following instructions on page 8-26.

5. The *View Palette* appears in the *task pane*. Views can be dragged from the *View Palette* onto the drawing sheet to create a base drawing view. Click on the **Isometric** view in the *View Palette* as shown.

6. Hold the **left-mouse-button** down and **drag** to place the **isometric view** as shown.

7. In the *Projected View Property Manager*, select the **Hidden Lines Removed** option for the *Display Style*.

8. Left-click on the **OK** icon in the *Drawing View Property Manager* to accept the view.

9. In the *Feature Manager Design Tree*, **right-click** on the **Sheet** icon to open the pop-up option menu and select **Properties**.

10. In the Sheet Properties window, set the scale to **1:1** and click **OK**.

Creating a Bill of Materials

A *Bill of Materials (BOM)*, or parts list, can be automatically inserted into a drawing using SolidWorks. A Bill of Materials is an example of a *SolidWorks Annotation Table*. A SolidWorks Annotation Table can be located in the drawing by clicking in the graphics area or by using a Table Anchor.

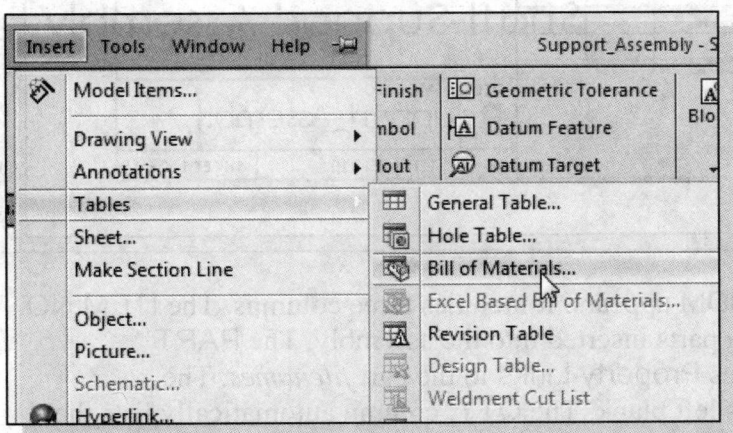

1. Under the **Insert** pull-down menu, select **Tables**, then **Bill of Materials**.

2. The message *"Select a drawing view to specify the model for creating the Bill of Materials"* appears in the *Bill of Materials Property Manager*. Select on the **shaft-support assembly view** in the graphics area by clicking on it once with the **left-mouse-button**.

3. Click on **OK** in the *Bill of Materials Property Manager* to insert the BOM. Locate the BOM so that it is aligned with the right border and the top of the title block as shown. Click the left-mouse-button to insert the BOM.

4. On your own, adjust the size and location of the inserted BOM by drag and drop with the control box as shown.

ITEM NO.	PART NUMBER	DESCRIPTION	QTY.
1	Base-Plate		1
2	Bearing		1
3	Collar		1
4	Cap-Screw		2

UNLESS OTHERWISE SPECIFIED:

DIMENSIONS ARE IN INCHES
TOLERANCES:
ANGULAR MACH ±01°
TWO PLACE DECIMAL   ±001
THREE PLACE DECIMAL ±0.001

DRAWN A.smith 00/23/13
CHECKED
ENG APPR
MFG APPR
Q A
COMMENTS:

Oregon Institue of Technology

TITLE:

Shaft-Support Assembly

SIZE **B** DWG. NO. Support_Assembly REV

SCALE: 1:1   WEIGHT: SHEET 1 OF 1

❖ The default SolidWorks BOM appears. It includes three columns. The ITEM NO. column lists the individual parts inserted into the assembly. The PART NUMBER column includes Property Links to the part *filenames*. The DESCRIPTION column is left blank. The QTY. column automatically lists the quantity of each part included in the assembly.

Editing the Bill of Materials

There are many ways in which the BOM table can be modified. We will add an additional Material column. This could be done simply by entering text. However, we will use SolidWorks Property Links. We will first set the material for each part in the part files. Then we will place the appropriate Property Links in the BOM.

1. Click once with the **left-mouse-button** on the **Open** icon on the *Menu Bar*.

2. Select the *Base-Plate* design (part file: **Base-Plate.sldprt**) in the browser, and click on the **Open** button to retrieve the model.

3. In the *Feature Manager Design Tree* for the part, *right click* on the *Material* icon, then select **Edit Material**.

4. In the *Material* pop-up window, expand the **Steel** folder of the selection tree, and select **Alloy Steel**.

5. Click **Apply** in the *Material* pop-up window to accept the setting.

6. Select **Close** to close the window.

❖ The material has been selected for the *Base-Plate*, and is defined as a SolidWorks user-defined custom property.

7. Select **Properties** from the *File* pull-down menu.

• The *Summary Information* window appears with the table of *Custom Properties* blank.

8. Click in the box under *Property Name* and enter **Material**.

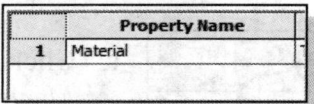

	Property Name
1	Material

9. Click in the box under *Value/Text Expression* and use the pull-down option list to select **Material**.

Value / Text Expression
Material
Mass
Density

❖ Notice the **Material** custom property appears and the **Evaluated Value** in the table automatically becomes **Alloy Steel**, the material selected for the part.

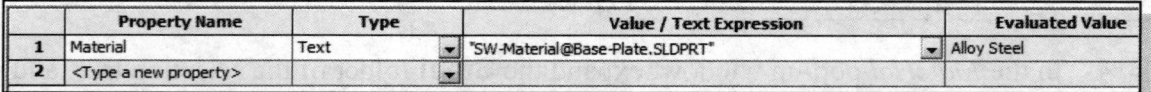

	Property Name	Type	Value / Text Expression	Evaluated Value
1	Material	Text	"SW-Material@Base-Plate.SLDPRT"	Alloy Steel
2	<Type a new property>			

10. Click **OK** in the *Summary Information* window to accept the settings.

11. On your own, **save** and **close** the *Base-Plate* part file. If the SolidWorks window appears, select **Yes**.

12. On your own, repeat the steps above to set the **Material** and the **Material Custom Property** for the *Bearing*, *Collar*, and *Cap-Screw* parts. Use the following: *Bearing* – Grey Cast Iron; *Collar* – Tin Bearing Bronze; *Cap-Screw* – Alloy Steel.

❖ The SolidWorks custom property **Material** for each part is now available for use in **Property Links**. We will now use the **Property Links** in the BOM.

13. Move the cursor over the top of the third column in the BOM. When the **Column** icon appears, **right-click** to open the *option menu*.

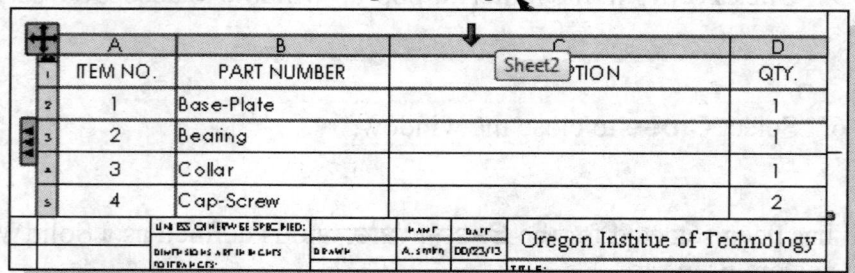

14. Select Insert → Column Right to add a new column to the right side.

15. In the Column type dialog box, choose Material as the Custom Property Name as shown.

16. Click on the sheet, away from the *Column Property* panel to accept the settings.

➤ Notice the corresponding material appears for each part due to the property link.

17. **Double-click** on the note entry Material in the new BOM.

18. Type over the word in all caps.

19. Press [**Enter**] to accept the change.

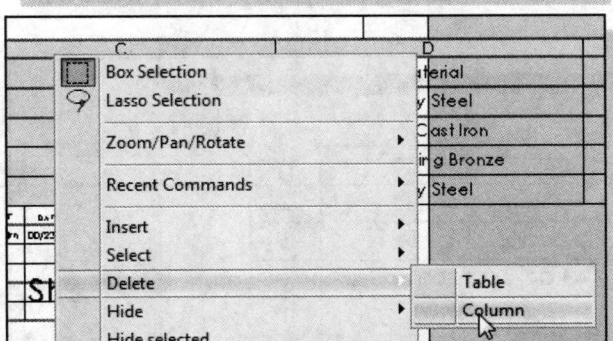

20. Click on the Description cell and delete the entire Column as shown.

21. On your own, adjust, reposition and resize the BOM so that it is as shown in the below figure.

ITEM NO.	PART NUMBER	MATERIAL	QTY.
1	Base-Plate	Alloy Steel	1
2	Bearing	Gray Cast Iron	1
3	Collar	Tin Bearing Bronze	1
4	Cap-Screw	Alloy Steel	2

UNLESS OTHERWISE SPECIFIED:		NAME	DATE	Oregon Institue of Technology
DIMENSIONS ARE IN INCHES TOLERANCES:	DRAWN	A. smkn	DD/23/13	

22. Select the BOM table by clicking on the upper left corner as shown in the figure.

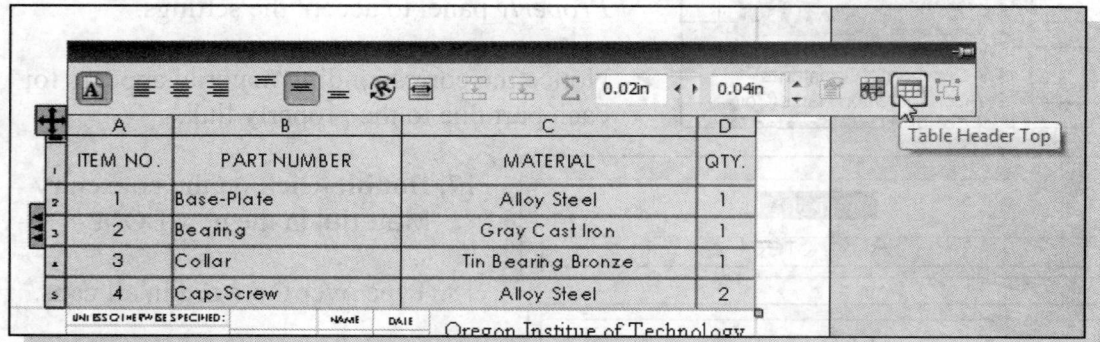

23. In the *popup toolbar*, click on the **Table Header Top** icon to set the location of the *Table Header*

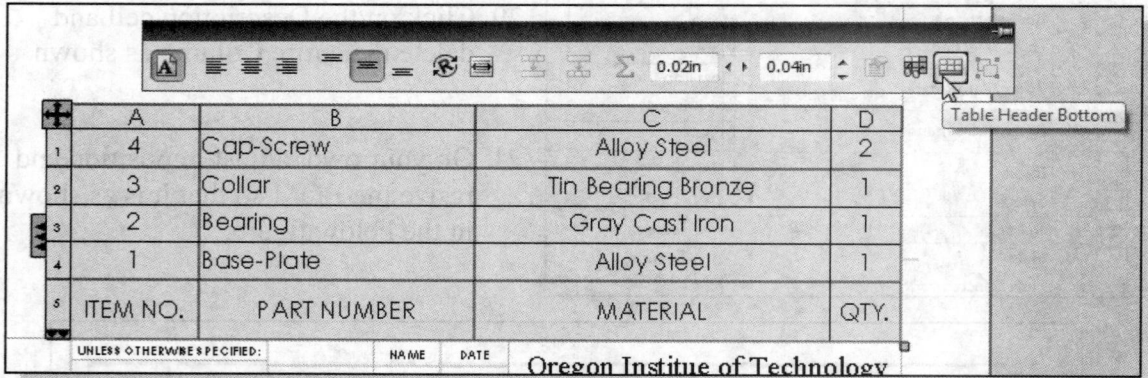

- The Table Header has been adjusted to the bottom and the Item Numbers are also adjusted accordingly as shown.

24. Click on the drawing sheet to exit the edit BOM table mode as shown.

Completing the Assembly Drawing

1. Press the [F] key to fit the drawing to the graphics area.

2. In the *Annotation* toolbar, click on the **AutoBalloon** button.

3. In the *AutoBalloon Property-Manager*, the message "*Select drawing sheet/view(s) to insert Auto Balloon*" is displayed. Click on the assembly view in the graphics area.

4. Select **1 Character** for the *Size* option on the *Balloon Setting* panel in the *Property Manager*.

5. Click **OK** in the *Property Manager* to create the balloons.

6. Move the cursor over the balloon labeling the *Collar* part. Click and drag with the **left-mouse-button** to move the balloon to the new location shown in the figure.

7. Click and drag to move the arrow head to the new location shown in the figure.

8. On your own, repeat the above steps to reposition the balloons as shown.

9. On your own, use the **Save As** command and save the drawing with the filename **MECH 212-05**. Notice the new filename appears in the title block.

10. If the SolidWorks window appears, select **Save All**.

Sheet (Sheet2)
  Edit Sheet Format
  Lock Sheet Focus
  Add Sheet...
  Copy
  Delete
  Properties...

  Relations/Snaps Options...

11. Move the cursor into the graphics area and **right-click** to open the pop-up option menu.

12. Select **Edit Sheet Format** from the pop-up option menu to change to *Edit Sheet Format* mode.

13. On your own, edit the title block to appear as shown in the figure.

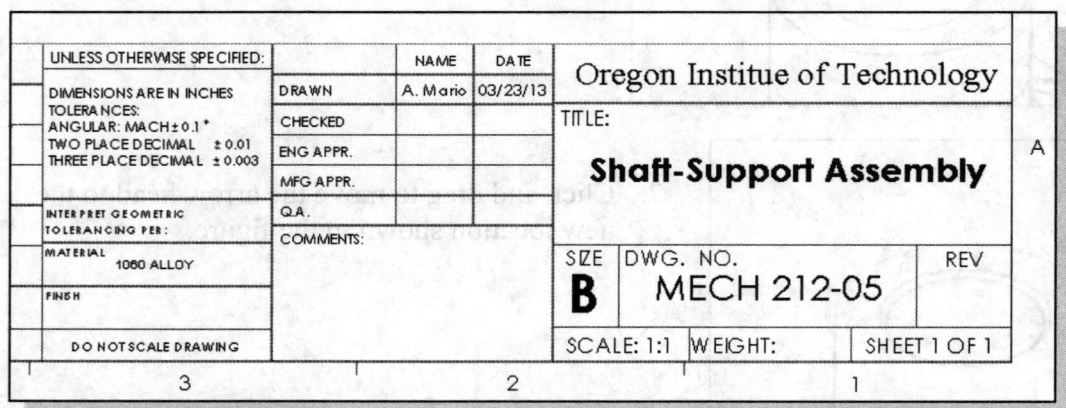

UNLESS OTHERWISE SPECIFIED:		NAME	DATE	Oregon Institue of Technology	
DIMENSIONS ARE IN INCHES	DRAWN	A. Mario	03/23/13		
TOLERANCES: ANGULAR: MACH±0.1°	CHECKED			TITLE:	
TWO PLACE DECIMAL ±0.01 THREE PLACE DECIMAL ±0.003	ENG APPR.			**Shaft-Support Assembly**	A
	MFG APPR.				
INTERPRET GEOMETRIC TOLERANCING PER:	Q.A.				
	COMMENTS:				
MATERIAL 1060 ALLOY				SIZE **B**	DWG. NO. MECH 212-05	REV
FINISH					
DO NOT SCALE DRAWING				SCALE: 1:1 WEIGHT:	SHEET 1 OF 1
3		2		1	

14. On your own, return to *Edit Sheet* mode.

Exporting the Bill of Materials

❖ The bill of materials can be exported as an *Excel* file.

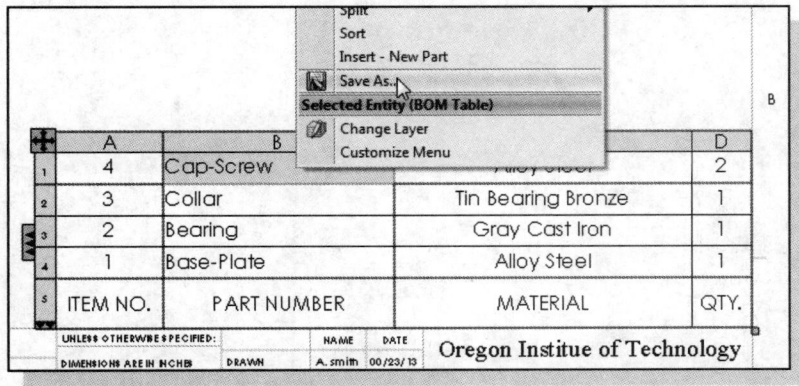

1. Right click the bill of materials on the drawing sheet.

2. Select **Save As** from the *option* menu.

3. Select **Excel** or another appropriate Excel file type for the *Save as type:* option.

4. Enter a *File name* and click **Save**.

5. On your own, open the file using *Microsoft Excel* and examine the BOM.

Questions:

1. What is an *assembly drawing*? What are the basic differences between an assembly drawing and a detail drawing?

2. What is the purpose of using **assembly mates**?

3. List three of the commonly used **assembly mates**.

4. Describe the difference between the **Aligned** option and the **Anti-aligned** option.

5. In an assembly, can we place more than one copy of a part? How is it done?

6. How should we determine the assembly order of different parts in an assembly model?

7. How do we adjust the information listed in the **Bill of Materials** of an assembly drawing?

8. How do we add an additional column in the **Bill of Materials** of an assembly drawing?

Exercises:

1. **Wheel Assembly** (Create a set of detail and assembly drawings. All dimensions are in mm.)

2. **Leveling Assembly** (Create a set of detail and assembly drawings. All dimensions are in mm.)

(a) Base Plate

(b) Sliding Block (Rounds & Fillets: R3)

(c) Lifting Block (Rounds & Fillets: R3)

(d) Adjusting Screw (M10 X 1.5)

Hex Socket
flat to flat 10
depth 9

Chamfer 45° X 1

12   11   5

Ø 14

Ø 16

A 2

Ø 10

72

Chapter 15
CSWA Exam Preparation

Learning Objectives

- Control Part Orientation
- Create a New View Orientation
- Use the SolidWorks Mass Properties Tool
- Obtain the Mass and Center of Mass of a Part
- Obtain the Mass and Center of Mass of an Assembly
- Use Distance and Angle Mates
- Create and Use Reference Axes

Certified SolidWorks Associate Exam Objectives Coverage

Tips about Taking the Certified SolidWorks Associate (CSWA) Examination

1. **Study**: The first step to maximize your potential on an exam is to sufficiently prepare for it. You need to be familiar with the SolidWorks package, and this can only be achieved by doing designs and exploring the different commands available. The Certified SolidWorks Associate (CSWA) exam is designed to measure your familiarity with the SolidWorks software. You must be able to perform the given task and answer the exam questions correctly and quickly.

2. **Make Notes**: Take notes of what you learn either while attending classroom sessions or going through study material. Use these notes as a review guide before taking the actual test.

3. **Time Management**: The examination has a time limit. Manage the time you spend on each question. Always remember you do not need to score 100% to pass the exam. Also keep in mind that some questions are weighed more heavily and may take more time to answer. You can flip back and forth to view different problems during the test time by using the arrow buttons. If you encounter a question you cannot answer in a reasonable amount of time, use the *Save As* feature in SolidWorks to save a copy of the file, and move on to the next question. You can return to any question and enter or change the answer as long as you do not hit the [**End Examination**] button.

4. **Use the *SolidWorks Help System***: If you get confused and can't think of the answer, remember the *SolidWorks Help System* is a great tool to confirm your considerations. In preparing for the exam, familiarize yourself with the help utility organization (e.g., Contents, Index, Search options).

5. **Use Internet Search**: Use of an internet search utility is allowed during the test. If a test question requires general knowledge, for example definitions of engineering or drafting concepts (stress, yield strength, auxiliary view, etc.), remember the internet is available as a tool to assist in your considerations.

6. **Use Common Sense**: If you are unable to get the correct answer and unable to eliminate all distracters, then you need to select the best answer from the remaining selections. This may be a task of selecting the best answer from amongst several correct answers, or it may be selecting the least incorrect answer from amongst several poor answers.

7. **Be Cautious and Don't Act in Haste**: Devote some time to ponder and think of the correct answer. Ensure that you interpret all the options correctly before selecting from available choices. Don't go into panic mode while taking a test. Use the *Arrow Buttons* to review each question. When you are confident that you have answered all questions, end the examination using the [**End Examination**] button to submit your answers for scoring. You will receive a score report once you have submitted your answers.

8. **Relax before exam**: In order to avoid last minute stress, make sure that you arrive 10 to 15 minutes early and relax before taking the exam.

Introduction

In this lesson, we will create and examine part and assembly files in a manner consistent with the format of the CSWA exam. This is a multiple choice exam. You are asked to build complex models and assemblies and your work is assessed in a multiple choice format by asking the value of parameters such as the mass or center of mass. These can be retrieved using the SolidWorks **Mass Properties** tool. In answering questions related to the location of the center of mass, it is important to ensure that the origin and coordinate system axes are consistent between your model and the exam problem as posed.

We will first create a part based on a dimensioned drawing with the origin and coordinate axes annotated. We will create the part, apply the correct material properties, and retrieve the mass and center of mass data. In building the model, we will ensure that it is oriented relative to the default coordinate system in the manner indicated in the problem. While the part is relatively simple, the procedure – taking care to locate the part, applying material properties, and retrieving mass properties – is the same as should be followed for many CSWA exam questions. The part requires the creation of an inclined **Reference Plane** to use in creating a sketch.

We will then create an assembly using multiple copies of two mating parts. The assembly will require the use of **Distance** and **Angle** mates, based on the dimensions given in the problem. In this case, we will not orient the parts or assembly based on the problem definition. Instead, after the assembly has been completed, we will create **Reference Axes** to match those in the problem statement and use these reference axes when retrieving the center of mass.

The Part Problem

We will model the part shown below and use the **Mass Properties** tool to determine the mass and center of mass of the part. The problem is presented below in a manner similar to that encountered on the CSWA exam.

Build the part shown below.
Unit system: MMGS (millimeter, gram, second)
Part origin: As shown.
Part material: Ductile iron   Density: 0.0071 g/mm^3

(1) What is the overall mass of the part in grams?
(2) Where is the center of mass of the part?

Before starting to build the model, it is important to select a strategy for controlling the origin and orientation of the X, Y, and Z axes since the center of mass must be defined relative to a known reference system. In this case the axis directions are defined in the drawing. We can either (1) build the part aligned to the default or global coordinate system as specified in the figure, or (2) build the part independent of this constraint and, after the part is complete, create a reference coordinate system with axes aligned with the part as shown in the figure. We will use the first strategy for the part problem. The second strategy will be used in the assembly problem to be done later in the chapter.

Strategy for Aligning the Part to the Default Axis System

The first feature to be created will be the base feature of the part. We must determine which plane to use to define the first sketch in order to align the part correctly. In the dimensioned drawing defining the part, we can see that the base rests on the X-Z plane (i.e., the **Top Plane**) with the positive X-axis aligned with the long dimension and the positive Z-axis aligned with the short dimension. We therefore want to create the base feature as shown below, with the origin located at the * and the X, Y and Z axes aligned as shown.

Creating the Base Feature

1. Select the **SolidWorks** option on the *Start* menu or select the **SolidWorks** icon on the desktop to start SolidWorks. The SolidWorks main window will appear on the screen.

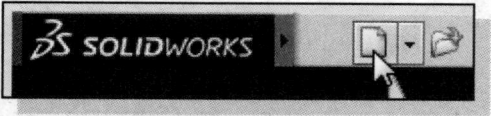

2. Select the **New** icon with a single click of the left-mouse-button on the *Menu Bar*.

3. Select the **Part** icon with a single click of the left-mouse-button in the *New SolidWorks Document* dialog box.

4. Select **OK** in the *New SolidWorks Document* dialog box to start a new part document.

5. Select the **Options** icon from the *Menu Bar* to open the *Options* dialog box.

6. Select the **Document Properties** tab.

7. Select **ANSI** in the pull-down selection window under the *Overall drafting standard* panel as shown.

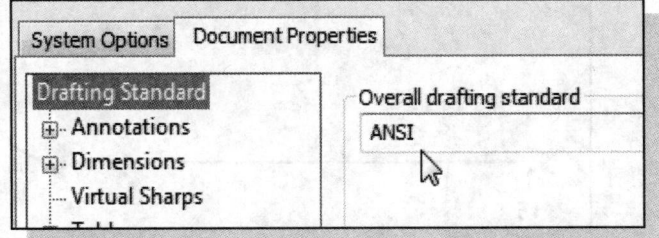

8. Click on the **Units** option. We will use the default **MMGS (millimeter, gram, second)** unit system as instructed in the problem definition.

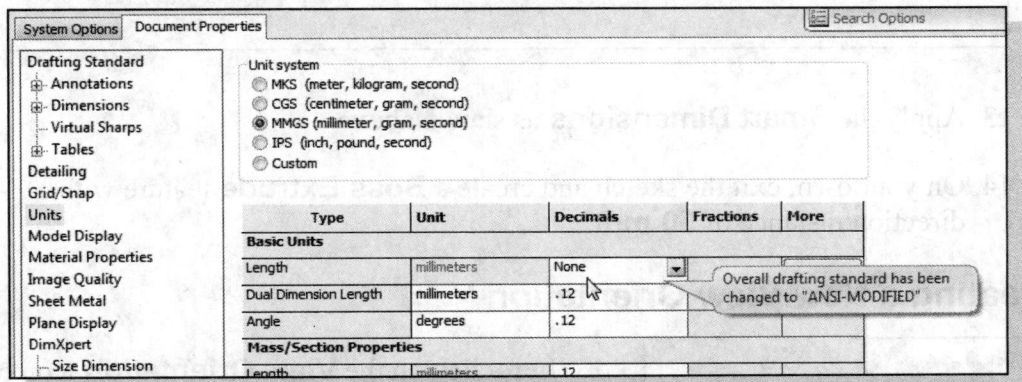

9. Select **None** in the *Decimals* spin box for the *Length units* as shown to define the display of digits after the decimal point. Click **OK** to accept the settings.

10. Select the **Extruded Boss/Base** button on the *Features* toolbar to create a new extruded feature.

11. Select the **Front** (XY) **Plane** as the sketch plane for the new sketch.

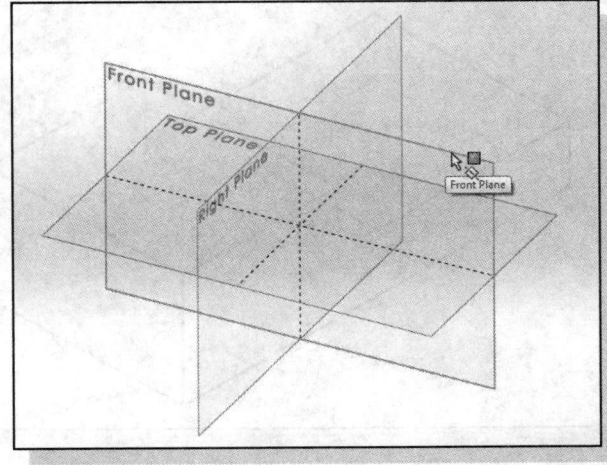

12. On your own, create the sketch with the lower left corner coincident with the origin, the long edge aligned with the positive X-axis, and the short edge aligned with the positive Y-axis as shown below.

13. Apply the **Smart Dimensions** as shown above.

14. On your own, exit the sketch and create a **Boss Extrude** feature with a Z-direction distance of **50 mm**.

Creating a New View Orientation

1. Left-click on the **View Orientation** icon on the *Heads-up View* toolbar to reveal the *View Orientation* pull-down menu. Select the **Isometric** command.

2. If necessary, use the *Hide/Show* pull-down menu on the *Heads-up View* toolbar to turn *ON* the **origin**'s visibility.

➤ Notice the axes are aligned correctly relative to the part, but the default isometric view does not correspond to the view orientation used in defining the problem. We will create a new view orientation which better matches the view used in defining the problem (page 15-5).

3. Left-click on the **View Orientation** icon on the *Heads-up View* toolbar to reveal the *View Orientation* pull-down menu. Select the **Front** command.

4. Hit the right arrow button [→] three times to rotate the view 45º.

5. Hit the down arrow button [↓] three times to rotate the view 45º.

➢ The view should appear as shown here. This view orientation corresponds to the one in the problem definition. We will want to return to this view as we continue working on the part. SolidWorks allows the user to define a new view orientation for this purpose.

6. Select **New View** in the *Heads-up View* display toolbar as shown.

7. Enter **Custom** as the name for the new view and click **OK**.

8. Left-click on the **View Orientation** icon on the *Heads-up View* toolbar to reveal the *View Orientation* pull-down menu. Notice the *Custom* view we created now appears as an option.

Completing the Part

➤ We will now create the reference geometry needed to create the inclined feature. To create an inclined reference plane, we must select an existing plane and an axis of rotation. The strategy we will use for creating the inclined reference plane involves three steps: (1) create a vertical reference plane offset from the left face by 30 mm; (2) create a reference axis at the intersection of the offset plane and the top face of the base feature; and (3) create the inclined reference plane by rotating the top face of the base feature about the reference axis.

1. Select the **Reference Geometry** command from the *Features* toolbar, and select the **Plane** option from the pull-down menu.

2. Move the cursor over the left face of the base feature as shown below. Click once with the **left-mouse-button** to select the face.

3. Notice the face, called **Face<1>**, appears in the *First Reference* panel of the *Plane Property Manager*, and the **Offset Distance** option is automatically selected.

4. Check the **Flip** option box and enter **30 mm** as the offset distance.

5. Click **OK** in the *Property Manager* to accept the settings and create the new reference plane.

6. Press the **[Esc]** key to unselect the new plane.

7. In the *Features* toolbar, select the **Reference Geometry** command by left-clicking the icon.

8. In the pull-down option menu of the Reference Geometry command, select the **Axis** option.

9. In the *Selections* panel of the *Axis Property Manager*, select the **Two Planes** option. (We will define the reference axis as the intersection of the offset reference plane and top face of the base feature.)

10. Select the offset reference plane, **Plane1**, in the *Design Tree* (expand the *Design Tree* in the graphics area if necessary) and the **top face of the base feature** in the graphics area.

11. Click **OK** in the *Property Manager* to create the new reference axis.

12. Press the [**Esc**] key to ensure no features are selected.

13. Select the **Reference Geometry** command from the *Features* toolbar, and select the **Plane** option from the pull-down menu.

14. Select **Axis1** (the reference axis created above) as the *First Reference* and the **top face of the base feature** as the *Second Reference*.

15. In the *Second Reference* panel of the *Plane Property Manager*, select the **At Angle** option button.

16. Enter **45 deg** as the angle in the *Property Manager*. The preview of the new plane should appear as in the figure below.

17. Click **OK** in the *Property Manager* to create the new reference plane.

➢ We now have the correct inclined reference plane on which to sketch the inclined feature.

18. On your own, create an **Extruded Boss/Base** feature, with the sketch shown, using the inclined reference plane, **Plane2**, as the sketch plane. (**NOTE:** Use the **Normal to** view orientation to view the sketch plane as shown.)

19. Left-click on the **View Orientation** icon on the *Heads-up View* toolbar to reveal the *View Orientation* pull-down menu. Select the **Custom** view that we created earlier.

20. On your own, complete an **Extruded Boss** feature as shown below. (**NOTE:** Use the **Reverse Direction** option if necessary. Use the **Up To Next** option for the *end condition*.)

21. On your own, create another **Extruded Boss** feature with the sketch as shown using the inclined face as the sketch plane.

22. Complete the 10 mm **Extruded Boss** feature as shown below.

23. On your own, create the extruded cut features necessary to complete the part. (See page 15-5 for dimensions.)

24. On your own, save the part with the filename *Problem1.SLDPRT*.

Selecting the Material and Viewing the Mass Properties

1. Right-click on the **Material** icon in the *Feature Manger Design Tree* and select **Edit Material** from the pop-up menu.

2. In the *Material* pop-up window, select **Ductile Iron** (in the Iron folder) as the material type. Notice the density listed in the *Material Property* table is 0.0071 g/mm³, as required in the problem statement.

3. Click **Apply** to select the material and **Close** the *Material* window.

4. Select the **Mass Properties** option on the *Tools* pull-down menu.

> ➢ The *Mass Properties* window is displayed. Notice the *Output coordinate system* is the **default** system.

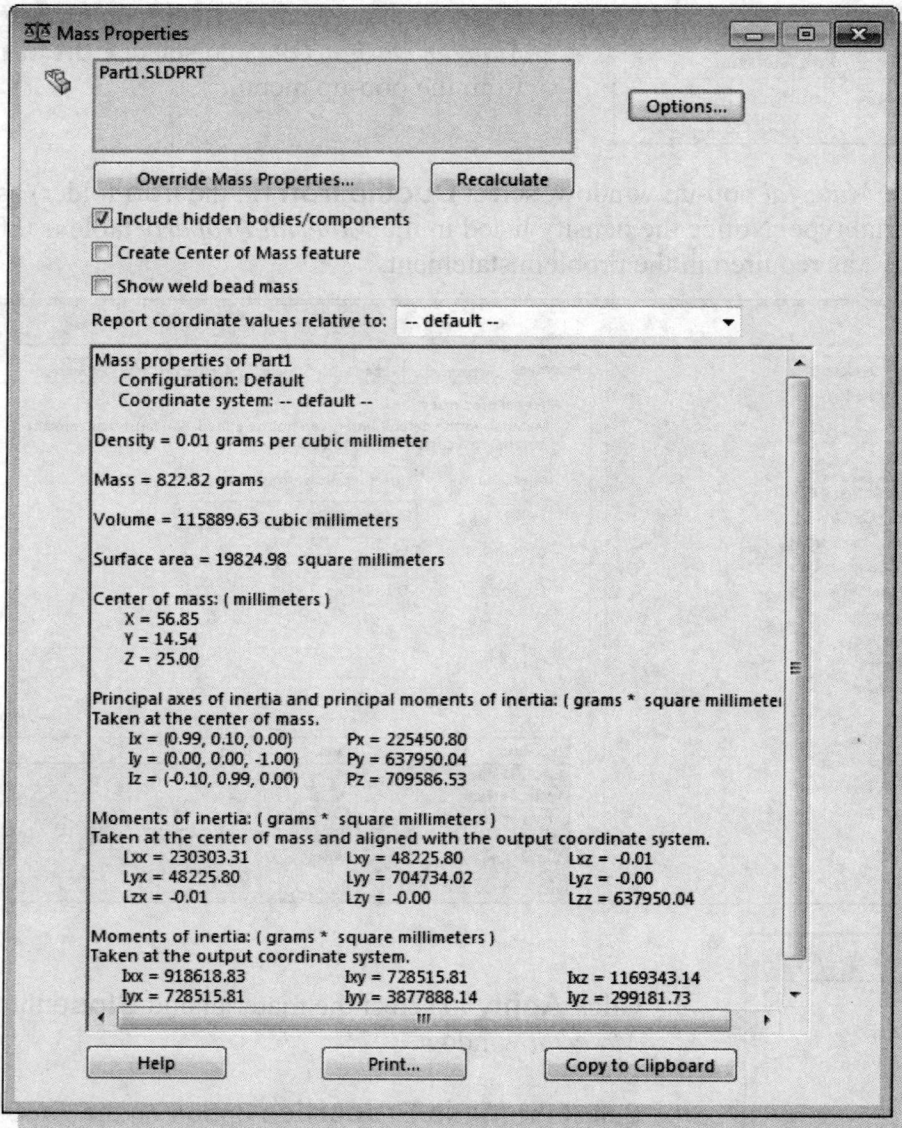

> ➢ Notice the *Mass* is **822.82 grams**.

> ➢ Notice the *Center of mass* is:
> **X = 56.85 mm**
> **Y = 14.54 mm**
> **Z = 25.00 mm**

> ➢ Look again at the problem on page 15-5. Note that the *Center of mass* coordinates above are based on the correct origin and along the correct X, Y, Z directions.

> ➢ Notice that *Moments of Inertia* are also reported.

➤ Look at the part in the graphics area. (Minimize the *Mass Properties* window if necessary.)

➤ Notice the center of mass and the principal axes are displayed. On your own, view the part from different directions and observe the location of the center of mass.

➤ Also displayed are the origin and coordinate axes used as the basis for the calculated properties. Verify that we have successfully created our part in the correct orientation based on the problem statement. The values for the center of mass in the *Mass Properties* dialog box therefore represent the correct values for the problem as stated.

5. **Close** the *Mass Properties* window.

6. On your own, save the part with the filename ***Problem1.SLDPRT***.

➤ We have successfully completed the problem. The part was created using the coordinate axes defined in the problem statement and the mass and center of mass were obtained. The SolidWorks **Mass Properties** tool provides an efficient method to obtain properties of parts and/or assemblies with complex shapes.

The Assembly Problem

We will model the assembly shown below and use the **Mass Properties** tool to determine the mass and center of mass of the assembly. The problem is presented below in a manner similar to that encountered on the CSWA exam.

Build the assembly shown.

It contains two **Brackets** and two **Rods**.

Unit system: MMGS (millimeter, gram, second)

Assembly origin: as shown.

Brackets: A dimensioned figure appears to the right (holes through all). The 1 mm radius notch is semicircular and located with its center 25 mm from the bottom edge of the bracket. Material: 1060 Alloy; Density = 0.0027 g/mm^3.

Rods: 10 mm in diameter and 150 mm long, with 1mm x 45° chamfers at each end. Material: 201 Annealed Stainless Steel (SS); Density = 0.00786 g/mm^3.

Questions:

    (1) What is the overall mass of the assembly in grams?

    (2) What is the center of mass of the assembly?

➢ Before starting to build the model, it is important to select a strategy for controlling the origin and orientation of the X, Y, and Z axes since the center of mass must be defined relative to a known reference system. The axis directions are defined in the drawing. We will build the part independent of this constraint and, after the part is complete, create a **reference coordinate system** aligned with the part as shown in the figure.

Creating the Parts

1. On your own, start a new part file using the default **Part** template in the *SolidWorks* Templates folder.

2. Select the **Options** icon from the *Menu Bar* to open the *Options* dialog box. Select the **Document Properties** tab.

3. On your own, set the *Overall drafting standard* to **ANSI** and the *Units* to the default **MMGS (millimeter, gram, second)** unit system as instructed in the problem definition.

4. On your own, create the *Bracket* using the dimensions shown in the figure in the previous section. Build the part so that the isometric view appears as shown.

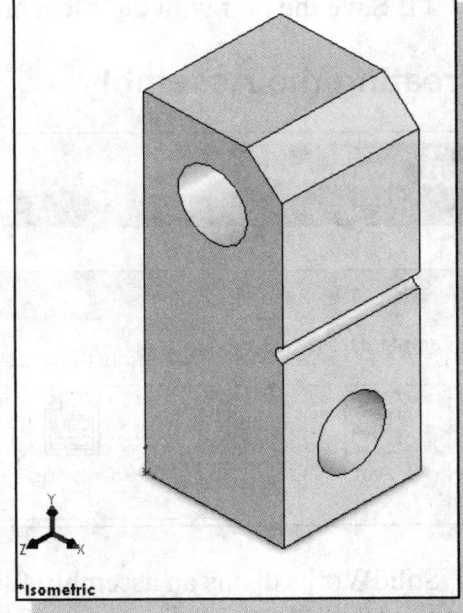

➢ Note the axis alignment is intentionally set to the lower left corner, which is not matching the problem definition. We will address this later using the **Reference Coordinate System** tool.

5. Right-click on the **Material** icon in the *Feature Manger Design Tree* and select **Edit Material** from the pop-up menu.

6. In the *Material* pop-up window, select **1060 Alloy** (in the Aluminum Alloys folder) as the material type.

7. Save the part with the filename **Bracket.SLDPRT**.

8. On your own, start a new part file using the default **Part** template in the SolidWorks Templates folder, set the *Overall drafting standard* to **ANSI** and the *Units* to the default **MMGS (millimeter, gram, second)** unit system.

9. On your own, create the *Rod* using the description in the previous section. Build the part so that the isometric view appears as shown. (**HINT:** Draw a circle on the Front Plane and extrude.)

*Isometric

10. On your own, set the material to **201 Annealed Stainless Steel (SS)** (in the Steel folder).

11. Save the part with the filename **Rod.SLDPRT**.

Creating the Assembly

1. Select the **New** icon with a single click of the left-mouse-button on the *Menu Bar*. The *New SolidWorks Document* dialog box appears.

2. Select the **Templates** tab and select the **Assembly** icon as shown.

3. Click **OK** to open the new Assembly file.

> SolidWorks opens an assembly file, and automatically opens the *Begin Assembly Property Manager*. The message "*Select a part or assembly to insert ...*" appears in the *Property Manager*. SolidWorks expects you to insert the first component.

> The *Part/Assembly to Insert* panel displays *Open documents*, including the *Bracket* and *Rod* parts.

4. Select the *Bracket* part as the base part for the assembly by clicking on **Bracket** in the *Part/Assembly to Insert* panel. (**NOTE:** If you have closed the *Bracket* part, it will not appear. In that case, click the Browse button and use the browser to open the *Bracket* part file.)

5. By default, the component is automatically aligned to the origin of the assembly coordinates. Click **OK** in the *Property Manager* to place the *Bracket* at the origin.

6. On your own, set the *Overall drafting standard* to **ANSI** and the *Units* to the default **MMGS (millimeter, gram, second)** unit system.
(**HINT**: Select Tools → Option → Document Properties.)

7. In the *Assembly* toolbar, select the **Insert Component** command by left-mouse-clicking the icon.

8. Select the *Rod* part in the *Part/Assembly to Insert* panel. (**NOTE:** If you have closed the *Rod* part, it will not appear. In that case, click the **Browse** button and use the browser to open the *Rod* part file.)

9. Place the *Rod* in the graphics area as shown in the figure. Click once with the **left-mouse-button** to place the component.

10. In the *Assembly* toolbar, select the **Mate** command by left-mouse-clicking once on the icon.

11. Select the **external cylindrical face** of the *Rod* as the first surface for the Mate, and the **interior cylindrical race** of the *Bracket* as the second face for the Mate, as shown.

12. A Concentric mate is applied by default. Click the **OK** button in the *Property Manager* to accept the settings and create the **Concentric** mate.

❖ We will now add a **Distance** mate to define the position of the *Rod* relative to the *Bracket* as defined in the problem statement.

13. Rotate the view (e.g., using the arrow keys) to display the reverse side of the *Rod* and *Bracket* as shown below.

14. Select the **edge face** of the *Rod* and the **side face** of the **Bracket** as shown below.

➢ SolidWorks will apply a **Coincident** mate by default. We want to apply a mate which is offset by a specific distance (30 mm as defined by the problem statement).

15. Select the *Distance* option by clicking the **Distance** button in the *Standard Mates* panel of the *Property Manager*.

16. Enter **30 mm** as the distance.

17. Click the **OK** button in the *Property Manager* to accept the settings and create the **Distance** mate.

18. Click **OK** again (or hit the [**Esc**] key) to exit the **Mate** command.

19. On your own, return to the **Isometric** view.

20. In the *Assembly* toolbar, select the **Insert Component** command by left-clicking the icon.

21. Select the *Bracket* part as the base part for the assembly by clicking on **Bracket** in the *Part/Assembly to Insert* panel.

22. Place the *Bracket* in the graphics area as shown in the figure. Click once with the **left-mouse-button** to place the component.

23. In the *Assembly* toolbar, select the **Mate** command by left-clicking once on the icon.

24. Select the **external cylindrical face** of the *Rod* as the first surface for the Mate, and the **interior cylindrical race** of *Bracket<2>* as the second face for the Mate, as shown.

25. An Anti-Aligned Concentric mate is applied by default. On your own, select the **Aligned** option at the bottom of the *Standard Mates* panel and observe the effect on the assembly.

26. Select the **Anti-Aligned** option. Look at the drawing in the problem statement to verify that it is the Anti-Aligned option that is required.

27. Click the **OK** button in the *Property Manager* to accept the settings and create the **Anti-Aligned Concentric** mate.

❖ We will now add a Distance mate to define the position of *Bracket<2>* relative to *Bracket<1>* as defined in the problem statement.

28. Select the **face** of *Bracket<1>* as shown.

29. Rotate the view and select the **face** of *Bracket<2>* as shown.

30. Select the *Distance* option by clicking the **Distance** button in the *Standard Mates* panel of the *Property Manager*.

31. Enter **50 mm** as the distance.

32. Click the **OK** button in the *Property Manager* to accept the settings and create the **Distance** mate.

❖ We will now add an Angle mate to define the angular orientation of *Bracket<2>* relative to *Bracket<1>* as defined in the problem statement.

33. Select the **face** of *Bracket<1>* as shown.

34. Select the *Angle* option by clicking the **Angle** button in the *Standard Mates* panel of the *Property Manager*.

35. Enter **60°** as the angle.

36. Select the **face** of *Bracket<1>* as shown, check the **Flip dimension** box **if necessary** to set the angle as shown in the figure below.

37. Click the **OK** button in the *Property Manager* to accept the settings and create the **Angle** mate as shown.

38. Click **OK** again (or hit the [**Esc**] key) to exit the Mate command.

39. On your own, use the **Insert Component** command to insert a second *Rod* part.

40. On your own, create a **concentric** mate to align the *Rod* to *Bracket<2>*.

41. On your own, create a **Distance-100mm** mate to define the position of *Rod<2>* relative to *Bracket<2>* as defined in the problem statement.

42. Compare the assembly to the drawing in the problem statement. Note that the locations and orientations of the brackets (particularly the locations of the chamfers and notches) and rods are correct.

43. On your own, save the assembly with the filename *Problem2.SLDASM*.

Creating a Reference Coordinate System

We have created the assembly without aligning it with the origin and coordinate axes defined in the problem statement. In order to calculate the center of mass relative to the correct origin and coordinate axes we will create a Reference Coordinate System.

➤ The Reference Coordinate System will be defined to be aligned with the edges of the base bracket (*Bracket<1>* in our assembly) as shown in the figure defining the problem.

1. In the *Assembly* toolbar, select the **Reference Geometry** command by left-clicking the icon.

2. In the pull-down option menu of the Reference Geometry command, select the **Coordinate System** option.

3. The *Coordinate System Property Manager* opens with the *Origin* selection window active. Select the **lower right corner** of *Bracket<1>* as the origin, as shown.

➤ The origin selection appears in the *Property-Manager* as **Vertex<1>@Bracket-1**.

4. The *X-axis* selection window is now active. We want to align the X-axis with the **bottom edge on the right face** of *Bracket<1>*. Move the cursor over the edge and click once with the left-mouse-button to **select** it.

➤ The X-axis selection appears in the *Property Manager* as Edge<1>@Bracket-1. Look at the coordinate icon which is now attached to the newly defined reference origin. Notice the X-axis in the figure is aligned with the correct edge, but the positive X-axis points in the wrong direction.

5. In the *Property Manager*, select the **Reverse X Axis Direction** option by clicking once with the left-mouse-button on the toggle button located to the left of the *X axis* selection window (if necessary).

6. Verify that the X-axis is now aligned with the correct edge and points in the correct direction.

7. The *Y-axis* selection window is now active. We want to align the Y-axis with the **right edge of the right face** of **Bracket<1>**. Move the cursor over the edge and click once with the left-mouse-button to **select** it.

8. The Y-axis selection appears in the *Property Manager* as Edge<2>@Bracket-1. Verify that the Y-axis is aligned with the correct edge, and the positive Y-axis points in the correct direction. (If the positive Y-axis points in the wrong direction, use the Reverse Y Axis Direction option to correct it.)

9. The origin and coordinate axes are now aligned as defined in the problem statement. Click **OK** in the *Property Manager* to accept the setting and create the **Reference Coordinate System**.

➤ Notice the **Reference Coordinate System** appears in the *Feature Manager Design Tree* as **Coordinate System1**, and that the reference axes correspond to the axes defined in the problem statement. We are now ready to calculate the *mass properties*.

View the Mass Properties

1. Select the **Mass Properties** option on the *Tools* pull-down menu.

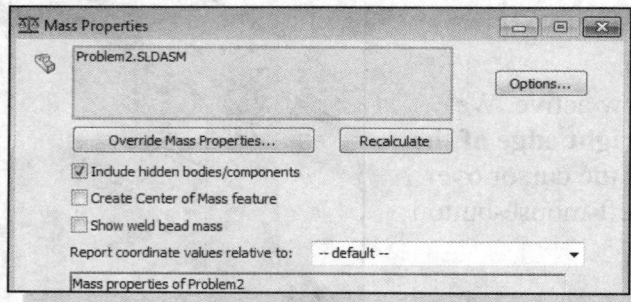

2. The *Mass Properties* window is displayed. Notice the *Report coordinate system* is the **default** system.

➤ In the graphics area, the **default** coordinate system in shown. The values appearing in the *Mass Properties* window were calculated relative to this coordinate system. These are **not** the results we need for the solution to the problem.

➤ We must change the *Report coordinate system* to the **Reference Coordinate System** we created.

3. Inside the *Mass Property* window, **left-click** on the arrow at the right end of the *Report coordinate system:* selection window, and select **Coordinate System1** from the selection list.

➤ Coordinate System1 is now the basis for the mass property calculations. Notice the calculated values for the center of mass (and other properties) change to those for the new coordinate system.

➤ Notice the coordinate system displayed in the graphics area is the correct system for the problem.

➤ Notice the *Mass* is **274.25 grams**.

➤ Notice the *Center of mass* is:

X = -56.76 mm
Y = 53.95 mm
Z = -14.95 mm

4. **Close** the *Mass Properties* window.

5. On your own, save the part with the filename ***Problem2.SLDASM***.

➤ We have successfully completed the problem. The correct alignment of the coordinate system was accomplished through the creation of a Reference Coordinate System. The SolidWorks **Reference Coordinate System** and **Mass Properties** tools can be used in combination to obtain mass properties of complex parts and assemblies relative to a specific coordinate system.

Questions:

1. How do we save a new *View Orientation* for future use?

2. Describe the effect of using the *Up to Next* end condition for an extruded boss feature.

3. How can we view the mass of a part or assembly?

4. Describe the steps in creating a **Reference Coordinate System**.

5. What mass properties are dependent on the selection of the output coordinate system?

6. What mass properties are independent of the selection of the output coordinate system?

7. How do we control the output coordinate system used in calculating mass properties?

8. How can we apply an assembly mate establishing an offset distance between two planes or faces?

Exercises:

1. Build the part shown below.
   Unit system: IPS (inch, pound, second)
   Part origin: As shown.
   Part material: AISI 1020
   Density: 0.285406 lb/in^3

What is the overall mass of the part in pounds?

What is the center of mass of the part?

Answer:

Mass:
   18.58 pounds

Center of mass:
   X = -6.07 inches
   Y = 1.91 inches
   Z = -1.98 inches

2. Build the assembly in SolidWorks. The assembly includes 8 components – 1 base, 1 jaw, 2 keys, 1 screw, 1 handle rod, 2 handle knobs.
    Use the IPS (inch, pound, second) unit system.

Base: A dimensioned figure appears to the right. The 1.5 inch wide and 1.25 inch wide slots are cut through the entire base.
Material: Gray Cast Iron
Density = 0.260116 lb/in³

Jaw: A dimensioned figure appears to the right. The shoulder of the jaw rests on the flat surface of the base and the jaw opening is set to 1.5 inches.
Material: Gray Cast Iron
Density = 0.260116 lb/in^3

Key: 0.1875 inch H x 0.375 inch W x 1.75 inch L. The keys fit into the slots on the jaw with the edge faces flush as shown in the sub-assembly to the right.
Material: Alloy Steel
Density = 0.27818 lb/in^3.

Screw: A dimensioned figure appears to the right. There is one chamfered edge (0.0625 inch x 45°). The flat ⌀ 0.75″ edge of the screw is flush with the corresponding recessed ⌀ 0.75 face on the jaw.
Material: Alloy Steel
Density = 0.27818 lb/in^3

Handle Rod: $\emptyset$ 0.375″ x 5.0″ L. The handle rod passes through the hole in the screw and is rotated to an angle of 30° with the horizontal as shown in the assembly view. The flat $\emptyset$ 0.375″ edges of the handle rod are flush with the corresponding recessed $\emptyset$ 0.735 faces on the handle knobs.
Material: Alloy Steel
Density = 0.27818 lb/in³.

Handle Knob: A dimensioned figure appears to the right. There are two chamfered edges (0.0625 inch x 45°). The handle knobs are attached to each end of the handle rod. The resulting overall length of the handle with knobs is 5.50″. The handle is aligned with the screw so that the outer edge of the upper knob is 2.0″ from the central axis of the screw.
Material: Alloy Steel
Density = 0.27818 lb/in³

What is the mass of the assembly?

What is the center of mass of the assembly with respect to the coordinate system illustrated in the assembly view?

Answer:

Mass:
    17.52 pounds

Center of mass:
    X = 1.74 inches
    Y = 1.75 inches
    Z = 3.98 inches

APPENDIX A

Running and Sliding Fits – American National Standard

Basic Hole System, Limits are in thousandths of an inch.
Limits for hole and shaft are applied to the basic size to obtain
the limits of sizes for the parts.

Nominal Size Range, Inches Over To	Class RC1 Limits of Clearance	Standard Limits Hole H5	Shaft g4	Class RC2 Limits of Clearance	Standard Limits Hole H6	Shaft g5	Class RC3 Limits of Clearance	Standard Limits Hole H7	Shaft f6	Class RC4 Limits of Clearance	Standard Limits Hole H8	Shaft f7
0 – 0.12	0.1 0.45	+0.2 +0	-0.1 -0.25	0.1 0.55	+0.25 0	-0.1 -0.3	0.3 0.95	+0.4 0	-0.3 -0.55	0.3 1.3	+0.6 0	-0.3 -0.7
0.12 – 0.24	0.15 0.5	+0.2 0	-0.15 -0.3	0.15 0.65	+0.3 0	-0.15 -0.35	0.4 1.12	+0.5 0	-0.4 -0.7	0.4 1.6	+0.7 0	-0.4 -0.9
0.24 – 0.40	0.2 0.6	+0.25 0	-0.2 -0.35	0.2 0.85	+0.4 0	-0.2 -0.45	0.5 1.5	+0.6 0	-0.5 -0.9	0.5 2.0	+0.9 0	-0.5 -1.1
0.40 – 0.71	0.25 0.75	+0.3 +0	-0.25 -0.45	0.25 0.95	+0.4 0	-0.25 -0.55	0.6 1.7	+0.7 0	-0.6 -1.0	0.6 2.3	+1.0 0	-0.6 -1.3
0.71 – 1.19	0.3 0.95	+0.4 0	-0.3 -0.55	0.3 1.2	+0.5 0	-0.3 -0.7	0.8 2.1	+0.8 0	-0.8 -1.3	0.8 2.8	+1.2 0	-0.8 -1.6
1.19 – 1.97	0.4 1.1	+0.4 0	-0.4 -0.7	0.4 1.4	+0.6 0	-0.4 -0.8	1.0 2.6	+1.0 0	-1.0 -1.6	1.0 3.6	+1.6 0	-1.0 -2.0
1.97 – 3.15	0.4 1.2	+0.5 0	-0.4 -0.7	0.4 1.6	+0.7 0	-0.4 -0.9	1.2 3.1	+1.2 0	-1.2 -1.9	1.2 4.2	+1.8 0	-1.2 -2.4
3.15 – 4.73	0.5 1.5	+0.6 0	-0.5 -0.9	0.5 2.0	+0.9 0	-0.5 -1.1	1.4 3.7	+1.4 0	-1.4 -2.3	1.4 5.0	+2.2 0	-1.4 -2.8
4.73 – 7.09	0.6 1.8	+0.7 0	-0.6 -1.1	0.6 2.3	+1.0 0	-0.6 -1.3	1.6 4.2	+1.6 0	-1.6 -2.6	1.6 5.7	+2.5 0	-1.6 -3.2
7.09 – 9.85	0.6 2.0	+0.8 0	-0.6 -1.2	0.6 2.6	+1.2 0	-0.6 -1.4	2.0 5.0	+1.8 0	-2.0 -3.2	2.0 6.6	+2.8 0	-2.0 -3.8
9.85 – 12.41	0.8 2.3	+0.9 0	-0.8 -1.4	0.8 2.9	+1.2 0	-0.7 -1.6	2.5 5.7	+2.0 0	-2.5 -3.7	2.5 7.5	+3.0 0	-2.2 -4.2
12.41 – 15.75	1.0 2.7	+1.0 0	-1.0 -1.7	1.0 3.4	+1.4 0	-0.7 -1.7	3.0 6.6	+2.2 0	-3.0 -4.4	3.0 8.7	+3.5 0	-2.5 -4.7
15.75 – 19.69	1.2 3.0	+1.0 0	-1.2 -2.0	0.8 3.4	+1.6 0	-0.8 -1.8	4.0 8.1	+2.5 0	-4.0 -5.6	2.8 9.3	+4.0 0	-2.8 -5.3

USAS/ASME B4.1 – 1967 (R2004) Standard. For larger diameters, see the standard. ASME/ANSI B18.3.5M – 1986 (R2002) Standard. Reprinted from the standard listed by permission of the American Society of Mechanical Engineers. All rights reserved.

APPENDIX A (Continued)

Running and Sliding Fits – American National Standard

Basic Hole System, Limits are in thousandths of an inch.
Limits for hole and shaft are applied to the basic size to obtain
the limits of sizes for the parts.

Nominal size Range, Inches Over To	Class RC5			Class RC6			Class RC7			Class RC8			Class RC9		
	Limits of Clearance	Standard Limits		Limits of Clearance	Standard Limits		Limits of Clearance	Standard Limits		Limits of Clearance	Standard Limits		Limits of Clearance	Standard Limits	
		Hole H8	Shaft e7		Hole H9	Shaft e8		Hole H9	Shaft d8		Hole H10	Shaft C9		Hole H11	Shaft
0 – 0.12	0.6 1.6	+0.6 0	-0.6 -1.0	0.6 2.2	+1.0 0	+0.6 -1.2	1.0 2.6	+1.0 0	-1.0 -1.6	2.5 5.1	+1.6 0	-2.5 -3.5	4.0 8.1	+2.5 0	-4.0 -5.6
0.12 – 0.24	0.8 2.0	+0.7 0	-0.8 -1.3	0.8 2.7	+1.2 0	-0.8 -1.5	1.2 3.1	+1.2 0	-1.2 -1.9	2.8 5.8	+1.8 0	-2.8 -4.0	4.5 9.0	+3.0 0	-4.5 -6.0
0.24 – 0.40	1.0 2.5	+0.9 0	-1.0 -1.6	1.0 3.3	+1.4 0	-1.0 -1.9	1.6 3.9	+1.4 0	-1.6 -2.5	3.0 6.6	+2.2 0	-3.0 -4.4	5.0 10.7	+3.5 0	-5.0 -7.2
0.40 – 0.71	1.2 2.9	+1.0 0	-1.2 -1.9	1.2 3.8	+1.6 0	-1.2 -2.2	2.0 4.6	+1.6 0	-2.0 -3.0	3.5 7.9	+2.8 0	-3.5 -5.1	6.0 12.8	+4.0 0	-6.0 -8.8
0.71 – 1.19	1.6 3.6	+1.2 0	-1.6 -2.4	1.6 4.8	+2.0 0	-1.6 -2.8	2.5 5.7	+2.0 0	-2.5 -3.7	4.5 10.0	+3.5 0	-4.5 -6.5	7.0 15.5	+5.0 0	-7.0 -10.5
1.19 – 1.97	2.0 4.6	+1.6 0	-2.0 -3.0	2.0 6.1	+2.5 0	-2.0 -3.6	3.0 7.1	+2.5 0	-3.0 -4.6	5.0 11.5	+4.0 0	-5.0 -7.5	8.0 18.0	+6.0 0	-8.0 12.0
1.97 – 3.15	2.5 5.5	+1.8 0	-2.5 -3.7	2.5 7.3	+3.0 0	-2.5 -4.3	4.0 8.8	+3.0 0	-4.0 -5.8	6.0 13.5	+4.5 0	-6.0 -9.0	9.0 20.5	+7.0 0	-9.0 -13.5
3.15 – 4.73	3.0 6.6	+2.2 0	-3.0 -4.4	3.0 8.7	+3.5 0	-3.0 -5.2	5.0 10.7	+3.5 0	-5.0 -7.2	7.0 15.5	+5.0 0	-7.0 -10.5	10.0 24.0	+9.0 0	-10.0 -15.0
4.73 – 7.09	3.5 7.6	+2.5 0	-3.5 -5.1	3.5 10.0	+4.0 0	-3.5 -6.0	6.0 12.5	+4.0 0	-6.0 -8.5	8.0 18.0	+6.0 0	-8.0 -12.0	12.0 28.0	+10.0 0	-12.0 -18.0
7.09 – 9.85	4.0 8.6	+2.8 0	-4.0 -5.8	4.0 11.3	+4.5 0	-4.0 -6.8	7.0 14.3	+4.5 0	-7.0 -9.8	10.0 21.5	+7.0 0	-10.0 -14.5	15.0 34.0	+12.0 0	-15.0 -22.0
9.85–12.41	5.0 10.0	+3.0 0	-5.0 -7.0	5.0 13.0	+5.0 0	-5.0 -8.0	8.0 16.0	+5.0 0	-8.0 -11	12.0 25.0	+8.0 0	-12.0 -17.0	18.0 38.0	+12.0 0	-18.0 -26.0
12.41– 15.75	6.0 11.7	+3.5 0	-6.0 -8.2	6.0 15.5	+6.0 0	-6.0 -9.5	10.0 19.5	+6.0 0	-10 -13.5	14.0 29.0	+9.0 0	-14.0 -20.0	22.0 45.0	+14.0 0	-22.0 -31.0
15.75– 19.69	8.0 14.5	+4.0 0	-8.0 -10.5	8.0 18.0	+6.0 0	-8.0 -12.0	12.0 22.0	+6.0 0	-12.0 -16.0	16.0 32.0	+10.0 0	-16.0 -22.0	25.0 51.0	+16.0 0	-25.0 -35.0

APPENDIX B – METRIC LIMITS AND FITS

Hole Basis Clearance Fits

Preferred Hole Basis Clearance Fits. Dimensions in mm.

Basic Size	Loose Running		Free Running		Close Running		Sliding		Locational Clearance	
	Hole H11	Shaft c11	Hole H9	Shaft d9	Hole H8	Shaft f7	Hole H7	Shaft g6	Hole H7	Shaft h6
1 max	1.060	0.940	1.025	0.980	1.014	0.994	1.010	0.998	1.010	1.000
min	1.000	0.880	1.000	0.955	1.000	0.984	1.000	0.992	1.000	0.994
1.2 max	1.260	0.940	1.225	1.180	1.214	1.194	1.210	1.198	1.210	1.200
min	1.200	0.880	1.200	1.155	1.200	1.184	1.200	1.192	1.200	1.194
1.6 max	1.660	1.540	1.625	1.580	1.614	1.594	1.610	1.598	1.610	1.600
min	1.600	1.480	1.600	1.555	1.600	1.584	1.600	1.592	1.600	1.594
2 max	2.060	1.940	2.025	1.980	2.014	1.994	2.010	1.998	2.010	2.000
min	2.000	1.880	2.000	1.955	2.000	1.984	2.000	1.992	2.000	1.994
2.5 max	2.560	2.440	2.525	2.480	2.514	2.494	2.510	2.498	2.510	2.500
min	2.500	2.380	2.500	2.455	2.500	2.484	2.500	2.492	2.500	2.494
3 max	3.060	2.940	3.025	2.980	3.014	2.994	3.010	2.998	3.010	3.000
min	3.000	2.880	3.000	2.955	3.000	2.984	3.000	2.992	3.000	2.994
4 max	4.075	3.930	4.030	3.970	4.018	3.990	4.012	3.996	4.012	4.000
min	4.000	3.855	4.000	3.940	4.000	3.987	4.000	3.988	4.000	3.992
5 max	5.075	4.930	5.030	4.970	5.018	4.990	5.012	4.998	5.012	5.000
min	5.000	4.855	5.000	4.940	5.000	4.978	5.000	4.988	5.000	4.992
6 max	6.075	5.930	6.030	5.970	6.018	5.990	6.012	5.996	6.012	6.000
min	6.000	5.855	6.000	5.940	6.000	5.978	6.000	5.988	6.000	5.992
8 max	8.090	7.920	8.036	7.960	8.022	7.987	8.015	7.995	8.015	8.000
min	8.000	7.830	8.000	7.924	8.000	7.972	8.000	7.986	8.000	7.991
10 max	10.090	9.920	10.036	9.960	10.022	9.987	10.015	9.995	10.015	10.000
min	10.000	9.830	10.000	9.924	10.000	9.972	10.000	9.986	10.000	9.991
12 max	12.110	11.905	12.043	11.950	12.027	11.984	12.018	11.994	12.018	12.000
min	12.000	11.795	12.000	11.907	12.000	11.966	12.000	11.983	12.000	11.989
16 max	16.110	15.905	16.043	15.950	16.027	15.984	16.018	15.994	16.018	16.000
min	16.000	15.795	16.000	15.907	16.000	15.966	16.000	15.983	16.000	15.989
20 max	20.130	19.890	20.052	19.935	20.033	19.980	20.021	19.993	20.021	20.000
min	20.000	19.760	20.000	19.883	20.000	19.959	20.000	19.980	20.000	19.987
25 max	25.130	24.890	25.052	24.935	25.033	24.980	24.993	25.021	25.021	25.000
min	25.000	24.760	25.000	24.883	25.000	24.959	24.980	25.000	25.000	24.987
30 max	30.130	29.890	30.052	29.935	30.033	29.980	30.021	29.993	30.021	30.000
min	30.000	29.760	30.000	29.883	30.000	29.959	30.000	29.980	30.000	29.987
40 max	40.160	39.880	40.062	39.920	40.039	39.975	40.025	39.991	40.025	40.000
min	40.000	39.720	40.000	39.858	40.000	39.950	40.000	39.975	40.000	39.984

APPENDIX B – METRIC LIMITS AND FITS (Continued)

Hole Basis Transition and Interference Fits

Preferred Hole Basis Clearance Fits. Dimensions in mm.

Basic Size		Locational Transition		Locational Transition		Locational Transition		Medium Drive		Force	
		Hole H7	Shaft k6	Hole H7	Shaft n6	Hole H7	Shaft p6	Hole H7	Shaft s6	Hole H7	Shaft u6
1	max	1.010	1.006	1.010	1.010	1.010	1.012	1.010	1.020	1.010	1.024
	min	1.000	1.000	1.000	1.004	1.000	1.006	1.000	1.014	1.000	1.018
1.2	max	1.210	1.206	1.210	1.210	1.210	1.212	1.210	1.220	1.210	1.224
	min	1.200	1.200	1.200	1.204	1.200	1.206	1.200	1.214	1.200	1.218
1.6	max	1.610	1.606	1.610	1.610	1.610	1.612	1.610	1.620	1.610	1.624
	min	1.600	1.600	1.600	1.604	1.600	1.606	1.600	1.614	1.600	1.618
2	max	2.010	2.006	2.010	2.020	2.010	2.012	2.010	2.020	2.010	2.024
	min	2.000	2.000	2.000	2.004	2.000	2.006	2.000	1.014	2.000	2.018
2.5	max	2.510	2.510	2.510	2.510	2.510	2.512	2.510	2.520	2.510	2.524
	min	2.500	2.500	2.500	2.504	2.500	2.506	2.500	2.514	2.500	2.518
3	max	3.010	3.010	3.010	3.010	3.010	3.012	3.010	3.020	3.010	3.024
	min	3.000	3.000	3.000	3.004	3.000	3.006	3.000	3.014	3.000	3.018
4	max	4.012	4.012	4.012	4.016	4.012	4.020	4.012	4.027	4.012	4.031
	min	4.000	4.000	4.000	4.008	4.000	4.012	4.000	4.019	4.000	4.023
5	max	5.012	5.009	5.012	5.016	5.012	5.020	5.012	5.027	5.012	5.031
	min	5.000	5.001	5.000	5.008	5.000	5.012	5.000	5.019	5.000	5.023
6	max	6.012	6.009	6.012	6.016	6.012	6.020	6.012	6.027	6.012	6.031
	min	6.000	6.001	6.000	6.008	6.000	6.012	6.000	6.019	6.000	6.023
8	max	8.015	8.010	8.015	8.019	8.015	8.024	8.015	8.032	8.015	8.037
	min	8.000	8.001	8.000	8.010	8.000	8.015	8.000	8.023	8.000	8.028
10	max	10.015	10.010	10.015	10.019	10.015	10.024	10.015	10.032	10.015	10.037
	min	10.000	10.001	10.000	10.010	10.000	10.015	10.000	10.023	10.000	10.028
12	max	12.018	12.012	12.018	12.023	12.018	12.029	12.018	12.039	12.018	12.044
	min	12.000	12.001	12.000	12.012	12.000	12.018	12.000	12.028	12.000	12.033
16	max	16.018	16.012	16.018	16.023	16.018	16.029	16.018	16.039	16.018	16.044
	min	16.000	16.001	16.000	16.012	16.000	16.018	16.000	16.028	16.000	16.033
20	max	20.021	20.015	20.021	20.028	20.021	20.035	20.021	20.048	20.021	20.054
	min	20.000	20.002	20.000	20.015	20.000	20.022	20.000	20.035	20.000	20.041
25	max	25.021	25.015	25.021	25.028	25.021	25.035	25.021	25.048	25.021	25.061
	min	25.000	25.002	25.000	25.015	25.000	25.022	25.000	25.035	25.000	25.048
30	max	30.021	30.015	30.021	30.028	30.021	30.035	30.021	30.048	30.021	30.061
	min	30.000	30.002	30.000	30.015	30.000	30.022	30.000	30.035	30.000	30.048
40	max	40.025	40.018	40.025	40.033	40.025	40.042	40.025	40.059	40.025	40.076
	min	40.000	40.002	40.000	40.017	40.000	40.026	40.000	40.043	40.000	40.060

APPENDIX B – METRIC LIMITS AND FITS (Continued)

Shaft Basis Clearance Fits

Preferred Shaft Basis Clearance Fits. Dimensions in mm.

Basic Size	Loose Running Hole C11	Shaft h11	Free Running Hole D9	Shaft h9	Close Running Hole F8	Shaft h7	Sliding Hole G7	Shaft h6	Locational Clearance Hole H7	Shaft h6
1 max	1.120	1.000	1.045	1.000	1.020	1.000	1.012	1.000	1.010	1.000
min	1.060	0.940	1.020	0.975	1.006	0.990	1.002	0.994	1.000	0.994
1.2 max	1.320	1.200	1.245	1.200	1.220	1.200	1.212	1.200	1.210	1.200
min	1.260	1.140	1.220	1.175	1.206	1.190	1.202	1.194	1.200	1.194
1.6 max	1.720	1.600	1.645	1.600	1.620	1.600	1.612	1.600	1.610	1.600
min	1.660	1.540	1.620	1.575	1.606	1.590	1.602	1.594	1.600	1.594
2 max	2.120	2.000	2.045	2.000	2.020	2.000	2.012	2.000	2.010	2.000
min	2.060	1.940	2.020	1.975	2.006	1.990	2.002	1.994	2.000	1.994
2.5 max	2.620	2.500	2.545	2.500	2.520	2.500	2.512	2.500	2.510	2.500
min	2.560	2.440	2.520	2.475	2.506	2.490	2.502	2.494	2.500	2.494
3 max	3.120	3.000	3.045	3.000	3.020	3.000	3.012	3.000	3.010	3.000
min	3.060	2.940	3.020	2.975	3.006	2.990	3.002	2.994	3.000	2.994
4 max	4.145	4.000	4.060	4.000	4.028	4.000	4.016	4.000	4.012	4.000
min	4.070	3.925	4.030	3.970	4.010	3.988	4.004	3.992	4.000	3.992
5 max	5.145	5.000	5.060	5.000	5.028	5.000	5.016	5.000	5.012	5.000
min	5.070	4.925	5.030	4.970	5.010	4.988	5.004	4.992	5.000	4.992
6 max	6.145	6.000	6.060	6.000	6.028	6.000	6.016	6.000	6.012	6.000
min	6.070	5.925	6.030	5.970	6.010	5.988	6.004	5.992	6.000	5.992
8 max	8.170	8.000	8.076	8.000	8.035	8.000	8.020	8.000	8.015	8.000
min	8.080	7.910	8.040	7.964	8.013	7.985	8.005	7.991	8.000	7.991
10 max	10.170	10.000	10.076	10.000	10.035	10.000	10.020	10.000	10.015	10.000
min	10.080	9.910	10.040	9.964	10.013	9.985	10.005	9.991	10.000	9.991
12 max	12.205	12.000	12.093	12.000	12.043	12.000	12.024	12.000	12.018	12.000
min	12.095	11.890	12.050	11.957	12.016	11.982	12.006	11.989	12.000	11.989
16 max	16.205	16.000	16.093	16.000	16.043	16.000	16.024	16.000	16.018	16.000
min	16.095	15.890	16.050	15.957	16.016	15.982	16.006	15.989	16.000	15.989
20 max	20.240	20.000	20.117	20.000	20.053	20.000	20.028	20.000	20.021	20.000
min	20.110	19.870	20.065	19.948	20.020	19.979	20.007	19.987	20.000	19.987
25 max	25.240	25.000	25.117	25.000	25.053	25.000	25.028	25.000	25.021	25.000
min	25.110	24.870	25.065	24.948	25.020	24.979	25.007	24.987	25.000	24.987
30 max	30.240	30.000	30.117	30.000	30.053	30.000	30.028	30.000	30.021	30.000
min	30.110	29.870	30.065	29.948	30.020	29.979	30.007	29.987	30.000	29.987
40 max	40.280	40.000	40.142	40.000	40.064	40.000	40.034	40.000	40.025	40.000
min	40.120	39.840	40.080	39.938	40.025	39.975	40.009	39.984	40.000	39.984

APPENDIX B - METRIC LIMITS AND FITS (Continued)

Shaft Basis Transition and Interference Fits

Preferred Shaft Basis Transition and Interference Fits. Dimensions in mm.

Basic Size	Locational Transition		Locational Transition		Locational Interference		Medium Drive		Force	
	Hole K7	Shaft h6	Hole N7	Shaft h6	Hole P7	Shaft h6	Hole S7	Shaft h6	Hole U7	Shaft h6
1 max	1.000	1.000	0.996	1.000	0.994	1.000	0.986	1.000	0.982	1.000
min	0.990	0.994	0.986	0.994	0.984	0.994	0.976	0.994	0.972	0.994
1.2 max	1.200	1.200	1.196	1.200	1.194	1.200	1.186	1.200	1.182	1.200
min	1.190	1.194	1.186	1.194	1.184	1.194	1.176	1.194	1.172	1.194
1.6 max	1.600	1.600	1.596	1.600	1.594	1.600	1.586	1.600	1.582	1.600
min	1.590	1.594	1.586	1.594	1.584	1.594	1.576	1.594	1.572	1.594
2 max	2.000	2.000	1.996	2.000	1.994	2.000	1.986	2.000	1.982	2.000
min	1.990	1.994	1.986	1.994	1.984	1.994	1.976	1.994	1.972	1.994
2.5 max	2.500	2.500	2.496	2.500	2.494	2.500	2.486	2.500	2.482	2.500
min	2.490	2.494	2.486	2.494	2.484	2.494	2.476	2.494	2.472	2.494
3 max	3.000	3.000	2.996	3.000	2.994	3.000	2.986	3.000	2.982	3.000
min	2.990	2.994	2.986	2.994	2.984	2.994	2.976	2.994	2.972	2.994
4 max	4.003	4.000	3.996	4.000	3.992	4.000	3.985	4.000	3.981	4.000
min	3.991	5.992	3.984	5.992	3.980	5.992	3.973	5.992	3.969	5.992
5 max	5.003	5.000	4.996	5.000	4.992	5.000	4.985	5.000	4.981	5.000
min	4.991	4.992	4.984	4.992	4.980	4.992	4.973	4.992	4.969	4.992
6 max	6.003	6.000	5.996	6.000	5.992	6.000	5.985	6.000	5.981	6.000
min	5.991	5.992	5.984	5.992	5.980	5.992	5.973	5.992	5.969	5.992
8 max	8.005	8.000	7.996	8.000	7.991	8.000	7.983	8.000	7.978	8.000
min	7.990	7.991	7.981	7.991	7.976	7.991	7.968	7.991	7.963	7.991
10 max	10.005	10.000	9.996	10.000	9.991	10.000	9.983	10.000	9.978	10.000
min	9.990	9.991	9.981	9.991	9.976	9.991	9.968	9.991	9.963	9.991
12 max	12.006	12.000	11.995	12.000	11.989	12.000	11.979	12.000	11.974	12.000
min	11.988	11.989	11.977	11.989	11.971	11.989	11.961	11.989	11.956	11.989
16 max	16.006	16.000	15.995	16.000	15.989	16.000	15.979	16.000	15.974	16.000
min	15.988	15.989	15.977	15.989	15.971	15.989	15.961	15.989	15.956	15.989
20 max	20.006	20.000	19.993	20.000	19.986	20.000	19.973	20.000	19.967	20.000
min	19.985	19.987	19.972	19.987	19.965	19.987	19.952	19.987	19.946	19.987
25 max	25.006	25.000	24.993	25.000	24.986	25.000	24.973	25.000	24.960	25.000
min	24.985	24.987	24.972	24.987	24.965	24.987	24.952	24.987	24.939	24.987
30 max	30.006	30.000	29.993	30.000	29.986	30.000	29.973	30.000	29.960	30.000
min	29.985	29.987	29.972	29.987	29.965	29.987	29.952	29.987	29.939	29.987
40 max	40.007	40.000	39.992	40.000	39.983	40.000	39.966	40.000	39.949	40.000
min	39.982	39.984	39.967	39.984	39.958	39.984	39.941	39.984	39.924	39.984

ANSI B4.2 – 1978 (R2004) Standard. ASME/ANSI B18.3.5M – 1986 (R2002) Standard. Reprinted from the standard listed by permission of the American Society of Mechanical Engineers. All rights reserved.

APPENDIX C – UNIFIED NATIONAL THREAD FORM

(External Threads) Approximate Minor diameter = D – 1.0825P   P = Pitch

Nominal Size, in.	Basic Major Diameter (D)	Coarse UNC		Fine UNF		Extra Fine UNEF	
		Thds. Per in.	Tap Drill Dia.	Thds Per in.	Tap Drill. Dia.	Thds. Per in.	Tap Drill Dia.
#0	0.060	…	…	80	3/64	…	…
#1	0.0730	64	0.0595	72	0.0595	…	…
#2	0.0860	56	0.0700	64	0.0700	…	…
#3	0.0990	48	0.0785	56	0.0820	…	…
#4	0.1120	40	0.0890	48	0.0935	…	…
#5	0.1250	40	0.1015	44	0.1040	…	…
#6	0.1380	32	0.1065	40	0.1130	…	…
#8	0.1640	32	0.1360	36	0.1360	…	…
#10	0.1900	24	0.1495	32	0.1590	…	…
#12	0.2160	24	0.1770	28	0.1820	32	0.1850
1/4	0.2500	20	0.2010	28	0.2130	32	7/32
5/16	0.3125	18	0.257	24	0.272	32	9/32
3/8	0.3750	16	5/16	24	0.332	32	11/32
7/16	0.4375	14	0.368	20	25/64	28	13/32
1/2	0.5000	13	27/64	20	29/64	28	15/32
9/16	0.5625	12	31/64	18	33/64	24	33/64
5/8	0.6250	11	17/32	18	37/64	24	37/64
11/16	0.675	…	…	…	…	24	41/64
3/4	0.7500	10	21/32	16	11/16	20	45/64
13/16	0.8125	…	…	…	…	20	49/64
7/8	0.8750	9	49/64	14	13/16	20	53/64
15/16	0.9375	…	…	…	…	20	57/64
1	1.0000	8	7/8	12	59/64	20	61/64
1 1/8	1.1250	7	63/64	12	1 3/64	18	1 5/64
1 1/4	1.2500	7	1 7/64	12	1 11/64	18	1 3/16
1 3/8	1.3750	6	1 7/32	12	1 19/64	18	1 5/16
1 1/2	1.5000	6	1 11/32	12	1 27/64	18	1 7/16
1 5/8	1.6250	…	…	…	…	18	1 9/16
1 3/4	1.7500	5	1 9/16	…	…	…	…
1 7/8	1.8750	…	…	…	…	…	…
2	2.0000	4 1/2	1 25/32	…	…	…	…
2 1/4	2.2500	4 1/2	2 1/32	…	…	…	…
2 1/2	2.5000	4	2 1/4	…	…	…	…
2 3/4	2.7500	4	2 1/2	…	…	…	…

APPENDIX D – METRIC THREAD FORM

(External Threads) Approximate Minor diameter = D – 1.2075P   P = Pitch
Preferred sizes for commercial threads and fasteners are shown in boldface type.

Coarse (general purpose)		Fine	
Nominal Size & Thread Pitch	Tap Drill Diameter, mm	Nominal Size & Thread Pitch	Tap Drill Diameter, mm
M1.6 x 0.35	1.25	---	---
M1.8 x 0.35	1.45	---	---
M2 x 0.4	1.6	---	---
M2.2 x 0.45	1.75	---	---
M2.5 x 0.45	2.05	---	---
M3 x 0.5	2.5	---	---
M3.5 x 0.6	2.9	---	---
M4 x 0.7	3.3	---	---
M4.5 x 0.75	3.75	---	---
M5 x 0.8	4.2	---	---
M6 x 1	5.0	---	---
M7 x 1	6.0	---	---
M8 x 1.25	6.8	**M8 x 1**	7.0
M9 x 1.25	7.75	---	---
M10 x 1.5	8.5	**M10 x 1.25**	8.75
M11 x 1.5	9.50	---	---
M12 x 1.75	10.30	**M12 x 1.25**	10.5
M14 x 2	12.00	**M14 x 1.5**	12.5
M16 x 2	14.00	**M16 x 1.5**	14.5
M18 x 2.5	15.50	**M18 x 1.5**	16.5
M20 x 2.5	17.5	**M20 x 1.5**	18.5
M22 x 2.5*	19.5	**M22 x 1.5**	20.5
M24 x 3	21.0	**M24 x 2**	22.0
M27 x 3*	24.0	**M27 x 2**	25.0
M30 x 3.5	26.5	**M30 x 2**	28.0
M33 x 3.5	29.5	M33 x 2	31.0
M36 x 4	32.0	**M36 x 2**	33.0
M39 x 4	35.0	M39 x 2	36.0
M42 x 4.5	37.5	**M42 x 2**	39.0
M45 x 4.5	40.5	M45 x 1.5	42.0
M48 x 5	43.0	**M48 x 2**	45.0
M52 x 5	47.0	M52 x 2	49.0
M56 x 5.5	50.5	**M56 x 2**	52.0
M60 x 5.5	54.5	M60 x 1.5	56.0
M64 x 6	58.0	**M64 x 2**	60.0
M68 x 6	62.0	M68 x 2	64.0
M72 x 6	66.0	**M72 x 2**	68.0
M80 x 6	74.0	**M80 x 2**	76.0
M90 x 6	84.0	**M90 x 2**	86.0
M100 x 6	94.0	**M100 x 2**	96.0

*Only for high strength structural steel fasteners
ASME B1.13M – 2001 Standard. Reprinted from the standard listed by permission of the American Society of Mechanical Engineers. All rights reserved.

APPENDIX E – FASTENERS (INCH SERIES)

Important! All fastener dimensions have a tolerance; each dimension has a maximum and minimum value. Only one size for each dimension is given in this appendix. Refer to the standards noted for the complete listing of values.

Regular Hex Head Bolts

Size (D)	Head Height Basic	Width Across Flats Basic Adjust to sixteenths	Width Across Corners Max.	Thread Length 6 in. or shorter	Over 6 in.
1/4	H = 0.625 D + 0.016	F = 1.500 D + 0.062		0.75	1.00
5/16 – 7/16	H = 0.625 D + 0.016			1.00	1.25
1/2 – 7/8	H = 0.625 D + 0.031		G = 1.1547 F	1.25	1.50
1 – 1 7/8	H = 0.625 D + 0.062	F = 1.500 D		2.50	2.75
2 – 3 3/4	H = 0.625 D + 0.125			5.25	5.50
4	H = 0.25 D + 0.188			6.25	6.50

- Radius of Fillet: D less than ½ in.: R 0.01~0.03,
  D larger than ½ in. but less than 1 in.: R 0.02~0.06
  D larger than 1 in.: R 0.03~0.09

Heavy Hex Head Bolts

Size (D)	Head Height Basic[*]	Width Across Flats Basic Adjust to sixteenth	Width Across Corners Max.
1/2 – 3	Same as for regular hex head bolts.	F = 1.500 D + 0.125	Max. G =1.1547 F

[*]Size to 1 in. adjusted to sixty-fourths. 1 1/8 through 2 1/2 in. sizes adjusted upward to thirty-seconds. 2 3/4 thru 4 in. sizes adjusted upward to sixteenths.

ASME B18.2.1 - 1996 Standard. Reprinted from the standard listed by permission of the American Society of Mechanical Engineers. All rights reserved.

Hex Nuts and Hex Jam Nuts

Hex Nuts   Hex Jam Nuts

Nut Size (D)	Nut Thickness Basic	Width Across Flats Basic (Adjust to Sixteenths)	Width Across Corners (Max.)
1/4	H = 0.875D	F=1.500 D + 0.062	Max. G = 1.1547 F
5/6 – 5/8	H = 0.875D		
3/4 – 1 1/8	H = 0.875D – 0.016	F = 1.500 D	
1 1/4 – 1 1/2	H = 0.875D – 0.031		

Hex Thick Nuts

Nut Size (D)	Width Across Flats Basic (Adjust to Sixteenths)	Width Across Corners (Max.)	Nut Thickness Basic
¼	F = 1.500 D + 0.062	Max. G = 1.1547 F	See Table
5/6 – 5/8	F = 1.500 D		
3/4 – 1 ½	F = 1.500 D		

Nut Size (D)	1/4	5/16	3/8	7/16	1/2	9/16	5/8
Nut Thickness Basic	9/32	21/64	13/32	29/64	9/16	39/64	23/32

Nut Size (D)	3/4	7/8	1	1 1/8	1 1/4	1 3/8	1 1/2
Nut Thickness Basic	13/16	29/32	1	1 5/32	1 1/4	1 3/8	1 1/2

Hex Jam Nut

Nut Size (D)	Nut Thickness Basic	Width Across Flats Basic (Adjust to Sixteenths)	Width Across Corners (Max.)
1/4	See Table	F=1.500 D + 0.062	Max. G = 1.1547 F
5/6 – 5/8	See Table		
3/4 – 1 1/8	H = 0.500D – 0.047	F = 1.500 D	
1 1/4 – 1 1/2	H = 0.500D – 0.094		

Nut Size (D)	1/4	5/16	3/8	7/16	1/2	9/16	5/8
Nut Thickness Basic	5/32	3/16	7/32	1/4	5/16	5/16	3/8

ASME/ANSI B18.2.2 -1987 (R1999) Standard. Reprinted from the standard listed by permission of the American Society of Mechanical Engineers. All rights reserved.

APPENDIX E – FASTENERS (INCH SERIES) Continued

Hexagon and Spline Socket Head Cap Screws

Screw Size (D)	Head Diameter	Head Height
# 0 — # 10	See Table	Max. H = D
1/4 – 1 1/2	Max. A = 1.50 D	

Screw Size (D)	# 0	# 1	# 2	# 3	# 4	#5	# 6	# 8	# 10
Max. Head Diameter	0.096	0.018	0.140	0.161	0.183	0.205	0.226	0.270	0.312

Hexagon and Spline Socket Flat Countersunk Head Cap Screws

82 deg.
±2 deg.

Screw Size (D)	Head Diameter (A) Theor. Sharp	Head Height (H)
# 0 — # 10	See Table	
# 4 — 3/8	Max. A = 2 D + 0.031	Max.H = 0.5 (Max. A – D) x cot(41°)
7/16	Max. A = 2 D – 0.031	
1/2 – 1 1/2	Max. A = 2 D – 0.062	

APPENDIX E – FASTENERS (INCH SERIES) Continued

Drill and Counterbore Sizes for Socket Head Cap Screws

Nominal Size of Screw (D)	Nominal Drill Size (A)		Counterbore Diameter (B)	Countersink (C)
	Close Fit	Normal Fit		
#0 (0.0600)	(#51) 0.067	(#49) 0.073	1/8	0.074
#1 (0.0730)	(#46) 0.081	(#43) 0.089	5/32	0.087
#2 (0.0860)	3/32	(#36) 0.106	3/16	0.102
#3 (0.0990)	(#36) 0.106	(#31) 0.120	7/32	0.115
#4 (0.1120)	1/8	(#29) 0.136	7/32	0.130
#5 (0.1250)	9/64	(#23) 0.154	1/4	0.145
#6 (0.1380)	(#23) 0.154	(#18) 0.170	9/32	0.158
#8 (0.1640)	(#15) 0.180	(#10) 0.194	5/16	0.188
#10 (0.1900)	(#5) 0.206	(#2) 0.221	3/8	0.218
1/4	17/64	9/32	7/16	0.278
5/16	21/64	11/32	17/32	0.346
3/8	25/64	13/32	5/8	0.415
7/16	29/64	15/32	23/32	0.483
1/2	33/64	17/32	13/16	0.552
5/8	41/64	21/32	1	0.689
3/4	49/64	25/32	1 3/16	0.828
7/8	57/64	29/32	1 3/8	0.963
1	1 1/64	1 1/32	1 5/8	1.100
1 1/4	1 9/32	1 5/16	2	1.370
1 1/2	1 17/32	1 9/16	2 3/8	1.640
1 3/4	1 25/32	1 13/16	2 3/4	1.910
2	2 1/32	2 1/16	3 1/8	2.180

(1) Countersink. It is considered good practice to countersink or break the edges of holes that are smaller than F (max.) in parts having a hardness which approaches, equals, or exceeds the screw hardness. The countersink or corner relief, however, should not be larger than is necessary to insure that the fillet on the screw is cleared. Normally, the diameter of countersink does not have to exceed F (max.). Countersinks or corner reliefs in excess of this diameter reduce the effective bearing area and introduce the possibility of imbedment or brinnelling or flaring of the heads of the screws.

(2) Close Fit. The close fit is normally limited to holes for those lengths of screws that are threaded to the head in assemblies where only one screw is to be used or where two or more screws are to be used and the mating holes are to be produced either at assembly or by matched and coordinated tooling.

(3) Normal Fit. The normal fit is intended for screws of relatively long length or for assemblies involving two or more screws where the mating holes are to be produced by conventional tolerancing methods. It provides for the maximum allowable eccentricity of the longest standard screws and for certain variations in the parts to be fastened, such as: deviations in hole straightness, angularity between the axis of the tapped hole and that of the hole for the shank, differences in center distances of the mating holes, etc.

ASME B18.3 -2003 Standard. Reprinted from the standard listed by permission of the American Society of Mechanical Engineers. All rights reserved.

APPENDIX E – FASTENERS (INCH SERIES) Continued

Slotted Flat Countersunk Head Cap Screws

Screw Size (D)	Head Diameter (A) Theor. Sharp	Head Height (H)
1/4 through 3/8	Max. A = 2.000 D	Max. H = 0.596 D
7/16	Max. A = 2.000 D – 0.063	Max. H = 0.596 D – 0.0375
1/4 through 3/8	Max. A = 2.000 D – 0.125	Max. H = 0.596 D – 0.075
1 1/8 through 1 1/2	Max. A = 2.000 D – 0.188	Max. H = 0.596 D – 0.112

ASME B18.6.2 – 1998 Standard. Reprinted from the standard listed by permission of the American Society of Mechanical Engineers. All rights reserved.

Slotted Round Head Cap Screws

Screw Size (D)	Head Diameter (A) Theor. Sharp	Head Height (H)
1/4 through 5/16	Max. A = 2.000 D – 0.063	Max. H = 0.875 D – 0.028
3/8 through 7/16	Max. A = 2.000 D – 0.125	Max. H = 0.875 D – 0.055
1/2 through 9/16	Max. A = 2.000 D – 0.1875	Max. H = 0.875 D – 0.083
5/8 through 3/4	Max. A = 2.000 D – 0.250	Max. H = 0.875 D – 0.110

ASME B18.6.2 – 1998 Standard. Reprinted from the standard listed by permission of the American Society of Mechanical Engineers. All rights reserved.

APPENDIX E – FASTENERS (INCH SERIES) Continued

Preferred Sizes of Type A Plain Washers

Nominal Washer Size [*]	Inside Diameter (A) Basic	Outside Diameter (B) Basic	Thickness (C)	Nominal Washer Size [*]	Inside Diameter (A) Basic	Outside Diameter (B) Basic	Thickness (C)
	0.078	0.188	0.020	1 N	1.062	2.000	0.134
	0.094	0.250	0.020	1 W	1.062	2.500	0.165
	0.125	0.312	0.032	1 1/8 N	1.250	2.250	0.134
#6 (0.138)	0.156	0.375	0.049	1 1/8 W	1.250	2.750	0.165
#8 (0.164)	0.188	0.438	0.049	1 1/4 N	1.375	2.500	0.165
#10 (0.190)	0.219	0.500	0.049	1 1/4 W	1.375	3.000	0.165
3/16	0.250	0.562	0.049	1 3/8 N	1.500	2.750	0.165
#12 (0.216)	0.250	0.562	0.065	1 3/8 W	1.500	3.250	0.180
1/4 N	0.281	0.625	0.065	1 1/2 N	1.625	3.000	0.165
1/4 W	0.312	0.734	0.065	1 1/2 W	1.625	3.500	0.180
5/16 N	0.344	0.688	0.065	1 5/8	1.750	3.750	0.180
5/16 W	0.375	0.875	0.083	1 3/4	1.875	4.000	0.180
3/8 N	0.406	0.812	0.065	1 7/8	2.000	4.250	0.180
3/8 W	0.438	1.000	0.083	2	2.125	4.500	0.180
7/16 N	0.469	0.922	0.065	2 1/4	2.375	4.750	0.220
7/16 W	0.500	1.250	0.083	2 1/2	2.625	5.000	0.238
1/2 N	0.531	1.062	0.095	2 3/4	2.875	5.250	0.259
1/2 W	0.562	1.375	0.109	3	3.125	5.500	0.284
9/16 N	0.594	1.156	0.095				
9/16 W	0.625	1.469	0.109				
5/8 N	0.656	1.312	0.095				
5/8 W	0.688	1.750	0.134				
3/4 N	0.812	1.469	0.134				
3/4 W	0.812	2.000	0.148				
7/8 N	0.938	1.750	0.134				
7/8 W	0.938	2.250	0.165				

[*]Nominal washer sizes are intended for use with comparable nominal screw or bolt sizes.
ANSI B18.22.1 - 1965 (R2003) Standard. Reprinted from the standard listed by permission of the
American Society of Mechanical Engineers. All rights reserved.

APPENDIX E – FASTENERS (INCH SERIES) Continued

Regular Helical Spring-Lock Washers

Enlarged Section

Nominal Washer Size	Min. Inside Diameter (A)	Max. Outside Diameter (B)	Mean Section Thickness (T)	Min. Section Width (W)	Min. Bearing Width (BW)
#2 (0.086)	0.088	0.172	0.020	0.035	0.024
#3 (0.099)	0.101	0.195	0.025	0.040	0.028
#4 (0.112)	0.114	0.209	0.025	0.040	0.028
#5 (0.125)	0.127	0.236	0.031	0.047	0.033
#6 (.0138)	0.141	0.250	0.031	0.047	0.033
#8 (0.164)	0.167	0.293	0.040	0.055	0.038
#10 (0.190)	0.193	0.334	0.047	0.062	0.043
#12 (0.216)	0.220	0.377	0.056	0.070	0.049
1/4	0.252	0.487	0.062	0.109	0.076
5/16	0.314	0.583	0.078	0.125	0.087
3/8	0.377	0.680	0.094	0.141	0.099
7/16	0.440	0.776	0.109	0.156	0.109
1/2	0.502	0.869	0.125	0.171	0.120
9/16	0.564	0.965	0.141	0.188	0.132
5/8	0.628	1.073	0.156	0.203	0.142
11/16	0.691	1.170	0.172	0.219	0.153
3/4	0.753	1.265	0.188	0.234	0.164
13/16	0.816	1.363	0.203	0.250	0.175
7/8	0.787	1.459	0.219	0.266	0.186
15/16	0.941	1.556	0.234	0.281	0.197
1	1.003	1.656	0.250	0.297	0.208
1 1/16	1.066	1.751	0.266	0.312	0.218
1 1/8	1.129	1.847	0.281	0.328	0.230
1 3/16	1.192	1.943	0.297	0.344	0.241
1 1/4	1.254	2.036	0.312	0.359	0.251
1 5/16	1.317	2.133	0.328	0.375	0.262
1 3/8	1.379	2.219	0.344	0.391	0.274
1 7/16	1.442	2.324	0.359	0.406	0.284
1 1/2	1.504	2.419	0.375	0.422	0.295
1 5/8	1.633	2.553	0.389	0.424	0.297
1 3/4	1.758	2.679	0.389	0.424	0.297
1 7/8	1.883	2.811	0.422	0.427	0.299
2	2.008	2.936	0.422	0.427	0.299
2 1/4	2.262	3.221	0.440	0.442	0.309
2 1/2	2.512	3.471	0.440	0.422	0.309
2 3/4	2.762	3.824	0.458	0.491	0.344
3	3.012	4.074	0.458	0.491	0.344

ASME B18.21.1 -1999 Standard. Reprinted by permission of the ASME. All rights reserved.

APPENDIX F – METRIC FASTENERS

Metric Hex Bolts

D	Ds	S	E	K	Da	Thread Length (B)		
Nominal Bolt Diameter And Thread Pitch	Max. Body Dia.	Max. Width Across Flats	Max. Width Across Corners	Max. Head Height	Fillet Transition Diameter	Bolt Lengths ≤ 125	Bolt Lengths > 125 and ≤ 200	Bolt Lengths >200
M5 x 0.8	5.48	8.00	9.24	3.88	5.7	16	22	35
M6 x 1	6.19	10.00	11.55	4.38	6.8	18	24	37
M8 x 1.25	8.58	13.00	15.01	5.68	9.2	22	28	41
M10 x 1.5	10.58	16.00	18.48	6.85	11.2	26	32	45
M12 x 1.75	12.70	18.00	20.78	7.95	13.7	30	36	49
M14 x 2	14.70	21.00	24.25	9.25	15.7	34	40	53
M16 x 2	16.70	24.00	27.71	10.75	17.7	38	44	57
M20 x 2.5	20.84	30.00	34.64	13.40	22.4	46	52	65
M24 x 3	24.84	36.00	41.57	15.90	26.4	54	60	73
M30 x 3.5	30.84	46.00	53.12	19.75	33.4	66	72	85
M36 x 4	37.00	55.00	63.51	23.55	39.4	78	84	97
M42 x 4.5	43.00	65.00	75.06	27.05	45.4	90	96	109
M48 x 5	49.00	75.00	86.60	31.07	52.0	102	108	121
M56 x 5.5	57.00	85.00	98.15	36.20	62.0		124	137
M64 x 6	65.52	95.00	109.70	41.32	70.0		140	153
M72 x 6	73.84	105.00	121.24	46.45	78.0		156	169
M80 x 6	82.16	115.00	132.79	51.58	86.0		172	185
M90 x 6	92.48	130.00	150.11	57.74	96.0		192	205
M100 x 6	102.80	145.00	167.43	63.90	107.0		212	225

ASME B18.3 - 2003 Standard. Reprinted from the standard listed by permission of the American Society of Mechanical Engineers. All rights reserved.

APPENDIX F – METRIC FASTENERS (Continued)

Drill and Counterbore Sizes for Socket Head Cap Screws

D	S	E	M	DW	C
Nominal Bolt Diameter and Thread Pitch	Max. Width Across Flats	Max. Width Across Corners	Max. Thickness	Min. Bearing Face Diameter	Max. Washer Face Thickness
M1.6 x 0.35	3.20	3.70	1.30	2.3	
M2 x 0.4	4.00	4.62	1.60	3.1	
M2.5 x 0.45	5.00	5.77	2.00	4.1	
M3 x 0.5	5.50	6.35	2.40	4.6	
M3.5 x 0.6	6.00	6.93	2.80	5.1	
M4 x 0.7	7.00	8.08	3.20	6.0	
M5 x 0.8	8.00	9.24	4.70	7.0	
M6 x 1	10.00	11.55	5.20	8.9	
M8 x 1.25	13.00	15.01	6.80	11.6	
M10 x 1.5	15.00	17.32	9.10	13.6	
M10 x 1.5	16.00	18.45	8.40	14.6	
M12 x 1.75	18.00	20.78	10.80	16.6	
M14 x 2	21.00	24.25	12.80	19.4	
M16 x 2	24.00	27.71	14.80	22.4	
M20 x 2.5	30.00	34.64	18.00	27.9	0.8
M24 x 3	36.00	41.57	21.50	32.5	0.8
M30 x 3.5	46.00	53.12	25.60	42.5	0.8
M36 x 4	55.00	63.51	31.00	50.8	0.8

ASME B18.2.4.1M - 2002 Standard. Reprinted from the standard listed by permission of the American Society of Mechanical Engineers. All rights reserved.

APPENDIX F – METRIC FASTENERS (Continued)

Metric Socket Head Cap Screws

Screw Size (D)	Head Diameter (A)	Head Height (H)
1.6 through 2.5	See Table	
3 through 8	Max. A = 1.5 D + 1	Max. H = D
> 10	Max. A = 1.5 D	

Screw Size (D)	1.6	2	2.5
Max. Head Diameter (A)	3.00	3.80	4.50

ASME/ANSI B18.3.1M - 1986 (R2002) Standard. Reprinted from the standard listed by permission of the American Society of Mechanical Engineers. All rights reserved.

Metric Countersunk Socket Head Cap Screws

Basic Screw Diameter and Thread Pitch	Head Diameter (A) Theor. Sharp	Head Height (H)
M3 x 0.5	6.72	1.86
M4 x 0.7	8.96	2.48
M5 x 0.8	11.20	3.10
M6 x 1	13.44	3.72
M8 x 1.25	17.92	4.96
M10 x 1.5	22.40	6.20
M12 x 1.75	26.88	7.44
M14 x 2	30.24	8.12
M16 x 2	33.60	8.80
M20 x 2.5	40.32	10.16

ASME/ANSI B18.3.5M - 1986 (R2002) Standard. Reprinted from the standard listed by permission of the American Society of Mechanical Engineers. All rights reserved.

APPENDIX F – METRIC FASTENERS (Continued)

Drill and Counterbore Sizes for Socket Head Cap Screws

Nominal Size or Basic Screw Diameter	A		X	Y
	Nominal Drill Size		Counterbore Diameter	Countersink Diameter
	Close Fit	Normal Fit		
M1.6	1.80	1.95	3.50	2.0
M2	2.20	2.40	4.40	2.6
M2.5	2.70	3.00	5.40	3.1
M3	3.40	3.70	6.50	3.6
M4	4.40	4.80	8.25	4.7
M5	5.40	5.80	9.75	5.7
M6	6.40	6.80	11.25	6.8
M8	8.40	8.80	14.25	9.2
M10	10.50	10.80	17.25	11.2
M12	12.50	12.80	19.25	14.2
M14	14.50	14.75	22.25	16.2
M16	16.50	16.75	25.50	18.2
M20	20.50	20.75	31.50	22.4
M24	24.50	24.75	37.50	26.4
M30	30.75	31.75	47.50	33.4
M36	37.00	37.50	56.50	39.4
M42	43.00	44.00	66.00	45.6
M48	49.00	50.00	75.00	52.6

APPENDIX F – METRIC FASTENERS (Continued)

Drill and Countersink Sizes for Flat Countersunk Head Cap Screws

D	A	Y
Nominal Screw Size	Nominal Hole Diameter	Min. Countersink Diameter
M3	3.5	6.72
M4	4.6	8.96
M5	6.0	11.20
M6	7.0	13.44
M8	9.0	17.92
M10	11.5	22.40
M12	13.5	26.88
M14	16.0	30.24
M16	18.0	33.60
M20	22.4	40.32

APPENDIX G – FASTENERS

BOLT AND SCREW CLEARANCE HOLES

(1) Inch Clearance Holes

| Nominal Screw Size | Fit Classes | | |
| | Normal | Close | Loose |
	Nominal Drill Size		
#0 (0.06)	#48 (0.0760)	#51 (0.0670)	3/32
#1 (0.073)	#43 (0.0890)	#46 (0.0810)	#37 (0.1040)
#2 (0.086)	#38 (0.1015)	3/32	#32 (0.1160)
#3 (0.099)	#32 (0.1160)	#36 (0.1065)	#30 (0.1285)
#4 (0.112)	#30 (0.1285)	#31 (0.1200)	#27 (0.1440)
#5 (0.125)	5/32	9/64	11/64
#6 (0.138)	#18 (0.1695)	#23 (0.1540)	#13 (0.1850)
#8 (0.164)	#9 (0.1960)	#15 (0.1800)	#3 (0.2130)
#10 (0.190)	#2 (0.2210)	#5 (0.2055)	B (0.238)
1/4	9/32	17/64	19/64
5/16	11/32	21/64	23/64
3/8	13/32	25/64	27/64
7/16	15/32	29/64	31/64
1/2	9/16	17/32	39/64
5/8	11/16	21/32	47/64
3/4	13/16	25/32	29/32
7/8	15/16	29/32	1 1/32
1	1 3/32	1 1/32	1 5/32
1 1/8	1 7/32	1 5/32	1 5/16
1 1/4	1 11/32	1 9/32	1 7/16
1 3/8	1 1/2	1 7/16	1 39/64
1 1/2	1 5/8	1 9/16	1 47/64

APPENDIX G – FASTENERS

BOLT AND SCREW CLEARANCE HOLES (Continued)

(2) Metric Clearance Holes

Nominal Screw Size	Fit Classes		
	Normal	Close	Loose
	Nominal Drill Size		
M1.6	1.8	1.7	2
M2	2.4	2.2	2.6
M2.5	2.9	2.7	3.1
M3	3.4	3.2	3.6
M4	4.5	4.3	4.8
M5	5.5	5.3	5.8
M6	6.6	6.4	7
M8	9	8.4	10
M10	11	10.5	12
M12	13.5	13	14.5
M14	15.5	15	16.5
M16	17.5	17	18.5
M20	22	21	24
M24	26	25	28
M30	33	31	35
M36	39	37	42
M42	45	43	48
M48	52	50	56
M56	62	58	66
M64	70	66	74
M72	78	74	82
M80	86	82	91
M90	96	93	101
M100	107	104	112

APPENDIX H – REFERENCES

- ASME B1.1 - 2003: Unified Inch Screw Threads (UN and UNR Thread Form)
- ASME B1.13M - 2001: Metric Screw Threads: M Profile
- USAS/ASME B4.1 - 1967 (R2004): Preferred Limits and Fits for Cylindrical Parts
- ANSI B4.2 - 1978 (R2004): Preferred Metric Limits and Fits
- ASME B18.2.1 - 1996: Square and Hex Bolts and Screws (Inch Series)
- ASME/ANSI B18.2.2 - 1987 (R1999): Square and Hex Nuts (Inch Series)
- ANSI B18.2.3.5M - 1979 (R2001): Metric Hex Bolts
- ASME B18.2.4.1M - 2002: Metric Hex Nuts, Style 1
- ASME B18.2.8 - 1999: Clearance Holes for Bolts, Screws, and Studs
- ASME B18.3 - 2003: Socket Cap, Shoulder, and Set Screws, Hex and Spline Keys (Inch Series)
- ASME/ANSI B18.3.1M - 1986 (R2002): Socket Head Cap Screws (Metric Series)
- ASME/ANSI B18.3.5M - 1986 (R2002): Hexagon Socket Flat Countersunk Head Cap Screws (Metric Series)
- ASME 18.6.2 - 1998: Slotted Head Cap Screws, Square Head Set Screws, and Slotted Headless Set Screws (Inch Series)
- ASME B18.21.1 - 1999: Lock Washers (Inch Series)
- ANSI B18.22.1 - 1965 (R2003): Plain Washers
- ASME Y14.2M - 1992 (R2003): Line Conventions and Lettering
- ASME Y14.3 - 2003: Multiview and Sectional view Drawings
- ASME Y14.4M - 1989 (R1999): Pictorial Drawings
- ASME Y14.5M - 1994: Dimensioning and Tolerancing
- ASME Y14.6 - 2001: Screw Thread Representation
- ASME Y14.100 - 2000: Engineering Drawing Practices

Notes:

INDEX

Advanced
Modern
Engineering
Mathematics

Modern Applications of Mathematics

Consulting Editors   **Glyn James**
Coventry University

Richard Clements
University of Bristol

Other titles in the series

Modern Engineering Mathematics   *Glyn James*
Transforms in Signals and Systems   *Peter Kraniauskas*
Engineering Mathematics: A Modern Foundation for Electronic, Electrical and
   Control Engineers   *Anthony Croft, Robert Davison and Martin Hargreaves*

EDITOR IN CHIEF: Sarah Mallen
DEVELOPMENT EDITORS: Laurice Suess and Lynne Balfe
PRODUCTION EDITOR: Susan Keany
PRODUCTION MANAGER: Stephen Bishop
PRODUCTION CONTROLLER: Jim Allman

Advanced Modern Engineering Mathematics

GLYN JAMES Coventry University

and

DAVID BURLEY   University of Sheffield
PHIL DYKE   University of Plymouth
JOHN SEARL   University of Edinburgh
NIGEL STEELE   Coventry University
JERRY WRIGHT   University of Bristol

 ADDISON-WESLEY PUBLISHING COMPANY

Wokingham, England · Reading, Massachusetts · Menlo Park, California · New York
Don Mills, Ontario · Amsterdam · Bonn · Sydney · Singapore
Tokyo · Madrid · San Juan · Milan · Paris · Mexico City · Seoul · Taipei

The programs presented in this book have been included for their instructional value. They have been tested with care but are not guaranteed for any particular purpose. The publisher does not offer any warranties or representations, nor does it accept any liabilities with respect to the programs.

Many of the designations used by manufacturers and sellers to distinguish their products are claimed as trademarks. Addison-Wesley has made every attempt to supply trademark information about manufacturers and their products mentioned in this book. Mathematica is a trademark of Wolfram Research Incorporated.
MATLAB is a trademark of The Mathworks Inc.
Maple is a registered trademark of Waterloo Maple Software

Text designed by Valerie O'Donnell
Illustrations: PanTek Arts
Typesetters: AFS (Glasgow) Ltd
Printed in Great Britain by The Bath Press, Avon

First printed 1993

British Library Cataloguing in Publication Data
A catalogue record for this book is available from the British Library.

Library of Congress Cataloging in Publication Data applied for

Acknowledgements
The publishers wish to thank Ove Arup Partnership, London and Intergraph (UK) Ltd, Swindon for permission to reproduce material on the opening pages of each chapter; and McGraw-Hill Publishers, The Biometrika Trustees and Pergamon Press for material used in this book.

Cover designed by Chris Eley, incorporating the following photographs: the Canary Wharf Tower, part of the major development of London's docklands, courtesy of Olympia & York Canary Wharf Ltd; modern assembly techniques at Honda's Swindon car plant, courtesy of Honda (UK); Rolls-Royce aero-engines, where quality of construction is paramount, courtesy of Rolls-Royce plc; CADCAM: a typical screen appearance generated by a window manager, reproduced by permission of Hewlett-Packard Limited; the Channel Tunnel, one of the largest construction projects in Europe, © Eurotunnel, reproduced courtesy of QA Photos Ltd.

About the Authors

Glyn James is Professor and Head of the School of Mathematical and Information Sciences at Coventry University. He graduated from the University College of Wales, Cardiff, in the late fifties, obtaining first class honours degrees in both Mathematics and Chemistry. He obtained a PhD in Engineering Science in 1971 as an external student of the University of Warwick. He has been a member of the Mathematics Department at Coventry University since 1964, being Head of the Department until 1992. His current research interests are in control theory and its application to industrial problems. He also has a keen interest in mathematical education, particularly in relation to the teaching of engineering mathematics and mathematical modelling. He was co-chairman of the European Mathematics Working Group established by the European Society for Engineering Education (SEFI) in 1982, a past chairman of the Education Committee of the Institute of Mathematics and its Applications (IMA), and member of the Royal Society Mathematics Education subcommittee. He is also a member of the editorial/advisory board of three mathematical education journals. He has published numerous papers and is co-editor of five books on various aspects of mathematical modelling. He is a member of the Council and past Vice-President of the IMA and has also served a period as Honorary Secretary of the Institute. He is a Chartered Mathematician and a Fellow of the IMA.

David Burley is Reader in the Department of Applied and Computational Mathematics at Sheffield University. He graduated in mathematics from King's College, University of London in 1955 and obtained his PhD in Mathematical Physics. After working in the University of Glasgow, he has spent most of his academic career in the University of Sheffield, and was Head of Department for six years. He has long experience of teaching engineering students and is particularly interested in teaching through mathematical models of physical and biological phenomena. His research work has ranged through statistical mechanics, optimization and fluid flows, and he has published extensively. Current interests involve the flow of molten glass and porewaters and their application in the glass industry and the oil industry.

Phil Dyke   is Head of the School of Mathematics and Statistics and Professor of Applied Mathematics at the University of Plymouth. After graduating with first class honours in Mathematics from the University of London in 1969, he gained a PhD in coastal sea modelling at Reading in 1972. Since then, Phil Dyke has been a full-time academic, initially at Heriot-Watt University teaching engineers followed by a brief spell at Sunderland. He still engages in teaching and is actively involved in building mathematical models relevant to environmental issues. He is a Chartered Mathematician and a Fellow of the Institute of Mathematics and its Applications.

John Searl   is director of the Edinburgh Centre for Mathematical Education at the University of Edinburgh. As well as lecturing on mathematical education, he teaches service courses for engineers and scientists. His current research concerns the development of learning environments that make for the effective learning of mathematics for 16–20 year olds. As an applied mathematician who has worked collaboratively with (among others) engineers, physicists, biologists and pharma-cologists, he is keen to develop the problem-solving skills of his students and to encourage them to think for themselves.

Jerry Wright   is Senior Lecturer in Engineering Mathematics and Deputy Director of the Centre for Communications Research at the University of Bristol. He graduated in Engineering (BSc and PhD at the University of Southampton) and in Mathematics (MSc at the University of London), all in the 1970s, and worked for a time at the National Physical Laboratory. He moved to Bristol in 1978, and now has wide experience of teaching mathematics to students of engineering. He has conducted research in nonlinear stochastic systems, and is currently working on the application of probabilistic language models to continuous speed recognition. He is a Fellow of the Institute of Mathematics and its Applications, and a Chartered Mathematician.

Nigel Steele   is Chair of the Division of Mathematics at Coventry University. He graduated in Mathematics from Southampton University in 1967, receiving his Master's degree in 1969. He has been a member of the Mathematics Department at Coventry University since 1968. He has a particular interest in teaching Engineering Mathematics, and is joint editor of the European Society for Engineering Education (SEFI) report 'A Common Core Curriculum in Mathematics for the European Engineer'. He has published numerous papers and one previous book, *Mathematics in Communication Theory*, with R. H. Jones. His current research interests are in the application of neurocomputing techniques, and in control theory. He is a Member of the Royal Aeronautical Society, a Chartered Mathematician and a Fellow of the Institute of Mathematics and its Applications.

Contents

Chapter 4   283
Fourier Series

Chapter 7   **551**

Vector Calculus

Chapter 8   615
Partial Differential Equations

Preface

Throughout the course of history, engineering and mathematics have developed in parallel. All branches of engineering depend on mathematics for their description and there has been a steady flow of ideas and problems from engineering that has stimulated and sometimes initiated branches of mathematics. Thus it is vital that engineering students receive a thorough grounding in mathematics, with the treatment related to their interests and problems. This has been the motivation in the production of this book – a companion text to *Modern Engineering Mathematics*, which was designed to provide a first-level core studies course in mathematics for undergraduate programmes in all engineering disciplines.

Skills development

Although the pace of this book is at a somewhat more advanced level than *Modern Engineering Mathematics* the philosophy of learning by doing is retained with continuing emphasis on the development of students' ability to use mathematics with understanding to solve engineering problems.

Examples and Exercises

The book contains over 320 fully worked examples and more than 750 exercises, with answers to all the questions given. There are copious review exercises at the end of each chapter and these are designed both to reinforce understanding and to extend the range of topics included. In many areas hand-worked exercises can be checked using a suitable software package. It is strongly recommended that this is done whenever possible, not simply to increase confidence, but also to gain insight into the use and the performance of such packages. By this means the student will rapidly develop an appreciation of the need to have a good understanding of the underpinning mathematical theory and of computational problems such as the sensitivity of eigenvalue calculation to rounding errors.

Applications

Recognizing the growing importance of mathematical modelling in engineering practice, each chapter contains specific sections on engineering applications. As in *Modern Engineering Mathematics*, these sections form an ideal framework for individual, or group, case study assignments leading to a written report and/or oral presentation, thereby helping to reinforce the skills of mathematical modelling, which are seen as essential if engineers are to tackle the increasingly complex systems they are being called upon to analyse and design. Also, recognizing the increased use of numerical methods in problem solving, the treatment of numerical methods is integrated with the analytical work throughout the book. Algorithms are written in pseudocode and, therefore, are readily transferable to any specific language by the user.

Building on the foundations laid in *Modern Engineering Mathematics*, this book gives an extensive treatment of some of the more advanced areas of mathematics that have applications in various fields of engineering, particularly as tools for computer-based system modelling, analysis and design. In making the choice of material to be included, the authoring team have recognized the increasing importance of digital techniques and statistics in engineering practice. It is believed that the content is sufficiently broad to provide the necessary second-level core studies for most engineering studies, where in each case a selection of the material may be made.

Content

Chapter 1 is designed to develop an understanding of the standard techniques associated with functions of a complex variable which are still seen as an important component of a practising engineer's mathematical 'tool-kit'. The level of treatment recognizes the increasing emphasis in engineering practice on the use of computational methods that has led to less emphasis on the teaching of complex variable theory on engineering undergraduate courses. **Chapters 2 and 3** are devoted to Laplace and *z* transforms, which provide the necessary mathematical foundation for the frequency domain analysis and design of continuous- and discrete-time systems respectively. While Laplace transforms have traditionally been a component of most engineering undergraduate courses, the more recent inclusion of the *z* transform reflects the increased impact of digital signal processing in many areas of engineering. **Chapters 4 and 5** deal with Fourier analysis, which is central to many areas of applications in engineering, particularly in the analysis of signals and systems, with discrete Fourier transforms providing one of the key methods for discrete signal analysis and widely used in fields such as communications theory and speech and image processing.

Matrix techniques provide the framework for much of the developments in modern engineering. **Chapter 6** extends the introductory work on matrix algebra covered in *Modern Engineering Mathematics* to embrace the eigenvalue problem which arises naturally in many fields. In addition, the chapter develops the techniques of matrix analysis, which are used extensively in control and systems engineering among others. **Chapter 7** provides a basic introduction to vector calculus, which is seen as necessary to ensure that engineers have a good understanding of the mathematical tools they bring to their tasks when using software packages for the modelling of engineering problems in more than one dimension. Many physical processes fundamental to engineering, such as heat transfer and wave propagation, are governed by partial differential equations; **Chapter 8** is devoted to such equations with recognition given to the increasing emphasis on numerical solutions. Optimization, which is dealt with in **Chapter 9**, is a rapidly developing field that has taken full advantage of numerical methods and developments in computer technology. Indeed, many complex and practical optimization tasks have only become tractable in the last few years. The book concludes with **Chapter 10**, which is devoted to probability and statistics. In almost all branches of engineering, data from experiments have to be analysed and conclusions drawn, decisions have to be made, production and distribution need to be organized and monitored, and quality has to be controlled. In all these activities, probability and statistics have at least a supporting role to play, and sometimes a central one.

Acknowledgements

A number of individuals have contributed to the development of this book and it is a pleasure to acknowledge their contribution. In particular, the contribution of Dick Clements of Bristol University has been significant, the continuing support and enthusiasm for the project of Sarah Mallen (former development director at Addison-Wesley) has been an inspiration, and the comments and suggestions made by many reviewers during the preparation of the manuscript were extremely valuable. The authoring team also wish to acknowledge the many sources from which exercises have been drawn over many years. Again the authoring team have been fortunate in having an excellent production team at Addison-Wesley. The team wish to thank sincerely all those concerned, in particular the production editor Susan Keany; without her considerable effort the book would not have been completed. Finally, I would like to thank my wife, Dolan, for her full support throughout the preparation of this book.

Glyn James
Coventry
August 1993

1

Functions of a Complex Variable

CONTENTS

1.1 Introduction

In Chapter 2 of *Modern Engineering Mathematics* we saw that complex numbers are very useful in solving problems in various fields of engineering. In the theory of alternating currents, the application of quantities such as complex impedance involves functions having complex numbers as independent variables. There are many other areas in engineering where this is the case; for example the motion of fluids, the transfer of heat or the processing of signals. Some of these applications are discussed later in this book.

Traditionally, complex variable techniques have been important, and extensively used, in a wide variety of engineering situations. This has been especially the case in areas such as electromagnetic and electrostatic field theory, fluid dynamics, aerodynamics and elasticity. With the rapid developments in computer technology and the consequential use of sophisticated algorithms for analysis and design in engineering there has, in recent years, been less emphasis on the use of complex variable techniques and a shift towards numerical techniques applied directly to the underlying full partial differential equations model of the situation being investigated. However, even when this is the case there is still considerable merit in having an analytical solution, possibly for an idealized model, in order both to develop a better understanding of the behaviour of the solution and to give confidence in numerical estimates for the solution of enhanced models. An example of where the theory has made a significant contribution is the design of aerofoil sections for aircraft and other lifting bodies. The strength of the theory in such applications is its ability to generate mappings which transform complicated shapes, such as an aerofoil section, into a simpler shape, typically a circle in the case of an aerofoil. The idealized airflow around the transformed shape (the circle) is relatively easy to calculate and by reversing the transformation the flow around the aerofoil, and hence its lifting capabilities, can be deduced. An application at the end of the chapter illustrates the technique applied to simplifying the geometry for the solution of a problem in the flow of heat.

Throughout engineering, transforms in one form or another play a major role in analysis and design. An area of continuing importance is the use of Laplace, z, Fourier and other transforms in areas such as control, communication and signal processing. Such transforms are considered later in this book, where it will be seen that functions of a complex variable play a key role. This chapter is devoted to developing an understanding of the standard techniques of complex variables so as to enable the reader to apply them with confidence in application areas.

1.2 Complex functions and mappings

In *Modern Engineering Mathematics* we saw that the concept of a function involved two sets X and Y and a rule that assigns to each element x in the set X (written $x \in X$) precisely one element $y \in Y$. Whenever this situation arises, we say that there is a **function** f that **maps** the set X to the set Y, and represent this symbolically by

$$y = f(x) \quad (x \in X)$$

Schematically we illustrate a function as in Figure 1.1. While x can take any value

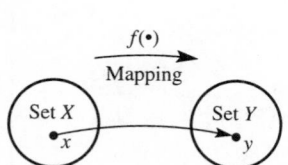

Figure 1.1 Real mapping $y = f(x)$.

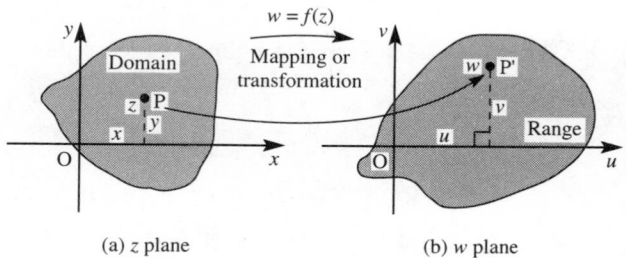

(a) z plane   (b) w plane

Figure 1.2 Complex mapping $w = f(z)$.

in the set X, the variable $y = f(x)$ depends on the particular element chosen for x. We therefore refer to x as the **independent** variable and y as the **dependent** variable. The set X is called the **domain** of the function, and the set of all images $y = f(x)$ $(x \in X)$ is called the **image set** or **range** of f. Previously we were concerned with real functions, so that x and y were real numbers. If the independent variable is a complex variable $z = x + jy$, where x and y are real and $j = \sqrt{(-1)}$, then the function $f(z)$ of z will in general also be complex. For example, if $f(z) = z^2$ then, replacing z by $x + jy$ and expanding, we have

$$f(z) = (x + jy)^2 = (x^2 - y^2) + j2xy = u + jv \quad \text{(say)}$$

where u and v are real. Such a function $f(z)$ is called a **complex function**, and we write

$$w = f(z)$$

where, in general, the dependent variable $w = u + jv$ is also complex.

The reader will recall that a complex number $z = x + jy$ can be represented on a plane called the **Argand diagram**, as illustrated in Figure 1.2(a). However, we cannot plot the values of x, y and $f(z)$ on one set of axes, as we were able to do for real functions $y = f(x)$. We therefore represent the values of

$$w = f(z) = u + jv$$

on a second plane as illustrated in Figure 1.2(b). The plane containing the independent variable z is called the z plane and the plane containing the dependent variable w is called the w plane. Thus the complex function $w = f(z)$ may be regarded as a **mapping** or **transformation** of points P within a region in the z plane (called the **domain**) to corresponding image points P′ within a region in the w plane (called the **range**).

It is this facility for mapping that gives the theory of complex functions much of its application in engineering. In most useful mappings the entire z plane is mapped onto the entire w plane, except perhaps for isolated points. Throughout this chapter the domain will be taken to be the entire z plane (that is, the set of all complex numbers, denoted by $\mathbb{C}$). This is analogous, for real functions, to the domain being the entire real line (that is, the set of all real numbers $\mathbb{R}$). If this is not the case then the complex function is termed 'not well defined'. In contrast, as for real functions, the range of the complex function may well be a proper subset of $\mathbb{C}$.

EXAMPLE 1.1   Find the image in the w plane of the straight line $y = 2x + 4$ in the z plane, $z = x + jy$, under the mapping

$$w = 2z + 6$$

Solution   Writing $w = u + jv$, where u and v are real, the mapping becomes

$$w = u + jv = 2(x + jy) + 6$$

or

$$u + jv = (2x + 6) + j2y$$

Equating real and imaginary parts then gives

$$u = 2x + 6, \qquad v = 2y \tag{1.1}$$

which, on solving for x and y, leads to

$$x = \tfrac{1}{2}(u - 6), \qquad y = \tfrac{1}{2}v$$

Thus the image of the straight line

$$y = 2x + 4$$

in the z plane is represented by

$$\tfrac{1}{2}v = 2 \times \tfrac{1}{2}(u - 6) + 4$$

or

$$v = 2u - 4$$

which corresponds to a straight line in the w plane. The given line in the z plane and the mapped image line in the w plane are illustrated in Figures 1.3(a) and (b) respectively.

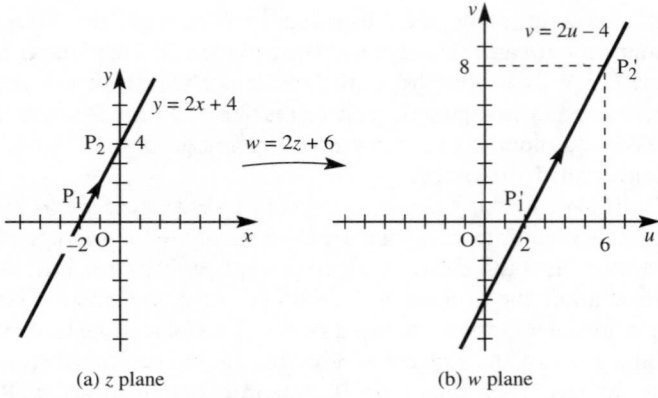

(a) z plane   (b) w plane

Figure 1.3 The mapping of Example 1.1.

Note from (1.1) that, in particular, the point $P_1(-2 + j0)$ in the z plane is mapped to the point $P'_1(2 + j0)$ in the w plane, and that the point $P_2(0 + j4)$ in the z plane is mapped to the point $P'_2(6 + j8)$ in the w plane. Thus, as the point P moves from P_1 to P_2 along the line $y = 2x + 4$ in the z plane, the mapped point P′ moves from P'_1 to P'_2 along the line $v = 2u - 4$ in the w plane. It is usual to indicate this with the arrowheads as illustrated in Figure 1.3.

1.2.1   Linear mappings

The mapping $w = 2z + 6$ in Example 1.1 is a particular example of a mapping corresponding to the general complex linear function

$$w = \alpha z + \beta \qquad (1.2)$$

where w and z are complex-valued variables, and α and β are complex constants. In this section we shall investigate mappings of the z plane onto the w plane corresponding to (1.2) for different choices of the constants α and β. In so doing we shall also introduce some general properties of mappings.

Case (a) $\alpha = 0$

Letting $\alpha = 0$ (or $\alpha = 0 + j0$) in (1.2) gives

$$w = \beta$$

which implies that $w = \beta$, no matter what the value of z. This is quite obviously a degenerate mapping, with the entire z plane being mapped onto the one point $w = \beta$ in the w plane. If nothing else, this illustrates the point made earlier in this section, that the image set may only be part of the entire w plane. In this particular case the image set is a single point. Since the whole of the z plane maps onto $w = \beta$, it follows that, in particular, $z = \beta$ maps to $w = \beta$. The point β is thus a **fixed point** in this mapping, which is a useful concept in helping us to understand a particular mapping. A further question of interest when considering mappings is that of whether, given a point in the w plane, we can tell from which point in the z plane it came under the mapping. If it is possible to get back to a unique point in the z plane then the mapping is said to have an **inverse mapping**. Clearly, for an inverse mapping $z = g(w)$ to exist, the point in the w plane has to be in the image set of the original mapping $w = f(z)$. Also, from the definition of a mapping, each point w in the w plane image set must lead to a single point z in the z plane under the inverse mapping $z = g(w)$. (Note the similarity to the requirements for the existence of an inverse function $f^{-1}(x)$ of a real function $f(x)$.) For the particular mapping $w = \beta$ considered here the image set is the single point $w = \beta$ in the w

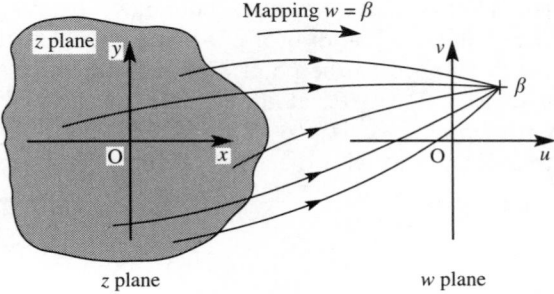

Figure 1.4 The degenerate mapping $w = \beta$.

plane, and it is clear from Figure 1.4 that there is no way of getting back to just a single point in the z plane. Thus the mapping $w = \beta$ has no inverse.

Case (b) $\beta = 0$, $\alpha \neq 0$

With such a choice for the constants α and β, the mapping corresponding to (1.2) becomes

$$w = \alpha z$$

Under this mapping, the origin is the only fixed point, there being no other fixed points that are finite. Also, in this case there exists an inverse mapping

$$z = \frac{1}{\alpha} w$$

that enables us to return from the w plane to the z plane to the very same point from which we started under $w = \alpha z$. To illustrate this mapping at work, let us choose $\alpha = 1 + j$, so that

$$w = (1 + j)z \tag{1.3}$$

and consider what happens to a general point z_0 in the z plane under this mapping. In general, there are two ways of doing this. We can proceed as in Example 1.1 and split both z and w into real and imaginary parts, equate real and imaginary parts and hence find the image curves in the w plane to specific curves (usually the lines $\mathrm{Re}\,(z) = $ constant, $\mathrm{Im}\,(z) = $ constant) in the z plane. Alternatively, we can rearrange the expression for w and deduce the properties of the mapping directly. The former course of action, as we shall see in this chapter, is the one most frequently used. Here, however, we shall take the latter approach and write $\alpha = 1 + j$ in polar form as

$$1 + j = \sqrt{2}\,e^{j\pi/4}$$

Then, if

$$z = r\,e^{j\theta}$$

Figure 1.5 The mapping $w = (1+\mathrm{j})z$.

in polar form it follows from (1.3) that

$$w = r\sqrt{2}\,\mathrm{e}^{\mathrm{j}(\theta + \pi/4)} \tag{1.4}$$

We can then readily deduce from (1.4) what the mapping does. The general point in the z plane with modulus r and argument θ is mapped onto an image point w, with modulus $r\sqrt{2}$ and argument $\theta + \frac{1}{4}\pi$ in the w plane as illustrated in Figure 1.5.

It follows that in general the mapping

$$w = \alpha z$$

maps the origin in the z plane to the origin in the w plane (fixed point), but effects an expansion by $|\alpha|$ and an anticlockwise rotation by $\arg \alpha$. Of course, $\arg \alpha$ need not be positive, and indeed it could even be zero (corresponding to α being real). The mapping can be loosely summed up in the phrase 'magnification and rotation, but no translation'. Certain geometrical properties are also preserved, the most important being that straight lines in the z plane will be transformed to straight lines in the w plane. This is readily confirmed by noting that the equation of any straight line in the z plane can always be written in the form

$$|z - a| = |z - b|$$

where a and b are complex constants (it was shown in Chapter 2 of *Modern Engineering Mathematics* that this is the equation of the perpendicular bisector of the join of the two points representing a and b on the Argand diagram). Under the mapping $w = \alpha z$, the equation maps to

$$\left| \frac{w}{\alpha} - a \right| = \left| \frac{w}{\alpha} - b \right| \quad (\alpha \neq 0)$$

or

$$|w - a\alpha| = |w - b\alpha|$$

in the w plane, which is clearly another straight line.

We now return to the general linear mapping (1.2) and rewrite it in the form

$$w - \beta = \alpha z$$

This can be looked upon as two successive mappings: first,

$$\zeta = \alpha z$$

Figure 1.6 The mapping $w = \zeta + \beta$.

identical to $w = \alpha z$ considered earlier, but this time mapping points from the z plane to points in the ζ plane; secondly,

$$w = \zeta + \beta \tag{1.5}$$

mapping points in the ζ plane to points in the w plane. Elimination of ζ regains equation (1.2). The mapping (1.5) represents a translation in which the origin in the ζ plane is mapped to the point $w = \beta$ in the w plane, and the mapping of any other point in the ζ plane is obtained by adding β to the coordinates to obtain the equivalent point in the w plane. Geometrically, the mapping (1.5) is as if the ζ plane is picked up and, without rotation, the origin placed over the point β. The original axes then represent the w plane as illustrated in Figure 1.6. Obviously *all* curves, in particular straight lines, are preserved under this translation.

We are now in a position to interpret (1.2), the general linear mapping, geometrically as a combination of mappings that can be regarded as fundamental, namely

- translation
- rotation, and
- magnification

that is,

$$z \underset{\text{rotation}}{\longrightarrow} e^{j\theta}z \underset{\text{magnification}}{\longrightarrow} |\alpha|e^{j\theta}z \underset{\text{translation}}{\longrightarrow} |\alpha|e^{j\theta}z + \beta = \alpha z + \beta = w$$

It clearly follows that a straight line in the z plane is mapped onto a corresponding straight line in the w plane under the linear mapping $w = \alpha z + \beta$. A second useful property of the linear mapping is that circles are mapped onto circles. To confirm this, consider the general circle

$$|z - z_0| = r$$

in the z plane, having the complex number z_0 as its centre and the real number r as its radius. Rearranging the mapping equation $w = \alpha z + \beta$ gives

$$z = \frac{w}{\alpha} - \frac{\beta}{\alpha} \quad (\alpha \neq 0)$$

so that

$$z - z_0 = \frac{w}{\alpha} - \frac{\beta}{\alpha} - z_0 = \frac{1}{\alpha}(w - w_0)$$

where $w_0 = \alpha z_0 + \beta$. Hence

$$|z - z_0| = r$$

implies

$$|w - w_0| = |\alpha|r$$

which is a circle, with centre w_0 given by the image of z_0 in the w plane and with radius $|\alpha|r$ given by the radius of the z plane circle magnified by $|\alpha|$.

We conclude this section by considering examples of linear mappings.

EXAMPLE 1.2 Examine the mapping

$$w = (1 + j)z + 1 - j$$

as a succession of fundamental mappings: translation, rotation and magnification.

Solution The linear mapping can be regarded as the following sequence of simple mappings:

$$z \xrightarrow{} e^{j\pi/4}z \xrightarrow{} \sqrt{2}\,e^{j\pi/4}z \xrightarrow{} \sqrt{2}\,e^{j\pi/4} + 1 - j = w$$

rotation   magnification   translation
anticlockwise by $\sqrt{2}$ $0 \to 1 - j$ or
by $\frac{1}{4}\pi$ $(0,0) \to (1, -1)$

Figure 1.7 illustrates this process diagramatically. The shading in Figure 1.7 helps to identify how the z plane moves, turns and expands under this mapping. For example, the line joining the points $0 + j2$ and $1 + j0$ in the z plane has the cartesian equation

$$\tfrac{1}{2}y + x = 1$$

Taking $w = u + jv$ and $z = x + jy$, the mapping

$$w = (1 + j)z + 1 - j$$

becomes

$$u + jv = (1 + j)(x + jy) + 1 - j = (x - y + 1) + j(x + y - 1)$$

Equating real and imaginary parts then gives

$$u = x - y + 1, \qquad v = x + y - 1$$

which on solving for x and y gives

$$2x = u + v, \qquad 2y = v - u + 2$$

Substituting for x and y into the equation $\tfrac{1}{2}y + x = 1$ then gives the image of this line in the w plane as the line

$$3v + u = 2$$

which crosses the real axis in the w plane at 2 and the imaginary axis at $\frac{2}{3}$. Both lines are shown dashed, in the z and w planes respectively, in Figure 1.7.

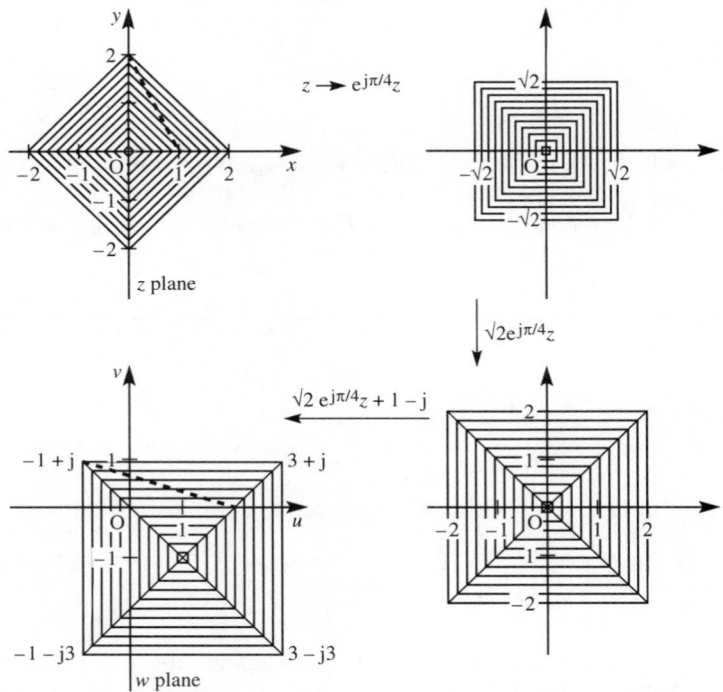

Figure 1.7 The mapping $w = (1+\mathrm{j})z + 1 - \mathrm{j}$.

EXAMPLE 1.3   The mapping $w = \alpha z + \beta$ (α, β constant complex numbers) maps the point $z = 1 + \mathrm{j}$ to the point $w = \mathrm{j}$, and the point $z = 1 - \mathrm{j}$ to the point $w = -1$.

(a) Determine α and β.

(b) Find the region in the w plane corresponding to the right half-plane $\mathrm{Re}\,(z) \geqslant 0$ in the z plane.

(c) Find the region in the w plane corresponding to the interior of the unit circle $|z| < 1$ in the z plane.

(d) Find the fixed point(s) of the mapping.

In (b)–(d) use the values of α and β determined in (a).

Solution   (a) The two values of z and w given as corresponding under the given linear mapping provides two equations for α and β as follows: $z = 1 + \mathrm{j}$ mapping to

$w = \mathrm{j}$ implies

$$\mathrm{j} = \alpha(1 + \mathrm{j}) + \beta$$

while $z = 1 - \mathrm{j}$ mapping to $w = -1$ implies

$$-1 = \alpha(1 - \mathrm{j}) + \beta$$

Substituting these two equations in α and β gives

$$\mathrm{j} + 1 = \alpha(1 + \mathrm{j}) - \alpha(1 - \mathrm{j})$$

so that

$$\alpha = \frac{1 + \mathrm{j}}{\mathrm{j}2} = \tfrac{1}{2}(1 - \mathrm{j})$$

Substituting back for β then gives

$$\beta = \mathrm{j} - (1 + \mathrm{j})\alpha = \mathrm{j} - \tfrac{1}{2}(1 - \mathrm{j}^2) = \mathrm{j} - 1$$

so that

$$w = \tfrac{1}{2}(1 - \mathrm{j})z + \mathrm{j} - 1 = (1 - \mathrm{j})(\tfrac{1}{2}z - 1)$$

(b) The best way to find specific image curves in the w plane is first to express $z\,(= x + \mathrm{j}y)$ in terms of $w\,(= u + \mathrm{j}v)$ and then, by equating real and imaginary parts, to express x and y in terms of u and v. We have

$$w = (1 - \mathrm{j})(\tfrac{1}{2}z - 1)$$

which, on dividing by $1 - \mathrm{j}$, gives

$$\frac{w}{1 - \mathrm{j}} = \tfrac{1}{2}z - 1$$

Taking $w = u + \mathrm{j}v$ and $z = x + \mathrm{j}y$ and then rationalizing the left-hand side, we have

$$\tfrac{1}{2}(u + \mathrm{j}v)(1 + \mathrm{j}) = \tfrac{1}{2}(x + \mathrm{j}y) - 1$$

Equating real and imaginary parts then gives

$$u - v = x - 2, \qquad u + v = y \tag{1.6}$$

The first of these can be used to find the image of $x \geqslant 0$. It is $u - v \geqslant -2$, which is also a region bordered by the straight line $u - v = 2$ and shown in Figure 1.8. Pick one point in the right half of the z plane, say $z = 2$, and the mapping gives $w = 0$ as the image of this point. This allays any doubts about which side of $u - v = -2$ corresponds to the right half of the z plane, $x \geqslant 0$. The two corresponding regions are shown 'hatched' in Figure 1.8.

Note that the following is always true, although we shall not prove it here. If a curve cuts the z plane in two then the corresponding curve in the w plane also cuts the w plane in two, and, further, points in one of the two distinct sets of the z plane partitioned by the curve correspond to points in just one of the similarly partitioned sets in the w plane.

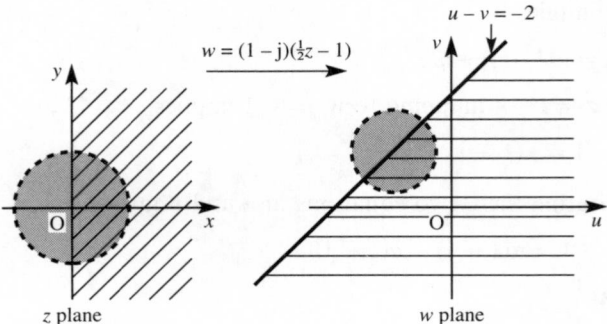

Figure 1.8 The mappings of Example 1.3.

(c) In cartesian form, with $z = x + jy$, the equation of the unit circle $|z| = 1$ is

$$x^2 + y^2 = 1$$

Substituting for x and y from the mapping relationships (1.6) gives the image of this circle as

$$(u - v + 2)^2 + (u + v)^2 = 1$$

or

$$u^2 + v^2 + 2u - 2v + \tfrac{3}{2} = 0$$

which, on completing the squares, leads to

$$(u + 1)^2 + (v - 1)^2 = \tfrac{1}{2}$$

As expected, this is a circle, having in this particular case centre $(-1, 1)$ and radius $\sqrt{\tfrac{1}{2}}$. If $x^2 + y^2 < 1$ then $(u + 1)^2 + (v - 1)^2 < \tfrac{1}{2}$, so the region inside the circle $|z| = 1$ in the z plane corresponds to the region inside its image circle in the w plane. Corresponding regions are shown shaded in Figure 1.8.

(d) The fixed point(s) of the mapping are obtained by putting $w = z$ in $w = \alpha z + \beta$, leading to

$$z = (\tfrac{1}{2}z - 1)(1 - j)$$

that is,

$$z = \tfrac{1}{2}z - \tfrac{1}{2}jz - 1 + j$$

so that

$$z = \frac{-1 + j}{\tfrac{1}{2} + \tfrac{1}{2}j} = j2$$

is the only fixed point.

    One final point is in order before we leave this example. In Figure 1.8 the images of $x = 0$ and $x^2 + y^2 = 1$ can also be seen in the context of translation, rotation (the line in Figure 1.8 rotates about $z = 2j$) and magnification (in fact, shrinkage, as can be seen by the decrease in diameter of the circle compared with its image in the w plane).

1.2.2   Exercises

1 Find in the cartesian form $y = mx + c$ (m and c real constants) the equations of the following straight lines in the z plane, $z = x + jy$:

(a) $|z - 2 + j| = |z - j + 3|$

(b) $z + z* + 4j(z - z*) = 6$

where * denotes the complex conjugate.

2 Find the point of intersection and the angle of intersection of the straight lines

$$|z - 1 - j| = |z - 3 + j|$$
$$|z - 1 + j| = |z - 3 - j|$$

3 The function $w = jz + 4 - 3j$ is a combination of translation and rotation. Show this diagramatically, following the procedure used in Example 1.2. Find the image of the line $6x + y = 22$ ($z = x + jy$) in the w plane under this mapping.

4 Show that the mapping $w = (1 - j)z$, where $w = u + jv$ and $z = x + jy$, maps the region $y > 1$ in the z plane onto the region $u + v > 2$ in the w plane. Illustrate the regions in a diagram.

5 Under the mapping $w = jz + j$, where $w = u + jv$ and $z = x + jy$, show that the half-plane $x > 0$ in the z plane maps onto the half-plane $v > 0$ in the w plane.

6 For $z = x + jy$ find the image region in the w plane corresponding to the semi-infinite strip $x > 0, 0 < y < 2$ in the z plane under the mapping $w = jz + 1$. Illustrate the regions in both planes.

7 Find the images of the following curves under the mapping

$$w = (j + \sqrt{3})z + j\sqrt{3} - 1$$

(a) $y = 0$ (b) $x = 0$

(c) $x^2 + y^2 = 1$

(d) $x^2 + y^2 + 2y = 1$

where $z = x + jy$.

8 The mapping $w = \alpha z + \beta$ (α, β both constant complex numbers) maps the point $z = 1 + j$ to the point $w = j$ and the point $z = -1$ to the point $w = 1 + j$.

(a) Determine α and β.

(b) Find the region in the w plane corresponding to the upper half-plane $\text{Im}(z) > 0$ and illustrate diagrammatically.

(c) Find the region in the w plane corresponding to the disc $|z| < 2$ and illustrate diagrammatically.

(d) Find the fixed point(s) of the mapping.

In (b)–(d) use the values of α and β determined in (a).

1.2.3   Inversion

The inversion mapping is of the form

$$w = \frac{1}{z} \tag{1.7}$$

and in this subsection we shall consider the image of circles and straight lines in the z plane under such a mapping. Clearly, under this mapping the image in the w plane of the general circle

$$|z - z_0| = r$$

in the z plane, with centre at z_0 and radius r, is given by

$$\left| \frac{1}{w} - z_0 \right| = r \tag{1.8}$$

but it is not immediately obvious what shaped curve this represents in the w plane. To investigate, we take $w = u + jv$ and $z_0 = x_0 + jy_0$ in (1.8), giving

$$\left| \frac{u - jv}{u^2 + v^2} - x_0 - jy_0 \right| = r$$

Squaring we have

$$\left(\frac{u}{u^2 + v^2} - x_0 \right)^2 + \left(\frac{v}{u^2 + v^2} + y_0 \right)^2 = r^2$$

which on expanding leads to

$$\frac{u^2}{(u^2 + v^2)^2} - \frac{2ux_0}{u^2 + v^2} + x_0^2 + \frac{v^2}{(u^2 + v^2)^2} + \frac{2vy_0}{(u^2 + v^2)} + y_0^2 = r^2$$

or

$$\frac{u^2 + v^2}{(u^2 + v^2)^2} + \frac{2vy_0 - 2ux_0}{u^2 + v^2} = r^2 - x_0^2 - y_0^2$$

so that

$$(u^2 + v^2)(r^2 - x_0^2 - y_0^2) + 2ux_0 - 2vy_0 = 1 \tag{1.9}$$

The expression is a quadratic in u and v, with the coefficients of u^2 and v^2 equal and no term in uv. It therefore represents a circle, unless the coefficient of $u^2 + v^2$ is itself zero, which occurs when

$$x_0^2 + y_0^2 = r^2, \quad \text{or} \quad |z_0| = r$$

and we have

$$2ux_0 - 2vy_0 = 1$$

which represents a straight line in the w plane.

Summarizing, the inversion mapping $w = 1/z$ maps the circle $|z - z_0| = r$ in the z plane onto another circle in the w plane unless $|z_0| = r$, in which case the circle is mapped onto a straight line in the w plane that does not pass through the origin. When $|z_0| \neq r$, we can divide the equation of the circle (1.9) in the w plane by the factor $r^2 - x_0^2 - y_0^2$ to give

$$u^2 + v^2 + \frac{2x_0 u}{r^2 - x_0^2 - y_0^2} - \frac{2y_0 v}{r^2 - x_0^2 - y_0^2} = \frac{1}{r^2 - x_0^2 - y_0^2}$$

which can be written in the form

$$(u - u_0)^2 + (v - v_0)^2 = R^2$$

where (u_0, v_0) are the coordinates of the centre and R the radius of the w plane circle. It is left as an exercise for the reader to show that

$$(u_0, v_0) = \left(-\frac{x_0}{r^2 - |z_0|^2}, \frac{y_0}{r^2 - |z_0|^2} \right), \quad R = \frac{r}{r^2 - |z_0|^2}$$

Next we consider the general straight line

$$|z - a_1| = |z - a_2|$$

in the z plane, where a_1 and a_2 are constant complex numbers with $a_1 \neq a_2$. Under the mapping (1.7), this becomes the curve in the w plane represented by the equation

$$\left| \frac{1}{w} - a_1 \right| = \left| \frac{1}{w} - a_2 \right| \tag{1.10}$$

Again, it is not easy to identify this curve, so we proceed as before and take

$$w = u + jv, \qquad a_1 = p + jq, \qquad a_2 = r + js$$

where p, q, r and s are real constants. Substituting in (1.10) and squaring both sides, we have

$$\left(\frac{u}{u^2 + v^2} - p \right)^2 + \left(\frac{v}{u^2 + v^2} + q \right)^2 = \left(\frac{u}{u^2 + v^2} - r \right)^2 + \left(\frac{v}{u^2 + v^2} + s \right)^2$$

Expanding out each term, the squares of $u/(u^2 + v^2)$ and $v/(u^2 + v^2)$ cancel, giving

$$-\frac{2up}{u^2 + v^2} + p^2 + \frac{2vq}{u^2 + v^2} + q^2 = -\frac{2ur}{u^2 + v^2} + r^2 + \frac{2vs}{u^2 + v^2} + s^2$$

which on rearrangement becomes

$$(u^2 + v^2)(p^2 + q^2 - r^2 - s^2) + 2u(r - p) + 2v(q - s) = 0 \tag{1.11}$$

Again this represents a circle *through the origin* in the w plane, unless

$$p^2 + q^2 = r^2 + s^2$$

which implies $|a_1| = |a_2|$, when it represents a straight line, also through the origin, in the w plane. The algebraic form of the coordinates of the centre of the circle and its radius can be deduced from (1.11).

We can therefore make the important conclusion that the inversion mapping $w = 1/z$ takes circles or straight lines in the z plane onto circles or straight lines in the w plane. Further, since we have carried out the algebra, we can be more specific. If the circle in the z plane passes through the origin (that is $|z_0| = r$ in (1.9)) then it is mapped onto a straight line that does *not* pass through the origin in the w plane. If the straight line in the z plane passes through the origin ($|a_1| = |a_2|$ in (1.11)) then it is mapped onto a straight line through the origin in the w plane. Figure 1.9 summarizes these conclusions.

To see why this is the case, we first note that the fixed points of the mapping, determined by putting $w = z$, are

$$z = \frac{1}{z}, \qquad \text{or} \quad z^2 = 1$$

so that $z = \pm 1$.

We also note that $z = 0$ is mapped to infinity in the w plane and $w = 0$ is mapped to infinity in the z plane and vice versa in both cases. Further, if we apply

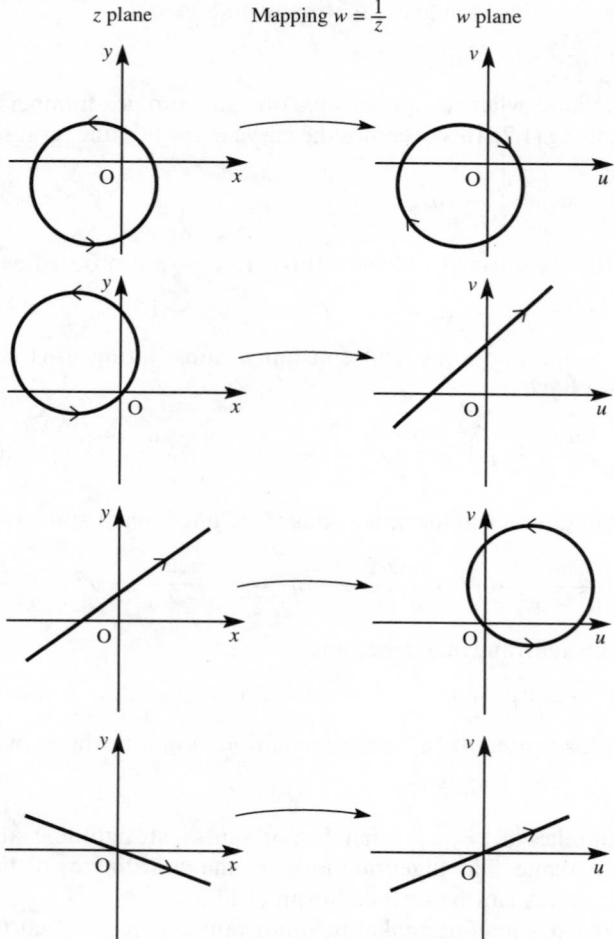

Figure 1.9 The inversion mapping $w = \dfrac{1}{z}$.

the mapping a second time, we get the identity mapping. That is, if

$$w = \frac{1}{z}, \quad \text{and} \quad \zeta = \frac{1}{w}$$

then

$$\zeta = \frac{1}{1/z} = z$$

which is the identity mapping.

The inside of the unit circle in the z plane, $|z| < 1$, is mapped onto $|1/w| < 1$ or $|w| > 1$, the outside of the unit circle in the w plane. By the same token, therefore, the outside of the unit circle in the z plane $|z| > 1$ is mapped onto $|1/w| > 1$ or

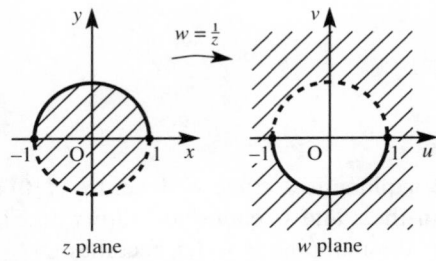

Figure 1.10 Mapping of the unit circle under $w = \dfrac{1}{z}$.

$|w| < 1$, the inside of the unit circle in the w plane. Points actually on $|z| = 1$ in the z plane are mapped to points on $|w| = 1$ in the w plane, with ± 1 staying fixed, as already shown. Figure 1.10 summarizes this property.

It is left as an exercise for the reader to show that the top half-boundary of $|z| = 1$ is mapped onto the bottom half-boundary of $|w| = 1$.

For any point z_0 in the z plane the point $1/z_0$ is called the **inverse of z_0 with respect to the circle** $|z| = 1$; this is the reason for the name of the mapping. (Note the double meaning of inverse; here it means the reciprocal function and not the 'reverse' mapping.) The more general definition of inverse is that for any point z_0 in the z plane the point r^2/z_0 is the inverse of z_0 with respect to the circle $|z| = r$, where r is a real constant.

EXAMPLE 1.4   Determine the image path in the w plane corresponding to the circle $|z - 3| = 2$ in the z plane under the mapping $w = 1/z$. Sketch the paths in both the z and w planes and shade the region in the w plane corresponding to the region inside the circle in the z plane.

Solution   The image in the w plane of the circle $|z - 3| = 2$ in the z plane under the mapping $w = 1/z$ is given by

$$\left| \frac{1}{w} - 3 \right| = 2$$

which, on taking $w = u + jv$, gives

$$\left| \frac{u - jv}{u^2 + v^2} - 3 \right| = 2$$

Squaring both sides, we then have

$$\left(\frac{u}{u^2 + v^2} - 3 \right)^2 + \left(\frac{-v}{u^2 + v^2} \right)^2 = 4$$

or

$$\frac{u^2 + v^2}{(u^2 + v^2)^2} - \frac{6u}{u^2 + v^2} + 5 = 0$$

which reduces to

$$1 - 6u + 5(u^2 + v^2) = 0$$

or

$$(u - \tfrac{3}{5})^2 + v^2 = \tfrac{4}{25}$$

Thus the image in the w plane is a circle with centre $(\tfrac{3}{5}, 0)$ and radius $\tfrac{2}{5}$. The corresponding circles in the z and w planes are shown in Figure 1.11.

Taking $z = x + jy$, the mapping $w = 1/z$ becomes

$$u + jv = \frac{1}{x + jy} = \frac{x - jy}{x^2 + y^2}$$

which, on equating real and imaginary parts, gives

$$u = \frac{x}{x^2 + y^2}, \qquad v = \frac{-y}{x^2 + y^2}$$

We can now use these two relationships to determine the images of particular points under the mapping. In particular, the centre $(3, 0)$ of the circle in the z plane is mapped onto the point $u = \tfrac{1}{3}$, $v = 0$ in the w plane, which is inside the mapped circle. Thus, under the mapping, the region inside the circle in the z plane is mapped onto the region inside the circle in the w plane.

Further, considering three sample points $A(1 + j0)$, $B(3 - j2)$ and $C(5 + j0)$ on the circle in the z plane, we find that the corresponding image points on the circle in the w plane are $A'(1, 0)$, $B'(\tfrac{3}{13}, \tfrac{2}{13})$ and $C'(\tfrac{1}{5}, 0)$. Thus, as the point z traverses the circle in the z plane in an anticlockwise direction, the corresponding point w in the w plane will also traverse the mapped circle in an anticlockwise direction as indicated in Figure 1.11.

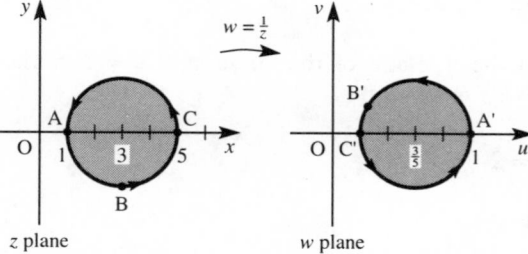

Figure 1.11 The mapping of Example 1.4.

1.2.4   Bilinear mappings

A **bilinear mapping** is a mapping of the form

$$w = \frac{az + b}{cz + d}$$

(1.12)

where a, b, c and d are prescribed complex constants. It is called the bilinear mapping in z and w since it can be written in the form $Awz + Bw + Cz + D = 0$, which is linear in both z and w.

Clearly the bilinear mapping (1.12) is more complicated than the linear mapping given by (1.2). In fact, the general linear mapping is a special case of the bilinear mapping, since setting $c = 0$ and $d = 1$ in (1.12) gives (1.2). In order to investigate the bilinear mapping, we rewrite the right-hand side of (1.12) as follows:

$$w = \frac{az + b}{cz + d} = \frac{\dfrac{a}{c}(cz + d) - \dfrac{ad}{c} + b}{cz + d}$$

so that

$$w = \frac{a}{c} + \frac{bc - ad}{c(cz + d)} \tag{1.13}$$

This mapping clearly degenerates to $w = a/c$ unless we demand that $bc - ad \neq 0$. We therefore say that (1.12) represents a bilinear mapping provided the determinant

$$\begin{vmatrix} a & b \\ c & d \end{vmatrix} = ad - bc$$

is non-zero. This is sometimes referred to as the **determinant of the mapping**. When the condition holds, the inverse mapping

$$z = \frac{-dw + b}{cw - a}$$

obtained by rearranging (1.12), is also bilinear, since

$$\begin{vmatrix} -d & b \\ c & -a \end{vmatrix} = da - cb \neq 0$$

Renaming the constants so that $\lambda = a/c$, $\mu = bc - ad$, $\alpha = c^2$ and $\beta = cd$, (1.13) becomes

$$w = \lambda + \frac{\mu}{\alpha z + \beta}$$

and we can break the mapping down into three steps as follows:

$$z_1 = \alpha z + \beta$$

$$z_2 = \frac{1}{z_1}$$

$$w = \lambda + \mu z_2$$

The first and third of these steps are linear mappings as considered in Section 1.2.1, while the second is the inversion mapping considered in Section 1.2.3. The bilinear mapping (1.12) can thus be generated from the following elementary mappings:

$$z \xrightarrow[\substack{\text{rotation} \\ \text{and} \\ \text{magnification}}]{} \alpha z \xrightarrow[\text{translation}]{} \alpha z + \beta \xrightarrow[\text{inversion}]{} \frac{1}{\alpha z + \beta}$$

$$\xrightarrow[\substack{\text{magnification} \\ \text{and} \\ \text{rotation}}]{} \frac{\mu}{\alpha z + \beta} \xrightarrow[\text{translation}]{} \lambda + \frac{\mu}{\alpha z + \beta} = w$$

We saw in Section 1.2.1 that the general linear transformation $w = \alpha z + \beta$ does not change the shape of the curve being mapped from the z plane onto the w plane. Also, in Section 1.2.3 we saw that the inversion mapping $w = 1/z$ maps circles or straight lines in the z plane onto circles or straight lines in the w plane. It follows that the bilinear mapping also exhibits this important property, in that it also will map circles or straight lines in the z plane onto circles or straight lines in the w plane.

EXAMPLE 1.5   Investigate the mapping

$$w = \frac{z - 1}{z + 1}$$

by finding the images in the w plane of the lines $\mathrm{Re}\,(z) = $ constant and $\mathrm{Im}\,(z) = $ constant. Find the fixed points of the mapping.

Solution   Since we are seeking specific image curves in the w plane, we first express z in terms of w and then express x and y in terms of u and v, where $z = x + \mathrm{j}y$ and $w = u + \mathrm{j}v$. Rearranging

$$w = \frac{z - 1}{z + 1}$$

gives

$$z = \frac{1 + w}{1 - w}$$

Taking $z = x + \mathrm{j}y$ and $w = u + \mathrm{j}v$, we have

$$x + \mathrm{j}y = \frac{1 + u + \mathrm{j}v}{1 - u - \mathrm{j}v}$$

$$= \frac{1 + u + \mathrm{j}v}{1 - u - \mathrm{j}v} \frac{1 - u + \mathrm{j}v}{1 - u + \mathrm{j}v}$$

which reduces to

$$x + \mathrm{j}y = \frac{1 - u^2 - v^2}{(1 - u)^2 + v^2} + \mathrm{j} \frac{2v}{(1 - u)^2 + v^2}$$

Equating real and imaginary parts then gives

$$x = \frac{1 - u^2 - v^2}{(1 - u)^2 + v^2} \qquad\qquad \text{(1.14a)}$$

$$y = \frac{2v}{(1 - u)^2 + v^2} \qquad\qquad \text{(1.14b)}$$

It follows from (1.14a) that the lines $\text{Re}(z) = x = c_1$, which are parallel to the imaginary axis in the z plane, correspond to the curves

$$c_1 = \frac{1 - u^2 - v^2}{(1 - u)^2 + v^2}$$

where c_1 is a constant, in the w plane. Rearranging this leads to

$$c_1(1 - 2u + u^2 + v^2) = 1 - u^2 - v^2$$

or, assuming that $1 + c_1 \neq 0$,

$$u^2 + v^2 - \frac{2c_1 u}{1 + c_1} + \frac{c_1 - 1}{c_1 + 1} = 0$$

which, on completing squares, gives

$$\left(u - \frac{c_1}{1 + c_1}\right)^2 + v^2 = \left(\frac{1}{1 + c_1}\right)^2$$

It is now clear that the corresponding curve in the w plane is a circle, centre $(u = c_1/(1 + c_1), v = 0)$ and radius $(1 + c_1)^{-1}$.

In the algebraic manipulation we assumed that $c_1 \neq -1$, in order to divide by $1 + c_1$. In the exceptional case $c_1 = -1$, we have $u = 1$, and the mapped curve is a straight line in the w plane parallel to the imaginary axis.

Similarly, it follows from (1.14b) that the lines $\text{Im}(z) = y = c_2$, which are parallel to the imaginary axis in the z plane, correspond to the curves

$$c_2 = \frac{2v}{(1 - u)^2 + v^2}$$

where c_2 is a constant, in the w plane. Again, this usually represents a circle in the w plane, but exceptionally will represent a straight line. Rearranging the equation we have

$$(1 - u)^2 + v^2 = \frac{2v}{c_2}$$

provided that $c_2 \neq 0$. Completing the square then leads to

$$(u - 1)^2 + \left(v - \frac{1}{c_2}\right)^2 = \frac{1}{c_2^2}$$

which represents a circle in the w plane, centre $(u = 1, v = 1/c_2)$ and radius $1/c_2$.

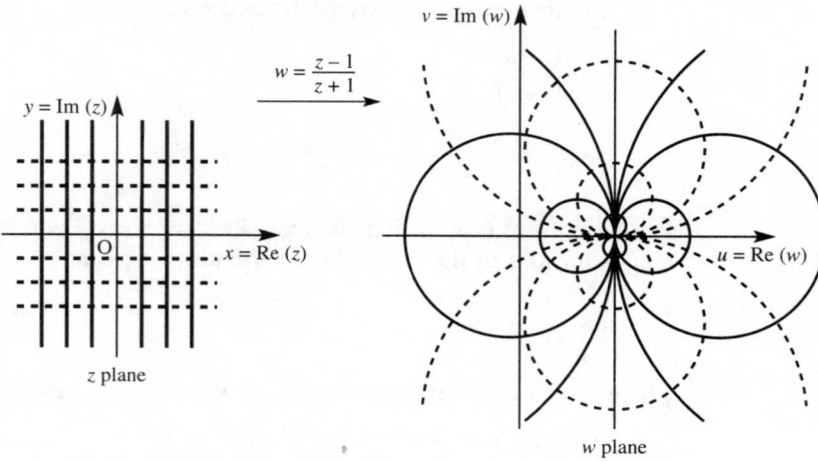

Figure 1.12 The mapping $w = (z-1)/(z+1)$.

In the exceptional case $c_2 = 0$, $v = 0$ and we see that the real axis $y = 0$ in the z plane maps onto the real axis $v = 0$ in the w plane.

Putting a sequence of values to c_1 and then to c_2, say -10 to $+10$ in steps of $+1$, enables us to sketch the mappings shown in Figure 1.12. The fixed points of the mapping are given by

$$z = \frac{z-1}{z+1}$$

that is,

$$z^2 = -1, \quad \text{or} \quad z = \pm j$$

In general, all bilinear mappings will have two fixed points. However, although there are mathematically interesting properties associated with particular mappings having coincident fixed points, they do not impinge on engineering applications, so they only deserve passing reference here.

EXAMPLE 1.6 Find the image in the w plane of the circle $|z| = 2$ in the z plane under the bilinear mapping

$$w = \frac{z-j}{z+j}$$

Sketch the curves in both the z and w planes and shade the region in the w plane corresponding to the region inside the circle in the z plane.

Solution Rearranging the transformation, we have

$$z = \frac{jw + j}{1 - w}$$

so that the image in the w plane of the circle $|z| = 2$ in the z plane is determined by

$$\left| \frac{jw + j}{1 - w} \right| = 2 \qquad\qquad (1.15)$$

One possible way of proceeding now is to put $w = u + jv$ and proceed as in Example 1.4, but the algebra becomes a little messy. An alternative approach is to use the property of complex numbers that $|z_1/z_2| = |z_1|/|z_2|$, so that (1.15) becomes

$$|jw + j| = 2|1 - w|$$

Taking $w = u + jv$ then gives

$$|-v + j(u + 1)| = 2|(1 - u) - jv|$$

which on squaring both sides leads to

$$v^2 + (1 + u)^2 = 4[(1 - u)^2 + v^2]$$

or

$$u^2 + v^2 - \tfrac{10}{3}u + 1 = 0$$

Completing the square of the u term then gives

$$(u - \tfrac{5}{3})^2 + v^2 = \tfrac{16}{9}$$

indicating that the image curve in the w plane is a circle centre ($u = \tfrac{5}{3}$, $v = 0$) and radius $\tfrac{4}{3}$. The corresponding circles in the z and w planes are illustrated in Figure 1.13. To identify corresponding regions, we consider the mapping of the point $z = 0 + j0$ inside the circle in the z plane. Under the given mapping, this maps to the point

$$w = \frac{0 - j}{0 + j} = -1 + j0$$

in the w plane. It then follows that the region inside the circle $|z| = 2$ in the z plane maps onto the region outside the mapped circle in the w plane.

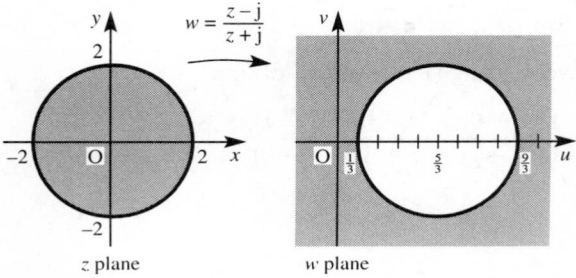

Figure 1.13 The mapping $w = (z - j)/(z + j)$.

An interesting property of (1.12) is that there is just one bilinear transformation that maps three given distinct points z_1, z_2 and z_3 in the z plane onto three specified distinct points w_1, w_2 and w_3 respectively in the w plane. It is left as an exercise for the reader to show that the bilinear transformation is given by

$$\frac{(w - w_1)(w_2 - w_3)}{(w - w_3)(w_2 - w_1)} = \frac{(z - z_1)(z_2 - z_3)}{(z - z_3)(z_2 - z_1)} \qquad \textbf{(1.16)}$$

The right-hand side of (1.16) is called the cross-ratio of z_1, z_2, z_3 and z. We shall illustrate with an example.

EXAMPLE 1.7   Find the bilinear transformation that maps the three points $z = 0$, $-j$ and -1 onto the three points $w = j$, 1, 0 respectively in the w plane.

Solution   Taking the transformation to be

$$w = \frac{az + b}{cz + d}$$

on using the given information on the three pairs of corresponding points we have

$$j = \frac{a(0) + b}{c(0) + d} = \frac{b}{d} \qquad \textbf{(1.17a)}$$

$$1 = \frac{a(-j) + b}{c(-j) + d} \qquad \textbf{(1.17b)}$$

$$0 = \frac{a(-1) + b}{c(-1) + d} \qquad \textbf{(1.17c)}$$

From (1.17c) $a = b$; then from (1.17a)

$$d = \frac{b}{j} = -jb = -ja$$

and from (1.17b) $c = ja$. Thus

$$w = \frac{az + a}{jaz - ja} = \frac{1}{j}\frac{z + 1}{z - 1} = -j\frac{z + 1}{z - 1}$$

Alternatively, using (1.16) we can obtain

$$\frac{(w - j)(1 - 0)}{(w - 0)(1 - j)} = \frac{(z - 0)(-j + 1)}{(z + 1)(-j - 0)}$$

or

$$w = -j\frac{z + 1}{z - 1}$$

as before.

1.2.5   Exercises

9 Show that if $z = x + jy$, the image of the half-plane $y > c$ (c constant) under the mapping $w = 1/z$ is the interior of a circle, provided that $c > 0$. What is the image when $c = 0$ and when $c < 0$? Illustrate with sketches in the w plane.

10 Determine the image in the w plane of the circle
$$|z + \tfrac{3}{4} + j| = \tfrac{7}{4}$$
under the inversion mapping $w = 1/z$.

11 Show that the mapping $w = 1/z$ maps the circle $|z - a| = a$, with a being a positive real constant, onto a straight line in the w plane. Sketch the corresponding curves in the z and w planes, indicating the region onto which the interior of the circle in the z plane is mapped.

12 Find a bilinear mapping that maps $z = 0$ to $w = j$, $z = -j$ to $w = 1$ and $z = -1$ to $w = 0$. Hence sketch the mapping by finding the images in the w plane of the lines $\text{Re}(z) = \text{constant}$ and $\text{Im}(z) = \text{constant}$ in the z plane. Verify that $z = \tfrac{1}{2}(j - 1)(-1 \pm \sqrt{3})$ are fixed points of the mapping.

13 The two complex variables w and z are related through the inverse mapping
$$w = \frac{1 + j}{z}$$
(a) Find the images of the points $z = 1$, $1 - j$ and 0 in the w plane.

(b) Find the region of the w plane corresponding to the interior of the unit circle $|z| < 1$ in the z plane.

(c) Find the curves in the w plane corresponding to the straight lines $x = y$ and $x + y = 1$ in the z plane.

(d) Find the fixed points of the mapping.

14 Given the complex mapping
$$w = \frac{z + 1}{z - 1}$$
where $w = u + jv$ and $z = x + jy$, determine the image curve in the w plane corresponding to the

semicircular arc $x^2 + y^2 = 1$ ($x \leqslant 0$) described from the point $(0, -1)$ to the point $(0, 1)$.

15 (a) Map the region in the z plane ($z = x + jy$) that lies between the lines $x = y$ and $y = 0$, with $x < 0$, onto the w plane under the bilinear mapping
$$w = \frac{z + j}{z - 3}$$
(*Hint*: Consider the point $w = \tfrac{2}{3}$ to help identify corresponding regions.)

(b) Show that, under the same mapping as in (a), the straight line $3x + y = 4$ in the z plane corresponds to the unit circle $|w| = 1$ in the w plane and that the point $w = 1$ does not correspond to a finite value of z.

16 If $w = (z - j)/(z + j)$, find and sketch the image in the w plane corresponding to the circle $|z| = 2$ in the z plane.

17 Show that the bilinear mapping
$$w = e^{j\theta_0} \frac{z - z_0}{z - z_0^*}$$
where θ_0 is a real constant $0 \leqslant \theta_0 < 2\pi$, z_0 a fixed complex number and z_0^* its conjugate, maps the upper half of the z plane ($\text{Im}(z) > 0$) onto the inside of the unit circle in the w plane ($|w| < 1$). Find the values of z_0 and θ_0 if $w = 0$ corresponds to $z = j$ and $w = -1$ corresponds to $z = \infty$.

18 Show that, under the mapping
$$w = \frac{2jz}{z + j}$$
circular arcs or the straight line through $z = 0$ and $z = j$ in the z plane are mapped onto circular arcs or the straight line through $w = 0$ and $w = j$ in the w plane. Find the images of the regions $|z - \tfrac{1}{2}| < \tfrac{1}{2}$ and $|z| < |z - j|$ in the w plane.

19 Find the most general bilinear mapping that maps the unit circle $|z| = 1$ in the z plane onto the unit circle $|w| = 1$ in the w plane and the point $z = z_0$ in the z plane to the origin $w = 0$ in the w plane.

1.2.6 The mapping $w = z^2$

There are a number of other mappings that are used by engineers. For example, in dealing with Laplace and z transforms, the subjects of Chapters 2 and 3 respectively, we are concerned with the polynomial mapping

$$w = a_0 + a_1 z + \ldots + a_n z^n$$

where $a_0, a_1, \ldots, a_n$ are complex constants, the rational function

$$w = \frac{P(z)}{Q(z)}$$

where P and Q are polynomials in z, and the exponential mapping

$$w = a e^{bz}$$

where $e = 2.71828\ldots$, the base of natural logarithms. As is clear from the bilinear mapping in Section 1.2.4, even elementary mappings can be cumbersome to analyse. Fortunately, we have two factors on our side. First, very detailed tracing of specific curves and their images is not required, only images of points. Secondly, by using complex differentiation, the subject of Section 1.3, various facets of these more complicated mappings can be understood without lengthy algebra. As a prelude, in this subsection we analyse the mapping $w = z^2$, which is the simplest polynomial mapping.

EXAMPLE 1.8   Investigate the mapping $w = z^2$ by plotting the images on the w plane of the lines $x =$ constant and $y =$ constant in the z plane.

Solution   There is some difficulty in inverting this mapping to get z as a function of w, since square roots lead to problems of uniqueness. However, there is no need to invert here, for taking $w = u + jv$ and $z = x + jy$, the mapping becomes

$$w = u + jv = (x + jy)^2 = (x^2 - y^2) + j2xy$$

which, on taking real and imaginary parts, gives

$$u = x^2 - y^2$$

$$v = 2xy \tag{1.18}$$

If $x = \alpha$, a real constant, then (1.18) becomes

$$u = \alpha^2 - y^2, \qquad v = 2\alpha y$$

which, on eliminating y, gives

$$u = \alpha^2 - \frac{v^2}{4\alpha^2}$$

or

$$4\alpha^2 u = 4\alpha^4 - v^2$$

so that

$$v^2 = 4\alpha^4 - 4\alpha^2 u$$
$$= 4\alpha^2(\alpha^2 - u)$$

This represents a parabola in the w plane, and, since the right-hand side must be positive, $\alpha^2 \geqslant u$ so the 'nose' of the parabola is at $u = \alpha^2$ on the positive real axis in the w plane.

If $y = \beta$, a real constant, then (1.18) becomes

$$u = x^2 - \beta^2, \qquad v = 2x\beta$$

which, on eliminating x, gives

$$u = \frac{v^2}{4\beta^2} - \beta^2$$

or

$$4\beta^2 = v^2 - 4\beta^4$$

so that

$$v^2 = 4\beta^2 u + 4\beta^4$$
$$= 4\beta^2(u + \beta^2)$$

This is also a parabola, but pointing in the opposite direction. The right-hand side, as before, must be positive, so that $u > -\beta^2$ and the 'nose' of the parabola is on the negative real axis. These curves are drawn in Figure 1.14.

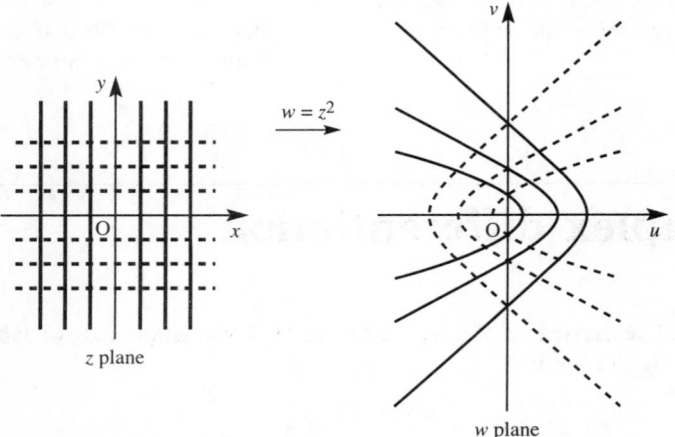

Figure 1.14 The mapping $w = z^2$.

We shall not dwell further on the finer points of the mapping $w = z^2$. Instead, we note that in general it is extremely difficult to plot images of curves in the z plane, even the straight lines parallel to the axes, under polynomial mappings. We also note that we do not often need to do so, and that we have done it only as an aid to understanding.

The exercises that follow should also help in understanding this topic. We shall then return to examine polynomial, rational and exponential mappings in Section 1.3.4, after introducing complex differentiation.

1.2.7 Exercises

20 Find the image region in the w plane corresponding to the region inside the triangle in the z plane having vertices at $0 + j0$, $2 + j0$ and $0 + j2$ under the mapping $w = z^2$. Illustrate with sketches.

21 Find the images of the lines $y = x$ and $y = -x$ under the mapping $w = z^2$. Also find the image of the general line through the origin $y = mx$. By putting $m = \tan \theta_0$, deduce that straight lines intersecting at the origin in the z plane map onto lines intersecting at the origin in the w plane, but that the angle between these image lines is double that between the original lines.

22 Consider the mapping $w = z^n$, where n is an integer (a generalization of the mapping $w = z^2$). Use the polar representation of complex numbers to show that

(a) Circles centred at the origin in the z plane are mapped onto circles centred at the origin in the w plane.

(b) Straight lines passing through the origin intersecting with angle θ_0 in the z plane are mapped onto straight lines passing through the origin in the w plane but intersecting at an angle $n\theta_0$.

23 If the complex function

$$w = \frac{1 + z^2}{z}$$

is represented by a mapping from the z plane onto the w plane, find u in terms of x and y, and v in terms of x and y, where $z = x + jy$, $w = u + jv$. Find the image of the unit circle $|z| = 1$ in the w plane. Show that the circle centred at the origin, of radius r, in the z plane ($|z| = r$) is mapped onto the curve

$$\left(\frac{r^2 u}{r^2 + 1} \right)^2 + \left(\frac{r^2 v}{r^2 - 1} \right)^2 = r^2 \quad (r \neq 1)$$

in the w plane. What kind of curves are these? What happens for very large r?

1.3 Complex differentiation

The derivative of a real function $f(x)$ of a single real variable x at $x = x_0$ is given by the limit

$$f'(x_0) = \lim_{x \to x_0} \left[\frac{f(x) - f(x_0)}{x - x_0} \right]$$

Here, of course, x_0 is a real number and so can be represented by a single point on the real line. The point representing x can then approach the fixed x_0 either from the left or from the right along this line. Let us now turn to complex variables and functions depending on them. We know that a plane is required to represent complex numbers, so z_0 is now a fixed point in the Argand diagram, somewhere in the plane. The definition of the derivative of the function $f(z)$ of the complex variable z at the point z_0 will thus be

$$f'(z_0) = \lim_{z \to z_0} \left[\frac{f(z) - f(z_0)}{z - z_0} \right]$$

It may appear that if we merely exchange z for x, the rest of this section will follow similar lines to the differentiation of functions of real variables. For real variables, taking the limit could only be done from the left or from the right, and the existence of a unique limit was not difficult to establish. For complex variables, however, the point that represents the fixed complex number z_0 can be approached along an infinite number of curves in the z plane. The existence of a unique limit is thus a very stringent requirement. That most complex functions can be differentiated in the usual way is a remarkable property of the complex variable. Since $z = x + \mathrm{j}y$, and x and y can vary independently, there are some connections with the calculus of functions of two real variables, but we shall not pursue this connection here.

Rather than use the word 'differentiable' to describe complex functions for which a derivative exists, if the function $f(z)$ has a derivative $f'(z)$ that exists at all points of a region R of the z plane then $f(z)$ is called **analytic** in R. Other terms such as **regular** or **holomorphic** are also used as alternatives to analytic. (Strictly, functions that have a power series expansion – see Section 1.4.1 – are called **analytic functions**. Since differentiable functions have a power series expansion they are referred to as analytic functions. However, there are examples of analytic functions that are not differentiable.)

1.3.1   Cauchy–Riemann equations

The following result is an important property of the analytic function.

If $z = x + \mathrm{j}y$ and $f(z) = u(x, y) + \mathrm{j}v(x, y)$, and $f(z)$ is analytic in some region R of the z plane, then the two equations

$$\frac{\partial u}{\partial x} = \frac{\partial v}{\partial y}, \qquad \frac{\partial u}{\partial y} = -\frac{\partial v}{\partial x} \tag{1.19}$$

known as the **Cauchy–Riemann equations**, hold throughout R.

It is instructive to prove this result. Since $f'(z)$ exists at any point z_0 in R,

$$f'(z_0) = \lim_{z \to z_0} \left[\frac{f(z) - f(z_0)}{z - z_0} \right]$$

where z can tend to z_0 along any path within R. Examination of (1.19) suggests that we might choose paths parallel to the x direction and parallel to the y direction, since these will lead to partial derivatives with respect to x and y. Thus, choosing $z - z_0 = \Delta x$, a real path, we see that

$$f'(z_0) = \lim_{\Delta x \to 0} \left[\frac{f(z_0 + \Delta x) - f(z_0)}{\Delta x} \right]$$

Since $f(z) = u + jv$, this means that

$$f'(z_0) = \lim_{\Delta x \to 0} \left[\frac{u(x_0 + \Delta x, y_0) + jv(x_0 + \Delta x, y_0) - u(x_0, y_0) - jv(x_0, y_0)}{\Delta x} \right]$$

or, on splitting into real and imaginary parts,

$$f'(z_0) = \lim_{\Delta x \to 0} \left[\frac{u(x_0 + \Delta x, y_0) - u(x_0, y_0)}{\Delta x} + j \frac{v(x_0 + \Delta x, y_0) - v(x_0, y_0)}{\Delta x} \right]$$

giving

$$f'(z_0) = \left[\frac{\partial u}{\partial x} + j \frac{\partial v}{\partial x} \right]_{x = x_0, \, y = y_0} \tag{1.20}$$

Starting again from the definition of $f'(z_0)$, but this time choosing $z - z_0 = j \Delta y$ for the path parallel to the y axis, we obtain

$$f'(z_0) = \lim_{j \Delta y \to 0} \left[\frac{f(z_0 + j \Delta y) - f(z_0)}{j \Delta y} \right]$$

Once again, using $f(z) = u + jv$ and splitting into real and imaginary parts, we see that

$$f'(z_0) = \lim_{j \Delta y \to 0} \left[\frac{u(x_0, y_0 + \Delta y) + jv(x_0, y_0 + \Delta y) - u(x_0, y_0) - jv(x_0, y_0)}{j \Delta y} \right]$$

$$= \lim_{\Delta y \to 0} \left[\frac{1}{j} \frac{u(x_0, y_0 + \Delta y) - u(x_0, y_0)}{\Delta y} + \frac{v(x_0, y_0 + \Delta y) - v(x_0, y_0)}{\Delta y} \right]$$

giving

$$f'(z_0) = \left[\frac{1}{j} \frac{\partial u}{\partial y} + \frac{\partial v}{\partial y} \right]_{x = x_0, \, y = y_0} \tag{1.21}$$

Since $f'(z_0)$ must be the same no matter what path is followed, the two values obtained in (1.20) and (1.21) must be equal. Hence

$$\frac{\partial u}{\partial x} + j \frac{\partial v}{\partial x} = \frac{1}{j} \frac{\partial u}{\partial y} + \frac{\partial v}{\partial y}$$

$$= -j \frac{\partial u}{\partial y} + \frac{\partial v}{\partial y}$$

Equating real and imaginary parts then gives the required Cauchy–Riemann equations

$$\frac{\partial u}{\partial x} = \frac{\partial v}{\partial y}, \qquad \frac{\partial v}{\partial x} = -\frac{\partial u}{\partial y}$$

at the point $z = z_0$. However, z_0 is an arbitrarily chosen point in the region R; hence the Cauchy–Riemann equations hold throughout R, and we have thus proved the required result.

It is tempting to think that should we choose more paths along which to let $z - z_0$ tend to zero, we could derive more relationships along the same lines as the Cauchy–Riemann equations. It turns out, however, that we merely reproduce them or expressions derivable from them, and it is possible to prove that satisfaction of the Cauchy–Riemann equations (1.19) is a necessary condition for a function $f(z) = u(x, y) + jv(x, y)$, $z = x + jy$, to be analytic in a specified region. At points where $f'(z)$ exists it may be obtained from either (1.20) or (1.21) as

$$f'(z) = \frac{\partial u}{\partial x} + j\frac{\partial v}{\partial x}$$

or

$$f'(z) = \frac{\partial v}{\partial y} - j\frac{\partial u}{\partial y}$$

If z is given in the polar form $z = r\,e^{j\theta}$ then

$$f(z) = u(r, \theta) + jv(r, \theta)$$

and the corresponding polar forms of the Cauchy–Riemann equations are

$$\frac{\partial u}{\partial r} = \frac{1}{r}\frac{\partial v}{\partial \theta}, \qquad \frac{\partial v}{\partial r} = -\frac{1}{r}\frac{\partial u}{\partial \theta} \qquad \textbf{(1.22)}$$

At points where $f'(z)$ exists it may be obtained from either of

$$f'(z) = e^{-j\theta}\left(\frac{\partial u}{\partial r} + j\frac{\partial v}{\partial r}\right) \qquad \textbf{(1.23a)}$$

or

$$f'(z) = e^{-j\theta}\left(\frac{1}{r}\frac{\partial v}{\partial \theta} - \frac{j}{r}\frac{\partial u}{\partial \theta}\right) \qquad \textbf{(1.23b)}$$

EXAMPLE 1.9   Verify that the function $f(z) = z^2$ satisfies the Cauchy–Riemann equations, and determine the derivative $f'(z)$.

Solution   Since $z = x + jy$, we have

$$f(z) = z^2 = (x + jy)^2 = (x^2 - y^2) + j2xy$$

so if $f(z) = u(x, y) + jv(x, y)$ then

$$u = x^2 - y^2, \qquad v = 2xy$$

giving the partial derivatives as

$$\frac{\partial u}{\partial x} = 2x, \qquad \frac{\partial u}{\partial y} = -2y$$

$$\frac{\partial v}{\partial x} = 2y, \qquad \frac{\partial v}{\partial y} = 2x$$

It is readily seen that the Cauchy–Riemann equations

$$\frac{\partial u}{\partial x} = \frac{\partial v}{\partial y}, \qquad \frac{\partial u}{\partial y} = -\frac{\partial v}{\partial x}$$

are satisfied.

The derivative $f'(z)$ is then given by

$$f'(z) = \frac{\partial u}{\partial x} + j\frac{\partial v}{\partial x} = 2x + j2y = 2z$$

as expected.

EXAMPLE 1.10   Verify that the exponential function $f(z) = e^{\alpha z}$, where α is a constant, satisfies the Cauchy–Riemann equations, and show that $f'(z) = \alpha e^{\alpha z}$.

Solution

$$f(z) = u + jv = e^{\alpha z} = e^{\alpha(x + jy)} = e^{\alpha x}\, e^{j\alpha y}$$
$$= e^{\alpha x}(\cos \alpha y + j \sin \alpha y)$$

so, equating real and imaginary parts,

$$u = e^{\alpha x} \cos \alpha y, \qquad v = e^{\alpha x} \sin \alpha y$$

The partial derivatives are

$$\frac{\partial u}{\partial x} = \alpha\, e^{\alpha x} \cos \alpha y, \qquad \frac{\partial v}{\partial x} = \alpha\, e^{\alpha x} \sin \alpha y$$

$$\frac{\partial u}{\partial y} = -\alpha\, e^{\alpha x} \sin \alpha y, \qquad \frac{\partial v}{\partial y} = \alpha\, e^{\alpha x} \cos \alpha y$$

confirming that the Cauchy–Riemann equations are satisfied. The derivative $f'(z)$ is then given by

$$f'(z) = \frac{\partial u}{\partial x} + j\frac{\partial v}{\partial x} = \alpha\, e^{\alpha x}(\cos \alpha y + j \sin \alpha y) = \alpha\, e^{\alpha z}$$

so that

$$\frac{\mathrm{d}}{\mathrm{d}z} e^{\alpha z} = \alpha\, e^{\alpha z} \tag{1.24}$$

As in the real variable case, we have

$$e^{jz} = \cos z + j \sin z \qquad (1.25)$$

(Section 1.4.3), so that $\cos z$ and $\sin z$ may be expressed as

$$\left. \begin{aligned} \cos z &= \frac{e^{jz} + e^{-jz}}{2} \\ \sin z &= \frac{e^{jz} - e^{-jz}}{2j} \end{aligned} \right\} \qquad (1.26a)$$

Using result (1.24) from Example 1.10, it is then readily shown that

$$\frac{d}{dz}(\sin z) = \cos z$$

$$\frac{d}{dz}(\cos z) = -\sin z$$

Similarly, we define the hyperbolic functions $\sinh z$ and $\cosh z$ by

$$\left. \begin{aligned} \sinh z &= \frac{e^z - e^{-z}}{2} = -j \sin jz \\ \cosh z &= \frac{e^z + e^{-z}}{2} = \cos jz \end{aligned} \right\} \qquad (1.26b)$$

from which, using (1.24), it is readily deduced that

$$\frac{d}{dz}(\sinh z) = \cosh z$$

$$\frac{d}{dz}(\cosh z) = \sinh z$$

We note from above that e^z has the following real and imaginary parts:

$$\text{Re}(e^z) = e^x \cos y$$

$$\text{Im}(e^z) = e^x \sin y$$

In real variables the exponential and circular functions are contrasted, one being monotonic, the other oscillatory. In complex variables, however, the real and imaginary parts of e^z are (two-variable) combinations of exponential and circular functions, which might seem surprising for an exponential function. Similarly, the circular functions of a complex variable have unfamiliar properties. For example, it is easy to see that $|\cos z|$ and $|\sin z|$ are unbounded for complex z by using the above relationships between circular and hyperbolic functions of complex variables. Contrast this with $|\cos x| \leqslant 1$ and $|\sin x| \leqslant 1$ for a real variable x.

In a similar way to the method adopted in Examples 1.9 and 1.10 it can be shown that the derivatives of the majority of functions $f(x)$ of a real variable x

carry over to the complex variable case $f(z)$ at points where $f(z)$ is analytic. Thus, for example,

$$\frac{d}{dz} z^n = nz^{n-1}$$

for all z in the z plane, and

$$\frac{d}{dz} \ln z = \frac{1}{z}$$

for all z in the z plane except for points on the non-positive real axis, where $\ln z$ is non-analytic.

It can also be shown that the rules associated with derivatives of a function of a real variable, such as the sum, product, quotient and chain rules, carry over to the complex variable case. Thus,

$$\frac{d}{dz} [f(z) + g(z)] = \frac{df(z)}{dz} + \frac{dg(z)}{dz}$$

$$\frac{d}{dz} [f(z)g(z)] = f(z)\frac{dg(z)}{dz} + \frac{df(z)}{dz} g(z)$$

$$\frac{d}{dz} f(g(z)) = \frac{df}{dg} \frac{dg}{dz}$$

$$\frac{d}{dz} \left[\frac{f(z)}{g(z)} \right] = \frac{g(z)f'(z) - f(z)g'(z)}{[g(z)]^2}$$

1.3.2 Conjugate and harmonic functions

A pair of functions $u(x, y)$ and $v(x, y)$ of the real variables x and y that satisfy the Cauchy–Riemann equations (1.19) are said to be **conjugate functions**. (Note here the different use of the word 'conjugate' to that used in complex number work, where $z^* = x - jy$ is the complex conjugate of $z = x + jy$.) Conjugate functions satisfy the orthogonality property in that the curves in the (x, y) plane defined by $u(x, y) = $ constant and $v(x, y) = $ constant are orthogonal curves. This follows since the gradient at any point on the curve $u(x, y) = $ constant is given by

$$\left[\frac{dy}{dx} \right]_u = -\frac{\partial u}{\partial y} \bigg/ \frac{\partial u}{\partial x}$$

and the gradient at any point on the curve $v(x, y) = $ constant is given by

$$\left[\frac{dy}{dx} \right]_v = -\frac{\partial v}{\partial y} \bigg/ \frac{\partial v}{\partial x}$$

It follows from the Cauchy–Riemann equations (1.19) that

$$\left[\frac{dy}{dx}\right]_u \left[\frac{dy}{dx}\right]_v = -1$$

so the curves are orthogonal.

A function that satisfies Laplace's equation in two dimensions is said to be **harmonic**; that is, $u(x, y)$ is a harmonic function if

$$\frac{\partial^2 u}{\partial x^2} + \frac{\partial^2 u}{\partial y^2} = 0$$

It is readily shown (see Example 1.12) that if $f(z) = u(x, y) + jv(x, y)$ is analytic, so that the Cauchy–Riemann equations are satisfied, then both u and v are **harmonic** functions. Therefore u and v are **conjugate harmonic functions**. Harmonic functions have applications in such areas as stress analysis in plates, inviscid two-dimensional fluid flow and electrostatics.

EXAMPLE 1.11   Given $u(x, y) = x^2 - y^2 + 2x$, find the conjugate function $v(x, y)$ such that $f(z) = u(x, y) + jv(x, y)$ is an analytic function of z throughout the z plane.

Solution   We are given $u(x, y) = x^2 - y^2 + 2x$, and, since $f(z) = u + jv$ is to be analytic, the Cauchy–Riemann equations must hold. Thus, from (1.19),

$$\frac{\partial v}{\partial y} = \frac{\partial u}{\partial x} = 2x + 2$$

Integrating this with respect to y gives

$$v = 2xy + 2y + F(x)$$

where $F(x)$ is an arbitrary function of x, since the integration was performed holding x constant. Differentiating v partially with respect to x gives

$$\frac{\partial v}{\partial x} = 2y + \frac{dF}{dx}$$

but this equals $-\partial u/\partial y$ by the second of the Cauchy–Riemann equations (1.19). Hence

$$\frac{\partial u}{\partial y} = -2y - \frac{dF}{dx}$$

But since $u = x^2 - y^2 + 2x$, $\partial u/\partial y = -2y$, and comparison yields $F(x) = $ constant. This constant is set equal to zero, since no conditions have been given by which it can be determined. Hence

$$u(x, y) + jv(x, y) = x^2 - y^2 + 2x + j(2xy + 2y)$$

To confirm that this is a function of z, note that $f(z)$ is $f(x + jy)$, and becomes just $f(x)$ if we set $y = 0$. Therefore we set $y = 0$ to obtain

$$f(x + j0) = f(x) = u(x, 0) + jv(x, 0) = x^2 + 2x$$

and it follows that

$$f(z) = z^2 + 2z$$

which can be easily checked by separation into real and imaginary parts.

EXAMPLE 1.12   Show that the real and imaginary parts $u(x, y)$ and $v(x, y)$ of a complex analytic function $f(z)$ are harmonic.

Solution   Since

$$f(z) = u(x, y) + jv(x, y)$$

is analytic, the Cauchy–Riemann equations

$$\frac{\partial v}{\partial x} = -\frac{\partial u}{\partial y}, \qquad \frac{\partial u}{\partial x} = \frac{\partial v}{\partial y}$$

are satisfied. Differentiating the first with respect to x gives

$$\frac{\partial^2 v}{\partial x^2} = -\frac{\partial^2 u}{\partial x\,\partial y} = -\frac{\partial^2 u}{\partial y\,\partial x} = -\frac{\partial}{\partial y}\left(\frac{\partial u}{\partial x}\right)$$

which is $-\partial^2 v/\partial y^2$, by the second Cauchy–Riemann equation. Hence

$$\frac{\partial^2 v}{\partial x^2} = -\frac{\partial^2 v}{\partial y^2}, \qquad \text{or} \qquad \frac{\partial^2 v}{\partial x^2} + \frac{\partial^2 v}{\partial y^2} = 0$$

and v is a harmonic function.
Similarly,

$$\frac{\partial^2 u}{\partial y^2} = -\frac{\partial^2 v}{\partial y\,\partial x} = -\frac{\partial}{\partial x}\left(\frac{\partial v}{\partial y}\right) = -\frac{\partial^2 u}{\partial x^2}$$

so that

$$\frac{\partial^2 u}{\partial x^2} + \frac{\partial^2 u}{\partial y^2} = 0$$

and u is also a harmonic function. We have assumed that both u and v have continuous second-order partial derivatives, so that

$$\frac{\partial^2 u}{\partial x\,\partial y} = \frac{\partial^2 u}{\partial y\,\partial x}, \qquad \frac{\partial^2 v}{\partial x\,\partial y} = \frac{\partial^2 v}{\partial y\,\partial x}$$

1.3.3   Exercises

24 Determine whether the following functions are analytic, and find the derivative where appropriate:

(a) $z\,e^z$ (b) $\sin 4z$
(c) zz^* (d) $\cos 2z$

25 Determine the constants a and b in order that

$$w = x^2 + ay^2 - 2xy + j(bx^2 - y^2 + 2xy)$$

be analytic. For these values of a and b find the derivative of w, and express both w and dw/dz as functions of $z = x + jy$.

26 Find a function $v(x, y)$ such that, given $u = 2x(1 - y)$, $f(z) = u + jv$ is analytic in z.

27 Show that $\phi(x, y) = e^x(x \cos y - y \sin y)$ is a harmonic function, and find the conjugate harmonic function $\psi(x, y)$. Write $\phi(x, y) + j\psi(x, y)$ as a function of $z = x + jy$ only.

28 Show that $u(x, y) = \sin x \cosh y$ is harmonic. Find the harmonic conjugate $v(x, y)$ and express $w = u + jv$ as a function of $z = x + jy$.

29 Find the orthogonal trajectories of the following families of curves:

(a) $x^3 y - xy^3 = \alpha$ (constant α)

(b) $e^{-x} \cos y + xy = \alpha$ (constant α)

30 Find the real and imaginary parts of the functions

(a) $z^2 e^{2z}$ (b) $\sin 2z$

Verify that they are analytic and find their derivatives.

31 Give a definition of the inverse sine function $\sin^{-1} z$ for complex z. Find the real and imaginary parts of $\sin^{-1} z$. (*Hint:* put $z = \sin w$, split into real and imaginary parts, and with $w = u + jv$ and $z = x + jy$ solve for u and v in terms of x and y.) Is $\sin^{-1} z$ analytic? If so, what is its derivative?

32 Establish that if $z = x + jy$, $|\sinh y| \leqslant |\sin z| \leqslant \cosh y$.

1.3.4   Mappings revisited

In Section 1.2 we examined mappings from the z plane to the w plane, where in the main the relationship between w and z, $w = f(z)$ was linear or bilinear. There is an important property of mappings, hinted at in Example 1.8 when considering the mapping $w = z^2$. A mapping $w = f(z)$ that preserves angles is called **conformal**. Under such a mapping, the angle between two intersecting curves in the z plane is the same as the angle between the corresponding intersecting curves in the w plane. The sense of the angle is also preserved. That is, if θ is the angle between curves 1 and 2 taken in the anticlockwise sense in the z plane then θ is also the angle between the image of curve 1 and the image of curve 2 in the w plane, and it too is taken in the anticlockwise sense. Figure 1.15 should make the idea of a conformal mapping clearer. If $f(z)$ is analytic then $w = f(z)$ defines a conformal mapping except at points where the derivative $f'(z)$ is zero.

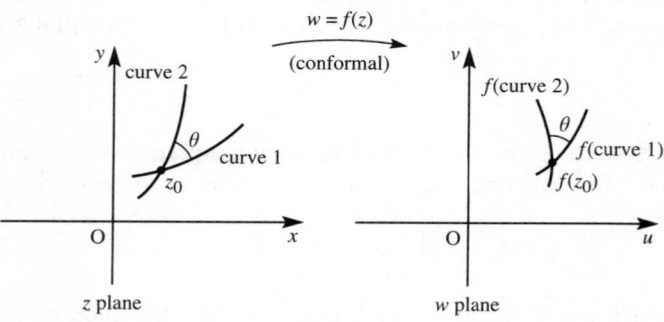

Figure 1.15 Conformal mappings.

Clearly the linear mappings

$$w = \alpha z + \beta \quad (\alpha \neq 0)$$

are conformal everywhere, since $dw/dz = \alpha$ and is not zero for any point in the z plane. Bilinear mappings given by (1.12) are not so straightforward to check. However, as we saw in Section 1.2.4, (1.12) can be rearranged as

$$w = \lambda + \frac{\mu}{\alpha z + \beta} \quad (\alpha, \mu \neq 0)$$

Thus

$$\frac{dw}{dz} = -\frac{\mu\alpha}{(\alpha z + \beta)^2}$$

which again is never zero for any point in the z plane. In fact, the only mapping we have considered so far that has a point at which it is not conformal everywhere is $w = z^2$ (cf. Example 1.8), which is not conformal at $z = 0$.

EXAMPLE 1.13   Determine the points at which the mapping $w = z + 1/z$ is not conformal and demonstrate this by considering the image in the w plane of the real axis in the z plane.

Solution   Taking $z = x + jy$ and $w = u + jv$, we have

$$w = u + jv = x + jy + \frac{x - jy}{x^2 + y^2}$$

which, on equating real and imaginary parts, gives

$$u = x + \frac{x}{x^2 + y^2}$$

$$v = y - \frac{y}{x^2 + y^2}$$

The real axis, $y = 0$, in the z plane corresponds to $v = 0$, the real axis in the w plane. Note, however, that the fixed point of the mapping is given by

$$z = z + \frac{1}{z}$$

or $z = \infty$. From the Cauchy–Riemann equations it is readily shown that w is analytic everywhere except at $z = 0$. Also, $dw/dz = 0$ when

$$1 - \frac{1}{z^2} = 0, \quad \text{that is,} \quad z = \pm 1$$

which are both on the real axis. Thus the mapping fails to be conformal at $z = 0$ and $z = \pm 1$. The image of $z = 1$ is $w = 2$, and the image of $z = -1$ is

$w = -2$. Consideration of the image of the real axis is therefore perfectly adequate, since this is a curve passing through each point where $w = z + 1/z$ fails to be conformal. It would be satisfying if we could analyse this mapping in the same manner as we did with $w = z^2$ in Example 1.8. Unfortunately, we cannot do this, because the algebra gets unwieldy (and, indeed, our knowledge of algebraic curves is also too scanty). Instead, let us look at the image of the point $z = 1 + \varepsilon$, where ε is a small real number. $\varepsilon > 0$ corresponds to the point Q just to the right of $z = 1$ on the real axis in the z plane, and the point P just to the left of $z = 1$ corresponds to $\varepsilon < 0$ (Figure 1.16).

If $z = 1 + \varepsilon$ then

$$w = 1 + \varepsilon + \frac{1}{1 + \varepsilon}$$

$$= 1 + \varepsilon + (1 + \varepsilon)^{-1}$$

$$= 1 + \varepsilon + 1 - \varepsilon + \varepsilon^2 - \varepsilon^3 + \ldots$$

$$\simeq 2 + \varepsilon^2$$

if $|\varepsilon|$ is much smaller than 1 (we shall discuss the validity of the power series expansion in Section 1.4). Whether ε is positive or negative, the point $w = 2 + \varepsilon^2$ is to the right of $w = 2$ in the w plane as indicated by the point R in Figure 1.16. Therefore, as $\varepsilon \to 0$, a curve (the real axis) that passes through $z = 1$ in the z plane making an angle $\theta = \pi$ corresponds to a curve (again the real axis) that approaches $w = 2$ in the w plane along the real axis from the right making an angle $\theta = 0$. Non-conformality has thus been confirmed. The treatment of $z = -1$ follows in an identical fashion, so the details are omitted. Note that when $y = 0$ ($v = 0$), $u = x + 1/x$ so, as the real axis in the z plane is traversed from $x = -\infty$ to $x = 0$, the real axis in the w plane is traversed from $u = -\infty$ to -2 *and back to* $u = -\infty$ *again* (when $x = -1$, u reaches 2). As the real axis in the z plane is traversed from $x = 0$ through $x = 1$ to $x = +\infty$, so the real axis in the w plane is traversed from $u = +\infty$ to $u = +2$ ($x = 1$) *back to* $u = \infty$ *again*. Hence the points on the real axis in the w plane in the range $-2 < u < 2$ do not correspond to real values of z. Solving $u = x + 1/x$ for x gives

$$x = \tfrac{1}{2}[u \pm \sqrt{(u^2 - 4)}]$$

which makes this point obvious. Figure 1.17 shows the image in the w plane of the real axis in the z plane. This mapping is very rich in interesting properties,

Figure 1.16 Image of $z = 1 + \varepsilon$ of Example 1.13.

Figure 1.17 Image in w plane of the real axis in the z plane for Example 1.13.

but we shall not pursue it further here. Aeronautical engineers may well meet it again if they study the flow around an aerofoil in two dimensions, for this mapping takes circles centred at the origin in the z plane onto meniscus (lens-shaped) regions in the w plane, and only a slight alteration is required before these images become aerofoil-shaped.

EXAMPLE 1.14   Examine the mapping

$$w = e^z$$

by (a) finding the images in the w plane of the lines $x = $ constant and $y = $ constant into the z plane, and (b) finding the image in the w plane of the left half-plane $(x < 0)$ in the z plane.

Solution   Taking $z = x + \mathrm{j}y$ and $w = u + \mathrm{j}v$, for $w = e^z$ we have

$$u = e^x \cos y$$

$$v = e^x \sin y$$

Squaring and adding these two equations, we obtain

$$u^2 + v^2 = e^{2x}$$

On the other hand, dividing the two equations gives

$$\frac{v}{u} = \tan y$$

We can now tackle the questions.

(a) Since $u^2 + v^2 = e^{2x}$, putting $x = $ constant shows that the lines parallel to the imaginary axis in the z plane correspond to circles centred at the origin in

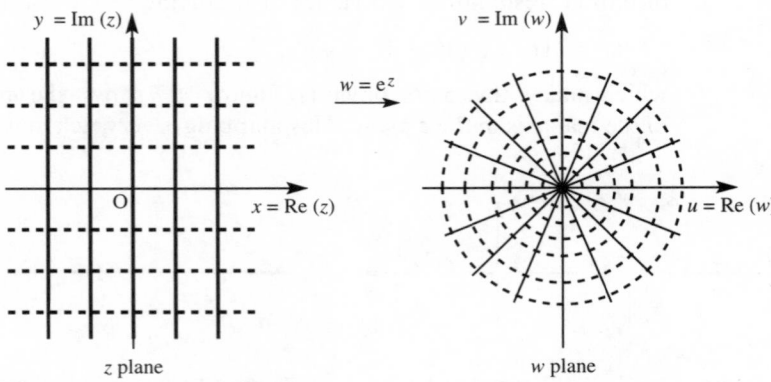

Figure 1.18 Mapping of lines under $w = e^z$.

the w plane. The equation

$$\frac{v}{u} = \tan y$$

shows that the lines parallel to the real axis in the z plane correspond to straight lines through the origin in the w plane ($v = u \tan \alpha$ if $y = \alpha$, a constant). Figure 1.18 shows the general picture.

(b) Since $u^2 + v^2 = e^{2x}$, if $x = 0$ then $u^2 + v^2 = 1$, so the imaginary axis in the z plane corresponds to the unit circle in the w plane. If $x < 0$ then $e^{2x} < 1$, and as $x \to -\infty$, $e^{2x} \to 0$, so the left half of the z plane corresponds to the interior of the unit circle in the w plane, as illustrated in Figure 1.19.

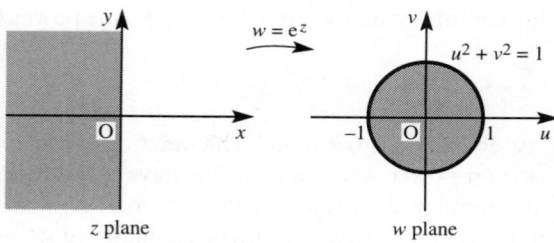

Figure 1.19 Mapping of half plane under $w = e^z$.

1.3.5   Exercises

33 Determine the points at which the following mappings are *not* conformal:

(a) $w = z^2 - 1$

(b) $w = 2z^3 - 21z^2 + 72z + 6$

(c) $w = 8z + \dfrac{1}{2z^2}$

34 Follow Example 1.13 for the mapping $w = z - 1/z$. Again determine the points at which the mapping is not conformal, but this time demonstrate this by looking at the image of the *imaginary* axis.

35 Find the region of the w plane corresponding to the following regions of the z plane under the exponential mapping $w = e^z$:

(a) $0 \leqslant x < \infty$

(b) $0 \leqslant x \leqslant 1, \ 0 \leqslant y \leqslant 1$

(c) $\frac{1}{2}\pi \leqslant y \leqslant \pi, \ 0 \leqslant x < \infty$

36 Consider the mapping $w = \sin z$. Determine the points at which the mapping is not conformal. By finding the images in the w plane of the lines $x = \text{constant}$ and $y = \text{constant}$ in the z plane ($z = x + \mathrm{j}y$), draw the mapping along similar lines to Figures 1.14 and 1.18.

37 Show that the transformation

$$z = \zeta + \frac{a^2}{\zeta}$$

where $z = x + \mathrm{j}y$ and $\zeta = R\,\mathrm{e}^{\mathrm{j}\theta}$ maps a circle, with centre at the origin and radius a, in the ζ plane, onto a straight line segment in the z plane. What is the length of the line? What happens if the circle in the ζ plane is centred at the origin but of radius b, where $b \neq a$?

1.4   Complex series

In *Modern Engineering Mathematics* we saw that there were distinct advantages in being able to express a function $f(x)$, such as the exponential, trigonometric and logarithmic functions, of a real variable x in terms of its power series expansion

$$f(x) = \sum_{n=0}^{\infty} a_n x^n = a_0 + a_1 x + a_2 x^2 + \ldots + a_r x^r + \ldots \qquad (1.27)$$

Power series are also very important in dealing with complex functions. In fact, any real function $f(x)$ which has a power series of the form in (1.27) has a corresponding complex function $f(z)$ having the same power series expansion, that is

$$f(z) = \sum_{n=0}^{\infty} a_n z^n = a_0 + a_1 z + a_2 z^2 + \ldots + a_r z^r + \ldots \qquad (1.28)$$

This property enables us to extend real functions to the complex case, so that methods based on power series expansions have a key role to play in formulating the theory of complex functions. In this section we shall consider some of the properties of the power series expansion of a complex function by drawing, wherever possible, an analogy with the power series expansion of the corresponding real function.

1.4.1   Power series

A series having the form

$$\sum_{n=0}^{\infty} a_n (z - z_0)^n = a_0 + a_1(z - z_0) + a_2(z - z_0)^2 + \ldots + a_r(z - z_0)^r + \ldots$$

$$\qquad (1.29)$$

in which the coefficients a_r are real or complex and z_0 is a fixed point in the complex z plane is called a **power series** about z_0 or a power series centred on z_0. Where $z_0 = 0$, the series (1.29) reduces to the series (1.28), which is a power series centred at the origin. In fact, on making the change of variable $z' = z - z_0$, (1.29) takes the form (1.28), so there is no loss of generality in considering the latter below.

Tests for the convergence or divergence of complex power series are similar to those used for power series of a real variable in *Modern Engineering Mathematics*. However, in complex series it is essential that the modulus $|a_n|$ be used. For example, the geometric series

$$\sum_{n=0}^{\infty} z^n$$

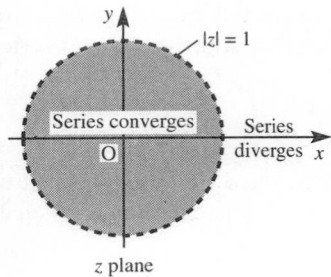

Figure 1.20 Region of convergence of $\sum_{n=0}^{\infty} z^n$.

has a sum to N terms

$$S_N = \sum_{n=0}^{N} z^n = \frac{1 - z^{N+1}}{1 - z}$$

and converges, if $|z| < 1$, to the limit $1/(1 - z)$ as $N \to \infty$. If $|z| \geqslant 1$, the series diverges. These results appear to be identical with the requirement that $|x| < 1$ to ensure convergence of the real power series

$$\frac{1}{1 - x} = \sum_{n=0}^{\infty} x^n$$

However, in the complex case the geometrical interpretation is different in that the condition $|z| < 1$ implies that z lies inside the circle centred at the origin and radius 1 in the z plane. Thus the series $\Sigma_{n=0}^{\infty} z^n$ converges if z lies inside this circle and diverges if z lies on or outside it. The situation is illustrated in Figure 1.20.

The existence of such a circle leads to an important concept in that in general there exists a circle centred at the origin and of radius R such that the series

$$\sum_{n=0}^{\infty} a_n z^n \qquad \begin{cases} \text{converges if} & |z| < R \\ \text{diverges if} & |z| > R \end{cases}$$

The radius R is called the **radius of convergence** of the power series. What happens when $|z| = R$ is normally investigated as a special case?

We have introduced the radius of convergence based on a circle centred at the origin, while the concept obviously does not depend on the location of the centre of the circle. If the series is centred on z_0 as in (1.29) then the convergence circle would be centred on z_0. Indeed it could even be centred at infinity, when the power series becomes

$$\sum_{n=0}^{\infty} a_n z^{-n} = a_0 + \frac{a_1}{z} + \frac{a_2}{z^2} + \ldots + \frac{a_r}{z^r} + \ldots$$

which we shall consider further in Section 1.4.5.

In order to determine the radius of convergence R for a given series, various tests for convergence, such as those introduced in *Modern Engineering Mathematics* for real series, may be applied. In particular, using d'Alembert's ratio test, it can be shown that the radius of convergence R of the complex series $\sum_{n=0}^{\infty} a_n z^n$ is given by

$$R = \lim_{n \to \infty} \left| \frac{a_n}{a_{n+1}} \right| \tag{1.30}$$

provided that the limit exists. Then the series is convergent within the disc $|z| < R$. In general, of course, the limit may not exist, and in such cases an alternative method must be used.

EXAMPLE 1.15   Find the power series, in the form indicated, representing the function $1/(z - 3)$ in the following three regions:

(a) $|z| < 3;$ $\displaystyle\sum_{n=0}^{\infty} a_n z^n$

(b) $|z - 2| < 1;$ $\displaystyle\sum_{n=0}^{\infty} a_n (z - 2)^n$

(c) $|z| > 3;$ $\displaystyle\sum_{n=0}^{\infty} \frac{a_n}{z^n}$

and sketch these regions on an Argand diagram.

Solution   We know that the binomial series expansion

$$(1 + z)^n = 1 + nz + \frac{n(n - 1)}{2!} z^2$$

$$+ \ldots + \frac{n(n - 1)(n - 2) \cdots (n - r + 1)}{r!} z^r + \ldots$$

is valid for $|z| < 1$. To solve the problem, we exploit this result by expanding the function $1/(z - 3)$ in three different ways:

(a) $\dfrac{1}{z - 3} = \dfrac{-\frac{1}{3}}{1 - \frac{1}{3}z} = -\frac{1}{3}(1 - \frac{1}{3}z)^{-1}$

$$= -\tfrac{1}{3}[1 + \tfrac{1}{3}z + (\tfrac{1}{3}z)^2 + \ldots + (\tfrac{1}{3}z)^n + \ldots]$$

for $|\frac{1}{3}z| < 1$, that is $|z| < 3$, giving the power series

$$\frac{1}{z - 3} = -\tfrac{1}{3} - \tfrac{1}{9}z - \tfrac{1}{27}z^2 - \ldots \quad (|z| < 3)$$

(b) $\dfrac{1}{z - 3} = \dfrac{1}{(z - 2) - 1} = [(z - 2) - 1]^{-1}$

$$= -[1 + (z - 2) + (z - 2)^2 + \ldots] \quad (|z - 2| < 1)$$

giving the power series

$$\frac{1}{z-3} = -1 - (z-2) - (z-2)^2 - \ldots \quad (|z-2| < 1)$$

(c) $\dfrac{1}{z-3} = \dfrac{1/z}{1-3/z} = \dfrac{1}{z}\left[1 + \dfrac{3}{z} + \left(\dfrac{3}{z}\right)^2 + \ldots\right]$

giving the power series

$$\frac{1}{z-3} = \frac{1}{z} + \frac{3}{z^2} + \frac{9}{z^3} + \ldots \quad (|z| > 3)$$

The three regions are sketched in Figure 1.21. Note that none of the regions include the point $z = 3$, which is termed a **singularity** of the function, a concept we shall discuss in Section 1.5.1.

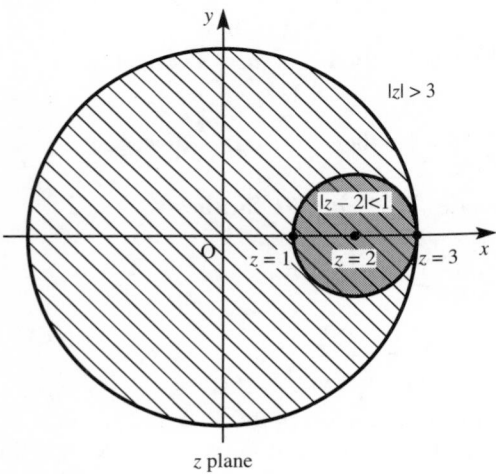

Figure 1.21 Regions of convergence for the series in Example 1.15.

In Example 1.15 the whole of the circle $|z| = 3$ was excluded from the three regions where the power series converge. In fact, it is possible to include any selected point in the z plane as a centre of the circle in which to define a power series that converges to $1/(z - 3)$ everywhere inside the circle, with the exception of the point $z = 3$. For example, the point $z = 4j$ would lead to the expansion of

$$\frac{1}{z - 4j + 4j - 3} = \frac{1}{4j - 3}\,\frac{1}{\dfrac{z - 4j}{4j - 3} + 1}$$

in a binomial series in powers of $(z - 4j)/(4j - 3)$, which converges to $1/(z - 3)$

inside the circle

$$|z - 4j| = |4j - 3| = \sqrt{(16 + 9)} = 5$$

We should not expect the point $z = 3$ to be included in any of the circles, since the function $1/(z - 3)$ is infinite there and hence not defined.

EXAMPLE 1.16   Prove that both the power series $\sum_{n=0}^{\infty} a_n z^n$ and the corresponding series of derivatives $\sum_{n=0}^{\infty} n a_n z^{n-1}$ have the same radius of convergence.

Solution   Let R be the radius of convergence of the power series $\sum_{n=0}^{\infty} a_n z^n$. Since $\lim_{n \to \infty} (a_n z_0^n) = 0$ (otherwise the series has no chance of convergence), if $|z_0| < R$ for some complex number z_0 then it is always possible to choose

$$|a_n| < |z_0|^{-n}$$

for $n > N$, with N a fixed integer. We now use d'Alembert's ratio test, namely

$$\text{if} \quad \lim_{n \to \infty} \left| \frac{a_{n+1}}{a_n} \right| < 1 \quad \text{then} \quad \sum_{n=0}^{\infty} a_n z^n \quad \text{converges}$$

$$\text{if} \quad \lim_{n \to \infty} \left| \frac{a_{n+1}}{a_n} \right| > 1 \quad \text{then} \quad \sum_{n=0}^{\infty} a_n z^n \quad \text{diverges}$$

The differential series $\sum_{n=1}^{\infty} n a_n z^{n-1}$ satisfies

$$\sum_{n=1}^{\infty} |n a_n z^{n-1}| < \sum_{n=1}^{\infty} n |a_n| |z|^{n-1}$$

$$< \sum_{n=1}^{\infty} n \frac{|z|^{n-1}}{|z_0|^n}$$

which, by the ratio test, converges if $0 < |z_0| < R$, since $|z| < |z_0|$ and $|z_0|$ can be as close to R as we choose. If, however, $|z| > R$ then $\lim_{n \to \infty} (a_n z^n) \neq 0$ and thus $\lim_{n \to \infty} (n a_n z^{n-1}) \neq 0$ too. Hence R is also the radius of convergence of the differentiated series $\sum_{n=1}^{\infty} n a_n z^{n-1}$.

The result obtained in Example 1.16 is important, since if the complex function

$$f(z) = \sum_{n=0}^{\infty} a_n z^n$$

that converges in $|z| < R$ then the derivative

$$f'(z) = \sum_{n=1}^{\infty} n a_n z^{n-1}$$

also converges in $|z| < R$. We can go on differentiating $f(z)$ through its power series and be sure that the differentiated function and the differentiated power series are equal inside the circle of convergence.

1.4.2   Exercises

38 Find the power series representation for the function $1/(z - j)$ in the regions

(a) $|z| < 1$ (b) $|z| > 1$

(c) $|z - 1 - j| < \sqrt{2}$

Deduce that the radius of convergence of the power series representation of this function is $|z_0 - j|$, where $z = z_0$ is the centre of the circle of convergence $(z_0 \neq j)$.

39 Find the power series representation of the function

$$f(z) = \frac{1}{z^2 + 1}$$

in the disc $|z| < 1$. Use Example 1.16 to deduce the power series for

(a) $\dfrac{1}{(z^2 + 1)^2}$ (b) $\dfrac{1}{(z^2 + 1)^3}$

valid in this same disc.

1.4.3   Taylor series

In *Modern Engineering Mathematics* we introduced the Taylor series expansion

$$f(x + a) = f(a) + \frac{x}{1!} f^{(1)}(a) + \frac{x^2}{2!} f^{(2)}(a) + \ldots = \sum_{n=0}^{\infty} \frac{x^n}{n!} f^{(n)}(a) \tag{1.31}$$

of a function $f(x)$ of a real variable x about $x = a$ and valid within the interval of convergence of the power series. For the engineer the ability to express a function in such a power series expansion is seen to be particularly useful in the development of numerical methods and the assessment of errors. The ability to express a complex function as a Taylor series is also important to engineers in many fields of applications, such as control and communications theory. The form of the Taylor series in the complex case is identical with that of (1.31).

If $f(z)$ is a complex function analytic inside and on a simple closed curve C (usually a circle) in the z plane then it follows from Example 1.16 that the higher derivatives of $f(z)$ also exist inside C. If z_0 and $z_0 + h$ are two fixed points inside C then

$$f(z_0 + h) = f(z_0) + h f^{(1)}(z_0) + \frac{h^2}{2!} f^{(2)}(z_0) + \ldots + \frac{h^n}{n!} f^{(n)}(z_0) + \ldots$$

where $f^{(k)}(z_0)$ is the kth derivative of $f(z)$ evaluated at $z = z_0$. Normally, $z = z_0 + h$ is introduced so that $h = z - z_0$, and the series expansion then becomes

$$f(z) = f(z_0) + (z - z_0) f^{(1)}(z_0) + \frac{(z - z_0)^2}{2!} f^{(2)}(z_0) + \ldots + \frac{(z - z_0)^n}{n!} f^{(n)}(z_0) + \ldots$$

$$= \sum_{n=0}^{\infty} \frac{(z - z_0)^n}{n!} f^{(n)}(z_0) \tag{1.32}$$

The power series expansion (1.32) is called the **Taylor series expansion** of the complex function $f(z)$ about z_0. The region of convergence of this series is

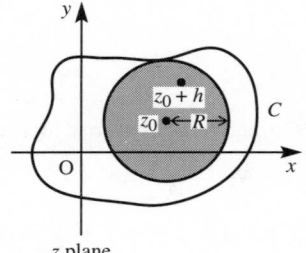

Figure 1.22 Region of convergence of the Taylor series.

z plane

$|z - z_0| < R$, a disc centred on $z = z_0$ and of radius R, the radius of convergence. Figure 1.22 illustrates the region of convergence. When $z_0 = 0$, as in real variables, the series expansion about the origin is often called a **Maclaurin series expansion**.

Since the proof of the Taylor series expansion does not add to our understanding of how to apply the result to the solution of engineering problems, we omit it at this stage.

EXAMPLE 1.17   Determine the Taylor series expansion of the function

$$f(z) = \frac{1}{z(z - 2j)}$$

about the point $z = j$:

(a) directly up to the term $(z - j)^4$,
(b) using the binomial expansion.

Determine the radius of convergence.

Solution   (a) The disadvantage with functions other than the most straightforward is that obtaining their derivatives is prohibitively complicated in terms of algebra. It is easier in this particular case to resolve the given function into partial fractions as

$$f(z) = \frac{1}{z(z - 2j)} = \frac{1}{2j}\left(\frac{1}{z - 2j} - \frac{1}{z}\right)$$

The right-hand side is now far easier to differentiate repeatedly. Proceeding to determine $f^{(k)}(j)$, we have

$$f(z) = \frac{1}{2j}\left(\frac{1}{z - 2j} - \frac{1}{z}\right), \qquad \text{so that} \quad f(j) = 1$$

$$f^{(1)}(z) = \frac{1}{2j}\left[-\frac{1}{(z - 2j)^2} + \frac{1}{z^2}\right], \qquad \text{so that} \quad f^{(1)}(j) = 0$$

$$f^{(2)}(z) = \frac{1}{2j}\left[\frac{2}{(z - 2j)^3} - \frac{2}{z^3}\right], \qquad \text{so that} \quad f^{(2)}(j) = -2$$

$$f^{(3)}(z) = \frac{1}{2j}\left[-\frac{6}{(z-2j)^4} + \frac{6}{z^4}\right], \qquad \text{so that} \quad f^{(3)}(j) = 0$$

$$f^{(4)}(z) = \frac{1}{2j}\left[\frac{24}{(z-2j)^5} - \frac{24}{z^5}\right], \qquad \text{so that} \quad f^{(4)}(j) = 24$$

leading from (1.32) to the Taylor series expansion

$$\frac{1}{z(z-2j)} = 1 - \frac{2}{2!}(z-j)^2 + \frac{24}{4!}(z-j)^4 + \dots$$

$$= 1 - (z-j)^2 + (z-j)^4 + \dots$$

(b) To use the binomial expansion, we first express $z(z-2j)$ as $(z-j+j)(z-j-j)$, which, being the difference of two squares $((z-j)^2 - j^2)$, leads to

$$f(z) = \frac{1}{z(z-2j)} = \frac{1}{(z-j)^2 + 1} = [1 + (z-j)^2]^{-1}$$

Use of the binomial expansion then gives

$$f(z) = 1 - (z-j)^2 + (z-j)^4 - (z-j)^6 + \dots$$

valid for $|z-j| < 1$, so the radius of convergence is 1.

The points where $f(z)$ is infinite (its singularities) are precisely at distance 1 away from $z = j$, so this value for the radius of convergence comes as no surprise.

EXAMPLE 1.18   Suggest a function to represent the power series

$$1 + z + \frac{z^2}{2!} + \frac{z^3}{3!} + \dots + \frac{z^n}{n!} + \dots$$

and determine its radius of convergence.

Solution   Set

$$f(z) = 1 + z + \frac{z^2}{2!} + \frac{z^3}{3!} + \dots = \sum_{n=0}^{\infty} \frac{z^n}{n!}$$

Assuming we can differentiate the series for $f(z)$ term by term, we obtain

$$f'(z) = \sum_{n=1}^{\infty} \frac{nz^{n-1}}{n!} = \sum_{n=1}^{\infty} \frac{z^{n-1}}{(n-1)!} = f(z)$$

Hence $f(z)$ is its own derivative. Since e^x is its own derivative in real variables, and is the only such function, it seems sensible to propose that

$$f(z) = \sum_{n=0}^{\infty} \frac{z^n}{n!} = e^z \tag{1.33}$$

the complex exponential function. Indeed the complex exponential e^z is defined by the power series (1.33). According to d'Alembert's ratio test the series $\Sigma_{n=0}^{\infty} a_n$ is convergent if $|a_{n+1}/a_n| \to L < 1$ as $n \to \infty$, where L is a real constant. If

$a_n = z^n/n!$ then $|a_{n+1}/a_n| = |z|/(n+1)$ which is less than unity for sufficiently large n, no matter how big $|z|$ is. Hence $\sum_{n=0}^{\infty} z^n/n!$ is convergent for *all* z and so has an infinite radius of convergence. Note that this is confirmed from (1.30). Such functions are called **entire**.

In the same way as we define the exponential function e^z by the power series expansion (1.31), we can define the circular functions $\sin z$ and $\cos z$ by the power series expansions

$$\sin z = z - \frac{z^3}{3!} + \frac{z^5}{5!} - \frac{z^7}{7!} + \ldots + (-1)^n \frac{z^{2n+1}}{(2n+1)!} + \ldots$$

$$\cos z = 1 - \frac{z^2}{2!} + \frac{z^4}{4!} - \frac{z^6}{6!} + \ldots + (-1)^n \frac{z^{2n}}{(2n)!} + \ldots$$

both of which are valid for all z. Using these power series definitions, we can readily prove the result (1.25), namely

$$e^{jz} = \cos z + j \sin z$$

1.4.4 Exercises

40 Find the first four non-zero terms of the Taylor series expansions of the following functions about the points indicated, and determine the radius of convergence in each case:

(a) $\dfrac{1}{1+z}$ $(z = 1)$

(b) $\dfrac{1}{z(z-4j)}$ $(z = 2j)$

(c) $\dfrac{1}{z^2}$ $(z = 1+j)$

41 Find the Maclaurin series expansion of the function

$$f(z) = \frac{1}{1 + z + z^2}$$

up to and including the term in z^3.

42 Without explicitly finding each Taylor series expansion, find the radius of convergence of the function

$$f(z) = \frac{1}{z^4 - 1}$$

about the three points $z = 0, z = 1 + j$ and $z = 2 + 2j$. Why is there no Taylor series expansion of this function about $z = j$?

43 Determine a Taylor series expansion of $f(z) = \tan z$. What is its radius of convergence?

1.4.5 Laurent series

Let us now examine more closely the solution of Example 1.15(c), where the power series obtained was

$$\frac{1}{z-3} = \frac{1}{z} + \frac{3}{z^2} + \frac{9}{z^3} + \dots$$

valid for $|z| > 3$. In the context of the definition, this is a power series about '$z = \infty$', the 'point at infinity'. Some readers, quite justifiably, may not be convinced that there is a single unique point at infinity. Figure 1.23 shows what is termed the **Riemann sphere**. A sphere lies on the complex z plane, with the contact point at the origin O. Let O$'$ be the top of the sphere, at the diametrically opposite point to O. Now, for any arbitrarily chosen point P in the z plane, by joining O$'$ and P we determine a unique point P$'$ where the line O$'$P intersects the sphere. There is thus exactly one point P$'$ on the sphere corresponding to each P in the z plane. The point O$'$ itself is the only point on the sphere that does not have a corresponding point on the (finite) z plane; we therefore say it corresponds to the **point at infinity** on the z plane.

Returning to consider power series, we know that, inside the radius of convergence, a given function and its Taylor series expansion are identically equal. Points at which a function fails to be analytic are called **singularities**, which we shall discuss in Section 1.5.1. No Taylor series expansion is possible about a singularity. Indeed, a Taylor series expansion about a point z_0 at which a function is analytic is only valid within a circle, centre z_0, up to the nearest singularity. Thus all singularities must be excluded in any Taylor series consideration. The Laurent series representation includes (or at least takes note of) the behaviour of the function in the vicinity of a singularity.

If $f(z)$ is a complex function analytic on concentric circles C_1 and C_2 of radii r_1 and r_2 (with $r_2 < r_1$), centred at z_0, and also analytic throughout the region between the circles (that is, an annular region), then for each point z within the annulus (Figure 1.24) $f(z)$ may be represented by the **Laurent series**

$$f(z) = \sum_{n=-\infty}^{\infty} c_n(z - z_0)^n$$

$$= \dots + \frac{c_{-r}}{(z - z_0)^r} + \frac{c_{-r+1}}{(z - z_0)^{r-1}} + \dots + \frac{c_{-1}}{z - z_0} + c_0$$

$$+ c_1(z - z_0) + \dots + c_r(z - z_0)^r + \dots \tag{1.34}$$

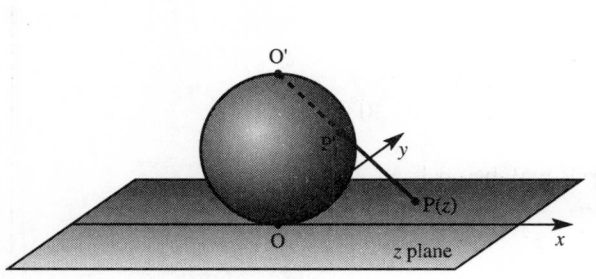

Figure 1.23 The Riemann sphere.

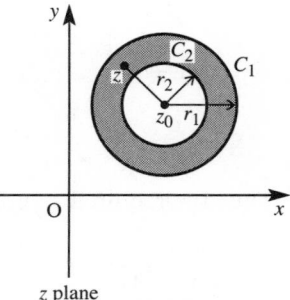

Figure 1.24 Region of validity of the Laurent series.

where in general the coefficients c_r are complex. The annular shape of the region is necessary in order to exclude the point $z = z_0$, which may be a singularity of $f(z)$, from consideration. If $f(z)$ is analytic at $z = z_0$ then $c_n = 0$ for $n = -1, -2, \ldots, -\infty$, and the Laurent series reduces to the Taylor series.

The Laurent series (1.34) for $f(z)$ may be written as

$$f(z) = \sum_{n=-\infty}^{-1} c_n(z - z_0)^n + \sum_{n=0}^{\infty} c_n(z - z_0)^n$$

and the first sum on the right-hand side, the 'non-Taylor' part is called the **principal part** of the Laurent series.

Of course, we can seldom actually sum a series to infinity. There is therefore often more than theoretical interest in the so-called 'remainder terms', these being the difference between the first n terms of a power series and the exact value of the function. For both Taylor and Laurent series these remainder terms are expressed, as in the case of real variable, in terms of the $(n+1)$th derivative of the function itself. For Laurent series in complex variables these derivatives can be expressed in terms of contour integrals (Section 1.6), which may be amenable to simple computation. Many of the details are outside the scope of this book, but there is some introductory material in Section 1.6.

EXAMPLE 1.19   For $f(z) = 1/z^2(z + 1)$ find the Laurent series expansion about (a) $z = 0$ and (b) $z = -1$. Determine the region of validity in each case.

Solution   As with Example 1.15, problems such as this are tackled by making use of the binomial series expansion

$$(1 + z)^n = 1 + nz + \frac{n(n-1)}{2!}z^2$$

$$+ \ldots + \frac{n(n-1)(n-2)\ldots(n-r+1)}{r!}z^r + \ldots$$

provided that $|z| < 1$.

(a) In this case $z_0 = 0$, so we need a series in powers of z. Thus

$$\frac{1}{z^2(1 + z)} = \frac{1}{z^2}(1 + z)^{-1}$$

$$= \frac{1}{z^2}(1 - z + z^2 - z^3 + z^4 - \ldots) \quad (0 < |z| < 1)$$

Thus the required Laurent series expansion is

$$\frac{1}{z^2(z + 1)} = \frac{1}{z^2} - \frac{1}{z} + 1 - z + z^2 \ldots$$

valid for $0 < |z| < 1$. The value $z = 0$ must be excluded because of the first two terms of the series. The region $0 < |z| < 1$ is an example of a **punctured disc**, a common occurrence in this branch of mathematics.

(b) In this case $z_0 = -1$, so we need a series in powers of $(z + 1)$. Thus

$$\frac{1}{z^2(z + 1)} = \frac{1}{(z + 1)}(z + 1 - 1)^{-2}$$

$$= \frac{1}{(z + 1)}[1 - (z + 1)]^{-2}$$

$$= \frac{1}{(z + 1)}[1 + 2(z + 1) + 3(z + 1)^2 + \ldots]$$

$$= \frac{1}{z + 1} + 2 + 3(z + 1) + 4(z + 1)^2 + \ldots$$

valid for $0 < |z + 1| < 1$. Note that in a meniscus-shaped region (that is, the region of overlap between the two circular regions $|z| < 1$ and $|z + 1| < 1$) both Laurent series are simultaneously valid. This is quite typical, and not a cause for concern.

EXAMPLE 1.20   Determine the Laurent series expansions of

$$f(z) = \frac{1}{(z + 1)(z + 3)}$$

valid for

(a) $1 < |z| < 3$
(b) $|z| > 3$
(c) $0 < |z + 1| < 2$
(d) $|z| < 1$

Solution   (a) Resolving into partial functions,

$$f(z) = \frac{1}{2}\left(\frac{1}{z + 1}\right) - \frac{1}{2}\left(\frac{1}{z + 3}\right)$$

Since $|z| > 1$ and $|z| < 3$, we express this as

$$f(z) = \frac{1}{2z}\left(\frac{1}{1 + 1/z}\right) - \frac{1}{6}\left(\frac{1}{1 + \frac{1}{3}z}\right)$$

$$= \frac{1}{2z}\left(1 + \frac{1}{z}\right)^{-1} - \frac{1}{6}(1 + \frac{1}{3}z)^{-1}$$

$$= \frac{1}{2z}\left(1 - \frac{1}{z} + \frac{1}{z^2} - \frac{1}{z^3} + \ldots\right) - \frac{1}{6}(1 - \frac{1}{3}z + \frac{1}{9}z^2 - \frac{1}{27}z^3 + \ldots)$$

$$= \ldots - \frac{1}{2z^4} + \frac{1}{2z^3} - \frac{1}{2z^2} + \frac{1}{2z} - \frac{1}{6} + \frac{1}{18}z - \frac{1}{54}z^2 + \frac{1}{162}z^3 - \ldots$$

(b) $f(z) = \dfrac{1}{2}\left(\dfrac{1}{z+1}\right) - \dfrac{1}{2}\left(\dfrac{1}{z+3}\right)$

Since $|z| > 3$, we express this as

$$f(z) = \frac{1}{2z}\left(\frac{1}{1 + 1/z}\right) - \frac{1}{2z}\left(\frac{1}{1 + 3/z}\right)$$

$$= \frac{1}{2z}\left(1 + \frac{1}{z}\right)^{-1} - \frac{1}{2z}\left(1 + \frac{3}{z}\right)^{-1}$$

$$= \frac{1}{2z}\left(1 - \frac{1}{z} + \frac{1}{z^2} - \frac{1}{z^3} + \dots\right) - \frac{1}{2z}\left(1 - \frac{3}{z} + \frac{9}{z^2} - \frac{27}{z^3} + \dots\right)$$

$$= \frac{1}{z^2} - \frac{4}{z^3} + \frac{13}{z^4} - \frac{40}{z^5} + \dots$$

(c) We can proceed as in Example 1.18. Alternatively, we can take $z + 1 = u$; then $0 < |u| < 2$ and

$$f(u) = \frac{1}{u(u+2)} = \frac{1}{2u(1 + \frac{1}{2}u)}$$

$$= \frac{1}{2u}(1 - \tfrac{1}{2}u + \tfrac{1}{4}u^2 - \tfrac{1}{8}u^3 + \dots)$$

giving

$$f(z) = \frac{1}{2(z+1)} - \tfrac{1}{4} + \tfrac{1}{8}(z+1) - \tfrac{1}{16}(z+1)^2 + \dots$$

(d) $f(z) = \dfrac{1}{2(z+1)} - \dfrac{1}{2(z+3)}$

Since $|z| < 1$, we express this as

$$f(z) = \frac{1}{2(1+z)} - \frac{1}{6(1 + \frac{1}{3}z)}$$

$$= \tfrac{1}{2}(1 + z)^{-1} - \tfrac{1}{6}(1 + \tfrac{1}{3}z)^{-1}$$

$$= \tfrac{1}{2}(1 - z + z^2 - z^3 + \dots) - \tfrac{1}{6}(1 - \tfrac{1}{3}z + \tfrac{1}{9}z^2 - \tfrac{1}{27}z^3 + \dots)$$

$$= \tfrac{1}{3} - \tfrac{4}{9}z + \tfrac{13}{27}z^2 - \tfrac{40}{81}z^3 + \dots$$

EXAMPLE 1.21   Determine the Laurent series expansion of the function $f(z) = z^3 \, e^{1/z}$ about

(a) $z = 0$

(b) $z = a$, a finite, non-zero complex number

(c) $z = \infty$

Solution   (a) From (1.33),

$$e^z = 1 + z + \frac{z^2}{2!} + \ldots \quad (0 \leqslant |z| < \infty)$$

Substituting $1/z$ for z, we obtain

$$e^{1/z} = 1 + \frac{1}{z} + \frac{1}{2!\,z^2} + \ldots \quad (0 < |z| \leqslant \infty)$$

so that

$$z^3 e^{1/z} = z^3 + z^2 + \frac{z}{2!} + \frac{1}{3!} + \frac{1}{4!\,z} + \frac{1}{5!\,z^2} + \ldots \quad (0 < |z| \leqslant \infty)$$

This series has infinitely many terms in its principal part, but stops at z^3 (it is written back to front). Series with never-ending principal parts are a problem, and fortunately are uncommon in engineering. Note also that the series is valid in an infinite punctured disc.

(b) The value of $f(a)$ must be $a^3 e^{1/a}$, which is not infinite since $a \neq 0$. Therefore $f(z)$ has a Taylor series expansion

$$f(z) = f(a) + (z - a)f^{(1)}(a) + \frac{(z - a)^2}{2!} f^{(2)}(a) + \ldots$$

about $z = a$. We have

$$f^{(1)}(z) = \frac{\mathrm{d}}{\mathrm{d}z}(z^3 e^{1/z}) = 3z^2 e^{1/z} - z e^{1/z}$$

$$f^{(2)}(z) = \frac{\mathrm{d}}{\mathrm{d}z}(3z^2 e^{1/z} - z e^{1/z}) = 6z e^{1/z} - 4 e^{1/z} + \frac{1}{z^2} e^{1/z}$$

giving the series as

$$z^3 e^{1/z} = a^3 e^{1/a} + (z - a)(3a^2 e^{1/a} - a e^{1/a})$$
$$+ \frac{1}{2!}(z - a)^2 \left(6a e^{1/a} - 4 e^{1/a} + \frac{1}{a^2} e^{1/a} \right) + \ldots$$

which is valid in the region $|z - a| < R$, where R is the distance between the origin, where $f(z)$ is not defined, and the point a; hence $R = |a|$. Thus the region of validity for this Taylor series is the disc $|z - a| < |a|$.

(c) To expand about $z = \infty$, let $w = 1/z$, so that

$$f(z) = \frac{1}{w^3} e^w$$

Expanding about $w = 0$ then gives

$$f\left(\frac{1}{w}\right) = \frac{1}{w^3} \left(1 + w + \frac{w^2}{2!} + \frac{w^3}{3!} + \ldots \right)$$

$$= \frac{1}{w^3} + \frac{1}{w^2} + \frac{1}{2!\,w} + \frac{1}{3!} + \frac{w}{4!} + \dots \quad (0 < |w| < \infty)$$

Note that this time there are only three terms in the principal part of $f(z)\,(= f(1/w))$.

1.4.6   Exercises

44 Determine the Laurent series expansion of
$$f(z) = \frac{1}{z(z-1)^2}$$
about (a) $z = 0$ and (b) $z = 1$, and specify the region of validity for each.

45 Determine the Laurent series expansion of the function
$$f(z) = z^2 \sin\frac{1}{z}$$
about the points

(a) $z = 0$ (b) $z = \infty$
(c) $z = a$, a finite non-zero complex number
(For (c), do *not* calculate the coefficients explicitly.)

46 Expand
$$f(z) = \frac{z}{(z-1)(2-z)}$$
in a Laurent series expansion valid for

(a) $|z| < 1$ (b) $1 < |z| < 2$ (c) $|z| > 2$
(d) $|z - 1| > 1$ (e) $0 < |z - 2| < 1$

1.5   Singularities, zeros and residues

1.5.1   Singularities and zeros

As indicated in Section 1.4.5 a **singularity** of a complex function $f(z)$ is a point of the z plane where $f(z)$ ceases to be analytic. Normally, this means $f(z)$ is infinite at such a point, but it can also mean that there is a choice of values, and it is not possible to pick a particular one. In this chapter we shall be mainly concerned with singularities at which $f(z)$ has an infinite value. A **zero** of $f(z)$ is a point in the z plane at which $f(z) = 0$.

Singularities can be classified in terms of the Laurent series expansion of $f(z)$ about the point in question. If $f(z)$ has a Taylor series expansion, that is a Laurent series expansion with zero principal part, about the point $z = z_0$, then z_0 is a **regular point** of $f(z)$. If $f(z)$ has a Laurent series expansion with only a finite number of terms in its principal part, for example

$$f(z) = \frac{a_{-m}}{(z-z_0)^m} + \ldots + \frac{a_{-1}}{(z-z_0)} + a_0 + a_1(z-z_0) + \ldots + a_m(z-z_0)^m + \ldots$$

then $f(z)$ has a singularity at $z = z_0$ called a **pole**. If there are m terms in the principal part, as in this example, then the pole is said to be of **order** m. Another way of defining this is to say that z_0 is a pole of order m if

$$\lim_{z \to z_0} (z-z_0)^m f(z) = a_{-m} \qquad (1.35)$$

where a_{-m} is finite and non-zero. If the principal part of the Laurent series for $f(z)$ at $z = z_0$ has infinitely many terms, which means that the above limit does not exist for any m, then $z = z_0$ is called an **essential singularity** of $f(z)$.

If $f(z)$ appears to be singular at $z = z_0$, but it turns out to be possible to define a Taylor series expansion there, then $z = z_0$ is called a **removable singularity**. The following examples illustrate these cases.

(a) $f(z) = z^{-1}$ has a pole of order one, called a **simple pole**, at $z = 0$.

(b) $f(z) = (z-1)^{-3}$ has a pole of order three at $z = 1$.

(c) $f(z) = e^{1/(z-j)}$ has an essential singularity at $z = j$.

(d) The function

$$f(z) = \frac{z-1}{(z+2)(z-3)^2}$$

has a zero at $z = 1$, a simple pole at $z = -2$ and a pole of order two at $z = 3$.

(e) The function

$$f(z) = \frac{\sin z}{z}$$

is not defined at $z = 0$, and appears to be singular there. However, defining

$$\text{sinc } z = \begin{cases} (\sin z)/z & (z \neq 0) \\ 1 & (z = 0) \end{cases}$$

gives a function having a Taylor series expansion

$$\text{sinc } z = 1 - \frac{z^2}{3!} + \frac{z^4}{5!} - \ldots$$

that is regular at $z = 0$. Therefore the (apparent) singularity at $z = 0$ has been removed, and thus $f(z) = (\sin z)/z$ has a removable singularity at $z = 0$.

Functions whose only singularities are poles are called **meromorphic** and, by and large, in engineering applications of complex variables most functions are meromorphic. To help familiarize the reader with these definitions, the following example should prove instructive.

EXAMPLE 1.22   Find the singularities and zeros of the following complex functions:

(a) $\dfrac{1}{z^4 - z^2(1 + j) + j}$ (b) $\dfrac{z - 1}{z^4 - z^2(1 + j) + j}$

(c) $\dfrac{\sin(z - 1)}{z^4 - z^2(1 + j) + j}$ (d) $\dfrac{1}{[z^4 - z^2(1 + j) + j]^3}$

Solution   (a) For

$$f(z) = \frac{1}{z^4 - z^2(1 + j) + j}$$

the numerator is never zero, and the denominator is only infinite when z is infinite. Thus $f(z)$ has no zeros in the finite z plane. The denominator is zero when

$$z^4 - z^2(1 + j) + j = 0$$

which factorizes to give

$$(z^2 - 1)(z^2 - j) = 0$$

leading to

$$z^2 = 1 \text{ or } j$$

so that the singularities are at

$$z = +1, \ -1, \ (1 + j)/\sqrt{2}, \ (1 - j)/\sqrt{2} \tag{1.36}$$

all of which are simple poles since none of the roots are repeated.

(b) The function

$$f(z) = \frac{z - 1}{z^4 - z^2(1 + j) + j}$$

is similar to $f(z)$ in (a), except that it has the additional term $z - 1$ in the numerator. Therefore, at first glance, it seems that the singularities are as in (1.36). However, a closer look indicates that $f(z)$ can be rewritten as

$$f(z) = \frac{z - 1}{(z - 1)(z + 1)[z - \sqrt{\tfrac{1}{2}}(1 + j)][z - \sqrt{\tfrac{1}{2}}(1 - j)]}$$

and the factor $z - 1$ cancels, rendering $z = 1$ a removable singularity, and reducing $f(z)$ to

$$f(z) = \frac{1}{(z + 1)[z - \sqrt{\tfrac{1}{2}}(1 + j)][z - \sqrt{\tfrac{1}{2}}(1 - j)]}$$

which has no (finite) zeros and $z = -1$, $\sqrt{\tfrac{1}{2}}(1 + j)$ and $\sqrt{\tfrac{1}{2}}(1 - j)$ as simple poles.

(c) In the case of

$$f(z) = \frac{\sin(z-1)}{z^4 - z^2(1+j) + j}$$

the function may be rewritten as

$$f(z) = \frac{\sin(z-1)}{z-1} \cdot \frac{1}{(z+1)[z - \sqrt{\tfrac{1}{2}}(1+j)][z - \sqrt{\tfrac{1}{2}}(1-j)]}$$

Now

$$\frac{\sin(z-1)}{z-1} \to 1 \quad \text{as } z \to 1$$

so once again $z = 1$ is a removable singularity. Also, as in (b), $z = -1$, $\sqrt{\tfrac{1}{2}}(1+j)$ and $\sqrt{\tfrac{1}{2}}(1-j)$ are simple poles and the only singularities. However,

$$\sin(z-1) = 0$$

has the general solution $z = 1 + N\pi$ $(N = 0, \pm1, \pm2, \ldots)$. Thus, apart from $N = 0$, all of these are zeros of $f(z)$.

(d) For

$$f(z) = \frac{1}{[z^4 - z^2(1+j) + j]^3}$$

factorizing as in (b), we have

$$f(z) = \frac{1}{(z-1)^3(z+1)^3[z - \sqrt{\tfrac{1}{2}}(1+j)]^3[z - \sqrt{\tfrac{1}{2}}(1-j)]^3}$$

so -1, $+1$, $\sqrt{\tfrac{1}{2}}(1+j)$ and $\sqrt{\tfrac{1}{2}}(1-j)$ are still singularities, but this time they are triply repeated. Hence they are all poles of order three. There are no zeros.

1.5.2   Exercises

47 Determine the location of, and classify, the singularities and zeros of the following functions. Specify also any zeros that may exist.

(a) $\dfrac{\cos z}{z^2}$

(b) $\dfrac{1}{(z+j)^2(z-j)}$

(c) $\dfrac{z}{z^4 - 1}$

(d) $\coth z$

(e) $\dfrac{\sin z}{z^2 + \pi^2}$

(f) $e^{z/(1-z)}$

(g) $\dfrac{z-1}{z^2+1}$

(h) $\dfrac{z+j}{(z+2)^3(z-3)}$

(i) $\dfrac{1}{z^2(z^2 - 4z + 5)}$

48 Expand each of the following functions in a Laurent series about $z = 0$, and give the type of singularity (if any) in each case:

(a) $\dfrac{1 - \cos z}{z}$

(b) $\dfrac{e^{z^2}}{z^3}$

(c) $z^{-1}\cosh z^{-1}$

(d) $\tan^{-1}(z^2 + 2z + 2)$

49 Show that if $f(z)$ is the ratio of two polynomials then it cannot have an essential singularity.

1.5.3   Residues

If a complex function $f(z)$ has a pole at the point $z = z_0$ then the coefficient a_{-1} of the term $1/(z - z_0)$ in the Laurent series expansion of $f(z)$ about $z = z_0$ is called the **residue** of $f(z)$ at the point $z = z_0$. The importance of residues will become apparent when we discuss integration in Section 1.6. Here we shall concentrate on efficient ways of calculating them, usually without finding the Laurent series expansion explicitly. However, experience and judgement are sometimes the only help in finding the easiest way of calculating residues. First let us consider the case when $f(z)$ has a simple pole at $z = z_0$. This implies, from the definition of a simple pole, that

$$f(z) = \frac{a_{-1}}{z - z_0} + a_0 + a_1(z - z_0) + \ldots$$

in an appropriate annulus $S < |z - z_0| < R$. Multiplying by $z - z_0$ gives

$$(z - z_0)f(z) = a_{-1} + a_0(z - z_0) + \ldots$$

which is a Taylor series expansion of $(z - z_0)f(z)$. If we let z approach z_0, we then obtain the result

$$\text{residue at a} \atop \text{simple pole } z_0 \quad = \lim_{z \to z_0} [(z - z_0)f(z)] = a_{-1} \tag{1.37}$$

Hence this limit gives a way of calculating the residue at a simple pole.

EXAMPLE 1.23   Determine the residues of

$$f(z) = \frac{2z}{(z^2 + 1)(2z - 1)}$$

at each of its poles in the finite z plane.

Solution   Factorizing the denominator, we have

$$f(z) = \frac{2z}{(z - j)(z + j)(2z - 1)}$$

so that $f(z)$ has simple poles at $z = j$, $-j$ and $\frac{1}{2}$. Using (1.37) then gives

$$\text{residue} \atop \text{at } z = j \quad = \lim_{z \to j} (z - j)\frac{2z}{(z - j)(z + j)(2z - 1)}$$

$$= \frac{2j}{2j(2j - 1)} = -\frac{1 + 2j}{5}$$

$$\text{residue} \atop \text{at } z = -j \quad = \lim_{z \to -j} (z - j)\frac{2z}{(z - j)(z + j)(2z - 1)}$$

$$= \frac{-2j}{-2j(-2j - 1)} = -\frac{1 - 2j}{5}$$

$$\text{residue} \atop \text{at } z = \tfrac{1}{2} \quad = \lim_{z \to \frac{1}{2}} (z - \tfrac{1}{2})\frac{z}{(z - j)(z + j)(z - \tfrac{1}{2})}$$

$$= \frac{\tfrac{1}{2}}{(\tfrac{1}{2} - j)(\tfrac{1}{2} + j)} = \tfrac{2}{5}$$

Note in this last case the importance of expressing $2z - 1$ as $2(z - \tfrac{1}{2})$.

EXAMPLE 1.24 Determine the residues of the function $1/(1 + z^4)$ at each of its poles in the finite z plane.

Solution The function $1/(1 + z^4)$ has poles where

$$1 + z^4 = 0$$

that is, at the points where

$$z^4 = -1 = e^{\pi j + 2\pi n j}$$

with n an integer. Recalling how to determine the roots of a complex number, these points are

$$z = e^{\pi j/4 + \pi j n/2} \quad (n = 0, 1, 2, 3)$$

that is

$$z = e^{\pi j/4}, \ e^{3\pi j/4}, \ e^{5\pi j/4}, \ e^{7\pi j/4}$$

or

$$z = (1 + j)/\sqrt{2}, \ (-1 + j)/\sqrt{2}, \ (-1 - j)/\sqrt{2}, \ (1 - j)/\sqrt{2}$$

To find the residue at the point z_0, we use (1.37), giving

$$\text{residue} \atop \text{at } z_0 \quad = \lim_{z \to z_0} \left(\frac{z - z_0}{1 + z^4}\right)$$

where z_0 is one of the above roots of $z^4 = -1$. It pays to use L'Hôpital's rule (Chapter 8 of *Modern Engineering Mathematics*) before substituting for a particular z_0. This is justified since $(z - z_0)/(1 + z_4)$ is of the indeterminate form $0/0$ at each of the four simple poles. Differentiating numerator and denominator gives

$$\lim_{z \to z_0} \left(\frac{z - z_0}{1 + z^4}\right) = \lim_{z \to z_0} \left(\frac{1}{4z^3}\right)$$

$$= \frac{1}{4z_0^3}$$

since $4z^3$ is not zero at any of the poles. $1/4z_0^3$ is thus the value of each residue at $z = z_0$. Substituting for the four values $(\pm 1 \pm j)/\sqrt{2}$ gives the following:

residue
at $z = (1 + j)/\sqrt{2}$ $\qquad = \dfrac{1}{4(\sqrt{\tfrac{1}{2}})^3(1 + j)^3} = -(1 + j)/4\sqrt{2}$

residue
at $z = (1 - j)/\sqrt{2}$ $\qquad = \dfrac{1}{4(\sqrt{\tfrac{1}{2}})^3(1 - j)^3} = (-1 + j)/4\sqrt{2}$

residue
at $z = (-1 + j)/\sqrt{2}$ $\qquad = \dfrac{1}{4(\sqrt{\tfrac{1}{2}})^3(-1 + j)^3} = (1 - j)/4\sqrt{2}$

residue
at $z = (-1 - j)/\sqrt{2}$ $\qquad = \dfrac{1}{4(\sqrt{\tfrac{1}{2}})^3(-1 - j)^3} = (1 + j)/4\sqrt{2}$

Finding each Laurent series for the four poles explicitly would involve far more difficult manipulation. However, the enthusiastic reader may like to check at least one of the above residues.

Next suppose that we have a pole of order two at $z = z_0$. The function $f(z)$ then has a Laurent series expansion of the form

$$f(z) = \frac{a_{-2}}{(z - z_0)^2} + \frac{a_{-1}}{z - z_0} + a_0 + a_1(z - z_0) + \ldots$$

Again, we are only interested in isolating the residue a_{-1}. This time we cannot use (1.37). Instead, we multiply $f(z)$ by $(z - z_0)^2$ to obtain

$$(z - z_0)^2 f(z) = a_{-2} + a_{-1}(z - z_0) + a_0(z - z_0)^2 + \ldots$$

and we differentiate to eliminate the unwanted a_{-2}:

$$\frac{d}{dz}[(z - z_0)^2 f(z)] = a_{-1} + 2a_0(z - z_0) + \ldots$$

Letting z tend to z_0 then gives

$$\lim_{z \to z_0} \left[\frac{d}{dz}(z - z_0)^2 f(z) \right] = a_{-1}$$

the required residue.

We now have the essence of finding residues, so let us recapitulate and generalize. If $f(z)$ has a pole of order m at $z - z_0$, we first multiply $f(z)$ by $(z - z_0)^m$. If $m \geqslant 2$, we then need to differentiate as many times as it takes (that is, $m - 1$ times) to make a_{-1} the leading term, without the multiplying factor $z - z_0$. The general formula for the residue at a pole of order m is thus

$$\frac{1}{(m-1)!} \lim_{z \to z_0} \left\{ \frac{d^{m-1}}{dz^{m-1}} [(z - z_0)^m f(z)] \right\} \tag{1.38}$$

where the factor $(m-1)!$ arises when the term $a_{-1}(z - z_0)^{m-1}$ is differentiated $m - 1$ times. This formula looks as difficult to apply as finding the Laurent series expansion directly. This indeed is often so; and hence experience and judgement are required. A few examples will help to decide on which way to calculate residues. A word of warning is in order here: a common source of error is confusion between the derivative in the formula for the residue, and the employment of L'Hôpital's rule to find the resulting limit.

EXAMPLE 1.25   Determine the residues of

$$f(z) = \frac{z^2 - 2z}{(z + 1)^2 (z^2 + 4)}$$

at each of its poles in the finite z plane.

Solution   Factorizing the denominator gives

$$f(z) = \frac{z^2 - 2z}{(z + 1)^2 (z - 2j)(z + 2j)}$$

so that $f(z)$ has simple poles at $z = 2j$ and $z = -2j$ and a pole of order two at $z = -1$. Using (1.37),

$$\begin{aligned}
\text{residue} \atop \text{at } z = 2j \quad &= \lim_{z \to 2j} (z - 2j) \frac{z^2 - 2z}{(z + 1)^2 (z - 2j)(z + 2j)} \\[2mm]
&= \frac{-4 - 4j}{(2j + 1)^2 (4j)} = \tfrac{1}{25}(7 + j)
\end{aligned}$$

$$\begin{aligned}
\text{residue} \atop \text{at } z = -2j \quad &= \lim_{z \to -2j} (z + 2j) \frac{z^2 - 2z}{(z + 1)^2 (z - 2j)(z + 2j)} \\[2mm]
&= \frac{-4 + 4j}{(-2j + 1)^2 (-4j)} = \tfrac{1}{25}(7 - j)
\end{aligned}$$

Using (1.38) with $m = 2$ we know that

$$\begin{aligned}
\text{residue} \atop \text{at } z = -1 \quad &= \frac{1}{1!} \lim_{z \to -1} \frac{d}{dz} \left[(z + 1)^2 \frac{z^2 - 2z}{(z + 1)^2 (z^2 + 4)} \right] \\[2mm]
&= \lim_{z \to -1} \frac{(z^2 + 4)(2z - 2) - (z^2 - 2z)(2z)}{(z^2 + 4)^2} \\[2mm]
&= \frac{(5)(-4) - (3)(-2)}{25} = -\tfrac{14}{25}
\end{aligned}$$

EXAMPLE 1.26   Determine the residues of the following functions at the points indicated:

(a) $\dfrac{e^z}{(1+z^2)^2}$ $(z=j)$

(b) $\left(\dfrac{\sin z}{z^2}\right)^3$ $(z=0)$

(c) $\dfrac{z^4}{(z+1)^3}$ $(z=-1)$

Solution   (a) Since

$$\frac{e^z}{(z^2+1)^2} = \frac{e^z}{(z+j)^2(z-j)^2}$$

and e^z is regular at $z=j$, it follows that $z=j$ is a pole of order two. Thus, from (1.38),

$$\text{residue} = \lim_{z\to j}\frac{d}{dz}\left[(z-j)^2\frac{e^z}{(z+j)^2(z-j)^2}\right]$$

$$= \lim_{z\to j}\left\{\frac{d}{dz}\left[\frac{e^z}{(z+j)^2}\right]\right\}$$

$$= \lim_{z\to j}\frac{(z+j)^2 e^z - 2(z+j)e^z}{(z+j)^4}$$

$$= \frac{(2j)^2 e^j - 2(2j)e^j}{(2j)^4}$$

$$= -\tfrac{1}{4}(1+j)e^j$$

Since $e^j = \cos 1 + j\sin 1$, we calculate the residue at $z=j$ as $0.075 - j0.345$.

(b) The function $[(\sin z)/z^2]^3$ has a pole at $z=0$, and, since $(\sin z/z)\to 1$ as $z\to 0$, $(\sin^2 z)/z^2$ may also be defined as 1 at $z=0$. Therefore, since

$$\left(\frac{\sin z}{z^2}\right)^3 = \frac{\sin^3 z}{z^3}\frac{1}{z^3}$$

the singularity at $z=0$ must be a pole of order three. We could use (1.38) to obtain the residue, which would involve determining the second derivative, but it is easier in this case to derive the coefficient of $1/z$ from the Laurent series expansion

$$\frac{\sin z}{z} = 1 - \frac{z^2}{3!} + \frac{z^4}{5!} - \cdots$$

giving

$$\frac{\sin z}{z^2} = \frac{1}{z} - \tfrac{1}{6}z + \tfrac{1}{120}z^3 - \cdots$$

Taking the cube of this series, we have

$$\left(\frac{\sin z}{z^2}\right)^3 = \left(\frac{1}{z} - \frac{1}{6}z + \frac{1}{120}z^3 - \dots\right)^3$$

$$= \frac{1}{z^3} - 3\frac{1}{z^2}\frac{z}{6} + \dots$$

$$= \frac{1}{z^3} - \frac{1}{2z} + \dots$$

Hence the residue at $z = 0$ is $-\frac{1}{2}$.

(c) The function $z^4/(z+1)^3$ has a triple pole at $z = -1$, so, using (1.38),

$$\text{residue} = \lim_{z \to -1} \left\{\frac{1}{2}\frac{d^2}{dz^2}\left[(z+1)^3 \frac{z^4}{(z+1)^3}\right]\right\}$$

$$= \lim_{z \to -1} \left[\frac{1}{2}\frac{d^2}{dz^2}(z^4)\right]$$

$$= \lim_{z \to -1} \frac{1}{2} \times 4 \times 3z^2 = 6(-1)^2 = 6$$

Residues are sometimes difficult to calculate using (1.38), especially if circular functions are involved and the pole is of order three or more. In such cases direct calculation of the Laurent series expansion using the standard series for $\sin z$ and $\cos z$ together with the binomial series, as in Example 1.26(b), is the best procedure.

1.5.4   Exercises

50 Determine the residues of the following rational functions at each pole in the finite z plane:

(a) $\dfrac{2z + 1}{z^2 - z - 2}$

(b) $\dfrac{1}{z^2(1 - z)}$

(c) $\dfrac{3z^2 + 2}{(z - 1)(z^2 + 9)}$

(d) $\dfrac{z^3 - z^2 + z - 1}{z^3 + 4z}$

(e) $\dfrac{z^6 + 4z^4 + z^3 + 1}{(z - 1)^5}$

(f) $\left(\dfrac{z + 1}{z - 1}\right)^2$

(g) $\dfrac{z + 1}{(z - 1)^2(z + 3)}$

(h) $\dfrac{3 + 4z}{z^3 + 3z^2 + 2z}$

51 Calculate the residues at the simple poles indicated of the following functions:

(a) $\dfrac{\cos z}{z}$ $(z = 0)$

(b) $\dfrac{\sin z}{z^4 + z^2 + 1}$ $(z = e^{\pi j/3})$

(c) $\dfrac{z^4 - 1}{z^4 + 1}$ $(z = e^{\pi j/4})$

(d) $\dfrac{z}{\sin z}$ $(z = \pi)$

(e) $\dfrac{1}{(z^2 + 1)^2}$ $(z = j)$

52 The following functions have poles at the points indicated. Determine the order of the pole and the residue there.

(a) $\dfrac{\cos z}{z^3}$ $(z = 0)$

(b) $\dfrac{z^2 - 2z}{(z + 1)^2(z^2 + 4)}$ $(z = -1)$

(c) $\dfrac{e^z}{\sin^2 z}$ $(z = n\pi, n \text{ an integer})$

(*Hint:* use $\lim_{u \to 0}(\sin u)/u = 1$ $(u = z - n\pi)$, after differentiating, to replace $\sin u$ by u under the limit.)

1.6 Contour integration

Consider the definite integral

$$\int_{z_1}^{z_2} f(z)\,\mathrm{d}z$$

of the function $f(z)$ of a complex variable z, in which z_1 and z_2 are a pair of complex numbers. This implies that we evaluate the integral as z takes values, in the z plane, from the point z_1 to the point z_2. Since these are two points in a plane, it follows that to evaluate the definite integral we require that some path from z_1 to z_2 be defined. It is therefore clear that a definite integral of a complex function $f(z)$ is in fact a **line integral**, as introduced in Chapter 9 of *Modern Engineering Mathematics*.

Line integrals will be considered again in Section 7.4 of this book. Briefly, for now, a line integral in the (x, y) plane, of the real variables x and y, is an integral of the form

$$\int_C [P(x, y)\,\mathrm{d}x + Q(x, y)\,\mathrm{d}y] \tag{1.39}$$

where C denotes the path of integration between two points A and B in the plane. In the particular case when

$$\frac{\partial P}{\partial y} = \frac{\partial Q}{\partial x} \tag{1.40}$$

the integrand $P(x, y)\,\mathrm{d}x + Q(x, y)\,\mathrm{d}y$ is a total differential, and the line integral is independent of the path C joining A and B.

In this section we introduce **contour integration**, which is the term used for evaluating line integrals in the complex plane.

1.6.1 Contour integrals

Let $f(z)$ be a complex function that is continuous at all points of a simple curve C in the z plane that is of finite length and joins two points a and b. (We have not gone into great detail regarding the question of continuity for complex variables. Suffice it to say that the intuitive concepts described in Chapter 6 of *Modern Engineering Mathematics* for real variables carry over to the case of complex variables.) Subdivide the curve into n parts by the points $z_1, z_2, \ldots, z_{n-1}$, taking $z_0 = a$ and $z_n = b$ (Figure 1.25). On each arc joining z_{k-1} to z_k $(k = 1, \ldots, n)$ choose a point $\tilde{z}_k$. Form the sum

$$S_n = f(\tilde{z}_1)(z_1 - z_0) + f(\tilde{z}_2)(z_2 - z_1) + \ldots + f(\tilde{z}_n)(z_n - z_{n-1})$$

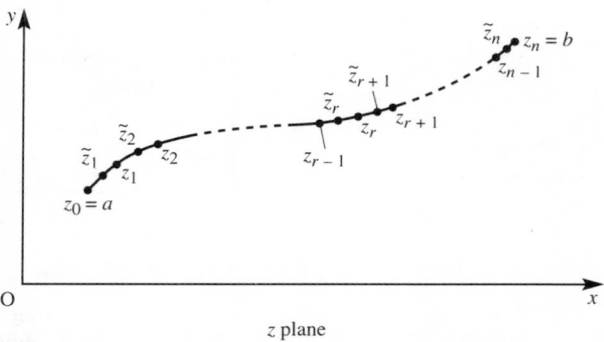

Figure 1.25 Partitioning of the curve C.

Then, writing $z_k - z_{k-1} = \Delta z_k$, S_n becomes

$$S_n = \sum_{k=1}^{n} f(\tilde{z}_k) \Delta z_k$$

If we let n increase in such a way that the largest of the chord lengths $|\Delta z_k|$ approaches zero then the sum S_n approaches a limit that does not depend on the mode of subdivision of the curve. We call this limit the **contour integral** of $f(z)$ along the curve C:

$$\int_C f(z)\,\mathrm{d}z = \lim_{|\Delta z_k| \to 0} \sum_{k=1}^{n} f(\tilde{z}_k)\Delta z_k \tag{1.41}$$

If we take $z = x + \mathrm{j}y$ and express $f(z)$ as

$$f(z) = u(x, y) + \mathrm{j}v(x, y)$$

then it can be shown from (1.41) that

$$\int_C f(z)\,\mathrm{d}z = \int_C [u(x, y) + \mathrm{j}v(x, y)]\,(\mathrm{d}x + \mathrm{j}\,\mathrm{d}y)$$

or

$$\int_C f(z)\,\mathrm{d}z = \int_C [u(x, y)\,\mathrm{d}x - v(x, y)\,\mathrm{d}y] + \mathrm{j}\int_C [v(x, y)\,\mathrm{d}x + u(x, y)\,\mathrm{d}y] \tag{1.42}$$

Both of the integrals on the right-hand side of (1.42) are real line integrals of the form (1.39), and can therefore be evaluated using the methods developed for such integrals.

EXAMPLE 1.27   Evaluate the contour integral $\int_C z^2\,\mathrm{d}z$ along the path C from $-1 + \mathrm{j}$ to $5 + \mathrm{j}3$ and composed of the two straight line segments, the first from $-1 + \mathrm{j}$ to $5 + \mathrm{j}$ and the second from $5 + \mathrm{j}$ to $5 + \mathrm{j}3$.

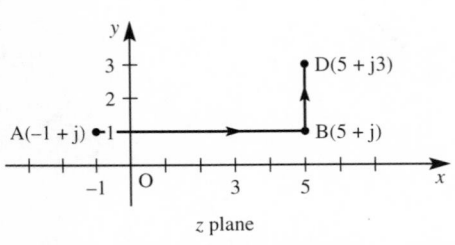

Figure 1.26 Path of integration for Example 1.27.   **Figure 1.27** Path of integration for Example 1.28.

Solution   The path of integration C is shown in Figure 1.26. Since $z^2 = (x + jy)^2 = (x^2 - y^2) + j2xy$, it follows from (1.42) that

$$I = \int_C z^2 \, dz = \int_C [(x^2 - y^2) \, dx - 2xy \, dy] + j \int_C [2xy \, dx + (x^2 - y^2) \, dy]$$

Along AB, $y = 1$ and $dy = 0$, so that

$$I_{AB} = \int_{-1}^{5} (x^2 - 1) \, dx + j \int_{-1}^{5} 2x \, dx$$

$$= [\tfrac{1}{3}x^3 - x]_{-1}^{5} + j[x^2]_{-1}^{5}$$

$$= 36 + j24$$

Along BD, $x = 5$ and $dx = 0$, so that

$$I_{BD} = \int_{1}^{3} -10y \, dy + j \int_{1}^{3} (25 - y^2) \, dy$$

$$= [-5y^2]_{1}^{3} + j[25y - \tfrac{1}{3}y^3]_{1}^{3}$$

$$= -40 + j\tfrac{124}{3}$$

Thus

$$\int_C z^2 \, dz = I_{AB} + I_{BD} = (36 + j24) + (-40 + j\tfrac{124}{3}) = -4 + j\tfrac{196}{3}$$

EXAMPLE 1.28   Show that $\int_C (z + 1) \, dz = 0$, where C is the boundary of the square with vertices at $z = 0$, $z = 1 + j0$, $z = 1 + j1$ and $z = 0 + j1$.

Solution   The path of integration C is shown in Figure 1.27.
Since $z + 1 = (x + 1) + jy$, it follows from (1.42) that

$$I = \int_C (z + 1) \, dz = \int_C [(x + 1) \, dx - y \, dy] + j \int_C [y \, dx + (x + 1) \, dy]$$

Along OA, $y = 0$ and $dy = 0$, so that

$$I_{OA} = \int_{0}^{1} (x + 1) \, dx = \tfrac{3}{2}$$

Along AB, $x = 1$ and $dx = 0$, so that

$$I_{AB} = \int_0^1 -y\,dy + j \int_0^1 2\,dy = -\tfrac{1}{2} + j2$$

Along BD, $y = 1$ and $dy = 0$, so that

$$I_{BD} = \int_1^0 (x + 1)\,dx + j \int_1^0 dx = -\tfrac{3}{2} - j$$

Along DO, $x = 0$ and $dx = 0$, so that

$$I_{DO} = \int_1^0 -y\,dy + j \int_1^0 dy = \tfrac{1}{2} - j$$

Thus

$$\int_C (z + 1)\,dz = I_{OA} + I_{AB} + I_{BD} + I_{DO} = 0$$

1.6.2   Cauchy's theorem

The most important result in the whole of complex variable theory is called Cauchy's theorem and it provides the foundation on which the theory of integration with respect to a complex variable is based. The theorem may be stated as follows.

THEOREM 1.1   Cauchy's theorem

If $f(z)$ is an analytic function with derivative $f'(z)$ that is continuous at all points inside and on a simple closed curve C then

$$\oint_C f(z)\,dz = 0$$

(Note the use of the symbol $\oint_C$ to denote integration around a closed curve, with the convention being that the integral is evaluated travelling round C in the positive or anticlockwise direction.)

Proof   To prove the theorem, we make use of **Green's theorem** in a plane, which will be introduced in Section 7.4.5. At this stage a statement of the theorem is sufficient.

If C is a simple closed curve enclosing a region A in a plane, and $P(x, y)$ and $Q(x, y)$ are continuous functions with continuous partial derivatives, then

$$\oint_C (P\,dx + Q\,dy) = \iint_A \left(\frac{\partial Q}{\partial x} - \frac{\partial P}{\partial y} \right) dx\,dy \tag{1.43}$$

Returning to the contour integral and taking

$$f(z) = u(x, y) + jv(x, y), \qquad z = x + jy$$

we have from (1.42)

$$\oint_C f(z)\,dz = \oint_C (u\,dx - v\,dy) + j\oint_C (v\,dx + u\,dy) \qquad \textbf{(1.44)}$$

Since $f(z)$ is analytic, the Cauchy–Riemann equations

$$\frac{\partial u}{\partial x} = \frac{\partial v}{\partial y}, \qquad \frac{\partial v}{\partial x} = -\frac{\partial u}{\partial y}$$

are satisfied on C and within the region R enclosed by C.

Since $u(x, y)$ and $v(x, y)$ satisfy the conditions imposed on $P(x, y)$ and $Q(x, y)$ in Green's theorem, we can apply (1.43) to both integrals on the right-hand side of (1.44) to give

$$\oint_C f(z)\,dz = \iint_R \left(-\frac{\partial v}{\partial x} - \frac{\partial u}{\partial y} \right) dx\,dy + j\iint_R \left(\frac{\partial u}{\partial x} - \frac{\partial v}{\partial y} \right) dx\,dy$$

$$= 0 + j0$$

by the Cauchy–Riemann equations. Thus

$$\oint_C f(z)\,dz = 0$$

as required.

In fact, the restriction in Cauchy's theorem that $f'(z)$ has to be continuous on C can be removed and so make the theorem applicable to a wider class of functions. A revised form of Theorem 1.1, with the restriction removed, is referred to as the **fundamental theorem of complex integration**. Since the proof that $f'(z)$ need not be continuous on C was first proposed by Goursat, the fundamental theorem is also sometimes referred to as the **Cauchy–Goursat theorem**. We shall not pursue the consequences of relaxation of this restriction any further in this book.

In practice, we frequently need to evaluate contour integrals involving functions such as

$$f_1(z) = \frac{1}{z - 2}, \qquad f_2(z) = \frac{z}{(z - 3)^2(z + 2)}$$

that have singularities associated with them. Since the function ceases to be analytic at such points, how do we accommodate for a singularity if it is inside the contour of integration? To resolve the problem the singularity is removed by **deforming the contour**.

First let us consider the case when the complex function $f(z)$ has a single isolated singularity at $z = z_0$ inside a closed curve C. To remove the singularity,

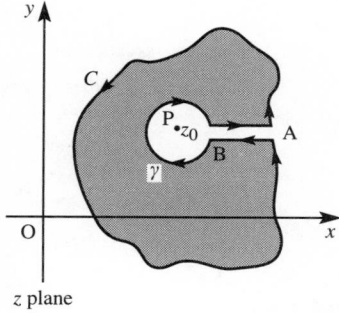

y

C

P $\cdot z_0$

B

A

γ

O

x

z plane

Figure 1.28 Deformed contour for an isolated singularity.

we surround it by a circle γ, of radius ρ, and then cut the region between the circle and the outer contour C by a straight line AB. This leads to the deformed contour indicated by the arrows in Figure 1.28. In the figure the line linking the circle γ to the contour C is shown as a narrow channel in order to enable us to distinguish between the path A to B and the path B to A. The region inside this deformed contour is shown shaded in the figure (recall that the region inside a closed contour is the region on the left as we travel round it). Since this contains no singularities, we can apply Cauchy's theorem and write

$$\oint_C f(z)\,dz + \int_{AB} f(z)\,dz + \oint_\gamma f(z)\,dz + \int_{BA} f(z)\,dz = 0$$

Since

$$\oint_{BA} = -\oint_{AB}, \quad \text{and} \quad \oint_\gamma = -\oint_\gamma$$

this reduces to

$$\oint_C f(z)\,dz = \oint_{\gamma^+} f(z)\,dz \tag{1.45}$$

with the $+$ indicating the change of sense from clockwise to anticlockwise around the circle γ.

EXAMPLE 1.29 Evaluate the integral

$$\oint_C \frac{dz}{z}$$

around

(a) any contour containing the origin;

(b) any contour not containing the origin.

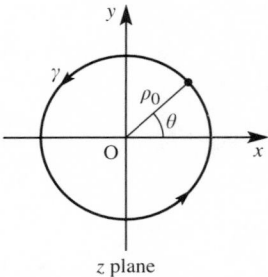

Figure 1.29 A circle of radius ρ_0 centred at the origin.

Solution   (a) $f(z) = 1/z$ has a singularity (a simple pole) at $z = 0$. Hence, using (1.45), the integral around any contour enclosing the origin is the same as the integral around a circle γ, centred at the origin and of radius ρ_0. We thus need to evaluate

$$\oint_\gamma \frac{1}{z}\,dz$$

As can be seen from Figure 1.29, on the circle γ

$$z = \rho_0\,e^{j\theta} \quad (0 \leqslant \theta < 2\pi)$$

so

$$dz = j\rho_0\,e^{j\theta}\,d\theta$$

leading to

$$\oint_\gamma \frac{1}{z}\,dz = \int_0^{2\pi} \frac{j\rho_0\,e^{j\theta}}{\rho_0\,e^{j\theta}}\,d\theta$$
$$= \int_0^{2\pi} j\,d\theta = 2\pi j$$

Hence if C encloses the origin then

$$\oint_C \frac{dz}{z} = 2\pi j$$

(b) If C does not enclose the origin then, by Cauchy's theorem,

$$\oint_C \frac{dz}{z} = 0$$

since $1/z$ is analytic inside and on any curve that does not enclose the origin.

EXAMPLE 1.30   Generalize the result of Example 1.29 by evaluating

$$\oint_C \frac{dz}{z^n}$$

where n is an integer, around any contour containing the origin.

Solution   If $n \leqslant 0$, we can apply Cauchy's theorem straight away (or evaluate the integral directly) to show the integral is zero. If $n > 1$, we proceed as in Example 1.29 and evaluate the integral around a circle, centred at the origin. Taking $z = \rho_0 \, e^{j\theta}$ as in Example 1.29, we have

$$\oint_C \frac{dz}{z^n} = \int_0^{2\pi} \frac{j\rho_0 \, e^{j\theta}}{\rho_0^n \, e^{nj\theta}} \, d\theta$$

where ρ_0 is once more the radius of the circle. If $n \neq 1$,

$$\oint_C \frac{dz}{z^n} = j \int_0^{2\pi} \frac{d\theta}{\rho_0^{n-1} \, e^{(n-1)j\theta}}$$

$$= j\rho_0^{1-n} \left[\frac{e^{(1-n)j\theta}}{(1-n)j} \right]_0^{2\pi}$$

$$= \frac{\rho_0^{1-n}}{1-n} (e^{(1-n)2\pi j} - 1)$$

$$= 0$$

since $e^{2\pi jN} = 1$ for any integer N. Hence

$$\oint_C \frac{dz}{z^n} = 0 \quad (n \neq 1)$$

In Examples 1.29 and 1.30 we have thus established the perhaps surprising result that if C is a contour containing the origin then

$$\int_C \frac{dz}{z^n} = \begin{cases} 2\pi j & (n = 1) \\ 0 & (n \text{ any other integer}) \end{cases}$$

If C does not contain the origin, the integral is of course zero by Cauchy's theorem.

EXAMPLE 1.31   Evaluate the integral

$$\oint_C \frac{dz}{z - 2 - j}$$

around any contour C containing the point $z = 2 + j$.

Solution   The function

$$f(z) = \frac{1}{z - 2 - j}$$

has a singularity (simple pole) at $z = 2 + j$. Hence, using (1.45), the integral around any contour C enclosing the point $z = 2 + j$ is the same as the integral around a circle γ centred at $z = 2 + \mathrm{j}$ and of radius ρ. Thus we need to evaluate

$$\oint_\gamma \frac{\mathrm{d}z}{z - 2 - \mathrm{j}}$$

As can be seen from Figure 1.30, on the circle γ

$$z = (2 + \mathrm{j}) + \rho\,\mathrm{e}^{\mathrm{j}\theta} \quad (0 \leqslant \theta < 2\pi)$$

$$\mathrm{d}z = \mathrm{j}\rho\,\mathrm{e}^{\mathrm{j}\theta}\,\mathrm{d}\theta$$

leading to

$$\oint_\gamma \frac{\mathrm{d}z}{z - 2 - \mathrm{j}} = \int_0^{2\pi} \frac{\mathrm{j}\rho\,\mathrm{e}^{\mathrm{j}\theta}}{\rho\,\mathrm{e}^{\mathrm{j}\theta}}\,\mathrm{d}\theta = \int_0^{2\pi} \mathrm{j}\,\mathrm{d}\theta = \mathrm{j}2\pi$$

Hence if C encloses the point $z = 2 + \mathrm{j}$ then

$$\oint_C \frac{\mathrm{d}z}{z - 2 - \mathrm{j}} = \pi\mathrm{j}2$$

Compare this with the answer to Example 1.29.

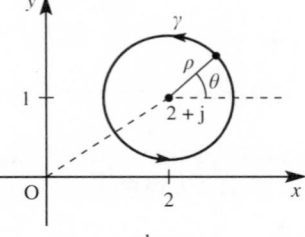

Figure 1.30 A circle of radius ρ centred at $2+\mathrm{j}$.

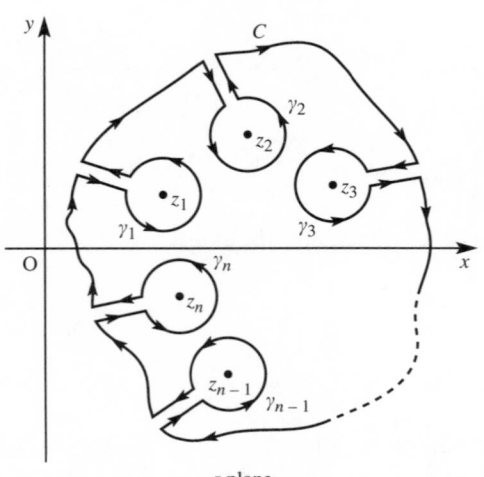

Figure 1.31 Deformed contour for n singularities.

So far we have only considered functions having a single singularity inside the closed contour C. The method can be extended to accommodate any finite number of singularities. If the function $f(z)$ has a finite number of singularities at $z = z_1, z_2, \ldots, z_n$, inside a closed contour C then we can deform the latter by introducing n circles $\gamma_1, \gamma_2, \ldots, \gamma_n$ to surround each of the singularities as shown in Figure 1.31. It is then readily shown that

$$\oint_C f(z)\,dz = \oint_{\gamma_1} f(z)\,dz + \oint_{\gamma_2} f(z)\,dz + \ldots + \oint_{\gamma_n} f(z)\,dz \qquad (1.46)$$

EXAMPLE 1.32   Evaluate the contour integral

$$\oint_C \frac{z\,dz}{(z-1)(z+2j)}$$

where C is

(a) any contour enclosing both the points $z = 1$ and $z = -2j$;

(b) any contour enclosing $z = -2j$ but excluding the point $z = 1$.

Solution   The function

$$f(z) = \frac{z}{(z-1)(z+2j)}$$

has singularities at both $z = 1$ and $z = -2j$.

(a) Since the contour encloses both singularities, we need to evaluate the integrals around circles γ_1 and γ_2 of radii ρ_1 and ρ_2 surrounding the points $z = 1$ and $z = -2j$ respectively. Alternatively, we can resolve $f(z)$ into partial fractions as

$$f(z) = \frac{\frac{1}{3}(1 - j2)}{z - 1} + \frac{\frac{1}{5}(4 + 2j)}{z + 2j}$$

and consider

$$I = \oint_C \frac{z\,dz}{(z-1)(z-2j)} = \tfrac{1}{3}(1 - 2j)\oint_C \frac{dz}{z-1} + \tfrac{1}{5}(4 + 2j)\oint_C \frac{dz}{z+2j}$$

$$= I_1 + I_2$$

The integrand of I_1 has a single singularity at $z = 1$, and we simply need to evaluate it around the circle γ_1 of radius ρ_1 about $z = 1$ to give

$$I_1 = 2\pi j$$

Similarly, I_2 has a single singularity at $z = -2j$, and we evaluate it around the circle γ_2 to give

$$I_2 = 2\pi j$$

Then

$$I = \tfrac{1}{3}(1 - j2)2\pi j + \tfrac{1}{5}(4 + j2)2\pi j = 2\pi j(\tfrac{17}{15} - j\tfrac{4}{15})$$

Thus if the contour C contains both the singularities then

$$\oint_C \frac{z\,dz}{(z - 1)(z + j2)} = 2\pi j(\tfrac{17}{15} - j\tfrac{4}{15})$$

(b) If the contour C only contains the singularity $z = -2j$ then

$$\oint_C \frac{z\,dz}{(z - 1)(z + 2j)} = I_2 = 2\pi j(\tfrac{4}{5} + j\tfrac{2}{5})$$

In Examples 1.29–1.32 we can note some similarity in the answers, with the common occurrence of the term $2\pi j$. It therefore appears that it may be possible to obtain some general results to assist in the evaluation of contour integrals. Indeed, this is the case, and such general results are contained in the **Cauchy integral theorem**.

THEOREM 1.2 Cauchy integral theorem

Let $f(z)$ be an analytic function within and on a simple closed contour C. If z_0 is any point in C then

$$\oint_C \frac{f(z)}{z - z_0}\,dz = 2\pi j f(z_0) \tag{1.47}$$

If we differentiate repeatedly n times with respect to z under the integral sign then it also follows that

$$\oint_C \frac{f(z)}{(z - z_0)^{n+1}}\,dz = \frac{2\pi j}{n!} f^{(n)}(z_0) \tag{1.48}$$

$\square$

Note that (1.48) implies that if $f'(z)$ exists at $z = z_0$ so does $f^{(n)}(z)$ for all n, as predicted earlier in the observations following Example 1.16.

EXAMPLE 1.33 Evalute the contour integral

$$\oint_C \frac{2z}{(z - 1)(z + 2)(z + j)}\,dz$$

where C is a contour that includes the three points $z = 1, z = -2$ and $z = -j$.

Solution   Since

$$f(z) = \frac{2z}{(z-1)(z+2)(z+j)}$$

has singularities at the points $z = 1$, $z = -2$ and $z = -j$ inside the contour, it follows from (1.46) that

$$\oint_C f(z)\,dz = \oint_{\gamma_1} f(z)\,dz + \oint_{\gamma_2} f(z)\,dz + \oint_{\gamma_3} f(z)\,dz \tag{1.49}$$

where γ_1, γ_2 and γ_3 are circles centred at the singularities $z = 1$, $z = -2$ and $z = -j$ respectively. In order to make use of the Cauchy integral theorem, (1.49) is written as

$$\oint_C f(z)\,dz = \oint_{\gamma_1} \frac{\left[\dfrac{2z}{(z+2)(z+j)}\right]}{z-1}\,dz + \oint_{\gamma_2} \frac{\left[\dfrac{2z}{(z-1)(z+j)}\right]}{z+2}\,dz$$

$$+ \oint_{\gamma_3} \frac{\left[\dfrac{2z}{(z-1)(z+2)}\right]}{z+j}\,dz$$

$$= \oint_{\gamma_1} \frac{f_1(z)}{z-1}\,dz + \oint_{\gamma_2} \frac{f_2(z)}{z+2}\,dz + \oint_{\gamma_3} \frac{f_3(z)}{z+j}\,dz$$

Since $f_1(z)$, $f_2(z)$ and $f_3(z)$ are analytic within and on the circles γ_1, γ_2 and γ_3 respectively, it follows from (1.47) that

$$\oint_C f(z)\,dz = 2\pi j[f_1(1) + f_2(-2) + f_3(-j)]$$

$$= 2\pi j\left[\frac{3}{2(1+j)} + \frac{-4}{(-3)(-2+j)} + \frac{-2j}{(-j-1)(-j+2)}\right]$$

so that

$$\oint_C \frac{2z\,dz}{(z-1)(z+2)(z+j)} = 0$$

EXAMPLE 1.34   Evaluate the contour integral

$$\oint_C \frac{z^4}{(z-1)^3}\,dz$$

where the contour C encloses the point $z = 1$.

Solution   Since $f(z) = z^4/(z-1)^3$ has a pole of order three at $z = 1$, it follows that

$$\oint_C f(z)\,dz = \oint_{\gamma} \frac{z^4}{(z-1)^3}\,dz$$

where γ is a circle centred at $z = 1$. Writing $f_1(z) = z^4$, then

$$\oint_C f(z)\,dz = \oint_\gamma \frac{f_1(z)}{(z-1)^3}\,dz$$

and, since $f_1(z)$ is analytic within and on the circle γ, it follows from (1.48) that

$$\oint_C f(z)\,dz = 2\pi j \frac{1}{2!}\left[\frac{d^2}{dz^2}f_1(z)\right]_{z=1}$$

$$= \pi j(12z^2)_{z=1}$$

so that

$$\oint_C \frac{z^4}{(z-1)^3}\,dz = 12\pi j$$

1.6.3   Exercises

53 Evaluate $\int_C (z^2 + 3z)\,dz$ along the following contours C in the complex z plane:

(a) the straight line joining $2 + j0$ to $0 + j2$;

(b) the straight lines from $2 + j0$ to $2 + j2$ and then to $0 + j2$;

(c) the circle $|z| = 2$ from $2 + j0$ to $0 + j2$ in an anticlockwise direction.

54 Evaluate $\oint_C (5z^4 - z^3 + 2)\,dz$ around the following closed contours C in the z plane:

(a) the circle $|z| = 1$;

(b) the square with vertices at $0 + j0$, $1 + j0$, $1 + j1$ and $1 + j0$;

(c) the curve consisting of the parabolas $y = x^2$ from $0 + j0$ to $1 + j1$ and $y^2 = x$ from $1 + j$ to $0 + j0$.

55 Generalize the result of Example 1.30, and show that

$$\int_C \frac{dz}{(z-z_0)^n} = \begin{cases} j2\pi & (n=1) \\ 0 & (n \neq 1) \end{cases}$$

where C is a simple closed contour surrounding the point $z = z_0$.

56 Evaluate the contour integral

$$\oint_C \frac{dz}{z-4}$$

where C is any simple closed curve and $z = 4$ is

(a) outside C (b) inside C

57 Using the Cauchy integral theorem, evaluate the contour integral

$$\oint_C \frac{2z\,dz}{(2z-1)(z+2)}$$

where C is

(a) the circle $|z| = 1$ (b) the circle $|z| = 3$

58 Using the Cauchy integral theorem, evaluate the contour integral

$$\oint_C \frac{5z\,dz}{(z+1)(z-2)(z+4j)}$$

where C is

(a) the circle $|z| = 3$ (b) the circle $|z| = 5$

59 Using the Cauchy integral theorem, evaluate the following contour integrals:

(a) $\oint_C \frac{z^3 + z}{(2z+1)^3}\,dz$

where C is the unit circle $|z| = 1$;

(b) $\oint_C \frac{4z}{(z-1)(z+2)^2}\,dz$

where C is the circle $|z| = 3$.

1.6.4 The residue theorem

This theorem draws together the theories of differentiation and integration of a complex function. It is concerned with the evaluation of the contour integral

$$I = \oint_C f(z)\,\mathrm{d}z$$

where the complex function $f(z)$ has a finite number n of isolated singularities at $z_1, z_2, \ldots, z_n$ inside the closed contour C. Defining the contour C as in Figure 1.31, we have as in (1.46) that

$$I = \oint_C f(z)\,\mathrm{d}z = \oint_{\gamma_1} f(z)\,\mathrm{d}z + \oint_{\gamma_2} f(z)\,\mathrm{d}z + \ldots + \oint_{\gamma_n} f(z)\,\mathrm{d}z \qquad \textbf{(1.46)}$$

If we assume that $f(z)$ has a pole of order m at $z = z_i$ then it can be represented by the Laurent series expansion

$$f(z) = \frac{a_{-m}^{(i)}}{(z - z_i)^m} + \ldots + \frac{a_{-1}^{(i)}}{z - z_i} + a_0^{(i)} + a_1^{(i)}(z - z_i) + \ldots + a_m^{(i)}(z - z_i)^m + \ldots$$

valid in the annulus $r_i < |z - z_i| < R_i$. If the curve C lies entirely within this annulus then, by Cauchy's theorem, (1.46) becomes

$$I = \oint_C f(z)\,\mathrm{d}z = \oint_{\gamma_i} f(z)\,\mathrm{d}z$$

Substituting the Laurent series expansion of $f(z)$, which we can certainly do since we are within the annulus of convergence, we obtain

$$\oint_{\gamma_i} f(z)\,\mathrm{d}z = \oint_{\gamma_i} \left[\frac{a_{-m}^{(i)}}{(z - z_i)^m} + \ldots + \frac{a_{-1}^{(i)}}{z - z_i} + a_0^{(i)} + a_1^{(i)}(z - z_i) + \ldots \right.$$

$$\left. + a_m^{(i)}(z - z_i)^m + \ldots \right] \mathrm{d}z$$

$$= a_{-m}^{(i)} \oint_{\gamma_i} \frac{\mathrm{d}z}{(z - z_i)^m} + \ldots + a_{-1}^{(i)} \oint_{\gamma_i} \frac{\mathrm{d}z}{z - z_i}$$

$$+ \oint_{\gamma_i} \mathrm{d}z + a_1^{(i)} \oint_{\gamma_i} (z - z_i)\,\mathrm{d}z + \ldots$$

Using the result from Exercise 55, all of these integrals are zero, except the one multiplying $a_{-1}^{(i)}$, the residue, which has the value $2\pi\mathrm{j}$. We have therefore shown that

$$\oint_{\gamma_i} f(z)\,\mathrm{d}z = 2\pi\mathrm{j}a_{-1}^{(i)} = 2\pi\mathrm{j} \times \text{residue at } z = z_i$$

This clearly generalizes, so that (1.46) becomes

$$I = \oint_C f(z)\, dz = 2\pi j \sum_{i=1}^{n} (\text{residue at } z = z_i)$$

$$= 2\pi j \times (\text{sum of residues inside } C)$$

Thus we have the following general result.

THEOREM 1.3 The residue theorem

If $f(z)$ is an analytic function within and on a simple closed curve C, apart from a finite number of poles, then

$$\oint_C f(z)\, dz = 2\pi j \times [\text{sum of residues of } f(z) \text{ at the poles inside } C] \qquad \square$$

This is quite a remarkable result in that it enables us to evaluate the contour integral $\oint_C f(z)\, dz$ by simply evaluating one coefficient of the Laurent series expansion of $f(z)$ at each of its singularities inside C.

EXAMPLE 1.35 Evaluate the contour integral

$$\oint_C \frac{dz}{z(1 + z)}$$

if C is

(a) the circle $|z| = \frac{1}{2}$;

(b) the circle $|z| = 2$.

Solution The singularities of $1/z(1 + z)$ are at $z = 0$ and -1. Evaluating the residues using (1.37), we have

$$\begin{matrix} \text{residue} \\ \text{at } z = 0 \end{matrix} = \lim_{z \to 0} z\, \frac{1}{z(1 + z)} = 1$$

$$\begin{matrix} \text{residue} \\ \text{at } z = -1 \end{matrix} = \lim_{z \to -1} (z + 1)\, \frac{1}{z(1 + z)} = -1$$

(a) If C is $|z| = \frac{1}{2}$ then it contains the pole at $z = 0$, but *not* the pole at $z = -1$. Hence, by the residue theorem,

$$\int_C \frac{dz}{z(z + 1)} = 2\pi j \times (\text{residue at } z = 0) = 2\pi j$$

(b) If C is $|z| = 2$ then both poles are inside C. Hence, by the residue theorem,

$$\int_C \frac{dz}{z(z+1)} = 2\pi j(1-1) = 0$$

EXAMPLE 1.36 Evaluate the contour integral

$$\int_C \frac{z^3 - z^2 + z - 1}{z^3 + 4z} dz$$

where C is

(a) $|z| = 1$
(b) $|z| = 3$

Solution The rational function

$$\frac{z^3 - z^2 + z - 1}{z^3 + 4z}$$

has poles at $z = 0$ and $\pm 2j$. Evaluating the residues using (1.37) gives

$$\begin{array}{ll} \text{residue} \\ \text{at } z = 0 \end{array} = \lim_{z \to 0} \frac{z(z^3 - z^2 + z - 1)}{z(z^2 + 4)} = -\tfrac{1}{4}$$

$$\begin{array}{ll} \text{residue} \\ \text{at } z = 2j \end{array} = \lim_{z \to 2j} \frac{(z - 2j)(z^3 - z^2 + z - 1)}{z(z - 2j)(z + 2j)} = -\tfrac{3}{8} + \tfrac{3}{4}j$$

$$\begin{array}{ll} \text{residue} \\ \text{at } z = -2j \end{array} = \lim_{z \to -2j} \frac{(z + 2j)(z^3 - z^2 + z - 1)}{z(z - 2j)(z + 2j)} = -\tfrac{3}{8} - \tfrac{3}{4}j$$

(Note that these have been evaluated in Exercise 50(d).)

(a) If C is $|z| = 1$ then only the pole at $z = 0$ is inside the contour, so only the residue there is taken into account in the residue theorem, and

$$\oint_C \frac{z^3 - z^2 + z - 1}{z^3 + 4z} dz = 2\pi j(-\tfrac{1}{4}) = -\tfrac{1}{2}\pi j$$

(b) If C is $|z| = 3$ then all the poles are inside the contour. Hence, by the residue theorem,

$$\oint_C \frac{z^3 - z^2 + z - 1}{z^3 + 4z} dz = 2\pi j(-\tfrac{1}{4} - \tfrac{3}{8} + \tfrac{3}{4}j - \tfrac{3}{8} - \tfrac{3}{4}j) = -2\pi j$$

EXAMPLE 1.37 Evaluate the contour integral

$$\int_C \frac{dz}{z^3(z^2 + 2z + 2)}$$

where C is the circle $|z| = 3$.

Solution   The poles of $1/z^3(z^2 + 2z + 2)$ are as follows: a pole of order three at $z = 0$, and two simple poles where $z^2 + 2z + 2 = 0$, that is at $z = -1 \pm j$. All of these poles lie inside the contour C.

From (1.38), the residue at $z = 0$ is given by

$$\lim_{z \to 0} \frac{1}{2!} \frac{d^2}{dz^2} \left[\frac{1}{z^2 + 2z + 2} \right]$$

$$= \lim_{z \to 0} \frac{1}{2} \frac{d}{dz} \left[\frac{-(2z + 2)}{(z^2 + 2z + 2)^2} \right]$$

$$= \lim_{z \to 0} \frac{d}{dz} \left[\frac{-(z + 1)}{(z^2 + 2z + 2)^2} \right]$$

$$= \lim_{z \to 0} \frac{-(z^2 + 2z + 2)^2 + (z + 1)2(z^2 + 2z + 2)(2z + 2)}{(z^2 + 2z + 2)^4}$$

$$= \frac{-4 + 2 \times 2 \times 2}{2^4} = \tfrac{1}{4}$$

From (1.37), the residue at $z = -1 - j$ is

$$\lim_{z \to -1-j} (z + 1 + j) \frac{1}{z^3(z + 1 + j)(z + 1 - j)}$$

$$= \lim_{z \to -1-j} \frac{1}{z^3(z + 1 - j)}$$

$$= \frac{1}{(-1 - j)^3(-2j)} = \frac{1}{(1 + j)^3 2j} = \frac{1}{(-2 + 2j)2j}$$

using $(1 + j)^3 = 1 + 3j + 3j^2 + j^3 = -2 + 2j$. Hence

$$\begin{matrix} \text{residue} \\ \text{at } z = -1 - j \end{matrix} = \tfrac{1}{4} \frac{1}{-1 - j} = -\tfrac{1}{4} \frac{1 - j}{2} = \tfrac{1}{8}(-1 + j)$$

Also, using (1.37),

$$\begin{matrix} \text{residue} \\ \text{at } z = -1 + j \end{matrix} = \lim_{z \to -1+j} (z + 1 - j) \frac{1}{z^3(z + 1 + j)(z + 1 - j)}$$

which is precisely the complex conjugate of the residue at $z = -1 - j$. Hence we can take a short cut with the algebra and state the residue as $\tfrac{1}{8}(-1 - j)$.

The sum of the residues is

$$\tfrac{1}{4} + \tfrac{1}{8}(-1 + j) + \tfrac{1}{8}(-1 - j) = 0$$

so, by the residue theorem,

$$\int_C \frac{dz}{z^3(z^2 + 2z + 2)} = 2\pi j(0) = 0$$

1.6.5 Evaluation of definite real integrals

The evaluation of definite integrals is often achieved by using the residue theorem together with a suitable complex function $f(z)$ and a suitable closed contour C. In this section we shall briefly consider two of the most common types of real integrals that can be evaluated in this way.

Type 1: Infinite real integrals of the form

$$\int_{-\infty}^{\infty} f(x)\,dx$$

where $f(x)$ is a rational function of the real variable x

To evaluate such integrals we consider the contour integral

$$\oint_C f(z)\,dz$$

where C is the closed contour illustrated in Figure 1.32, consisting of the real axis from $-R$ to $+R$ and the semicircle Γ, of radius R, in the upper half z plane. Since $z = x$ on the real axis,

$$\oint_C f(z)\,dz = \int_{-R}^{R} f(x)\,dx + \int_{\Gamma} f(z)\,dz$$

Then, provided that $\lim_{R \to \infty} \int_{\Gamma} f(z)\,dz = 0$, taking $R \to \infty$ gives

$$\oint_C f(z)\,dz = \int_{-\infty}^{\infty} f(x)\,dx$$

On the semicircular path Γ, $z = R\,e^{j\theta}$ $(0 \leqslant \theta \leqslant \frac{1}{2}\pi)$, giving

$$dz = jR\,e^{j\theta}\,d\theta$$

and

$$\int_{\Gamma} f(z)\,dz = \int_0^{\pi/2} f(R\,e^{j\theta})jR\,e^{j\theta}\,d\theta$$

For this to tend to zero as $R \to \infty$, $|f(R\,e^{j\theta})|$ must decrease at least as rapidly as R^{-2}, implying that the degree of the denominator of the rational function $f(x)$ must be at least two more than the degree of the numerator. Thus, provided that this condition is satisfied, this approach may be used to calculate the infinite real integral $\int_{-\infty}^{\infty} f(x)\,dx$. Note that if $f(x)$ is an even function of x then the same approach can also be used to evaluate $\int_0^{\infty} f(x)\,dx$, since if $f(x)$ is even, it follows that

$$\int_{-\infty}^{\infty} f(x)\,dx = 2\int_0^{\infty} f(x)\,dx$$

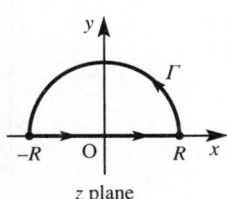

Figure 1.32 The closed contour for evaluating

$$\int_{-\infty}^{\infty} f(x)\,dx.$$

EXAMPLE 1.38 Using contour integration, show that

$$\int_{-\infty}^{\infty} \frac{dx}{(x^2 + 4)^2} = \tfrac{1}{16}\pi$$

Solution Consider the contour integral

$$I = \oint_C \frac{dz}{(z^2 + 4)^2}$$

where C is the closed semicircular contour shown in Figure 1.32. The integrand $1/(z^2 + 4)^2$ has poles of order two at $z = \pm 2j$. However, the only singularity inside the contour C is the double pole at $z = 2j$. From (1.38),

$$\begin{aligned} \text{residue} \atop \text{at } z = 2j \end{aligned} = \lim_{z \to 2j} \frac{1}{1!} \frac{d}{dz} (z - 2j)^2 \frac{1}{(z - 2j)^2 (z + 2j)^2}$$

$$= \lim_{z \to 2j} \frac{-2}{(z + 2j)^3}$$

$$= \frac{-2}{(4j)^3} = -\tfrac{1}{32}j$$

so, by the residue theorem,

$$\oint_C \frac{dz}{(z^2 + 4)^2} = 2\pi j(-\tfrac{1}{32}j) = \tfrac{1}{16}\pi$$

Since

$$\oint_C \frac{dz}{(z^2 + 4)^2} = \int_{-R}^{R} \frac{dx}{(x^2 + 4)^2} + \int_{\Gamma} \frac{dz}{(z^2 + 4)^2}$$

letting $R \to \infty$, and noting that the second integral becomes zero, gives

$$\oint_C \frac{dz}{(z^2 + 4)^2} = \int_{-\infty}^{\infty} \frac{dx}{(x^2 + 4)^2} = \tfrac{1}{16}\pi$$

Note that in this particular case we could have evaluated the integral without using contour integration. Making the substitution $x = 2\tan\theta$, $dx = 2\sec^2\theta\, d\theta$ gives

$$\int_{-\infty}^{\infty} \frac{dx}{(x^2 + 4)^2} = \int_{-\pi/2}^{\pi/2} \frac{2\sec^2\theta\, d\theta}{(4\sec^2\theta)^2}$$

$$= \tfrac{1}{8} \int_{-\pi/2}^{\pi/2} \cos^2\theta\, d\theta = \tfrac{1}{16}[\tfrac{1}{2}\sin 2\theta + \theta]_{-\pi/2}^{\pi/2} = \tfrac{1}{16}\pi$$

Type 2: Real integrals of the form

$$I = \int_0^{2\pi} G(\sin\theta, \cos\theta)\, d\theta$$

where G is a rational function of $\sin\theta$ and $\cos\theta$

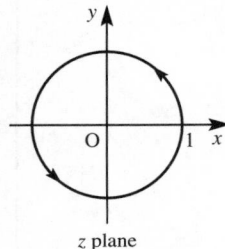

Figure 1.33 The unit-circle contour for evaluating $\int_0^{2\pi} G(\sin\theta, \cos\theta)\, d\theta$.

We take $z = e^{j\theta}$, so that

$$\sin\theta = \frac{1}{2j}\left(z - \frac{1}{z}\right), \qquad \cos\theta = \tfrac{1}{2}\left(z + \frac{1}{z}\right)$$

and

$$dz = j e^{j\theta}\, d\theta, \qquad \text{or} \quad d\theta = \frac{dz}{jz}$$

On substituting back, the integral I becomes

$$I = \oint_C f(z)\, dz$$

where C is the unit circle $|z| = 1$ shown in Figure 1.33.

EXAMPLE 1.39   Using contour integration, evaluate

$$I = \int_0^{2\pi} \frac{d\theta}{2 + \cos\theta}$$

Solution   Take $z = e^{j\theta}$, so that

$$\cos\theta = \tfrac{1}{2}\left(z + \frac{1}{z}\right), \qquad d\theta = \frac{dz}{jz}$$

On substituting, the integral becomes

$$I = \oint_C \frac{dz}{jz[2 + \tfrac{1}{2}(z + 1/z)]}$$

$$= \frac{2}{j} \oint_C \frac{dz}{z^2 + 4z + 1}$$

where C is the unit circle $|z| = 1$ shown in Figure 1.33. The integrand has singularities at

$$z^2 + 4z + 1 = 0$$

that is, at $z = -2 \pm \sqrt{3}$. The only singularity inside the contour C is the simple pole at $z = -2 + \sqrt{3}$. From (1.37),

$$\begin{array}{c} \text{residue} \\ \text{at } z = -2 + \sqrt{3} \end{array} = \lim_{z \to -2+\sqrt{3}} \left[\frac{2}{j}(z + 2 - \sqrt{3})\frac{1}{(z + 2 - \sqrt{3})(z + 2 + \sqrt{3})} \right]$$

$$= \frac{2}{j}\frac{1}{2\sqrt{3}} = \frac{1}{j\sqrt{3}}$$

so, by the residue theorem,

$$I = 2\pi j \left(\frac{1}{j\sqrt{3}} \right) = \frac{2\pi}{\sqrt{3}}$$

Thus

$$\int_0^{2\pi} \frac{d\theta}{2 + \cos\theta} = \frac{2\pi}{\sqrt{3}}$$

1.6.6   Exercises

60 Evaluate the integral

$$\oint_C \frac{z \, dz}{z^2 + 1}$$

where C is

(a) the circle $|z| = \frac{1}{2}$ (b) the circle $|z| = 2$

61 Evaluate the integral

$$\oint_C \frac{z^2 + 3jz - 2}{z^3 + 9z} dz$$

where C is

(a) the circle $|z| = 1$ (b) the circle $|z| = 4$

62 Calculate the residues at all the poles of the function

$$f(z) = \frac{(z^2 + 2)(z^2 + 4)}{(z^2 + 1)(z^2 + 6)}$$

Hence calculate the integral

$$\oint_C f(z) \, dz$$

where C is

(a) the circle $|z| = 2$ (b) the circle $|z - j| = 1$
(c) the circle $|z| = 4$

63 Evaluate the integral

$$\oint_C \frac{dz}{z^2(1 + z^2)^2}$$

where C is

(a) the circle $|z| = \frac{1}{2}$ (b) the circle $|z| = 2$

64 Using the residue theorem, evaluate the following contour integrals:

(a) $\oint_C \frac{(3z^2 + 2) \, dz}{(z - 1)(z^2 + 4)}$,

where C is $\begin{cases} \text{(i) the circle } |z - 2| = 2 \\ \text{(ii) the circle } |z| = 4 \end{cases}$

(b) $\oint_C \frac{(z^2 - 2z) \, dz}{(z + 1)^2(z^2 + 4)}$,

where C is $\begin{cases} \text{(i) the circle } |z| = 3 \\ \text{(ii) the circle } |z + j| = 2 \end{cases}$

(c) $\oint_C \frac{dz}{(z + 1)^3(z - 1)(z - 2)}$,

where C is $\begin{cases} \text{(i) the circle } |z| = \frac{1}{2} \\ \text{(ii) the circle } |z + 1| = 1 \\ \text{(iii) the rectangle with vertices} \\ \qquad \text{at } \pm j, \, 3 \pm j \end{cases}$

(d) $\displaystyle\oint_C \frac{(z-1)\,dz}{(z^2-4)(z+1)^4},$

where C is $\begin{cases} \text{(i) the circle } |z| = \frac{1}{2} \\ \text{(ii) the circle } |z + \frac{3}{2}| = 2 \\ \text{(iii) the triangle with vertices} \\ \qquad \text{at } -\frac{3}{2}+j,\ -\frac{3}{2}-j,\ 3+j0 \end{cases}$

65 Using a suitable contour integral, evaluate the following real integrals:

(a) $\displaystyle\int_{-\infty}^{\infty} \frac{dx}{x^2 + x + 1}$

(b) $\displaystyle\int_{-\infty}^{\infty} \frac{dx}{(x^2 + 1)^2}$

(c) $\displaystyle\int_0^{\infty} \frac{dx}{(x^2 + 1)(x^2 + 4)^2}$

(d) $\displaystyle\int_0^{2\pi} \frac{\cos 3\theta}{5 - 4\cos\theta}\,d\theta$

(e) $\displaystyle\int_0^{2\pi} \frac{4\,d\theta}{5 + 4\sin\theta}$

(f) $\displaystyle\int_{-\infty}^{\infty} \frac{x^2\,dx}{(x^2 + 1)^2(x^2 + 2x + 2)}$

(g) $\displaystyle\int_0^{2\pi} \frac{d\theta}{3 - 2\cos\theta + \sin\theta}$

(h) $\displaystyle\int_0^{\infty} \frac{dx}{x^4 + 1}$

(i) $\displaystyle\int_{-\infty}^{\infty} \frac{dx}{(x^2 + 4x + 5)^2}$

(j) $\displaystyle\int_0^{2\pi} \frac{\cos\theta}{3 + 2\cos\theta}\,d\theta$

1.7   Engineering application: analysing AC circuits

Figure 1.34 AC circuit of Section 1.7.

If in the circuit shown in Figure 1.34 we wish to find the variation in impedance Z and admittance Y as the capacitance C of the capacitor varies from 0 to ∞. Here

$$\frac{1}{Z} = \frac{1}{R} + j\omega C, \qquad Y = \frac{1}{Z}$$

Writing

$$\frac{1}{Z} = \frac{1 + j\omega CR}{R}$$

we clearly have

$$Z = \frac{R}{1 + j\omega CR} \qquad\qquad (1.50)$$

Equation (1.50) can be interpreted as a bilinear mapping with Z and C as the two variables. We examine what happens to the real axis in the C plane (C varies from 0 to ∞ and, of course, is real) under the inverse of the mapping given by (1.50). Rearranging (1.50), we have

$$C = \frac{R - Z}{j\omega RZ} \qquad\qquad (1.51)$$

Taking $Z = x + jy$

$$C = \frac{R - x - jy}{j\omega R(x + jy)}$$

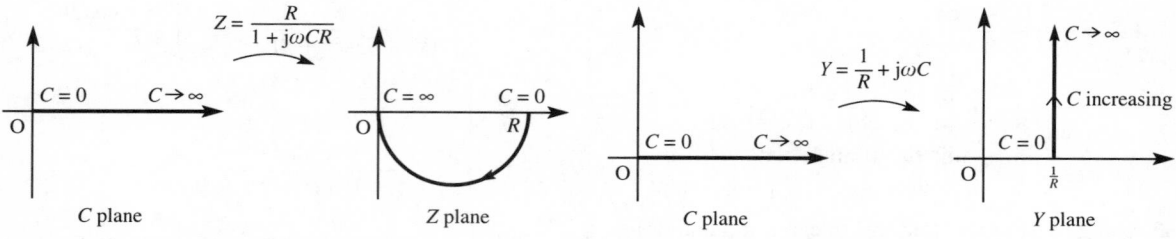

Figure 1.35 Mapping for the impedance Z.

Figure 1.36 Mapping for the admittance Y.

$$= \frac{x + jy - R}{\omega R(y - jx)}$$

$$= \frac{(x + jy - R)(y + jx)}{\omega R(x^2 + y^2)} \tag{1.52}$$

Equating imaginary parts, and remembering that C is real, gives

$$0 = x^2 + y^2 - Rx \tag{1.53}$$

which represents a circle, with centre at $(\frac{1}{2}R, 0)$ and of radius $\frac{1}{2}R$. Thus the real axis in the C plane is mapped onto the circle given by (1.53) in the Z plane. Of course, C is positive. If $C = 0$, (1.53) indicates that $Z = R$. The circuit of Figure 1.34 confirms that the impedance is R in this case. If $C \to \infty$ then $Z \to 0$, so the positive real axis in the plane is mapped onto either the upper or lower half of the circle. Equating real parts in (1.52) gives

$$C = \frac{-y}{\omega(x^2 + y^2)}$$

so $C > 0$ gives $y < 0$, implying that the lower half of the circle is the image in the Z plane of the positive real axis in the C plane, as indicated in Figure 1.35. A diagram such as Figure 1.35 gives an immediate visual impression of how the impedance Z varies as C varies.

The admittance $Y = 1/Z$ is given by

$$Y = \frac{1}{R} + j\omega C$$

which represents a linear mapping as shown in Figure 1.36.

1.8   Engineering application: use of harmonic functions

In this section we discuss two engineering applications where use is made of the properties of harmonic functions.

1.8.1   A heat transfer problem

We saw in Section 1.3.2 that every analytic function generates a pair of harmonic functions. The problem of finding a function that is harmonic in a specified region and satisfies prescribed boundary conditions is one of the oldest and most important problems in science-based engineering. Sometimes the solution can be found by means of a conformal mapping defined by an analytic function. This, essentially, is a consequence of the 'function of a function' rule of calculus, which implies that every harmonic function of x and y transforms into a harmonic function of u and v under the mapping

$$w = u + jv = f(x + jy) = f(z)$$

where $f(z)$ is analytic. Furthermore, the level curves of the harmonic function in the z plane are mapped onto corresponding level curves in the w plane, so that a harmonic function that has a constant value along part of the boundary of a region or has a zero normal derivative along part of the boundary is mapped onto a harmonic function with the same property in the w plane.

For heat transfer problems the level curves of the harmonic function correspond to isotherms, and a zero normal derivative corresponds to thermal insulation. To illustrate these ideas, consider the simple steady-state heat transfer problem shown schematically in Figure 1.37. There is a cylindrical pipe with an offset cylindrical cavity through which steam passes at 100 °C. The outer temperature of the pipe is 0 °C. The radius of the inner circle is $\frac{3}{10}$ of that of the outer circle, so by choosing the outer radius as the unit of length the problem can be stated as that of finding a harmonic function $T(x, y)$ such that

$$\frac{\partial^2 T}{\partial x^2} + \frac{\partial^2 T}{\partial y^2} = 0$$

in the region between the circles $|z| = 1$ and $|z - 0.3| = 0.3$, and $T = 0$ on $|z| = 1$ and $T = 100$ on $|z - 0.3| = 0.3$.

The mapping

$$w = \frac{z - 3}{3z - 1}$$

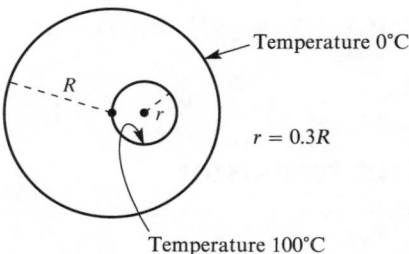

Temperature 0°C

R

r

$r = 0.3R$

Temperature 100°C

Figure 1.37 Schematic diagram of heat transfer problem.

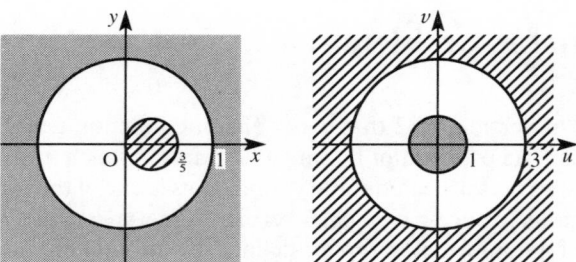

Figure 1.38 The mapping $w = (z-3)/(3z-1)$.

transforms the circle $|z| = 1$ onto the circle $|w| = 1$ and the circle $|z - 0.3| = 0.3$ onto the circle $|w| = 3$ as shown in Figure 1.38. Thus the problem is transformed into the axially symmetric problem in the w plane of finding a harmonic function $T(u, v)$ such that $T(u, v) = 100$ on $|w| = 1$ and $T(u, v) = 0$ on $|w| = 3$. Harmonic functions with such axial symmetry have the general form

$$T(u, v) = A \ln (u^2 + v^2) + B$$

where A and B are constants.

Here we require, in addition to the axial symmetry, that $T(u, v) = 100$ on $u^2 + v^2 = 1$ and $T(u, v) = 0$ on $u^2 + v^2 = 9$. Thus $B = 100$ and $A = -100 \ln 9$, and the solution on the w plane is

$$T(u, v) = \frac{100[1 - \ln (u^2 + v^2)]}{\ln 9}$$

We need the solution on the z plane, which means in general we have to obtain u and v in terms of x and y. Here, however, it is a little easier, since $u^2 + v^2 = |w|^2$ and

$$|w|^2 = \left| \frac{z - 3}{3z - 1} \right|^2$$

$$= \frac{|z - 3|^2}{|3z - 1|^2}$$

$$= \frac{(x - 3)^2 + y^2}{(3x - 1)^2 + 9y^2}$$

Thus

$$T(x, y) = \frac{100}{\ln 9} \{1 - \ln [(x - 3)^2 + y^2] - \ln [(3x - 1)^2 + 9y^2]\}$$

1.8.2   Current in a field-effect transistor

The fields (E_x, E_y) in an insulated-gate field-effect transistor are harmonic conjugates that satisfy a non-linear boundary condition. For the transistor shown schematically

Figure 1.39 (a) Schematic diagram for an insulated-gate field-effect transistor; (b) an appropriate coordinate system for the application.

in Figure 1.39 we have

$$\frac{\partial E_y}{\partial x} = \frac{\partial E_x}{\partial y}, \qquad \frac{\partial E_y}{\partial y} = \frac{-\partial E_x}{\partial x}$$

with conditions

$$E_x = 0 \quad \text{on the electrodes}$$

$$E_x\left(E_y + \frac{V_0}{h}\right) = -\frac{I}{2\mu\varepsilon_0\varepsilon_r} \quad \text{on the channel}$$

$$E_y \to \frac{V_g}{h} \quad \text{as } x \to -\infty \quad (0 < y < h)$$

$$E_y \to \frac{V_d - V_g}{h} \quad \text{as } x \to \infty \quad (0 < y < h)$$

where V_0 is a constant with dimensions of potential, h is the insulator thickness, I is the current in the channel, which is to be found, μ, ε_0 and ε_r have their usual meanings, and the gate potential V_g and the drain potential V_d are taken with respect to the source potential.

The key to the solution of this problem is the observation that the non-linear boundary condition

$$2E_x\left(E_y + \frac{V_0}{h}\right) = -\frac{I}{\mu\varepsilon_0\varepsilon_r}$$

contains the harmonic function (now of E_x and E_y)

$$H(E_x, E_y) = 2E_x\left(E_y + \frac{V_0}{h}\right)$$

A harmonic conjugate of H is the function

$$G(E_x, E_y) = \left(E_y + \frac{V_0}{h}\right)^2 - E_x^2$$

Since E_x and E_y are harmonic conjugates with respect to x and y, so are G and H. Thus the problem may be restated as that of finding harmonic conjugates G and H such that

$$H = 0 \quad \text{on the electrodes}$$

$$H = -\frac{I}{\mu\varepsilon_0\varepsilon_r} \quad \text{on the channel}$$

$$G \to \left(\frac{V_0 - V_g}{h}\right)^2 \quad \text{as } x \to \infty \quad (0 < y < h)$$

$$G \to \left(\frac{V_0 + V_d - V_g}{h}\right)^2 \quad \text{as } x \to -\infty \quad (0 < y < h)$$

Using the sequence of mappings shown in Figure 1.40, which may be composed into the single formula

$$w = \frac{ae^{bz} - a^2}{ae^{bz} - 1}$$

where $a = e^{bL/2}$ and $b = \pi/h$, the problem is transformed into finding harmonic-conjugate functions G and H (on the w plane) such that

$$H = 0 \quad \text{on } v = 0 \quad (u > 0) \tag{1.54}$$

$$H = -\frac{I}{\mu\varepsilon_0\varepsilon_r} \quad \text{on } v = 0 \quad (u < 0) \tag{1.55}$$

$$G = \left(\frac{V_0 - V_g}{h}\right)^2 \quad \text{at } w = e^{bL} \tag{1.56}$$

$$G = \left(\frac{V_0 + V_d - V_g}{h}\right)^2 \quad \text{at } w = 1 \tag{1.57}$$

The conditions (1.54), (1.55) and (1.57) are sufficient to determine H and G completely

$$H = -\frac{I \arg(w)}{\pi\mu\varepsilon_0\varepsilon_r}$$

$$G = -\frac{I \ln|w|}{\pi\mu\varepsilon_0\varepsilon_r} + \left(\frac{V_0 + V_d - V_g}{h}\right)^2$$

while the condition (1.56) determines the values of I

$$I = \frac{\mu\varepsilon_0\varepsilon_r}{Lh}(2V_0 - 2V_g + V_d)V_d$$

This example shows the power of complex variable methods for solving difficult problems arising in engineering mathematics. The following exercises give some simpler examples for the reader to investigate.

Figure 1.40 Sequence of mappings to simplify the problem.

1.8.3   Exercises

66 Show that the transformation $w = 1/z$, $w = u + jv$, $z = x + jy$, transforms the circle $x^2 + y^2 = 2ax$ in the z plane into the straight line $u = 1/2a$ in the w plane. Two long conducting wires of radius a are

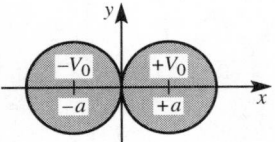

Figure 1.41 Conducting wires of Exercise 66.

placed adjacent and parallel to each other, so that their cross-section appears as in Figure 1.41. The wires are separated at O by an insulating gap of negligible dimensions, and carry potentials $\pm V_0$ as indicated. Find an expression for the potential at a general point (x, y) in the plane of the cross-section and sketch the equipotentials.

67 Find the images under the mapping

$$w = \frac{z + 1}{1 - z}$$

$z = x + jy$, of

(a) the points $A(-1, 0)$, $B(0, 1)$, $C(\frac{24}{25}, \frac{7}{25})$ and $D(\frac{3}{4}, 0)$ in the z plane,

(b) the straight line $y = 0$,

(c) the circle $x^2 + y^2 = 1$.

Illustrate your answer with a diagram showing the z and w planes and shade on the w plane the region corresponding to $x^2 + y^2 < 1$.

A semicircular disc of unit radius, $[(x, y): x^2 + y^2 \leqslant 1, y \geqslant 0]$, has its straight boundary at temperature $0\,^\circ C$ and its curved boundary at $100\,^\circ C$. Prove that the temperature at the point (x, y) is

$$T = \frac{200}{\pi} \tan^{-1} \left(\frac{2y}{1 - x^2 - y^2} \right)$$

68 (a) Show that the function

$$G(x, y) = 2x(1 - y)$$

satisfies the Laplace equation and construct its harmonic conjugate $H(x, y)$ that satisfies $H(0, 0) = 0$. Hence obtain, in terms of z, where $z = x + jy$, the function F such that $W = F(z)$ where $W = G + jH$.

(b) Show that under the mapping $w = \ln z$, the harmonic function $G(x, y)$ defined in (a) is mapped into the function

$$G(u, v) = 2e^u \cos v - e^{2u} \sin 2v$$

Verify that $G(u, v)$ is harmonic.

(c) Generalize the result (b) to prove that under the

mapping $w = f(z)$, where $f'(z)$ exists, a harmonic function of (x, y) is transformed into a harmonic function of (u, v).

69 Show that if $w = (z + 3)/(z - 3)$, $w = u + jv$, $z = x + jy$, the circle $u^2 + v^2 = k^2$ in the w plane is the image of the circle

$$x^2 + y^2 + 6\frac{1 + k^2}{1 - k^2}x + 9 = 0 \quad (k^2 \neq 1)$$

in the z plane.

Two long cylindrical wires, each of radius $4\,mm$, are placed parallel to each other with their axes $10\,mm$ apart, so that their cross-section appears as in Figure 1.42. The wires carry potentials $\pm V_0$ as shown. Show that the potential $V(x, y)$ at the point (x, y) is given by

$$V = \frac{V_0}{\ln 4} \{\ln [(x + 3)^2 + y^2] - \ln [(x - 3)^2 + y^2]\}$$

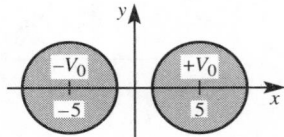

Figure 1.42 Cylindrical wires of Exercise 69.

70 Find the image under the mapping

$$w = \frac{j(1 - z)}{1 + z}$$

$z = x + jy$, $w = u + jv$, of

(a) the points $A(1, 0)$, $B(0, 1)$, $C(0, -1)$ in the z plane,

(b) the straight line $y = 0$,

(c) the circle $x^2 + y^2 = 1$.

A circular plate of unit radius, $[(x, y): x^2 + y^2 \leqslant 1]$, has one half (with $y > 0$) of its rim, $x^2 + y^2 = 1$, at temperature $0\,^\circ C$ and the other half (with $y < 0$) at temperature $100\,^\circ C$. Using the above mapping, prove that the steady-state temperature at the point (x, y) is

$$T = \frac{100}{\pi} \tan^{-1} \left(\frac{1 - x^2 - y^2}{2y} \right)$$

71 The problem shown schematically in Figure 1.43 arose during a steady-state heat transfer investigation. T is the temperature. By applying the successive

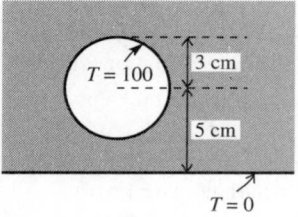

Figure 1.43 Schematic representation of Exercise 71.

mappings

$$z_1 = \frac{z + j4}{z - j4}, \qquad w = \ln z_1$$

show that the temperature at the point (x, y) in the shaded region in the figure is given by

$$T(x, y) = \frac{50}{\ln 3} \ln\left[\frac{x^2 + (4 + y)^2}{x^2 + (4 - y)^2}\right]$$

72 The functions

$$w = z + \frac{1}{z}, \qquad w = \frac{z + 1}{z - 1}$$

perform the mappings shown in Figure 1.44. A long bar of semicircular cross-section has the temperature of the part of its curved surface corresponding to the arc PQ in Figure 1.45 kept at 100 °C while the rest of the surface is kept at 0 °C. Show that the temperature T at the point (x, y) is given by

$$T = \frac{100}{\pi}[\arg(z^2 + z + 1) - \arg(z^2 - z + 1)]$$

Figure 1.44 Mappings of Exercise 72.

Figure 1.45 Cross-section of bar of Exercise 72.

1.9   Review exercises (1–24)

1 Find the images of the following points under the mappings given:

(a) $z = 1 + j$ under $w = (1 + j)z + j$

(b) $z = 1 - j2$ under $w = j3z + j + 1$

(c) $z = 1$ under $w = \frac{1}{2}(1 - j)z + \frac{1}{2}(1 + j)$

(d) $z = j2$ under $w = \frac{1}{2}(1 - j)z + \frac{1}{2}(1 + j)$

2 Under each of the mappings given in Review exercise 1, find the images in the w plane of the two straight lines

(a) $y = 2x$ (b) $x + y = 1$

in the z plane, $z = x + jy$.

3 The linear mapping $w = \alpha z + \beta$, where α and β are complex constants, maps the point $z = 2 - j$ in the

z plane to the point $w = 1$ in the w plane, and the point $z = 0$ to the point $w = 3 + j$.

(a) Determine α and β.

(b) Find the region in the w plane corresponding to the left half-plane $\mathrm{Re}\,(z) = 0$ in the z plane.

(c) Find the region in the w plane corresponding to the circle $5|z| \leqslant 1$ in the z plane.

(d) Find the fixed point of the mapping.

4 Map the following straight lines from the z plane, $z = x + jy$, to the w plane under the inverse mapping $w = j/z$:

(a) $x = y + 1$ (b) $y = 3x$

(c) the line joining $A(1 + j)$ to $B(2 + j3)$ in the z plane

(d) $y = 4$

In each case sketch the image curve.

5 Two complex variables w and z are related by the mapping

$$w = \frac{z + 1}{z - 1}$$

Sketch this mapping by finding the images in the w plane of the lines $\mathrm{Re}\,(z) = \text{constant}$ and $\mathrm{Im}\,(z) = \text{constant}$. Find the fixed points of the mapping.

6 The mapping

$$w = \frac{1 - z^2}{z}$$

takes points from the z plane to the w plane. Find the fixed points of the mapping, and show that the circle of radius r with centre at the origin in the z plane is transformed to the ellipse

$$\left(\frac{ur^2}{r^2 - 1}\right)^2 + \left(\frac{vr^2}{r^2 + 1}\right)^2 = r^2$$

in the w plane, where $w = u + jv$. Investigate what happens when $r = 1$.

7 Find the real and imaginary parts of the complex function $w = z^3$, and verify the Cauchy–Riemann equations.

8 Find a function $v(x, y)$ such that, given

$$u(x, y) = x \sin x \cosh y - y \cos x \sinh y$$

$f(z) = u + jv$ is an analytic function of z ($f(0) = 0$).

9 Find the bilinear transformation that maps the three

points $z = 0$, j and $\frac{1}{2}(1 + j)$ in the z plane to the three points $w = \infty$, $-j$ and $1 - j$ respectively in the w plane. Check that the transformation will map

(a) the lower half of the z plane onto the upper half of the w plane

(b) the interior of the circle with centre $z = j\frac{1}{2}$ and radius $\frac{1}{2}$ in the z plane onto the half-plane $\mathrm{Im}\,(w) < -1$ in the w plane.

10 Show that the mapping

$$z = \zeta + \frac{a^2}{4\zeta}$$

where $z = x + jy$ and $\zeta = R\mathrm{e}^{j\theta}$ maps the circle $R = \text{constant}$ in the ζ plane onto an ellipse in the z plane. Suggest a possible use for this mapping.

11 Find the power series representation of the function

$$\frac{1}{1 + z^3}$$

in the disc $|z| < 1$. Deduce the power series for

$$\frac{1}{(1 + z^3)^2}$$

valid in the same disc.

12 Find the first four non-zero terms of the Taylor series expansion of the following functions about the point indicated, and determine the radius of convergence of each:

(a) $\dfrac{1 - z}{1 + z}$ $(z = 0)$ (b) $\dfrac{1}{z^2 + 1}$ $(z = 1)$

(c) $\dfrac{z}{z + 1}$ $(z = j)$

13 Find the radius of convergence of each Taylor series expansion of the following function about the points indicated, *without* finding the series itself:

$$f(z) = \frac{1}{z(z^2 + 1)}$$

at the points $z = 1$, -1, $1 + j$, $1 + j\frac{1}{2}$ and $2 + j3$.

14 Determine the Laurent series expansion of the function

$$f(z) = \frac{1}{(z^2 + 1)z}$$

about the points (a) $z = 0$ and (b) $z = 1$, and determine the region of validity of each.

15 Find the Laurent series expansion of the function

$$f(z) = e^z \sin\left(\frac{1}{1-z}\right)$$

about (a) $z = 0$, (b) $z = 1$ and (c) $z = \infty$, indicating the range of validity in each case. (Do *not* find terms explicitly, indicate only the form of the principal part.)

16 Find the real and imaginary parts of the functions

(a) $e^z \sinh z$ (b) $\cos 2z$

(c) $\dfrac{\sin z}{z}$ (d) $\tan z$

17 Determine whether the following mappings are conformal, and, if not, find the non-conformal points:

(a) $w = \dfrac{1}{z^2}$

(b) $w = 2z^3 + 3z^2 + 6(1-j)z + 1$

(c) $w = 64z + \dfrac{1}{z^3}$

18 Consider the mapping $w = \cos z$. Determine the points where the mapping is not conformal. By finding the images in the w plane of the lines $x = $ constant and $y = $ constant in the z plane ($z = x + jy$), draw the mapping similarly to Figures 1.14 and 1.18.

19 Determine the location of and classify the singularities of the following functions:

(a) $\dfrac{\sin z}{z^2}$ (b) $\dfrac{1}{(z^3 - 8)^2}$

(c) $\dfrac{z+1}{z^4 - 1}$ (d) $\mathrm{sech}\, z$

(e) $\sinh z$ (f) $\sin\left(\dfrac{1}{z}\right)$ (g) z^z

20 Find the residues of the following functions at the points indicated:

(a) $\dfrac{e^{2z}}{(1+z)^2}$ $(z = -1)$ (b) $\dfrac{\cos z}{2z - \pi}$ $(z = \tfrac{1}{2}\pi)$

(c) $\dfrac{\tan z}{2z - \pi}$ $(z = \tfrac{1}{2}\pi)$ (d) $\dfrac{z}{(z+8)^3}$ $(z = -8)$

21 Find the poles and zeros, and determine all the residues, of the rational function

$$f(z) = \frac{(z^2 - 1)(z^2 + 3z + 5)}{z(z^4 + 1)}$$

22 Determine the residue of the rational function

$$\frac{z^7 + 6z^5 - 30z^4}{(z - 1 - j)^3}$$

23 Evaluate the following contour integrals along the circular paths indicated:

(a) $\displaystyle\oint_C \frac{z\,dz}{z^2 + 7z + 6}$,   where C is $|z| = 2$

(b) $\displaystyle\oint_C \frac{(z^2 + 1)(z^2 + 3)}{(z^2 + 9)(z^2 + 4)}dz$,   where C is $|z| = 4$

(c) $\displaystyle\oint_C \frac{dz}{z^2(1 - z^2)^2}$,   where $\begin{cases}\text{(i)} \ \ C \text{ is } |z| = \tfrac{1}{2} \\ \text{(ii)} \ C \text{ is } |z| = 2\end{cases}$

(d) $\displaystyle\oint_C \frac{dz}{(2z - 3j)(z + j)}$,   where $\begin{cases}\text{(i)} \ \ C \text{ is } |z| = 2 \\ \text{(ii)} \ C \text{ is } |z - 1| = 1\end{cases}$

(e) $\displaystyle\oint_C \frac{z^3\,dz}{(z^2 + 1)(z^2 + z + 1)}$,

where C is $|z - j| = \tfrac{1}{2}$

(f) $\displaystyle\oint_C \frac{(z - 1)\,dz}{z(z - 2)^2(z - 3)}$,   where $\begin{cases}\text{(i)} \ \ C \text{ is } |z| = 1 \\ \text{(ii)} \ C \text{ is } |z| = \tfrac{5}{2}\end{cases}$

24 Using a suitable contour integral, evaluate the following real integrals:

(a) $\displaystyle\int_{-\infty}^{\infty} \frac{x^2\,dx}{(x^2 + 1)^2(x^2 + 2x + 2)}$

(b) $\displaystyle\int_0^{\infty} \frac{x^2\,dx}{x^4 + 16}$

(c) $\displaystyle\int_0^{2\pi} \frac{\sin^2\theta\,d\theta}{5 + 4\cos\theta}$

(d) $\displaystyle\int_0^{2\pi} \frac{\cos 2\theta\,d\theta}{5 - 4\cos\theta}$

2

Laplace Transforms

CONTENTS

2.1 Introduction

Laplace transform methods have a key role to play in the modern approach to the analysis and design of engineering systems. The stimulus for developing these methods was the pioneering work of the English electrical engineer Oliver Heaviside (1850–1925) in developing a method for the systematic solution of ordinary differential equations with constant coefficients. Heaviside was concerned with solving practical problems, and his method was based mainly on intuition, lacking mathematical rigour: consequently it was frowned upon by theoreticians at the time. However, Heaviside himself was not concerned with rigorous proofs, and was satisfied that his method gave the correct results. Using his ideas, he was able to solve important practical problems that could not be dealt with using classical methods. This led to many new results in fields such as the propagation of currents and voltages along transmission lines.

Because it worked in practice, Heaviside's method was widely accepted by engineers. As its power for problem-solving became more and more apparent, the method attracted the attention of mathematicians, who set out to justify it. This provided the stimulus for rapid developments in many branches of mathematics, including improper integrals, asymptotic series and transform theory. Research on the problem continued for many years before it was eventually recognized that an integral transform developed by the French mathematician Pierre Simon de Laplace (1749–1827) almost a century before provided a theoretical foundation for Heaviside's work. It was also recognized that the use of this integral transform provided a more systematic alternative for investigating differential equations than the method proposed by Heaviside. It is this alternative approach that is the basis of the **Laplace transform method**.

We have already come across instances where a mathematical transformation has been used to simplify the solution of a problem. For example, the logarithm is used to simplify multiplication and division problems. To multiply or divide two numbers, we transform them into their logarithms, add or subtract these, and then perform the inverse transformation (that is, the antilogarithm) to obtain the product or quotient of the original numbers. The purpose of using a transformation is to create a new domain in which it is easier to handle the problem being investigated. Once results have been obtained in the new domain, they can be inverse-transformed to give the desired results in the original domain.

The Laplace transform is an example of a class called **integral transforms**, and it takes a function $f(t)$ of one variable t (which we shall refer to as **time**) into a function $F(s)$ of another variable s (the **complex frequency**). Another integral transform widely used by engineers is the **Fourier transform**, which is dealt with in Chapter 5. The attraction of the Laplace transform is that it transforms *differential* equations in the t (time) domain into *algebraic* equations in the s (frequency) domain. Solving differential equations in the t domain therefore reduces to solving algebraic equations in the s domain. Having done the latter for the desired unknowns, their values as functions of time may be found by taking inverse transforms. Another advantage of using the Laplace transform for solving differential equations is that initial conditions play an essential role in the transformation process, so they are automatically incorporated into the solution. This contrasts with the classical approach considered in Chapters 10 and 11 of *Modern Engineering Mathematics*, where the initial conditions are only introduced when the unknown constants of integration are determined. The Laplace transform is therefore an ideal tool for solving initial-value problems such as those occurring in the investigation of electrical circuits and mechanical vibrations.

The Laplace transform finds particular application in the field of signals and linear systems analysis. A distinguishing feature of a system is that when it is subjected to an excitation (input), it produces a response (output). When the input $u(t)$ and output $x(t)$ are functions of a single variable t, representing time, it is

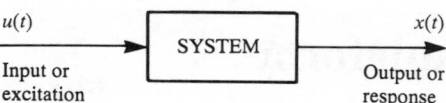

Figure 2.1 Schematic representation of a system.

normal to refer to them as **signals**. Schematically, a system may be represented as in Figure 2.1. The problem facing the engineer is that of determining the system output $x(t)$ when it is subjected to an input $u(t)$ applied at some instant of time, which we can take to be $t = 0$. The relationship between output and input is determined by the laws governing the behaviour of the system. If the system is linear and time-invariant then the output is related to the input by a linear differential equation with constant coefficients, and we have a standard initial-value problem, which is amenable to solution using the Laplace transform.

While many of the problems considered in this chapter can be solved by the classical approach of Chapters 10 and 11 of *Modern Engineering Mathematics*, the Laplace transform leads to a more unified approach and provides the engineer with greater insight into system behaviour. In practice, the input signal $u(t)$ may be a discontinuous or periodic function, or even a pulse, and in such cases the use of the Laplace transform has distinct advantages over the classical approach. Also, more often than not, an engineer is interested not only in system analysis but also in system synthesis or design. Consequently, an engineer's objective in studying a system's response to specific inputs is frequently to learn more about the system with a view to improving or controlling it so that it satisfies certain specifications. It is in this area that the use of the Laplace transform is attractive, since by considering the system response to particular inputs, such as a sinusoid, it provides the engineer with powerful graphical methods for system design that are relatively easy to apply and widely used in practice.

In modelling the system by a differential equation, it has been assumed that both the input and output signals can vary at any instant of time; that is, they are functions of a continuous time variable (note that this does not mean that the signals themselves have to be continuous functions of time). Such systems are called **continuous-time systems**, and it is for investigating these that the Laplace transform is best suited. With the introduction of computer control into system design, signals associated with a system may only change at discrete instants of time. In such cases the system is said to be a **discrete-time system**, and is modelled by a difference equation rather than a differential equation. Such systems are dealt with using the z transform considered in Chapter 3.

2.2   The Laplace transform

2.2.1   Definition and notation

We define the Laplace transform of a function $f(t)$ by the expression

$$\mathcal{L}\{f(t)\} = \int_0^\infty e^{-st} f(t)\, dt \tag{2.1}$$

where s is a complex variable and e^{-st} is called the **kernel** of the transformation.

It is usual to represent the Laplace transform of a function by the corresponding capital letter, so that we write

$$\mathcal{L}\{f(t)\} = F(s) = \int_0^\infty e^{-st} f(t)\, dt \tag{2.2}$$

An alternative notation in common use is to denote $\mathcal{L}\{f(t)\}$ by $\bar{f}(s)$ or simply $\bar{f}$.

Before proceeding, there are a few observations relating to the definition (2.2) worthy of comment.

(a) The symbol $\mathcal{L}$ denotes the **Laplace transform operator**; when it operates on a function $f(t)$, it transforms it into a function $F(s)$ of the complex variable s. We say that the operator transforms the function $f(t)$ in the t domain (usually called the **time domain**) into the function $F(s)$ in the s domain (usually called the **complex frequency domain**, or simply the **frequency domain**). This relationship is depicted graphically in Figure 2.2, and it is usual to refer to $f(t)$ and $F(s)$ as a **Laplace transform pair**, written as $\{f(t), F(s)\}$.

(b) Because the upper limit in the integral is infinite, the domain of integration is infinite. Thus the integral is an example of an *improper integral*, as introduced in Section 8.3 of *Modern Engineering Mathematics*; that is,

$$\int_0^\infty e^{-st} f(t)\, dt = \lim_{T \to \infty} \int_0^T e^{-st} f(t)\, dt$$

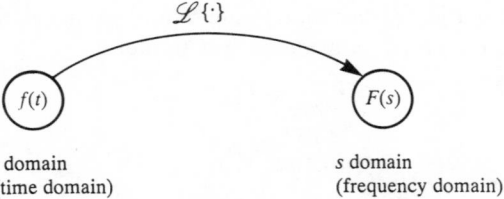

Figure 2.2 The Laplace transform operator.

This immediately raises the question of whether or not the integral converges, an issue we shall consider in Section 2.2.3.

(c) Because the lower limit in the integral is zero, it follows that when taking the Laplace transform, the behaviour of $f(t)$ for negative values of t is ignored or suppressed. This means that $F(s)$ contains information on the behaviour of $f(t)$ only for $t \geqslant 0$, so that the Laplace transform is not a suitable tool for investigating problems in which values of $f(t)$ for $t < 0$ are relevant. In most engineering applications this does not cause any problems, since we are then concerned with physical systems for which the functions we are dealing with vary with time t. An attribute of physically realizable systems is that they are **non-anticipatory** in the sense that there is no output (or response) until an input (or excitation) is applied. Because of this causal relationship between the input and output, we define a function $f(t)$ to be **causal** if $f(t) = 0$ $(t < 0)$. In general, however, unless the domain is clearly specified, a function $f(t)$ is normally interpreted as being defined for all real values, both positive and negative, of t. Making use of the Heaviside unit step function $H(t)$ (see also Section 2.5.1), where

$$H(t) = \begin{cases} 0 & (t < 0) \\ 1 & (t \geqslant 0) \end{cases}$$

we have

$$f(t)H(t) = \begin{cases} 0 & (t < 0) \\ f(t) & (t \geqslant 0) \end{cases}$$

Thus the effect of multiplying $f(t)$ by $H(t)$ is to convert it into a causal function. Graphically, the relationship between $f(t)$ and $f(t)H(t)$ is as shown in Figure 2.3.

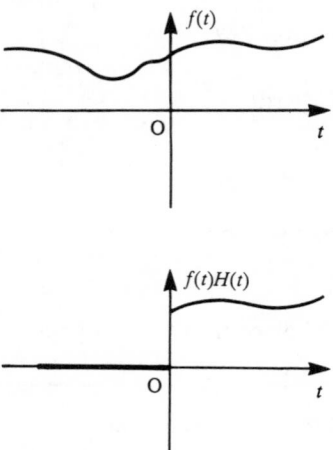

Figure 2.3 Graphs of $f(t)$ and its causal equivalent function.

It follows that the corresponding Laplace transform $F(s)$ contains full information on the behaviour of $f(t)H(t)$. While the presence of the step function is not necessary for the determination of $\mathscr{L}\{f(t)\}$, it is required if we are to recover the original function from a knowledge of its transform. Consequently, it is normal to refer to $\{f(t)H(t), F(s)\}$ rather than $\{f(t), F(s)\}$ as being a Laplace transform pair. Throughout this chapter it will be assumed that all functions are causal, with $f(t)$, for example, being interpreted as $f(t)H(t)$. Thus the presence of the step function will be assumed, and we shall refer to $\{f(t), F(s)\}$ as being a Laplace transform pair.

(d) If the behaviour of $f(t)$ for $t < 0$ is of interest then we need to use the alternative **two-sided** or **bilateral Laplace transform** of the function $f(t)$, defined by

$$\mathscr{L}_{\mathrm{B}}\{f(t)\} = \int_{-\infty}^{\infty} \mathrm{e}^{-st} f(t)\,\mathrm{d}t \tag{2.3}$$

The Laplace transform defined by (2.2), with lower limit zero, is sometimes referred to as the **one-sided** or **unilateral Laplace transform** of the function $f(t)$. In this chapter we shall concern ourselves only with the latter transform, and refer to it simply as the Laplace transform of the function $f(t)$. Note that when $f(t)$ is a causal function,

$$\mathscr{L}_{\mathrm{B}}\{f(t)\} = \mathscr{L}\{f(t)\}$$

(e) Another issue concerning the lower limit of zero is the interpretation of $f(0)$ when $f(t)$ has a discontinuity at the origin. The question then arises as to whether or not we should include the discontinuity and take the lower limit as $0-$ or exclude the discontinuity and take the lower limit as $0+$ (as in Section 6.4.1 of *Modern Engineering Mathematics*, $0-$ and $0+$ denote values of t just to the left and right of the origin respectively). Provided we are consistent, we can take either, both interpretations being adopted in practice. In order to accommodate any peculiarities that may occur at $t = 0$, such as an impulse applied at $t = 0$, we take $0-$ as the lower limit and interpret (2.2) as

$$\mathscr{L}\{f(t)\} = F(s) = \int_{0-}^{\infty} \mathrm{e}^{-st} f(t)\,\mathrm{d}t \tag{2.4}$$

2.2.2   Transforms of simple functions

In this section we obtain the Laplace transforms of some simple functions.

EXAMPLE 2.1   Determine the Laplace transform of the function

$$f(t) = c$$

where c is a constant.

Solution   Using the definition (2.2),

$$\mathcal{L}(c) = \int_0^\infty e^{-st} c \, dt$$

$$= \lim_{T \to \infty} \int_0^T e^{-st} c \, dt$$

$$= \lim_{T \to \infty} \left[-\frac{c}{s} e^{-st} \right]_0^T = \frac{c}{s} \left(1 - \lim_{T \to \infty} e^{-sT} \right)$$

Taking $s = \sigma + j\omega$, where σ and ω are real,

$$\lim_{T \to \infty} e^{-sT} = \lim_{T \to \infty} (e^{-(\sigma + j\omega)T}) = \lim_{T \to \infty} e^{-\sigma T} (\cos \omega T + j \sin \omega T)$$

A finite limit exists provided that $\sigma = \text{Re}\,(s) > 0$, when the limit is zero. Thus, provided that $\text{Re}\,(s) > 0$, the Laplace transform is

$$\mathcal{L}(c) = \frac{c}{s}, \quad \text{Re}\,(s) > 0$$

so that

$$\left. \begin{aligned} f(t) &= c \\ F(s) &= \frac{c}{s} \end{aligned} \right\} \quad \text{Re}\,(s) > 0 \tag{2.5}$$

constitute an example of a Laplace transform pair.

EXAMPLE 2.2   Determine the Laplace transform of the ramp function

$$f(t) = t$$

Solution   From the definition (2.2),

$$\mathcal{L}\{t\} = \int_0^\infty e^{-st} t \, dt = \lim_{T \to \infty} \int_0^T e^{-st} t \, dt$$

$$= \lim_{T \to \infty} \left[-\frac{t}{s} e^{-st} - \frac{e^{-st}}{s^2} \right]_0^T$$

$$= \frac{1}{s^2} - \lim_{T \to \infty} \frac{T e^{-sT}}{s} - \lim_{T \to \infty} \frac{e^{-sT}}{s^2}$$

Following the same procedure as in Example 2.1, limits exist provided that $\text{Re}\,(s) > 0$, when

$$\lim_{T \to \infty} \frac{T e^{-sT}}{s} = \lim_{T \to \infty} \frac{e^{-sT}}{s^2} = 0$$

Thus, provided that $\mathrm{Re}\,(s) > 0$,

$$\mathscr{L}\{t\} = \frac{1}{s^2}$$

giving us the Laplace transform pair

$$\left.\begin{array}{l} f(t) = t \\[2mm] F(s) = \dfrac{1}{s^2} \end{array}\right\} \quad \mathrm{Re}\,(s) > 0 \tag{2.6}$$

EXAMPLE 2.3   Determine the Laplace transform of the one-sided exponential function

$$f(t) = \mathrm{e}^{kt}$$

Solution   The definition (2.2) gives

$$\mathscr{L}\{\mathrm{e}^{kt}\} = \int_0^\infty \mathrm{e}^{-st}\mathrm{e}^{kt}\,\mathrm{d}t = \lim_{T\to\infty}\int_0^T \mathrm{e}^{-(s-k)t}\,\mathrm{d}t$$

$$= \lim_{T\to\infty}\frac{-1}{s-k}[\mathrm{e}^{-(s-k)t}]_0^T$$

$$= \frac{1}{s-k}\left(1 - \lim_{T\to\infty}\mathrm{e}^{-(s-k)T}\right)$$

Writing $s = \sigma + \mathrm{j}\omega$, where σ and ω are real, we have

$$\lim_{T\to\infty}\mathrm{e}^{-(s-k)T} = \lim_{T\to\infty}\mathrm{e}^{-(\sigma-k)T}\mathrm{e}^{\mathrm{j}\omega T}$$

If k is real, then, provided that $\sigma = \mathrm{Re}\,(s) > k$, the limit exists, and is zero. If k is complex, say $k = a + \mathrm{j}b$, then the limit will also exist, and be zero, provided that $\sigma > a$ (that is, $\mathrm{Re}\,(s) > \mathrm{Re}\,(k)$). Under these conditions, we then have

$$\mathscr{L}\{\mathrm{e}^{kt}\} = \frac{1}{s-k}$$

giving us the Laplace transform pair

$$\left.\begin{array}{l} f(t) = \mathrm{e}^{kt} \\[2mm] F(s) = \dfrac{1}{s-k} \end{array}\right\} \quad \mathrm{Re}\,(s) > \mathrm{Re}\,(k) \tag{2.7}$$

EXAMPLE 2.4   Determine the Laplace transforms of the sine and cosine functions

$$f(t) = \sin at, \qquad g(t) = \cos at$$

where a is a real constant.

Solution   Since

$$e^{jat} = \cos at + j \sin at$$

we may write

$$f(t) = \sin at = \mathrm{Im}\, e^{jat}$$
$$g(t) = \cos at = \mathrm{Re}\, e^{jat}$$

Using this formulation, the required transforms may be obtained from the result

$$\mathscr{L}\{e^{kt}\} = \frac{1}{s-k}, \quad \mathrm{Re}(s) > \mathrm{Re}(k)$$

of Example 2.3.

Taking $k = ja$ in this result gives

$$\mathscr{L}\{e^{jat}\} = \frac{1}{s-ja}, \quad \mathrm{Re}(s) > 0$$

or

$$\mathscr{L}\{e^{jat}\} = \frac{s+ja}{s^2+a^2}, \quad \mathrm{Re}(s) > 0$$

Thus, equating real and imaginary parts,

$$\mathscr{L}\{\sin at\} = \mathrm{Im}\, \mathscr{L}\{e^{jat}\} = \frac{a}{s^2+a^2}, \quad \mathrm{Re}(s) > 0$$

$$\mathscr{L}\{\cos at\} = \mathrm{Re}\, \mathscr{L}\{e^{jat}\} = \frac{s}{s^2+a^2}, \quad \mathrm{Re}(s) > 0$$

giving us the Laplace transform pairs

$$\mathscr{L}\{\sin at\} = \frac{a}{s^2+a^2}, \quad \mathrm{Re}(s) > 0 \tag{2.8}$$

$$\mathscr{L}\{\cos at\} = \frac{s}{s^2+a^2}, \quad \mathrm{Re}(s) > 0 \tag{2.9}$$

2.2.3   Existence of the Laplace transform

Clearly, from the definition (2.2), the Laplace transform of a function $f(t)$ exists if and only if the improper integral in the definition converges for at least some values of s. The examples of Section 2.2.2 suggest that this relates to the boundedness of the function, with the factor e^{-st} in the transform integral acting like a convergence factor in that the allowed values of $\text{Re}(s)$ are those for which the integral converges. In order to be able to state sufficient conditions on $f(t)$ for the existence of $\mathcal{L}\{f(t)\}$, we first introduce the definition of a function of exponential order.

DEFINITION 2.1

A function $f(t)$ is said to be of **exponential order** as $t \rightarrow \infty$ if there exists a real number σ and positive constants M and T such that

$$|f(t)| < Me^{\sigma t}$$

for all $t > T$.

What this definition tells us is that a function $f(t)$ is of exponential order if it does not grow faster than some exponential function of the form $Me^{\sigma t}$. Fortunately, most functions of practical significance satisfy this requirement, and are therefore of exponential order. There are, however, functions that are not of exponential order, an example being e^{t^2}, since this grows more rapidly than $Me^{\sigma t}$ as $t \rightarrow \infty$, whatever the values of M and σ.

EXAMPLE 2.5   The function $f(t) = e^{3t}$ is of exponential order, with $\sigma \geqslant 3$.

EXAMPLE 2.6   Show that the function $f(t) = t^3$ $(t \geqslant 0)$ is of exponential order.

Solution   Since

$$e^{\alpha t} = 1 + \alpha t + \tfrac{1}{2}\alpha^2 t^2 + \tfrac{1}{6}\alpha^3 t^3 + \ldots$$

it follows that for any $\alpha > 0$

$$t^3 < \frac{6}{\alpha^3}e^{\alpha t}$$

so that t^3 is of exponential order, with $\sigma > 0$.

It follows from Examples 2.5 and 2.6 that the choice of σ in Definition 2.1 is not unique for a particular function. For this reason, we define the greatest lower bound σ_c of the set of possible values of σ to be the **abscissa of convergence** of $f(t)$. Thus, in the case of the function $f(t) = e^{3t}$, $\sigma_c = 3$, while in the case of the function $f(t) = t^3$, $\sigma_c = 0$.

Returning to the definition of the Laplace transform given by (2.2), it follows that if $f(t)$ is a continuous function and is also of exponential order with abscissa of convergence σ_c, so that

$$|f(t)| < Me^{\sigma_c t}$$

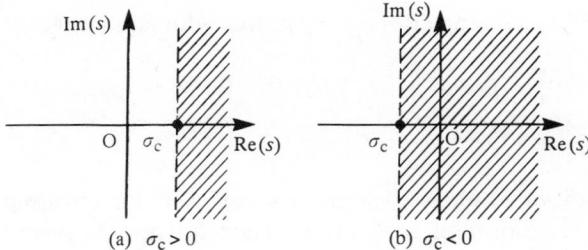

Figure 2.4 Region of convergence for $\mathscr{L}\{f(t)\}$; σ_{c} is the abscissa of convergence for $f(t)$.

then, taking $T = 0$ in Definition 2.1,

$$|F(s)| = \left| \int_0^\infty \mathrm{e}^{-st} f(t)\,\mathrm{d}t \right| \leqslant \int_0^\infty |\mathrm{e}^{-st}|\,|f(t)|\,\mathrm{d}t$$

Writing $s = \sigma + \mathrm{j}\omega$, where σ and ω are real, since $|\mathrm{e}^{-\mathrm{j}\omega t}| = 1$, we have

$$|\mathrm{e}^{-st}| = |\mathrm{e}^{-\sigma t}|\,|\mathrm{e}^{-\mathrm{j}\omega t}| = |\mathrm{e}^{-\sigma t}| = \mathrm{e}^{-\sigma t}$$

so that

$$|F(s)| \leqslant \int_0^\infty \mathrm{e}^{-\sigma t} |f(t)|\,\mathrm{d}t$$

$$\leqslant M \int_0^\infty \mathrm{e}^{-\sigma t}\, \mathrm{e}^{\sigma_{\mathrm{c}} t}\,\mathrm{d}t$$

$$= M \int_0^\infty \mathrm{e}^{-(\sigma - \sigma_{\mathrm{c}})t}\,\mathrm{d}t$$

This last integral is finite whenever $\sigma = \mathrm{Re}(s) > \sigma_{\mathrm{c}}$, so we can conclude that a continuous function $f(t)$ of exponential order, with abscissa of convergence σ_{c}, has a Laplace transform; that is,

$$\mathscr{L}\{f(t)\} = F(s), \quad \mathrm{Re}(s) > \sigma_{\mathrm{c}}$$

where the region of convergence is as shown in Figure 2.4.

In fact, the requirement that $f(t)$ be continuous is not essential, and may be relaxed to $f(t)$ being piecewise-continuous, as defined in Section 7.6.1 of *Modern Engineering Mathematics*; that is, $f(t)$ must have only a finite number of finite discontinuities, being elsewhere continuous and bounded.

We conclude this section by stating a theorem that ensures the existence of a Laplace transform.

THEOREM 2.1   Existence of Laplace transform

If the causal function $f(t)$ is piecewise-continuous on $[0, \infty]$ and is of exponential order, with abscissa of convergence σ_{c}, then its Laplace transform exists, with region of convergence $\mathrm{Re}\,(s) > \sigma_c$ in the s domain; that is,

$$\mathscr{L}\{f(t)\} = F(s) = \int_0^\infty \mathrm{e}^{-st} f(t)\,\mathrm{d}t, \quad \mathrm{Re}\,(s) > \sigma_c \qquad \square$$

The conditions of this theorem are *sufficient* for ensuring the existence of the Laplace transform of a function. They do not, however, constitute *necessary* conditions for the existence of such a transform, and it does not follow that if the conditions are violated then a transform does not exist. In fact, the conditions are more restrictive than necessary, since there exist functions with infinite discontinuities that possess Laplace transforms.

2.2.4   Properties of the Laplace transform

In this section we consider some of the properties of the Laplace transform that will enable us to find further transform pairs $\{f(t), F(s)\}$ without having to compute them directly using the definition. Further properties will be developed in later sections when the need arises.

Property 2.1: The linearity property

A fundamental property of the Laplace transform is its linearity, which may be stated as follows:

> If $f(t)$ and $g(t)$ are functions having Laplace transforms and if α and β are any constants then
>
> $$\mathscr{L}\{\alpha f(t) + \beta g(t)\} = \alpha \mathscr{L}\{f(t)\} + \beta \mathscr{L}\{g(t)\}$$

As a consequence of this property, we say that the Laplace transform operator $\mathscr{L}$ is a **linear operator**. A proof of the property follows readily from the definition (2.2), since

$$\mathscr{L}\{\alpha f(t) + \beta g(t)\} = \int_0^\infty [\alpha f(t) + \beta g(t)] \mathrm{e}^{-st}\,\mathrm{d}t$$

$$= \int_0^\infty \alpha f(t) \mathrm{e}^{-st}\,\mathrm{d}t + \int_0^\infty \beta g(t) \mathrm{e}^{-st}\,\mathrm{d}t$$

$$= \alpha \int_0^\infty f(t) \mathrm{e}^{-st}\,\mathrm{d}t + \beta \int_0^\infty g(t) \mathrm{e}^{-st}\,\mathrm{d}t$$

$$= \alpha \mathscr{L}\{f(t)\} + \beta \mathscr{L}\{g(t)\}$$

Regarding the region of convergence, if $f(t)$ and $g(t)$ have abscissae of convergence σ_1 and σ_2, respectively, then

$$|f(t)| < M_1 e^{\sigma_1 t}, \qquad |g(t)| < M_2 e^{\sigma_2 t}$$

It follows that

$$|\alpha f(t) + \beta g(t)| \leqslant |\alpha|\,|f(t)| + |\beta|\,|g(t)|$$
$$\leqslant |\alpha| M_1 e^{\sigma_1 t} + |\beta| M_2 e^{\sigma_2 t}$$
$$\leqslant (|\alpha| M_1 + |\beta| M_2) e^{\sigma t}$$

where $\sigma = \max(\sigma_1, \sigma_2)$, so that the abscissa of convergence of the linear sum $\alpha f(t) + \beta g(t)$ is the maximum of those for $f(t)$ and $g(t)$.

This linearity property may clearly be extended to a linear combination of any finite number of functions, and may even be extended to an infinite number of functions – provided that their sum is convergent.

EXAMPLE 2.7   Determine $\mathscr{L}\{3t + 2e^{3t}\}$.

Solution   Using the results given in (2.6) and (2.7),

$$\mathscr{L}\{t\} = \frac{1}{s^2}, \quad \mathrm{Re}\,(s) > 0$$

$$\mathscr{L}\{e^{3t}\} = \frac{1}{s-3}, \quad \mathrm{Re}\,(s) > 3$$

so, by the linearity property,

$$\mathscr{L}\{3t + 2e^{3t}\} = 3\mathscr{L}\{t\} + 2\mathscr{L}\{e^{3t}\}$$
$$= \frac{3}{s^2} + \frac{2}{s-3}, \quad \mathrm{Re}\,(s) > \max\{0, 3\}$$
$$= \frac{3}{s^2} + \frac{2}{s-3}, \quad \mathrm{Re}\,(s) > 3$$

EXAMPLE 2.8   Determine $\mathscr{L}\{5 - 3t + 4\sin 2t - 6e^{4t}\}$.

Solution   Using the results given in (2.5)–(2.7),

$$\mathscr{L}\{5\} = \frac{5}{s}, \quad \mathrm{Re}\,(s) > 0$$

$$\mathscr{L}\{t\} = \frac{1}{s^2}, \quad \mathrm{Re}\,(s) > 0$$

$$\mathcal{L}\{\sin 2t\} = \frac{2}{s^2 + 4}, \quad \mathrm{Re}\,(s) > 0$$

$$\mathcal{L}\{e^{4t}\} = \frac{1}{s - 4}, \quad \mathrm{Re}\,(s) > 4$$

so, by the linearity property,

$$\mathcal{L}\{5 - 3t + 4\sin 2t - 6e^{4t}\} = \mathcal{L}\{5\} - 3\mathcal{L}\{t\} + 4\mathcal{L}\{\sin 2t\} - 6\mathcal{L}\{e^{4t}\}$$

$$= \frac{5}{s} - \frac{3}{s^2} + \frac{8}{s^2 + 4} - \frac{6}{s - 4}, \quad \mathrm{Re}\,(s) > \max\{0, 4\}$$

$$= \frac{5}{s} - \frac{3}{s^2} + \frac{8}{s^2 + 4} - \frac{6}{s - 4}, \quad \mathrm{Re}\,(s) > 4$$

The first shift property is another property that enables us to add more combinations to our repertoire of Laplace transform pairs. As with the linearity property, it will prove to be of considerable importance in our later discussions, particularly when considering the inversion of Laplace transforms.

Property 2.2: The first shift property

The property is contained in the following theorem, commonly referred to as the **first shift theorem** or sometimes as the **exponential modulation theorem**.

THEOREM 2.2   **The first shift theorem**

If $f(t)$ is a function having Laplace transform $F(s)$, with $\mathrm{Re}\,(s) > \sigma_c$, then the function $e^{at} f(t)$ also has a Laplace transform, given by

$$\mathcal{L}\{e^{at} f(t)\} = F(s - a), \quad \mathrm{Re}\,(s) > \sigma_c + \mathrm{Re}\,(a)$$

Proof   A proof of the theorem follows directly from the definition of the Laplace transform, since

$$\mathcal{L}\{e^{at} f(t)\} = \int_0^\infty e^{at} f(t) e^{-st} \, dt$$

$$= \int_0^\infty f(t) e^{-(s-a)t} \, dt$$

Then, since

$$\mathcal{L}\{f(t)\} = F(s) = \int_0^\infty f(t) e^{-st} \, dt, \quad \mathrm{Re}\,(s) > \sigma_c$$

we see that the last integral above is in structure exactly the Laplace transform of $f(t)$ itself, except that $s - a$ takes the place of s, so that

$$\mathscr{L}\{e^{at}f(t)\} = F(s-a), \quad \text{Re}\,(s-a) > \sigma_c$$

or

$$\mathscr{L}\{e^{at}f(t)\} = F(s-a), \quad \text{Re}\,(s) > \sigma_c + \text{Re}\,(a) \qquad\qquad \square$$

An alternative way of expressing the result of Theorem 2.2, which may be found more convenient in application, is as

$$\mathscr{L}\{e^{at}f(t)\} = [\mathscr{L}\{f(t)\}]_{s\to s-a} = [F(s)]_{s\to s-a}$$

In other words, the theorem says that the Laplace transform of e^{at} times a function $f(t)$ is equal to the Laplace transform of $f(t)$ itself, with s replaced by $s - a$.

EXAMPLE 2.9   Determine $\mathscr{L}\{te^{-2t}\}$.

Solution   From the result given in (2.6),

$$\mathscr{L}\{t\} = F(s) = \frac{1}{s^2}, \quad \text{Re}\,(s) > 0$$

so, by the first shift theorem,

$$\mathscr{L}\{te^{-2t}\} = F(s+2) = [F(s)]_{s\to s+2}, \quad \text{Re}\,(s) > 0 - 2$$

that is,

$$\mathscr{L}\{te^{-2t}\} = \frac{1}{(s+2)^2}, \quad \text{Re}\,(s) > -2$$

EXAMPLE 2.10   Determine $\mathscr{L}\{e^{-3t}\sin 2t\}$.

Solution   From the result (2.8),

$$\mathscr{L}\{\sin 2t\} = F(s) = \frac{2}{s^2 + 4}, \quad \text{Re}\,(s) > 0$$

so, by the first shift theorem,

$$\mathscr{L}\{e^{-3t}\sin 2t\} = F(s+3) = [F(s)]_{s\to s+3}, \quad \text{Re}\,(s) > 0 - 3$$

that is,

$$\mathscr{L}\{e^{-3t}\sin 2t\} = \frac{2}{(s+3)^2 + 4} = \frac{2}{s^2 + 6s + 13}, \quad \text{Re}\,(s) > -3$$

The function $e^{-3t}\sin 2t$ in Example 2.10 is a member of a general class of functions called **damped sinusoids**. These play an important role in the study of engineering systems, particularly in the analysis of vibrations. For this reason, we add the following two general members of the class to our standard library of Laplace transform pairs:

$$\mathscr{L}\{e^{-kt}\sin at\} = \frac{a}{(s+k)^2 + a^2}, \quad \text{Re}(s) > -k \tag{2.10}$$

$$\mathscr{L}\{e^{-kt}\cos at\} = \frac{s+k}{(s+k)^2 + a^2}, \quad \text{Re}(s) > -k \tag{2.11}$$

where in both cases k and a are real constants.

Property 2.3: Derivative-of-transform property

This property relates operations in the time domain to those in the transformed s domain, but initially we shall simply look upon it as a method of increasing our repertoire of Laplace transform pairs. The property is also sometimes referred to as the **multiplication-by-t** property. A statement of the property is contained in the following theorem.

THEOREM 2.3   **Derivative of transform**

If $f(t)$ is a function having Laplace transform

$$F(s) = \mathscr{L}\{f(t)\}, \quad \text{Re}(s) > \sigma_c$$

then the functions $t^n f(t)$ $(n = 1, 2, \ldots)$ also have Laplace transforms, given by

$$\mathscr{L}\{t^n f(t)\} = (-1)^n \frac{d^n F(s)}{ds^n}, \quad \text{Re}(s) > \sigma_c$$

Proof   By definition,

$$\mathscr{L}\{f(t)\} = F(s) = \int_0^\infty e^{-st} f(t)\, dt$$

so that

$$\frac{d^n F(s)}{ds^n} = \frac{d^n}{ds^n} \int_0^\infty e^{-st} f(t)\, dt$$

Owing to the convergence properties of the improper integral involved, we can interchange the operations of differentiation and integration and differentiate with respect to s under the integral sign. Thus

$$\frac{d^n F(s)}{ds^n} = \int_0^\infty \frac{\partial^n}{\partial s^n} [e^{-st} f(t)]\, dt$$

which, on carrying out the repeated differentiation, gives

$$\frac{d^n F(s)}{ds^n} = (-1)^n \int_0^\infty e^{-st} t^n f(t) \, dt$$

$$= (-1)^n \mathcal{L}\{t^n f(t)\}, \quad \text{Re}(s) > \sigma_c$$

the region of convergence remaining unchanged. $\square$

In other words, Theorem 2.3 says that differentiating the transform of a function with respect to s is equivalent to multiplying the function itself by $-t$. As with the previous properties, we can now use this result to add to our list of Laplace transform pairs.

EXAMPLE 2.11 Determine $\mathcal{L}\{t \sin 3t\}$.

Solution Using the result (2.8),

$$\mathcal{L}\{\sin 3t\} = F(s) = \frac{3}{s^2 + 9}, \quad \text{Re}(s) > 0$$

so, by the derivative theorem,

$$\mathcal{L}\{t \sin 3t\} = -\frac{dF(s)}{ds} = \frac{6s}{(s^2 + 9)^2}, \quad \text{Re}(s) > 0$$

EXAMPLE 2.12 Determine $\mathcal{L}\{t^2 e^t\}$.

Solution From the result (2.7),

$$\mathcal{L}\{e^t\} = F(s) = \frac{1}{s - 1}, \quad \text{Re}(s) > 1$$

so, by the derivative theorem,

$$\mathcal{L}\{t^2 e^t\} = (-1)^2 \frac{d^2 F(s)}{ds^2} = (-1)^2 \frac{d^2}{ds^2}\left(\frac{1}{s-1}\right)$$

$$= (-1)\frac{d}{ds}\left(\frac{1}{(s-1)^2}\right)$$

$$= \frac{2}{(s-1)^3}, \quad \text{Re}(s) > 1$$

EXAMPLE 2.13 Determine $\mathscr{L}\{t^n\}$, where n is a positive integer.

Solution Using the result (2.5),

$$\mathscr{L}\{1\} = \frac{1}{s}, \quad \text{Re}\,(s) > 0$$

so, by the derivative theorem,

$$\mathscr{L}\{t^n\} = (-1)^n \frac{d^n}{ds^n}\left(\frac{1}{s}\right)$$

$$= \frac{n!}{s^{n+1}}, \quad \text{Re}\,(s) > 0$$

2.2.5   Table of Laplace transforms

It is appropriate at this stage to draw together the results proved to date for easy access. This is done in the form of two short tables. Figure 2.5(a) lists some Laplace transform pairs and Figure 2.5(b) lists the properties already considered.

2.2.6   Exercises

1 Use the definition of the Laplace transform to obtain the transforms of $f(t)$ when $f(t)$ is given by
(a) $\cosh 2t$ (b) t^2 (c) $3 + t$ (d) te^{-t}
stating the region of convergence in each case.

2 What are the abscissae of convergence for the following functions?
(a) e^{5t}
(b) e^{-3t}
(c) $\sin 2t$
(d) $\sinh 3t$
(e) $\cosh 2t$
(f) t^4
(g) $e^{-5t} + t^2$
(h) $3\cos 2t - t^3$
(i) $3e^{2t} - 2e^{-2t} + \sin 2t$
(j) $\sinh 3t + \sin 3t$

3 Using the results shown in Figure 2.5, obtain the Laplace transforms of the following functions, stating the region of convergence:
(a) $5 - 3t$
(b) $7t^3 - 2\sin 3t$
(c) $3 - 2t + 4\cos 2t$
(d) $\cosh 3t$
(e) $\sinh 2t$
(f) $5e^{-2t} + 3 - 2\cos 2t$
(g) $4te^{-2t}$
(h) $2e^{-3t}\sin 2t$
(i) $t^2 e^{-4t}$
(j) $6t^3 - 3t^2 + 4t - 2$
(k) $2\cos 3t + 5\sin 3t$
(l) $t\cos 2t$
(m) $t^2\sin 3t$
(n) $t^2 - 3\cos 4t$
(o) $t^2 e^{-2t} + e^{-t}\cos 2t + 3$

2.2.7   The inverse transform

The symbol $\mathscr{L}^{-1}\{F(s)\}$ denotes a causal function $f(t)$ whose Laplace transform is $F(s)$; that is,

(a)

$f(t)$	$\mathscr{L}\{f(t)\} = F(s)$	Region of convergence
c, c a constant	$\dfrac{c}{s}$	$\mathrm{Re}\,(s) > 0$
t	$\dfrac{1}{s^2}$	$\mathrm{Re}\,(s) > 0$
t^n, n a positive integer	$\dfrac{n!}{s^{n+1}}$	$\mathrm{Re}\,(s) > 0$
e^{kt}, k a constant	$\dfrac{1}{s-k}$	$\mathrm{Re}\,(s) > \mathrm{Re}\,(k)$
$\sin at$, a a real constant	$\dfrac{a}{s^2+a^2}$	$\mathrm{Re}\,(s) > 0$
$\cos at$, a a real constant	$\dfrac{s}{s^2+a^2}$	$\mathrm{Re}\,(s) > 0$
$\mathrm{e}^{-kt}\sin at$, k and a real constants	$\dfrac{a}{(s+k)^2+a^2}$	$\mathrm{Re}\,(s) > -k$
$\mathrm{e}^{-kt}\cos at$, k and a real constants	$\dfrac{s+k}{(s+k)^2+a^2}$	$\mathrm{Re}\,(s) > -k$

(b)

$$\mathscr{L}\{f(t)\} = F(s), \quad \mathrm{Re}\,(s) > \sigma_1 \quad \text{and} \quad \mathscr{L}\{g(t)\} = G(s), \quad \mathrm{Re}\,(s) > \sigma_2$$

Linearity: $\mathscr{L}\{\alpha f(t) + \beta g(t)\} = \alpha F(s) + \beta G(s), \quad \mathrm{Re}\,(s) > \max(\sigma_1, \sigma_2)$

First shift theorem: $\mathscr{L}\{\mathrm{e}^{at}f(t)\} = F(s-a), \quad \mathrm{Re}\,(s) > \sigma_1 + \mathrm{Re}\,(a)$

Derivative of transform:

$$\mathscr{L}\{t^n f(t)\} = (-1)^n \frac{\mathrm{d}^n F(s)}{\mathrm{d}s^n}, \quad (n = 1, 2, \ldots), \, \mathrm{Re}\,(s) > \sigma_1$$

Figure 2.5 (a) Table of Laplace transform pairs. (b) Some properties of the Laplace transform.

$$\text{if} \quad \mathscr{L}\{f(t)\} = F(s) \quad \text{then} \quad f(t) = \mathscr{L}^{-1}\{F(s)\}$$

This correspondence between the functions $F(s)$ and $f(t)$ is called the **inverse Laplace transformation**, $f(t)$ being the **inverse transform** of $F(s)$, and $\mathscr{L}^{-1}$ being referred to as the **inverse Laplace transform operator**. These relationships are depicted in Figure 2.6.

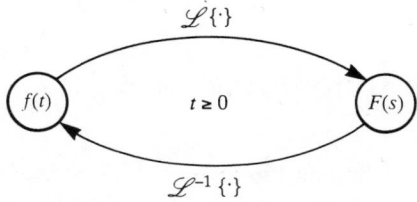

Figure 2.6 The Laplace transform and its inverse.

As was pointed out in observation (c) of Section 2.2.1, the Laplace transform $F(s)$ only determines the behaviour of $f(t)$ for $t \geqslant 0$. Thus $\mathscr{L}^{-1}\{F(s)\} = f(t)$ only for $t \geqslant 0$. As indicated before, we are assuming throughout this chapter that we are dealing with causal functions, so that when writing $\mathscr{L}^{-1}\{F(s)\} = f(t)$, it is assumed that $t \geqslant 0$. Strictly speaking, we should write

$$\mathscr{L}^{-1}\{F(s)\} = f(t)H(t) \tag{2.12}$$

EXAMPLE 2.14 Since

$$\mathscr{L}\{e^{at}\} = \frac{1}{s-a}$$

it follows that

$$\mathscr{L}^{-1}\left\{\frac{1}{s-a}\right\} = e^{at}$$

EXAMPLE 2.15 Since

$$\mathscr{L}\{\sin \omega t\} = \frac{\omega}{s^2 + \omega^2}$$

it follows that

$$\mathscr{L}^{-1}\left\{\frac{\omega}{s^2 + \omega^2}\right\} = \sin \omega t$$

The linearity property for the Laplace transform (Property 2.1), states that if α and β are any constants then

$$\mathscr{L}\{\alpha f(t) + \beta g(t)\} = \alpha \mathscr{L}\{f(t)\} + \beta \mathscr{L}\{g(t)\}$$
$$= \alpha F(s) + \beta G(s)$$

It then follows from the above definition that

$$\mathscr{L}^{-1}\{\alpha F(s) + \beta G(s)\} = \alpha f(t) + \beta g(t)$$
$$= \alpha \mathscr{L}^{-1}\{F(s)\} + \beta \mathscr{L}^{-1}\{G(s)\}$$

so that the inverse Laplace transform operator $\mathscr{L}^{-1}$ is also a linear operator.

2.2.8 Evaluation of inverse transforms

The most obvious way of finding the inverse transform of the function $F(s)$ is to make use of a table of transforms such as that given in Figure 2.5. Sometimes it is possible to write down the inverse transform directly from the table, but more often than not it is first necessary to carry out some algebraic manipulation on $F(s)$. In particular, we frequently need to determine the inverse transform of a rational function of the form $p(s)/q(s)$, where $p(s)$ and $q(s)$ are polynomials in s. In such cases the procedure is first to resolve the function into partial fractions and then to use the table of transforms.

EXAMPLE 2.16 Find

$$\mathscr{L}^{-1}\left\{\frac{1}{(s+3)(s-2)}\right\}$$

Solution First $1/(s+3)(s+2)$ is resolved into partial fractions, giving

$$\frac{1}{(s+3)(s-2)} = \frac{-\frac{1}{5}}{s+3} + \frac{\frac{1}{5}}{s-2}$$

Then, using the result $\mathscr{L}^{-1}\{1/(s+a)\} = e^{-at}$ together with the linearity property, we have

$$\mathscr{L}^{-1}\left\{\frac{1}{(s+3)(s-2)}\right\} = -\tfrac{1}{5}\mathscr{L}^{-1}\left\{\frac{1}{s+3}\right\} + \tfrac{1}{5}\mathscr{L}^{-1}\left\{\frac{1}{s-2}\right\}$$

$$= -\tfrac{1}{5}e^{-3t} + \tfrac{1}{5}e^{2t}$$

EXAMPLE 2.17 Find

$$\mathscr{L}^{-1}\left\{\frac{s+1}{s^2(s^2+9)}\right\}$$

Solution Resolving $(s+1)/s^2(s^2+9)$ into partial fractions gives

$$\frac{s+1}{s^2(s^2+9)} = \frac{\frac{1}{9}}{s} + \frac{\frac{1}{9}}{s^2} - \frac{1}{9}\frac{s+1}{s^2+9}$$

$$= \frac{\frac{1}{9}}{s} + \frac{\frac{1}{9}}{s^2} - \frac{1}{9}\frac{s}{s^2+3^2} - \frac{1}{27}\frac{3}{s^2+3^2}$$

Using the results in Figure 2.5, together with the linearity property, we have

$$\mathscr{L}^{-1}\left\{\frac{s+1}{s^2(s^2+9)}\right\} = \tfrac{1}{9} + \tfrac{1}{9}t - \tfrac{1}{9}\cos 3t - \tfrac{1}{27}\sin 3t$$

2.2.9   Inversion using the first shift theorem

In Theorem 2.2 we saw that if $F(s)$ is the Laplace transform of $f(t)$ then, for a scalar a, $F(s-a)$ is the Laplace transform of $e^{at}f(t)$. This theorem normally causes little difficulty when used to obtain the Laplace transforms of functions, but it does frequently lead to problems when used to obtain inverse transforms. Expressed in the inverse form, the theorem becomes

$$\mathscr{L}^{-1}\{F(s-a)\} = e^{at}f(t)$$

The notation

$$\mathscr{L}^{-1}\{[F(s)]_{s \to s-a}\} = e^{at}[f(t)]$$

where $F(s) = \mathscr{L}\{f(t)\}$ and $[F(s)]_{s \to s-a}$ denotes that s in $F(s)$ is replaced by $s - a$, may make the relation clearer.

EXAMPLE 2.18 Find

$$\mathscr{L}^{-1}\left\{\frac{1}{(s+2)^2}\right\}$$

Solution

$$\frac{1}{(s+2)^2} = \left[\frac{1}{s^2}\right]_{s \to s+2}$$

and, since $1/s^2 = \mathscr{L}\{t\}$, the shift theorem gives

$$\mathscr{L}^{-1}\left\{\frac{1}{(s+2)^2}\right\} = te^{-2t}$$

EXAMPLE 2.19 Find

$$\mathscr{L}^{-1}\left\{\frac{2}{s^2 + 6s + 13}\right\}$$

Solution

$$\frac{2}{s^2 + 6s + 13} = \frac{2}{(s+3)^2 + 4} = \left[\frac{2}{s^2 + 2^2}\right]_{s \to s+3}$$

and, since $2/(s^2 + 2^2) = \mathscr{L}\{\sin 2t\}$, the shift theorem gives

$$\mathscr{L}^{-1}\left\{\frac{2}{s^2 + 6s + 13}\right\} = e^{-3t}\sin 2t$$

EXAMPLE 2.20 Find

$$\mathscr{L}^{-1}\left\{\frac{s+7}{s^2 + 2s + 5}\right\}$$

Solution

$$\frac{s+7}{s^2+2s+5}=\frac{s+7}{(s+1)^2+4}=\frac{(s+1)}{(s+1)^2+4}+3\frac{2}{(s+1)^2+4}$$

$$=\left[\frac{s}{s^2+2^2}\right]_{s\to s+1}+3\left[\frac{2}{s^2+2^2}\right]_{s\to s+1}$$

Since $s/(s^2+2^2)=\mathscr{L}\{\cos 2t\}$ and $2/(s^2+2^2)=\mathscr{L}\{\sin 2t\}$, the shift theorem gives

$$\mathscr{L}^{-1}\left\{\frac{s+7}{s^2+2s+5}\right\}=\mathrm{e}^{-t}\cos 2t+3\mathrm{e}^{-t}\sin 2t$$

EXAMPLE 2.21 Find

$$\mathscr{L}^{-1}\left\{\frac{1}{(s+1)^2(s^2+4)}\right\}$$

Solution Resolving $1/(s+1)^2(s^2+4)$ into partial fractions gives

$$\frac{1}{(s+1)^2(s^2+4)}=\frac{\frac{2}{25}}{s+1}+\frac{\frac{1}{5}}{(s+1)^2}-\frac{1}{25}\frac{2s+3}{s^2+4}$$

$$=\frac{\frac{2}{25}}{s+1}+\frac{1}{5}\left[\frac{1}{s^2}\right]_{s\to s+1}-\frac{2}{25}\frac{s}{s^2+2^2}-\frac{3}{50}\frac{2}{s^2+2^2}$$

Since $1/s^2=\mathscr{L}\{t\}$, the shift theorem, together with the results in Figure 2.5, gives

$$\mathscr{L}^{-1}\left\{\frac{1}{(s+1)^2(s^2+4)}\right\}=\tfrac{2}{25}\mathrm{e}^{-t}+\tfrac{1}{5}\mathrm{e}^{-t}t-\tfrac{2}{25}\cos 2t-\tfrac{3}{50}\sin 2t$$

2.2.10 Exercises

4 Find $\mathscr{L}^{-1}\{F(s)\}$ when $F(s)$ is given by

(a) $\dfrac{1}{(s+3)(s+7)}$

(b) $\dfrac{s+5}{(s+1)(s-3)}$

(c) $\dfrac{s-1}{s^2(s+3)}$

(d) $\dfrac{2s+6}{s^2+4}$

(e) $\dfrac{1}{s^2(s^2+16)}$

(f) $\dfrac{s+8}{s^2+4s+5}$

(g) $\dfrac{s+1}{s^2(s^2+4s+8)}$

(h) $\dfrac{4s}{(s-1)(s+1)^2}$

(i) $\dfrac{s+7}{s^2+2s+5}$

(j) $\dfrac{3s^2-7s+5}{(s-1)(s-2)(s-3)}$

(k) $\dfrac{5s-7}{(s+3)(s^2+2)}$

(l) $\dfrac{s}{(s-1)(s^2+2s+2)}$

(m) $\dfrac{s-1}{s^2+2s+5}$

(n) $\dfrac{s-1}{(s-2)(s-3)(s-4)}$

(o) $\dfrac{3s}{(s-1)(s^2-4)}$

(p) $\dfrac{36}{s(s^2+1)(s^2+9)}$

(q) $\dfrac{2s^2+4s+9}{(s+2)(s^2+3s+3)}$

(r) $\dfrac{1}{(s+1)(s+2)(s^2+2s+10)}$

2.3 Solution of differential equations

We first consider the Laplace transforms of derivatives and integrals, and then apply these to the solution of differential equations.

2.3.1 Transforms of derivatives

If we are to use Laplace transform methods to solve differential equations, we need to find convenient expressions for the Laplace transforms of derivatives such as $\mathrm{d}f/\mathrm{d}t$, $\mathrm{d}^2f/\mathrm{d}t^2$ or, in general, $\mathrm{d}^nf/\mathrm{d}t^n$. By definition,

$$\mathscr{L}\left\{\frac{\mathrm{d}f}{\mathrm{d}t}\right\} = \int_0^\infty \mathrm{e}^{-st}\frac{\mathrm{d}f}{\mathrm{d}t}\,\mathrm{d}t$$

Integrating by parts, we have

$$\mathscr{L}\left\{\frac{\mathrm{d}f}{\mathrm{d}t}\right\} = [\mathrm{e}^{-st}f(t)]_0^\infty + s\int_0^\infty \mathrm{e}^{-st}f(t)\,\mathrm{d}t$$

$$= -f(0) + sF(s)$$

that is,

$$\mathscr{L}\left\{\frac{\mathrm{d}f}{\mathrm{d}t}\right\} = sF(s) - f(0) \tag{2.13}$$

The advantage of using the Laplace transform when dealing with differential equations can readily be seen, since it enables us to replace the operation of differentiation in the time domain by a simple algebraic operation in the s domain.

Note that to deduce the result (2.13), we have assumed that $f(t)$ is continuous, with a piecewise-continuous derivative $\mathrm{d}f/\mathrm{d}t$, for $t \geqslant 0$ and that it is also of exponential order as $t \to \infty$.

Likewise, if both $f(t)$ and $\mathrm{d}f/\mathrm{d}t$ are continuous on $t \geqslant 0$ and are of exponential order as $t \to \infty$, and $\mathrm{d}^2f/\mathrm{d}t^2$ is piecewise-continuous for $t \geqslant 0$, then

$$\mathscr{L}\left\{\frac{\mathrm{d}^2f}{\mathrm{d}t^2}\right\} = \int_0^\infty \mathrm{e}^{-st}\frac{\mathrm{d}^2f}{\mathrm{d}t^2}\,\mathrm{d}t$$

$$= \left[\mathrm{e}^{-st}\frac{\mathrm{d}f}{\mathrm{d}t}\right]_0^\infty + s\int_0^\infty \mathrm{e}^{-st}\frac{\mathrm{d}f}{\mathrm{d}t}\,\mathrm{d}t$$

$$= -\left[\frac{\mathrm{d}f}{\mathrm{d}t}\right]_{t=0} + s\mathscr{L}\left\{\frac{\mathrm{d}f}{\mathrm{d}t}\right\}$$

which, on using (2.12), gives

$$\mathscr{L}\left\{\frac{\mathrm{d}^2 f}{\mathrm{d}t^2}\right\} = -\left[\frac{\mathrm{d}f}{\mathrm{d}t}\right]_{t=0} + s[sF(s) - f(0)]$$

leading to the result

$$\mathscr{L}\left\{\frac{\mathrm{d}^2 f}{\mathrm{d}t^2}\right\} = s^2 F(s) - sf(0) - \left[\frac{\mathrm{d}f}{\mathrm{d}t}\right]_{t=0} = s^2 F(s) - sf(0) - f^{(1)}(0) \qquad \textbf{(2.14)}$$

Clearly, provided that $f(t)$ and its derivative satisfy the required conditions, this procedure may be extended to obtain the Laplace transform of $f^{(n)}(t) = \mathrm{d}^n f/\mathrm{d}t^n$ in the form

$$\mathscr{L}\{f^{(n)}(t)\} = s^n F(s) - s^{n-1}f(0) - s^{n-2}f^{(1)}(0) - \ldots - f^{(n-1)}(0)$$

$$= s^n F(s) - \sum_{i=1}^{n} s^{n-1}f^{(i-1)}(0) \qquad \textbf{(2.15)}$$

a result that may be readily proved by induction.

Since we have interpreted the lower limit in the definition of the Laplace transform to be $0-$, $f(0)$ and $f^{(i)}(0)$ ($i = 1, 2, \ldots, n-1$) should be interpreted as the values of $f(t)$ and $f^{(i)}(t)$ ($i = 1, 2, \ldots, n-1$) as $t \to 0$ from below; that is, $t \to 0$ through negative values of t. This is particularly important when dealing with problems involving switching transients, when $f(0-) \neq f(0+)$.

2.3.2   Transforms of integrals

In some applications the behaviour of a system may be represented by an **integro-differential equation**, which is an equation containing both derivatives and integrals of the unknown variable. For example, the current i in a series electrical circuit consisting of a resistance R, an inductance L and capacitance C, and subject to an applied voltage E, is given by

$$L\frac{\mathrm{d}i}{\mathrm{d}t} + iR + \frac{1}{C}\int_0^t i(\tau)\,\mathrm{d}\tau = E$$

To solve such equations directly, it is convenient to be able to obtain the Laplace transform of integrals such as $\int_0^t f(\tau)\,\mathrm{d}\tau$.

Writing

$$g(t) = \int_0^t f(\tau)\,\mathrm{d}\tau$$

we have

$$\frac{\mathrm{d}g}{\mathrm{d}t} = f(t), \qquad g(0) = 0$$

Taking Laplace transforms,

$$\mathscr{L}\left\{\frac{dg}{dt}\right\} = \mathscr{L}\{f(t)\}$$

which, on using (2.13), gives

$$sG(s) = F(s)$$

or

$$\mathscr{L}\{g(t)\} = G(s) = \frac{1}{s}F(s) = \frac{1}{s}\mathscr{L}\{f(t)\}$$

leading to the result

$$\mathscr{L}\left\{\int_0^t f(\tau)\,dt\right\} = \frac{1}{s}\mathscr{L}\{f(t)\} = \frac{1}{s}F(s) \qquad (2.16)$$

EXAMPLE 2.22   Obtain

$$\mathscr{L}\left\{\int_0^t (\tau^3 + \sin 2\tau)\,d\tau\right\}$$

In this case $f(\tau) = \tau^3 + \sin 2\tau$, giving

$$F(s) = \mathscr{L}\{f(t)\} = \mathscr{L}\{t^3\} + \mathscr{L}\{\sin 2t\}$$

$$= \frac{6}{s^4} + \frac{2}{s^2 + 4}$$

so, by (2.16),

$$\mathscr{L}\left\{\int_0^t (\tau^3 + \sin 2\tau)\,d\tau\right\} = \frac{1}{s}F(s)$$

$$= \frac{6}{s^5} + \frac{2}{s(s^2 + 4)}$$

2.3.3   Ordinary differential equations

Having obtained expressions for the Laplace transforms of derivatives, we are now in a position to use Laplace transform methods to solve ordinary linear differential equations with constant coefficients, which were introduced in Section 11.3 of *Modern Engineering Mathematics*. To illustrate this, consider the general second-order linear differential equation

$$a\frac{d^2x}{dt^2} + b\frac{dx}{dt} + cx = u(t) \quad (t \geqslant 0) \tag{2.17}$$

subject to the initial conditions $x(0) = x_0$, $\dot{x}(0) = v_0$ where as usual a dot denotes differentiation with respect to time, t. Such a differential equation may model the dynamics of some system for which the variable $x(t)$ determines the **response** of the system to the **forcing** or **excitation** term $u(t)$. The terms **system input** and **system output** are also frequently used for $u(t)$ and $x(t)$ respectively. Since the differential equation is linear and has constant coefficients, a system characterized by such a model is said to be a **linear time-invariant system**.

Taking Laplace transforms of each term in (2.17) gives

$$a\mathscr{L}\left\{\frac{d^2x}{dt^2}\right\} + b\mathscr{L}\left\{\frac{dx}{dt}\right\} + c\mathscr{L}\{x\} = \mathscr{L}\{u(t)\}$$

which on using (2.13) and (2.14) leads to

$$a[s^2X(s) - sx(0) - \dot{x}(0)] + b[X(s) - x(0)] + cX(s) = U(s)$$

Rearranging gives

$$(as^2 + bs + c)X(s) = U(s) + (as + b)x_0 + av_0$$

so that

$$X(s) = \frac{U(s) + (as + b)x_0 + av_0}{as^2 + bs + c} \tag{2.18}$$

Equation (2.18) determines the Laplace transform $X(s)$ of the response, from which, by taking the inverse transform, the desired time response $x(t)$ may be obtained.

Before considering specific examples, there are a few observations worth noting at this stage.

(a) As we have already noted in Section 2.3.1, a distinct advantage of using the Laplace transform is that it enables us to replace the operation of differentiation by an algebraic operation. Consequently, by taking the Laplace transform of each term in a differential equation, it is converted into an algebraic equation in the variable s. This may then be rearranged using algebraic rules to obtain an expression for the Laplace transform of the response; the desired time response is then obtained by taking the inverse transform.

(b) The Laplace transform method yields the complete solution of the linear differential equation, with the initial conditions automatically included. This contrasts with the classical approach adopted in Section 11.3.2 of *Modern Engineering Mathematics*, in which the general solution consists of two components, the **complementary function** and the **particular integral**, with the initial conditions determining the undetermined constants associated with the complementary function. When the solution is expressed in the general form (2.18), upon inversion the term involving $U(s)$ leads to the particular integral while that involving x_0 and v_0 gives the complementary function. A useful side issue is that an explicit solution for the transient is obtained that reflects the initial conditions.

(c) The Laplace transform method is ideally suited for solving initial-value problems; that is, linear differential equations in which all the initial conditions $x(0)$, $\dot{x}(0)$, and so on, at time $t = 0$ are specified. The method is less attractive for boundary-value problems, when the conditions on $x(t)$ and its derivatives are not all specified at $t = 0$, but some are specified at other values of the independent variable. It is still possible, however, to use the Laplace transform method by assigning arbitrary constants to one or more of the initial conditions and then determining their values using the given boundary conditions.

(d) It should be noted that the denominator of the right-hand side of (2.18) is the left-hand side of (2.17) with the operator d/dt replaced by s. The denominator equated to zero also corresponds to the auxiliary equation or characteristic equation used in the classical approach. Given a specific initial-value problem, the process of obtaining a solution using Laplace transform methods is fairly straightforward, and is illustrated by Example 2.23.

EXAMPLE 2.23   Solve the differential equation

$$\frac{d^2x}{dt^2} + 5\frac{dx}{dt} + 6x = 2e^{-t} \quad (t \geqslant 0)$$

subject to the initial conditions $x = 1$ and dx/d$t = 0$ at $t = 0$.

Solution   Taking Laplace transforms

$$\mathscr{L}\left\{\frac{d^2x}{dt^2}\right\} + 5\mathscr{L}\left\{\frac{dx}{dt}\right\} + 6\mathscr{L}\{x\} = 2\mathscr{L}\{e^{-t}\}$$

leads to the transformed equation

$$[s^2X(s) - sx(0) - \dot{x}(0)] + 5[sX(s) - x(0)] + 6X(s) = \frac{2}{s+1}$$

which on rearrangement gives

$$(s^2 + 5s + 6)X(s) = \frac{2}{s+1} + (s+5)x(0) + \dot{x}(0)$$

Incorporating the given initial conditions $x(0) = 1$ and $\dot{x}(0) = 0$ leads to

$$(s^2 + 5s + 6)X(s) = \frac{2}{s+1} + s + 5$$

That is,

$$X(s) = \frac{2}{(s+1)(s+2)(s+3)} + \frac{s+5}{(s+3)(s+2)}$$

Resolving the rational terms into partial fractions gives

$$X(s) = \frac{1}{s+1} - \frac{2}{s+2} + \frac{1}{s+3} + \frac{3}{s+2} - \frac{2}{s+3}$$

$$= \frac{1}{s+1} + \frac{1}{s+2} - \frac{1}{s+3}$$

Taking inverse transforms gives the desired solution

$$x(t) = e^{-t} + e^{-2t} - e^{-3t} \quad (t \geq 0)$$

In principle the procedure adopted in Example 2.23 for solving a second-order linear differential equation with constant coefficients is readily carried over to higher-order differential equations. A general nth-order linear differential equation may be written as

$$a_n \frac{d^n x}{dt^n} + a_{n-1} \frac{d^{n-1} x}{dt^{n-1}} + \ldots + a_0 x = u(t) \quad (t \geq 0) \tag{2.19}$$

where $a_n, a_{n-1}, \ldots, a_0$ are constants, with $a_n \neq 0$. This may be written in the more concise form

$$q(D)x(t) = u(t) \tag{2.20}$$

where D denotes the operator d/dt and $q(D)$ is the polynomial

$$q(D) = \sum_{r=0}^{n} a_r D^r$$

The objective is then to determine the response $x(t)$ for a given forcing function $u(t)$ subject to the given set of initial conditions

$$D^r x(0) = \left[\frac{d^r x}{dt^r}\right]_{t=0} = c_r \quad (r = 0, 1, \ldots, n-1)$$

Taking Laplace transforms in (2.20) and proceeding as before leads to

$$X(s) = \frac{p(s)}{q(s)}$$

where

$$p(s) = U(s) + \sum_{r=0}^{n-1} c_r \sum_{i=r+1}^{n} a_i s^{i-r-1}$$

Then, in principle, by taking the inverse transform, the desired response $x(t)$ may be obtained as

$$x(t) = \mathcal{L}^{-1}\left\{\frac{p(s)}{q(s)}\right\}$$

For high-order differential equations the process of performing this inversion may prove to be rather tedious, and matrix methods may be used as indicated in Chapter 6.

To conclude this section, further worked examples are developed in order to help consolidate understanding of this method for solving linear differential equations.

EXAMPLE 2.24   Solve the differential equation

$$\frac{d^2x}{dt^2} + 6\frac{dx}{dt} + 9x = \sin t \quad (t \geqslant 0)$$

subject to the initial conditions $x = 0$ and $dx/dt = 0$ at $t = 0$.

Solution   Taking Laplace transforms

$$\mathscr{L}\left\{\frac{d^2x}{dt^2}\right\} + 6\mathscr{L}\left\{\frac{dx}{dt}\right\} + 9\mathscr{L}\{x\} = \mathscr{L}\{\sin t\}$$

leads to the equation

$$[s^2 X(s) - sx(0) - \dot{x}(0)] + 6[sX(s) - x(0)] + 9X(s) = \frac{1}{s^2 + 1}$$

which on rearrangement gives

$$(s^2 + 6s + 9)X(s) = \frac{1}{s^2 + 1} + (s + 6)x(0) + \dot{x}(0)$$

Incorporating the given initial conditions $x(0) = \dot{x}(0) = 0$ leads to

$$X(s) = \frac{1}{(s^2 + 1)(s + 3)^2}$$

Resolving into partial fractions gives

$$X(s) = \tfrac{3}{50}\frac{1}{s + 3} + \tfrac{1}{10}\frac{1}{(s + 3)^2} + \tfrac{2}{25}\frac{1}{s^2 + 1} - \tfrac{3}{50}\frac{s}{s^2 + 1}$$

that is,

$$X(s) = \tfrac{3}{50}\frac{1}{s + 3} + \tfrac{1}{10}\left[\frac{1}{s^2}\right]_{s \to s + 3} + \tfrac{2}{25}\frac{1}{s^2 + 1} - \tfrac{3}{50}\frac{s}{s^2 + 1}$$

Taking inverse transforms, using the shift theorem, leads to the desired solution

$$x(t) = \tfrac{3}{50}e^{-3t} + \tfrac{1}{10}te^{-3t} + \tfrac{2}{25}\sin t - \tfrac{3}{50}\cos t \quad (t \geqslant 0)$$

EXAMPLE 2.25   Solve the differential equation

$$\frac{d^3x}{dt^3} + 5\frac{d^2x}{dt^2} + 17\frac{dx}{dt} + 13x = 1 \quad (t \geqslant 0)$$

subject to the initial conditions $x = dx/dt = 1$ and $d^2x/dt^2 = 0$ at $t = 0$.

Solution Taking Laplace transforms

$$\mathscr{L}\left\{\frac{d^3x}{dt^3}\right\} + 5\mathscr{L}\left\{\frac{d^2x}{dt^2}\right\} + 17\mathscr{L}\left\{\frac{dx}{dt}\right\} + 13\mathscr{L}\{x\} = \mathscr{L}\{1\}$$

leads to the equation

$$s^3 X(s) - s^2 x(0) - s\dot{x}(0) - \ddot{x}(0) + 5[s^2 X(s) - sx(0) - \dot{x}(0)]$$

$$+ 17[sX(s) - x(0)] + 13X(s) = \frac{1}{s}$$

which on rearrangement gives

$$(s^3 + 5s^2 + 17s + 13)X(s) = \frac{1}{s} + (s^2 + 5s + 17)x(0) + (s + 5)\dot{x}(0) + \ddot{x}(0)$$

Incorporating the given initial conditions $x(0) = \dot{x}(0) = 1$ and $\ddot{x}(0) = 0$ leads to

$$X(s) = \frac{s^3 + 6s^2 + 22s + 1}{s(s^3 + 5s^2 + 17s + 13)}$$

Clearly $s + 1$ is a factor of $s^3 + 5s^2 + 17s + 13$, and by algebraic division we have

$$X(s) = \frac{s^3 + 6s^2 + 22s + 1}{s(s + 1)(s^2 + 4s + 13)}$$

Resolving into partial fractions,

$$X(s) = \frac{\frac{1}{13}}{s} + \frac{\frac{8}{5}}{s + 1} - \frac{1}{65}\frac{44s + 7}{s^2 + 4s + 13}$$

$$= \frac{\frac{1}{13}}{s} + \frac{\frac{8}{5}}{s + 1} - \frac{1}{65}\frac{44(s + 2) - 27(3)}{(s + 2)^2 + 3^2}$$

Taking inverse transforms, using the shift theorem, leads to the solution

$$x(t) = \tfrac{1}{13} + \tfrac{8}{5}e^{-t} - \tfrac{1}{65}e^{-2t}(44\cos 3t - 27\sin 3t) \quad (t \geqslant 0)$$

2.3.4   Simultaneous differential equations

In engineering we frequently encounter systems whose characteristics are modelled by a set of simultaneous linear differential equations with constant coefficients. The method of solution is essentially the same as that adopted in Section 2.3.3 for solving a single differential equation in one unknown. Taking Laplace transforms throughout, the system of simultaneous differential equations is transformed into a system of simultaneous algebraic equations, which are then solved for the transformed variables; inverse transforms then give the desired solutions.

EXAMPLE 2.26 Solve for $t \geqslant 0$ the simultaneous first-order differential equations

$$\frac{dx}{dt} + \frac{dy}{dt} + 5x + 3y = e^{-t} \tag{2.21}$$

$$2\frac{dx}{dt} + \frac{dy}{dt} + x + y = 3 \tag{2.22}$$

subject to the initial conditions $x = 2$ and $y = 1$ at $t = 0$.

Solution Taking Laplace transforms in (2.21) and (2.22) gives

$$sX(s) - x(0) + sY(s) - y(0) + 5X(s) + 3Y(s) = \frac{1}{s+1}$$

$$2[sX(s) - x(0)] + sY(s) - y(0) + X(s) + Y(s) = \frac{3}{s}$$

Rearranging and incorporating the given initial conditions $x(0) = 2$ and $y(0) = 1$ leads to

$$(s+5)X(s) + (s+3)Y(s) = 3 + \frac{1}{s+1} = \frac{3s+4}{s+1} \tag{2.23}$$

$$(2s+1)X(s) + (s+1)Y(s) = 5 + \frac{3}{s} = \frac{5s+3}{s} \tag{2.24}$$

Hence, by taking Laplace transforms, the pair of simultaneous differential equations (2.21) and (2.22) in $x(t)$ and $y(t)$ has been transformed into a pair of simultaneous algebraic equations (2.23) and (2.24) in the transformed variables $X(s)$ and $Y(s)$. These algebraic equations may now be solved simultaneously for $X(s)$ and $Y(s)$ using standard algebraic techniques.

Solving first for $X(s)$ gives

$$X(s) = \frac{2s^2 + 14s + 9}{s(s+2)(s-1)}$$

Resolving into partial fractions,

$$X(s) = -\frac{\frac{9}{2}}{s} - \frac{\frac{11}{6}}{s+2} + \frac{\frac{25}{3}}{s-1}$$

which on inversion gives

$$x(t) = -\tfrac{9}{2} - \tfrac{11}{6}e^{-2t} + \tfrac{25}{3}e^{t} \quad (t \geqslant 0) \tag{2.25}$$

Likewise, solving for $Y(s)$ gives

$$Y(s) = \frac{s^3 - 22s^2 - 39s - 15}{s(s+1)(s+2)(s-1)}$$

Resolving into partial fractions,

$$Y(s) = \frac{\frac{15}{2}}{s} + \frac{\frac{1}{2}}{s+1} + \frac{\frac{11}{2}}{s+2} - \frac{\frac{25}{2}}{s-1}$$

which on inversion gives

$$y(t) = \tfrac{15}{2} + \tfrac{1}{2}e^{-t} + \tfrac{11}{2}e^{-2t} - \tfrac{25}{2}e^{t} \quad (t \geq 0)$$

Thus the solution to the given pair of simultaneous differential equations is

$$\left. \begin{array}{l} x(t) = -\tfrac{9}{2} - \tfrac{11}{6}e^{-2t} + \tfrac{25}{3}e^{t} \\ y(t) = \tfrac{15}{2} + \tfrac{1}{2}e^{-t} + \tfrac{11}{2}e^{-2t} - \tfrac{25}{2}e^{t} \end{array} \right\} \quad (t \geq 0)$$

Note When solving a pair of first-order simultaneous differential equations such as (2.21) and (2.22), an alternative approach to obtaining the value of $y(t)$ having obtained $x(t)$ is to use (2.21) and (2.22) directly.
Eliminating dy/dt from (2.21) and (2.22) gives

$$2y = \frac{dx}{dt} - 4x - 3 + e^{-t}$$

Substituting the solution obtained in (2.25) for $x(t)$ gives

$$2y = (\tfrac{15}{3}e^{-2t} + \tfrac{25}{3}e^{t}) - 4(-\tfrac{9}{2} - \tfrac{11}{6}e^{-2t} + \tfrac{25}{3})e^{t} - 3 + e^{-t}$$

leading as before to the solution

$$y = \tfrac{15}{2} + \tfrac{1}{2}e^{-t} + \tfrac{11}{2}e^{-2t} - \tfrac{25}{2}e^{t}$$

A further alternative is to express (2.23) and (2.24) in matrix form and solve for $X(s)$ and $Y(s)$ using Gaussian elimination.

In principle, the same procedure as used in Example 2.26 can be employed to solve a pair of higher-order simultaneous differential equations or a larger system of differential equations involving more unknowns. However, the algebra involved can become quite complicated, and matrix methods are usually preferred, as indicated in Chapter 6.

2.3.5 Exercises

5 Using Laplace transform methods, solve for $t \geq 0$ the following differential equations, subject to the specified initial conditions:

(a) $\dfrac{dx}{dt} + 3x = e^{-2t}$ subject to $x = 2$ at $t = 0$

(b) $3\dfrac{dx}{dt} - 4x = \sin 2t$ subject to $x = \tfrac{1}{3}$ at $t = 0$

(c) $\dfrac{d^2x}{dt^2} + 2\dfrac{dx}{dt} + 5x = 1$

subject to $x = 0$ and $\dfrac{dx}{dt} = 0$ at $t = 0$

(d) $\dfrac{d^2y}{dt^2} + 2\dfrac{dy}{dt} + y = 4\cos 2t$

subject to $y = 0$ and $\dfrac{dy}{dt} = 2$ at $t = 0$

(e) $\dfrac{d^2x}{dt^2} - 3\dfrac{dx}{dt} + 2x = 2e^{-4t}$

subject to $x = 0$ and $\dfrac{dx}{dt} = 1$ at $t = 0$

(f) $\dfrac{d^2x}{dt^2} + 4\dfrac{dx}{dt} + 5x = 3e^{-2t}$

subject to $x = 4$ and $\dfrac{dx}{dt} = -7$ at $t = 0$

(g) $\dfrac{d^2x}{dt^2} + \dfrac{dx}{dt} - 2x = 5e^{-t}\sin t$

subject to $x = 1$ and $\dfrac{dx}{dt} = 0$ at $t = 0$

(h) $\dfrac{d^2y}{dt^2} + 2\dfrac{dy}{dt} + 3y = 3t$

subject to $y = 0$ and $\dfrac{dy}{dt} = 1$ at $t = 0$

(i) $\dfrac{d^2x}{dt^2} + 4\dfrac{dx}{dt} + 4x = t^2 + e^{-2t}$

subject to $x = \frac{1}{2}$ and $\dfrac{dx}{dt} = 0$ at $t = 0$

(j) $9\dfrac{d^2x}{dt^2} + 12\dfrac{dx}{dt} + 5x = 1$

subject to $x = 0$ and $\dfrac{dx}{dt} = 0$ at $t = 0$

(k) $\dfrac{d^2x}{dt^2} + 8\dfrac{dx}{dt} + 16x = 16\sin 4t$

subject to $x = -\frac{1}{2}$ and $\dfrac{dx}{dt} = 1$ at $t = 0$

(l) $9\dfrac{d^2y}{dt^2} + 12\dfrac{dy}{dt} + 4y = e^{-t}$

subject to $y = 1$ and $\dfrac{dy}{dt} = 1$ at $t = 0$

(m) $\dfrac{d^3x}{dt^3} - 2\dfrac{d^2x}{dt^2} - \dfrac{dx}{dt} + 2x = 2 + t$

subject to $x = 0$, $\dfrac{dx}{dt} = 1$ and $\dfrac{d^2x}{dt^2} = 0$ at $t = 0$

(n) $\dfrac{d^3x}{dt^3} + \dfrac{d^2x}{dt^2} + \dfrac{dx}{dt} + x = \cos 3t$

subject to $x = 0$, $\dfrac{dx}{dt} = 1$ and $\dfrac{d^2x}{dt^2} = 1$ at $t = 0$

6 Using Laplace transform methods, solve for $t \geqslant 0$ the following simultaneous differential equations subject to the given initial conditions:

(a) $2\dfrac{dx}{dt} - 2\dfrac{dy}{dt} - 9y = e^{-2t}$

$2\dfrac{dx}{dt} + 4\dfrac{dy}{dt} + 4x - 37y = 0$

subject to $x = 0$ and $y = \frac{1}{4}$ at $t = 0$

(b) $\dfrac{dx}{dt} + 2\dfrac{dy}{dt} + x - y = 5\sin t$

$2\dfrac{dx}{dt} + 3\dfrac{dy}{dt} + x - y = e^t$

subject to $x = 0$ and $y = 0$ at $t = 0$

(c) $\dfrac{dx}{dt} + \dfrac{dy}{dt} + 2x + y = e^{-3t}$

$\dfrac{dy}{dt} + 5x + 3y = 5e^{-2t}$

subject to $x = -1$ and $y = 4$ at $t = 0$

(d) $3\dfrac{dx}{dt} + 3\dfrac{dy}{dt} - 2x = e^t$

$\dfrac{dx}{dt} + 2\dfrac{dy}{dt} - y = 1$

subject to $x = 1$ and $y = 1$ at $t = 0$

(e) $3\dfrac{dx}{dt} + \dfrac{dy}{dt} - 2x = 3\sin t + 5\cos t$

$2\dfrac{dx}{dt} + \dfrac{dy}{dt} + y = \sin t + \cos t$

subject to $x = 0$ and $y = -1$ at $t = 0$

(f) $\dfrac{dx}{dt} + \dfrac{dy}{dt} + y = t$

$\dfrac{dx}{dt} + 4\dfrac{dy}{dt} + x = 1$

subject to $x = 1$ and $y = 0$ at $t = 0$

(g) $2\dfrac{dx}{dt} + 3\dfrac{dy}{dt} + 7x = 14t + 7$

$5\dfrac{dx}{dt} - 3\dfrac{dy}{dt} + 4x + 6y = 14t - 14$

subject to $x = y = 0$ at $t = 0$

(h) $\dfrac{d^2x}{dt^2} = y - 2x$

$\dfrac{d^2y}{dt^2} = x - 2y$

subject to $x = 4$, $y = 2$, $dx/dt = 0$ and $dy/dt = 0$ at $t = 0$

(i) $5\dfrac{d^2x}{dt^2} + 12\dfrac{d^2y}{dt^2} + 6x = 0$

$5\dfrac{d^2x}{dt^2} + 16\dfrac{d^2y}{dt^2} + 6y = 0$

subject to $x = \frac{7}{4}, y = 1, dx/dt = 0$ and $dy/dt = 0$ at $t = 0$

(j) $2\dfrac{d^2x}{dt^2} - \dfrac{d^2y}{dt^2} - \dfrac{dx}{dt} - \dfrac{dy}{dt} = 3y - 9x$

$2\dfrac{d^2x}{dt^2} - \dfrac{d^2y}{dt^2} + \dfrac{dx}{dt} + \dfrac{dy}{dt} = 5y - 7x$

subject to $x = dx/dt = 1$ and $y = dy/dt = 0$ at $t = 0$

2.4 Engineering applications: electrical circuits and mechanical vibrations

To illustrate the use of Laplace transforms, we consider here their application to the analysis of electrical circuits and vibrating mechanical systems. Since initial conditions are automatically taken into account in the transformation process, the Laplace transform is particularly attractive for examining the transient behaviour of such systems. Although electrical circuits and mechanical vibrations were considered in Section 11.4 of *Modern Engineering Mathematics*, we shall review here the modelling aspects in each case.

2.4.1 Electrical circuits

Passive electrical circuits are constructed of three basic elements: **resistors** (having resistance R, measured in ohms Ω), **capacitors** (having capacitance C, measured in farads F) and **inductors** (having inductance L, measured in henries H), with the associated variables being **current** $i(t)$ (measured in amperes A) and **voltage** $v(t)$ (measured in volts V). The current flow in the circuit is related to the charge $q(t)$ (measured in coulombs C) by the relationship

$$i = \dfrac{dq}{dt}$$

Conventionally, the basic elements are represented symbolically as in Figure 2.7.

(a) Resistor   (b) Capacitor   (c) Inductor

Figure 2.7 Constituent elements of an electrical circuit.

The relationship between the flow of current $i(t)$ and the voltage drops $v(t)$ across these elements at time t are

voltage drop across resistor $= Ri$ (Ohm's law)

voltage drop across capacitor $= \dfrac{1}{C} \displaystyle\int i \, dt = \dfrac{q}{C}$

The interaction between the individual elements making up an electrical circuit is determined by **Kirchhoff's laws**:

Law 1

The algebraic sum of all the currents entering any junction (or node) of a circuit is zero.

Law 2

The algebraic sum of the voltage drops around any closed loop (or path) in a circuit is zero.

Use of these laws leads to the circuit equations, which may then be analysed using Laplace transform techniques.

EXAMPLE 2.27 The *LCR* circuit of Figure 2.8 consists of a resistor R, a capacitor C and an inductor L connected in series together with a voltage source $e(t)$. Prior to closing the switch at time $t = 0$, both the charge on the capacitor and the resulting current in the circuit are zero. Determine the charge $q(t)$ on the capacitor and the resulting current $i(t)$ in the circuit at time t given that $R = 160\,\Omega$, $L = 1\,\text{H}$, $C = 10^{-4}\,\text{F}$ and $e(t) = 20\,\text{V}$.

Solution Applying Kirchhoff's second law to the circuit of Figure 2.8 gives

$$Ri + L\frac{di}{dt} + \frac{1}{C}\int i\,dt = e(t) \tag{2.26}$$

or, using $i = dq/dt$,

$$L\frac{d^2q}{dt^2} + R\frac{dq}{dt} + \frac{1}{C}q = e(t)$$

Figure 2.8 *LCR* circuit of Example 2.27.

Substituting the given values for L, R, C and $e(t)$ gives

$$\frac{d^2q}{dt^2} + 160\frac{dq}{dt} + 10^4q = 20$$

Taking Laplace transforms throughout leads to the equation

$$(s^2 + 160s + 10^4)Q(s) = [sq(0) + \dot{q}(0)] + 160q(0) + \frac{20}{s}$$

where $Q(s)$ is the transform of $q(t)$. We are given that $q(0) = 0$ and $\dot{q}(0) = i(0) = 0$, so that this reduces to

$$(s^2 + 160s + 10^4)Q(s) = \frac{20}{s}$$

that is,

$$Q(s) = \frac{20}{s(s^2 + 160s + 10^4)}$$

Resolving into partial fractions gives

$$Q(s) = \frac{\frac{1}{500}}{s} - \frac{1}{500}\frac{s + 160}{s^2 + 160s + 10^4}$$

$$= \frac{1}{500}\left[\frac{1}{s} - \frac{(s + 80) + \frac{4}{3}(60)}{(s + 80)^2 + (60)^2}\right]$$

$$= \frac{1}{500}\left[\frac{1}{s} - \left[\frac{s + \frac{4}{3} \times 60}{s^2 + 60^2}\right]_{s \to s + 80}\right]$$

Taking inverse transforms, making use of the shift theorem (Theorem 2.2), gives

$$q(t) = \tfrac{1}{500}(1 - e^{-80t}\cos 60t - \tfrac{4}{3}e^{-80t}\sin 60t)$$

The resulting current $i(t)$ in the circuit is then given by

$$i(t) = \frac{dq}{dt} = \tfrac{1}{3}e^{-80t}\sin 60t$$

Note that we could have determined the current by taking Laplace transforms in (2.26). Substituting the given values for L, R, C and $e(t)$ and using (2.16) leads to the transformed equation

$$160I(s) + sI(s) + \frac{10^4}{s}I(s) = \frac{20}{s}$$

that is,

$$I(s) = \frac{20}{(s^2 + 80)^2 + 60^2}$$

which, on taking inverse transforms, gives as before

$$i(t) = \tfrac{1}{3}e^{-80t}\sin 60t$$

EXAMPLE 2.28 In the parallel network of Figure 2.9 there is no current flowing in either loop prior to closing the switch at time $t = 0$. Deduce the currents $i_1(t)$ and $i_2(t)$ flowing in the loops at time t.

Figure 2.9 Parallel circuit of Example 2.28.

Solution Applying Kirchhoff's first law to node X gives

$$i = i_1 + i_2$$

Applying Kirchhoff's second law to each of the two loops in turn gives

$$R_1(i_1 + i_2) + L_1 \frac{d}{dt}(i_1 + i_2) + R_2 i_1 = 200$$

$$L_2 \frac{di_2}{dt} + R_3 i_2 - R_2 i_1 = 0$$

Substituting the given values for the resistances and inductances gives

$$\left. \begin{array}{l} \dfrac{di_1}{dt} + \dfrac{di_2}{dt} + 56i_1 + 40i_2 = 400 \\[3mm] \dfrac{di_2}{dt} - 8i_1 + 10i_2 = 0 \end{array} \right\} \qquad (2.27)$$

Taking Laplace transforms and incorporating the initial conditions $i_1(0) = i_2(0) = 0$ leads to the transformed equations

$$(s + 56)I_1(s) + (s + 40)I_2(s) = \frac{400}{s} \qquad (2.28)$$

$$-8I_1(s) + (s + 10)I_2(s) = 0 \qquad (2.29)$$

Hence

$$I_2(s) = \frac{3200}{s(s^2 + 74s + 880)} = \frac{3200}{s(s + 59.1)(s + 14.9)}$$

Resolving into partial fractions gives

$$I_2(s) = \frac{3.64}{s} + \frac{1.22}{s + 59.1} - \frac{4.86}{s + 14.9}$$

which, on taking inverse transforms, leads to

$$i_2(t) = 3.64 + 1.22e^{-59.1t} - 4.86e^{-14.9t}$$

From (2.27),

$$i_1(t) = \tfrac{1}{8}\left(10i_2 + \frac{di_2}{dt}\right)$$

that is,

$$i_1(t) = 4.54 - 7.49e^{-59.1t} + 2.98e^{-14.9t}$$

Note that as $t \to \infty$, the currents $i_1(t)$ and $i_2(t)$ approach the constant values 4.54 and 3.63 A respectively.

EXAMPLE 2.29   A voltage $e(t)$ is applied to the primary circuit at time $t = 0$, and mutual induction M drives the current $i_2(t)$ in the secondary circuit of Figure 2.10. If, prior to closing the switch, the currents in both circuits are zero, determine the induced current $i_1(t)$ in the secondary circuit at time t when $R_1 = 4\,\Omega$, $R_2 = 10\,\Omega$, $L_1 = 2\,\text{H}$, $L_2 = 8\,\text{H}$, $M = 2\,\text{H}$ and $e(t) = 28 \sin 2t$ V.

Figure 2.10 Circuit of Example 2.29.

Solution   Applying Kirchhoff's second law to the primary and secondary circuits respectively gives

$$R_1 i_1 + L_1 \frac{di_1}{dt} + M \frac{di_2}{dt} = e(t)$$

$$R_2 i_2 + L_2 \frac{di_2}{dt} + M \frac{di_1}{dt} = 0$$

Substituting the given values for the resistances, inductances and applied voltage leads to

$$2\frac{di_1}{dt} + 4i_1 + 2\frac{di_2}{dt} = 28 \sin 2t$$

$$2\frac{di_1}{dt} + 8\frac{di_2}{dt} + 10i_2 = 0$$

Taking Laplace transforms and noting that $i_1(0) = i_2(0) = 0$ leads to the equations

$$(s + 2)I_1(s) + sI_2(s) = \frac{28}{s^2 + 4} \qquad (2.30)$$

$$sI_1(s) + (4s + 5)I_2(s) = 0 \qquad (2.31)$$

Solving for $I_2(s)$ yields

$$I_2(s) = -\frac{28s}{(3s + 10)(s + 1)(s^2 + 4)}$$

Resolving into partial fractions gives

$$I_2(s) = -\frac{\frac{45}{17}}{3s + 10} + \frac{\frac{4}{5}}{s + 1} + \frac{7}{85}\frac{s - 26}{s^2 + 4}$$

Taking inverse Laplace transforms gives the current in the secondary circuit as

$$i_2(t) = \tfrac{4}{5}e^{-t} - \tfrac{15}{17}e^{-10t/3} + \tfrac{7}{85}\cos 2t - \tfrac{91}{85}\sin 2t$$

As $t \to \infty$, the current will approach the sinusoidal response

$$i_2(t) = \tfrac{7}{85}\cos 2t - \tfrac{91}{85}\sin 2t$$

2.4.2 Mechanical vibrations

Mechanical translational systems may be used to model many situations, and involve three basic elements: **masses** (having mass M, measured in kg), **springs** (having spring stiffness K, measured in $\mathrm{N\,m^{-1}}$) and **dampers** (having damping coefficient B, measured in $\mathrm{N\,s\,m^{-1}}$). The associated variables are **displacement** $x(t)$ (measured in m) and **force** $F(t)$ (measured in N). Conventionally, the basic elements are represented symbolically as in Figure 2.11.

Assuming we are dealing with ideal springs and dampers (that is, assuming that they behave linearly), the relationships between the forces and displacements at time t are

mass: $\qquad F = M\dfrac{\mathrm{d}^2x}{\mathrm{d}t^2} = M\ddot{x} \qquad$ (Newton's law)

(a) Mass (b) Spring (c) Damper

Figure 2.11 Constituent elements of a translational mechanical system.

spring: $\qquad F = K(x_2 - x_1) \qquad$ (Hooke's law)

damper: $\qquad F = B\left(\dfrac{dx_2}{dt} - \dfrac{dx_1}{dt}\right) = B(\dot{x}_2 - \dot{x}_1)$

Using these relationships leads to the system equations, which may then be analysed using Laplace transform techniques.

EXAMPLE 2.30 The mass of the mass–spring–damper system of Figure 2.12(a) is subjected to an externally applied periodic force $F(t) = 4 \sin \omega t$ at time $t = 0$. Determine the resulting displacement $x(t)$ of the mass at time t, given that $x(0) = \dot{x}(0) = 0$, for the two cases

(a) $\omega = 2$ (b) $\omega = 5$

In the case $\omega = 5$, what would happen to the response if the damper were missing?

Solution As indicated in Figure 2.12(b), the forces acting on the mass M are the applied forces $F(t)$ and the restoring forces F_1 and F_2 due to the spring and damper respectively. Thus, by Newton's law,

$$M\ddot{x}(t) = F(t) - F_1(t) - F_2(t)$$

Since $M = 1$, $F(t) = 4 \sin \omega t$, $F_1(t) = Kx(t) = 25x(t)$ and $F_2(t) = B\dot{x}(t) = 6\dot{x}(t)$, this gives

$$\ddot{x}(t) + 6\dot{x}(t) + 25x(t) = 4 \sin \omega t \qquad \textbf{(2.32)}$$

as the differential equation representing the motion of the system.

Taking Laplace transforms throughout in (2.32) gives

$$(s^2 + 6s + 25)X(s) = [sx(0) + \dot{x}(0)] + 6x(0) + \frac{4\omega}{s^2 + \omega^2}$$

where $X(s)$ is the transform of $x(t)$. Incorporating the given initial conditions

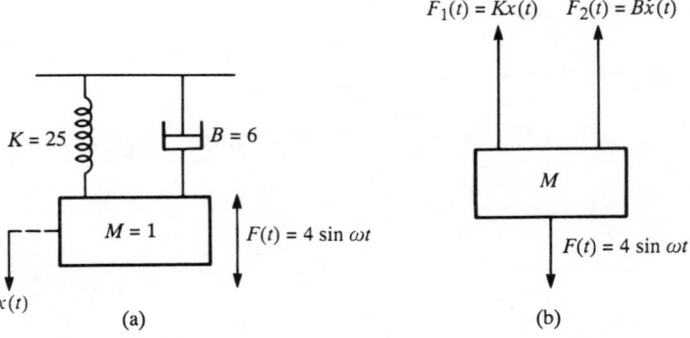

(a)   (b)

Figure 2.12 Mass–spring–damper system of Example 2.30.

$x(0) = \dot{x}(0) = 0$ leads to

$$X(s) = \frac{4\omega}{(s^2 + \omega^2)(s^2 + 6s + 25)} \qquad (2.33)$$

In case (a), with $\omega = 2$, (2.33) gives

$$X(s) = \frac{8}{(s^2 + 4)(s^2 + 6s + 25)}$$

which, on resolving into partial fractions, leads to

$$X(s) = \tfrac{4}{195} \frac{-4s + 14}{s^2 + 4} + \tfrac{2}{195} \frac{8s + 20}{s^2 + 6s + 25}$$

$$= \tfrac{4}{195} \frac{-4s + 14}{s^2 + 4} + \tfrac{2}{195} \frac{8(s + 3) - 4}{(s + 3)^2 + 16}$$

Taking inverse Laplace transforms gives the required response

$$x(t) = \tfrac{4}{195}(7 \sin 2t - 4 \cos 2t) + \tfrac{2}{195}e^{-3t}(8 \cos 4t - \sin 4t) \qquad (2.34)$$

In case (b), with $\omega = 5$, (2.33) gives

$$X(s) = \frac{20}{(s^2 + 25)(s^2 + 6s + 25)} \qquad (2.35)$$

that is,

$$X(s) = \frac{-\tfrac{2}{15}s}{s^2 + 25} + \tfrac{1}{15} \frac{2(s + 3) + 6}{(s + 3)^2 + 16}$$

which, on taking inverse Laplace transforms, gives the required response

$$x(t) = -\tfrac{2}{15} \cos 5t + \tfrac{1}{15}e^{-3t}(2 \cos 4t + \tfrac{3}{2} \sin 4t) \qquad (2.36)$$

If the damping term were missing then (2.35) would become

$$X(s) = \frac{20}{(s^2 + 25)^2} \qquad (2.37)$$

By Theorem 2.3,

$$\mathcal{L}\{t \cos 5t\} = -\frac{d}{ds}\mathcal{L}\{\cos 5t\} = -\frac{d}{ds}\left(\frac{s}{s^2 + 25}\right)$$

that is,

$$\mathcal{L}\{t \cos 5t\} = -\frac{1}{s^2 + 25} + \frac{2s^2}{(s^2 + 25)^2} = \frac{1}{s^2 + 25} - \frac{50}{(s^2 + 25)^2}$$

$$= \tfrac{1}{5}\mathcal{L}\{\sin 5t\} - \frac{50}{(s^2 + 25)^2}$$

Thus, by the linearity property (2.11),

$$\mathscr{L}\{\tfrac{1}{5}\sin 5t - t\cos 5t\} = \frac{50}{(s^2 + 25)^2}$$

so that taking inverse Laplace transforms in (2.37) gives the response as

$$x(t) = \tfrac{2}{25}(\sin 5t - 5t\cos 5t)$$

Because of the term $t\cos 5t$, the response $x(t)$ is unbounded as $t \to \infty$. This arises because in this case the applied force $F(t) = 4\sin 5t$ is in **resonance** with the system (that is, the vibrating mass), whose natural oscillating frequency is $\tfrac{2}{5}\pi$, equal to that of the applied force. Even in the presence of damping, the amplitude of the system response is maximized when the applied force is approaching resonance with the system. (It is left as an exercise to check that the amplitude of response in (2.36) is greater than that in (2.34).) In the absence of damping we have the limiting case of **pure resonance**, leading to an unbounded response. As noted in Section 11.4.3 of *Modern Engineering Mathematics*, resonance is of practical importance, since, for example, it can lead to large and strong structures collapsing under what appears to be a relatively small force.

EXAMPLE 2.31 Consider the mechanical system of Figure 2.13(a), which consists of two masses $M_1 = 1$ and $M_2 = 2$, each attached to a fixed base by a spring, having constants $K_1 = 1$ and $K_3 = 2$ respectively, and attached to each other by a third spring having constant $K_2 = 2$. The system is released from rest at time $t = 0$ in a position in which M_1 is displaced 1 unit to the left of its equilibrium position and M_2 is displaced 2 units to the right of its equilibrium position. Neglecting all frictional effects, determine the positions of the masses at time t.

Solution Let $x_1(t)$ and $x_2(t)$ denote the displacements of the masses M_1 and M_2 respectively from their equilibrium positions. Since frictional effects are neglected, the only forces acting on the masses are the restoring forces due to the springs, as shown in Figure 2.13(b). Applying Newton's law to the motions of M_1 and

Figure 2.13 Two-mass system of Example 2.31.

M_2 respectively gives

$$M_1\ddot{x}_1 = F_2 - F_1 = K_2(x_2 - x_1) - K_1 x_1$$
$$M_2\ddot{x}_2 = -F_3 - F_2 = -K_3 x_2 - K_2(x_2 - x_1)$$

which, on substituting the given values for M_1, M_2, K_1, K_2 and K_3, gives

$$\ddot{x}_1 + 3x_1 - 2x_2 = 0 \tag{2.38}$$
$$2\ddot{x}_2 + 4x_2 - 2x_1 = 0 \tag{2.39}$$

Taking Laplace transforms leads to the equations

$$(s^2 + 3)X_1(s) - 2X_2(s) = sx_1(0) + \dot{x}_1(0)$$
$$-X_1(s) + (s^2 + 2)X_2(s) = sx_2(0) + \dot{x}_2(0)$$

Since $x_1(t)$ and $x_2(t)$ denote displacements to the right of the equilibrium positions, we have $x_1(0) = -1$ and $x_2(0) = 2$. Also, the system is released from rest, so that $\dot{x}_1(0) = \dot{x}_2(0) = 0$. Incorporating these initial conditions, the transformed equations become

$$(s^2 + 3)X_1(s) - 2X_2(s) = -s \tag{2.40}$$
$$-X_1(s) + (s^2 + 2)X_2(s) = 2s \tag{2.41}$$

Hence

$$X_2(s) = \frac{2s^3 + 5s}{(s^2 + 4)(s^2 + 1)}$$

Resolving into partial fractions gives

$$X_2(s) = \frac{s}{s^2 + 1} + \frac{s}{s^2 + 4}$$

which, on taking inverse Laplace transforms, leads to the response

$$x_2(t) = \cos t + \cos 2t$$

Substituting for $x_2(t)$ in (2.39) gives

$$x_1(t) = 2x_2(t) + \ddot{x}_2(t)$$
$$= 2\cos t + 2\cos 2t - \cos t - 4\cos 2t$$

that is,

$$x_1(t) = \cos t - 2\cos 2t$$

Thus the positions of the masses at time t are

$$x_1(t) = \cos t - 2\cos 2t$$
$$x_2(t) = \cos t + \cos 2t$$

2.4.3   Exercises

7 Use the Laplace transform technique to find the transforms $I_1(s)$ and $I_2(s)$ of the respective currents flowing in the circuit of Figure 2.14, where $i_1(t)$ is that through the capacitor and $i_2(t)$ that through the resistance. Hence determine $i_2(t)$. (Initially, $i_1(0) = i_2(0) = q_1(0) = 0$.) Sketch $i_2(t)$ for large values of t.

Figure 2.14 Circuit of Exercise 7.

8 At time $t = 0$, with no currents flowing, a voltage $v(t) = 10 \sin t$ is applied to the primary circuit of a transformer that has a mutual inductance of 1 H, as shown in Figure 2.15. Denoting the current flowing at time t in the secondary circuit by $i_2(t)$, show that

$$\mathscr{L}\{i_2(t)\} = \frac{10s}{(s^2 + 7s + 6)(s^2 + 1)}$$

and deduce that

$$i_2(t) = -e^{-t} + \tfrac{12}{37}e^{-6t} + \tfrac{25}{37}\cos t + \tfrac{35}{37}\sin t$$

9 In the circuit of Figure 2.16 there is no energy stored (that is, there is no charge on the capacitors and no current flowing in the inductances) prior to the closure of the switch at time $t = 0$. Determine $i_1(t)$ for $t > 0$ for a constant applied voltage $E_0 = 10$ V.

10 Determine the displacements of the masses M_1 and M_2 in Figure 2.13 at time $t > 0$ when

$$M_1 = M_2 = 1$$
$$K_1 = 1, \; K_2 = 3 \quad \text{and} \quad K_3 = 9$$

What are the natural frequencies of the system?

11 When testing the landing-gear unit of a space vehicle, drop tests are carried out. Figure 2.17 is a schematic model of the unit at the instant when it first touches the ground. At this instant the spring is fully extended and the velocity of the mass is

Figure 2.15 Circuit of Exercise 8.

Figure 2.16 Circuit of Exercise 9.

Figure 2.17 Landing-gear of Exercise 11.

Figure 2.18 Mechanical system of Exercise 12.

$\sqrt{(2gh)}$, where h is the height from which the unit has been dropped. Obtain the equation representing the displacement of the mass at time $t > 0$ when $M = 50\,\text{kg}$, $B = 180\,\text{N s m}^{-1}$ and $K = 474.5\,\text{N m}^{-1}$, and investigate the effects of different dropping heights h. (g is the acceleration due to gravity, and may be taken as $9.8\,\text{m s}^{-2}$.)

12 Consider the mass–spring–damper system of Figure 2.18, which may be subject to two input forces $u_1(t)$ and $u_2(t)$. Show that the displacements $x_1(t)$ and $x_2(t)$ of the two masses are given by

$$x_1(t) = \mathscr{L}^{-1}\left\{\frac{M_1 s^2 + Bs + K_2}{\Delta}U_1(s) + \frac{B_1 s}{\Delta}U_2(s)\right\}$$

$$x_2(t) = \mathscr{L}^{-1}\left\{\frac{B_1 s}{\Delta}U_1(s)\right.$$

$$\left. + \frac{M_1 s^2 + B_1 s + K_1}{\Delta}U_2(s)\right\}$$

where

$$\Delta = (M_1 s^2 + B_1 s + K_1)(M_2 s^2 + B_1 s + K_2) - B_1^2 s^2$$

2.5 Step and impulse functions

2.5.1 The Heaviside step function

In Sections 2.3 and 2.4 we considered linear differential equations in which the forcing function was continuous. In many engineering applications the forcing function may frequently be discontinuous, for example a square wave resulting from an on/off switch. In order to accommodate such discontinuous functions, we use the Heaviside unit step function $H(t)$, which, as we saw in Section 2.2.1, is defined by

$$H(t) = \begin{cases} 0 & (t < 0) \\ 1 & (t \geqslant 0) \end{cases}$$

Figure 2.19 Heaviside unit step function.

and is illustrated graphically in Figure 2.19(a). The Heaviside function is also frequently referred to simply as the **unit step function**. A function representing a unit step at $t = a$ may be obtained by a horizontal translation of duration a. This is depicted graphically in Figure 2.19(b), and defined by

$$H(t - a) = \begin{cases} 0 & (t < a) \\ 1 & (t \geqslant a) \end{cases}$$

The product function $f(t)H(t - a)$ takes values

$$f(t)H(t - a) = \begin{cases} 0 & (t < a) \\ f(t) & (t \geqslant a) \end{cases}$$

so the function $H(t - a)$ may be interpreted as a device for 'switching on' the function $f(t)$ at $t = a$. In this way the unit step function may be used to write a concise formulation of piecewise-continuous functions. To illustrate this, consider the piecewise-continuous function $f(t)$ illustrated in Figure 2.20 and defined by

$$f(t) = \begin{cases} f_1(t) & (0 \leqslant t < t_1) \\ f_2(t) & (t_1 \leqslant t < t_2) \\ f_3(t) & (t \geqslant t_2) \end{cases}$$

To construct this function $f(t)$, we could use the following 'switching' operations:

(a) switch on the function $f_1(t)$ at $t = 0$;

(b) switch on the function $f_2(t)$ at $t = t_1$ and at the same time switch off the function $f_1(t)$;

Figure 2.20 Piecewise-continuous function.

(c) switch on the function $f_3(t)$ at $t = t_2$ and at the same time switch off the function $f_2(t)$.

In terms of the unit step function, the function $f(t)$ may thus be expressed as

$$f(t) = f_1(t)H(t) + [f_2(t) - f_1(t)]H(t - t_1) + [f_3(t) - f_2(t)]H(t - t_2)$$

Alternatively, $f(t)$ may be constructed using the **top hat function** $H(t - a) - H(t - b)$. Clearly,

$$H(t - a) - H(t - b) = \begin{cases} 1 & (a \leqslant t < b) \\ 0 & \text{otherwise} \end{cases} \tag{2.42}$$

which, as illustrated in Figure 2.21, gives

$$f(t)[H(t - a) - H(t - b)] = \begin{cases} f(t) & (a \leqslant t < b) \\ 0 & \text{otherwise} \end{cases}$$

Using this approach, the function $f(t)$ of Figure 2.20 may be expressed as

$$f(t) = f_1(t)[H(t) - H(t - t_1)] + f_2(t)[H(t - t_1) - H(t - t_2)] + f_3(t)H(t - t_2)$$

giving, as before,

$$f(t) = f_1(t)H(t) + [f_2(t) - f_1(t)]H(t - t_1) + [f_3(t) - f_2(t)]H(t - t_2)$$

It is easily checked that this corresponds to the previous formulation, since for $0 \leqslant t < t_1$

$$H(t) = 1, \quad H(t - t_1) = H(t - t_2) = 0$$

giving

$$f(t) = f_1(t) \quad (0 \leqslant t < t_1)$$

while for $t_1 \leqslant t < t_2$

$$H(t) = H(t - t_1) = 1, \quad H(t - t_2) = 0$$

giving

$$f(t) = f_1(t) + [f_2(t) - f_1(t)] = f_2(t) \quad (t_1 \leqslant t \leqslant t_2)$$

and finally for $t \geqslant t_2$

$$H(t) = H(t - t_1) = H(t - t_2) = 1$$

Figure 2.21 Top hat function.

giving

$$f(t) = f_1(t) + [f_2(t) - f_1(t)] + [f_3(t) - f_2(t)] = f_3(t) \quad (t \geqslant t_2)$$

EXAMPLE 2.32   Express in terms of the unit step functions the piecewise-continuous causal function

$$f(t) \begin{cases} 2t^2 & (0 \leqslant t < 3) \\ t + 4 & (3 \leqslant t < 5) \\ 9 & (t \geqslant 5) \end{cases}$$

Figure 2.22 Piecewise-continuous function of Example 2.32.

Solution $f(t)$ is depicted graphically in Figure 2.22, and in terms of unit step functions it may be expressed as

$$f(t) = 2t^2 H(t) + (t + 4 - 2t^2)H(t - 3) + (9 - t - 4)H(t - 5)$$

That is,

$$f(t) = 2t^2 H(t) + (4 + t - 2t^2)H(t - 3) + (5 - t)H(t - 5)$$

EXAMPLE 2.33   Express in terms of unit step functions the piecewise-continuous causal function

$$f(t) = \begin{cases} 0 & (t < 1) \\ 1 & (1 \leqslant t < 3) \\ 3 & (3 \leqslant t < 5) \\ 2 & (5 \leqslant t < 6) \\ 0 & (t \geqslant 6) \end{cases}$$

Solution $f(t)$ is depicted graphically in Figure 2.22, and in terms of unit step functions it may be expressed as

$$f(t) = 1H(t - 1) + (3 - 1)H(t - 3) + (2 - 3)H(t - 5) + (0 - 2)H(t - 6)$$

That is,

$$f(t) = 1H(t - 1) + 2H(t - 3) - 1H(t - 5) - 2H(t - 6)$$

Figure 2.23 Piecewise-continuous function of Example 2.33.

2.5.2   Laplace transform of unit step function

By definition of the Laplace transform, the transform of $H(t - a)$, $a \geqslant 0$, is given by

$$\mathcal{L}\{H(t - a)\} = \int_0^\infty H(t - a)\,\mathrm{e}^{-st}\,\mathrm{d}t$$

$$= \int_0^a 0\mathrm{e}^{-st}\,\mathrm{d}t + \int_a^\infty 1\mathrm{e}^{-st}\,\mathrm{d}t$$

$$= \left[\frac{\mathrm{e}^{-st}}{-s}\right]_a^\infty = \frac{\mathrm{e}^{-as}}{s}$$

That is,

$$\mathcal{L}\{H(t - a)\} = \frac{\mathrm{e}^{-as}}{s} \quad (a \geqslant 0) \tag{2.43}$$

and in the particular case of $a = 0$

$$\mathcal{L}\{H(t)\} = \frac{1}{s} \tag{2.44}$$

EXAMPLE 2.34   Determine the Laplace transform of the rectangular pulse

$$f(t) = \begin{cases} 0 & (t < a) \\ K & (a \leqslant t < b) \\ 0 & (t \geqslant b) \end{cases} \qquad K \text{ constant}, \quad b > a > 0$$

Solution   The pulse is depicted graphically in Figure 2.24. In terms of unit step functions, it may be expressed, using the top hat function, as

$$f(t) = K[H(t - a) - H(t - b)]$$

Figure 2.24 Rectangular pulse.

Then, taking Laplace transforms,

$$\mathcal{L}\{f(t)\} = K\mathcal{L}\{H(t-a)\} - K\mathcal{L}\{H(t-b)\}$$

which, on using the result (2.24), gives

$$\mathcal{L}\{f(t)\} = K\frac{e^{-as}}{s} - K\frac{e^{-bs}}{s}$$

That is,

$$\mathcal{L}\{f(t)\} = \frac{K}{s}(e^{-as} - e^{-bs})$$

EXAMPLE 2.35 Determine the Laplace transform of the piecewise-constant function $f(t)$ shown in Figure 2.23.

Solution From Example 2.33 $f(t)$ may be expressed as

$$f(t) = 1H(t-1) + 2H(t-3) - 1H(t-5) - 2H(t-6)$$

Taking Laplace transforms,

$$\mathcal{L}\{f(t)\} = 1\mathcal{L}\{H(t-1)\} + 2\mathcal{L}\{H(t-3)\} - 1\mathcal{L}\{H(t-5)\} - 2\mathcal{L}\{H(t-6)\}$$

which, on using the result (2.43), gives

$$\mathcal{L}\{f(t)\} = \frac{e^{-s}}{s} + 2\frac{e^{-3s}}{s} - \frac{e^{-5s}}{s} - 2\frac{e^{-6s}}{s}$$

That is,

$$\mathcal{L}\{f(t)\} = \frac{1}{s}(e^{-s} + 2e^{-3s} - e^{-5s} - 2e^{-6s})$$

2.5.3 The second shift theorem

This theorem is dual to the first shift theorem given as Theorem 2.2, and is sometimes referred to as the **Heaviside** or **delay theorem**.

THEOREM 2.4   If $\mathscr{L}\{f(t)\} = F(s)$ then for a positive constant a

$$\mathscr{L}\{f(t-a)H(t-a)\} = \mathrm{e}^{-as}F(s)$$

Proof   By definition,

$$\mathscr{L}\{f(t-a)H(t-a)\} = \int_0^\infty f(t-a)H(t-a)\mathrm{e}^{-st}\,\mathrm{d}t$$

$$= \int_a^\infty f(t-a)\mathrm{e}^{-st}\,\mathrm{d}t$$

Making the substitution $T = t - a$,

$$\mathscr{L}\{f(t-a)H(t-a)\} = \int_0^\infty f(T)\mathrm{e}^{-s(T+a)}\,\mathrm{d}T$$

$$= \mathrm{e}^{-sa}\int_0^\infty f(T)\mathrm{e}^{-sT}\,\mathrm{d}T$$

Since $F(s) = \mathscr{L}\{f(t)\} = \int_0^\infty f(T)\mathrm{e}^{-sT}$, it follows that

$$\mathscr{L}\{f(t-a)H(t-a)\} = \mathrm{e}^{-as}F(s) \qquad\qquad \square$$

It is important to distinguish between the two functions $f(t)H(t-a)$ and $f(t-a)H(t-a)$. As we saw earlier, $f(t)H(t-a)$ simply indicates that the function $f(t)$ is 'switched on' at time $t = a$, so that

$$f(t)H(t-a) = \begin{cases} 0 & (t < a) \\ f(t) & (t \geqslant a) \end{cases}$$

On the other hand, $f(t-a)H(t-a)$ represents a translation of the function $f(t)$ by a units to the right (to the right, since $a > 0$), so that

$$f(t-a)H(t-a) = \begin{cases} 0 & (t < a) \\ f(t-a) & (t \geqslant a) \end{cases}$$

The difference between the two is illustrated graphically in Figure 2.25. $f(t-a)H(t-a)$ may be interpreted as representing the function $f(t)$ delayed in time by a units. Thus, when considering its Laplace transform $\mathrm{e}^{-as}F(s)$, where $F(s)$ denotes the

Figure 2.25 Illustration of $f(t-a)H(t-a)$.

Laplace transform of $f(t)$, the component e^{-as} may be interpreted as a delay operator on the transform $F(s)$, indicating that the response of the system characterized by $F(s)$ will be delayed in time by a units. Since many practically important systems have some form of delay inherent in their behaviour, it is clear that the result of this theorem is very useful.

EXAMPLE 2.36   Determine the Laplace transform of the causal function $f(t)$ defined by

$$f(t) = \begin{cases} t & (0 \leqslant t < b) \\ 0 & (t \geqslant b) \end{cases}$$

Figure 2.26 Sawtooth pulse.

Solution $f(t)$ is illustrated graphically in Figure 2.26, and is seen to characterize a sawtooth pulse of duration b. In terms of unit step functions,

$$f(t) = tH(t) - tH(t - b)$$

In order to apply the second shift theorem, each term must be rearranged to be of the form $f(t - a)H(t - a)$; that is, the time argument $t - a$ of the function must be the same as that of the associated step function. In this particular example this gives

$$f(t) = tH(t) - (t - b)H(t - b) - bH(t - b)$$

Taking Laplace transforms,

$$\mathscr{L}\{f(t)\} = \mathscr{L}\{tH(t)\} - \mathscr{L}\{(t - b)H(t - b)\} - b\mathscr{L}\{H(t - b)\}$$

which, on using Theorem 2.4, leads to

$$\mathscr{L}\{f(t)\} = \frac{1}{s^2} - \mathrm{e}^{-bs}\mathscr{L}(t) - b\frac{\mathrm{e}^{-bs}}{s}$$

$$= \frac{1}{s^2} - \frac{\mathrm{e}^{-bs}}{s^2} - b\frac{\mathrm{e}^{-bs}}{s}$$

giving

$$\mathscr{L}\{f(t)\} = \frac{1}{s^2}(1 - \mathrm{e}^{-bs}) - \frac{b}{s}\mathrm{e}^{-bs}$$

It should be noted that this result could have been obtained without the use of the second shift theorem, since, directly from the definition of the Laplace transform,

$$\mathscr{L}\{f(t)\} = \int_0^\infty f(t)\,\mathrm{e}^{-st}\,\mathrm{d}t = \int_0^b t\,\mathrm{e}^{-st}\,\mathrm{d}t + \int_0^\infty 0\,\mathrm{e}^{-st}\,\mathrm{d}t$$

$$= \left[-\frac{t\mathrm{e}^{-st}}{s} \right]_0^b + \int_0^b \frac{\mathrm{e}^{-st}}{s}\,\mathrm{d}t$$

$$= \left[-\frac{t\mathrm{e}^{-st}}{s} - \frac{\mathrm{e}^{-st}}{s^2} \right]_0^b$$

$$= \left(-\frac{b\mathrm{e}^{-sb}}{s} - \frac{\mathrm{e}^{-sb}}{s^2} \right) - \left(-\frac{1}{s^2} \right)$$

$$= \frac{1}{s^2}(1 - \mathrm{e}^{-bs}) - \frac{b}{s}\mathrm{e}^{-bs}$$

as before.

EXAMPLE 2.37   Obtain the Laplace transform of the piecewise-continuous causal function

$$f(t) = \begin{cases} 2t^2 & (0 \leqslant t < 3) \\ t + 4 & (3 \leqslant t < 5) \\ 9 & (t \geqslant 5) \end{cases}$$

considered in Example 2.32.

Solution   In Example 2.32 we saw that $f(t)$ may be expressed in terms of unit step functions as

$$f(t) = 2t^2 H(t) - (2t^2 - t - 4)H(t - 3) - (t - 5)H(t - 5)$$

Before we can find $\mathscr{L}\{f(t)\}$, the function $2t^2 - t - 4$ must be expressed as a function of $t - 3$. This may be readily achieved as follows. Let $z = t - 3$. Then

$$2t^2 - t - 4 = 2(z + 3)^2 - (z + 3) - 4$$

$$= 2z^2 + 11z + 11$$

$$= 2(t - 3)^2 + 11(t - 3) + 11$$

Hence

$$f(t) = 2t^2 H(t) - [2(t - 3)^2 + 11(t - 3) + 11]H(t - 3) - (t - 5)H(t - 5)$$

Taking Laplace transforms,

$$\mathscr{L}\{f(t)\} = 2\mathscr{L}\{t^2 H(t)\} - \mathscr{L}\{[2(t - 3)^2 + 11(t - 3) + 11]H(t - 3)\}$$
$$- \mathscr{L}\{(t - 5)H(t - 5)\}$$

which, on using Theorem 2.4, leads to

$$\mathcal{L}\{f(t)\} = 2\frac{2}{s^3} - e^{-3s}\mathcal{L}\{2t^2 + 11t + 11\} - e^{-5s}\mathcal{L}\{t\}$$

$$= \frac{4}{s^3} - e^{-3s}\left(\frac{4}{s^3} + \frac{11}{s^2} + \frac{11}{s}\right) - \frac{e^{-5s}}{s^2}$$

Again this result could have been obtained directly from the definition of the Laplace transform, but in this case the required integration by parts is a little more tedious.

2.5.4 Inversion using the second shift theorem

We have seen in Examples 2.34 and 2.35 that, to obtain the Laplace transforms of piecewise-continuous functions, use of the second shift theorem could be avoided, since it is possible to obtain such transforms directly from the definition of the Laplace transform.

In practice, the importance of the theorem lies in determining *inverse* transforms, since, as indicated earlier, delays are inherent in most practical systems and engineers are interested in knowing how these influence the system response. Consequently, by far the most useful form of the second shift theorem is

$$\mathcal{L}^{-1}\{e^{-as}F(s)\} = f(t - a)H(t - a) \tag{2.45}$$

Comparing (2.45) with the result (2.12), namely

$$\mathcal{L}^{-1}\{F(s)\} = f(t)H(t)$$

we see that

$$\mathcal{L}^{-1}\{e^{-as}F(s)\} = [f(t)H(t)] \quad \text{with } t \text{ replaced by } t - a$$

indicating that the response $f(t)$ has been delayed in time by a units. This is why the theorem is sometimes called the delay theorem.

EXAMPLE 2.38 Determine $\mathcal{L}^{-1}\left\{\dfrac{4e^{-4s}}{s(s + 2)}\right\}$.

Solution This may be written as $\mathcal{L}^{-1}\{e^{-4s}F(s)\}$, where

$$F(s) = \frac{4}{s(s + 2)}$$

First we obtain the inverse transform $f(t)$ of $F(s)$. Resolving into partial fractions,

$$F(s) = \frac{2}{s} - \frac{2}{s + 2}$$

which, on inversion, gives

$$f(t) = 2 - 2e^{-2t}$$

a graph of which is shown in Figure 2.27(a). Then, using (2.45), we have

$$\mathcal{L}^{-1}\left\{e^{-4s}\frac{4}{s(s + 2)}\right\} = \mathcal{L}^{-1}\{e^{-4s}F(s)\}$$

$$= f(t - 4)H(t - 4)$$

$$= (2 - 2e^{-2(t-4)})H(t - 4)$$

giving

$$\mathcal{L}^{-1}\left\{\frac{4e^{-4s}}{s(s + 2)}\right\} = \begin{cases} 0 & (t < 4) \\ 2(1 - e^{-2(t-4)}) & (t \geqslant 4) \end{cases}$$

which is plotted in Figure 2.27(b).

(a) Graph of $f(t)$

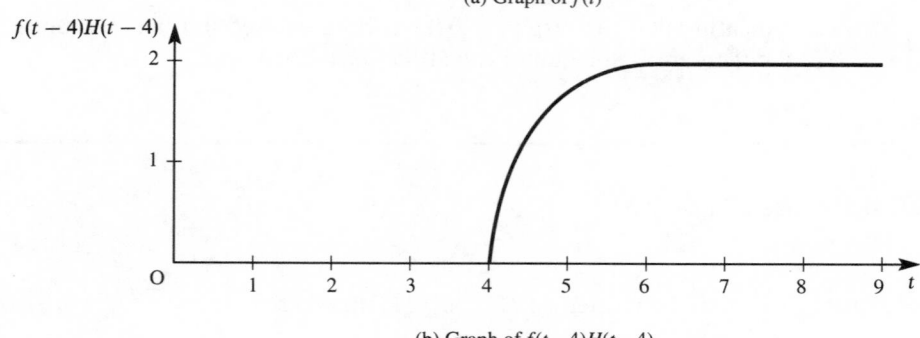

(b) Graph of $f(t - 4)H(t - 4)$

Figure 2.27 Inverse transforms of Example 2.38.

EXAMPLE 2.39   Determine $\mathscr{L}^{-1}\left\{\dfrac{e^{-s\pi}(s+3)}{s(s^2+1)}\right\}$.

Solution   This may be written as $\mathscr{L}^{-1}\{e^{-s\pi}F(s)\}$, where

$$F(s) = \frac{s+3}{s(s^2+1)}$$

Resolving into partial fractions,

$$F(s) = \frac{3}{s} - \frac{3s}{s^2+1} + \frac{1}{s^2+1}$$

which, on inversion, gives

$$f(t) = 3 - 3\cos t + \sin t$$

a graph of which is shown in Figure 2.28(a). Then, using (2.45), we have

$$\mathscr{L}^{-1}\left\{\frac{e^{-s\pi}(s+3)}{s(s^2+1)}\right\} = \mathscr{L}^{-1}\{e^{-s\pi}F(s)\}$$

$$= f(t-\pi)H(t-\pi)$$

$$= [3 - 3\cos(t-\pi) + \sin(t-\pi)]H(t-\pi)$$

$$= (3 + 3\cos t - \sin t)H(t-\pi)$$

(a)

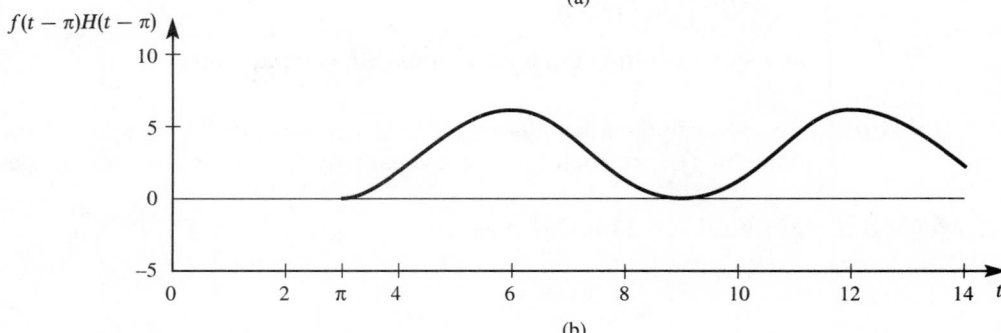

(b)

Figure 2.28 Inverse transforms of Example 2.39.

giving

$$\mathscr{L}^{-1}\left\{\frac{e^{-s\pi}(s+3)}{s(s^2+1)}\right\} = \begin{cases} 0 & (t < \pi) \\ 3 + 3\cos t - \sin t & (t \geqslant \pi) \end{cases}$$

which is plotted in Figure 2.28(b).

2.5.5   Differential equations

We now return to the solution of linear differential equations for which the forcing function $f(t)$ is piecewise-continuous, like that illustrated in Figure 2.20. One approach to solving a differential equation having such a forcing function is to solve it separately for each of the continuous components $f_1(t)$, $f_2(t)$, and so on, comprising $f(t)$, using the fact that in this equation all the derivatives, except the highest, must remain continuous so that values at the point of discontinuity provide the initial conditions for the next section. This approach is obviously rather tedious, and a much more direct one is to make use of Heaviside step functions to specify $f(t)$. Then the method of solution follows that used in Section 2.3, and we shall simply illustrate it by examples.

EXAMPLE 2.40   Obtain the solution $x(t)$, $t \geqslant 0$, of the differential equation

$$\frac{d^2x}{dt^2} + 5\frac{dx}{dt} + 6x = f(t) \tag{2.46}$$

where $f(t)$ is the pulse function

$$f(t) = \begin{cases} 3 & (0 \leqslant t < 6) \\ 0 & (t \geqslant 6) \end{cases}$$

and subject to the initial conditions $x(0) = 0$ and $\dot{x}(0) = 2$.

Solution   To illustrate the advantage of using a step function formulation of the forcing function $f(t)$, we shall first solve separately for each of the time ranges.

Method 1   For $0 \leqslant t < 6$, (2.46) becomes

$$\frac{d^2x}{dt^2} + 5\frac{dx}{dt} + 6x = 3$$

with $x(0) = 0$ and $\dot{x}(0) = 2$.

Taking Laplace transforms gives

$$(s^2 + 5s + 6)X(s) = sx(0) + \dot{x}(0) + 5x(0) + \frac{3}{s} = 2 + \frac{3}{s}$$

That is,

$$X(s) = \frac{2s + 3}{s(s + 2)(s + 3)} = \frac{\frac{1}{2}}{s} + \frac{\frac{1}{2}}{s + 2} - \frac{1}{s + 3}$$

which, on inversion, gives

$$x(t) = \tfrac{1}{2} + \tfrac{1}{2}e^{-2t} - e^{-3t} \quad (0 \leqslant t < 6)$$

We now determine the values of $x(6)$ and $\dot{x}(6)$ in order to provide the initial conditions for the next stage:

$$x(6) = \tfrac{1}{2} + \tfrac{1}{2}e^{-12} - e^{-18} = \alpha, \quad \dot{x}(6) = -e^{-12} + 3e^{-18} = \beta$$

For $t \geqslant 6$ we make the change of independent variable $T = t - 6$, whence (2.46) becomes

$$\frac{d^2 x}{dT^2} + 5\frac{dx}{dT} + 6x = 0$$

subject to $x(T = 0) = \alpha$ and $\dot{x}(T = 0) = \beta$.

Taking Laplace transforms gives

$$(s^2 + 5s + 6)X(s) = sx(T = 0) + \dot{x}(T = 0) + 5x(T = 0)$$

$$= \alpha s + 5\alpha + \beta$$

That is,

$$X(s) = \frac{\alpha s + 5\alpha + \beta}{(s + 2)(s + 3)}$$

$$= \frac{\beta + 3\alpha}{s + 2} - \frac{\beta + 2\alpha}{s + 3}$$

which, on taking inverse transforms, gives

$$x(T) = (\beta + 3\alpha)e^{-2T} - (\beta + 2\alpha)e^{-3T}$$

Substituting the values of α and β and reverting to the independent variable t gives

$$x(t) = (\tfrac{3}{2} + \tfrac{1}{2}e^{-12})e^{-2(t-6)} - (1 + e^{-18})e^{-3(t-6)} \quad (t \geqslant 6)$$

That is,

$$x(t) = (\tfrac{1}{2}e^{-2t} - e^{-3t}) + (\tfrac{3}{2}e^{-2(t-6)} - e^{-3(t-6)}) \quad (t \geqslant 6)$$

Thus the solution of the differential equation is

$$x(t) = \begin{cases} \tfrac{1}{2} + \tfrac{1}{2}e^{-2t} - e^{-3t} & (0 \leqslant t < 6) \\ (\tfrac{1}{2}e^{-2t} - e^{-3t}) + (\tfrac{3}{2}e^{-2(t-6)} - e^{-3(t-6)}) & (t \geqslant 6) \end{cases}$$

Figure 2.29 Forcing function and response of Example 2.40.

The forcing function $f(t)$ and response $x(t)$ are shown in Figures 2.29(a) and (b) respectively.

Method 2   In terms of Heaviside step functions,

$$f(t) = 3H(t) - 3H(t - 6)$$

so that, using (2.43),

$$\mathscr{L}\{f(t)\} = \frac{3}{s} - \frac{3}{s}e^{-6s}$$

Taking Laplace transforms in (2.46) then gives

$$(s^2 + 5s + 6)X(s) = sx(0) + \dot{x}(0) + 5x(0) + \mathscr{L}\{f(t)\}$$

$$= 2 + \frac{3}{s} - \frac{3}{s}e^{-6s}$$

That is,

$$X(s) = \frac{2s + 3}{s(s + 2)(s + 3)} - e^{-6s}\frac{3}{s(s + 2)(s + 3)}$$

$$= \left(\frac{\frac{1}{2}}{s} + \frac{\frac{1}{2}}{s+2} - \frac{1}{s+3}\right) - e^{-6s}\left(\frac{\frac{1}{2}}{s} - \frac{\frac{3}{2}}{s+2} + \frac{1}{s+3}\right)$$

Taking inverse Laplace transforms and using the result (2.45) gives

$$x(t) = \left(\tfrac{1}{2} + \tfrac{1}{2}e^{-2t} - e^{-3t}\right) - \left(\tfrac{1}{2} - \tfrac{3}{2}e^{-2(t-6)} + e^{-3(t-6)}\right)H(t-6)$$

which is the required solution. This corresponds to that obtained in Method 1, since, using the definition of $H(t-6)$, it may be written as

$$x(t) = \begin{cases} \tfrac{1}{2} + \tfrac{1}{2}e^{-2t} - e^{-3t} & (0 \leqslant t < 6) \\ \left(\tfrac{1}{2}e^{-2t} - e^{-3t}\right) + \left(\tfrac{3}{2}e^{-2(t-6)} - e^{-3(t-6)}\right) & (t \geqslant 6) \end{cases}$$

This approach is clearly less tedious, since the initial conditions at the discontinuities are automatically taken account of in the solution.

EXAMPLE 2.41   Determine the solution $x(t)$, $t \geqslant 0$, of the differential equation

$$\frac{d^2 x}{dt^2} + 2\frac{dx}{dt} + 5x = f(t) \tag{2.47}$$

where

$$f(t) = \begin{cases} t & (0 \leqslant t \leqslant \pi) \\ 0 & (t \geqslant \pi) \end{cases}$$

and subject to the initial conditions $x(0) = 0$ and $\dot{x}(0) = 3$.

Solution   Following the procedures of Example 2.36, we have

$$f(t) = tH(t) - tH(t - \pi)$$
$$= tH(t) - (t - \pi)H(t - \pi) - \pi H(t - \pi)$$

so that, using Theorem 2.4,

$$\mathscr{L}\{f(t)\} = \frac{1}{s^2} - \frac{e^{-\pi s}}{s^2} - \frac{\pi e^{-\pi s}}{s}$$

$$= \frac{1}{s^2} - e^{-\pi s}\left(\frac{1}{s^2} + \frac{\pi}{s}\right)$$

Taking Laplace transforms in (2.47) then gives

$$(s^2 + 2s + 5)X(s) = sx(0) + \dot{x}(0) + 2x(0) + \mathscr{L}\{f(t)\}$$

$$= 3 + \frac{1}{s^2} - e^{-\pi s}\left(\frac{1}{s^2} + \frac{\pi}{s}\right)$$

using the given initial conditions.
Thus

$$X(s) = \frac{3s^2 + 1}{s^2(s^2 + 2s + 5)} - e^{-\pi s}\frac{1 + s\pi}{s^2(s^2 + 2s + 5)}$$

which, on resolving into partial fractions, leads to

$$X(s) = \tfrac{1}{25}\left[-\frac{2}{s} + \frac{5}{s^2} + \frac{2s + 74}{(s + 1)^2 + 4}\right]$$

$$-\frac{e^{-\pi s}}{25}\left[\frac{5\pi - 2}{s} + \frac{5}{s^2} - \frac{(5\pi - 2)s + (10\pi + 1)}{(s + 1)^2 + 4}\right]$$

$$= \tfrac{1}{25}\left[-\frac{2}{s} + \frac{5}{s^2} + \frac{2(s + 1) + 72}{(s + 1)^2 + 4}\right]$$

$$-\frac{e^{-\pi s}}{25}\left[\frac{5\pi - 2}{s} + \frac{5}{s^2} - \frac{(5\pi - 2)(s + 1) + (5\pi + 3)}{(s + 1)^2 + 4}\right]$$

Taking inverse Laplace transforms and using (2.45) gives the desired solution:

$$x(t) = \tfrac{1}{25}(-2 + 5t + 2e^{-t}\cos 2t + 36e^{-t}\sin 2t)$$

$$-\tfrac{1}{25}[(5\pi - 2) + 5(t - \pi) - (5\pi - 2)e^{-(t - \pi)}\cos 2(t - \pi)$$

$$-\tfrac{1}{2}(5\pi + 3)e^{-(t - \pi)}\sin 2(t - \pi)]H(t - \pi)$$

That is,

$$x(t) = \tfrac{1}{25}[5t - 2 + 2e^{-t}(\cos 2t + 18\sin 2t)]$$

$$-\tfrac{1}{25}\{5t - 2 - e^{\pi}e^{-t}[(5\pi - 2)\cos 2t + \tfrac{1}{2}(5\pi + 3)\sin 2t]\}H(t - \pi)$$

or, in alternative form,

$$x(t) = \begin{cases} \tfrac{1}{25}[5t - 2 + 2e^{-t}(\cos 2t + 18\sin 2t)] & (0 \leqslant t < \pi) \\ \tfrac{1}{25}e^{-t}\{(2 + (5\pi - 2)e^{\pi})\cos 2t + [36 + \tfrac{1}{2}(5\pi + 3)e^{\pi}]\sin 2t\} & (t \geqslant \pi) \end{cases}$$

2.5.6   Periodic functions

We have already determined the Laplace transforms of periodic functions, such as $\sin \omega t$ and $\cos \omega t$, which are smooth (differentiable) continuous functions. In many engineering applications, however, one frequently encounters periodic functions that exhibit discontinuous behaviour. Examples of typical periodic functions of practical importance are shown in Figure 2.30.

Such periodic functions may be represented as infinite series of terms involving step functions; once expressed in such a form, the result (2.43) may then be used to obtain their Laplace transforms.

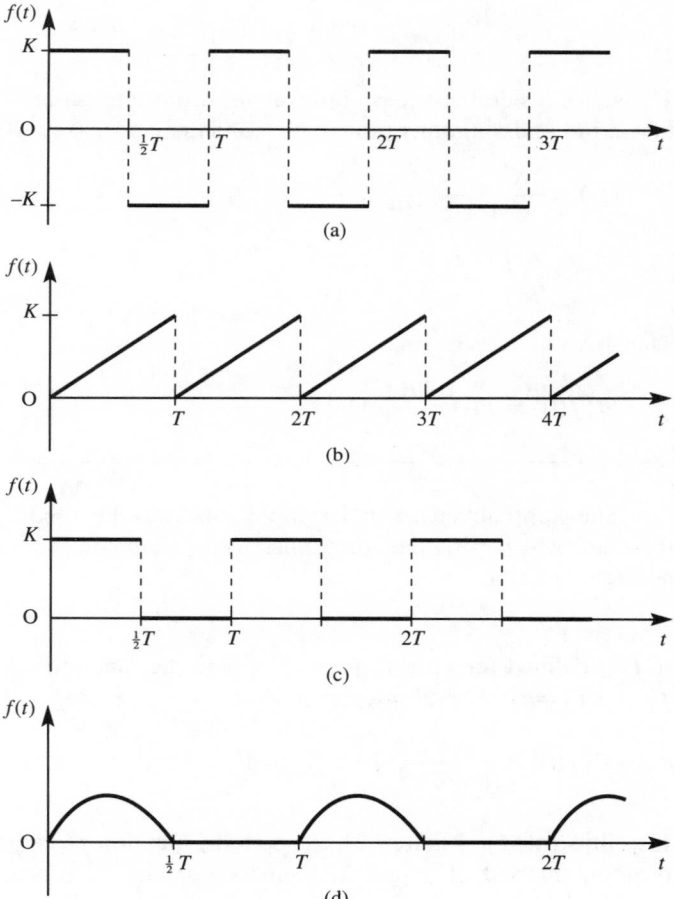

Figure 2.30 Typical practically important periodic functions: (a) square wave; (b) sawtooth wave; (c) repeated pulse wave; (d) half-wave rectifier.

EXAMPLE 2.42   Obtain the Laplace transform of the square wave illustrated in Figure 2.30(a).

Solution   In terms of step functions, the square wave may be expressed in the form

$$f(t) = KH(t) - 2KH(t - \tfrac{1}{2}T) + 2KH(t - T) - 2KH(t - \tfrac{3}{2}T)$$
$$+ 2KH(t - 2T) + \ldots$$
$$= K[H(t) - 2H(t - \tfrac{1}{2}T) + 2H(t - T) - 2H(t - \tfrac{3}{2}T) + 2H(t - 2T) + \ldots]$$

Taking Laplace transforms and using the result (2.43) gives

$$\mathscr{L}\{f(t)\} = F(s) = K\left(\frac{1}{s} - \frac{2}{s}e^{-sT/2} + \frac{2}{s}e^{-sT} - \frac{2}{s}e^{-3sT/2} + \frac{2}{s}e^{-2sT} + \ldots\right)$$

$$= \frac{2K}{s}[1 - \mathrm{e}^{-sT/2} + (\mathrm{e}^{-sT/2})^2 - (\mathrm{e}^{-sT/2})^3 + (\mathrm{e}^{-sT/2})^4 - \cdots] - \frac{K}{S}$$

The series inside the square brackets is an infinite geometric progression with first term 1 and common ratio $-\mathrm{e}^{-sT/2}$, and therefore has sum $(1 + \mathrm{e}^{-sT/2})^{-1}$. Thus,

$$F(s) = \frac{2K}{s}\frac{1}{1 + e^{-sT/2}} - \frac{K}{s}$$

$$= \frac{K}{s}\frac{1 - \mathrm{e}^{-sT/2}}{1 + \mathrm{e}^{-sT/2}}$$

That is,

$$\mathcal{L}\{f(t)\} = F(s) = \frac{K}{s}\tanh\tfrac{1}{4}sT$$

The approach used in Example 2.42 may be used to prove the following theorem, which provides an explicit expression for the Laplace transform of a periodic function.

THEOREM 2.5 If $f(t)$, defined for all positive t, is a periodic function with period T, that is, $f(t + nT) = f(t)$ for all integers n, then

$$\mathcal{L}\{f(t)\} = \frac{1}{1 - \mathrm{e}^{-sT}}\int_0^T \mathrm{e}^{-st}f(t)\,\mathrm{d}t$$

Proof If, as illustrated in Figure 2.31, the periodic function $f(t)$ is piecewise-continuous over an interval of length T, then its Laplace transform exists and can be expressed as a series of integrals over successive periods; that is,

$$\mathcal{L}\{f(t)\} = \int_0^\infty f(t)\,\mathrm{e}^{-st}\,\mathrm{d}t$$

$$= \int_0^T f(t)\,\mathrm{e}^{-st}\,\mathrm{d}t + \int_T^{2T} f(t)\,\mathrm{e}^{-st}\,\mathrm{d}t + \int_{2T}^{3T} f(t)\,\mathrm{e}^{-st}\,\mathrm{d}t + \cdots$$

$$+ \int_{(n-1)T}^{nT} f(t)\,\mathrm{e}^{-st}\,\mathrm{d}t + \cdots$$

Figure 2.31 Periodic function having period T.

If in successive integrals we make the substitutions

$$t = \tau + nT \quad (n = 0, 1, 2, 3, \ldots)$$

then

$$\mathcal{L}\{f(t)\} = \sum_{n=0}^{\infty} \int_{0}^{T} f(\tau + nT) e^{-s(\tau + nT)} \, d\tau$$

Since $f(t)$ is periodic with period T,

$$f(\tau + nT) = f(t) \quad (n = 0, 1, 2, 3, \ldots)$$

so that

$$\mathcal{L}\{f(t)\} = \sum_{n=0}^{\infty} \int_{0}^{T} f(\tau) e^{-s\tau} e^{-snT} \, d\tau$$

$$= \left(\sum_{n=0}^{\infty} e^{-snT} \right) \int_{0}^{T} f(\tau) e^{-s\tau} \, d\tau$$

The series $\sum_{n=0}^{\infty} e^{-snT} = 1 + e^{-sT} + e^{-2sT} + e^{-3sT} + \ldots$ is an infinite geometric progression with first term 1 and common ratio e^{-sT}. Its sum is given by $(1 - e^{-sT})^{-1}$, so that

$$\mathcal{L}\{f(t)\} = \frac{1}{1 - e^{-sT}} \int_{0}^{T} f(\tau) e^{-s\tau} \, d\tau$$

Since, within the integral, τ is a 'dummy' variable, it may be replaced by t to give the desired result.   □

We note that, in terms of the Heaviside step function, Theorem 2.5 may be stated as follows:

If $f(t)$, defined for all positive t, is a periodic function with period T and

$$f_1(t) = f(t)(H(t) - H(t - T))$$

then

$$\mathcal{L}\{f(t)\} = (1 - e^{-sT})^{-1} \mathcal{L}\{f_1(t)\}$$

This formulation follows since $f(t)$ is periodic and $f_1(t) = 0$ for $t > T$. For the periodic function $f(t)$ shown in Figure 2.31 the corresponding function $f_1(t)$ is shown in Figure 2.32. We shall see from the following examples that this formulation simplifies the process of obtaining Laplace transforms of periodic functions.

Figure 2.32 Plot of periodic function within one period.

EXAMPLE 2.43   Confirm the result obtained in Example 2.42 using Theorem 2.5.

Solution   For the square wave $f(t)$ illustrated in Figure 2.30(a), $f(t)$ is defined over the period $0 < t < T$ by

$$f(t) = \begin{cases} K & (0 < t < \tfrac{1}{2}T) \\ -K & (\tfrac{1}{2}T < t < T) \end{cases}$$

Hence we can write $f_1(t) = K[H(t) - 2H(t - \tfrac{1}{2}T) + H(t - T)]$, and thus

$$\mathcal{L}\{f_1(t)\} = K\left(\frac{1}{s} - \frac{2}{s}e^{-sT/2} + \frac{1}{s}e^{-sT}\right)$$

$$= \frac{K}{s}(1 - e^{-sT/2})^2$$

Using the result of Theorem 2.5,

$$\mathcal{L}\{f(t)\} = \frac{K(1 - e^{-sT/2})^2}{s(1 - e^{-sT})} = \frac{K(1 - e^{-sT/2})^2}{s(1 - e^{-sT/2})(1 + e^{-sT/2})}$$

$$= \frac{K}{s}\frac{1 - e^{-sT/2}}{1 + e^{-sT/2}} = \frac{K}{s}\tanh\tfrac{1}{4}sT$$

confirming the result obtained in Example 2.42.

EXAMPLE 2.44   Determine the Laplace transform of the rectified half-wave defined by

$$f(t) = \begin{cases} \sin \omega t & (0 < t < \pi/\omega) \\ 0 & (\pi/\omega < t < 2\pi/\omega) \end{cases}$$

$$f(t + 2n\pi/\omega) = f(t) \quad \text{for all integers } n$$

Solution $f(t)$ is illustrated in Figure 2.30(d), with $T = 2\pi/\omega$. We can express $f_1(t)$ as

$$f_1(t) = \sin \omega t\,[H(t) - H(t - \pi/\omega)]$$

$$= \sin \omega t\, H(t) + \sin \omega(t - \pi/\omega)\, H(t - \pi/\omega)$$

So

$$\mathcal{L}\{f_1(t)\} = \frac{\omega}{s^2 + \omega^2} + e^{-s\pi/\omega}\frac{\omega}{s^2 + \omega^2}$$

$$= \frac{\omega}{s^2 + \omega^2}(1 + e^{-s\pi/\omega})$$

Then, by the result of Theorem 2.5,

$$\mathcal{L}\{f(t)\} = \frac{\omega}{s^2 + \omega^2}\frac{1 + e^{-s\pi/\omega}}{1 - e^{-2s\pi/\omega}} = \frac{\omega}{(s^2 + \omega^2)(1 - e^{-s\pi/\omega})}$$

2.5.7   Exercises

13 A function $f(t)$ is defined by

$$f(t) = \begin{cases} t & (0 \leqslant t \leqslant 1) \\ 0 & (t > 1) \end{cases}$$

Express $f(t)$ in terms of Heaviside unit step functions and show that

$$\mathcal{L}\{f(t)\} = \frac{1}{s^2}(1 - e^{-s}) - \frac{1}{s}e^{-s}$$

14 Express in terms of Heaviside unit step functions the following piecewise-continuous causal functions. In each case obtain the Laplace transform of the function.

(a)

$$f(t) = \begin{cases} 3t^2 & (0 < t \leqslant 4) \\ 2t - 3 & (4 < t < 6) \\ 5 & (t > 6) \end{cases}$$

(b)

$$g(t) = \begin{cases} t & (0 \leqslant t < 1) \\ 2 - t & (1 < t < 2) \\ 0 & (t > 2) \end{cases}$$

15 Obtain the inverse Laplace transforms of the following:

(a) $\dfrac{e^{-5s}}{(s - 2)^4}$ (b) $\dfrac{3e^{-2s}}{(s + 3)(s + 1)}$

(c) $\dfrac{s + 1}{s^2(s^2 + 1)}e^{-s}$ (d) $\dfrac{s + 1}{s^2 + s + 1}e^{-\pi s}$

(e) $\dfrac{s}{s^2 + 25}e^{-4\pi s/5}$ (f) $\dfrac{e^{-s}(1 - e^{-s})}{s^2(s^2 + 1)}$

16 Given that $x = 0$ when $t = 0$, obtain the solution of the differential equation

$$\frac{dx}{dt} + x = f(t) \quad (t \geqslant 0)$$

where $f(t)$ is the function defined in Exercise 13. Sketch a graph of the solution.

17 Given that $x = 1$ and $dx/dt = 0$, obtain the solution of the differential equation

$$\frac{d^2x}{dt^2} + \frac{dx}{dt} + x = g(t) \quad (t \geqslant 0)$$

where $g(t)$ is the piecewise-continuous function defined in Exercise 14(b).

18 Show that the function

$$f(t) = \begin{cases} 0 & (0 \leqslant t < \tfrac{1}{2}\pi) \\ \sin t & (t \geqslant \tfrac{1}{2}\pi) \end{cases}$$

may be expressed in the form $f(t) = \cos(t - \tfrac{1}{2}\pi)$ $H(t - \tfrac{1}{2}\pi)$, where $H(t)$ is the Heaviside unit step function. Hence solve the differential equation

$$\frac{d^2x}{dt^2} + 3\frac{dx}{dt} + 2x = f(t)$$

where $f(t)$ is given above, and $x = 1$ and $dx/dt = -1$ when $t = 0$.

19 Express the function

$$f(t) = \begin{cases} 3 & (0 \leqslant t < 4) \\ 2t - 5 & (t \geqslant 4) \end{cases}$$

in terms of Heaviside unit step functions and obtain its Laplace transform. Obtain the response of the harmonic oscillator

$$\ddot{x} + x = f(t)$$

to such a forcing function, given that $x = 1$ and $dx/dt = 0$ when $t = 0$.

20 The response $\theta_o(t)$ of a system to a forcing function $\theta_i(t)$ is determined by the second-order differential equation

$$\ddot{\theta}_o + 6\dot{\theta}_o + 10\theta_o = \theta_i \quad (t \geqslant 0)$$

Suppose that $\theta_i(t)$ is a constant stimulus applied for a limited period and characterized by

$$\theta_i(t) = \begin{cases} 3 & (0 \leqslant t < a) \\ 0 & (t \geqslant a) \end{cases}$$

determine the response of the system at time t given that the system was initially in a quiescent state. Show that the transient response at time T ($> a$) is

$$-\tfrac{3}{10}e^{-3T}\{\cos T + 3\sin T$$
$$- e^{3a}[\cos(T - a) + 3\sin(T - a)]\}$$

21 The input $\theta_i(t)$ and output $\theta_o(t)$ of a servomechanism are related by the differential equation

$$\ddot{\theta}_o + 8\dot{\theta}_o + 16\theta_o = \theta_i \quad (t \geqslant 0)$$

and initially $\theta_o(0) = \dot{\theta}_o(0) = 0$. For $\theta_i = f(t)$, where

$$f(t) = \begin{cases} 1 - t & (0 < t < 1) \\ 0 & (t > 1) \end{cases}$$

show that

$$\mathcal{L}\{\theta_i(t)\} = \frac{s-1}{s^2} + \frac{1}{s^2}e^{-s}$$

and hence obtain an expression for the response of the system at time t.

22 During the time interval t_1 to t_2, a constant electromotive force e_0 acts on the series RC circuit shown in Figure 2.33. Assuming that the circuit is

Figure 2.33 Circuit of Exercise 22.

initially in a quiescent state, show that the current in the circuit at time t is

$$i(t) = \frac{e_0}{R}[e^{-(t-t_1)/RC}H(t-t_1) - e^{-(t-t_2)/RC}H(t-t_2)]$$

Sketch this as a function of time.

23 A periodic function $f(t)$, with period 4 units, is defined within the interval $0 \leqslant t < 4$ by

$$f(t) = \begin{cases} 3t & (0 \leqslant t < 2) \\ 6 & (2 \leqslant t < 4) \end{cases}$$

Sketch a graph of the function for $0 \leqslant t < 12$ and obtain its Laplace transform.

24 Obtain the Laplace transform of the periodic sawtooth wave with period T, illustrated in Figure 2.30(b).

2.5.8 The impulse function

In many engineering applications we are interested in seeking the responses of systems to forcing functions that are applied suddenly but only for a very short time. These functions are known as **impulsive forces**. Mathematically, such forcing functions are idealized by the **impulse function**, which is a function whose total value is concentrated at one point. To develop a mathematical formulation of the impulse function and obtain some insight into its physical interpretation, consider the pulse function $\phi(t)$ defined by

$$\phi(t) = \begin{cases} 0 & (0 < t < a - \tfrac{1}{2}T) \\ A/T & (a - \tfrac{1}{2}T \leqslant t < a + \tfrac{1}{2}T) \\ 0 & (t \geqslant a + \tfrac{1}{2}T) \end{cases}$$

and illustrated in Figure 2.34(a). Since the height of the pulse is A/T and its duration (or width) is T, the area under the pulse is A; that is,

$$\int_{-\infty}^{\infty} \phi(t)\,dt = \int_{a-T/2}^{a+T/2} \frac{A}{T}\,dt = A$$

If we now consider the limiting process in which the duration of the pulse approaches zero, in such a way that the area under the pulse remains A, then we obtain a formulation of the impulse function of magnitude A occurring at time $t = a$. It is important to appreciate that the magnitude of the impulse function is measured by its area.

The impulse function whose magnitude is unity is called the **unit impulse function** or **Dirac delta function**. The unit impulse occurring at $t = a$ is the limiting

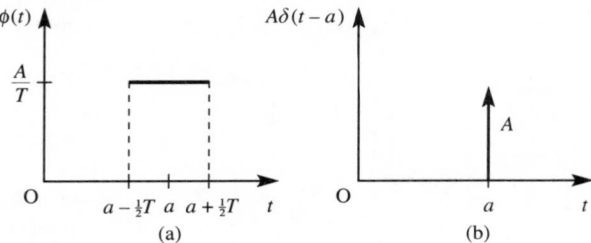

Figure 2.34 Impulse function.

case of the pulse $\phi(t)$ of Figure 2.34(a) with A having the value unity. It is denoted by $\delta(t - a)$ and has the properties

$$\delta(t - a) = 0 \quad (t \neq a)$$

$$\int_{-\infty}^{\infty} \delta(t - a)\,\mathrm{d}t = 1$$

Likewise, an impulse function of magnitude A occurring at $t = a$ is denoted by $A\delta(t - a)$ and may be represented diagrammatically as in Figure 2.34(b).

An impulse function is not a function in the usual sense, but is an example of a class of what are called **generalized functions**, which may be analysed using the theory of **generalized calculus**. (It may also be regarded mathematically as a **distribution** and investigated using the **theory of distributions**.) However, its properties are such that, used with care, it can lead to results that have physical or practical significance and which in many cases cannot be obtained by any other method. In this context it provides engineers with an important mathematical tool. Although, clearly, an impulse function is not physically realizable, it follows from the above formulation that physical signals can be produced that closely approximate it.

We noted that the magnitude of the impulse function is determined by the area under the limiting pulse. The actual shape of the limiting pulse is not really important, provided that the area contained within it remains constant as its duration approaches zero. Physically, therefore, the unit impulse function at $t = a$ may equally well be regarded as the pulse $\phi_1(t)$ of Figure 2.35 in the limiting case as T approaches zero.

In some applications we need to consider a unit impulse function at time $t = 0$. This is denoted by $\delta(t)$ and is defined as the limiting case of the pulse $\phi_2(t)$

Figure 2.35 Approximation to a unit pulse.

Figure 2.36 Pulse at the origin.

illustrated in Figure 2.36 as T approaches zero. It has the properties

$$\delta(t) = 0 \quad (t \neq 0)$$

$$\int_{-\infty}^{\infty} \delta(t)\,dt = 1$$

2.5.9   The sifting property

An important property of the unit impulse function that is of practical significance is the so-called **sifting property**, which states that if $f(t)$ is continuous at $t = a$ then

$$\int_{-\infty}^{\infty} f(t)\delta(t - a)\,dt = f(a) \tag{2.48}$$

This is referred to as the sifting property because it provides a method of isolating, or sifting out, the value of a function at any particular point.

For theoretical reasons it is convenient to use infinite limits in (2.48), while in reality finite limits can be substituted. This follows since for $\alpha < a < \beta$, where α and β are constants,

$$\int_{\alpha}^{\beta} f(t)\delta(t - a)\,dt = f(a) \tag{2.49}$$

For example,

$$\int_{0}^{2\pi} \cos t\, \delta(t - \tfrac{1}{3}\pi)\,dt = \cos \tfrac{1}{3}\pi = \tfrac{1}{2}$$

2.5.10   Laplace transforms of impulse functions

By the definition of the Laplace transform, we have for any $a > 0$

$$\mathscr{L}\{\delta(t-a)\} = \int_0^\infty \delta(t-a)\,e^{-st}\,dt$$

which, using the sifting property, gives the important result

$$\mathscr{L}\{\delta(t-a)\} = e^{-as} \tag{2.50}$$

or, in terms of the inverse transform,

$$\mathscr{L}^{-1}\{e^{-as}\} = \delta(t-a) \tag{2.51}$$

As mentioned earlier, in many applications we may have an impulse function $\delta(t)$ at $t = 0$, and it is in order to handle such a function that we must carefully specify whether the lower limit in the Laplace integral defined in Section 2.2.1 is $0-$ or $0+$. Adopting the notation

$$\mathscr{L}_+\{f(t)\} = \int_{0+}^\infty f(t)\,e^{-st}\,dt$$

$$\mathscr{L}_-\{f(t)\} = \int_{0-}^\infty f(t)\,e^{-st}\,dt$$

we have

$$\mathscr{L}_-\{f(t)\} = \int_{0-}^{0+} f(t)\,e^{-st}\,dt + \int_{0+}^\infty f(t)\,e^{-st}\,dt$$

If $f(t)$ does not involve an impulse function at $t = 0$ then clearly $\mathscr{L}_+\{f(t)\} = \mathscr{L}_-\{f(t)\}$. However, if $f(t)$ does involve an impulse function at $t = 0$ then

$$\int_{0-}^{0+} f(t)\,dt \neq 0$$

and it follows that

$$\mathscr{L}_+\{f(t)\} \neq \mathscr{L}_-\{f(t)\}$$

In Section 2.2.1 we adopted the definition

$$\mathscr{L}\{f(t)\} = \mathscr{L}_-\{f(t)\}$$

so that (2.50) and (2.51) hold for $a = 0$, giving

$$\mathscr{L}\{\delta(t)\} = \int_{0-}^\infty \delta(t)\,e^{-st}\,dt = e^{-s0} = 1$$

so that

$$\mathscr{L}\{\delta(t)\} = 1 \tag{2.52}$$

or, in inverse form,

$$\mathscr{L}^{-1}\{1\} = \delta(t) \tag{2.53}$$

EXAMPLE 2.45   Determine $\mathscr{L}^{-1}\left\{\dfrac{s^2}{s^2+4}\right\}$.

Solution   Since

$$\frac{s^2}{s^2+4} = \frac{s^2+4-4}{s^2+4} = 1 - \frac{4}{s^2+4}$$

we have

$$\mathscr{L}^{-1}\left\{\frac{s^2}{s^2+4}\right\} = \mathscr{L}^{-1}\{1\} - \mathscr{L}^{-1}\left\{\frac{4}{s^2+4}\right\}$$

giving

$$\mathscr{L}^{-1}\left\{\frac{s^2}{s^2+4}\right\} = \delta(t) - 2\sin 2t$$

EXAMPLE 2.46   Determine the solution of the differential equation

$$\frac{d^2x}{dt^2} + 3\frac{dx}{dt} + 2x = 1 + \delta(t-4) \qquad\qquad (2.54)$$

subject to the initial conditions $x(0) = \dot{x}(0) = 0$.

Solution   Taking Laplace transforms in (2.54) gives

$$[s^2 X(s) - sx(0) - \dot{x}(0)] + 3[sX(s) - x(0)] + 2X(s) = \mathscr{L}\{1\} + \mathscr{L}\{\delta(t-4)\}$$

which, on incorporating the given initial conditions and using (2.50), leads to

$$(s^2 + 3s + 2)X(s) = \frac{1}{s} + e^{-4s}$$

giving

$$X(s) = \frac{1}{s(s+2)(s+1)} + e^{-4s}\frac{1}{(s+2)(s+1)}$$

Resolving into partial fractions, we have

$$X(s) = \tfrac{1}{2}\left(\frac{1}{s} + \frac{1}{s+2} - \frac{2}{s+1}\right) + e^{-4s}\left(\frac{1}{s+1} - \frac{1}{s+2}\right)$$

which, on taking inverse transforms and using the result (2.45), gives the required response:

$$x(t) = \tfrac{1}{2}(1 + e^{-2t} - 2e^{-t}) + (e^{-(t-4)} - e^{-2(t-4)})H(t-4)$$

or, in an alternative form,

$$x(t) = \begin{cases} \frac{1}{2}(1 + e^{-2t} - 2e^{-t}) & (0 \leqslant t < 4) \\ \frac{1}{2} + (e^4 - 1)e^{-t} - (e^8 - \frac{1}{2})e^{-2t} & (t \geqslant 4) \end{cases}$$

We note that, although the response $x(t)$ is continuous at $t = 4$, the consequence of the impulsive input at $t = 4$ is a step change in the derivative $\dot{x}(t)$.

2.5.11 Relationship between Heaviside step and impulse functions

From the definitions of $H(t)$ and $\delta(t)$, it can be argued that

$$H(t) = \int_{-\infty}^{t} \delta(\tau)\,\mathrm{d}\tau \qquad\qquad (2.55)$$

since the interval of integration contains zero if $t > 0$ but not if $t < 0$. Conversely, (2.55) may be written as

$$\delta(t) = \frac{\mathrm{d}}{\mathrm{d}t}H(t) = H'(t) \qquad\qquad (2.56)$$

which expresses the fact that $H'(t)$ is zero everywhere except at $t = 0$, when the jump in $H(t)$ occurs.

While this argument may suffice in practice, since we are dealing with generalized functions a more formal proof requires the development of some properties of generalized functions. In particular, we need to define what is meant by saying that two generalized functions are equivalent.

One method of approach is to use the concept of a **test function** $\theta(t)$, which is a continuous function that has continuous derivatives of all orders and that is zero outside a finite interval. One class of testing function, adopted by R. R. Gabel and R. A. Roberts (*Signals and Linear Systems*, Wiley, New York, 1973), is

$$\theta(t) = \begin{cases} e^{-d^2/(d^2 - t^2)} & (|t| < d), \qquad \text{where } d = \text{constant} \\ 0 & \text{otherwise} \end{cases}$$

For a generalized function $g(t)$ the integral

$$G(\theta) = \int_{-\infty}^{\infty} \theta(t)g(t)\,\mathrm{d}t$$

is evaluated. This integral assigns the number $G(\theta)$ to each function $\theta(t)$, so that $G(\theta)$ is a generalization of the concept of a function: it is a **linear functional** on the space of test functions $\theta(t)$. For example, if $g(t) = \delta(t)$ then

$$G(\theta) = \int_{-\infty}^{\infty} \theta(t)\delta(t)\,\mathrm{d}t = \theta(0)$$

so that in this particular case, for each weighting function $\theta(t)$, the value $\theta(0)$ is assigned to $G(\theta)$.

We can now use the concept of a test function to define what is meant by saying that two generalized functions are equivalent or 'equal'.

DEFINITION 2.2: The equivalence property

If $g_1(t)$ and $g_2(t)$ are two generalized functions then $g_1(t) = g_2(t)$ if and only if

$$\int_{-\infty}^{\infty} \theta(t)g_1(t)\, \mathrm{d}t = \int_{-\infty}^{\infty} \theta(t)g_2(t)\, \mathrm{d}t$$

for all test functions $\theta(t)$ for which the integrals exist.

The test function may be regarded as a 'device' for examining the generalized function. Gabel and Roberts draw a rough parallel with the role of using the output of a measuring instrument to deduce properties about what is being measured. In such an analogy $g_1(t) = g_2(t)$ if the measuring instrument can detect no differences between them.

Using the concept of a test function $\theta(t)$, the Dirac delta function $\delta(t)$ may be defined in the generalized form

$$\int_{-\infty}^{\infty} \theta(t)\delta(t)\, \mathrm{d}t = \theta(0)$$

Interpreted as an ordinary integral, this has no meaning. The integral and the function $\delta(t)$ are merely defined by the number $\theta(0)$. In this sense we can handle $\delta(t)$ as if it were an ordinary function, except that we never talk about the value of $\delta(t)$; rather we talk about the value of integrals involving $\delta(t)$.

Using the equivalence property, we can now confirm the result (2.56), namely that

$$\delta(t) = \frac{\mathrm{d}}{\mathrm{d}t} H(t) = H'(t)$$

To prove this, we must show that

$$\int_{-\infty}^{\infty} \theta(t)\delta(t)\, \mathrm{d}t = \int_{-\infty}^{\infty} \theta(t)H'(t)\, \mathrm{d}t \qquad (2.57)$$

Integrating the right-hand side of (2.57) by parts, we have

$$\int_{-\infty}^{\infty} \theta(t)H'(t)\, \mathrm{d}t = [H(t)\theta(t)]_{-\infty}^{\infty} - \int_{-\infty}^{\infty} H(t)\theta'(t)\, \mathrm{d}t$$

$$= 0 - \int_{0}^{\infty} \theta'(t)\, \mathrm{d}t \qquad \text{(by the definitions of } \theta(t) \text{ and } H(t))$$

$$= -[\theta(t)]_{0}^{\infty} = \theta(0)$$

Since the left-hand side of (2.57) is also $\theta(0)$, the equivalence of $\delta(t)$ and $H'(t)$ is proved.

Figure 2.37 Piecewise-continuous function with jump discontinuities.

Likewise, it can be shown that

$$\delta(t - a) = \frac{d}{dt} H(t - a) = H'(t - a) \tag{2.58}$$

The results (2.56) and (2.58) may be used to obtain the **generalized derivatives** of piecewise-continuous functions having jump discontinuities $d_1, d_2, \ldots, d_n$ at times $t_1, t_2, \ldots, t_n$ respectively, as illustrated in Figure 2.37. On expressing $f(t)$ in terms of Heaviside step functions as in Section 2.5.1, and differentiating using the product rule, use of (2.56) and (2.58) leads to the result

$$f'(t) = g'(t) + \sum_{i=1}^{n} d_i \delta(t - t_i) \tag{2.59}$$

where $g'(t)$ denotes the ordinary derivative of $f(t)$ where it exists. The result (2.59) tells us that the derivative of a piecewise-continuous function with jump discontinuities is the ordinary derivative where it exists plus the sum of delta functions at the discontinuities multiplied by the magnitudes of the respective jumps.

By the magnitude d_i of a jump in a function $f(t)$ at a point t_i, we mean the difference between the right-hand and left-hand limits of $f(t)$ at t_i; that is,

$$d_i = f(t_i + 0) - f(t_i - 0)$$

It follows that an upward jump, such as d_1 and d_2 in Figure 2.37, is positive, while a downward jump, such as d_3 in Figure 2.37, is negative.

The result (2.59) gives an indication as to why the use of differentiators in practical systems is not encouraged, since the introduction of impulses means that derivatives increase noise levels in signal reception. In contrast, integrators have a smoothing effect on signals, and are widely used.

EXAMPLE 2.47   Obtain the generalized derivative of the piecewise-continuous function

$$f(t) = \begin{cases} 2t^2 + 1 & (0 \leqslant t < 3) \\ t + 4 & (3 \leqslant t < 5) \\ 4 & (t \geqslant 5) \end{cases}$$

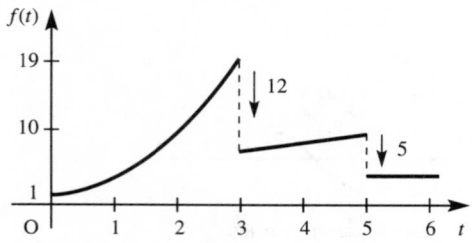

Figure 2.38 Piecewise-continuous function of Example 2.47.

Solution $f(t)$ is depicted graphically in Figure 2.38, and it has jump discontinuities of magnitudes 1, -12 and -5 at times $t = 0$, 3 and 5 respectively. Using (2.59), the generalized derivative is

$$f'(t) = g'(t) + 1\delta(t) - 12\delta(t - 3) - 5\delta(t - 5)$$

where

$$g'(t) = \begin{cases} 4t & (0 \leqslant t < 3) \\ 1 & (3 \leqslant t < 5) \\ 0 & (t \geqslant 5) \end{cases}$$

EXAMPLE 2.48   A system is characterized by the differential equation model

$$\frac{d^2x}{dt^2} + 5\frac{dx}{dt} + 6x = u + 3\frac{du}{dt} \tag{2.60}$$

Determine the response of the system to a forcing function $u(t) = e^{-t}$ applied at time $t = 0$, given that it was initially in a quiescent state.

Solution   Since the system is initially in a quiescent state, and there is no input at time $t = 0$, the transformed equation corresponding to (2.60) is

$$(s^2 + 5s + 6)X(s) = (3s + 1)U(s)$$

giving

$$X(s) = \frac{3s + 1}{s^2 + 5s + 6}U(s)$$

In the particular case when $u(t) = e^{-t}$, $U(s) = 1/(s + 1)$, so that

$$X(s) = \frac{(3s + 1)}{(s + 1)(s + 2)(s + 3)} = \frac{-1}{s + 1} + \frac{5}{s + 2} - \frac{4}{s + 3}$$

which, on taking inverse transforms, gives the desired response as

$$x(t) = -e^{-t} + 5e^{-2t} - 4e^{-3t} \quad (t \geqslant 0)$$

One might have been tempted to adopt a different approach and substitute for

$u(t)$ directly in (2.60) before taking Laplace transforms. This leads to

$$\frac{d^2x}{dt^2} + 5\frac{dx}{dt} + 6x = e^{-t} - 3e^{-t} = -2e^{-t}$$

which, on taking Laplace transforms, leads to

$$(s^2 + 5s + 6)X(s) = -\frac{2}{s+1}$$

giving

$$X(s) = \frac{-2}{(s+1)(s+2)(s+3)} = \frac{-1}{s+1} + \frac{2}{s+2} - \frac{1}{s+3}$$

which, on inversion, gives

$$x(t) = -e^{-t} + 2e^{-2t} - e^{-3t} \quad (t \geq 0)$$

Clearly this approach results in a different solution, and therefore appears to lead to a paradox. However, this apparent paradox can be resolved by noting that the second approach is erroneous in that it ignores the important fact that we are dealing with causal functions. Strictly speaking,

$$u(t) = e^{-t}H(t)$$

and, when determining du/dt, the product rule of differential calculus should be employed, giving

$$\frac{du}{dt} = -e^{-t}H(t) + e^{-t}\frac{d}{dt}H(t)$$

$$= -e^{-t}H(t) + e^{-t}\delta(t)$$

Substituting this into (2.60) and taking Laplace transforms gives

$$(s^2 + 5s + 6)X(s) = \frac{1}{s+1} + 3\left(-\frac{1}{s+1} + 1\right)$$

$$= \frac{3s+1}{s+1}$$

That is,

$$X(s) = \frac{3s+1}{(s+1)(s^2+5s+6)}$$

leading to the same response

$$x(t) = -e^{-t} + 5e^{-2t} - 4e^{-3t} \quad (t \geq 0)$$

as in the first approach above.

The differential equation used in Example 2.48 is of a form that occurs frequently in practice, so it is important that the causal nature of the forcing term be recognized.

The derivative $\delta'(t)$ of the delta function is also a generalized function, and, using the equivalence property, it is readily shown that

$$\int_{-\infty}^{\infty} f(t)\delta'(t)\,dt = -f'(0)$$

or, more generally,

$$\int_{-\infty}^{\infty} f(t)\delta'(t-a)\,dt = -f'(a)$$

provided that $f'(t)$ is continuous at $t = a$.

Likewise, the nth derivative satisfies

$$\int_{-\infty}^{\infty} f(t)\delta^n(t-a)\,dt = (-1)^n f^{(n)}(a)$$

provided that $f^{(n)}(t)$ is continuous at $t = a$.

Using the definition of the Laplace transforms, it follows that

$$\mathcal{L}\{\delta^{(n)}(t-a)\} = s^n\,e^{-as}$$

and, in particular,

$$\mathcal{L}\{\delta^{(n)}(t)\} = s^n \tag{2.61}$$

2.5.12   Exercises

25 Obtain the inverse Laplace transforms of the following:

(a) $\dfrac{2s^2 + 1}{(s+2)(s+3)}$ (b) $\dfrac{s^2 - 1}{s^2 + 4}$ (c) $\dfrac{s^2 + 2}{s^2 + 2s + 5}$

26 Solve for $t \geqslant 0$ the following differential equations, subject to the specified initial conditions:

(a) $\dfrac{d^2x}{dt^2} + 7\dfrac{dx}{dt} + 12x = 2 + \delta(t-2)$

    subject to $x = 0$ and $\dfrac{dx}{dt} = 0$ at $t = 0$

(b) $\dfrac{d^2x}{dt^2} + 6\dfrac{dx}{dt} + 13x = \delta(t-2\pi)$

    subject to $x = 0$ and $\dfrac{dx}{dt} = 0$ at $t = 0$

(c) $\dfrac{d^2x}{dt^2} + 7\dfrac{dx}{dt} + 12x = \delta(t-3)$

    subject to $x = 1$ and $\dfrac{dx}{dt} = 1$ at $t = 0$

27 Obtain the generalized derivatives of the following piecewise-continuous functions:

(a)
$$f(t) = \begin{cases} 3t^2 & (0 \leqslant t < 4) \\ 2t - 3 & (4 \leqslant t < 6) \\ 5 & (t \geqslant 6) \end{cases}$$

(b)
$$g(t) = \begin{cases} t & (0 \leqslant t < 1) \\ 2 - t & (1 \leqslant t < 2) \\ 0 & (t \geqslant 2) \end{cases}$$

(c)
$$f(t) = \begin{cases} 2t + 5 & (0 \leqslant t < 2) \\ 9 - 3t & (2 \leqslant t < 4) \\ t^2 - t & (t \geqslant 4) \end{cases}$$

28 Solve for $t \geqslant 0$ the differential equation

$$\frac{d^2x}{dt^2} + 7\frac{dx}{dt} + 10x = 2u + 3\frac{du}{dt}$$

subject to $x = 0$ and $dx/dt = 2$ at $t = 0$ and where $u(t) = e^{-2t}H(t)$.

29 A periodic function $f(t)$ is an infinite train of unit impulses at $t = 0$ and repeated at intervals of $t = T$. Show that

$$\mathcal{L}\{f(t)\} = \frac{1}{1 - e^{-sT}}$$

The response of a harmonic oscillator to such a periodic stimulus is determined by the differential equation

$$\frac{d^2x}{dt^2} + \omega^2x = f(t) \quad (t \geqslant 0)$$

Show that

$$x(t) = \frac{1}{\omega} \sum_{n=0}^{\infty} H(t - nT) \sin \omega(t - nT) \quad (t \geqslant 0)$$

and sketch the responses from $t = 0$ to $t = 6\pi/\omega$ for the two cases (a) $T = \pi/\omega$ and (b) $T = 2\pi/\omega$.

30 An impulse voltage $E\delta(t)$ is applied at time $t = 0$ to a circuit consisting of a resistor R, a capacitor C and an inductor L connected in series. Prior to application of this voltage, both the charge on the capacitor and the resulting current in the circuit are zero. Determine the charge $q(t)$ on the capacitor and the resulting current $i(t)$ in the circuit at time t.

2.5.13 Bending of beams

So far, we have considered examples in which Laplace transform methods have been used to solve initial-value-type problems. These methods may also be used to solve boundary-value problems, and, to illustrate, we consider in this section the application of Laplace transform methods to determine the transverse deflection of a uniform thin beam due to loading.

Consider a thin uniform beam of length l and let $y(x)$ be its transverse displacement, at distance x measured from one end, from the original position due to loading. The situation is illustrated in Figure 2.39, with the displacement measured upwards. Then, from the elementary theory of beams, we have

$$EI\frac{d^4y}{dx^4} = -W(x) \tag{2.62}$$

where $W(x)$ is the transverse force per unit length, with a downwards force taken to be positive, and EI is the flexural rigidity of the beam (E is Young's modulus

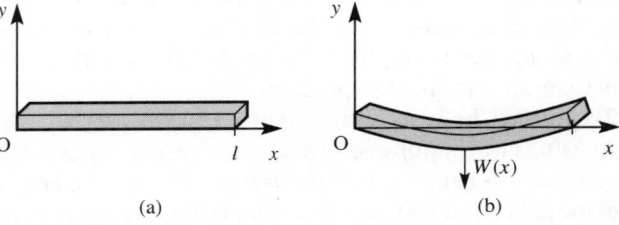

Figure 2.39 Transverse deflection of a beam: (a) initial position; (b) displaced position.

of elasticity and I is the moment of inertia of the beam about its central axis). It is assumed that the beam has uniform elastic properties and a uniform cross-section over its length, so that both E and I are taken to be constants.

Equation (2.62) is sometimes written as

$$EI\frac{d^4y}{dx^4} = W(x)$$

where $y(x)$ is the transverse displacement measured downwards and not upwards as in (2.62).

In cases when the loading is uniform along the full length of the beam, that is, $W(x) = $ constant, (2.62) may be readily solved by the normal techniques of integral calculus. However, when the loading is non-uniform, the use of Laplace transform methods has a distinct advantage, since by making use of Heaviside unit functions and impulse functions, the problem of solving (2.62) independently for various sections of the beam may be avoided.

Taking Laplace transforms throughout in (2.62) gives

$$EI[s^4Y(s) - s^3y(0) - s^2y_1(0) - sy_2(0) - y_3(0)] = -W(s) \qquad \textbf{(2.63)}$$

where

$$y_1(0) = \left(\frac{dy}{dx}\right)_{x=0}, \qquad y_2(0) = \left(\frac{d^2y}{dx^2}\right)_{x=0}, \qquad y_3(0) = \left(\frac{d^3y}{dx^3}\right)_{x=0}$$

and may be interpreted physically as follows:

$EIy_3(0)$ is the shear at $x = 0$

$EIy_2(0)$ is the bending moment at $x = 0$

$y_1(0)$ is the slope at $x = 0$

$y(0)$ is the deflection at $x = 0$

Solving (2.63) for $y(s)$ leads to

$$Y(s) = -\frac{W(s)}{EIs^4} + \frac{y(0)}{s} + \frac{y_1(0)}{s^2} + \frac{y_2(0)}{s^3} + \frac{y_3(0)}{s^4} \qquad \textbf{(2.64)}$$

Thus four boundary conditions need to be found, and ideally they should be the shear, bending moment, slope and deflection at $x = 0$. However, in practice these boundary conditions are not often available. While some of them are known, other boundary conditions are specified at points along the beam other than at $x = 0$, for example conditions at the far end, $x = l$, or conditions at possible points of support along the beam. That is, we are faced with a boundary-value problem rather than an initial-value problem.

To proceed, known conditions at $x = 0$ are inserted, while the other conditions among $y(0)$, $y_1(0)$, $y_2(0)$ and $y_3(0)$ that are not specified are carried forward as undetermined constants. Inverse transforms are taken throughout in (2.45) to obtain the deflection $y(x)$, and the outstanding undetermined constants are obtained using the boundary conditions specified at points along the beam other than at $x = 0$.

The boundary conditions are usually embodied in physical conditions such as the following:

(a) The beam is freely, or simply, supported at both ends, indicating that both the bending moments and deflection are zero at both ends, so that $y = d^2y/dx^2 = 0$ at both $x = 0$ and $x = l$.

(b) At both ends the beam is clamped, or built into a wall. Thus the beam is horizontal at both ends, so that $y = dy/dx = 0$ at both $x = 0$ and $x = l$.

(c) The beam is a cantilever with one end free (that is, fixed horizontally at one end, with the other end free). At the fixed end (say $x = 0$)

$$y = \frac{dy}{dx} = 0 \quad \text{at } x = 0$$

and at the free end ($x = l$), since both the shearing force and bending moment are zero,

$$\frac{d^2y}{dx^2} = \frac{d^3y}{dx^3} = 0 \quad \text{at } x = l$$

If the load is not uniform along the full length of the beam, use is made of Heaviside step functions and impulse functions in specifying $W(x)$ in (2.62). For example, a uniform load w per unit length over the portion of the beam $x = x_1$ to $x = x_2$ is specified as $wH(x - x_1) - wH(x - x_2)$, and a point load w at $x = x_1$ is specified as $w\delta(x - x_1)$.

EXAMPLE 2.49   Figure 2.40 illustrates a uniform beam of length l, freely supported at both ends, bending under uniformly distributed self-weight W and a concentrated point load P at $x = \frac{1}{3}l$. Determine the transverse deflection $y(x)$ of the beam.

Solution   As in Figure 2.39, the origin is taken at the left-hand end of the beam, and the deflection $y(x)$ measured upwards from the horizontal at the level of the supports. The deflection $y(x)$ is then given by (2.62), with the force function $W(x)$ having contributions from the weight W, the concentrated load P and the support reactions R_1 and R_2. However, since we are interested in solving (2.62) for $0 \leqslant x \leqslant l$, point loads or reactions at the end $x = l$ may be omitted from the force function.

Figure 2.40 Loaded beam of Example 2.49.

As a preliminary, we need to determine R_1. This is done by taking static moments about the end $x = l$, assuming the weight W to be concentrated at the centroid $x = \frac{1}{2}l$, giving

$$R_1 l = \tfrac{1}{2}Wl + P\tfrac{2}{3}l$$

or

$$R_1 = \tfrac{1}{2}W + \tfrac{2}{3}P$$

The force function $W(x)$ may then be expressed as

$$W(x) = \frac{W}{l}H(x) + P\delta(x - \tfrac{1}{3}l) - (\tfrac{1}{2}W + \tfrac{2}{3}P)\delta(x)$$

with a Laplace transform

$$W(s) = \frac{W}{ls} + Pe^{-ls/3} - (\tfrac{1}{2}W + \tfrac{2}{3}P)$$

Since the beam is freely supported at both ends, the deflection and bending moments are zero at both ends, so we take the boundary conditions as

$$y = 0 \quad \text{at } x = 0 \text{ and } x = l$$

$$\frac{d^2 y}{dx^2} = 0 \quad \text{at } x = 0 \text{ and } x = l$$

The transformed equation (2.64) becomes

$$Y(s) = \frac{1}{EI}\left[\frac{W}{ls^5} + \frac{P}{s^4}e^{-ls/3} - (\tfrac{1}{2}W + \tfrac{2}{3}P)\frac{1}{s^4}\right] + \frac{y_1(0)}{s^2} + \frac{y_3(0)}{s^4}$$

Taking inverse transforms, making use of the second shift theorem (Theorem 2.4), gives the deflection $y(x)$ as

$$y(x) = -\frac{1}{EI}\left[\frac{1}{24}\frac{W}{l}x^4 + \tfrac{1}{6}P(x - \tfrac{1}{3}l)^3 H(x - \tfrac{1}{3}l) - \tfrac{1}{6}(\tfrac{1}{2}W + \tfrac{2}{3}P)x^3\right]$$
$$+ y_1(0)x + \tfrac{1}{6}y_3(0)x^3$$

To obtain the value of the undetermined constants $y_1(0)$ and $y_3(0)$, we employ the unused boundary conditions at $x = l$, namely $y(l) = 0$ and $y_2(l) = 0$. For $x > \tfrac{1}{3}l$

$$y(x) = -\frac{1}{EI}\left[\frac{1}{24}\frac{W}{l}x^4 + \tfrac{1}{6}P(x - \tfrac{1}{3}l)^3 - \tfrac{1}{6}(\tfrac{1}{2}W + \tfrac{2}{3}P)x^3\right] + y_1(0)x + \tfrac{1}{6}y_3(0)x^3$$

$$\frac{d^2 y}{dx^2} = y_2(x) = -\frac{1}{EI}\left[\frac{Wx^2}{2l} + P(x - \tfrac{1}{3}l) - \left(\tfrac{1}{3}W + \frac{2P}{3}\right)x\right] + y_3(0)x$$

Thus taking $y_2(l) = 0$ gives $y_3(0) = 0$, and taking $y(l) = 0$ gives

$$-\frac{1}{EI}(\tfrac{1}{24}Wl^3 + \tfrac{4}{8}Pl^3 - \tfrac{1}{12}Wl^3 - \tfrac{1}{3}Pl^3) + y_1(0)l = 0$$

so that

$$y_1(0) = -\frac{l^2}{EI}(\tfrac{1}{24}W + \tfrac{5}{81}P)$$

Substituting back, we find that the deflection $y(x)$ is given by

$$y(x) = -\frac{W}{EI}\left(\frac{x^4}{24l} - \tfrac{1}{12}x^3 + \tfrac{1}{24}l^2x\right) - \frac{P}{EI}(\tfrac{5}{81}l^2x - \tfrac{1}{9}x^3)$$

$$-\frac{P}{6EI}(x - \tfrac{1}{3}l)^3 H(x - \tfrac{1}{3}l)$$

or, for the two sections of the beam,

$$y(x) = \begin{cases} -\dfrac{W}{EI}\left(\dfrac{x}{24l} - \tfrac{1}{12}x^3 + \tfrac{1}{24}l^2x\right) - \dfrac{P}{EI}(\tfrac{5}{81}l^2x - \tfrac{1}{9}x^3) & (0 < x < \tfrac{1}{3}l) \\[2ex] -\dfrac{W}{EI}\left(\dfrac{x^4}{24l} - \tfrac{1}{12}x^3 + \tfrac{1}{24}l^2x\right) \\[2ex] \quad -\dfrac{P}{EI}(\tfrac{19}{162}l^2x + \tfrac{1}{18}x^3 - \tfrac{1}{6}x^2l - \tfrac{1}{162}l^3) & (\tfrac{1}{3}l < x < l) \end{cases}$$

2.5.14 Exercises

31 Find the deflection of a beam simply supported at its ends $x = 0$ and $x = l$, bending under a uniformly distributed self-weight M and a concentrated load W at $x = \tfrac{1}{2}l$.

32 A cantilever beam of negligible weight and of length l is clamped at the end $x = 0$. Determine the deflection of the beam when it is subjected to a load

per unit length, w, over the section $x = x_1$ to $x = x_2$. What is the maximum deflection if $x_1 = 0$ and $x_2 = l$?

33 A uniform cantilever beam of length l is subjected to a concentrated load W at a point distance b from the fixed end. Determine the deflection of the beam, distinguishing between the sections $0 < x \leqslant b$ and $b < x \leqslant l$.

2.6 Transfer functions

2.6.1 Definitions

The **transfer function** of a linear time-invariant system is defined to be the ratio of the Laplace transform of the system output (or response function) to the Laplace transform of the system input (or forcing function), *under the assumption that all the initial conditions are zero* (that is, the system is initially in a **quiescent state**).

Transfer functions are frequently used in engineering to characterize the input–output relationships of linear time-invariant systems, and play an important role in the analysis and design of such systems.

Consider a linear time-invariant system characterized by the differential equation

$$a_n \frac{\mathrm{d}^n x}{\mathrm{d}t^n} + a_{n-1} \frac{\mathrm{d}^{n-1} x}{\mathrm{d}t^{n-1}} + \dots + a_0 x = b_m \frac{\mathrm{d}^m u}{\mathrm{d}t^m} + \dots + b_0 u \tag{2.65}$$

where $n \geqslant m$, the as and bs are constant coefficients, and $x(t)$ is the system response or output to the input or forcing term $u(t)$ applied at time $t = 0$. Taking Laplace transforms throughout in (2.65) will lead to the transformed equation. Since all the initial conditions are assumed to be zero, we see from (2.15) that, in order to obtain the transformed equation, we simply replace $\mathrm{d}/\mathrm{d}t$ by s, giving

$$(a_n s^n + a_{n-1} s^{n-1} + \dots + a_0) X(s) = (b_m s^m + \dots + b_0) U(s)$$

where $X(s)$ and $U(s)$ denote the Laplace transforms of $x(t)$ and $u(t)$ respectively.

The system transfer function $G(s)$ is then defined to be

$$G(s) = \frac{X(s)}{U(s)} = \frac{b_m s^m + \dots + b_0}{a_n s^n + \dots + a_0} \tag{2.66}$$

and the system may be represented diagrammatically by the operation box of Figure 2.41. This representation is referred to as the **input–output block diagram** representation of the system.

Writing

$$P(s) = b_m s^m + \dots + b_0$$

$$Q(s) = a_n s^n + \dots + a_0$$

Figure 2.41 Transfer function block diagram.

the transfer function may be expressed as

$$G(s) = \frac{P(s)}{Q(s)}$$

where, in order to make the system physically realizable, the degrees m and n of the polynomials $P(s)$ and $Q(s)$ must be such that $n \geqslant m$. This is because it follows from (2.61) that if $m > n$ then the system response $x(t)$ to a realistic input $u(t)$ will involve impulses.

The equation $Q(s) = 0$ is called the **characteristic equation** of the system; its order determines the **order of the system**, and its roots are referred to as the **poles** of the transfer function. Likewise, the roots of $P(s) = 0$ are referred to as the **zeros** of the transfer function.

It is important to realize that, in general, a transfer function is only used to characterize a linear time-invariant system. It is a property of the system itself, and is independent of both system input and output.

Although the transfer function characterizes the dynamics of the system, it provides no information concerning the actual physical structure of the system, and in fact systems that are physically different may have identical transfer functions; for example, the mass–spring–damper system of Figure 2.12 and the *LCR* circuit of Figure 2.8 both have the transfer function

$$G(s) = \frac{X(s)}{U(s)} = \frac{1}{\alpha s^2 + \beta s + \gamma}$$

In the mass–spring–damper system $X(s)$ determines the displacement $x(t)$ of the mass and $U(s)$ represents the applied force $F(t)$, while α denotes the mass, β the damping coefficient and γ the spring constant. On the other hand, in the *LCR* circuit $X(s)$ determines the charge $q(t)$ on the condenser and $U(s)$ represents the applied emf $e(t)$, while α denotes the inductance, β the resistance and γ the reciprocal of the capacitance.

In practice, an overall system may be made up of a number of components each characterized by its own transfer function and related operation box. The overall system input–output transfer function is then obtained by the rules of **block diagram algebra**.

Since $G(s)$ may be written as

$$G(s) = \frac{b_m}{a_m} \frac{(s - z_1)(s - z_2)\cdots(s - z_m)}{(s - p_1)(s - p_2)\cdots(s - p_n)}$$

where the z_is and p_is are the transfer function zeros and poles respectively, we observe that $G(s)$ is known, apart from a constant factor, if the positions of all the poles and zeros are known. Consequently, a plot of the poles and zeros of $G(s)$ is often used as an aid in the graphical analysis of the transfer function (a common convention is to mark the position of a zero by a circle $\circ$ and that of a pole by a cross $\times$). Since the coefficients of the polynomials $P(s)$ and $Q(s)$ are real, all complex roots always occur in complex conjugate pairs, so that the **pole–zero plot** is symmetrical about the real axis.

EXAMPLE 2.50 The response $x(t)$ of a system to a forcing function $u(t)$ is determined by the differential equation

$$9\frac{d^2x}{dt^2} + 12\frac{dx}{dt} + 13x = 2\frac{du}{dt} + 3u$$

(i) Determine the transfer function characterizing the system.

(ii) Write down the characteristic equation of the system. What is the order of the system?

(iii) Determine the transfer function poles and zeros, and illustrate them diagrammatically in the s plane.

Solution (i) Assuming all the initial conditions to be zero, taking Laplace transforms throughout in the differential equation

$$9\frac{d^2x}{dt^2} + 12\frac{dx}{dt} + 13x = 2\frac{du}{dt} + 3u$$

leads to

$$(9s^2 + 12s + 13)X(s) = (2s + 3)U(s)$$

so that the system transfer function is given by

$$G(s) = \frac{X(s)}{U(s)} = \frac{2s + 3}{9s^2 + 12s + 13}$$

(ii) The characteristic equation of the system is

$$9s^2 + 12s + 13 = 0$$

and the system is of order 2.

(iii) The transfer function poles are the roots of the characteristic equation

$$9s^2 + 12s + 13 = 0$$

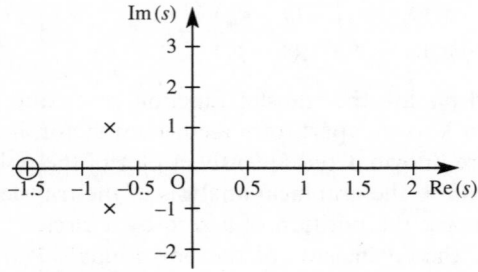

Figure 2.42 Pole ($\times$)–zero ($\bigcirc$) plot for Example 2.50.

which are

$$s = \frac{-12 \pm \sqrt{(144 - 468)}}{18} = -\frac{2 \pm j3}{3}$$

That is, the transfer function has simple poles at

$$s = -\tfrac{2}{3} + j \quad \text{and} \quad s = -\tfrac{2}{3} - j$$

The transfer function zeros are determined by equating the numerator polynomial $2s + 3$ to zero; that is,

$$2s + 3 = 0$$

so that the transfer function has a single zero at

$$s = -\tfrac{3}{2}$$

The corresponding pole–zero plot in the s plane is shown in Figure 2.42.

2.6.2   Stability

The stability of a system is a property of vital importance to engineers. Intuitively, we may regard a stable system as one that will remain at rest unless it is excited by an external source, and will return to rest if all such external influences are removed. Thus a stable system is one whose response, in the absence of an input, will approach zero as time approaches infinity. This then ensures that any bounded input produces a bounded output; this property is frequently taken to be the definition of a **stable linear system**.

Clearly, stability is a property of the system itself, and does not depend on the system input or forcing function. Since a system may be characterized in the s domain by its transfer function $G(s)$, it should be possible to use the transfer function to specify conditions for the system to be stable.

In considering the time response of

$$X(s) = G(s)U(s), \quad G(s) = \frac{P(s)}{Q(s)}$$

to any given input $u(t)$, it is necessary to factorize the denominator polynomial

$$Q(s) = a_n s^n + a_{n-1} s^{n-1} + \ldots + a_0$$

and various forms of factors can be involved.

Simple factor of the form s + α, with α real

This corresponds to a simple pole at $s = -\alpha$, and will in the partial-fractions expansion of $G(s)$ lead to a term of the form $c/(s + \alpha)$ having corresponding time response $c\,\mathrm{e}^{-\alpha t}H(t)$, using the strict form of the inverse given in (2.12). If $\alpha > 0$, so that the pole is in the left half of the s plane, the time response will tend to zero as $t \to \infty$. If $\alpha < 0$, so that the pole is in the right half of the s plane, the time response will increase without bound as $t \to \infty$. It follows that a stable system must have real-valued simple poles of $G(s)$ in the left half of the s plane.

$\alpha = 0$ corresponds to a simple pole at the origin, having a corresponding time response that is a step $cH(t)$. A system having such a pole is said to be **marginally stable**; this does not ensure that a bounded input will lead to a bounded output, since, for example, if such a system has an input that is a step d applied at time $t = 0$ then the response will be a ramp $cdtH(t)$, which is unbounded as $t \to \infty$.

Repeated simple factors of the form $(s + \alpha)^n$, with α real

This corresponds to a multiple pole at $s = -\alpha$, and will lead in the partial-fractions expansion of $G(s)$ to a term of the form $c/(s + \alpha)^n$ having corresponding time response $[c/(n - 1)!]t^{n-1}\,\mathrm{e}^{-\alpha t}H(t)$. Again the response will decay to zero as $t \to \infty$ only if $\alpha > 0$, indicating that a stable system must have all real-valued repeated poles of $G(s)$ in the left half of the s plane.

Quadratic factors of the form $(s + \alpha)^2 + \beta^2$, with α and β real

This corresponds to a pair of complex conjugate poles at $s = -\alpha + \mathrm{j}\beta, s = -\alpha - \mathrm{j}\beta$, and will lead in the partial-fractions expansion of $G(s)$ to a term of the form

$$\frac{c(s + \alpha) + d\beta}{(s + \alpha)^2 + \beta^2}$$

having corresponding time response

$$\mathrm{e}^{-\alpha t}(c \cos \beta t + d \sin \beta t) \equiv A\mathrm{e}^{-\alpha t}\sin(\beta t + \gamma)$$

where $A = \sqrt{(c^2 + d^2)}$ and $\gamma = \tan^{-1}(c/d)$.

Again we see that poles in the left half of the s plane (corresponding to $\alpha > 0$) have corresponding time responses that die away, in the form of an exponentially damped sinusoid, as $t \to \infty$. A stable system must therefore have complex conjugate poles located in the left half of the s plane; that is, all complex poles must have a negative real part.

If $\alpha = 0$, the corresponding time response will be a periodic sinusoid, which will not die away as $t \to \infty$. Again this corresponds to a marginally stable system, and will, for example, give rise to a response that increases without bound as $t \to \infty$ when the input is a sinusoid at the same frequency β.

A summary of the responses corresponding to the various types of poles is given in Figure 2.43.

The concept of stability may be expressed in the form of Definition 2.3.

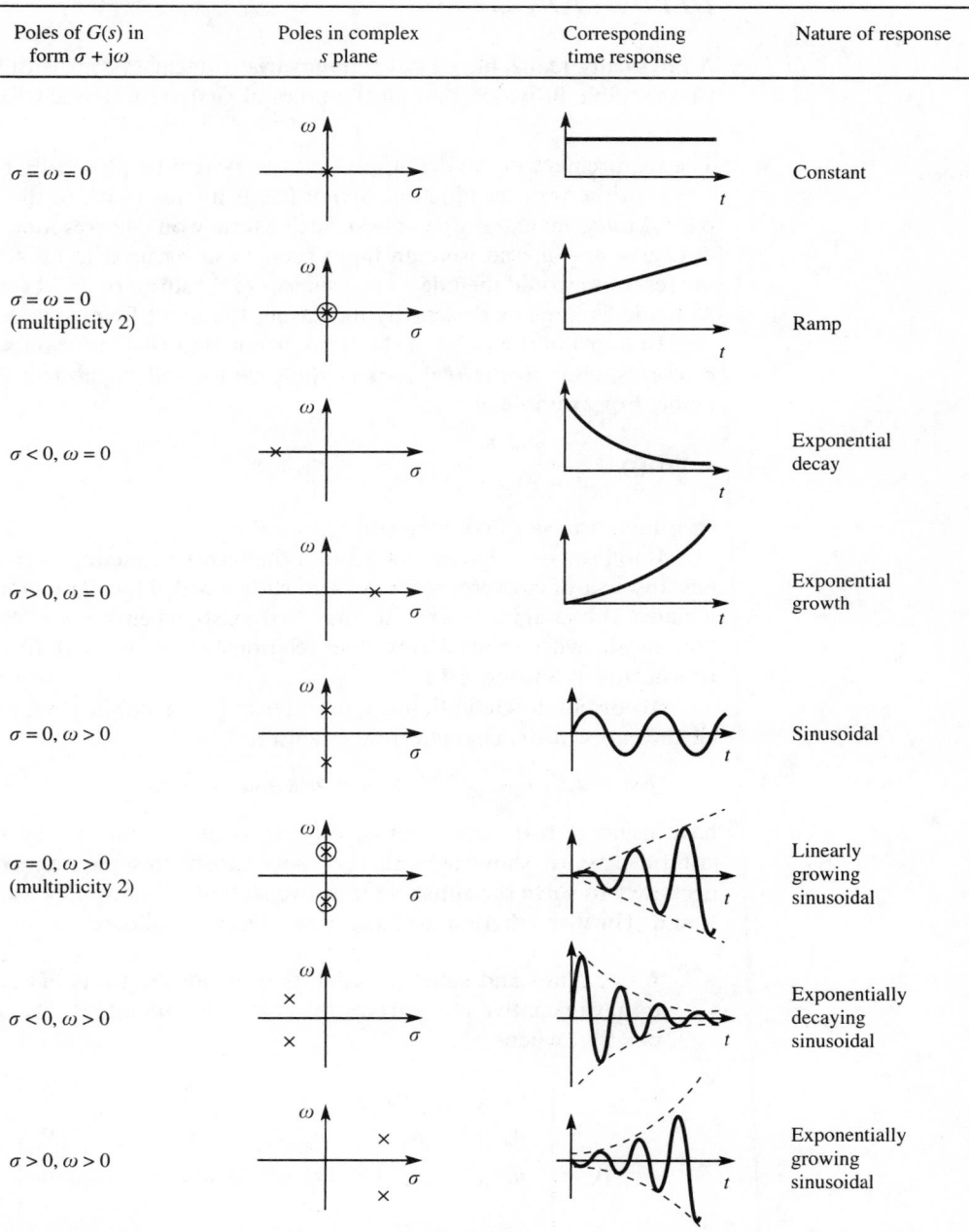

Poles of $G(s)$ in form $\sigma + j\omega$	Poles in complex s plane	Corresponding time response	Nature of response
$\sigma = \omega = 0$			Constant
$\sigma = \omega = 0$ (multiplicity 2)			Ramp
$\sigma < 0, \omega = 0$			Exponential decay
$\sigma > 0, \omega = 0$			Exponential growth
$\sigma = 0, \omega > 0$			Sinusoidal
$\sigma = 0, \omega > 0$ (multiplicity 2)			Linearly growing sinusoidal
$\sigma < 0, \omega > 0$			Exponentially decaying sinusoidal
$\sigma > 0, \omega > 0$			Exponentially growing sinusoidal

Figure 2.43 Relationship between transfer function poles and time response.

DEFINITION 2.3

A physically realizable causal time-invariant linear system with transfer function $G(s)$ is stable provided that all the poles of $G(s)$ are in the left half of the s plane.

The requirement in the definition that the system be physically realizable, that is, $n \geqslant m$ in the transfer function $G(s)$ of (2.66), avoids terms of the form s^{m-n} in the partial-fractions expansion of $G(s)$. Such a term would correspond to differentiation of degree $m - n$, and were an input such as $\sin \omega t$ used to excite the system then the response would include a term such as $\omega^{m-n} \sin \omega t$ or $\omega^{m-n} \cos \omega t$, which could be made as large as desired by increasing the input frequency ω.

In terms of the poles of the transfer function $G(s)$, its abscissa of convergence σ_c corresponds to the real part of the pole located furthest to the right in the s plane. For example, if

$$G(s) = \frac{s + 1}{(s + 3)(s + 2)}$$

then the abscissa of convergence $\sigma_c = -2$.

It follows from Definition 2.3 that the transfer function $G(s)$ of a stable system has abscissa of convergence $\sigma_c = -\alpha$, with $\alpha > 0$. Thus its region of convergence includes the imaginary axis, so that $G(s)$ exists when $s = j\omega$. We shall return to this result when considering the relationship between Laplace and Fourier transforms in Section 5.4.1.

According to Definition 2.3, in order to prove stability, we need to show that all the roots of the characteristic equation

$$Q(s) = a_n s^n + a_{n-1} s^{n-1} + \ldots + a_1 s + a_0 = 0 \tag{2.67}$$

have negative real parts (that is, they lie in the left half of the s plane). Various criteria exist to show that all the roots satisfy this requirement, and it is not necessary to solve the equation to prove stability. One widely used criterion is the **Routh–Hurwitz criterion**, which can be stated as follows:

A necessary and sufficient condition for all the roots of equation (2.67) to have negative real parts is that the determinants $\Delta_1, \Delta_2, \ldots, \Delta_n$ are all positive, where

$$\Delta_r = \begin{vmatrix} a_{n-1} & a_n & 0 & 0 & \cdots & 0 \\ a_{n-3} & a_{n-2} & a_{n-1} & a_n & \cdots & 0 \\ a_{n-5} & a_{n-4} & a_{n-3} & a_{n-2} & \cdots & 0 \\ \vdots & \vdots & \vdots & \vdots & & \vdots \\ a_{n-(2r-1)} & a_{n-2r} & a_{n-2r-1} & a_{n-2r-2} & \cdots & a_{n-r} \end{vmatrix} \tag{2.68}$$

it being understood that in each determinant all the as with subscripts that are either negative or greater than n are to be replaced by zero.

EXAMPLE 2.51   Show that the roots of the characteristic equation

$$s^4 + 9s^3 + 33s^2 + 51s + 26 = 0$$

all have negative real parts.

Solution   In this case $n = 4$, $a_0 = 26$, $a_1 = 51$, $a_2 = 33$, $a_3 = 9$, $a_4 = 1$ and $a_r = 0$ $(r > 4)$. The determinants of the Routh–Hurwitz criterion are

$$\Delta_1 = |a_{n-1}| = |a_3| = |9| = 9 > 0$$

$$\Delta_2 = \begin{vmatrix} a_{n-1} & a_n \\ a_{n-3} & a_{n-2} \end{vmatrix} = \begin{vmatrix} a_3 & a_4 \\ a_1 & a_2 \end{vmatrix} = \begin{vmatrix} 9 & 1 \\ 51 & 33 \end{vmatrix} = 246 > 0$$

$$\Delta_3 = \begin{vmatrix} a_{n-1} & a_n & 0 \\ a_{n-3} & a_{n-2} & a_{n-1} \\ a_{n-5} & a_{n-4} & a_{n-3} \end{vmatrix} = \begin{vmatrix} a_3 & a_4 & 0 \\ a_1 & a_2 & a_3 \\ a_{-1} & a_0 & a_1 \end{vmatrix} = \begin{vmatrix} 9 & 1 & 0 \\ 51 & 33 & 9 \\ 0 & 26 & 51 \end{vmatrix} = 10\,440 > 0$$

$$\Delta_4 = \begin{vmatrix} a_{n-1} & a_n & 0 & 0 \\ a_{n-3} & a_{n-2} & a_{n-1} & a_n \\ a_{n-5} & a_{n-4} & a_{n-3} & a_{n-2} \\ a_{n-7} & a_{n-6} & a_{n-5} & a_{n-4} \end{vmatrix} = \begin{vmatrix} a_3 & a_4 & 0 & 0 \\ a_1 & a_2 & a_3 & a_4 \\ a_{-1} & a_0 & a_1 & a_2 \\ a_{-3} & a_{-2} & a_{-1} & a_0 \end{vmatrix}$$

$$= \begin{vmatrix} 9 & 1 & 0 & 0 \\ 51 & 33 & 9 & 1 \\ 0 & 26 & 51 & 37 \\ 0 & 0 & 0 & 26 \end{vmatrix} = 26\Delta_3 > 0$$

Thus $\Delta_1 > 0$, $\Delta_2 > 0$, $\Delta_3 > 0$ and $\Delta_4 > 0$, so that all the roots of the given characteristic equation have negative real parts. This is readily checked, since the roots are -2, -1, $-3 + j2$ and $-3 - j2$.

EXAMPLE 2.52   The steady motion of a steam-engine governor is modelled by the differential equations

$$m\ddot{\eta} + b\dot{\eta} + d\eta - e\omega = 0 \tag{2.69}$$

$$I_0\dot{\omega} = -f\eta \tag{2.70}$$

where η is a small fluctuation in the angle of inclination, ω a small fluctuation in the angular velocity of rotation, and m, b, d, e, f and I_0 are all positive constants. Show that the motion of the governor is stable provided that

$$\frac{bd}{m} > \frac{ef}{I_0}$$

Solution   Differentiating (2.69) gives

$$m\ddot{\eta} + b\ddot{\eta} + d\dot{\eta} - e\dot{\omega} = 0$$

which, on using (2.70), leads to

$$m\ddot{\eta} + b\ddot{\eta} + d\dot{\eta} + \frac{ef}{I_0}\eta = 0$$

for which the corresponding characteristic equation is

$$ms^3 + bs^2 + ds + \frac{ef}{I_0} = 0$$

This is a cubic polynomial, so the parameters of (2.67) are

$$n = 3, \quad a_0 = \frac{ef}{I_0}, \quad a_1 = d, \quad a_2 = b, \quad a_3 = m \quad (a_r = 0, r > 3)$$

The determinants (2.68) of the Routh–Hurwitz criterion are

$$\Delta_1 = |a_2| = b > 0$$

$$\Delta_2 = \begin{vmatrix} a_2 & a_3 \\ a_0 & a_1 \end{vmatrix} = \begin{vmatrix} b & m \\ ef/I_0 & d \end{vmatrix} = bd - \frac{mef}{I_0}$$

(and so $\Delta_2 > 0$ provided that $bd - mef/I_0 > 0$ or $bd/m > ef/I_0$), and

$$\Delta_3 = \begin{vmatrix} a_2 & a_3 & 0 \\ a_0 & a_1 & a_2 \\ 0 & 0 & a_0 \end{vmatrix} = a_0\Delta_2 > 0 \quad \text{if } \Delta_2 > 0$$

Thus the action of the governor is stable provided that $\Delta_2 > 0$; that is,

$$\frac{bd}{m} > \frac{ef}{I_0}$$

2.6.3   Impulse response

From (2.66), we find that for a system having transfer function $G(s)$ the response $x(t)$ of the system, initially in a quiescent state, to an input $u(t)$ is determined by the transformed relationship

$$X(s) = G(s)U(s)$$

If the input $u(t)$ is taken to be the unit impulse function $\delta(t)$ then the system response will be determined by

$$X(s) = G(s)\mathscr{L}\{\delta(t)\} = G(s)$$

Taking inverse Laplace transforms leads to the corresponding time response $h(t)$, which is called the **impulse response** of the system (it is also sometimes referred to as the **weighting function** of the system); that is, the impulse response is given by

$$h(t) = \mathscr{L}^{-1}\{X(s)\} = \mathscr{L}^{-1}\{G(s)\} \tag{2.71}$$

We therefore have the following definition.

DEFINITION 2.4: Impulse response

The impulse response $h(t)$ of a linear time-invariant system is the response of the system to a unit impulse applied at time $t = 0$ when all the initial conditions are zero. It is such that $\mathscr{L}\{h(t)\} = G(s)$, where $G(s)$ is the system transfer function.

Since the impulse response is the inverse Laplace transform of the transfer function, it follows that both the impulse response and the transfer function carry the same information about the dynamics of a linear time-invariant system. Theoretically, therefore, it is possible to determine the complete information about the system by exciting it with an impulse and measuring the response. For this reason, it is common practice in engineering to regard the transfer function as being the Laplace transform of the impulse response, since this places greater emphasis on the parameters of the system when considering system design.

We saw in Section 2.6.2 that, since the transfer function $G(s)$ completely characterizes a linear time-invariant system, it can be used to specify conditions for system stability, which are that all the poles of $G(s)$ lie in the left half of the s plane. Alternatively, characterizing the system by its impulse response, we can say that the system is stable provided that its impulse response decays to zero as $t \rightarrow \infty$.

EXAMPLE 2.53   Determine the impulse response of the linear system whose response $x(t)$ to an input $u(t)$ is determined by the differential equation

$$\frac{d^2 x}{dt^2} + 5\frac{dx}{dt} + 6x = 5u(t) \tag{2.72}$$

Solution   The impulse response $h(t)$ is the system response to $u(t) = \delta(t)$ when all the initial conditions are zero. It is therefore determined as the solution of the differential equation

$$\frac{d^2 h}{dt^2} + 5\frac{dh}{dt} + 6h = 5\delta(t) \tag{2.73}$$

subject to the initial conditions $h(0) = \dot{h}(0) = 0$. Taking Laplace transforms in (2.73) gives

$$(s^2 + 5s + 6)H(s) = 5\mathscr{L}\{\delta(t)\} = 5$$

so that

$$H(s) = \frac{5}{(s+3)(s+2)} = \frac{5}{s+2} - \frac{5}{s+3}$$

which, on inversion, gives the desired impulse response

$$h(t) = 5(e^{-2t} - e^{-3t})$$

Alternatively, the transfer function $G(s)$ of the system determined by (2.72) is

$$G(s) = \frac{5}{s^2 + 5s + 6}$$

so that $h(t) = \mathscr{L}^{-1}\{G(s)\} = 5(e^{-2t} - e^{-3t})$ as before.

2.6.4   Initial- and final-value theorems

The initial- and final-value theorems are two useful theorems that enable us to predict system behaviour as $t \to 0$ and $t \to \infty$ without actually inverting Laplace transforms.

THEOREM 2.6   The initial-value theorem

If $f(t)$ and $f'(t)$ are both Laplace-transformable and if $\lim_{s \to \infty} sF(s)$ exists then

$$\lim_{t \to 0+} f(t) = f(0+) = \lim_{s \to \infty} sF(s)$$

Proof   From (2.13),

$$\mathscr{L}\{f'(t)\} = \int_{0-}^{\infty} f'(t) e^{-st}\, dt = sF(s) - f(0-)$$

where we have highlighted the fact that the lower limit is $0-$. Hence

$$\lim_{s \to \infty} [sF(s) - f(0-)] = \lim_{s \to \infty} \int_{0-}^{\infty} f'(t) e^{-st}\, dt$$

$$= \lim_{s \to \infty} \int_{0-}^{0+} f'(t) e^{-st}\, dt + \lim_{s \to \infty} \int_{0+}^{\infty} f'(t) e^{-st}\, dt \quad \textbf{(2.74)}$$

If $f(t)$ is discontinuous at the origin, so that $f(0+) \neq f(0-)$, then, from (2.59), $f'(t)$ contains an impulse term $[f(0+) - f(0-)]\delta(t)$, so that

$$\lim_{s \to \infty} \int_{0-}^{0+} f'(t) e^{-st}\, dt = f(0+) - f(0-)$$

Also, since the Laplace transform of $f'(t)$ exists, it is of exponential order and we have

$$\lim_{s \to \infty} \int_{0+}^{\infty} f'(t)\,e^{-st}\,dt = 0$$

so that (2.74) becomes

$$\lim_{s \to \infty} sF(s) - f(0-) = f(0+) - f(0-)$$

giving the required result:

$$\lim_{s \to \infty} sF(s) = f(0+)$$

If $f(t)$ is continuous at the origin then $f'(t)$ does not contain an impulse term, and the right-hand side of (2.74) is zero, giving

$$\lim_{s \to \infty} sF(s) = f(0-) = f(0+) \qquad \square$$

It is important to recognize that the initial-value theorem does not give the initial value $f(0-)$ used when determining the Laplace transform, but rather gives the value of $f(t)$ as $t \to 0+$. This distinction is highlighted in the following example.

EXAMPLE 2.54   The circuit of Figure 2.44 consists of a resistance R and a capacitance C connected in series together with constant voltage source E. Prior to closing the switch at time $t = 0$, both the charge on the capacitor and the resulting current in the circuit are zero. Determine the current $i(t)$ in the circuit at time t after the switch is closed, and investigate the use of the initial-value theorem.

Solution   Applying Kirchhoff's law to the circuit of Figure 2.44, we have

$$Ri + \frac{1}{C} \int i\,dt = E_0$$

which, on taking Laplace transforms, gives the transformed equation

$$RI(s) + \frac{1}{c}\frac{I(s)}{s} = \frac{E_0}{s}$$

Therefore

$$I(s) = \frac{E_0/R}{s + 1/RC}$$

Figure 2.44 RC circuit of Example 2.54.

Taking inverse transforms gives the current $i(t)$ at $t \geq 0$ as

$$i(t) = \frac{E_0}{R} e^{-t/RC} \qquad (2.75)$$

Applying the initial-value theorem,

$$\lim_{t \to 0+} i(t) = \lim_{s \to \infty} sI(s) = \lim_{s \to \infty} \frac{sE_0/R}{s + 1/RC}$$

$$= \lim_{s \to \infty} \frac{E_0/R}{1 + 1/RCs} = \frac{E_0}{R}$$

That is,

$$i(0+) = \frac{E_0}{R}$$

a result that is readily confirmed by allowing $t \to 0+$ in (2.75). We note that this is not the same as the initial state $i(0) = 0$ owing to the fact that there is a step change in $i(t)$ at $t = 0$.

THEOREM 2.7   The final-value theorem

If $f(t)$ and $f'(t)$ are both Laplace-transformable and $\lim_{t \to \infty} f(t)$ exists then

$$\lim_{t \to \infty} f(t) = \lim_{s \to 0} sF(s)$$

Proof   From (2.13),

$$\mathscr{L}\{f'(t)\} = \int_{0-}^{\infty} f'(t) e^{-st} \, dt = sF(s) - f(0-)$$

Taking limits, we have

$$\lim_{s \to 0} [sF(s) - f(0-)] = \lim_{s \to 0} \int_{0-}^{\infty} f'(t) e^{-st} \, dt$$

$$= \int_{0-}^{\infty} f'(t) \, dt = [f(t)]_{0-}^{\infty}$$

$$= \lim_{t \to \infty} f(t) - f(0-)$$

giving the required result:

$$\lim_{t \to \infty} f(t) = \lim_{s \to 0} sF(s) \qquad \square$$

The restriction that $\lim_{t \to \infty} f(t)$ must exist means that the theorem does not hold for functions such as e^t, which tends to infinity as $t \to \infty$, or $\sin \omega t$, whose limit is undefined. Since in practice the final-value theorem is used to obtain the behaviour of $f(t)$ as $t \to \infty$ from knowledge of the transform $F(s)$, it is more common to express the restriction in terms of restrictions on $F(s)$, which are that $sF(s)$ must have all its poles in the left half of the s plane; that is, $sF(s)$ must represent a stable transfer function. It is important that the theorem be used with caution and that this restriction be fully recognized, since the existence of $\lim_{s \to 0} sF(s)$ does *not* imply that $f(s)$ has a limiting value as $t \to \infty$.

EXAMPLE 2.55   Investigate the application of the final-value theorem to the transfer function

$$F(s) = \frac{1}{(s+2)(s-3)} \tag{2.76}$$

Solution $$\lim_{s \to \infty} sF(s) = \lim_{s \to \infty} \frac{s}{(s+2)(s-3)} = 0$$

so the use of the final-value theorem implies that for the time function $f(t)$ corresponding to $F(s)$ we have

$$\lim_{t \to \infty} f(t) = 0$$

However, taking inverse transforms in (2.76) gives

$$f(t) = \frac{1}{s}(e^{3t} - e^{-2t})$$

implying that $f(t)$ tends to infinity as $t \to \infty$. This implied contradiction arises since the theorem is not valid in this case. Although $\lim_{s \to 0} sF(s)$ exists, $sF(s)$ has a pole at $s = 3$, which is not in the left half of the s plane.

The final-value theorem provides a useful vehicle for determining a system's **steady-state gain (SSG)** and the **steady-state errors**, or **offsets**, in feedback control systems, both of which are important features in control system design.

The SSG of a stable system is the system's steady-state response, that is, the response as $t \to \infty$, to a unit step input. For a system with transfer function $G(s)$ we have, from (2.66), that its response $x(t)$ is related to the input $u(t)$ by the transformed equation

$$X(s) = G(s)U(s)$$

For a unit step input

$$u(t) = 1H(t)$$

giving

$$U(s) = \frac{1}{s}$$

so that

$$X(s) = \frac{G(s)}{s}$$

From the final-value theorem, the steady-state gain is

$$\text{SSG} = \lim_{t \to \infty} x(t) = \lim_{s \to 0} sX(s) = \lim_{s \to 0} G(s)$$

EXAMPLE 2.56   Determine the steady-state gain of a system having transfer function

$$G(s) = \frac{20(1 + 3s)}{s^2 + 7s + 10}$$

Solution   The response $x(t)$ to a unit step input $u(t) = 1H(t)$ is given by the transformed equation

$$X(s) = G(s)U(s)$$
$$= \frac{20(1 + 3s)}{s^2 + 7s + 10} \frac{1}{s}$$

Then, by the final-value theorem, the steady-state gain is given by

$$\text{SSG} = \lim_{t \to \infty} x(t) = \lim_{s \to 0} sX(s)$$
$$= \lim_{s \to 0} \frac{20(1 + 3s)}{s^2 + 7s + 10} = 2$$

Note that for a step input of magnitude K, that is, $u(t) = KH(t)$, the steady-state response will be $\lim_{s \to 0} kG(s) = 2K$; that is,

steady-state response to step input = SSG × magnitude of step input

---

A unity feedback control system having forward-path transfer function $G(s)$, reference input or desired output $r(t)$ and actual output $x(t)$ is illustrated by the block diagram of Figure 2.45. Defining the error to be $e(t) = r(t) - y(t)$, it follows that

$$G(s)E(s) = X(s) = R(s) - E(s)$$

Figure 2.45 Unity feedback control system.

giving

$$E(s) = \frac{R(s)}{1 + G(s)}$$

Thus, from the final-value theorem, the steady-state error (SSE) is

$$\text{SSE} = \lim_{t \to \infty} e(t) = \lim_{s \to 0} sE(s) = \lim_{s \to 0} \frac{sR(s)}{1 + G(s)} \qquad (2.77)$$

EXAMPLE 2.57   Determine the SSE for the system of Figure 2.45 when $G(s)$ is the same as in Example 2.50 and $r(t)$ is a step of magnitude K.

Solution   Since $r(t) = KH(t)$, we have $R(s) = K/s$, so, using (2.77),

$$\text{SSE} = \lim_{s \to 0} \frac{sK/s}{1 + G(s)} = \frac{K}{1 + \text{SSG}}$$

where SSG $= 2$ as determined in Example 2.56. Thus

$$\text{SSE} = \tfrac{1}{2}K$$

It is clear from Example 2.57 that if we are to reduce the SSE, which is clearly desirable in practice, then the SSG needs to be increased. However, such an increase could lead to an undesirable transient response, and in system design a balance must be achieved. Detailed design techniques for alleviating such problems are not considered here; for such a discussion the reader is referred to specialist texts (see for example J. Schwarzenbach and K. F. Gill, *System Modelling and Control*, Edward Arnold, London, 1984).

2.6.5   Exercises

34 The response $x(t)$ of a system to a forcing function $u(t)$ is determined by the differential equation model

$$\frac{d^2x}{dt^2} + 2\frac{dx}{dt} + 5x = 3\frac{du}{dt} + 2u$$

(a) Determine the transfer function characterizing the system.

(b) Write down the characteristic equation of the system. What is the order of the system?

(c) Determine the transfer function poles and zeros, and illustrate them diagrammatically in the s plane.

35 Repeat Exercise 34 for a system whose response $x(t)$ to an input $u(t)$ is determined by the differential equation

$$\frac{d^3x}{dt^3} + 5\frac{d^2x}{dt^2} + 17\frac{dx}{dt} + 13x = \frac{d^2u}{dt^2} + 5\frac{du}{dt} + 6$$

36 Which of the following transfer functions represent stable systems and which represent unstable systems?

(a) $\dfrac{s - 1}{(s + 2)(s^2 + 4)}$ (b) $\dfrac{(s + 2)(s - 2)}{(s + 1)(s - 1)(s + 4)}$

(c) $\dfrac{s-1}{(s+2)(s+4)}$ (d) $\dfrac{6}{(s^2+s+1)(s+1)^2}$

(e) $\dfrac{5(s+10)}{(s+5)(s^2-s+10)}$

37 Which of the following characteristic equations are representative of stable systems?

(a) $s^2 - 4s + 13 = 0$

(b) $5s^3 + 13s^2 + 31s + 15 = 0$

(c) $s^3 + s^2 + s + 1 = 0$

(d) $24s^4 + 11s^3 + 26s^2 + 45s + 36 = 0$

(e) $s^3 + 2s^2 + 2s + 1 = 0$

38 The differential equation governing the motion of a mass–spring–damper system with controller is

$$m\frac{d^3x}{dt^3} + c\frac{d^2x}{dt^2} + k\frac{dx}{dt} + Krx = 0$$

where m, c, K and r are constants. Show that the motion of the system is stable provided that $r < c/m$.

39 The behaviour of a system having a gain controller is characterized by the characteristic equation

$$s^4 + 2s^3 + (K+2)s^2 + 7s + K = 0$$

where K is the controller gain. Show that the system is stable provided that $K > 2.1$.

40 A feedback control system has characteristic equation

$$s^3 + 15Ks^2 + (2K-1)s + 5K = 0$$

where K is a constant gain factor. Determine the range of positive values of K for which the system will be stable.

41 Determine the impulse responses of the linear systems whose response $x(t)$ to an input $u(t)$ is determined by the following differential equations:

(a) $\dfrac{d^2x}{dt^2} + 15\dfrac{dx}{dt} + 56x = 3u(t)$

(b) $\dfrac{d^2x}{dt^2} + 8\dfrac{dx}{dt} + 25x = u(t)$

(c) $\dfrac{d^2x}{dt^2} - 2\dfrac{dx}{dt} - 8x = 4u(t)$

(d) $\dfrac{d^2x}{dt^2} - 4\dfrac{dx}{dt} + 13x = u(t)$

What can be said about the stability of each of the systems?

42 The response of a given system to a unit step $u(t) = 1H(t)$ is given by

$$x(t) = 1 - \tfrac{7}{3}e^{-t} + \tfrac{3}{2}e^{-2t} - \tfrac{1}{6}e^{-4t}$$

What is the transfer function of the system?

43 Verify the initial-value theorem for the functions

(a) $2 - 3\cos t$ (b) $(3t-1)^2$ (c) $t + 3\sin 2t$

44 Verify the final-value theorem for the functions

(a) $1 + 3e^{-t}\sin 2t$ (b) t^2e^{-2t}

(c) $3 - 2e^{-3t} + e^{-t}\cos 2t$

45 Using the final-value theorem, check the value obtained for $i_2(t)$ as $t \to \infty$ for the circuit of Example 2.27.

46 Discuss the applicability of the final-value theorem for obtaining the value of $i_2(t)$ as $t \to \infty$ for the circuit of Example 2.28.

47 Use the initial- and final-value theorems to find the jump at $t = 0$ and the limiting value as $t \to \infty$ for the solution of the initial-value problem

$$7\frac{dy}{dt} + 5y = 4 + e^{-3t} + 2\delta(t)$$

with $y(0-) = -1$.

2.6.6   Convolution

Convolution is a useful concept that has many applications in various fields of engineering. In Section 2.6.7 we shall use it to obtain the response of a linear system to any input in terms of the impulse response.

DEFINITION 2.5: *Convolution*

Given two piecewise-continuous functions $f(t)$ and $g(t)$, the **convolution** of $f(t)$ and $g(t)$, denoted by $f * g(t)$, is defined as

$$f * g(t) = \int_{-\infty}^{\infty} f(\tau)g(t - \tau)\,d\tau$$

In the particular case when $f(t)$ and $g(t)$ are causal functions

$$f(\tau) = g(\tau) = 0 \quad (\tau < 0), \qquad g(t - \tau) = 0 \quad (\tau > t)$$

and we have

$$f * g(t) = \int_0^t f(\tau)g(t - \tau)\,d\tau \tag{2.78}$$

The notation $f * g(t)$ indicates that the convolution $f * g$ is a function of t; that is, it could also be written as $(f * g)(t)$. The integral $\int_{-\infty}^{\infty} f(\tau)g(t - \tau)\,d\tau$ is called the **convolution integral**. Alternative names are the **superposition integral**, **Duhamel integral**, **folding integral** and **faltung integral**.

Convolution can be considered as a generalized function, and as such it has many of the properties of multiplication. In particular, the commutative law is satisfied, so that

$$f * g(t) = g * f(t)$$

or, for causal functions,

$$\int_0^t f(\tau)g(t - \tau)\,d\tau = \int_0^t f(t - \tau)g(\tau)\,d\tau \tag{2.79}$$

This means that the convolution can be evaluated by time-shifting either of the two functions. The result (2.79) is readily proved, since by making the substitution $\tau_1 = t - \tau$ in (2.78) we obtain

$$f * g(t) = \int_t^0 f(t - \tau_1)g(\tau_1)(-d\tau_1)$$

$$= \int_0^t f(t - \tau_1)g(\tau_1)\,d\tau_1 = g * f(t)$$

EXAMPLE 2.58   For the two causal functions

$$f(t) = tH(t), \qquad g(t) = \sin 2t\, H(t)$$

show that $f * g(t) = g * f(t)$.

Solution
$$f * g(t) = \int_0^t f(\tau)g(t - \tau)\,d\tau$$

$$= \int_0^t \tau \sin 2(t - \tau)\,d\tau$$

Integrating by parts gives

$$f * g(t) = [\tfrac{1}{2}\tau \cos 2(t - \tau) + \tfrac{1}{4}\sin 2(t - \tau)]_0^t$$
$$= \tfrac{1}{2}t - \tfrac{1}{4}\sin 2t$$

$$g * f(t) = \int_0^t f(t - \tau)g(\tau)\,d\tau$$

$$= \int_0^t (t - \tau)\sin 2\tau\,d\tau$$

$$= [-\tfrac{1}{2}(t - \tau)\cos 2\tau - \tfrac{1}{4}\sin 2\tau]_0^t$$
$$= \tfrac{1}{2}t - \tfrac{1}{4}\sin 2t$$

so that $f * g(t) = g * f(t)$.

The importance of convolution in Laplace transform work is that it enables us to obtain the inverse transform of the product of two transforms. The necessary result for doing this is contained in the following theorem.

THEOREM 2.8   Convolution theorem for Laplace transforms

If $f(t)$ and $g(t)$ are of exponential order σ, piecewise-continuous on $t \geq 0$ and have Laplace transforms $F(s)$ and $G(s)$ respectively, then, for $s > \sigma$

$$\mathcal{L}\left\{\int_0^t f(t)g(t - \tau)\,dt\right\} = \mathcal{L}\{f * g(t)\} = F(s)G(s)$$

or, in the more useful inverse form,

$$\mathcal{L}^{-1}\{F(s)G(s)\} = f * g(t) \tag{2.80}$$

Proof   By definition,

$$F(s)G(s) = \mathcal{L}\{f(t)\}\mathcal{L}\{g(t)\} = \left[\int_0^\infty e^{-sx}f(x)\,dx\right]\left[\int_0^\infty e^{-sy}g(y)\,dy\right]$$

where we have used the 'dummy' variables x and y, rather than t, in the integrals to avoid confusion. This may now be expressed in the form of the double integral

$$F(s)G(s) = \int_0^\infty \int_0^\infty e^{-s(x+y)}f(x)g(y)\,dx\,dy$$

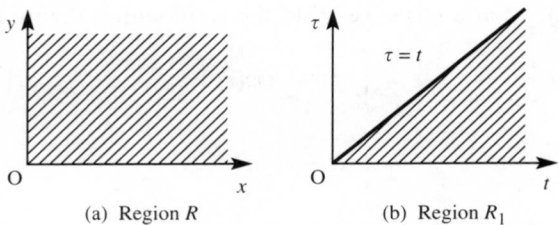

(a) Region R　　　　　(b) Region R_1

Figure 2.46 Regions of integration.

$$= \iint\limits_{R} e^{-s(x+y)} f(x)g(y)\,dx\,dy$$

where R is the the first quadrant in the (x, y) plane, as shown in Figure 2.46(a). On making the substitution

$$x + y = t, \qquad y = \tau$$

the double integral is transformed into

$$F(s)G(s) = \iint\limits_{R_1} e^{-st} f(t - \tau)g(\tau)\,dt\,d\tau$$

where R_1 is the semi-infinite region in the (τ, t) plane bounded by the lines $\tau = 0$ and $\tau = t$, as shown in Figure 2.46(b). This may be written as

$$F(s)G(s) = \int_0^\infty e^{-st} \left(\int_0^t f(t - \tau)g(\tau)\,d\tau \right) dt$$

$$= \int_0^\infty e^{-st} [g * f(t)]\,dt$$

$$= \mathscr{L}\{g * f(t)\}$$

and, since convolution is commutative, we may write this as

$$F(s)G(s) = \mathscr{L}\{f * g(t)\}$$

which concludes the proof.　　　　　　　　　　　　　　　　　　$\square$

EXAMPLE 2.59　Using the convolution theorem, determine $\mathscr{L}^{-1}\left\{\dfrac{1}{s^2(s + 2)^2}\right\}$.

Solution　We express $1/s^2(s + 2)^2$ as $(1/s^2)[1/(s + 2)^2]$; then, since

$$\mathscr{L}\{t\} = \frac{1}{s^2}, \qquad \mathscr{L}\{t\,e^{-2t}\} = \frac{1}{(s + 2)^2}$$

taking $f(t) = t$ and $g(t) = t\,e^{-2t}$ in the convolution theorem gives

$$\mathscr{L}^{-1}\left\{\frac{1}{s^2}\frac{1}{(s+2)^2}\right\} = \int_0^t f(t-\tau)g(\tau)\,\mathrm{d}\tau$$

$$= \int_0^t (t-\tau)\tau\,e^{-2\tau}\,\mathrm{d}\tau$$

which on integration by parts gives

$$\mathscr{L}^{-1}\left\{\frac{1}{s^2}\frac{1}{(s+2)^2}\right\} = [-\tfrac{1}{2}e^{-2\tau}[(t-\tau)\tau + \tfrac{1}{2}(t-2\tau) - \tfrac{1}{2}]]_0^t$$

$$= \tfrac{1}{4}[t - 1 + (t+1)e^{-2t}]$$

We can check this result by first expressing the given transform in partial-fractions form and then inverting to give

$$\frac{1}{s^2(s+2)^2} = \frac{-\tfrac{1}{4}}{s} + \frac{\tfrac{1}{4}}{s^2} + \frac{\tfrac{1}{4}}{s+2} + \frac{\tfrac{1}{4}}{(s+2)^2}$$

so that

$$\mathscr{L}^{-1}\left\{\frac{1}{s^2(s+2)^2}\right\} = -\tfrac{1}{4} + \tfrac{1}{4}t + \tfrac{1}{4}e^{-2t} + \tfrac{1}{4}t\,e^{-2t} = \tfrac{1}{4}[t - 1 + (t+1)e^{-2t}]$$

as before.

2.6.7 System response to an arbitrary input

The impulse response of a linear time-invariant system is particularly useful in practice in that it enables us to obtain the response of the system to an arbitrary input using the convolution integral. This provides engineers with a powerful approach to the analysis of dynamical systems.

Let us consider a linear system characterized by its impulse response $h(t)$. Then we wish to determine the response $x(t)$ of the system to an arbitrary input

(a)   (b)

Figure 2.47 Approximation to a continuous input.

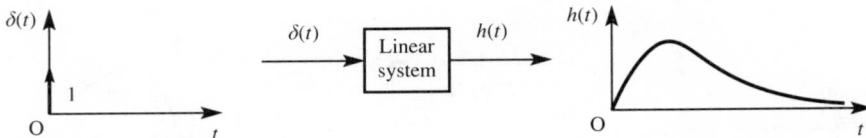

Figure 2.48 Impulse response of a linear system.

$u(t)$ such as that illustrated in Figure 2.47(a). We first approximate the continuous function $u(t)$ by an infinite sequence of impulses of magnitude $u(n \, \Delta T), n = 0, 1, 2, \ldots$, as shown in Figure 2.47(b). This approximation for $u(t)$ may be written as

$$u(t) \simeq \sum_{n=0}^{\infty} u(n \, \Delta T)\delta(t - n \, \Delta T) \, \Delta T \tag{2.81}$$

Since the system is linear, the **principle of superposition** holds, so that the response of the system to the sum of the impulses is equal to the sum of the responses of the system to each of the impulses acting separately. Depicting the impulse response $h(t)$ of the linear system by Figure 2.48, the responses due to the individual impulses forming the sum in (2.81) are illustrated in the sequence of plots in Figure 2.49.

Summing the individual responses, we find that the response due to the sum of the impulses is

$$\sum_{n=0}^{\infty} u(n \, \Delta T)h(t - n \, \Delta T) \, \Delta T \tag{2.82}$$

Allowing $\Delta T \to 0$, so that $n \, \Delta T$ approaches a continuous variable τ, the above sum will approach an integral that will be representative of the system response $x(t)$ to the continuous input $u(t)$. Thus

$$x(t) = \int_0^{\infty} u(\tau)h(t - \tau) \, d\tau$$

$$= \int_0^{t} u(\tau)h(t - \tau) \, d\tau \qquad \text{(since } h(t) \text{ is a causal function)}$$

That is,

$$x(t) = u * h(t)$$

Since convolution is commutative, we may also write

$$x(t) = h * u(t) = \int_0^{t} h(\tau)u(t - \tau) \, d\tau$$

In summary, we have the result that if the impulse response of a linear time-invariant system is $h(t)$ then its response to an arbitrary input $u(t)$ is

$$x(t) = \int_0^{t} u(\tau)h(t - \tau) \, d\tau = \int_0^{t} h(\tau)u(t - \tau) \, d\tau \tag{2.83}$$

Figure 2.49 Responses due to individual impulses.

It is important to realize that this is the response of the system to the input $u(t)$ assuming it to be initially in a quiescent state.

EXAMPLE 2.60

The response $\theta_o(t)$ of a system to a driving force $\theta_i(t)$ is given by the linear differential equation

$$\frac{d^2\theta_o}{dt^2} + \frac{2d\theta_o}{dt} + 5\theta_o = \theta_i$$

Determine the impulse response of the system. Hence, using the convolution integral, determine the response of the system to a unit step input at time $t = 0$, assuming that it is initially in a quiescent state. Confirm this latter result by direct calculation.

Solution   The impulse response $h(t)$ is the solution of

$$\frac{d^2 h}{dt^2} + 2\frac{dh}{dt} + 5h = \delta(t)$$

subject to the initial conditions $h(0) = \dot{h}(0) = 0$. Taking Laplace transforms gives

$$(s^2 + 2s + 5)H(s) = \mathcal{L}\{\delta(t)\} = 1$$

so that

$$H(s) = \frac{1}{s^2 + 2s + 5} = \tfrac{1}{2}\frac{2}{(s+1)^2 + 2^2}$$

which, on inversion, gives the impulse response as

$$h(t) = \tfrac{1}{2}e^{-t}\sin 2t$$

Using the convolution integral

$$\theta_o(t) = \int_0^t h(\tau)\theta_i(t - \tau)\,d\tau$$

with $\theta_i(t) = 1H(t)$ gives the response to the unit step as

$$\theta_o(t) = \tfrac{1}{2}\int_0^t e^{-\tau}\sin 2\tau\,d\tau$$

Integrating by parts twice gives

$$\theta_o(t) = -\tfrac{1}{2}e^{-t}\sin 2t - e^{-t}\cos 2t + 1 - 2\int_0^t e^{-\tau}\sin 2\tau\,d\tau$$

$$= -\tfrac{1}{2}e^{-t}\sin 2t - e^{-t}\cos 2t + 1 - 4\theta_o(t)$$

Hence

$$\theta_o(t) = \tfrac{1}{5}(1 - e^{-t}\cos 2t - \tfrac{1}{2}e^{-t}\sin 2t)$$

(Note that in this case, because of the simple form of $\theta_i(t)$, the convolution integral $\int_0^t h(\tau)\theta_i(t - \tau)\,d\tau$ is taken in preference to $\int_0^t \theta_i(\tau)h(t - \tau)\,d\tau$.)

To obtain the step response directly, we need to solve for $t \geqslant 0$ the differential equation

$$\frac{d^2 \theta_o}{dt^2} + 2\frac{d\theta_o}{dt} + 5\theta_o = 1$$

subject to the initial conditions $\theta_o(0) = \dot{\theta}_o(0) = 0$. Taking Laplace transforms gives

$$(s^2 + 2s + 5)\Theta(s) = \frac{1}{s}$$

so that

$$\Theta = \frac{1}{s(s^2 + 2s + 5)}$$

$$= \frac{\frac{1}{5}}{s} - \frac{1}{5}\frac{s+2}{(s+1)^2 + 4}$$

which, on inversion, gives

$$\theta_o(t) = \tfrac{1}{5} - \tfrac{1}{5}e^{-t}(\cos 2t + \tfrac{1}{2}\sin 2t)$$

$$= \tfrac{1}{5}(1 - e^{-t}\cos 2t - \tfrac{1}{2}e^{-t}\sin 2t)$$

confirming the previous result.

We therefore see that a linear time-invariant system may be characterized in the frequency domain (or s domain) by its transfer function $G(s)$ or in the time domain by its impulse response $h(t)$, as depicted in Figures 2.50(a) and (b) respectively. The response in the frequency domain is obtained by algebraic multiplication, while the time-domain response involves a convolution. This equivalence of the operation of convolution in the time domain with algebraic multiplication in the frequency domain is clearly a powerful argument for the use of frequency-domain techniques in engineering design.

Figure 2.50 (a) Frequency-domain and (b) time-domain representations of a linear time-invariant system.

2.6.8 Exercises

48 For the following pairs of causal functions $f(t)$ and $g(t)$ show that $f * g(t) = g * f(t)$:

(a) $f(t) = t$, $g(t) = \cos 3t$

(b) $f(t) = t + 1$, $g(t) = e^{-2t}$

(c) $f(t) = t^2$, $g(t) = \sin 2t$

(d) $f(t) = e^{-t}$, $g(t) = \sin t$

49 Using the convolution theorem, determine the following inverse Laplace transforms. Check your results by first expressing the given transform in partial-fractions form and then inverting using the standard results.

(a) $\mathcal{L}^{-1}\left\{\dfrac{1}{s(s+3)^3}\right\}$ (b) $\mathcal{L}^{-1}\left\{\dfrac{1}{(s-2)^2(s+3)^2}\right\}$

(c) $\mathcal{L}^{-1}\left\{\dfrac{1}{s^2(s+4)}\right\}$

50 Taking $f(\lambda) = \lambda$ and $g(\lambda) = e^{-\lambda}$, use the inverse form (2.80) of the convolution theorem to show that the solution of the integral equation

$$y(t) = \int_0^t \lambda e^{-(t-\lambda)}\,d\lambda$$

is

$$y(t) = (t - 1) + e^{-t}.$$

51 Find the impulse response of the system characterized by the differential equation

$$\frac{d^2x}{dt^2} + 7\frac{dx}{dt} + 12x = u(t)$$

and hence find the response of the system to the pulse input $u(t) = A[H(t) - H(t - T)]$, assuming that it is initially in a quiescent state.

52 The response $\theta_o(t)$ of a servomechanism to a driving force $\theta_i(t)$ is given by the second-order differential

equation

$$\frac{d^2\theta_o}{dt^2} + 4\frac{d\theta_o}{dt} + 5\theta_o = \theta_i \quad (t \geqslant 0)$$

Determine the impulse response of the system, and hence, using the convolution integral, obtain the response of the servomechanism to a unit step driving force, applied at time $t = 0$, given that the system is initially in a quiescent state.

Check your answer by directly solving the differential equation

$$\frac{d^2\theta_o}{dt^2} + 4\frac{d\theta_o}{dt} + 5\theta_o = 1$$

subject to the initial conditions $\theta_o = \dot{\theta}_o = 0$ when $t = 0$.

2.7   Engineering application: frequency response

Frequency-response methods provide a graphical approach for the analysis and design of systems. Traditionally these methods have evolved from practical considerations, and as such are still widely used by engineers, providing tremendous insight into overall system behaviour. In this section we shall illustrate how the frequency response can be readily obtained from the system transfer function $G(s)$ by simply replacing s by $j\omega$. Methods of representing it graphically will also be considered.

Consider the system depicted in Figure 2.41, with transfer function

$$G(s) = \frac{K(s - z_1)(s - z_2)\cdots(s - z_m)}{(s - p_1)(s - p_2)\cdots(s - p_n)} \quad (m \leqslant n) \tag{2.84}$$

When the input is the sinusoidally varying signal

$$u(t) = A \sin \omega t$$

applied at time $t = 0$, the system response $x(t)$ for $t \geqslant 0$ is determined by

$$X(s) = G(s)\mathscr{L}\{A \sin \omega t\}$$

That is,

$$X(s) = G(s)\frac{A\omega}{s^2 + \omega^2}$$

$$= \frac{KA\omega(s - z_1)(s - z_2)\cdots(s - z_m)}{(s - p_1)(s - p_2)\cdots(s - p_n)(s - j\omega)(s + j\omega)}$$

which, on expanding in partial fractions, gives

$$X(s) = \frac{\alpha_1}{s - j\omega} + \frac{\alpha_2}{s + j\omega} + \sum_{i=1}^{n} \frac{\beta_i}{s - p_i}$$

where $\alpha_1, \alpha_2, \beta_1, \beta_2, \ldots, \beta_n$ are constants. Here the first two terms in the summation are generated by the input and determine the steady-state response, while the remaining terms are generated by the transfer function and determine the system transient response.

Taking inverse Laplace transforms, the system response $x(t)$, $t \geqslant 0$, is given by

$$x(t) = \alpha_1 e^{j\omega t} + \alpha_2 e^{-j\omega t} + \sum_{i=1}^{n} \beta_i e^{p_i t} \quad (t \geqslant 0)$$

In practice we are generally concerned with systems that are stable, for which the poles p_i, $i = 1, 2, \ldots, n$, of the transfer function $G(s)$ lie in the left half of the s plane. Consequently, for practical systems the time-domain terms $\beta_i e^{p_i t}$, $i = 1, 2, \ldots, n$, decay to zero as t increases, and will not contribute to the steady-state response $x_{ss}(t)$ of the system. Thus for stable linear systems the latter is determined by the first two terms as

$$x_{ss}(t) = \alpha_1 e^{j\omega t} + \alpha_2 e^{-j\omega t}$$

Using the 'cover-up' rule for determining the coefficients α_1 and α_2 in the partial-fraction expansions gives

$$\alpha_1 = \left[\frac{(s - j\omega)G(s)A\omega}{(s - j\omega)(s + j\omega)} \right]_{s = j\omega} = \frac{A}{2j} G(j\omega)$$

$$\alpha_2 = \left[\frac{(s + j\omega)G(s)A\omega}{(s - j\omega)(s + j\omega)} \right]_{s = -j\omega} = -\frac{A}{2j} G(-j\omega)$$

so that the steady-state response becomes

$$x_{ss}(t) = \frac{A}{2j} G(j\omega) e^{j\omega t} - \frac{A}{2j} G(-j\omega) e^{-j\omega t} \tag{2.85}$$

$G(j\omega)$ can be expressed in the polar form

$$G(j\omega) = |G(j\omega)| e^{j \arg G(j\omega)}$$

where $|G(j\omega)|$ denotes the magnitude (or modulus) of $G(j\omega)$. (Note that both the magnitude and argument vary with frequency ω.) Then, assuming that the system has real parameters,

$$G(-j\omega) = |G(j\omega)| e^{-j \arg G(j\omega)}$$

and the steady-state response (2.85) becomes

$$x_{ss}(t) = \frac{A}{2j} [|G(j\omega)| e^{j \arg G(j\omega)}] e^{j\omega t} - \frac{A}{2j} [|G(j\omega)| e^{-j \arg G(j\omega)}] e^{-j\omega t}$$

$$= \frac{A}{2j} |G(j\omega)| [e^{j[\omega t + \arg G(j\omega)]} - e^{-j[\omega t + \arg G(j\omega)]}]$$

That is,

$$x_{ss}(t) = A|G(j\omega)| \sin [\omega t + \arg G(j\omega)] \tag{2.86}$$

This indicates that if a stable linear system with transfer function $G(s)$ is subjected to a sinusoidal input then

(a) the steady-state system response is also a sinusoid having the same frequency ω as the input;

(b) the amplitude of this response is $|G(j\omega)|$ times the amplitude A of the input sinusoid; the input is said to be **amplified** if $|G(j\omega)| > 1$ and **attenuated** if $|G(j\omega)| < 1$;

(c) the phase shift between input and output is $\arg G(j\omega)$. The system is said to **lead** if $\arg G(j\omega) > 0$ and **lag** if $\arg G(j\omega) < 0$.

The variations in both the magnitude $|G(j\omega)|$ and argument $\arg G(j\omega)$ as the frequency ω of the input sinusoid is varied constitute the **frequency response of the system**, the magnitude $|G(j\omega)|$ representing the **amplitude gain** or **amplitude ratio** of the system for sinusoidal input with frequency ω, and the argument $\arg G(j\omega)$ representing the **phase shift**.

The result (2.86) implies that the function $G(j\omega)$ may be found experimentally by subjecting a system to sinusoidal excitations and measuring the amplitude gain and phase shift between output and input as the input frequency is varied over the range $0 < \omega < \infty$. In principle, therefore, frequency-response measurements may be used to determine the system transfer function $G(s)$.

In Chapters 4 and 5, dealing with Fourier series and Fourier transforms, we shall see that most functions can be written as sums of sinusoids, and consequently the response of a linear system to almost any input can be deduced in the form of the corresponding sinusoidal responses. It is important, however, to appreciate that the term 'response' in the expression 'frequency response' only relates to the steady-state response behaviour of the system.

The information contained in the system frequency response may be conveniently displayed in graphical form. In practice it is usual to represent it by two graphs: one showing how the amplitude $|G(j\omega)|$ varies with frequency and one showing how the phase shift $\arg G(j\omega)$ varies with frequency.

EXAMPLE 2.61   Determine the frequency response of the RC filter shown in Figure 2.51. Sketch the amplitude and phase-shift plots.

Figure 2.51 RC filter.

Solution The input–output relationship is given by

$$E_o(s) = \frac{1}{RCs + 1} E_i(s)$$

so that the filter is characterized by the transfer function

$$G(s) = \frac{1}{RCs + 1}$$

Therefore

$$G(j\omega) = \frac{1}{RCj\omega + 1} = \frac{1 - jRC\omega}{1 + R^2C^2\omega^2}$$

$$= \frac{1}{1 + R^2C^2\omega^2} - j\frac{RC\omega}{1 + R^2C^2\omega^2}$$

giving the frequency-response characteristics

$$\text{amplitude ratio} = |G(j\omega)| = \sqrt{\left[\frac{1}{(1 + R^2C^2\omega^2)^2} + \frac{R^2C^2\omega^2}{(1 + R^2C^2\omega^2)^2}\right]}$$

$$= \frac{1}{\sqrt{(1 + R^2C^2\omega^2)}}$$

$$\text{phase shift} = \arg G(j\omega) = -\tan^{-1}(RC\omega)$$

Note that for $\omega = 0$

$$|G(j\omega)| = 1, \qquad \arg G(j\omega) = 0$$

and as $\omega \to \infty$

$$|G(j\omega)| \to 0, \qquad \arg G(j\omega) \to -\tfrac{1}{2}\pi$$

Plots of the amplitude and phase-shift curves are shown in Figures 2.52(a) and (b) respectively.

(a)

(b)

Figure 2.52 Frequency-response plots for Example 2.61: (a) amplitude plot; (b) phase-shift plot.

For the simple transfer function of Example 2.61, plotting the amplitude and phase-shift characteristics was relatively easy. For higher-order transfer functions it can be a rather tedious task, and it would be far more efficient to use a suitable computer package. However, to facilitate the use of frequency-response techniques in system design, engineers adopt a different approach, making use of **Bode plots** to display the relevant information. This approach is named after H. W. Bode, who developed the techniques at the Bell Laboratories in the late 1930s. Again it involves drawing separate plots of amplitude and phase shift, but in this case on semilogarithmic graph paper, with frequency plotted on the horizontal logarithmic axis and amplitude, or phase, on the vertical linear axis. It is also normal to express the amplitude gain in decibels (dB); that is,

$$\text{amplitude gain in dB} = 20 \log |G(j\omega)|$$

and the phase shift $\arg G(j\omega)$ in degrees. Thus the Bode plots consist of

(a) a plot of amplitude in decibels versus $\log \omega$, and

(b) a plot of phase shift in degrees versus $\log \omega$.

Note that with the amplitude gain measured in decibels, the input signal will be amplified if the gain is greater than zero and attenuated if it is less than zero.

The advantage of using Bode plots is that the amplitude and phase information can be obtained from the constituent parts of the transfer function by graphical addition. It is also possible to make simplifying approximations in which curves can be replaced by straight-line asymptotes. These can be drawn relatively quickly, and provide sufficient information to give an engineer a 'feel' for the system behaviour. Desirable system characteristics are frequently specified in terms of frequency-response behaviour, and since the approximate Bode plots permit quick determination of the effect of changes, they provide a good test for the system designer.

EXAMPLE 2.62   Draw the approximate Bode plots corresponding to the transfer function

$$G(s) = \frac{4 \times 10^3 (5 + s)}{s(100 + s)(20 + s)} \tag{2.87}$$

Solution   First we express the transfer function in what is known as the **standard form**, namely

$$G(s) = \frac{10(1 + 0.2s)}{s(1 + 0.01s)(1 + 0.05s)}$$

giving

$$G(j\omega) = \frac{10(1 + j0.2\omega)}{j\omega(1 + j0.01\omega)(1 + j0.05\omega)}$$

Taking logarithms to base 10,

$$20 \log |G(j\omega)| = 20 \log 10 + 20 \log |1 + j0.2\omega| - 20 \log |j\omega|$$

$$- 20 \log |1 + j0.01\omega| - 20 \log |1 + j0.05\omega|$$

$$\arg G(j\omega) = \arg 10 + \arg(1 + j0.2\omega) - \arg j\omega - \arg(1 + j0.01\omega)$$

$$- \arg(1 + j0.05\omega) \tag{2.88}$$

The transfer function involves constituents that are again a simple zero and simple poles (including one at the origin). We shall now illustrate how the Bode plots can be built up from those of the constituent parts.

Consider first the amplitude gain plot, which is a plot of $20 \log |G(j\omega)|$ versus $\log \omega$:

(a) for a simple gain k a plot of $20 \log k$ is a horizontal straight line, being above the $0\,\text{dB}$ axis if $k > 1$ and below it if $k < 1$;

(b) for a simple pole at the origin a plot of $-20 \log \omega$ is a straight line with slope $-20\,\text{dB/decade}$ and intersecting the $0\,\text{dB}$ axis at $\omega = 1$;

(c) for a simple zero or pole not at the origin we see that

$$20 \log |1 + j\tau\omega| \to \begin{cases} 0 & \text{as } \omega \to 0 \\ 20 \log \tau\omega = 20 \log \omega - 20 \log(1/\tau) & \text{as } \omega \to \infty \end{cases}$$

Note that the graph of $20 \log \tau\omega$ is a straight line with slope $20\,\text{dB/decade}$ and intersecting the $0\,\text{dB}$ axis at $\omega = 1/\tau$. Thus the plot of $20 \log |1 + j\tau\omega|$ may be approximated by two straight lines: one for $\omega < 1/\tau$ and one for $\omega > 1/\tau$. The frequency at intersection $\omega = 1/\tau$ is called the **breakpoint** or **corner frequency**; here $|1 + j\tau\omega| = \sqrt{2}$, enabling the true curve to be indicated at this frequency. Using this approach, straight-line approximations to the amplitude plots of a simple zero and a simple pole, neither at zero, are shown in Figures 2.53(a) and (b) respectively (actual plots are also shown).

Figure 2.53 Straight-line approximations to Bode amplitude plots: (a) simple zero; (b) simple pole.

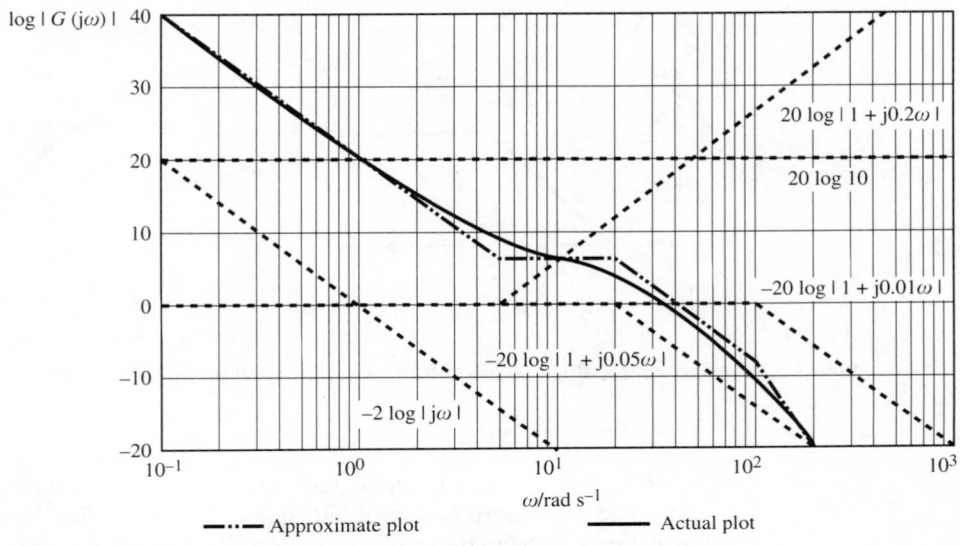

Figure 2.54 Amplitude Bode plots for the $G(s)$ of Example 2.62.

Using the approximation plots for the constituent parts as indicated in (a)–(c) earlier, we can build up the approximate amplitude gain plot corresponding to (2.87) by graphical addition as indicated in Figure 2.54. The actual amplitude gain plot, produced using a software package, is also shown.

The idea of using asymptotes can also be used to draw the phase-shift Bode plots; again taking account of the accumulated effects of the individual components making up the transfer function, namely that

(i) the phase shift associated with a constant gain k is zero;

(ii) the phase shift associated with a simple pole or zero at the origin is $+90°$ or $-90°$ respectively;

(iii) for a simple zero or pole not at the origin

$$\tan^{-1}(\omega\tau) \to \begin{cases} 0 & \text{as } \omega \to 0 \\ 90° & \text{as } \omega \to \infty \end{cases}$$

$$\tan^{-1}(\omega\tau) = 45° \quad \text{when } \omega\tau = 1$$

With these observations in mind, the following approximations are made. For frequencies ω less than one-tenth of the corner frequency $\omega = 1/\tau$ (that is, for $\omega < 1/10\tau$) the phase shift is assumed to be $0°$, and for frequencies greater than ten times the corner frequency (that is, for $\omega > 10/\tau$) the phase shift is assumed to be $\pm 90°$. For frequencies between these limits (that is, $1/10\tau < \pi < 10/\tau$) the phase-shift plot is taken to be a straight line that passes through $0°$ at

Figure 2.55 Approximate Bode phase-shift plots: (a) simple zero; (b) simple pole.

$\omega = 1/10\tau$, $\pm 45°$ at $\omega = 1/\tau$, and $\pm 90°$ at $\omega = 10/\tau$. In each case the plus sign is associated with a zero and the minus sign with a pole. With these assumptions, straight-line approximations to the phase-shift plots for a simple zero and pole, neither located at the origin, are shown in Figures 2.55(a) and (b) respectively (the actual plots are represented by the broken curves).

Using these approximations, a straight-line approximate phase-gain plot corresponding to (2.88) is shown in Figure 2.56. Again, the actual phase-gain plot, produced using a software package, is shown.

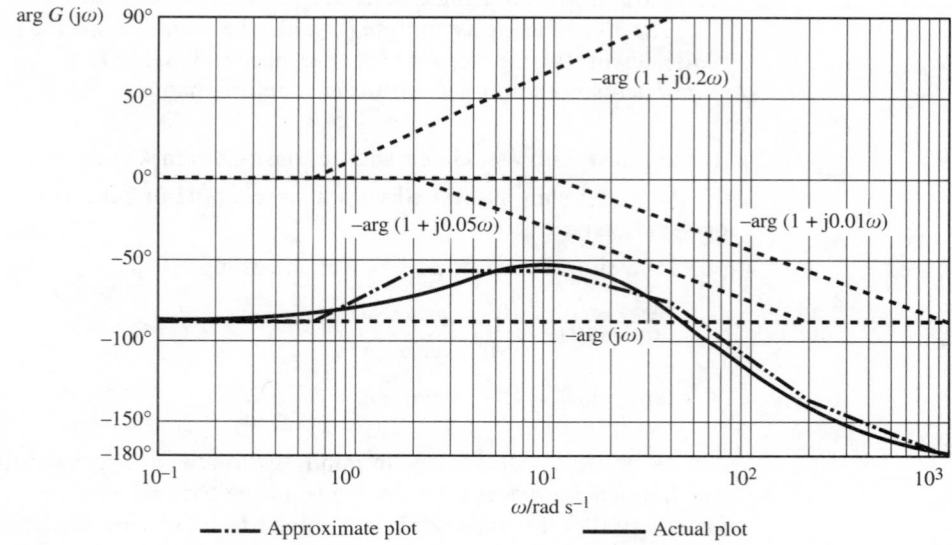

Figure 2.56 Phase-shift Bode plot for the $G(s)$ of Example 2.62.

In the graphical approach adopted in this section, separate plots of amplitude gain and phase shift versus frequency have been drawn. It is also possible to represent the frequency response graphically using only one plot. When this is done using the pair of polar coordinates $(|G(j\omega)|, \arg G(j\omega))$ and allowing the frequency ω to vary, the resulting Argand diagram is referred to as the **polar plot** or **frequency-response plot**. Such a graphical representation of the transfer function forms the basis of the **Nyquist approach** to the analysis of feedback systems. In fact, the main use of frequency-response methods in practice is in the analysis and design of closed-loop control systems. For the unity feedback system of Figure 2.45 the frequency-response plot of the forward-path transfer function $G(s)$ is used to infer overall closed-loop system behaviour. The Bode plots are perhaps the quickest plots to construct, especially when straight-line approximations are made, and are useful when attempting to estimate a transfer function from a set of physical frequency-response measurements. Other plots used in practice are the **Nichols diagram** and the **inverse Nyquist** (or **polar**) **plot**, the first of these being useful for designing feedforward compensators and the second for designing feedback compensators. Although there is no simple mathematical relationship, it is also worth noting that transient behaviour may also be inferred from the various frequency-response plots. For example, the reciprocal of the inverse M circle centred on the -1 point in the inverse Nyquist plot gives an indication of the peak overshoot in the transient behaviour (see, for example, G. Franklin, D. Powell and A. Naeini-Emami (1986), *Feedback Control of Dynamic Systems*, Reading, MA: Addison-Wesley).

2.8 Review exercises (1–30)

1 Solve, using Laplace transforms, the following differential equations:

(a) $\dfrac{d^2x}{dt^2} + 4\dfrac{dx}{dt} + 5x = 8\cos t$

subject to $x = \dfrac{dx}{dt} = 0$ at $t = 0$

(b) $5\dfrac{d^2x}{dt^2} - 3\dfrac{dx}{dt} - 2x = 6$

subject to $x = 1$ and $\dfrac{dx}{dt} = 1$ at $t = 0$

2 (a) Find the inverse Laplace transform of

$$\frac{1}{(s+1)(s+2)(s^2+2s+2)}$$

(b) A voltage source $Ve^{-t}\sin t$ is applied across a series LCR circuit with $L = 1$, $R = 3$ and $C = \frac{1}{2}$.

Show that the current $i(t)$ in the circuit satisfies the differential equation

$$\frac{d^2i}{dt^2} + 3\frac{di}{dt} + 2i = Ve^{-t}\sin t$$

Find the current $i(t)$ in the circuit at time $t \geqslant 0$ if $i(t)$ satisfies the initial conditions $i(0) = 1$ and $(di/dt)(0) = 2$.

3 Use Laplace transform methods to solve the simultaneous differential equations

$$\frac{d^2x}{dt^2} - x + 5\frac{dy}{dt} = t$$

$$\frac{d^2y}{dt^2} - 4y - 2\frac{dx}{dt} = -2$$

subject to $x = y = \dfrac{dx}{dt} = \dfrac{dy}{dt} = 0$ at $t = 0$.

4 Solve the differential equation

$$\frac{d^2x}{dt^2} + 2\frac{dx}{dt} + 2x = \cos t$$

subject to the initial conditions $x = x_0$ and $dx/dt = x_1$ at $t = 0$. Identify the steady-state and transient solutions. Find the amplitude and phase shift of the steady-state solution.

5 Resistors of 5 and 20 Ω are connected to the primary and secondary coils of a transformer with inductances as shown in Figure 2.57. At time $t = 0$, with no currents flowing, a voltage $E = 100\,V$ is applied to the primary circuit. Show that subsequently the current in the secondary circuit is

$$\frac{20}{\sqrt{41}}(e^{-(11+\sqrt{41})t/2} - e^{-(11-\sqrt{41})t/2})$$

Figure 2.57 Circuit of Review exercise 5.

6 (a) Find the Laplace transforms of
  (i) $\cos(\omega t + \phi)$ (ii) $e^{-\omega t}\sin(\omega t + \phi)$
 (b) Using Laplace transform methods, solve the differential equation

$$\frac{d^2x}{dt^2} + 4\frac{dx}{dt} + 8x = \cos 2t$$

given that $x = 2$ and $dx/dt = 1$ when $t = 0$.

7 (a) Find the inverse Laplace transform of

$$\frac{s-4}{s^2 + 4s + 13}$$

 (b) Solve using Laplace transforms the differential equation

$$\frac{dy}{dt} + 2y = 2(2 + \cos t + 2\sin t)$$

given that $y = -3$ when $t = 0$.

8 Using Laplace transforms, solve the simultaneous differential equations

$$\frac{dx}{dt} + 5x + 3y = 5\sin t - 2\cos t$$

$$\frac{dy}{dt} + 3y + 5x = 6\sin t - 3\cos t$$

where $x = 1$ and $y = 0$ when $t = 0$.

9 The charge q on a capacitor in an inductive circuit is given by the differential equation

$$\frac{d^2q}{dt^2} + 300\frac{dq}{dt} + 2 \times 10^4 q = 200\sin 100t$$

and it is also known that both q and dq/dt are zero when $t = 0$. Use the Laplace transform method to find q. What is the phase difference between the steady-state component of the current dq/dt and the applied emf $200\sin 100t$ to the nearest half-degree?

10 Use Laplace transforms to find the value of x given that

$$4\frac{dx}{dt} + 6x + y = 2\sin 2t$$

$$\frac{d^2x}{dt^2} + x - \frac{dy}{dt} = 3e^{-2t}$$

and that $x = 2$ and $dx/dt = -2$ when $t = 0$.

11 (a) Use Laplace transforms to solve the differential equation

$$\frac{d^2\theta}{dt^2} + 8\frac{d\theta}{dt} + 16\theta = \sin 2t$$

given that $\theta = 0$ and $d\theta/dt = 0$ when $t = 0$.
 (b) Using Laplace transforms, solve the simultaneous differential equations

$$\frac{di_1}{dt} + 2i_1 + 6i_2 = 0$$

$$i_1 + \frac{di_2}{dt} - 3i_2 = 0$$

given that $i_1 = 1$, $i_2 = 0$ when $t = 0$.

12 The terminals of a generator producing a voltage V are connected through a wire of resistance R and a coil of inductance L (and negligible resistance). A capacitor of capacitance C is connected in parallel with the resistance R as shown in Figure 2.58. Show that the current i flowing through the resistance R is given by

$$LCR\frac{d^2i}{dt^2} + L\frac{di}{dt} + Ri = V$$

Figure 2.58 Circuit of Review exercise 12.

Suppose that
(i) $V = 0$ for $t < 0$ and $V = E$ (constant) for $t \geqslant 0$
(ii) $L = 2R^2C$
(iii) $CR = 1/2n$

and show that the equation reduces to

$$\frac{d^2i}{dt^2} + 2n\frac{di}{dt} + 2n^2i = 2n^2\frac{E}{R}$$

Hence, assuming that $i = 0$ and $di/dt = 0$ when $t = 0$, use Laplace transforms to obtain an expression for i in terms of t.

13 Show that the currents in the coupled circuits of Figure 2.59 are determined by the simultaneous differential equations

$$L\frac{di_1}{dt} + R(i_1 - i_2) + Ri_1 = E$$

$$L\frac{di_2}{dt} + Ri_2 - R(i_1 - i_2) = 0$$

Find i_1 in terms of t, L, E and R, given that $i_1 = 0$ and $di_1/dt = E/L$ at $t = 0$, and show that $i_1 \simeq \frac{2}{3}E/R$ for large t. What does i_2 tend to for large t?

Figure 2.59 Circuit of Review exercise 13.

14 A system consists of two unit masses lying in a straight line on a smooth surface and connected together to two fixed points by three springs. When a sinusoidal force is applied to the system, the displacements $x_1(t)$ and $x_2(t)$ of the respective masses

from their equilibrium positions satisfy the equations

$$\frac{d^2x_1}{dt^2} = x_2 - 2x_1 + \sin 2t$$

$$\frac{d^2x_2}{dt^2} = -2x_2 + x_1$$

Given that the system is initially at rest in the equilibrium position ($x_1 = x_2 = 0$), use the Laplace transform method to solve the equations for $x_1(t)$ and $x_2(t)$.

15 (a) Obtain the inverse Laplace transforms of

(i) $\dfrac{s + 4}{s^2 + 2s + 10}$ (ii) $\dfrac{s - 3}{(s - 1)^2(s - 2)}$

(b) Use Laplace transforms to solve the differential equation

$$\frac{d^2y}{dt^2} + 2\frac{dy}{dt} + y = 3te^{-t}$$

given that $y = 4$ and $dy/dt = 2$ when $t = 0$.

16 (a) Determine the inverse Laplace transform of

$$\frac{5}{s^2 - 14s + 53}$$

(b) The equation of motion of the moving coil of a galvanometer when a current i is passed through it is of the form

$$\frac{d^2\theta}{dt^2} + 2K\frac{d\theta}{dt} + n^2\theta = \frac{n^2i}{K}$$

where θ is the angle of deflection from the 'no-current' position and n and K are positive constants. Given that i is a constant and $\theta = 0 = d\theta/dt$ when $t = 0$, obtain an expression for the Laplace transform of θ.

In constructing the galvanometer, it is desirable to have it critically damped (that is, $n = K$). Use the Laplace transform method to solve the differential equation in this case, and sketch the graph of θ against t for positive values of t.

17 (a) Given that α is a positive constant, use the second shift theorem to

(i) show that the Laplace transform of $\sin t\, H(t - \alpha)$ is

$$e^{-\alpha s}\frac{\cos \alpha + s\sin \alpha}{s^2 + 1}$$

(ii) find the inverse transform of

$$\frac{s\, e^{-\alpha s}}{s^2 + 2s + 5}$$

(b) Solve the differential equation

$$\frac{d^2y}{dt^2} + 2\frac{dy}{dt} + 5y = \sin t - \sin t\, H(t - \pi)$$

given that $y = dy/dt = 0$ when $t = 0$.

18 Show that the Laplace transform of the voltage $v(t)$, with period T, defined by

$$v(t) = \begin{cases} 1 & (0 \leqslant t < \tfrac{1}{2}T) \\ -1 & (\tfrac{1}{2}T \leqslant t < T) \end{cases} \quad v(t + T) = v(t)$$

is

$$V(s) = \frac{1}{s}\frac{1 - e^{-sT/2}}{1 + e^{-sT/2}}$$

This voltage is applied to a capacitor of $100\,\mu\text{F}$ and a resistor of $250\,\Omega$ in series, with no charge initially on the capacitor. Show that the Laplace transform $I(s)$ of the current $i(t)$ flowing, for $t \geqslant 0$, is

$$I(s) = \frac{1}{250(s + 40)}\frac{1 - e^{-sT/2}}{1 + e^{-sT/2}}$$

and give an expression, involving Heaviside step functions, for $i(t)$ where $0 \leqslant t \leqslant 2T$. For $T = 10^{-3}\,\text{s}$, is this a good representation of the steady-state response of the circuit? Briefly give a reason for your answer.

19 The response $x(t)$ of a control system to a forcing term $u(t)$ is given by the differential equation

$$\frac{d^2x}{dt^2} + 2\frac{dx}{dt} + 2x = u(t) \quad (t \geqslant 0)$$

Determine the impulse response of the system, and hence, using the convolution integral, obtain the response of the system to a unit step $u(t) = 1H(t)$ applied at $t = 0$, given that initially the system is in a quiescent state. Check your solution by directly solving the differential equation

$$\frac{d^2x}{dt^2} + 2\frac{dx}{dt} + 2x = 1 \quad (t \geqslant 0)$$

with $x = dx/dt = 0$ at $t = 0$.

20 A light horizontal beam, of length 5 m and constant flexural rigidity EI, built in at the left-hand end $x = 0$, is simply supported at the point $x = 4\,\text{m}$ and carries a distributed load with density function

$$W(x) = \begin{cases} 12\,\text{kN m}^{-1} & (0 < x < 4) \\ 24\,\text{kN m}^{-1} & (4 < x < 5) \end{cases}$$

Write down the fourth-order boundary-value problem satisfied by the deflection $y(x)$. Solve this problem to determine $y(x)$, and write down the resulting

expressions for $y(x)$ for the cases $0 \leqslant x \leqslant 4$ and $4 \leqslant x \leqslant 5$. Calculate the end reaction and moment by evaluating appropriate derivatives of $y(x)$ at $x = 0$. Check that your results satisfy the equation of equilibrium for the beam as a whole.

21 (a) Sketch the function defined by

$$f(t) = \begin{cases} 0 & (0 \leqslant t < 1) \\ 1 & (1 \leqslant t < 2) \\ 0 & (t > 2) \end{cases}$$

Express $f(t)$ in terms of Heaviside step functions, and use the Laplace transform to solve the differential equation

$$\frac{dx}{dt} + x = f(t)$$

given that $x = 0$ at $t = 0$.

(b) The Laplace transform $I(s)$ of the current $i(t)$ in a certain circuit is given by

$$I(s) = \frac{E}{s[Ls + R/(1 + Cs)]}$$

where E, L, R and C are positive constants. Determine (i) $\lim_{t \to 0} i(t)$ and (ii) $\lim_{t \to \infty} i(t)$.

22 Show that the Laplace transform of the half-rectified sine-wave function

$$v(t) = \begin{cases} \sin t & (0 \leqslant t \leqslant \pi) \\ 0 & (\pi \leqslant t \leqslant 2\pi) \end{cases}$$

of period 2π, is

$$\frac{1}{(1 + s^2)(1 - e^{-\pi s})}$$

Such a voltage $v(t)$ is applied to a $1\,\Omega$ resistor and a $1\,\text{H}$ inductor connected in series. Show that the resulting current, initially zero, is $\sum_{n=0}^{\infty} f(t - n\pi)$, where $f(t) = (\sin t - \cos t + e^{-t})H(t)$. Sketch a graph of the function $f(t)$.

23 (a) Find the inverse Laplace transform of $1/s^2(s + 1)^2$ by writing the expression in the form $(1/s^2)[1/(s + 1)^2]$ and using the convolution theorem.

(b) Use the convolution theorem to solve the integral equation

$$y(t) = t + 2\int_0^t y(u)\cos(t - u)\,du$$

and the integro-differential equation

$$\int_0^t y''(u)y'(t - u)\,du = y(t)$$

where $y(0) = 0$ and $y'(0) = y_1$. Comment on the solution of the second equation.

24 A beam of negligible weight and length $3l$ carries a point load W at a distance l from the left-hand end. Both ends are clamped horizontally at the same level. Determine the equation governing the deflection of the beam. If, in addition, the beam is now subjected to a load per unit length, w, over the shorter part of the beam, what will then be the differential equation determining the deflection?

25 (a) Using Laplace transforms, solve the differential equation

$$\frac{\mathrm{d}^2x}{\mathrm{d}t^2} - 3\frac{\mathrm{d}x}{\mathrm{d}t} + 3x = H(t - a) \quad (a > 0)$$

where $H(t)$ is the Heaviside unit step function, given that $x = 0$ and $\mathrm{d}x/\mathrm{d}t = 0$ at $t = 0$.

(b) The output $x(t)$ from a stable linear control system with input $\sin \omega t$ and transfer function $G(s)$ is determined by the relationship

$$X(s) = G(s)\mathcal{L}\{\sin \omega t\}$$

where $X(s) = \mathcal{L}\{x(t)\}$. Show that, after a long time t, the output approaches $x_s(t)$, where

$$x_s(t) = \mathrm{Re}\left(\frac{\mathrm{e}^{\mathrm{j}\omega t}G(\mathrm{j}\omega)}{\mathrm{j}}\right)$$

26 Consider the feedback system of Figure 2.60, where K is a constant feedback gain.

(a) In the absence of feedback (that is, $K = 0$) is the system stable?

(b) Write down the transfer function $G_1(s)$ for the overall feedback system.

(c) Plot the locus of poles of $G_1(s)$ in the s plane for both positive and negative values of K.

(d) From the plots in (c), specify for what range of values of K the feedback system is stable.

(e) Confirm your answer to (d) using the Routh–Hurwitz criterion.

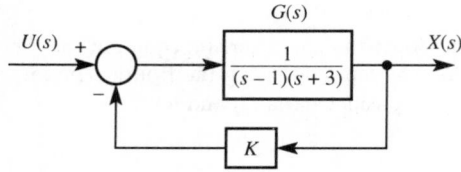

Figure 2.60 Feedback system of Review exercise 26.

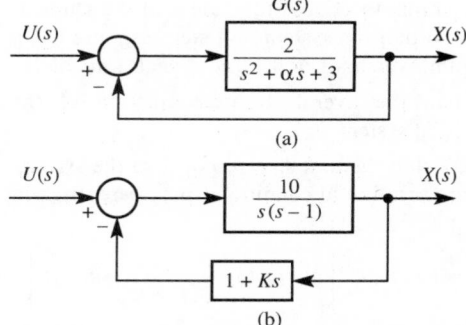

Figure 2.61 Feedback control systems of Review exercise 27.

27 (a) For the feedback control system of Figure 2.61(a) it is known that the impulse response is $h(t) = 2\mathrm{e}^{-2t}\sin t$. Use this to determine the value of the parameter α.

(b) Consider the control system of Figure 2.61(b), having both proportional and rate feedback. Determine the critical value of the gain K for stability of the closed loop system.

28 (An extended problem) The transient response of a practical control system to a unit step input often exhibits damped oscillations before reaching steady-state. The following properties are some of those used to specify the transient response characteristics of an underdamped system:

   rise time, the time required for the response to rise from 0 to 100% of its final value;

   peak time, the time required for the response to reach the first peak of the overshoot;

   settling time, the time required for the response curve to reach and stay within a range about the final value of size specified by an absolute percentage of the final value (usually 2% or 5%);

   maximum overshoot, the maximum peak value of the response measured from unity.

Consider the feedback control system of Figure 2.62 having both proportional and derivative feedback.

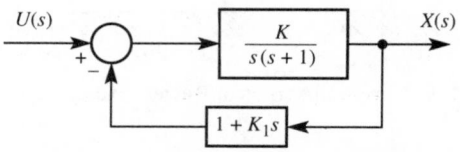

Figure 2.62 Feedback control system of Review exercise 28.

It is desirable to choose the values of the gains K and K_1 so that the system unit step response has a maximum overshoot of 0.2 and a peak time of 1 s.

(a) Obtain the overall transfer function of the closed-loop system.

(b) Show that the unit step response of the system, assuming zero initial conditions, may be written in the form

$$x(t) = 1 - e^{-\omega_n \xi t} \left[\cos \omega_d t + \frac{\xi}{\sqrt{(1 - \xi^2)}} \sin \omega_d t \right]$$

$$(t \geqslant 0)$$

where $\omega_d = \omega_n \sqrt{(1 - \xi^2)}$, $\omega_n = K$ and $2\omega_n \xi = 1 + KK_1$.

(c) Determine the values of the gains K and K_1 so that the desired characteristics are achieved.

(d) With these values of K and K_1, determine the rise time and settling time, comparing both the 2% and 5% criteria for the latter.

29 (An extended problem) The mass M_1 of the mechanical system of Figure 2.63(a) is subjected to a harmonic forcing term $\sin \omega t$. Determine the steady-state response of the system.

It is desirable to design a vibration absorber to absorb the steady-state oscillations so that in the steady state $x(t) \equiv 0$. To achieve this, a secondary system is attached as illustrated in Figure 2.63(b).

(a) Show that, with an appropriate choice of M_2 and K_2, the desired objective may be achieved.

(a)   (b)

Figure 2.63 Vibration absorber of Review exercise 29.

(b) What is the corresponding steady-state motion of the mass M_2?

(c) Comment on the practicality of your design.

30 (An extended problem) The electronic amplifier of Figure 2.64 has open-loop transfer function $G(s)$ with the following characteristics: a low-frequency gain of 120 dB and simple poles at 1 MHz, 10 MHz and 25 MHz. It may be assumed that the amplifier is ideal, so that $K/(1 + K\beta) \simeq 1/\beta$, where β is the feedback gain and K the steady-state gain associated with $G(s)$.

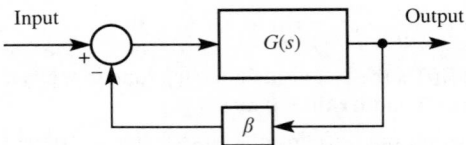

Figure 2.64 Electronic amplifier of Review exercise 30.

(a) Construct the magnitude versus log frequency and phase versus log frequency plots (Bode plots) for the open-loop system.

(b) Determine from the Bode plots whether or not the system is stable in the case of unity feedback (that is, $\beta = 1$).

(c) Determine the value of β for marginal stability, and hence the corresponding value of the closed-loop low-frequency gain.

(d) Feedback is now applied to the amplifier to reduce the overall closed loop gain at low frequencies to 100 dB. Determine the gain and phase margin corresponding to this closed-loop configuration.

(e) Using the given characteristics, express $G(s)$ in the form

$$G(s) = \frac{K}{(1 + s\tau_1)(1 + s\tau_2)(1 + s\tau_3)}$$

and hence obtain the input–output transfer function for the amplifier.

(f) Write down the characteristic equation for the closed-loop system and, using the Routh–Hurwitz criterion, reconsider parts (b) and (c).

3

The z Transform

CONTENTS

3.1 Introduction

In this chapter we focus attention on discrete- (time) processes. With the advent of fast and cheap digital computers, there has been renewed emphasis on the analysis and design of digital systems, which represent a major class of engineering systems. The main thrust of this chapter will be in this direction. However, it is a mistake to believe that the mathematical basis of this area of work is of such recent vintage. The first comprehensive text in English dealing with difference equations was *The Treatise of the Calculus of Finite Differences* due to George Boole and published in 1860. Much of the early impetus for the **finite calculus** was due to the need to carry out interpolation and to approximate derivatives and integrals. Later, numerical methods for the solution of differential equations were devised, many of which were based on **finite difference methods**, involving the approximation of the derivative terms to produce a **difference equation**. The underlying idea in each case so far discussed is some form of approximation of an underlying continuous function or continuous-time process. There are situations, however, where it is more appropriate to propose a discrete-time model from the start.

Digital systems operate on digital signals, which are usually generated by **sampling** a continuous-time signal, that is, a signal defined for every instant of a possibly infinite time interval. The sampling process generates a **discrete-time signal**, defined only at the instants when sampling takes place so that a digital sequence is generated. After processing by a computer, the output digital signal may be used to construct a new continuous-time signal, perhaps by the use of a **zero-order hold** device, and this in turn might be used to control a plant or process. Digital signal processing devices have made a major impact in many areas of engineering, as well as in the home. For example, many readers will have heard the significantly improved reproduction quality available from compact disc players, which operate using digital technology.

We have seen in Chapter 2 that the Laplace transform was a valuable aid in the analysis of continuous-time systems, and in this chapter we develop the *z* transform, which will perform the same task for discrete-time systems. We introduce the transform in connection with the solution of difference equations, and later we show how difference equations arise as discrete-time system models.

The chapter includes two engineering applications. The first is on the design of digital filters, and highlights one of the major applications of transform methods as a design tool. It may be expected that whenever sampling is involved, performance will improve as sampling rate is increased. Engineers have found that this is not the full story, and the second application deals with some of the problems encountered. This leads on to an introduction to the unifying concept of the $\mathscr{D}$ transform, which brings together the theories of the Laplace and *z* transforms.

3.2   The *z* transform

Since *z* transforms relate to sequences, we first review the notation associated with sequences, which were considered in more detail in Chapter 6 of *Modern Engineering Mathematics*. A finite sequence $\{x_k\}_0^n$ is an ordered set of $n + 1$ real or complex numbers:

$$\{x_k\}_0^n = \{x_0, x_1, x_2, \ldots, x_n\}$$

Note that the set of numbers is ordered so that position in the sequence is important. The position is identified by the position index k, where k is an integer. If the number of elements in the set is infinite then this leads to the **infinite sequence**

$$\{x_k\}_0^\infty = \{x_0, x_1, x_2, \ldots\}$$

When dealing with sampled functions of time t, it is necessary to have a means of allowing for $t < 0$. To do this, we allow the sequence of numbers to extend to infinity on both sides of the initial position x_0, and write

$$\{x_k\}_{-\infty}^\infty = \{\ldots, x_{-2}, x_{-1}, x_0, x_1, x_2, \ldots\}$$

Sequences $\{x_k\}_{-\infty}^\infty$ for which $x_k = 0 \ (k < 0)$ are called **causal sequences**, by analogy with continuous-time causal functions $f(t)H(t)$ defined in Section 2.2.1 as

$$f(t)H(t) = \begin{cases} 0 & (t < 0) \\ f(t) & (t \geqslant 0) \end{cases}$$

While for some finite sequences it is possible to specify the sequence by listing all the elements of the set, it is normally the case that a sequence is specified by giving a formula for its general element x_k.

3.2.1   Definition and notation

The z **transform** of a sequence $\{x_k\}_{-\infty}^\infty$ is defined in general as

$$\mathscr{Z}\{x_k\}_{-\infty}^\infty = X(z) = \sum_{k=-\infty}^\infty \frac{x_k}{z^k} \tag{3.1}$$

whenever the sum exists and where z is a complex variable, as yet undefined.

The process of taking the z transform of a sequence thus produces a function of a complex variable z, whose form depends upon the sequence itself. The symbol $\mathscr{Z}$ denotes the **z-transform operator**; when it operates on a sequence $\{x_k\}$ it transforms the latter into the function $X(z)$ of the complex variable z. It is usual to refer to $\{x_k\}$, $X(z)$ as a **z-transform pair**, which is sometimes written as $\{x_k\} \leftrightarrow X(z)$. Note the similarity to obtaining the Laplace transform of a function in Section 2.2.1. We shall return to consider the relationship between Laplace and z transforms in Section 3.7.

For sequences $\{x_k\}_{-\infty}^\infty$ that are *causal*, that is

$$x_k = 0 \quad (k < 0)$$

the z transform given in (3.1) reduces to

$$\mathscr{Z}\{x_k\}_0^\infty = X(z) = \sum_{k=0}^\infty \frac{x_k}{z^k} \tag{3.2}$$

In this chapter we shall be concerned with causal sequences, and so the definition given in (3.2) will be the one that we shall use henceforth. We shall therefore from now on take $\{x_k\}$ to denote $\{x_k\}_0^\infty$. Non-causal sequences, however, are of importance, and arise particularly in the field of digital image processing, among others.

EXAMPLE 3.1   Determine the *z* transform of the sequence

$$\{x_k\} = \{2^k\} \quad (k \geqslant 0)$$

Solution   From the definition (3.2),

$$\mathscr{L}\{2^k\} = \sum_{k=0}^{\infty} \frac{2^k}{z^k}$$

$$= \sum_{k=0}^{\infty} \left(\frac{2}{z}\right)^k$$

which we recognize as a geometric series, with common ratio $r = 2/z$ between successive terms. The series thus converges for $|z| > 2$, when

$$\sum_{k=0}^{\infty} \left(\frac{2}{z}\right)^k = \lim_{k \to \infty} \frac{1 - (2/z)^k}{1 - 2/z}$$

$$= \frac{1}{1 - 2/z}$$

leading to

$$\mathscr{L}\{2^k\} = \frac{z}{z-2} \quad (|z| > 2) \tag{3.3}$$

so that

$$\left.\begin{array}{r} \{x_k\} = \{2^k\} \\[2mm] X(z) = \dfrac{z}{z-2} \end{array}\right\}$$

is an example of a *z*-transform pair.

From Example 3.1, we see that the *z* transform of the sequence $\{2^k\}$ exists provided that we restrict the complex variable *z* so that it lies outside the circle $|z| = 2$ in the *z* plane. From another point of view, the function

$$X(z) = \frac{z}{z-2} \quad (|z| > 2)$$

may be thought of as a **generating function** for the sequence $\{2^k\}$, in the sense that the coefficient of z^{-k} in the expansion of $X(z)$ in powers of $1/z$ *generates* the *k*th term of the sequence $\{2^k\}$. This can easily be verified, since

$$\frac{z}{z-2} = \frac{1}{1-2/z} = \left(1-\frac{2}{z}\right)^{-1}$$

and, since $|z| > 2$, we can expand this as

$$\left(1-\frac{2}{z}\right)^{-1} = 1 + \frac{2}{z} + \left(\frac{2}{z}\right)^2 + \ldots + \left(\frac{2}{z}\right)^k + \ldots$$

and we see that the coefficient of z^{-k} is indeed 2^k, as expected.

We can generalize the result (3.3) in an obvious way to determine $\mathscr{L}\{a^k\}$, the z transform of the sequence $\{a^k\}$, where a is a real or complex constant. At once

$$\mathscr{L}\{a^k\} = \sum_{k=0}^{\infty} \frac{a^k}{z^k}$$

$$= \frac{1}{1-a/z} \quad (|z| > |a|)$$

so that

$$\mathscr{L}\{a^k\} = \frac{z}{z-a} \quad (|z| > |a|) \tag{3.4}$$

EXAMPLE 3.2   Show that

$$\mathscr{L}\{(-\tfrac{1}{2})^k\} = \frac{2z}{2z+1} \quad (|z| > \tfrac{1}{2})$$

Solution   Taking $a = -\tfrac{1}{2}$ in (3.4), we have

$$\mathscr{L}\{(-\tfrac{1}{2})^k\} = \sum_{k=0}^{\infty} \frac{(-\tfrac{1}{2})^k}{z^k}$$

$$= \frac{z}{z-(-\tfrac{1}{2})} \quad (|z| > \tfrac{1}{2})$$

so that

$$\mathscr{L}\{(-\tfrac{1}{2})^k\} = \frac{2z}{2z+1} \quad (|z| > \tfrac{1}{2})$$

Further z-transform pairs can be obtained from (3.4) by formally differentiating with respect to a, which for the moment we regard as a parameter. This gives

$$\frac{d}{da}\mathscr{L}\{a^k\} = \mathscr{L}\left\{\frac{da^k}{da}\right\} = \frac{d}{da}\left(\frac{z}{z-a}\right)$$

leading to

$$\mathscr{L}\{ka^{k-1}\} = \frac{z}{(z-a)^2} \quad (|z| > |a|) \tag{3.5}$$

In the particular case $a = 1$ this gives

$$\mathscr{L}\{k\} = \frac{z}{(z-1)^2} \quad (|z| > 1) \tag{3.6}$$

EXAMPLE 3.3   Find the z transform of the sequence

$$\{2k\} = \{0, 2, 4, 6, 8, \ldots\}$$

From (3.6),

$$\mathscr{L}\{k\} = \mathscr{L}\{0, 1, 2, 3, \ldots\}$$

$$= \sum_{k=0}^{\infty} \frac{k}{z^k} = \frac{z}{(z-1)^2}$$

Using the definition (3.1),

$$\mathscr{L}\{0, 2, 4, 6, 8, \ldots\} = 0 + \frac{2}{z} + \frac{4}{z^2} + \frac{6}{z^3} + \frac{8}{z^4} + \cdots$$

$$= 2 \sum_{k=0}^{\infty} \frac{k}{z^k}$$

so that

$$\mathscr{L}\{2k\} = 2\mathscr{L}\{k\} = \frac{2z}{(z-1)^2} \tag{3.7}$$

Example 3.3 demonstrates the 'linearity' property of the z transform, which we shall consider further in Section 3.3.1.

A sequence of particular importance is the **unit pulse** or **impulse** sequence

$$\{\delta_k\} = \{1\} = \{1, 0, 0, \ldots\}$$

It follows directly from the definition (3.4) that

$$\mathscr{L}\{\delta_k\} = 1 \tag{3.8}$$

3.2.2   Sampling: a first introduction

Sequences are often generated in engineering applications through the sampling of continuous-time signals, described by functions $f(t)$ of a continuous-time variable

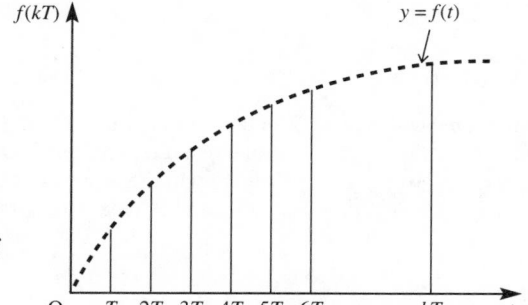

Figure 3.1 Sampling of a continuous-time signal.

t. Here we shall not discuss the means by which a signal is sampled, but merely suppose this to be possible in idealized form.

Figure 3.1 illustrates the idealized sampling process in which a continuous-time signal $f(t)$ is sampled instantaneously and perfectly at uniform intervals T, the **sampling interval**. The idealized sampling process generates the sequence

$$\{f(kT)\} = \{f(0), f(T), f(2T), \ldots, f(nT), \ldots\} \tag{3.9}$$

Using the definition (3.1), we can take the z transform of the sequence (3.9) to give

$$\mathscr{Z}\{f(kT)\} = \sum_{k=0}^{\infty} \frac{f(kT)}{z^k} \tag{3.10}$$

whenever the series converges. This idea is simply demonstrated by an example.

EXAMPLE 3.4   The signal $f(t) = e^{-t} H(t)$ is sampled at intervals T. What is the z transform of the resulting sequence of samples?

Solution   Sampling the causal function $f(t)$ generates the sequence

$$\{f(kT)\} = \{f(0), f(T), f(2T), \ldots, f(nT), \ldots\}$$
$$= \{1, e^{-T}, e^{-2T}, e^{-3T}, \ldots, e^{-nT}, \ldots\}$$

Then, using (3.1),

$$\mathscr{Z}\{f(kT)\} = \sum_{k=0}^{\infty} \frac{e^{-kT}}{z^k} = \sum_{k=0}^{\infty} \left(\frac{e^{-T}}{z}\right)^k$$

so that

$$\mathscr{Z}\{e^{-kT}\} = \frac{z}{z - e^{-T}} \quad (|z| > e^{-T}) \tag{3.11}$$

It is important to note in Example 3.4 that the region of convergence depends on the sampling interval T.

3.2.3   Exercises

1 Calculate the z transform of the following sequences, stating the region of convergence in each case:

(a) $\{(\frac{1}{4})^k\}$ (b) $\{3^k\}$ (c) $\{(-2)^k\}$ (d) $\{-(2^k)\}$

(e) $\{3k\}$

2 The continuous-time signal $f(t) = e^{-2\omega t}$, where ω is a real constant, is sampled when $t \geqslant 0$ at intervals T. Write down the general term of the sequence of samples, and calculate the z transform of the sequence.

3.3   Properties of the z transform

In this section we establish the basic properties of the z transform that will enable us to develop further z-transform pairs, without having to compute them directly using the definition.

3.3.1   The linearity property

As for Laplace transforms, a fundamental property of the z transform is its linearity, which may be stated as follows.

If $\{x_k\}$ and $\{y_k\}$ are sequences having z transforms $X(z)$ and $Y(z)$ respectively and if α and β are any constants, real or complex then

$$\mathscr{L}\{\alpha x_k + \beta y_k\} = \alpha \mathscr{L}\{x_k\} + \beta \mathscr{L}\{y_k\} = \alpha X(z) + \beta Y(z) \qquad (3.12)$$

As a consequence of this property, we say that the z-transform operator $\mathscr{L}$ is a **linear operator**. A proof of the property follows readily from the definition (3.4), since

$$\mathscr{L}\{\alpha x_k + \beta y_k\} = \sum_{k=0}^{\infty} \frac{\alpha x_k + \beta y_k}{z^k}$$

$$= \alpha \sum_{k=0}^{\infty} \frac{x_k}{z^k} + \beta \sum_{k=0}^{\infty} \frac{y_k}{z^k}$$

$$= \alpha X(z) + \beta Y(z)$$

The region of existence of the z transform, in the z plane, of the linear sum will be the intersection of the regions of existence (that is, the region common to both) of the individual z transforms $X(z)$ and $Y(z)$.

EXAMPLE 3.5   The continuous-time function $f(t) = \cos \omega t \, H(t)$, ω a constant, is sampled in the idealized sense at intervals T to generate the sequence $\{\cos k\omega T\}$. Determine the z transform of the sequence.

Solution   Using the result $\cos k\omega T = \frac{1}{2}(e^{jk\omega T} + e^{-jk\omega T})$ and the linearity property, we have

$$\mathscr{L}\{\cos k\omega T\} = \mathscr{L}\{\tfrac{1}{2}e^{jk\omega T} + \tfrac{1}{2}e^{-jk\omega T}\}$$

$$= \tfrac{1}{2}\mathscr{L}\{e^{jk\omega T}\} + \tfrac{1}{2}\mathscr{L}\{e^{-jk\omega T}\}$$

Using (3.7) and noting that $|e^{jk\omega T}| = |e^{-jk\omega T}| = 1$ gives

$$\mathscr{L}\{\cos k\omega T\} = \tfrac{1}{2}\frac{z}{z - e^{j\omega T}} + \tfrac{1}{2}\frac{z}{z - e^{-j\omega T}} \quad (|z| > 1)$$

$$= \tfrac{1}{2}\frac{z(z - e^{-j\omega T}) + z(z - e^{j\omega T})}{z^2 - (e^{j\omega T} + e^{-j\omega T})z + 1}$$

leading to the z-transform pair

$$\mathscr{L}(\cos k\omega T) = \frac{z(z - \cos \omega T)}{z^2 - 2z\cos \omega T + 1} \quad (|z| > 1) \tag{3.13}$$

In a similar manner to Example 3.5, we can verify the z-transform pair

$$\mathscr{L}\{\sin k\omega T\} = \frac{z \sin \omega T}{z^2 - 2z\cos \omega T + 1} \quad (|z| > 1) \tag{3.14}$$

and this is left as an exercise for the reader (see Exercise 3).

3.3.2   The first shift property (delaying)

In this and the next section we introduce two properties relating the z transform of a sequence to the z transform of a shifted version of the same sequence. In this section we consider a delayed version of the sequence $\{x_k\}$, denoted by $\{y_k\}$, with

$$y_k = x_{k-k_0}$$

Here k_0 is the number of steps in the delay; for example, if $k_0 = 2$ then $y_k = x_{k-2}$, so that

$$y_0 = x_{-2}, \qquad y_1 = x_{-1}, \qquad y_2 = x_0, \qquad y_3 = x_1$$

and so on. Thus the sequence $\{y_k\}$ is simply the sequence $\{x_k\}$ moved backward,

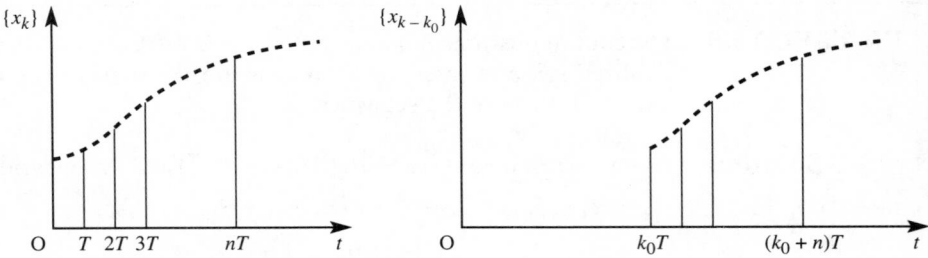

Figure 3.2 Sequence and its shifted form.

or delayed, by two steps. From the definition (3.1),

$$\mathscr{Z}\{y_k\} = \sum_{k=0}^{\infty} \frac{y_k}{z^k}$$

$$= \sum_{k=0}^{\infty} \frac{x_{k-k_0}}{z^k}$$

$$= \sum_{p=k_0}^{\infty} \frac{x_p}{z^{p+k_0}}$$

where we have written $p = k - k_0$. If $\{x_k\}$ is a causal sequence, so that $x_p = 0$ $(p < 0)$, then

$$\mathscr{Z}\{y_k\} = \sum_{p=0}^{\infty} \frac{x_p}{z^{p+k_0}} = \frac{1}{z^{k_0}} \sum_{p=0}^{\infty} \frac{x_p}{z^p}$$

$$= \frac{1}{z^{k_0}} X(z)$$

where $X(z)$ is the z transform of $\{x_k\}$.

We therefore have the result

$$\mathscr{Z}\{x_{k-k_0}\} = \frac{1}{z^{k_0}} \mathscr{Z}\{x_k\} \tag{3.15}$$

which is referred to as the **first shift property** of z transforms.

If $\{x_k\}$ represents the sampled form, with uniform sampling interval T, of the continuous signal $x(t)$ then $\{x_{k-k_0}\}$ represents the sampled form of the continuous signal $x(t - k_0 T)$ which, as illustrated in Figure 3.2, is the signal $x(t)$ delayed by a multiple k_0 of the sampling interval T. The reader will find it of interest to compare this result with the first shift property of Laplace transforms (Theorem 2.2).

EXAMPLE 3.6   The causal sequence $\{x_k\}$ is generated by

$$x_k = (\tfrac{1}{2})^k \quad (k \geqslant 0)$$

Determine the z transform of the shifted sequence $\{x_{k-2}\}$.

Solution By the first shift property,

$$\mathscr{L}\{x_{k-2}\} = \frac{1}{z^2}\mathscr{L}\{(\tfrac{1}{2})^k\}$$

which, on using (3.4), gives

$$\mathscr{L}\{x_{k-2}\} = \frac{1}{z^2}\frac{z}{z-\frac{1}{2}} \quad (|z| > \tfrac{1}{2})$$

$$= \frac{1}{z^2}\frac{2z}{2z-1}$$

$$= \frac{2}{z(2z-1)} \quad (|z| > \tfrac{1}{2})$$

We can confirm this result by direct use of the definition (3.1). From this, and the fact that $\{x_k\}$ is a causal sequence,

$$\{x_{k-2}\} = \{x_{-2}, x_{-1}, x_0, x_1, \ldots\}$$

$$= \{0, 0, 1, \tfrac{1}{2}, \tfrac{1}{4}, \ldots\}$$

Thus,

$$\mathscr{L}\{x_{k-2}\} = 0 + 0 + \frac{1}{z^2} + \frac{1}{2z^3} + \frac{1}{4z^4} + \cdots$$

$$= \frac{1}{z^2}\left(1 + \frac{1}{2z} + \frac{1}{4z^2} + \cdots\right)$$

$$= \frac{1}{z^2}\frac{z}{z-\frac{1}{2}} \quad (|z| > \tfrac{1}{2})$$

$$= \frac{2}{z(2z-1)} \quad (|z| > \tfrac{1}{2})$$

3.3.3   The second shift property (advancing)

In this section we seek a relationship between the z transform of an advanced version of a sequence and that of the original sequence. First we consider a single-step advance. If $\{y_k\}$ is the single-step advanced version of the sequence $\{x_k\}$ then $\{y_k\}$ is generated by

$$y_k = x_{k+1} \quad (k \geqslant 0)$$

Then

$$\mathscr{Z}\{y_k\} = \sum_{k=0}^{\infty} \frac{y_k}{z^k} = \sum_{k=0}^{\infty} \frac{x_{k+1}}{z^k}$$

$$= z \sum_{k=0}^{\infty} \frac{x_{k+1}}{z^{k+1}}$$

and putting $p = k + 1$ gives

$$\mathscr{Z}\{y_k\} = z \sum_{p=1}^{\infty} \frac{x_p}{z^p} = z\left(\sum_{p=0}^{\infty} \frac{x_p}{z^p} - x_0 \right)$$

$$= zX(z) - zx_0$$

where $X(z)$ is the z transform of $\{x_k\}$.

We therefore have the result

$$\mathscr{Z}\{x_{k+1}\} = zX(z) - zx_0 \tag{3.16}$$

In a similar manner it is readily shown that for a two-step advanced sequence $\{x_{k+2}\}$

$$\mathscr{Z}\{x_{k+2}\} = z^2 X(z) - z^2 x_0 - z x_1 \tag{3.17}$$

Note the similarity in structure between (3.16) and (3.17) on the one hand and those for the Laplace transforms of first and second derivatives (Section 2.3.1). In general, it is readily proved by induction that for a k_0-step advanced sequence $\{x_{k+k_0}\}$

$$\mathscr{Z}\{x_{k+k_0}\} = z^{k_0} X(z) - \sum_{n=0}^{k_0-1} x_n z^{k_0-n} \tag{3.18}$$

In Section 3.5.2 we shall use these results to solve difference equations.

3.3.4 Some further properties

In this section we shall state some further useful properties of the z transform, leaving their verification to the reader as Exercises 9 and 10.

(i) Multiplication by a^k

If $Z\{x_k\} = X(z)$ then for a constant a

$$\mathscr{Z}\{a^k x_k\} = X(a^{-1}z) \tag{3.19}$$

(ii) Multiplication by k^n

If $\mathscr{Z}\{x_k\} = X(z)$ then for a positive integer n

$$\mathscr{Z}\{k^n x_k\} = \left(-z \frac{\mathrm{d}}{\mathrm{d}z} \right)^n X(z) \tag{3.20}$$

Note that in (3.20) the operator $-z\,\mathrm{d}/\mathrm{d}z$ means 'first differentiate with respect to z and then multiply by $-z$'. Raising to the power of n means 'repeat the operation n times'.

(iii) Initial-value theorem

If $\{x_k\}$ is a sequence with z transform $X(z)$ then the initial-value theorem states that

$$\lim_{z\to\infty} X(z) = x_0 \tag{3.21}$$

(iv) Final-value theorem

If $\{x_k\}$ is a sequence with z transform $X(z)$ then the final-value theorem states that

$$\lim_{k\to\infty} x_k = \lim_{z\to1}(1 - z^{-1})X(z) \tag{3.22}$$

provided that $\lim_{k\to\infty} x_k$ exists.

3.3.5   Table of *z* transforms

It is appropriate at this stage to draw together the results proved so far for easy access. This is done in the form of a table in Figure 3.3.

$\{x_k\}\ (k \geqslant 0)$	$\mathscr{Z}\{x_k\}$	Region of existence
$x_k = \begin{cases}1 & (k=0)\\ 0 & (k>0)\end{cases}$ (unit pulse sequence)	1	All z
$x_k = 1$ (unit step sequence)	$\dfrac{z}{z-1}$	$\|z\|>1$
$x_k = a^k$ (a constant)	$\dfrac{z}{z-a}$	$\|z\|>\|a\|$
$x_k = k$	$\dfrac{z}{(z-1)^2}$	$\|z\|>1$
$x_k = ka^{k-1}$ (a constant)	$\dfrac{z^2}{(z-a)^2}$	$\|z\|>a$
$x_k = \mathrm{e}^{-kT}$ (T constant)	$\dfrac{z}{z-\mathrm{e}^{-T}}$	$\|z\|>\mathrm{e}^{-T}$
$x_k = \cos k\omega T$ (ω, T constants)	$\dfrac{z(z-\cos\omega T)}{z^2-2z\cos\omega T+1}$	$\|z\|>1$
$x_k = \sin k\omega T$ (ω, T constants)	$\dfrac{z\sin\omega T}{z^2-2z\cos\omega T+1}$	$\|z\|>1$

Figure 3.3 A short table of z transforms.

3.3.6   Exercises

3 Use the method of Example 3.5 to confirm (3.14), namely

$$\mathscr{L}\{\sin k\omega T\} = \frac{z \sin \omega T}{z^2 - 2z \cos \omega T + 1}$$

where ω and T are constants.

4 Use the first shift property to calculate the z transform of the sequence $\{y_k\}$, with

$$y_k = \begin{cases} 0 & (k < 3) \\ x_k & (k \geqslant 3) \end{cases}$$

where $\{x_k\}$ is causal and $x_k = (\frac{1}{2})^k$. Confirm your result by direct evaluation of $\mathscr{L}\{y_k\}$ using the definition of the z transform.

5 Determine the z transforms of the sequences

(a) $\{(-\frac{1}{5})^k\}$ (b) $\{\cos k\pi\}$

6 Determine $\mathscr{L}\{(\frac{1}{2})^k\}$. Using (3.6), obtain the z transform of the sequence $\{k(\frac{1}{2})^k\}$.

7 Show that for a constant α

(a) $\mathscr{L}\{\sinh k\alpha\} = \dfrac{z \sinh \alpha}{z^2 - 2z \cosh \alpha + 1}$

(b) $\mathscr{L}\{\cosh k\alpha\} = \dfrac{z^2 - z \cosh \alpha}{z^2 - 2z \cosh \alpha + 1}$

8 Sequences are generated by sampling a causal continuous-time signal $u(t)$ $(t \geqslant 0)$ at uniform intervals T. Write down an expression for u_k, the general term of the sequence, and calculate the corresponding z transform when $u(t)$ is

(a) e^{-4t} (b) $\sin t$ (c) $\cos 2t$

9 Prove the initial- and final-value theorems given in (3.21) and (3.22).

10 Prove the multiplication properties given in (3.19) and (3.20).

3.4   The inverse z transform

In this section we consider the problem of recovering a causal sequence $\{x_k\}$ from knowledge of its z transform $X(z)$. As we shall see, the work on the inversion of Laplace transforms in Section 2.2.7 will prove a valuable asset for this task.

Formally the symbol $\mathscr{L}^{-1}[X(z)]$ denotes a causal sequence $\{x_k\}$ whose z transform is $X(z)$; that is,

$$\text{if} \quad \mathscr{L}\{x_k\} = X(z) \quad \text{then} \quad \{x_k\} = \mathscr{L}^{-1}[X(z)]$$

This correspondence between $X(z)$ and $\{x_k\}$ is called the **inverse z transformation**, $\{x_k\}$ being the **inverse transform** of $X(z)$, and $\mathscr{L}^{-1}$ being referred to as the **inverse z-transform operator**.

As for the Laplace transforms in Section 2.2.8, the most obvious way of finding the inverse transform of $X(z)$ is to make use of a table of transforms such as that given in Figure 3.3. Sometimes it is possible to write down the inverse transform directly from the table, but more often than not it is first necessary to carry out some algebraic manipulation on $X(z)$. In particular, we frequently need to determine the inverse transform of a rational expression of the form $P(z)/Q(z)$, where $P(z)$ and $Q(z)$ are polynomials in z. In such cases the procedure, as for Laplace transforms, is first to resolve the expression, or a revised form of the expression, into partial fractions and then to use the table of transforms. We shall now illustrate the approach through some examples.

3.4.1   Inverse techniques

EXAMPLE 3.7   Find

$$\mathscr{Z}^{-1}\left[\frac{z}{z-2}\right]$$

Solution   From Figure 3.3, we see that $z/(z-2)$ is a special case of the transform $z/(z-a)$, with $a = 2$. Thus

$$\mathscr{Z}^{-1}\left[\frac{z}{z-2}\right] = \{2^k\}$$

EXAMPLE 3.8   Find

$$\mathscr{Z}^{-1}\left[\frac{z}{(z-1)(z-2)}\right]$$

Solution   Guided by our work on Laplace transforms, we might attempt to resolve

$$Y(z) = \frac{z}{(z-1)(z-2)}$$

into partial fractions. This approach does produce the correct result, as we shall show later. However, we notice that most of the entries in Figure 3.3 contain a factor z in the numerator of the transform. We therefore resolve

$$\frac{Y(z)}{z} = \frac{1}{(z-1)(z-2)}$$

into partial fractions, as

$$\frac{Y(z)}{z} = \frac{1}{z-2} - \frac{1}{z-1}$$

so that

$$Y(z) = \frac{z}{z-2} - \frac{z}{z-1}$$

Then using the result $\mathscr{Z}^{-1}[z/(z-a)] = \{a^k\}$ together with the linearity property, we have

$$\mathscr{L}^{-1}[Y(z)] = \mathscr{L}^{-1}\left(\frac{z}{z-2} - \frac{z}{z-1}\right)$$

$$= \mathscr{L}^{-1}\left(\frac{z}{z-2}\right) - \mathscr{L}^{-1}\left(\frac{z}{z-1}\right)$$

$$= \{2^k\} - \{1^k\} \quad (k \geqslant 0)$$

so that

$$\mathscr{L}^{-1}\left[\frac{z}{(z-1)(z-2)}\right] = \{2^k - 1\} \quad (k \geqslant 0) \tag{3.23}$$

Suppose that in Example 3.8 we had not thought so far ahead and we had simply resolved $Y(z)$, rather than $Y(z)/z$, into partial fractions. Would the result be the same? The answer of course is 'yes', as we shall now show. Resolving

$$Y(z) = \frac{z}{(z-1)(z-2)}$$

into partial fractions gives

$$Y(z) = \frac{2}{z-2} - \frac{1}{z-1}$$

which may be written as

$$Y(z) = \frac{1}{z}\frac{2z}{z-2} - \frac{1}{z}\frac{z}{z-1}$$

Since

$$\mathscr{L}^{-1}\left[\frac{2z}{z-2}\right] = 2\mathscr{L}^{-1}\left(\frac{z}{z-2}\right) = 2\{2^k\}$$

it follows from the first shift property (3.15) that

$$\mathscr{L}^{-1}\left[\frac{1}{z}\frac{2z}{z-2}\right] = \begin{cases} \{2 \cdot 2^{k-1}\} & (k > 0) \\ 0 & (k = 0) \end{cases}$$

Similarly,

$$\mathscr{L}^{-1}\left[\frac{1}{z}\frac{z}{z-1}\right] = \begin{cases} \{1^{k-1}\} = \{1\} & (k > 0) \\ 0 & (k = 0) \end{cases}$$

Combining these last two results, we have

$$\mathscr{L}^{-1}[Y(z)] = \mathscr{L}^{-1}\left[\frac{1}{z}\frac{2z}{z-2}\right] - \mathscr{L}^{-1}\left[\frac{1}{z}\frac{z}{z-1}\right]$$

$$= \begin{cases} \{2^k - 1\} & (k > 0) \\ 0 & (k = 0) \end{cases}$$

which, as expected, is in agreement with the answer obtained in Example 3.8.

We can see that adopting this latter approach, while producing the correct result, involved extra effort in the use of a shift theorem. When possible, we avoid this by 'extracting' the factor z as in Example 3.8, but of course this is not always possible, and recourse must be made to the shift property, as the following example illustrates.

EXAMPLE 3.9   Find

$$\mathscr{Z}^{-1}\left[\frac{2z + 1}{(z + 1)(z - 3)}\right]$$

Solution   In this case there is no factor z available in the numerator, and so we must resolve

$$Y(z) = \frac{2z + 1}{(z + 1)(z - 3)}$$

into partial fractions, giving

$$Y(z) = \tfrac{1}{4}\frac{1}{z + 1} + \tfrac{7}{4}\frac{1}{z - 3}$$

$$= \tfrac{1}{4}\frac{1}{z}\frac{z}{z + 1} + \tfrac{7}{4}\frac{1}{z}\frac{z}{z - 3}$$

Since

$$\mathscr{Z}^{-1}\left[\frac{z}{z + 1}\right] = \{(-1)^k\} \quad (k \geqslant 0)$$

$$\mathscr{Z}^{-1}\left[\frac{z}{z - 3}\right] = \{3^k\} \quad (k \geqslant 0)$$

it follows from the first shift property (3.15) that

$$\mathscr{Z}^{-1}\left[\frac{1}{z}\frac{z}{z + 1}\right] = \begin{cases} \{(-1)^{k-1}\} & (k > 0) \\ 0 & (k = 0) \end{cases}$$

$$\mathscr{Z}^{-1}\left[\frac{1}{z}\frac{z}{z - 3}\right] = \begin{cases} 3^{k-1} & (k > 0) \\ 0 & (k = 0) \end{cases}$$

Then, from the linearity property

$$\mathscr{Z}^{-1}[Y(z)] = \tfrac{1}{4}\mathscr{Z}^{-1}\left[\frac{1}{z}\frac{z}{z + 1}\right] + \tfrac{7}{4}\mathscr{Z}^{-1}\left[\frac{1}{z}\frac{z}{z - 3}\right]$$

giving

$$\mathscr{Z}^{-1}\left[\frac{2z + 1}{(z + 1)(z - 3)}\right] = \begin{cases} \{\tfrac{1}{4}(-1)^{k-1} + \tfrac{7}{4}3^{k-1}\} & (k > 0) \\ 0 & (k = 0) \end{cases}$$

It is often the case that the rational function $P(z)/Q(z)$ to be inverted has a quadratic term in the denominator. Unfortunately, in this case there is nothing resembling the first shift theorem of the Laplace transform which, as we saw in Section 2.2.9, proved so useful in similar circumstances. Looking at Figure 3.3, the only two transforms with quadratic terms in the denominator are those associated with the sequences $\{\cos k\omega T\}$ and $\{\sin k\omega T\}$. In practice these prove difficult to apply in the inverse form, and a 'first principles' approach is more appropriate. We illustrate this with two examples, demonstrating that all that is really required is the ability to handle complex numbers at the stage of resolution into partial fractions.

EXAMPLE 3.10   Invert the z transform

$$Y(z) = \frac{z}{z^2 + a^2}$$

where a is a real constant.

Solution   In view of the factor z in the numerator, we resolve $Y(z)/z$ into partial fractions, giving

$$\frac{Y(z)}{z} = \frac{1}{z^2 + a^2}$$

$$= \frac{1}{(z + ja)(z - ja)}$$

$$= \frac{1}{j2a} \frac{1}{z - ja} - \frac{1}{j2a} \frac{1}{z + ja}$$

That is

$$Y(z) = \frac{1}{j2a} \left(\frac{z}{z - ja} - \frac{z}{z + ja} \right)$$

Using the result $\mathcal{Z}^{-1}[z/(z - a)] = \{a^k\}$, we have

$$\mathcal{Z}^{-1}\left[\frac{z}{z - ja} \right] = \{(ja)^k\} = \{j^k a^k\}$$

$$\mathcal{Z}^{-1}\left[\frac{z}{z + ja} \right] = \{(-ja)^k\} = \{(-j)^k a^k\}$$

From the relation $e^{j\theta} = \cos\theta + j\sin\theta$, we have

$$j = e^{j\pi/2}, \qquad -j = e^{-j\pi/2}$$

so that

$$\mathcal{Z}^{-1}\left[\frac{z}{z - ja} \right] = \{a^k(e^{j\pi/2})^k\} = \{a^k e^{jk\pi/2}\}$$

$$= \{a^k(\cos\tfrac{1}{2}k\pi + j\sin\tfrac{1}{2}k\pi)\}$$

$$\mathscr{L}^{-1}\left[\frac{z}{z+ja}\right] = \{a^k(\cos\tfrac{1}{2}k\pi - j\sin\tfrac{1}{2}k\pi)\}$$

The linearity property then gives

$$\mathscr{L}^{-1}[Y(z)] = \left\{\frac{a^k}{j2a}(\cos\tfrac{1}{2}k\pi + j\sin\tfrac{1}{2}k\pi - \cos\tfrac{1}{2}k\pi + j\sin\tfrac{1}{2}k\pi)\right\}$$

$$= \{a^{k-1}\sin\tfrac{1}{2}k\pi\}$$

EXAMPLE 3.11   Invert

$$Y(z) = \frac{z}{z^2 - z + 1}$$

Solution   The denominator of the transform may be factorized as

$$z^2 - z + 1 = \left(z - \tfrac{1}{2} - j\frac{\sqrt{3}}{2}\right)\left(z - \tfrac{1}{2} + j\frac{\sqrt{3}}{2}\right)$$

In exponential form we have $\tfrac{1}{2} \pm j\tfrac{1}{2}\sqrt{3} = e^{\pm j\pi/3}$, so the denominator may be written as

$$z^2 - z + 1 = (z - e^{j\pi/3})(z - e^{-j\pi/3})$$

We then have

$$\frac{Y(z)}{z} = \frac{1}{(z - e^{j\pi/3})(z - e^{-j\pi/3})}$$

which can be resolved into partial fractions as

$$\frac{Y(z)}{z} = \frac{1}{e^{j\pi/3} - e^{-j\pi/3}}\frac{1}{z - e^{j\pi/3}} + \frac{1}{e^{-j\pi/3} - e^{j\pi/3}}\frac{1}{z - e^{-j\pi/3}}$$

Noting that $\sin\theta = (e^{j\theta} - e^{-j\theta})/j2$, this reduces to

$$\frac{Y(z)}{z} = \frac{1}{j2\sin\tfrac{1}{3}\pi}\frac{z}{z - e^{j\pi/3}} - \frac{1}{j2\sin\tfrac{1}{3}\pi}\frac{z}{z - e^{-j\pi/3}}$$

$$= \frac{1}{j\sqrt{3}}\frac{z}{z - e^{j\pi/3}} - \frac{1}{j\sqrt{3}}\frac{z}{z - e^{-j\pi/3}}$$

Using the result $\mathscr{L}^{-1}[z/(z - a)] = \{a^k\}$, this gives

$$\mathscr{L}^{-1}[Y(z)] = \frac{1}{j\sqrt{3}}(e^{jk\pi/3} - e^{-jk\pi/3})$$

$$= \{2\sqrt{\tfrac{1}{3}}\sin\tfrac{1}{3}k\pi\}$$

We conclude this section with two further examples, illustrating the inversion technique applied to frequently occurring transform types.

EXAMPLE 3.12   Find the sequence whose z transform is

$$F(z) = \frac{z^3 + 2z^2 + 1}{z^3}$$

Solution $F(z)$ is unlike any z transform treated so far in the examples. However, it is readily expanded in a power series in z^{-1} as

$$F(z) = 1 + \frac{2}{z} + \frac{1}{z^3}$$

Using (3.4), it is then apparent that

$$\mathscr{Z}^{-1}[F(z)] = \{f_k\} = \{1, 2, 1, 0, 0, \ldots\}$$

EXAMPLE 3.13   Find $\mathscr{Z}^{-1}[G(z)]$ where

$$G(z) = \frac{z(1 - e^{-aT})}{(z - 1)(z - e^{-aT})}$$

where a and T are positive constants.

Solution   Resolving into partial fractions,

$$\frac{G(z)}{z} = \frac{1}{z - 1} - \frac{1}{z - e^{-aT}}$$

giving

$$G(z) = \frac{z}{z - 1} - \frac{z}{z - e^{-aT}}$$

Using the result $\mathscr{Z}^{-1}[z/(z - a)] = \{a^k\}$, we have

$$\mathscr{Z}^{-1}[G(z)] = \{(1 - e^{-akT})\} \quad (k \geqslant 0)$$

In this particular example $G(z)$ is the z transform of a sequence derived by sampling the continuous-time signal

$$f(t) = 1 - e^{-at}$$

at intervals T.

3.4.2   Exercises

11 Invert the following z transforms. Give the general term of the sequence in each case.

(a) $\dfrac{z}{z - 1}$ (b) $\dfrac{z}{z + 1}$

(c) $\dfrac{z}{z - \frac{1}{2}}$ (d) $\dfrac{z}{3z + 1}$

(e) $\dfrac{z}{z - j}$ (f) $\dfrac{z}{z + j\sqrt{2}}$

(g) $\dfrac{1}{z - 1}$ (h) $\dfrac{z + 2}{z + 1}$

12 By first resolving $Y(z)/z$ into partial fractions, find $\mathscr{Z}^{-1}[Y(z)]$ when $Y(z)$ is given by

(a) $\dfrac{z}{(z - 1)(z + 2)}$ (b) $\dfrac{z}{(2z + 1)(z - 3)}$

(c) $\dfrac{z^2}{(2z + 1)(z - 1)}$ (d) $\dfrac{2z}{2z^2 + z - 1}$

(e) $\dfrac{z}{z^2 + 1}$ [*Hint:* $z^2 + 1 = (z + j)(z - j)$]

(f) $\dfrac{z}{z^2 - 2\sqrt{3}\,z + 4}$ (g) $\dfrac{2z^2 - 7z}{(z - 1)^2(z - 3)}$

(h) $\dfrac{z^2}{(z - 1)^2(z^2 - z + 1)}$

13 Find $\mathscr{Z}^{-1}[Y(z)]$ when $Y(z)$ is given by

(a) $\dfrac{1}{z} + \dfrac{2}{z^7}$ (b) $1 + \dfrac{3}{z^2} - \dfrac{2}{z^9}$

(c) $\dfrac{3z + z^2 + 5z^5}{z^5}$ (d) $\dfrac{1 + z}{z^3} + \dfrac{3z}{3z + 1}$

(e) $\dfrac{2z^3 + 6z^2 + 5z + 1}{z^2(2z + 1)}$ (f) $\dfrac{2z^2 - 7z + 7}{(z - 1)^2(z - 2)}$

(g) $\dfrac{z - 3}{z^2 - 3z + 2}$

3.5 Discrete-time systems and difference equations

In Chapter 2 the Laplace transform technique was examined, first as a method for solving differential equations, then as a way of characterizing a continuous-time system. In fact, much could be deduced concerning the behaviour of the system and its properties by examining its transform-domain representation, without looking for specific time-domain responses at all. In this section we shall discuss the idea of a linear discrete-time system and its model, a **difference equation**. Later we shall see that the z transform plays an analogous role to the Laplace transform for such systems, by providing a transform-domain representation of the system.

3.5.1 Difference equations

First we illustrate the motivation for studying difference equations by means of an example.

Suppose that a sequence of observations $\{x_k\}$ is being recorded and we receive observation x_k at (time) step or index k. We might attempt to process (for example smooth or filter) this sequence of observations $\{x_k\}$ using the discrete-time feedback system illustrated in Figure 3.4. At time step k the observation x_k enters the system

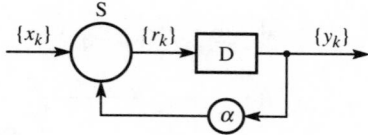

Figure 3.4 Discrete-time signal processing system.

as an input, and, after combination with the 'feedback' signal at the summing junction S, proceeds to the block labelled D. This block is a unit delay block, and its function is to hold its input signal until the 'clock' advances one step, to step $k + 1$. At this time the input signal is passed without alteration to become the signal y_{k+1}, the $(k + 1)$th member of the output sequence $\{y_k\}$. At the same time this signal is fed back through a scaling block of amplitude α to the summing junction S. This process is instantaneous, and at S the feedback signal is subtracted from the next input observation x_{k+1} to provide the next input to the delay block D. The process then repeats at each 'clock' step.

To analyse the system, let $\{r_k\}$ denote the sequence of input signals to D; then, owing to the delay action of D, we have

$$y_{k+1} = r_k$$

Also, owing to the feedback action,

$$r_k = x_k - \alpha y_k$$

where α is the feedback gain. Combining the two expressions gives

$$y_{k+1} = x_k - \alpha y_k$$

or

$$y_{k+1} + \alpha y_k = x_k \tag{3.24}$$

Equation (3.24) is an example of a first-order difference equation, and it relates adjacent members of the sequence $\{y_k\}$ to each other and to the input sequence $\{x_k\}$.

A solution of the difference equation (3.24) is a formula for y_k, the general term of the output sequence $\{y_k\}$, and this will depend on both k and the input sequence $\{x_k\}$ as well as, in this case, the feedback gain α.

EXAMPLE 3.14   Find a difference equation to represent the system shown in Figure 3.5, having input and output sequences $\{x_k\}$ and $\{y_k\}$ respectively, where D is the unit delay block and a and b are constant feedback gains.

Figure 3.5 The system for Example 3.14.

Solution Introducing intermediate signal sequences $\{r_k\}$ and $\{v_k\}$ as shown in Figure 3.5, at each step the outputs of the delay blocks are

$$y_{k+1} = v_k \tag{3.25}$$

$$v_{k+1} = r_k \tag{3.26}$$

and at the summing junction

$$r_k = x_k - av_k + by_k \tag{3.27}$$

From (3.25),

$$y_{k+2} = v_{k+1}$$

which on using (3.26) gives

$$y_{k+2} = r_k$$

Substituting for r_k from (3.27) then gives

$$y_{k+2} = x_k - av_k + by_k$$

which on using (3.25) becomes

$$y_{k+2} = x_k - ay_{k+1} + by_k$$

Rearranging this gives

$$y_{k+2} + ay_{k+1} - by_k = x_k \tag{3.28}$$

as the difference equation representing the system.

The difference equation (3.28) is an example of a second-order linear constant-coefficient difference equation, and there are strong similarities between this and a second-order linear constant-coefficient differential equation. It is of second order because the term involving the greatest shift of the $\{y_k\}$ sequence is the term in y_{k+2}, implying a shift of two steps. As demonstrated by Example 3.14, the degree of shift, or the order of the equation, is closely related to the number of delay blocks in the block diagram.

3.5.2 The solution of difference equations

Difference equations arise in a variety of ways, sometimes from the direct modelling of systems in discrete time or as an approximation to a differential equation describing the behaviour of a system modelled as a continuous-time system. We do not discuss this further here; rather we restrict ourselves to the technique of solution but examples of applications will be apparent from the exercises. The z-transform method is based upon the second shift property (Section 3.3.3), and it will quickly emerge as a technique almost identical to the Laplace transform method for ordinary differential equations introduced in Section 2.3.3. We shall introduce the method by means of an example.

EXAMPLE 3.15 If in Example 3.14, $a = 1$, $b = 2$ and the input sequence $\{x_k\}$ is the unit step sequence $\{1\}$, solve the resulting difference equation (3.28).

Solution Substituting for a, b and $\{x_k\}$ in (3.28) leads to the difference equation

$$y_{k+2} + y_{k+1} - 2y_k = 1 \quad (k \geqslant 0) \tag{3.29}$$

Taking z transforms throughout in (3.29) gives

$$\mathscr{Z}\{y_{k+2} + y_{k+1} - 2y_k\} = \mathscr{Z}\{1, 1, 1, \ldots\}$$

which, on using the linearity property and the result $\mathscr{Z}\{1\} = z/(z - 1)$, may be written as

$$\mathscr{Z}\{y_{k+2}\} + \mathscr{Z}\{y_{k+1}\} - 2\mathscr{Z}\{y_k\} = \frac{z}{z - 1}$$

Using (3.16) and (3.17) then gives

$$[z^2 Y(z) - z^2 y_0 - z y_1] + [z Y(z) - z y_0] - 2Y(z) = \frac{z}{z - 1}$$

which on rearranging leads to

$$(z^2 + z - 2)Y(z) = \frac{z}{z - 1} + z^2 y_0 + z(y_1 + y_0) \tag{3.30}$$

To proceed, we need some further information, namely the first and second terms y_0 and y_1 of the solution sequence $\{y_k\}$. Without this additional information, we cannot find a unique solution. As we saw in Section 2.3.3, this compares with the use of the Laplace transform method to solve second-order differential equations, where the values of the solution and its first derivative at time $t = 0$ are required.

Suppose that we know (or are given) that

$$y_0 = 0, \qquad y_1 = 1$$

Then (3.30) becomes

$$(z^2 + z - 2)Y(z) = z + \frac{z}{z - 1}$$

or

$$(z + 2)(z - 1)Y(z) = z + \frac{z}{z - 1}$$

and solving for $Y(z)$ gives

$$z(z-1) + z =$$

$$Y(z) = \frac{z}{(z+2)(z-1)} + \frac{z}{(z+2)(z-1)^2}$$

$$= \frac{z^2}{(z+2)(z-1)^2} \tag{3.31}$$

To obtain the solution sequence $\{y_k\}$, we must take the inverse transform in (3.31). Proceeding as in Section 3.4, we resolve $Y(z)/z$ into partial fractions as

$$\frac{Y(z)}{z} = \frac{z}{(z+2)(z-1)^2}$$

$$= \tfrac{1}{3}\frac{1}{(z-1)^2} + \tfrac{2}{9}\frac{1}{z-1} - \tfrac{2}{9}\frac{1}{z+2}$$

and so

$$Y(z) = \tfrac{1}{3}\frac{z}{(z-1)^2} + \tfrac{2}{9}\frac{z}{z-1} - \tfrac{2}{9}\frac{z}{z+2}$$

Using the results $\mathcal{Z}^{-1}[z/(z-a)] = \{a^k\}$ and $\mathcal{Z}^{-1}[z/(z-1)^2] = \{k\}$ from Figure 3.3, we obtain

$$\{y_k\} = \{\tfrac{1}{3}k + \tfrac{2}{9} - \tfrac{2}{9}(-2)^k\} \quad (k \geqslant 0)$$

as the solution sequence for the difference equation satisfying the conditions $y_0 = 0$ and $y_1 = 1$.

The method adopted in Example 3.15 is called the **z-transform method for solving linear constant-coefficient difference equations**, and is analogous to the Laplace transform method for solving linear constant-coefficient differential equations.

To conclude this section, two further examples are given to help consolidate understanding of the method.

EXAMPLE 3.16   Solve the difference equation

$$8y_{k+2} - 6y_{k+1} + y_k = 9 \quad (k \geqslant 0)$$

given that $y_0 = 1$ and $y_1 = \tfrac{3}{2}$.

Solution   Taking z transforms

$$8\mathcal{Z}\{y_{k+2}\} - 6\mathcal{Z}\{y_{k+1}\} + \mathcal{Z}\{y_k\} = 9\mathcal{Z}\{1\}$$

Using (3.16) and (3.17) and the result $\mathcal{Z}\{1\} = z/(z-1)$ gives

$$8[z^2 Y(z) - z^2 y_0 - zy_1] - 6[zY(z) - zy_0] + Y(z) = \frac{9z}{z-1}$$

which on rearranging leads to

$$(8z^2 - 6z + 1)Y(z) = 8z^2 y_0 + 8z y_1 - 6z y_0 + \frac{9z}{z - 1}$$

We are given that $y_0 = 1$ and $y_1 = \frac{3}{2}$, so

$$(8z^2 - 6z + 1)Y(z) = 8z^2 + 6z + \frac{9z}{z - 1}$$

or

$$\frac{Y(z)}{z} = \frac{8z + 6}{(4z - 1)(2z - 1)} + \frac{9}{(4z - 1)(2z - 1)(z - 1)}$$

$$= \frac{z + \frac{3}{4}}{(z - \frac{1}{4})(z - \frac{1}{2})} + \frac{\frac{9}{8}}{(z - \frac{1}{4})(z - \frac{1}{2})(z - 1)}$$

Resolving into partial fractions gives

$$\frac{Y(z)}{z} = \frac{5}{z - \frac{1}{2}} - \frac{4}{z - \frac{1}{4}} + \frac{6}{z - \frac{1}{4}} - \frac{9}{z - \frac{1}{2}} + \frac{3}{z - 1}$$

$$= \frac{2}{z - \frac{1}{4}} - \frac{4}{z - \frac{1}{2}} + \frac{3}{z - 1}$$

and so

$$Y(z) = \frac{2z}{z - \frac{1}{4}} - \frac{4z}{z - \frac{1}{2}} + \frac{3z}{z - 1}$$

Using the result $\mathscr{Z}^{-1}\{z/(z - a)\} = \{a^k\}$ from Figure 3.3, we take inverse transforms, to obtain

$$\{y_k\} = \{2(\tfrac{1}{4})^k - 4(\tfrac{1}{2})^k + 3\} \quad (k \geqslant 0)$$

as the required solution.

EXAMPLE 3.17   Solve the difference equation

$$y_{k+2} + 2y_k = 0 \quad (k \geqslant 0)$$

given that $y_0 = 1$ and $y_1 = \sqrt{2}$.

Solution   Taking *z* transforms, we have

$$[z^2 Y(z) - z^2 y_0 - z y_1] + 2Y(z) = 0$$

and substituting the given values of y_0 and y_1 gives

$$z^2 Y(z) - z^2 - \sqrt{2}\, z + 2Y(z) = 0$$

or

$$(z^2 + 2)Y(z) = z^2 + \sqrt{2}\, z$$

Resolving $Y(z)/z$ into partial fractions gives

$$\frac{Y(z)}{z} = \frac{z + \sqrt{2}}{z^2 + \sqrt{2}} = \frac{z + \sqrt{2}}{(z + j\sqrt{2})(z - j\sqrt{2})}$$

Following the approach adopted in Example 3.13, we write

$$j\sqrt{2} = \sqrt{2}\,e^{j\pi/2}, \qquad -j\sqrt{2} = \sqrt{2}\,e^{-j\pi/2}$$

$$\frac{Y(z)}{z} = \frac{z + \sqrt{2}}{(z - \sqrt{2}\,e^{j\pi/2})(z - \sqrt{2}\,e^{-j\pi/2})}$$

$$= \frac{(1 + j)/j2}{z - \sqrt{2}\,e^{j\pi/2}} - \frac{(1 - j)/j2}{z - \sqrt{2}\,e^{-j\pi/2}}$$

Thus

$$Y(z) = \frac{1}{j2}\left[(1 + j)\frac{z}{z - \sqrt{2}\,e^{j\pi/2}} - (1 - j)\frac{z}{z - \sqrt{2}\,e^{-j\pi/2}} \right]$$

which on taking inverse transforms gives

$$\{y_k\} = \left\{ \frac{2^{k/2}}{j2}\left[(1 + j)\,e^{jk\pi/2} - (1 - j)\,e^{-jk\pi/2} \right] \right\}$$

$$= \{2^{k/2}(\cos\tfrac{1}{2}k\pi + \sin\tfrac{1}{2}k\pi)\} \quad (k \geqslant 0)$$

as the required solution.

The solution in Example 3.17 was found to be a real-valued sequence, and this comes as no surprise because the given difference equation and the 'starting' values y_0 and y_1 involved only real numbers. This observation provides a useful check on the algebra when complex partial fractions are involved.

3.5.3 Exercises

14 Find difference equations representing the discrete-time systems shown in Figure 3.6.

15 Using z-transform methods, solve the following difference equations:

(a) $y_{k+2} - 2y_{k+1} + y_k = 0$ subject to $y_0 = 0, y_1 = 1$

(b) $y_{n+2} - 8y_{n+1} - 9y_n = 0$ subject to $y_0 = 2, y_1 = 1$

(c) $y_{k+2} + 4y_k = 0$ subject to $y_0 = 0, y_1 = 1$

(d) $2y_{k+2} - 5y_{k+1} - 3y_k = 0$ subject to $y_0 = 3, y_1 = 2$

Figure 3.6 The systems for Exercise 14.

16 Using *z*-transform methods, solve the following difference equations:

(a) $6y_{k+2} + 5y_{k+1} - y_k = 5$ subject to $y_0 = y_1 = 0$

(b) $y_{k+2} - 5y_{k+1} + 6y_k = 5$ subject to $y_0 = 0, y_1 = 1$

(c) $y_{n+2} - 5y_{n+1} + 6y_n = (\frac{1}{2})^n$ subject to $y_0 = y_1 = 0$

(d) $y_{n+2} - 3y_{n+1} + 3y_n = 1$ subject to $y_0 = 1, y_1 = 0$

(e) $2y_{n+2} - 3y_{n+1} - 2y_n = 6n + 1$ subject to $y_0 = 1, y_1 = 2$

(f) $y_{n+2} - 4y_n = 3n - 5$ subject to $y_0 = y_1 = 0$

17 A person's capital at the beginning, and expenditure during, a given year k are denoted by C_k and E_k respectively, and satisfy the difference equations

$$C_{k+1} = 1.5C_k - E_k$$
$$E_{k+1} = 0.21C_k + 0.5E_k$$

(a) Show that eventually the person's capital grows at 20% per annum.

(b) If the capital at the beginning of year 1 is £6000 and the expenditure during year 1 is £3720 then find the year in which the expenditure is a minimum and the capital at the beginning of that year.

18 The dynamics of a discrete-time system is determined by the difference equation

$$y_{k+2} - 5y_{k+1} + 6y_k = u_k$$

Determine the response of the system to the unit step input

$$u_k = \begin{cases} 0 & (k < 0) \\ 1 & (k \geqslant 0) \end{cases}$$

given that $y_0 = y_1 = 1$.

19 As a first attempt to model the national economy, it is assumed that the national income I_k at year k is given by

$$I_k = C_k + P_k + G_k$$

where C_k is the consumer expenditure, P_k is private investment and G_k is government expenditure. It is also assumed that the consumer spending is proportional to the national income in the previous year, so that

$$C_k = aI_{k-1} \quad (0 < a < 1)$$

It is further assumed that private investment is proportional to the change in consumer spending over the previous year, so that

$$P_k = b(C_k - C_{k-1}) \quad (0 < b \leqslant 1)$$

Show that under these assumptions the national income I_k is determined by the difference equation

$$I_{k+2} - a(1 + b)I_{k+1} + abI_k = G_{k+2}$$

If $a = \frac{1}{2}, b = 1$, government spending is at a constant level (that is, $G_k = G$ for all k) and $I_0 = 2G, I_1 = 3G$, show that

$$I_k = 2[1 + (\tfrac{1}{2})^{k/2} \sin \tfrac{1}{4}k\pi]G$$

Discuss what happens as $k \to \infty$.

20 The difference equation for current in a particular ladder network of N loops is

$$R_1 i_{n+1} + R_2(i_{n+1} - i_n) + R_2(i_{n+1} - i_{n+2}) = 0$$
$$(0 \leqslant n \leqslant N - 2)$$

where i_n is the current in the $(n + 1)$th loop, and R_1 and R_2 are constant resistors.

(a) Show that this may be written as

$$i_{n+2} - 2\cosh \alpha \, i_{n+1} + i_n = 0 \quad (0 \leqslant n \leqslant N - 2)$$

where

$$\alpha = \cosh^{-1}\left(1 + \frac{R_1}{2R_2}\right)$$

(b) By solving the equation in (a), show that

$$i_n = \frac{i_1 \sinh n\alpha - i_0 \sinh (n - 1)\alpha}{\sinh \alpha} \quad (2 \leqslant n \leqslant N)$$

3.6 Discrete linear systems: characterization

In this section we examine the concept of a discrete-time linear system and its difference equation model. Ideas developed in Chapter 2 for continuous-time system modelling will be seen to carry over to discrete-time systems, and we shall see that the *z* transform is the key to the understanding of such systems.

3.6.1   *z* transfer functions

In Section 2.6, when considering continuous-time linear systems modelled by differential equations, we introduced the concept of the system (Laplace) transfer function. This is a powerful tool in the description of such systems, since it contains all the information on system stability and also provides a method of calculating the response to an arbitrary input signal using a convolution integral. In the same way, we can identify a z transfer function for a discrete-time linear time-invariant system modelled by a difference equation, and we can arrive at results analogous to those of Chapter 2.

Let us consider the general linear constant-coefficient difference equation model for a linear time-invariant system, with input sequence $\{u_k\}$ and output sequence $\{y_k\}$. Both $\{u_k\}$ and $\{y_k\}$ are causal sequences throughout. Such a difference equation model takes the form

$$a_n y_{k+n} + a_{n-1} y_{k+n-1} + a_{n-2} y_{k+n-2} + \ldots + a_0 y_k = b_m u_{k+m} + b_{m-1} u_{k+m-1}$$
$$+ b_{m-2} u_{k+m-2} + \ldots + b_0 u_k$$

$$(3.32)$$

where $k \geqslant 0$ and n, m (with $n \geqslant m$) are positive integers and the a_i and b_j are constants. The difference equation (3.32) differs in one respect from the examples considered in Section 3.5 in that the possibility of delayed terms in the input sequence $\{u_k\}$ is also allowed for. The order of the difference equation is n if $a_n \neq 0$, and for the system to be physically realizable, $n \geqslant m$.

Assuming the system to be initially in a quiescent state, we take z transforms throughout in (3.32) to give

$$(a_n z^n + a_{n-1} z^{n-1} + \ldots + a_0) Y(z) = (b_m z^m + b_{m-1} z^{m-1} + \ldots + b_0) U(z)$$

where $Y(z) = \mathscr{L}\{y_k\}$ and $U(z) = \mathscr{L}\{u_k\}$. The **system discrete** or z **transfer function** $G(z)$ is defined as

$$G(z) = \frac{Y(z)}{U(z)} = \frac{b_m z^m + b_{m-1} z^{m-1} + \ldots + b_0}{a_n z^n + a_{n-1} z^{n-1} + \ldots + a_0} \qquad (3.33)$$

and is normally rearranged (by dividing numerator and denominator by a_n) so that the coefficient of z^n in the denominator is 1. In deriving $G(z)$ in this form, we have assumed that the system was initially in a quiescent state. This assumption is certainly valid for the system (3.32) if

$$y_0 = y_1 = \ldots = y_{n-1} = 0$$
$$u_0 = u_1 = \ldots = u_{m-1} = 0$$

This is not the end of the story, however, and we shall use the term 'quiescent' to mean that no non-zero values are stored on the delay elements before the initial time.

On writing

$$P(z) = b_m z^m + b_{m-1} z^{m-1} + \ldots + b_0$$

$$Q(z) = a_n z^n + a_{n-1} z^{n-1} + \ldots + a_0$$

the discrete transfer function may be expressed as

$$G(z) = \frac{P(z)}{Q(z)}$$

As for the continuous model in Section 2.6.1, the equation $Q(z) = 0$ is called the **characteristic equation** of the discrete system, its order n determines the **order of the system**, and its roots are referred to as the **poles** of the discrete transfer function. Likewise, the roots of $P(z) = 0$ are referred to as the **zeros** of the discrete transfer function.

EXAMPLE 3.18   Draw a block diagram to represent the system modelled by the difference equation

$$y_{k+2} + 3y_{k+1} - y_k = u_k \qquad (3.34)$$

and find the corresponding z transfer function.

Solution   The difference equation may be thought of as a relationship between adjacent members of the solution sequence $\{y_k\}$. Thus at each time step k we have from (3.34)

$$y_{k+2} = -3y_{k+1} + y_k + u_k \qquad (3.35)$$

which provides a formula for y_{k+2} involving y_k, y_{k+1} and the input u_k. The structure shown in Figure 3.7(a) illustrates the generation of the sequence $\{y_k\}$ from $\{y_{k+2}\}$ using two delay blocks.

We now use (3.35) as a prescription for generating the sequence $\{y_{k+2}\}$ and arrange for the correct combination of signals to be formed at each step k at the input summing junction S of Figure 3.7(a). This leads to the structure shown in Figure 3.7(b), which is the required block diagram.

We can of course produce a block diagram in the z-transform domain, using a similar process. Taking the z transform throughout in (3.34), under the assumption of a quiescent initial state, we obtain

$$z^2 Y(z) + 3z Y(z) - Y(z) = U(z) \qquad (3.36)$$

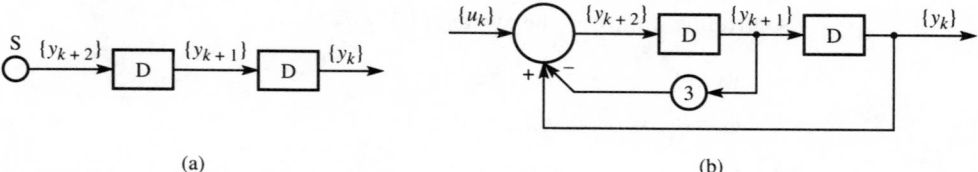

(a)   (b)

Figure 3.7 (a) The basic second-order block diagram substructure.   (b) Block diagram representation of (3.34).

or

$$z^2 Y(z) = -3z Y(z) + Y(z) + U(z) \tag{3.37}$$

The representation (3.37) is the transform domain version of (3.35), and the z-transform domain basic structure corresponding to the time-domain structure of Figure 3.7(a) is shown in Figure 3.8(a).

The unit delay blocks, labelled D in Figure 3.7(a), become '$1/z$' elements in the z-transform domain diagram, in line with the first shift property (3.15), where a number k_0 of delay steps involves multiplication by z^{-k_0}.

It is now a simple matter to construct the 'signal' transform $z^2 Y(z)$ from (3.37) and arrange for it to be available at the input to the summing junction S in Figure 3.8(a). The resulting block diagram is shown in Figure 3.8(b).

The z transfer function follows at once from (3.36) as

$$G(z) = \frac{Y(z)}{U(z)} = \frac{1}{z^2 + 3z - 1} \tag{3.38}$$

(a)   (b)

Figure 3.8 (a) The z-transform domain basic second-order block diagram substructure.   (b) The z-transform domain block diagram representation of (3.34).

EXAMPLE 3.19   A system is specified by its z transfer function

$$G(z) = \frac{z - 1}{z^2 + 3z + 2}$$

What is the order n of the system? Can it be implemented using only n delay elements? Illustrate this.

Solution   If $\{u_k\}$ and $\{y_k\}$ denote respectively the input and output sequences to the system then

$$G(z) = \frac{Y(z)}{U(z)} = \frac{z - 1}{z^2 + 3z + 2}$$

so that

$$(z^2 + 3z + 2)Y(z) = (z - 1)U(z)$$

Taking inverse transforms, we obtain the corresponding difference equation model assuming the system is initially in a quiescent state

$$y_{k+2} + 3y_{k+1} + 2y_k = u_{k+1} - u_k \tag{3.39}$$

The difference equation (3.39) has a more complex right-hand side than the difference equation (3.34) considered in Example 3.18. This results from the existence of z terms in the numerator of the transfer function. By definition, the order of the difference equation (3.39) is still 2. However, realization of the system with two delay blocks is not immediately apparent, although this can be achieved, as we shall now illustrate.

Introduce a new signal sequence $\{r_k\}$ such that

$$(z^2 + 3z + 2)R(z) = U(z) \tag{3.40}$$

where $R(z) = \mathcal{Z}\{r_k\}$. In other words, $\{r_k\}$ is the output of the system having transfer function $1/(z^2 + 3z + 2)$.

Multiplying both sides of (3.40) by z, we obtain

$$z(z^2 + 3z + 2)R(z) = zU(z)$$

or

$$(z^2 + 3z + 2)zR(z) = zU(z) \tag{3.41}$$

Subtracting (3.40) from (3.41) we have

$$(z^2 + 3z + 2)zR(z) - (z^2 + 3z + 2)R(z) = zU(z) - U(z)$$

giving

$$(z^2 + 3z + 2)[zR(z) - R(z)] = (z - 1)U(z)$$

Finally, choosing

$$Y(z) = zR(z) - R(z) \tag{3.42}$$

$$(z^2 + 3z + 2)Y(z) = (z - 1)U(z)$$

which is a realization of the given transfer function.

To construct a block diagram realization of the system, we first construct a block diagram representation of (3.40) as in Figure 3.9(a). We now 'tap-off'

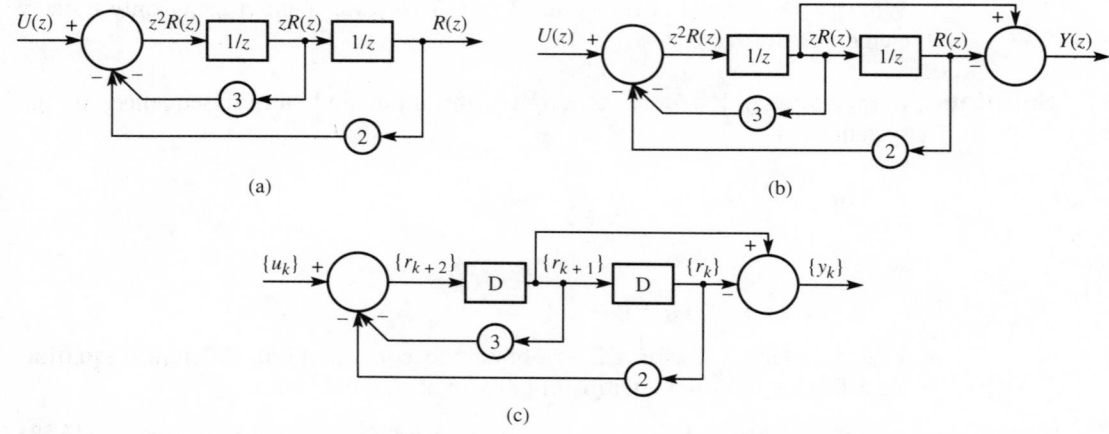

(a)

(b)

(c)

Figure 3.9 The z-transform block diagrams for the systems (3.40) (a) and (3.39) (b), and the time-domain realization (c) of the system in Example 3.19.

appropriate signals to generate $Y(z)$ according to (3.42) to construct a block diagram representation of the specified system. The resulting block diagram is shown in Figure 3.9(b).

In order to implement the system, we must exhibit a physically realizable time-domain structure, that is, one containing only D elements. Clearly, since Figure 3.9(b) contains only '$1/z$' blocks, we can immediately produce a realizable time-domain structure as shown in Figure 3.9(c), where, as before, D is the unit delay block.

EXAMPLE 3.20   A system is specified by its z transfer function

$$G(z) = \frac{z}{z^2 + 0.3z + 0.02}$$

Draw a block diagram to illustrate a time-domain realization of the system. Find a second structure that also implements the system.

Solution   We know that if $\mathscr{Z}\{u_k\} = U\{z\}$ and $\mathscr{Z}\{y_k\} = Y(z)$ are the z transforms of the input and output sequences respectively then, by definition,

$$G(z) = \frac{Y(z)}{U(z)} = \frac{z}{z^2 + 0.3z + 0.02} \tag{3.43}$$

which may be rewritten as

$$(z^2 + 0.3z + 0.02)Y(z) = zU(z)$$

Noting the presence of the factor z on the right-hand side, we follow the procedure of Example 3.19 and consider the system

$$(z^2 + 0.3z + 0.02)R(z) = U(z) \tag{3.44}$$

Multiplying both sides by z, we have

$$(z^2 + 0.3z + 0.02)zR(z) = zU(z)$$

and so, if the output $Y(z) = zR(z)$ is extracted from the block diagram corresponding to (3.44), we have the block diagram representation of the given system (3.43). This is illustrated in Figure 3.10(a), with the corresponding time-domain implementation shown in Figure 3.10(b).

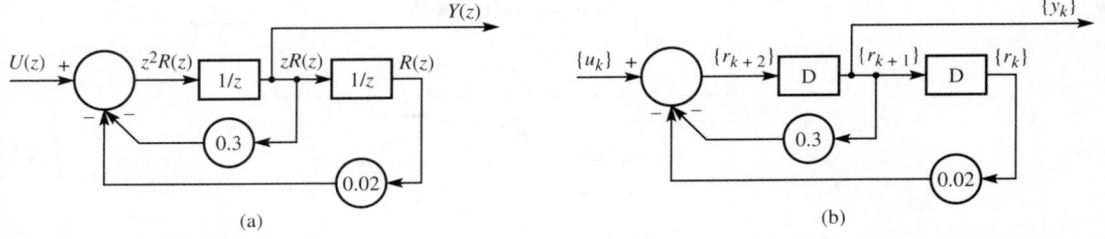

(a)   (b)

Figure 3.10 (a) The z-transform block diagram for the system of Example 3.20.   (b) The time-domain implementation of (a).

To discover a second form of time-domain implementation, note that

$$G(z) = \frac{z}{z^2 + 0.3z + 0.02} = \frac{2}{z + 0.2} - \frac{1}{z + 0.1}$$

We may therefore write

$$Y(z) = G(z)U(z) = \left(\frac{2}{z + 0.2} - \frac{1}{z + 0.1} \right) U(z)$$

so that

$$Y(z) = R_1(z) - R_2(z)$$

where

$$R_1(z) = \frac{2}{z + 0.2} U(z) \qquad\qquad (3.45a)$$

$$R_2(z) = \frac{1}{z + 0.1} U(z) \qquad\qquad (3.45b)$$

From (3.45a), we have

$$(z + 0.2)R_1(z) = 2U(z)$$

which can be represented by the block diagram shown in Figure 3.11(a). Likewise, (3.45b) may be represented by the block diagram shown in Figure 3.11(b).

Recalling that $Y(z) = R_1(z) - R_2(z)$, it is clear that the given system can be represented and then implemented by an obvious coupling of the two subsystems

Figure 3.11 The block diagrams for the subsystems (3.45a) and (3.45b), and an alternative z-transform block diagram (c) for the system of Example 3.20.

represented by (3.45a, b). The resulting z-transform block diagram is shown in Figure 3.11(c). The time-domain version is readily obtained by replacing the '$1/z$' blocks by D and the transforms $U(z)$ and $Y(z)$ by their corresponding sequences $\{u_k\}$ and $\{y_k\}$ respectively.

3.6.2 The impulse response

In Example 3.20 we saw that two quite different realizations were possible for the same transfer function $G(z)$, and others are possible. Whichever realization of the transfer function is chosen, however, when presented with the same input sequence $\{u_k\}$, the same output sequence $\{y_k\}$ will be produced. Thus we identify the system as characterized by its transfer function as the key concept, rather than any particular implementation. This idea is reinforced when we consider the impulse response sequence for a discrete-time linear time-invariant system, and its role in convolution sums.

Consider the sequence

$$\{\delta_k\} = \{1, 0, 0, \ldots\}$$

that is, the sequence consisting of a single 'pulse' at $k = 0$, followed by a train of zeros. As we saw in Section 3.2.1, the z transform of this sequence is easily found from the definition (3.1) as

$$\mathscr{Z}\{\delta_k\} = 1 \tag{3.46}$$

The sequence $\{\delta_k\}$ is called the **impulse sequence**, by analogy with the continuous-time counterpart $\delta(t)$, the impulse function. The analogy is perhaps clearer on considering the transformed version (3.46). In continuous-time analysis, using Laplace transform methods, we observed that $\mathscr{L}\{\delta(t)\} = 1$, and (3.46) shows that the 'entity' with z transform equal to unity is the sequence $\{\delta_k\}$. It is in fact the property that $\mathscr{Z}\{\delta_k\} = 1$ that makes the impulse sequence of such great importance.

Consider a system with transfer function $G(z)$, so that the z transform $Y(z)$ of the output sequence $\{y_k\}$ corresponding to an input sequence $\{u_k\}$ with z transform $U(z)$ is

$$Y(z) = G(z)U(z) \tag{3.47}$$

If the input sequence $\{y_k\}$ is the impulse sequence $\{\delta_k\}$ and the system is initially quiescent, then the output sequence $\{y_{\delta_k}\}$ is called the impulse response of the system. Hence

$$\mathscr{Z}\{y_{\delta_k}\} = Y_\delta(z) = G(z) \tag{3.48}$$

That is, the z transfer function of the system is the z transform of the impulse response. Alternatively, we can say that the impulse response of a system is the inverse z transform of the system transfer function. This compares with the definition of the impulse response for continuous systems given in Section 2.6.3.

Substituting (3.48) into (3.47), we have

$$Y(z) = Y_\delta(z)U(z) \qquad\qquad (3.49)$$

Thus the z transform of the system output in response to any input sequence $\{u_k\}$ is the product of the transform of the input sequence with the transform of the system impulse response. The result (3.49) shows the underlying relationship between the concepts of impulse response and transfer function, and explains why the impulse response (or the transfer function) is thought of as characterizing a system. In simple terms, if either of these is known then we have all the information about the system for any analysis we may wish to do.

EXAMPLE 3.21   Find the impulse response of the system with z transfer function

$$G(z) = \frac{z}{z^2 + 3z + 2}$$

Solution   Using (3.48),

$$Y_\delta(z) = \frac{z}{z^2 + 3z + 2} = \frac{z}{(z+2)(z+1)}$$

Resolving $Y_\delta(z)/z$ into partial fractions gives

$$\frac{Y_\delta(z)}{z} = \frac{1}{(z+2)(z+1)} = \frac{1}{z+1} - \frac{1}{z+2}$$

which on inversion gives the impulse response sequence

$$\{y_{\delta_k}\} = \mathscr{Z}^{-1}\left[\frac{z}{z+1} - \frac{z}{z+2}\right]$$

$$= \{(-1)^k - (2^k)\} \quad (k \geqslant 0)$$

EXAMPLE 3.22   A system has the impulse response sequence

$$\{y_{\delta_k}\} = \{a^k - 0.5^k\}$$

where $a > 0$ is a real constant. What is the nature of this response when (a) $a = 0.4$, (b) $a = 1.2$? Find the step response of the system in both cases.

Solution   When $a = 0.4$

$$\{y_{\delta_k}\} = \{0.4^k - 0.5^k\}$$

and, since both $0.4^k \to 0$ as $k \to \infty$ and $0.5^k \to 0$ as $k \to \infty$, we see that the terms of the impulse response sequence go to zero as $k \to \infty$.

On the other hand, when $a = 1.2$, since $(1.2)^k \to \infty$ as $k \to \infty$, we see that in this case the impulse response sequence terms become unbounded, implying that the system 'blows up'.

In order to calculate the step response, we first determine the system transfer function $G(z)$, using (3.48), as

$$G(z) = Y_\delta(z) = \mathscr{L}\{a^k - 0.5^k\}$$

giving

$$G(z) = \frac{z}{z - a} - \frac{z}{z - 0.5}$$

The system step response is the system response to the unit step sequence $\{h_k\} = \{1, 1, 1, \ldots\}$ which, from Figure 3.3, has z transform

$$\mathscr{L}\{h_k\} = \frac{z}{z - 1}$$

Hence, from (3.46), the step response is determined by

$$Y(z) = G(z)\mathscr{L}\{h_k\}$$

$$= \left(\frac{z}{z - a} - \frac{z}{z - 0.5}\right)\frac{z}{z - 1}$$

so that

$$\frac{Y(z)}{z} = \frac{z}{(z - a)(z - 1)} - \frac{z}{(z - 0.5)(z - 1)}$$

$$= \frac{a}{a - 1}\frac{1}{z - a} - \frac{1}{z - 0.5} + \left(2 + \frac{1}{1 - a}\right)\frac{1}{z - 1}$$

giving

$$Y(z) = \frac{a}{a - 1}\frac{z}{z - a} - \frac{z}{z - 0.5} + \left(2 + \frac{1}{1 - a}\right)\frac{z}{z - 1}$$

which on taking inverse transforms gives the step response as

$$\{y_k\} = \left\{\frac{a}{a - 1}a^k - (0.5)^k + \left(2 + \frac{1}{1 - a}\right)\right\} \tag{3.50}$$

Considering the output sequence (3.50), we see that when $a = 0.4$, since $(0.4)^k \to 0$ as $k \to \infty$ (and $(0.5)^k \to 0$ as $k \to \infty$), the output sequence terms tend to the constant value

$$2 + \frac{1}{1 - 0.4} = 3.6667$$

In the case of $a = 1.2$, since $(1.2)^k \to \infty$ as $k \to \infty$, the output sequence is unbounded, and again the system 'blows up'.

3.6.3   Stability

Example 3.22 illustrated the concept of system stability for discrete systems. When $a = 0.4$, the impulse response decayed to zero with increasing k, and we observed that the step response remained bounded (in fact, the terms of the sequence approached a constant limiting value). However, when $a = 1.2$, the impulse response became unbounded, and we observed that the step response also increased without limit. In fact, as we saw for continuous systems in Section 2.6.3, a linear constant-coefficient discrete-time system is stable provided that its impulse response goes to zero as $t \to \infty$. As for the continuous case, we can relate this definition to the poles of the system transfer function

$$G(z) = \frac{P(z)}{Q(z)}$$

As we saw in Section 3.6.1, the system poles are determined as the n roots of its characteristic equation

$$Q(z) = a_n z^n + a_{n-1} z^{n-1} + \ldots + a_0 = 0 \tag{3.51}$$

For instance, in Example 3.19 we considered a system with transfer function

$$G(z) = \frac{z - 1}{z^2 + 3z + 2}$$

having poles determined by $z^2 + 3z + 2 = 0$, that is poles at $z = -1$ and $z = -2$. Since the impulse response is the inverse transform of $G(z)$, we expect this system to 'blow up' or rather, be unstable, because its impulse response sequence would be expected to contain terms of the form $(-1)^k$ and $(-2)^k$, neither of which goes to zero as $k \to \infty$. (Note that the term in $(-1)^k$ neither blows up nor goes to zero, simply alternating between $+1$ and -1; however, $(-2)^k$ certainly becomes unbounded as $k \to \infty$.) On the other hand, in Example 3.20 we encountered a system with transfer function

$$G(z) = \frac{z}{z^2 + 0.3z + 0.02}$$

having poles determined by

$$Q(z) = z^2 + 0.3z + 0.02 = (z + 0.2)(z + 0.1) = 0$$

that is poles at $z = -0.2$ and $z = -0.1$. Clearly, this system is stable, since its impulse response contains terms in $(-0.2)^k$ and $(-0.1)^k$, both of which go to zero as $k \to \infty$.

Both of these illustrative examples gave rise to characteristic polynomials $Q(z)$ that were quadratic in form and that had real coefficients. More generally, $Q(z) = 0$ gives rise to a polynomial equation of order n, with real coefficients. From the theory of polynomial equations, we know that $Q(z) = 0$ has n roots α_i $(i = 1, 2, \ldots, n)$, which may be real or complex (with complex roots occurring in conjugate pairs).

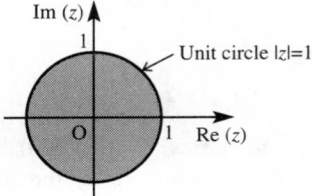

Figure 3.12 Region of stability in the z plane.

Hence the characteristic equation may be written in the form

$$Q(z) = a_n(z - \alpha_1)(z - \alpha_2) \cdots (z - \alpha_n) = 0 \qquad (3.52)$$

The system poles α_i $(i = 1, 2, \ldots, n)$ determined by (3.52) may be expressed in the polar form

$$\alpha_i = r_i e^{j\theta_i} \quad (i = 1, 2, \ldots, n)$$

where $\theta_i = 0$ or π if α_i is real. From the interpretation of the impulse response as the inverse transform of the transfer function $G(z) = P(z)/Q(z)$, it follows that the impulse response sequence of the system will contain terms in

$$r_1^k e^{jk\theta_1}, r_2^k e^{jk\theta_2}, \ldots, r_n^k e^{jk\theta_n}$$

Since, for stability, terms in the impulse response sequence must tend to zero as $k \to \infty$, it follows that a system having characteristic equation $Q(z) = 0$ will be stable provided that

$$r_i < 1 \quad \text{for } i = 1, 2, \ldots, n$$

Therefore a linear constant-coefficient discrete-time system with transfer function $G(z)$ is stable if and only if all the poles of $G(z)$ lie within the unit circle $|z| < 1$ in the complex z plane, as illustrated in Figure 3.12. If one or more poles lie outside this unit circle then the system will be unstable. If one or more distinct poles lie on the unit circle $|z| = 1$, with all the other poles inside, then the system is said to be **marginally stable**.

EXAMPLE 3.23   Which of the following systems, specified by their transfer function $G(z)$, are stable?

(a) $G(z) = \dfrac{1}{z + 0.25}$

(b) $G(z) = \dfrac{z}{z^2 - z + 0.5}$

(c) $G(z) = \dfrac{z^2}{z^3 - 3z^2 + 2.5z - 1}$

Solution (a) The single pole is at $z = -0.25$, so $r_1 = 0.25 < 1$, and the system is stable.

(b) The system poles are determined by

$$z^2 - z + 0.5 = [z - 0.5(1 + j)][z - 0.5(1 - j)] = 0$$

giving the poles as the conjugate pair $z_1 = 0.5(1 + j)$, $z_2 = 0.5(1 - j)$. The amplitudes $r_1 = r_2 = 0.707 < 1$, and again the system is stable.

(c) The system poles are determined by

$$z^3 - 3z^2 + 2.5z - 1 = (z - 2)[z - 0.5(1 + j)][z - 0.5(1 - j)]$$

giving the poles as $z_1 = 2$, $z_2 = 0.5(1 + j)$, $z_3 = 0.5(1 - j)$, and so their amplitudes are $r_1 = 2, r_2 = r_3 = 0.707$. Since $r_1 > 1$, it follows that the system is unstable.

According to our definition, it follows that to prove stability we must show that all the roots of the characteristic equation

$$Q(z) = z^n + a_{n-1}z^{n-1} + \ldots + a_0 = 0 \tag{3.53}$$

lie within the unit circle $|z| = 1$ (note that for convenience we have arranged for the coefficient of z^n to be unity in (3.53)). Many mathematical criteria have been developed to test for this property. One such method, widely used in practice, is the **Jury stability criterion** introduced by E. I. Jury in 1963. This procedure gives necessary and sufficient conditions for the polynomial equation (3.53) to have all its roots inside the unit circle $|z| = 1$.

The first step in the procedure is to set up a table as in Figure 3.13 using information from the given polynomial equation (3.53) and where

Row	z^n	z^{n-1}	z^{n-2}	...	z^{n-k}	...	z^2	z^1	z^0
1	1	a_{n-1}	a_{n-2}	...	a_{n-k}	...	a_2	a_1	a_0
2	a_0	a_1	a_2	...	a_k	...	a_{n-2}	a_{n-1}	1
3	$\Delta_1 = b_0$	b_1	b_2	...	b_k	...	b_{n-2}	b_{n-1}	
4	b_{n-1}	b_{n-2}	b_{n-3}	...	b_{n-1-k}	...	b_1	b_0	
5	$\Delta_2 = c_0$	c_1	c_2	...	c_k	...	c_{n-2}		
6	c_{n-2}	c_{n-3}	c_{n-4}	...	c_{n-2-k}	...	c_0		
7	$\Delta_3 = d_0$	d_1	d_2	...	d_k	...			
8	d_{n-3}	d_{n-4}	d_{n-5}	...	d_{n-3-k}	...			
⋮									
⋮									
$2n-5$	$\Delta_{n-3} = s_0$	s_1	s_2	s_3					
$2n-4$	s_3	s_2	s_1	s_0					
$2n-3$	$\Delta_{n-2} = r_0$	r_1	r_2						
$2n-2$	r_2	r_1	r_0						
$2n-1$	$\Delta_{n-1} = t_0$								

Figure 3.13 Jury stability table for the polynomial equation (3.53).

$$b_k = \begin{vmatrix} 1 & a_k \\ a_0 & a_{n-k} \end{vmatrix}, \quad c_k = \begin{vmatrix} b_0 & b_{n-1-k} \\ b_{n-1} & b_k \end{vmatrix}, \quad d_k = \begin{vmatrix} c_0 & c_{n-2-k} \\ c_{n-2} & c_k \end{vmatrix}$$

$$\ldots, \quad t_0 = \begin{vmatrix} r_0 & r_2 \\ r_2 & r_0 \end{vmatrix}$$

Note that the elements of row $2j + 2$ consist of the elements of row $2j + 1$ written in the reverse order for $j = 0, 1, 2, \ldots, n$; that is, the elements of the even rows consist of the elements of the odd rows written in reverse order. Necessary and sufficient conditions for the polynomial equation (3.53) to have all its roots inside the unit circle $|z| = 1$ are then given by

(i) $F(1) > 0, \quad (-1)^n F(-1) > 0$

(ii) $\Delta_1 > 0, \quad \Delta_2 > 0, \quad \Delta_3 > 0, \quad \ldots, \quad \Delta_{n-2} > 0, \quad \Delta_{n-1} > 0$ **(3.54)**

EXAMPLE 3.24   Show that all the roots of the polynomial equation

$$F(z) = z^3 + \tfrac{1}{3}z^2 - \tfrac{1}{4}z - \tfrac{1}{12} = 0$$

lie within the unit circle $|z| = 1$.

Solution   The corresponding Jury stability table is shown in Figure 3.14. In this case

(i) $F(1) = 1 + \tfrac{1}{3} - \tfrac{1}{4} - \tfrac{1}{12} > 0$

         $(-1)^n F(-1) = (-1)^3 (-1 + \tfrac{1}{3} + \tfrac{1}{4} - \tfrac{1}{12}) > 0$

(ii) $\Delta_1 = \tfrac{143}{144} > 0, \quad \Delta_2 = (\tfrac{143}{144})^2 - \tfrac{4}{81} > 0$

Thus, by the criteria (3.54), all the roots lie within the unit circle. In this case this is readily confirmed, since the polynomial $F(z)$ may be factorized as

$$F(z) = (z - \tfrac{1}{2})(z + \tfrac{1}{2})(z + \tfrac{1}{3}) = 0$$

So the roots are $z_1 = \tfrac{1}{2}$, $z_2 = -\tfrac{1}{2}$ and $z_3 = -\tfrac{1}{3}$.

Row	z^3	z^2	z^1	z^0
1	1	$\tfrac{1}{3}$	$-\tfrac{1}{4}$	$-\tfrac{1}{12}$
2	$-\tfrac{1}{12}$	$-\tfrac{1}{4}$	$\tfrac{1}{3}$	1
3	$\Delta_1 = \begin{vmatrix} 1 & -\tfrac{1}{12} \\ -\tfrac{1}{12} & 1 \end{vmatrix}$	$\begin{vmatrix} 1 & -\tfrac{1}{4} \\ -\tfrac{1}{12} & \tfrac{1}{3} \end{vmatrix}$	$\begin{vmatrix} 1 & \tfrac{1}{3} \\ -\tfrac{1}{12} & -\tfrac{1}{4} \end{vmatrix}$	
	$= \tfrac{143}{144}$	$= \tfrac{5}{16}$	$= -\tfrac{2}{9}$	
4	$-\tfrac{2}{9}$	$\tfrac{5}{16}$	$\tfrac{143}{144}$	
5	$\Delta_2 = \begin{vmatrix} \tfrac{143}{144} & -\tfrac{2}{9} \\ -\tfrac{2}{9} & \tfrac{143}{144} \end{vmatrix}$			
	$= 0.936\,78$			

Figure 3.14 Jury stability table for Example 3.24.

The Jury stability table may also be used to determine how many roots of the polynomial equation (3.53) lie outside the unit circle. The number of such roots is determined by the number of changes in sign in the sequence

$$1, \quad \Delta_1, \quad \Delta_2, \quad \dots, \quad \Delta_{n-1}$$

EXAMPLE 3.25 Show that the polynomial equation

$$F(z) = z^3 - 3z^2 - \tfrac{1}{4}z + \tfrac{3}{4} = 0$$

has roots that lie outside the unit circle $|z| = 1$. Determine how many such roots there are.

Solution The corresponding Jury stability table is shown in Figure 3.15. Hence, in this case

$$F(1) = 1 - 3 - \tfrac{1}{4} + \tfrac{3}{4} = -\tfrac{3}{2}$$

$$(-1)^n F(-1) = (-1)^3(-1 - 3 + \tfrac{1}{4} + \tfrac{3}{4}) = 3$$

As $F(1) < 0$, it follows from (3.54) that the polynomial equation has roots outside the unit circle $|z| = 1$. From Figure 3.15, the sequence $1, \Delta_1, \Delta_2$ is $1, \tfrac{7}{16}, -\tfrac{15}{16}$, and since there is only one sign change in the sequence, it follows that one root lies outside the unit circle. Again this is readily confirmed, since $F(z)$ may be factorized as

$$F(z) = (z - \tfrac{1}{2})(z + \tfrac{1}{2})(z - 3) = 0$$

showing that there is indeed one root outside the unit circle at $z = 3$.

Row	z^3	z^2	z^1	z^0
1	1	-3	$-\tfrac{1}{4}$	$\tfrac{3}{4}$
2	$\tfrac{3}{4}$	$-\tfrac{1}{4}$	-3	1
3	$\Delta_1 = \tfrac{7}{16}$	$-\tfrac{45}{16}$	2	
4	2	$-\tfrac{45}{16}$	$\tfrac{7}{16}$	
5	$\Delta_2 = -\tfrac{15}{16}$			

Figure 3.15 Jury stability table for Example 3.25.

3.6.4 Convolution

Here we shall briefly extend the concept of convolution introduced in Section 2.6.6 to discrete-time systems. From (3.45), for an initially quiescent system with an impulse response sequence $\{y_{\delta_k}\}$ with z transform $Y_\delta(z)$, the z transform $Y(z)$ of the output sequence $\{y_k\}$ in response to an input sequence $\{u_k\}$ with z transform $U(z)$ is given by

$$Y(z) = Y_\delta(z)U(z) \tag{3.49}$$

For the purposes of solving a particular problem, the best approach to determining $\{y_k\}$ for a given $\{u_k\}$ is to invert the right-hand side of (3.49) as an ordinary z transform with no particular thought as to its structure. However, to understand more of the theory of linear systems in discrete time, it is worth exploring the general situation a little further. To do this, we revert to the time domain.

Suppose that a linear discrete-time time-invariant system has impulse response sequence $\{y_{\delta_k}\}$, and suppose that we wish to find the system response $\{y_k\}$ to an input sequence $\{u_k\}$, with the system initially in a quiescent state. First we express the input sequence

$$\{u_k\} = \{u_0, u_1, u_2, \ldots u_n, \ldots\} \tag{3.55}$$

as

$$\{u_k\} = u_0\{\delta_k\} + u_1\{\delta_{k-1}\} + u_2\{\delta_{k-2}\} + \ldots + u_n\{\delta_{k-n}\} + \ldots \tag{3.56}$$

where

$$\delta_{k-j} = \begin{cases} 0 & (k \neq j) \\ 1 & (k = j) \end{cases}$$

In other words, $\{\delta_{k-j}\}$ is simply an impulse sequence with the pulse shifted to $k = j$. Thus, in going from (3.55) to (3.56), we have decomposed the input sequence $\{u_k\}$ into a weighted sum of shifted impulse sequences. Under the assumption of an initially quiescent system, linearity allows us to express the response $\{y_k\}$ to the input sequence $\{u_k\}$ as the appropriately weighted sum of shifted impulse responses. Thus, since the impulse response is $\{y_{\delta_k}\}$, the response to the shifted impulse sequence $\{\delta_{k-j}\}$ will be $\{y_{\delta_{k-j}}\}$, and the response to the weighted impulse sequence $u_j\{\delta_{k-j}\}$ will be simply $u_j\{y_{\delta_{k-j}}\}$. Summing the contributions from all the sequences in (3.56), we obtain

$$\{y_k\} = \sum_{j=0}^{\infty} u_j\{y_{\delta_{k-j}}\} \tag{3.57}$$

as the response of the system to the input sequence $\{u_k\}$. Expanding (3.57), we have

$$\begin{aligned}
\{y_k\} &= u_0\{y_{\delta_k}\} + u_1\{y_{\delta_{k-1}}\} + \ldots + u_j\{y_{\delta_{k-j}}\} + \ldots \\
&= u_0\{y_{\delta_0}, y_{\delta_1}, y_{\delta_2}, \ldots, \quad y_{\delta_n}, \ldots\} \\
&\quad + u_1\{0, y_{\delta_0}, y_{\delta_1}, \ldots, \quad y_{\delta_{n-1}}, \ldots\} \\
&\quad + u_2\{0, 0, y_{\delta_0}, \ldots, \quad y_{\delta_{n-2}}, \ldots\} \\
&\quad \vdots \\
&\quad + u_h\{0, 0, 0, \quad \ldots, 0, y_{\delta_0}, y_{\delta_1}, \ldots\} \\
&\quad + \ldots \qquad\qquad\qquad \underset{h\text{th position}}{\uparrow}
\end{aligned}$$

From this expansion, we find that the hth term of the output sequence is determined by

$$y_h = \sum_{j=0}^{h} u_j y_{\delta_{h-j}} \tag{3.58}$$

That is,

$$\{y_k\} = \left\{ \sum_{j=0}^{k} u_j y_{\delta_{k-j}} \right\} \tag{3.59}$$

The expression (3.58) is called the **convolution sum**, and the result (3.59) is analogous to (2.83) for continuous systems.

EXAMPLE 3.26   A system has z transfer function

$$G(z) = \frac{z}{z + \frac{1}{2}}$$

What is the system step response? Verify the result using (3.59).

Solution   From (3.46), the system step response is

$$Y(z) = G(z)\mathscr{Z}\{h_k\}$$

where $\{h_k\} = \{1, 1, 1, \ldots\}$. From Figure 3.3, $\mathscr{Z}\{h_k\} = z/(z-1)$, so

$$Y(z) = \frac{z}{z + \frac{1}{2}} \frac{z}{z-1}$$

Resolving $Y(z)/z$ into partial fractions gives

$$\frac{Y(z)}{z} = \frac{z}{(z + \frac{1}{2})(z-1)} = \frac{2}{3}\frac{1}{z-1} + \frac{1}{3}\frac{1}{z + \frac{1}{2}}$$

so

$$Y(z) = \frac{2}{3}\frac{z}{z-1} + \frac{1}{3}\frac{z}{z + \frac{1}{2}}$$

Taking inverse transforms then gives the step response as

$$\{y_k\} = \left\{\frac{2}{3} + \frac{1}{3}(-\frac{1}{2})^k\right\}$$

Using (3.59), we first have to find the impulse response, which, from (3.48), is given by

$$\{y_{\delta_k}\} = \mathscr{Z}^{-1}[G(z)]$$

$$= \mathscr{Z}^{-1}\left[\frac{z}{z + \frac{1}{2}}\right]$$

so that

$$\{y_{\delta_k}\} = \{(-\frac{1}{2})^k\}$$

Taking $\{u_k\}$ to be the unit step sequence $\{h_k\}$, where $h_k = 1$ $(k \geqslant 0)$, the step response may then be determined from (3.59) as

$$\{y_k\} = \left\{\sum_{j=0}^{k} u_j y_{\delta_{k-j}}\right\}$$

$$= \left\{\sum_{j=0}^{k} 1 \cdot (-\tfrac{1}{2})^{k-j}\right\}$$

$$= \left\{(-\tfrac{1}{2})^k \sum_{j=0}^{k} (-\tfrac{1}{2})^{-j}\right\} = \left\{(-\tfrac{1}{2})^k \sum_{j=0}^{k} (-2)^j\right\}$$

Recognizing the sum as the sum to $k+1$ terms of a geometric series with common ratio -2, we have

$$\{y_k\} = \left\{(-\tfrac{1}{2})^k \frac{1 - (-2)^{k+1}}{1 - (-2)}\right\}$$

$$= \{\tfrac{1}{3}((-\tfrac{1}{2})^k + 2)\} = \{\tfrac{2}{3} + \tfrac{1}{3}(-\tfrac{1}{2})^k\}$$

which concurs with the sequence obtained by direct evaluation.

Example 3.26 reinforces the remark made earlier that the easiest approach to obtaining the response is by direct inversion of (3.32). However, (3.59), together with the argument leading to it, provides a great deal of insight into the way in which the response sequence $\{y_k\}$ is generated. It also serves as a useful 'closed form' for the output of the system, and readers should consult specialist texts on signals and systems for a full discussion (P. Kraniauskas, *Transforms in Signals and Systems*, Addison-Wesley, Wokingham, 1992).

The astute reader will recall that we commenced this section by suggesting that we were about to study the implications of the input–output relationship (3.49), namely

$$Y(z) = Y_\delta(z)U(z)$$

We have in fact explored the time-domain input–output relationship for a linear system, and we now proceed to link this approach with our work in the transform domain. By definition,

$$U(z) = \sum_{k=0}^{\infty} u_k z^{-k} = u_0 + \frac{u_1}{z} + \frac{u_2}{z^2} + \ldots + \frac{u_k}{z^k} + \ldots$$

$$Y_\delta(z) = \sum_{k=0}^{\infty} y_{\delta_k} z^{-k} = y_{\delta_0} + \frac{y_{\delta_1}}{z} + \frac{y_{\delta_2}}{z^2} + \ldots + \frac{y_{\delta_k}}{z^k} + \ldots$$

so

$$Y_\delta(z)U(z) = u_0 y_{\delta_0} + (u_0 y_{\delta_1} + u_1 y_{\delta_0})\frac{1}{z} + (u_0 y_{\delta_2} + u_1 y_{\delta_1} + u_2 y_{\delta_0})\frac{1}{z^2} + \ldots \quad \textbf{(3.60)}$$

Considering the kth term of (3.60), we see that the coefficient of z^{-k} is simply

$$\sum_{j=0}^{k} u_j y_{\delta k - j}$$

However, by definition, since $Y(z) = Y_\delta(z)U(z)$, this is also $y(k)$, the kth term of the output sequence, so that the latter is

$$\{y_k\} = \left\{ \sum_{j=0}^{k} u_j y_{\delta k - j} \right\}$$

as found in (3.59). We have thus shown that the time-domain and transform-domain approaches are equivalent, and, in passing, we have established the z transform of the convolution sum as

$$\mathcal{Z}\left\{ \sum_{j=0}^{k} u_j v_{k-j} \right\} = U(z)V(z) \qquad (3.61)$$

where

$$\mathcal{Z}\{u_k\} = U(z), \qquad \mathcal{Z}\{v_k\} = V(z)$$

Putting $p = k - j$ in (3.61) shows that

$$\sum_{j=0}^{k} u_j v_{k-j} = \sum_{p=0}^{k} u_{k-p} v_p \qquad (3.62)$$

confirming that the convolution process is commutative.

3.6.5   Exercises

21 Find the transfer functions of each of the following discrete-time systems, given that the system is initially in a quiescent state:

(a) $y_{k+2} - 3y_{k+1} + 2y_k = u_k$

(b) $y_{k+2} - 3y_{k+1} + 2y_k = u_{k+1} - u_k$

(c) $y_{k+3} - y_{k+2} + 2y_{k+1} + y_k = u_k + u_{k-1}$

22 Draw a block diagram representing the discrete-time system

$$y_{k+2} + 0.5y_{k+1} + 0.25y_k = u_k$$

Hence find a block diagram representation of the system

$$y_{k+2} + 0.5y_{k+1} + 0.25y_k = u_k - 0.6u_{k+1}$$

23 Find the impulse response for the systems with z transfer function

(a) $\dfrac{z}{8z^2 + 6z + 1}$

(b) $\dfrac{z^2}{z^2 - 3z + 3}$

(c) $\dfrac{z^2}{z^2 - 0.2z - 0.08}$

(d) $\dfrac{5z^2 - 12z}{z^2 - 6z + 8}$

24 Obtain the impulse response for the systems of Exercises 21(a, b).

25 Which of the following systems are stable?

(a) $9y_{k+2} + 9y_{k+1} + 2y_k = u_k$

(b) $9y_{k+2} - 3y_{k+1} - 2y_k = u_k$

(c) $2y_{k+2} - 2y_{k+1} + y_k = u_{k+1} - u_k$

(d) $2y_{k+2} + 3y_{k+1} - y_k = u_k$

(e) $4y_{k+2} - 3y_{k+1} - y_k = u_{k+1} - 2u_k$.

26 Use the method of Example 3.26 to calculate the step response of the system with transfer function

$$\frac{z}{z - \frac{1}{2}}$$

Verify the result by direct calculation.

27 A sampled data system described by the difference equation

$$y_{n+1} - y_n = u_n$$

is controlled by making the input u_n proportional to the previous error according to

$$u_n = K\left(\frac{1}{2^n} - y_{n-1}\right)$$

where K is a positive gain. Determine the range of values of K for which the system is stable. Taking $K = \frac{2}{9}$, determine the response of the system given $y_0 = y_1 = 0$.

28 Show that the system

$$y_{n+2} + 2y_{n+1} + 2y_n = u_{n+1} \quad (n \geq 0)$$

has a transfer function

$$D(z) = \frac{z}{z^2 + 2z + 2}$$

Show that the poles of the system are at $z = -1 + j$ and $z = -1 - j$. Hence show that the impulse response of the system is given by

$$h_n = \mathscr{L}^{-1}D(z) = 2^{n/2}\sin\tfrac{3}{4}n\pi$$

3.7 The relationship between Laplace and z transforms

Throughout this chapter we have attempted to highlight similarities, where they occur, between results in Laplace transform theory and those for z transforms. In this section we take a closer look at the relationship between the two transforms. In Section 3.2.2 we introduced the idea of sampling a continuous-time signal $f(t)$ instantaneously at uniform intervals T to produce the sequence

$$\{f(nT)\} = \{f(0), f(T), f(2T), \ldots, f(nT), \ldots\} \tag{3.63}$$

An alternative way of representing the sampled function is to define the continuous-time sampled version of $f(t)$ as $\hat{f}(t)$ where

$$\hat{f}(t) = \sum_{n=0}^{\infty} f(t)\,\delta(t - nT)$$

$$= \sum_{n=0}^{\infty} f(nT)\,\delta(t - nT) \tag{3.64}$$

The representation (3.64) may be interpreted as defining a row of impulses located at the sampling points and weighted by the appropriate sampled values (as illustrated in Figure 3.16). Taking the Laplace transform of $\hat{f}(t)$, following the results of Section 2.5.10, we have

$$\mathscr{L}\{\hat{f}(t)\} = \int_{0-}^{\infty}\left[\sum_{k=0}^{\infty} f(kT)\,\delta(t - kT)\right]e^{-st}\,dt$$

Figure 3.16 Sampled function $f(t)$.

$$= \sum_{k=0}^{\infty} f(kT) \int_{0-}^{\infty} \delta(t - kT) e^{-st} \, dt$$

giving

$$\mathscr{L}\{\hat{f}(t)\} = \sum_{k=0}^{\infty} f(kT) e^{-ksT} \tag{3.65}$$

Making the change of variable $z = e^{sT}$ in (3.65) leads to the result

$$\mathscr{L}\{\hat{f}(t)\} = \sum_{k=0}^{\infty} f(kT) z^{-k} = F(z) \tag{3.66}$$

where, as in (3.10), $F(z)$ denotes the z transform of the sequence $\{f(kT)\}$. We can therefore view the z transform of a sequence of samples in discrete time as the Laplace transform of the continuous-time sampled function $\hat{f}(t)$ with an appropriate change of variable

$$z = e^{sT} \quad \text{or} \quad s = \frac{1}{T} \ln z$$

In Chapter 1 we saw that under this transformation the left half of the s plane, $\text{Re}(s) < 0$, is mapped onto the region inside the unit circle in the z plane, $|z| < 1$. This is consistent with our stability criteria in the s and z domains.

3.8   Engineering application: design of discrete-time systems

An important development in many areas of modern engineering is the replacement of analogue devices by digital ones. Perhaps the most widely known example is the compact disc player, in which mechanical transcription followed by analogue signal processing has been superseded by optical technology and digital signal processing. There are other examples in many fields of engineering, particularly where automatic control is employed.

3.8.1   Analogue filters

At the centre of most signal processing applications are **filters**. These have the effect of changing the spectrum of input signals, that is, attentuating components of signals by an amount depending on the frequency of the component. For example, an analogue **ideal low-pass filter** passes without attenuation all signal components at frequencies less than a critical frequency $\omega = \omega_c$ say. The amplitude of the frequency response $|G(j\omega)|$ (see Section 2.7) of such an ideal filter is shown in Figure 3.17.

One class of analogue filters whose frequency response approximates that of the ideal low-pass filter comprises what are known as **Butterworth filters**. As well as having 'good' characteristics, these can be implemented using a network as illustrated in Figure 3.18 for the second-order filter.

It can be shown (see R. H. Jones and N. C. Steele, *Mathematics in Communication Theory*, Ellis Horwood, Chichester, 1989), that the transfer function $G_n(s)$ of the nth-order filter is

$$G_n(s) = \frac{1}{B_n(x)}$$

where

$$B_n(x) = \sum_{k=0}^{n} a_k x^k$$

with

$$x = \frac{s}{\omega_c}, \qquad a_k = \prod_{r=1}^{k} \frac{\cos(r-1)\alpha}{\sin r\alpha}, \qquad \alpha = \frac{\pi}{2n}$$

Using these relations, it is readily shown that

$$G_2(s) = \frac{\omega_c^2}{s^2 + \sqrt{2}\,\omega_c s + \omega_c^2} \tag{3.67}$$

Figure 3.17 Amplitude response for an ideal low-pass filter.

Figure 3.18 *LCR* network for implementing a second-order Butterworth filter.

$$G_3(s) = \frac{\omega_c^3}{s^3 + 2\omega_c s^2 + 2\omega_c^2 s + \omega_c^3} \tag{3.68}$$

and so on. On sketching the amplitudes of the frequency responses $G_n(j\omega)$, it becomes apparent that increasing n improves the approximation to the response of the ideal low-pass filter of Figure 3.17.

3.8.2   Designing a digital replacement filter

Suppose that we now wish to design a discrete-time system, to operate on samples taken from an input signal, that will operate in a similar manner to a Butterworth filter. We shall assume that the input signal $u(t)$ and the output signal $y(t)$ of the analogue filter are both sampled at the same intervals T to generate the input sequence $\{u(kT)\}$ and the output sequence $\{y(kT)\}$ respectively. Clearly, we need to specify what is meant by 'operate in a similar manner'. In this case, we shall select as our design strategy a method that matches the impulse response sequence of the digital design with a sequence of samples, drawn at the appropriate instants T from the impulse response of an analogue 'prototype'. We shall select the prototype from one of the Butterworth filters discussed in Section 3.8.1, although there are many other possibilities.

Let us select the first-order filter, with cut-off frequency ω_c, as our prototype. Then the first step is to calculate the impulse response of this filter. The Laplace transfer function of the filter is

$$G(s) = \frac{\omega_c}{s + \omega_c}$$

So, from (2.71), the impulse response is readily obtained as

$$h(t) = \omega_c e^{-\omega_c t} \quad (t \geqslant 0) \tag{3.69}$$

Next, we sample this response at intervals T to generate the sequence

$$\{h(kT)\} = \{\omega_c e^{-\omega_c kT}\}$$

which on taking the z transform, gives

$$\mathscr{Z}\{h(kT)\} = H(z) = \omega_c \frac{z}{z - e^{-\omega_c T}}$$

Finally, we choose $H(z)$ to be the transfer function of our digital system. This means simply that the input–output relationship for the design of the digital system will be

$$Y(z) = H(z)U(z)$$

Figure 3.19 Block diagram for the digital replacement filter, $\alpha = k\omega_c$, $\beta = e^{-\omega_c t}$.

where $Y(z)$ and $U(z)$ are the z transforms of the output and input sequences $\{y(kT)\}$ and $\{u(kT)\}$ respectively. Thus we have

$$Y(z) = \omega_c \frac{z}{z - e^{-\omega_c T}} U(z) \tag{3.70}$$

Our digital system is now defined, and we can easily construct the corresponding difference equation model of the system as

$$(z - e^{-\omega_c T})Y(z) = \omega_c z U(z)$$

that is

$$z Y(z) - e^{-\omega_c T} Y(z) = \omega_c z U(z)$$

Under the assumption of zero initial conditions, we can take inverse transforms to obtain the first-order difference equation model

$$y(k + 1) - e^{-\omega_c T} y(k) = \omega_c u(k + 1) \tag{3.71}$$

A block diagram implementation of (3.71) is shown in Figure 3.19.

3.8.3   Possible developments

The design method we have considered is called the **impulse invariant technique**, and is only one of many available. The interested reader may develop this study in various ways:

(1) Write a computer program to evaluate the sequence generated by (3.71) with $\omega_c = 1$, and compare with values obtained at the sampling instants for the impulse response (3.69) of the prototype analogue filter.

(2) Repeat the design process for the second-order Butterworth filter.

(3) By setting $s = j\omega$ in the Laplace transfer function of the prototype, and $z = e^{j\omega T}$ in the z transfer function of the digital design, compare the amplitude of the frequency responses in both cases. For an explanation of the results obtained, see Chapter 5.

(4) An alternative design strategy is to replace s in the Laplace transfer function with

$$\frac{2}{T}\frac{z-1}{z+1}$$

(this is a process that makes use of the trapezoidal method of approximate integration). Design alternative digital filters using this technique.

(5) Show that filters designed using either of these techniques will be stable provided that the prototype design is itself stable.

3.9   Engineering application: the delta operator and the $\mathscr{D}$ transform

3.9.1   Introduction

In recent years, sampling rates for digital systems have increased many-fold, and traditional model formulations based on the z transform have produced unsatisfactory results in some applications. It is beyond the scope of this text to describe this situation in detail, but it is possible to give a brief introduction to the problem and to suggest an approach to the solution. For further details see R. M. Middleton and G. C. Goodwin, *Digital Control and Estimation, A Unified Approach* (Prentice-Hall, Englewood Cliffs, NJ, 1990) or W. Forsythe and R. M. Goodall, *Digital Control* (Macmillan, London, 1991). The contribution of Colin Paterson (Division of Mathematics, Coventry University) to the development of this application is gratefully acknowledged.

3.9.2   The q or shift operator and the δ operator

In the time domain we define the shift operator q in terms of its effect on a sequence $\{x_k\}$ as

$$q\{x_k\} = \{x_{k+1}\}$$

That is, the effect of the shift operator is to shift the sequence by one position, so that the kth term of the new sequence is the $(k+1)$th term of the original sequence. It is then possible to write the difference equation

$$y_{k+2} + 2y_{k+1} + 5y_k = u_{k+1} - u_k$$

as

$$q^2 y_k + 2q\, y_k + 5y_k = qu_k - u_k$$

or

$$(q^2 + 2q + 5)y_k = (q - 1)u_k \qquad (3.72)$$

Note that if we had taken the z transform of the difference equation, with an initially quiescent system, we would have obtained

$$(z^2 + 2z + 5)Y(z) = (z - 1)U(z)$$

We see at once the correspondence between the time-domain q operator and the z-transform operator $\mathcal{Z}$.

The next step is to introduce the δ operator, defined as

$$\delta = \frac{q - 1}{\Delta}$$

where Δ has the dimensions of time and is often chosen as the sampling period T. Note that

$$\delta y_k = \frac{(q - 1)y_k}{\Delta} = \frac{y_{k+1} - y_k}{\Delta}$$

so that if $\Delta = T$ then, in the limit of rapid sampling,

$$\delta y_k \simeq \frac{dy}{dt}$$

Solving for q we see that

$$q = 1 + \Delta\delta$$

The difference equation (3.72) can thus be written as

$$((1 + \Delta\delta)^2 + 2(1 + \Delta\delta) + 5)y_k = [(1 + \Delta\delta) - 1]u_k$$

or

$$[(\Delta\delta)^2 + 4\Delta\delta + 8]y_k = \Delta\delta u_k$$

or, finally, as

$$\left(\delta^2 + \frac{4\delta}{\Delta} + \frac{8}{\Delta^2}\right)y_k = \frac{\delta}{\Delta}u_k$$

3.9.3 Constructing a discrete-time system model

So far, we have simply demonstrated a method of rewriting a difference equation in an alternative form. We now examine the possible advantages of constructing discrete-time system models using the δ operator. To do this, we consider a particular example, in which we obtain two different discrete-time forms of the second-order Butterworth filter, both based on the bilinear transform method, sometimes known as **Tustin's method**. This method has its origins in the trapezoidal approximation to the integration process; full details are given in R. H. Jones and N. C. Steele, *Mathematics in Communication Theory* (Ellis Horwood, Chichester, 1989).

The continuous-time second-order Butterworth filter with cut-off frequency $\omega_c = 1$ is modelled, as indicated by (3.67), by the differential equation

$$\frac{d^2y}{dt^2} + 1.414\,21\frac{dy}{dt} + y = u(t) \tag{3.73}$$

where $u(t)$ is the input and $y(t)$ the filter response. Taking Laplace transforms throughout on the assumption of quiescent initial conditions, that is, $y(0) = (dy/dt)(0) = 0$, we obtain the transformed equation

$$(s^2 + 1.414\,21s + 1)Y(s) = U(s) \tag{3.74}$$

This represents a stable system, since the system poles, given by

$$s^2 + 1.414\,21s + 1 = 0$$

are located at $s = -0.707\,10 \pm j0.707\,10$ and thus lie in the left half-plane of the complex s plane.

We now seek a discrete-time version of the differential equation (3.73). To do this, we first transform (3.74) into the z domain using the **bilinear transform method**, which involves replacing s by

$$\frac{2}{T}\frac{z-1}{z+1}$$

Equation (3.74) then becomes

$$\left[\frac{4}{T^2}\left(\frac{z-1}{z+1}\right)^2 + 1.414\,21\frac{2}{T}\left(\frac{z-1}{z+1}\right) + 1\right]Y(z) = U(z)$$

or

$$[(\tfrac{1}{4}T^2 + 1.414\,21 \times \tfrac{1}{2}T + 4)z^2 + (\tfrac{1}{2}T^2 - 8)z + \tfrac{1}{4}T^2 - 1.414\,21 \times \tfrac{1}{2}T + 4]Y(z)$$
$$= \tfrac{1}{4}T^2(z^2 + 2z + 1)U(z) \tag{3.75}$$

We can now invert this transformed equation to obtain the time-domain model

$$(\tfrac{1}{4}T^2 + 1.414\,21 \times \tfrac{1}{2}T + 4)y_{k+2} + (\tfrac{1}{2}T^2 - 8)y_{k+1} + (\tfrac{1}{4}T^2 - 1.414\,21 \times \tfrac{1}{2}T + 4)y_k$$
$$= \tfrac{1}{4}T^2(u_{k+2} + 2u_{k+1} + u_k) \tag{3.76}$$

For illustrative purposes we set $T = 0.1\,\text{s}$ in (3.76) to obtain

$$4.073\,21y_{k+2} - 7.995\,00y_{k+1} + 3.931\,79y_k = 0.025\,00(u_{k+2} + 2u_{k+1} + u_k)$$

Note that the roots of the characteristic equation have modulus of about 0.9825, and are thus quite close to the stability boundary.

When $T = 0.01$ s, (3.76) becomes

$$4.007\,10 y_{k+2} - 7.999\,95 y_{k+1} + 3.992\,95 y_k = 0.000\,03(u_{k+2} + 2u_{k+1} + u_k)$$

In this case the roots have modulus of about 0.9982, and we see that increasing the sampling rate has moved them even closer to the stability boundary, and that *high accuracy in the coefficients is essential*, thus adding to the expense of implementation.

An alternative method of proceeding is to avoid the intermediate stage of obtaining the z-domain model (3.75) and to proceed directly to a discrete-time representation from (3.73), using the transformation

$$s \rightarrow \frac{2}{T} \frac{q-1}{q+1}$$

leading to the same result as in (3.76). Using the δ operator instead of the shift operator q, noting that $q = 1 + \Delta\delta$, we make the transformation

$$s \rightarrow \frac{2}{T} \frac{\Delta\delta}{2 + \Delta\delta}$$

or, if $T = \Delta$, the transformation

$$s \rightarrow \frac{2\delta}{2 + \Delta\delta}$$

in (3.74), which becomes

$$[\delta^2 + 1.414\,21 \times \tfrac{1}{2}\delta(2 + \Delta\delta) + \tfrac{1}{4}(2 + \Delta\delta)^2]y_k = \tfrac{1}{4}(2 + \Delta\delta)^2 u_k$$

Note that in this form it is easy to see that in the limit as $\Delta \rightarrow 0$ (that is, as sampling becomes very fast) we regain the original differential equation model. Rearranging this equation, we have

$$\left[\delta^2 + \frac{(1.414\,21 + \Delta)}{(1 + 1.414\,21 \times \tfrac{1}{2}\Delta + \tfrac{1}{4}\Delta^2)}\delta + \frac{1}{(1 + 1.414\,21 \times \tfrac{1}{2}\Delta + \tfrac{1}{4}\Delta^2)}\right]y_k$$

$$= \frac{(2 + \Delta\delta)^2}{4(1 + 1.414\,21 \times \tfrac{1}{2}\Delta + \tfrac{1}{4}\Delta^2)}u_k \qquad (3.77)$$

In order to assess stability, it is helpful to introduce a transform variable γ associated with the δ operator. This is achieved by defining γ in terms of z as

$$\gamma = \frac{z-1}{\Delta}$$

The region of stability in the z plane, $|z| < 1$, thus becomes

$$|1 + \Delta\gamma| < 1$$

or

$$\left|\frac{1}{\Delta} + \gamma\right| < \frac{1}{\Delta} \qquad (3.78)$$

This corresponds to a circle in the γ domain, centre $(-1/\Delta, 0)$ and radius $1/\Delta$. As $\Delta \to 0$, we see that this circle expands in such a way that the stability region is the entire open left half-plane, and coincides with the stability region for continuous-time systems.

Let us examine the pole locations for the two cases previously considered, namely $T = 0.1$ and $T = 0.01$. With $\Delta = T = 0.1$, the characteristic equation has the form

$$\gamma^2 + 1.410\,92\gamma + 0.931\,78 = 0$$

with roots, corresponding to poles of the system, at $-0.705\,46 \pm \mathrm{j}0.658\,87$. The centre of the circular stability region is now at $-1/0.1 = -10$, with radius 10, and these roots lie at a radial distance of about 9.3178 from this centre. Note that the distance of the poles from the stability boundary is just less than 0.7. The poles of the original continuous-time model were also at about this distance from the appropriate boundary, and we observe the sharp contrast from our first discretized model, when the discretization process itself moved the pole locations very close to the stability boundary. In that approach the situation became exacerbated when the sampling rate was increased, to $T = 0.01$, and the poles moved nearer to the boundary. Setting $T = 0.01$ in the new formulation, we find that the characteristic equation becomes

$$\gamma^2 + 1.414\,13\gamma + 0.992\,95 = 0$$

with roots at $-0.707\,06 \pm \mathrm{j}0.702\,14$. The stability circle is now centred at -100, with radius 100, and the radial distance of the poles is about 99.2954. Thus the distance from the boundary remains at about 0.7. Clearly, in the limit as $\Delta \to 0$, the pole locations become those of the continuous-time model, with the stability circle enlarging to become the entire left half of the complex γ plane.

3.9.4   Implementing the design

The discussion so far serves to demonstrate the utility of the δ operator formulation, but the problem of implementation of the design remains. It is possible to construct a δ^{-1} block based on delay or $1/z$ blocks, as shown in Figure 3.20. Systems can be realized using these structures in cascade or otherwise, and simulation studies have produced successful results. An alternative approach is to make use of the **state-space form** of the system model (see Section 6.8). We demonstrate this

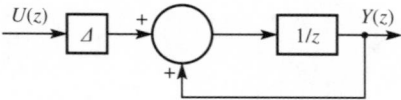

Figure 3.20 The δ^{-1} block.

approach again for the case $T = 0.01$, when, with $T = \Delta = 0.01$, (3.77) becomes

$$(\delta^2 + 1.414\,13\delta + 0.992\,95)y_k = (0.000\,02\delta^2 + 0.009\,30\delta + 0.992\,95)u_k \quad \textbf{(3.79)}$$

We now define state variables $x_{1,k}$ and $x_{2,k}$ by

$$x_{1,k} = y_k, \qquad x_{2,k} = \delta y_k$$

so that

$$\delta x_{1,k} = x_{2,k}$$
$$\delta x_{2,k} = -0.992\,95x_{1,k} - 1.414\,13x_{2,k} + u_k$$

and

$$y_k = 0.992\,93x_{1,k} + 0.009\,72x_{2,k} + 0.000\,02u_k$$

Defining the vectors $x_k = [x_{1,k} \quad x_{2,k}]^{\mathrm{T}}$ and $\delta x_k = [\delta x_{1,k} \quad \delta x_{2,k}]^{\mathrm{T}}$, these equations can be represented in matrix form as

$$\delta x_k = \begin{bmatrix} 0 & 1 \\ -0.992\,95 & -1.414\,13 \end{bmatrix} x_k + \begin{bmatrix} 0 \\ 1 \end{bmatrix} u_k \qquad \textbf{(3.80a)}$$

and

$$y_k = [0.992\,93 \quad 0.009\,72]x_k + 0.000\,02u_k \qquad \textbf{(3.80b)}$$

We now return to the q form to implement the system. Recalling that $\delta = (q - 1)/\Delta$, (3.80a) becomes

$$qx_k = x_{k+1} = x_k + \Delta\left(\begin{bmatrix} 0 & 1 \\ -0.992\,95 & -1.414\,13 \end{bmatrix} x_k + \begin{bmatrix} 0 \\ 1 \end{bmatrix} u_k\right) \qquad \textbf{(3.81)}$$

with (3.80b) remaining the same and where $\Delta = 0.01$, in this case. Equations (3.81) and (3.80b) may be expressed in the vector–matrix form

$$x_{k+1} = x_k + \Delta[A(\Delta)x_k + bu_k]$$
$$y = c^{\mathrm{T}}(\Delta)x_k + d(\Delta)u_k$$

This matrix difference equation can now be implemented without difficulty using standard delay blocks, and has a form similar to the result of applying a simple Euler discretization of the original continuous-time model expressed in state-space form.

3.9.5   The $\mathscr{D}$ transform

In Section 3.9.3 we introduced a transform variable

$$\gamma = \frac{z - 1}{\Delta}$$

The purpose of this was to enable us to analyse the stability of systems described in the δ form. We now define a transform in terms of the z transform using the notation given by R. M. Middleton and G. C. Goodwin, *Digital Control and Estimation, A Unified Approach* (Prentice-Hall, Englewood Cliffs, NJ, 1990). Let the sequence $\{f_k\}$ have z transform $F(z)$; then the new transform is given by

$$F'_\Delta(\gamma) = F(z)|_{z = \Delta\gamma + 1}$$

$$= \sum_{k=0}^{\infty} \frac{f_k}{(1 + \Delta\gamma)^k}$$

The $\mathscr{D}$ transform is formally defined as a slight modification to this form, as

$$\mathscr{D}(f_k) = F_\Delta(\gamma) = \Delta F'_\Delta(\gamma) = \Delta \sum_{k=0}^{\infty} \frac{f_k}{(1 + \Delta\gamma)^k}$$

The purpose of this modification is to permit the construction of a *unified theory of transforms* encompassing both continuous- and discrete-time models in the same structure. These developments are beyond the scope of the text, but may be pursued by the interested reader in the reference given above. We conclude the discussion with an example to illustrate the ideas. The ramp sequence $\{u_k\} = \{k\Delta\}$ can be obtained by sampling the continuous-time function $f(t) = t$ at intervals Δ. This sequence has z transform

$$U(z) = \frac{\Delta z}{(z - 1)^2}$$

and the corresponding $\mathscr{D}$ transform is then

$$\Delta U'_\Delta(\gamma) = \frac{1 + \Delta\gamma}{\gamma^2}$$

Note that on setting $\Delta = 0$ and $\gamma = s$ one recovers the Laplace transform of $f(t)$.

3.9.6   Exercises

29 A continuous-time system having input $y(t)$ and output $y(t)$ is defined by its transfer function

$$H(s) = \frac{1}{(s + 1)(s + 2)}$$

Use the methods described above to find the q and δ form of the discrete-time system model obtained using the transformation

$$s \to \frac{2}{\Delta}\frac{z - 1}{z + 1}$$

where Δ is the sampling interval. Examine the stability of the original system and that of the

discrete-time systems when $\Delta = 0.1$ and when $\Delta = 0.01$.

30 Use the formula in equation (3.68) to obtain the transfer function of the third-order Butterworth filter with $\omega_c = 1$, and obtain the corresponding δ form discrete-time system when $T = \Delta$.

31 Make the substitution

$$x_1(t) = y(t)$$

$$x_2(t) = \frac{dy(t)}{dt}$$

in Exercise 29 to obtain the state-space form of the system model,

$$\dot{x}(t) = \mathbf{A}x(t) + \mathbf{b}u(t)$$
$$y(t) = \mathbf{c}^{\mathrm{T}}x(t) + du(t)$$

The **Euler discretization technique** replaces $\dot{x}(t)$ by

$$\frac{x((k+1)\varDelta) - x(k\varDelta)}{\varDelta}$$

Show that this corresponds to the model obtained above with $\mathbf{A} = \mathbf{A}(0)$, $\mathbf{c} = \mathbf{c}(0)$ and $d = d(0)$.

32 The discretization procedure used in Section 3.9.3 has been based on the bilinear transform method, derived from the trapezoidal approximation to the integration process. An alternative approximation

is the Adams–Bashforth procedure, and it can be shown that this means that we should make the transformation

$$s \to \frac{12}{\varDelta} \frac{z^2 - z}{5z^2 + 8z - 1}$$

where $\varDelta$ is the sampling interval (see W. Forsythe and R. M. Goodall, *Digital Control* (Macmillan, London, 1991). Use this transformation to discretize the system given by

$$H(s) = \frac{s}{s+1}$$

when $\varDelta = 0.1$ in

(a) the z form, and
(b) the γ form.

3.10 Review exercises (1–16)

1 The signal $f(t) = t$ is sampled at intervals T to generate the sequence $\{f(kT)\}$. Show that

$$\mathscr{Z}\{f(kT)\} = \frac{Tz}{(z-1)^2}$$

2 Show that

$$\mathscr{Z}\{a^k \sin k\omega\} = \frac{az \sin \omega}{z^2 - 2az \cos \omega + a^2} \quad (a > 0)$$

3 Show that

$$\mathscr{Z}\{k^2\} = \frac{z(z+1)}{(z-1)^3}$$

4 Find the impulse response for the system with transfer function

$$H(z) = \frac{(3z^2 - z)}{z^2 - 2z + 1}$$

5 Calculate the step response for the system with transfer function

$$H(z) = \frac{1}{z^2 + 3z + 2}$$

6 A process with Laplace transfer function $H(s) = 1/(s+1)$ is in cascade with a zero-order hold

device with Laplace transfer function $G(s) = (1 - e^{-sT})/s$. The overall transfer function is then

$$\frac{1 - e^{-sT}}{s(s+1)}$$

Write $F(s) = 1/s(s+1)$, and find $f(t) = \mathscr{L}^{-1}\{F(s)\}$. Sample $f(t)$ at intervals T to produce the sequence $\{f(kT)\}$ and find $\tilde{F}(z) = \mathscr{Z}\{f(kT)\}$. Deduce that

$$e^{-sT}F(s) \to \frac{1}{z}\tilde{F}(z)$$

and hence show that the overall z transfer function for the process and zero-order hold is

$$\frac{1 - e^{-T}}{z - e^{-T}}$$

7 A system has Laplace transfer function

$$H(s) = \frac{s+1}{(s+2)(s+3)}$$

Calculate the impulse response, and obtain the z transform of this response when sampled at intervals T.

8 It can be established that if $X(z)$ is the z transform of the sequence $\{x_n\}$ then the general term of that sequence is given by

$$x_n = \frac{1}{j2\pi} \oint_C X(z)z^{n-1} dz$$

where C is any closed contour containing all the sigularities of $X(z)$. If we assume that all the singularities of $X(z)$ are poles located within a circle of finite radius then it is an easy application of the residue theorem to show that

$$x_n = \sum [\text{residues of } X(z)z^{n-1} \text{ at poles of } X(z)]$$

(a) Let $X(z) = z/(z-a)(z-b)$, with a and b real. Where are the poles of $X(z)$? Calculate the residues of $z^{n-1}X(z)$, and hence invert the transform to obtain $\{x_n\}$.

(b) Use the residue method to find

(i) $\mathscr{L}^{-1}\left\{\dfrac{z}{(z-3)^2}\right\}$ (ii) $\mathscr{L}^{-1}\left\{\dfrac{z}{z^2-z+1}\right\}$

9 The impulse response of a certain discrete-time system is $\{(-1)^k - 2^k\}$. What is the step response?

10 A discrete-time system has transfer function

$$H(z) = \frac{z^2}{(z+1)(z-1)}$$

Find the response to the sequence $\{1, -1, 0, 0, \ldots\}$.

11 Show that the response of the second-order system with transfer function

$$\frac{z^2}{(z-\alpha)(z-\beta)}$$

to the input $\{1, -(\alpha+\beta), \alpha\beta, 0, 0, 0, \ldots\}$ is

$$\{\delta_k\} = \{1, 0, 0, \ldots\}$$

Deduce that the response of the system

$$\frac{z}{(z-\alpha)(z-\beta)}$$

to the same input will be

$$\{\delta_{k-1}\} = \{0, 1, 0, 0, \ldots\}$$

12 A system is specified by its Laplace transfer function

$$H(s) = \frac{s}{(s+1)(s+2)}$$

Calculate the impulse response $y_\delta(t) = \mathscr{L}^{-1}\{H(s)\}$, and show that if this response is sampled at intervals T to generate the sequence $\{y_\delta(nT)\}$ $(n = 0, 1, 2, \ldots)$ then

$$D(z) = \mathscr{L}\{y_\delta(nT)\} = \frac{2z}{z - e^{-2T}} - \frac{z}{z - e^{-T}}$$

A discrete-time system is now constructed so that

$$Y(z) = TD(z)X(z)$$

where $X(z)$ is the z transform of the input sequence $\{x_n\}$ and $Y(z)$ that of the output sequence $\{y_n\}$, with $x_n = x(nT)$ and $y_n = y(nT)$. Show that if $T = 0.5\,\text{s}$ then the difference equation governing the system is

$$y_{n+2} - 0.9744y_{n+1} + 0.2231y_n = 0.5x_{n+2}$$
$$- 0.4226x_{n+1}$$

Sketch a block diagram for the discrete-time system modelled by the difference equation

$$p_{n+2} - 0.9744p_{n+1} + 0.2231p_n = x_n$$

and verify that the signal y_n, as defined above, is generated by taking $y_n = 0.5p_{n+2} - 0.4226p_{n+1}$ as output.

13 In a discrete-time position-control system the position y_n satisfies the difference equation

$$y_{n+1} = y_n + av_n \quad (a \text{ constant})$$

where v_n and u_n satisfy the difference equations

$$v_{n+1} = v_n + bu_n \quad (b \text{ constant})$$
$$u_n = k_1(x_n - y_n) - k_2v_n \quad (k_1, k_2 \text{ constants})$$

(a) Show that if $k_1 = 1/4ab$ and $k_2 = 1/b$ then the z transfer function of the system is

$$\frac{Y(z)}{X(z)} = \frac{1}{(1-2z)^2}$$

where $Y(z) = \mathscr{L}\{y_n\}$ and $X(z) = \mathscr{L}\{x_n\}$.

(b) If also $x_n = A$ (where A is a constant), determine the response sequence $\{y_n\}$ given that $y_0 = y_1 = 0$.

14 The step response of a continuous-time system is modelled by the differential equation

$$\frac{d^2y}{dt^2} + 3\frac{dy}{dt} + 2y = 1 \quad (t \geq 0)$$

with $y(0) = \dot{y}(0) = 0$. Use the backward-difference approximation

$$\frac{dy}{dt} \simeq \frac{y_k - y_{k-1}}{T}$$

$$\frac{d^2y}{dt^2} \simeq \frac{y_k - 2y_{k-1} + y_{k-2}}{T^2}$$

to show that this differential equation may be approximated by

$$\frac{y_k - 2y_{k-1} + y_{k-2}}{T^2} + 3\frac{y_k - y_{k-1}}{T} + 2y_k = 1$$

Take the z transform of this difference equation, and

show that the system poles are at

$$z = \frac{1}{1 + T}, \qquad z = \frac{1}{1 + 2T}$$

Deduce that the general solution is thus

$$y_k = \alpha \left(\frac{1}{1 + T}\right)^k + \beta \left(\frac{1}{1 + 2T}\right)^k + \gamma$$

Show that $\gamma = \frac{1}{2}$ and, noting that the initial conditions $y(0) = 0$ and $\dot{y}(0) = 0$ imply $y_0 = y_{-1} = 0$, deduce that

$$y_k = \frac{1}{2}\left[\left(\frac{1}{1 + 2T}\right)^k - 2\left(\frac{1}{1 + T}\right)^k + 1\right]$$

Note that the z-transform method could be used to obtain this result if we redefine $\mathscr{Z}\{y_k\} = \sum_{j=-1}^{\infty}(y_j/z^j)$, with appropriate modifications to the formulae for $\mathscr{Z}\{y_{k+1}\}$ and $\mathscr{Z}\{y_{k+2}\}$.

Explain why the calculation procedure is always stable in theory, but note the pole locations for very small T.

Finally, verify that the solution of the differential equation is

$$y(t) = \frac{1}{2}(e^{-2t} - 2e^{-t} + 1)$$

and plot graphs of the exact and approximate solutions with $T = 0.1\,\text{s}$ and $T = 0.05\,\text{s}$.

15 Again consider the step response of the system modelled by the differential equation

$$\frac{d^2 y}{dt^2} + 3\frac{dy}{dt} + 2y = 1 \quad (t \geqslant 0)$$

with $y(0) = \dot{y}(0) = 0$. Now discretize using the bilinear transform method, that is, take the Laplace transform

and make the transformation

$$s \rightarrow \frac{2}{T}\frac{z - 1}{z + 1}$$

where T is the sampling interval. Show that the poles of the resulting z transfer function are at

$$z = \frac{1 - T}{1 + T}, \qquad z = \frac{2 - T}{2 + T}$$

Deduce that the general solution is then

$$y_k = \alpha \left(\frac{1 - T}{1 + T}\right)^k + \beta \left(\frac{2 - T}{2 + T}\right)^k + \gamma$$

Deduce that $\gamma = \frac{1}{2}$ and, using the conditions $y_0 = y_{-1} = 0$, show that

$$y_k = \frac{1}{2}\left[(1 - T)\left(\frac{1 - T}{1 + T}\right)^k - (2 - T)\left(\frac{2 - T}{2 + T}\right)^k + 1\right]$$

Plot graphs to illustrate the exact solution and the approximate solution when $T = 0.1\,\text{s}$ and $T = 0.05\,\text{s}$.

16 Show that the z transform of the sampled version of the signal $f(t) = t^2$ is

$$F(z) = \frac{z(z + 1)\Delta^2}{(z - 1)^3}$$

where Δ is the sampling interval. Verify that the $\mathscr{D}$ transform is then

$$\frac{(1 + \Delta v)(2 + \Delta v)}{v^3}$$

4

Fourier Series

CONTENTS

4.1   Introduction

The representation of a function in the form of a series is fairly common practice in mathematics. Probably the most familiar expansions are power series of the form

$$f(x) = \sum_{n=0}^{\infty} a_n x^n$$

which were introduced in Chapter 6 of *Modern Engineering Mathematics* and in which the resolved components or **base set** comprise the power functions

$$1, x, x^2, x^3, \ldots, x^n, \ldots$$

For example, we recall that the exponential function may be represented by the infinite series

$$e^x = 1 + x + \frac{x^2}{2!} + \frac{x^3}{3!} + \ldots + \frac{x^n}{n!} + \ldots = \sum_{n=0}^{\infty} \frac{x^n}{n!}$$

There are frequently advantages in expanding a function in such a series, since the first few terms of a good approximation are easy to deal with. For example, term-by-term integration or differentiation may be applied or suitable function approximations can be made.

Power functions comprise only one example of a base set for the expansion of functions: a number of other base sets may be used. In particular, a **Fourier series** is an expansion of a periodic function $f(t)$ of period $T = 2\pi/\omega$ in which the base set is the set of sine functions, giving an expanded representation of the form

$$f(t) = A_0 + \sum_{n=1}^{\infty} A_n \sin(n\omega t + \phi_n)$$

Although the idea of expanding a function in the form of such a series had been used by Bernoulli, D'Alembert and Euler (*c.* 1750) to solve problems associated with the vibration of strings, it was Joseph Fourier (1768–1830) who developed the approach to a stage where it was generally useful. Fourier, a French physicist, was interested in heat-flow problems: given an initial temperature at all points of a region, he was concerned with determining the change in the temperature distribution over time. When Fourier postulated in 1807 that an arbitrary function $f(x)$ could be represented by a trigonometric series of the form

$$\sum_{n=0}^{\infty} (A_n \cos nkx + B_n \sin nkx)$$

the result was considered so startling that it met considerable opposition from the leading mathematicians of the time, notably Laplace, Poisson and, more significantly, Lagrange, who is regarded as one of the greatest mathematicians of all time. They questioned his work because of its lack of rigour, and it was probably this opposition that delayed the publication of Fourier's work, his classic text *Théorie Analytique de la Chaleur* (The Analytical Theory of Heat) not appearing until 1822. This text has since become the source for the modern methods of solving practical problems associated with partial differential equations subject to prescribed boundary conditions. In addition to heat flow, this class of problems includes structural vibrations, wave propagation and diffusion, which are discussed in Chapter 8. The task of giving Fourier's work a more rigorous mathematical underpinning was undertaken later by Dirichlet (*c.* 1830) and subsequently Riemann, his successor at the University of Göttingen.

In addition to its use in solving boundary-value problems associated with partial differential equations, Fourier series analysis is central to many other applications in engineering. In Chapter 2 we saw how the frequency response of a dynamical system, modelled by a linear differential equation with constant coefficients, is readily determined and the role that it plays in both system analysis and design. In such cases the frequency response, being the steady-state response to a sinusoidal input signal $A \sin \omega t$, is also a sinusoid having the same frequency as the input signal. As mentioned in Section 2.5.6, periodic functions, which are not purely sinusoidal, frequently occur as input signals in engineering applications, particularly in electrical engineering, since many electrical sources of practical value, such as electronic rectifiers, generate non-sinusoidal periodic waveforms. Fourier series provide the ideal framework for analysing the steady-state response to such periodic input signals, since they enable us to represent the signals as infinite sums of sinusoids. The steady-state response due to each sinusoid can then be determined as in Section 2.7, and, because of the linear character of the system, the desired steady-state response can be determined as the sum of the individual responses. As the Fourier series expansion will consist of sinusoids having frequencies $n\omega$ that are multiples of the input signal frequency ω, the steady-state response will also have components having such frequencies. If one of the multiple frequencies $n\omega$ happens to be close in value to the natural oscillating frequency of the system, then it will resonate with the system, and the component at this frequency will dominate the steady-state response. Thus a distinction of significant practical interest between a non-sinusoidal periodic input signal and a sinusoidal input signal is that although the signal may have a frequency considerably lower than the natural frequency of the system, serious problems can still arise owing to resonance. A Fourier series analysis helps to identify such a possibility.

In Chapter 5 we shall illustrate how Fourier series analysis may be extended to aperiodic functions by the use of Fourier transforms. The discrete versions of such transforms provide one of the most advanced methods for discrete signal analysis, and are widely used in such fields as communications theory and speech and image processing.

An introduction to Fourier series techniques is given in Chapter 12 of *Modern Engineering Mathematics*. In order to make the present chapter self-contained, the introductory material is first revisited and then extended to include the consideration of frequency spectra, oscillating and nonlinear systems, complex representation and generalized Fourier analysis. Applications to boundary-value problems are considered in Chapter 8, and the Fourier analysis of aperiodic signals is dealt with in Chapter 5, where numerical procedures are also considered.

4.2   Fourier series expansion

In this section we develop the Fourier series expansion of periodic functions and discuss how closely they approximate the functions. We also indicate how symmetrical properties of the function may be taken advantage of in order to reduce the amount of mathematical manipulation involved in determining the Fourier series.

4.2.1   Periodic functions

A function $f(t)$ is said to be **periodic** if its image values are repeated at regular intervals in its domain. Thus the graph of a periodic function can be divided into 'vertical strips' that are replicas of each other, as illustrated in Figure 4.1. The interval between two successive replicas is called the **period** of the function. We therefore say that a function $f(t)$ is periodic with period T if, for all its domain values t,

$$f(t + mT) = f(t)$$

for any integer m.

To provide a measure of the number of repetitions per unit of t, we define the **frequency** of a periodic function to be the reciprocal of its period, so that

$$\text{frequency} = \frac{1}{\text{period}} = \frac{1}{T}$$

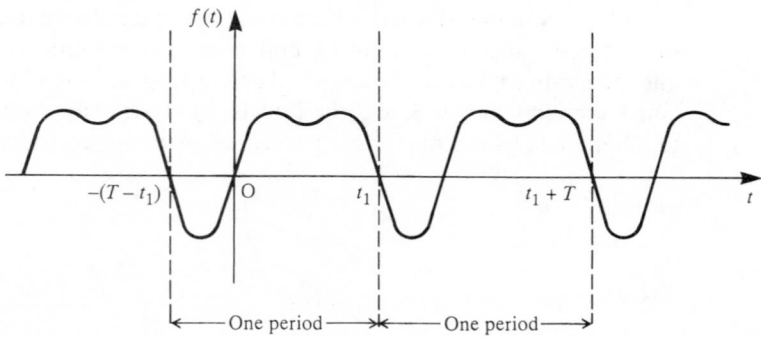

Figure 4.1 A periodic function with period T.

The term **circular frequency** is also used in engineering, and is defined by

$$\text{circular frequency} = 2\pi \times \text{frequency} = \frac{2\pi}{T}$$

and is measured in radians per second. It is common to drop the term 'circular' and refer to this simply as the frequency when the context is clear.

4.2.2   Fourier's theorem

This theorem states that a periodic function that satisfies certain conditions can be expressed as the sum of a number of sine functions of different amplitudes, phases and periods. That is, if $f(t)$ is a periodic function with period T then

$$f(t) = A_0 + A_1 \sin(\omega t + \phi_1) + A_2 \sin(2\omega t + \phi_2) + \dots$$
$$+ A_n \sin(n\omega t + \phi_n) + \dots \tag{4.1}$$

where the As and ϕs are constants and $\omega = 2\pi/T$ is the frequency of $f(t)$. The term $A_1 \sin(\omega t + \phi_1)$ is called the **first harmonic** or the **fundamental mode**, and it has the same frequency ω as the parent function $f(t)$. The term $A_n \sin(n\omega t + \phi_n)$ is called the **nth harmonic**, and it has frequency $n\omega$, which is n times that of the fundamental. A_n denotes the **amplitude** of the nth harmonic and ϕ_n is its **phase angle**, measuring the lag or lead of the nth harmonic with reference to a pure sine wave of the same frequency.

Since

$$A_n \sin(n\omega t + \phi_n) \equiv (A_n \cos \phi_n) \sin n\omega t + (A_n \sin \phi_n) \cos n\omega t$$

$$\equiv b_n \sin \omega t + a_n \cos n\omega t$$

where

$$b_n = A_n \cos \phi_n, \qquad a_n = A_n \sin \phi_n \tag{4.2}$$

the expansion (4.1) may be written as

$$f(t) = \tfrac{1}{2} a_0 + \sum_{n=1}^{\infty} a_n \cos n\omega t + \sum_{n=1}^{\infty} b_n \sin n\omega t \tag{4.3}$$

where $a_0 = 2A_0$ (we shall see later that taking the first term as $\tfrac{1}{2} a_0$ rather than a_0 is a convenience that enables us to make a_0 fit a general result). The expansion (4.3) is called the **Fourier series expansion** of the function $f(t)$, and the as and bs are called the **Fourier coefficients**. In electrical engineering it is common practice to refer to a_n and b_n respectively as the **in-phase** and **phase quadrature components** of the nth harmonic, this terminology arising from the use of the phasor notation $e^{jn\omega t} = \cos n\omega t + j\sin n\omega t$. Clearly, (4.1) is an alternative representation of the

Fourier series with the amplitude and phase of the nth harmonic being determined from (4.2) as

$$A_n = \sqrt{(a_n^2 + b_n^2)}, \qquad \phi_n = \tan^{-1}\left(\frac{a_n}{b_n}\right)$$

with care being taken over choice of quadrant.

4.2.3   The Fourier coefficients

Before proceeding to evaluate the Fourier coefficients, we first recall the following integrals, in which $T = 2\pi/\omega$:

$$\int_d^{d+T} \cos n\omega t \, dt = \begin{cases} 0 & (n \neq 0) \\ T & (n = 0) \end{cases} \tag{4.4}$$

$$\int_d^{d+T} \sin n\omega t \, dt = 0 \quad \text{(all } n) \tag{4.5}$$

$$\int_d^{d+T} \sin m\omega t \sin n\omega t \, dt = \begin{cases} 0 & (m \neq n) \\ \tfrac{1}{2}T & (m = n \neq 0) \end{cases} \tag{4.6}$$

$$\int_d^{d+T} \cos m\omega t \cos n\omega t \, dt = \begin{cases} 0 & (m \neq n) \\ \tfrac{1}{2}T & (m = n \neq 0) \end{cases} \tag{4.7}$$

$$\int_d^{d+T} \cos m\omega t \sin n\omega t \, dt = 0 \quad \text{(all } m \text{ and } n) \tag{4.8}$$

The results (4.4)–(4.8) constitute the **orthogonality relations** for sine and cosine functions, and show that the set of functions

$$\{1, \cos \omega t, \cos 2\omega t, \ldots, \cos n\omega t, \sin \omega t, \sin 2\omega t, \ldots, \sin n\omega t\}$$

is an orthogonal set of functions on the interval $d \leqslant t \leqslant d + T$. The choice of d is arbitrary in these results, it only being necessary to integrate over a period of duration T.

Integrating the series (4.3) with respect to t over the period $t = d$ to $t = d + T$, and using (4.4) and (4.5), we find that each term on the right-hand side is zero except for the term involving a_0; that is, we have

$$\int_d^{d+T} f(t) \, dt = \tfrac{1}{2}a_0 \int_d^{d+T} dt + \sum_{n=1}^{\infty}\left(a_n \int_d^{d+T} \cos n\omega t \, dt + b_n \int_d^{d+T} \sin n\omega t \, dt\right)$$

$$= \tfrac{1}{2}a_0(T) + \sum_{n=1}^{\infty} [a_n(0) + b_n(0)]$$

$$= \tfrac{1}{2}Ta_0$$

Thus

$$\tfrac{1}{2}a_0 = \frac{1}{T} \int_d^{d+T} f(t)\, dt$$

and we can see that the constant term $\tfrac{1}{2}a_0$ in the Fourier series expansion represents the mean value of the function $f(t)$ over one period. For an electrical signal it represents the bias level or DC (direct current) component. Hence

$$a_0 = \frac{2}{T} \int_d^{d+T} f(t)\, dt \qquad (4.9)$$

To obtain this result, we have assumed that term-by-term integration of the series (4.3) is permissible. This is indeed so because of the convergence properties of the series – its validity is discussed in detail in more advanced texts.

To obtain the Fourier coefficient a_n $(n \neq 0)$, we multiply (4.3) throughout by $\cos m\omega t$ and integrate with respect to t over the period $t = d$ to $t = d + T$, giving

$$\int_d^{d+T} f(t) \cos m\omega t\, dt = \tfrac{1}{2}a_0 \int_d^{d+T} \cos m\omega t\, dt + \sum_{n=1}^{\infty} a_n \int_d^{d+T} \cos n\omega t \cos m\omega t\, dt$$

$$+ \sum_{n=1}^{\infty} b_n \int_d^{d+T} \cos m\omega t \sin n\omega t\, dt$$

Assuming term-by-term integration to be possible, and using (4.4), (4.7) and (4.8), we find that, when $m \neq 0$, the only non-zero integral on the right-hand side is the one that occurs in the first summation when $n = m$. That is, we have

$$\int_d^{d+T} f(t) \cos m\omega t\, dt = a_m \int_d^{d+T} \cos m\omega t \cos m\omega t\, dt = \tfrac{1}{2}a_m T$$

giving

$$a_m = \frac{2}{T} \int_d^{d+T} f(t) \cos m\omega t\, dt$$

which, on replacing m by n, gives

$$a_n = \frac{2}{T} \int_d^{d+T} f(t) \cos n\omega t\, dt \qquad (4.10)$$

The value of a_0 given in (4.9) may be obtained by taking $n = 0$ in (4.10), so that we may write

$$a_n = \frac{2}{T} \int_d^{d+T} f(t) \cos n\omega t\, dt \quad (n = 0, 1, 2, \ldots) \qquad (4.11)$$

This explains why the constant term in the Fourier series expansion was taken as $\tfrac{1}{2}a_0$ and not a_0, since this ensures compatibility of the results (4.9) and (4.10). Although a_0 and a_n satisfy the same formula, it is usually safer to work them out separately.

Finally, to obtain the Fourier coefficients b_n, we multiply (4.3) throughout by $\sin m\omega t$ and integrate with respect to t over the period $t = d$ to $t = d + T$, giving

$$\int_d^{d+T} f(t)\sin m\omega t\, dt = \tfrac{1}{2}a_0 \int_d^{d+T} \sin m\omega t\, dt$$

$$+ \sum_{n=1}^{\infty} \left(a_n \int_d^{d+T} \sin m\omega t \cos n\omega t\, dt + b_n \int_t^{d+T} \sin m\omega t \sin n\omega t\, dt \right)$$

Assuming term-by-term integration to be possible, and using (4.5), (4.6) and (4.8), we find that the only non-zero integral on the right-hand side is the one that occurs in the second summation when $m = n$. That is, we have

$$\int_d^{d+T} f(t)\sin m\omega t\, dt = b_m \int_d^{d+T} \sin m\omega t \sin m\omega t\, dt = \tfrac{1}{2}b_m T$$

giving, on replacing m by n,

$$b_n = \frac{2}{T} \int_d^{d+T} f(t)\sin n\omega t\, dt \quad (n = 1, 2, 3, \ldots) \tag{4.12}$$

The equations (4.11) and (4.12) giving the Fourier coefficients are known as **Euler's formulae**.

Summary

In summary, we have shown that if a periodic function $f(t)$ of period $T = 2\pi/\omega$ can be expanded as a Fourier series then that series is given by

$$f(t) = \tfrac{1}{2}a_0 + \sum_{n=1}^{\infty} a_n \cos n\omega t + \sum_{n=1}^{\infty} b_n \sin n\omega t \tag{4.3}$$

where the coefficients are given by the Euler formulae

$$a_n = \frac{2}{T} \int_d^{d+T} f(t)\cos n\omega t\, dt \quad (n = 0, 1, 2, \ldots) \tag{4.11}$$

$$b_n = \frac{2}{T} \int_d^{d+T} f(t)\sin n\omega t\, dt \quad (n = 1, 2, 3, \ldots) \tag{4.12}$$

The limits of integration in Euler's formulae may be specified over any period, so that the choice of d is arbitrary, and may be made in such a way as to help in the calculation of a_n and b_n. In practice, it is common to specify $f(t)$ over either the period $-\tfrac{1}{2}T < t < \tfrac{1}{2}T$ or the period $0 < t < T$, leading respectively to the limits of integration being $-\tfrac{1}{2}T$ and $\tfrac{1}{2}T$ (that is, $d = -\tfrac{1}{2}T$) or 0 and T (that is, $d = 0$).

It is also worth noting that an alternative approach may simplify the calculation of a_n and b_n. Using the formula

$$e^{jn\omega t} = \cos n\omega t + j\sin n\omega t$$

we have

$$a_n + \mathrm{j}b_n = \frac{2}{T} \int_d^{d+T} f(t)\,\mathrm{e}^{\mathrm{j}n\omega t}\,\mathrm{d}t \tag{4.13}$$

Evaluating this integral and equating real and imaginary parts on each side gives the values of a_n and b_n. This approach is particularly useful when only the amplitude $|a_n + \mathrm{j}b_n|$ of the nth harmonic is required.

4.2.4 Functions of period 2π

If the period T of the periodic function $f(t)$ is taken to be 2π then $\omega = 1$, and the series (4.3) becomes

$$f(t) = \tfrac{1}{2}a_0 + \sum_{n=1}^{\infty} a_n \cos nt + \sum_{n=1}^{\infty} b_n \sin nt \tag{4.14}$$

with the coefficients given by

$$a_n = \frac{1}{\pi} \int_d^{d+2\pi} f(t)\cos nt\,\mathrm{d}t \quad (n = 0, 1, 2, \dots) \tag{4.15}$$

$$b_n = \frac{1}{\pi} \int_d^{d+2\pi} f(t)\sin nt\,\mathrm{d}t \quad (n = 1, 2, \dots) \tag{4.16}$$

While a unit frequency may rarely be encountered in practice, consideration of this particular case reduces the amount of mathematical manipulation involved in determining the coefficients a_n and b_n. Also, there is no loss of generality in considering this case, since if we have a function $f(t)$ of period T, we may write $t_1 = 2\pi t/T$, so that

$$f(t) \equiv f\left(\frac{Tt_1}{2\pi}\right) \equiv F(t_1)$$

where $F(t_1)$ is a function of period 2π. That is, by a simple change of variable, a periodic function $f(t)$ of period T may be transformed into a periodic function $F(t_1)$ of period 2π. Thus, in order to develop an initial understanding and to discuss some of the properties of Fourier series, we shall first consider functions of period 2π, returning to functions of period other than 2π in Section 4.2.10.

EXAMPLE 4.1   Obtain the Fourier series expansion of the periodic function $f(t)$ of period 2π defined by

$$f(t) = t \quad (0 < t < 2\pi)$$
$$f(t) = f(t + 2\pi)$$

Figure 4.2 Sawtooth wave of Example 4.1.

Solution   A sketch of the function $f(t)$ over the interval $-4\pi < t < 4\pi$ is shown in Figure 4.2. Since the function is periodic we only need to sketch it over one period, the pattern being repeated for other periods. Using (4.15) to evaluate the Fourier coefficients a_0 and a_n gives

$$a_0 = \frac{1}{\pi} \int_0^{2\pi} f(t)\, dt = \frac{1}{\pi} \int_0^{2\pi} t\, dt$$

$$= \frac{1}{\pi} \left[\frac{t^2}{2} \right]_0^{2\pi} = 2\pi$$

and

$$a_n = \frac{1}{\pi} \int_0^{2\pi} f(t) \cos nt\, dt \quad (n = 1, 2, \ldots)$$

$$= \frac{1}{\pi} \int_0^{2\pi} t \cos nt\, dt$$

which, on integration by parts, gives

$$a_n = \frac{1}{\pi} \left[t\, \frac{\sin nt}{n} + \frac{\cos nt}{n^2} \right]_0^{2\pi}$$

$$= \frac{1}{\pi} \left(\frac{2\pi}{n} \sin 2n\pi + \frac{1}{n^2} \cos 2n\pi - \frac{\cos 0}{n^2} \right)$$

$$= 0$$

since $\sin 2n\pi = 0$ and $\cos 2n\pi = \cos 0 = 1$. Note the need to work out a_0 separately from a_n in this case. The formula (4.16) for b_n gives

$$b_n = \frac{1}{n} \int_0^{2\pi} f(t) \sin nt\, dt \quad (n = 1, 2, \ldots)$$

$$= \frac{1}{\pi} \int_0^{2\pi} t \sin nt\, dt$$

which, on integration by parts, gives

$$b_n = \frac{1}{\pi}\left[-\frac{t}{n}\cos nt + \frac{\sin nt}{n^2}\right]_0^{2\pi}$$

$$= \frac{1}{\pi}\left(-\frac{2\pi}{n}\cos 2n\pi\right) \qquad \text{(since } \sin 2n\pi = \sin 0 = 0\text{)}$$

$$= -\frac{2}{n} \qquad \text{(since } \cos 2n\pi = 1\text{)}$$

Hence from (4.14) the Fourier series expansion of $f(t)$ is

$$f(t) = \pi - \sum_{n=1}^{\infty}\frac{2}{n}\sin nt$$

or, in expanded form,

$$f(t) = \pi - 2\left(\sin t + \frac{\sin 2t}{2} + \frac{\sin 3t}{3} + \ldots + \frac{\sin nt}{n} + \ldots\right)$$

EXAMPLE 4.2   As period function $f(t)$ with period 2π is defined by

$$f(t) = t^2 + t \quad (-\pi < t < \pi)$$

$$f(t) = f(t + 2\pi)$$

Sketch a graph of the function $f(t)$ for values of t from $t = -3\pi$ to $t = 3\pi$ and obtain a Fourier series expansion of the function.

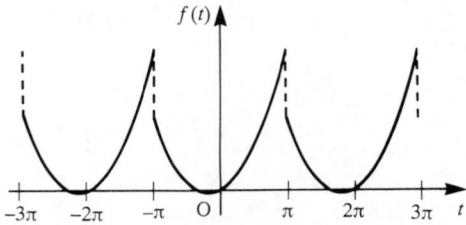

Figure 4.3 Graph of the function $f(t)$ of Example 4.2.

Solution   A graph of the function $f(t)$ for $-3\pi < t < 3\pi$ is shown in Figure 4.3. From (4.15) we have

$$a_0 = \frac{1}{\pi}\int_{-\pi}^{\pi}f(t)\,\mathrm{d}t = \frac{1}{\pi}\int_{-\pi}^{\pi}(t^2 + t)\,\mathrm{d}t = \tfrac{2}{3}\pi^2$$

and

$$a_n = \frac{1}{\pi}\int_{-\pi}^{\pi}f(t)\cos nt\,\mathrm{d}t \quad (n = 1, 2, 3, \ldots)$$

$$= \frac{1}{\pi}\int_{-\pi}^{\pi}(t^2 + t)\cos nt\,\mathrm{d}t$$

which, on integration by parts, gives

$$a_n = \frac{1}{\pi}\left[\frac{t^2}{n}\sin nt + \frac{2t}{n^2}\cos nt - \frac{2}{n^3}\sin nt + \frac{t}{n}\sin nt + \frac{1}{n^2}\cos nt\right]_{-\pi}^{\pi}$$

$$= \frac{1}{\pi}\frac{4\pi}{n^2}\cos n\pi \qquad \left(\text{since } \sin n\pi = 0 \text{ and } \left[\frac{1}{n^2}\cos nt\right]_{-\pi}^{\pi} = 0\right)$$

$$= \frac{4}{n^2}(-1)^n \qquad (\text{since } \cos n\pi = (-1)^n)$$

From (4.16)

$$b_n = \frac{1}{\pi}\int_{-\pi}^{\pi} f(t)\sin nt\, dt \quad (n = 1, 2, 3, \ldots)$$

$$= \frac{1}{\pi}\int_{-\pi}^{\pi} (t^2 + t)\sin nt\, dt$$

which, on integration by parts, gives

$$b_n = \frac{1}{\pi}\left[-\frac{t^2}{n}\sin nt + \frac{2t}{n^2}\sin nt + \frac{2}{n^3}\cos nt - \frac{t}{n}\cos nt + \frac{1}{n^2}\sin nt\right]_{-\pi}^{\pi}$$

$$= -\frac{2}{n}\cos n\pi = -\frac{2}{n}(-1)^n \qquad (\text{since } \cos n\pi = (-1)^n)$$

Hence from (4.14) the Fourier series expansion of $f(t)$ is

$$f(t) = \tfrac{1}{3}\pi^3 + \sum_{n=1}^{\infty}\frac{4}{n^2}(-1)^n\cos nt - \sum_{n=1}^{\infty}\frac{2}{n}(-1)^n\sin nt$$

or, in expanded form,

$$f(t) = \tfrac{1}{3}\pi^3 + 4\left(-\cos t + \frac{\cos 2t}{2^2} - \frac{\cos 3t}{3^2} + \cdots\right)$$

$$+ 2\left(\sin t - \frac{\sin 2t}{2} + \frac{\sin 3t}{3}\cdots\right)$$

To illustrate the alternative approach, using (4.13) gives

$$a_n + jb_n = \frac{1}{\pi}\int_{-\pi}^{\pi} f(t)\,e^{jnt}\, dt$$

$$= \frac{1}{\pi}\int_{-\pi}^{\pi} (t^2 + t)\,e^{jnt}\, dt$$

$$= \frac{1}{\pi}\left(\left[\frac{t^2 + t}{jn}e^{jnt}\right]_{-\pi}^{\pi} - \int_{-\pi}^{\pi}\frac{2t + 1}{jn}e^{jnt}\, dt\right)$$

$$= \frac{1}{\pi}\left[\frac{t^2 + t}{jn}e^{jnt} - \frac{2t + 1}{(jn)^2}e^{jnt} + \frac{2e^{jnt}}{(jn)^3}\right]_{-\pi}^{\pi}$$

Since

$$e^{jn\pi} = \cos n\pi + j \sin n\pi = (-1)^n$$

$$e^{-jn\pi} = \cos n\pi - j \sin n\pi = (-1)^n$$

and

$$1/j = -j$$

$$a_n + jb_n = \frac{(-1)^n}{\pi}\left(-j\frac{\pi^2 + \pi}{n} + \frac{2\pi + 1}{n^2} + \frac{j2}{n^3} + j\frac{\pi^2 - \pi}{n} - \frac{1 - 2\pi}{n^2} - \frac{j2}{n^3}\right)$$

$$= (-1)^n\left(\frac{4}{n^2} - j\frac{2}{n}\right)$$

Equating real and imaginary parts gives, as before,

$$a_n = \frac{4}{n^2}(-1)^n, \qquad b_n = -\frac{2}{n}(-1)^n$$

A periodic function $f(t)$ may be specified in a piecewise fashion over a period, or, indeed, it may only be piecewise-continuous over a period, as illustrated in Figure 4.4. In order to calculate the Fourier coefficients in such cases, it is necessary to break up the range of integration in the Euler formulae to correspond to the various components of the function. For example, for the function shown in Figure 4.4, $f(t)$ is defined in the interval $-\pi < t < \pi$ by

$$f(t) = \begin{cases} f_1(t) & (-\pi < t < -p) \\ f_2(t) & (-p < t < q) \\ f_3(t) & (q < t < \pi) \end{cases}$$

and is periodic elsewhere. The Euler formulae (4.15) and (4.16) for the Fourier

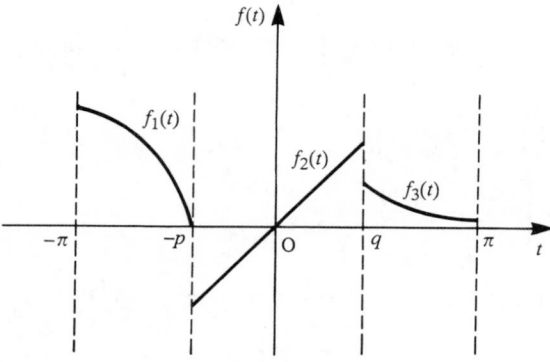

Figure 4.4 Piecewise-continuous function over a period.

coefficients become

$$a_n = \frac{1}{\pi}\left[\int_{-\pi}^{-p} f_1(t)\cos nt\,dt + \int_{-p}^{q} f_2(t)\cos nt\,dt + \int_{q}^{\pi} f_3(t)\cos nt\,dt \right]$$

$$b_n = \frac{1}{\pi}\left[\int_{-\pi}^{-p} f_1(t)\sin nt\,dt + \int_{-p}^{q} f_2(t)\sin nt\,dt + \int_{q}^{\pi} f_3(t)\sin nt\,dt \right]$$

EXAMPLE 4.3 A periodic function $f(t)$ of period 2π is defined within the period $0 \leqslant t \leqslant 2\pi$ by

$$f(t) = \begin{cases} t & (0 \leqslant t \leqslant \tfrac{1}{2}\pi) \\ \tfrac{1}{2}\pi & (\tfrac{1}{2}\pi \leqslant t \leqslant \pi) \\ \pi - \tfrac{1}{2}t & (\pi \leqslant t \leqslant 2\pi) \end{cases}$$

Sketch a graph of $f(t)$ for $-2\pi \leqslant t \leqslant 3\pi$ and find a Fourier series expansion of it.

Figure 4.5 Graph of the function $f(t)$ of Example 4.3.

Solution A graph of the function $f(t)$ for $-2\pi \leqslant t \leqslant 3\pi$ is shown in Figure 4.5. From (4.15),

$$a_0 = \frac{1}{\pi}\int_0^{2\pi} f(t)\,dt$$

$$= \frac{1}{\pi}\left[\int_0^{\pi/2} t\,dt + \int_{\pi/2}^{\pi} \tfrac{1}{2}\pi\,dt + \int_{\pi}^{2\pi} (\pi - \tfrac{1}{2}t)\,dt \right]$$

$$= \tfrac{5}{8}\pi$$

and

$$a_n = \frac{1}{\pi}\int_0^{2\pi} f(t)\cos nt\,dt \quad (n = 1, 2, 3, \ldots)$$

$$= \frac{1}{\pi}\left[\int_0^{\pi/2} t\cos nt\,dt + \int_{\pi/2}^{\pi} \tfrac{1}{2}\pi \cos nt\,dt + \int_{\pi}^{2\pi} (\pi - \tfrac{1}{2}t)\cos nt\,dt \right]$$

$$= \frac{1}{\pi}\left(\left[\frac{t}{n}\sin nt + \frac{\cos nt}{n^2} \right]_0^{\pi/2} + \left[\frac{\pi}{2n}\sin nt \right]_{\pi/2}^{\pi} \right.$$

$$\left. + \left[\frac{2\pi - t}{2}\frac{\sin nt}{n} - \frac{\cos nt}{2n^2} \right]_{\pi}^{2\pi} \right)$$

$$= \frac{1}{\pi}\left(\frac{\pi}{2n}\sin \tfrac{1}{2}n\pi + \frac{1}{n^2}\cos \tfrac{1}{2}n\pi - \frac{1}{n^2} - \frac{\pi}{2n}\sin \tfrac{1}{2}n\pi - \frac{1}{2n^2} + \frac{1}{2n^2}\cos n\pi \right)$$

$$= \frac{1}{2\pi n^2}(2\cos \tfrac{1}{2}n\pi - 3 + \cos n\pi)$$

that is,

$$a_n = \begin{cases} \dfrac{1}{\pi n^2}\left[(-1)^{n/2} - 1\right] & \text{(even } n\text{)} \\[3mm] -\dfrac{2}{\pi n^2} & \text{(odd } n\text{)} \end{cases}$$

From (4.16),

$$b_n = \frac{1}{\pi}\int_0^{2\pi} f(t)\sin nt\,\mathrm{d}t \quad (n = 1,2,3,\ldots)$$

$$= \frac{1}{\pi}\left[\int_0^{\pi/2} t\sin nt\,\mathrm{d}t + \int_{\pi/2}^{\pi} \tfrac{1}{2}\pi\sin nt\,\mathrm{d}t + \int_{\pi}^{2\pi}(\pi - \tfrac{1}{2}t)\sin nt\,\mathrm{d}t\right]$$

$$= \frac{1}{\pi}\left(\left[-\frac{t}{n}\cos nt + \frac{1}{n^2}\sin nt\right]_0^{\pi/2} + \left[-\frac{\pi}{2n}\cos nt\right]_{\pi/2}^{\pi}\right.$$

$$\left. + \left[\frac{t-2\pi}{2n}\cos nt - \frac{1}{n^2}\sin nt\right]_{\pi}^{2\pi}\right)$$

$$= \frac{1}{\pi}\left(-\frac{\pi}{2n}\cos\tfrac{1}{2}n\pi + \frac{1}{n^2}\sin\tfrac{1}{2}n\pi - \frac{\pi}{2n}\cos n\pi + \frac{\pi}{2n}\cos\tfrac{1}{2}n\pi + \frac{\pi}{2n}\cos n\pi\right)$$

$$= \frac{1}{\pi n^2}\sin\tfrac{1}{2}n\pi$$

$$= \begin{cases} 0 & \text{(even } n\text{)} \\[3mm] \dfrac{(-1)^{(n-1)/2}}{\pi n^2} & \text{(odd } n\text{)} \end{cases}$$

Hence from (4.14) the Fourier series expansion of $f(t)$ is

$$f(t) = \tfrac{5}{16}\pi - \frac{2}{\pi}\left(\cos t + \frac{\cos 3t}{3^2} + \frac{\cos 5t}{5^2} + \cdots\right)$$

$$- \frac{2}{\pi}\left(\frac{\cos 2t}{2^2} + \frac{\cos 6t}{6^2} + \frac{\cos 10t}{10^2} + \cdots\right)$$

$$+ \frac{1}{\pi}\left(\sin t - \frac{\sin 3t}{3^2} + \frac{\sin 5t}{5^2} - \frac{\sin 7t}{7^2} + \cdots\right)$$

4.2.5   Even and odd functions

Noting that a particular function possesses certain symmetrical properties enables us both to tell which terms are absent from a Fourier series expansion of the function and to simplify the expressions determining the remaining coefficients. In this section we consider even and odd function symmetries, while in Section 4.2.6 we shall consider symmetry due to even and odd harmonics.

First we consider the properties of even and odd functions that are useful for determining the Fourier coefficients. If $f(t)$ is an even function then $f(t) = f(-t)$ for all t, and the graph of the function is symmetrical about the vertical axis as illustrated in Figure 4.6(a). From the definition of integration, it follows that if $f(t)$ is an even function then

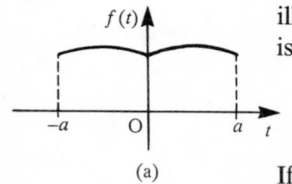

(a)

$$\int_{-a}^{a} f(t)\,dt = 2\int_{0}^{a} f(t)\,dt$$

If $f(t)$ is an odd function then $f(t) = -f(-t)$ for all t, and the graph of the function is symmetrical about the origin; that is, there is opposite-quadrant symmetry, as illustrated in Figure 4.6(b). It follows that if $f(t)$ is an odd function then

(b)

$$\int_{-a}^{a} f(t)\,dt = 0$$

Figure 4.6 Graphs of (a) an even function and (b) an odd function.

The following properties of even and odd functions are also useful for our purposes:

(a) the *sum* of two (or more) *odd* functions is an *odd* function;

(b) the *product* of two *even* functions is an *even* function;

(c) the *product* of two *odd* functions is an *even* function;

(d) the *product* of an *odd* and an *even* function is an *odd* function;

(e) the *derivative* of an *even* function is an *odd* function;

(f) the *derivative* of an *odd* function is an *even* function.

Using these properties, and taking $d = \frac{1}{2}T$ in (4.11) and (4.12), we have the following:

(i) If $f(t)$ is an *even* periodic function of period T then

$$a_n = \frac{2}{T}\int_{-T/2}^{T/2} f(t)\cos n\omega t\,dt = \frac{4}{T}\int_{0}^{T/2} f(t)\cos n\omega t\,dt$$

using property (b), and

$$b_n = \frac{2}{T}\int_{-T/2}^{T/2} f(t)\sin n\omega t\,dt = 0$$

using property (d). Thus the Fourier series expansion of an even periodic function $f(t)$ with period T consists of cosine terms only and, from (4.3), is given by

$$f(t) = \tfrac{1}{2}a_0 + \sum_{n=1}^{\infty} a_n \cos n\omega t \tag{4.17}$$

with

$$a_n = \frac{4}{T}\int_{0}^{T/2} f(t)\cos n\omega t \quad (n = 0, 1, 2, \ldots) \tag{4.18}$$

(ii) If $f(t)$ is an *odd* periodic function of period T then

$$a_n = \frac{2}{T} \int_{-T/2}^{T/2} f(t) \cos n\omega t \, dt = 0$$

using property (d), and

$$b_n = \frac{2}{T} \int_{-T/2}^{T/2} f(t) \sin n\omega t \, dt = \frac{4}{T} \int_{0}^{T/2} f(t) \sin n\omega t \, dt$$

using property (c). Thus the Fourier series expansion of an odd periodic function $f(t)$ with period T consists of sine terms only and, from (4.3), is given by

$$f(t) = \sum_{n=1}^{\infty} b_n \sin n\omega t \tag{4.19}$$

with

$$b_n = \frac{4}{T} \int_{0}^{T/2} f(t) \sin n\omega t \, dt \quad (n = 1, 2, 3, \ldots) \tag{4.20}$$

EXAMPLE 4.4 A periodic function $f(t)$ with period 2π is defined within the period $-\pi < t < \pi$ by

$$f(t) = \begin{cases} -1 & (-\pi < t < 0) \\ 1 & (0 < t < \pi) \end{cases}$$

Find its Fourier series expansion.

Solution A sketch of the function $f(t)$ over the interval $-4\pi < t < 4\pi$ is shown in Figure 4.7. Clearly $f(t)$ is an odd function of t, so that its Fourier series expansion consists of sine terms only. Taking $T = 2\pi$, that is $\omega = 1$, in (4.19) and (4.20), the Fourier series expansion is given by

$$f(t) = \sum_{n=1}^{\infty} b_n \sin nt$$

with

$$b_n = \frac{2}{\pi} \int_{0}^{\pi} f(t) \sin nt \, dt \quad (n = 1, 2, 3, \ldots)$$

$$= \frac{2}{\pi} \int_{0}^{\pi} 1 \sin nt \, dt = \frac{2}{\pi} \left[-\frac{1}{n} \cos nt \right]_{0}^{\pi}$$

$$= \frac{2}{n\pi} (1 - \cos n\pi) = \frac{2}{n\pi} [1 - (-1)^n]$$

$$= \begin{cases} 4/n\pi & (\text{odd } n) \\ 0 & (\text{even } n) \end{cases}$$

Figure 4.7 Square wave of Example 4.4.

Thus the Fourier series expansion of $f(t)$ is

$$f(t) = \frac{4}{\pi}(\sin t + \tfrac{1}{3}\sin 3t + \tfrac{1}{5}\sin 5t + \ldots)$$

$$= \frac{4}{\pi} \sum_{n=1}^{\infty} \frac{\sin (2n-1)t}{2n-1} \tag{4.21}$$

EXAMPLE 4.5   A periodic function $f(t)$ with period 2π is defined as

$$f(t) = t^2 \quad (-\pi < t < \pi)$$
$$f(t) = f(t + 2\pi)$$

Obtain a Fourier series expansion for it.

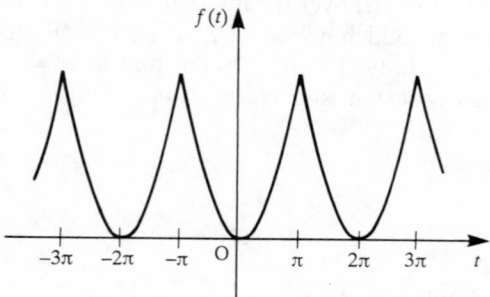

Figure 4.8 The function $f(t)$ of Example 4.5.

Solution   A sketch of the function $f(t)$ over the interval $-3\pi < t < 3\pi$ is shown in Figure 4.8. Clearly, $f(t)$ is an even function of t, so that its Fourier series expansion consists of cosine terms only. Taking $T = 2\pi$, that is $\omega = 1$, in (4.17) and (4.18), the Fourier series expansion is given by

$$f(t) = \tfrac{1}{2}a_0 + \sum_{n=1}^{\infty} a_n \cos nt$$

with

$$a_0 = \frac{2}{\pi} \int_0^\pi f(t)\,dt = \frac{2}{\pi} \int_0^\pi t^2\,dt = \tfrac{2}{3}\pi^2$$

and

$$a_n = \frac{2}{\pi} \int_0^\pi f(t) \cos nt\,dt \quad (n = 1, 2, 3, \ldots)$$

$$= \frac{2}{\pi} \int_0^\pi t^2 \cos nt\,dt$$

$$= \frac{2}{\pi} \left[\frac{t^2}{n} \sin nt + \frac{2t}{n^2} \cos nt - \frac{2}{n^3} \sin nt \right]_0^\pi$$

$$= \frac{2}{\pi} \left(\frac{2\pi}{n^2} \cos n\pi \right) = \frac{4}{n^2} (-1)^n$$

since $\sin n\pi = 0$ and $\cos n\pi = (-1)^n$. Thus the Fourier series expansion of $f(t) = t^2$ is

$$f(t) = \tfrac{1}{3}\pi^3 + 4 \sum_{n=1}^{\infty} \frac{(-1)^n}{n^2} \cos nt \qquad (4.22)$$

or, writing out the first few terms,

$$f(t) = \tfrac{1}{3}\pi^3 - 4 \cos t + \cos 2t - \tfrac{4}{9} \cos 3t + \ldots$$

4.2.6 Even and odd harmonics

In this section we consider types of symmetry that can be identified in order to eliminate terms from the Fourier series expansion having even values of n (including $n = 0$) or odd values of n.

(a) If a periodic function $f(t)$ with period T is such that

$$f(t + \tfrac{1}{2}T) = f(t)$$

then only even harmonics are present in its Fourier series expansion. For even n we have

$$a_n = \frac{4}{T} \int_0^{T/2} f(t) \cos n\omega t\,dt \qquad (4.23)$$

$$b_n = \frac{4}{T} \int_0^{T/2} f(t) \sin n\omega t\,dt \qquad (4.24)$$

An example of such a function is given in Figure 4.9(a).

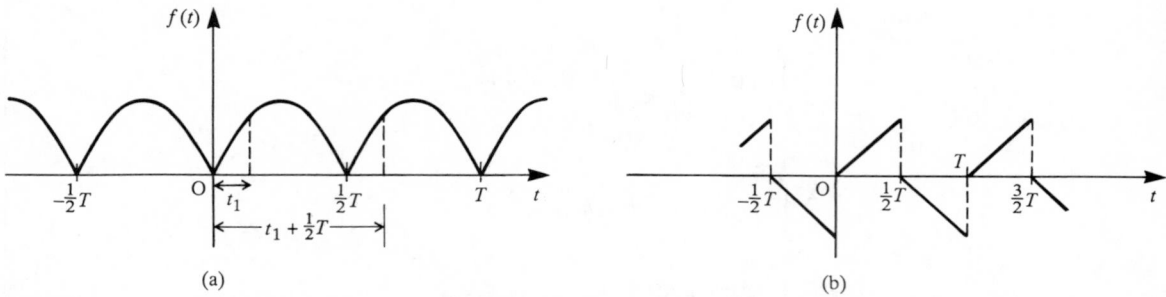

Figure 4.9 Functions having Fourier series with (a) only even harmonics and (b) only odd harmonics.

(b) If a periodic function $f(t)$ with period T is such that

$$f(t + \tfrac{1}{2}T) = -f(t)$$

then only odd harmonics are present in its Fourier series expansion. For odd n

$$a_n = \frac{4}{T} \int_0^{T/2} f(t) \cos n\omega t \, dt \qquad (4.25)$$

$$b_n = \frac{4}{T} \int_0^{T/2} f(t) \sin n\omega t \, dt \qquad (4.26)$$

An example of such a function is shown in Figure 4.9(b).

The square wave of Example 4.4 is such that $f(t + \pi) = -f(t)$, so that, from (b), its Fourier series expansion consists of only odd harmonics. Since it is also an odd function, it follows that its Fourier series expansion consists only of odd-harmonic sine terms, which is confirmed by the result (4.21).

EXAMPLE 4.6   Obtain the Fourier series expansion of the rectified sine wave

$$f(t) = |\sin t|$$

Solution   A sketch of the wave over the interval $-\pi < t < 2\pi$ is shown in Figure 4.10. Taking the period to be 2π, it also follows that $f(t + \pi) = f(t)$, so that only even harmonics are present in the Fourier series expansion. Since the function is also an even function of t, it follows that the Fourier series expansion will

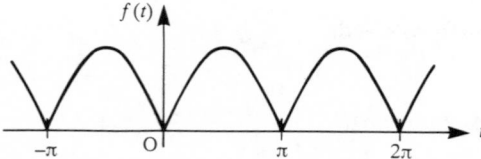

Figure 4.10 Rectified wave $f(t) = |\sin t|$.

consist only of even-harmonic cosine terms. Taking $T = 2\pi$, that is $\omega = 1$, in (4.23), the coefficients of the even harmonics are given by

$$a_n = \frac{2}{\pi} \int_0^\pi f(t) \cos nt \quad (\text{even } n)$$

$$= \frac{2}{\pi} \int_0^\pi \sin t \cos nt \, dt$$

$$= \frac{2}{\pi} \int_0^\pi [\sin (n + 1)t - \sin (n - 1)t] \, dt$$

$$= \frac{1}{\pi} \left[-\frac{\cos (n + 1)t}{n + 1} + \frac{\cos (n - 1)t}{n - 1} \right]_0^\pi$$

Since both $n + 1$ and $n - 1$ are odd when n is even,

$$\cos (n + 1)\pi = \cos (n - 1)\pi = -1$$

so that

$$a_n = \frac{1}{\pi} \left[\left(\frac{1}{n + 1} - \frac{1}{n - 1} \right) - \left(-\frac{1}{n + 1} + \frac{1}{n - 1} \right) \right]$$

$$= -\frac{4}{\pi} \frac{1}{n^2 - 1}$$

Thus the Fourier series expansion of $f(t)$ is

$$f(t) = \tfrac{1}{2} a_0 + \sum_{\substack{n=2 \\ (n \text{ even})}}^{\infty} a_n \cos nt$$

$$= \frac{2}{\pi} - \frac{4}{\pi} \sum_{\substack{n=2 \\ (n \text{ even})}}^{\infty} \frac{1}{n^2 - 1} \cos nt$$

$$= \frac{2}{\pi} - \frac{4}{\pi} \sum_{n=1}^{\infty} \frac{1}{4n^2 - 1} \cos 2nt$$

or, writing out the first few terms,

$$f(t) = \frac{2}{\pi} - \frac{4}{\pi} (\tfrac{1}{3} \cos 2t + \tfrac{1}{15} \cos 4t + \tfrac{1}{35} \cos 6t + \ldots)$$

4.2.7   Linearity property

The linearity property as applied to Fourier series may be stated in the form of the following theorem.

THEOREM 4.1   If $f(t) = g(t) + h(t)$, where $g(t)$ and $h(t)$ are periodic functions of period T, then $f(t)$ has a Fourier series expansion in which the coefficients are the sums of the coefficients in the Fourier series expansions of $g(t)$ and $h(t)$.

Proof   Clearly $f(t)$ is periodic with period T. If the Fourier series expansions of $g(t)$ and $h(t)$ are

$$g(t) = \tfrac{1}{2}a_0 + \sum_{n=1}^{\infty} a_n \cos n\omega t + \sum_{n=1}^{\infty} b_n \sin n\omega t$$

$$h(t) = \tfrac{1}{2}\alpha_0 + \sum_{n=1}^{\infty} \alpha_n \cos n\omega t + \sum_{n=1}^{\infty} \beta_n \sin n\omega t$$

then, using (4.11) and (4.12), the Fourier coefficients in the expansion of $f(t)$ are

$$A_n = \frac{2}{T} \int_{d}^{d+T} f(t) \cos n\omega t \, dt = \frac{2}{T} \int_{d}^{d+T} [g(t) + h(t)] \cos n\omega t \, dt$$

$$= \frac{2}{T} \int_{d}^{d+T} g(t) \cos n\omega t \, dt + \frac{2}{T} \int_{d}^{d+T} h(t) \cos n\omega t \, dt$$

$$= a_n + \alpha_n$$

and

$$B_n = \frac{2}{T} \int_{d}^{d+T} f(t) \sin n\omega t \, dt = \frac{2}{T} \int_{d}^{d+T} g(t) \sin n\omega t \, dt + \frac{2}{T} \int_{d}^{d+T} h(t) \sin n\omega t \, dt$$

$$= b_n + \beta_n$$

confirming that the Fourier series expansion of $f(t)$ is

$$f(t) = \tfrac{1}{2}(a_0 + \alpha_0) + \sum_{n=1}^{\infty} (a_n + \alpha_n) \cos n\omega t + \sum_{n=1}^{\infty} (b_n + \beta_n) \sin n\omega t \qquad \square$$

EXAMPLE 4.7   Suppose that $g(t)$ and $h(t)$ are periodic functions of period 2π and are defined within the period $-\pi < t < \pi$ by

$$g(t) = t^2, \qquad h(t) = t$$

Determine the Fourier series expansions of both $g(t)$ and $h(t)$ and use the linearity property to confirm the expansion obtained in Example 4.2 for the periodic function $f(t)$ defined within the period $-\pi < t < \pi$ by $f(t) = t^2 + t$.

Solution   The Fourier series of $g(t)$ is given by (4.22) as

$$g(t) = \tfrac{1}{3}\pi^2 + 4 \sum_{n=1}^{\infty} \frac{(-1)^n}{n^2} \cos nt$$

Recognizing that $h(t) = t$ is an odd function of t, we find, taking $T = 2\pi$ and $\omega = 1$ in (4.19) and (4.20), that its Fourier series expansion is

$$h(t) = \sum_{n=1}^{\infty} b_n \sin nt$$

where

$$b_n = \frac{2}{\pi} \int_0^{\pi} h(t) \sin nt \, dt \quad (n = 1, 2, 3, \ldots)$$

$$= \frac{2}{\pi} \int_0^{\pi} t \sin nt \, dt = \frac{2}{\pi} \left[-\frac{t}{n} \cos nt + \frac{\sin nt}{n^2} \right]_0^{\pi}$$

$$= -\frac{2}{n}(-1)^n$$

recognizing again that $\cos n\pi = (-1)^n$ and $\sin n\pi = 0$. Thus the Fourier series expansion of $h(t) = t$ is

$$h(t) = -2 \sum_{n=1}^{\infty} \frac{(-1)^n}{n} \sin nt \qquad (4.27)$$

Using the linearity property, we find, by combining (4.12) and (4.27), that the Fourier series expansion of $f(t) = g(t) + h(t) = t^2 + t$ is

$$f(t) = \tfrac{1}{3}\pi^2 + 4 \sum_{n=1}^{\infty} \frac{(-1)^n}{n^2} \cos nt - 2 \sum_{n=1}^{\infty} \frac{(-1)^n}{n} \sin nt$$

which conforms with the series obtained in Example 4.2.

4.2.8   Convergence of the Fourier series

So far we have concentrated our attention on determining the Fourier series expansion corresponding to a given periodic function $f(t)$. In reality, this is an exercise in integration, since we merely have to compute the coefficients a_n and b_n using Euler's formulae (4.11) and (4.12) and then substitute these values into (4.3). We have not yet considered the question of whether or not the Fourier series thus obtained is a valid representation of the periodic function $f(t)$. It should not be assumed that the existence of the coefficients a_n and b_n in itself implies that the associated series converges to the function $f(t)$.

A full discussion of the convergence of a Fourier series is beyond the scope of this book and we shall confine ourselves to simply stating a set of conditions that $f(t)$ must satisfy in order that it have a convergent Fourier series expansion. These conditions, known as **Dirichlet's conditions**, may be stated in the form of Theorem 4.2.

THEOREM 4.2   Dirichlet's conditions

If $f(t)$ is a bounded periodic function that in any period has

(a) a finite number of isolated maxima and minima, and

(b) a finite number of points of finite discontinuity

then the Fourier series expansion of $f(t)$ converges to $f(t)$ at all points where $f(t)$ is continuous and to the average of the right- and left-hand limits of $f(t)$ at points where $f(t)$ is discontinuous (that is, to the mean of the discontinuity). □

EXAMPLE 4.8   Give reasons why the functions

(a) $\dfrac{1}{3-t}$ (b) $\sin\left(\dfrac{1}{t-2}\right)$

do not satisfy Dirichlet's conditions in the interval $0 < t < 2\pi$.

Solution   (a) The function $f(t) = 1/(3-t)$ has an infinite discontinuity at $t = 3$, which is within the interval, and therefore does not satisfy the condition that $f(t)$ must only have *finite* discontinuities within a period.

(b) The function $f(t) = \sin[1/(t-2)]$ has an infinite number of maxima and minima in the neighbourhood of $t = 2$, which is within the interval, and therefore does not satisfy the requirement that $f(t)$ must have only a finite number of isolated maxima and minima within one period.

The conditions of Theorem 4.2 are sufficient to ensure that a representative Fourier series expansion of $f(t)$ exists. However, they are not necessary conditions for convergence, and it does not follow that a representative Fourier series does not exist if they are not satisfied. Indeed, necessary conditions on $f(t)$ for the existence of a convergent Fourier series are not yet known. In practice, this does not cause any problems, since for almost all conceivable practical applications the functions that are encoutered satisfy the conditions of Theorem 4.2 and therefore have representative Fourier series.

Another issue of importance in practical applications is the rate of convergence of a Fourier series, since this is an indication of how many terms must be taken in the expansion in order to obtain a realistic approximation to the function $f(t)$ it represents. Obviously, this is determined by the coefficients a_n and b_n of the Fourier series and the manner in which these decrease as n increases.

In an example, such as Example 4.1, in which the function $f(t)$ is only piecewise-continuous, exhibiting jump discontinuities, the Fourier coefficients decrease as $1/n$, and it may be necessary to include a large number of terms to obtain an adequate approximation to $f(t)$. In an example, such as Example 4.3,

Figure 4.11 Plots of $f_N(t)$ for a square wave: (a) $N = 1$; (b) 2; (c) 3; (d) 20.

in which the function is a continuous function but has discontinuous first derivatives (owing to the sharp corners), the Fourier coefficients decrease as $1/n^2$, and so one would expect the series to converge more rapidly. Indeed, this argument applies in general, and we may summarize as follows:

(a) if $f(t)$ is only piecewise-continuous then the coefficients in its Fourier series representation decrease as $1/n$;

(b) if $f(t)$ is continuous everywhere but has discontinuous first derivatives then the coefficients in its Fourier series representation decrease as $1/n^2$;

(c) if $f(t)$ and all its derivatives up to that of the rth order are continuous but the $(r + 1)$th derivative is discontinuous then the coefficients in its Fourier series representation decrease as $1/n^r$.

These observations are not surprising, since they simply tell us that the smoother the function $f(t)$, the more rapidly will its Fourier series representation converge.

To illustrate some of these issues related to convergence we return to Example 4.4, in which the Fourier series (4.21) was obtained as a representation of the square wave of Figure 4.7.

Since (4.21) is an infinite series, it is clearly not possible to plot a graph of the result. However, by considering finite partial sums, it is possible to plot graphs of approximations to the series. Denoting the sum of the first N terms in the infinite series by $f_N(t)$, that is

$$f_N(t) = \frac{4}{\pi} \sum_{n=1}^{N} \frac{\sin(2n - 1)t}{2n - 1} \tag{4.28}$$

the graphs of $f_N(t)$ for $N = 1, 2, 3$ and 20 are as shown in Figure 4.11. It can be seen that at points where $f(t)$ is continuous the approximation of $f(t)$ by $f_N(t)$ improves as N increases, confirming that the series converges to $f(t)$ at all such points. It can also be seen that at points of discontinuity of $f(t)$, which occur at $t = \pm n\pi$ ($n = 0, 1, 2, \ldots$) the series converges to the mean value of the discontinuity, which in this particular example is $\frac{1}{2}(-1 + 1) = 0$. As a consequence, the equality sign in (4.21) needs to be interpreted carefully. Although such use may be acceptable, in the sense that the series converges to $f(t)$ for values of t where $f(t)$ is continuous, this is not so at points of discontinuity. To overcome this problem, the symbol $\sim$ (read as 'behaves as' or 'represented by') rather than $=$ is frequently used in the Fourier series representation of a function $f(t)$, so that (4.21) is often written as

$$f(t) \sim \sum_{n=1}^{\infty} \frac{\sin(2n-1)t}{2n-1}$$

In Section 4.7.3 it is shown that the Fourier series converges to $f(t)$ in the sense that the integral of the square of the difference between $f(t)$ and $f_N(t)$ is minimized.

We note that convergence of the Fourier series is slowest near a point of discontinuity, such as the one that occurs at $t = 0$. Although the series does converge to the mean value of the discontinuity (namely zero) at $t = 0$, there is, as indicated in Figure 4.11(d), an undershoot at $t = 0-$ (that is, just to the left of $t = 0$) and an overshoot at $t = 0+$ (that is, just to the right of $t = 0$). This non-smooth convergence of the Fourier series leading to the occurrence of an undershoot and an overshoot at points of discontinuity of $f(t)$ is a characteristic of all Fourier series representing discontinuous functions, not only that of the square wave of Example 4.4, and is known as **Gibbs' phenomenon** after the American physicist J. W. Gibbs (1839–1903). The magnitude of the undershoot/overshoot does not diminish as $N \to \infty$ in (4.28), but simply gets 'sharper' and 'sharper', tending to a spike. In general, the magnitude of the undershoot and overshoot together amount to about 18% of the magnitude of the discontinuity (that is, the difference in the values of the function $f(t)$ to the left and right of the discontinuity). It is important that the existence of this phenomenon be recognized, since in certain practical applications these spikes at discontinuities have to be suppressed by using appropriate smoothing factors.

Theoretically, we can use the series (4.21) to obtain an approximation to π. This is achieved by taking $t = \frac{1}{2}\pi$, when $f(t) = 1$; (4.21) then gives

$$1 = \frac{4}{\pi} \sum_{n=1}^{\infty} \frac{\sin\frac{1}{2}(2n-1)\pi}{2n-1}$$

leading to

$$\pi = 4(1 - \tfrac{1}{3} + \tfrac{1}{5} - \tfrac{1}{7} + \ldots) = 4 \sum_{n=1}^{\infty} \frac{(-1)^{n+1}}{2n-1}$$

For practical purposes, however, this is not a good way of obtaining an approximation to π, because of the slow rate of convergence of the series.

4.2.9   Exercises

1 In each of the following a periodic function $f(t)$ of period 2π is specified over one period. In each case sketch a graph of the function for $-4\pi \leqslant t \leqslant 4\pi$ and obtain a Fourier series representation of the function.

(a) $f(t) = \begin{cases} -\pi & (-\pi < t < 0) \\ t & (0 < t < \pi) \end{cases}$

(b) $f(t) = \begin{cases} t + \pi & (-\pi < t < 0) \\ 0 & (0 < t < \pi) \end{cases}$

(c) $f(t) = 1 - \dfrac{t}{\pi}$ $(0 \leqslant t \leqslant 2\pi)$

(d) $f(t) = \begin{cases} 0 & (-\pi \leqslant t \leqslant -\frac{1}{2}\pi) \\ 2\cos t & (-\frac{1}{2}\pi \leqslant t \leqslant \frac{1}{2}\pi) \\ 0 & (\frac{1}{2}\pi \leqslant t \leqslant \pi) \end{cases}$

(e) $f(t) = \cos\frac{1}{2}t$ $(-\pi < t < \pi)$

(f) $f(t) = |t|$ $(-\pi < t < \pi)$

(g) $f(t) = \begin{cases} 0 & (-\pi \leqslant t \leqslant 0) \\ 2t - \pi & (0 < t \leqslant \pi) \end{cases}$

(h) $f(t) = \begin{cases} -t + e^t & (-\pi \leqslant t < 0) \\ t + e^t & (0 \leqslant t < \pi) \end{cases}$

2 Obtain the Fourier series expansion of the periodic function $f(t)$ of period 2π defined over the period $0 \leqslant t \leqslant 2\pi$ by

$$f(t) = (\pi - t)^2 \quad (0 \leqslant t \leqslant 2\pi)$$

Use the Fourier series to show that

$$\tfrac{1}{12}\pi^2 = \sum_{n=1}^{\infty} \frac{(-1)^{n+1}}{n^2}$$

3 The charge $q(t)$ on the plates of a capacitor at time t is as shown in Figure 4.12. Express $q(t)$ as a Fourier series expansion.

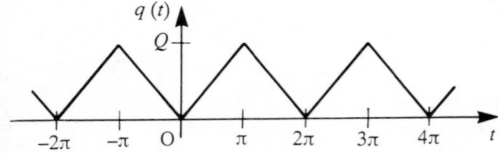

Figure 4.12 Plot of the charge $q(t)$ in Exercise 3.

4 The clipped response of a half-wave rectifier is the periodic function $f(t)$ of period 2π defined over the period $0 \leqslant t \leqslant 2\pi$ by

$$f(t) = \begin{cases} 5\sin t & (0 \leqslant t \leqslant \pi) \\ 0 & (\pi \leqslant t \leqslant 2\pi) \end{cases}$$

Express $f(t)$ as a Fourier series expansion.

5 Show that the Fourier series representing the periodic function $f(t)$, where

$$f(t) = \begin{cases} \pi^2 & (-\pi < t < 0) \\ (t - \pi)^2 & (0 < t < \pi) \end{cases}$$

$$f(t + 2\pi) = f(t)$$

is

$$f(t) = \tfrac{2}{3}\pi^2 + \sum_{n=1}^{\infty} \left[\frac{2}{n^2}\cos nt + \frac{(-1)^n}{n}\pi\sin nt \right]$$

$$- \frac{4}{\pi}\sum_{n=1}^{\infty} \frac{\sin(2n-1)t}{(2n-1)^3}$$

Use this result to show that

(a) $\displaystyle\sum_{n=1}^{\infty} \frac{1}{n^2} = \tfrac{1}{6}\pi^2$ (b) $\displaystyle\sum_{n=1}^{\infty} \frac{(-1)^{n+1}}{n^2} = \tfrac{1}{12}\pi^2$

6 A periodic function $f(t)$ of period 2π is defined within the domain $0 \leqslant t \leqslant \pi$ by

$$f(t) = \begin{cases} t & (0 \leqslant t \leqslant \frac{1}{2}\pi) \\ \pi - t & (\frac{1}{2}\pi \leqslant t \leqslant \pi) \end{cases}$$

Sketch a graph of $f(t)$ for $-2\pi < t < 4\pi$ for the two cases where

(a) $f(t)$ is an even function

(b) $f(t)$ is an odd function

Find the Fourier series expansion that represents the even function for all values of t, and use it to show that

$$\tfrac{1}{8}\pi^2 = \sum_{n=1}^{\infty} \frac{1}{(2n-1)^2}$$

7 A periodic function $f(t)$ of period 2π is defined within the period $0 \leqslant t \leqslant 2\pi$ by

$$f(t) = \begin{cases} 2 - t/\pi & (0 \leqslant t \leqslant \pi) \\ t/\pi & (\pi \leqslant t \leqslant 2\pi) \end{cases}$$

Draw a graph of the function for $-4\pi \leqslant t \leqslant 4\pi$ and obtain its Fourier series expansion.

By replacing t by $t - \frac{1}{2}\pi$ in your answer, show that the periodic function $f(t - \frac{1}{2}\pi) - \frac{3}{2}$ is represented by a sine series of odd harmonics.

4.2.10   Functions of period T

Although all the results have been related to periodic functions having period T, all the examples we have considered so far have involved periodic functions of period 2π. This was done primarily for ease of manipulation in determining the Fourier coefficients while becoming acquainted with Fourier series. As mentioned in Section 4.2.4, functions having unit frequency (that is, of period 2π) are rarely encountered in practice, and in this section we consider examples of periodic functions having periods other than 2π.

EXAMPLE 4.9   A periodic function $f(t)$ of period 4 (that is, $f(t+4) = f(t)$) is defined in the range $-2 < t < 2$ by

$$f(t) = \begin{cases} 0 & (-2 < t < 0) \\ 1 & (0 < t < 2) \end{cases}$$

Sketch a graph of $f(t)$ for $-6 \leqslant t \leqslant 6$ and obtain a Fourier series expansion for the function.

Solution   A graph of $f(t)$ for $-6 \leqslant t \leqslant 6$ is shown in Figure 4.13. Taking $T = 4$ in (4.11) and (4.12), we have

$$a_0 = \tfrac{1}{2} \int_{-2}^{2} f(t)\,dt = \tfrac{1}{2}\left(\int_{-2}^{0} 0\,dt + \int_{0}^{2} 1\,dt \right) = 1$$

$$a_n = \tfrac{1}{2} \int_{-2}^{2} f(t) \cos \tfrac{1}{2}n\pi t\,dt \quad (n = 1, 2, 3, \ldots)$$

$$= \tfrac{1}{2}\left(\int_{-2}^{0} 0\,dt + \int_{0}^{2} \cos \tfrac{1}{2}n\pi t\,dt \right) = 0$$

and

$$b_n = \tfrac{1}{2} \int_{-2}^{2} f(t) \sin \tfrac{1}{2}n\pi t\,dt \quad (n = 1, 2, 3, \ldots)$$

$$= \tfrac{1}{2}\left(\int_{-2}^{0} 0\,dt + \int_{0}^{2} \sin \tfrac{1}{2}n\pi t\,dt \right)$$

$$= \frac{1}{n\pi}(1 - \cos n\pi) = \frac{1}{n\pi}[1 - (-1)^n]$$

$$= \begin{cases} 0 & (\text{even } n) \\ 2/n\pi & (\text{odd } n) \end{cases}$$

Thus, from (4.10), the Fourier series expansion of $f(t)$ is

$$f(t) = \tfrac{1}{2} + \frac{2}{\pi}(\sin\tfrac{1}{2}\pi t + \tfrac{1}{3}\sin\tfrac{3}{2}\pi t + \tfrac{1}{5}\sin\tfrac{5}{2}\pi t + \ldots)$$

$$= \tfrac{1}{2} + \frac{2}{\pi}\sum_{n=1}^{\infty}\frac{1}{2n-1}\sin\tfrac{1}{2}(2n-1)\pi t$$

Figure 4.13 The function $f(t)$ of Example 4.9.

Figure 4.14 The function $f(t)$ of Example 4.10.

EXAMPLE 4.10   A periodic function $f(t)$ of period 2 is defined by

$$f(t) = \begin{cases} 3t & (0 < t < 1) \\ 3 & (1 < t < 2) \end{cases}$$

$$f(t+2) = f(t)$$

Sketch a graph of $f(t)$ for $-4 \leqslant t \leqslant 4$ and determine a Fourier series expansion for the function.

Solution   A graph of $f(t)$ for $-4 \leqslant t \leqslant 4$ is shown in Figure 4.14. Taking $T = 2$ in (4.11) and (4.12), we have

$$a_0 = \frac{2}{2}\int_0^2 f(t)\,\mathrm{d}t = \int_0^1 3t\,\mathrm{d}t + \int_1^2 3\,\mathrm{d}t = \tfrac{7}{2}$$

$$a_n = \frac{2}{2}\int_0^2 f(t)\cos\frac{n\pi t}{1}\,\mathrm{d}t \quad (n = 1, 2, 3, \ldots)$$

$$= \int_0^1 3t\cos n\pi t\,\mathrm{d}t + \int_1^2 3\cos n\pi t\,\mathrm{d}t$$

$$= \left[\frac{3t\sin n\pi t}{n\pi} + \frac{3\cos n\pi t}{(n\pi)^2}\right]_0^1 + \left[\frac{3\sin n\pi t}{n\pi}\right]_1^2$$

$$= \frac{3}{(n\pi)^2}(\cos n\pi - 1)$$

$$= \begin{cases} 0 & (\text{even } n) \\ -6/(n\pi)^2 & (\text{odd } n) \end{cases}$$

and

$$b_n = \frac{2}{2} \int_0^2 f(t) \sin \frac{n\pi t}{1} \, dt \quad (n = 1, 2, 3, \ldots)$$

$$= \int_0^1 3t \sin n\pi t \, dt + \int_1^2 3 \sin n\pi t \, dt$$

$$= \left[-\frac{3 \cos n\pi t}{n\pi} + \frac{3 \sin n\pi t}{(n\pi)^2} \right]_0^1 + \left[-\frac{3 \cos n\pi t}{n\pi} \right]_1^2$$

$$= -\frac{3}{n\pi} \cos 2n\pi = -\frac{3}{n\pi}$$

Thus, from (4.10), the Fourier series expansion of $f(t)$ is

$$f(t) = \frac{7}{4} - \frac{6}{\pi^2} (\cos \pi t + \tfrac{1}{9} \cos 3\pi t + \tfrac{1}{25} \cos 5\pi t + \ldots)$$

$$- \frac{3}{\pi} (\sin \pi t + \tfrac{1}{2} \sin 2\pi t + \tfrac{1}{3} \sin 3\pi t + \ldots)$$

$$= \frac{7}{4} - \frac{6}{\pi^2} \sum_{n=1}^{\infty} \frac{\cos(2n-1)\pi t}{(2n-1)^2} - \frac{3}{\pi} \sum_{n=1}^{\infty} \frac{\sin n\pi t}{n}$$

4.2.11 Exercises

8 Find a Fourier series expansion of the periodic function

$$f(t) = t \quad (-l < t < l)$$
$$f(t + 2l) = f(t)$$

9 A periodic function $f(t)$ of period $2l$ is defined over one period by

$$f(t) = \begin{cases} -\dfrac{K}{l}(l+t) & (-l < t < 0) \\[2mm] \dfrac{K}{l}(l-t) & (0 < t < l) \end{cases}$$

Determine its Fourier series expansion and illustrate graphically for $-3l < t < 3l$.

10 A periodic function of period 10 is defined within the period $-5 < t < 5$ by

$$f(t) = \begin{cases} 0 & (-5 < t < 0) \\ 3 & (0 < t < 5) \end{cases}$$

Determine its Fourier series expansion and illustrate graphically for $-12 < t < 12$.

11 Passing a sinusoidal voltage $A \sin \omega t$ through a half-wave rectifier produces the clipped sine wave shown in Figure 4.15. Determine a Fourier series expansion of the rectified wave.

Figure 4.15 Rectified sine wave of Exercise 11.

12 Obtain a Fourier series expansion of the periodic function

$$f(t) = t^2 \quad (-T < t < T)$$

$$f(t + 2T) = f(t)$$

and illustrate graphically for $-3T < t < 3T$.

13 Determine a Fourier series representation of the periodic voltage $e(t)$ shown in Figure 4.16.

Figure 4.16 Voltage $e(t)$ of Exercise 13.

4.3   Functions defined over a finite interval

One of the requirements of Fourier's theorem is that the function to be expanded be periodic. Therefore a function $f(t)$ that is not periodic cannot have a Fourier series representation that converges to it *for all values* of t. However, we can obtain a Fourier series expansion that represents a *non-periodic* function $f(t)$ that is defined only over a finite time interval $0 \leqslant t \leqslant \tau$. This is a facility that is frequently used to solve problems in practice, particularly boundary-value problems involving partial differential equations, such as the consideration of heat flow along a bar or the vibrations of a string. Various forms of Fourier series representations of $f(t)$, valid only in the interval $0 \leqslant t \leqslant \tau$, are possible, including series consisting of cosine terms only or series consisting of sine terms only. To obtain these, various periodic extensions of $f(t)$ are formulated.

4.3.1   Full-range series

Suppose the given function $f(t)$ is defined only over the finite time interval $0 \leqslant t \leqslant \tau$. Then, to obtain a full-range Fourier series representation of $f(t)$ (that is, a series consisting of both cosine and sine terms), we define the **periodic extension** $\phi(t)$ of $f(t)$ by

$$\phi(t) = f(t) \quad (0 < t < \tau)$$

$$\phi(t + \tau) = \phi(t)$$

The graphs of a possible $f(t)$ and its periodic extension $\phi(t)$ are shown in Figures 4.17(a) and (b) respectively.

Provided that $f(t)$ satisfies Dirichlet's conditions in the interval $0 \leqslant t \leqslant \tau$, the new function $\phi(t)$, of period τ, will have a convergent Fourier series expansion.

(a)   (b)

Figure 4.17 Graphs of a function defined only over a finite interval $0 \leqslant t \leqslant \tau$ (a) and its periodic extension (b).

Since, within the particular period $0 < t < \tau$, $\phi(t)$ is identical with $f(t)$, it follows that this Fourier series expansion of $\phi(t)$ will be representative of $f(t)$ within this interval.

EXAMPLE 4.11   Find a full-range Fourier series expansion of $f(t) = t$ valid in the finite interval $0 < t < 4$. Draw graphs of both $f(t)$ and the periodic function represented by the Fourier series obtained.

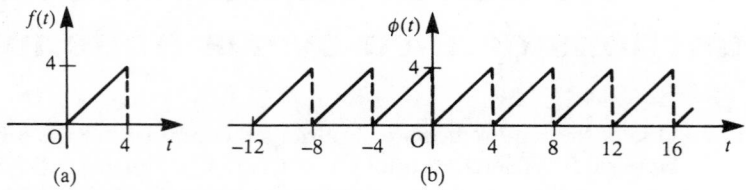

Figure 4.18 The functions $f(t)$ and $\phi(t)$ of Example 4.11.

Solution   Define the periodic function $\phi(t)$ by

$$\phi(t) = f(t) = t \quad (0 < t < 4)$$

$$\phi(t + 4) = \phi(t)$$

Then the graphs of $f(t)$ and its periodic extension $\phi(t)$ are as shown in Figures 4.18(a) and (b) respectively. Since $\phi(t)$ is a periodic function with period 4, it has a convergent Fourier series expansion. Taking $T = 4$ in (4.11) and (4.12), the Fourier coefficients are determined as

$$a_0 = \tfrac{1}{2} \int_0^4 f(t)\,\mathrm{d}t = \tfrac{1}{2} \int_0^4 t\,\mathrm{d}t = 4$$

$$a_n = \tfrac{1}{2} \int_0^4 f(t) \cos \tfrac{1}{2} n\pi t\,\mathrm{d}t \quad (n = 1, 2, 3, \ldots)$$

$$= \tfrac{1}{2} \int_0^4 t \cos \tfrac{1}{2} n\pi t\,\mathrm{d}t$$

$$= \tfrac{1}{2} \left[\frac{2t}{n\pi} \sin \tfrac{1}{2} n\pi t + \frac{4}{(n\pi)^2} \cos \tfrac{1}{2} n\pi t \right]_0^4 = 0$$

and

$$b_n = \tfrac{1}{2} \int_0^4 f(t) \sin \tfrac{1}{2} n\pi t\,\mathrm{d}t \quad (n = 1, 2, 3, \ldots)$$

$$= \tfrac{1}{2} \int_0^4 t \sin \tfrac{1}{2} n\pi t\,\mathrm{d}t$$

$$= \tfrac{1}{2} \left[-\frac{2t}{n\pi} \cos \tfrac{1}{2} n\pi t + \frac{4}{(n\pi)^2} \sin \tfrac{1}{2} n\pi t \right]_0^4 = -\frac{4}{n\pi}$$

Thus, by (4.10), the Fourier series expansion of $\phi(t)$ is

$$\phi(t) = 2 - \frac{4}{\pi}(\sin\tfrac{1}{2}\pi t + \tfrac{1}{2}\sin \pi t + \tfrac{1}{3}\sin\tfrac{3}{2}\pi t + \tfrac{1}{4}\sin 2t + \tfrac{1}{5}\sin\tfrac{5}{2}\pi t + \ldots)$$

$$= 2 - \frac{4}{\pi}\sum_{n=1}^{\infty}\frac{1}{n}\sin\tfrac{1}{2}n\pi t$$

Since $\phi(t) = f(t)$ for $0 < t < 4$, it follows that this Fourier series is representative of $f(t)$ within this interval, so that

$$f(t) = t = 2 - \frac{4}{\pi}\sum_{n=1}^{\infty}\frac{1}{n}\sin\tfrac{1}{2}n\pi t \quad (0 < t < 4) \tag{4.29}$$

It is important to appreciate that this series converges to t only within the interval $0 < t < 4$. For values of t outside this interval it converges to the periodic extended function $\phi(t)$. Again convergence is to be interpreted in the sense of Theorem 4.2, so that at the end points $t = 0$ and $t = 4$ the series does not converge to t but to the mean of the discontinuity in $\phi(t)$, namely the value 2.

4.3.2   Half-range cosine and sine series

Rather than develop the periodic extensions $\phi(t)$ of $f(t)$ as in Section 4.3.1, it is possible to formulate periodic extensions that are either even or odd functions, so that the resulting Fourier series of the extended periodic functions consist either of cosine terms only or sine terms only.

For a function $f(t)$ defined only over the finite interval $0 \leqslant t \leqslant \tau$ its **even periodic extension** $F(t)$ is the even periodic function defined by

$$F(t) = \begin{cases} f(t) & (0 < t < \tau) \\ f(-t) & (-\tau < t < 0) \end{cases}$$

$$F(t + 2\tau) = f(t)$$

As an illustration, the even periodic extension $F(t)$ of the function $f(t)$ shown in Figure 4.17(a) (redrawn in Figure 4.19a) is shown in Figure 4.19(b).

Provided that $f(t)$ satisfies Dirichlet's conditions in the interval $0 < t < \tau$, since it is an even function of period 2τ, it follows from Section 4.2.5 that the

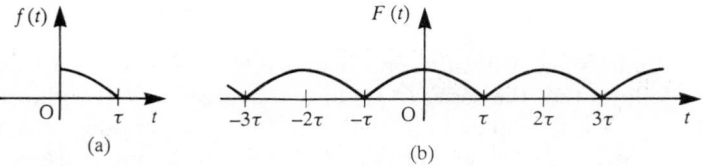

Figure 4.19 (a) A function $f(t)$. (b) Its even periodic extension $F(t)$.

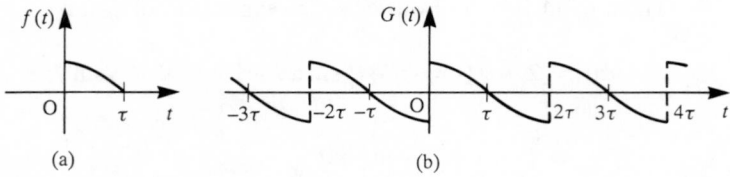

Figure 4.20 (a) A function $f(t)$. (b) Its odd periodic extension $G(t)$.

even periodic extension $F(t)$ will have a convergent Fourier series representation consisting of cosine terms only and given by

$$F(t) = \tfrac{1}{2}a_0 + \sum_{n=1}^{\infty} a_n \cos \frac{n\pi t}{\tau} \tag{4.30}$$

where

$$a_n = \frac{2}{\tau} \int_0^{\tau} f(t) \cos \frac{n\pi t}{\tau} \, dt \quad (n = 0, 1, 2, \ldots) \tag{4.31}$$

Since, within the particular interval $0 < t < \tau$, $F(t)$ is identical with $f(t)$, it follows that the series (4.30) also converges to $f(t)$ within this interval.

For a function $f(t)$ defined only over the finite interval $0 \leqslant t \leqslant \tau$, its **odd periodic extension** $G(t)$ is the odd periodic function defined by

$$G(t) = \begin{cases} f(t) & (0 < t < \tau) \\ -f(-t) & (-\tau < t < 0) \end{cases}$$

$$G(t + 2\tau) = G(t)$$

Again, as an illustration, the odd periodic extension $G(t)$ of the function $f(t)$ shown in Figure 4.17(a) (redrawn in Figure 4.20a) is shown in Figure 4.20(b).

Provided that $f(t)$ satisfies Dirichlet's conditions in the interval $0 < t < \tau$, since it is an odd function of period 2τ, it follows from Section 4.2.5 that the odd periodic extension $G(t)$ will have a convergent Fourier series representation consisting of sine terms only and given by

$$G(t) = \sum_{n=1}^{\infty} b_n \sin \frac{n\pi t}{\tau} \tag{4.32}$$

where

$$b_n = \frac{2}{\tau} \int_0^{\tau} f(t) \sin \frac{n\pi t}{\tau} \, dt \quad (n = 1, 2, 3, \ldots) \tag{4.33}$$

Again, since, within the particular interval $0 < t < \tau$, $G(t)$ is identical with $f(t)$, it follows that the series (4.32) also converges to $f(t)$ within this interval.

We note that both the even and odd periodic extensions $F(t)$ and $G(t)$ are of period 2τ, which is twice the length of the interval over which $f(t)$ is defined. However, the resulting Fourier series (4.30) and (4.32) are based only on the function $f(t)$, and for this reason are called the **half-range Fourier series expansions** of $f(t)$. In particular, the even half-range expansion $F(t)$, (4.30), is called the **half-range cosine series expansion** of $f(t)$, while the odd half-range expansion $G(t)$, (4.32), is called the **half-range sine series expansion** of $f(t)$.

EXAMPLE 4.12   For the function $f(t) = t$ defined only in the interval $0 < t < 4$, and considered in Example 4.11, obtain

(a) a half-range cosine series expansion

(b) a half-range sine series expansion.

Draw graphs of $f(t)$ and of the periodic functions represented by the two series obtained for $-20 < t < 20$.

Solution   (a) *Half-range cosine series.* Define the periodic function $F(t)$ by

$$F(t) = \begin{cases} f(t) = t & (0 < t < 4) \\ f(-t) = -t & (-4 < t < 0) \end{cases}$$

$$F(t + 8) = F(t)$$

Then, since $F(t)$ is an even periodic function with period 8, it has a convergent Fourier series expansion given by (4.30). Taking $\tau = 4$ in (4.31), we have

$$a_0 = \tfrac{2}{4} \int_0^4 f(t)\,\mathrm{d}t = \tfrac{1}{2} \int_0^4 t\,\mathrm{d}t = 4$$

$$a_n = \tfrac{2}{4} \int_0^4 f(t) \cos \tfrac{1}{4} n\pi t \,\mathrm{d}t \quad (n = 1, 2, 3, \ldots)$$

$$= \tfrac{1}{2} \int_0^4 t \cos \tfrac{1}{4} n\pi t \,\mathrm{d}t$$

$$= \tfrac{1}{2} \left[\frac{4t}{n\pi} \sin \tfrac{1}{4} n\pi t + \frac{16}{(n\pi)^2} \cos \tfrac{1}{4} n\pi t \right]_0^4$$

$$= \frac{8}{(n\pi)^2} (\cos n\pi - 1)$$

$$= \begin{cases} 0 & (\text{even } n) \\ -16/(n\pi)^2 & (\text{odd } n) \end{cases}$$

Then, by (4.30), the Fourier series expansion of $F(t)$ is

$$F(t) = 2 - \frac{16}{\pi^2} \left(\cos \tfrac{1}{4}\pi t + \frac{1}{3^2} \cos \tfrac{3}{4}\pi t + \frac{1}{5^2} \cos \tfrac{5}{4}\pi t + \ldots \right)$$

or

$$F(t) = 2 - \frac{16}{\pi^2} \sum_{n=1}^{\infty} \frac{1}{(2n-1)^2} \cos \tfrac{1}{4}(2n-1)\pi t$$

Since $F(t) = f(t)$ for $0 < t < 4$, it follows that this Fourier series is representative of $f(t)$ within this interval. Thus the half-range cosine series expansion of $f(t)$ is

$$f(t) = t = 2 - \frac{16}{\pi^2} \sum_{n=1}^{\infty} \frac{1}{(2n-1)^2} \cos \tfrac{1}{4}(2n-1)\pi t \quad (0 < t < 4) \tag{4.34}$$

(b) *Half-range sine series.* Define the periodic function $G(t)$ by

$$G(t) = \begin{cases} f(t) = t & (0 < t < 4) \\ -f(-t) = t & (-4 < t < 0) \end{cases}$$

$$G(t + 8) = G(t)$$

Then, since $G(t)$ is an odd periodic function with period 8, it has a convergent Fourier series expansion given by (4.32). Taking $\tau = 4$ in (4.3), we have

$$b_n = \tfrac{2}{4} \int_0^4 f(t) \sin \tfrac{1}{4} n\pi t \, dt \quad (n = 1, 2, 3, \ldots)$$

$$= \tfrac{1}{2} \int_0^4 t \sin \tfrac{1}{4} n\pi t \, dt$$

$$= \tfrac{1}{2} \left[-\frac{4t}{n\pi} \cos \tfrac{1}{4} n\pi t + \frac{16}{(n\pi)^2} \sin \tfrac{1}{4} n\pi t \right]_0^4$$

$$= -\frac{8}{n\pi} \cos n\pi = -\frac{8}{n\pi}(-1)^n$$

Thus, by (4.32), the Fourier series expansion of $G(t)$ is

$$G(t) = \frac{8}{\pi}(\sin \tfrac{1}{4}\pi t - \tfrac{1}{2}\sin \tfrac{1}{2}\pi t + \tfrac{1}{3}\sin \tfrac{3}{4}\pi t - \ldots)$$

$$= \frac{8}{\pi} \sum_{n=1}^{\infty} \frac{(-1)^{n+1}}{n} \sin \tfrac{1}{4} n\pi t$$

Since $G(t) = g(t)$ for $0 < t < 4$, it follows that this Fourier series is representative of $f(t)$ within this interval. Thus the half-range sine series expansion of $f(t)$ is

$$f(t) = t = \frac{8}{\pi} \sum_{n=1}^{\infty} \frac{(-1)^{n+1}}{n} \sin \tfrac{1}{4} n\pi t \quad (0 < t < 4) \tag{4.35}$$

Graphs of the given function $f(t)$ and of the even and odd periodic expansions $F(t)$ and $G(t)$ are given in Figures 4.21(a), (b) and (c) respectively.

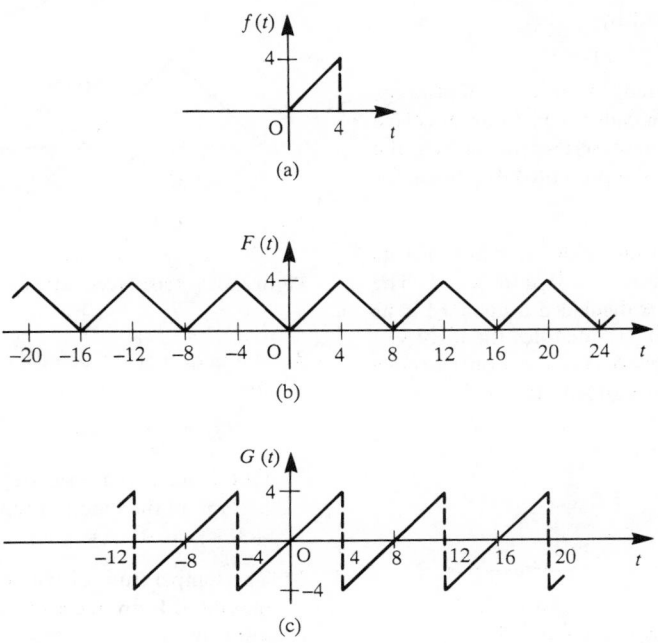

Figure 4.21 The functions $f(t)$, $F(t)$ and $G(t)$ of Example 4.12.

It is important to realize that the three different Fourier series representations (4.29), (4.34) and (4.35) are representative of the function $f(t) = t$ only within the defined interval $0 < t < 4$. Outside this interval the three Fourier series converge to the three different functions $\phi(t)$, $F(t)$ and $G(t)$, illustrated in Figures 4.18(b), 4.21(b) and 4.21(c) respectively.

4.3.3   Exercises

14 Show that the half-range Fourier sine series expansion of the function $f(t) = 1$, valid for $0 < t < \pi$, is

$$f(t) = \frac{4}{\pi} \sum_{n=1}^{\infty} \frac{\sin(2n+1)t}{2n+1} \quad (0 < t < \pi)$$

Sketch the graphs of both $f(t)$ and the periodic function represented by the series expansion for $-3\pi < t < 3\pi$.

15 Determine the half-range cosine series expansion of the function $f(t) = 2t - 1$, valid for $0 < t < 1$. Sketch

the graphs of both $f(t)$ and the periodic function represented by the series expansion for $-2 < t < 2$.

16 The function $f(t) = 1 - t^2$ is to be represented by a Fourier series expansion over the finite interval $0 < t < 1$. Obtain a suitable

(a) full-range series expansion,

(b) half-range sine series expansion,

(c) half-range cosine series expansion.

Draw graphs of $f(t)$ and of the periodic functions represented by each of the three series for $-4 < t < 4$.

17 A function $f(t)$ is defined by

$$f(t) = \pi t - t^2 \quad (0 \leqslant t \leqslant \pi)$$

and is to be represented by either a half-range Fourier sine series or a half-range Fourier cosine series. Find both of these series and sketch the graphs of the functions represented by them for $-2\pi < t < 2\pi$.

18 A tightly stretched flexible uniform string has its ends fixed at the points $x = 0$ and $x = l$. The midpoint of the string is displaced a distance a, as shown in Figure 4.22. If $f(x)$ denotes the displaced profile of the string, express $f(x)$ as a Fourier series expansion consisting only of sine terms.

Figure 4.22 Displaced string of Exercise 18.

19 Repeat Exercise 18 for the case where the displaced profile of the string is as shown in Figure 4.23.

20 A function $f(t)$ is defined on $0 \leqslant t \leqslant \pi$ by

$$f(t) = \begin{cases} \sin t & (0 \leqslant t < \frac{1}{2}\pi) \\ 0 & (\frac{1}{2}\pi \leqslant t \leqslant \pi) \end{cases}$$

Find a half-range Fourier series expansion of $f(t)$ on this interval. Sketch a graph of the function represented by the series for $-2\pi \leqslant t \leqslant 2\pi$.

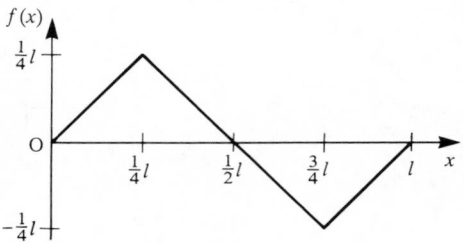

Figure 4.23 Displaced string of Exercise 19.

21 A function $f(x)$ is defined on the interval $-l \leqslant x \leqslant l$ by

$$f(x) = \frac{A}{l}(|x| - l)$$

Obtain a Fourier series expansion of $f(x)$ and sketch a graph of the function represented by the series for $-3l \leqslant x \leqslant 3l$.

22 The temperature distribution $T(x)$ at a distance x, measured from one end, along a bar of length L is given by

$$T(x) = Kx(L - x) \quad (0 \leqslant x \leqslant L), \quad K = \text{constant}$$

Express $T(x)$ as a Fourier series expansion consisting of sine terms only.

23 Find the Fourier sine series expansion of the function $f(t)$ valid for $-1 < t < 1$, where

$$f(t) = \begin{cases} 1 & (-1 < t < 0) \\ \cos \pi t & (0 < t < 1) \end{cases}$$

To what value does this series converge when $t = 1$?

4.4 Differentiation and integration of Fourier series

It is inevitable that the desire to obtain the derivative or the integral of a Fourier series will arise in some applications. Since the smoothing effects of the integration process tend to eliminate discontinuities, whereas the process of differentiation has the opposite effect, it is not surprising that the integration of a Fourier series is more likely to be possible than its differentiation. We shall not pursue the theory in depth here; rather we shall state, without proof, two theorems concerned with the term-by-term integration and differentiation of Fourier series, and make some observations on their use.

4.4.1   Integration of a Fourier series

THEOREM 4.3   A Fourier series expansion of a periodic function $f(t)$ that satisfies Dirichlet's conditions may be integrated term by term, and the integrated series converges to the integral of the function $f(t)$.   □

According to this theorem, if $f(t)$ satisfies Dirichlet's conditions in the interval $-\pi \leqslant t \leqslant \pi$ and has a Fourier series expansion

$$f(t) = \tfrac{1}{2}a_0 + \sum_{n=1}^{\infty} (a_n \cos nt + b_n \sin nt)$$

then for $-\pi \leqslant t_1 < t \leqslant \pi$

$$\int_{t_1}^{t} f(t)\,dt = \int_{t_1}^{t} \tfrac{1}{2}a_0\,dt + \sum_{n=1}^{\infty} \int_{t_1}^{t} (a_n \cos nt + b_n \sin nt)\,dt$$

$$= \tfrac{1}{2}a_0(t - t_1) + \sum_{n=1}^{\infty} \left[\frac{b_n}{n}(\cos nt_1 - \cos nt) \right. $$

$$\left. + \frac{a_n}{n}(\sin nt - \sin nt_1) \right]$$

Because of the presence of the term $\tfrac{1}{2}a_0 t$ on the right-hand side, this is clearly not a Fourier series expansion of the integral on the left-hand side. However, the result can be rearranged to be a Fourier series expansion of the function

$$g(t) = \int_{t_1}^{t} f(t)\,dt - \tfrac{1}{2}a_0 t$$

Example 4.13 serves to illustrate this process. Note also that the Fourier coefficients in the new Fourier series are $-b_n/n$ and a_n/n, so, from the observations made in Section 4.2.8, the integrated series converges faster than the original series for $f(t)$. If the given function $f(t)$ is piecewise-continuous, rather than continuous, over the interval $-\pi \leqslant t \leqslant \pi$ then care must be taken to ensure that the integration process is carried out properly over the various subintervals. Again, Example 4.14 serves to illustrate this point.

EXAMPLE 4.13   From Example 4.5, the Fourier series expansion of the function

$$f(t) = t^2 \quad (-\pi \leqslant t \leqslant \pi)$$

$$f(t + 2\pi) = f(\pi)$$

is

$$t^2 = \tfrac{1}{3}\pi^2 + 4 \sum_{n=1}^{\infty} \frac{(-1)^n \cos nt}{n^2} \quad (-\pi \leqslant t \leqslant \pi)$$

Integrating this result between the limits $-\pi$ and t gives

$$\int_{-\pi}^{t} t^2 \, dt = \int_{-\pi}^{t} \tfrac{1}{3}\pi^2 \, dt + 4 \sum_{n=1}^{\infty} \int_{-\pi}^{t} \frac{(-1)^n \cos nt}{n^2} \, dt$$

that is,

$$\tfrac{1}{3}t^3 = \tfrac{1}{3}\pi^2 t + 4 \sum_{n=1}^{\infty} \frac{(-1)^n \sin nt}{n^3} \quad (-\pi \leqslant t \leqslant \pi)$$

Because of the term $\tfrac{1}{3}\pi^2 t$ on the right-hand side, this is clearly not a Fourier series expansion. However, rearranging, we have

$$t^3 - \pi^2 t = 12 \sum_{n=1}^{\infty} \frac{(-1)^n \sin nt}{n^2}$$

and now the right-hand side may be taken to be the Fourier series expansion of the function

$$g(t) = t^3 - \pi^2 t \quad (-\pi \leqslant t \leqslant \pi)$$

$$g(t + 2\pi) = g(t)$$

EXAMPLE 4.14   Integrate term by term the Fourier series expansion obtained in Example 4.4 for the square wave

$$f(t) = \begin{cases} -1 & (-\pi < t < 0) \\ 1 & (0 < t < \pi) \end{cases}$$

$$f(t + 2\pi) = f(t)$$

illustrated in Figure 4.7.

Solution   From (4.21), the Fourier series expansion for $f(t)$ is

$$f(t) = \frac{4}{\pi} \frac{\sin(2n-1)t}{2n-1}$$

We now need to integrate between the limits $-\pi$ and t and, owing to the discontinuity in $f(t)$ at $t = 0$, we must consider separately values of t in the intervals $-\pi < t < 0$ and $0 \leqslant t \leqslant \pi$.

Case (i), interval $-\pi < t < 0$. Integrating (4.21) term by term, we have

$$\int_{-\pi}^{t} (-1) \, dt = \frac{4}{\pi} \sum_{n=1}^{\infty} \int_{-\pi}^{t} \frac{\sin(2n-1)t}{(2n-1)} \, dt$$

that is,

$$-(t + \pi) = -\frac{4}{\pi} \sum_{n=1}^{\infty} \left[\frac{\cos(2n-1)t}{(2n-1)^2} \right]_{-\pi}^{t}$$

$$= -\frac{4}{\pi} \left[\sum_{n=1}^{\infty} \frac{\cos(2n-1)t}{(2n-1)^2} + \sum_{n=1}^{\infty} \frac{1}{(2n-1)^2} \right]$$

It can be shown that

$$\sum_{n=1}^{\infty} \frac{2}{(2n-1)^2} = \tfrac{1}{8}\pi^2$$

(see Exercise 6), so that the above simplifies to

$$-t = \tfrac{1}{2}\pi - \frac{4}{\pi} \sum_{n=1}^{\infty} \frac{\cos(2n-1)t}{(2n-1)^2} \quad (-\pi < t < 0) \tag{4.36}$$

Case (ii), interval $0 < t < \pi$. Integrating (4.21) term by term, we have

$$\int_{-\pi}^{0} (-1)\,dt + \int_{0}^{t} 1\,dt = \frac{4}{\pi} \sum_{n=1}^{\infty} \int_{-\pi}^{t} \frac{\sin(2n-1)t}{(2n-1)}\,dt$$

giving

$$t = \tfrac{1}{2}\pi - \frac{4}{\pi} \sum_{n=1}^{\infty} \frac{\cos(2n-1)t}{(2n-1)^2} \quad (0 < t < \pi) \tag{4.37}$$

Taking (4.36) and (4.37) together, we find that the function

$$g(t) = |t| = \begin{cases} -t & (-\pi < t < 0) \\ t & (0 < t < \pi) \end{cases}$$

$$g(t + 2\pi) = g(t)$$

has a Fourier series expansion

$$g(t) = |t| = \tfrac{1}{2}\pi - \frac{4}{\pi} \sum_{n=1}^{\infty} \frac{\cos(2n-1)t}{(2n-1)^2}$$

4.4.2   Differentiation of a Fourier series

THEOREM 4.4   If $f(t)$ is a periodic function that satisfies Dirichlet's conditions then its derivative $f'(t)$, wherever it exists, may be found by term-by-term differentiation of the Fourier series of $f(t)$ if and only if the function $f(t)$ is continuous everywhere and the function $f'(t)$ has a Fourier series expansion (that is, $f'(t)$ satisfies Dirichlet's conditions). $\qquad\square$

It follows from Theorem 4.4 that if the Fourier series expansion of $f(t)$ is differentiable term by term then $f(t)$ must be periodic at the end points of a period (owing to the condition that $f(t)$ must be continuous everywhere). Thus, for example, if we are dealing with a function $f(t)$ of period 2π and defined in the range $-\pi < t < \pi$ then we must have $f(-\pi) = f(\pi)$. To illustrate this point, consider the Fourier series expansion of the function

$$f(t) = t \quad (-\pi < t < \pi)$$

$$f(t + 2\pi) = f(t)$$

which, from Example 4.7, is given by

$$f(t) = 2(\sin t - \tfrac{1}{2}\sin 2t + \tfrac{1}{3}\sin 3t - \tfrac{1}{4}\sin 4t + \ldots)$$

Differentiating term by term, we have

$$f'(t) = 2(\cos t - \cos 2t + \cos 3t - \cos 4t + \ldots)$$

If this differentiation process is valid then $f'(t)$ must be equal to unity for $-\pi < t < \pi$. Clearly this is not the case, since the series on the right-hand side does not converge for any value of t. This follows since the nth term of the series is $2(-1)^{n+1}\cos nt$ and does not tend to zero as $n \to \infty$.

If $f(t)$ is continuous everywhere and has a Fourier series expansion

$$f(t) = \tfrac{1}{2}a_0 + \sum_{n=1}^{\infty} (a_n \cos nt + b_n \sin nt)$$

then, from Theorem 4.4, provided that $f'(t)$ satisfies the required conditions, its Fourier series expansion is

$$f'(t) = \sum_{n=1}^{\infty} (nb_n \cos nt - na_n \sin nt)$$

In this case the Fourier coefficients of the derived expansion are nb_n and na_n, so, in contrast to the integrated series, the derived series will converge more slowly than the original series expansion for $f(t)$.

EXAMPLE 4.15 Consider the process of differentiating term by term the Fourier series expansion of the function

$$f(t) = t^2 \quad (-\pi \leqslant t \leqslant \pi)$$

$$f(t + 2\pi) = f(t)$$

Solution From Example 4.5, the Fourier series expansion of $f(t)$ is

$$t^2 = \tfrac{1}{3}\pi^2 + 4\sum_{n=1}^{\infty} \frac{(-1)^n \cos nt}{n^2} \quad (-\pi \leqslant t \leqslant \pi)$$

Since $f(t)$ is continuous within and at the end points of the interval $-\pi \leqslant t \leqslant \pi$,

we may apply Theorem 4.4 to obtain

$$2t = 4 \sum_{n=1}^{\infty} -\frac{n(-1)^n}{n^2} \sin nt$$

that is,

$$t = 2 \sum_{n=1}^{\infty} \frac{(-1)^{n+1} \sin nt}{n} \quad (-\pi \leqslant t \leqslant \pi)$$

which conforms with the Fourier series expansion obtained for the function

$$f(t) = t \quad (-\pi < t < \pi)$$

$$f(t + 2\pi) = f(t)$$

in Example 4.7.

4.4.3   Coefficients in terms of jumps at discontinuities

For periodic functions that, within a period, are piecewise polynomials and exhibit jump discontinuities, the Fourier coefficients may be determined in terms of the magnitude of the jumps and those of derived functions. This method is useful for determining describing functions (see Section 4.8) for nonlinear characteristics in control engineering, where only the fundamental component of the Fourier series is important; this applies particularly to the case of multivalued nonlinearities.

Consider a periodic function $f(t)$, of period T, having within the time interval $-\frac{1}{2}T \leqslant t \leqslant \frac{1}{2}T$ a finite number $(m + 1)$ of jump discontinuities $d_0, d_1, \ldots, d_m$ at times $t_0, t_1, \ldots t_m$, with $t_0 = -\frac{1}{2}T$ and $t_m = \frac{1}{2}T$. Furthermore, within the interval $t_{s-1} < t < t_s$ $(s = 1, 2, \ldots, m)$ let $f(t)$ be represented by polynomial functions $P_s(t)$ $(s = 1, 2, \ldots, m)$, as illustrated in Figure 4.24. If $f(t)$ is to be represented in terms of the Fourier series

$$f(t) = \tfrac{1}{2}a_0 + \sum_{n=1}^{\infty} a_n \cos n\omega t + \sum_{n=1}^{\infty} b_n \sin n\omega t$$

Figure 4.24 Piecewise polynomial periodic function exhibiting jump discontinuities.

then, from (4.11),

$$a_n = \frac{2}{T} \sum_{s=1}^{m} \int_{t_{s-1}}^{t_s} P_s(t) \cos n\omega t \, dt$$

Defining the magnitude of the jump discontinuities as in Section 2.5.11, namely

$$d_i = f(t_i + 0) - f(t_i - 0)$$

and noting that $t_0 = -\frac{1}{2}T$ and $t_m = \frac{1}{2}T$, integration by parts and summation gives

$$a_n = -\frac{1}{n\pi} \sum_{s=1}^{m} \left[d_s \sin n\omega t_s + \int_{t_{s-1}}^{t_s} P_s^{(1)}(t) \sin n\omega t \, dt \right] \qquad (4.38)$$

where $P_s^{(1)}(t)$ denotes the piecewise components of the derivative $f^{(1)}(t) \equiv f'(t)$ in the generalized sense of (2.59).

In a similar manner the integral terms of (4.38) may be expressed as

$$\sum_{s=1}^{m} \int_{t_{s-1}}^{t_s} P_s^{(1)} \sin n\omega t \, dt = \frac{1}{n\omega} \sum_{s=1}^{m} \left[d_s^{(1)} \cos n\omega t + \int_{t_{s-1}}^{t_s} P_s^{(2)}(t) \cos n\omega t \, dt \right]$$

where $d_s^{(1)}$ ($s = 1, 2, \ldots, m$) denotes the magnitude of the jump discontinuities in the derivative $f^{(1)}(t)$.

Continuing in this fashion, integrals involving higher derivatives may be obtained. However, since all $P_s(t)$ ($s = 1, 2, \ldots, m$) are polynomials, a stage is reached when all the integrals vanish. If the degree of $P_s(t)$ is less than or equal to N for $s = 1, 2, \ldots, m$ then

$$a_n = \frac{1}{n\pi} \sum_{s=1}^{m} \sum_{r=0}^{N} (-1)^{r+1} (n\omega)^{-2r} [d_s^{(2r)} \sin n\omega t_s + (n\omega)^{-1} d_s^{(2r+1)} \cos n\omega t_s]$$
$$(n \neq 0) \qquad (4.39)$$

where $d_s^{(r)}$ denotes the magnitudes of the jump discontinuities in the rth derivative of $f(t)$ according to (2.59).

Similarly, it may be shown that

$$b_n = \frac{1}{n\pi} \sum_{s=1}^{m} \sum_{r=0}^{N} (-1)^{r} (n\omega)^{-2r} [d_s^{(2r)} \cos n\omega t_s - (n\omega)^{-1} d_s^{(2r+1)} \sin n\omega t_s] \qquad (4.40)$$

and the coefficient a_0 is found by direct integration of the corresponding Euler formula

$$a_0 = \frac{2}{T} \int_{-T/2}^{T/2} f(t) \, dt \qquad (4.41)$$

EXAMPLE 4.16 Using (4.39)–(4.41), obtain the Fourier series expansion of the periodic function $f(t)$ defined by

$$f(t) = \begin{cases} t^2 & (-\pi < t < 0) \\ -2 & (0 < t < \pi) \end{cases}$$

$$f(t + 2\pi) = f(t)$$

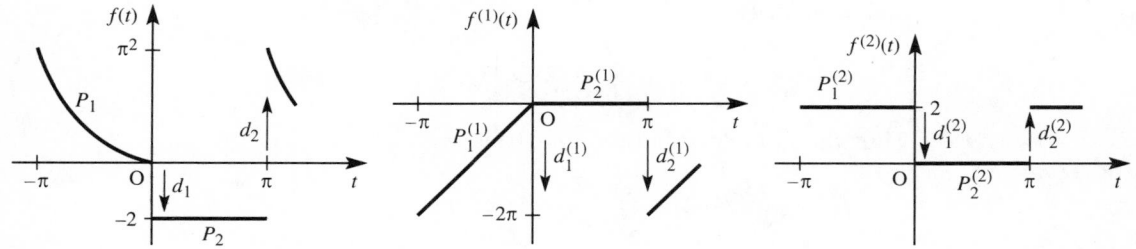

Figure 4.25 $f(t)$, $f^{(1)}(t)$, $f^{(2)}(t)$ of Example 4.16.

Solution   In this case $N = 2$, and the graphs of $f(t)$ together with those of its first two derivatives are shown in Figure 4.25.

Jump discontinuities occur at $t = -\pi, 0$ and π, so that $m = 2$. The piecewise polynomials involved and the corresponding jump discontinuities are

(a) $P_1(t) = t^2$, $P_2(t) = -2$

$\quad\quad d_1 = -2$, $d_2 = \pi^2 + 2$

(b) $P_1^{(1)}(t) = 2t$ $P_2^{(1)}(t) = 0$

$\quad\quad d_1^{(1)} = 0$ $d_2^{(1)} = -2\pi$

(c) $P_1^{(2)}(t) = 2$, $P_2^{(2)}(t) = 0$

$\quad\quad d_1^{(2)} = -2$ $d_2^{(2)} = 2$

with $d_1^{(r)} = d_2^{(r)} = 0$ for $r > 2$.

Taking $\omega = 1$ (since $T = 2\pi$) in (4.39) gives

$$a_n = \frac{1}{n\pi}\left(-\sum_{s=1}^{2} d_s \sin nt_s - \frac{1}{n}\sum_{s=1}^{2} d_s^{(1)} \cos nt_s + \frac{1}{n^2}\sum_{s=1}^{2} d_s^{(2)} \sin nt_s\right)$$

Since $t_1 = 0$, $t_2 = \pi$, $\sin 0 = \sin n\pi = 0$, $\cos 0 = 1$ and $\cos n\pi = (-1)^n$, we have

$$a_n = \frac{2}{n^2}(-1)^n \quad (n = 1, 2, 3, \dots)$$

Likewise, from (4.40),

$$b_n = \frac{1}{n\pi}\left(\sum_{s=1}^{2} d_s \cos nt_s - \frac{1}{n}\sum_{s=1}^{2} d_s^{(1)} \sin nt_s - \frac{1}{n^2}\sum_{s=1}^{2} d_s^{(2)} \cos nt_s\right)$$

$$= \frac{1}{n\pi}\left\{-2 + (\pi^2 + 2)(-1)^n - \frac{1}{n^2}[-2 + 2(-1)^n]\right\}$$

$$= \frac{1}{n\pi}\left\{\left(\frac{2}{n^2} - 2\right)[1 - (-1)^n] + \pi^2(-1)^n\right\} \quad (n = 1, 2, 3, \dots)$$

and, from (4.41),

$$a_0 = \frac{1}{\pi}\left[\int_{-\pi}^{0} t^2\,dt + \int_{0}^{\pi} (-2)\,dt\right] = \tfrac{1}{3}\pi^2 - 2$$

Thus the Fourier expansion for $f(t)$ is

$$f(t) = (\tfrac{1}{6}\pi^2 - 1) + \sum_{n=1}^{\infty} \frac{2}{n^2}(-1)^n \cos nt$$

$$+ \sum_{n=1}^{\infty} \frac{1}{n\pi}\left\{\left(\frac{2}{n^2} - 2\right)[1 - (-1)^n] + \pi^2(-1)^n\right\} \sin nt$$

4.4.4   Exercises

24 Show that the periodic function

$$f(t) = t \quad (-T < t < T)$$
$$f(t + 2T) = f(t)$$

has a Fourier series expansion

$$f(t) = \frac{2T}{\pi}\left(\sin\frac{\pi t}{T} - \tfrac{1}{2}\sin\frac{2\pi t}{T} + \tfrac{1}{3}\sin\frac{3\pi t}{T}\right.$$
$$\left. - \tfrac{1}{4}\sin\frac{4\pi t}{T} + \ldots\right)$$

By term-by-term integration of this series, show that the periodic function

$$g(t) = t^2 \quad (-T < t < T)$$
$$g(t + 2T) = g(t)$$

has a Fourier series expansion

$$g(t) = \tfrac{1}{3}T^2 - \frac{4T^2}{\pi^2}\left(\cos\frac{\pi t}{T} - \frac{1}{2^2}\cos\frac{2\pi t}{T}\right.$$
$$\left. + \frac{1}{3^2}\cos\frac{3\pi t}{T} - \frac{1}{4^2}\cos\frac{4\pi t}{T} + \ldots\right)$$

(*Hint*: A constant of integration must be introduced; it may be evaluated as the mean value over a period.)

25 The periodic function

$$h(t) = \pi^2 - t^2 \quad (-\pi < t < \pi)$$
$$h(t + 2\pi) = h(t)$$

has a Fourier series expansion

$$h(t) = \tfrac{2}{3}\pi^2 + 4\left(\cos t - \frac{1}{2^2}\cos 2t + \frac{1}{3^2}\cos 3t \ldots\right)$$

By term-by-term differentiation of this series, confirm the series obtained for $f(t)$ in Exercise 24 for the case when $T = \pi$.

26 (a) Suppose that the derivative $f'(t)$ of a periodic function $f(t)$ of period 2π has a Fourier series expansion

$$f'(t) = \tfrac{1}{2}A_0 + \sum_{n=1}^{\infty} A_n \cos nt + \sum_{n=1}^{\infty} B_n \sin nt$$

Show that

$$A_0 = \frac{1}{n}[f(\pi_-) - f(-\pi_+)]$$
$$A_n = (-1)^n A_0 + nb_n$$
$$B_n = -na_n$$

where a_0, a_n and b_n are the Fourier coefficients of the function $f(t)$.

(b) In Example 4.7 we saw that the periodic function

$$f(t) = t^2 + t \quad (-\pi < t < \pi)$$
$$f(t + 2\pi) = f(t)$$

has a Fourier series expansion

$$f(t) = \tfrac{1}{3}\pi^2 + \sum_{n=1}^{\infty} \frac{4}{n^2}(-1)^n \cos nt$$
$$- \sum_{n=1}^{\infty} \frac{2}{n}(-1)^n \sin nt$$

Differentiate this series term by term, and explain why it is not a Fourier expansion of the periodic function

$$g(t) = 2t + 1 \quad (-\pi < t < \pi)$$
$$g(t + 2\pi) = g(t)$$

(c) Use the results of (a) to obtain the Fourier series expansion of $g(t)$ and confirm your solution by direct evaluation of the coefficients using Euler's formulae.

27 Using (4.39)–(4.41), confirm the following Fourier series expansions:

(a) (4.21) for the square wave of Example 4.4;

(b) the expansion obtained in Example 4.1 for the sawtooth wave;

(c) the expansion obtained for the piecewise-continuous function $f(t)$ of Example 4.3.

28 Consider the periodic function

$$f(t) = \begin{cases} 0 & (-\pi < t < -\tfrac{1}{2}\pi) \\ \pi + 2t & (-\tfrac{1}{2}\pi < t < 0) \\ \pi - 2t & (0 < t < \tfrac{1}{2}\pi) \\ 0 & (\tfrac{1}{2}\pi < t < \pi) \end{cases}$$

$$f(t + 2\pi) = f(t)$$

(a) Sketch a graph of the function for $-4\pi < t < 4\pi$.

(b) Use (4.39)–(4.41) to obtain the Fourier series expansion

$$f(t) = \tfrac{1}{4}\pi + \frac{4}{\pi} \sum_{n=1}^{\infty} \frac{1}{n} \cos\left(\tfrac{1}{2}n\pi - 1\right) \cos nt$$

and write out the first 10 terms of this series. (*Note:* Although the function $f(t)$ itself has no jump discontinuities, the method may be used since the derivative does have jump discontinuities.)

29 Use the method of Section 4.4.3 to obtain the Fourier series expansions for the following periodic functions:

(a) $f(t) = \begin{cases} 0 & (-\pi < t < 0) \\ t^2 & (0 < t < \pi) \end{cases}$

$\quad f(t + 2\pi) = f(t)$

(b) $f(t) = \begin{cases} 2 & (-\pi < t < -\tfrac{1}{2}\pi) \\ t^3 & (-\tfrac{1}{2}\pi < t < \tfrac{1}{2}\pi) \\ -2 & (\tfrac{1}{2}\pi < t < \pi) \end{cases}$

$\quad f(t + 2\pi) = f(t)$

(c) $f(t) = \begin{cases} t & (0 < t < 1) \\ 1 - t & (1 < t < 2) \end{cases}$

$\quad f(t + 2) = f(t)$

(d) $f(t) = \begin{cases} \tfrac{1}{2} + t & (-\tfrac{1}{2} < t < 0) \\ \tfrac{1}{2} - t & (0 < t < \tfrac{1}{2}) \end{cases}$

$\quad f(t + 1) = f(t)$

4.5   Engineering application: frequency response and oscillating systems

4.5.1   Response to periodic input

In Section 2.7 we showed that the frequency response, defined as the steady-state response to a sinusoidal input $A \sin \omega t$, of a stable linear system having a transfer function $G(s)$ is given by (2.86) as

$$x_{ss}(t) = A|G(j\omega)| \sin\left[\omega t + \arg G(j\omega)\right] \tag{4.42}$$

By employing a Fourier series expansion, we can use this result to determine the steady-state response of a stable linear system to a non-sinusoidal periodic input. For a stable linear system having a transfer function $G(s)$, let the input be a periodic function $P(t)$ of period $2T$ (that is, one having frequency $\omega = \pi/T$ in rad s^{-1}). From (4.21), $P(t)$ may be expressed in the form of the Fourier series expansion

$$P(t) = \tfrac{1}{2}a_0 + \sum_{n=1}^{\infty} A_n \sin(n\omega t + \phi_n) \qquad (4.43)$$

where A_n and ϕ_n are defined as in Section 4.2.1. The steady-state response to each term in the series expansion (4.43) may be obtained using (4.42). Since the system is linear, the principle of superposition holds, so that the steady-state response to the periodic input $P(t)$ may be obtained as the sum of the steady-state responses to the individual sinusoids comprising the sum in (4.43). Thus the steady-state response to the input $P(t)$ is

$$x_{ss}(t) = \tfrac{1}{2}a_0 G(0) + \sum_{n=1}^{\infty} A_n |G(j\omega n)| \sin[n\omega t + \phi_n + \arg G(j\omega n)] \qquad (4.44)$$

There are two issues related to this steady-state response that are worthy of note.

(a) For practical systems $|G(j\omega)| \to 0$ as $\omega \to \infty$, so that $|G(j\omega n)| \to 0$ as $n \to \infty$ in (4.44). As a consequence, the Fourier series representation of the steady-state response $x_{ss}(t)$ converges more rapidly than the Fourier series representation of the periodic input $P(t)$. From a practical point of view, this is not surprising, since it is a consequence of the smoothing action of the system (that is, as indicated in Section 4.4, integration is a 'smoothing' operation).

(b) There is a significant difference between the steady-state response (4.44) to a non-sinusoidal periodic input of frequency ω and the steady-state response (4.41) to a pure sinusoid at the same frequency. As indicated in (4.42), in the case of a sinusoidal input at frequency ω the steady-state response is also a sinusoid at the same frequency ω. However, for a non-sinusoidal periodic input $P(t)$ at frequency ω the steady-state response (4.44) is no longer at the same frequency; rather it comprises an infinite sum of sinusoids having frequencies $n\omega$ that are integer multiples of the input frequency ω. This clearly has important practical implications, particularly when considering the responses of oscillating or vibrating systems. If the frequency $n\omega$ of one of the harmonics in (4.44) is close to the natural oscillating frequency of an underdamped system then the phenomenon of **resonance** will arise.

To someone unfamiliar with the theory, it may seem surprising that a practical system may resonate at a frequency much higher than that of the input. As indicated in Example 2.30, the phenomenon of resonance is important in practice, and it is therefore important that engineers have some knowledge of the theory associated with Fourier series, so that the possible dominance of a system response by one of the higher harmonics, rather than the fundamental, may be properly interpreted.

EXAMPLE 4.17   The mass–spring–damper system of Figure 4.26(a) is initially at rest in a position of equilibrium. Determine the steady-state response of the system when the mass is subjected to an externally applied periodic force $P(t)$ having the form of the square wave shown in Figure 4.26(b).

Figure 4.26 (a) System and (b) input for Example 4.17.

Solution From Newton's law, the displacement $x(t)$ of the mass at time t is given by

$$M\frac{\mathrm{d}^2x}{\mathrm{d}t^2} + B\frac{\mathrm{d}x}{\mathrm{d}t} + Kx = P(t) \tag{4.45}$$

so that the system may be represented by the block diagram of Figure 4.27. Thus the system transfer function is

$$G(s) = \frac{1}{Ms^2 + Bs + K} \tag{4.46}$$

From Example 4.4, the Fourier series expansion for the square wave $P(t)$ is

$$P(t) = \frac{40}{\pi}\left[\sin t + \frac{\sin 3t}{3} + \frac{\sin 5t}{5} + \ldots + \frac{\sin(2n-1)t}{2n-1} + \ldots\right]$$

that is,

$$P(t) = u_1(t) + u_2(t) + u_3(t) + \ldots + u_n(t) + \ldots \tag{4.47}$$

where

$$u_n(t) = \frac{40}{\pi}\frac{\sin(2n-1)t}{2n-1} \tag{4.48}$$

Substituting the given values for M, B and K, the transfer function (4.46) becomes

$$G(s) = \frac{1}{10s^2 + 0.5s + 250}$$

Thus

$$G(j\omega) = \frac{1}{-10\omega^2 + 0.5j\omega + 250} = \frac{250 - 10\omega^2}{D} - j\frac{0.5\omega}{D}$$

$$\xrightarrow{P(s)}\boxed{\dfrac{1}{Ms^2 + Bs + K}}\xrightarrow{X(s)}$$

Figure 4.27 Block diagram for the system of Figure 4.26.

where $D = (250 - 10\omega^2)^2 + 0.25\omega^2$, so that

$$|G(j\omega)| = \sqrt{\left[\frac{(250 - 10\omega^2)^2 + 0.25\omega^2}{D^2} \right]}$$

$$= \frac{1}{\sqrt{D}} = \frac{1}{\sqrt{[(250 - 10\omega^2)^2 + 0.25\omega^2]}} \qquad (4.49)$$

$$\arg G(j\omega) = -\tan^{-1}\left(\frac{0.5\omega}{250 - 10\omega^2} \right) \qquad (4.50)$$

Using (4.42), the steady-state response of the system to the nth harmonic $u_n(t)$ given by (4.48) is

$$x_{ssn}(t) = \frac{40}{\pi(2n-1)} |G(j(2n-1))| \sin\left[(2n-1)t + \arg G(j(2n-1)) \right] \qquad (4.51)$$

where $|G(j\omega)|$ and $\arg G(j\omega)$ are given by (4.49) and (4.50) respectively. The steady-state response $x_{ss}(t)$ of the system to the square-wave input $P(t)$ is then determined as the sum of the steady-state responses due to the individual harmonics in (4.47); that is,

$$x_{ss}(t) = \sum_{n=1}^{\infty} x_{ssn}(t) \qquad (4.52)$$

where $x_{ssn}(t)$ is given by (4.51).

Evaluating the first few terms of the response (4.52), we have

$$x_{ss1}(t) = \frac{40}{\pi} \frac{1}{\sqrt{[(250 - 10)^2 + 0.25]}} \sin\left[t - \tan^{-1}\left(\frac{0.5}{240} \right) \right]$$

$$= 0.053 \sin(t - 0.003)$$

$$x_{ss2}(t) = \frac{40}{3\pi} \frac{1}{\sqrt{[(250 - 90)^2 + 2.25]}} \sin\left[3t - \tan^{-1}\left(\frac{1.5}{160} \right) \right]$$

$$= 0.027 \sin(3t - 0.009)$$

$$x_{ss3}(t) = \frac{40}{5\pi} \frac{1}{\sqrt{(6.25)}} \sin\left[5t - \tan^{-1}\left(\frac{2.5}{0} \right) \right]$$

$$= 1.02 \sin(5t - \tfrac{1}{2}\pi)$$

$$x_{ss4}(t) = \frac{40}{7\pi} \frac{1}{\sqrt{[(250 - 490)^2 + 12.25]}} \sin\left[7t - \tan^{-1}\left(\frac{3.5}{-240} \right) \right]$$

$$= 0.0076 \sin(7t - 3.127)$$

Thus a good approximation to the steady-state response (4.52) is

$$x_{ss}(t) \simeq 0.053 \sin(t - 0.003) + 0.027 \sin(3t - 0.54) + 1.02 \sin(5t - \tfrac{1}{2}\pi)$$

$$+ 0.0076 \sin(7t - 3.127) \qquad (4.53)$$

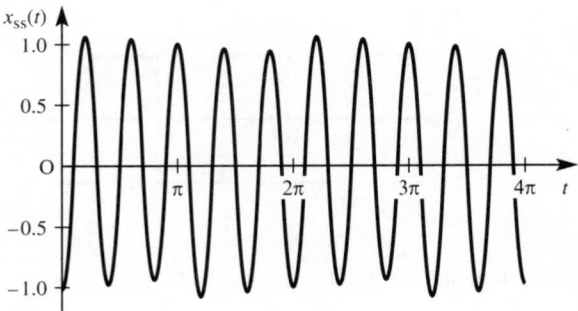

Figure 4.28 Steady-state response of system of Figure 4.26.

The graph of this displacement is shown in Figure 4.28, and it appears from this that the response has a frequency about five times that of the input. This is because the term $1.02 \sin(5t - \frac{1}{2}\pi)$ dominates in the response (4.53); this is a consequence of the fact that the natural frequency of oscillation of the system is $\sqrt{(K/M)} = 5\,\text{rad s}^{-1}$, so that it is in resonance with this particular harmonic.

In conclusion, it should be noted that it was not essential to introduce transfer functions to solve this problem. Alternatively, by determining the particular integral (see Chapter 11 of *Modern Engineering Mathematics*) of the differential equation (4.45), the steady-state response to an input $A \sin \omega t$ is determined as

$$x_{ss}(t) = \frac{A \sin(\omega t - \alpha)}{\sqrt{[(K - M\omega^2)^2 + B^2\omega^2]}}, \qquad \tan \alpha = \frac{\omega B}{K - M\omega^2}$$

giving $x_{ssn}(t)$ as in (4.52). The solution then proceeds as before.

4.5.2   Exercises

30 Determine the steady-state current in the circuit of Figure 4.29(a) as a result of the applied periodic voltage shown in Figure 4.29(b).

(a)

Figure 4.29 (a) Circuit of Exercise 30.

(b)

Figure 4.29 (b) Applied voltage.

31 Determine the steady-state response of the mass–spring–damper system of Figure 4.30(a) when the

(a)   **(b)**

Figure 4.30 (a) Mass–spring–damper system of Exercise 31. (b) Applied force.

mass is subjected to the externally applied periodic force $f(t)$ shown in Figure 4.30(b).

What frequency dominates the response, and why?

32 Determine the steady-state motion of the mass of Figure 4.31(a) when it is subjected to the externally applied force of Figure 4.31(b).

33 Determine the steady-state current in the circuit shown in Figure 4.32(a) when the applied voltage is of the form shown in Figure 4.32(b).

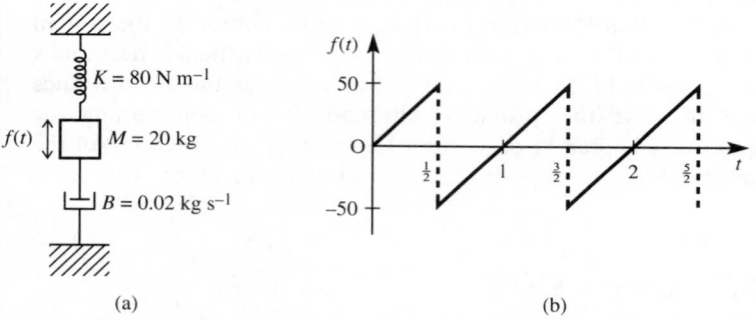

(a)   **(b)**

Figure 4.31 (a) Mass–spring–damper system of Exercise 32. (b) Applied force.

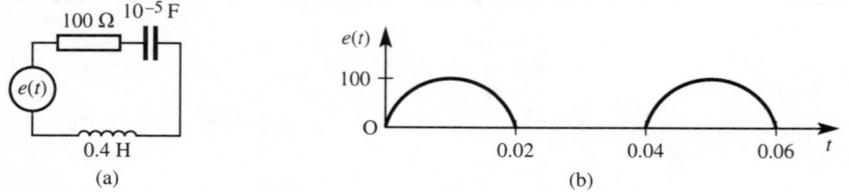

(a)   **(b)**

Figure 4.32 (a) Circuit of Exercise 33. (b) Applied voltage.

4.6 Complex form of Fourier series

An alternative to the trigonometric form of the Fourier series considered so far is the complex or exponential form. As a result of the properties of the exponential function, this form is easily manipulated mathematically. It is widely used by engineers in practice, particularly in work involving signal analysis, and provides a smoother transition from the consideration of Fourier series for dealing with periodic signals to the consideration of Fourier transforms for dealing with aperiodic signals, which will be dealt with in Chapter 5.

4.6.1 Complex representation

To develop the complex form of the Fourier series

$$f(t) = \tfrac{1}{2}a_0 + \sum_{n=1}^{\infty} a_n \cos n\omega t + \sum_{n=1}^{\infty} b_n \sin n\omega t \qquad (4.54)$$

representing a periodic function $f(t)$ of period T, we proceed as follows. Substituting the results

$$\sin n\omega t = \frac{1}{2j}(e^{jn\omega t} - e^{-jn\omega t})$$

$$\cos n\omega t = \tfrac{1}{2}(e^{jn\omega t} + e^{-jn\omega t})$$

into (4.54) gives

$$f(t) = \tfrac{1}{2}a_0 + \sum_{n=1}^{\infty} a_n \frac{e^{jn\omega t} + e^{-jn\omega t}}{2} + \sum_{n=1}^{\infty} b_n \frac{e^{jn\omega t} - e^{-jn\omega t}}{2j}$$

$$= \tfrac{1}{2}a_0 + \sum_{n=1}^{\infty} \tfrac{1}{2}a_n(e^{jn\omega t} + e^{-jn\omega t}) + \sum_{n=1}^{\infty} -j\tfrac{1}{2}b_n(e^{jn\omega t} - e^{-jn\omega t})$$

$$= \tfrac{1}{2}a_0 + \sum_{n=1}^{\infty} [\tfrac{1}{2}(a_n - jb_n)e^{jn\omega t} + \tfrac{1}{2}(a_n + jb_n)e^{-jn\omega t}] \qquad (4.55)$$

Writing

$$c_0 = \tfrac{1}{2}a_0, \qquad c_n = \tfrac{1}{2}(a_n - jb_n), \qquad c_{-n} = c_n^* = \tfrac{1}{2}(a_n + jb_n) \qquad (4.56)$$

(4.55) becomes

$$f(t) = c_0 + \sum_{n=1}^{\infty} c_n e^{jn\omega t} + \sum_{n=1}^{\infty} c_{-n} e^{-jn\omega t}$$

$$= c_0 + \sum_{n=1}^{\infty} c_n e^{jn\omega t} + \sum_{n=-1}^{-\infty} c_n e^{jn\omega t}$$

$$= \sum_{n=-\infty}^{\infty} c_n e^{jn\omega t}, \qquad \text{since} \quad c_0 e^0 = c_0$$

Thus the Fourier series (4.54) becomes simply

$$f(t) = \sum_{n=-\infty}^{\infty} c_n e^{jn\omega t} \qquad (4.57)$$

which is referred to as the **complex** or **exponential form** of the Fourier series expansion of the function $f(t)$.

In order that we can apply this result directly, it is necessary to obtain a formula for calculating the complex coefficients c_n. To do this, we incorporate the Euler formulae (4.11) and (4.12) into the definitions given in (4.56), leading to

$$c_0 = \tfrac{1}{2}a_0 = \frac{1}{T}\int_d^{d+T} f(t)\,dt \tag{4.58}$$

$$c_n = \tfrac{1}{2}(a_n - jb_n) = \frac{1}{T}\left[\int_d^{d+T} f(t)\cos n\omega t\,dt - j\int_d^{d+T} f(t)\sin n\omega t\,dt\right]$$

$$= \frac{1}{T}\int_d^{d+T} f(t)(\cos n\omega t - j\sin n\omega t)\,dt$$

$$= \frac{1}{T}\int_d^{d+T} f(t)\,e^{-jn\omega t}\,dt \tag{4.59}$$

$$c_{-n} = \tfrac{1}{2}(a_n + jb_n) = \frac{1}{T}\int_d^{d+T} f(t)(\cos n\omega t + j\sin n\omega t)\,dt$$

$$= \frac{1}{T}\int_d^{d+T} f(t)\,e^{jn\omega t}\,dt \tag{4.60}$$

From (4.58)–(4.60), it is readily seen that for all values of n

$$c_n = \frac{1}{T}\int_d^{d+T} f(t)\,e^{-jn\omega t}\,dt \tag{4.61}$$

In summary, the complex form of the Fourier series expansion of a periodic function $f(t)$, of period T, is

$$f(t) = \sum_{n=-\infty}^{\infty} c_n\,e^{jn\omega t} \tag{4.57}$$

where

$$c_n = \frac{1}{T}\int_d^{d+T} f(t)\,e^{-jn\omega t}\,dt \quad (n = 0, \pm 1, \pm 2, \ldots) \tag{4.61}$$

In general the coefficients c_n ($n = 0, \pm 1, \pm 2, \ldots$) are complex, and may be expressed in the form

$$c_n = |c_n|\,e^{j\phi_n}$$

where $|c_n|$, the magnitude of c_n, is given from the definitions (4.56) by

$$|c_n| = \sqrt{[(\tfrac{1}{2}a_n)^2 + (\tfrac{1}{2}b_n)^2]} = \tfrac{1}{2}\sqrt{(a_n^2 + b_n^2)}$$

so that $2|c_n|$ is the amplitude of the nth harmonic. The argument ϕ_n of c_n is related to the phase of the nth harmonic.

EXAMPLE 4.18   Find the complex form of the Fourier series expansion of the periodic function $f(t)$ defined by

$$f(t) = \cos \tfrac{1}{2}t \quad (-\pi < t < \pi)$$

$$f(t + 2\pi) = f(t)$$

Figure 4.33 Function $f(t)$ of Example 4.18.

Solution   A graph of the function $f(t)$ over the interval $-3\pi \leqslant t \leqslant 3\pi$ is shown in Figure 4.33. Here the period T is 2π, so from (4.61) the complex coefficients c_n are given by

$$c_n = \frac{1}{2\pi} \int_{-\pi}^{\pi} \cos \tfrac{1}{2}t\, e^{-jnt}\, dt = \frac{1}{4\pi} \int_{-\pi}^{\pi} (e^{jt/2} + e^{-jt/2}) e^{-jnt}\, dt$$

$$= \frac{1}{4\pi} \int_{-\pi}^{\pi} (e^{-j(n-1/2)t} + e^{-j(n+1/2)t})\, dt$$

$$= \frac{1}{4\pi} \left[\frac{-2e^{-j(2n-1)t/2}}{j(2n-1)} - \frac{2e^{-j(2n+1)t/2}}{j(2n+1)} \right]_{-\pi}^{\pi}$$

$$= \frac{j}{2\pi} \left[\left(\frac{e^{-jn\pi} e^{j\pi/2}}{2n-1} + \frac{e^{-jn\pi} e^{-j\pi/2}}{2n+1} \right) - \left(\frac{e^{jn\pi} e^{-j\pi/2}}{2n-1} + \frac{e^{jn\pi} e^{j\pi/2}}{2n+1} \right) \right]$$

Now $e^{j\pi/2} = \cos \tfrac{1}{2}\pi + j \sin \tfrac{1}{2}\pi = j$, $e^{-j\pi/2} = -j$ and $e^{jn\pi} = e^{-jn\pi} = \cos n\pi = (-1)^n$, so that

$$c_n = \frac{j}{2\pi} \left(\frac{j}{2n-1} - \frac{j}{2n+1} + \frac{j}{2n-1} - \frac{j}{2n+1} \right)(-1)^n$$

$$= \frac{(-1)^n}{\pi} \left(\frac{1}{2n+1} - \frac{1}{2n-1} \right) = \frac{-2(-1)^n}{(4n^2-1)\pi}$$

Note that in this case c_n is real, which is as expected, since the function $f(t)$ is an even function of t.

From (4.57), the complex Fourier series expansion for $f(t)$ is

$$f(t) = \sum_{n=-\infty}^{\infty} \frac{2(-1)^{n+1}}{(4n^2-1)\pi} e^{jnt}$$

This may readily be converted back to the trigonometric form, since, from the definitions (4.56),

$$a_0 = 2c_0, \qquad a_n = c_n + c_n^*, \qquad b_n = j(c_n - c_n^*)$$

so that in this particular case

$$a_0 = \frac{4}{\pi}$$

$$a_n = 2\left[\frac{2}{\pi}\frac{(-2)^{n+1}}{4n^2+1}\right] = \frac{4}{\pi}\frac{(-1)^{n+1}}{4n^2-1}$$

$$b_n = 0$$

Thus the trigonometric form of the Fourier series is

$$f(t) = \frac{2}{\pi} + \frac{4}{\pi}\sum_{n=1}^{\infty}\frac{(-1)^{n+1}}{4n^2-1}\cos nt$$

which corresponds to the solution to Exercise 1(e).

EXAMPLE 4.19 Obtain the complex form of the Fourier series of the sawtooth function $f(t)$ defined by

$$f(t) = \frac{2t}{T} \quad (0 < t < 2T)$$

$$f(t + 2T) = f(t)$$

Solution A graph of the function $f(t)$ over the interval $-6T < t < 6T$ is shown in Figure 4.34. Here the period is $2T$, that is, $\omega = \pi/T$, so from (4.61) the complex coefficients c_n are given by

$$c_n = \frac{1}{2T}\int_0^{2T}f(t)e^{-jn\pi t/T}\,dt = \frac{1}{2T}\int_0^{2T}\frac{2}{T}te^{-jn\pi t/T}\,dt$$

$$= \frac{1}{T^2}\left[\frac{Tt}{-jn\pi}e^{-jn\pi t/T} - \frac{T^2}{(jn\pi)^2}e^{-jn\pi t/T}\right]_0^{2T} \quad (n \neq 0)$$

Now $e^{-jn2\pi} = e^{-j0} = 1$, so

$$c_n = \frac{1}{T^2}\left[\frac{2T^2}{-jn\pi} + \frac{T^2}{(n\pi)^2} - \frac{T^2}{(n\pi)^2}\right] = \frac{j2}{n\pi} \quad (n \neq 0)$$

In the particular case $n = 0$

$$c_0 = \frac{1}{2T}\int_0^{2T}f(t)\,dt = \frac{1}{2T}\int_0^{2T}\frac{2t}{T}\,dt = \frac{1}{T^2}[\tfrac{1}{2}t^2]_0^{2T} = 2$$

Figure 4.34 Function of $f(t)$ of Example 4.19.

Thus from (4.57) the complex form of the Fourier series expansion of $f(t)$ is

$$f(t) = 2 + \sum_{n=-\infty}^{-1} \frac{j2}{n\pi} e^{jn\pi t/T} + \sum_{n=1}^{\infty} \frac{j2}{n\pi} e^{jn\pi t/T}$$

$$= 2 + \sum_{\substack{n=-\infty \\ n \neq 0}}^{\infty} \frac{j2}{n\pi} e^{jn\pi t/T}$$

Noting that $j = e^{j\pi/2}$, this result may also be written in the form

$$f(t) = 2 + \frac{2}{\pi} \sum_{\substack{n=-\infty \\ n \neq 0}}^{\infty} \frac{1}{n} e^{j(n\pi t/T + \pi/2)}$$

As in Example 4.18, the Euler coefficients in the corresponding trigonometric series are

$$a_0 = 2c_0 = 4$$

$$a_n = c_n + c_n^* = 0$$

$$b_n = j(c_n + c_n^*) = j\left(\frac{2j}{n\pi} + \frac{2j}{n\pi}\right) = -\frac{4}{n\pi}$$

so that the corresponding trigonometric Fourier series expansion of $f(t)$ is

$$f(t) = 2 - \frac{4}{\pi} \sum_{n=1}^{\infty} \frac{1}{n} \sin \frac{n\pi t}{T}$$

which corresponds to the solution of Example 4.11 when $T = 2$.

4.6.2   The multiplication theorem and Parseval's theorem

Two useful results, particularly in the application of Fourier series to signal analysis, are the **multiplication theorem** and **Parseval's theorem**. The multiplication theorem enables us to write down the mean value of the product of two periodic functions over a period in terms of the coefficients of their Fourier series expansions, while Parseval's theorem enables us to write down the mean square value of a periodic function, which, as we will see in Section 4.6.4, determines the power spectrum of the function.

THEOREM 4.5   The multiplication theorem

If $f(t)$ and $g(t)$ are two periodic functions having the same period T then

$$\frac{1}{T} \int_c^{c+T} f(t)g(t)\,dt = \sum_{n=-\infty}^{\infty} c_n d_n^* \qquad \text{(4.62)}$$

where the c_n and d_n are the coefficients in the complex Fourier series expansions of $f(t)$ and $g(t)$ respectively.

Proof   Let $f(t)$ and $g(t)$ have complex Fourier series given by

$$f(t) = \sum_{n=-\infty}^{\infty} c_n e^{jn2\pi t/T} \tag{4.63a}$$

with

$$c_n = \frac{1}{T} \int_c^{c+T} f(t) e^{-jn2\pi t/T} \, dT \tag{4.63b}$$

and

$$g(t) = \sum_{n=-\infty}^{\infty} d_n e^{jn2\pi t/T} \tag{4.64a}$$

with

$$d_n = \frac{1}{T} \int_c^{c+T} g(t) e^{-jn2\pi t/T} \, dt \tag{4.64b}$$

Then

$$\frac{1}{T} \int_c^{c+T} f(t)g(t) \, dt = \frac{1}{T} \int_c^{c+T} \left(\sum_{n=-\infty}^{\infty} c_n e^{jn2\pi t/T} \right) g(t) \, dt \qquad \text{using (4.63a)}$$

$$= \sum_{n=-\infty}^{\infty} c_n \left[\frac{1}{T} \int_c^{c+T} g(t) e^{jn2\pi t/T} \, dt \right] \qquad \begin{array}{l} \text{assuming term-} \\ \text{by-term integra-} \\ \text{tion is possible} \end{array}$$

$$= \sum_{n=-\infty}^{\infty} c_n d_{-n} \qquad \text{using (4.64b)}$$

Since $d_{-n} = d_n^*$, the complex conjugate of d_n, this reduces to the required result:

$$\frac{1}{T} \int_c^{c+T} f(t)g(t) \, dt = \sum_{n=-\infty}^{\infty} c_n d_n^* \qquad \qquad \square$$

In terms of the real coefficients a_n, b_n and α_n, β_n of the corresponding trigonometric Fourier series expansions of $f(t)$ and $g(t)$,

$$f(t) = \tfrac{1}{2}a_0 + \sum_{n=1}^{\infty} a_n \cos\left(\frac{n2\pi t}{T} \right) + \sum_{n=1}^{\infty} b_n \sin\left(\frac{n2\pi t}{T} \right)$$

$$g(t) = \tfrac{1}{2}\alpha_0 + \sum_{n=1}^{\infty} \alpha_n \cos\left(\frac{n2\pi t}{T} \right) + \sum_{n=1}^{\infty} \beta_n \sin\left(\frac{n2\pi t}{T} \right)$$

and using the definitions (4.56), the multiplication theorem result (4.62) reduces to

$$\frac{1}{T} \int_c^{c+T} f(t)g(t) \, dt = \sum_{n=1}^{\infty} c_{-n} d_n + c_0 d_0 + \sum_{n=1}^{\infty} c_n d_{-n}$$

$$= \tfrac{1}{4}\alpha_0 a_0 + \tfrac{1}{4} \sum_{n=1}^{\infty} [(a_n - jb_n)(\alpha_n + j\beta_n) + (a_n + jb_n)(\alpha_n - j\beta_n)]$$

giving

$$\frac{1}{T} \int_c^{c+T} f(t)g(t)\,\mathrm{d}t = \tfrac{1}{4}\alpha_0 a_0 + \tfrac{1}{2} \sum_{n=1}^{\infty} (a_n\alpha_n + b_n\beta_n)$$

THEOREM 4.6 Parseval's theorem

If $f(t)$ is a periodic function with period T then

$$\frac{1}{T} \int_c^{c+T} [f(t)]^2\,\mathrm{d}t = \sum_{n=-\infty}^{\infty} c_n c_n^* = \sum_{n=-\infty}^{\infty} |c_n|^2 \qquad (4.65)$$

where the c_n are the coefficients in the complex Fourier series expansion of $f(t)$.

Proof This result follows from the multiplication theorem, since, taking $g(t) = f(t)$ in (4.62), we obtain

$$\frac{1}{T} \int_c^{c+T} [f(t)]^2\,\mathrm{d}t = \sum_{n=-\infty}^{\infty} c_n c_n^* = \sum_{n=-\infty}^{\infty} |c_n|^2 \qquad \square$$

Using (4.60), Parseval's theorem may be written in terms of the real coefficients a_n and b_n of the trigonometric Fourier series expansion of the function $f(t)$ as

$$\frac{1}{T} \int_c^{c+T} [f(t)]^2\,\mathrm{d}t = \tfrac{1}{4}a_0^2 + \tfrac{1}{2} \sum_{n=1}^{\infty} (a_n^2 + b_n^2) \qquad (4.66)$$

The **root mean square (RMS)** value of a periodic function $f(t)$ of period T, defined by

$$f_{\mathrm{RMS}} = \frac{1}{T} \int_c^{c+T} [f(t)]^2\,\mathrm{d}t$$

may therefore be expressed in terms of the Fourier coefficients using (4.65) or (4.66).

EXAMPLE 4.20 By applying Parseval's theorem to the function

$$f(t) = \frac{2t}{T} \quad (0 < t < T)$$

$$f(t + 2T) = f(t)$$

considered in Example 4.19, show that

$$\tfrac{1}{6}\pi^2 = \sum_{n=1}^{\infty} \frac{1}{n^2}$$

Solution From Example 4.19, the coefficients of the complex Fourier series expansion of $f(t)$ are

$$c_0 = 2, \qquad c_n = \frac{\mathrm{j}2}{n\pi} \quad (n \neq 0)$$

Thus, applying the Parseval's theorem result (4.65), noting that the period in this case is $2T$, we obtain

$$\frac{1}{2T} \int_0^{2T} [f(t)]^2 \, dt = c_0^2 + \sum_{n=-\infty}^{-1} |c_n|^2 + \sum_{n=1}^{\infty} |c_n|^2$$

giving

$$\frac{1}{2T} \int_0^{2T} \frac{4t^2}{T^2} \, dt = 4 + 2 \sum_{n=1}^{\infty} \left(\frac{2}{n\pi}\right)^2$$

which reduces to

$$\tfrac{16}{3} = 4 + \sum_{n=1}^{\infty} \frac{8}{n^2\pi^2}$$

leading to the required result

$$\tfrac{1}{6}\pi^2 = \sum_{n=1}^{\infty} \frac{1}{n^2}$$

4.6.3 Discrete frequency spectra

In expressing a periodic function $f(t)$ by its Fourier series expansion, we are decomposing the function into its **harmonic** or **frequency components**. We have seen that if $f(t)$ is of period T then it has frequency components at frequencies

$$\omega_n = \frac{n2\pi}{T} = n\omega_0 \quad (n = 1, 2, 3, \ldots) \tag{4.67}$$

where ω_0 is the frequency of the parent function $f(t)$. (All frequencies here are measured in rad s^{-1}.)

A Fourier series may therefore be interpreted as constituting a **frequency spectrum** of the periodic function $f(t)$, and provides an alternative representation of the function to its time-domain waveform. This frequency spectrum is often displayed by plotting graphs of both the amplitudes and phases of the various harmonic components against angular frequency ω_n. A plot of amplitude against angular frequency is called the **amplitude spectrum**, while that of phase against angular frequency is called the **phase spectrum**. For a periodic function $f(t)$, of period T, harmonic components only occur at discrete frequencies ω_n, given by (4.63), so that these spectra are referred to as **discrete frequency spectra** or **line spectra**. In Chapter 5 Fourier transforms will be used to define continuous spectra for aperiodic functions. With the growing ability to process signals digitally, the representation of signals by their corresponding spectra is an approach widely used in almost all branches of engineering, especially electrical engineering, when

Figure 4.35 Real discrete frequency spectrum.

considering topics such as filtering and modulation. An example of the use of a discrete spectral representation of a periodic function is in distortion measurements on amplifiers, where the harmonic content of the output, measured digitally, to a sinusoidal input provides a measure of the distortion.

If the Fourier series expansion of a periodic function $f(t)$, with period T, has been obtained in the trigonometric form

$$f(t) = \tfrac{1}{2}a_0 + \sum_{n=1}^{\infty} a_n \cos\left(\frac{n2\pi t}{T}\right) + \sum_{n=1}^{\infty} b_n \sin\left(\frac{n2\pi t}{T}\right)$$

then, as indicated in Section 4.2.2, this may be expressed in terms of the various harmonic components as

$$f(t) = A_0 + \sum_{n=1}^{\infty} A_n \sin\left(\frac{n2\pi t}{T} + \phi_n\right) \tag{4.68}$$

where

$$A_0 = \tfrac{1}{2}a_0, \qquad A_n = \sqrt{(a_n^2 + b_n^2)}$$

and the ϕ_n are determined by

$$\sin\phi_n = \frac{b_n}{A_n}, \qquad \cos\phi_n = \frac{a_n}{A_n}$$

In this case a plot of A_n against angular frequency ω_n will constitute the amplitude spectrum and that of ϕ_n against ω_n the phase spectrum. These may be incorporated in the same graph by indicating the various phases on the amplitude spectrum as illustrated in Figure 4.35. It can be seen that the amplitude spectrum consists of a series of equally spaced vertical lines whose lengths are proportional to the amplitudes of the various harmonic components making up the function $f(t)$. Clearly the trigonometric form of the Fourier series does not in general lend itself to the plotting of the discrete frequency spectrum, and the amplitudes A_n and phases ϕ_n must first be determined from the values of a_n and b_n previously determined.

In work on signal analysis it is much more common to use the complex form of the Fourier series. For a periodic function $f(t)$, of period T, this is given by (4.57), with the complex coefficients being given by

$$c_n = |c_n|\,\mathrm{e}^{\mathrm{j}\phi_n} \quad (n = 0, \pm1, \pm2, \ldots)$$

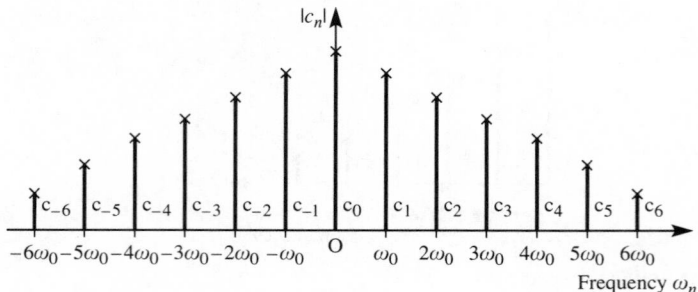

Figure 4.36 Complex form of the amplitude spectrum.

in which $|c_n|$ and ϕ_n denote the magnitude and argument of c_n respectively. Since in general c_n is a complex quantity, we need two line spectra to determine the discrete frequency spectrum; the amplitude spectrum being a plot of $|c_n|$ against ω_n and the phase spectrum that of ϕ_n against ω_n. In cases where c_n is real a single spectrum may be used to represent the function $f(t)$. Since $|c_{-n}| = |c_n^*| = |c_n|$, the amplitude spectrum will be symmetrical about the vertical axis, as illustrated in Figure 4.36.

Note that in the complex form of the discrete frequency spectrum we have components at the discrete frequencies $0, \pm\omega_0, \pm 2\omega_0, \pm 3\omega_0, \dots$; that is, both positive and negative discrete frequencies are involved. Clearly signals having negative frequencies are not physically realizable, and have been introduced for mathematical convenience. At frequency $n\omega_0$ we have the component $e^{jn\omega_0 t}$, which in itself is not a physical signal; to obtain a physical signal, we must consider this alongside the corresponding component $e^{-jn\omega_0 t}$ at the frequency $-n\omega_0$, since then we have

$$e^{jn\omega_0 t} + e^{-jn\omega_0 t} = 2\cos n\omega_0 t \tag{4.69}$$

EXAMPLE 4.21   Plot the discrete amplitude and phase spectra for the periodic function

$$f(t) = \frac{2t}{T} \quad (0 < t < 2T)$$

$$f(t + 2T) = f(t)$$

of Example 4.19. Consider both complex and real forms.

Solution   In Example 4.19 the complex coefficients were determined as

$$c_0 = 2$$

$$c_n = \frac{j2}{n\pi} \quad (n = \pm 1, \pm 2, \pm 3, \dots)$$

Thus

$$|c_n| = \begin{cases} 2/n\pi & (n = 1, 2, 3, \dots) \\ -2/n\pi & (n = -1, -2, -3, \dots) \end{cases}$$

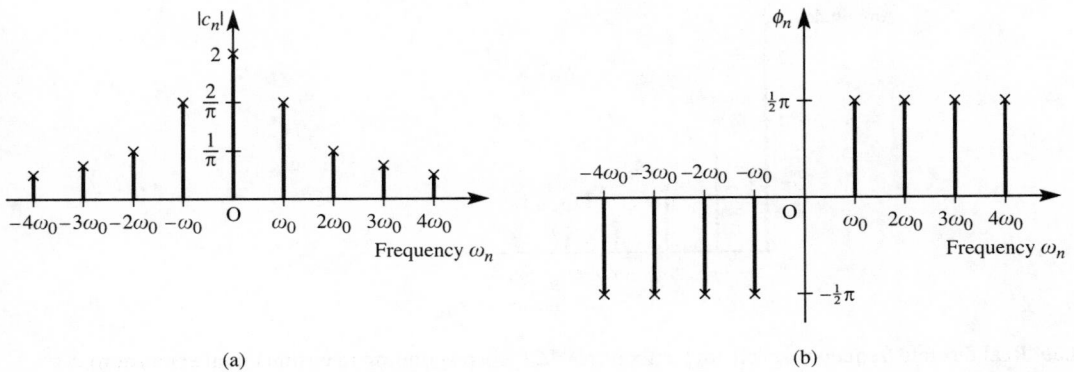

(a)   (b)

Figure 4.37 Complex discrete frequency spectra for Example 4.21, with $\omega_0 = \pi/T$:
(a) amplitude spectrum; (b) phase spectrum.

$$\phi_n = \arg c_n = \begin{cases} \frac{1}{2}\pi & (n = 1, 2, 3, \ldots) \\ -\frac{1}{2}\pi & (n = -1, -2, -3, \ldots) \end{cases}$$

The corresponding amplitude and phase spectra are shown in Figures 4.37(a)
and (b) respectively.

In Example 4.19 we saw that the coefficients in the trigonometric form of
the Fourier series expansion of $f(t)$ are

$$a_0 = 4, \qquad a_n = 0, \qquad b_n = -\frac{4}{n\pi}$$

so that the amplitude coefficients in (4.67) are

$$A_0 = 2, \qquad A_n = \frac{4}{n\pi} \quad (n = 1, 2, 3, \ldots)$$

leading to the real discrete frequency spectrum of Figure 4.38.

Figure 4.38 Real discrete frequency spectrum for Example 4.21 (corresponding to sinusoidal
expansion).

Figure 4.39 Real discrete frequency spectrum for Example 4.21 (corresponding to cosinusoidal expansion).

Since $|c_n| = \frac{1}{2}\sqrt{(a_n^2 + b_n^2)} = \frac{1}{2}A_n$, the amplitude spectrum lines in the complex form (Figure 4.37) are, as expected, halved in amplitude relative to those in the real representation (Figure 4.38), the other half-value being allocated to the corresponding negative frequency. In the complex representation the phases at negative frequencies (Figure 4.37b) are the negatives of those at the corresponding positive frequencies. In our particular representation (4.68) of the real form the phases at positive frequencies differ by $\frac{1}{2}\pi$ between the real and complex form. Again this is not surprising, since from (4.69) we see that combining positive and negative frequencies in the complex form leads to a cosinusoid at that frequency rather than a sinusoid. In order to maintain equality of the phases at positive frequencies between the complex and real representations, a cosinusoidal expansion

$$f(t) = A_0 + \sum_{n=1}^{\infty} A_n \cos\left(\frac{n\pi t}{T} + \phi_n\right) \tag{4.70}$$

of the real Fourier series is frequently adopted as an alternative to the sinusoidal series expansion (4.68). Taking (4.70), the amplitude spectrum will remain the same as for (4.68), but the phase spectrum will be determined by

$$\sin \phi_n = -\frac{b_n}{A_n}, \qquad \cos \phi_n = \frac{a_n}{A_n}$$

showing a phase shift of $\frac{1}{2}\pi$ from that of (4.68). Adopting the real representation (4.70), the corresponding real discrete frequency spectrum for the function $f(t)$ of Example 4.21 is as illustrated in Figure 4.39.

EXAMPLE 4.22   Determine the complex form of the Fourier series expansion of the periodic (period $2T$) infinite train of identical rectangular pulses of magnitude A and duration $2d$ illustrated in Figure 4.40. Draw the discrete frequency spectrum in the particular case when $d = \frac{1}{10}$ and $T = \frac{1}{2}$.

Figure 4.40 Infinite train of rectangular pulses of Example 4.22.

Solution   Over one period $-T < t < T$ the function $f(t)$ representing the train is expressed as

$$f(t) = \begin{cases} 0 & (-T < t < -d) \\ A & (-d < t < d) \\ 0 & (d < t < T) \end{cases}$$

From (4.61), the complex coefficients c_n are given by

$$c_n = \frac{1}{2T} \int_{-T}^{T} f(t) e^{-jn\pi t/T} \, dt$$

$$= \frac{1}{2T} \int_{-d}^{d} A e^{-jn\pi t/T} \, dt = \frac{A}{2T} \left[\frac{-T}{jn\pi} e^{-jn\pi t/T} \right]_{-d}^{d} \quad (n \neq 0)$$

$$= \frac{A}{n\pi} \frac{e^{jn\pi d/T} - e^{-jn\pi d/T}}{j2}$$

$$= \frac{A}{n\pi} \sin\left(\frac{n\pi d}{T} \right)$$

$$= \frac{Ad}{T} \frac{\sin(n\pi d/T)}{n\pi d/T} \quad (n = \pm 1, \pm 2, \ldots)$$

In the particular case when $n = 0$

$$c_0 = \frac{1}{2T} \int_{-T}^{T} f(t) \, dt = \frac{1}{2T} \int_{-d}^{d} A \, dt = \frac{Ad}{T}$$

so that

$$c_n = \frac{Ad}{T} \operatorname{sinc}\left(\frac{n\pi d}{T} \right) \quad (n = 0, \pm 1, \pm 2, \ldots)$$

where the **sinc function** is defined by

$$\operatorname{sinc} t = \begin{cases} \dfrac{\sin t}{t} & (t \neq 0) \\ 1 & (t = 0) \end{cases}$$

Thus from (4.57) the complex Fourier series expansion for the infinite train of

pulses $f(t)$ is

$$f(t) = \sum_{n=-\infty}^{\infty} \frac{Ad}{T} \operatorname{sinc}\left(\frac{n\pi d}{T}\right) e^{jn\pi t/T}$$

As expected, since $f(t)$ is an even function, c_n is real, so we need only plot the discrete amplitude spectrum to represent $f(t)$. Since the amplitude spectrum is a plot of $|c_n|$ against frequency $n\omega_0$, with $\omega_0 = \pi/T$, it will only take values at the discrete frequency values

$$0, \ \pm\frac{\pi}{T}, \ \pm\frac{2\pi}{7}, \ \pm\frac{3\pi}{7}, \ \ldots$$

In the particular case $d = \frac{1}{10}$, $T = \frac{1}{2}$, $\omega_0 = 2\pi$ the amplitude spectrum will only exist at frequency values

$$0, \ \pm 2\pi, \ \pm 4\pi, \ldots$$

Since in this case

$$c_n = \tfrac{1}{5} A \operatorname{sinc} \tfrac{1}{5} n\pi \quad (n = 0, \pm 1, \pm 2, \ldots)$$

noting that $\operatorname{sinc} \tfrac{1}{5} n\pi = 0$ when $\tfrac{1}{5} n\pi = m\pi$ or $n = 5m$ $(m = \pm 1, \pm 2, \ldots)$, the spectrum is as shown in Figure 4.41.

Figure 4.41 Discrete amplitude spectrum for an infinite train of pulses when $d = \frac{1}{10}$ and $T = \frac{1}{2}$.

As we will see in Chapter 5, the sinc function $\operatorname{sinc} t = (\sin t)/t$ plays an important role in signal analysis, and it is sometimes referred to as the **sampling function**. A graph of $\operatorname{sinc} t$ is shown in Figure 4.42, and it is clear that the function oscillates

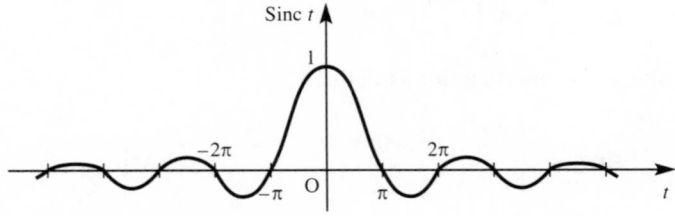

Figure 4.42 Graph of sinc t.

over intervals of length 2π and decreases in amplitude with increasing t. Note also that the function has zeros at $t = \pm n\pi$ ($n = 1, 2, 3, \ldots$).

4.6.4   Power spectrum

The **average power** P associated with a periodic signal $f(t)$, of period T, is defined as the mean square value; that is,

$$P = \frac{1}{T} \int_d^{d+T} [f(t)]^2 \, dt \qquad (4.71)$$

For example, if $f(t)$ represents a voltage waveform applied to a resistor then P represents the average power, measured in watts, dissipated by a $1\,\Omega$ resistor.

By Parseval's theorem (Theorem 4.6),

$$P = \tfrac{1}{4}a_0^2 + \tfrac{1}{2} \sum_{n=1}^{\infty} (a_n^2 + b_n^2) \qquad (4.72)$$

Since

$$\frac{1}{T} \int_d^{d+T} \left[a_n \cos\left(\frac{2n\pi t}{T}\right) \right]^2 dt = \tfrac{1}{2}a_n^2$$

$$\frac{1}{T} \int_d^{d+T} \left[b_n \cos\left(\frac{2n\pi t}{T}\right) \right]^2 dt = \tfrac{1}{2}b_n^2$$

the power in the nth harmonic is

$$P_n = \tfrac{1}{2}(a_n^2 + b_n^2) \qquad (4.73)$$

and it follows from (4.72) that the power of the periodic function $f(t)$ is the sum of the power of the individual harmonic components contained in $f(t)$.

In terms of the complex Fourier coefficients, Parseval's theorem gives

$$P = \sum_{n=-\infty}^{\infty} |c_n|^2 \qquad (4.74)$$

As discussed in Section 4.6.3, the component $e^{jn\omega_0 t}$ at frequency $\omega_n = n\omega_0$, $\omega_0 = 2\pi/T$, must be considered alongside the component $e^{-jn\omega_0 t}$ at the corresponding negative frequency $-\omega_n$ in order to form the actual nth harmonic component of the function $f(t)$. Since $|c_{-n}|^2 = |c_n^*|^2 = |c_n|^2$, it follows that the power associated with the nth harmonic is the sum of the power associated with $e^{jn\omega_0 t}$ and $e^{-jn\omega_0 t}$; that is,

$$P_n = 2|c_n|^2 \qquad (4.75)$$

which, since $|c_n| = \tfrac{1}{2}\sqrt{(a_n^2 + b_n^2)}$, corresponds to (4.73). Thus in the complex form half the power of the nth harmonic is associated with the positive frequency and half with the negative frequency.

Since the total power of a periodic signal is the sum of the power associated with each of the harmonics of which the signal is composed, it is again useful to consider a spectral representation, and a plot of $|c_n|^2$ against angular frequency ω_n is called the **power spectrum** of the function $f(t)$. Clearly such a spectrum is readily deduced from the discrete amplitude spectrum of $|c_n|$ against angular frequency ω_n.

EXAMPLE 4.23   For the spectrum of the infinite train of rectangular pulses shown in Figure 4.40, determine the percentage of the total power contained within the frequency band up to the first zero value (called the **zero crossing** of the spectrum) at 10π rad s^{-1}.

Solution   From (4.71), the total power associated with the infinite train of rectangular pulses $f(t)$ is

$$P = \frac{1}{2T} \int_{-T}^{T} [f(t)]^2 \, dt = \frac{1}{2T} \int_{-d}^{d} A^2 \, dt$$

which in the particular case when $d = \frac{1}{10}$ and $T = \frac{1}{2}$ becomes

$$P = \int_{-1/10}^{1/10} A^2 \, dt = \tfrac{1}{5} A^2$$

The power contained in the frequency band up to the first zero crossing at 10π rad s^{-1} is

$$P_1 = c_0^2 + 2(c_1^2 + c_2^2 + c_3^2 + c_4^2)$$

where

$$c_n = \tfrac{1}{5} A \operatorname{sinc} \tfrac{1}{5} n\pi$$

That is,

$$P_1 = \tfrac{1}{25} A^2 + \tfrac{2}{25} A^2 (\operatorname{sinc}^2 \tfrac{1}{5}\pi + \operatorname{sinc}^2 \tfrac{2}{5}\pi + \operatorname{sinc}^2 \tfrac{3}{5}\pi + \operatorname{sinc}^2 \tfrac{4}{5}\pi)$$

$$= \tfrac{1}{25} A^2 [1 + 2(0.875 + 0.756 + 0.255 + 0.055)]$$

$$= \tfrac{1}{5} A^2 (0.976)$$

Thus $P_1 = 0.976P$, so that approximately 97.6% of the total power associated with $f(t)$ is contained in the frequency band up to the first zero crossing at 10π rad s^{-1}.

Suppose that a periodic voltage $v(t)$, of period T, applied to a linear circuit, results in a corresponding current $i(t)$, having the same period T. Then, given the Fourier series representation of both the voltage and current at a pair of terminals, we can use the multiplication theorem (Theorem 4.5) to obtain an expression for the average power P at the terminals. Thus, given

$$v(t) = \sum_{n=-\infty}^{\infty} c_n e^{j2n\pi t/T}$$

$$i(t) = \sum_{n=-\infty}^{\infty} d_n \, e^{j2n\pi t/T}$$

the instantaneous power at the terminals is vi and the average power is

$$P = \frac{1}{T} \int_d^{d+T} vi \, dt = \sum_{n=-\infty}^{\infty} c_n d_n^*$$

or, in terms of the corresponding trigonometric Fourier series coefficients a_n, b_n and α_n, β_n

$$P = \tfrac{1}{4}\alpha_0 \beta_0 + \tfrac{1}{2} \sum_{n=1}^{\infty} (a_n \alpha_n + b_n \beta_n)$$

4.6.5   Exercises

34 Show that the complex form of the Fourier series expansion of the periodic function

$$f(t) = t^2 \quad (-\pi < t < \pi)$$
$$f(t + 2\pi) = f(t)$$

is

$$f(t) = \sum_{n=-\infty}^{\infty} \frac{2}{n^2}(-1)^n e^{jnt}$$

Using (4.56), obtain the corresponding trigonometric series and check with the series obtained in Example 4.5.

35 Obtain the complex form of the Fourier series expansion of the square wave

$$f(t) = \begin{cases} 0 & (-2 < t < 0) \\ 1 & (0 < t < 2) \end{cases}$$
$$f(t + 4) = f(t)$$

Using (4.56), obtain the corresponding trigonometric series and check with the series obtained in Example 4.9.

36 Obtain the complex form of the Fourier series expansion of the following periodic functions.

(a) $f(t) = \begin{cases} \pi & (-\pi < t < 0) \\ t & (0 < t < \pi) \end{cases}$

$f(t + 2\pi) = f(t)$

(b) $f(t) = \begin{cases} a \sin \omega t & (0 < t < \tfrac{1}{2}\pi) \\ 0 & (\tfrac{1}{2}\pi < t < T) \end{cases}$

$f(t + T) = f(t), \qquad T = 2\pi/\omega$

(c) $f(t) = \begin{cases} 2 & (-\pi < t < 0) \\ 1 & (0 < t < \pi) \end{cases}$

$f(t + 2\pi) = f(t)$

(d) $f(t) = |\sin t| \quad (-\pi < t < \pi)$

$f(t + 2\pi) = f(t)$

37 A periodic function $f(t)$, of period 2π, is defined within the period $-\pi < t < \pi$ by

$$f(t) = \begin{cases} 0 & (-\pi < t < 0) \\ 1 & (0 < t < \pi) \end{cases}$$

Using the Fourier coefficients of $f(t)$, together with Parseval's theorem, show that

$$\sum_{n=1}^{\infty} \frac{1}{(2n-1)^2} = \tfrac{1}{8}\pi^2$$

(*Note*: The Fourier coefficients may be deduced from Example 4.9 or Exercise 35.)

38 (a) Show that the Fourier series expansion of the periodic function

$$f(t) = \tfrac{1}{2}\pi t \quad (0 < t < 20)$$
$$f(t + 20) = f(t)$$

may be expressed as

$$f(t) = 5\pi - 10 \sum_{n=1}^{\infty} \frac{1}{n} \sin 100\pi t$$

(b) Using (4.66), estimate the RMS value of $f(t)$ by
    (i) using the first four terms of the Fourier series;
    (ii) using the first eight terms of the Fourier series.

(c) Obtain the true RMS value of $f(t)$, and hence determine the percentage errors in the estimated values obtained in (b).

39 A periodic voltage $v(t)$ (in V) of period 5 ms and specified by

$$v(t) = \begin{cases} 60 & (0 < t < 1.25\,\text{ms}) \\ 0 & (1.25\,\text{ms} < t < 5\,\text{ms}) \end{cases}$$

$$v(t + 5\,\text{ms}) = v(t)$$

is applied across the terminals of a 15 Ω resistor.

(a) Obtain expressions for the coefficients c_n of the complex Fourier series representation of $v(t)$, and write down the values of the first five non-zero terms.

(b) Calculate the power associated with each of the first five non-zero terms of the Fourier expansion.

(c) Calculate the total power delivered to the 15 Ω resistor.

(d) What is the percentage of the total power delivered to the resistor by the first five non-zero terms of the Fourier series?

4.7   Orthogonal functions

As was noted in Section 4.2.3, the fact that the set of functions $\{1, \cos \omega t, \sin \omega t, \ldots, \cos n\omega t, \sin n\omega t, \ldots\}$ is an orthogonal set of functions on the interval $d \leqslant t \leqslant d + T$ was crucial in the evaluation of the coefficient in the Fourier series expansion of a function $f(t)$. It is natural to ask whether it is possible to express the function $f(t)$ as a series expansion in other sets of functions. In the case of periodic functions $f(t)$ there is no natural alternative, but if we are concerned with representing a function $f(t)$ only in a finite interval $t_1 \leqslant t \leqslant t_2$ then a variety of other possibilities exist. These possibilities are drawn from a class of functions called **orthogonal functions**, of which the trigonometric set $\{1, \cos \omega t, \sin \omega t, \ldots, \cos n\omega t, \sin n\omega t\}$ is a particular example.

4.7.1   Definitions

Two real functions $f(t)$ and $g(t)$ that are piecewise-continuous in the interval $t_1 \leqslant t \leqslant t_2$ are said to be **orthogonal** in this interval if

$$\int_{t_1}^{t_2} f(t)g(t)\,dt = 0$$

A set of real functions $\phi_1(t), \phi_2(t), \ldots \equiv \{\phi_n(t)\}$, each of which is piecewise-continuous on $t_1 \leqslant t \leqslant t_2$, is said to be an **orthogonal set** on this interval if $\phi_n(t)$ and $\phi_m(t)$ are orthogonal for each pair of distinct indices n, m; that is, if

$$\int_{t_1}^{t_2} \phi_n(t)\phi_m(t)\,dt = 0 \quad (n \neq m) \tag{4.76}$$

We shall also assume that no member of the set $\{\phi_n(t)\}$ is identically zero except at a finite number of points, so that

$$\int_{t_1}^{t_2} \phi_m^2(t)\, dt = \gamma_m \quad (m = 1, 2, 3, \ldots) \tag{4.77}$$

where γ_m $(m = 1, 2, \ldots)$ are all non-zero constants.

An orthogonal set $\{\phi_n(t)\}$ is said to be **orthonormal** if each of its components is also normalized; that is, $\gamma_m = 1$ $(m = 1, 2, 3, \ldots)$. We note that any orthogonal set $\{\phi_n(t)\}$ can be converted into an orthonormal set by dividing each member $\phi_m(t)$ of the set by $\sqrt{\gamma_m}$.

EXAMPLE 4.24   Since (4.4)–(4.8) hold,

$$\{1, \cos t, \sin t, \cos 2t, \sin 2t, \ldots, \cos nt, \sin nt\}$$

is an orthogonal set on the interval $d \leqslant t \leqslant d + 2\pi$, while the set

$$\left\{ \frac{1}{\sqrt{(2\pi)}}, \frac{\cos t}{\sqrt{\pi}}, \frac{\sin t}{\sqrt{\pi}}, \ldots, \frac{\cos nt}{\sqrt{\pi}}, \frac{\sin nt}{\sqrt{\pi}} \right\}$$

forms an orthonormal set on the same interval.

The latter follows since

$$\int_d^{d+2\pi} \left[\frac{1}{\sqrt{(2\pi)}} \right]^2 dt = 1$$

$$\int_d^{d+2\pi} \left(\frac{\cos nt}{\sqrt{\pi}} \right)^2 dt = \int_d^{d+2\pi} \left(\frac{\sin nt}{\sqrt{\pi}} \right)^2 dt = 1 \quad (n = 1, 2, 3, \ldots)$$

The definition of orthogonality considered so far applies to real functions, and has to be amended somewhat if members of the set $\{\phi_n(t)\}$ are complex functions of the real variable t. In such a case the set $\{\phi_n(t)\}$ is said to be an orthogonal set on the interval $t_1 \leqslant t \leqslant t_2$ if

$$\int_{t_1}^{t_2} \phi_n(t) \phi_m^*(t)\, dt = \begin{cases} 0 & (n \neq m) \\ \gamma & (n = m) \end{cases} \tag{4.78}$$

where $\phi_m^*(t)$ denotes the complex conjugate of $\phi(t)$.

EXAMPLE 4.25   Verify that the set of complex exponential functions

$$\{e^{jn\pi t/T}\} \quad (n = 0, \pm 1, \pm 2, \pm 3, \ldots)$$

used in the complex representation of the Fourier series is an orthogonal set on the interval $0 \leqslant t \leqslant 2T$.

Solution First,

$$\int_0^{2T} e^{jn\pi t/T} 1 \, dt = \left[\frac{T}{jn\pi} e^{jn\pi t/T} \right]_0^{2T} = 0 \quad (n \neq 0)$$

since $e^{j2n\pi} = e^0 = 1$. Secondly,

$$\int_0^{2T} e^{jn\pi t/T} (e^{jm\pi t/T})^* \, dt = \int_0^{2T} e^{j(n-m)\pi t/T} \, dt$$

$$= \left[\frac{T}{j(n-m)\pi} e^{j(n-m)\pi t/T} \right]_0^{2T} = 0 \quad (n \neq m)$$

and, when $n = m$,

$$\int_0^{2T} e^{jn\pi t/T} (e^{jn\pi t/T})^* \, dt = \int_0^{2T} 1 \, dt = 2T$$

Thus

$$\int_0^{2T} e^{jn\pi t/T} 1 \, dt = 0 \quad (n \neq 0)$$

$$\int_0^{2T} e^{jn\pi t/T} (e^{jm\pi t/T})^* \, dt = \begin{cases} 0 & (n \neq m) \\ 2T & (n = m) \end{cases}$$

and, from (4.78), the set is an orthogonal set on the interval $0 \leqslant t \leqslant 2T$.

The trigonometric and exponential sets are examples of orthogonal sets that we have already used in developing the work on Fourier series. Examples of other sets of orthogonal functions that are widely used in practice are Legendre polynomials, Bessel functions, Hermite polynomials, Lagurre polynomials, Jacobi polynomials, Tchebyshev (sometimes written as Chebyshev) polynomials and Walsh functions.

4.7.2 Generalized Fourier series

Let $\{\phi_n(t)\}$ be an orthogonal set on the interval $t_1 \leqslant t \leqslant t_2$ and suppose that we wish to represent the piecewise-continuous function $f(t)$ in terms of this set within this interval. Following the Fourier series development, suppose that it is possible to express $f(t)$ as a series expansion of the form

$$f(t) = \sum_{n=1}^{\infty} c_n \phi_n(t) \tag{4.79}$$

We now wish to determine the coefficients c_n, and to do so we again follow the Fourier series development. Multiplying (4.79) throughout by $\phi_m(t)$ and integrating term by term, we obtain

$$\int_{t_1}^{t_2} f(t)\phi_m(t)\,dt = \sum_{n=1}^{\infty} c_n \int_{t_1}^{t_2} \phi_m(t)\phi_n(t)\,dt$$

which, on using (4.76) and (4.77), reduces to

$$\int_{t_1}^{t_2} f(t)\phi_n(t)\,dt = c_n\gamma_n$$

giving

$$c_n = \frac{1}{\gamma_n} \int_{t_1}^{t_2} f(t)\phi_n(t)\,dt \quad (n = 1, 2, 3, \ldots) \tag{4.80}$$

Summarizing, if $f(t)$ is a piecewise-continuous function on the interval $t_1 \leqslant t \leqslant t_2$ and $\{\phi_n(t)\}$ is an orthogonal set on this interval then the series

$$f(t) = \sum_{n=1}^{\infty} c_n\phi_n(t)$$

is called the **generalized Fourier series** of $f(t)$ with respect to the basis set $\{\phi_n(t)\}$, and the coefficients c_n, given by (4.80), are called the **generalized Fourier coefficients** with respect to the same basis set.

A parallel can be drawn between a generalized Fourier series expansion of a function $f(t)$ with respect to an orthogonal basis set of functions $\{\phi_n(t)\}$ and the representation of a vector f in terms of an orthogonal basis set of vectors $v_1, v_2, \ldots, v_n$ as

$$\boldsymbol{f} = \alpha_1\boldsymbol{v}_1 + \ldots + \alpha_n\boldsymbol{v}_n$$

where

$$\alpha_i = \frac{\boldsymbol{f}\cdot\boldsymbol{v}_i}{\boldsymbol{v}_i\cdot\boldsymbol{v}_i} = \frac{\boldsymbol{f}\cdot\boldsymbol{v}_i}{|\boldsymbol{v}_i|^2}$$

There is clearly a similarity between this pair of results and the pair (4.79)–(4.80).

4.7.3   Convergence of generalized Fourier series

As in the case of a Fourier series expansion, partial sums of the form

$$F_N(t) = \sum_{n=1}^{N} c_n\phi_n(t) \tag{4.81}$$

can be considered, and we wish this representation to be, in some sense, a 'close approximation' to the parent function $f(t)$. This question arises when considering such a partial sum as to whether choosing the coefficients c_n as the generalized

Fourier coefficients (4.80) leads to the 'best' approximation. Defining the **mean square error** E_N between the actual value of $f(t)$ and the approximation $F_N(t)$ as

$$E_N = \frac{1}{t_2 - t_1} \int_{t_1}^{t_2} [f(t) - F_N(t)]^2 \, dt$$

it can be shown that E_N is minimized, for all N, when the coefficients c_n are chosen according to (4.80). Thus in this sense the finite generalized Fourier series gives the best approximation.

To verify this result, assume, for convenience, that the set $\{\phi_n(t)\}$ is orthonormal, and consider the Nth partial sum

$$F_N(t) = \sum_{n=1}^{N} \tilde{c}_n \phi_n(t)$$

where the $\tilde{c}_n$ are to be chosen in order to minimize the mean square error E_N. Now

$$(t_2 - t_1)E_N = \int_{t_1}^{t_2} \left[f(t) - \sum_{n=1}^{N} \tilde{c}_n \phi_n(t) \right]^2 dt$$

$$= \int_{t_1}^{t_2} f^2(t) \, dt - 2 \sum_{n=1}^{N} \tilde{c}_n \int_{t_1}^{t_2} f(t) \phi_n(t) \, dt + \sum_{n=1}^{N} \tilde{c}_n^2 \int_{t_1}^{t_2} \phi_n^2(t) \, dt$$

$$= \int_{t_1}^{t_2} f^2(t) \, dt - 2 \sum_{n=1}^{N} \tilde{c}_n c_n + \sum_{n=1}^{N} \tilde{c}_n^2$$

since $\{\phi_n(t)\}$ is an orthonormal set. That is,

$$(t_2 - t_1)E_N = \int_{t_1}^{t_2} f^2(t) \, dt - \sum_{n=1}^{N} c_n^2 + \sum_{n=1}^{N} (\tilde{c}_n - c_n)^2 \tag{4.82}$$

which is clearly minimized when $\tilde{c}_n = c_n$.

Taking $\tilde{c}_n = c_n$ in (4.82), the mean square error E_N in approximating $f(t)$ by $F_N(t)$ of (4.77) is given by

$$E_N = \frac{1}{t_2 - t_1} \left[\int_{t_1}^{t_2} f^2(t) \, dt - \sum_{n=1}^{N} c_n^2 \right]$$

if the set $\{\phi_n(t)\}$ is orthonormal, and is given by

$$E_N = \frac{1}{t_2 - t_1} \left[\int_{t_1}^{t_2} f^2(t) \, dt - \sum_{n=1}^{N} \gamma_n c_n^2 \right] \tag{4.83}$$

if the set $\{\phi_n(t)\}$ is orthogonal.

Since, by definition, E_N is non-negative, it follows from (4.83) that

$$\int_{t_1}^{t_2} f^2(t) \, dt \geqslant \sum_{n=1}^{N} \gamma_n c_n^2 \tag{4.84}$$

a result known as **Bessel's inequality**. The question that arises in practice is whether or not $E_N \to 0$ as $N \to \infty$, indicating that the sum

$$\sum_{n=1}^{N} c_n \phi_n(t)$$

converges to the function $f(t)$. If this were the case then, from (4.83),

$$\int_{t_1}^{t_2} f^2(t)\, dt = \sum_{n=1}^{\infty} \gamma_n c_n^2 \tag{4.85}$$

which is the **generalized form of Parseval's theorem**, and the set $\{\phi_n(t)\}$ is said to be complete. Strictly speaking, the fact that Parseval's theorem holds ensures that the partial sum $F_N(t)$ converges in the mean to the parent function $f(t)$ as $N \to \infty$, and this does not necessarily guarantee convergence at any particular point. In engineering applications, however, this distinction may be overlooked, since for the functions met in practice convergence in the mean also ensures pointwise convergence at points where $f(t)$ is convergent, and convergence to the mean of the discontinuity at points where $f(t)$ is discontinuous.

EXAMPLE 4.26

The set $\{1, \cos t, \sin t, \ldots, \cos nt, \sin nt\}$ is a complete orthogonal set in the interval $d \leqslant t \leqslant d + 2\pi$. Following the same argument as above, it is readily shown that for a function $f(t)$ that is piecewise-continuous on $d \leqslant t \leqslant d + 2\pi$ the mean square error between $f(t)$ and the finite Fourier series

$$F_N(t) = \tfrac{1}{2}\tilde{a}_0 + \sum_{n=1}^{N} \tilde{a}_n \cos nt + \sum_{n=1}^{N} \tilde{b}_n \sin nt$$

is minimized when $\tilde{a}_0$, $\tilde{a}_n$ and $\tilde{b}_n$ $(n = 1, 2, 3, \ldots)$ are equal to the corresponding Fourier coefficients a_0, a_n and b_n $(n = 1, 2, 3, \ldots)$ determined using (4.11) and (4.12). In this case the mean square error E_N is given by

$$E_N = \frac{1}{2\pi}\left[\int_d^{d+2\pi} f^2(t)\, dt - \pi\left[\tfrac{1}{2}a_0^2 + \sum_{n=1}^{N}(a_n^2 + b_n^2) \right] \right]$$

Bessel's inequality (4.84) becomes

$$\int_d^{d+2\pi} f^2(t)\, dt \geqslant \pi\left[\tfrac{1}{2}a_0^2 + \sum_{n=1}^{N}(a_n^2 + b_n^2) \right]$$

and Parseval's theorem (4.85) reduces to

$$\frac{1}{2\pi}\int_d^{d+2\pi} f^2(t) = \tfrac{1}{4}a_0^2 + \tfrac{1}{2}\sum_{n=1}^{\infty}(a_n^2 + b_n^2)$$

which conforms with (4.66). Since, in this case, the basis set is complete, Parseval's theorem holds, and the Fourier series converges to $f(t)$ in the sense discussed above.

4.7.4 Exercises

40 The Fourier series expansion for the periodic square
wave

$$f(t) = \begin{cases} -1 & (-\pi < t < 0) \\ 1 & (0 < t < \pi) \end{cases}$$

$$f(t + 2\pi) = f(t)$$

is

$$f(t) = \sum_{n=1}^{\infty} \frac{4}{\pi(2n-1)} \sin(2n-1)t$$

Determine the mean square error corresponding to
approximations to $f(t)$ based on the use of one term,
two terms and three terms respectively in the series
expansion.

41 The Legendre polynomials $P_n(t)$ are generated by
the formula

$$P_n(t) = \frac{1}{2^n n!} \frac{d^n}{dt^n} (t^2 - 1)^n \quad (n = 0, 1, 2, \ldots)$$

and satisfy the recurrence relationship

$$nP_n(t) = (2n-1)tP_{n-1}(t) - (n-1)P_{n-2}(t)$$

(a) Deduce that

$$P_0(t) = 1, \qquad P_1(t) = t$$
$$P_2(t) = \tfrac{1}{2}(3t^2 - 1), \qquad P_3(t) = \tfrac{1}{2}(5t^3 - 3t)$$

(b) Show that the polynomials form an orthogonal
set on the interval $(-1, 1)$ and, in particular, that

$$\int_{-1}^{1} P_m(t) P_n(t) \, dt$$

$$= \begin{cases} 0 & (n \neq m) \\ 2/(2n+1) & (n = m; \ m = 0, 1, 2, \ldots) \end{cases}$$

(c) Given that the function

$$f(t) = \begin{cases} -1 & (-1 < t < 0) \\ 0 & (t = 0) \\ 1 & (0 < t < 1) \end{cases}$$

is expressed as a Fourier–Legendre series expansion

$$f(t) = \sum_{r=0}^{\infty} c_r P_r(t)$$

determine the values of c_0, c_1, c_2 and c_3.

(d) Plot graphs to illustrate convergence of the series
obtained in (c), and compare the mean square error
with that of the corresponding Fourier series
expansion.

42 Repeat parts (c) and (d) of Exercise 41 for the function

$$f(x) = \begin{cases} 0 & (-1 < x < 0) \\ x & (0 < x < 1) \end{cases}$$

43 Lagurre polynomials $L_n(t)$ are generated by the
formula

$$L_n(t) = e^t \frac{d^n}{dt^n} (t^n e^{-t}) \quad (n = 0, 1, 2, \ldots)$$

and satisfy the recurrence relation

$$L_n(t) = (2n - 1 - t)L_{n-1}(t) - (n-1)^2 L_{n-2}(t)$$
$$(n = 2, 3, \ldots)$$

These polynomials are orthogonal on the interval
$0 \leqslant t < \infty$ with respect to the weighting function
e^{-t}, so that

$$\int_0^{\infty} e^{-t} L_n(t) L_m(t) \, dt = \begin{cases} 0 & (n \neq m) \\ (n!)^2 & (n = m) \end{cases}$$

(a) Deduce that

$$L_0(t) = 1, \qquad L_1(t) = 1 - t$$
$$L_2(t) = 2 - 4t + t^2$$
$$L_3(t) = 6 - 18t + 9t^2 - t^3$$

(b) Confirm the above orthogonality result in the
case of L_0, L_1, L_2 and L_3.

(c) Given that the function $f(t)$ is to be approximated
over the interval $0 \leqslant t < \infty$ by

$$f(t) = \sum_{r=0}^{\infty} c_r L_r(t)$$

show that

$$c_r = \frac{1}{(r!)^2} \int_0^{\infty} f(t) e^{-t} L_r(t) \, dt \quad (r = 0, 1, 2, \ldots)$$

(*Note:* Lagurre polynomials are of particular
importance to engineers, since they can be generated
as the impulse responses of relatively simple networks.)

44 Hermite polynomials $H_n(t)$ are generated by the
formula

$$H_n(t) = (-1)^n e^{t^2/2} \frac{d^n}{dt^n} e^{-t^2/2} \quad (n = 0, 1, 2, \ldots)$$

and satisfy the recurrence relationship

$$H_n(t) = 2tH_{n-1}(t) - 2(n-1)H_{n-2}(t) \quad (n = 2, 3, \ldots)$$

The polynomials are orthogonal on the interval $-\infty < t < \infty$ with respect to the weighting function $e^{-t^2/2}$, so that

$$\int_{-\infty}^{\infty} e^{-t^2/2} H_n(t) H_m(t)\, dt = \begin{cases} 0 & (n \neq m) \\ \sqrt{(2\pi)}n! & (n = m) \end{cases}$$

(a) Deduce that

$$H_0(t) = 1, \qquad H_1(t) = t$$
$$H_2(t) = t^2 - 1 \qquad H_3(t) = t^3 - 3t$$
$$H_4(t) = t^4 - 6t^2 + 3$$

(b) Confirm the above orthogonality result for H_0, H_1, H_2 and H_3.

(c) Given that the function $f(t)$ is to be approximated over the interval $-\infty < t < \infty$ by

$$f(t) = \sum_{r=0}^{\infty} c_r H_r(t)$$

show that

$$c_r = \frac{1}{r!\sqrt{\pi}} \int_{-\infty}^{\infty} e^{-t^2} f(t) H_r(t)\, dt \quad (r = 0, 1, \ldots)$$

45 Tchebyshev polynomials $T_n(t)$ are generated by the formula

$$T_n(t) = \cos(n \cos^{-1} t) \quad (n = 0, 1, 2, \ldots)$$

or

$$T_n(t) = \sum_{r=0}^{[n/2]} (-1)^r \frac{n!}{(2r)!(n-2r)!} (1-t^2)^r t^{n-2r}$$

$$(n = 0, 1, 2, \ldots)$$

where

$$[n/2] = \begin{cases} n/2 & (\text{even } n) \\ (n-1)/2 & (\text{odd } n) \end{cases}$$

They also satisfy the recurrence relationship

$$T_n(t) = 2tT_{n-1}(t) - T_{n-2}(t) \quad (n = 2, 3, \ldots)$$

and are orthogonal on the interval $-1 \leq t \leq 1$ with respect to the weighting function $1/\sqrt{(1-t^2)}$, so that

$$\int_{-1}^{1} \frac{T_n(t)T_m(t)}{\sqrt{(1-t^2)}}\, dt = \begin{cases} 0 & (m \neq n) \\ \tfrac{1}{2}\pi & (m = n \neq 0) \\ \pi & (m = n = 0) \end{cases}$$

(a) Deduce that

$$T_0(t) = 1, \qquad T_1(t) = t$$
$$T_2(t) = 2t^2 - 1, \qquad T_3(t) = 4t^3 - 3t$$
$$T_4(t) = 8t^4 - 8t^2 + 1$$
$$T_5(t) = 16t^5 - 20t^3 + 5t$$

(b) Confirm the above orthogonality result for T_0, T_1, T_2 and T_3.

(c) Given that the function $f(t)$ is to be approximated over the interval $-1 \leq t \leq 1$ by

$$f(t) = \sum_{r=0}^{\infty} c_r T_r(t)$$

show that

$$c_0 = \frac{1}{\pi} \int_{-1}^{1} \frac{f(t)T_0(t)}{\sqrt{(1-t^2)}}\, dt$$

$$c_r = \frac{2}{\pi} \int_{-1}^{1} \frac{f(t)T_r(t)}{\sqrt{(1-t^2)}}\, dt \quad (r = 1, 2, \ldots)$$

46 With developments in digital techniques, Walsh functions $W_n(t)$ have become of considerable importance in practice, since they are so easily generated by digital logic circuitry. The first four Walsh functions may be defined on the interval $0 \leq t \leq T$ by

$$W_0(t) = \frac{1}{\sqrt{T}} \quad (0 \leq t \leq T)$$

$$W_1(t) = \begin{cases} 1/\sqrt{T} & (0 \leq t < \tfrac{1}{2}T) \\ -1/\sqrt{T} & (\tfrac{1}{2}T < t \leq T) \end{cases}$$

$$W_2(t) = \begin{cases} 1/\sqrt{T} & (0 \leq t < \tfrac{1}{4}T,\ \tfrac{3}{4}T < t \leq T) \\ -1/\sqrt{T} & (\tfrac{1}{4}T < t < \tfrac{3}{4}T) \end{cases}$$

$$W_3(t) =$$
$$\begin{cases} 1/\sqrt{T} & (0 \leq t < \tfrac{1}{8}T,\ \tfrac{3}{8}T < t < \tfrac{5}{8}T,\ \tfrac{7}{8}T < t \leq T) \\ -1/\sqrt{T} & (\tfrac{1}{8}T < t < \tfrac{3}{8}T,\ \tfrac{5}{8}T < t < \tfrac{7}{8}T) \end{cases}$$

(a) Plot graphs of the functions $W_0(t)$, $W_1(t)$, $W_2(t)$ and $W_3(t)$, and show that they are orthonormal on the interval $0 \leq t \leq T$. Write down an expression for $W_n(t)$.

(b) The Walsh functions may be used to obtain a Fourier–Walsh series expansion for a function $f(t)$, over the interval $0 \leq t \leq T$, in the form

$$f(t) = \sum_{r=0}^{\infty} c_r W_r(t)$$

Illustrate this for the square wave of Exercise 40. What is the corresponding mean square error? Comment on your answer.

4.8   Engineering application: describing functions

Many control systems containing a nonlinear element may be represented by the block diagram of Figure 4.43. In practice, describing function techniques are used to analyse and design such control systems. Essentially the method involves replacing the nonlinearity by an equivalent gain N and then using the techniques developed for linear systems, such as the frequency response methods of Section 2.7. If the nonlinear element is subjected to a sinusoidal input $e(t) = X \sin \omega t$ then its output $z(t)$ may be represented by the Fourier series expansion

$$z(t) = \tfrac{1}{2}a_0 + \sum_{n=1}^{\infty} a_n \cos n\omega t + \sum_{n=1}^{\infty} b_n \sin n\omega t$$

$$= \tfrac{1}{2}a_0 + \sum_{n=1}^{\infty} A_n \sin(n\omega t + \phi_n)$$

with $A_n = \sqrt{(a_n^2 + b_n^2)}$ and $\phi_n = \tan^{-1}(a_n/b_n)$.

The **describing function** $N(X)$ of the nonlinear element is then defined to be the complex ratio of the fundamental component of the output to the input; that is,

$$N(X) = \frac{A_1}{X} e^{j\phi_1}$$

with $N(X)$ being independent of the input frequency ω if the nonlinear element is memory-free.

Having determined the describing function, the behaviour of the closed loop system is then determined by the characteristic equation

$$1 + N(X)G(j\omega) = 0$$

If a combination of X and ω can be found to satisfy this equation then the system is capable of sustained oscillations at that frequency and magnitude; that is, the

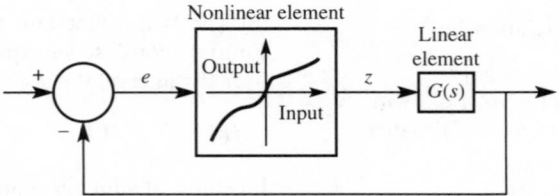

Figure 4.43 Nonlinear control system.

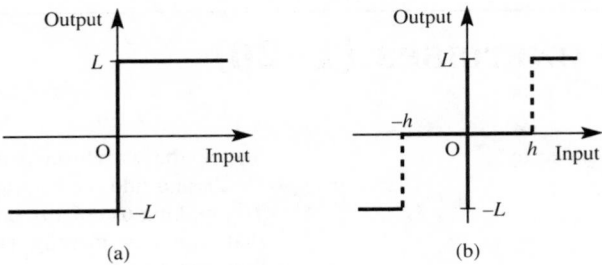

Figure 4.44 (a) Relay.   (b) Relay with dead zone.

system exhibits **limit-cycle behaviour**. In general, more than one combination can be found, and the resulting oscillations can be a stable or unstable limit cycle.

Normally the characteristic equation is investigated graphically by plotting $G(j\omega)$ and $-1/N(X)$, for all values of X, on the same polar diagram. Limit cycles then occur at frequencies and amplitudes corresponding to points of intersection of the curves. Sometimes plotting can be avoided by calculating the maximum value of $N(X)$ and hence the value of the gain associated with $G(s)$ that will just cause limit cycling to occur.

Using this background information, the following investigation is left as an exercise for the reader to develop.

(a) Show that the describing functions $N_1(X)$ and $N_2(X)$ corresponding respectively to the relay (on–off nonlinearity) of Figure 4.44(a) and the relay with dead zone of Figure 4.44(b) are

$$N_1(X) = \frac{4L}{\pi X}, \qquad N_2(X) = \frac{4L}{\pi X} \sqrt{\left[1 - \left(\frac{h}{X} \right)^2 \right]}$$

(b) For the system of Figure 4.45 show that a limit cycle exists when the nonlinearity is the relay of Figure 4.44(a) with $L = 1$. Determine the amplitude and frequency of this limit cycle.

In an attempt to eliminate the limit-cycle oscillation, the relay is replaced by the relay with dead zone illustrated in Figure 4.44(b), again with $L = 1$. Show that this allows our objective to be achieved provided that $h > 10/3\pi$.

Figure 4.45 Nonlinear system of exercise.

4.9   Review exercises (1–20)

1 A periodic function $f(t)$ is defined by

$$f(t) = \begin{cases} t^2 & (0 \leqslant t < \pi) \\ 0 & (\pi < t \leqslant 2\pi) \end{cases}$$

$$f(t + 2\pi) = f(t)$$

Obtain a Fourier series expansion of $f(t)$ and deduce that

$$\tfrac{1}{6}\pi^2 = \sum_{r=1}^{\infty} \frac{1}{r^2}$$

2 Determine the full-range Fourier series expansion of the even function $f(t)$ of period 2π defined by

$$f(t) = \begin{cases} \tfrac{2}{3}t & (0 \leqslant t \leqslant \tfrac{1}{3}\pi) \\ \tfrac{1}{3}(\pi - t) & (\tfrac{1}{3}\pi \leqslant t \leqslant \pi) \end{cases}$$

To what value does the series converge at $t = \tfrac{1}{3}\pi$?

3 A function $f(t)$ is defined for $0 \leqslant t \leqslant \tfrac{1}{2}T$ by

$$f(t) = \begin{cases} t & (0 \leqslant t \leqslant \tfrac{1}{4}T) \\ \tfrac{1}{2}T - t & (\tfrac{1}{4}T \leqslant t \leqslant \tfrac{1}{2}T) \end{cases}$$

Sketch odd and even functions that have a period T and are equal to $f(t)$ for $0 \leqslant t \leqslant \tfrac{1}{2}T$.

(a) Find the half-range Fourier sine series of $f(t)$.

(b) To what value will the series converge for $t = -\tfrac{1}{4}T$?

(c) What is the sum of the following series?

$$S = \sum_{r=1}^{\infty} \frac{1}{(2r-1)^2}$$

4 Prove that if $g(x)$ is an odd function and $f(x)$ an even function of x, the product $g(x)[c + f(x)]$ is an odd function if c is a constant.

A periodic function with period 2π is defined by

$$F(\theta) = \tfrac{1}{12}\theta(\pi^2 - \theta^2)$$

in the interval $-\pi \leqslant \theta \leqslant \pi$. Show that the Fourier series representation of the function is

$$F(\theta) = \sum_{n=1}^{\infty} \frac{(-1)^{n+1}}{n^3} \sin n\theta$$

5 A repeating waveform of period 2π is described by

$$f(t) = \begin{cases} \pi + t & (-\pi \leqslant t \leqslant -\tfrac{1}{2}\pi) \\ -t & (-\tfrac{1}{2}\pi \leqslant t \leqslant \tfrac{1}{2}\pi) \\ t - \pi & (\tfrac{1}{2}\pi \leqslant t \leqslant \pi) \end{cases}$$

Sketch the waveform over the range $t = -2\pi$ to $t = 2\pi$ and find the Fourier series representation of $f(t)$, making use of any properties of the waveform that you can identify before any integration is performed.

6 A function $f(x)$ is defined in the interval $-1 \leqslant x \leqslant 1$ by

$$f(x) = \begin{cases} 1/2\varepsilon & (-\varepsilon < x < \varepsilon) \\ 0 & (1 \leqslant x < -\varepsilon; \; \varepsilon < x \leqslant 1) \end{cases}$$

Sketch a graph of $f(x)$ and show that a Fourier series expansion of $f(x)$ valid in the interval $-1 \leqslant x \leqslant 1$ is given by

$$f(x) = \tfrac{1}{2} + \sum_{n=1}^{\infty} \frac{\sin n\pi\varepsilon}{n\pi\varepsilon} \cos n\pi x$$

7 Show that the half-range Fourier sine series for the function

$$f(t) = \left(1 - \frac{t}{\pi}\right)^2 \quad (0 \leqslant t \leqslant \pi)$$

is

$$f(t) = \sum_{n=1}^{\infty} \frac{2}{n\pi} \left\{ 1 - \frac{2}{n^2\pi^2}[1 - (-1)^n] \right\} \sin nt$$

8 Find a half-range Fourier sine and Fourier cosine series for $f(x)$ valid in the interval $0 < x < \pi$ when $f(x)$ is defined by

$$f(x) = \begin{cases} x & (0 \leqslant x \leqslant \tfrac{1}{2}\pi) \\ \pi - x & (\tfrac{1}{2}\pi \leqslant x \leqslant \pi) \end{cases}$$

Sketch the graph of the Fourier series obtained for $-2\pi < x \leqslant 2\pi$.

9 A function $f(x)$ is periodic of period 2π and is defined by $f(x) = e^x \, (-\pi < x < \pi)$. Sketch the graph of $f(x)$ from $x = -2\pi$ to $x = 2\pi$ and prove that

$$f(x) = \frac{2\sinh\pi}{\pi} \left[\tfrac{1}{2} + \sum_{n=1}^{\infty} \frac{(-1)^n}{1+n^2}(\cos nx - n\sin nx) \right]$$

10 A function $f(t)$ is defined on $0 < t < \pi$ by

$$f(t) = \pi - t$$

Find

(a) a half-range Fourier sine series, and

(b) a half-range Fourier cosine series

for $f(t)$ valid for $0 < t < \pi$.
   Sketch the graphs of the functions represented by each series for $-2\pi < t < 2\pi$.

11 Show that the Fourier series

$$\tfrac{1}{2}\pi - \frac{4}{\pi}\sum_{n=1}^{\infty}\frac{\cos(2n-1)t}{(2n-1)^2}$$

represents the function $f(t)$, of period 2π, given by

$$f(t) = \begin{cases} t & (0 \leqslant t \leqslant \pi) \\ -t & (-\pi \leqslant t \leqslant 0) \end{cases}$$

Deduce that, apart from a transient component (that is, a complementary function that dies away as $t \to \infty$), the differential equation

$$\frac{dx}{dt} + x = f(t)$$

has the solution

$$x = \tfrac{1}{2}\pi - \frac{4}{\pi}\sum_{n=1}^{\infty}\frac{\cos(2n-1)t + (2n-1)\sin(2n-1)t}{(2n-1)^2[1+(2n-1)^2]}$$

12 Show that if $f(t)$ is a periodic function of period 2π and

$$f(t) = \begin{cases} t/T & (0 < t < \pi) \\ (2\pi - t)/\pi & (\pi < t < 2\pi) \end{cases}$$

then

$$f(t) = \tfrac{1}{2} - \frac{4}{\pi^2}\sum_{n=1}^{\infty}\frac{\cos(2n+1)t}{(2n+1)^2}$$

Show also that, when ω is not an integer,

$$y = \frac{1}{2\omega^2}(1 - \cos\omega t)$$

$$- \frac{4}{\pi^2}\sum_{n=1}^{\infty}\frac{\cos(2n+1)t - \cos\omega t}{(2n+1)^2[\omega^2 - (2n+1)^2]}$$

satisfies the differential equation

$$\frac{d^2y}{dt^2} + \omega y = f(t)$$

subject to the initial conditions $y = dy/dt = 0$ at $t = 0$.

13 (a) A periodic function $f(t)$, of period 2π, is defined in $-\pi \leqslant t \leqslant \pi$ by

$$f(t) = \begin{cases} -t & (-\pi \leqslant t \leqslant 0) \\ t & (0 \leqslant t \leqslant \pi) \end{cases}$$

Obtain a Fourier series expansion for $f(t)$, and from it, using Parseval's theorem, deduce that

$$\tfrac{1}{96}\pi^4 = \sum_{n=1}^{\infty}\frac{1}{(2n-1)^4}$$

(b) By formally differentiating the series obtained in (a), obtain the Fourier series expansion of the periodic square wave

$$g(t) = \begin{cases} -1 & (-\pi < t < 0) \\ 0 & (t = 0) \\ 1 & (0 < t < \pi) \end{cases}$$

$$g(t + 2\pi) = g(t)$$

Check the validity of your result by determining directly the Fourier series expansion of $g(t)$.

14 A periodic function $f(t)$, of period 2π, is defined in the range $-\pi < t < \pi$ by

$$f(t) = \sin\tfrac{1}{2}t$$

Show that the complex form of the Fourier series expansion for $f(t)$ is

$$f(t) = \sum_{n=-\infty}^{\infty}\frac{j4n(-1)^n}{\pi(4n^2 - 1)}e^{jnt}$$

15 (a) Find the Fourier series expansion of the voltage $v(t)$ represented by the half-wave rectified sine wave

$$v(t) = \begin{cases} 10\sin(2\pi t/T) & (0 < t < \tfrac{1}{2}T) \\ 0 & (\tfrac{1}{2}T < t < T) \end{cases}$$

$$v(t + T) = v(t)$$

(b) If the voltage $v(t)$ in (a) is applied to a $10\,\Omega$ resistor, what is the total average power delivered to the resistor? What percentage of the total power is carried by the second-harmonic component of the voltage?

16 The periodic waveform $f(t)$ shown in Figure 4.46

Figure 4.46 Waveform $f(t)$ of Review exercise 4.16.

may be written as

$$f(t) = 1 + g(t)$$

where $g(t)$ represents an odd function.

(a) Sketch the graph of $g(t)$.

(b) Obtain the Fourier series expansion for $g(t)$, and hence write down the Fourier series expansion for $f(t)$.

17 Show that the complex Fourier series expansion for the periodic function

$$f(t) = t \quad (0 < t < 2\pi)$$
$$f(t + 2\pi) = f(t)$$

is

$$f(t) = \pi + \sum_{\substack{n=-\infty \\ n \neq 0}}^{\infty} \frac{j e^{jnt}}{n}$$

18 (a) A square-wave voltage $v(t)$ of period T is defined by

$$f(t) = \begin{cases} -1 & (-\tfrac{1}{2}T < t < 0) \\ 1 & (0 < t < \tfrac{1}{2}T) \end{cases}$$

$$v(t + T) = v(t)$$

Show that its Fourier series expansion is given by

$$v(t) = \frac{4}{\pi} \sum_{n=1}^{\infty} \frac{\sin\left[(4n-2)\pi t/T\right]}{2n-1}$$

(b) Find the steady-state response of the circuit shown in Figure 4.47 to the sinusoidal input voltage

$$v_\omega(t) = \sin \omega t$$

and hence write down the Fourier series expansion

of the circuit's steady-state response to the square-wave voltage $v(t)$ in (a).

19 (a) Defining the nth Tchebyshev polynomial by

$$T_n(t) = \cos(n \cos^{-1} t)$$

use Euler's formula $\cos\theta = \tfrac{1}{2}(e^{j\theta} + e^{-j\theta})$ to obtain the expansions of t^{2k} and t^{2k+1} in Tchebyshev polynomials, where k is a positive integer.

(b) Establish the recurrence relation

$$T_n(t) = 2t T_{n-1}(t) - T_{n-2}(t)$$

(c) Write down the values of $T_0(t)$ and $T_1(t)$ from the definition, and then use (b) to find $T_2(t)$ and $T_3(t)$.

(d) Express $t^5 - 5t^4 + 7t^3 + 6t - 8$ in Tchebyshev polynomials.

(e) Find the cubic polynomial that approximates to

$$t^5 - 5t^4 + 7t^3 + 6t - 8$$

over the interval $(-1, 1)$ with the smallest maximum error. Give an upper bound for this error. Is there a value of t for which this upper bound is attained?

20 The relationship between the input and output of a relay with a dead zone Δ and no hysteresis is shown in Figure 4.48. Show that the describing function is

$$N(x_i) = \frac{4M}{\pi x_i}\left[1 - \left(\frac{\Delta}{2x_i}\right)^2\right]^{1/2}$$

for an input amplitude x_i.

If this relay is used in the forward path of the

Figure 4.47 Circuit of Review exercise 4.18.

Figure 4.48 Relay with dead zone of Review exercise 4.20.

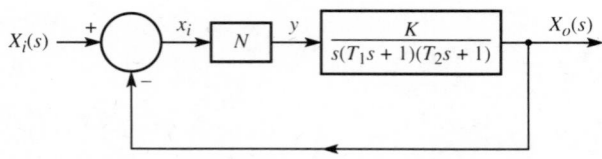

Figure 4.49 Positional control system of Review exercise 4.20.

on–off positional control system shown in Figure 4.49, where the transfer function

$$\frac{K}{s(T_1 s + 1)(T_2 s + 1)}$$

characterizes the time constant of the servo-motor, and the inertia and viscous damping of the load, show that a limit-cycle oscillation will not occur provided that the dead zone in the relay is such that

$$\Delta > \frac{4MK}{\pi} \frac{T_1 T_2}{T_1 + T_2}$$

5

The Fourier Transform

CONTENTS

5.1 Introduction

In Chapter 4 we saw how Fourier series provided an ideal framework for analysing the steady-state response of systems to a periodic input signal. In this chapter we extend the ideas of Fourier analysis to deal with non-periodic functions. We do this through the introduction of the Fourier transform. As the theory develops, we shall see how the complex exponential form of the Fourier series representation of a periodic function emerges as a special case of the Fourier transform. Similarities between the transform and the Laplace transform, discussed in Chapter 2, will also be highlighted.

While Fourier transforms first found most application in the solution of partial differential equations, it is probably true to say that today Fourier-transform methods are most heavily used in the analysis of signals and systems. This chapter is therefore developed with such applications in mind, and its main aim is to develop an understanding of the underlying mathematics as a preparation for a specialist study of application areas in various branches of engineering.

Throughout this book we draw attention to the impact of digital computers on engineering and thus on the mathematics required to understand engineering concepts. While much of the early work on signal analysis was implemented using analogue devices, the bulk of modern equipment exploits digital technology. In Chapter 2 we developed the Laplace transform as an aid to the analysis and design of continuous-time systems while in Chapter 3 we introduced the z and $\mathcal{D}$ transforms to assist with the analysis and design of discrete-time systems. In this chapter the frequency-domain analysis introduced in Chapter 2 for continuous-time systems is consolidated and then extended to provide a framework for the frequency-domain description of discrete-time systems through the introduction of discrete Fourier transforms. These discrete transforms provide one of the most advanced methods for discrete signal analysis, and are widely used in such fields as communications theory and speech and image processing. In practice, the computational aspects of the work assume great importance, and the use of appropriate computational algorithms for the calculation of the discrete Fourier transform is essential. For this reason we have included an introduction to the fast Fourier transform algorithm, based on the pioneering work of J. W. Cooley and J. W. Tukey published in 1965, which it is hoped will serve the reader with the necessary understanding for progression to the understanding of specialist engineering applications.

5.2   The Fourier transform

5.2.1   The Fourier integral

In Chapter 4 we saw how Fourier series methods provided a technique for the frequency-domain representation of periodic functions. As indicated in Section 4.6.3, in expressing a function as its Fourier series expansion we are decomposing the function into its harmonic or frequency components. Thus a periodic function $f(t)$, of period T', has frequency components at discrete frequencies

$$\omega_n = \frac{2\pi n}{T'} = n\omega_0 \quad (n = 0, 1, 2, 3, \ldots)$$

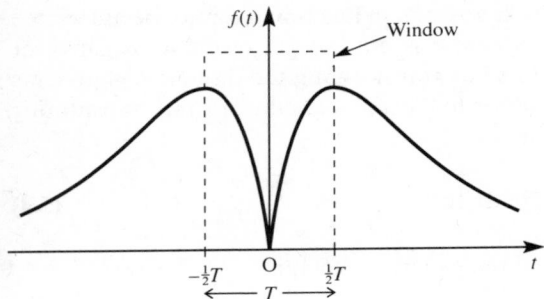

Figure 5.1 The view of $f(t)$ through a window of length T.

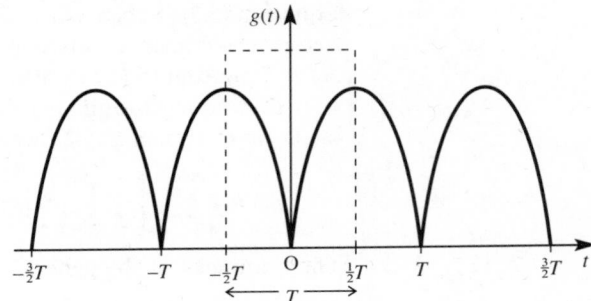

Figure 5.2 The periodic function $g(t)$ based on the 'windowed' view of $f(t)$.

where ω_0 is the fundamental frequency, that is, the frequency of the parent function $f(t)$. Consequently we were able to interpret a Fourier series as constituting a **discrete frequency spectrum** of the periodic function $f(t)$, thus providing an alternative frequency-domain representation of the function to its time-domain waveform. However, not all functions are periodic and so we need to develop an approach that will give a similar representation for non-periodic functions, defined on $-\infty < t < \infty$. One way of achieving this is to look at a portion of a non-periodic function $f(t)$ over an interval T, by imagining that we are looking at a graph of $f(t)$ through a 'window' of length T, and then to consider what happens as T gets larger.

Figure 5.1 depicts this situation, with the window placed symmetrically about the origin. We could now concentrate only on the 'view through the window' and carry out a Fourier series development based on that portion of $f(t)$ alone. Whatever the behaviour of $f(t)$ outside the window, the Fourier series thus generated would represent the periodic function defined by

$$g(t) = \begin{cases} f(t) & (|t| < \tfrac{1}{2}T) \\ f(t - nT) & (\tfrac{1}{2}(2n - 1)T < |t| < \tfrac{1}{2}(2n + 1)T) \end{cases}$$

Figure 5.2 illustrates $g(t)$, and we can see that the graphs of $f(t)$ and $g(t)$ agree on the interval $(-\tfrac{1}{2}T, \tfrac{1}{2}T)$. Note that this approach corresponds to the one adopted in Section 4.3 to obtain the Fourier series expansion of functions defined over a finite interval.

Using the complex or exponential form of the Fourier series expansion, we have from (4.57) and (4.61) that

$$g(t) = \sum_{n=-\infty}^{\infty} G_n e^{jn\omega_0 t} \tag{5.1}$$

with

$$G_n = \frac{1}{T} \int_{-T/2}^{T/2} g(t) e^{-jn\omega_0 t} \, dt \tag{5.2}$$

and where

$$\omega_0 = 2\pi/T \tag{5.3}$$

Equation (5.2) in effect *transforms* the time-domain function $g(t)$ into the associated frequency-domain components G_n, where n is any integer (positive, negative or zero). Equation (5.1) can also be viewed as transforming the discrete components G_n in the frequency-domain representation to the time-domain form $g(t)$. Substituting for G_n in (5.1), using (5.2), we obtain

$$g(t) = \sum_{n=-\infty}^{\infty} \left[\frac{1}{T} \int_{-T/2}^{T/2} g(\tau) e^{-jn\omega_0 \tau} \, d\tau \right] e^{jn\omega_0 t} \tag{5.4}$$

The frequency of the general term in the expansion (5.4) is

$$\frac{2\pi n}{T} = n\omega_0 = \omega_n$$

and so the difference in frequency between successive terms is

$$\frac{2\pi}{T}[(n+1) - n] = \frac{2\pi}{T} = \Delta\omega$$

Since $\Delta\omega = \omega_0$, we can express (5.4) as

$$g(t) = \sum_{n=\infty}^{\infty} \left[\frac{1}{2\pi} \int_{-T/2}^{T/2} g(\tau) e^{-j\omega_n \tau} \, d\tau \right] e^{j\omega_n t} \Delta\omega \tag{5.5}$$

Defining $G(j\omega)$ as

$$G(j\omega) = \int_{-T/2}^{T/2} g(\tau) e^{-j\omega_n \tau} \, d\tau \tag{5.6}$$

we have

$$g(t) = \frac{1}{2\pi} \sum_{n=-\infty}^{\infty} e^{j\omega_n t} G(j\omega_n) \Delta\omega \tag{5.7}$$

As $T \to \infty$, our window widens, so that $g(t) = f(t)$ everywhere and $\Delta\omega \to 0$. Since we also have

$$\lim_{\Delta\omega \to 0} \frac{1}{2\pi} \sum_{n=-\infty}^{\infty} e^{j\omega_n t} G(j\omega_n) \Delta\omega = \frac{1}{2\pi} \int_{-\infty}^{\infty} e^{j\omega t} G(j\omega) \, d\omega$$

it follows from (5.7) and (5.6) that

$$f(t) = \int_{-\infty}^{\infty} \left[\frac{1}{2\pi} e^{j\omega t} \int_{-\infty}^{\infty} f(\tau) e^{-j\omega \tau} \, d\tau \right] d\omega \tag{5.8}$$

The result (5.8) is known as the **Fourier integral representation** of $f(t)$. A set of conditions that are sufficient for the existence of the Fourier integral is a revised form of Dirichlet's conditions for Fourier series, contained in Theorem 4.2. These conditions may be stated in the form of Theorem 5.1.

THEOREM 5.1   Dirichlet's conditions for the Fourier integral

If the function $f(t)$ is such that

(a) it is absolutely integrable, so that

$$\int_{-\infty}^{\infty} |f(t)| \, dt < \infty$$

(that is, the integral is finite), and

(b) it has at most a finite number of maxima and minima and a finite number of discontinuities in any finite interval

then the Fourier integral representation of $f(t)$, given in (5.8), converges to $f(t)$ at all points where $f(t)$ is continuous and to the average of the right- and left-hand limits of $f(t)$ where $f(t)$ is discontinuous (that is, to the mean of the discontinuity).   □

As was indicated in Section 4.2.8 for Fourier series, the use of the equality sign in (5.8) must be interpreted carefully because of the non-convergence to $f(t)$ at points of discontinuity. Again the symbol $\sim$ (read as 'behaves as' or 'represented by') rather than $=$ is frequently used.

The absolute integrable condition (a) of Theorem 5.1 implies that the absolute area under the graph of $y = f(t)$ is finite. Clearly this is so if $f(t)$ decays sufficiently fast with time. However, in general the condition seems to imply a very tight constraint on the nature of $f(t)$, since clearly functions of the form $f(t) = $ constant, $f(t) = e^{at}$, $f(t) = e^{-at}$, $f(t) = \sin \omega t$, and so on, defined for $-\infty < t < \infty$, do not meet the requirement. In practice, however, signals are usually causal and do not last for ever (that is, they only exist for a finite time). Also, in practice no signal amplitude goes to infinity, so consequently no **practical signal** $f(t)$ can have an infinite area under its graph $y = f(t)$. Thus for practical signals the integral in (5.8) exists.

To obtain the trigonometric (or real) form of the Fourier integral, we substitute

$$e^{-j\omega(\tau - t)} = \cos \omega(\tau - t) - j \sin \omega(\tau - t)$$

in (5.8) to give

$$f(t) = \frac{1}{2\pi} \int_{-\infty}^{\infty} \int_{-\infty}^{\infty} f(\tau)[\cos \omega(\tau - t) - j \sin \omega(\tau - t)] \, d\tau \, d\omega$$

Since $\sin \omega(\tau - t)$ is an odd function of ω, this reduces to

$$f(t) = \frac{1}{2\pi} \int_{-\infty}^{\infty} \int_{-\infty}^{\infty} f(\tau) \cos \omega(\tau - t) \, d\tau \, d\omega$$

which, on noting that the integrand is an even function of ω, reduces further to

$$f(t) = \frac{1}{\pi} \int_{0}^{\infty} d\omega \int_{-\infty}^{\infty} f(\tau) \cos \omega(\tau - t) \, d\tau \tag{5.9}$$

The representation (5.9) is then the required trigonometric form of the Fourier integral.

If $f(t)$ is either an odd function or an even function then further simplifications of (5.9) are possible. Detailed calculations are left as an exercise for the reader, and we shall simply quote the results.

(a) If $f(t)$ is an even function then (5.9) reduces to

$$f(t) = \frac{2}{\pi} \int_0^\infty \int_0^\infty f(\tau) \cos \omega \tau \cos \omega t \, d\tau \, d\omega \qquad (5.10)$$

which is referred to as the **Fourier cosine integral**.

(b) If $f(t)$ is an odd function then (5.9) reduces to

$$f(t) = \frac{2}{\pi} \int_0^\infty \int_0^\infty f(\tau) \sin \omega \tau \sin \omega t \, d\tau \, d\omega \qquad (5.11)$$

which is referred to as the **Fourier sine integral**.

In the case of the Fourier series representation of a periodic function it was a matter of some interest to determine how well the first few terms of the expansion represented the function. The corresponding problem in the non-periodic case is to investigate how well the Fourier integral represents a function when only the components in the lower part of the (continuous) frequency range are taken into account. To illustrate, consider the rectangular pulse of Figure 5.3 given by

$$f(t) = \begin{cases} 1 & (|t| \leqslant 1) \\ 0 & (|t| > 1) \end{cases}$$

Figure 5.3
Rectangular pulse
$$f(t) = \begin{cases} 1 & (|t| \leqslant 1) \\ 0 & (|t| > 1) \end{cases}.$$

This is clearly an even function, so from (5.10) its Fourier integral is

$$f(t) = \frac{2}{\pi} \int_0^\infty \int_0^1 1 \cos \omega \tau \cos \omega t \, d\tau \, d\omega$$

$$= \frac{2}{\pi} \int_0^\infty \frac{\cos \omega t \sin \omega}{\omega} \, d\omega$$

An elementary evaluation of this integral is not possible, so we consider frequencies $\omega < \omega_0$, when

$$f(t) \simeq \frac{2}{\pi} \int_0^{\omega_0} \frac{\cos \omega t \sin \omega}{\omega} \, d\omega$$

$$= \frac{1}{\pi} \int_0^{\omega_0} \frac{\sin \omega(t + 1)}{\omega} \, d\omega - \frac{1}{\pi} \int_0^{\omega_0} \frac{\sin \omega(t - 1)}{\omega} \, d\omega$$

$$= \frac{1}{\pi} \int_0^{\omega_0(t + 1)} \frac{\sin u}{u} \, du - \frac{1}{\pi} \int_0^{\omega_0(t - 1)} \frac{\sin u}{u} \, du$$

The integral

$$\mathrm{Si}\,(x) = \int_0^x \frac{\sin u}{u} \, du \quad (x \geqslant 0)$$

occurs frequently, and it can be shown that

$$\mathrm{Si}\,(x) = \sum_{n=0}^\infty \frac{(-1)^n x^{2n+1}}{(2n + 1)(2n + 1)!}$$

Figure 5.4 Plot of (5.12): (a) $\omega_0 = 4$; (b) $\omega_0 = 8$; (c) $\omega_0 = 16$.

Its values have been tabulated (see for example L. Rade and B. Westergren, *Beta Mathematics Handbook*, Chartwell-Bratt Ltd, 1990). Thus

$$f(t) \simeq \mathrm{Si}(\omega_0(t + 1)) - \mathrm{Si}(\omega_0(t - 1)) \tag{5.12}$$

This has been plotted for $\omega_0 = 4$, 8 and 16, and the responses are shown in Figures 5.4(a), (b) and (c) respectively. Physically, these responses describe the output of an ideal low-pass filter, cutting out all frequencies $\omega > \omega_0$, when the input signal is the rectangular pulse of Figure 5.3. The reader will no doubt note the similarities with the Fourier series discussion of Section 4.2.8 and the continuing existence of the Gibbs phenomenon.

5.2.2   The Fourier transform pair

We note from (5.6) and (5.7) that the Fourier integral (5.8) may be written in the form of the pair of equations

$$F(j\omega) = \int_{-\infty}^{\infty} f(t)\,e^{-j\omega t}\,dt \tag{5.13}$$

$$f(t) = \frac{1}{2\pi} \int_{-\infty}^{\infty} F(j\omega)\,e^{j\omega t}\,d\omega \tag{5.14}$$

$F(j\omega)$ as defined by (5.13) is called the **Fourier transform** of $f(t)$, and it provides a frequency-domain representation of the non-periodic function $f(t)$, whenever the integral in (5.13) exists. Note that we have used the notation $F(j\omega)$ for the Fourier transform of $f(t)$ rather than the alternative $F(\omega)$, which is also in common use. The reason for this choice is a consequence of the relationship between the Fourier and Laplace transforms, which will emerge later in Section 5.4.1. We stress that this is a *choice* that we have made, but the reader should have no difficulty in using either form, provided that once the choice has been made it is then adhered to. Equation (5.14) then provides us with a way of reconstructing $f(t)$ if we know its Fourier transform $F(j\omega)$.

A word of caution is in order here regarding the scaling factor $1/2\pi$ in (5.14). Although the convention that we have adopted here is fairly standard, some authors associate the factor $1/2\pi$ with (5.13) rather than (5.14), while others associate a factor of $(2\pi)^{-1/2}$ with each of (5.13) and (5.14). In all cases the pair combine to give the Fourier integral (5.8). We could overcome this possible confusion by measuring the frequency in cycles per second or hertz rather than in radians per second, this being achieved using the substitution $f = 2\pi/\omega$, where f is in hertz and ω is in radians per second. We have not adopted this approach, since ω is so widely used by engineers.

In line with our notation for Laplace transforms in Chapter 2, we introduce the symbol $\mathscr{F}$ to denote the Fourier transform operator. Then from (5.13) the Fourier transform $\mathscr{F}\{f(t)\}$ of a function $f(t)$ is defined by

$$\mathscr{F}\{f(t)\} = F(j\omega) = \int_{-\infty}^{\infty} f(t)\,e^{-j\omega t}\,dt \tag{5.15}$$

whenever the integral exists. Similarly, using (5.14), we define the inverse Fourier transform of $G(j\omega)$ as

$$\mathscr{F}^{-1}\{G(j\omega)\} = g(t) = \frac{1}{2\pi} \int_{-\infty}^{\infty} G(j\omega)\,e^{j\omega t}\,d\omega \tag{5.16}$$

whenever the integral exists. The relations (5.15) and (5.16) together constitute the **Fourier transform pair**, and they provide a pathway between the time- and frequency-domain representations of a function. Equation (5.15) expresses $f(t)$ in the frequency domain, and is analogous to resolving it into harmonic components with a continuously varying frequency ω. This contrasts with a Fourier series representation of a periodic function, where the resolved frequencies take discrete values.

The conditions for the existence of the Fourier transform $F(j\omega)$ of the function $f(t)$ are Dirichlet's conditions (Theorem 5.1). Corresponding trigonometric forms of the Fourier transform pair may be readily written down from (5.9), (5.10) and (5.11).

EXAMPLE 5.1   Does the function

$$f(t) = 1 \quad (-\infty < t < \infty)$$

have a Fourier transform representation?

Solution   Since the area under the curve of $y = f(t)$ $(-\infty < t < \infty)$ is infinite, it follows that $\int_{-\infty}^{\infty} |f(t)|\, dt$ is unbounded, so by Theorem 5.1 a Fourier transform representation does not exist. We can confirm this directly from the definition (5.15). We have

$$\int_{-\infty}^{\infty} 1\,e^{-j\omega t}\, dt = \lim_{\alpha \to \infty} \int_{-\alpha}^{\alpha} e^{-j\omega t}\, dt$$

$$= \lim_{\alpha \to \infty} \left[-\frac{1}{j\omega}(e^{-j\omega\alpha} - e^{j\omega\alpha}) \right]$$

$$= \lim_{\alpha \to \infty} \frac{2\sin\omega\alpha}{\omega}$$

Since this last limit does not exist, we conclude that $f(t) = 1$ $(-\infty < t < \infty)$ does not have a Fourier transform representation.

It is clear, using integration by parts, that $f(t) = t$ $(-\infty < t < \infty)$ does not have a Fourier transform, nor indeed does $f(t) = t^n$ $(n > 1$, an integer; $-\infty < t < \infty)$.

While neither e^{at} nor e^{-at} $(a > 0)$ has a Fourier transform, when we consider the causal signal $f(t) = H(t)e^{-at}$ $(a > 0)$, we do at last obtain a transform.

EXAMPLE 5.2   Find the Fourier transform of the one-sided exponential function

$$f(t) = H(t)e^{-at} \quad (a > 0)$$

where $f(t)$ is the Heaviside unit step function.

Solution   The graph of $f(t)$ is shown in Figure 5.5, and since $f(t) \to 0$ as $t \to \infty$, it is clear that the area under the graph is bounded. Hence, by Theorem 5.1, a Fourier

Figure 5.5 The 'one-sided' exponential function $f(t) = H(t)e^{-at}$ $(a > 0)$.

transform exists. Using the definition (5.15), we have

$$\mathscr{F}\{f(t)\} = \int_{-\infty}^{\infty} H(t)\,e^{-at}\,e^{-j\omega t}\,dt \quad (a > 0)$$

$$= \int_{0}^{\infty} e^{-(a+j\omega)t}\,dt$$

$$= \left[-\frac{e^{-(a+j\omega)t}}{a + j\omega} \right]_{0}^{\infty}$$

so that

$$\mathscr{F}\{H(t)\,e^{-at}\} = \frac{1}{a + j\omega} \tag{5.17}$$

EXAMPLE 5.3   Calculate the Fourier transform of the rectangular pulse

$$f(t) = \begin{cases} A & (|t| \leqslant T) \\ 0 & (|t| > T) \end{cases}$$

Solution   The graph of $f(t)$ is shown in Figure 5.6, and since the area under it is finite, a Fourier transform exists. From the definition (5.15), we have

$$\mathscr{F}\{f(t)\} = \int_{-T}^{T} A\,e^{-j\omega t}\,dt = \left[-\frac{A}{j\omega}e^{-j\omega t} \right]_{-T}^{T}$$

$$= \frac{2A}{\omega}\sin\omega T = 2AT\,\text{sinc}\,\omega T$$

where $\text{sinc}\,x$ is defined, as in Example 4.22, by

$$\text{sinc}\,x = \begin{cases} \dfrac{\sin x}{x} & (x \neq 0) \\ 1 & (x = 0) \end{cases}$$

Figure 5.6 The
rectangular pulse

$$f(t) = \begin{cases} A & (|t| \leqslant T) \\ 0 & (|t| > T) \end{cases}.$$

By direct use of the definition (5.15), we can, as in Examples 5.2 and 5.3, determine the Fourier transforms of some standard functions. A brief table of transforms in given in Figure 5.7.

$f(t)$	$\mathscr{F}\{f(t)\} = \displaystyle\int_{-\infty}^{\infty} f(t)\,\mathrm{e}^{-\mathrm{j}\omega t}\,\mathrm{d}t$
$\mathrm{e}^{-at}H(t) \quad (a > 0)$	$\dfrac{1}{a + \mathrm{j}\omega}$
$t\,\mathrm{e}^{-at}H(t) \quad (a > 0)$	$\dfrac{1}{(a + \mathrm{j}\omega)^2}$
$\begin{cases} A & (\lvert t \rvert \leqslant T) \\ 0 & (\lvert t \rvert > T) \end{cases}$	$2AT\,\mathrm{sinc}\,\omega T$
$\mathrm{e}^{-a\lvert t \rvert} \quad (a > 0)$	$\dfrac{2a}{a^2 + \omega^2}$

Figure 5.7 A brief table of Fourier transforms.

5.2.3 The continuous Fourier spectra

From Figure 5.7, it is clear that Fourier transforms are generally complex-valued functions of the real frequency variable ω. If $\mathscr{F}\{f(t)\} = F(\mathrm{j}\omega)$ is the Fourier transform of the signal $f(t)$ then $F(\mathrm{j}\omega)$ is also known as the **(complex) frequency spectrum** of $f(t)$. Writing $F(\mathrm{j}\omega)$ in the exponential form

$$F(\mathrm{j}\omega) = \lvert F(\mathrm{j}\omega) \rvert\, \mathrm{e}^{\mathrm{j}\arg F(\mathrm{j}\omega)}$$

plots of $\lvert F(\mathrm{j}\omega) \rvert$ and $\arg F(\mathrm{j}\omega)$, which are both real-valued functions of ω, are called the amplitude and phase spectra respectively of the signal $f(t)$. These two spectra represent the **frequency-domain portrait** of the signal $f(t)$. In contrast to the situation when $f(t)$ was periodic, where (as shown in Section 4.6.3) the amplitude and phase spectra were defined only at discrete values of ω, we now see that both spectra are defined for all values of the continuous variable ω.

EXAMPLE 5.4   Determine the amplitude and phase spectra of the causal signal

$$f(t) = \mathrm{e}^{-at}H(t) \quad (a > 0)$$

and plot their graphs.

Solution   From (5.17),

$$\mathscr{F}\{f(t)\} = F(\mathrm{j}\omega) = \frac{1}{a + \mathrm{j}\omega} \quad = \frac{a}{a^2 + \omega^2} - \mathrm{j}\,\frac{\omega}{a^2 + \omega^2}$$

Thus the amplitude and argument of $F(\mathrm{j}\omega)$ are

$$\lvert F(\mathrm{j}\omega) \rvert = \frac{1}{\sqrt{(a^2 + \omega^2)}} \tag{5.18}$$

$$\arg F(j\omega) = \tan^{-1}(1) - \tan^{-1}\left(\frac{\omega}{a}\right)$$

$$= -\tan^{-1}\left(\frac{\omega}{a}\right) \tag{5.19}$$

These are the amplitude and phase spectra of $f(t)$, and are plotted in Figure 5.8.

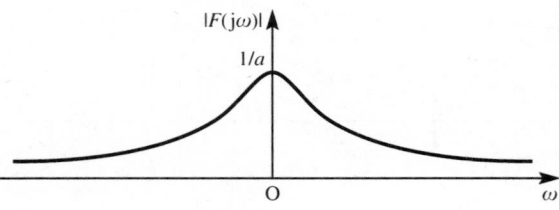

Figure 5.8 Amplitude and phase spectra of the one-sided exponential function $f(t) = e^{-at}H(t)$ $(a > 0)$.

Generally, as we have observed, the Fourier transform and thus the frequency spectrum are complex-valued quantities. In some cases, as for instance in Example 5.3, the spectrum is purely real. In Example 5.3 we found that the transform of the pulse illustrated in Figure 5.6 was

$$F(j\omega) = 2AT \operatorname{sinc} \omega T$$

where

$$\operatorname{sinc} \omega T = \begin{cases} \dfrac{\sin \omega T}{\omega T} & (\omega \neq 0) \\ 1 & (\omega = 0) \end{cases}$$

is an even function of ω, taking both positive and negative values. In this case the amplitude and phase spectra are given by

$$|F(j\omega)| = 2AT|\operatorname{sinc} \omega T| \tag{5.20}$$

$$\arg F(j\omega) = \begin{cases} 0 & (\operatorname{sinc} \omega T \geqslant 0) \\ \pi & (\operatorname{sinc} \omega T < 0) \end{cases} \tag{5.21}$$

with corresponding graphs shown in Figure 5.9.

Figure 5.9 (a) Amplitude and (b) spectra of the pulse

$$f(t) = \begin{cases} A & (|t| \leqslant T) \\ 0 & (|t| > T) \end{cases}$$

In fact, when the Fourier transform is a purely real-valued function, we can plot all the information on a single frequency spectrum of $F(j\omega)$ versus ω. For the rectangular pulse of Figure 5.6 the resulting graph is shown in Figure 5.10.

From Figure 5.7, we can see that the Fourier transforms discussed so far have two properties in common. First, the amplitude spectra are even functions of the frequency variable ω. This is always the case when the time signal $f(t)$ is real, that is, loosely speaking, a consequence of the fact that we have decomposed, or analysed $f(t)$, relative to complex exponentials rather than real-valued sines and cosines. The second point to note is that all the amplitude spectra decrease rapidly as ω increases. This means that most of the information concerning the 'shape' of the signal $f(t)$ is contained in a fairly small interval of the frequency axis around $\omega = 0$.

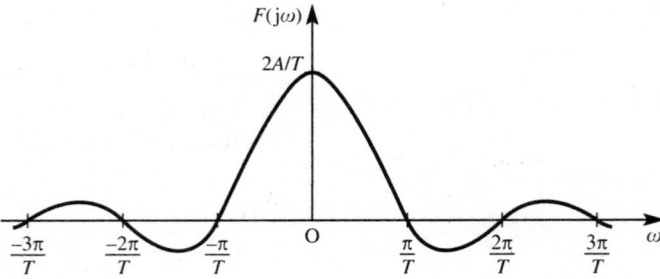

Figure 5.10 Frequency spectrum (real-valued) of the pulse

$$f(t) = \begin{cases} A & (|t| \leqslant T) \\ 0 & (|t| > T) \end{cases}$$

From another point of view, we see that a device capable of passing signals of frequencies up to about $\omega = 3\pi/T$ would pass a reasonably accurate version of the rectangular pulse of Example 5.3.

5.2.4 Exercises

1 Calculate the Fourier transform of the two-sided exponential pulse given by

$$f(t) = \begin{cases} e^{at} & (t \leqslant 0) \\ e^{-at} & (t > 0) \end{cases} \quad (a > 0)$$

2 Determine the Fourier transform of the 'on–off' pulse shown in Figure 5.11.

Figure 5.11 The 'on–off' pulse.

3 A triangular pulse is defined by

$$f(t) = \begin{cases} (A/T)t + A & (-T \leqslant t \leqslant 0) \\ (-A/T)t + A & (0 < t \leqslant T) \end{cases}$$

Sketch $f(t)$ and determine its Fourier transform. What is the relationship between this pulse and that of Exercise 2?

4 Determine the Fourier transforms of

$$f(t) = \begin{cases} 2K & (|t| \leqslant 2) \\ 0 & (|t| > 2) \end{cases}$$

$$g(t) = \begin{cases} K & (|t| \leqslant 1) \\ 0 & (|t| > 1) \end{cases}$$

Sketch the function $h(t) = f(t) - g(t)$ and determine its Fourier transform.

5 Calculate the Fourier transform of the 'off–on–off' pulse $f(t)$ defined by

$$f(t) = \begin{cases} 0 & (t < -2) \\ -1 & (-2 \leqslant t < -1) \\ 1 & (-1 \leqslant t \leqslant 1) \\ -1 & (1 < t \leqslant 2) \\ 0 & (t > 2) \end{cases}$$

6 Show that the Fourier transform of

$$f(t) = \begin{cases} \sin at & (|t| \leqslant \pi/a) \\ 0 & (|t| > \pi/a) \end{cases}$$

is

$$\frac{j2a \sin (\pi\omega/a)}{\omega^2 - a^2}$$

7 Calculate the Fourier transform of

$$f(t) = e^{-at} \sin \omega_0 t \, H(t)$$

8 Based on (5.10) and (5.11), define the **Fourier sine transform** as

$$F_s(x) = \int_0^\infty f(t) \sin xt \, dt$$

and the **Fourier cosine transform** as

$$F_c(x) = \int_0^\infty f(t) \cos xt \, dt$$

Show that

$$f(t) = \begin{cases} 0 & (t < 0) \\ \cos at & (0 \leqslant t \leqslant a) \\ 0 & (t > a) \end{cases}$$

has Fourier cosine transform

$$\frac{1}{2} \left[\frac{\sin (1 + x)a}{1 + x} + \frac{\sin (1 - x)a}{1 - x} \right]$$

9 Show that the Fourier sine and cosine transforms of

$$f(t) = \begin{cases} 0 & (t < 0) \\ 1 & (0 \leqslant t \leqslant a) \\ 0 & (t > a) \end{cases}$$

are

$$\frac{1 - \cos xa}{x}, \qquad \frac{\sin xa}{x}$$

respectively.

10 Find the sine and cosine transforms of $f(t) = e^{-at} H(t)$ $(a > 0)$.

5.3   Properties of the Fourier transform

In this section we establish some of the properties of the Fourier transform that allow its use as a practical tool in system analysis and design.

5.3.1   The linearity property

Linearity is a fundamental property of the Fourier transform, and may be stated as follows.

> If $f(t)$ and $g(t)$ are functions having Fourier transforms $F(j\omega)$ and $G(j\omega)$ respectively, and if α and β are constants then
>
> $$\mathscr{F}\{\alpha f(t) + \beta g(t)\} = \alpha \mathscr{F}\{f(t)\} + \beta \mathscr{F}\{g(t)\} = \alpha F(j\omega) + \beta G(j\omega) \qquad \textbf{(5.22)}$$

As a consequence of this, we say that the Fourier transform operator $\mathscr{F}$ is a **linear operator**. The proof of this property follows readily from the definition (5.15), since

$$\mathscr{F}\{\alpha f(t) + \beta g(t)\} = \int_{-\infty}^{\infty} [\alpha f(t) + \beta g(t)] e^{-j\omega t}\, dt$$

$$= \alpha \int_{-\infty}^{\infty} f(t) e^{-j\omega t}\, dt + \beta \int_{-\infty}^{\infty} g(t) e^{-j\omega t}\, dt$$

$$= \alpha F(j\omega) + \beta G(j\omega)$$

Clearly the linearity property also applies to the inverse transform operator $\mathscr{F}^{-1}$.

5.3.2   Time-differentiation property

If the function $f(t)$ has a Fourier transform $F(j\omega)$ then, by (5.16),

$$f(t) = \frac{1}{2\pi} \int_{-\infty}^{\infty} F(j\omega) e^{j\omega t}\, d\omega$$

Differentiating with respect to t gives

$$\frac{df}{dt} = \frac{1}{2\pi} \int_{-\infty}^{\infty} \frac{\partial}{\partial t} [F(j\omega) e^{j\omega t}]\, d\omega = \frac{1}{2\pi} \int_{-\infty}^{\infty} (j\omega) F(j\omega) e^{j\omega t}\, d\omega$$

implying that the time signal df/dt is the inverse Fourier transform of $(j\omega) F(j\omega)$.

In other words

$$\mathscr{F}\left\{\frac{df}{dt}\right\} = (j\omega)F(j\omega)$$

Repeating the argument n times, it follows that

$$\mathscr{F}\left\{\frac{d^n f}{dt^n}\right\} = (j\omega)^n F(j\omega) \tag{5.23}$$

The result (5.23) is referred to as the **time-differentiation property**, and may be used to obtain frequency-domain representations of differential equations.

EXAMPLE 5.5   Show that if the time signals $y(t)$ and $u(t)$ have Fourier transforms $Y(j\omega)$ and $U(j\omega)$ respectively, and if

$$\frac{d^2 y(t)}{dt^2} + 3\frac{dy(t)}{dt} + 7y(t) = 3\frac{du(t)}{dt} + 2u(t) \tag{5.24}$$

then $Y(j\omega) = G(j\omega)U(j\omega)$ for some function $G(j\omega)$.

Solution   Taking Fourier transforms throughout in (5.24), we have

$$\mathscr{F}\left\{\frac{d^2 y(t)}{dt^2} + 3\frac{dy(t)}{dt} + 7y(t)\right\} = \mathscr{F}\left\{3\frac{du(t)}{dt} + 2u(t)\right\}$$

which, on using the linearity property (5.22), reduces to

$$\mathscr{F}\left\{\frac{d^2 y(t)}{dt^2}\right\} + 3\mathscr{F}\left\{\frac{dy(t)}{dt}\right\} + 7\mathscr{F}\{y(t)\} = 3\mathscr{F}\left\{\frac{du(t)}{dt}\right\} + 2\mathscr{F}\{u(t)\}$$

Then, from (5.23),

$$(j\omega)^2 Y(j\omega) + 3(j\omega)Y(j\omega) + 7Y(j\omega) = 3(j\omega)U(j\omega) + 2U(j\omega)$$

that is,

$$(-\omega^2 + j3\omega + 7)Y(j\omega) = (j3\omega + 2)U(j\omega)$$

giving

$$Y(j\omega) = G(j\omega)U(j\omega)$$

where

$$G(j\omega) = \frac{2 + j3\omega}{7 - \omega^2 + j3\omega}$$

The reader may at this stage be fearing that we are about to propose yet *another* method for solving differential equations. This is not the idea! Rather, we shall show that the Fourier transform provides an essential tool for the analysis (and synthesis) of linear systems from the viewpoint of the frequency domain.

5.3.3   Time-shift property

If a function $f(t)$ has Fourier transform $F(j\omega)$ then what is the Fourier transform of the shifted version of $f(\tau)$, defined by $g(t) = f(t - \tau)$? From the definition (5.15),

$$\mathscr{F}\{g(t)\} = \int_{-\infty}^{\infty} g(t)\,e^{-j\omega t}\,dt = \int_{-\infty}^{\infty} f(t - \tau)\,e^{-j\omega t}\,dt$$

Making the substitution $x = t - \tau$, we have

$$\mathscr{F}\{g(t)\} = \int_{-\infty}^{\infty} f(x)\,e^{-j\omega(x+\tau)}\,dx$$

$$= e^{-j\omega\tau} \int_{-\infty}^{\infty} f(x)\,e^{-j\omega x}\,dx$$

$$= e^{-j\omega\tau} F(j\omega)$$

that is,

$$\mathscr{F}\{f(t - \tau)\} = e^{-j\omega\tau} F(j\omega) \tag{5.25}$$

The result (5.25) is known as the **time-shift property**, and implies that delaying a signal by a time τ causes its Fourier transform to be multiplied by $e^{-j\omega\tau}$.
Since

$$|e^{-j\omega\tau}| = |\cos \omega\tau - j\sin \omega\tau| = |\sqrt{(\cos^2 \omega\tau + \sin^2 \omega\tau)}|$$

$$= 1$$

we have

$$|e^{-j\omega\tau} F(j\omega)| = |F(j\omega)|$$

indicating that the amplitude spectrum of $f(t - \tau)$ is identical with that of $f(t)$. However,

$$\arg\,[e^{j\omega\tau} F(j\omega)] = \arg F(j\omega) - \arg e^{j\omega\tau}$$

$$= \arg F(j\omega) - \omega\tau$$

indicating that each frequency component is shifted by an amount proportional to its frequency ω.

EXAMPLE 5.6   Determine the Fourier transform of the rectangular pulse $f(t)$ shown in Figure 5.12.

Figure 5.12
Rectangular pulse of
Example 5.6.

Solution   This is just the pulse of Example 5.3 (shown in Figure 5.6), delayed by T. The pulse of Example 5.3 had a Fourier transform $2AT \operatorname{sinc} \omega T$, and so, using the shift property (5.25) with $\tau = T$, we have

$$\mathcal{F}\{f(t)\} = F(j\omega) = e^{-j\omega T} 2AT \operatorname{sinc} \omega T$$

$$= 2ATe^{-j\omega T} \operatorname{sinc} \omega T$$

5.3.4   Frequency-shift property

Suppose that a function $f(t)$ has Fourier transform $F(j\omega)$. Then, from the definition (5.15), the Fourier transform of the related function $g(t) = e^{j\omega_0 t} f(t)$ is

$$\mathcal{F}\{g(t)\} = \int_{-\infty}^{\infty} e^{j\omega_0 t} f(t) e^{-j\omega t} \, dt$$

$$= \int_{-\infty}^{\infty} f(t) e^{-j(\omega - \omega_0)t} \, dt$$

$$= \int_{-\infty}^{\infty} f(t) e^{-j\tilde{\omega} t} \, dt, \qquad \text{where } \tilde{\omega} = \omega - \omega_0$$

$$= F(j\tilde{\omega}), \qquad \text{by definition}$$

Thus

$$\mathcal{F}\{e^{j\omega_0 t} f(t)\} = F(j(\omega - \omega_0)) \tag{5.26}$$

The result (5.26) is known as the **frequency-shift property**, and indicates that multiplication by $e^{j\omega_0 t}$ simply shifts the spectrum of $f(t)$ so that it is centred on the point $\omega = \omega_0$ in the frequency domain. This phenomena is the mathematical foundation for the process of **modulation** in communication theory, illustrated in Example 5.7.

EXAMPLE 5.7   Determine the frequency spectrum of the signal $g(t) = f(t) \cos \omega_c t$.

Solution   Since $\cos \omega_c t = \frac{1}{2}(e^{j\omega_c t} + e^{-j\omega_c t})$, it follows, using the linearity property (5.22), that

$$\mathcal{F}\{g(t)\} = \mathcal{F}\{\tfrac{1}{2}f(t)(e^{j\omega_c t} + e^{-j\omega_c t})\}$$

$$= \tfrac{1}{2}\mathcal{F}\{f(t) e^{j\omega_c t}\} + \tfrac{1}{2}\mathcal{F}\{f(t) e^{-j\omega_c t}\}$$

If $\mathcal{F}\{f(t)\} = F(j\omega)$ then, using (5.26),

$$\mathcal{F}\{f(t) \cos \omega_c t\} = \mathcal{F}\{g(t)\}$$

$$= \tfrac{1}{2}F(j(\omega - \omega_c)) + \tfrac{1}{2}F(j(\omega + \omega_c))$$

The effect of multiplying the signal $f(t)$ by the **carrier signal** $\cos \omega_c t$ is thus to produce a signal whose spectrum consists of two (scaled) versions of $F(j\omega)$, the spectrum of $f(t)$; one centred on $\omega = \omega_c$ and the other on $\omega = -\omega_c$. The carrier signal $\cos \omega_c t$ is said to be modulated by the signal $f(t)$.

5.3.5 The symmetry property

From the definition of the transform pair (5.15) and (5.16) it is apparent that there is some symmetry of structure in relation to the variables t and ω. We can establish the exact form of this symmetry as follows. From (5.16),

$$f(t) = \frac{1}{2\pi} \int_{-\infty}^{\infty} F(j\omega) e^{j\omega t} d\omega$$

or, equivalently, by changing the 'dummy' variable in the integration,

$$2\pi f(t) = \int_{-\infty}^{\infty} F(jy) e^{jyt} dy$$

so that

$$2\pi f(-t) = \int_{-\infty}^{\infty} F(jy) e^{-jyt} dy$$

or, on replacing t by ω,

$$2\pi f(-\omega) = \int_{-\infty}^{\infty} F(jy) e^{-jy\omega} dy \qquad \textbf{(5.27)}$$

The right-hand side of (5.27) is simply the definition (5.15) of the Fourier transform of $F(jt)$, with the integration variable t replaced by y. We therefore conclude that

$$\mathscr{F}\{F(jt)\} = 2\pi f(-\omega) \qquad \textbf{(5.28a)}$$

given that

$$\mathscr{F}\{f(t)\} = F(j\omega) \qquad \textbf{(5.28b)}$$

What (5.28) tells us is that if $f(t)$ and $F(j\omega)$ form a Fourier transform pair then $F(jt)$ and $2\pi f(-\omega)$ also form a Fourier transform pair. This property is referred to as the **symmetry property of Fourier transforms**. It is also sometimes referred to as the **duality property**.

EXAMPLE 5.8 Determine the Fourier transform of the signal

$$g(t) = C \operatorname{sinc} at = \begin{cases} \dfrac{C \sin at}{at} & (t \neq 0) \\ C & (t = 0) \end{cases} \qquad \textbf{(5.29)}$$

Solution From Example 5.3, we know that if

$$f(t) = \begin{cases} A & (|t| \leqslant T) \\ 0 & (|t| > T) \end{cases} \tag{5.30}$$

then

$$\mathcal{F}\{f(t)\} = F(j\omega) = 2AT \operatorname{sinc} \omega T$$

Thus, by the symmetry property (5.28), $F(jt)$ and $2\pi f(-\omega)$ are also a Fourier transform pair. In this case

$$F(jt) = 2AT \operatorname{sinc} tT$$

and so, choosing $T = a$ and $A = C/2a$ to correspond to (5.29), we see that

$$F(jt) = C \operatorname{sinc} at = g(t)$$

has Fourier transform $2\pi f(-\omega)$. Rewriting (5.30), we find that, since $|\omega| = |-\omega|$,

$$\mathcal{F}\{C \operatorname{sinc} at\} = \begin{cases} 2\pi C/2a & (|\omega| \leqslant a) \\ 0 & (|\omega| > a) \end{cases}$$

$$= \begin{cases} \pi C/a & (|\omega| \leqslant a) \\ 0 & (|\omega| > a) \end{cases}$$

A graph of $g(t)$ and its Fourier transform $G(j\omega) = 2\pi f(-\omega)$ is shown in Figure 5.13.

Figure 5.13 The Fourier transform pair $g(t)$ and $G(j\omega)$ of Example 5.8.

5.3.6 Exercises

11 Use the linearity property to verify the result in Exercise 4.

12 If $y(t)$ and $u(t)$ are signals with Fourier transforms $Y(j\omega)$ and $U(j\omega)$ respectively, and

$$\frac{d^2y(t)}{dt^2} + 3\frac{dy(t)}{dt} + y(t) = u(t)$$

show that $Y(j\omega) = H(j\omega)U(j\omega)$ for some function $H(j\omega)$. What is $H(j\omega)$?

13 Use the time-shift property to calculate the Fourier transform of the double pulse defined by

$$f(t) = \begin{cases} 1 & (1 \leqslant |t| \leqslant 2) \\ 0 & (\text{otherwise}) \end{cases}$$

14 Calculate the Fourier transform of the windowed cosine function

$$f(t) = \cos \omega_0 t \left[H(t + \tfrac{1}{2}T) - H(t - \tfrac{1}{2}T)\right]$$

15 Find the Fourier transform of the shifted form of the windowed cosine function

$$g(t) = \cos \omega_0 t \left[H(t) - H(t - T)\right]$$

16 Calculate the Fourier transform of the windowed sine function

$$f(t) = \sin 2t \left[H(t + 1) - H(t - 1)\right]$$

5.4 The frequency response

In this section we first consider the relationship between the Fourier and Laplace transforms, and then proceed to consider the frequency response in terms of the Fourier transform.

5.4.1 Relationship between Fourier and Laplace transforms

The differences between the Fourier and Laplace transforms are quite subtle. At first glance it appears that to obtain the Fourier transform from the Laplace transform we merely write $j\omega$ for s, and that the difference ends there. This is true in some cases, but not in all. Strictly, the Fourier and Laplace transforms are distinct, and neither is a generalization of the other.

Writing down the defining integrals, we have

The Fourier transform

$$\mathscr{F}\{f(t)\} = \int_{-\infty}^{\infty} f(t)e^{-j\omega t}\,dt \tag{5.31}$$

The bilateral Laplace transform

$$\mathscr{L}_B\{f(t)\} = \int_{-\infty}^{\infty} f(t)e^{-st}\,dt \tag{5.32}$$

The unilateral Laplace transform

$$\mathscr{L}\{f(t)\} = \int_{0_-}^{\infty} f(t)e^{-st}\,dt \tag{5.33}$$

There is an obvious structural similarity between (5.31) and (5.32), while the connection with (5.33) is not so clear in view of the lower limit of integration. In the Laplace transform definitions recall that s is a complex variable, and may be written as

$$s = \sigma + j\omega \tag{5.34}$$

where σ and ω are real variables. We can then interpret (5.31), the Fourier transform of $f(t)$, as a special case of (5.32), when $\sigma = 0$, provided that the Laplace transform exists when $\sigma = 0$, or equivalently when $s = j\omega$ (that is, s describes the imaginary axis in the s plane). If we restrict our attention to causal functions, that is, functions (or signals) that are zero whenever $t < 0$, the bilateral Laplace transform (5.32) is identical with the unilateral Laplace transform (5.33). The Fourier transform can thus be regarded as a special case of the unilateral Laplace transform for causal functions, provided again that the unilateral Laplace transform exists on the imaginary axis $s = j\omega$.

The next part of the story is concerned with a class of time signals $f(t)$ whose Laplace transforms do exist on the imaginary axis $s = j\omega$. Recall from (2.71) that a causal linear time-invariant system with Laplace transfer function $G(s)$ has an impulse response $h(t)$ given by

$$h(t) = \mathscr{L}^{-1}\{G(s)\} = g(t)H(t), \quad \text{say} \tag{5.35}$$

Furthermore, if the system is stable then all the poles of $G(s)$ are in the left half-plane, implying that $g(t)H(t) \rightarrow 0$ as $t \rightarrow \infty$. Let the pole locations of $G(s)$ be

$$p_1, p_2, \ldots, p_n$$

where

$$p_k = -a_k^2 + jb_k$$

in which a_k, b_k are real and $a_k \neq 0$ for $k = 1, 2, \ldots, n$. Examples of such poles are illustrated in Figure 5.14, where we have assumed that $G(s)$ is the transfer function of a real system so that poles that do not lie on the real axis occur in conjugate pairs. As indicated in Section 2.2.3, the Laplace transfer function $G(s)$ will exist in the shaded region of Figure 5.14 defined by

$$\text{Re}(s) \geqslant -c^2$$

Figure 5.14 Pole locations for $G(s)$ and the region of existence of $G(s)$.

where $-c^2$ is the abscissa of convergence and is such that

$$0 < c^2 < \min_k a_k^2$$

The important conclusion is that for such systems $G(s)$ always exists on the imaginary axis $s = j\omega$, and so $h(t) = g(t)H(t)$ always has a Fourier transform. In other words, we have demonstrated that the impulse response function $h(t)$ of a *stable causal*, linear time-invariant system always has a Fourier transform. Moreover, we have shown that this can be found by evaluating the Laplace transform on the imaginary axis, that is, by putting $s = j\omega$ in the Laplace transform. We have thus established that Fourier transforms exist for a significant class of useful signals; this knowledge will be used in Section 5.4.2.

EXAMPLE 5.9   Which of the following causal time-invariant systems have impulse responses that possess Fourier transforms? Find the latter when they exist.

(a) $\dfrac{d^2 y(t)}{dt^2} + 3\dfrac{dy(t)}{dt} + 2y(t) = u(t)$

(b) $\dfrac{d^2 y(t)}{dt^2} + \omega^2 y(t) = u(t)$

(c) $\dfrac{d^2 y(t)}{dt^2} + \dfrac{dy(t)}{dt} + y(t) = 2u(t) + \dfrac{du(t)}{dt}$

Solution   Assuming that the systems are initially in a quiescent state when $t < 0$, taking Laplace transforms gives

(a) $Y(s) = \dfrac{1}{s^2 + 3s + 2} U(s) = G_1(s)U(s)$

(b) $Y(s) = \dfrac{1}{s^2 + \omega^2} U(s) = G_2(s)U(s)$

(c) $Y(s) = \dfrac{s + 2}{s^2 + s + 1} U(s) = G_3(s)U(s)$

In case (a) the poles of $G_1(s)$ are at $s = -1$ and $s = -2$, so the system is stable and the impulse response has a Fourier transform given by

$$G_1(j\omega) = \left.\frac{1}{s^2 + 3s + 2}\right|_{s=j\omega} = \frac{1}{2 - \omega^2 + j3\omega}$$

$$= \frac{2 - \omega^2 - j3\omega}{(2 - \omega^2)^2 + 9\omega^2} = \frac{(2 - \omega^2) - j3\omega}{\omega^4 + 5\omega^2 + 4}$$

In case (b) we find that the poles of $G_2(s)$ are at $s = j\omega$ and $s = -j\omega$, that is, on the imaginary axis. The system is not stable (notice that the impulse response does not decay to zero), and the impulse response does not possess a Fourier transform.

In case (c) the poles of $G_3(s)$ are at $s = -\frac{1}{2} + j\frac{1}{2}\sqrt{3}$ and $s = -\frac{1}{2} - j\frac{1}{2}\sqrt{3}$. Since these are in the left half-plane, $\text{Re}(s) < 0$, we conclude that the system is stable. The Fourier transform of the impulse response is then

$$G_3(j\omega) = \frac{2 + j\omega}{1 - \omega^2 + j\omega}$$

5.4.2 The frequency response

For a linear time-invariant system, initially in a quiescent state, having a Laplace transfer function $G(s)$, the response $y(t)$ to an input $u(t)$ is given in (2.66) as

$$Y(s) = G(s)U(s) \tag{5.36}$$

where $Y(s)$ and $U(s)$ are the Laplace transforms of $y(t)$ and $u(t)$ respectively. In Section 2.7 we saw that, subject to the system being stable, the steady-state response $y_{ss}(t)$ to a sinusoidal input $u(t) = A \sin \omega t$ is given by (2.86) as

$$y_{ss}(t) = A|G(j\omega)| \sin [\omega t + \arg G(j\omega)] \tag{5.37}$$

That is, the steady-state response is also sinusoidal, with the same frequency as the input signal but having an amplitude gain $|G(j\omega)|$ and a phase shift $\arg G(j\omega)$.

More generally, we could have taken the input to be the complex sinusoidal signal

$$u(t) = A\,e^{j\omega t}$$

and, subject to the stability requirement, showed that the steady-state response is

$$y_{ss}(t) = AG(j\omega)\,e^{j\omega t} \tag{5.38}$$

or

$$y_{ss}(t) = A|G(j\omega)|\,e^{j[\omega t + \arg G(j\omega)]} \tag{5.39}$$

As before, $|G(j\omega)|$ and $\arg G(j\omega)$ are called the amplitude gain and phase shift respectively. Both are functions of the real frequency variable ω, and their plots versus ω constitute the **system frequency response**, which, as we saw in Section 2.7, characterizes the behaviour of the system. Note that taking imaginary parts throughout in (5.39) leads to the sinusoidal response (5.37).

We note that the steady-state response (5.38) is simply the input signal $A\,e^{j\omega t}$ multiplied by the Fourier transform $G(j\omega)$ of the system's impulse response. Consequently $G(j\omega)$ is called the **frequency transfer function** of the system. Therefore if the system represented in (5.36) is stable, so that $G(j\omega)$ exists as the Fourier transform of its impulse response, and the input $u(t) = \mathscr{L}^{-1}\{U(s)\}$ has a Fourier transform $U(j\omega)$ then we may represent the system in terms of the frequency transfer function as

$$Y(j\omega) = G(j\omega)U(j\omega) \tag{5.40}$$

Equation (5.40) thus determines the Fourier transform of the system output, and can be used to determine the frequency spectrum of the output from that of the input. This means that both the amplitude and phase spectra of the output are available, since

$$|Y(j\omega)| = |G(j\omega)||U(j\omega)| \tag{5.41a}$$

$$\arg Y(j\omega) = \arg G(j\omega) + \arg U(j\omega) \tag{5.41b}$$

We shall now consider an example that will draw together both these and some earlier ideas which serve to illustrate the relevance of this material in the communications industry.

EXAMPLE 5.10   A signal $f(t)$ consists of two components:

(a) a symmetric rectangular pulse of duration 2π (see Example 5.3) and

(b) a second pulse, also of duration 2π (that is a copy of (a)), modulating a signal with carrier frequency $\omega_0 = 3$ (the process of modulation was introduced in Section 5.3.4).

Write down an expression for $f(t)$ and illustrate its amplitude spectrum. Describe the amplitude spectrum of the output signal if $f(t)$ is applied to a stable causal system with a Laplace transfer function

$$G(s) = \frac{1}{s^2 + \sqrt{2}s + 1}$$

Solution   Denoting the pulse of Example 5.3, with $T = \pi$, by $P_\pi(t)$, and noting the use of the term 'carrier signal' in Example 5.7, we have

$$f(t) = P_\pi(t) + (\cos 3t)P_\pi t$$

From Example 5.3,

$$\mathscr{F}\{P_\pi(t)\} = 2\pi \operatorname{sinc} \omega\pi$$

so, using the result of Example 5.7, we have

$$\mathscr{F}\{f(t)\} = F(j\omega) = 2\pi \operatorname{sinc} \omega\pi + \tfrac{1}{2}[2\pi \operatorname{sinc}(\omega - 3)\pi + 2\pi \operatorname{sinc}(\omega + 3)\pi]$$

The corresponding amplitude spectrum obtained by plotting $|F(j\omega)|$ versus ω is illustrated in Figure 5.15.

Since the system with transfer function

$$G(s) = \frac{1}{s^2 + \sqrt{2}s + 1}$$

Figure 5.15 Amplitude spectrum of the signal $P_\pi(t) + (\cos 3t)P_\pi(t)$.

is stable and causal, it has a frequency transfer function

$$G(j\omega) = \frac{1}{1 - \omega^2 + j\sqrt{2}\,\omega}$$

so that its amplitude gain is

$$|G(j\omega)| = \frac{1}{\sqrt{(\omega^4 + 1)}}$$

The amplitude spectrum of the output signal $|Y(j\omega)|$ when the input is $f(t)$ is then obtained from (5.41a) as the product of $|F(j\omega)|$ and $|G(j\omega)|$. Plots of both the amplitude gain spectrum $|G(j\omega)|$ and the output amplitude spectrum $|Y(j\omega)|$ are shown in Figures 5.16(a) and (b) respectively. Note from Figure 5.16(b) that we have a reasonably good copy of the amplitude spectrum of $P_\pi(t)$ (see Figure 5.8a). However, the second element of $f(t)$ has effectively vanished. Our system has 'filtered out' this latter component while 'passing' an almost intact version of the first. Examination of the time-domain response would show that the first

Figure 5.16 (a) Amplitude gain spectrum of the system with $G(s) = 1/(s^2 + \sqrt{2}s + 1)$.   (b) Amplitude spectrum of the output signal $|Y(j\omega)|$ of Example 5.10.

component does in fact experience some 'smoothing', which, roughly speaking, consists of rounding of the sharp edges. The system considered here is a second-order 'low-pass' Butterworth filter (introduced in Section 3.8.1).

5.4.3   Exercises

17 Find the impulse response of systems (a) and (c) of Example 5.9. Calculate the Fourier transform of each using the definition (5.15), and verify the results given in Example 5.9.

18 Use the time-shift property to calculate the Fourier transform of the double rectangular pulse $f(t)$ illustrated in Figure 5.17.

Figure 5.17 The double rectangular pulse of Exercise 18.

19 The system with transfer function

$$G(s) = \frac{1}{s^2 + \sqrt{2}\,s + 1}$$

was discussed in Example 5.10. Make a transformation

$$s \rightarrow \frac{1}{s'}$$

and write down $G(s')$. Examine the frequency response of a system with transfer function $G(s')$ and in particular find the amplitude response when $\omega = 0$ and as $\omega \rightarrow \infty$. How would you describe such a system?

20 Use the symmetry property, and the result of Exercise 1 to calculate the Fourier transform of

$$f(t) = \frac{1}{a^2 + t^2}$$

Sketch $f(t)$ and its transform (which is real).

21 Using the results of Examples 5.3 and 5.7, calculate the Fourier transform of the pulse-modulated signal

$$f(t) = P_T(t) \cos \omega_0 t$$

where

$$P_T(t) = \begin{cases} 1 & (|t| \leqslant T) \\ 0 & (|t| > T) \end{cases}$$

is the pulse of duration $2T$.

5.5   Transforms of the step and impulse functions

In this section we consider the application of Fourier transforms to the concepts of energy, power and convolution. In so doing, we shall introduce the Fourier transform of the Heaviside unit step function $H(t)$ and the impulse function $\delta(t)$.

5.5.1 Energy and power

In Section 4.6.4 we introduced the concept of the power spectrum of a periodic signal and found that it enabled us to deduce useful information relating to the latter. In this section we define two quantities associated with time signals $f(t)$, defined for $-\infty < t < \infty$, namely signal energy and signal power. Not only are these important quantities in themselves, but, as we shall see, they play an important role in characterizing signal types.

The total **energy** associated with the signal $f(t)$ is defined as

$$E = \int_{-\infty}^{\infty} [f(t)]^2 \, dt \tag{5.42}$$

If $f(t)$ has a Fourier transform $F(j\omega)$, so that, from (5.16),

$$f(t) = \frac{1}{2\pi} \int_{-\infty}^{\infty} F(j\omega) \, e^{j\omega t} \, d\omega$$

then (5.42) may be expressed as

$$E = \int_{-\infty}^{\infty} f(t) f(t) \, dt$$

$$= \int_{-\infty}^{\infty} f(t) \left[\frac{1}{2\pi} \int_{-\infty}^{\infty} F(j\omega) \, e^{j\omega t} \, d\omega \right] dt$$

On changing the order of integration, this becomes

$$E = \frac{1}{2\pi} \int_{-\infty}^{\infty} F(j\omega) \left[\int_{-\infty}^{\infty} f(t) \, e^{j\omega t} \, dt \right] d\omega \tag{5.43}$$

From the defining integral (5.15) for $F(j\omega)$, we recognize the part of the integrand within the square brackets as $F(-j\omega)$, which, if $f(t)$ is real, is such that $F(-j\omega) = F^*(j\omega)$, where $F^*(j\omega)$ is the complex conjugate of $F(j\omega)$. Thus (5.43) becomes

$$E = \frac{1}{2\pi} \int_{-\infty}^{\infty} F(j\omega) F^*(j\omega) \, d\omega$$

so that

$$E = \int_{-\infty}^{\infty} [f(t)]^2 \, dt = \frac{1}{2\pi} \int_{-\infty}^{\infty} |F(j\omega)|^2 \, d\omega \tag{5.44}$$

Equation (5.44) relates the total energy of the signal $f(t)$ to the integral over all frequencies of $|F(j\omega)|^2$. For this reason, $|F(j\omega)|^2$ is called the **energy spectral density**, and a plot of $|F(j\omega)|^2$ versus ω is called the **energy spectrum** of the signal $f(t)$. The result (5.44) is called **Parseval's theorem**, and is an extension of the result contained in Theorem 4.6 for periodic signals.

EXAMPLE 5.11   Determine the energy spectral densities of

(a) the one-sided exponential function $f(t) = e^{-at} H(t) \ (a > 0)$,

(b) the rectangular pulse of Figure 5.6.

Solution   (a) From (5.17), the Fourier transform of $f(t)$ is

$$F(j\omega) = \frac{a - j\omega}{a^2 + \omega^2}$$

The energy spectral density of the function is therefore

$$|F(j\omega)|^2 = F(j\omega)F^*(j\omega) = \frac{a - j\omega}{a^2 + \omega^2} \frac{a + j\omega}{a^2 + \omega^2}$$

that is,

$$|F(j\omega)|^2 = \frac{1}{a^2 + \omega^2}$$

(b) From Example 5.3, the Fourier transform $F(j\omega)$ of the rectangular pulse is

$$F(j\omega) = 2AT \operatorname{sinc} \omega T$$

Thus the energy spectral density of the pulse is

$$|F(j\omega)|^2 = 4A^2T^2 \operatorname{sinc}^2 \omega T$$

There are important signals $f(t)$, defined in general for $-\infty < t < \infty$, for which the integral $\int_{-\infty}^{\infty} [f(t)]^2 \, dt$ in (5.42) is either unbounded (that is, it becomes infinite) or does not converge to a finite limit; for example, $\sin t$. For such signals, instead of considering energy, we consider the average power P, frequently referred to as the **power** of the signal. This is defined by

$$P = \lim_{T \to \infty} \frac{1}{T} \int_{-T/2}^{T/2} [f(t)]^2 \, dt \tag{5.45}$$

Note that for signals that satisfy the Dirichlet conditions (Theorem 5.1) the integral in (5.42) exists and, since in (5.45) we divide by the signal duration, it follows that such signals have zero power associated with them.

In order to obtain a frequency-domain representation of (5.45), leading to the concept of a **power density function**, we need to obtain some form of Fourier transform representation of functions $f(t)$ that do not satisfy the Dirichlet conditions.

We begin by considering the Fourier transform of the generalized function $\delta(t)$, the Dirac delta function introduced in Section 2.5.8. Recall from (2.49) that $\delta(t)$ satisfies the sifting property; that is, for a continuous function $g(t)$,

$$\int_a^b g(t)\, \delta(t - c)\, dt = \begin{cases} g(c) & (a < c < b) \\ 0 & \text{otherwise} \end{cases}$$

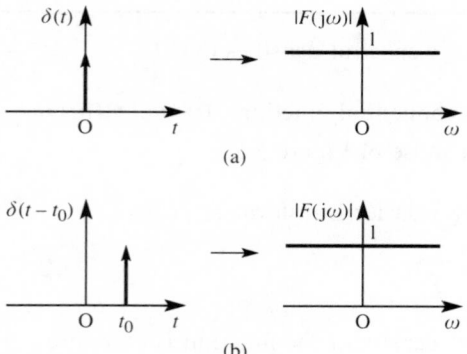

Figure 5.18 (a) $\delta(t)$ and its amplitude spectrum. (b) $\delta(t-t_0)$ and its amplitude spectrum.

Using the defining integral (5.15), we readily obtain the following two Fourier transforms:

$$\mathscr{F}\{\delta(t)\} = \int_{-\infty}^{\infty} \delta(t)\,\mathrm{e}^{-\mathrm{j}\omega t}\,\mathrm{d}t = 1 \tag{5.46}$$

$$\mathscr{F}\{\delta(t - t_0)\} = \int_{-\infty}^{\infty} \delta(t - t_0)\,\mathrm{e}^{-\mathrm{j}\omega t}\,\mathrm{d}t = \mathrm{e}^{-\mathrm{j}\omega t_0} \tag{5.47}$$

These two transforms are, by now, unremarkable, and, noting that $|\mathrm{e}^{-\mathrm{j}\omega t_0}| = 1$, we illustrate the signals and their spectra in Figure 5.18.

We now depart from the definition of the Fourier transform given in (5.15) and seek new transform pairs based on (5.46) and (5.47). Using the symmetry (duality) property of Section 5.3.5, we deduce from (5.46) that

$$1 \quad \text{and} \quad 2\pi\delta(-\omega) = 2\pi\delta(\omega) \tag{5.48}$$

is another Fourier transform pair. Likewise, from (5.47), we deduce that

$$\mathrm{e}^{-\mathrm{j}t_0 t} \quad \text{and} \quad 2\pi\delta(-\omega - t_0)$$

is also a Fourier transform pair. Substituting $t_0 = -\omega_0$ into the latter, we have

$$\mathrm{e}^{\mathrm{j}\omega_0 t} \quad \text{and} \quad 2\pi\delta(\omega_0 - \omega) = 2\pi\delta(\omega - \omega_0) \tag{5.49}$$

as another Fourier transform pair.

We are thus claiming that in (5.48) and (5.49) that $f_1(t) = 1$ and $f_2(t) = \mathrm{e}^{\mathrm{j}\omega_0 t}$, which do not have 'ordinary' Fourier transforms as defined by (5.15), actually *do* have **'generalized' Fourier transforms** given by

$$F_1(\mathrm{j}\omega) = 2\pi\delta(\omega) \tag{5.50}$$

$$F_2(\mathrm{j}\omega) = 2\pi\delta(\omega - \omega_0) \tag{5.51}$$

respectively. The term 'generalized' has been used because the two transforms contain the generalized functions $\delta(\omega)$ and $\delta(\omega - \omega_0)$. Let us now test our conjecture that (5.50) and (5.51) are Fourier transforms of $f_1(t)$ and $f_2(t)$ respectively. If (5.50) and (5.51) really are Fourier transforms then their time-domain images $f_1(t)$ and $f_2(t)$ respectively should reappear via the inverse transform (5.16). Substituting $F_1(j\omega)$ from (5.50) into (5.16), we have

$$\mathscr{F}^{-1}\{F_1(j\omega)\} = \frac{1}{2\pi} \int_{-\infty}^{\infty} F_1(j\omega)\, e^{j\omega t}\, d\omega$$

$$= \frac{1}{2\pi} \int_{-\infty}^{\infty} 2\pi\delta(\omega)\, e^{j\omega t}\, d\omega = 1$$

so $f_1(t) = 1$ is recovered.

Similarly, using (5.51), we have

$$\mathscr{F}^{-1}\{F_2(j\omega)\} = \frac{1}{2\pi} \int_{-\infty}^{\infty} 2\pi\delta(\omega - \omega_0)\, e^{j\omega t}\, d\omega = e^{j\omega_0 t}$$

so that $f_2(t) = e^{j\omega_0 t}$ is also recovered.

Our approach has therefore been successful, and we do indeed have a way of generating new pairs of transforms. We shall therefore use the approach to find generalized Fourier transforms for the signals

$$f_3(t) = \cos\omega_0 t, \qquad f_4(t) = \sin\omega_0 t$$

Since

$$f_3(t) = \cos\omega_0 t = \tfrac{1}{2}(e^{j\omega_0 t} + e^{-j\omega_0 t})$$

the linearity property (5.22) gives

$$\mathscr{F}\{f_3(t)\} = \tfrac{1}{2}\mathscr{F}\{e^{j\omega_0 t}\} + \tfrac{1}{2}\mathscr{F}\{e^{-j\omega_0 t}\}$$

which, on using (5.49), leads to the generalized Fourier transform pair

$$\mathscr{F}\{\cos\omega_0 t\} = \pi[\delta(\omega - \omega_0) + \delta(\omega + \omega_0)] \tag{5.52}$$

Likewise, we deduce the generalized Fourier transform pair

$$\mathscr{F}\{\sin\omega_0 t\} = j\pi[\delta(\omega + \omega_0) - \delta(\omega - \omega_0)] \tag{5.53}$$

The development of (5.53) and the verification that both (5.52) and (5.53) invert correctly using the inverse transform (5.16) is left as an exercise for the reader.

It is worth noting at this stage that defining the Fourier transform $\mathscr{F}\{f(t)\}$ of $f(t)$ in (5.15) as

$$\mathscr{F}\{f(t)\} = \int_{-\infty}^{\infty} f(t)\, e^{-j\omega t}\, dt$$

whenever the integral exists does not preclude the existence of other Fourier transforms, such as the generalized one just introduced, defined by other means.

It is clear that the total energy

$$E = \int_{-\infty}^{\infty} \cos^2\omega_0 t\, dt$$

associated with the signal $f_3(t) = \cos \omega_0 t$ is unbounded. However, from (5.45), we can calculate the power associated with the signal as

$$P = \lim_{T \to \infty} \frac{1}{T} \int_{-T/2}^{T/2} \cos^2 \omega_0 t \, dt$$

$$= \lim_{T \to \infty} \frac{1}{T} \left[t + \frac{1}{2\omega_0} \sin 2 \omega_0 t \right]_{-T/2}^{T/2}$$

$$= \tfrac{1}{2}$$

Thus, while the signal $f_3(t) = \cos \omega_0 t$ has unbounded energy associated with it, its power content is $\tfrac{1}{2}$. Signals whose associated energy is finite, for example $f(t) = e^{-at} H(t)$ $(a > 0)$ are sometimes called **energy signals**, while those whose associated energy is unbounded but whose total power is finite are known as **power signals**. The concepts of power signals and power spectral density are important in the analysis of random signals, which we shall not consider in this text.

EXAMPLE 5.12   Suppose that a periodic function $f(t)$, defined on $-\infty < t < \infty$, may be expanded in a Fourier series having exponential form

$$f(t) = \sum_{n=-\infty}^{\infty} F_n e^{jn\omega_0 t}$$

What is the (generalized) Fourier transform of $f(t)$?

Solution   From the definition,

$$\mathscr{F}\{f(t)\} = \mathscr{F} \left\{ \sum_{n=-\infty}^{\infty} F_n e^{jn\omega_0 t} \right\}$$

$$= \sum_{n=-\infty}^{\infty} F_n \mathscr{F}\{e^{jn\omega_0 t}\}$$

which, on using (5.49), gives

$$\mathscr{F}\{f(t)\} = \sum_{n=-\infty}^{\infty} F_n 2\pi\delta(\omega - n\omega_0)$$

That is,

$$\mathscr{F}\{f(t)\} = 2\pi \sum_{n=-\infty}^{\infty} F_n \delta(\omega - n\omega_0)$$

where F_n $(-\infty < n < \infty)$ are the coefficients of the exponential form of the Fourier series representation of $f(t)$.

EXAMPLE 5.13   Use the result of Example 5.12 to verify the Fourier transform of $f(t) = \cos \omega_0 t$ given in (5.52).

Solution   Since

$$f(t) = \cos \omega_0 t = \tfrac{1}{2} e^{j\omega_0 t} + \tfrac{1}{2} e^{-j\omega_0 t}$$

the F_n of Example 5.12 are

$$F_{-1} = F_1 = \tfrac{1}{2}$$

$$F_n = 0 \quad (n \neq \pm 1)$$

Thus, using the result

$$\mathscr{F}\{f(t)\} = 2\pi \sum_{n=-\infty}^{\infty} F_n \delta(\omega - \omega_0)$$

we have

$$\mathscr{F}\{\cos \omega_0 t\} = 2\pi F_{-1} \delta(\omega + \omega_0) + 2\pi F_1 \delta(\omega - \omega_0)$$

$$= \pi[\delta(\omega + \omega_0) + \delta(\omega - \omega_0)]$$

in agreement with (5.52).

EXAMPLE 5.14   Determine the (generalized) Fourier transform of the periodic 'sawtooth' function, defined by

$$f(t) = \frac{2t}{T} \quad (0 < t < 2T)$$

$$f(t + 2T) = f(t)$$

Solution   In Example 4.19 we saw that the exponential form of the Fourier series representation of $f(t)$ is

$$f(t) = \sum_{n=-\infty}^{\infty} F_n e^{jn\omega_0 t}$$

with

$$\omega_0 = \frac{2\pi}{2T} = \frac{\pi}{T}$$

$$F_0 = 2$$

$$F_n = \frac{j2}{n\pi} \quad (n \neq 0)$$

It follows from Example 5.12 that the Fourier transform $\mathscr{F}\{f(t)\}$ is

$$\mathscr{F}\{f(t)\} = F(j\omega) = 4\pi\delta(\omega) + \sum_{\substack{n=-\infty \\ n \neq 0}}^{\infty} j\frac{4}{n} \delta(\omega - n\omega_0)$$

$$= 4\pi\delta(\omega) + j4 \sum_{\substack{n=-\infty \\ n \neq 0}}^{\infty} \frac{1}{n} \delta\left(\omega - \frac{n\pi}{T}\right)$$

Thus we see that the amplitude spectrum simply consists of pulses located at integer multiples of the fundamental frequency $\omega_0 = \pi/T$. The discrete line spectra obtained via the exponential form of the Fourier series for this periodic function is thus reproduced, now with a scaling factor of 2π.

EXAMPLE 5.15 Determine the (generalized) Fourier transform of the unit impulse train $f(t) = \sum_{n=-\infty}^{\infty} \delta(t - nT)$ shown symbolically in Figure 5.19.

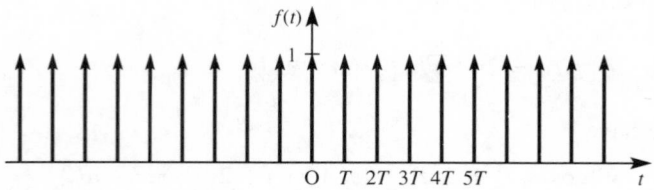

Figure 5.19 Unit impulse train $f(t) = \sum_{n=-\infty}^{\infty} \delta(t - nT)$.

Solution Although $f(t)$ is a generalized function, and not a function in the ordinary sense, it follows that since

$$f(t + kT) = \sum_{n=-\infty}^{\infty} \delta(t + (k - n)T) \quad (k \text{ an integer})$$

$$= \sum_{m=-\infty}^{\infty} \delta(t - mT) \quad (m = n - k)$$

$$= f(t)$$

it is periodic, with period T. Moreover, we can formally expand $f(t)$ as a Fourier series

$$f(t) = \sum_{n=-\infty}^{\infty} F_n e^{jn\omega_0 t} \quad \left(\omega_0 = \frac{2\pi}{T}\right)$$

with

$$F_n = \frac{1}{T} \int_{-T/2}^{T/2} f(t) e^{-jn\omega_0 t}\, dt$$

$$= \frac{1}{T} \int_{-T/2}^{T/2} \delta(t) e^{-jn\omega_0 t}\, dt$$

$$= \frac{1}{T} \quad \text{for all } n$$

It follows from Example 5.12 that

$$\mathscr{F}\{f(t)\} = 2\pi \sum_{n=-\infty}^{\infty} \frac{1}{T} \delta(\omega - n\omega_0)$$

$$= \omega_0 \sum_{n=-\infty}^{\infty} \delta(\omega - n\omega_0)$$

Thus we have shown that

$$\mathscr{F}\left\{\sum_{n=-\infty}^{\infty} \delta(t - nT)\right\} = \omega_0 \sum_{n=-\infty}^{\infty} \delta(\omega - n\omega_0) \qquad (5.54)$$

where $\omega_0 = 2\pi/T$. That is, the time-domain impulse train has another impulse train as its transform. We shall see in Section 5.6.4 that this result is of particular importance in dealing with sampled time signals.

Following our successful hunt for generalized Fourier transforms, we are led to consider the possibility that the Heaviside unit step function $H(t)$ defined in Section 2.5.1 may have a transform in this sense. Recall from (2.56) that if

$$f(t) = H(t)$$

then

$$\frac{\mathrm{d}f(t)}{\mathrm{d}t} = \delta(t)$$

From the time-differentiation property (5.23), we might expect that if

$$\mathscr{F}\{H(t)\} = \bar{H}(\mathrm{j}\omega)$$

then

$$(\mathrm{j}\omega)\bar{H}(\mathrm{j}\omega) = \mathscr{F}\{\delta(t)\} = 1 \qquad (5.55)$$

Equation (5.55) suggests that a candidate for $\bar{H}(\mathrm{j}\omega)$ might be $1/\mathrm{j}\omega$, but this is not the case, since inversion using (5.16) does not give $H(t)$ back. Using (5.16) and complex variable techniques, it can be shown that

$$\mathscr{F}^{-1}\left\{\frac{1}{\mathrm{j}\omega}\right\} = \frac{1}{2\pi} \int_{-\infty}^{\infty} \frac{\mathrm{e}^{\mathrm{j}\omega t}}{\mathrm{j}\omega}\,\mathrm{d}\omega = \begin{cases} \frac{1}{2} & (t > 0) \\ 0 & (t = 0) \\ -\frac{1}{2} & (t < 0) \end{cases}$$

$$= \tfrac{1}{2}\operatorname{sgn}(t)$$

where $\operatorname{sgn}(t)$ is the **signum function**, defined by

$$\operatorname{sgn}(t) = \begin{cases} 1 & (t > 0) \\ 0 & (t = 0) \\ -1 & (t < 0) \end{cases}$$

However, we note that (5.55) is also satisfied by

$$\bar{H}(\mathrm{j}\omega) = \frac{1}{\mathrm{j}\omega} + c\delta(\omega) \qquad (5.56)$$

where c is a constant. This follows from the equivalence property (see Definition

2.2) $f(\omega)\delta(\omega) = f(0)\delta(\omega)$ with $f(\omega) = j\omega$, which gives

$$(j\omega)\bar{H}(j\omega) = 1 + (j\omega)c\delta(\omega) = 1$$

Inverting (5.56) using (5.16), we have

$$g(t) = \mathscr{F}^{-1}\left\{\frac{1}{j\omega} + c\delta(\omega)\right\} = \frac{1}{2\pi}\int_{-\infty}^{\infty}\left[\frac{1}{j\omega} + c\delta(\omega)\right]e^{j\omega t}\,d\omega$$

$$= \begin{cases} c/2\pi + \frac{1}{2} & (t > 0) \\ c/2\pi & (t = 0) \\ c/2\pi - \frac{1}{2} & (t < 0) \end{cases}$$

and, choosing $c = \pi$, we have

$$g(t) = \begin{cases} 1 & (t > 0) \\ \frac{1}{2} & (t = 0) \\ 0 & (t < 0) \end{cases}$$

Thus we have (almost) recovered the step function $H(t)$. Here $g(t)$ takes the value $\frac{1}{2}$ at $t = 0$, but this is not surprising in view of the convergence of the Fourier integral at points of discontinuity as given in Theorem 5.1. With this proviso, we have shown that

$$\bar{H}(j\omega) = \mathscr{F}\{H(t)\} = \frac{1}{j\omega} + \pi\delta(\omega) \tag{5.57}$$

We must confess to having made an informed guess as to what additional term to add in (5.56) to produce the Fourier transform (5.57). We could instead have chosen $c\delta(k\omega)$ with k a constant as an additional term. While it is possible to show that this would not lead to a different result, proving uniqueness is not trivial and is beyond the scope of this book.

5.5.2 Convolution

In Section 2.6.6 we saw that the convolution integral, in conjuction with the Laplace transform, provided a useful tool for *discussing* the nature of the solution of a differential equation, although it was not perhaps the most efficient way of evaluating the solution to a particular problem. As the reader may now have come to expect, in view of the duality between time and frequency domains, there are two convolution results involving the Fourier transform.

Convolution in time

Suppose that

$$\mathscr{F}\{u(t)\} = U(j\omega) = \int_{-\infty}^{\infty} u(t)\,e^{-j\omega t}\,dt$$

$$\mathscr{F}\{v(t)\} = V(j\omega) = \int_{-\infty}^{\infty} v(t)\,e^{-j\omega t}\,dt$$

then the Fourier transform of the convolution

$$y(t) = \int_{-\infty}^{\infty} u(\tau)v(t-\tau)\,d\tau = u(t)*v(t) \tag{5.58}$$

is

$$\mathscr{F}\{y(t)\} = Y(j\omega) = \int_{-\infty}^{\infty} e^{-j\omega t}\left[\int_{-\infty}^{\infty} u(\tau)v(t-\tau)\,d\tau\right]dt$$

$$= \int_{-\infty}^{\infty} u(\tau)\left[\int_{-\infty}^{\infty} e^{-j\omega t}v(t-\tau)\,dt\right]d\tau$$

Introducing the change of variables $z \rightarrow t - \tau$, $\tau \rightarrow \tau$ and following the procedure for change of variable from Section 2.6.6, the transform can be expressed as

$$Y(j\omega) = \int_{-\infty}^{\infty} u(\tau)\left[\int_{-\infty}^{\infty} v(z)\,e^{-j\omega(z+\tau)}\,dz\right]d\tau$$

$$= \int_{-\infty}^{\infty} u(\tau)\,e^{-j\omega\tau}\,d\tau \int_{-\infty}^{\infty} v(z)\,e^{-j\omega z}\,dz$$

so that

$$Y(j\omega) = U(j\omega)V(j\omega) \tag{5.59}$$

That is,

$$\mathscr{F}\{u(t)*v(t)\} = \mathscr{F}\{v(t)*u(t)\} = U(j\omega)V(j\omega) \tag{5.60}$$

indicating that a convolution in the time domain is transformed into a product in the frequency domain.

Convolution in frequency

If

$$\mathscr{F}\{u(t)\} = U(j\omega), \quad \text{with } u(t) = \frac{1}{2\pi}\int_{-\infty}^{\infty} U(j\omega)\,e^{j\omega t}\,d\omega$$

$$\mathscr{F}\{v(t)\} = V(j\omega), \quad \text{with } v(t) = \frac{1}{2\pi}\int_{-\infty}^{\infty} V(j\omega)\,e^{j\omega t}\,d\omega$$

then the inverse transform of the convolution

$$U(j\omega)*V(j\omega) = \int_{-\infty}^{\infty} U(jy)V(j(\omega-y))\,dy$$

is given by

$$\mathscr{F}^{-1}\{U(j\omega) * V(j\omega)\} = \frac{1}{2\pi} \int_{-\infty}^{\infty} e^{j\omega t} \left[\int_{-\infty}^{\infty} U(jy)V(j(\omega - y)) \, dy \right] d\omega$$

$$= \frac{1}{2\pi} \int_{-\infty}^{\infty} U(jy) \left[\int_{-\infty}^{\infty} V(j(\omega - y)) e^{j\omega t} \, d\omega \right] dy$$

A change of variable $z \to \omega - y$, $\omega \to \omega$ leads to

$$\mathscr{F}^{-1}\{U(j\omega) * V(j\omega)\} = \frac{1}{2\pi} \int_{-\infty}^{\infty} U(jy) \left[\int_{-\infty}^{\infty} V(jz) e^{j(z+y)t} \, dz \right] dy$$

$$= \frac{1}{2\pi} \int_{-\infty}^{\infty} U(jy) e^{jyt} \, dy \int_{-\infty}^{\infty} V(jz) e^{jzt} \, dz$$

$$= 2\pi u(t)v(t)$$

That is,

$$\mathscr{F}\{u(t)v(t)\} = \frac{1}{2\pi} U(j\omega) * V(j\omega) \tag{5.61}$$

and thus multiplication in the time domain corresponds to convolution in the frequency domain (subject to the scaling factor $1/(2\pi)$).

EXAMPLE 5.16   Suppose that $f(t)$ has a Fourier transform $F(j\omega)$. Find an expression for the Fourier transform of $g(t)$, where

$$g(t) = \int_{-\infty}^{t} f(\tau) \, d\tau$$

Solution   Since

$$H(t - \tau) = \begin{cases} 1 & (\tau \leqslant t) \\ 0 & (\tau > t) \end{cases}$$

we can write

$$g(t) = \int_{-\infty}^{\infty} f(\tau)H(t - \tau) \, d\tau = f(t) * H(t)$$

the convolution of $g(t)$ and $H(t)$. Then, using (5.60),

$$\mathscr{F}\{g(t)\} = G(j\omega) = F(j\omega)\bar{H}(j\omega)$$

which, on using the expression for $\bar{H}(j\omega)$ from (5.57), gives

$$G(j\omega) = \frac{F(j\omega)}{j\omega} + \pi F(j\omega)\delta(\omega)$$

so that

$$G(j\omega) = \frac{F(j\omega)}{j\omega} + \pi F(0)\delta(\omega) \tag{5.62}$$

5.5.3 Exercises

22 Verify that $\mathscr{F}^{-1}\{\pi[\delta(\omega - \omega_0) + \delta(\omega + \omega_0)]\} = \cos \omega_0 t$.

23 Show that $\mathscr{F}\{\sin \omega_0 t\} = j\pi[\delta(\omega + \omega_0) - \delta(\omega - \omega_0)]$. Use (5.16) to verify that

$$\mathscr{F}^{-1}\{j\pi[\delta(\omega + \omega_0) - \delta(\omega - \omega_0)]\} = \sin \omega_0 t$$

24 Suppose that $f(t)$ and $g(t)$ have Fourier transforms $F(j\omega)$ and $G(j\omega)$ respectively, defined in the 'ordinary' sense (that is, using (5.15)), and show that

$$\int_{-\infty}^{\infty} f(t)G(jt)\,dt = \int_{-\infty}^{\infty} F(jt)g(t)\,dt$$

This result is known as **Parseval's formula**.

25 Use the results of Exercise 24 and the symmetry property to show that

$$\int_{-\infty}^{\infty} f(t)g(t)\,dt = \frac{1}{2\pi}\int_{-\infty}^{\infty} F(j\omega)G(-j\omega)\,d\omega$$

26 Use the convolution result in the frequency domain to obtain $\mathscr{F}\{H(t)\sin \omega_0 t\}$.

27 Calculate the exponential form of the Fourier series for the periodic pulse train shown in Figure 5.20. Hence show that

$$\mathscr{F}\{f(t)\} = \frac{2\pi Ad}{T}\sum_{n=-\infty}^{\infty} \mathrm{sinc}\left(\frac{n\pi d}{T}\right)\delta(\omega - n\omega_0)$$

$(\omega_0 = 2\pi/T)$.

Figure 5.20 Periodic pulse train of Exercise 27.

5.6 The Fourier transform in discrete time

5.6.1 Introduction

The earlier sections of this chapter have discussed the Fourier transform of signals defined as functions of the continuous-time variable t. We have seen that a major area of application is in the analysis of signals in the frequency domain, leading to the concept of the frequency response of a linear system. In Chapter 4 we considered signals defined at discrete-time instants, together with linear systems modelled by difference equations. There we found that in system analysis the z transform plays a role similar to that of the Laplace transform for continuous-time systems. We now attempt to develop a theory of Fourier analysis to complement that for continuous-time systems, and then consider the problem of estimating the continuous-time Fourier transform in a form suitable for computer execution.

5.6.2   A Fourier transform for sequences

First we return to our work on Fourier series and write down the exponential form of the Fourier series representation for the periodic function $F(e^{j\theta})$ of period 2π. Writing $\theta = \omega t$, we infer from (4.57) and (4.61) that

$$F(e^{j\theta}) = \sum_{n=-\infty}^{\infty} f_n e^{jn\theta} \tag{5.63}$$

where

$$f_n = \frac{1}{2\pi} \int_{-\pi}^{\pi} F(e^{j\theta}) e^{-jn\theta} \, d\theta \tag{5.64}$$

Thus the operation has generated a sequence of numbers $\{f_n\}$ from the periodic function $F(e^{j\theta})$ of the continuous variable θ. Let us reverse the process and imagine that we *start* with a sequence $\{g_k\}$ and use (5.63) to *define* a periodic function $\tilde{G}'(e^{j\theta})$ such that

$$\tilde{G}'(e^{j\theta}) = \sum_{n=-\infty}^{\infty} g_n e^{jn\theta} \tag{5.65}$$

We have thus defined a transformation from the sequence $\{g_k\}$ to $\tilde{G}'(e^{j\theta})$. This transformation can be inverted, since, from (5.64),

$$g_k = \frac{1}{2\pi} \int_{-\pi}^{\pi} \tilde{G}'(e^{j\theta}) e^{-jk\theta} \, d\theta \tag{5.66}$$

and we recover the terms of the sequence $\{g_k\}$ from $\tilde{G}'(e^{j\theta})$.

It is convenient for our later work if we modify the definition slightly, defining the Fourier transform of the sequence $\{g_k\}$ as

$$\mathcal{F}\{g_k\} = G(e^{j\theta}) = \sum_{n=-\infty}^{\infty} g_n e^{-jn\theta} \tag{5.67}$$

whenever the series converges. The inverse transform is then given from (5.66), by

$$g_k = \frac{1}{2\pi} \int_{-\pi}^{\pi} G(e^{j\theta}) e^{jk\theta} \, d\theta \tag{5.68}$$

The results (5.67) and (5.68) thus constitute the Fourier transform pair for the sequence $\{g_k\}$. Note that $G(e^{j\theta})$ is a function of the continuous variable θ, and since it is a function of $e^{j\theta}$ it is periodic (with a period of at most 2π), irrespective of whether or not the sequence $\{g_k\}$ is periodic.

Note that we have adopted the notation $G(e^{j\theta})$ rather than $G(\theta)$ for the Fourier transform, similarly to our use of $F(j\omega)$ rather than $F(\omega)$ in the case of continuous-time signals. In the present case we shall be concerned with the relationship with the z transform of Chapter 3, where $z = r e^{j\theta}$, and the significance of our choice will soon emerge.

EXAMPLE 5.17   Find the transform of the sequence $\{g_k\}_{-\infty}^{\infty}$, where $g_0 = 2$, $g_2 = g_{-2} = 1$ and $g_k = g_{-k} = 0$ for $k \neq 1$ or 2.

Solution   From the definition (5.67),

$$\mathscr{F}\{g_k\} = G(e^{j\theta}) = \sum_{n=-\infty}^{\infty} g_n e^{-jn\theta}$$

$$= g_{-2} e^{j2\theta} + g_0 1 + g_2 e^{-j2\theta} = e^{j2\theta} + 2 + e^{-j2\theta}$$

$$= 2(1 + \cos 2\theta) = 4 \cos^2 \theta$$

In this particular case the transform is periodic of period π, rather than 2π. This is because $g_1 = g_{-1} = 0$, so that $\cos\theta$ does not appear in the transform. Since $G(e^{j\theta})$ is purely real, we may plot the transform as in Figure 5.21.

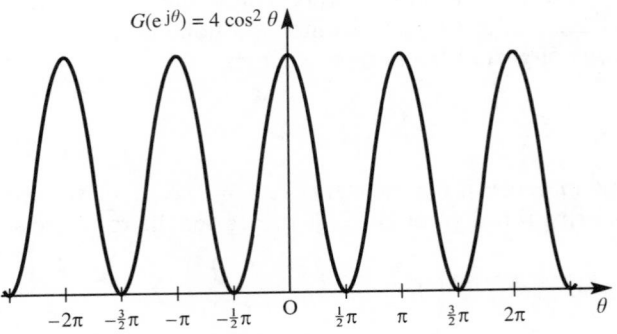

Figure 5.21 Transform of the sequence of Example 5.17.

Having defined a Fourier transform for sequences, we now wish to link it to the frequency response of discrete-time systems. In Section 5.4.2 the link between frequency responses and the Fourier transforms of continuous-time systems was established using the Laplace transform. We suspect therefore that the z transform should yield the necessary link for discrete-time systems. Indeed, the argument follows closely that of Section 5.4.2.

For a causal linear time-invariant discrete-time system with z transfer function $G(z)$ the relationship between the input sequence $\{u_k\}$ and output sequence $\{y_k\}$ in the transform domain is given from Section 3.6.1 by

$$Y(z) = G(z)U(z) \tag{5.69}$$

where $U(z) = \mathscr{Z}\{u_k\}$ and $Y(z) = \mathscr{Z}\{y_k\}$.

To investigate the system frequency response, we seek the output sequence corresponding to an input sequence

$$\{u_k\} = \{A\,e^{j\omega kT}\} = \{A\,e^{jk\theta}\}, \qquad \theta = \omega T \tag{5.70}$$

which represents samples drawn, at equal intervals T, from the continuous-time complex sinusoidal signal $e^{j\omega t}$.

The frequency response of the discrete-time system is then its steady-state response to the sequence $\{u_k\}$ given in (5.70). As for the continuous-time case (Section 5.4.2), the complex form $e^{j\omega t}$ is used in order to simplify the algebra, and the steady-state sinusoidal response is easily recovered by taking imaginary parts, if necessary.

From Figure 3.3, we see that

$$\mathscr{L}\{A\, e^{jk\theta}\} = \mathscr{L}\{A\,(e^{j\theta})^k\} = \frac{Az}{z - e^{j\theta}}$$

so, from (5.69), the response of the system to the input sequence (5.70) is determined by

$$Y(z) = G(z)\frac{Az}{z - e^{j\theta}} \tag{5.71}$$

Taking the system to be of order n, and under the assumption that the n poles p_r $(r = 1, 2, \ldots, n)$ of $G(z)$ are distinct and none is equal to $e^{j\theta}$, we can expand $Y(z)/z$ in terms of partial fractions to give

$$\frac{Y(z)}{z} = \frac{c}{z - e^{j\theta}} + \sum_{r=1}^{n} \frac{c_r}{z - p_r} \tag{5.72}$$

where, in general, the constants c_r $(r = 1, 2, \ldots, n)$ are complex. Taking inverse z transforms throughout in (5.72) then gives the response sequence as

$$\{y_k\} = \mathscr{L}^{-1}\{Y(z)\} = \mathscr{L}^{-1}\left\{\frac{zc}{z - e^{j\theta}}\right\} + \sum_{r=1}^{n} \mathscr{L}^{-1}\left\{\frac{zc_r}{z - p_r}\right\}$$

that is,

$$\{y^k\} = c\{e^{jk\theta}\} + \sum_{r=1}^{n} c_r\{p_r^k\} \tag{5.73}$$

If the transfer function $G(z)$ corresponds to a stable discrete-time system then all its poles p_r $(r = 1, 2, \ldots, n)$ lie within the unit circle $|z| < 1$, so that all the terms under the summation sign in (5.73) tend to zero as $k \to \infty$. This is clearly seen by expressing p_r in the form $p_r = |p_r|e^{j\phi_r}$ and noting that if $|p_r| < 1$ then $|p_r|^k \to 0$ as $k \to \infty$. Consequently, for stable systems the steady-state response corresponding to (5.73) is

$$\{y_{k_{ss}}\} = c\{e^{jk\theta}\}$$

Using the 'cover-up' rule for partial fractions, the constant c is readily determined from (5.71) as

$$c = AG(e^{j\theta})$$

so that the steady-state response becomes

$$\{y_{k_{ss}}\} = AG(e^{j\theta})\{e^{jk\theta}\} \tag{5.74}$$

We have assumed that the poles of $G(z)$ are distinct in order to simplify the algebra. Extending the development to accommodate multiple poles is readily accomplished, leading to the same steady-state response as given in (5.74).

The result (5.74) corresponds to (5.38) for continuous-time systems, and indicates that the steady-state response sequence is simply the input sequence with each term multiplied by $G(e^{j\theta})$. Consequently $G(e^{j\theta})$ is called the **frequency transfer function** of the discrete-time system and, as for the continuous case, it characterizes the system's frequency response. Clearly $G(e^{j\theta})$ is simply $G(z)$, the z transfer function, with $z = e^{j\theta}$, and so we are simply evaluating the z transfer function around the unit circle $|z| = 1$. The z transfer function $G(z)$ will exist on $|z| = 1$ if and only if the system is stable, and thus the result is the exact analogue of the result for continuous-time systems in Section 5.4.2, where the Laplace transfer function was evaluated along the imaginary axis to yield the frequency response of a stable linear continuous-time system.

To complete the analogy with continuous-time systems, we need one further result. From Section 3.6.2, the impulse response of the linear causal discrete-time system with z transfer function $G(z)$ is

$$\{y_{k_\delta}\} = \mathcal{Z}^{-1}\{G(z)\} = \{g_k\}_{k=0}^{\infty}, \qquad \text{say}$$

Taking inverse transforms then gives

$$G(z) = \sum_{k=0}^{\infty} g_k z^{-k} = \sum_{k=-\infty}^{\infty} g_k z^{-k}$$

since $g_k = 0$ $(k < 0)$ for a causal system. Thus

$$G(e^{j\theta}) = \sum_{k=-\infty}^{\infty} g_k e^{-jk\theta}$$

and we conclude from (5.67) that $G(e^{j\theta})$ is simply the Fourier transform of the sequence $\{g_k\}$. Therefore the discrete-time frequency transfer function $G(e^{j\theta})$ is the Fourier transform of the impulse response sequence.

EXAMPLE 5.18   Determine the frequency transfer function of the causal discrete-time system shown in Figure 5.22 and plot its amplitude spectrum.

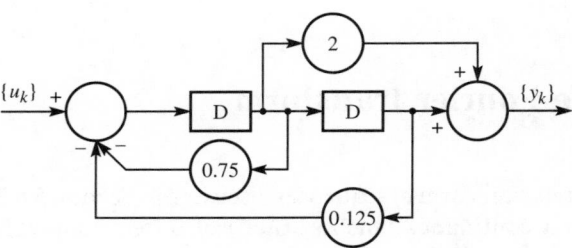

Figure 5.22 Discrete-time system of Example 5.18.

Solution Using the methods of Section 3.6.1, we readily obtain the z transfer function as

$$G(z) = \frac{2z + 1}{z^2 + 0.75z + 0.125}$$

Next we check for system stability. Since $z^2 + 0.75 + 0.125 = (z + 0.5)(z + 0.25)$, the poles of $G(z)$ are at $p_1 = -0.5$ and $p_2 = -0.25$, and since both are inside the unit circle $|z| = 1$, the system is stable. The frequency transfer function may then be obtained as $G(e^{j\theta})$, where

$$G(e^{j\theta}) = \frac{2e^{j\theta} + 1}{e^{j2\theta} + 0.75e^{j\theta} + 0.125}$$

To determine the amplitude spectrum, we evaluate $|G(e^{j\theta})|$ as

$$|G(e^{j\theta})| = \frac{|2e^{j\theta} + 1|}{|e^{j2\theta} + 0.75e^{j\theta} + 0.125|}$$

$$= \frac{\sqrt{(5 + 4\cos\theta)}}{\sqrt{(1.578 + 1.688\cos\theta + 0.25\cos 2\theta)}}$$

A plot of $|G(e^{j\theta})|$ versus θ then leads to the amplitude spectrum of Figure 5.23.

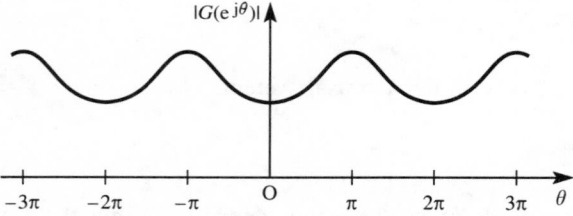

Figure 5.23 Amplitude spectrum of the system of Example 5.18.

In Example 5.18 we note the periodic behaviour of the amplitude spectrum, which is inescapable when discrete-time signals and systems are concerned. Note, however, that the periodicity is in the variable $\theta = \omega T$ and that we may have control over the choice of T, the time between samples of our input signal.

5.6.3 The discrete Fourier transform

The Fourier transform of sequences discussed in Section 5.6.2 transforms a sequence $\{g_k\}$ into a continuous function $G(e^{j\theta})$ of a frequency variable θ, where $\theta = \omega T$ and T is the time between signal samples. In this section, with an eye to computer requirements, we look at the implications of sampling $G(e^{j\theta})$. The overall operation will have commenced with samples of a time signal $\{g_k\}$ and proceeded via a Fourier transformation process, finally producing a sequence $\{G_k\}$ of samples drawn from the frequency-domain image $G(e^{j\theta})$ of $\{g_k\}$.

Suppose that we have a sequence $\{g_k\}$ of N samples drawn from a continuous-time signal $g(t)$, at equal intervals T; that is,

$$\{g_k\} = \{g(kT)\}_{k=0}^{N-1}$$

Using (5.67), the Fourier transform of this sequence is

$$\mathscr{F}\{g_k\} = G(e^{j\theta}) = \sum_{n=-\infty}^{\infty} g_n e^{-jn\theta} \tag{5.75}$$

when $g_k = 0$ ($k \notin [0, N-1]$). Then, with $\theta = \omega T$, we may write (5.75) as

$$G(e^{j\omega T}) = \sum_{n=0}^{N-1} g_n e^{-jn\omega T} \tag{5.76}$$

We now sample this transform $G(e^{j\omega T})$ at intervals $\Delta\omega$ in such a way as to create N samples spread equally over the interval $0 \leqslant \theta \leqslant 2\pi$, that is, over one period of the essentially periodic function $G(e^{j\theta})$. We then have

$$N\,\Delta\theta = 2\pi$$

where $\Delta\theta$ is the normalized frequency spacing. Since $\theta = \omega T$ and T is a constant such that $\Delta\theta = T\,\Delta\omega$, we deduce that

$$\Delta\omega = \frac{2\pi}{NT} \tag{5.77}$$

Sampling (5.76) at intervals $\Delta\omega$ produces the sequence

$$\{G_k\}_{k=0}^{N-1}, \qquad \text{where } G_k = \sum_{n=0}^{N-1} g_n e^{-jnk\,\Delta\omega\,T} \tag{5.78}$$

Since

$$G_{k+N} = \sum_{n=0}^{N-1} g_n e^{-jn(k+N)\,\Delta\omega\,T}$$

$$= \sum_{n=0}^{N-1} g_n e^{-jnk\,\Delta\omega\,T} e^{-jn2\pi}, \qquad \text{using (5.77)}$$

$$= \sum_{n=0}^{N-1} g_n e^{-jnk\,\Delta\omega\,T} = G_k$$

it follows that the sequence $\{G_k\}_{-\infty}^{\infty}$ is periodic, with period N. We have therefore generated a sequence of samples in the frequency domain that in some sense represents the spectrum of the underlying continuous-time signal. We shall postpone the question of the exact nature of this representation for the moment, but as the reader will have guessed, it is crucial to the purpose of this section. First, we consider the question of whether, from knowledge of the sequence $\{G_k\}_{k=0}^{N-1}$ of (5.78), we can recover the original sequence $\{g_n\}_{n=0}^{N-1}$. To see how this can be achieved, consider a sum of the form

$$S_r = \sum_{k=0}^{N-1} G_k e^{-jkr\Delta\omega T} \tag{5.79}$$

Substituting for G_k from (5.78), we have

$$S_r = \sum_{k=0}^{N-1} \left(\sum_{m=0}^{N-1} g_m e^{-jmk\Delta\omega T} \right) e^{-jkr\Delta\omega T}$$

$$= \sum_{k=0}^{N-1} \sum_{m=0}^{N-1} g_m e^{-jk\Delta\omega(m+r)T}$$

That is, on interchanging the order of integration,

$$S_r = \sum_{m=0}^{N-1} g_m \sum_{k=0}^{N-1} e^{-jk\Delta\omega(m+r)T} \tag{5.80}$$

Now

$$\sum_{k=0}^{N-1} e^{-jk\Delta\omega(m+r)T}$$

is a geometric progression with first term $e^0 = 1$ and common ratio $e^{-j\Delta\omega(m+r)T}$, and so the sum to N terms is thus

$$\sum_{k=0}^{N-1} e^{-jk\Delta\omega(m+r)T} = \frac{1 - e^{-j\Delta\omega(m+r)NT}}{1 - e^{-j\Delta\omega(m+r)T}}$$

$$= \frac{1 - e^{-j(m+r)2\pi}}{1 - e^{-j\Delta\omega(m+r)T}}$$

$$= 0 \quad (m \neq -r)$$

When $m = -r$

$$\sum_{k=0}^{N-1} e^{-jk\Delta\omega(m+r)T} = \sum_{k=0}^{N-1} 1 = N$$

Thus

$$\sum_{k=0}^{N-1} e^{-jk\Delta\omega(m+r)T} = N\delta_{m,-r} \tag{5.81}$$

where δ_{ij} is the Kronecker delta defined by

$$\delta_{ij} = \begin{cases} 1 & (i = j) \\ 0 & (i \neq j) \end{cases}$$

Substituting (5.81) into (5.80), we have

$$S_r = N \sum_{m=0}^{N-1} g_m \delta_{m,-r}$$

$$= Ng_{-r}$$

Returning to (5.79) and substituting for S_r, we see that

$$g_{-r} = \frac{1}{N} \sum_{k=0}^{N-1} G_k e^{-jkr\Delta\omega T}$$

which on taking $n = -r$ gives

$$g_n = \frac{1}{N} \sum_{k=0}^{N-1} G_k e^{jkn\Delta\omega T} \tag{5.82}$$

Thus (5.82) allows us to determine the members of the sequence

$$\{g_n\}_{n=0}^{N-1}$$

that is, it enables us to recover the time-domain samples from the frequency-domain samples *exactly*.

The relations

$$G_k = \sum_{n=0}^{N-1} g_n e^{-jnk\Delta\omega T} \tag{5.78}$$

$$g_n = \frac{1}{N} \sum_{k=0}^{N-1} G_k e^{jnk\Delta\omega T} \tag{5.82}$$

with $\Delta\omega = 2\pi/NT$, between the time- and frequency-domain sequences $\{g_n\}_{n=0}^{N-1}$ and $\{G_k\}_{k=0}^{N-1}$ define the **discrete Fourier transform (DFT)** pair. The pair provide pathways between time and frequency domains for discrete-time signals in exactly the same sense that (5.15) and (5.16) defined similar pathways for continuous-time signals. It should be stressed again that, whatever the properties of the sequences $\{g_n\}$ and $\{G_k\}$ on the right-hand sides of (5.78) and (5.82), the sequences generated on the left-hand sides will be periodic, with period N.

EXAMPLE 5.19   The sequence $\{g_k\}_{k=0}^{2} = \{1, 2, 1\}$ is generated by sampling a time signal $g(t)$ at intervals with $T = 1$. Determine the discrete Fourier transform of the sequence, and verify that the sequence can be recovered exactly from its transform.

Solution   From (5.78), the discrete Fourier transform sequence $\{G_k\}_{k=0}^{2}$ is generated by

$$G_k = \sum_{n=0}^{2} g_n e^{-jkn\Delta\omega T} \quad (k = 0, 1, 2)$$

In this case $T = 1$ and, with $N = 3$, (5.77) gives

$$\Delta\omega = \frac{2\pi}{3 \times 1} = \tfrac{2}{3}\pi$$

Thus

$$G_0 = \sum_{n=0}^{2} g_n e^{-jn \times 0 \times 2\pi/3} = \sum_{n=0}^{2} g_n$$

$$= g_0 + g_1 + g_2 = 1 + 2 + 1 = 4$$

$$G_1 = \sum_{n=0}^{2} g_n e^{-jn \times 1 \times 2\pi/3}$$

$$= g_0 e^0 + g_1 e^{-j2\pi/3} + g_2 e^{-j4\pi/3}$$

$$= 1 + 2e^{-j2\pi/3} + 1e^{-j4\pi/3}$$

$$= e^{-j2\pi/3}(e^{j2\pi/3} + 2 + e^{-j2\pi/3})$$

$$= 2e^{-j2\pi/3}(1 + \cos \tfrac{2}{3}\pi) = e^{-j2\pi/3}$$

$$G_2 = \sum_{n=0}^{2} g_n e^{-jn \times 2 \times 2\pi/3} = \sum_{n=0}^{2} g_n e^{-jn4\pi/3}$$

$$= g_0 e^0 + g_1 e^{-j4\pi/3} + g_2 e^{-j8\pi/3}$$

$$= e^{-j4\pi/3}[e^{j4\pi/3} + 2 + e^{-j4\pi/3}]$$

$$= 2e^{-j4\pi/3}(1 + \cos \tfrac{4}{3}\pi) = e^{-j4\pi/3}$$

Thus

$$\{G_k\}_{k=0}^{2} = \{4, e^{-j2\pi/3}, e^{-j4\pi/3}\}$$

We must now show that use of (5.82) will recover the original sequence $\{g_k\}_{k=0}^{2}$. From (5.82), the inverse transform of $\{G_k\}_{k=0}^{2}$ is given by

$$\tilde{g}_n = \frac{1}{N} \sum_{k=0}^{N-1} G_k e^{jkn\Delta\omega T}$$

again with $T = 1$, $\Delta\omega = \tfrac{2}{3}\pi$ and $N = 3$. Thus

$$\tilde{g}_0 = \tfrac{1}{3} \sum_{k=0}^{2} G_k e^{jk \times 0 \times 2\pi/3} = \tfrac{1}{3} \sum_{k=0}^{2} G_k$$

$$= \tfrac{1}{3}(4 + e^{-j2\pi/3} + e^{-j4\pi/3})$$

$$= \tfrac{1}{3}[4 + e^{-j\pi}(e^{j\pi/3} + e^{-j\pi/3})]$$

$$= \tfrac{1}{3}(4 - 2\cos \tfrac{1}{3}\pi) = 1$$

$$\tilde{g}_1 = \tfrac{1}{3} \sum_{k=0}^{2} G_k e^{jk \times 1 \times 2\pi/3}$$

$$= \tfrac{1}{3}(G_0 + G_1 e^{j2\pi/3} + G_2 e^{j4\pi/3})$$

$$= \tfrac{1}{3}(4 + 1 + 1) = 2$$

$$\tilde{g}_2 = \tfrac{1}{3} \sum_{k=0}^{2} G_k e^{jk \times 2 \times 2\pi/3}$$

$$= \tfrac{1}{3}(G_0 + G_1 e^{j4\pi/3} + G_2 e^{j8\pi/3})$$

$$= \tfrac{1}{3}[4 + e^{j\pi}(e^{j\pi/3} + e^{-j\pi/3})]$$

$$= \tfrac{1}{3}(4 - 2\cos \tfrac{1}{3}\pi) = 1$$

That is

$$\{\tilde{g}_n\}_{n=0}^{2} = \{1, 2, 1\} = \{g_k\}_{k=0}^{2}$$

and thus the original sequence has been recovered exactly from its transform.

We see from Example 5.19 that the operation of calculating N terms of the transformed sequence involved $N \times N = N^2$ multiplications and $N(N-1)$ summations, all of which are operations involving complex numbers in general. The computation of the discrete Fourier transform in this direct manner is thus said to be a computation of complexity N^2. Such computations rapidly become impossible as N increases, owing to the time required for this execution.

5.6.4   Estimation of the continuous Fourier transform

We saw in Section 5.4.2 that the continuous Fourier transform provides a means of examining the frequency response of a stable linear time-invariant *continuous*-time system. Similarly, we saw in Section 5.6.2 how a discrete-time Fourier transform could be developed that allows examination of the frequency response of a stable linear time-invariant *discrete*-time system. By sampling this latter transform, we developed the discrete Fourier transform itself. Why did we do this? First we have found a way (at least in theory) of involving the computer in our efforts. Secondly, as we shall now show, we can use the discrete Fourier transform to estimate the continuous Fourier transform of a continuous-time signal. To see how this is done, let us first examine what happens when we sample a continuous-time signal.

Suppose that $f(t)$ is a non-periodic continuous-time signal, a portion of which is shown in Figure 5.24(a). Let us sample the signal at equal intervals T, to generate the sequence

$$\{f(0), f(T), \ldots, f(nT), \ldots\}$$

as shown in Figure 5.24(b). Imagine now that each of these samples is presented in turn, at the appropriate instant, as the input to a continuous linear time-invariant system with impulse response $h(t)$. The output would then be, from Section 2.6.6,

$$y(t) = \int_{-\infty}^{\infty} h(t-\tau) f(0)\delta(\tau) \, d\tau + \int_{-\infty}^{\infty} h(t-\tau) f(T)\delta(\tau - T) \, d\tau$$

$$+ \ldots + \int_{-\infty}^{\infty} h(t-\tau) f(nT)\delta(\tau - nT) \, d\tau + \ldots$$

$$= \int_{-\infty}^{\infty} h(t-\tau) \sum_{k=0}^{\infty} f(kT)\delta(\tau - kT) \, d\tau$$

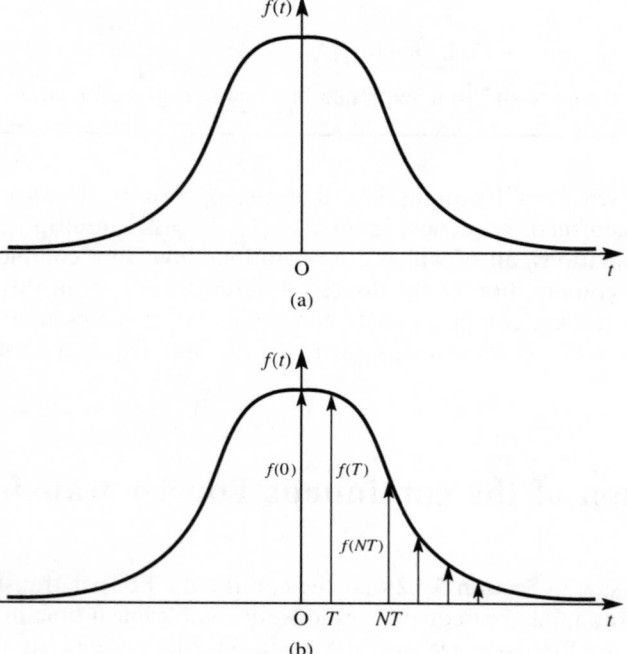

Figure 5.24 (a)
Continuous-time
signal $f(t)$.   (b)
Samples drawn from
$f(t)$.

Thus

$$y(t) = \int_{-\infty}^{\infty} h(t - \tau) f_s(\tau)\, d\tau \qquad (5.83)$$

where

$$f_s(t) = \sum_{k=0}^{\infty} f(kT)\delta(t - kT)$$

$$= f(t) \sum_{k=0}^{\infty} \delta(t - kT) \qquad (5.84)$$

which we identify as a 'continuous-time' representation of the sampled version of $f(t)$. We are thus lead to picture $f_s(t)$ as in Figure 5.25.

Figure 5.25
Visualization of $f_s(t)$
defined in (5.84).

In order to admit the possibility of signals that are non-zero for $t < 0$, we can generalize (5.84) slightly by allowing in general that

$$f_s(t) = f(t) \sum_{k=-\infty}^{\infty} \delta(t - kT) \tag{5.85}$$

We can now use convolution to find the Fourier transform $F_s(j\omega)$ of $f_s(t)$. Using the representation (5.85) for $f_s(t)$, we have

$$F_s(j\omega) = \mathscr{F}\{f_s(t)\} = \mathscr{F}\left\{ f(t) \sum_{k=-\infty}^{\infty} \delta(t - kT) \right\}$$

which, on using (5.61), leads to

$$F_s(j\omega) = \frac{1}{2\pi} F(j\omega) * \mathscr{F}\left\{ \sum_{k=-\infty}^{\infty} \delta(t - kT) \right\} \tag{5.86}$$

where

$$\mathscr{F}\{f(t)\} = F(j\omega)$$

From (5.54),

$$\mathscr{F}\left\{ \sum_{k=-\infty}^{\infty} \delta(t - kT) \right\} = \frac{2\pi}{T} \sum_{k=-\infty}^{\infty} \delta\left(\omega - \frac{2\pi k}{T} \right)$$

so that, assuming the interchange of the order of integration and summation to be possible, (5.86) becomes

$$F_s(j\omega) = \frac{1}{2\pi} F(j\omega) * \frac{2\pi}{T} \sum_{k=-\infty}^{\infty} \delta\left(\omega - \frac{2\pi k}{T} \right)$$

$$= \frac{1}{T} \int_{-\infty}^{\infty} F(j[\omega - \omega']) \sum_{k=-\infty}^{\infty} \delta\left(\omega' - \frac{2\pi k}{T} \right) d\omega'$$

$$= \frac{1}{T} \sum_{k=-\infty}^{\infty} \int_{-\infty}^{\infty} F(j[\omega - \omega']) \delta\left(\omega' - \frac{2\pi k}{T} \right) d\omega'$$

$$= \frac{1}{T} \sum_{k=-\infty}^{\infty} F\left(j\left(\omega - \frac{2\pi k}{T} \right) \right)$$

Thus

$$F_s(j\omega) = \frac{1}{T} \sum_{k=-\infty}^{\infty} F(j[\omega - k\omega_0]), \qquad \omega_0 = \frac{2\pi}{T} \tag{5.87}$$

Examining (5.87), we see that the spectrum $F_s(j\omega)$ of the sampled version $f_s(t)$ of $f(t)$ consists of repeats of the spectrum $F(j\omega)$ of $f(t)$ scaled by a factor $1/T$, these repeats being spaced at intervals $\omega_0 = 2\pi/T$ apart. Figure 5.26(a) shows the amplitude spectrum $|F(j\omega)|$ of a band-limited signal $f(t)$, that is, a signal whose spectrum is zero for $|\omega| > \omega_m$. Figures 5.26(b–e) show the amplitude spectrum $|F_s(j\omega)|$ of the sampled version for increasing values of the sampling interval T. Clearly, as T increases, the spectrum of $F(j\omega)$, as observed using $|F_s(j\omega)|$ in

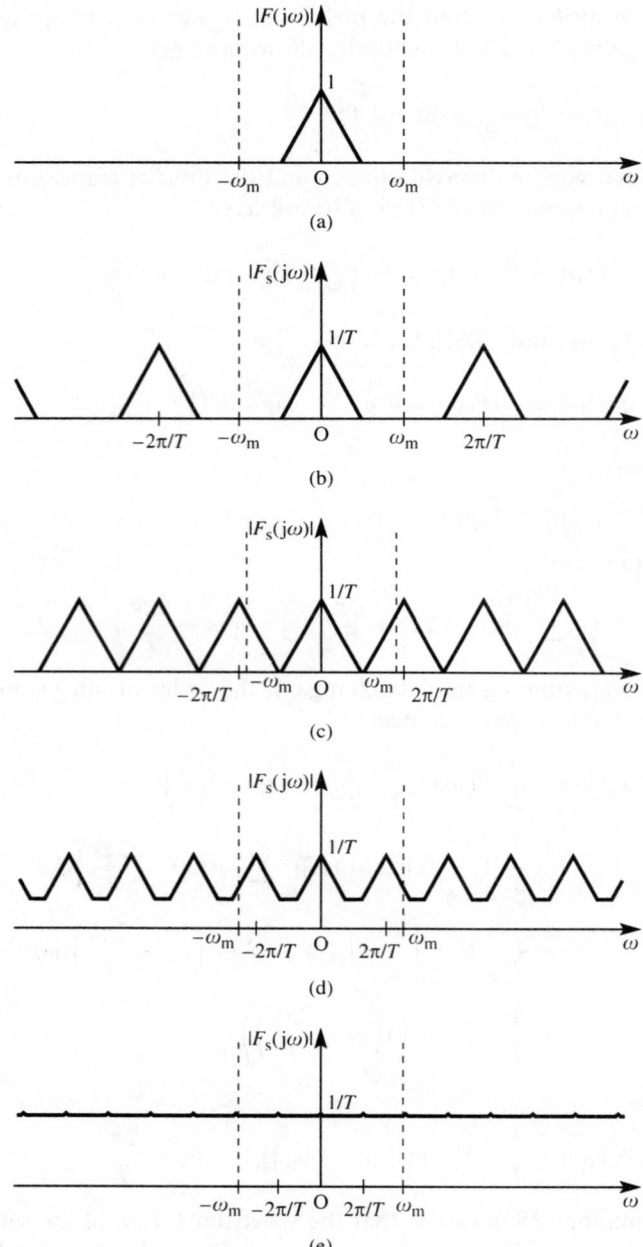

Figure 5.26 (a)
Amplitude spectrum
of a band-limited
signal $f(t)$. (b)–(e)
Amplitude spectrum
$|F_s(j\omega)|$ of $f_s(t)$,
showing periodic
repetition of $|F_s(j\omega)|$
and interaction effects
as T increases.

$-\omega_m < \omega < \omega_m$, becomes more and more misleading because of 'interaction' from neighbouring copies.

As we saw in Section 5.6.2, the periodicity in the amplitude spectrum $|F_s(j\omega)|$ of $f_s(t)$ is inevitable as a consequence of the sampling process, and ways have to be found to minimize the problems it causes. The interaction observed in Figure 5.26 between the periodic repeats is known as **aliasing error**, and it is clearly essential to minimize this effect. This can be achieved in an obvious way if the original unsampled signal $f(t)$ is band-limited as in Figure 5.26(a). It is apparent that we must arrange that the periodic repeats of $|F(j\omega)|$ be far enough apart to prevent interaction between the copies. This implies that we have

$$\omega_0 \geqslant 2\omega_m$$

at an absolute (and impractical!) minimum. Since $\omega_0 = 2\pi/T$, the constraint implies that

$$T \leqslant \pi/\omega_m$$

where T is the interval between samples. The minimum time interval allowed is

$$T_{min} = \pi/\omega_m$$

which is known as the **Nyquist interval** and we have in fact deduced a form of the **Nyquist–Shannon sampling theorem**. If $T < T_{min}$ then the 'copies' of $F(j\omega)$ are isolated from each other, and we can focus on just one copy, either for the purpose of signal reconstruction, or for the purposes of the estimation of $F(j\omega)$ itself. Here we are concerned only with the latter problem. Basically, we have established a condition under which the spectrum of the samples of the band-limited signal $f(t)$, that is, the spectrum of $f_s(t)$, can be used to estimate $F(j\omega)$.

Suppose we have drawn N samples from a continuous signal $f(t)$ at intervals T, in accordance with the Nyquist criterion, as in Figure 5.27. We then consider

$$f_s(t) = \sum_{k=0}^{N-1} f(kT)\delta(t - kT)$$

or equivalently, the sequence

$$\{f_k\}_{k=0}^{N-1}, \qquad \text{where } f_k = f(kT)$$

Figure 5.27 Sampling in a continuous-time signal.

Note that

$$f_s(t) = 0 \quad (t > (N-1)T)$$

so that

$$f_k = 0 \quad (k > N-1)$$

The Fourier transform of $f_s(t)$ is

$$
\begin{aligned}
F_s(j\omega) &= \int_{-\infty}^{\infty} f_s(t)\,e^{-j\omega t}\,dt \\
&= \int_{-\infty}^{\infty} \sum_{k=0}^{N-1} f(kT)\delta(t-kT)\,e^{-j\omega t}\,dt \\
&= \sum_{k=0}^{N-1} \int_{-\infty}^{\infty} f(kT)\delta(t-kT)\,e^{-j\omega t}\,dt \\
&= \sum_{k=0}^{N-1} f(kT)\,e^{-j\omega kT} = \sum_{k=0}^{N-1} f_k\,e^{-j\omega kT}
\end{aligned}
\tag{5.88}
$$

The transform in (5.88) is a function of the continuous variable ω, so, as in (5.78), we must now sample the continuous spectrum $F_s(j\omega)$ to permit computer evaluation.

We chose N samples to represent $f(t)$ in the time domain, and for this reason we also choose N samples in the frequency domain to represent $F(j\omega)$. Thus we sample (5.88) at intervals $\Delta\omega$, to generate the sequence

$$\{F_s(jn\,\Delta\omega)\}_{n=0}^{N-1} \tag{5.89a}$$

where

$$F_s(jn\,\Delta\omega) = \sum_{k=0}^{N-1} f_k\,e^{-jkn\Delta\omega\,T} \tag{5.89b}$$

We must now choose the frequency-domain sampling interval $\Delta\omega$. To see how to do this, recall that the sampled spectrum $F_s(j\omega)$ consisted of repeats of $F(j\omega)$, spaced at intervals $2\pi/T$ apart. Thus to sample just one copy in its entirety, we should choose

$$N\,\Delta\omega = 2\pi/T$$

or

$$\Delta\omega = 2\pi/NT \tag{5.90}$$

Note that the resulting sequence, defined outside $0 \leqslant n \leqslant N-1$, is periodic, as we should expect. However, note also that, following our discussion in Section 5.6, the process of recovering a time signal from samples of its spectrum will result in a periodic waveform, whatever the nature of the original time signal. We should not be surprised by this, since it is exactly in accordance with our introductory discussion in Section 5.1.

In view of the scaling factor $1/T$ in (5.90), our estimate of the Fourier transform

$F(j\omega)$ of $f(t)$ over the interval

$$0 \leqslant t \leqslant (N-1)T$$

will from (5.89), be the sequence of samples

$$\{TF_s(jn\,\Delta\omega)\}_{n=0}^{N-1}$$

where

$$TF_s(jn\,\Delta\omega) = T\sum_{k=0}^{N-1} f_k e^{-jkn\Delta\omega\,T}$$

which, from the definition of the discrete Fourier transform in (5.78), gives

$$TF_s(jn\,\Delta\omega) = T \times \mathrm{DFT}\{f_k\}$$

where DFT $\{f_k\}$ is the discrete Fourier transform of the sequence $\{f_k\}$. We illustrate the use of this estimate in Example 5.20.

EXAMPLE 5.20   The delayed triangular pulse $f(t)$ is as illustrated in Figure 5.28. Estimate its Fourier transform using 10 samples and compare with the exact values.

Figure 5.28 The delayed triangular pulse.

Solution   Using $N = 10$ samples at intervals $T = 0.2\,\text{s}$, we generate the sequence

$$\{f_k\}_{k=0}^9 = \{f(0), f(0.2), f(0.4), f(0.6), f(0.8), f(1.0), f(1.2), f(1.4), f(1.6), f(1.8)\}$$

Clearly, from Figure 5.28, we can express the continuous function $f(t)$ as

$$f(t) = \begin{cases} t & (0 \leqslant t \leqslant 0.5) \\ 1 - t & (0.5 < t < 1) \\ 0 & (t \geqslant 1) \end{cases}$$

and so

$$\{f_k\}_{k=0}^9 = \{0, 0.2, 0.4, 0.4, 0.2, 0, 0, 0, 0, 0\}$$

Using (5.78), the discrete Fourier transform $\{F_n\}_{n=0}^9$ of the sequence $\{f_k\}_{k=0}^9$ is generated by

$$F_n = \sum_{k=0}^9 f_k e^{-jkn\Delta\omega\,T}, \qquad \text{where } \Delta\omega = \frac{2\pi}{NT} = \frac{2\pi}{10 \times 0.2} = \pi$$

That is,

$$F_n = \sum_{k=0}^{9} f_k e^{-jkn(0.2\pi)}$$

or, since $f_0 = f_5 = f_6 = f_7 = f_8 = f_9 = 0$,

$$F_n = \sum_{k=1}^{4} f_k e^{-jnk(0.2\pi)}$$

The estimate of the Fourier transform, also based on $N = 10$ samples, is then the sequence

$$\{TF_n\}_{n=0}^{9} = \{0.2F_n\}_{n=0}^{9}$$

We thus have 10 values representing the Fourier transform at

$$\omega = n\,\Delta\omega \quad (n = 0, 1, 2, \ldots, 9)$$

or since $\Delta\omega = 2\pi/NT$

$$\omega = 0, \pi, 2\pi, \ldots, 9\pi$$

At $\omega = \pi$, corresponding to $n = 1$, our estimate is

$$0.2F_1 = 0.2 \sum_{k=1}^{4} f_k e^{-jk(0.2\pi)}$$

$$= 0.2[0.2\,e^{-j(0.2\pi)} + 0.4(e^{-j(0.4\pi)} + e^{-j(0.6\pi)}) + 0.2\,e^{-j(0.8\pi)}]$$

$$= -0.1992j$$

At $\omega = 2\pi$, corresponding to $n = 2$, our estimate is

$$0.2F_2 = 0.2 \sum_{k=1}^{4} f_k e^{-jk(0.4\pi)}$$

$$= 0.2[0.2\,e^{-j(0.4\pi)} + 0.4(e^{-j(0.8\pi)} + e^{-j(1.2\pi)}) + 0.2\,e^{-j(1.6\pi)}]$$

$$= -0.1047$$

Continuing in this manner, we compute the sequence

$$\{0.2F_0, 0.2F_1, \ldots, 0.2F_n\}$$

as

$$\{0.2400, -0.1992j, -0.1047, 0.0180j, -0.0153, 0, -0.0153, -0.0180j, -0.1047,$$
$$0.1992j\}$$

This then represents the estimate of the Fourier transform of the continuous function $f(t)$. The exact value of the Fourier transform of $f(t)$ is easily computed by direct use of the definition (5.15) as

$$F(j\omega) = \mathcal{F}\{f(t)\} = \tfrac{1}{4}e^{-j\omega/2}\operatorname{sinc}^2 \tfrac{1}{4}\omega$$

which we can use to examine the validity of our result. The comparison is shown in Figure 5.29 and illustrated graphically in Figure 5.30.

ω	Exact $F(j\omega)$	DFT estimate	$|F(j\omega)|$	|DFT estimate|	% error
0	0.2500	0.2400	0.2500	0.2400	4%
π	$-0.2026j$	$-0.1992j$	0.2026	0.1992	1.7%
2π	-0.1013	-0.1047	0.1013	0.1047	3.2%
3π	$0.0225j$	$0.1080j$	0.0225	0.0180	20%
4π	0	-0.0153	0	0.0153	—
5π	$-0.0081j$	0	0.0081	0	—
6π	-0.0113	-0.0153	0.0113	0.0153	—
7π	0.0041	$-0.0180j$	0.0041	0.0180	—
8π	0	-0.1047	0	0.1047	—
9π	$-0.0025j$	$0.1992j$	0.0025	0.1992	—

Figure 5.29 Comparison of exact results and DFT estimate for the amplitude spectrum of the signal of Example 5.20.

Figure 5.30 Exact result $|F(j\omega)|$ (✱) and DFT estimate TF_n(□) of the Fourier transform in Example 5.20.

From the Nyquist–Shannon sampling theorem, with $T = 0.2\,\text{s}$, we deduce that our results will be completely accurate if the original signal $f(t)$ is band-limited with a zero spectrum for $|\omega| > |\omega_m| = 5\pi$. Our signal is not strictly band-limited in this way, and we thus expect to observe some error in our results, particularly near $\omega = 5\pi$, because of the effects of aliasing. The estimate obtained is satisfactory at $\omega = 0, \pi, 2\pi$, but begins to lose accuracy at $\omega = 3\pi$. Results obtained above $\omega = 5\pi$ are seen to be images of those obtained for values below $\omega = 5\pi$, and this is to be expected owing to the periodicity of the DFT. In our calculation the DFT sequence will be periodic, with period $N = 10$; thus, for example,

$$|TF_7| = |TF_{7-10}| = |TF_{-3}| = T|F_{-3}|$$

As we have seen many times, for a real signal the amplitude spectrum is symmetric about $\omega = 0$. Thus $|F_{-3}| = |F_3|$, $|F_{-5}| = |F_5|$, and so on, and the effects of the symmetry are apparent in Figure 5.29. It is perhaps worth observing that if we had calculated (say) $\{TF_{-4}, TF_{-3}, \ldots, TF_0, TF_1, \ldots, TF_5\}$, we should have obtained a 'conventional' plot, with the right-hand portion, beyond $\omega = 5\pi$, translated to the left of the origin. However, using the plot of the amplitude spectrum in the chosen form does highlight the source of error due to aliasing.

In this section we have discussed a method by which Fourier transforms can be estimated numerically, at least in theory. It is apparent, though, that the amount of labour involved is significant, and as we observed in Section 5.6.3 an algorithm based on this approach is in general prohibitive in view of the amount of computing time required. The next section gives a brief introduction to a method of overcoming this problem.

5.6.5   The fast Fourier transform

The calculation of a discrete Fourier transform based on N sample values requires, as we have seen, N^2 complex multiplications and $N(N-1)$ summations. For real signals, symmetry can be exploited, but for large N, $\frac{1}{2}N^2$ does not represent a significant improvement over N^2 for the purposes of computation. In fact, a totally new approach to the problem was required before the discrete Fourier transform could become a practical engineering tool. In 1965 Cooley and Tukey introduced the **fast Fourier transform (FFT)** in order to reduce the computational complexity (J. W. Cooley and J. W. Tukey, An algorithm for the machine computation of complex Fourier series, *Mathematics of Computation* **19** (1965) 297–301). We shall briefly introduce their approach in this section: for a full discussion see E. O. Brigham, *The Fast Fourier Transform* (Prentice-Hall, Englewood Cliffs, NJ, 1974), whose treatment is similar to that adopted here.

We shall restrict ourselves to the situation where $N = 2^\gamma$ for some integer γ, and, rather than examine the general case, we shall focus on a particular value of γ. In proceeding in this way, the idea should be clear and the extension to other values of γ appear credible. We can summarize the approach as being in three stages:

(a) matrix formulation;

(b) matrix factorization; and, finally,

(c) rearranging.

We first consider a matrix formulation of the DFT. From (5.78), the Fourier transform sequence $\{G_k\}_{k=0}^{N-1}$ of the sequence $\{g_n\}_{n=0}^{N-1}$ is generated by

$$G_k = \sum_{n=0}^{N-1} g_n e^{-j2\pi nk/N} \quad (k = 0, 1, \ldots, N-1) \tag{5.91}$$

We shall consider the particular case when $\gamma = 2$ (that is, $N = 2^2 = 4$), and define

$$W = e^{-j2\pi/N} = e^{-j\pi/2}$$

so that (5.91) becomes

$$G_k = \sum_{n=0}^{N-1} g_n W^{nk} = \sum_{n=0}^{3} g_n W^{nk} \quad (k = 0, 1, 2, 3)$$

Writing out the terms of the transformed sequence, we have

$$G_0 = g_0 W^0 + g_1 W^0 + g_2 W^0 + g_3 W^0$$
$$G_1 = g_0 W^0 + g_1 W^1 + g_2 W^2 + g_3 W^3$$
$$G_2 = g_0 W^0 + g_1 W^2 + g_2 W^4 + g_3 W^6$$
$$G_3 = g_0 W^0 + g_1 W^3 + g_2 W^6 + g_3 W^9$$

which may be expressed in the vector–matrix form

$$
\begin{bmatrix} G_0 \\ G_1 \\ G_2 \\ G_3 \end{bmatrix}
=
\begin{bmatrix}
W^0 & W^0 & W^0 & W^0 \\
W^0 & W^1 & W^2 & W^3 \\
W^0 & W^2 & W^4 & W^6 \\
W^0 & W^3 & W^6 & W^9
\end{bmatrix}
\begin{bmatrix} g_0 \\ g_1 \\ g_2 \\ g_3 \end{bmatrix}
\tag{5.92}
$$

or, more generally, as

$$G_k = \boldsymbol{W}^{nk} \boldsymbol{g}_n$$

where the vectors $\boldsymbol{G}_k$ and $\boldsymbol{g}_n$ and the square matrix $\boldsymbol{W}^{nk}$ are defined as in (5.92). The next step relates to the special properties of the entries in the matrix $\boldsymbol{W}^{nk}$. Note that $W^{nk} = W^{nk+pN}$, where p is an integer, and so,

$$W^4 = W^0 = 1$$
$$W^6 = W^2$$
$$W^9 = W^1$$

Thus (5.92) becomes

$$
\begin{bmatrix} G_0 \\ G_1 \\ G_2 \\ G_3 \end{bmatrix}
=
\begin{bmatrix}
1 & 1 & 1 & 1 \\
1 & W^1 & W^2 & W^3 \\
1 & W^2 & W^0 & W^2 \\
1 & W^3 & W^2 & W^1
\end{bmatrix}
\begin{bmatrix} g_0 \\ g_1 \\ g_2 \\ g_3 \end{bmatrix}
\tag{5.93}
$$

Equation (5.93) is the end of the first stage of the development. In fact, we have so far only made use of the properties of the Nth roots of unity. Stage two involves the factorization of a matrix, the details of which will be explained later.

Note that

$$
\begin{bmatrix}
1 & W^0 & 0 & 0 \\
1 & W^2 & 0 & 0 \\
0 & 0 & 1 & W^1 \\
0 & 0 & 1 & W^3
\end{bmatrix}
=
\begin{bmatrix}
1 & 0 & W^0 & 0 \\
0 & 1 & 0 & W^0 \\
1 & 0 & W^2 & 0 \\
0 & 1 & 0 & W^2
\end{bmatrix}
\begin{bmatrix}
1 & 1 & 1 & 1 \\
1 & W^2 & W^0 & W^2 \\
1 & W^1 & W^2 & W^3 \\
1 & W^3 & W^2 & W^1
\end{bmatrix}
\tag{5.94}
$$

where we have used $W^5 = W^1$ and $W^0 = 1$ (in the top row). The matrix on the right-hand side of (5.94) is the coefficient matrix of (5.93), *but with rows 2 and 3 interchanged.* Thus we can write (5.93) as

$$
\begin{bmatrix} G_0 \\ G_2 \\ G_1 \\ G_3 \end{bmatrix} = \begin{bmatrix} 1 & W^0 & 0 & 0 \\ 1 & W^2 & 0 & 0 \\ 0 & 0 & 1 & W^1 \\ 0 & 0 & 1 & W^3 \end{bmatrix} \begin{bmatrix} 1 & 0 & W^0 & 0 \\ 0 & 1 & 0 & W^0 \\ 1 & 0 & W^2 & 0 \\ 0 & 1 & 0 & W^2 \end{bmatrix} \begin{bmatrix} g_0 \\ g_1 \\ g_2 \\ g_3 \end{bmatrix}
\tag{5.95}
$$

We now define a vector $\boldsymbol{g}'$ as

$$
\boldsymbol{g}' = \begin{bmatrix} g_0' \\ g_1' \\ g_2' \\ g_3' \end{bmatrix} = \begin{bmatrix} 1 & 0 & W^0 & 0 \\ 0 & 1 & 0 & W^0 \\ 1 & 0 & W^2 & 0 \\ 0 & 1 & 0 & W^2 \end{bmatrix} \begin{bmatrix} g_0 \\ g_1 \\ g_2 \\ g_3 \end{bmatrix}
\tag{5.96}
$$

It then follows from (5.96) that

$$
g_0' = g_0 + W^0 g_2
$$
$$
g_1' = g_1 + W^0 g_3
$$

so that g_0' and g_1' are each calculated by one complex multiplication and one addition. Of course, in this special case, since $W^0 = 1$, the multiplication is unnecessary, but we are attempting to infer the general situation. For this reason, W^0 has not been replaced by 1.

Also, it follows from (5.96) that

$$
g_2' = g_0 + W^2 g_2
$$
$$
g_3' = g_1 + W^2 g_3
$$

and, since $W^2 = -W^0$, the computation of the pair g_2' and g_3' can make use of the computations of $W^0 g_2$ and $W^0 g_3$, with one further addition in each case. Thus the vector $\boldsymbol{g}'$ is determined by a total of four complex additions and two complex multiplications.

To complete the calculation of the transform, we return to (5.95), and rewrite it in the form

$$
\begin{bmatrix} G_0 \\ G_2 \\ G_1 \\ G_3 \end{bmatrix} = \begin{bmatrix} 1 & W^0 & 0 & 0 \\ 1 & W^2 & 0 & 0 \\ 0 & 0 & 1 & W^1 \\ 0 & 0 & 1 & W^3 \end{bmatrix} \begin{bmatrix} g_0' \\ g_1' \\ g_2' \\ g_3' \end{bmatrix}
\tag{5.97}
$$

It then follows from (5.97) that

$$
G_0 = g_0' + W^0 g_1'
$$
$$
G_2 = g_0' + W^2 g_1'
$$

and we see that G_0 is determined by one complex multiplication and one complex addition. Furthermore, because $W^2 = -W^0$, G_2 follows after one further complex addition.

Similarly, it follows from (5.97) that

$$G_1 = g_2' + W^1 g_3'$$

$$G_3 = g_2' + W^3 g_3'$$

and, since $W^3 = -W^1$, a total of one further complex multiplication and two further additions are required to produce the re-ordered transform vector

$$[G_0 \quad G_2 \quad G_1 \quad G_3]^T$$

Thus the total number of operations required to generate the (re-ordered) transform is four complex multiplications and eight complex additions. Direct calculation would have required $N^2 = 16$ complex multiplications and $N(N-1) = 12$ complex additions. Even with a small value of N, these savings are significant, and, interpreting computing time requirements as being proportional to the number of complex multiplications involved, it is easy to see why the FFT algorithm has become an essential tool for computational Fourier analysis. When $N = 2^\gamma$, the FFT algorithm is effectively a procedure for producing γ $N \times N$ matrices of the form (5.94). Extending our ideas, it is possible to see that generally the FFT algorithm, when $N = 2^\gamma$, will require $\frac{1}{2}N\gamma$ (four, when $N = 2^2 = 4$) complex multiplications and $N\gamma$ (eight, when $N = 4$) complex additions. Since

$$\gamma = \log_2 N$$

the demands of the FFT algorithm in terms of computing time, estimated on the basis of the number of complex multiplications, is often given as about $N \log_2 N$, as opposed to N^2 for the direct evaluation of the transform. This completes the second stage of our task, and we are only left with the problem of rearrangement of our transform vector into 'natural' order.

The means by which this is achieved is most elegant. Instead of indexing G_0, G_1, G_2, G_3 in decimal form, an alternative binary notation is used, and $[G_0 \quad G_1 \quad G_2 \quad G_3]^T$ becomes

$$[G_{00} \quad G_{01} \quad G_{10} \quad G_{11}]^T$$

The process of 'bit reversal' means rewriting a binary number with its bits or digits in reverse order. Applying this process to $[G_{00} \quad G_{01} \quad G_{10} \quad G_{11}]^T$ yields

$$[G_{00} \quad G_{10} \quad G_{01} \quad G_{11}]^T = [G_0 \quad G_2 \quad G_1 \quad G_3]^T$$

with decimal labelling. This latter form is exactly the one obtained at the end of the FFT calculation, and we see that the natural order can easily be recovered by rearranging the output on the basis of bit reversal of the binary indexed version.

We have now completed our introduction to the fast Fourier transform. We shall now consider an example to illustrate the ideas discussed here. We shall then conclude by considering in greater detail the matrix factorization process used in the second stage.

EXAMPLE 5.21 Use the method of the FFT algorithm to compute the Fourier transform of the sequence

$$\{g_n\}_{n=0}^3 = \{1, 2, 1, 0\}$$

Solution In this case $N = 4 = 2^2$, and we begin by computing the vector $\boldsymbol{g}_n' = [g_0' \quad g_1' \quad g_2' \quad g_3']^T$, which, from (5.96), is given by

$$\boldsymbol{g}_n' = \begin{bmatrix} 1 & 0 & W^0 & 0 \\ 0 & 1 & 0 & W^0 \\ 1 & 0 & W^2 & 0 \\ 0 & 1 & 0 & W^2 \end{bmatrix} \begin{bmatrix} g_0 \\ g_1 \\ g_2 \\ g_3 \end{bmatrix}$$

For $N = 4$

$$W^n = (e^{-j2\pi/4})^n = e^{-jn\pi/2}$$

and so

$$\boldsymbol{g}_n' = \begin{bmatrix} 1 & 0 & 1 & 0 \\ 0 & 1 & 0 & 1 \\ 1 & 0 & -1 & 0 \\ 0 & 1 & 0 & -1 \end{bmatrix} \begin{bmatrix} 1 \\ 2 \\ 1 \\ 0 \end{bmatrix} = \begin{bmatrix} 2 \\ 2 \\ 0 \\ 2 \end{bmatrix}$$

Next, we compute the 'bit-reversed' order transform vector $\boldsymbol{G}'$, say, which, from (5.97), is given by

$$\boldsymbol{G}' = \begin{bmatrix} 1 & W^0 & 0 & 0 \\ 1 & W^2 & 0 & 0 \\ 0 & 0 & 1 & W^1 \\ 0 & 0 & 1 & W^3 \end{bmatrix} \begin{bmatrix} g_0' \\ g_1' \\ g_2' \\ g_3' \end{bmatrix}$$

or, in this particular case,

$$\boldsymbol{G}' = \begin{bmatrix} G_{00} \\ G_{10} \\ G_{01} \\ G_{11} \end{bmatrix} = \begin{bmatrix} 1 & 1 & 0 & 0 \\ 1 & -1 & 0 & 0 \\ 0 & 0 & 1 & -j \\ 0 & 0 & 1 & j \end{bmatrix} \begin{bmatrix} 2 \\ 2 \\ 0 \\ 2 \end{bmatrix} = \begin{bmatrix} 4 \\ 0 \\ -2j \\ 2j \end{bmatrix} \tag{5.98}$$

Finally, we recover the transform vector $\boldsymbol{G} = [G_0 \quad G_1 \quad G_2 \quad G_3]^T$ as

$$\boldsymbol{G} = \begin{bmatrix} 4 \\ -2j \\ 0 \\ 2j \end{bmatrix}$$

and we have thus established the Fourier transform of the sequence $\{1, 2, 1, 0\}$ as the sequence

$$\{4, -2j, 0, 2j\}$$

It is interesting to compare the labour involved in this calculation with that in Example 5.19.

To conclude this section, we reconsider the matrix factorization operation, which is at the core of the process of calculating the fast Fourier transform. In a book of this nature it is not appropriate to reproduce a proof of the validity of the algorithm for any N of the form $N = 2^\gamma$. Rather, we shall illustrate how the factorization we introduced in (5.94) was obtained. The factored form of the matrix will not be generated in any calculation: what actually happens is that the various summations are performed using their structural properties.

From (5.91), with $W = e^{-j2\pi/N}$, we wish to calculate the sums

$$G_k = \sum_{n=0}^{N-1} g_n W^{nk} \quad k = 0, 1, \ldots, N - 1 \tag{5.99}$$

In the case $N = 4$, $\gamma = 2$ we see that k and n take only the values 0, 1, 2 and 3, so we can represent both k and n using two-digit binary numbers; in general γ-digit binary numbers will be required.

We write $k = k_1 k_0$ and $n = n_1 n_0$, where k_0, k_1, n_0 and n_1 may take the values 0 or 1 only. For example, $k = 3$ becomes $k = 11$ and $n = 2$ becomes $n = 10$. The decimal form can always be recovered easily as $k = 2k_1 + k_0$ and $n = 2n_1 + n_0$.

Using binary notation, we can write (5.99) as

$$G_{k_1 k_0} = \sum_{n_0=0}^{1} \sum_{n_1=0}^{1} g_{n_1 n_0} W^{(2n_1 + n_0)(2k_1 + k_0)} \tag{5.100}$$

The single summation of (5.99) is now replaced, when $\gamma = 2$, by two summations. Again we see that for the more general case with $N = 2^\gamma$ a total of γ summations replaces the single sum of (5.99).

The matrix factorization operation with which we are concerned is now achieved by considering the term

$$W^{(2n_1 + n_0)(2k_1 + k_0)}$$

in (5.100). Expanding gives

$$W^{(2n_1 + n_0)(2k_1 + k_0)} = W^{(2k_1 + k_0)2n_1} W^{(2k_1 + k_0)n_0}$$

$$= W^{4n_1 k_1} W^{2n_1 k_0} W^{(2k_1 + k_0)n_0} \tag{5.101}$$

Since $W = e^{-j2\pi/N}$, and $N = 4$ in this case, the leading term in (5.101) becomes

$$W^{4n_1 k_1} = (e^{-j2\pi/4})^{4n_1 k_1} = (e^{-j2\pi})^{n_1 k_1}$$

$$= 1^{n_1 k_1} = 1$$

Again we observe that in the more general case such a factor will always emerge.

Thus (5.101) can be written as

$$W^{(2n_1+n_0)(2k_1+k_0)} = W^{2n_1k_0}W^{(2k_1+k_0)n_0}$$

so that (5.100) becomes

$$G_{k_1k_0} = \sum_{n_0=0}^{1} \left[\sum_{n_1=0}^{1} g_{n_1n_0}W^{2n_1k_0} \right] W^{(2k_1+k_0)n_0} \qquad (5.102)$$

which is the required matrix factorization. This can be seen by writing

$$g'_{k_0n_0} = \sum_{n_1=0}^{1} g_{n_1n_0}W^{2n_1k_0} \qquad (5.103)$$

so that the sum in the square brackets in (5.102) defines the four relations

$$\left.\begin{aligned}
g'_{00} &= g_{00}W^{2,0,0} + g_{10}W^{2,1,0} = g_{00} + g_{10}W^0\\
g'_{01} &= g_{01}W^{2,0,0} + g_{11}W^{2,1,0} = g_{01} + g_{11}W^0\\
g'_{10} &= g_{00}W^{2,0,1} + g_{10}W^{2,1,1} = g_{00} + g_{10}W^2\\
g'_{11} &= g_{01}W^{2,0,1} + g_{11}W^{2,1,1} = g_{01} + g_{11}W^2
\end{aligned}\right\} \qquad (5.104)$$

which, in matrix form, becomes

$$\begin{bmatrix} g'_{00} \\ g'_{01} \\ g'_{10} \\ g'_{11} \end{bmatrix} = \begin{bmatrix} 1 & 0 & W^0 & 0 \\ 0 & 1 & 0 & W^0 \\ 1 & 0 & W^2 & 0 \\ 0 & 1 & 0 & W^2 \end{bmatrix} \begin{bmatrix} g_{00} \\ g_{01} \\ g_{10} \\ g_{11} \end{bmatrix} \qquad (5.105)$$

and we see that we have re-established the system of equations (5.96), this time with binary indexing. Note that in (5.104) and (5.105) we distinguished between terms in W^0 depending on how the zero is generated. When the zero is generated through the value of the summation index (that is, when $n_1 = 0$ and thus a zero will always be generated whatever the value of γ) we replace W^0 by 1. When the index is zero because of the value of k_0, we maintain W^0 as an aid to generalization.

The final stage of the factorization appears when we write the outer summation of (5.102) as

$$G'_{k_0k_1} = \sum_{n_0=0}^{1} g'_{k_0n_0}W^{(2k_1+k_0)n_0} \qquad (5.106)$$

which, on writing out in full, gives

$$G'_{00} = g'_{00}W^{0,0} + g'_{01}W^{0,1} = g'_{00} + g'_{01}W^0$$
$$G'_{01} = g'_{00}W^{2,0} + g'_{01}W^{2,1} = g'_{00} + g'_{01}W^2$$
$$G'_{10} = g'_{10}W^{1,0} + g'_{11}W^{1,1} = g'_{10} + g'_{11}W^1$$
$$G'_{11} = g'_{10}W^{3,0} + g'_{11}W^{3,1} = g'_{10} + g'_{11}W^3$$

or, in matrix form,

$$
\begin{bmatrix} G'_{00} \\ G'_{01} \\ G'_{10} \\ G'_{11} \end{bmatrix} = \begin{bmatrix} 1 & W^0 & 0 & 0 \\ 1 & W^2 & 0 & 0 \\ 0 & 0 & 1 & W^1 \\ 0 & 0 & 1 & W^3 \end{bmatrix} \begin{bmatrix} g'_{00} \\ g'_{01} \\ g'_{10} \\ g'_{11} \end{bmatrix}
\tag{5.107}
$$

The matrix in (5.107) is exactly that of (5.97), and we have completed the factorization process as we intended. Finally, to obtain the transform in a natural order, we must carry out the bit-reversal operation. From (5.102) and (5.105), we achieve this by simply writing

$$
G_{k_1 k_0} = G'_{k_0 k_1}
\tag{5.108}
$$

We can therefore summarize the Cooley–Tukey algorithm for the fast Fourier transform for the case $N = 4$ by the three relations (5.103), (5.106) and (5.108), that is,

$$
g'_{k_0 n_0} = \sum_{n_1 = 0}^{1} g_{n_1 n_0} W^{2 n_1 k_0}
$$

$$
G'_{k_0 k_1} = \sum_{n_0 = 0}^{1} g'_{k_0 n_0} W^{(2 k_1 + k_0) n_0}
$$

$$
G_{k_1 k_0} = G'_{k_0 k_1}
$$

The evaluation of these three relationships is equivalent to the matrix factorization process together with the bit-reversal procedure discussed above.

The fast Fourier transform is essentially a computer-orientated algorithm and highly efficient codes are available in software libraries, usually requiring a simple subroutine call for their implementation. The interested reader who would prefer to produce 'home-made' code may find listings in the textbook by Brigham quoted at the beginning of this section, as well as elsewhere.

5.6.6   Exercises

28 Calculate directly the discrete Fourier transform of the sequence

$\{1, 0, 1, 0\}$

using the methods of Section 5.6.3 (see Example 5.19).

29 Use the fast Fourier transform method to calculate the transform of the sequence of Exercise 28 (follow Example 5.21).

30 Use the FFT algorithm implemented on a computer to improve the experiment with the estimation of the spectrum of the signal of Example 5.20.

31 Derive an FFT algorithm for $N = 2^3 = 8$ points.

Work from (5.99), writing

$k = 4k_2 + 2k_1 + k_0, \qquad k_i = 0$ or 1 for all i

$n = 4n_2 + 2n_1 + n_0, \qquad n_i = 0$ or 1 for all i

to show that

$$
g'_{k_0 n_1 n_0} = \sum_{n_2 = 0}^{1} g_{n_2 n_1 n_0} W^{4 k_0 n_2}
$$

$$
g''_{k_0 k_1 n_0} = \sum_{n_1 = 0}^{1} g'_{k_0 n_1 n_0} W^{(2 k_1 + k_0) 2 n_1}
$$

$$
G'_{k_0 k_1 k_2} = \sum_{n_0 = 0}^{1} g''_{k_0 k_1 n_0} W^{(4 k_2 + 2 k_1 + k_0) n_0}
$$

$$
G_{k_2 k_1 k_0} = G'_{k_0 k_1 k_2}
$$

5.7   Engineering application: the design of analogue filters

In this section we explore the ideas of mathematical design or synthesis. We shall express in mathematical form the desired performance of a system, and, utilizing the ideas we have developed, produce a system design.

This chapter has been concerned with the frequency-domain representation of signals and systems, and the system we shall design will operate on input signals to produce output signals with specific frequency-domain properties. In Figure 5.31 we illustrate the amplitude response of an ideal low-pass filter. This filter passes perfectly signals, or components of signals, at frequencies less than the cut-off frequency ω_c. Above ω_c, attenuation is perfect, meaning that signals above this frequency are not passed by this filter.

The amplitude response of this ideal device is given by

Figure 5.31
Amplitude response of an ideal low-pass filter.

$$|H'(j\omega)| = \begin{cases} 1 & (|\omega| \leqslant \omega_c) \\ 0 & (|\omega| > \omega_c) \end{cases}$$

Such an ideal response cannot be attained by a real analogue device, and our design problem is to approximate this response to an acceptable degree using a system that can be constructed. A class of functions whose graphs resemble that of Figure 5.31 is the set

$$|H_B(j\omega)| = \frac{1}{\sqrt{[1 + (\omega/\omega_c)^{2n}]}}$$

and we see from Figure 5.32, which corresponds to $\omega_c = 1$, that, as n increases, the graph approaches the ideal response. This particular approximation is known as the **Butterworth approximation**, and is only one of a number of possibilities.

To explore this approach further, we must ask the question whether such a response could be obtained as the frequency response of a realizable, stable linear

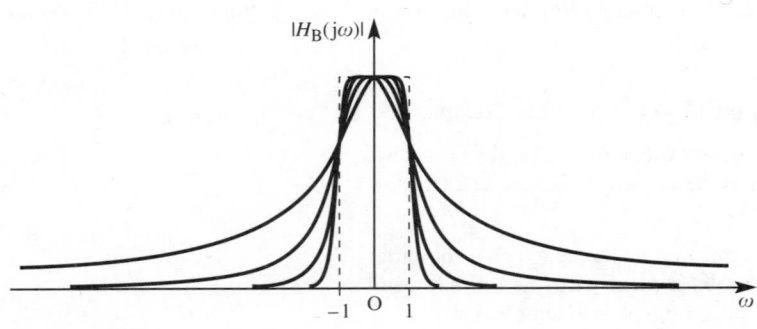

Figure 5.32 Amplitude responses of the Butterworth filters.

system. We assume that it can, although if our investigation leads to the opposite conclusion then we shall have to abandon this approach and seek another. If $H_B(j\omega)$ is the frequency response of such a system then it will have been obtained by replacing s with $j\omega$ in the system Laplace transfer function. This is at least possible since, by assumption, we are dealing with a stable system. Now

$$|H_B(j\omega)|^2 = \frac{1}{1 + (j\omega/j\omega_c)^{2n}}$$

where $|H_B(j\omega)|^2 = H_B(j\omega)H_B^*(j\omega)$. If $H_B(s)$ is to have real coefficients, and thus be realizable, then we must have $H_B^*(j\omega) = H(-j\omega)$. Thus

$$H_B(j\omega)H_B(-j\omega) = \frac{1}{1 + (\omega/\omega_c)^{2n}}$$

$$= \frac{1}{1 + (j\omega/j\omega_c)^{2n}}$$

and we see that the response could be obtained by setting $s = j\omega$ in

$$H_B(s)H_B(-s) = \frac{1}{1 + (s/j\omega_c)^{2n}}$$

Our task is now to attempt to separate $H_B(s)$ from $H_B(-s)$ in such a way that $H_B(s)$ represents the transfer function of a stable system. To do this, we solve the equation

$$1 + (s/j\omega_c)^{2n} = 0$$

to give the poles of $H_B(s)H_B(-s)$ as

$$s = \omega_c\, e^{j[(2k+1)\pi/2n + \pi/2]} \quad (k = 0, 1, 2, 3, \ldots) \tag{5.109}$$

Figure 5.33 shows the pole locations for the cases $n = 1, 2, 3$ and 5. The important observations that we can make from this figure are that in each case there are $2n$ poles equally spaced around the circle of radius ω_c in the Argand diagram, and that there are no poles on the imaginary axis. If $s = s_1$ is a pole of $H_B(s)H_B(-s)$

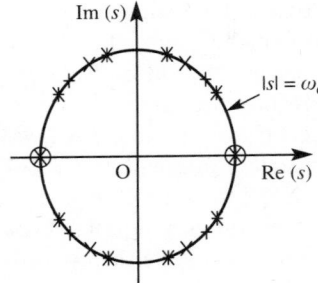

Figure 5.33 Pole locations for the Butterworth filters: $\bigcirc$, $n = 1$; $+$, $n = 2$; $\times$, $n = 3$; $*$, $n = 5$.

then so is $s = -s_1$, and we can thus select as poles for the transfer function $H_B(s)$ those lying in the left half-plane. The remaining poles are then those of $H_B(-s)$. By this procedure, we have generated a stable transfer function $H_B(s)$ for our filter design.

The transfer function that we have generated from the frequency-domain specification of system behaviour must now be related to a real system, and this is the next step in the design process. The form of the transfer function for the filter of order n can be shown to be

$$H_B(s) = \frac{\omega_c^n}{(s - s_1)(s - s_2)\cdots(s - s_n)}$$

where $s_1, s_2, \ldots, s_n$ are the stable poles generated by (5.109). The reader is invited to show that the second-order Butterworth filter has transfer function

$$H_B(s) = \frac{\omega_c^2}{s^2 + \sqrt{2}\,\omega_c s + \omega_c^2}$$

Writing $Y(s) = H_B(s)U(s)$, with $H_B(s)$ as above, we obtain

$$Y(s) = \frac{\omega_c^2}{s^2 + \sqrt{2}\,\omega_c s + \omega_c^2}\, U(s)$$

or

$$(s^2 + \sqrt{2}\,\omega_c s + \omega_c^2)Y(s) = \omega_c^2 U(s) \tag{5.110}$$

If we assume that all initial conditions are zero then (5.110) represents the Laplace transform of the differential equation

$$\frac{d^2 y(t)}{dt^2} + \sqrt{2}\,\omega_c \frac{dy(t)}{dt} + \omega_c^2 y(t) = \omega_c^2 u(t) \tag{5.111}$$

This step completes the mathematical aspect of the design exercise. It is possible to show that a system whose behaviour is modelled by this differential equation can be constructed using elementary circuit components, and the specification of such a circuit would complete the design. For a fuller treatment of the subject the interested reader could consult R. H. Jones and N. C. Steele, *Mathematics in Communication Theory* (Ellis Horwood, Chichester, 1989).

To appreciate the operation of this filter, the use of a dynamic simulation package is recommended. After setting the cut-off frequency ω_c, at 4 for example, the output of the system $y(t)$ corresponding to an input signal $u(t) = \sin t + \sin 10t$ will demonstrate the almost-perfect transmission of the low-frequency ($\omega = 1$) term, with nearly total attenuation of the high-frequency ($\omega = 10$) signal. As an extension to this exercise, the differential equation to represent the third- and fourth-order filters should be obtained, and the responses compared. Using a simulation package and an FFT coding, it is possible to investigate the operation of such devices from the viewpoint of the frequency domain by examining the spectrum of samples drawn from both input and output signals.

5.8 Engineering application: modulation, demodulation and frequency-domain filtering

5.8.1 Introduction

In this section we demonstrate the practical implementation of modulation, demodulation and frequency-domain filtering. These are the processes by which an information-carrying signal can be combined with others for transmission along a channel, with the signal subsequently being recovered so that the transmitted information can be extracted. When a number of signals have to be transmitted along a single channel at the same time, one solution is to use the method of **amplitude modulation** as described in Section 5.3.4. We assume that the channel is 'noisy', so that the received signal contains noise, and this signal is then cleaned and demodulated using **frequency-domain filtering** techniques. This idea is easy to describe and to implement, but cannot usually be performed on-line in view of the heavy computational requirements. Our filtering operations are carried out on the frequency-domain version of the signal, and this is generated using the fast Fourier transform algorithm. Use is made of the **MATLAB package**, which has become almost a standard requirement for engineers, and is available in a student version (*The Student Edition of MATLAB*, Prentice-Hall, Englewood Cliffs, NJ, 1992). A MATLAB M-file demonstrating frequency-domain filtering is shown in Figure 5.34. It can be used with current versions of the package. (Note that in this figure, i is used instead of j to represent $\sqrt{-1}$, as this is normal practice when using MATLAB.) Readers without access to MATLAB should find it fairly easy to interpret this file for the production of their own code.

Figure 5.34
'MATLAB' M-file demonstrating frequency-domain filtering using the fast Fourier transform.

```
% Demonstration of frequency domain filtering using the FFT.
%
%
% Some MATLAB housekeeping to prevent memory problems!
clear
clg
%
% Select a value of N for the number of samples to be taken.
% Make a selection by adding or removing % symbols.
% N must be a power of 2.
%N = 512;
N = 1024;
%N = 2048;
%N = 4096;
```

```
%N =  8192;
%
% T is the sampling interval and the choice of N determines the
% interval over which the signal is processed. Also, if
% N frequency domain values are to be produced the resolution
% is determined.
T= 0.001;
t=0:T:(N−1)*T;
delw =2*pi/(T*N);
%
% Generate the 'information'
f =t.*exp(−t/2);
%
% Set the frequency of the carriers, wc is the carrier which
% will be modulated.
wc = 2*pi*50;
wca = 2*pi*120;
%
% Perform the modulation...
x=f.*cos(wc*t) + cos(wca*t);
%
% ...and add channel noise here
nfac = 0.2;
rand('normal');
x = x + nfac*rand(t);
%
% Plot the 'received" time signal
plot(t,x)
title('The time signal, modulated carrier and noise if added')
xlabel('time, t')
ylabel('x(t)')
pause
%
% Calculate the DFT using the FFT algorithm...
y=fft(x);
z=T*abs(y);
w=0:delw:(N−1)*delw;
%
% ... and plot the amplitude spectrum.
plot(w,z)
title('The amplitude spectrum. Spikes at frequencies of carriers')
xlabel('frequency, w')
ylabel('amplitude')
pause
%
% Construct a filter to isolate the information-bearing carrier.
%
% 2*hwind + 1 is the length of the filter 'window'.
% Set ffac to a value less than 1.0 ffac = 0.5 gives a filter
% of half length wc/2 where wc is frequency of carrier. Don't
```

Figure 5.34—*continued*

```
% exceed a value of 0.95!
ffac = 0.5;
hwind = round(ffac*wc/delw);
1 = 2*hwind+1;
%
% Set the centre of the window at peak corresponding to wc.
% Check this is ok by setting l = 1!
l1 = round(wc/delw) − hwind;
%
% Remember that we must have both ends of the filter!
mask = [zeros(1,l1),ones(1,l),zeros(1,N−(2*l+2*l1−1)),ones(1,l),zeros(1,l1−1)];
%
% Do the frequency domain filtering...
zz = mask.*y;
%
% ...and calculate the inverse DFT
yya =ifft(zz);
%
% Remove rounding errors...it is real!
yy=0.5*(yya + conj(yya));
%
% Plot the 'cleaned' spectrum with only lower carrier present.
plot(w,T*abs(zz))
title('Upper carrier eliminated and noise reduced')
xlabel('frequency, w')
ylabel('amplitude')
pause
%
% Now the signal is cleaned but needs demodulating so
% form the product with 2*carrier signal...
dem = yy.*cos(wc*t);
dem = 2*dem;
%
% ...and take the DFT.
demft = fft(dem);
%
% Use a low-pass filter on the result, the length is llp.
% The same factor is used as before!
llp = round(ffac*wc/delw);
masklp = [ones(1,llp),zeros(1,N−(2*llp−1)),ones(1,llp−1)];
%
% Carry out the filtering...
op = masklp.*demft;
%
% ...and plot the DFT of filtered signal.
plot(w,T*abs(op))
title('Result of demodulation and low-pass filtering')
xlabel('frequency, w')
ylabel('amplitude')
pause
```

Figure 5.34—*continued*

```
%
% Return to the time domain...
opta =ifft(op);
opt=0.5*(opta + conj(opta));
act = f;
vp = N;
% ...and finally plot the extracted signal vs the original.
plot(t(1:vp),opt(1:vp),'—',t(1:vp),act(1:vp),':');
title('The extracted signal, with original')
xlabel('time, t')
ylabel('f(t)')
pause
%
% Clean-up...
clg
clear
%
% ...but responsibly!
i = sqrt(−1);
home
```

Figure 5.34—*concluded.*

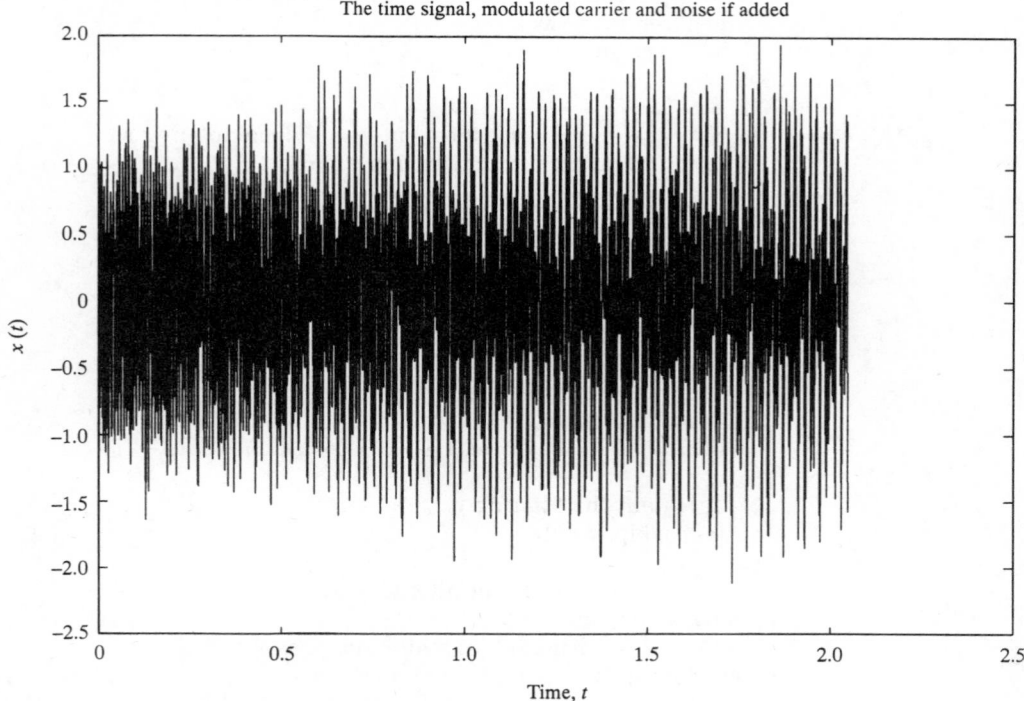

Figure 5.35 Time-domain version of signal, modulated carrier and noise if added.

5.8.2   Modulation and transmission

We suppose that our 'information' consists of samples from the system $f(t) = t e^{-t/2}$, taken at intervals $T = 0.001$ s. This signal, or more correctly, data sequence, will be used to modulate the carrier signal $\cos(50 * 2 * \pi * t)$. A second carrier signal is given by $\cos(120 * 2 * \pi * t)$, and this can be thought of as carrying the signal $f(t) = 1$. We combine these two signals and add 'white noise' to represent the action of the channel. This part of the exercise corresponds to the signal generation and transmission part of the overall process, and Figure 5.35 shows the time-domain version of the resulting signal.

5.8.3   Identification and isolation of the information-carrying signal

Here we begin the signal-processing operations. The key to this is Fourier analysis, and we make use of the fast Fourier transform algorithm to perform the necessary transforms and their inverses. First we examine the spectrum of the received signal, shown in Figure 5.36. We immediately see two spikes corresponding to the carrier

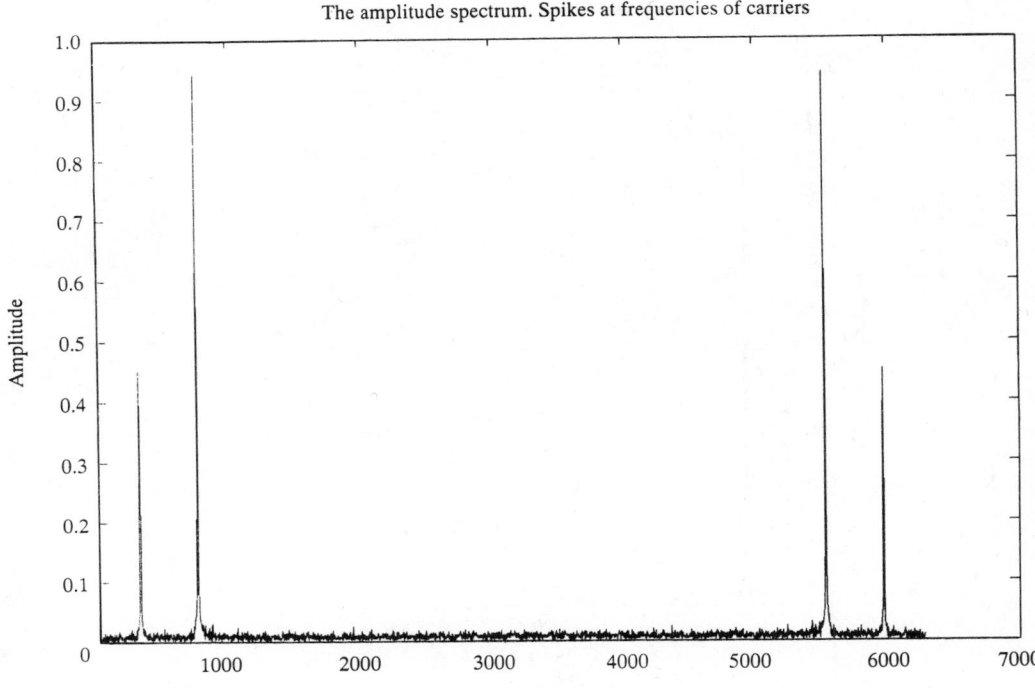

Figure 5.36
Spectrum of
received signal.

signals, and we know that the lower one is carrying the signal we wish to extract. We must design a suitable filter to operate in the frequency domain for the isolation of the selected carrier wave before using the demodulation operation to extract the information. To do this, we simply mask the transformed signal, multiplying by 1 those components we wish to pass, and by 0 those we wish to reject. Obviously we want to pass the carrier-wave frequency component itself, but we must remember that the spectrum of the information signal is centred on this frequency, and so we must pass a band of frequencies around this centre frequency. Again a frequency-domain filter is constructed. We thus have to construct a bandpass filter of suitable bandwidth to achieve this, and moreover, we must remember to include the right-hand half of the filter! There are no problems here with the Nyquist frequency – at first glance we simply need to avoid picking up the second carrier wave. However, the larger the bandwidth we select, the more noise we shall pass, and so a compromise has to be found between the necessary width for good signal recovery and noise elimination. Obviously, since we *know* the bandwidth of our information signal in this case, we could make our choice based on this knowledge. This, however, would be cheating, because usually the exact nature of the transmitted information is not known in advance: if it were, there would be little point in sending it! In the M file we have set the half-length of the filter to be a fraction of the carrier frequency. The carrier frequency ω_c represents the maximum

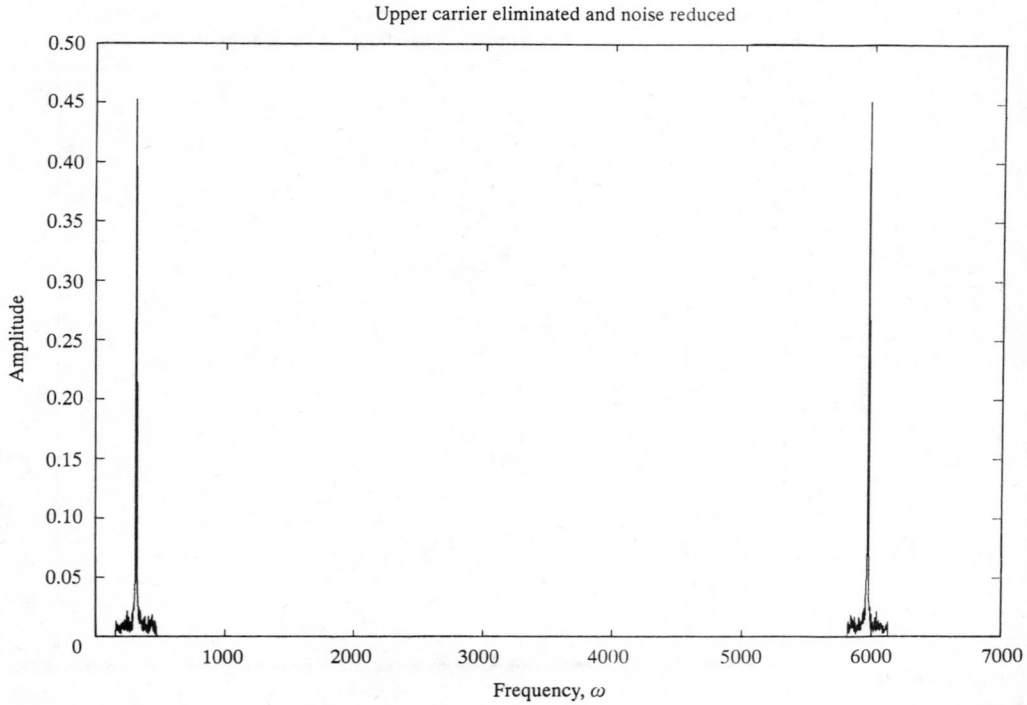

Figure 5.37 Spectrum after application of bandpass filter.

possible channel bandwidth, and in practice a channel would have a specified maximum bandwidth associated with it. Figure 5.37 shows the resulting spectrum after application of the bandpass filter, with a bandwidth less than ω_c.

5.8.4   Demodulation stage

The purpose of this operation is to extract the information from the carrier wave, and it can be shown that multiplying the time signal by $\cos \omega_c T$, where ω_c is the frequency of the carrier wave, has the effect of shifting the spectrum of the modulating signal so that it is again centred on the origin. To perform the multiplication operation, we have to return to the time domain, and this is achieved by using the inverse FFT algorithm. In the frequency-domain representation of the demodulated signal there are also copies of the spectrum of the modulating signal present, centred at higher frequencies $(2\omega_c, 4\omega_c)$, and so we must perform a final low-pass filtering operation on the demodulated signal. To do this, we return to the frequency domain using the FFT algorithm again. The result of the demodulation and low-pass filtering operations is shown in Figure 5.38.

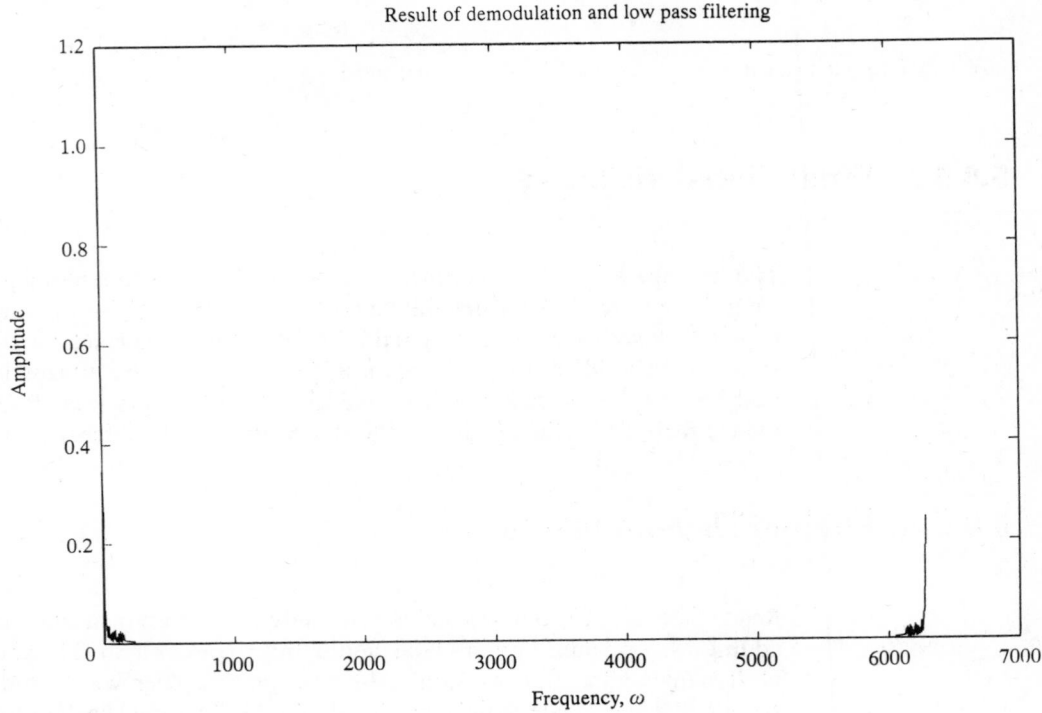

Figure 5.38 Result of demodulation and low-pass filtering operations.

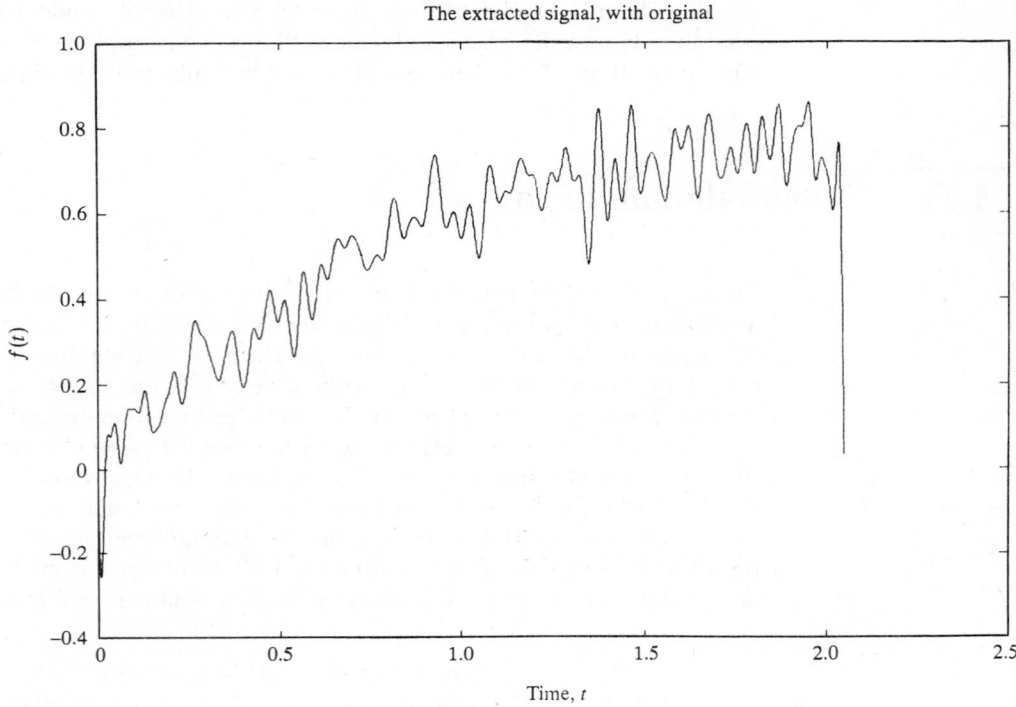

Figure 5.39 Extracted signal, shown together with the original signal.

5.8.5   Final signal recovery

The last operation to be performed is to return to the time domain to examine what we have achieved. After calling the inverse FFT routine, the extracted signal is plotted together with the original for comparison. The results with a fairly low value for the added noise are shown in Figure 5.39. If the process is carried out in the absence of noise altogether, excellent signal recovery is achieved, except for the characteristic 'ringing' due to the sharp edges of the filters.

5.8.6   Further developments

Readers are invited to develop this case study to increase their understanding. Try adding a second information signal modulating the second carrier wave, and extract both signals after 'transmission'. Also add more carrier waves and modulating signals, and investigate signal recovery. If information signal bandwidths are limited to a fixed value, how many signals can be transmitted and recovered satisfactorily?

What happens if T is altered? Can the 'ringing' effect be reduced by smoothing the transition from the string of ones to the string of zeros in the filter masks? Seek references to various **window functions** in signal-processing texts to assist in resolving this question.

5.9 Review exercises (1–25)

1 Calculate the Fourier sine transform of the causal function $f(t)$ defined by

$$f(t) = \begin{cases} t & (0 \leqslant t \leqslant 1) \\ 1 & (1 < t \leqslant 2) \\ 0 & (t > 2) \end{cases}$$

2 Show that if $\mathscr{F}\{f(t)\} = F(j\omega)$ then $\mathscr{F}\{f(-t)\} = F(-j\omega)$. Show also that

$$\mathscr{F}\{f(-t-a)\} = e^{ja\omega} F(-j\omega)$$

where a is real and positive.
Find $\mathscr{F}\{f(t)\}$ when

$$f(t) = \begin{cases} -\frac{1}{2}\pi & (t < -2) \\ \frac{1}{4}\pi t & (-2 \leqslant t \leqslant 2) \\ \frac{1}{2}\pi & (t > 2) \end{cases}$$

3 Use the result

$$\mathscr{F}[H(t + \tfrac{1}{2}T) - H(t - \tfrac{1}{2}T)] = T \operatorname{sinc} \tfrac{1}{2}\omega T$$

and the frequency convolution result to verify that the Fourier transform of the windowed cosine function

$$f(t) = \cos \omega_0 t \, [H(t + \tfrac{1}{2}T) - H(t - \tfrac{1}{2}T)]$$

is

$$\tfrac{1}{2}T[\operatorname{sinc} \tfrac{1}{2}(\omega - \omega_0)T + \operatorname{sinc} \tfrac{1}{2}(\omega + \omega_0)T]$$

4 Show that

$$\delta(t - t_1) * \delta(t - t_2) = \delta(t - (t_1 + t_2))$$

and hence show that

$$\mathscr{F}\{\cos \omega_0 t \, H(t)\} = \tfrac{1}{2}\pi[\delta(\omega + \omega_0) + \delta(\omega - \omega_0)]$$
$$+ \frac{j\omega}{\omega_0^2 - \omega^2}$$

5 Establish the demodulation property,

$$\mathscr{F}\{f(t)\cos \omega_0 t \cos \omega_0 t\}$$
$$= \tfrac{1}{2}F(j\omega) + \tfrac{1}{4}[F(j\omega + 2j\omega_0) + F(j\omega - 2j\omega_0)]$$

6 Use the result $\mathscr{F}\{H(t + T) - H(t - T)\} = 2T \operatorname{sinc} \omega T$ and the symmetry property to show that

$$\mathscr{F}\{\operatorname{sinc} t\} = \pi[H(\omega + 1) - H(\omega - 1)]$$

Check your result by use of the inversion integral.

7 For a wide class of frequently occurring Laplace transforms it is possible to deduce an inversion integral based on the Fourier inversion integral. If $X(s) = \mathscr{L}\{x(t)\}$ is such a transform, we have

$$x(t) = \frac{1}{j2\pi} \int_{\gamma - j\infty}^{\gamma + j\infty} X(s) e^{st} \, ds$$

where $\operatorname{Re}(s) = \gamma$, with γ real, defines a line in the s plane to the right of all the poles of $X(s)$. Usually the integral can be evaluated using the residue theorem, and we then have

$$x(t) = \sum \text{residues of } X(s) e^{st} \text{ at all poles of } X(s)$$

(a) Write down the poles for the transform

$$X(s) = \frac{1}{(s-a)(s-b)}$$

where a and b are real. Calculate the residues of $X(s) e^{st}$ at these poles and invert the transform.

(b) Calculate

(i) $\mathscr{L}^{-1}\left\{\dfrac{1}{(s-2)^2}\right\}$ (ii) $\mathscr{L}^{-1}\left\{\dfrac{1}{s^2(s+1)}\right\}$

(c) Show that

$$\mathscr{L}^{-1}\left\{\frac{2s}{(s^2+1)^2}\right\} = t \sin t$$

8 A linear system has impulse response $h(t)$, so that the output corresponding to an input $u(t)$ is

$$y(t) = \int_{-\infty}^{\infty} h(t - \tau)u(\tau) \, d\tau$$

When $u(t) = \cos \omega_0 t$, $y(t) = -\sin \omega_0 t$ $(\omega_0 \geqslant 0)$. Find the output when $u(t)$ is given by

(a) $\cos \omega_0 (t + \frac{1}{4}\pi)$

(b) $\sin \omega_0 t$

(c) $e^{j\omega_0 t}$

(d) $e^{-j\omega_0 t}$

This system is known as a **Hilbert transformer**.

9 In Section 5.5.1 we established that

$$\mathcal{F}^{-1}\left\{\frac{1}{j\omega}\right\} = \frac{1}{2}\,\text{sgn}\,(t)$$

where $\text{sgn}\,(t)$ is the signum function. Deduce that

$$\mathcal{F}\{\text{sgn}\,(t)\} = \frac{2}{j\omega}$$

and use the symmetry result to demonstrate that

$$\mathcal{F}\left\{-\frac{1}{\pi t}\right\} = j\,\text{sgn}\,(\omega)$$

10 The **Hilbert transform** of a signal $f(t)$ is defined by

$$F_{Hi}(x) = \mathcal{H}\{f(t)\} = \frac{1}{\pi}\int_{-\infty}^{\infty}\frac{f(\tau)}{\tau - x}\,d\tau$$

Show that the operation of taking the Hilbert transform is equivalent to the convolution

$$-\frac{1}{\pi t} * f(t)$$

and hence deduce that the Hilbert-transformed signal has an amplitude spectrum $F_{Hi}(j\omega)$ identical with $f(t)$. Show also that the phase of the transformed signal is changed by $\pm\frac{1}{2}\pi$, depending on the sign of ω.

11 Show that

$$\frac{t}{(t^2 + a^2)(t - x)}$$

$$= \frac{1}{x^2 + a^2}\left(\frac{a^2}{t^2 + a^2} + \frac{x}{t - x} - \frac{xt}{t^2 + a^2}\right)$$

Hence show that the Hilbert transform of

$$f(t) = \frac{t}{t^2 + a^2} \quad (a > 0)$$

is

$$\frac{a}{x^2 + a^2}$$

12 If $F_{Hi}(x) = \mathcal{H}\{f(t)\}$ is the Hilbert transform of $f(t)$, establish the following properties:

(a) $\mathcal{H}\{f(a + t)\} = F_{Hi}(x + a)$

(b) $\mathcal{H}\{f(at)\} = F_{Hi}(ax)$ $(a > 0)$

(c) $\mathcal{H}\{f(-at)\} = -F_{Hi}(-ax)$ $(a > 0)$

(d) $\mathcal{H}\left\{\dfrac{df}{dt}\right\} = \dfrac{d}{dx}F_{Hi}(x)$

(e) $\mathcal{H}\{tf(t)\} = xF_{Hi}(x) + \dfrac{1}{\pi}\displaystyle\int_{-\infty}^{\infty} f(t)\,dt$

13 Show that

$$f(t) = -\frac{1}{\pi}\int_{-\infty}^{\infty}\frac{F_{Hi}(x)}{x - t}\,dx$$

14 Define the **analytic signal** associated with the real signal $f(t)$ as

$$f_a(t) = f(t) - jF_{Hi}(t)$$

where $F_{Hi}(t)$ is the Hilbert transform of $f(t)$. Use the method of Review exercise 3 to show that

$$\mathcal{F}\{f_a(t)\} = F_a(j\omega) = \begin{cases} 2F(j\omega) & (\omega > 0) \\ 0 & (\omega < 0) \end{cases}$$

15 Use the result $\mathcal{F}\{H(t)\} = 1/j\omega + \pi\delta(\omega)$ and the symmetry property to show that

$$\mathcal{F}\{H(\omega)\} = \frac{1}{2}\delta(t) + \frac{j}{2\pi t}$$

(*Hint*: $H(-\omega) = 1 - H(\omega)$.)

Hence show that if $\hat{f}(t)$ is defined by $\mathcal{F}\{\hat{f}(t)\} = 2H(\omega)F(j\omega)$ then $\hat{f}(t) = f(t) - F_{Hi}(t)$, the analytic signal associated with $f(t)$, where $F(j\omega) = \mathcal{F}\{f(t)\}$ and $F_{Hi}(t) = \mathcal{H}\{f(t)\}$.

If $f(t) = \cos \omega_0 t$ $(\omega_0 > 0)$, find $\mathcal{F}\{f(t)\}$ and hence $\hat{f}(t)$. Deduce that

$$\mathcal{H}\{\cos \omega_0 t\} = -\sin \omega_0 t$$

By considering the signal $g(t) = \sin \omega_0 t$ $(\omega_0 > 0)$, show that

$$\mathcal{H}\{\sin \omega_0 t\} = \cos \omega_0 t$$

16 A causal system has impulse response $\bar{h}(t)$, where $\bar{h}(t) = 0$ $(t < 0)$. Define the even part $\bar{h}_e(t)$ of $\bar{h}(t)$ as

$$\bar{h}_e(t) = \frac{1}{2}[\bar{h}(t) + \bar{h}(-t)]$$

and the odd part $h_o(t)$ as

$$\bar{h}_o(t) = \frac{1}{2}[\bar{h}(t) - \bar{h}(-t)]$$

Deduce that if $\bar{h}(t) = 0$ $(t < 0)$ then

$$\bar{h}_o(t) = \mathrm{sgn}\,(t)\,\bar{h}_e(t)$$

and that

$$\bar{h}(t) = \bar{h}_e(t) + \mathrm{sgn}\,(t)\,\bar{h}_e(t) \quad \text{for all } t$$

Verify this result for $\bar{h}(t) = \sin t\, H(t)$. Take the Fourier transform of this result to establish that

$$\bar{H}(\mathrm{j}\omega) = \bar{H}_e(\mathrm{j}\omega) + \mathrm{j}\mathscr{H}\{\bar{H}_e(\mathrm{j}\omega)\}$$

Let $\bar{h}(t) = \mathrm{e}^{-at}H(t)$ be such a causal impulse response. By taking the Fourier transform, deduce the Hilbert transform pair

$$\mathscr{H}\left\{\frac{a}{a^2 + t^2}\right\} = -\frac{x}{a^2 + x^2}$$

Use the result

$$\mathscr{H}\{tf(t)\} = x\,\mathscr{H}\{f(t)\} + \frac{1}{\pi}\int_{-\infty}^{\infty} f(t)\,\mathrm{d}t$$

to show that

$$\mathscr{H}\left\{\frac{t}{a^2 + t^2}\right\} = \frac{a}{x^2 + a^2}$$

17 The **Hartley transform** is defined as

$$F_H(s) = H\{f(t)\} = \int_{-\infty}^{\infty} f(t)\,\mathrm{cas}\,2\pi st\,\mathrm{d}t$$

where $\mathrm{cas}\,t = \cos t + \sin t$. Find the Hartley transform of the functions

(a) $f(t) = \mathrm{e}^{-at}H(t) \quad (a > 0)$

(b) $f(t) = \begin{cases} 0 & (|t| > T) \\ 1 & (|t| \leqslant T) \end{cases}$

18 An alternative form of the Fourier transform pair is given by

$$F(\mathrm{j}p) = \int_{-\infty}^{\infty} f(t)\,\mathrm{e}^{-\mathrm{j}2\pi pt}\,\mathrm{d}t$$

$$g(t) = \int_{-\infty}^{\infty} G(\mathrm{j}p)\,\mathrm{e}^{\mathrm{j}2\pi pt}\,\mathrm{d}t$$

where the frequency p is now measured in hertz. Define the even part of the Hartley transform as

$$E(s) = \tfrac{1}{2}[F_H(s) + F_H(-s)]$$

and the odd part as

$$O(s) = \tfrac{1}{2}[F_H(s) - F_H(-s)]$$

Show that the Fourier transform of $f(t)$ is given by

$$F(\mathrm{j}p) = E(p) - \mathrm{j}O(p)$$

and confirm your result for $f(t) = \mathrm{e}^{-2t}H(t)$.

19 Prove the **time-shift result** for the Hartley transform in the form

$$F_H\{f(t - T)\} = \sin 2\pi T\, F_H(-s) + \cos 2\pi T\, F_H(s)$$

20 Using the alternative form of the Fourier transform given in Exercise 18, it can be shown that the Fourier transform of the Heaviside step function is

$$\mathscr{F}\{H(t)\} = \frac{1}{\mathrm{j}p\pi} + \tfrac{1}{2}\delta(p)$$

Show that the Hartley transform of $H(t)$ is then

$$\tfrac{1}{2}\delta(s) + \frac{1}{\mathrm{j}s\pi}$$

and deduce that the Hartley transform of $H(t - \tfrac{1}{2})$ is

$$\tfrac{1}{2}\delta(s) + \frac{\cos \pi s - \sin \pi s}{s\pi}$$

21 Show that $F_H\{\delta(t)\} = 1$ and deduce that $F_H\{1\} = \delta(s)$. Show also that $F_H\{\delta(t - t_0)\} = \mathrm{cas}\,2\pi st_0$ and that

$$F_H\{\mathrm{cas}\,2\pi s_0 t\} = F_H\{\cos 2\pi s_0 t\} + F_H\{\sin 2\pi s_0 t\}$$
$$= \delta(s - s_0)$$

22 Prove the Hartley transform **modulation theorem** in the form

$$F_H\{f(t)\cos 2\pi s_0 t\} = \tfrac{1}{2}F_H(s - s_0) + \tfrac{1}{2}F_H(s + s_0)$$

Hence show that

$$F_H\{\cos 2\pi s_0 t\} = \tfrac{1}{2}[\delta(s - s_0) + \delta(s + s_0)]$$
$$F_H\{\sin 2\pi s_0 t\} = \tfrac{1}{2}[\delta(s - s_0) - \delta(s + s_0)]$$

23 Show that

$$\mathscr{F}\{\tan^{-1} t\} = \frac{\pi \mathrm{e}^{-|\omega|}}{\mathrm{j}\omega}$$

$$\left(\text{Hint: Consider } \int_{-\infty}^{t} (1 + t^2)^{-1}\,\mathrm{d}t.\right)$$

24 Show that

$$x(t) = \tfrac{1}{2}(1 + \cos \omega_0 t)[H(t + \tfrac{1}{2}T) - H(t - \tfrac{1}{2}T)]$$

has Fourier transform

$$T[\mathrm{sinc}\,\omega + \tfrac{1}{2}\mathrm{sinc}\,(\omega - \omega_0) + \tfrac{1}{2}\mathrm{sinc}\,(\omega + \omega_0)]$$

25 The **discrete Hartley transform** of the sequence $\{f(r)\}_{r=0}^{N-1}$ is defined by

$$H(v) = \frac{1}{N}\sum_{r=0}^{N-1} f(r)\,\mathrm{cas}\left(\frac{2\pi vr}{N}\right) \quad (v = 0, 1, \ldots, N - 1)$$

The inverse transform is

$$f(r) = \sum_{v=0}^{N-1} H(v) \operatorname{cas}\left(\frac{2\pi v r}{N}\right) \quad (r = 0, \ldots, N-1)$$

Show that in the case $N = 4$,

$$\mathbf{H} = \boldsymbol{T}\boldsymbol{f}$$

$$\mathbf{H} = [H(0) \quad H(1) \quad H(2) \quad H(3)]^{\mathrm{T}}$$

$$\boldsymbol{f} = [f(0) \quad f(1) \quad f(2) \quad f(3)]^{\mathrm{T}}$$

$$\boldsymbol{T} = \frac{1}{4}\begin{bmatrix} 1 & 1 & 1 & 1 \\ 1 & 1 & -1 & -1 \\ 1 & -1 & 1 & -1 \\ 1 & -1 & -1 & 1 \end{bmatrix}$$

Hence compute the discrete Hartley transform of the sequence $\{1, 2, 3, 4\}$. Show that $\boldsymbol{T}^2 = \frac{1}{4}\boldsymbol{I}$ and hence that $\boldsymbol{T}^{-1} = 4\boldsymbol{T}$, and verify that applying the $\boldsymbol{T}^{-1}$ operator regains the original sequence.

6

Matrix Analysis

CONTENTS

6.1 Introduction

In this chapter we turn our attention again to matrices, first considered in Chapter 4 of *Modern Engineering Mathematics*, and their applications in engineering. As the reader will be aware, matrices are arrays of real or complex numbers, and have a special, but not exclusive, relationship with systems of linear equations. An (incorrect) initial impression often formed by users of mathematics is that mathematicians have something of an obsession with these systems and their solution. However, such systems occur quite naturally in the process of numerical solution of ordinary differential equations used to model everyday engineering processes. In Chapter 8 we shall see that they also occur in numerical methods for the solution of partial differential equations, for example those modelling the flow of a fluid or the transfer of heat. Systems of linear first-order differential equations with constant coefficients are at the core of the **state-space** representation of linear system models. Identification, analysis and indeed design of such systems can conveniently be performed in the state-space representation, with this form assuming a particular importance in the case of multivariable systems.

In all these areas it is convenient to use a matrix representation for the systems under consideration, since this allows the system model to be manipulated following the rules of matrix algebra. A particularly valuable type of manipulation is **simplification** in some sense. Such a simplification process is an example of a system transformation, carried out by the process of matrix multiplication. At the heart of many transformations are the **eigenvalues** and **eigenvectors** of a square matrix. In addition to providing the means by which simplifying transformations can be deduced, system eigenvalues provide vital information on system stability, fundamental frequencies, speed of decay and long-term system behaviour. For this reason, we devote a substantial amount of space to the process of their calculation, both by hand and by numerical means when necessary. Our treatment of numerical methods is intended to be purely indicative rather than complete, because a comprehensive matrix algebra computational tool kit is now part of the essential armoury of all serious users of mathematics.

In addition to developing the use of matrix algebra techniques, we also demonstrate the techniques and applications of matrix analysis, focusing on the state-space system model widely used in control and systems engineering. Here we encounter the idea of a function of a matrix, in particular the matrix exponential, and we see again the role of the eigenvalues in its calculation. We also highlight the use of transform methods in the calculation of functions of matrices, linking with our work on the Laplace and z transforms in Chapters 2 and 3.

6.2 The eigenvalue problem

A problem that leads to a concept of crucial importance in many branches of mathematics and its applications is that of seeking non-trivial solutions $x \neq 0$ to the matrix equation

$$\boldsymbol{A}x = \lambda x$$

This is referred to as the eigenvalue problem; values of the scalar λ for which non-trivial solutions exist are called **eigenvalues** and the corresponding solutions $x \neq 0$ are called the **eigenvectors**. Such problems arise naturally in many branches of engineering. For example, in vibrations the eigenvalues and eigenvectors describe the frequency and mode of vibration respectively, while in mechanics they represent principal stresses and the principal axes of stress in bodies subjected to external forces. In Section 6.10 we shall see that eigenvalues also play an important role in the stability analysis of dynamical systems.

6.2.1   The characteristic equation

The set of simultaneous equations

$$\boldsymbol{A}\boldsymbol{x} = \lambda\boldsymbol{x} \tag{6.1}$$

where $\boldsymbol{A}$ is an $n \times n$ matrix and $\boldsymbol{x} = [x_1 \quad x_2 \quad \ldots \quad x_n]^\mathrm{T}$ is an $n \times 1$ column vector can be written in the form

$$(\lambda\boldsymbol{I} - \boldsymbol{A})\boldsymbol{x} = 0 \tag{6.2}$$

where $\boldsymbol{I}$ is the identity matrix. The matrix equation (6.2) represents simply a set of homogeneous equations, and we know that a non-trivial solution exists if

$$c(\lambda) = |\lambda\boldsymbol{I} - \boldsymbol{A}| = 0 \tag{6.3}$$

Here $c(\lambda)$ is the expansion of the determinant and is a polynomial of degree n in λ, called the **characteristic polynomial** of $\boldsymbol{A}$. Thus

$$c(\lambda) = \lambda^n + c_{n-1}\lambda^{n-1} + c_{n-2}\lambda^{n-2} + \ldots + c_1\lambda + c_0$$

and the equation $c(\lambda) = 0$ is called the **characteristic equation** of $\boldsymbol{A}$. We note that this equation can be obtained just as well by evaluating $|\boldsymbol{A} - \lambda\boldsymbol{I}| = 0$; however, the form (6.3) is preferred for the definition of the characteristic equation, since the coefficient of λ^n is then always $+1$.

In many areas of engineering, particularly in those involving vibration or the control of processes, the determination of those values of λ for which (6.2) has a non-trivial solution (that is, a solution for which $\boldsymbol{x} \neq 0$) is of vital importance. These values of λ are precisely the values that satisfy the characteristic equation, and are called the eigenvalues of $\boldsymbol{A}$.

EXAMPLE 6.1   Find the characteristic equation for the matrix

$$\boldsymbol{A} = \begin{bmatrix} 1 & 1 & -2 \\ -1 & 2 & 1 \\ 0 & 1 & -1 \end{bmatrix}$$

Solution By (6.3), the characteristic equation for A is the cubic equation

$$c(\lambda) = \begin{vmatrix} \lambda - 1 & -1 & 2 \\ 1 & \lambda - 2 & -1 \\ 0 & -1 & \lambda + 1 \end{vmatrix} = 0$$

Expanding the determinant along the first column gives

$$c(\lambda) = (\lambda - 1)\begin{vmatrix} \lambda - 2 & -1 \\ -1 & \lambda + 1 \end{vmatrix} - \begin{vmatrix} -1 & 2 \\ -1 & \lambda + 1 \end{vmatrix}$$

$$= (\lambda - 1)[(\lambda - 2)(\lambda + 1) - 1] - [2 - (\lambda + 1)]$$

Thus

$$c(\lambda) = \lambda^3 - 2\lambda^2 - \lambda + 2 = 0$$

is the required characteristic equation.

For matrices of large order, determining the characteristic polynomial by direct expansion of $|\lambda I - A|$ is unsatisfactory in view of the large number of terms involved in the determinant expansion. Alternative procedures are available to reduce the amount of calculation, and that due to Faddeev may be stated as follows.

The method of Faddeev

If the characteristic polynomial of an $n \times n$ matrix A is written as

$$\lambda^n - p_1\lambda^{n-1} - \ldots - p_{n-1}\lambda - p_n \qquad\qquad (6.4)$$

then the coefficients $p_1, p_2, \ldots, p_n$ can be computed using

$$p_r = \frac{1}{r}\text{trace } A_r, \quad (r = 1, 2, \ldots, n)$$

where

$$A_r = \begin{cases} A & (r = 1) \\ AB_{r-1} & (r = 2, 3, \ldots, n) \end{cases}$$

and

$$B_r = A_r - p_r I, \qquad \text{where } I \text{ is the } n \times n \text{ identity matrix}$$

The calculations may be checked using the result that

$$B_n = A_n - p_n I \quad \text{must be the zero matrix}$$

EXAMPLE 6.2   Using the method of Faddeev, obtain the characteristic equation of the matrix A of Example 6.1.

Solution

$$A = \begin{bmatrix} 1 & 1 & -2 \\ -1 & 2 & 1 \\ 0 & 1 & -1 \end{bmatrix}$$

Let the characteristic equation be

$$c(\lambda) = \lambda^3 - p_1 \lambda^2 - p_2 \lambda - p_3$$

Then, following the procedure described above,

$$p_1 = \text{trace } A = (1 + 2 - 1) = 2$$

$$B_1 = A - 2I = \begin{bmatrix} -1 & 1 & -2 \\ -1 & 0 & 1 \\ 0 & 1 & -3 \end{bmatrix}$$

$$A_2 = AB_1 = \begin{bmatrix} -2 & -1 & 5 \\ -1 & 0 & 1 \\ -1 & -1 & 4 \end{bmatrix}$$

$$p_2 = \tfrac{1}{2}\,\text{trace } A_2 = \tfrac{1}{2}(-2 + 0 + 4) = 1$$

$$B_2 = A_2 - I = \begin{bmatrix} -3 & -1 & 5 \\ -1 & -1 & 1 \\ -1 & -1 & 3 \end{bmatrix}$$

$$A_3 = AB_2 = \begin{bmatrix} -2 & 0 & 0 \\ 0 & -2 & 0 \\ 0 & 0 & -2 \end{bmatrix}$$

$$p_3 = \tfrac{1}{3}\,\text{trace } A_3 = \tfrac{1}{3}(-2 - 2 - 2) = -2$$

Then, from (6.4), the characteristic polynomial of A is

$$c(\lambda) = \lambda^3 - 2\lambda^2 - \lambda + 2$$

in agreement with the result of Example 6.1. In this case, however, a check may be carried out on the computation, since

$$B_3 = A_3 + 2I = 0$$

as required.

6.2.2 Eigenvalues and eigenvectors

The roots of the characteristic equation (6.3) are called the eigenvalues of the matrix A (the terms latent roots, proper roots and characteristic roots are also sometimes used). By the Fundamental Theorem of Algebra, a polynomial equation of degree n has exactly n roots, so that the matrix A has exactly n eigenvalues λ_i, $i = 1, 2, \ldots, n$. These eigenvalues may be real or complex, and not necessarily distinct. Corresponding to each eigenvalue λ_i, there is a non-zero solution $x = e_i$ of (6.2); e_i is called the eigenvector of A corresponding to the eigenvalue λ_i. (Again the terms latent vector, proper vector and characteristic vector are sometimes seen, but are generally obsolete.) We note that if $x = e_i$ satisfies (6.2) then any scalar multiple $\beta_i e_i$ of e_i also satisfies (6.2), so that the eigenvector e_i may only be determined to within a scalar multiple.

EXAMPLE 6.3 Determine the eigenvalues and eigenvectors for the matrix A of Example 6.1.

Solution
$$A = \begin{bmatrix} 1 & 1 & -2 \\ -1 & 2 & 1 \\ 0 & 1 & -1 \end{bmatrix}$$

The eigenvalues λ_i of A satisfy the characteristic equation $c(\lambda) = 0$, and this has been obtained in Examples 6.1 and 6.2 as the cubic

$$\lambda^3 - 2\lambda^2 - \lambda + 2 = 0$$

which can be solved to obtain the eigenvalues λ_1, λ_2 and λ_3.

Alternatively, it may be possible, using the determinant form $|\lambda I - A|$, or indeed (as we often do when seeking the eigenvalues) the form $|A - \lambda I|$, by carrying out suitable row and/or column operations to factorize the determinant. In this case

$$|A - \lambda I| = \begin{vmatrix} 1 - \lambda & 1 & -2 \\ -1 & 2 - \lambda & 1 \\ 0 & 1 & -1 - \lambda \end{vmatrix} \tag{6.5}$$

and adding column 1 to column 3 gives

$$\begin{vmatrix} 1 - \lambda & 1 & -1 - \lambda \\ -1 & 2 - \lambda & 0 \\ 0 & 1 & -1 - \lambda \end{vmatrix} = -(1 + \lambda) \begin{vmatrix} 1 - \lambda & 1 & 1 \\ -1 & 2 - \lambda & 0 \\ 0 & 1 & 1 \end{vmatrix}$$

Subtracting row 3 from row 1 gives

$$-(1 + \lambda)\begin{vmatrix} 1 - \lambda & 0 & 0 \\ -1 & 2 - \lambda & 0 \\ 0 & 1 & 1 \end{vmatrix} = -(1 + \lambda)(1 - \lambda)(2 - \lambda)$$

Setting $|\mathbf{A} - \lambda \mathbf{I}| = 0$ gives the eigenvalues as $\lambda_1 = 2$, $\lambda_2 = 1$ and $\lambda_3 = -1$. The order in which they are written is arbitrary, but for consistency we shall adopt the convention of taking $\lambda_1, \lambda_2, \ldots, \lambda_n$ in decreasing order.

Having obtained the eigenvalues $\lambda_i (i = 1, 2, 3)$, the corresponding eigenvectors $\mathbf{e}_i$ are obtained by solving the appropriate homogeneous equations

$$(\mathbf{A} - \lambda_i \mathbf{I})\mathbf{e}_i = 0 \tag{6.6}$$

When $i = 1$, $\lambda_i = \lambda_1 = 2$ and (6.6) is

$$\begin{bmatrix} -1 & 1 & -2 \\ -1 & 0 & 1 \\ 0 & 1 & -3 \end{bmatrix} \begin{bmatrix} e_{11} \\ e_{12} \\ e_{13} \end{bmatrix} = 0$$

that is,

$$-e_{11} + e_{12} - 2e_{13} = 0$$
$$-e_{11} + 0e_{12} + e_{13} = 0$$
$$0e_{11} + e_{12} - 3e_{13} = 0$$

leading to the solution

$$\frac{e_{11}}{-1} = \frac{-e_{12}}{3} = \frac{e_{13}}{-1} = \beta_1$$

where β_1 is an arbitrary scalar. Thus the eigenvector $\mathbf{e}_1$ corresponding to the eigenvalue $\lambda_1 = 2$ is

$$\mathbf{e}_1 = \beta_1 [1 \quad 3 \quad 1]^T$$

As a check, we can compute

$$\mathbf{A}\mathbf{e}_1 = \begin{bmatrix} 1 & 1 & -2 \\ -1 & 2 & 1 \\ 0 & 1 & -1 \end{bmatrix} \begin{bmatrix} 1 \\ 3 \\ 1 \end{bmatrix} = \beta_1 \begin{bmatrix} 2 \\ 6 \\ 2 \end{bmatrix} = 2\beta_1 \begin{bmatrix} 1 \\ 3 \\ 1 \end{bmatrix} = \lambda_1 \mathbf{e}_1$$

and thus conclude that our calculation was correct.

When $i = 2$, $\lambda_i = \lambda_2 = 1$ and we have to solve

$$\begin{bmatrix} 0 & 1 & -2 \\ -1 & 1 & 1 \\ 0 & 1 & -2 \end{bmatrix} \begin{bmatrix} e_{21} \\ e_{22} \\ e_{23} \end{bmatrix} = 0$$

that is,

$$0e_{21} + e_{22} - 2e_{23} = 0$$
$$-e_{21} + e_{22} + e_{23} = 0$$
$$0e_{21} + e_{22} - 2e_{23} = 0$$

leading to the solution

$$\frac{e_{21}}{-3} = \frac{-e_{22}}{2} = \frac{e_{23}}{-1} = \beta_2$$

where β_2 is an arbitrary scalar. Thus the eigenvector e_2 corresponding to the eigenvalue $\lambda_2 = 1$ is

$$e_2 = \beta_2 [3 \quad 2 \quad 1]^{\mathrm{T}}$$

Again a check could be made by computing Ae_2.

Finally, when $i = 3$, $\lambda_i = \lambda_3 = -1$ and we obtain from (6.6)

$$\begin{bmatrix} 2 & 1 & -2 \\ -1 & 3 & 1 \\ 0 & 1 & 0 \end{bmatrix} \begin{bmatrix} e_{31} \\ e_{32} \\ e_{33} \end{bmatrix} = 0$$

that is,

$$2e_{31} + e_{32} - 2e_{33} = 0$$
$$-e_{31} + 3e_{32} + e_{33} = 0$$
$$0e_{31} + e_{32} + 0e_{33} = 0$$

and hence

$$\frac{e_{31}}{-1} = \frac{e_{32}}{0} = \frac{e_{33}}{-1} = \beta_3$$

Here again β_3 is an arbitrary scalar, and the eigenvector e_3 corresponding to the eigenvalue λ_3 is

$$e_3 = \beta_3 [1 \quad 0 \quad 1]^{\mathrm{T}}$$

The calculation can be checked as before. Thus we have found that the eigenvalues of the matrix A are 2, 1 and -1, with corresponding eigenvectors

$$\beta_1 [1 \quad 3 \quad 1]^{\mathrm{T}}, \quad \beta_2 [3 \quad 2 \quad 1]^{\mathrm{T}} \quad \text{and} \quad \beta_3 [1 \quad 0 \quad 1]^{\mathrm{T}}$$

respectively.

Since in Example 6.3 the β_i, $i = 1, 2, 3$, are arbitrary, it follows that there are an infinite number of eigenvectors, scalar multiples of each other, corresponding to each eigenvalue. Sometimes it is convenient to scale the eigenvectors according to some convention. A convention frequently adopted is to **normalize** the eigenvectors so that they are uniquely determined up to a scale factor of ± 1. The normalized form of an eigenvector $e = [e_1 \quad e_2 \quad \dots \quad e_n]^{\mathrm{T}}$ is denoted by $\hat{e}$ and is given by

$$\hat{e} = \frac{e}{|e|}$$

where

$$|e| = \sqrt{(e_1^2 + e_2^2 + \dots + e_n^2)}$$

For example, for the matrix A of Example 6.3, the normalized forms of the eigenvectors are

$$\hat{e}_1 = [1/\sqrt{11} \quad 3/\sqrt{11} \quad 1/\sqrt{11}]^{\mathrm{T}}, \quad \hat{e}_2 = [3/\sqrt{14} \quad 2/\sqrt{14} \quad 1/\sqrt{14}]^{\mathrm{T}}$$

and

$$\hat{e}_3 = [1/\sqrt{2} \quad 0 \quad 1/\sqrt{2}]^{\mathrm{T}}$$

However, throughout the text, unless otherwise stated, the eigenvectors will always be presented in their 'simplest' form, so that for the matrix of Example 6.3 we take $\beta_1 = \beta_2 = \beta_3 = 1$ and write

$$e_1 = [1 \quad 3 \quad 1]^{\mathrm{T}}, \quad e_2 = [3 \quad 2 \quad 1]^{\mathrm{T}} \quad \text{and} \quad e_3 = [1 \quad 0 \quad 1]^{\mathrm{T}}$$

EXAMPLE 6.4   Find the eigenvalues and eigenvectors of

$$A = \begin{bmatrix} \cos\theta & -\sin\theta \\ \sin\theta & \cos\theta \end{bmatrix}$$

Solution   Now

$$|\lambda I - A| = \begin{vmatrix} \lambda - \cos\theta & \sin\theta \\ -\sin\theta & \lambda - \cos\theta \end{vmatrix}$$

$$= \lambda^2 - 2\lambda\cos\theta + \cos^2\theta + \sin^2\theta$$

$$= \lambda^2 - 2\lambda\cos\theta + 1$$

So the eigenvalues are the roots of

$$\lambda^2 - 2\lambda\cos\theta + 1 = 0$$

that is,

$$\lambda = \cos\theta \pm \mathrm{j}\sin\theta$$

Solving for the eigenvectors as in Example 6.3, we obtain

$$e_1 = [1 \quad -\mathrm{j}]^{\mathrm{T}} \quad \text{and} \quad e_2 = [1 \quad \mathrm{j}]^{\mathrm{T}}$$

In Example 6.4 we see that eigenvalues can be complex numbers, and that the eigenvectors may have complex components. This situation arises when the characteristic equation has complex (conjugate) roots.

6.2.3 Exercises

1 Using the method of Faddeev, obtain the characteristic polynomials of the matrices

(a) $\begin{bmatrix} 3 & 2 & 1 \\ 4 & 5 & -1 \\ 2 & 3 & 4 \end{bmatrix}$

(b) $\begin{bmatrix} 2 & -1 & 1 & 2 \\ 0 & 1 & 1 & 0 \\ -1 & 1 & 1 & 1 \\ 1 & 1 & 1 & 0 \end{bmatrix}$

2 Find the eigenvalues and corresponding eigenvectors of the matrices

(a) $\begin{bmatrix} 1 & 1 \\ 1 & 1 \end{bmatrix}$

(b) $\begin{bmatrix} 1 & 2 \\ 3 & 2 \end{bmatrix}$

(c) $\begin{bmatrix} 1 & 0 & -4 \\ 0 & 5 & 4 \\ -4 & 4 & 3 \end{bmatrix}$

(d) $\begin{bmatrix} 1 & 1 & 2 \\ 0 & 2 & 2 \\ -1 & 1 & 3 \end{bmatrix}$

(e) $\begin{bmatrix} 5 & 0 & 6 \\ 0 & 11 & 6 \\ 6 & 6 & -2 \end{bmatrix}$

(f) $\begin{bmatrix} 1 & -1 & 0 \\ 1 & 2 & 1 \\ -2 & 1 & -1 \end{bmatrix}$

(g) $\begin{bmatrix} 4 & 1 & 1 \\ 2 & 5 & 4 \\ -1 & -1 & 0 \end{bmatrix}$

(h) $\begin{bmatrix} 1 & -4 & -2 \\ 0 & 3 & 1 \\ 1 & 2 & 4 \end{bmatrix}$

6.2.4 Repeated eigenvalues

In the examples considered so far the eigenvalues λ_i $(i = 1, 2, \ldots)$ of the matrix $\boldsymbol{A}$ have been distinct, and in such cases the corresponding eigenvectors have been linearly independent. The matrix $\boldsymbol{A}$ is then said to have a full set of linearly independent eigenvectors. It is clear that the roots of the characteristic equation $c(\lambda)$ may not all be distinct; and when $c(\lambda)$ has $p \leqslant n$ distinct roots, $c(\lambda)$ may be factorized as

$$c(\lambda) = (\lambda - \lambda_1)^{m_1}(\lambda - \lambda_2)^{m_2} \cdots (\lambda - \lambda_p)^{m_p}$$

indicating that the root $\lambda = \lambda_i, i = 1, 2, \ldots, p$, is a root of order m_i, where the integer m_i is called the **algebraic multiplicity** of the eigenvalue λ_i. Clearly $m_1 + m_2 + \ldots + m_p = n$. When a matrix $\boldsymbol{A}$ has repeated eigenvalues, the question arises as to whether it is possible to obtain a full set of linearly independent eigenvectors for $\boldsymbol{A}$. The concepts of linear independence and rank used in this section are discussed in Chapter 4 of *Modern Engineering Mathematics*. We first consider two examples to illustrate the situation.

EXAMPLE 6.5   Determine the eigenvalues and corresponding eigenvectors of the matrix

$$A = \begin{bmatrix} 3 & -3 & 2 \\ -1 & 5 & -2 \\ -1 & 3 & 0 \end{bmatrix}$$

Solution   We find the eigenvalues from

$$\begin{vmatrix} 3-\lambda & -3 & 2 \\ -1 & 5-\lambda & -2 \\ -1 & 3 & -\lambda \end{vmatrix} = 0$$

as $\lambda_1 = 4$, $\lambda_2 = \lambda_3 = 2$.

The eigenvectors are obtained from

$$(A - \lambda I)e_i = 0 \tag{6.7}$$

and when $\lambda = \lambda_1 = 4$, we obtain from (6.7)

$$e_1 = \begin{bmatrix} 1 & -1 & -1 \end{bmatrix}^T$$

When $\lambda = \lambda_2 = \lambda_3 = 2$, (6.7) becomes

$$\begin{bmatrix} 1 & -3 & 2 \\ -1 & 3 & -2 \\ -1 & 3 & -2 \end{bmatrix} \begin{bmatrix} e_{21} \\ e_{22} \\ e_{23} \end{bmatrix} = 0$$

so that the corresponding eigenvector is obtained from the single equation

$$e_{21} - 3e_{22} + 2e_{23} = 0 \tag{6.8}$$

Clearly we are free to choose any two of the components e_{21}, e_{22} or e_{23} at will, with the remaining one determined by (6.8). Suppose we set $e_{22} = \alpha$ and $e_{23} = \beta$; then (6.8) means that $e_{21} = 3\alpha - 2\beta$, and thus

$$e_2 = \begin{bmatrix} 3\alpha - 2\beta & \alpha & \beta \end{bmatrix}^T$$

$$= \alpha \begin{bmatrix} 3 \\ 1 \\ 0 \end{bmatrix} + \beta \begin{bmatrix} -2 \\ 0 \\ 1 \end{bmatrix} \tag{6.9}$$

Now $\lambda = 2$ is an eigenvalue of multiplicity 2, and we seek, if possible, two linearly independent eigenvectors defined by (6.9). Setting $\alpha = 1$ and $\beta = 0$ yields

$$e_2 = \begin{bmatrix} 3 & 1 & 0 \end{bmatrix}^T$$

and setting $\alpha = 0$ and $\beta = 1$ gives a second vector

$$e_3 = \begin{bmatrix} -2 & 0 & 1 \end{bmatrix}^T$$

These two vectors are linearly independent and of the form defined by (6.9), and it is clear that many other choices are possible. However, any other choices of the form (6.9) will be linear combinations of e_2 and e_3 as chosen above. For example, $e = [1 \quad 1 \quad 1]$ satisfies (6.9), but $e = e_2 + e_3$.

In this example, although there was a repeated eigenvalue of algebraic multiplicity 2, it was possible to construct two linearly independent eigenvectors corresponding to this eigenvalue. Thus the matrix A has three and only three linearly independent eigenvectors.

EXAMPLE 6.6   Determine the eigenvalues and corresponding eigenvectors for the matrix

$$A = \begin{bmatrix} 1 & 2 & 2 \\ 0 & 2 & 1 \\ -1 & 2 & 2 \end{bmatrix}$$

Solution   Solving $|A - \lambda I| = 0$ gives the eigenvalues as $\lambda_1 = \lambda_2 = 2, \lambda_3 = 1$. The eigenvector corresponding to the non-repeated or simple eigenvalue $\lambda_3 = 1$ is easily found as

$$e_3 = [1 \quad 1 \quad -1]^{\mathrm{T}}$$

When $\lambda = \lambda_1 = \lambda_2 = 2$, the corresponding eigenvector is given by

$$(A - 2I)e_1 = 0$$

that is, as the solution of

$$-e_{11} + 2e_{12} + 2e_{13} = 0 \tag{i}$$

$$e_{13} = 0 \tag{ii}$$

$$-e_{11} + 2e_{12} \qquad = 0 \tag{iii}$$

From (ii) we have $e_{13} = 0$, and from (i) and (ii) it follows that $e_{11} = 2e_{12}$. We deduce that there is only one linearly independent eigenvector corresponding to the repeated eigenvalue $\lambda = 2$, namely

$$e_1 = [2 \quad 1 \quad 0]^{\mathrm{T}}$$

and in this case the matrix A does not possess a full set of linearly independent eigenvectors.

We see from Examples 6.5 and 6.6 that if an $n \times n$ matrix A has repeated eigenvalues then a full set of n linearly independent eigenvectors may or may not exist. The number of linearly independent eigenvectors associated with a repeated eigenvalue λ_i of algebraic multiplicity m_i is given by the **nullity** q_i of the matrix $A - \lambda_i I$, where

$$q_i = n - \mathrm{rank}\,(A - \lambda_i I), \qquad \text{with} \quad 1 \leqslant q_i \leqslant m_i \tag{6.10}$$

q_i is sometimes referred to as the **degeneracy** of the matrix $A - \lambda_i I$ or the **geometric multiplicity** of the eigenvalue λ_i, since it determines the dimension of the space spanned by the corresponding eigenvector(s) e_i.

EXAMPLE 6.7   Confirm the findings of Examples 6.5 and 6.6 concerning the number of linearly independent eigenvectors found.

Solution   In Example 6.5, we had an eigenvalue $\lambda_2 = 2$ of algebraic multiplicity 2. Correspondingly,

$$A - \lambda_2 I = \begin{bmatrix} 3-2 & -3 & 2 \\ -1 & 5-2 & -2 \\ -1 & 3 & -2 \end{bmatrix} = \begin{bmatrix} 1 & -3 & 2 \\ -1 & 3 & -2 \\ -1 & 3 & -2 \end{bmatrix}$$

and performing the row operation of adding row 1 to rows 2 and 3 yields

$$\begin{bmatrix} 1 & -3 & 2 \\ 0 & 0 & 0 \\ 0 & 0 & 0 \end{bmatrix}$$

Adding 3 times column 1 to column 2 followed by subtracting 2 times column 1 from column 3 gives finally

$$\begin{bmatrix} 1 & 0 & 0 \\ 0 & 0 & 0 \\ 0 & 0 & 0 \end{bmatrix}$$

indicating a rank of 1. Then from (6.10) the nullity $q_2 = 3 - 1 = 2$, confirming that corresponding to the eigenvalue $\lambda = 2$ there are two linearly independent eigenvectors, as found in Example 6.5.

In Example 6.6 we again had a repeated eigenvalue $\lambda_1 = 2$ of algebraic multiplicity 2. Then

$$A - 2I = \begin{bmatrix} 1-2 & 2 & 2 \\ 0 & 2-2 & 1 \\ -1 & 2 & 2-2 \end{bmatrix} = \begin{bmatrix} -1 & 2 & 2 \\ 0 & 0 & 1 \\ -1 & 2 & 0 \end{bmatrix}$$

Performing row and column operations as before produces the matrix

$$\begin{bmatrix} -1 & 0 & 0 \\ 0 & 0 & 1 \\ 0 & 0 & 0 \end{bmatrix}$$

this time indicating a rank of 2. From (6.10) the nullity $q_1 = 3 - 2 = 1$, confirming that there is one and only one linearly independent eigenvector associated with this eigenvalue, as found in Example 6.6.

6.2.5 Exercises

3 Obtain the eigenvalues and corresponding eigenvectors of the matrices

(a) $\begin{bmatrix} 2 & 2 & 1 \\ 1 & 3 & 1 \\ 1 & 2 & 2 \end{bmatrix}$
(b) $\begin{bmatrix} 0 & -2 & -2 \\ -1 & 1 & 2 \\ -1 & -1 & 2 \end{bmatrix}$

(c) $\begin{bmatrix} 4 & 6 & 6 \\ 1 & 3 & 2 \\ -1 & -5 & -2 \end{bmatrix}$

(d) $\begin{bmatrix} 7 & -2 & -4 \\ 3 & 0 & -2 \\ 6 & -2 & -3 \end{bmatrix}$

4 Given that $\lambda = 1$ is a three-times repeated eigenvalue of the matrix

$$A = \begin{bmatrix} -3 & -7 & -5 \\ 2 & 4 & 3 \\ 1 & 2 & 2 \end{bmatrix}$$

using the concept of rank, determine how many linearly independent eigenvectors correspond to this value of λ. Determine a corresponding set of linearly independent eigenvectors.

5 Given that $\lambda = 1$ is a twice-repeated eigenvalue of the matrix

$$A = \begin{bmatrix} 2 & 1 & -1 \\ -1 & 0 & 1 \\ -1 & -1 & 2 \end{bmatrix}$$

how many linearly independent eigenvectors correspond to this value of λ? Determine a corresponding set of linearly independent eigenvectors.

6.2.6 Some useful properties of eigenvalues

The following basic properties of the eigenvalues $\lambda_1, \lambda_2, \ldots, \lambda_n$ of an $n \times n$ matrix A are sometimes useful. The results are readily proved from either the definition of eigenvalues as the values of λ satisfying (6.1), or by comparison of corresponding characteristic polynomials (6.3). Consequently, the proofs are left to Exercise 6.

Property 6.1

The sum of the eigenvalues A is

$$\sum_{i=1}^{n} \lambda_i = \text{trace } A = \sum_{i=1}^{n} a_{ii}$$

Property 6.2

The product of the eigenvalues of A is

$$\prod_{i=1}^{n} \lambda_i = \det \mathbf{A}$$

where $\det \mathbf{A}$ denotes the determinant of the matrix $\mathbf{A}$.

Property 6.3

The eigenvalues of the inverse matrix $\mathbf{A}^{-1}$, provided it exists, are

$$\frac{1}{\lambda_1}, \quad \frac{1}{\lambda_2}, \quad \ldots, \quad \frac{1}{\lambda_n}$$

Property 6.4

The eigenvalues of the transposed matrix $\mathbf{A}^T$ are

$$\lambda_1, \lambda_2, \ldots, \lambda_n$$

as for the matrix $\mathbf{A}$.

Property 6.5

If k is a scalar then the eigenvalues of $k\mathbf{A}$ are

$$k\lambda_1, \quad k\lambda_2, \quad \ldots, \quad k\lambda_n$$

Property 6.6

If k is a scalar and $\mathbf{I}$ the $n \times n$ identity (unit) matrix then the eigenvalues of $\mathbf{A} + k\mathbf{I}$ are respectively

$$\lambda_1 \pm k, \quad \lambda_2 \pm k, \quad \ldots, \quad \lambda_n \pm k$$

Property 6.7

If k is a positive integer then the eigenvalues of $\mathbf{A}^k$ are

$$\lambda_1^k, \quad \lambda_2^k, \quad \ldots, \quad \lambda_n^k$$

6.2.7   Symmetric matrices

A square matrix A is said to be **symmetric** if $A^T = A$. Such matrices form an important class and arise in a variety of practical situations. Two important results concerning the eigenvalues and eigenvectors of such matrices are

(a) the eigenvalues of a real symmetric matrix are real;

(b) for an $n \times n$ real symmetric matrix it is always possible to find n linearly independent eigenvectors $e_1, e_2, \ldots, e_n$ that are mutually orthogonal so that $e_i^T e_j = 0$ for $i \neq j$.

If the orthogonal eigenvectors of a symmetric matrix are normalized as

$$\hat{e}_1, \quad \hat{e}_2, \quad \ldots, \quad \hat{e}_n$$

then the **inner (scalar) product** is

$$\hat{e}_i^T \hat{e}_j = \delta_{ij} \quad (i, j = 1, 2, \ldots, n)$$

where δ_{ij} is the Kronecker delta:

$$\delta_{ij} = \begin{cases} 1 & (i = j) \\ 0 & (i \neq j) \end{cases}$$

The set of normalized eigenvectors of a symmetric matrix therefore form an orthonormal set (that is, they form a mutually orthogonal normalized set of vectors).

EXAMPLE 6.8   Obtain the eigenvalues and corresponding orthogonal eigenvectors of the symmetric matrix

$$A = \begin{bmatrix} 2 & 2 & 0 \\ 2 & 5 & 0 \\ 0 & 0 & 3 \end{bmatrix}$$

and show that the normalized eigenvectors form an orthonormal set.

Solution   The eigenvalues of A are $\lambda_1 = 6, \lambda_2 = 3$ and $\lambda_3 = 1$, with corresponding eigenvectors

$$e_1 = [1 \quad 2 \quad 0]^T, \qquad e_2 = [0 \quad 0 \quad 1]^T, \qquad e_3 = [-2 \quad 1 \quad 0]^T$$

which in normalized form are

$$\hat{e}_1 = [1 \quad 2 \quad 0]^T / \sqrt{5}$$

$$\hat{e}_2 = [0 \quad 0 \quad 1]^T$$

$$\hat{e}_3 = [-2 \quad 1 \quad 0]^T / \sqrt{5}$$

Evaluating the inner products, we see that, for example,

$$\hat{e}_1^T \hat{e}_1 = \tfrac{1}{5} + \tfrac{4}{5} + 0 = 1$$

$$\hat{e}_1^T \hat{e}_3 = -\tfrac{2}{5} + \tfrac{2}{5} + 0 = 0$$

and that

$$\hat{e}_i^T \hat{e}_j = \delta_{ij} \quad (i, j = 1, 2, 3)$$

confirming that the eigenvectors form an orthonormal set.

6.2.8   Exercises

6 Verify Properties 6.1–6.7 of Section 6.2.6.

7 Given that the eigenvalues of the matrix

$$A = \begin{bmatrix} 4 & 1 & 1 \\ 2 & 5 & 4 \\ -1 & -1 & 0 \end{bmatrix}$$

are 5, 3 and 1:

(a) confirm Properties 6.1–6.4 of Section 6.2.6.

(b) taking $k = 2$, confirm Properties 6.5–6.7 of Section 6.2.6.

8 Determine the eigenvalues and corresponding eigenvectors of the symmetric matrix

$$A = \begin{bmatrix} -3 & -3 & -3 \\ -3 & 1 & -1 \\ -3 & -1 & 1 \end{bmatrix}$$

and verify that the eigenvectors are mutually orthogonal.

9 The 3×3 symmetric matrix A has eigenvalues 6, 3 and 2. The eigenvectors corresponding to the eigenvalues 6 and 3 are $[1 \ \ 1 \ \ 2]^T$ and $[1 \ \ 1 \ \ -1]^T$ respectively. Find an eigenvector corresponding to the eigenvalue 2.

6.3   Numerical methods

In practice we may well be dealing with matrices whose elements are decimal numbers or with matrices of high orders. In order to determine the eigenvalues and eigenvectors of such matrices, it is necessary that we have numerical algorithms at our disposal.

6.3.1   The power method

Consider a matrix A having n distinct eigenvalues $\lambda_1, \lambda_2, \ldots, \lambda_n$ and corresponding n linearly independent eigenvectors $e_1, e_2, \ldots, e_n$. Taking this set of vectors as the basis, we can write any vector $x = [x_1 \quad x_2 \quad \ldots \quad x_n]^T$ as a linear combination in the form

$$x = \alpha_1 e_1 + \alpha_2 e_2 + \ldots + \alpha_n e_n = \sum_{i=1}^{n} \alpha_i e_i$$

Then, since $Ae_i = \lambda_i e_i$ for $i = 1, 2, \ldots, n,$

$$Ax = A \sum_{i=1}^{n} \alpha_i e_i = \sum_{i=1}^{n} \alpha_i \lambda_i e_i$$

and, for any positive integer $k,$

$$A^k x = \sum_{i=1}^{n} \alpha_i \lambda_i^k e_i$$

or

$$A^k x = \lambda_1^k \left[\alpha_1 e_1 + \sum_{i=2}^{n} \alpha_i \left(\frac{\lambda_i}{\lambda_1} \right)^k e_i \right] \tag{6.11}$$

Assuming that the eigenvalues are ordered such that

$$|\lambda_1| > |\lambda_2| > \ldots > |\lambda_n|$$

and that $\alpha_1 \neq 0$, we have from (6.11)

$$\lim_{k \to \infty} A^k x = \lambda_1^k \alpha_1 e_1 \tag{6.12}$$

since all the other terms inside the square brackets tend to zero. The eigenvalue λ_1 and its corresponding eigenvector e_1 are referred to as the **dominant** eigenvalue and eigenvector respectively. The other eigenvalues and eigenvectors are called **subdominant**.

Thus if we introduce the iterative process

$$x^{(k+1)} = Ax^{(k)} \quad (k = 0, 1, 2, \ldots)$$

starting with some arbitrary vector $x^{(0)}$ not orthogonal to e_1, it follows from (6.12) that

$$x^{(k)} = A^k x^{(0)}$$

will converge to the dominant eigenvector of A.

A clear disadvantage with this scheme is that if $|\lambda_1|$ is large then $A^k x^{(0)}$ will become very large, and computer overflow can occur. This can be avoided by scaling the vector $x^{(k)}$ after each iteration. The standard approach is to make the largest element of $x^{(k)}$ unity using the scaling factor $\max(x^{(k)})$, which represents the element of $x^{(k)}$ having the largest modulus.

Thus in practice we adopt the iterative process

$$y^{(k+1)} = Ax^{(k)}$$

$$x^{(k+1)} = \frac{y^{(k+1)}}{\max(y^{(k+1)})} \quad (k = 0, 1, 2, \ldots) \tag{6.13}$$

and it is common to take $x^{(0)} = [1 \quad 1 \quad \ldots \quad 1]^T$.

```
{read in x^T = [x₁ x₂ ... xₙ]}
  m ← 0
  repeat
    mold ← m
    {evaluate y = Ax}
    {find m = max(yᵢ)}
    {x^T = [y₁/m y₂/m ... yₙ/m]}
  until abs(m − mold) < tolerance
{write (results)}
```

Figure 6.1 Outline pseudocode program for power method to calculate the maximum eigenvalue.

Corresponding to (6.11), we have

$$x^{(k)} = A^k x^{(0)} = R\lambda_1^k \left[\alpha_1 e_1 + \sum_{i=2}^{n} \alpha_i \left(\frac{\lambda_i}{\lambda_1}\right)^k e_i \right]$$

where

$$R = [\max(y^{(1)}) \max(y^{(2)}) \cdots \max(y^{(k)})]^{-1}$$

Again we see that $x^{(k)}$ converges to a multiple of the dominant eigenvector e_1. Also, since $A x^{(k)} \rightarrow \lambda_1 x^{(k)}$, we have $y^{(k+1)} \rightarrow \lambda_1 x^{(k)}$, and since the largest element of $x^{(k)}$ is unity, it follows that the scaling factors $\max(y^{(k+1)})$ converge to the dominant eigenvalue λ_1. The **rate of convergence** depends primarily on the ratios

$$\left|\frac{\lambda_2}{\lambda_1}\right|, \quad \left|\frac{\lambda_3}{\lambda_1}\right|, \quad \dots, \quad \left|\frac{\lambda_n}{\lambda_1}\right|$$

The smaller these ratios, the faster the rate of convergence. The iterative process represents the simplest form of the **power method**, and a pseudocode for the basic algorithm is given in Figure 6.1.

EXAMPLE 6.9 Use the power method to find the dominant eigenvalue and the corresponding eigenvector of the matrix

$$A = \begin{bmatrix} 1 & 1 & -2 \\ -1 & 2 & 1 \\ 0 & 1 & -1 \end{bmatrix}$$

Solution Taking $x^{(0)} = \begin{bmatrix} 1 & 1 & 1 \end{bmatrix}^T$ in (6.13), we have

$$y^{(1)} = A x^{(0)} = \begin{bmatrix} 1 & 1 & -2 \\ -1 & 2 & 1 \\ 0 & 1 & -1 \end{bmatrix} \begin{bmatrix} 1 \\ 1 \\ 1 \end{bmatrix} = \begin{bmatrix} 0 \\ 2 \\ 0 \end{bmatrix}$$

$$= 2 \begin{bmatrix} 0 \\ 1 \\ 0 \end{bmatrix}; \qquad \lambda_1^{(1)} = 2$$

$$x^{(1)} = \tfrac{1}{2} y^{(1)} = \begin{bmatrix} 0 \\ 1 \\ 0 \end{bmatrix}$$

$$y^{(2)} = Ax^{(1)} = \begin{bmatrix} 1 & 1 & -2 \\ -1 & 2 & 1 \\ 0 & 1 & -1 \end{bmatrix} \begin{bmatrix} 0 \\ 1 \\ 0 \end{bmatrix} = \begin{bmatrix} 1 \\ 2 \\ 1 \end{bmatrix}$$

$$= 2 \begin{bmatrix} 0.5 \\ 1 \\ 0.5 \end{bmatrix}; \qquad \lambda_2^{(2)} = 2$$

$$x^{(2)} = \tfrac{1}{2} y^{(2)} = \begin{bmatrix} \tfrac{1}{2} \\ 1 \\ \tfrac{1}{2} \end{bmatrix}$$

$$y^{(3)} = Ax^{(2)} = \begin{bmatrix} 1 & 1 & -2 \\ -1 & 2 & 1 \\ 0 & 1 & -1 \end{bmatrix} \begin{bmatrix} \tfrac{1}{2} \\ 1 \\ \tfrac{1}{2} \end{bmatrix} = \begin{bmatrix} \tfrac{1}{2} \\ 2 \\ \tfrac{1}{2} \end{bmatrix}$$

$$= 2 \begin{bmatrix} 0.25 \\ 1 \\ 0.25 \end{bmatrix}; \qquad \lambda_3^{(2)} = 2$$

$$x^{(3)} = \begin{bmatrix} 0.25 \\ 1 \\ 0.25 \end{bmatrix}$$

Continuing with the process, we have

$$y^{(4)} = 2[0.375 \quad 1 \quad 0.375]^{\mathrm{T}}$$
$$y^{(5)} = 2[0.312 \quad 1 \quad 0.312]^{\mathrm{T}}$$
$$y^{(6)} = 2[0.344 \quad 1 \quad 0.344]^{\mathrm{T}}$$
$$y^{(7)} = 2[0.328 \quad 1 \quad 0.328]^{\mathrm{T}}$$
$$y^{(8)} = 2[0.336 \quad 1 \quad 0.336]^{\mathrm{T}}$$

Clearly $y^{(k)}$ is approaching the vector $2[\frac{1}{3} \quad 1 \quad \frac{1}{3}]^T$, so that the dominant eigenvalue is 2 and the corresponding eigenvector is $[\frac{1}{3} \quad 1 \quad \frac{1}{3}]^T$, which conforms with the answer obtained in Example 6.3.

EXAMPLE 6.10   Find the dominant eigenvalue of

$$A = \begin{bmatrix} 1 & 0 & -1 & 0 \\ 0 & 1 & 1 & 0 \\ -1 & 1 & 2 & 1 \\ 0 & 0 & 1 & -1 \end{bmatrix}$$

Solution   Starting with $x^{(0)} = [1 \quad 1 \quad 1 \quad 1]^T$, the iterations give the following:

Iteration k	1	2	3	4	5	6	7
Eigenvalue	—	3	2.6667	3.3750	3.0741	3.2048	3.1636	3.1642
$x_1^{(k)}$	1	0	−0.3750	−0.4074	−0.4578	−0.4549	−0.4621	−0.4621
$x_2^{(k)}$	1	0.6667	0.6250	0.4815	0.4819	0.4624	0.4621	0.4621
$x_3^{(k)}$	1	1	1	1	1	1	1	1
$x_4^{(k)}$	1	0	0.3750	0.1852	0.2651	0.2293	0.2403	0.2401

This indicates that the dominant eigenvalue is aproximately 3.16, with corresponding eigenvector $[-0.46 \quad 0.46 \quad 1 \quad 0.24]^T$.

The power method is suitable for obtaining the dominant eigenvalue and corresponding eigenvector of a matrix A having real distinct eigenvalues. The smallest eigenvalue, provided it is non-zero, can be obtained by using the same method on the inverse matrix A^{-1} when it exists. This follows since if $Ax = \lambda x$ then $A^{-1}x = \lambda^{-1}x$. To find the subdominant eigenvalue using this method the dominant eigenvalue must first be removed from the matrix using **deflation methods**. We shall illustrate such a method for symmetric matrices only.

Let A be a symmetric matrix having real eigenvalues $\lambda_1, \lambda_2, \ldots, \lambda_n$. Then, by result (b) of Section 6.2.7, it has n corresponding mutually orthogonal normalized eigenvectors $\hat{e}_1, \hat{e}_2, \ldots, \hat{e}_n$ such that

$$\hat{e}_i^T \hat{e}_j = \delta_{ij} \quad (i, j = 1, 2, \ldots, n)$$

Let λ_1 be the dominant eigenvalue and consider the matrix

$$A_1 = A - \lambda_1 \hat{e}_1 \hat{e}_1^T$$

which is such that

$$A_1 \hat{e}_1 = (A - \lambda_1 \hat{e}_1 \hat{e}_1^T)\hat{e}_1 = A\hat{e}_1 - \lambda_1 \hat{e}_1(\hat{e}_1^T \hat{e}_1)$$
$$= \lambda_1 \hat{e}_1 - \lambda_1 \hat{e}_1 = 0$$

$$A_1\hat{e}_2 = A\hat{e}_2 - \lambda_1\hat{e}_1(\hat{e}_1^T\hat{e}_2) = \lambda_2\hat{e}_2$$

$$A_1\hat{e}_3 = A\hat{e}_3 - \lambda_1\hat{e}_1(\hat{e}_1^T\hat{e}_3) = \lambda_3\hat{e}_3$$

$$\vdots$$

$$A_1\hat{e}_n = A\hat{e}_n - \lambda_1\hat{e}_1(\hat{e}_1^T\hat{e}_n) = \lambda_n\hat{e}_n$$

Thus the matrix A_1 has the same eigenvalues and eigenvectors as the matrix A, except that the eigenvalue corresponding to λ_1 is now zero. The power method can then be applied to the matrix A_1 to obtain the subdominant eigenvalue λ_2 and its corresponding eigenvector e_2. By repeated use of this technique, we can determine all the eigenvalues and corresponding eigenvectors of A.

EXAMPLE 6.11   Given that the symmetric matrix

$$A = \begin{bmatrix} 2 & 2 & 0 \\ 2 & 5 & 0 \\ 0 & 0 & 3 \end{bmatrix}$$

has a dominant eigenvalue $\lambda_1 = 6$ with corresponding normalized eigenvector $\hat{e}_1 = [1 \quad 2 \quad 0]^T/\sqrt{5}$, find the subdominant eigenvalue λ_2 and corresponding eigenvector $\hat{e}_2$.

Solution   Following the above procedure,

$$A_1 = A - \lambda_1\hat{e}_1\hat{e}_1^T$$

$$= \begin{bmatrix} 2 & 2 & 0 \\ 2 & 5 & 0 \\ 0 & 0 & 3 \end{bmatrix} - \frac{6}{5}\begin{bmatrix} 1 \\ 2 \\ 0 \end{bmatrix}[1 \quad 2 \quad 0]$$

$$= \begin{bmatrix} \frac{4}{5} & -\frac{2}{5} & 0 \\ -\frac{2}{5} & \frac{1}{5} & 0 \\ 0 & 0 & 3 \end{bmatrix}$$

Applying the power method procedure (6.13), with $x^{(0)} = [1 \quad 1 \quad 1]^T$, gives

$$y^{(1)} = A_1 x^{(0)} = \begin{bmatrix} \frac{2}{5} \\ -\frac{1}{5} \\ 3 \end{bmatrix}$$

$$= 3\begin{bmatrix} \frac{2}{15} \\ -\frac{1}{15} \\ 1 \end{bmatrix}; \qquad \lambda_2^{(1)} = 3$$

$$x^{(1)} = \begin{bmatrix} \frac{2}{15} \\ -\frac{1}{15} \\ 1 \end{bmatrix} = \begin{bmatrix} 0.133 \\ -0.133 \\ 1 \end{bmatrix}$$

$$y^{(2)} = A_1 x^{(1)} = \begin{bmatrix} \frac{2}{15} \\ -\frac{1}{15} \\ 3 \end{bmatrix}$$

$$= 3 \begin{bmatrix} \frac{2}{45} \\ -\frac{2}{45} \\ 1 \end{bmatrix}; \qquad \lambda_2^{(2)} = 3$$

$$x^{(2)} = \begin{bmatrix} \frac{2}{45} \\ -\frac{2}{45} \\ 1 \end{bmatrix} = \begin{bmatrix} 0.044 \\ -0.044 \\ 1 \end{bmatrix}$$

$$y^{(3)} = A_1 x^{(2)} = \begin{bmatrix} \frac{2}{45} \\ -\frac{2}{45} \\ 3 \end{bmatrix}$$

$$= 3 \begin{bmatrix} \frac{2}{135} \\ -\frac{2}{135} \\ 1 \end{bmatrix}; \qquad \lambda_2^{(2)} = 3$$

$$x^{(3)} = \begin{bmatrix} 0.015 \\ -0.015 \\ 1 \end{bmatrix}$$

Clearly the subdominant eigenvalue of A is $\lambda_2 = 3$, and a few more iterations confirms the corresponding normalized eigenvector is $\hat{e}_2 = [0 \quad 0 \quad 1]^T$. This is confirmed by the solution of Example 6.8. Note that the third eigenvalue may then be obtained using Property 6.1 of Section 6.2.6, since

$$\text{trace } A = 10 = \lambda_1 + \lambda_2 + \lambda_3 = 6 + 3 + \lambda_3$$

giving $\lambda_3 = 1$. Alternatively, λ_3 and $\hat{e}_3$ can be obtained by applying the power method to the matrix $A_2 = A_1 - \lambda_2 \hat{e}_2 \hat{e}_2^T$.

Although it is good as an illustration of the principles underlying iterative methods for evaluating eigenvalues and eigenvectors, the power method is of little practical importance, except possibly when dealing with large sparse matrices. In order to evaluate all the eigenvalues and eigenvectors of a matrix, including those with repeated eigenvalues, more sophisticated methods are required. Many of the numerical methods available, such as the **Jacobi** and **Householder methods**, are only applicable to symmetric matrices, and involve reducing the matrix to a special form so that its eigenvalues can be readily calculated. Analogous methods for non-symmetric matrices are the **LR** and **QR methods**. It is methods such as these, together with others based on the inverse iterative method, that form the basis of the algorithms that exist in modern software libraries. Such methods will not be pursued further here, and the interested reader is referred to specialist texts on numerical analysis.

6.3.2   Gerschgorin circles

In many engineering applications it is not necessary to obtain accurate approximations to the eigenvalues of a matrix. All that is often required are bounds on the eigenvalues. For example, when considering the stability of continuous- or discrete-time systems (see Sections 6.6–6.8), we are concerned as to whether the eigenvalues lie in the negative half-plane or within the unit circle in the complex plane. (Note that the eigenvalues of a non-symmetric matrix can be complex.) The Gerschgorin theorems often provide a quick method to answer such questions without the need for detailed calculations. These theorems may be stated as follows.

THEOREM 6.1   First Gerschgorin theorem

Every eigenvalue of the matrix $\boldsymbol{A} = [a_{ij}]$, of order n, lies inside at least one of the circles (called **Gerschgorin circles**) in the complex plane with centre a_{ii} and radii $r_i = \Sigma_{j=1, j \neq i}^{n} |a_{ij}| \, (i = 1, 2, \ldots, n)$. Expressed in another form, all the eigenvalues of the matrix $\boldsymbol{A} = [a_{ij}]$ lie in the union of the discs

$$|z - a_{ii}| \leqslant r_i = \sum_{\substack{j=1 \\ j \neq i}}^{n} |a_{ij}| \quad (i = 1, 2, \ldots, n) \tag{6.14}$$

in the complex z plane. □

THEOREM 6.2   Second Gerschgorin theorem

If the union of s of the Gerschgorin circles forms a connected region isolated from the remaining circles then exactly s of the eigenvalues lie within this region. □

Since the disc $|z - a_{ii}| \leqslant r_i$ is contained within the disc

$$|z| \leqslant |a_{ii}| + r_i = \sum_{j=1}^{n} |a_{ij}|$$

centred at the origin, we have a less precise but more easily applied criterion that all the eigenvalues of the matrix A lie within the disc

$$|z| \leqslant \max_i \left\{ \sum_{j=1}^{n} |a_{ij}| \right\} \quad (i = 1, 2, \ldots, n) \tag{6.15}$$

centred at the origin.

The **spectral radius** $\rho(A)$ of a matrix A is the modulus of its dominant eigenvalue; that is,

$$\rho(A) = \max \left\{ |\lambda_i| \right\} \quad (i = 1, 2, \ldots, n) \tag{6.16}$$

where $\lambda_1, \lambda_2, \ldots, \lambda_n$ are the eigenvalues of A. Geometrically, $\rho(A)$ is the radius of the smallest circle centred at the origin in the complex plane such that all the eigenvalues of A lie inside the circle. It follows from (6.15) that

$$\rho(A) \leqslant \max_i \left\{ \sum_{j=1}^{n} |a_{ij}| \right\} \quad (i = 1, 2, \ldots, n) \tag{6.17}$$

EXAMPLE 6.12   Draw the Gerschgorin circles corresponding to the matrix

$$A = \begin{bmatrix} 10 & -1 & 0 \\ -1 & 2 & 2 \\ 0 & 2 & 3 \end{bmatrix}$$

What can be concluded about the eigenvalues of A?

Solution   The three Gerschgorin circles are

(i) $|z - 10| = |-1| + 0 = 1$

(ii) $|z - 2| = |-1| + |2| = 3$

(iii) $|z - 3| = |2| = 2$

and are illustrated in Figure 6.2.

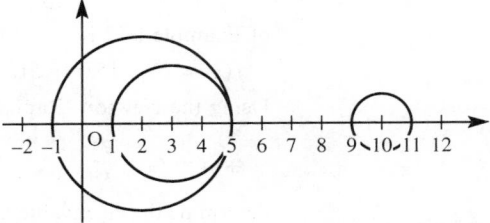

z plane

Figure 6.2 Gerschgorin circles for the matrix A of Example 6.12.

It follows from Theorem 6.2 that one eigenvalue lies within the circle centred $(10, 0)$ of radius 1, and two eigenvalues lie within the union of the other two circles; that is, within the circle centred at $(2, 0)$ of radius 3. Since the matrix $\boldsymbol{A}$ is symmetric, it follows from result (a) of Section 6.2.7 that the eigenvalues are real. Hence

$$9 < \lambda_1 < 11$$

$$-1 < \{\lambda_2, \lambda_3\} < 5$$

6.3.3   Exercises

10 Use the power method to estimate the dominant eigenvalue and its corresponding eigenvector for the matrix

$$\boldsymbol{A} = \begin{bmatrix} 4 & 3 & 2 \\ 3 & 5 & 2 \\ 2 & 2 & 1 \end{bmatrix}$$

Stop when you consider the eigenvalue estimate is correct to two decimal places.

11 Repeat Exercise 10 for the matrices

(a) $\boldsymbol{A} = \begin{bmatrix} 2 & 1 & 0 \\ 1 & 2 & 1 \\ 1 & 1 & 2 \end{bmatrix}$ (b) $\boldsymbol{A} = \begin{bmatrix} 3 & 0 & 1 \\ 2 & 2 & 2 \\ 4 & 2 & 5 \end{bmatrix}$

(c) $\boldsymbol{A} = \begin{bmatrix} 2 & -1 & 0 & 0 \\ -1 & 2 & -1 & 0 \\ 0 & -1 & 2 & -1 \\ 0 & 0 & -1 & 2 \end{bmatrix}$

12 The symmetric matrix

$$\boldsymbol{A} = \begin{bmatrix} 3 & 1 & 1 \\ 1 & 3 & 1 \\ 1 & 1 & 5 \end{bmatrix}$$

has dominant eigenvector $\boldsymbol{e}_1 = [1 \quad 1 \quad 2]^T$. Obtain the matrix

$$\boldsymbol{A}_1 = \boldsymbol{A} - \lambda_1 \hat{\boldsymbol{e}}_1 \hat{\boldsymbol{e}}_1^T$$

where λ_1 is the eigenvalue corresponding to the eigenvector $\boldsymbol{e}_1$. Using the deflation method, obtain the subdominant eigenvalue λ_2 and corresponding eigenvector $\boldsymbol{e}_2$ correct to two decimal places, taking $[1 \quad 1 \quad 1]^T$ as a first approximation to $\boldsymbol{e}_2$. Continue the process to obtain the third eigenvalue λ_3 and its corresponding eigenvector $\boldsymbol{e}_3$.

13 Draw the Gerschgorin circles corresponding to the matrix

$$\boldsymbol{A} = \begin{bmatrix} 5 & 1 & -1 \\ 1 & 0 & 1 \\ -1 & 1 & -5 \end{bmatrix}$$

and hence show that the three eigenvalues are such that

$$3 < \lambda_1 < 7, \quad -2 < \lambda_2 < 2, \quad -7 < \lambda_3 < -3$$

14 Show that the characteristic equation of the matrix

$$\boldsymbol{A} = \begin{bmatrix} 10 & -1 & 0 \\ -1 & 2 & 2 \\ 0 & 2 & 3 \end{bmatrix}$$

of Example 6.12 is

$$f(\lambda) = \lambda^3 - 15\lambda^2 + 51\lambda - 17 = 0$$

Using the Newton–Raphson iterative procedure

$$\lambda_{n+1} = \lambda_n - \frac{f(\lambda_n)}{f'(\lambda_n)}$$

determine the eigenvalue identified in Example 6.12 to lie in the interval $9 < \lambda < 11$, correct to three decimal places.

Using Properties 6.1 and 6.2 of Section 6.2.6,

determine the other two eigenvalues of $\boldsymbol{A}$ to the same approximation.

15 (a) If the eigenvalues of the $n \times n$ matrix $\boldsymbol{A}$ are

$$\lambda_1 > \lambda_2 > \lambda_3 > \cdots > \lambda_n \geqslant 0$$

show that the eigenvalue λ_n can be found by applying the power method to the matrix $k\boldsymbol{I} - \boldsymbol{A}$, where $\boldsymbol{I}$ is the identity matrix and $k \geqslant \lambda_1$.

(b) By considering the Gerschgorin circles, show that the eigenvalues of the matrix

$$\boldsymbol{A} = \begin{bmatrix} 2 & -1 & 0 \\ -1 & 2 & -1 \\ 0 & -1 & 2 \end{bmatrix}$$

satisfy the inequality

$$0 \leqslant \lambda \leqslant 4$$

Hence, using the result proved in (a), determine the smallest modulus eigenvalue of $\boldsymbol{A}$ correct to two decimal places.

6.4   Reduction to canonical form

In this section we examine the process of reduction of a matrix to **canonical form**. Specifically, we examine methods by which certain square matrices can be reduced or transformed into diagonal form. The process of transformation can be thought of as a change of system coordinates, with the new coordinate axes chosen in such a way that the system can be expressed in a simple form. The simplification may, for example, be a transformation to principal axes or a decoupling of system equations.

We will see that not all matrices can be reduced to diagonal form. In some cases we can only achieve the so-called Jordan canonical form, but many of the advantages of the diagonal form can be extended to this case as well.

The transformation to diagonal form is just one example of a **similarity** transform. Other such transforms exist, but, in common with the transformation to diagonal form, their purpose is usually that of simplifying the system model in some way.

6.4.1   Reduction to diagonal form

For an $n \times n$ matrix $\boldsymbol{A}$ possessing a full set of n linearly independent eigenvectors $e_1, e_2, \ldots, e_n$ we can write down a **modal matrix** $\boldsymbol{M}$ having the n eigenvectors as its columns:

$$\boldsymbol{M} = [e_1 \quad e_2 \quad e_3 \quad \cdots \quad e_n]$$

The diagonal matrix having the eigenvalues of $\boldsymbol{A}$ as its diagonal elements is called the **spectral matrix** corresponding to the modal matrix $\boldsymbol{M}$ of $\boldsymbol{A}$, often denoted by

Λ. That is

$$\Lambda = \begin{bmatrix} \lambda_1 & & & 0 \\ & \lambda_2 & & \\ & & \ddots & \\ 0 & & & \lambda_n \end{bmatrix}$$

with the ijth element being given by $\lambda_i \delta_{ij}$, where δ_{ij} is the Kronecker delta and $i, j = 1, 2, \ldots, n$. It is important in the work that follows that the pair of matrices M and Λ are written down correctly. If the ith column of M is the eigenvector e_i then the element in the (i, i) position in Λ must be λ_i, the eigenvalue corresponding to the eigenvector e_i.

EXAMPLE 6.13   Obtain a modal matrix and the corresponding spectral matrix for the matrix A of Example 6.3.

Solution

$$A = \begin{bmatrix} 1 & 1 & -2 \\ -1 & 2 & 1 \\ 0 & 1 & -1 \end{bmatrix}$$

having eigenvalues $\lambda_1 = 2, \lambda_2 = 1$ and $\lambda_3 = -1$, with corresponding eigenvectors

$$e_1 = [1 \quad 3 \quad 1]^T, \quad e_2 = [3 \quad 2 \quad 1]^T, \quad e_3 = [1 \quad 0 \quad 1]^T$$

Choosing as modal matrix $M = [e_1 \quad e_2 \quad e_3]^T$ gives

$$M = \begin{bmatrix} 1 & 3 & 1 \\ 3 & 2 & 0 \\ 1 & 1 & 1 \end{bmatrix}$$

The corresponding spectral matrix is

$$\Lambda = \begin{bmatrix} 2 & 0 & 0 \\ 0 & 1 & 0 \\ 0 & 0 & -1 \end{bmatrix}$$

Returning to the general case, if we premultiply the matrix M by A, we obtain

$$AM = A[e_1 \quad e_2 \quad \ldots \quad e_n]$$

$$= [Ae_1 \quad Ae_2 \quad \ldots \quad Ae_n]$$

$$= [\lambda_1 e_1 \quad \lambda_2 e_2 \quad \ldots \quad \lambda_n e_n]$$

so that

$$AM = M\Lambda \tag{6.18}$$

Since the n eigenvectors $e_1, e_2, \ldots, e_n$ are linearly independent, the matrix M is non-singular, so that M^{-1} exists. Thus premultiplying by M^{-1} gives

$$M^{-1}AM = M^{-1}M\Lambda$$

$$= \Lambda \tag{6.19}$$

indicating that the similarity transformation $M^{-1}AM$ reduces the matrix A to the **diagonal** or **canonical form** Λ. Thus a matrix A possessing a full set of linearly independent eigenvectors is reducible to diagonal form, and the reduction process is often referred to as the **diagonalization** of the matrix A. Since

$$A = M\Lambda M^{-1} \tag{6.20}$$

it follows that A is uniquely determined once the eigenvalues and corresponding eigenvectors are known. Note that knowledge of the eigenvalues and eigenvectors alone is not sufficient: in order to structure M and Λ correctly, the association of eigenvalues and the *corresponding* eigenvectors must also be known.

EXAMPLE 6.14   Verify results (6.19) and (6.20) for the matrix A of Example 6.13.

Solution   Since

$$M = \begin{bmatrix} 1 & 3 & 1 \\ 3 & 2 & 0 \\ 1 & 1 & 1 \end{bmatrix}$$

we have

$$M^{-1} = \frac{1}{6} \begin{bmatrix} -2 & 2 & 2 \\ 3 & 0 & -3 \\ -1 & -2 & 7 \end{bmatrix}$$

Taking

$$\Lambda = \begin{bmatrix} 2 & 0 & 0 \\ 0 & 1 & 0 \\ 0 & 0 & -1 \end{bmatrix}$$

matrix multiplication confirms the results

$$M^{-1}AM = \Lambda, \quad A = M\Lambda M^{-1}$$

For an $n \times n$ symmetric matrix A it follows, from result (b) of Section 6.2.7, that to the n real eigenvalues $\lambda_1, \lambda_2, \ldots, \lambda_n$ there correspond n linearly independent normalized eigenvectors $\hat{e}_1, \hat{e}_2, \ldots, \hat{e}_n$ that are mutually orthogonal so that

$$\hat{e}_i^{\mathrm{T}} \hat{e}_j = \delta_{ij} \quad (i, j = 1, 2, \ldots, n)$$

The corresponding modal matrix

$$\hat{M} = [\hat{e}_1 \quad \hat{e}_2 \quad \ldots \quad \hat{e}_n]$$

is then such that

$$\hat{M}^{\mathrm{T}} \hat{M} = \begin{bmatrix} \hat{e}_1^{\mathrm{T}} \\ \hat{e}_2^{\mathrm{T}} \\ \vdots \\ \hat{e}_n^{\mathrm{T}} \end{bmatrix} [\hat{e}_1 \quad \hat{e}_2 \quad \ldots \quad \hat{e}_n]$$

$$= \begin{bmatrix} \hat{e}_1^{\mathrm{T}} \hat{e}_1 & \hat{e}_1^{\mathrm{T}} \hat{e}_2 & \ldots & \hat{e}_1^{\mathrm{T}} \hat{e}_n \\ \hat{e}_2^{\mathrm{T}} \hat{e}_1 & \hat{e}_2^{\mathrm{T}} \hat{e}_2 & \ldots & \hat{e}_2^{\mathrm{T}} \hat{e}_n \\ \vdots & \vdots & & \vdots \\ \hat{e}_n^{\mathrm{T}} \hat{e}_1 & \hat{e}_n^{\mathrm{T}} \hat{e}_2 & \ldots & \hat{e}_n^{\mathrm{T}} \hat{e}_n \end{bmatrix}$$

$$= \begin{bmatrix} 1 & 0 & \ldots & 0 \\ 0 & 1 & \ldots & 0 \\ \vdots & \vdots & & \vdots \\ 0 & 0 & \ldots & 1 \end{bmatrix} = I$$

That is, $\hat{M}^{\mathrm{T}} \hat{M} = I$ and so $\hat{M}^{\mathrm{T}} = \hat{M}^{-1}$. Thus $\hat{M}$ is an **orthogonal matrix** (the term **orthonormal matrix** would be more appropriate, but the nomenclature is long established).

It follows from (6.19) that a symmetric matrix A can be reduced to diagonal form Λ using the orthogonal transformation

$$\hat{M}^{\mathrm{T}} A \hat{M} = \Lambda \tag{6.21}$$

EXAMPLE 6.15   For the symmetric matrix A considered in Example 6.8 write down the corresponding orthogonal modal matrix $\hat{M}$ and show that $\hat{M}^{\mathrm{T}} A \hat{M} = \Lambda$, where Λ is the spectral matrix.

Solution   From Example 6.8 the eigenvalues are $\lambda_1 = 6$, $\lambda_2 = 3$ and $\lambda_3 = 1$, with corresponding normalized eigenvectors

$$\hat{e}_1 = [1 \quad 2 \quad 0]^{\mathrm{T}} / \sqrt{5}$$

$$\hat{e}_2 = [0 \quad 0 \quad 1]^{\mathrm{T}}$$

$$\hat{e}_3 = [-2 \quad 1 \quad 0]^{\mathrm{T}}/\sqrt{5}$$

The corresponding modal matrix is

$$\hat{M} = \begin{bmatrix} \sqrt{\frac{1}{5}} & 0 & -2\sqrt{\frac{1}{5}} \\ 2\sqrt{\frac{1}{5}} & 0 & \sqrt{\frac{1}{5}} \\ 0 & 1 & 0 \end{bmatrix}$$

and, by matrix multiplication,

$$\hat{M}^{\mathrm{T}} A \hat{M} = \begin{bmatrix} 6 & 0 & 0 \\ 0 & 3 & 0 \\ 0 & 0 & 1 \end{bmatrix} = \Lambda$$

6.4.2   The Jordan canonical form

If an $n \times n$ matrix A does not possess a full set of linearly independent eigenvectors then it cannot be reduced to diagonal form using the similarity transformation $M^{-1}AM$. In such a case, however, it is possible to reduce A to a **Jordan canonical form**, making use of 'generalized' eigenvectors.

As indicated in (6.10), if a matrix A has an eigenvalue λ_i of algebraic multiplicity m_i and geometric multiplicity q_i, with $1 \leqslant q_i \leqslant m_i$, then there are q_i linearly independent eigenvectors corresponding to λ_i. Consequently, we need to generate $m_i - q_i$ generalized eigenvectors in order to produce a full set. To obtain these, we first obtain the q_i linearly independent eigenvectors by solving

$$(A - \lambda_i I)e_i = 0$$

Then for each of these vectors we try to construct a generalized eigenvector e_i^* such that

$$(A - \lambda_i I)e_i^* = e_i$$

If the resulting vector e_i^* is linearly independent of all the eigenvectors (and generalized eigenvectors) already found then it is a valid additional generalized eigenvector. If further generalized eigenvectors corresponding to λ_i are needed, we then repeat the process using

$$(A - \lambda_i I)e_i^{**} = e_i^*$$

and so on until sufficient vectors are found.

EXAMPLE 6.16   Obtain a generalized eigenvector corresponding to the eigenvalue $\lambda = 2$ of Example 6.6.

Solution   For

$$A = \begin{bmatrix} 1 & 2 & 2 \\ 0 & 2 & 1 \\ -1 & 2 & 2 \end{bmatrix}$$

we found in Example 6.6 that corresponding to the eigenvalue $\lambda_i = 2$ there was only one linearly independent eigenvector

$$e_1 = [2 \quad 1 \quad 0]^T$$

and we need to find a generalized eigenvector to produce a full set. To obtain the generalized eigenvector e_1^*, we solve

$$(A - 2I)e_1^* = e_1$$

that is, we solve

$$\begin{bmatrix} -1 & 2 & 2 \\ 0 & 0 & 1 \\ -1 & 2 & 0 \end{bmatrix} \begin{bmatrix} e_{11}^* \\ e_{12}^* \\ e_{13}^* \end{bmatrix} = \begin{bmatrix} 2 \\ 1 \\ 0 \end{bmatrix}.$$

At once, we have $e_{13}^* = 1$ and $e_{11}^* = 2e_{12}^*$, and so

$$e_1^* = [2 \quad 1 \quad 1]^T$$

Thus, by including generalized eigenvectors, we have a full set of eigenvectors for the matrix A given by

$$e_1 = [2 \quad 1 \quad 0]^T, \qquad e_2 = [2 \quad 1 \quad 1]^T, \qquad e_3 = [1 \quad -1 \quad 1]^T$$

If we include the generalized eigenvectors, it is always possible to obtain for an $n \times n$ matrix A a modal matrix M with n linearly independent columns $e_1, e_2, \ldots, e_n$. Corresponding to (6.18), we have

$$AM = MJ$$

where J is called the **Jordan form** of A. Premultiplying by M^{-1} then gives

$$M^{-1}AM = J \tag{6.22}$$

The process of reducing A to J is known as the **reduction** of A to its Jordan normal, or canonical form.

If A has p distinct eigenvalues then the matrix J is of the block-diagonal form

$$J = [J_1 \quad J_2 \quad \ldots \quad J_p]$$

where each submatrix J_i $(i = 1, 2, \ldots, p)$ is associated with the corresponding eigenvalue λ_i. The submatrix J_i will have λ_i as its leading diagonal elements, with zeros elsewhere except on the diagonal above the leading diagonal. On this diagonal the entries will have the value 1 or 0, depending on the number of generalized eigenvectors used and how they were generated. To illustrate this, suppose that A is a 7×7 matrix with eigenvalues $\lambda_1 = 1$, $\lambda_2 = 2$ (occurring twice), $\lambda_3 = 3$ (occurring four times), and suppose that the number of linearly independent eigenvectors generated in each case is

$\lambda_1 = 1,$ 1 eigenvector

$\lambda_2 = 2,$ 1 eigenvector

$\lambda_3 = 3,$ 2 eigenvectors

with one further generalized eigenvector having been determined for $\lambda_2 = 2$ and two more for $\lambda_3 = 3$.

Corresponding to $\lambda_1 = 1$, the Jordan block J_1 will be just $[1]$, while that corresponding to $\lambda_2 = 2$ will be

$$J_2 = \begin{bmatrix} 2 & 1 \\ 0 & 2 \end{bmatrix}$$

corresponding to $\lambda_3 = 3$, the Jordan block J_3 can take one of the two forms

$$J_{3,1} = \begin{bmatrix} \lambda_3 & 1 & 0 & \vdots & 0 \\ 0 & \lambda_3 & 1 & \vdots & 0 \\ 0 & 0 & \lambda_3 & \vdots & 0 \\ \cdots & \cdots & \cdots & \vdots & \cdots \\ 0 & 0 & 0 & \vdots & \lambda_3 \end{bmatrix}$$

or

$$J_{3,2} = \begin{bmatrix} \lambda_3 & 1 & \vdots & 0 & 0 \\ 0 & \lambda_3 & \vdots & 0 & 0 \\ \cdots & \cdots & \vdots & \cdots & \cdots \\ 0 & 0 & \vdots & \lambda_3 & 1 \\ 0 & 0 & \vdots & 0 & \lambda_3 \end{bmatrix}$$

depending on how the generalized eigenvectors are generated. Corresponding to $\lambda_3 = 3$, we had two linearly independent eigenvectors $e_{3,1}$ and $e_{3,2}$. If both generalized eigenvectors are generated from *one* of these vectors then J_3 will take the form $J_{3,1}$, whereas if one generalized eigenvector has been generated from each eigenvector then J_3 will take the form $J_{3,2}$.

EXAMPLE 6.17 Obtain the Jordan canonical form of the matrix A of Example 6.16, and show that $M^{-1}AM = J$ where M is a modal matrix that includes generalized eigenvectors.

Solution For

$$A = \begin{bmatrix} 1 & 2 & 2 \\ 0 & 2 & 1 \\ -1 & 2 & 2 \end{bmatrix}$$

from Example 6.16 we know that the eigenvalues of A are $\lambda_1 = 2$ (twice) and $\lambda_3 = 1$. The eigenvector corresponding to $\lambda_3 = 1$ has been determined as $e_3 = [1 \quad 1 \quad -1]^T$ in Example 6.6 and corresponding to $\lambda_1 = 2$ we found one linearly independent eigenvector $e_1 = [2 \quad 1 \quad 0]^T$ and a generalized eigenvector $e_1^* = [2 \quad 1 \quad 1]^T$. Thus the modal matrix including this generalized eigenvector is

$$M = \begin{bmatrix} 2 & 2 & 1 \\ 1 & 1 & 1 \\ 0 & 1 & -1 \end{bmatrix}$$

and the corresponding Jordan canonical form is

$$J = \begin{bmatrix} 2 & 1 & \vdots & 0 \\ 0 & 2 & \vdots & 0 \\ \cdots & \cdots & \vdots & \cdots \\ 0 & 0 & \vdots & 1 \end{bmatrix}$$

To check this result, we compute M^{-1} as

$$M^{-1} = \begin{bmatrix} 2 & -3 & -1 \\ -1 & 2 & 1 \\ -1 & 2 & 0 \end{bmatrix}$$

and, forming $M^{-1}AM$, we obtain J as expected.

6.4.3 Exercises

16 Show that the eigenvalues of the matrix

$$A = \begin{bmatrix} -1 & 6 & -12 \\ 0 & -13 & 30 \\ 0 & -9 & 20 \end{bmatrix}$$

are 5, 2 and -1. Obtain the corresponding eigenvectors. Write down the modal matrix M and spectral matrix Λ. Evaluate M^{-1} and show that $M^{-1}AM = \Lambda$.

17 Using the eigenvalues and corresponding eigenvectors of the symmetric matrix

$$A = \begin{bmatrix} 2 & 2 & 0 \\ 2 & 5 & 0 \\ 0 & 0 & 3 \end{bmatrix}$$

obtained in Example 6.8, verify that $\hat{M}^T A \hat{M} = \Lambda$ where $\hat{M}$ and Λ are respectively a normalized modal matrix and a spectral matrix of A.

18 Given

$$A = \begin{bmatrix} 5 & 10 & 8 \\ 10 & 2 & -2 \\ 8 & -2 & 11 \end{bmatrix}$$

find its eigenvalues and corresponding eigenvectors. Normalize the eigenvectors and write down the corresponding normalized modal matrix $\hat{M}$. Write down $\hat{M}^T$ and show that $\hat{M}^T A \hat{M} = \Lambda$, where Λ is the spectral matrix of A.

19 Determine the eigenvalues and corresponding eigenvectors of the matrix

$$A = \begin{bmatrix} 1 & 2 & 2 \\ 0 & 2 & 1 \\ -1 & 1 & 2 \end{bmatrix}$$

Write down the modal matrix M and spectral matrix Λ. Confirm that $M^{-1}AM = \Lambda$ and that $A = M\Lambda M^{-1}$.

20 Determine the eigenvalues and corresponding eigenvectors of the symmetric matrix

$$A = \begin{bmatrix} 3 & -2 & 4 \\ -2 & -2 & 6 \\ 4 & 6 & -1 \end{bmatrix}$$

Verify that the eigenvectors are orthogonal, and write down an orthogonal matrix L such that $L^T A L = \Lambda$, where Λ is the spectral matrix of A.

21 A 3×3 symmetric matrix A has eigenvalues 6, 3 and 1. The eigenvectors corresponding to the eigenvalues 6 and 1 are $\begin{bmatrix} 1 & 2 & 0 \end{bmatrix}^T$ and $\begin{bmatrix} -2 & 1 & 0 \end{bmatrix}^T$ respectively. Find the eigenvector corresponding to the eigenvalue 3, and hence determine the matrix A.

22 Given that $\lambda = 1$ is a thrice-repeated eigenvalue of the matrix

$$A = \begin{bmatrix} -3 & -7 & -5 \\ 2 & 4 & 3 \\ 1 & 2 & 2 \end{bmatrix}$$

use the nullity, given by (6.10), of a suitable matrix to show that there is only one corresponding linearly independent eigenvector. Obtain two further generalized eigenvectors, and write down the corresponding modal matrix M. Confirm that $M^{-1}AM = J$, where J is the appropriate Jordan matrix.

23 Show that the eigenvalues of the matrix

$$A = \begin{bmatrix} 1 & 0 & 0 & -3 \\ 0 & 1 & -3 & 0 \\ -0.5 & -3 & 1 & 0.5 \\ 3 & 0 & 0 & 1 \end{bmatrix}$$

are -2, -2, 4 and 4. Using the nullity, given by (6.10), of appropriate matrices, show that there are two linearly independent eigenvectors corresponding to the repeated eigenvalue -2 and only one corresponding to the repeated eigenvalue 4. Obtain a further generalized eigenvector corresponding to the eigenvalue 4. Write down the Jordan canonical form of A.

6.4.4 Quadratic forms

A **quadratic form** in n independent variables $x_1, x_2, \ldots, x_n$ is a homogeneous second-degree polynomial of the form

$$
\begin{aligned}
V(x_1, x_2, \ldots, x_n) &= \sum_{i=1}^{n} \sum_{j=1}^{n} a_{ij} x_i x_j \\
&= a_{11} x_1^2 + a_{12} x_1 x_2 + \ldots + a_{1n} x_1 x_n \\
&\quad + a_{21} x_2 x_1 + a_{22} x_2^2 + \ldots + a_{2n} x_2 x_n \\
&\quad \vdots \\
&\quad + a_{n1} x_n x_1 + a_{n2} x_n x_2 + \ldots + a_{nn} x_n^2
\end{aligned}
\tag{6.23}
$$

Defining the vector $x = [x_1 \quad x_2 \quad \dots \quad x_n]^T$ and the matrix

$$A = \begin{bmatrix} a_{11} & a_{12} & \dots & a_{1n} \\ a_{21} & a_{22} & \dots & a_{2n} \\ \vdots & \vdots & & \vdots \\ a_{n1} & a_{n2} & \dots & a_{nn} \end{bmatrix}$$

the quadratic form (6.23) may be written in the form

$$V(x) = x^T A x \tag{6.24}$$

The matrix A is referred to as the matrix of the quadratic form and the determinant of A is called the **discriminant** of the quadratic form.

Now a_{ij} and a_{ji} in (6.23) are both coefficients of the term $x_i x_j$ $(i \neq j)$, so that for $i \neq j$ the coefficient of the term $x_i x_j$ is $a_{ij} + a_{ji}$. By defining new coefficients a'_{ij} and a'_{ji} for $x_i x_j$ and $x_j x_i$ respectively, such that $a'_{ij} = a'_{ji} = \frac{1}{2}(a_{ij} + a_{ji})$, the matrix A associated with the quadratic form $V(x)$ may be taken to be symmetric. Thus for real quadratic forms we can, without loss of generality, consider the matrix A to be a symmetric matrix.

EXAMPLE 6.18   Find the real symmetric matrix corresponding to the quadratic form

$$V(x_1, x_2, x_3) = x_1^2 + 3x_2^2 - 4x_3^2 - 3x_1 x_2 + 2x_1 x_3 - 5x_2 x_3$$

Solution   If $x = [x_1 \quad x_2 \quad x_3]^T$, we have

$$V(x_1, x_2, x_3) = [x_1 \quad x_2 \quad x_3] \begin{bmatrix} 1 & -\frac{3}{2} & \frac{2}{2} \\ -\frac{3}{2} & 3 & -\frac{5}{2} \\ \frac{2}{2} & -\frac{5}{2} & -4 \end{bmatrix} \begin{bmatrix} x_1 \\ x_2 \\ x_3 \end{bmatrix}$$

$$= x^T A x$$

where the matrix of the quadratic form is

$$A = \begin{bmatrix} 1 & -\frac{3}{2} & 1 \\ -\frac{3}{2} & 3 & -\frac{5}{2} \\ 1 & -\frac{5}{2} & -4 \end{bmatrix}$$

In Section 6.4.1 we saw that a real symmetric matrix A can always be reduced to the diagonal form

$$\hat{M}^T A \hat{M} = \Lambda$$

where $\hat{M}$ is the normalized orthogonal modal matrix of A and Λ is its spectral matrix. Thus for a real quadratic form we can specify a change of variables

$$x = \hat{M}y$$

where $y = [y_1 \quad y_2 \quad \cdots \quad y_n]^T$, such that

$$V = x^T A x = y^T \hat{M}^T A \hat{M} y = y^T \Lambda y$$

giving

$$V = \lambda_1 y_1^2 + \lambda_2 y_2^2 + \cdots + \lambda_n y_n^2 \tag{6.25}$$

Hence the quadratic form $x^T A x$ may be reduced to the sum of squares by the transformation $x = \hat{M}y$, where $\hat{M}$ is the normalized modal matrix of A. The resulting form given in (6.25) is called the **canonical form** of the quadratic form V given in (6.24). The reduction of a quadratic form to its canonical form has many applications in engineering, particularly in stress analysis.

EXAMPLE 6.19   Find the canonical form of the quadratic form

$$V = x_1^2 + 5x_2^2 + 3x_3^2 + 4x_1 x_2$$

Can V take negative values for any values of x_1, x_2 and x_3?

Solution   At once, we have

$$V = x^T \begin{bmatrix} 2 & 2 & 0 \\ 2 & 5 & 0 \\ 0 & 0 & 3 \end{bmatrix} x = x^T A x$$

where

$$x = [x_1 \quad x_2 \quad x_3]^T, \qquad A = \begin{bmatrix} 2 & 2 & 0 \\ 2 & 5 & 0 \\ 0 & 0 & 3 \end{bmatrix}$$

The real symmetric matrix A is the matrix of Example 6.15, where we found the normalized orthogonal modal matrix $\hat{M}$ and spectral matrix Λ to be

$$\hat{M} = \begin{bmatrix} \sqrt{\tfrac{1}{5}} & 0 & -2\sqrt{\tfrac{1}{5}} \\ 2\sqrt{\tfrac{1}{5}} & 0 & \sqrt{\tfrac{1}{5}} \\ 0 & 1 & 0 \end{bmatrix}, \qquad \Lambda = \begin{bmatrix} 6 & 0 & 0 \\ 0 & 3 & 0 \\ 0 & 0 & 1 \end{bmatrix}$$

such that $\hat{M}^T A \hat{M} = \Lambda$. Thus, setting $x = \hat{M}y$, we obtain

$$V = y^T \hat{M}^T A \hat{M} y = y^T \begin{bmatrix} 6 & 0 & 0 \\ 0 & 3 & 0 \\ 0 & 0 & 1 \end{bmatrix} y$$

$$= 6y_1^2 + 3y_2^2 + y_3^2$$

as the required canonical form.

Clearly V is non-negative for all y_1, y_2 and y_3. Since $x = \hat{M}y$ and $\hat{M}$ is an orthogonal matrix it follows that $y = \hat{M}x$, so for all x there is a corresponding y. It follows that V cannot take negative values for any values of x_1, x_2 and x_3.

The quadratic form of Example (6.19) was seen to be non-negative for any vector x, and is positive provided that $x \neq 0$. Such a quadratic form $x^{\mathrm{T}}Ax$ is called a **positive-definite** quadratic form, and, by reducing to canonical form, we have seen that this property depends only on the eigenvalues of the real symmetric matrix A. This leads us to classify quadratic forms $V = x^{\mathrm{T}}Ax$, where $x = [x_1 \quad x_2 \quad \ldots \quad x_n]^{\mathrm{T}}$ in the following manner.

(a) V is **positive-definite**, that is, $V > 0$ for all vectors x except $x = 0$, if and only if all the eigenvalues of A are positive.

(b) V is **positive-semidefinite**, that is, $V \geqslant 0$ for all vectors x and $V = 0$ for at least one vector $x \neq 0$, if and only if all the eigenvalues of A are non-negative and at least one of the eigenvalues is zero.

(c) V is **negative-definite** if $-V$ is positive-definite, with a corresponding condition on the eigenvalues of $-A$.

(d) V is **negative-semidefinite** if $-V$ is positive-semidefinite, with a corresponding condition on the eigenvalues of $-A$.

(e) V is **indefinite**, that is, V takes at least one positive value and at least one negative value, if and only if the matrix A has both positive and negative eigenvalues.

Since the classification of a real quadratic form $x^{\mathrm{T}}Ax$ depends entirely on the location of the eigenvalues of the symmetric matrix A, it may be viewed as a property of A itself. For this reason, it is common to talk of positive-definite, positive-semidefinite, and so on, symmetric matrices without reference to the underlying quadratic form.

EXAMPLE 6.20 Classify the following quadratic forms:

(a) $3x_1^2 + 2x_2^2 + 3x_3^2 - 2x_1x_2 - 2x_2x_3$
(b) $7x_1^2 + x_2^2 + x_3^2 - 4x_1x_2 - 4x_1x_3 + 8x_2x_3$
(c) $-3x_1^2 - 5x_2^2 - 3x_3^2 + 2x_1x_2 + 2x_2x_3 - 2x_1x_3$
(d) $4x_1^2 + x_2^2 + 15x_3^2 - 4x_1x_2$

Solution (a) The matrix corresponding to the quadratic form is

$$A = \begin{bmatrix} 3 & -1 & 0 \\ -1 & 2 & -1 \\ 0 & -1 & 3 \end{bmatrix}$$

The eigenvalues of A are 4, 3 and 1, so the quadratic form is positive-definite.

(b) The matrix corresponding to the quadratic form is

$$A = \begin{bmatrix} 7 & -2 & -2 \\ -2 & 1 & 4 \\ -2 & 4 & 1 \end{bmatrix}$$

The eigenvalues of A are 9, 3 and -3, so the quadratic form is indefinite.

(c) The matrix corresponding to the quadratic form is

$$A = \begin{bmatrix} -3 & 1 & -1 \\ 1 & -5 & 1 \\ -1 & 1 & -3 \end{bmatrix}$$

The eigenvalues of A are -6, -3 and -2, so the quadratic form is negative-definite.

(d) The matrix corresponding to the quadratic form is

$$A = \begin{bmatrix} 4 & -2 & 0 \\ -2 & 1 & 0 \\ 0 & 0 & 15 \end{bmatrix}$$

The eigenvalues of A are 15, 5 and 0, so the quadratic form is positive-semidefinite.

In Example 6.20 classifying the quadratic forms involved determining the eigenvalues of A. If A contains one or more parameters then the task becomes difficult, if not impossible, even with the use of a symbolic algebra computer package. Frequently in engineering, particularly in stability analysis, it is necessary to determine the range of values of a parameter k, say, for which a quadratic form remains definite or at least semidefinite in sign. J. J. Sylvester determined criteria for the classification of quadratic forms (or the associated real symmetric matrix) that do not require the computation of the eigenvalues. These criteria are known as **Sylvester's conditions**, which we shall briefly discuss without proof.

In order to classify the quadratic form $x^T A x$ Sylvester's conditions involve consideration of the principal minors of A. A **principal minor** P_i of order i ($i = 1, 2, \ldots, n$) of an $n \times n$ square matrix A is the determinant of the submatrix, of order i, whose principal diagonal is part of the principal diagonal of A. Note that when $i = n$ the principal minor is det A. In particular, the **leading principal minors** of A are

$$D_1 = |a_{11}|, \quad D_2 = \begin{vmatrix} a_{11} & a_{12} \\ a_{21} & a_{22} \end{vmatrix}, \quad D_3 = \begin{vmatrix} a_{11} & a_{12} & a_{13} \\ a_{21} & a_{22} & a_{23} \\ a_{31} & a_{32} & a_{33} \end{vmatrix}, \ldots, D_n = \det A$$

EXAMPLE 6.21   Determine all the principal minors of the matrix

$$A = \begin{bmatrix} 1 & k & 0 \\ k & 2 & 0 \\ 0 & 0 & 5 \end{bmatrix}$$

and indicate which are the leading principal minors.

Solution   (a) The principal minor of order three is

$$P_3 = \det A = 5(2 - k^2) \qquad \text{(leading principal minor } D_3)$$

(b) The principal minors of order two are
   (i) deleting row 1 and column 1,

$$P_{21} = \begin{vmatrix} 2 & 0 \\ 0 & 5 \end{vmatrix} = 10$$

   (ii) deleting row 2 and column 2,

$$P_{22} = \begin{vmatrix} 1 & 0 \\ 0 & 5 \end{vmatrix} = 5$$

   (iii) deleting row 3 and column 3,

$$P_{23} = \begin{vmatrix} 1 & k \\ k & 2 \end{vmatrix} = 2 - k^2 \quad \text{(leading principal minor } D_2)$$

(c) The principal minors of order one are
   (i) deleting rows 1 and 2 and columns 1 and 2,

$$P_{11} = |5| = 5$$

   (ii) deleting rows 1 and 3 and columns 1 and 3,

$$P_{12} = |2| = 2$$

   (iii) deleting rows 2 and 3 and columns 2 and 3,

$$P_{13} = |1| = 1 \qquad \text{(leading principal minor } D_1)$$

Sylvester's conditions

These state that the quadratic form $x^T A x$, where A is an $n \times n$ real symmetric matrix, is

(a) **positive-definite** if and only if all the leading principal minors of A are positive; that is, $D_i > 0$ ($i = 1, 2, \ldots, n$);

(b) **negative-definite** if and only if the leading principal minors of A alternate in sign with $a_{11} < 0$; that is, $(-1)^i D_i > 0$ ($i = 1, 2, \ldots, n$);

(c) **positive-semidefinite** if and only if det $A = 0$ and *all* the principal minors of A are non-negative; that is, det $A = 0$ and $P_i \geq 0$ for *all* principal minors;

(d) **negative-semidefinite** if and only if det $A = 0$ and $(-1)^i P_i \geq 0$ for *all* principal minors.

EXAMPLE 6.22   For what values of k is the matrix A of Example 6.21 positive-definite?

Solution   The leading principal minors of A are

$$D_1 = 1, \qquad D_2 = 2 - k^2, \qquad D_3 = 5(2 - k^2)$$

These will be positive provided that $2 - k^2 > 0$, so the matrix will be positive-definite provided that $k^2 < 2$, that is, $-\sqrt{2} < k < \sqrt{2}$.

EXAMPLE 6.23   Using Sylvester's conditions, confirm the conclusions of Example 6.20.

Solution   (a) The matrix of the quadratic form is

$$A = \begin{bmatrix} 3 & -1 & 0 \\ -1 & 2 & -1 \\ 0 & -1 & 3 \end{bmatrix}$$

and its leading principal minors are

$$3, \quad \begin{vmatrix} 3 & -1 \\ -1 & 2 \end{vmatrix} = 5, \quad \det A = 12$$

Thus, by Sylvester's condition (a), the quadratic form is positive-definite.

(b) The matrix of the quadratic form is

$$A = \begin{bmatrix} 7 & -2 & -2 \\ -2 & 1 & 4 \\ -2 & 4 & 1 \end{bmatrix}$$

and its leading principal minors are

$$7, \quad \begin{vmatrix} 7 & -2 \\ -2 & 1 \end{vmatrix} = 3, \quad \det A = -81$$

Thus none of Sylvester's conditions can be satisfied, and the quadratic form is indefinite.

(c) The matrix of the quadratic form is

$$A = \begin{bmatrix} -3 & 1 & -1 \\ 1 & -5 & 1 \\ -1 & 1 & -3 \end{bmatrix}$$

and its leading principal minors are

$$-3, \quad \begin{vmatrix} -3 & 1 \\ 1 & -5 \end{vmatrix} = 14, \quad \det \boldsymbol{A} = -36$$

Thus, by Sylvester's condition (b), the quadratic form is negative-definite.

(d) The matrix of the quadratic form is

$$\boldsymbol{A} = \begin{bmatrix} 4 & -2 & 0 \\ -2 & 1 & 0 \\ 0 & 0 & 15 \end{bmatrix}$$

and its leading principal minors are

$$4, \quad \begin{vmatrix} 4 & -2 \\ -2 & 1 \end{vmatrix} = 0, \quad \det \boldsymbol{A} = 0$$

We therefore need to evaluate all the principal minors to see if the quadratic form is positive-semidefinite. The principal minors are

$$4, \quad 1, \quad 15, \quad \begin{vmatrix} 4 & -2 \\ -2 & 1 \end{vmatrix} = 0, \quad \begin{vmatrix} 1 & 0 \\ 0 & 15 \end{vmatrix} = 15, \quad \begin{vmatrix} 4 & 0 \\ 0 & 15 \end{vmatrix} = 60, \quad \det \boldsymbol{A} = 0$$

Thus, by Sylvester's condition (c), the quadratic form is positive-semidefinite.

6.4.5   Exercises

24 Classify the quadratic forms
(a) $x_1^2 + 2x_2^2 + 7x_3^2 - 2x_1x_2 + 4x_1x_3 - 2x_2x_3$
(b) $x_1^2 + 2x_2^2 + 5x_3^2 - 2x_1x_2 + 4x_1x_3 - 2x_2x_3$
(c) $x_1^2 + 2x_2^2 + 4x_3^2 - 2x_1x_2 + 4x_1x_3 - 2x_2x_3$

25 (a) Show that $ax_1^2 - 2bx_1x_2 + cx_2^2$ is positive-definite if and only if $a > 0$ and $ac > b^2$.
(b) Find inequalities that must be satisfied by a and b to ensure that $2x_1^2 + ax_2^2 + 3x_3^2 - 2x_1x_2 + 2bx_2x_3$ is positive-definite.

26 Evaluate the definiteness of the matrix

$$\boldsymbol{A} = \begin{bmatrix} 2 & 1 & -1 \\ 1 & 2 & 1 \\ -1 & 1 & 2 \end{bmatrix}$$

(a) by obtaining the eigenvalues;
(b) by evaluating the principal minors.

27 Determine the exact range of k for which the quadratic form
$$Q(x, y, z) = k(x^2 + y^2) + 2xy + z^2 + 2xz - 2yz$$
is positive-definite in x, y and z. What can be said about the definiteness of Q when $k = 2$?

28 Determine the minimum value of the constant a such that the quadratic form

$$\boldsymbol{x}^{\mathrm{T}} \begin{bmatrix} 3+a & 1 & 1 \\ 1 & a & 2 \\ 1 & 2 & a \end{bmatrix} \boldsymbol{x}$$

where $\boldsymbol{x} = [x_1 \ x_2 \ x_3]^{\mathrm{T}}$, is positive-definite.

29 Express the quadratic form
$$Q = x_1^2 + 4x_1x_2 - 4x_1x_3 - 6x_2x_3 + \lambda(x_2^2 + x_3^2)$$
in the form $\boldsymbol{x}^{\mathrm{T}}\boldsymbol{A}\boldsymbol{x}$, where $\boldsymbol{x} = [x_1 \ x_2 \ x_3]^{\mathrm{T}}$ and $\boldsymbol{A}$ is a symmetric matrix. Hence determine the range of values of λ for which Q is positive-definite.

6.5   Functions of a matrix

Let A be an $n \times n$ constant square matrix, so that

$$A^2 = AA, \quad A^3 = AA^2 = A^2A, \quad \text{and so on}$$

are all defined. We can then define a function $f(A)$ of the matrix A using a power series representation. For example,

$$f(A) = \sum_{r=0}^{p} \beta_r A^r = \beta_0 I + \beta_1 A + \ldots + \beta_p A^p \tag{6.26}$$

where we have interpreted A^0 as the $n \times n$ identity matrix I.

EXAMPLE 6.24   Given the 2×2 square matrix

$$A = \begin{bmatrix} 1 & -1 \\ 2 & 3 \end{bmatrix}$$

determine

$$f(A) = \sum_{r=0}^{2} \beta_r A^r$$

when $\beta_0 = 1$, $\beta_1 = -1$ and $\beta_2 = 3$.

Solution   Now

$$f(A) = \beta_0 I + \beta_1 A + \beta_2 A^2$$

$$= 1 \begin{bmatrix} 1 & 0 \\ 0 & 1 \end{bmatrix} - 1 \begin{bmatrix} 1 & -1 \\ 2 & 3 \end{bmatrix} + 3 \begin{bmatrix} -1 & -4 \\ 6 & 7 \end{bmatrix}$$

$$= \begin{bmatrix} -3 & -11 \\ 16 & 19 \end{bmatrix}$$

Note that A is a 2×2 matrix and $f(A)$ is another 2×2 matrix.

Suppose that in (6.26) we let $p \rightarrow \infty$, so that

$$f(A) = \sum_{r=0}^{\infty} \beta_r A^r$$

We can attach meaning to $f(A)$ in this case if the matrices

$$f_p(A) = \sum_{r=0}^{p} \beta_r A^r$$

tend to a constant $n \times n$ matrix in the limit as $p \rightarrow \infty$.

EXAMPLE 6.25   For the matrix

$$A = \begin{bmatrix} 1 & 0 \\ 0 & 1 \end{bmatrix}$$

using a computer and larger and larger values of p, we infer that

$$f(A) = \lim_{p \to \infty} \sum_{r=0}^{p} \frac{A^r}{r!}$$

$$\simeq \begin{bmatrix} 2.718\,28 & 0 \\ 0 & 2.718\,28 \end{bmatrix}$$

indicating that

$$f(A) = \begin{bmatrix} e & 0 \\ 0 & e \end{bmatrix}$$

What would be the corresponding results if

(a) $A = \begin{bmatrix} -1 & 0 \\ 0 & 1 \end{bmatrix}$,   (b) $A = \begin{bmatrix} -t & 0 \\ 0 & t \end{bmatrix}$?

Solution   (a) The computer will lead to the prediction

$$f(A) \simeq \begin{bmatrix} (2.718\,28)^{-1} & 0 \\ 0 & 2.718\,28 \end{bmatrix}$$

indicating that

$$f(A) = \begin{bmatrix} e^{-1} & 0 \\ 0 & e \end{bmatrix}$$

(b) The computer is of little help in this case. However, hand calculation shows that we are generating the matrix

$$f(A) = \begin{bmatrix} 1 - t + \frac{1}{2}t^2 - \frac{1}{6}t^3 + \ldots & 0 \\ 0 & 1 + t + \frac{1}{2}t^2 + \frac{1}{6}t^3 + \ldots \end{bmatrix}$$

indicating that

$$f(A) = \begin{bmatrix} e^{-t} & 0 \\ 0 & e^t \end{bmatrix}$$

By analogy with the definition of the scalar exponential function

$$e^{at} = 1 + at + \frac{a^2 t^2}{2!} + \ldots + \frac{a^r t^r}{r!} + \ldots = \sum_{r=0}^{\infty} \frac{(at)^r}{r!}$$

It is natural to define the matrix function e^{At}, where t is a scalar parameter, by the power series

$$f(\mathbf{A}) = \sum_{r=0}^{\infty} \frac{\mathbf{A}^r}{r!} t^r \qquad (6.27)$$

In fact the matrix in part (b) of Example 6.25 illustrates that this definition is reasonable.

In Example 6.25 we were able to spot the construction of the matrix $f(\mathbf{A})$, but this will not be the case when $\mathbf{A}$ is a general $n \times n$ square matrix. In order to overcome this limitation and generate a method that will not rely on our ability to 'spot' a closed form of the limiting matrix, we make use of the Cayley–Hamilton theorem, which may be stated as follows.

THEOREM 6.3   Cayley–Hamilton theorem

A square matrix $\mathbf{A}$ satisfies its own characteristic equation; that is, if

$$\lambda^n + c_{n-1}\lambda^{n-1} + c_{n-2}\lambda^{n-2} + \ldots + c_1\lambda + c_0 = 0$$

is the characteristic equation of an $n \times n$ matrix $\mathbf{A}$ then

$$\mathbf{A}^n + c_{n-1}\mathbf{A}^{n-1} + c_{n-2}\mathbf{A}^{n-2} + \ldots + c_1\mathbf{A} + c_0\mathbf{I} = \mathbf{0} \qquad (6.28)$$

where $\mathbf{I}$ is the $n \times n$ identity matrix.   ☐

The proof of this theorem is not trivial, and is not included here. We shall illustrate the theorem using a simple example.

EXAMPLE 6.26   Verify the Cayley–Hamilton theorem for the matrix

$$\mathbf{A} = \begin{bmatrix} 3 & 4 \\ 1 & 2 \end{bmatrix}$$

Solution   The characteristic equation of $\mathbf{A}$ is

$$\begin{vmatrix} 3 - \lambda & 4 \\ 1 & 2 - \lambda \end{vmatrix} = 0$$

or

$$\lambda^2 - 5\lambda + 2 = 0$$

Since

$$\mathbf{A}^2 = \begin{bmatrix} 3 & 4 \\ 1 & 2 \end{bmatrix}\begin{bmatrix} 3 & 4 \\ 1 & 2 \end{bmatrix} = \begin{bmatrix} 13 & 20 \\ 5 & 8 \end{bmatrix}$$

we have

$$\mathbf{A}^2 - 5\mathbf{A} + 2\mathbf{I} = \begin{bmatrix} 13 & 20 \\ 5 & 8 \end{bmatrix} - 5\begin{bmatrix} 3 & 4 \\ 1 & 2 \end{bmatrix} + 2\begin{bmatrix} 1 & 0 \\ 0 & 1 \end{bmatrix} = \mathbf{0}$$

thus verifying the validity of the Cayley–Hamilton theorem for this matrix.

In the particular case when A is a 2×2 matrix with characteristic equation

$$c(\lambda) = \lambda^2 + a_1\lambda + a_2 = 0 \qquad (6.29)$$

it follows from the Cayley–Hamilton theorem that

$$c(A) = A^2 + a_1 A + a_2 I = 0$$

The significance of this result for our present purposes begins to appear when we rearrange to give

$$A^2 = -a_1 A - a_2 I$$

This means that A^2 can be written in terms of A and $A^0 = I$. Moreover, multiplying by A gives

$$A^3 = -a_1 A^2 - a_2 A$$
$$= -a_1(-a_1 A - a_2 I) - a_2 A$$

Thus A^3 can also be expressed in terms of A and $A^0 = I$; that is, in terms of powers of A less than $n = 2$, the order of the matrix A in this case. It is clear that we could continue the process of multiplying by A and substituting A^2 for as long as we could manage the algebra. However, we can quickly convince ourselves that for any integer $r \geqslant n$

$$A^r = \alpha_0 I + \alpha_1 A \qquad (6.30)$$

where α_0 and α_1 are constants whose values will depend on r.

This is a key result deduced from the Cayley–Hamilton theorem, and the determination of the α_i $(i = 0, 1)$ is not as difficult as it might appear. To see how to perform the calculations, we use the characteristic equation of A itself. If we assume that the eigenvalues λ_1 and λ_2 of A are distinct then it follows from (6.29) that

$$c(\lambda_i) = \lambda_i^2 + a_1\lambda_i + a_2 = 0 \quad (i = 1, 2)$$

Thus we can write

$$\lambda_i^2 = -a_1\lambda_i - a_2$$

in which a_1 and a_2 are the same constants as in (6.29). Then, for $i = 1, 2$,

$$\lambda_i^3 = -a_1\lambda_i^2 - a_2\lambda_i$$
$$= -a_1(-a_1\lambda_i - a_2) - a_2\lambda_i$$

Proceeding in this way, we deduce that for each of the eigenvalues λ_1 and λ_2 we can write

$$\lambda_i^r = \alpha_0 + \alpha_1\lambda_i$$

with the same α_0 and α_1 as in (6.30). This therefore provides us with a procedure for the calculation of A^r when $r \geqslant n$ (the order of the matrix) is an integer.

EXAMPLE 6.27   If the matrix

$$A = \begin{bmatrix} 0 & 1 \\ -2 & -3 \end{bmatrix}$$

has eigenvalues $\lambda_1 = -1$ and $\lambda_2 = -2$ calculate A^5 and A^r, where r is an integer greater than 2.

Solution   Since A is a 2×2 square matrix, it follows from (6.30) that

$$A^5 = \alpha_0 I + \alpha_1 A$$

and for each eigenvalue λ_i ($i = 1, 2$) α_0 and α_1 satisfy

$$\lambda_i^5 = \alpha_0 + \alpha_1 \lambda_i$$

Substituting $\lambda_1 = -1$ and $\lambda_2 = -2$ leads to the following pair of simultaneous equations:

$$(-1)^5 = \alpha_0 + \alpha_1(-1)$$

$$(-2)^5 = \alpha_0 + \alpha_1(-2)$$

which can be solved for α_0 and α_1 to give

$$\alpha_0 = 2(-1)^5 - (-2)^5$$

$$\alpha_1 = (-1)^5 - (-2)^5$$

Then

$$A^5 = [2(-1)^5 - (-2)^5]\begin{bmatrix} 1 & 0 \\ 0 & 1 \end{bmatrix} + [(-1)^5 - (-2)^5]\begin{bmatrix} 0 & 1 \\ -2 & -3 \end{bmatrix}$$

$$= \begin{bmatrix} 2(-1)^5 - (-2)^5 & (-1)^5 - (-2)^5 \\ (-2)((-1)^5 - (-2)^5) & 2(-2)^5 - (-1)^5 \end{bmatrix}$$

$$= \begin{bmatrix} 30 & 31 \\ -62 & -63 \end{bmatrix}$$

Replacing the exponent 5 by the general value r, the algebra is identical, and it is easy to see that

$$A^r = \begin{bmatrix} 2(-1)^r - (-2)^r & (-1)^r - (-2)^r \\ -2((-1)^r - (-2)^r) & 2(-2)^r - (-1)^r \end{bmatrix}$$

To evaluate α_0 and α_1 in (6.27), we assumed that the matrix A had distinct eigenvalues λ_1 and λ_2, leading to a pair of simultaneous equations for α_0 and α_1. What happens if the 2×2 matrix A has a repeated eigenvalue so that $\lambda_1 = \lambda_2 = \lambda$, say? We shall apparently have just a single equation to determine the two constants α_0 and α_1. However, we can obtain a second equation by differentiating with respect to λ, as illustrated in Example 6.28.

EXAMPLE 6.28 Given that the matrix

$$A = \begin{bmatrix} 0 & 1 \\ -1 & -2 \end{bmatrix}$$

has eigenvalues $\lambda_1 = \lambda_2 = -1$, determine A^r, where r is an integer greater than 2.

Solution Since A is a 2×2 matrix, it follows from (6.30) that

$$A = \alpha_0 I + \alpha_1 A$$

with α_0 and α_1 satisfying

$$\lambda^r = \alpha_0 + \alpha_1 \lambda \tag{6.31}$$

Since in this case we have only one value of λ, namely $\lambda = -1$, we differentiate (6.31) with respect to λ, to obtain

$$r\lambda^{r-1} = \alpha_1 \tag{6.32}$$

Substituting $\lambda = -1$ in (6.31) and (6.32) leads to

$$\alpha_1 = (-1)^{r-1} r$$

$$\alpha_0 = (-1)^r + \alpha_1 = (1 - r)(-1)^r$$

giving

$$A^r = (1 - r)(-1)^r \begin{bmatrix} 1 & 0 \\ 0 & 1 \end{bmatrix} - r(-1)^r \begin{bmatrix} 0 & 1 \\ -1 & -2 \end{bmatrix}$$

$$= \begin{bmatrix} (1 - r)(-1)^r & -r(-1)^r \\ r(-1)^r & (1 + r)(-1)^r \end{bmatrix}$$

Having found a straightforward way of expressing any positive integer power of the 2×2 square matrix A we see that the same process could be used for each of the terms in (6.26) for $r \geqslant 2$. Thus, for a 2×2 matrix A and some α_0 and α_1,

$$f(A) = \sum_{r=0}^{p} \beta_r A^r = \alpha_0 I + \alpha_1 A$$

If, as $p \to \infty$,

$$f(A) = \lim_{p \to \infty} \sum_{r=0}^{p} \beta_r A^r$$

exists, that is, it is a 2×2 matrix with finite entries independent of p, then we may write

$$f(A) = \sum_{r=0}^{\infty} \beta_r A^r = \alpha_0 I + \alpha_1 A \tag{6.33}$$

We are now in a position to check the results of our computer experiment with the matrix

$$A = \begin{bmatrix} 1 & 0 \\ 0 & 1 \end{bmatrix}$$

of Example 6.25. We have defined

$$f(A) = e^{At} = \sum_{r=0}^{\infty} \frac{A^r}{r!} t^r$$

so we can write

$$e^{At} = \alpha_0 I + \alpha_1 A$$

Since A has repeated eigenvalue $\lambda = 1$, we adopt the method of Example 6.28 to give

$$e^t = \alpha_0 + \alpha_1$$
$$t e^t = \alpha_1$$

leading to

$$\alpha_1 = t e^t, \qquad \alpha_0 = (1 - t) e^t$$

Thus

$$e^{At} = (1 - t) e^t I + t e^t A = e^t I$$
$$= \begin{bmatrix} e^t & 0 \\ 0 & e^t \end{bmatrix}$$

Setting $t = 1$ confirms our inference in Example 6.25.

EXAMPLE 6.29   Calculate e^{At} and $\sin At$ when

$$A = \begin{bmatrix} 1 & -1 \\ 0 & 1 \end{bmatrix}$$

Solution   Again A has repeated eigenvalues, with $\lambda_1 = \lambda_2 = 1$. Thus for e^{At} we have

$$e^{At} = \alpha_0 + \alpha_1 A$$

with

$$e^t = \alpha_0 + \alpha_1$$
$$t e^t = \alpha_1$$

leading to

$$e^{At} = \begin{bmatrix} e^t & -t e^t \\ 0 & e^t \end{bmatrix}$$

Similarly,

$$\sin At = \alpha_0 I + \alpha_1 A$$

with

$$\sin \lambda t = \alpha_0 + \alpha_1$$

$$t \sin \lambda t = \alpha_1$$

leading to

$$\sin \boldsymbol{A}t = \begin{bmatrix} \sin t & -t \sin t \\ 0 & \sin t \end{bmatrix}$$

Although we have worked so far with 2×2 matrices, nothing in our development restricts us to this case. The Cayley–Hamilton theorem allows us to express positive integer powers of any $n \times n$ square matrix $\boldsymbol{A}$ in terms of powers of $\boldsymbol{A}$ up to $n - 1$. That is, if $\boldsymbol{A}$ is an $n \times n$ matrix and $p \geqslant n$ then

$$\boldsymbol{A}^p = \sum_{r=0}^{n-1} \beta_r \boldsymbol{A}^r$$

$$= \beta_0 \boldsymbol{I} + \beta_1 \boldsymbol{A} + \ldots + \beta_{n-1} \boldsymbol{A}^{n-1}$$

From this we can deduce that for an $n \times n$ matrix $\boldsymbol{A}$ we may write

$$f(\boldsymbol{A}) = \sum_{r=0}^{\infty} \beta_r \boldsymbol{A}^r$$

as

$$f(\boldsymbol{A}) = \sum_{r=0}^{n-1} \alpha_r \boldsymbol{A}^r \qquad (6.34a)$$

which generalizes the result (6.33). Again the coefficients $\alpha_0, \alpha_1, \ldots, \alpha_{n-1}$ are obtained by solving the n equations

$$f(\lambda_i) = \sum_{r=0}^{n-1} \alpha_r \lambda_i^r \quad (i = 1, 2, \ldots, n) \qquad (6.34b)$$

where $\lambda_1, \lambda_2, \ldots, \lambda_n$ are the eigenvalues of $\boldsymbol{A}$. If $\boldsymbol{A}$ has repeated eigenvalues, we differentiate as before, noting that if λ_i is an eigenvalue of multiplicity m then the first $m - 1$ derivatives

$$\frac{\mathrm{d}^k}{\mathrm{d}\lambda_i^k} f(\lambda_i) = \frac{\mathrm{d}^k}{\mathrm{d}\lambda_i^k} \sum_{r=0}^{n-1} \alpha_r \lambda_i^r \quad (k = 1, 2, \ldots, m - 1)$$

are also satisfied by λ_i.

Sometimes it is advantageous to use an alternative approach to evaluate

$$f(\boldsymbol{A}) = \sum_{r=0}^{p} \beta_r \boldsymbol{A}^r$$

If $\boldsymbol{A}$ possesses n linearly independent eigenvectors then there exists a modal matrix $\boldsymbol{M}$ and spectral matrix Λ such that

$$\boldsymbol{M}^{-1} \boldsymbol{A} \boldsymbol{M} = \Lambda = \mathrm{diag}(\lambda_1, \lambda_2, \ldots, \lambda_n)$$

Now

$$M^{-1}f(A)M = \sum_{r=0}^{p} \beta_r(M^{-1}A^rM) = \sum_{r=0}^{p} \beta_r(M^{-1}AM)^r$$

$$= \sum_{r=0}^{p} \beta_r \Lambda^r$$

$$= \sum_{r=0}^{p} \beta_r \operatorname{diag}(\lambda_1^r, \lambda_2^r, \ldots, \lambda_n^r)$$

$$= \operatorname{diag}\left(\sum_{r=0}^{p} \beta_r\lambda_1^r, \sum_{r=0}^{p} \beta_r\lambda_2^r, \ldots, \sum_{r=0}^{p} \beta_r\lambda_n^r\right)$$

$$= \operatorname{diag}(f(\lambda_1), f(\lambda_2), \ldots, f(\lambda_n))$$

This gives us a second method of computing functions of a square matrix, since we see that

$$f(A) = M \operatorname{diag}(f(\lambda_1), f(\lambda_2), \ldots, f(\lambda_n))M^{-1} \qquad (6.35)$$

EXAMPLE 6.30   Using the result (6.35), calculate A^k for the matrix

$$A = \begin{bmatrix} 0 & 1 \\ -2 & -3 \end{bmatrix}$$

of Example 6.27.

Solution A has eigenvalues $\lambda_1 = -1$ and $\lambda_2 = -2$ with corresponding eigenvectors

$$e_1 = [1 \quad -1]^T, \qquad e_2 = [1 \quad -2]^T$$

Thus a modal matrix M and corresponding spectral matrix Λ are

$$M = \begin{bmatrix} 1 & 1 \\ -1 & -2 \end{bmatrix}, \qquad \Lambda = \begin{bmatrix} -1 & 0 \\ 0 & -2 \end{bmatrix}$$

Clearly

$$M^{-1} = \begin{bmatrix} 2 & 1 \\ -1 & -1 \end{bmatrix}$$

Taking $f(A) = A^k$, we have

$$\operatorname{diag}(f(-1), f(-2)) = \operatorname{diag}((-1)^k, (-2)^k)$$

Thus, from (6.35),

$$f(A) = M\begin{bmatrix} (-1)^k & 0 \\ 0 & (-2)^k \end{bmatrix}M^{-1}$$

$$= \begin{bmatrix} 2(-1)^k - (-2)^k & (-1)^k - (-2)^k \\ 2((-2)^k - (-1)^k) & 2(-2)^k - (-1)^k \end{bmatrix}$$

as determined in Example 6.27.

Example 6.30 demonstrates a second approach to the calculation of a function of a matrix. There is little difference in the labour associated with each method, perhaps the only comment we should make is that each approach gives a different perspective on the construction of the matrix function either from powers of the matrix itself or from its spectral and modal matrices.

Later in this chapter we need to make use of some properties of the exponential matrix e^{At}, where A is a constant $n \times n$ square matrix. These are now briefly discussed. First, we have

$$\frac{d}{dt}(e^{At}) = A e^{At} = e^{At} A \tag{6.36}$$

which follows from the power series definition given in (6.27), and the proof is left as an exercise. Secondly,

$$e^{A(t_1 + t_2)} = e^{At_1} e^{At_2} \tag{6.37}$$

Although this property is true in general we shall illustrate its validity for the particular case when A has n linearly independent eigenvectors. Then, from (6.35),

$$e^{At_1} = M \operatorname{diag}(e^{\lambda_1 t_1}, e^{\lambda_2 t_1}, \dots, e^{\lambda_n t_1}) M^{-1}$$

$$e^{At_2} = M \operatorname{diag}(e^{\lambda_1 t_2}, e^{\lambda_2 t_2}, \dots, e^{\lambda_n t_2}) M^{-1}$$

so that

$$e^{At_1} e^{At_2} = M \operatorname{diag}(e^{\lambda_1 (t_1 + t_2)}, e^{\lambda_2 (t_1 + t_2)}, \dots, e^{\lambda_n (t_1 + t_2)}) M^{-1}$$

$$= e^{A(t_1 + t_2)}$$

It is important to note that in general

$$e^{At} e^{Bt} \neq e^{(A + B)t}$$

It follows from the series definition that

$$e^{At} e^{Bt} = e^{(A + B)t} \tag{6.38}$$

if and only if the matrices A and B commute, that is, if $AB = BA$.

To conclude this section we consider the derivative and integral of a matrix $A(t) = [a_{ij}(t)]$, whose elements $a_{ij}(t)$ are functions of t. The derivative and integral of $A(t)$ are defined respectively by

$$\frac{d}{dt} A(t) = \left[\frac{d}{dt} a_{ij}(t) \right] \tag{6.39}$$

and

$$\int A(t)\, dt = \left[\int a_{ij}(t)\, dt \right] \tag{6.40}$$

that is, each element of the matrix is differentiated or integrated as appropriate.

EXAMPLE 6.31   Evaluate $d\boldsymbol{A}/dt$ and $\int \boldsymbol{A}\, dt$ for the matrix

$$\begin{bmatrix} t^2 + 1 & t - 3 \\ 2 & t^2 + 2t - 1 \end{bmatrix}$$

Solution   Using (6.39),

$$\frac{d\boldsymbol{A}}{dt} = \begin{bmatrix} \dfrac{d}{dt}(t^2 + 1) & \dfrac{d}{dt}(t - 3) \\[2mm] \dfrac{d}{dt}(2) & \dfrac{d}{dt}(t^2 + 2t - 1) \end{bmatrix} = \begin{bmatrix} 2t & 1 \\ 0 & 2t + 2 \end{bmatrix}$$

Using (6.40),

$$\int \boldsymbol{A}\, dt = \begin{bmatrix} \displaystyle\int (t^2 + 1)\, dt & \displaystyle\int (t - 3)\, dt \\[3mm] \displaystyle\int 2\, dt & \displaystyle\int (t^2 + 2t - 1)\, dt \end{bmatrix}$$

$$= \begin{bmatrix} \frac{1}{3}t^3 + t + c_{11} & \frac{1}{2}t^2 - 3t + c_{12} \\[1mm] 2t + c_{21} & \frac{1}{3}t^3 + t^2 - t + c_{22} \end{bmatrix}$$

$$= \begin{bmatrix} \frac{1}{3}t^3 + t & \frac{1}{2}t^2 - 3t \\[1mm] 2t & \frac{1}{3}t^3 + t^2 - t \end{bmatrix} + \begin{bmatrix} c_{11} & c_{12} \\ c_{21} & c_{22} \end{bmatrix}$$

$$= \begin{bmatrix} \frac{1}{3}t^3 + t & \frac{1}{2}t^2 - 3t \\[1mm] 2t & \frac{1}{3}t^3 + t^2 - t \end{bmatrix} + \boldsymbol{C}$$

where $\boldsymbol{C}$ is a constant matrix.

From the basic definitions, it follows that for constants α and β

$$\frac{d}{dt}(\alpha \boldsymbol{A} + \beta \boldsymbol{B}) = \alpha \frac{d\boldsymbol{A}}{dt} + \beta \frac{d\boldsymbol{B}}{dt} \tag{6.41}$$

$$\int (\alpha \boldsymbol{A} + \beta \boldsymbol{B})\, dt = \alpha \int \boldsymbol{A}\, dt + \beta \int \boldsymbol{B}\, dt \tag{6.42}$$

$$\frac{d}{dt}(\boldsymbol{AB}) = \boldsymbol{A}\frac{d\boldsymbol{B}}{dt} + \frac{d\boldsymbol{A}}{dt}\boldsymbol{B} \tag{6.43}$$

Note in (6.43) that order is important, since in general $\boldsymbol{AB} \neq \boldsymbol{BA}$.
    Note that in general

$$\frac{d}{dt}[\boldsymbol{A}(t)]^n \neq n\boldsymbol{A}^{n-1}\frac{d\boldsymbol{A}}{dt}$$

6.5.1 Exercises

30 Show that the matrix

$$A = \begin{bmatrix} 5 & 6 \\ 2 & 3 \end{bmatrix}$$

satisfies its own characteristic equation.

31 Given

$$A = \begin{bmatrix} 1 & 2 \\ 1 & 1 \end{bmatrix}$$

use the Cayley–Hamilton theorem to evaluate

(a) A^2 (b) A^3 (c) A^4

32 The characteristic equation of an $n \times n$ matrix A is

$$c(\lambda) = \lambda^n + c_{n-1}\lambda^{n-1} + c_{n-2}\lambda^{n-2} + \ldots + c_1\lambda + c_0$$
$$= 0$$

so, by the Cayley–Hamilton theorem,

$$A^n + c_{n-1}A^{n-1} + c_{n-2}A^{n-2} + \ldots + c_1 A + c_0 I$$
$$= \mathbf{0}$$

If A is non-singular then every eigenvalue is non-zero, so $c_0 \neq 0$ and

$$I = \frac{1}{c_0}(A^n + c_{n-1}A^{n-1} + \ldots + c_1 A)$$

which on multiplying throughout by A^{-1} gives

$$A^{-1} = \frac{1}{c_0}(A^{n-1} + c_{n-1}A^{n-2} + \ldots + c_1 I] \quad \textbf{(6.44)}$$

(a) Using (6.44) find the inverse of the matrix

$$A = \begin{bmatrix} 2 & 1 \\ 1 & 2 \end{bmatrix}$$

(b) Show that the characteristic equation of the matrix

$$A = \begin{bmatrix} 1 & 1 & 2 \\ 3 & 1 & 1 \\ 2 & 3 & 1 \end{bmatrix}$$

is

$$\lambda^3 - 3\lambda^2 - 7\lambda - 11 = 0$$

Evaluate A^2 and, using (6.44), determine A^{-1}.

33 Given

$$A = \begin{bmatrix} 2 & 3 & 1 \\ 3 & 1 & 2 \\ 1 & 2 & 3 \end{bmatrix}$$

compute A^2 and, using the Cayley–Hamilton theorem, compute

$$A^7 - 3A^6 + A^4 + 3A^3 - 2A^2 + 3I$$

34 Evaluate e^{At} for

(a) $A = \begin{bmatrix} 1 & 0 \\ 1 & 1 \end{bmatrix}$ (b) $A = \begin{bmatrix} 1 & 0 \\ 1 & 2 \end{bmatrix}$

35 Given

$$A = \frac{\pi}{2}\begin{bmatrix} 2 & 0 & 0 \\ 0 & 1 & 1 \\ 0 & 0 & 1 \end{bmatrix}$$

show that

$$\sin A = \frac{4}{\pi}A - \frac{4}{\pi^2}A^2 = \begin{bmatrix} 0 & 0 & 0 \\ 0 & 1 & 0 \\ 0 & 0 & 1 \end{bmatrix}$$

36 Given

$$A = \begin{bmatrix} t^2 + 1 & 2t - 3 \\ 5 - t & t^2 - t + 3 \end{bmatrix}$$

evaluate

(a) $\dfrac{dA}{dt}$ (b) $\displaystyle\int_1^2 A\,dt$

37 Given

$$A = \begin{bmatrix} t^2 + 1 & t - 1 \\ 5 & 0 \end{bmatrix}$$

evaluate A^2 and show that

$$\frac{d}{dt}(A^2) \neq 2A\frac{dA}{dt}$$

6.6 State-space representation

In Section 2.3 we applied Laplace transform methods to obtain the response of a linear time-invariant system to a given input. It was noted at the time that the process of taking the inverse transform, to obtain the system response, could prove to be rather tedious for high-order systems. In this section we shall apply matrix techniques to obtain the response of such systems.

6.6.1 Single-input–single-output (SISO) systems

First let us consider the **single-input–single-output (SISO) system** characterized by the nth-order linear differential equation

$$a_n \frac{d^n y}{dt^n} + a_{n-1} \frac{d^{n-1} y}{dt^{n-2}} + \ldots + a_1 \frac{dy}{dt} + a_0 y = u(t) \tag{6.45}$$

where, as in (2.19), the coefficients a_i $(i = 0, 1, \ldots, n)$ are constants with $a_n \neq 0$ and it is assumed that the initial conditions $y(0)$, $y^{(1)}(0), \ldots, y^{(n-1)}(0)$ are known.

We introduce the n variables $x_1(t), x_2(t), \ldots, x_n(t)$ defined by

$$x_1(t) = y(t)$$

$$x_2(t) = \frac{dy}{dt} = \dot{x}_1(t)$$

$$x_3(t) = \frac{d^2 y}{dt^2} = \dot{x}_2(t)$$

$$\vdots$$

$$x_{n-1}(t) = \frac{d^{n-2} y}{dt^{n-2}} = \dot{x}_{n-2}(t)$$

$$x_n(t) = \frac{d^{n-1} y}{dt^{n-1}} = \dot{x}_{n-1}(t)$$

then, by substituting in (6.45), we have

$$a_n \dot{x}_n + a_{n-1} x_n + a_{n-2} x_{n-1} + \ldots + a_1 x_2 + a_0 x_1 = u(t)$$

giving

$$\dot{x}_n = -\frac{a_{n-1}}{a_n}x_n - \frac{a_{n-2}}{a_n}x_{n-1} - \dots - \frac{a_1}{a_n}x_2 - \frac{a_0}{a_n}x_1 + \frac{1}{a_n}u$$

Thus, we can represent (6.45) as a system of n simultaneous first-order differential equations

$$\dot{x}_1 = x_2$$
$$\dot{x}_2 = x_3$$
$$\vdots$$
$$\dot{x}_{n-1} = x_n$$
$$\dot{x}_n = -\frac{a_0}{a_n}x_1 - \frac{a_1}{a_n}x_2 - \dots - \frac{a_{n-1}}{a_n}x_n + \frac{1}{a_n}u$$

which may be written as the **vector–matrix differential equation**

$$\begin{bmatrix} \dot{x}_1 \\ \dot{x}_2 \\ \vdots \\ \dot{x}_{n-1} \\ \dot{x}_n \end{bmatrix} = \begin{bmatrix} 0 & 1 & 0 & \dots & 0 & 0 \\ 0 & 0 & 1 & \dots & 0 & 0 \\ \vdots & \vdots & \vdots & & \vdots & \vdots \\ 0 & 0 & 0 & \dots & 0 & 1 \\ -\frac{a_0}{a_n} & -\frac{a_1}{a_n} & -\frac{a_2}{a_n} & \dots & -\frac{a_{n-2}}{a_n} & -\frac{a_{n-1}}{a_n} \end{bmatrix} \begin{bmatrix} x_1 \\ x_2 \\ \vdots \\ x_{n-1} \\ x_n \end{bmatrix} + \begin{bmatrix} 0 \\ 0 \\ \vdots \\ 0 \\ \frac{1}{a_n} \end{bmatrix} u(t)$$

$$(6.46)$$

This may be written in the more concise form

$$\dot{x} = Ax + bu \qquad\qquad (6.47)$$

The vector $x(t)$ is called the system **state vector**, and it contains all the information that one needs to know about the behaviour of the system. Its components are the n **state variables** $x_1, x_2, \dots, x_n$, which may be considered as representing a set of coordinate axes in the n-dimensional coordinate space over which $x(t)$ ranges. This is referred to as the **state space**, and as time increases the state vector $x(t)$ will describe a locus in this space called a **trajectory**. In two dimensions the state space reduces to the **phase plane** used in Chapter 11 of *Modern Engineering Mathematics* to investigate second-order systems. The matrix A is called the **system matrix** and the particular form adopted in (6.46) is known as the **companion form**, which is widely adopted in practice. Equation (6.47) is referred to as the system **state equation**.

It is important to realize that the choice of state variables $x_1, x_2, \dots x_n$ is not unique. For example, for the system represented by (6.45) we could also take

$$x_1 = \frac{\mathrm{d}^{n-1}y}{\mathrm{d}t^{n-1}}, \quad x_2 = \frac{\mathrm{d}^{n-2}y}{\mathrm{d}t^{n-2}}, \quad \dots, \quad x_n = y$$

giving a state equation (6.47) with

$$A = \begin{bmatrix} -\dfrac{a_{n-1}}{a_n} & -\dfrac{a_{n-2}}{a_n} & \cdots & -\dfrac{a_1}{a_n} & -\dfrac{a_0}{a_n} \\ 1 & 0 & \cdots & 0 & 0 \\ 0 & 1 & \cdots & 0 & 0 \\ \vdots & \vdots & & \vdots & \vdots \\ 0 & 0 & \cdots & 1 & 0 \end{bmatrix}, \quad b = \begin{bmatrix} \dfrac{1}{a_n} \\ 0 \\ \vdots \\ 0 \end{bmatrix}$$

The output, or response, of the system determined by (6.45) is given by y, which in terms of the state variables is determined by x_1. Thus

$$y = \begin{bmatrix} 1 & 0 & \cdots & 0 \end{bmatrix} \begin{bmatrix} x_1 \\ x_2 \\ \vdots \\ x_n \end{bmatrix}$$

or, more precisely,

$$y = c^{\mathrm{T}} x \tag{6.48}$$

where $c = \begin{bmatrix} 1 & 0 & \cdots & 0 \end{bmatrix}^{\mathrm{T}}$.

We shall see later that, in contrast with the transform methods adopted in Chapters 2 and 3, which are generally applied to SISO systems, a distinct advantage of the vector–matrix approach is that it is applicable to multivariable (that is, multi-input–multi-output MIMO) systems. In such cases it is particularly important to distinguish between the system state variables and the system outputs, which, in general, are linear combinations of the state variables.

Together the pair of equations (6.47) and (6.48) in the form

$$\dot{x} = Ax + bu \tag{6.49a}$$

$$y = c^{\mathrm{T}} x \tag{6.49b}$$

constitute the **dynamic equations** of the system and are commonly referred to as the state-space model representation of the system. Such a representation forms the basis of the so-called 'modern approach' to the analysis and design of control systems in engineering. An obvious advantage of adopting the vector–matrix representation (6.49) is the compactness of the notation.

More generally the output y could be a linear combination of both the state and input, so that the more general form of the system dynamic equations (6.49) is

$$\dot{x} = Ax + bu \tag{6.50a}$$

$$y = c^{\mathrm{T}} x + du \tag{6.50b}$$

EXAMPLE 6.32   Obtain a state-space representation of the system characterized by the third-order differential equation

$$\frac{d^3y}{dt^3} + 3\frac{d^2y}{dt^2} + 2\frac{dy}{dt} - 4y = e^{-t} \tag{6.51}$$

Solution   Writing

$$x_1 = y$$

$$x_2 = \frac{dy}{dt} = \dot{x}_1$$

$$x_3 = \frac{d^2y}{dt^2} = \dot{x}_2$$

we have, from (6.51),

$$\dot{x}_3 = \frac{d^3y}{dt^3} = 4y - 2\frac{dy}{dt} - 3\frac{d^2y}{dt^2} + e^{-t}$$

$$= 4x_1 - 2x_2 - 3x_3 + e^{-t}$$

Thus the corresponding state equation is

$$\begin{bmatrix} \dot{x}_1 \\ \dot{x}_2 \\ \dot{x}_3 \end{bmatrix} = \begin{bmatrix} 0 & 1 & 0 \\ 0 & 0 & 1 \\ 4 & -2 & -3 \end{bmatrix} \begin{bmatrix} x_1 \\ x_2 \\ x_3 \end{bmatrix} + \begin{bmatrix} 0 \\ 0 \\ 1 \end{bmatrix} e^{-t}$$

with the output y being given by

$$y = x_1 = \begin{bmatrix} 1 & 0 & 0 \end{bmatrix} \begin{bmatrix} x_1 \\ x_2 \\ x_3 \end{bmatrix}$$

These two equations then constitute the state-space representation of the system.

We now proceed to consider the more general SISO system characterized by the differential equation

$$\frac{d^ny}{dt^n} + a_n\frac{d^{n-1}y}{dt^{n-1}} + \ldots + a_0y = b_m\frac{d^mu}{dt^m} + \ldots + b_0u \quad (m \leqslant n) \tag{6.52}$$

in which the input involves derivative terms. As we saw in (2.66), this system may be characterized by the transfer function

$$G(s) = \frac{b_ms^m + \ldots + b_0}{s^n + a_{n-1}s^{n-1} + \ldots + a_0} \tag{6.53}$$

depicted by the input–output block diagram of Figure 2.41.

Again there are various ways of representing (6.53) in the state-space form, depending on the choice of the state variables. As an illustration, we shall consider one possible approach, introducing others in the exercises.

We define A and b as in (6.46); that is, we take A to be the companion matrix of the left-hand side of (6.51) (or the companion matrix of the denominator in the transfer-function model (6.53)), giving

$$
A = \begin{bmatrix}
0 & 1 & 0 & \cdots & 0 & 0 \\
0 & 0 & 1 & & 0 & 0 \\
\vdots & \vdots & \vdots & & \vdots & \vdots \\
0 & 0 & 0 & \cdots & 0 & 1 \\
-a_0 & -a_1 & -a_2 & \cdots & -a_{n-2} & -a_{n-1}
\end{bmatrix}
$$

and we take $b = [0 \quad 0 \quad \cdots \quad 0 \quad 1]^T$. In order to achieve the desired response, the vector c is then chosen to be

$$
c = [b_0 \quad b_1 \quad \cdots \quad b_m \quad 0 \quad \cdots \quad 0]^T \tag{6.54}
$$

To confirm that this structure is appropriate, it is convenient to adopt Laplace transform notation. Taking

$$
X_1(s) = \frac{1}{s^n + a_{n-1}s^{n-1} + \ldots + a_0} U(s)
$$

we have

$$
X_2(s) = sX_1(s), \qquad X_3(s) = sX_2(s) = s^2 X_1(s), \qquad \cdots
$$

$$
X_n(s) = sX_{n-1}(s) = s^{n-1} X_1(s)
$$

so that

$$
Y(s) = c^T X(s) = b_0 X_1(s) + b_1 X_2(s) + \ldots + b_m X_{m+1}(s)
$$

$$
= \frac{b_0 + b_1 s + b_2 s^2 + \ldots + b_m s^m}{s^n + a_{n-1}s^{n-1} + \ldots + a_0}
$$

which confirms (6.54).

EXAMPLE 6.33   For the system characterized by the differential equation model

$$
\frac{d^3 y}{dt^3} + 6\frac{d^2 y}{dt^2} + 11\frac{dy}{dt} + 3y = 5\frac{d^2 u}{dt^2} + \frac{du}{dt} + u \tag{6.55}
$$

obtain

(a) a transfer-function model;

(b) a state-space model.

Solution (a) Assuming all initial conditions to be zero, taking Laplace transforms throughout in (6.55) leads to

$$(s^3 + 6s^2 + 11s + 3)\,Y(s) = (5s^2 + s + 1)\,U(s)$$

so that the transfer-function model is given by

$$G(s) = \frac{Y(s)}{U(s)} = \frac{5s^2 + s + 1}{s^3 + 6s^2 + 11s + 3} \qquad \begin{matrix} \leftarrow c \\ \leftarrow \boldsymbol{A} \end{matrix}$$

(b) Taking $\boldsymbol{A}$ to be the companion matrix of the left-hand side in (6.55)

$$\boldsymbol{A} = \begin{bmatrix} 0 & 1 & 0 \\ 0 & 0 & 1 \\ -3 & -11 & -6 \end{bmatrix}$$

and

$$\boldsymbol{b} = [0 \quad 0 \quad 1]^{\mathrm{T}}$$

we have, from (6.54),

$$\boldsymbol{c} = [1 \quad 1 \quad 5]^{\mathrm{T}}$$

(Note that the last row of $\boldsymbol{A}$ and c may be obtained from the transfer function in (a) by reading the coefficients of the denominator and numerator backwards, as indicated by the arrows, and negating those in the denominator.) Then from (6.49) the state-space model becomes

$$\dot{x} = \boldsymbol{A}x + \boldsymbol{b}u$$

$$y = \boldsymbol{c}^{\mathrm{T}}x$$

This model structure may be depicted by the block diagram of Figure 6.3. It provides an ideal model for simulation studies, with the state variables being the outputs of the various integrators involved.

Figure 6.3 Block diagram for the state-space model of Example 6.33.

A distinct advantage of this approach to obtaining the state-space model is that A, b and c are readily written down. A possible disadvantage in some applications is that the output y itself is not a state variable. An approach in which y is a state variable is developed in Exercise 43. In practice, it is also fairly common to choose the state variables from a physical consideration, as is illustrated in Example 6.34.

6.6.2 Multi-input–multi-output (MIMO) systems

Many practical systems are multivariable in nature, being characterized by having more than one input and/or more than one output. In general terms, the state-space model is similar to that in (6.50) for SISO systems, except that the input is now a vector $u(t)$ as is the output $y(t)$. Thus the more general form, corresponding to (6.50), of the state-space model representation of an nth-order **multi-input–multi-output (MIMO) system** subject to r inputs and l outputs is

$$\dot{x} = Ax + Bu \left.\right\} \qquad \text{(6.56a)}$$
$$y = Cx + Du \left.\right\} \qquad \text{(6.56b)}$$

where x is the n-state vector, u is the r-input vector, y is the l-output vector, A is the $n \times n$ system matrix, B is the $n \times r$ control (or input) matrix, and C and D are respectively $l \times n$ and $l \times r$ output matrices.

EXAMPLE 6.34 Obtain the state-space model representation characterizing the two-input–one-output parallel network shown in Figure 6.4 in the form

$$\dot{x} = Ax + Bu, \qquad y = c^{\mathrm{T}}x + d^{\mathrm{T}}u$$

where the elements x_1, x_2, x_3 of x and u_1, u_2 of u are as indicated in the figure, and the output y is the voltage drop across the inductor L_1 (v_C denotes the voltage drop across the capacitor C).

Figure 6.4 Parallel circuit of Example 6.34.

Solution   Applying Kirchhoff's second law to each of the two loops in turn gives

$$R_1 i_1 + L_1 \frac{di_1}{dt} + v_C = e_1 \tag{6.57}$$

$$L_2 \frac{di_2}{dt} + v_C = e_2 \tag{6.58}$$

The voltage drop v_C across the capacitor C is given by

$$\dot{v}_C = \frac{1}{C}(i_1 + i_2) \tag{6.59}$$

The output y, being the voltage drop across the inductor L_1, is given by

$$y = L_1 \frac{di_1}{dt}$$

which, using (6.57), gives

$$y = -R_1 i_1 - v_C + e_1 \tag{6.60}$$

Writing $x_1 = i_1$, $x_2 = i_2$, $x_3 = v_C$, $u_1 = e_1$ and $u_2 = e_2$, (6.57)–(6.60) give the state-space representation as

$$\begin{bmatrix} \dot{x}_1 \\ \dot{x}_2 \\ \dot{x}_3 \end{bmatrix} = \begin{bmatrix} -\dfrac{R_1}{L_1} & 0 & -\dfrac{1}{L_1} \\ 0 & 0 & -\dfrac{1}{L_2} \\ \dfrac{1}{C} & \dfrac{1}{C} & 0 \end{bmatrix} \begin{bmatrix} x_1 \\ x_2 \\ x_3 \end{bmatrix} + \begin{bmatrix} \dfrac{1}{L_1} & 0 \\ 0 & \dfrac{1}{L_2} \\ 0 & 0 \end{bmatrix} \begin{bmatrix} u_1 \\ u_2 \end{bmatrix}$$

$$y = [-R_1 \quad 0 \quad -1] \begin{bmatrix} x_1 \\ x_2 \\ x_3 \end{bmatrix} + [1 \quad 0] \begin{bmatrix} u_1 \\ u_2 \end{bmatrix}$$

which is of the required form

$$\dot{x} = Ax + Bu$$
$$y = c^T x + d^T u$$

6.6.3   Exercises

38 Obtain the state-space forms of the differential equations

(a) $\dfrac{d^3 y}{dt^3} + 4\dfrac{d^2 y}{dt^2} + 5\dfrac{dy}{dt} + 4y = u(t)$

(b) $\dfrac{d^4 y}{dt} + 2\dfrac{d^2 y}{dt^2} + 4\dfrac{dy}{dt} = 5u(t)$

using the companion form of the system matrix in each case.

39 Obtain the dynamic equations in state-space form for the systems having a transfer function models

(a) $\dfrac{s^2 + 3s + 5}{s^3 + 6s^2 + 5s + 7}$ (b) $\dfrac{s^2 + 3s + 2}{s^3 + 4s^2 + 3s}$

using the companion form of the system matrix in each case.

40 Obtain the state-space model of the single-input–single-input network system of Figure 6.5 in the form $\dot{x} = Ax + bu$, $y = c^Tx$, where u, y and the elements x_1, x_2, x_3 of x are as indicated.

Figure 6.5 Network of Exercise 40.

41 The mass–spring–damper system of Figure 6.6 models the suspension system of a quarter-car. Obtain a state-space model in which the output

Figure 6.6 Quarter-car suspension model of Exercise 41.

represents the body mass vertical movement y and the input represents the tyre vertical movement $u(t)$ due to the road surface. All displacements are measured from equilibrium positions.

42 Obtain the state-space model, in the form $\dot{x} = Ax + bu$, $y = Cx + d^Tu$ of the one-input–two-output network illustrated in Figure 6.7. The elements x_1, x_2 of the state vector x and y_1, y_2 of the output vector y are as indicated. If $R_1 = 1\,\text{k}\Omega$, $R_2 = 5\,\text{k}\Omega$, $R_3 = R_4 = 3\,\text{k}\Omega$, $C_1 = C_2 = 1\,\mu\text{F}$ calculate the eigenvalues of the system matrix A.

Figure 6.7 Network of Exercise 42.

43 It was noted in Section 6.6.1 that a possible disadvantage of the state-space model representation (6.54) for the transfer function model (6.53) is that the output y is not a state variable. Suppose we wish the output y to be the state variable x_1; that is, in the state-space representation (6.9) we take $c^T = [1 \quad 0 \quad \dots \quad 0]^T$. If A is again taken to be the companion matrix of the denominator then it can be shown that the coefficients $b_1, b_2, \dots, b_n$ of the vector b are determined as the first n coefficients in the series in s^{-1} obtained by dividing the denominator of the transfer function (6.53) into the numerator. Illustrate this approach for the transfer-function model of Figure 6.8.

Figure 6.8 Transfer-function model of Exercise 43.

6.7 **Solution of the state equation**

In this section we are concerned with seeking the solution of the state equation

$$\dot{x} = Ax + Bu \tag{6.61}$$

given the value of x at some initial time t_0 to be x_0. Having obtained the solution of this state equation, a system response y may then be readily written down from the linear transformation (6.56b). As mentioned in Section 6.6.1, an obvious advantage of adopting the vector–matrix notation of (6.61) is its compactness. In this section we shall see that another distinct advantage is that (6.61) behaves very much like the corresponding first-order scalar differential equation

$$\frac{dx}{dt} = ax + bu, \qquad x(t_0) = x_0 \tag{6.62}$$

6.7.1   Direct form of the solution

Before considering the nth-order system represented by (6.61), let us first briefly review the solution of (6.62). When the input u is zero, (6.62) reduces to the homogeneous equation

$$\frac{dx}{dt} = ax \tag{6.63}$$

which, by separation of variables,

$$\int_{x_0}^{x} \frac{dx}{x} = \int_{t_0}^{t} a\,dt$$

gives

$$\ln x - \ln x_0 = a(t - t_0)$$

leading to the solution

$$x = x_0\, e^{a(t - t_0)} \tag{6.64}$$

for the unforced system.

If we consider the nonhomogeneous equation (6.62) directly, a solution can be obtained by first multiplying throughout by the integrating factor e^{-at} to obtain

$$e^{-at}\left(\frac{dx}{dt} - ax\right) = e^{-at} bu(t)$$

or

$$\frac{d}{dt}(e^{-at} x) = e^{-at} bu(t)$$

which on integration gives

$$e^{-at} x - e^{-at_0} x_0 = \int_{t_0}^{t} e^{-a\tau} bu(\tau)\, d\tau$$

leading to the solution

$$x(t) = e^{a(t-t_0)} x_0 + \int_{t_0}^{t} e^{-a(t-\tau)} b u(\tau) \, d\tau \tag{6.65}$$

The first term of the solution, which corresponds to the solution of the unforced system, is the **complementary function**, while the convolution integral constituting the second term, which is dependent on the forcing function $u(t)$, is the **particular integral**.

Returning to (6.61), we first consider the unforced homogeneous system

$$\dot{x} = Ax, \qquad x(t_0) = x_0 \tag{6.66}$$

which represents the situation when the system is 'relaxing' from an initial state.

The solution is completely analogous to the solution (6.64) of the scalar equation (6.63), and is of the form

$$x = e^{A(t-t_0)} x_0 \tag{6.67}$$

It is readily shown that this is a solution of (6.66). Using (6.36), differentiation of (6.67) gives

$$\dot{x} = A e^{A(t-t_0)} x_0 = Ax$$

so that (6.66) is satisfied. Also, from (6.67),

$$x(t_0) = e^{A(t_0-t_0)} x_0 = I x_0 = x_0$$

using $e^0 = I$. Thus, since (6.67) satisfies the differential equation and the initial conditions, it represents a unique solution of (6.66).

Likewise, the nonhomogeneous equation (6.61) may be solved in an analogous manner to that used for solving (6.62). Premultiplying (6.61) throughout by e^{-At}, we obtain

$$e^{-At}(\dot{x} - Ax) = e^{At} B u(t)$$

or using (6.36),

$$\frac{d}{dt}(e^{-At} x) = e^{-At} B u(t)$$

Integration then gives

$$e^{-At} x(t) - e^{-At_0} x_0 = \int_{t_0}^{t} e^{-A\tau} B u(\tau) \, d\tau$$

leading to the solution

$$x(t) = e^{A(t-t_0)} x_0 + \int_{t_0}^{t} e^{A(t-\tau)} B u(\tau) \, d\tau \tag{6.68}$$

This is analogous to the solution given in (6.65) for the scalar equation (6.62). Again it contains two terms: one dependent on the initial state and corresponding to the solution of the unforced system, and one a convolution integral arising from the input. Having obtained the solution of the state equation, the system output $y(t)$ is then readily obtained from equation (6.56b).

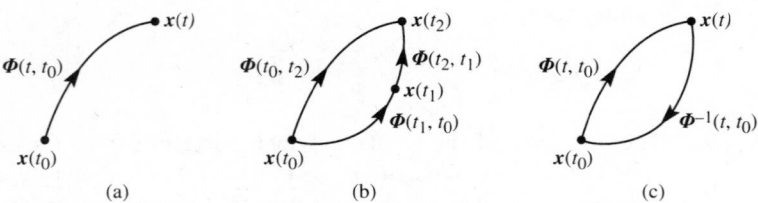

Figure 6.9 (a) Transition matrix $\boldsymbol{\Phi}(t, t_0)$. (b) The transition property. (c) The inverse $\boldsymbol{\Phi}^{-1}(t, t_0)$.

6.7.2   The transition matrix

The matrix exponential $e^{A(t-t_0)}$ is referred to as the **fundamental** or **transition matrix** and is frequently denoted by $\boldsymbol{\Phi}(t, t_0)$; so that (6.66) is written as

$$x(t) = \boldsymbol{\Phi}(t, t_0)x_0 \tag{6.69}$$

This is an important matrix, which can be used to characterize a linear system, and in the absence of any input it maps a given state x_0 at any time t_0 to the state $x(t)$ at any time t, as illustrated in Figure 6.9(a).

Using the properties of the exponential matrix given in Section 6.5, certain properties of the transition matrix may be deduced. From

$$e^{A(t_1 + t_2)} = e^{At_1} e^{At_2}$$

it follows that $\boldsymbol{\Phi}(t, t_0)$ satisfies the **transition property**

$$\boldsymbol{\Phi}(t_2, t_0) = \boldsymbol{\Phi}(t_2, t_1)\boldsymbol{\Phi}(t_1, t_0) \tag{6.70}$$

for any t_0, t_1 and t_2, as illustrated in Figure 6.9(b). From

$$e^{At} e^{-At} = I$$

it follows that the inverse $\boldsymbol{\Phi}^{-1}(t, t_0)$ of the transition matrix is obtained by replacing t by $-t$, so that

$$\boldsymbol{\Phi}^{-1}(t, t_0) = \boldsymbol{\Phi}(-t, t_0) = \boldsymbol{\Phi}(t_0, t) \tag{6.71}$$

for any t_0 and t, as illustrated in Figure 6.9(c).

6.7.3   Evaluating the transition matrix

Since, when dealing with time invariant systems, there is no loss of generality in taking $t_0 = 0$, we shall, for convenience, consider the evaluation of the transition matrix

$$\boldsymbol{\Phi}(t) = \boldsymbol{\Phi}(t, 0) = e^{At}$$

Clearly, methods of evaluating this are readily applicable to the evaluation of

$$\boldsymbol{\Phi}(t, \tau) = e^{\boldsymbol{A}(t-\tau)}$$

Indeed, since $\boldsymbol{A}$ is a constant matrix,

$$\boldsymbol{\Phi}(t, \tau) = \boldsymbol{\Phi}(t - \tau, 0)$$

so, having obtained $\boldsymbol{\Phi}(t)$, we can write down $\boldsymbol{\Phi}(t, \tau)$ by simply replacing t by $t - \tau$.

Since $\boldsymbol{A}$ is a constant matrix the methods discussed in Section 6.5 are applicable for evaluating the transition matrix. From (6.34a),

$$e^{\boldsymbol{A}t} = \alpha_0(t)\boldsymbol{I} + \alpha_1(t)\boldsymbol{A} + \alpha_2(t)\boldsymbol{A}^2 + \ldots + \alpha_{n-1}(t)\boldsymbol{A}^{n-1} \qquad \text{(6.72a)}$$

where, using (6.34b), the $\alpha_i(t)$ $(i = 0, 1, \ldots, n-1)$ are obtained by solving simultaneously the n equations

$$e^{\lambda_j t} = \alpha_0(t) + \alpha_1(t)\lambda_j + \alpha_2(t)\lambda_j^2 + \ldots + \alpha_{n-1}(t)\lambda_j^{n-1} \qquad \text{(6.72b)}$$

where λ_j $(j = 1, 2, \ldots, n)$ are the eigenvalues of $\boldsymbol{A}$. As in Section 6.5, if $\boldsymbol{A}$ has repeated eigenvalues then derivatives of $e^{\lambda t}$, with respect to λ, will have to be used.

EXAMPLE 6.35 A system is characterized by the state equation

$$\begin{bmatrix} \dot{x}_1(t) \\ \dot{x}_2(t) \end{bmatrix} = \begin{bmatrix} -1 & 0 \\ 1 & -3 \end{bmatrix} \begin{bmatrix} x_1(t) \\ x_2(t) \end{bmatrix} + \begin{bmatrix} 1 \\ 1 \end{bmatrix} u(t)$$

Given that the input is the unit step function

$$u(t) = H(t) = \begin{cases} 0 & (t < 0) \\ 1 & (t \geqslant 0) \end{cases}$$

and initially

$$x_1(0) = x_2(0) = 1$$

deduce the state $\boldsymbol{x}(t) = [x_1(t) \quad x_2(t)]^{\mathrm{T}}$ of the system at subsequent time t.

Solution From (6.68), the solution is given by

$$\boldsymbol{x}(t) = e^{\boldsymbol{A}t}\boldsymbol{x}(0) + \int_0^t e^{\boldsymbol{A}(t-\tau)}\boldsymbol{b}u(\tau)\,\mathrm{d}\tau \qquad \text{(6.73)}$$

where

$$\boldsymbol{A} = \begin{bmatrix} -1 & 0 \\ 1 & -3 \end{bmatrix}, \qquad \boldsymbol{b} = [1 \quad 1]^{\mathrm{T}}$$

Since $\boldsymbol{A}$ is a 2×2 matrix, it follows from (6.72a) that

$$e^{\boldsymbol{A}t} = \alpha_0(t)\boldsymbol{I} + \alpha_1(t)\boldsymbol{A}$$

The eigenvalues of $\boldsymbol{A}$ are $\lambda_1 = -1$ and $\lambda_2 = -3$, so, using (6.72), we have

$$\alpha_0(t) = \tfrac{1}{2}(3e^{-t} - e^{-3t}), \qquad \alpha_1(t) = \tfrac{1}{2}(e^{-t} - e^{-3t})$$

giving

$$e^{At} = \begin{bmatrix} e^{-t} & 0 \\ \frac{1}{2}(e^{-t} - e^{-3t}) & e^{-3t} \end{bmatrix}$$

Thus the first term in (6.73) becomes

$$e^{At}x(0) = \begin{bmatrix} e^{-t} & 0 \\ \frac{1}{2}(e^{-t} - e^{-3t}) & e^{-3t} \end{bmatrix}\begin{bmatrix} 1 \\ 1 \end{bmatrix} = \begin{bmatrix} e^{-t} \\ \frac{1}{2}(e^{-t} + e^{-3t}) \end{bmatrix}$$

and the second term is

$$\int_0^t e^{A(t-\tau)}bu(\tau)\,d\tau = \int_0^t \begin{bmatrix} e^{-(t-\tau)} & 0 \\ \frac{1}{2}(e^{-(t-\tau)} - e^{-3(t-\tau)}) & e^{-3(t-\tau)} \end{bmatrix}\begin{bmatrix} 1 \\ 1 \end{bmatrix}1\,d\tau$$

$$= \int_0^t \begin{bmatrix} e^{-(t-\tau)} \\ \frac{1}{2}(e^{-(t-\tau)} + e^{-3(t-\tau)}) \end{bmatrix}d\tau$$

$$= \begin{bmatrix} e^{-(t-\tau)} \\ \frac{1}{2}(e^{-(t-\tau)} + \frac{1}{3}e^{-3(t-\tau)}) \end{bmatrix}_0^t$$

$$= \begin{bmatrix} e^{-0} \\ \frac{1}{2}(e^{-0} + \frac{1}{3}e^{-0}) \end{bmatrix} - \begin{bmatrix} e^{-t} \\ \frac{1}{2}(e^{-t} + \frac{1}{3}e^{-3t}) \end{bmatrix}$$

$$= \begin{bmatrix} 1 - e^{-t} \\ \frac{2}{3} - \frac{1}{2}e^{-t} - \frac{1}{6}e^{-3t} \end{bmatrix}$$

Substituting back in (6.73) gives the required solution

$$x(t) = \begin{bmatrix} e^{-t} \\ \frac{1}{2}(e^{-t} + e^{-3t}) \end{bmatrix} + \begin{bmatrix} 1 - e^{-t} \\ \frac{2}{3} - \frac{1}{2}e^{-t} - \frac{1}{6}e^{-3t} \end{bmatrix}$$

$$= \begin{bmatrix} 1 \\ \frac{2}{3} + \frac{1}{3}e^{-3t} \end{bmatrix}$$

That is,

$$x_1(t) = 1, \qquad x_2(t) = \tfrac{2}{3} + \tfrac{1}{3}e^{-3t}$$

6.7.4 Exercises

44 Obtain the transition matrix $\boldsymbol{\Phi}(t)$ of the system

$$\dot{x} = Ax$$

where

$$A = \begin{bmatrix} 1 & 0 \\ 1 & 1 \end{bmatrix}$$

Verify that $\boldsymbol{\Phi}(t)$ has the following properties:
(a) $\boldsymbol{\Phi}(0) = I$;
(b) $\boldsymbol{\Phi}(t_2) = \boldsymbol{\Phi}(t_2 - t_1)\boldsymbol{\Phi}(t_1)$;
(c) $\boldsymbol{\Phi}^{-1}(t) = \boldsymbol{\Phi}(-t)$.

45 Writing $x_1 = y$ and $x_2 = dy/dt$ express the differential equation

$$\frac{d^2 y}{dt^2} + 2\frac{dy}{dt} + y = 0$$

in the vector–matrix form $\dot{x} = Ax$, $x = [x_1 \quad x_2]^T$. Obtain the transition matrix and hence solve the differential equation given that $y = dy/dt = 1$ when $t = 0$. Confirm your answer by direct solution of the second-order differential equation.

46 Solve

$$\dot{x} = \begin{bmatrix} \dot{x}_1 \\ \dot{x}_2 \end{bmatrix} = \begin{bmatrix} 1 & 0 \\ 1 & 1 \end{bmatrix} \begin{bmatrix} x_1 \\ x_2 \end{bmatrix}$$

subject to $x(0) = [1 \quad 1]^T$.

47 Find the solution of

$$\dot{x} = \begin{bmatrix} \dot{x}_1 \\ \dot{x}_2 \end{bmatrix} = \begin{bmatrix} 0 & 1 \\ -6 & -5 \end{bmatrix} \begin{bmatrix} x_1 \\ x_2 \end{bmatrix} + \begin{bmatrix} 0 \\ 6 \end{bmatrix} u(t) \quad (t \geq 0)$$

where $u(t) = 2$ and $x(0) = [1 \quad -1]^T$.

48 Using (6.68), find the response for $t \geq 0$ of the system

$$\dot{x}_1 = x_2 + 2u$$
$$\dot{x}_2 = -2x_1 - 3x_2$$

to an input $u(t) = e^{-t}$ and subject to the initial conditions $x_1(0) = 0$, $x_2(0) = 1$.

49 A system is governed by the vector–matrix differential equation

$$\dot{x}(t) = \begin{bmatrix} 3 & 4 \\ 2 & 1 \end{bmatrix} x(t) + \begin{bmatrix} 0 & 1 \\ 1 & 1 \end{bmatrix} u(t) \quad (t \geq 0)$$

where $x(t)$ and $u(t)$ are respectively the state and input vectors of the system. Determine the transition matrix of this system, and hence obtain an explicit expression for $x(t)$ for the input $u(t) = [4 \quad 3]^T$ and subject to the initial condition $x(0) = [1 \quad 2]^T$.

6.7.5   Laplace transform solution

Defining

$$\mathscr{L}\{x(t)\} = \begin{bmatrix} \mathscr{L}\{x_1(t)\} \\ \mathscr{L}\{x_2(t)\} \\ \vdots \\ \mathscr{L}\{x_n(t)\} \end{bmatrix} = \begin{bmatrix} X_1(s) \\ X_2(s) \\ \vdots \\ X_n(s) \end{bmatrix} = X(s)$$

$$\mathscr{L}\{u(t)\} = \begin{bmatrix} \mathscr{L}\{u_1(t)\} \\ \mathscr{L}\{u_2(t)\} \\ \vdots \\ \mathscr{L}\{u_r(t)\} \end{bmatrix} = \begin{bmatrix} U_1(s) \\ U_2(s) \\ \vdots \\ U_r(s) \end{bmatrix} = U(s)$$

and then taking Laplace transforms throughout in the state equation

$$\dot{x}(t) = Ax(t) + Bu(t)$$

gives

$$sX(s) - x(0) = AX(s) + BU(s)$$

which on rearranging gives

$$(sI - A)X(s) = x(0) + BU(s)$$

where I is the identity matrix. Premultiplying throughout by $(sI - A)^{-1}$ gives

$$X(s) = (sI - A)^{-1}x(0) + (sI - A)^{-1}BU(s) \tag{6.74}$$

which on taking inverse Laplace transforms gives the response as

$$x(t) = \mathcal{L}^{-1}\{(sI - A)^{-1}\}x(0) + \mathcal{L}^{-1}\{(sI - A)^{-1}BU(s)\} \tag{6.75}$$

On comparing the solution (6.75) with that given in (6.68), we find that the transition matrix $\boldsymbol{\Phi}(t) = e^{At}$ may also be written in the form

$$\boldsymbol{\Phi}(t) = \mathcal{L}^{-1}\{(sI - A)^{-1}\}$$

As mentioned in Section 6.7.3, having obtained $\boldsymbol{\Phi}(t)$,

$$\boldsymbol{\Phi}(t, t_0) = e^{A(t - t_0)}$$

may be obtained on simply replacing t by $t - t_0$.

EXAMPLE 6.36   Using the Laplace transform approach, obtain an expression for the state $x(t)$ of the system characterized by the state equation

$$\dot{x}(t) = \begin{bmatrix} \dot{x}_1(t) \\ \dot{x}_2(t) \end{bmatrix} = \begin{bmatrix} -1 & 0 \\ 1 & -3 \end{bmatrix} \begin{bmatrix} x_1(t) \\ x_2(t) \end{bmatrix} + \begin{bmatrix} 1 \\ 1 \end{bmatrix} u(t)$$

when the input $u(t)$ is the unit step function

$$u(t) = H(t) = \begin{cases} 0 & (t < 0) \\ 1 & (t \geqslant 0) \end{cases}$$

and subject to the initial condition $x(0) = [1 \quad 1]^{\mathrm{T}}$

Solution   In this case

$$A = \begin{bmatrix} -1 & 0 \\ 1 & -3 \end{bmatrix}, \qquad b = \begin{bmatrix} 1 \\ 1 \end{bmatrix}, \qquad u(t) = H(t)$$

$$x_0 = [1 \quad 1]^{\mathrm{T}}$$

Thus

$$sI - A = \begin{bmatrix} s + 1 & 0 \\ -1 & s + 3 \end{bmatrix}$$

$$\det(sI - A) = (s + 1)(s + 3)$$

giving

$$(sI - A)^{-1} = \frac{1}{(s + 1)(s + 3)} \begin{bmatrix} s + 3 & 0 \\ 1 & s + 1 \end{bmatrix}$$

$$= \begin{bmatrix} \dfrac{1}{s + 1} & 0 \\ \dfrac{1}{2(s + 1)} - \dfrac{1}{2(s - 3)} & \dfrac{1}{s + 3} \end{bmatrix}$$

which, on taking inverse transforms, gives the transition matrix as

$$e^{At} = \mathscr{L}^{-1}\{(sI - A)^{-1}\} = \begin{bmatrix} e^{-t} & 0 \\ \frac{1}{2}e^{-t} - \frac{1}{2}e^{-3t} & e^{-3t} \end{bmatrix}$$

so that the first term in the solution (6.75) becomes

$$\mathscr{L}^{-1}\{(sI - A)^{-1}\}x_0 = \begin{bmatrix} e^{-t} & 0 \\ \frac{1}{2}e^{-t} - \frac{1}{2}e^{-3t} & e^{-3t} \end{bmatrix}\begin{bmatrix} 1 \\ 1 \end{bmatrix} = \begin{bmatrix} e^{-t} \\ \frac{1}{2}e^{-t} + \frac{1}{2}e^{-3t} \end{bmatrix}$$

(6.76)

Since $U(s) = \mathscr{L}\{H(t)\} = 1/s$,

$$(sI - A)^{-1}bU(s) = \frac{1}{(s+1)(s+3)}\begin{bmatrix} s+3 & 0 \\ 1 & s+1 \end{bmatrix}\begin{bmatrix} 1 \\ 1 \end{bmatrix}\frac{1}{s}$$

$$= \frac{1}{s(s+1)(s+3)}\begin{bmatrix} s+3 \\ s+2 \end{bmatrix}$$

$$= \begin{bmatrix} \dfrac{1}{s} - \dfrac{1}{s+1} \\[2mm] \dfrac{2}{3s} - \dfrac{1}{2(s+1)} - \dfrac{1}{6(s+3)} \end{bmatrix}$$

so that the second term in (6.75) becomes

$$\mathscr{L}^{-1}\{(sI - A)^{-1}bU(s)\} = \begin{bmatrix} 1 - e^{-t} \\ \frac{2}{3} - \frac{1}{2}e^{-t} - \frac{1}{6}e^{-3t} \end{bmatrix}$$ (6.77)

Combining (6.76) and (6.77), the response $x(t)$ is given by

$$x(t) = \begin{bmatrix} e^{-t} \\ \frac{1}{2}e^{-t} + \frac{1}{2}e^{-3t} \end{bmatrix} + \begin{bmatrix} 1 - e^{-t} \\ \frac{2}{3} - \frac{1}{2}e^{-t} - \frac{1}{6}e^{-3t} \end{bmatrix} = \begin{bmatrix} 1 \\ \frac{2}{3} + \frac{1}{3}e^{-3t} \end{bmatrix}$$

Note that throughout the solution corresponds to that obtained in Example 6.35.

Again, having obtained an expression for the system state $x(t)$, its output, or response, $y(t)$ may be obtained from the linear transformation (6.56b).

We can also use the Laplace transform formulation to obtain the input–output transfer-function matrix for a multivariable system. Taking Laplace transforms throughout in (6.56b) gives

$$Y(s) = CX(s) + DU(s)$$ (6.78)

where $Y(s) = \mathscr{L}\{y(t)\}$. Assuming zero initial conditions in (6.74), we have

$$X(s) = (sI - A)^{-1}BU(s)$$

which on substituting in (6.78) gives the system input–output relationship

$$Y(s) = [C(sI - A)^{-1}B + D]U(s)$$

so that the system transfer function matrix for a multi-input–multi-output system is

$$G(s) = C(sI - A)^{-1}B + D \qquad (6.79)$$

EXAMPLE 6.37   (a) Obtain the state-space model characterizing the network of Figure 6.10. Take the inductor current and the voltage drop across the capacitor as the state variables, take the input variable to be the output of the voltage source, and take the output variables to be the currents through L and R_2 respectively.

(b) Find the transfer-function matrix relating the output variables y_1 and y_2 to the input variable u. Thus find the system response to the unit step $u(t) = H(t)$, assuming that the circuit is initially in a quiescent state.

Figure 6.10 Network of Example 6.37.

Solution   (a) The current i_C in the capacitor is given by

$$i_C = C\dot{v}_C = C\dot{x}_1$$

Applying Kirchhoff's second law to the outer loop gives

$$e = R_1(i_L + i_C) + v_C + R_2 i_C$$
$$= R_1(x_2 + C\dot{x}_1) + x_1 + R_2 C\dot{x}_1$$

leading to

$$\dot{x}_1 = -\frac{1}{C(R_1 + R_2)}x_1 - \frac{R_1}{C(R_1 + R_2)}x_2 + \frac{e}{C(R_1 + R_2)}$$

Applying Kirchhoff's second law to the left-hand loop gives

$$e = R_1(i_L + i_C) + L\dot{i}_L$$
$$= R_1(x_2 + C\dot{x}_1) + L\dot{x}_2$$

leading to

$$\dot{x}_2 = \frac{R_1}{L(R_1 + R_2)}x_1 - \frac{R_1 R_2}{L(R_1 + R_2)}x_2 + \frac{e}{L}\frac{R_2}{R_1 + R_2}$$

Also,

$$y_1 = x_2$$

$$y_2 = C\dot{x}_1 = -\frac{1}{R_1 + R_2}x_1 - \frac{1}{R_1 + R_2}x_2 + \frac{e}{R_1 + R_2}$$

Substituting the given parameter values leads to the state-space representation

$$\begin{bmatrix} \dot{x}_1 \\ \dot{x}_2 \end{bmatrix} = \begin{bmatrix} -2 & -4 \\ 2 & -11 \end{bmatrix}\begin{bmatrix} x_1 \\ x_2 \end{bmatrix} + \begin{bmatrix} 2 \\ \frac{11}{2} \end{bmatrix}u$$

$$\begin{bmatrix} y_1 \\ y_2 \end{bmatrix} = \begin{bmatrix} 0 & 1 \\ -\frac{2}{15} & -\frac{4}{15} \end{bmatrix}\begin{bmatrix} x_1 \\ x_2 \end{bmatrix} + \begin{bmatrix} 0 \\ \frac{2}{15} \end{bmatrix}u$$

which is of the standard form

$$\dot{x} = Ax + bu$$

$$y = Cx + du$$

(b) From (6.79), the transfer-function matrix $G(s)$ relating the output variables y_1 and y_2 to the input u is

$$G(s) = C(sI - A)^{-1}b + d$$

Now

$$sI - A = \begin{bmatrix} s + 2 & 4 \\ -2 & s + 11 \end{bmatrix}$$

giving

$$(sI - A)^{-1} = \frac{1}{(s + 3)(s + 10)}\begin{bmatrix} s + 11 & -4 \\ 2 & s + 2 \end{bmatrix}$$

$$C(sI - A)^{-1}b = \frac{1}{(s + 3)(s + 10)}\begin{bmatrix} 0 & 1 \\ -\frac{2}{15} & -\frac{4}{15} \end{bmatrix}\begin{bmatrix} s + 11 & -4 \\ 2 & s + 2 \end{bmatrix}\begin{bmatrix} 2 \\ \frac{11}{2} \end{bmatrix}$$

$$= \frac{1}{(s + 3)(s + 10)}\begin{bmatrix} \frac{11}{2}s + 15 \\ -\frac{26}{15}s - 4 \end{bmatrix}$$

so that

$$G(s) = \frac{1}{(s + 3)(s + 10)}\begin{bmatrix} \frac{11}{2}s + 15 \\ -\frac{26}{15}s - 4 \end{bmatrix} + \begin{bmatrix} 0 \\ \frac{2}{15} \end{bmatrix}$$

$$= \begin{bmatrix} \dfrac{\frac{11}{2}s + 15}{(s + 3)(s + 10)} \\ \dfrac{-\frac{26}{15}s - 4}{(s + 3)(s + 10)} + \frac{2}{15} \end{bmatrix}$$

The output variables y_1 and y_2 are then given by the inverse Laplace transform of

$$Y(s) = G(s)U(s)$$

where $U(s) = \mathcal{L}[u(t)] = \mathcal{L}[H(t)] = 1/s$; that is,

$$Y(s) = \begin{bmatrix} \dfrac{\frac{11}{2}s + 15}{s(s+3)(s+10)} \\[2ex] \dfrac{-\frac{26}{15}s - 4}{s(s+3)(s+10)} + \dfrac{2}{15s} \end{bmatrix} = \begin{bmatrix} \dfrac{\frac{1}{2}}{s} + \dfrac{\frac{1}{14}}{s+3} - \dfrac{\frac{4}{7}}{s+10} \\[2ex] -\dfrac{\frac{2}{15}}{s} - \dfrac{\frac{2}{35}}{s+3} + \dfrac{\frac{4}{21}}{s+10} + \dfrac{\frac{2}{15}}{s} \end{bmatrix}$$

which on taking inverse Laplace transforms gives the output variables as

$$\begin{bmatrix} y_1 \\ y_2 \end{bmatrix} = \begin{bmatrix} \frac{1}{2} + \frac{1}{14}e^{-3t} - \frac{4}{7}e^{-10t} \\[1ex] -\frac{2}{35}e^{-3t} + \frac{4}{21}e^{-10t} \end{bmatrix} \quad (t \geqslant 0)$$

6.7.6   Exercises

50 A system is governed by the vector–matrix differential equation

$$\dot{x}(t) = \begin{bmatrix} 3 & 4 \\ 2 & 1 \end{bmatrix} x(t) + \begin{bmatrix} 0 & 1 \\ 1 & 1 \end{bmatrix} u(t) \quad (t \geqslant 0)$$

where $x(t)$ and $u(t)$ are respectively the state and input vectors of the system. Use Laplace transforms to obtain the state vector $x(t)$ for the input $u(t) = [4 \quad 3]^T$ and subject to the initial condition $x(0) = [1 \quad 2]^T$. Compare with the answer to Exercise 49.

51 Given that the differential equations modelling a certain control system are

$$\dot{x}_1 = x_1 - 3x_2 + u$$
$$\dot{x}_2 = 2x_1 - 4x_2 + u$$

use (6.75) to determine the state vector $x = [x_1 \quad x_2]^T$ for the control input $u = e^{-3t}$, applied at time $t = 0$, given that $x_1 = x_2 = 1$ at time $t = 0$.

52 Determine the response $y = x_1$ of the system governed by the differential equations

$$\left. \begin{array}{l} \dot{x}_1 = -2x_2 + u_1 - u_2 \\ \dot{x}_2 = x_1 - 3x_2 + u_1 + u_2 \end{array} \right\} \quad (t \geqslant 0)$$

to an input $u = [u_1 \quad u_2]^T = [1 \quad t]^T$ and subject to the initial conditions $x_1(0) = 0$, $x_2(0) = 1$.

53 Using the Laplace transform approach, obtain an expression for the state $x(t)$ of the system characterized by the state equation

$$\dot{x} = \begin{bmatrix} \dot{x}_1 \\ \dot{x}_2 \end{bmatrix} = \begin{bmatrix} 0 & 1 \\ -2 & -3 \end{bmatrix} \begin{bmatrix} x_1 \\ x_2 \end{bmatrix} + \begin{bmatrix} 2 \\ 0 \end{bmatrix} u \quad (t \geqslant 0)$$

where the input is

$$u(t) = \begin{cases} 0 & (t < 0) \\ e^{-t} & (t \geqslant 0) \end{cases}$$

and subject to the initial condition $x(0) = [1 \quad 0]^T$.

6.7.7   Spectral representation of response

We first consider the unforced system

$$\dot{x}(t) = Ax(t) \tag{6.80}$$

with the initial state $x(t_0)$ at time t_0 given, and assume that the matrix A has n

distinct eigenvalues λ_i $(i = 1, 2, \ldots, n)$ corresponding to n linearly independent eigenvectors e_i $(i = 1, 2, \ldots, n)$. Since the n eigenvectors are linearly independent, they may be used as a basis for the n-dimensional state space, so that the system state $x(t)$ may be written as a linear combination in the form

$$x(t) = c_1(t)e_1 + \ldots + c_n(t)e_n \tag{6.81}$$

where, since the eigenvectors are constant, the time-varying nature of $x(t)$ is reflected in the coefficients $c_i(t)$. Substituting (6.81) into (6.80) gives

$$\dot{c}_1(t)e_i + \ldots + \dot{c}_n(t)e_n = A[c_1(t)e_1 + \ldots + c_n(t)e_n] \tag{6.82}$$

Since (λ_i, e_i) are **spectral pairs** (that is, eigenvalue–eigenvector pairs) for the matrix A,

$$Ae_i = \lambda_i e_i \quad (i = 1, 2, \ldots, n)$$

(6.82) may be written as

$$[\dot{c}_1(t) - \lambda_1 c_1(t)]e_1 + \ldots + [\dot{c}_n(t) - \lambda_n c_n(t)]e_n = 0 \tag{6.83}$$

Because the eigenvectors e_i are linearly independent, it follows from (6.83) that the system (6.80) is completely represented by the set of uncoupled differential equations

$$\dot{c}_i(t) - \lambda_i c_i(t) = 0 \quad (i = 1, 2, \ldots, n) \tag{6.84}$$

with solutions of the form

$$c_i(t) = e^{\lambda_i(t - t_0)} c_i(t_0)$$

Then, using (6.81), the system response is

$$x(t) = \sum_{i=1}^{n} c_i(t_0) e^{\lambda_i(t - t_0)} e_i \tag{6.85}$$

Using the given information about the initial state,

$$x(t_0) = \sum_{i=1}^{n} c_i(t_0)e_i \tag{6.86}$$

so that the constants $c_i(t_0)$ may be found from the given initial state using the **reciprocal basis vectors** r_i $(i = 1, 2, \ldots, n)$ defined by

$$r_i^T e_j = \delta_{ij}$$

where δ_{ij} is the Kronecker delta. Taking the scalar product of both sides of (6.86) with r_k, we have

$$r_k^T x(t_0) = \sum_{i=1}^{n} c_i(t_0) r_k^T e_i$$

$$= c_k(t_0) \quad (k = 1, 2, \ldots, n)$$

which on substituting in (6.85) gives the system response

$$x(t) = \sum_{i=1}^{n} r_i^T x(t_0) e^{\lambda_i(t - t_0)} e_i \tag{6.87}$$

which is referred to as the **spectral** or **modal form** of the response. The terms $r_i^T x(t_0) e^{\lambda_i(t-t_0)} e_i$ are called the **modes** of the system. Thus, provided that the system matrix A has n linearly independent eigenvectors, this approach has the advantage of enabling us to break down the general system response into the sum of its simple modal responses. The amount of excitation of each mode, represented by $r_i^T x(t_0)$, is dependent only on the initial conditions, so if, for example, the initial state $x(t_0)$ is parallel to the ith eigenvector e_i then only the ith mode will be excited.

It should be noted that if a pair of eigenvalues λ_1, λ_2 are complex conjugates then the modes associated with $e^{\lambda_1(t-t_0)}$ and $e^{\lambda_2(t-t_0)}$ cannot be separated from each other. The combined motion takes place in a plane determined by the corresponding eigenvectors e_1 and e_2 and is oscillatory.

By retaining only the dominant modes, the spectral representation may be used to approximate high-order systems by lower-order ones.

EXAMPLE 6.38 Obtain in spectral form the response of the second-order system

$$\begin{bmatrix} \dot{x}_1 \\ \dot{x}_2 \end{bmatrix} = \begin{bmatrix} -2 & 1 \\ 1 & -1 \end{bmatrix}\begin{bmatrix} x_1 \\ x_2 \end{bmatrix}, \quad x(0) = \begin{bmatrix} 1 \\ 2 \end{bmatrix}$$

and sketch the trajectory.

Solution The eigenvalues of the matrix

$$A = \begin{bmatrix} -2 & 1 \\ 1 & -2 \end{bmatrix}$$

are determined by

$$|A - \lambda I| = \lambda^2 + 4\lambda + 3 = 0$$

that is,

$$\lambda_1 = -1, \quad \lambda_2 = -3$$

with corresponding eigenvectors

$$e_1 = [1 \quad 1]^T, \quad e_2 = [1 \quad -1]^T$$

Denoting the reciprocal basis vectors by

$$r_1 = [r_{11} \quad r_{12}]^T, \quad r_2 = [r_{21} \quad r_{22}]^T$$

and using the relationships

$$r_i^T e_j = \delta_{ij} \quad (i, j = 1, 2)$$

we have

$$r_1^T e_1 = r_{11} + r_{12} = 1$$
$$r_1^T e_2 = r_{11} - r_{12} = 0$$

giving

$$r_{11} = \tfrac{1}{2}, \qquad r_{12} = \tfrac{1}{2}, \qquad \boldsymbol{r}_1 = [\tfrac{1}{2} \ \tfrac{1}{2}]^{\mathrm{T}}$$

and

$$\boldsymbol{r}_2^{\mathrm{T}} \boldsymbol{e}_2 = r_{21} + r_{22} = 0$$

$$\boldsymbol{r}_2^{\mathrm{T}} \boldsymbol{e}_2 = r_{21} - r_{22} = 1$$

giving

$$r_{21} = \tfrac{1}{2}, \qquad r_{22} = -\tfrac{1}{2}, \qquad \boldsymbol{r}_2 = [\tfrac{1}{2} \ \tfrac{1}{2}]^{\mathrm{T}}$$

Thus

$$\boldsymbol{r}_1^{\mathrm{T}} \boldsymbol{x}(0) = \tfrac{1}{2} + 1 = \tfrac{3}{2}, \qquad \boldsymbol{r}_2^{\mathrm{T}} \boldsymbol{x}(0) = \tfrac{1}{2} - 1 = -\tfrac{1}{2}$$

so that, from (6.87), the system response is

$$\boldsymbol{x}(t) = \sum_{i=1}^{2} \boldsymbol{r}_i^{\mathrm{T}} \boldsymbol{x}(0)\, \mathrm{e}^{\lambda_i t} \boldsymbol{e}_i$$

$$= \boldsymbol{r}_1^{\mathrm{T}} \boldsymbol{x}(0)\, \mathrm{e}^{\lambda_1 t} \boldsymbol{e}_1 + \boldsymbol{r}_2^{\mathrm{T}} \boldsymbol{x}(0)\, \mathrm{e}^{\lambda_2 t} \boldsymbol{e}_2$$

That is,

$$\boldsymbol{x}(t) = \tfrac{3}{2} \mathrm{e}^{-t} \boldsymbol{e}_1 - \tfrac{1}{2} \mathrm{e}^{-3t} \boldsymbol{e}_2$$

which is in the required spectral form.

To plot the response, we first draw axes corresponding to the eigenvectors $\boldsymbol{e}_1$ and $\boldsymbol{e}_2$, as shown in Figure 6.11. Taking these as coordinate axes, we are at the point $(\tfrac{3}{2}, -\tfrac{1}{2})$ at time $t = 0$. As t increases, the movement along the direction of $\boldsymbol{e}_2$ is much faster than that in the direction of $\boldsymbol{e}_1$, since e^{-3t} decreases more rapidly than e^{-t}. We can therefore guess the trajectory, without plotting, as sketched in Figure 6.11.

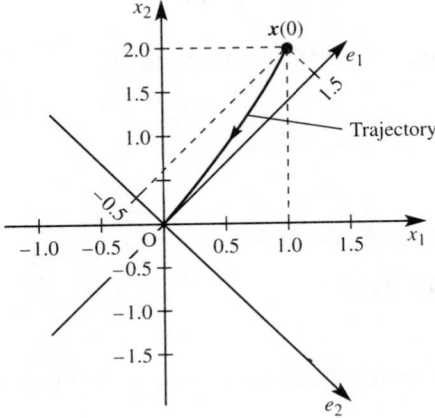

Figure 6.11 Trajectory for Example 6.38.

We can proceed in an analogous manner to obtain the spectral representation of the response to the forced system

$$\dot{x}(t) = Ax(t) + Bu(t)$$

with $x(t_0)$ given. Making the same assumption regarding the linear independence of the eigenvectors e_i $(i = 1, 2, \ldots, n)$ of the matrix A, the vector $Bu(t)$ may also be written as a linear combination of the form

$$Bu(t) = \sum_{i=1}^{n} \beta_i(t)e_i \tag{6.88}$$

so that, corresponding to (6.83), we have

$$[\dot{c}_1(t) - \lambda_1 c_1(t) - \beta_1(t)]e_1 + \ldots + [\dot{c}_n(t) - \lambda_n c_n(t) - \beta_n(t)]e_n = 0$$

As a consequence of the linear independence of the eigenvectors e_i this leads to the set of uncoupled differential equations

$$\dot{c}_i(t) - \lambda_i c_i(t) - \beta_i(t) = 0 \quad (i = 1, 2, \ldots, n)$$

which, using (6.65), have corresponding solutions

$$c_i(t) = e^{\lambda_i(t-t_0)}c_i(t_0) + \int_{t_0}^{t} e^{\lambda_i(t-\tau)}\beta_i(\tau)\,d\tau \tag{6.89}$$

As for $c_i(t_0)$, the reciprocal basis vectors r_i may be used to obtain the coefficients $\beta_i(\tau)$. Taking the scalar product of both sides of (6.88) with r_k and using the relationships $r_i^T e_j = \delta_{ij}$, we have

$$r_k^T Bu(t) = \beta_k(t) \quad (k = 1, 2, \ldots, n)$$

Thus, from (6.89),

$$c_i(t) = e^{\lambda_i(t-t_0)}r_i^T x(t_0) + \int_{t_0}^{t} e^{\lambda_i(t-\tau)}r_i^T Bu(\tau)\,d\tau$$

giving the spectral form of the system response as

$$x(t) = \sum_{i=1}^{n} c_i(t)e_i$$

6.7.8 Canonical representation

Consider the state-space representation given in (6.56), namely

$$\dot{x} = Ax + Bu \tag{6.56a}$$

$$y = Cx + Du \tag{6.56b}$$

Applying the transformation

$$x = Tz$$

where T is a non-singular matrix, leads to

$$T\dot{z} = ATz + Bu$$

$$y = CTz + Du$$

which may be written in the form

$$\dot{z} = \tilde{A}z + \tilde{B}u \qquad\qquad\qquad\text{(6.90a)}$$

$$y = \tilde{C}z + \tilde{D}u \qquad\qquad\qquad\text{(6.90b)}$$

where z is now a state vector and

$$\tilde{A} = T^{-1}AT, \qquad \tilde{B} = T^{-1}B, \qquad \tilde{C} = CT, \qquad \tilde{D} = D$$

From (6.79), the input–output transfer-function matrix corresponding to (6.90) is

$$\begin{aligned}
G_1(s) &= \tilde{C}(sI - \tilde{A})^{-1}\tilde{B} + \tilde{D} \\
&= CT(sI - T^{-1}AT)^{-1}T^{-1}B + D \\
&= CT(sT^{-1}IT - T^{-1}AT)^{-1}T^{-1}B + D \\
&= CT[T^{-1}(sI - A)T]^{-1}T^{-1}B + D \\
&= CT[T^{-1}(sI - A)^{-1}T]T^{-1}B + D \quad \text{(using the commutative property)} \\
&= C(sI - A)^{-1}B + D \\
&= G(s)
\end{aligned}$$

where $G(s)$ is the transfer-function matrix corresponding to (6.56).

Thus the system input–output relationship is unchanged by the transformation, and the linear systems (6.56) and (6.90) are said to be **equivalent**. As a consequence, the intrinsic properties of the system, such as stability, controllability and observability, which are of interest to the engineer, are preserved by the transformation, and there is merit in seeking a transformation leading to a system that is more easily analysed.

Since the transformation matrix T can be arbitrarily chosen, an infinite number of equivalent systems exist. Of particular interest is the case when T is taken to be the modal matrix M of the system matrix A; that is

$$T = M = [e_1 \quad e_2 \quad \cdots \quad e_n]$$

where e_i $(i = 1, 2, \ldots, n)$ are the eigenvectors of the matrix A. Under the assumption that the n eigenvalues are distinct,

$$\tilde{A} = M^{-1}AM = \Lambda, \qquad \text{the spectral matrix of } A$$

$$\tilde{B} = M^{-1}B$$

$$\tilde{C} = CM, \qquad \tilde{D} = D$$

so that (6.90) becomes

$$\dot{z} = \Lambda z + M^{-1} Bu \tag{6.91a}$$

$$y = CMz + Du \tag{6.91b}$$

Equation (6.91a) constitutes a system of uncoupled linear differential equations

$$\dot{z}_i = \lambda_i z_i + b_i^T u \quad (i = 1, 2, \ldots, n) \tag{6.92}$$

where $z = (z_1, z_2, \ldots, z_n)^T$ and b_i^T is the ith row of the matrix $M^{-1} B$. Thus, by reducing (6.56) to the equivalent form (6.91) using the transformation $x = Mz$, the modes of the system have been uncoupled, with the new state variables z_i $(i = 1, 2, \ldots, n)$ being associated with the ith mode only. The representation (6.91) is called the **normal** or **canonical representation** of the system equations.

From (6.65), the solution of (6.92) is

$$z_i = e^{\lambda_i(t-t_0)} x(t_0) + \int_{t_0}^{t} e^{\lambda_i(t-\tau)} b_i^T u(\tau) \, d\tau \quad (i = 1, \ldots, n)$$

so that the solution of (6.91a) may be written as

$$z(t) = e^{\Lambda(t-t_0)} z(t_0) + \int_{t_0}^{t} e^{\Lambda(t-\tau)} M^{-1} Bu(\tau) \, d\tau \tag{6.93}$$

where

$$e^{\Lambda(t-t_0)} = \begin{bmatrix} e^{\lambda_1(t-t_0)} & & 0 \\ & \ddots & \\ 0 & & e^{\lambda_n(t-t_0)} \end{bmatrix}$$

In terms of the original state vector $x(t)$, (6.93) becomes

$$x(t) = Mz = Me^{\Lambda(t-t_0)} M^{-1} x(t_0) + \int_{t_0}^{t} Me^{\Lambda(t-\tau)} M^{-1} Bu(\tau) \, d\tau \tag{6.94}$$

and the system response is then obtained from (6.56b) as

$$y(t) = Cx(t) + Du(t)$$

By comparing the response (6.94) with that in (6.68), we note that the transition matrix may be written as

$$\Phi(t, t_0) = e^{A(t-t_0)} = Me^{\Lambda(t-t_0)} M^{-1}$$

The representation (6.91) may be used to readily infer some system properties. If the system is stable then each mode must be stable, so, from (6.94), each λ_i $(i = 1, 2, \ldots, n)$ must have a negative real part. If, for example, the jth row of the matrix $M^{-1} B$ is zero then, from (6.92), $\dot{z}_j = \lambda_j z_j + 0$, so the input $u(t)$ has no influence on the jth mode of the system, and the mode is said to be **uncontrollable**. A system is said to be **controllable** if all of its modes are controllable.

If the jth column of the matrix CM is zero then, from (6.91b), the response y

is independent of z_j, so it is not possible to use information about the output to identify z_j. The state z_j is then said to be **unobservable**, and the overall system is not **observable**.

EXAMPLE 6.39   A third-order system is characterized by the state-space model

$$\dot{x} = \begin{bmatrix} 0 & 1 & 0 \\ 0 & 0 & 1 \\ 0 & -5 & -6 \end{bmatrix} x + \begin{bmatrix} 1 \\ -3 \\ 18 \end{bmatrix} u$$

$$y = [1 \quad 0 \quad 0]x$$

where $x = [x_1 \quad x_2 \quad x_3]^T$. Obtain the equivalent canonical representation of the model and then obtain the response of the system to a unit step $u(t) = H(t)$ given that initially $x(0) = [1 \quad 1 \quad 0]^T$.

Solution   The eigenvalues of the matrix

$$A = \begin{bmatrix} 0 & 1 & 0 \\ 0 & 0 & 1 \\ 0 & -5 & -6 \end{bmatrix}$$

are determined by

$$|A - \lambda I| = \begin{vmatrix} -\lambda & 1 & 0 \\ 0 & -\lambda & 1 \\ 0 & -5 & -6-\lambda \end{vmatrix} = 0$$

that is,

$$\lambda(\lambda^2 + 6\lambda + 5) = 0$$

giving $\lambda_1 = 0$, $\lambda_2 = -1$ and $\lambda_3 = -5$, with corresponding eigenvectors

$$e_1 = [1 \quad 0 \quad 0]^T, \qquad e_2 = [1 \quad -1 \quad 1]^T, \qquad e_3 = [1 \quad -5 \quad 25]^T$$

The corresponding modal and spectral matrices are

$$M = \begin{bmatrix} 1 & 1 & 1 \\ 0 & -1 & -5 \\ 0 & 1 & 25 \end{bmatrix}, \qquad \Lambda = \begin{bmatrix} 0 & 0 & 0 \\ 0 & -1 & 0 \\ 0 & 0 & -5 \end{bmatrix}$$

and the inverse modal matrix is determined to be

$$M^{-1} = \frac{1}{20} \begin{bmatrix} 20 & 25 & 4 \\ 0 & -25 & -5 \\ 0 & 1 & 1 \end{bmatrix}$$

In this case $\boldsymbol{B} = [1 \quad -3 \quad 18]^T$, so

$$\boldsymbol{M}^{-1}\boldsymbol{B} = \frac{1}{20} \begin{bmatrix} 20 & 24 & 4 \\ 0 & -25 & -5 \\ 0 & 1 & 1 \end{bmatrix} \begin{bmatrix} 1 \\ -3 \\ 18 \end{bmatrix} = \frac{1}{20} \begin{bmatrix} 20 \\ -15 \\ 15 \end{bmatrix} = \begin{bmatrix} 1 \\ -\frac{3}{4} \\ \frac{3}{4} \end{bmatrix}$$

Likewise, $\boldsymbol{C} = [1 \quad 0 \quad 0]$, giving

$$\boldsymbol{CM} = [1 \quad 0 \quad 0] \begin{bmatrix} 1 & 1 & 1 \\ 0 & -1 & -5 \\ 0 & 1 & 25 \end{bmatrix} = [1 \quad 1 \quad 1]$$

Thus, from (6.91), the equivalent canonical state-space representation is

$$\dot{z} = \begin{bmatrix} \dot{z}_1 \\ \dot{z}_2 \\ \dot{z}_3 \end{bmatrix} = \begin{bmatrix} 0 & 0 & 0 \\ 0 & -1 & 0 \\ 0 & 0 & -5 \end{bmatrix} \begin{bmatrix} z_1 \\ z_2 \\ z_3 \end{bmatrix} + \begin{bmatrix} 1 \\ -\frac{3}{4} \\ \frac{3}{4} \end{bmatrix} u \qquad (6.95a)$$

$$y = [1 \quad 1 \quad 1] \begin{bmatrix} z_1 \\ z_2 \\ z_3 \end{bmatrix} \qquad (6.95b)$$

When $u(t) = H(t)$, from (6.93) the solution of (6.95a) is

$$\dot{z} = \begin{bmatrix} e^{0t} & 0 & 0 \\ 0 & e^{-t} & 0 \\ 0 & 0 & e^{-5t} \end{bmatrix} z(0) + \int_0^t \begin{bmatrix} 1 & 0 & 0 \\ 0 & e^{-(t-\tau)} & 0 \\ 0 & 0 & e^{-5(t-\tau)} \end{bmatrix} \begin{bmatrix} 1 \\ -\frac{3}{4} \\ \frac{3}{4} \end{bmatrix} 1\, d\tau$$

where

$$z(0) = \boldsymbol{M}^{-1}x(0) = \frac{1}{20} \begin{bmatrix} 20 & 24 & 4 \\ 0 & -25 & -5 \\ 0 & 1 & 1 \end{bmatrix} \begin{bmatrix} 1 \\ 1 \\ 0 \end{bmatrix} = \begin{bmatrix} \frac{44}{20} \\ -\frac{25}{20} \\ \frac{1}{20} \end{bmatrix}$$

$$z = \begin{bmatrix} 1 & 0 & 0 \\ 0 & e^{-t} & 0 \\ 0 & 0 & e^{-5t} \end{bmatrix} \begin{bmatrix} \frac{11}{5} \\ -\frac{5}{4} \\ \frac{1}{20} \end{bmatrix} + \int_0^t \begin{bmatrix} 1 \\ -\frac{3}{4}e^{-(t-\tau)} \\ \frac{3}{4}e^{-5(t-\tau)} \end{bmatrix} d\tau$$

$$= \begin{bmatrix} \frac{11}{5} \\ -\frac{5}{4}e^{-t} \\ \frac{1}{20}e^{-5t} \end{bmatrix} + \begin{bmatrix} t \\ -\frac{3}{4} + \frac{3}{4}e^{-t} \\ \frac{3}{20} - \frac{3}{20}e^{-5t} \end{bmatrix} = \begin{bmatrix} t + \frac{11}{5} \\ -\frac{3}{4} - \frac{1}{2}e^{-t} \\ \frac{3}{20} - \frac{1}{10}e^{-5t} \end{bmatrix}$$

Then, from (6.95b),

$$y = z_1 + z_2 + z_3 = (t + \tfrac{11}{5}) + (-\tfrac{3}{4} - \tfrac{1}{2}e^{-t}) + (\tfrac{3}{20} - \tfrac{1}{10}e^{-5t})$$

$$= t + \tfrac{8}{5} - \tfrac{1}{2}e^{-t} - \tfrac{1}{10}e^{-5t}$$

If we drop the assumption that the eigenvalues of A are distinct then $\tilde{A} = M^{-1}AM$ is no longer diagonal, but may be represented by the corresponding Jordan canonical form J with M being made up of both eigenvectors and generalized eigenvectors of A. The equivalent canonical form in this case will be

$$\dot{z} = Jz + M^{-1}Bu$$

$$y = CMz + Du$$

with the solution corresponding to (6.93) being

$$x(t) = Me^{J(t-t_0)}M^{-1}x(t_0) + \int_{t_0}^{t} Me^{J(t-\tau)}M^{-1}Bu(\tau)\,d\tau$$

6.7.9   Exercises

54 Obtain in spectral form the response of the unforced second-order system

$$\dot{x}(t) = \begin{bmatrix} \dot{x}_1(t) \\ \dot{x}_2(t) \end{bmatrix} = \begin{bmatrix} -\tfrac{3}{2} & \tfrac{3}{4} \\ 1 & -\tfrac{5}{2} \end{bmatrix} x(t), \qquad x(0) = \begin{bmatrix} 2 \\ 4 \end{bmatrix}$$

Using the eigenvectors as the frame of reference, sketch the trajectory.

55 Using the spectral form of the solution given in (6.87), solve the second-order system

$$\dot{x}(t) = \begin{bmatrix} -2 & 2 \\ 2 & -5 \end{bmatrix} x(t), \qquad x(0) = \begin{bmatrix} 2 \\ 3 \end{bmatrix}$$

and sketch the trajectory.

56 Repeat Exercise 55 for the system

$$\dot{x}(t) = \begin{bmatrix} 0 & -4 \\ 2 & -4 \end{bmatrix} x(t), \qquad x(0) = \begin{bmatrix} 1 \\ 2 \end{bmatrix}$$

57 Determine the equivalent canonical representation of the third-order system

$$\dot{x} = \begin{bmatrix} 1 & 1 & -2 \\ -1 & 2 & 1 \\ 0 & 1 & -1 \end{bmatrix} x + \begin{bmatrix} -1 \\ 1 \\ -1 \end{bmatrix} u$$

$$y = [-2 \quad 1 \quad 0]x$$

58 The solution of a third-order linear system is given by

$$x = \alpha_0 e^{-t}e_0 + \alpha_1 e^{-2t}e_1 + \alpha_2 e^{-3t}e_2$$

where e_0, e_1 and e_2 are linearly independent vectors having values

$$e_0 = [1 \quad 1 \quad 0]^T, \qquad e_1 = [0 \quad 1 \quad 1]^T,$$
$$e_2 = [1 \quad 2 \quad 3]^T$$

Initially, at time $t = 0$ the system state is $x(0) = [1 \quad 1 \quad 1]^T$. Find α_0, α_1 and α_2 using the reciprocal basis method.

59 Obtain the eigenvalues and eigenvectors of the matrix

$$A = \begin{bmatrix} 5 & 4 \\ 1 & 2 \end{bmatrix}$$

Using a suitable transformation $x(t) = Mz(t)$, reduce $\dot{x}(t) = Ax(t)$ to the canonical form $\dot{z}(t) = \Lambda z(t)$, where Λ is the spectral matrix of A. Solve the decoupled canonical form for z, and hence solve for $x(t)$ given that $x(0) = [1 \quad 4]^T$.

60 A second-order system is governed by the state equation

$$\dot{x}(t) = \begin{bmatrix} 3 & 4 \\ 2 & 1 \end{bmatrix} x(t) + \begin{bmatrix} 0 & 1 \\ 1 & 1 \end{bmatrix} u(t) \quad (t \geq 0)$$

Using a suitable transformation $x(t) = Mz(t)$, reduce this to the canonical form

$$\dot{z}(t) = \Lambda z(t) + Bu(t)$$

where Λ is the spectral matrix of

$$\begin{bmatrix} 3 & 4 \\ 2 & 1 \end{bmatrix}$$

and B is a suitable 2×2 matrix.

For the input $u(t) = [4 \quad 3]^T$ solve the decoupled canonical form for z, and hence solve for $x(t)$ given that $x(0) = [1 \quad 2]^T$. Compare the answer with that for Exercises 49 and 50.

61 A third-order single-input–single-output system is characterized by the transfer-function model

$$\frac{Y(s)}{U(s)} = \frac{3s^2 + 2s + 1}{s^3 + 6s^2 + 11s + 6}$$

where $Y(s)$ and $U(s)$ are the Laplace transforms of the system output and input respectively. Express the system model in the state-space form

$$\dot{x} = Ax + bu \tag{6.96a}$$
$$y = c^T x \tag{6.96b}$$

where A is in the companion form. By making a suitable transformation $x = Mz$, reduce the state-space model to its canonical form, and comment on the stability, controllability and observability of the system.

Given that

(i) a necessary and sufficient condition for the system (6.96) to be controllable is that the rank of the **Kalman matrix** $[b \quad Ab \quad A^2b \quad \ldots \quad A^{n-1}b]$ be the same as the order of A, and

(ii) a necessary and sufficient condition for it to be observable is that the rank of the Kalman matrix $[c \quad A^Tc \quad (A^T)^2c \quad \ldots \quad (A^T)^{n-1}c]$ be the same as the order of A,

evaluate the ranks of the relevant Kalman matrices to confirm your earlier conclusions on the controllability and observability of the given system.

62 Repeat Exercise 61 for the system characterized by the transfer function model

$$\frac{s^2 + 3s + 5}{s^3 + 6s^2 + 5s}$$

6.8 Discrete-time systems

In Chapter 3 we considered the role of z transforms in providing a frequency-domain approach to the modelling of discrete-time systems, the analysis and design of which is a subject of increasing importance in many branches of engineering. In this section we consider the time-domain state-space model representation for such systems.

6.8.1 State-space model

Consider the nth-order linear time-invariant discrete-time system modelled by the difference equation

$$y_{k+n} + a_{n-1}y_{k+n-1} + a_{n-2}y_{k+n-2} + \ldots + a_0y_k = b_0u_k \tag{6.97}$$

which corresponds to (6.32), which represented the general case, with $b_i = 0$ $(i > 0)$. Recall that $\{y_k\}$ is the output sequence, with general term y_k, and $\{u_k\}$ the input sequence, with general term u_k. Following the procedure of Section 6.6.1, we introduce state variables $x_1(k), x_2(k), \ldots, x_n(k)$ for the system, defined by

$$x_1(k) = y_k$$
$$x_2(k) = y_{k+1}$$
$$\vdots \qquad\qquad\qquad\qquad\qquad (6.98)$$
$$x_n(k) = y_{k+n-1}$$

Note that we have used the notation $x_i(k)$ rather than the suffix notation $x_{i,k}$ for clarity. When needed, we shall adopt the same convention for the input term and write $u(k)$ for u_k in the interests of consistency. We now define the state vector corresponding to this choice of state variables as $x(k) = [x_1(k) \quad x_2(k) \quad \ldots \quad x_n(k)]^{\mathrm{T}}$. Examining the system of equations (6.98), we see that

$$x_1(k + 1) = y_{k+1} = x_2(k)$$
$$x_2(k + 1) = y_{k+2} = x_3(k)$$
$$\vdots$$
$$x_{n-1}(k + 1) = y_{k+n-1} = x_n(k)$$
$$x_n(k + 1) = y_{k+n}$$
$$= -a_{n-1}y_{k+n-1} - a_{n-2}y_{k+n-2} - \ldots - a_0 y_k + b_0 u_k$$
$$= -a_{n-1}x_n(k) - a_{n-2}x_{n-1}(k) - \ldots - a_0 x_1(k) + b_0 u(k)$$

using the alternative notation for u_k.

We can now write the system in the vector–matrix form

$$
x(k+1) = \begin{bmatrix} x_1(k+1) \\ x_2(k+1) \\ \vdots \\ \\ x_n(k+1) \end{bmatrix} = \begin{bmatrix} 0 & 1 & 0 & 0 & \cdots & 0 \\ 0 & 0 & 1 & 0 & \cdots & 0 \\ \vdots & \vdots & \vdots & \vdots & & \vdots \\ 0 & 0 & 0 & 0 & \cdots & 1 \\ -a_0 & -a_1 & -a_2 & -a_3 & \cdots & -a_{n-1} \end{bmatrix} \begin{bmatrix} x_1(k) \\ x_2(k) \\ \vdots \\ \\ x_n(k) \end{bmatrix} + \begin{bmatrix} 0 \\ 0 \\ \vdots \\ \\ b_0 \end{bmatrix} u(k)
$$
$$(6.99)$$

which corresponds to (6.46) for a continuous-time system. Again, we can write this more concisely as

$$x_{k+1} = Ax(k) + bu(k) \qquad\qquad\qquad\qquad (6.100)$$

where x_k, A and b are defined as in (6.99). The output of the system is the sequence

$\{y_k\}$, and the general term $y_k = x_1(k)$ can be recovered from the state vector $\mathbf{x}(k)$ as

$$y(k) = x_1(k) = [1 \quad 0 \quad 0 \quad \dots \quad 0]\mathbf{x}(k) = \mathbf{c}^T\mathbf{x}(k) \tag{6.101}$$

As in the continuous-time case, it may be that the output of the system is a combination of the state and the input sequence $\{u(k)\}$, in which case (6.101) becomes

$$y(k) = \mathbf{c}^T\mathbf{x}(k) + du(k) \tag{6.102}$$

Equations (6.100) and (6.102) constitute the state-space representation of the system, and we immediately note the similarity with (6.50a, b) derived for continuous-time systems. Likewise, for the multi-input–multi-output case the discrete-time state-space model corresponding to (6.56) is

$$\mathbf{x}(k + 1) = \mathbf{A}\mathbf{x}(k) + \mathbf{B}\mathbf{u}(k) \tag{6.103a}$$

$$y(k) = \mathbf{C}\mathbf{x}(k) + \mathbf{D}\mathbf{u}(k) \tag{6.103b}$$

EXAMPLE 6.40 Determine the state-space representation of the system modelled by the difference equation

$$y_{k+2} + 0.2y_{k+1} + 0.3y_k = u_k \tag{6.104}$$

Solution We choose as state variables

$$x_1(k) = y_k$$
$$x_2(k) = y_{k+1}$$

Thus

$$x_1(k + 1) = x_2(k)$$

and from (6.104),

$$x_2(k + 1) = -0.3x_1(k) - 0.2x_2(k) + u(k)$$

The state-space representation is then

$$\mathbf{x}(k + 1) = \mathbf{A}\mathbf{x}(k) + \mathbf{b}u(k)$$
$$y(k) = \mathbf{c}^T\mathbf{x}(k)$$

with

$$\mathbf{A} = \begin{bmatrix} 0 & 1 \\ -0.3 & -0.2 \end{bmatrix}, \qquad \mathbf{b} = \begin{bmatrix} 0 \\ 1 \end{bmatrix}, \qquad \mathbf{c}^T = [1 \quad 0]$$

We notice, from reference to Section 3.6.1, that the procedure used in Example 6.40 for establishing the state-space form of the system corresponds to labelling the output of each delay block in the system as a state variable. In the absence of any reason for an alternative choice, this is the logical approach. Section 3.6.1 also gives a clue towards a method of obtaining the state-space representation for systems described by the more general form of (6.32) with $b_i \neq 0$ $(i > 0)$. Example 3.19 illustrates such a system, with z transfer function

$$G(z) = \frac{z - 1}{z^2 + 3z + 2}$$

The block diagram for this system is shown in Figure 3.9(b), and we choose as state variables the outputs from each delay block. It is of course immaterial whether we start from the left- or the right-hand side of the diagram (obviously, different representations will be obtained depending on the choice we make, but the different forms will yield identical information on the system). Choosing to start on the right-hand side (that is, with $x_1(k)$ the output of the right-hand delay block and $x_2(k)$ that of the left-hand block), we obtain

$$x_1(k + 1) = x_2(k)$$
$$x_2(k + 1) = -3x_2(k) - 2x_1(k) + u(k)$$

From Figure 3.9(b) it is clear that the system output is given by

$$y(k) = -x_1(k) + x_2(k)$$

and thus the state-space form corresponding to our choice of state variables is

$$x(k + 1) = \boldsymbol{A}x(k) + \boldsymbol{b}u(k)$$
$$y(k) = \boldsymbol{c}^{\mathrm{T}}x(k)$$

with

$$\boldsymbol{A} = \begin{bmatrix} 0 & 1 \\ -2 & -3 \end{bmatrix}, \qquad \boldsymbol{b} = \begin{bmatrix} 0 \\ 1 \end{bmatrix}, \qquad \boldsymbol{c}^{\mathrm{T}} = \begin{bmatrix} -1 & 1 \end{bmatrix}$$

We notice that, in contrast with the system of Example 6.40, the row vector $\boldsymbol{c}^{\mathrm{T}} = \begin{bmatrix} -1 & 1 \end{bmatrix}$ now combines contributions from both state variables to form the output $y(k)$.

6.8.2 Solution of the discrete-time state equation

As in Section 6.7.1 for continuous-time systems, we first consider the unforced or homogeneous case

$$x(k + 1) = \boldsymbol{A}x(k) \tag{6.105}$$

in which the input $\boldsymbol{u}(k)$ is zero for all time instants k. Taking $k = 0$ in (6.105) gives

$$x(1) = \boldsymbol{A}x(0)$$

Likewise, taking $k = 1$ in (6.105) gives

$$x(2) = \mathbf{A}x(1) = \mathbf{A}^2 x(0)$$

and we readily deduce that in general

$$x(k) = \mathbf{A}^k x(0) \quad (k \geqslant 0) \tag{6.106}$$

Equation (6.106) represents the solution of (6.105), and is analogous to (6.67) for the continuous-time case. We define the **transition matrix** $\boldsymbol{\Phi}(k)$ of the discrete-time system (6.105) by

$$\boldsymbol{\Phi}(k) = \mathbf{A}^k$$

and it is a unique matrix satisfying

$$\boldsymbol{\Phi}(k + 1) = \mathbf{A}\boldsymbol{\Phi}(k), \qquad \boldsymbol{\Phi}(0) = \mathbf{I}$$

where $\mathbf{I}$ is the identity matrix.

Since $\mathbf{A}$ is a constant matrix, the methods discussed in Section 6.5 are applicable for evaluating the transition matrix. From (6.34a),

$$\mathbf{A}^k = \alpha_0(k)\mathbf{I} + \alpha_1(k)\mathbf{A} + \alpha_2(k)\mathbf{A}^2 + \ldots + \alpha_{n-1}(k)\mathbf{A}^{n-1} \tag{6.107}$$

where, using (6.34b), the $\alpha_i(k)$ $(k = 0, \ldots, n-1)$ are obtained by solving simultaneously the n equations

$$\lambda_j^k = \alpha_0(k) + \alpha_1(k)\lambda_j + \alpha_2(k)\lambda_j^2 + \ldots + \alpha_{n-1}(k)\lambda_j^{n-1} \tag{6.108}$$

where λ_j $(j = 1, 2, \ldots, n)$ are the eigenvalues of $\mathbf{A}$. As in Section 6.5, if $\mathbf{A}$ has repeated eigenvalues then derivatives of λ^k with respect to λ will have to be used. The method for determining $\mathbf{A}^k$ is thus very similar to that used for evaluating $e^{\mathbf{A}t}$ in Section 6.7.3.

EXAMPLE 6.41 Obtain the response of the second-order unforced discrete-time system

$$x(k + 1) = \begin{bmatrix} x_1(k) \\ x_2(k) \end{bmatrix} = \begin{bmatrix} \frac{1}{2} & 0 \\ -1 & \frac{1}{3} \end{bmatrix} x(k)$$

subject to $x(0) = [1 \quad 1]^{\mathrm{T}}$.

Solution In this case the system matrix is

$$\mathbf{A} = \begin{bmatrix} \frac{1}{2} & 0 \\ -1 & \frac{1}{3} \end{bmatrix}$$

having eigenvalues $\lambda_1 = \frac{1}{2}$ and $\lambda_2 = \frac{1}{3}$. Since $\mathbf{A}$ is a 2×2 matrix, it follows from (6.107) that

$$\mathbf{A}^k = \alpha_0(k)\mathbf{I} + \alpha_1(k)\mathbf{A}$$

with $\alpha_0(k)$ and $\alpha_1(k)$ given from (6.108),

$$\lambda_j^k = \alpha_0(k) + \alpha_1(k)\lambda_j \quad (j = 1, 2)$$

Solving the resulting two equations

$$(\tfrac{1}{2})^k = \alpha_0(k) + (\tfrac{1}{2})\alpha_1(k)$$

$$(\tfrac{1}{3})^k = \alpha_0(k) + (\tfrac{1}{3})\alpha_1(k)$$

for $\alpha_0(k)$ and $\alpha_1(k)$ gives

$$\alpha_0(k) = 3(\tfrac{1}{3})^k - 2(\tfrac{1}{2})^k$$

$$\alpha_1(k) = 6[(\tfrac{1}{2})^k - (\tfrac{1}{3})^k]$$

Thus the transition matrix is

$$\boldsymbol{\Phi}(k) = \boldsymbol{A}^k = \begin{bmatrix} (\tfrac{1}{2})^k & 0 \\ 6[(\tfrac{1}{3})^k - (\tfrac{1}{2})^k] & (\tfrac{1}{3})^k \end{bmatrix}$$

Note that $\boldsymbol{\Phi}(0) = \boldsymbol{I}$, as required.

Then from (6.106) the solution of the unforced system is

$$x(k + 1) = \begin{bmatrix} (\tfrac{1}{2})^k & 0 \\ 6[(\tfrac{1}{3})^k - (\tfrac{1}{2})^k] & (\tfrac{1}{3})^k \end{bmatrix} \begin{bmatrix} 1 \\ 1 \end{bmatrix} = \begin{bmatrix} (\tfrac{1}{2})^k \\ 7(\tfrac{1}{3})^k - 6(\tfrac{1}{2})^k \end{bmatrix}$$

Having determined the solution of the unforced system, it can be shown that the solution of the state equation (6.103a) for the forced system with input $u(k)$, analogous to the solution given in (6.68) for the continuous-time system

$$\dot{x} = \boldsymbol{A}x + \boldsymbol{B}u$$

is

$$x(k) = \boldsymbol{A}^k x(0) + \sum_{j=0}^{k-1} \boldsymbol{A}^{k-j-1} \boldsymbol{B}u(j) \tag{6.109}$$

Having obtained the solution of the state equation, the system output or response $y(k)$ is obtained from (6.103b) as

$$y(k) = \boldsymbol{C}\boldsymbol{A}^k x(0) + \boldsymbol{C} \sum_{j=0}^{k-1} \boldsymbol{A}^{k-j-1} \boldsymbol{B}u(j) + \boldsymbol{D}u(k) \tag{6.110}$$

In Section 6.7.5 we saw how the Laplace transform could be used to solve the state-space equations in the case of continuous-time systems. In a similar manner, z transforms can be used to solve the equations for discrete-time systems.

Defining $\mathscr{Z}\{x(k)\} = X(z)$ and $\mathscr{Z}\{u(k)\} = U(z)$ and taking z transforms throughout in the equation

$$x(k + 1) = \boldsymbol{A}x(k) + \boldsymbol{B}u(k)$$

gives

$$z X(z) - zx(0) = \boldsymbol{A}X(z) + \boldsymbol{B}U(z)$$

which, on rearranging gives

$$(z\boldsymbol{I} - \boldsymbol{A})X(z) = zx(0) + \boldsymbol{B}U(z)$$

where I is the identity matrix. Premultiplying by $(zI - A)^{-1}$ gives

$$X(z) = z(zI - A)^{-1}x(0) + (zI - A)^{-1}BU(z) \qquad (6.111)$$

Taking inverse z transforms gives the response as

$$x(k) = \mathcal{Z}^{-1}\{X(z)\} = \mathcal{Z}^{-1}\{z(zI - A)^{-1}\}x(0) + \mathcal{Z}^{-1}\{(zI - A)^{-1}BU(z)\} \qquad (6.112)$$

which corresponds to (6.75) in the continuous-time case.

On comparing the solution (6.112) with that given in (6.109), we see that the transition matrix $\Phi(t) = A^k$ may also be written in the form

$$\Phi(t) = A^k = \mathcal{Z}^{-1}\{z(zI - A)^{-1}\}$$

This is readily confirmed from (6.111), since on expanding $z(zI - A)^{-1}$ by the binomial theorem, we have

$$z(zI - A)^{-1} = I + \frac{A}{z} + \frac{A^2}{z^2} + \dots + \frac{A^r}{z^r} + \dots$$

$$= \sum_{r=0}^{\infty} \frac{A^r}{z^r}$$

$$= \mathcal{Z}\{A^k\}$$

EXAMPLE 6.42 Using the z-transform approach, obtain an expression for the state $x(k)$ of the system characterized by the state equation

$$x(k+1) = \begin{bmatrix} 2 & 5 \\ -3 & -6 \end{bmatrix} x(k) + \begin{bmatrix} 1 \\ 1 \end{bmatrix} u(k) \quad (k \geqslant 0)$$

when the input is the unit step function

$$u(k) = \begin{cases} 0 & (k < 0) \\ 1 & (k \geqslant 0) \end{cases}$$

and subject to the initial condition $x(0) = [1 \quad -1]^{\mathrm{T}}$.

Solution In this case

$$A = \begin{bmatrix} 2 & 5 \\ -3 & -6 \end{bmatrix}$$

so

$$zI - A = \begin{bmatrix} z-2 & -5 \\ 3 & z+6 \end{bmatrix}$$

giving

$$(zI - A)^{-1} = \frac{1}{(z+1)(z+3)} \begin{bmatrix} z+6 & 5 \\ -3 & z-2 \end{bmatrix}$$

$$= \begin{bmatrix} \dfrac{\frac{5}{2}}{z+1} - \dfrac{\frac{3}{2}}{z+3} & \dfrac{\frac{5}{2}}{z+1} - \dfrac{\frac{5}{2}}{z+3} \\[3mm] \dfrac{-\frac{3}{2}}{z+1} + \dfrac{\frac{3}{2}}{z+3} & \dfrac{-\frac{3}{2}}{z+1} + \dfrac{\frac{5}{2}}{z+3} \end{bmatrix}$$

Then

$$\mathscr{L}^{-1}\{z(z\boldsymbol{I} - \boldsymbol{A})^{-1}\} = \mathscr{L}^{-1} \begin{bmatrix} \frac{5}{2}\dfrac{z}{z+1} - \frac{3}{2}\dfrac{z}{z+3} & \frac{5}{2}\dfrac{z}{z+1} - \frac{5}{2}\dfrac{z}{z+3} \\[3mm] -\frac{3}{2}\dfrac{z}{z+1} + \frac{3}{2}\dfrac{z}{z+3} & -\frac{3}{2}\dfrac{z}{z+1} + \frac{5}{2}\dfrac{z}{z+3} \end{bmatrix}$$

$$= \begin{bmatrix} \frac{5}{2}(-1)^k - \frac{3}{2}(-3)^k & \frac{5}{2}(-1)^k - \frac{5}{2}(-3)^k \\[2mm] -\frac{3}{2}(-1)^k + \frac{3}{2}(-3)^k & -\frac{3}{2}(-1)^k + \frac{5}{2}(-3)^k \end{bmatrix}$$

so that, with $\boldsymbol{x}(0) = [1 \quad -1]^{\mathrm{T}}$, the first term in the solution (6.112) becomes

$$\mathscr{L}^{-1}\{z(z\boldsymbol{I} - \boldsymbol{A})^{-1}\}\boldsymbol{x}(0) = \begin{bmatrix} (-3)^k \\ -(-3)^k \end{bmatrix} \tag{6.113}$$

Since $U(z) = \mathscr{L}\{u(k)\} = z/(z-1)$,

$$(z\boldsymbol{I} - \boldsymbol{A})^{-1}\boldsymbol{B}U(z) = \frac{1}{(z+1)(z+3)}\begin{bmatrix} z+6 & 5 \\ -3 & z-2 \end{bmatrix}\begin{bmatrix} 1 \\ 1 \end{bmatrix}\frac{z}{z-1}$$

$$= \frac{z}{(z-1)(z+1)(z+3)}\begin{bmatrix} z+11 \\ z-5 \end{bmatrix}$$

$$= \begin{bmatrix} \frac{3}{2}\dfrac{z}{z-1} - \frac{5}{2}\dfrac{z}{z+1} + \dfrac{z}{z+3} \\[3mm] -\frac{1}{2}\dfrac{z}{z-1} + \frac{3}{2}\dfrac{z}{z+1} - \dfrac{z}{z+3} \end{bmatrix}$$

so that the second term in the solution (6.112) becomes

$$\mathscr{L}^{-1}\{(z\boldsymbol{I} - \boldsymbol{A})^{-1}\boldsymbol{B}U(z)\} = \begin{bmatrix} \frac{3}{2} - \frac{5}{2}(-1)^k + (-3)^k \\ -\frac{1}{2} + \frac{3}{2}(-1)^k - (-3)^k \end{bmatrix} \tag{6.114}$$

Combining (6.113) and (6.114), the response $\boldsymbol{x}(k)$ is given by

$$\boldsymbol{x}(k) = \begin{bmatrix} \frac{3}{2} - \frac{5}{2}(-1)^k + 2(-3)^k \\ -\frac{1}{2} + \frac{3}{2}(-1)^k - 2(-3)^k \end{bmatrix}$$

6.8.3 Exercises

63 Use z transforms to determine A^k for the matrices

(a) $\begin{bmatrix} 0 & 1 \\ 4 & 0 \end{bmatrix}$ (b) $\begin{bmatrix} -1 & 3 \\ 3 & -1 \end{bmatrix}$ (c) $\begin{bmatrix} -1 & 1 \\ 0 & -1 \end{bmatrix}$

64 Solve the discrete-time system specified by

$$x(k + 1) = -7x(k) + 4y(k)$$
$$y(k + 1) = -8x(k) + y(k)$$

with $x(0) = 1$ and $y(0) = 2$, by writing it in the form $x(k + 1) = Ax(k)$. Use your answer to calculate $x(1)$ and $x(2)$, and check your answers by calculating $x(1)$, $y(1)$, $x(2)$, $y(2)$ directly from the given difference equations.

65 Using the z-transform approach, obtain an expression for the state $x(k)$ of the system characterized by the state equation

$$x(k + 1) = \begin{bmatrix} 0 & 1 \\ -0.16 & 1 \end{bmatrix} x(k) + \begin{bmatrix} 1 \\ 1 \end{bmatrix} u(k)$$

when the input is the unit step function

$$u(k) = \begin{cases} 0 & (k < 0) \\ 1 & (k \geqslant 0) \end{cases}$$

and subject to the initial condition $x(0) = [1 \quad -1]^T$.

66 The difference equation

$$y(k + 2) = y(k + 1) + y(k)$$

with $y(0) = 0$, and $y(1) = 1$ generates the **Fibonacci sequence** $\{y(k)\}$, which occurs in many practical situations. Taking $x_1(k) = y(k)$ and $x_2(k) = y(k + 1)$, express the difference equation in state-space form and hence obtain a general expression for $y(k)$. Show that as $k \to \infty$ the ratio $y(k + 1)/y(k)$ tends to the constant $\frac{1}{2}(\sqrt{5} + 1)$. This is the so-called **Golden Ratio**, which has intrigued mathematicians for centuries because of its strong influence on art and architecture. The Golden rectangle, that is, one whose two sides are in this ratio, is one of the most visually satisfying of all geometric forms.

6.9   Engineering application: capacitor microphone

Many smaller portable tape recorders have a capacitor microphone built in, since such a system is simple and robust. It works on the principle that if the distance between the plates of a capacitor changes then the capacitance changes in a known manner, and these changes induce a current in an electric circuit. This current can can then be amplified or stored. The basic system is illustrated in Figure 6.12. There is a small air gap (about 0.02 mm) between the moving diaphragm and the fixed plate. Sound waves falling on the diaphragm cause vibrations and small variations in the capacitance C; these are certainly sufficiently small that the equations can be *linearized*.

We assume that the diaphragm has mass m and moves as a single unit so that its motion is one-dimensional. The housing of the diaphragm is modelled as a spring-and-dashpot system. The plates are connected through a simple circuit containing a resistance and an imposed steady voltage from a battery. Figure 6.13 illustrates the model. The distance $x(t)$ is measured from the position of zero spring tension, F is the imposed force and f is the force required to hold the moving

Figure 6.12 Capacitor microphone.

Figure 6.13 Capacitor microphone model.

plate in position against the electrical attraction. The mechanical motion is governed by Newton's equation

$$m\ddot{x} = -kx - \lambda\dot{x} - f + F \qquad (6.115)$$

and the electrical circuit equation gives

$$E = RI + \frac{q}{C}, \quad \text{with} \quad \frac{dq}{dt} = I \qquad (6.116)$$

The variation of capacitance C with x is given by the standard formula

$$C = \frac{C_0 a}{a + x}$$

where a is the equilibrium distance between the plates. The force f is not so obvious, but the following assumption is standard

$$f = \tfrac{1}{2}q^2 \frac{d}{dx}\left(\frac{1}{C}\right) = \tfrac{1}{2}\frac{q^2}{C_0 a}$$

It is convenient to write the equations in the first-order form

$$\dot{x} = v$$

$$m\dot{v} = -kx - \lambda v - \tfrac{1}{2}\frac{q^2}{C_0 a} + F(t)$$

$$R\dot{q} = -\frac{q(a + x)}{aC_0} + E$$

Furthermore, it is convenient to non-dimensionalize the equations. While it is obvious how to do this for the distance and velocity, for the time and the charge it is less so. There are three natural time scales in the problem: the electrical time $\tau_1 = RC_0$, the spring time $\tau_2^2 = m/k$ and the damping time $\tau_3 = m/\lambda$. Choosing to non-dimensionalize the time with respect to τ_1, the non-dimensionalization of the charge follows:

$$\tau = \frac{t}{\tau_1}, \qquad X = \frac{x}{a}, \qquad V = \frac{v}{ka/\lambda}, \qquad Q = \frac{q}{\sqrt{(2C_0 ka^2)}}$$

Then, denoting differentiation with respect to τ by a prime, the equations are

$$X' = \frac{RC_0 k}{\lambda} V$$

$$\frac{m}{\lambda RC_0} V' = -X - V - Q^2 + \frac{F}{ka}$$

$$Q' = -Q(1 + X) + \frac{EC_0}{\sqrt{(2C_0 ka^2)}}$$

There are four non-dimensional parameters: the external force divided by the spring force gives the first, $G = F/ka$; the electrical force divided by the spring force gives the second, $D^2 = (E^2 C_0/2a)/ka$; and the remaining two are

$$A = \frac{RC_0 k}{\lambda} = \frac{\tau_1 \tau_3}{\tau_2^2}$$

$$B = \frac{m}{\lambda RC_0} = \frac{\tau_3}{\tau_1}$$

The final equations are therefore

$$\left.\begin{aligned} X' &= AV \\ BV' &= -X - V - Q^2 + G \\ Q' &= -Q(1 + X) + D \end{aligned}\right\} \tag{6.117}$$

In equilibrium, with no driving force, $G = 0$ and $V = X' = V' = Q' = 0$, so that

$$\left.\begin{aligned} Q^2 + X &= 0 \\ Q(1 + X) - D &= 0 \end{aligned}\right\} \tag{6.118}$$

or, on eliminating Q,

$$X(1 + X)^2 = -D^2$$

From Figure 6.14, we see that there is always one solution for $X < -1$, or equivalently $x < -a$. The implication of this solution is that the plates have crossed. This is clearly impossible, so the solution is discarded on physical grounds. There are two other solutions if

$$D^2 < \tfrac{1}{3}(\tfrac{4}{3})^2 = \tfrac{4}{27}$$

Figure 6.14 Solutions to (6.118).

or

$$\frac{E^2 C_0}{2ka^2} < \frac{2}{3\sqrt{3}} \tag{6.119}$$

We can interpret this statement as saying that the electrical force must not be too strong, and (6.119) gives a precise meaning to what 'too strong' means. There are two physically satisfactory equilibrium solutions $-\frac{1}{3} < X_1 < 0$ and $-1 < X_2 < -\frac{1}{3}$, and the only question left is whether they are stable or unstable.

Stability is determined by small oscillations about the two values X_1 and X_2, where these values satisfy (6.118). Writing

$$X = X_i + \varepsilon$$
$$Q = Q_i + \eta$$
$$V = \theta$$

and substituting into (6.117), neglecting terms in ε^2, y^2, θ^2, $\varepsilon\theta$ and so on, gives

$$\left.\begin{array}{l} \varepsilon' = A\theta \\ B\theta' = -\varepsilon - \theta - 2Q_i\eta + G \\ \eta' = -Q_i\varepsilon - (1 + X_1)\eta \end{array}\right\} \tag{6.120}$$

Equations (6.120) are the linearized versions of (6.117) about the equilibrium values. To test for stability, we put $G = 0$ and $\varepsilon = Le^{\alpha\tau}$, $Q = Me^{\alpha\tau}$, $\eta = Ne^{\alpha\tau}$ into (6.120):

$$L\alpha = AM$$
$$BM\alpha = -L - M - 2Q_iN$$
$$N\alpha = -Q_iL - (1 + X_i)y$$

which can be written in the matrix form

$$\alpha \begin{bmatrix} L \\ M \\ N \end{bmatrix} = \begin{bmatrix} 0 & A & 0 \\ -1/B & -1/B & -2Q_i/B \\ -Q_i & 0 & -(1 + X_i) \end{bmatrix} \begin{bmatrix} L \\ M \\ N \end{bmatrix}$$

Thus the fundamental stability problem is an eigenvalue problem, a result common to all vibrational stability problems. The equations have non-trivial solutions if

$$0 = \begin{vmatrix} -\alpha & A & B \\ -1/B & -(1/B) - \alpha & -2Q_i/B \\ -Q_i & 0 & -(1 + X_i) - \alpha \end{vmatrix}$$

$$= [B\alpha^3 + (B(1 + X_i) + 1)\alpha^2 + (1 + X + A)\alpha + A(1 + X - 2Q^2)]/B$$

For stability, α must have a negative real part, so that the vibrations damp out, and the Routh–Hurwitz criteria (Section 2.6.2) gives the conditions for this to be the case. Each of the coefficients must be positive, and for the first three

$$B > 0, \qquad B(1 + X_i) + 1 > 0, \qquad 1 + X_i + A > 0$$

are obviously satisfied since $-1 < X_i < 0$. The next condition is

$$A(1 + X_i - 2Q_i^2) > 0$$

which, from (6.118), gives

$$1 + 3X_i > 0, \qquad \text{or} \quad X_i > -\tfrac{1}{3}$$

Thus the only solution that can possibly be stable is the one for which $X_i > -\tfrac{1}{3}$; the other solution is unstable. There is one final condition to check,

$$[B(1 + X_i) + 1](1 + X_i + A) - BA(1 + X_i - 2Q_i^2) > 0$$

or

$$B(1 + X_i)^2 + 1 + X_i + A + 2BAQ_2^2 > 0$$

Since all the terms are positive, the solution $X_i > \tfrac{1}{3}$ is indeed a stable solution.

Having established the stability of one of the positions of the capacitor diaphragm, the next step is to look at the response of the microphone to various inputs. The characteristics can most easily be checked by looking at the frequency response, which is the system response to an individual input $G = be^{j\omega t}$, as the frequency ω varies. This will give information of how the electrical output behaves and for which range of frequencies the response is reasonably flat.

The essential point of this example is to show that a practical vibrational problem gives a stability problem that involves eigenvalues and a response that involves a matrix inversion. The same behaviour is observed for more complicated vibrational problems.

6.10 Engineering application: pole placement

In Chapters 2 and 3 we examined the behaviour of linear systems in both continuous time and discrete time, concentrating on the transform-domain representation, using the Laplace or z transform as appropriate. In this chapter we have examined the same types of system, this time modelled in the form of vector–matrix differential or difference equations. So far we have concentrated on system *analysis*, that is, the question 'Given the system, how does it behave?' In this section we turn our attention briefly to consider the design or synthesis problem, and while it is not possible to produce an exhaustive treatment, it is intended to give the reader an appreciation of the role of mathematics in this task.

6.10.1   Poles and eigenvalues

By now the reader should be convinced that there is an association between system poles as deduced from the system transfer function and the eigenvalues of the system matrix in state-space form. Thus, for example, the system modelled by the second-order differential equation

$$\frac{d^2y}{dt^2} + \tfrac{1}{2}\frac{dy}{dt} - \tfrac{1}{2}y = u$$

has transfer function

$$G(s) = \frac{1}{s^2 + \tfrac{1}{2}s - \tfrac{1}{2}}$$

The system can also be represented in the state-space form

$$\dot{x} = Ax + bu, \qquad y = c^T x \tag{6.121}$$

where

$$x = [x_1 \quad x_2]^T, \qquad A = \begin{bmatrix} 0 & 1 \\ \tfrac{1}{2} & -\tfrac{1}{2} \end{bmatrix}$$

$$b = [0 \quad 1]^T, \qquad c = [1 \quad 0]^T$$

It is easy to check that the poles of the transfer function $G(s)$ are at $s = -1$ and $s = \tfrac{1}{2}$, and that these values are also the eigenvalues of the matrix A. Clearly this is an unstable system, with the pole or eigenvalue corresponding to $s = \tfrac{1}{2}$ located in the right-half of the complex plane. In Section 6.10.2 we examine a method of moving this unstable pole to a new location, thus providing a method of overcoming the stability problem.

6.10.2   The pole placement or eigenvalue location technique

We now examine the possibility of introducing **state feedback** into the system. To do this, we use as system input

$$u = k^T x + u_{ext}$$

where $k = [k_1 \quad k_2]^T$ and u_{ext} is the external input. The state equation in (6.121) then becomes

$$\dot{x} = \begin{bmatrix} 0 & 1 \\ \tfrac{1}{2} & -\tfrac{1}{2} \end{bmatrix} x + \begin{bmatrix} 0 \\ 1 \end{bmatrix} [(k_1 x_1 + k_2 x_2) + u_{ext}]$$

Figure 6.15 Feedback connections for eigenvalue location.

That is,

$$\dot{x} = \begin{bmatrix} 0 & 1 \\ k_1 + \frac{1}{2} & k_2 - \frac{1}{2} \end{bmatrix} x + \begin{bmatrix} 0 \\ 1 \end{bmatrix} u_{\text{ext}}$$

Calculating the characteristic equation of the new system matrix, we find that the eigenvalues are given by the roots of

$$\lambda^2 - (k_2 - \tfrac{1}{2})\lambda - (k_1 + \tfrac{1}{2}) = 0$$

Suppose that we not only wish to stabilize the system, but also wish to improve the response time. This could be achieved if both eigenvalues were located at (say) $\lambda = -5$, which would require the characteristic equation to be

$$\lambda^2 + 10\lambda + 25 = 0$$

In order to make this pole relocation, we should choose

$$-(k_2 - \tfrac{1}{2}) = 10$$
$$-(k_1 + \tfrac{1}{2}) = 25$$

indicating that we take $k_1 = -\frac{51}{2}$ and $k_2 = -\frac{19}{2}$. Figure 6.15 shows the original system and the additional state-feedback connections as dotted lines. We see that for this example at least, it is possible to locate the system poles or eigenvalues wherever we please in the complex plane, by a suitable choice of the vector k. This corresponds to the choice of feedback gain, and in practical situations we are of course constrained by the need to specify reasonable values for these. Nevertheless, this technique, referred to as **pole placement**, is a powerful method for system control. There are some questions that remain. For example, can we apply the technique to all systems? Also, can it be extended to systems with more than one input? The following exercises will suggest answers to these questions, and help to prepare the reader for the study of specialist texts.

6.10.3 Exercises

67 An unstable system has Laplace transfer function

$$H(s) = \frac{1}{(s + \tfrac{1}{2})(s - 1)}$$

Make an appropriate choice of state variables to represent this system in the form

$$\dot{x} = Ax + bu, \qquad y = c^{\mathsf{T}} x$$

where

$$x = [x_1 \quad x_2]^T, \qquad A = \begin{bmatrix} 0 & 1 \\ \frac{1}{2} & \frac{1}{2} \end{bmatrix}$$

$$b = [0 \quad 1]^T, \qquad c = [1 \quad 0]^T$$

This particular form of the state-space model in which A takes the companion form and b has a single 1 in the last row is called the **control canonical form** of the system equations, and pole placement is particularly straightforward in this case.

Find a state-variable feedback control of the form $u = k^T x$ that will relocate both system poles at $s = -4$, thus stabilizing the system.

68 Find the control canonical form of the state-space equations for the system characterized by the transfer function

$$G(s) = \frac{2}{(s + 1)(s + \frac{1}{4})}$$

Calculate or (better) simulate the step response of the system, and find a control law that relocates both poles at $s = -5$. Calculate or simulate the step response of the new system. How do the two responses differ?

69 The technique for pole placement can be adapted to multi-input systems in certain cases. Consider the system

$$\dot{x} = Ax + Bu, \qquad y = c^T x$$

where

$$x = [x_1 \quad x_2]^T, \qquad u = [u_1 \quad u_2]^T$$

$$A = \begin{bmatrix} 0 & 1 \\ 6 & 1 \end{bmatrix}, \qquad B = \begin{bmatrix} 1 & 0 \\ 1 & 1 \end{bmatrix}, \qquad c = [1 \quad 0]^T$$

Writing $Bu = b_1 u_1 + b_2 u_2$, where $b_1 = [1 \quad 1]^T$ and $b_2 = [0 \quad 1]^T$, enables us to work with each input separately. As a first step, use only the input u_1 to relocate both the system poles at $s = -5$. Secondly, use input u_2 only to achieve the same result. Note that we can use either or both inputs to obtain any pole locations we choose, subject of course to physical constraints on the size of the feedback gains.

70 The bad news is that it is not always possible to use the procedure described in Exercise 69. In the first place, it assumes that a full knowledge of the state vector $x(t)$ is available. This may not always be the

case; however, in many systems this problem can be overcome by the use of an **observer**. For details, a specialist text on control should be consulted.

There are also circumstances in which the system itself does not permit the use of the technique. Such systems are said to be **uncontrollable**, and the following example, which is more fully discussed in J. G. Reed, *Linear System Fundamentals* (McGraw-Hill, Tokyo, 1983) demonstrates the problem. Consider the system

$$\dot{x} = \begin{bmatrix} 0 & -2 \\ 1 & -3 \end{bmatrix} x + \begin{bmatrix} 2 \\ 1 \end{bmatrix} u$$

with

$$y = [0 \quad 1] x$$

Find the system poles and attempt to relocate both of them, at, say, $s = -2$. It will be seen that no gain vector k can be found to achieve this. Calculating the system transfer function gives a clue to the problem, but Exercise 71 shows how the problem could have been seen from the state-space form of the system.

71 In Exercise 62 it was stated that the system

$$\dot{x} = Ax + bu$$

$$y = c^T x$$

where A is an $n \times n$ matrix, is controllable provided that the Kalman matrix

$$M = [b \quad Ab \quad A^2 b \quad \cdots \quad A^{n-1} b]$$

is of rank n. This condition must be satisfied if we are to be able to use the procedure for pole placement. Calculate the Kalman controllability matrix for the system in Exercise 70 and confirm that it has rank less than $n = 2$. Verify that the system of Exercise 67 satisfies the controllability condition.

72 We have noted that when the system equations are expressed in control canonical form, the calculations for pole relocation are particularly easy. The following technique shows how to transform controllable systems into this form. Given the system

$$\dot{x} = Ax + bu, \qquad y = c^T x$$

calculate the Kalman controllability matrix M, defined in Exercise 71, and its inverse M^{-1}. Note that this will only exist for controllable systems. Set v^T as the last row of M^{-1} and form the transformation matrix

$$T = \begin{bmatrix} v^T \\ v^T A \\ \vdots \\ v^T A^{n-1} \end{bmatrix}$$

A transformation of state is now made by introducing the new state vector $z(t) = T x(t)$, and the resulting system will be in control canonical form. To illustrate the technique, carry out the procedure for the system

defined by

$$\dot{x} = \begin{bmatrix} 8 & -2 \\ 35 & -9 \end{bmatrix} x + \begin{bmatrix} 1 \\ 4 \end{bmatrix} u$$

and show that this leads to the system

$$\dot{z} = \begin{bmatrix} 0 & 1 \\ 2 & -1 \end{bmatrix} z + \begin{bmatrix} 0 \\ 1 \end{bmatrix} u$$

Finally, check that the two system matrices have the same eigenvalues, and show that this will always be the case.

6.11 Review exercises (1–22)

1 Obtain the eigenvalues and corresponding eigenvectors of the matrices

(a) $\begin{bmatrix} -1 & 6 & 12 \\ 0 & -13 & 30 \\ 0 & -9 & 20 \end{bmatrix}$ (b) $\begin{bmatrix} 2 & 0 & 1 \\ -1 & 4 & -1 \\ -1 & 2 & 0 \end{bmatrix}$

(c) $\begin{bmatrix} 1 & -1 & 0 \\ -1 & 2 & -1 \\ 0 & -1 & 1 \end{bmatrix}$

2 Find the principal stress values (eigenvalues) and the corresponding principal stress directions (eigenvectors) for the stress matrix

$$T = \begin{bmatrix} 3 & 2 & 1 \\ 2 & 3 & 1 \\ 1 & 1 & 4 \end{bmatrix}$$

Verify that the principal stress directions are mutually orthogonal.

3 Find the values of b and c for which the matrix

$$A = \begin{bmatrix} 2 & -1 & 0 \\ -1 & 3 & b \\ 0 & b & c \end{bmatrix}$$

has $[1 \ 0 \ 1]^T$ as an eigenvector. For these values of b and c calculate all the eigenvalues and corresponding eigenvectors of the matrix A.

4 Use Gerschgorin's theorem to show that the largest-modulus eigenvalue λ_1 of the matrix

$$A = \begin{bmatrix} 4 & -1 & 0 \\ -1 & 4 & -1 \\ 0 & -1 & 4 \end{bmatrix}$$

is such that $2 \leq |\lambda_1| \leq 6$.

Use the power method, with starting vector $x^{(0)} = [-1 \ 1 \ -1]^T$ to find λ_1 correct to one decimal place.

5 (a) Using the power method find the dominant eigenvalue and the corresponding eigenvector of the matrix

$$A = \begin{bmatrix} 2 & 1 & 1 \\ 1 & 2.5 & 1 \\ 1 & 1 & 3 \end{bmatrix}$$

starting with an initial vector $[1 \ 1 \ 1]^T$ and working to three decimal places.

(b) Given that another eigenvalue A is 1.19 correct to two decimal places, find the value of the third eigenvalue using a property of matrices.

(c) Having determined all the eigenvalues of $\boldsymbol{A}$, indicate which of these can be obtained by using the power method on the following matrices: (i) $\boldsymbol{A}^{-1}$; (ii) $\boldsymbol{A} - 3\boldsymbol{I}$.

6 Consider the differential equations

$$\frac{dx}{dt} = 4x + y + z$$

$$\frac{dy}{dt} = 2x + 5y + 4z$$

$$\frac{dz}{dt} = -x - y$$

Show that if it is assumed that there are solutions of the form $x = \alpha e^{\lambda t}$, $y = \beta e^{\lambda t}$ and $z = \gamma e^{\lambda t}$ then the system of equations can be transformed into the eigenvalue problem

$$\begin{bmatrix} 4 & 1 & 1 \\ 2 & 5 & 4 \\ -1 & -1 & 0 \end{bmatrix} \begin{bmatrix} \alpha \\ \beta \\ \gamma \end{bmatrix} = \lambda \begin{bmatrix} \alpha \\ \beta \\ \gamma \end{bmatrix}$$

Show that the eigenvalues for this problem are 5, 3 and 1, and find the eigenvectors corresponding to the smallest eigenvalue.

7 Find the eigenvalues and corresponding eigenvectors for the matrix

$$\boldsymbol{A} = \begin{bmatrix} 8 & -8 & -2 \\ 4 & -3 & -2 \\ 3 & -4 & 1 \end{bmatrix}$$

Write down the modal matrix $\boldsymbol{M}$ and spectral matrix Λ of $\boldsymbol{A}$, and confirm that

$$\boldsymbol{M}^{-1}\boldsymbol{A}\boldsymbol{M} = \Lambda$$

8 Show that the eigenvalues of the symmetric matrix

$$\boldsymbol{A} = \begin{bmatrix} 1 & 0 & -4 \\ 0 & 5 & 4 \\ -4 & 4 & 3 \end{bmatrix}$$

are 9, 3 and -3. Obtain the corresponding eigenvectors in normalized form, and write down the normalized modal matrix $\hat{\boldsymbol{M}}$. Confirm that

$$\hat{\boldsymbol{M}}^{\mathrm{T}}\boldsymbol{A}\hat{\boldsymbol{M}} = \Lambda$$

where Λ is the spectral matrix of $\boldsymbol{A}$.

9 In a radioactive series consisting of four different nuclides starting with the parent substance N_1 and ending with the stable product N_4 the amounts of each nuclide present at time t are given by the differential equations model

$$\frac{dN_1}{dt} = -6N_1$$

$$\frac{dN_2}{dt} = 6N_1 - 4N_2$$

$$\frac{dN_3}{dt} = 4N_2 - 2N_3$$

$$\frac{dN_4}{dt} = 2N_3$$

Express these in the vector–matrix form

$$\dot{N} = \boldsymbol{A}N$$

where $N = [N_1 \ \ N_2 \ \ N_3 \ \ N_4]^{\mathrm{T}}$. Find the eigenvalues and corresponding eigenvectors of $\boldsymbol{A}$. Using the spectral form of the solution, determine $N_4(t)$ given that at time $t = 0$, $N_t = C$ and $N_2 = N_3 = N_4 = 0$.

10 (a) Given

$$\boldsymbol{A} = \begin{bmatrix} 2 & 0 \\ 1 & 1 \end{bmatrix}$$

use the Cayley–Hamilton theorem to find

(i) $\boldsymbol{A}^7 - 3\boldsymbol{A}^6 + \boldsymbol{A}^4 + 3\boldsymbol{A}^3 - 2\boldsymbol{A}^2 + 3\boldsymbol{I}$

(ii) $\boldsymbol{A}^k$, where $k > 0$ is an integer

(b) Using the Cayley–Hamilton theorem, find $e^{\boldsymbol{A}t}$ when

$$\boldsymbol{A} = \begin{bmatrix} 0 & 1 \\ 0 & -2 \end{bmatrix}$$

11 Show that the matrix

$$\boldsymbol{A} = \begin{bmatrix} 1 & 2 & 3 \\ 0 & 1 & 4 \\ 0 & 0 & 1 \end{bmatrix}$$

has an eigenvalue $\lambda = 1$ with algebraic multiplicity 3. By considering the rank of a suitable matrix, show that there is only one corresponding linearly independent eigenvector e_1. Obtain the eigenvector e_1 and two further generalized eigenvectors. Write down the corresponding modal matrix $\boldsymbol{M}$ and confirm that $\boldsymbol{M}^{-1}\boldsymbol{A}\boldsymbol{M} = \boldsymbol{J}$, where $\boldsymbol{J}$ is the appropriate

Jordan matrix. (*Hint*: In this example care must be taken in applying the procedure to evaluate the generalized eigenvectors to ensure that the triad of vectors takes the form $\{T^2\omega, T\omega, \omega\}$, where $T = A - \lambda I$, with $T^2\omega = e_1$.)

12 The equations of motion of three equal masses connected by springs of equal stiffness are

$$\ddot{x} = -2x + y$$
$$\ddot{y} = x - 2y + z$$
$$\ddot{z} = y - 2z$$

Show that for normal modes of oscillation

$$x = X \cos \omega t, \qquad y = Y \cos \omega t, \qquad z = Z \cos \omega t$$

to exist then the condition on $\lambda = \omega^2$ is

$$\begin{bmatrix} \lambda - 2 & 1 & 0 \\ 1 & \lambda - 2 & 1 \\ 0 & 1 & \lambda - 2 \end{bmatrix} = 0$$

Find the three values of λ that satisfy this condition, and find the ratios $X:Y:Z$ in each case.

13 Classify the following quadratic forms:

(a) $2x^2 + y^2 + 2z^2 - 2xy - 2yz$
(b) $3x^2 + 7y^2 + 2z^2 - 4xy - 4xz$
(c) $16x^2 + 36y^2 + 17z^2 + 32xy + 32xz + 16yz$
(d) $-21x^2 + 30xy - 12xz - 11y^2 + 8yz - 2z^2$
(e) $-x^2 - 3y^2 - 5z^2 + 2xy + 2xz + 2yz$

14 Show that $e_1 = [1 \quad 2 \quad 3]^T$ is an eigenvector of the matrix

$$A = \begin{bmatrix} \frac{7}{2} & -\frac{1}{2} & -\frac{1}{2} \\ 4 & -1 & 0 \\ -\frac{3}{2} & \frac{3}{2} & \frac{1}{2} \end{bmatrix}$$

and find its corresponding eigenvalue. Find the other two eigenvalues and their corresponding eigenvectors.

Write down in spectral form the general solution of the system of differential equations

$$2\frac{dx}{dt} = 7x - y - z$$

$$\frac{dy}{dt} = 4x - y$$

$$2\frac{dz}{dt} = -3x + 3y + z$$

Hence show that if $x = 2$, $y = 4$ and $z = 6$ when $t = 0$ then the solution is

$$x = 2e^t, \qquad y = 4e^t, \qquad z = 6e^t$$

15 A continuous-time system is specified in state-space form as

$$\dot{x}(t) = Ax(t) + bu(t)$$
$$y(t) = c^T x(t)$$

where

$$A = \begin{bmatrix} 0 & 6 \\ -1 & -5 \end{bmatrix}, \qquad b = \begin{bmatrix} 0 \\ 1 \end{bmatrix}, \qquad c = \begin{bmatrix} 1 \\ 1 \end{bmatrix}$$

(a) Draw a block diagram to represent the system.
(b) Using Laplace transformations, show that the state transition matrix is given by

$$e^{At} = \begin{bmatrix} 3e^{-2t} - 2e^{-3t} & 6e^{-2t} - 6e^{-3t} \\ e^{-3t} - e^{-2t} & 3e^{-3t} - 2e^{-2t} \end{bmatrix}$$

(c) Calculate the impulse response of the system, and determine the response $y(t)$ of the system to an input $u(t) = 1$ $(t \geqslant 0)$, subject to the initial state $x(0) = [1 \quad 0]^T$.

16 Show that the eigenvalues of the matrix

$$A = \begin{bmatrix} 1 & 1 & -2 \\ -1 & 2 & 1 \\ 0 & 1 & -1 \end{bmatrix}$$

are 2, 1 and -1, and find the corresponding eigenvectors. Write down the modal matrix M and spectral matrix Λ of A, and verify that $M\Lambda = AM$.
    Deduce that the system of difference equations

$$x(k + 1) = Ax(k)$$

where $x(k) = [x_1(k) \quad x_2(k) \quad x_3(k)]^T$, has a solution

$$x(k) = My(k)$$

where $y(k) = \Lambda^k y(0)$. Find this solution, given $x(0) = [1 \quad 0 \quad 0]^T$.

17 A linear time-invariant system (A, b, c) is modelled by the state-space equations

$$\dot{x}(t) = Ax(t) + bu(t)$$
$$y(t) = c^T x(t)$$

where $x(t)$ is the n-dimensional state vector, and $u(t)$ and $y(t)$ are the system input and output respectively.

Given that the system matrix A has n distinct non-zero eigenvalues, show that the system equations may be reduced to the canonical form

$$\dot{\xi}(t) = \Lambda \xi(t) + b_1 u(t)$$

$$y(t) = c_1^T \xi(t)$$

where Λ is a diagonal matrix. What properties of this canonical form determine the controllability and observability of (A, b, c)?

Reduce to canonical form the system (A, b, c) having

$$A = \begin{bmatrix} 1 & 1 & -2 \\ -1 & 2 & 1 \\ 0 & 1 & -1 \end{bmatrix}$$

$$b = \begin{bmatrix} -1 \\ 1 \\ -1 \end{bmatrix} \qquad c = \begin{bmatrix} -2 \\ 1 \\ 0 \end{bmatrix}$$

and comment on its stability, controllability and observability by considering the ranks of the appropriate Kalman matrices $[b \quad Ab \quad A^2 b]$ and $[c \quad A^T c \quad (A^T)^2 c]$.

18 A single-input–single-output system is represented in state-space form, using the usual notation, as

$$\dot{x}(t) = Ax(t) + bu(t)$$

$$y(t) = c^T x(t)$$

For

$$A = \begin{bmatrix} -2 & -1 \\ 2 & 0 \end{bmatrix}, \qquad b = \begin{bmatrix} 1 \\ 0 \end{bmatrix}, \qquad c = \begin{bmatrix} 1 \\ 1 \end{bmatrix}$$

show that

$$e^{At} = \begin{bmatrix} e^{-t}(\cos t - \sin t) & -e^{-t}\sin t \\ 2e^{-t}\sin t & e^{-t}(\cos t + \sin t) \end{bmatrix}$$

and find $x(t)$ given that $x(0) = 0$ and $u(t) = 1$ $(t \geqslant 0)$.

Show that the Laplace transfer function of the system is

$$H(s) = \frac{Y(s)}{U(s)} = c(sI - A)^{-1} b$$

and find $H(s)$ for this system. What is the system impulse response?

19 The system shown in Figure 6.16 is a realization of a discrete-time system. Show that, with state variables $x_1(k)$ and $x_2(k)$ as shown, the system may be

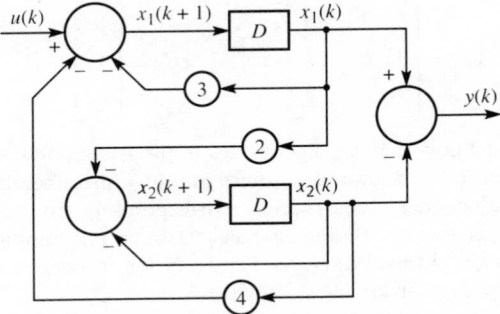

Figure 6.16 Discrete-time system of Review exercise 19

represented as

$$x(k + 1) = Ax(k) + bu(k)$$

$$y(k) = c^T x(k)$$

where

$$A = \begin{bmatrix} -3 & -4 \\ -2 & -1 \end{bmatrix}, \qquad b = \begin{bmatrix} 1 \\ 0 \end{bmatrix}, \qquad c = \begin{bmatrix} 1 \\ -1 \end{bmatrix}$$

Calculate the z transfer function of the system, $D(z)$, where

$$D(z) = c(zI - A)^{-1} b$$

Reduce the system to control canonical form by the following means:

(i) calculate the controllability matrix M_c, where $M_c = [b \quad Ab]$ is the matrix with columns b and Ab;

(ii) show that rank $(M_c) = 2$, and calculate M_c^{-1};

(iii) write down the vector v^T corresponding to the last row of M_c^{-1};

(iv) form the matrix $T = [v^T \quad v^T A]^T$, the matrix with rows v^T and $v^T A$;

(v) calculate T^{-1} and using this matrix T, show that the transformation $z(k) = Tx(k)$ produces the system

$$z(k + 1) = TAT^{-1}z(k) + Tbu(k)$$

$$= Cz(k) + b_c u(k)$$

where C is of the form

$$\begin{bmatrix} 0 & 1 \\ -\alpha & -\beta \end{bmatrix}$$

and $b_c = [0 \quad 1]^T$. Calculate α and β, and comment on the values obtained in relation to the transfer function $D(z)$.

20 The behaviour of an unforced mechanical system is governed by the differential equation

$$\dot{x}(t) = \begin{bmatrix} 5 & 2 & -1 \\ 3 & 6 & -9 \\ 1 & 1 & 1 \end{bmatrix} x(t), \qquad x(0) = \begin{bmatrix} 0 \\ 1 \\ 0 \end{bmatrix}$$

(a) Show that the eigenvalues of the system matrix are 6, 3, 3 and that there is only one linearly independent eigenvector corresponding to the eigenvalue 3. Obtain the eigenvectors corresponding to the eigenvalues 6 and 3 and a further generalized eigenvector for the eigenvalue 3.

(b) Write down a generalized modal matrix M and confirm that

$$AM = MJ$$

for an appropriate Jordan matrix J.

(c) Using the result

$$x(t) = M e^{Jt} M^{-1} x(0)$$

obtain the solution to the given differential equation.

21 A controllable linear plant that can be influenced by one input $u(t)$ is modelled by the differential equation

$$\dot{x}(t) = Ax(t) + bu(t)$$

where $x(t) = [x_1(t) \quad x_2(t) \quad \dots \quad x_n(t)]^T$ is the state vector, A is a constant matrix with distinct real eigenvalues $\lambda_1, \lambda_2, \dots, \lambda_n$ and $b = [b_1 \quad b_2 \quad \dots \quad b_n]^T$ is a constant vector. By the application of the feedback control

$$u(t) = K v_K^T x(t)$$

where v_K is the eigenvector of A^T corresponding to the eigenvalue λ_K of A^T (and hence of A), the eigenvalue λ_K can be changed to a new real value ρ_K without altering the other eigenvalues. To achieve this, the feedback gain K is chosen as

$$K = \frac{\rho_K - \lambda_K}{p_K}$$

where $p_K = v_K^T b$.

Show that the system represented by

$$\dot{x}(t) = \begin{bmatrix} 1 & 2 & 0 \\ 0 & -1 & 0 \\ -3 & -3 & -2 \end{bmatrix} x(t) + \begin{bmatrix} 0 \\ 1 \\ 0 \end{bmatrix} u(t)$$

is controllable, and find the eigenvalues and corresponding eigenvectors of the system matrix. Deduce that the system is unstable in the absence of control, and determine a control law that will relocate the eigenvalue corresponding to the unstable mode at the new value -5.

22 (Extended problem) Many vibrational systems are modelled by the vector–matrix differential equation

$$\ddot{x}(t) = Ax(t) \qquad (1)$$

where A is a constant $n \times n$ matrix and $x(t) = [x_1(t) \quad x_2(t) \quad \dots \quad x_n(t)]^T$. By substituting $x = e^{\lambda t} u$, show that

$$\lambda^2 u = Au \qquad (2)$$

and that non-trivial solutions for u exist provided that

$$|A - \lambda^2 I| = 0 \qquad (3)$$

Let $\lambda_1^2, \lambda_2^2, \dots, \lambda_n^2$ be the solutions of (3) and $u_1, u_2, \dots, u_n$ the corresponding solutions of (2). Define M to be the matrix having $u_1, u_2, \dots, u_n$ as its columns and S to be the diagonal matrix having $\lambda_1^2, \lambda_2^2, \dots, \lambda_n^2$ as its diagonal elements. By applying the transformation $x(t) = Mq(t)$, where $q(t) = [q_1(t) \quad q_2(t) \quad \dots \quad q_n(t)]^T$, to (1), show that

$$\ddot{q} = Sq \qquad (4)$$

and deduce that (4) has solutions of the form

$$q_i = C_i \sin(\omega_i t + \alpha_i) \qquad (5)$$

where c_i and α_i are arbitrary constants and $\lambda_i = j\omega_i$, with $j = \sqrt{(-1)}$.

The solutions λ_i^2 of (3) define the **natural frequencies** ω_i of the system. The corresponding solutions q_i given in (5) are called the **normal modes** of the system. The general solution of (1) is then obtained using $x(t) = Mq(t)$.

A mass–spring vibrating system is governed by the differential equations

$$\ddot{x}_1(t) = -3x_1(t) + 2x_2(t)$$
$$\ddot{x}_2(t) = x_1(t) - 2x_2(t)$$

with $x_1(0) = 1$ and $x_2(0) = \dot{x}_1(0) = \dot{x}_2(0) = 2$. Determine the natural frequencies and the corresponding normal modes of the system. Hence obtain the general displacement $x_1(t)$ and $x_2(t)$ at time $t \geq 0$. Plot graphs of both the normal modes and the general solutions.

7

Vector Calculus

CONTENTS

7.1 ## Introduction

In *Modern Engineering Mathematics* the basic ideas and techniques of the calculus of several variables were introduced, and were used in the solution of problems arising in engineering and technology. In this chapter we shall reconsider the ideas, and both specialize and extend them for the special case of functions of the space variable $r = xi + yj + zk = (x, y, z)$. Many applications involve functions like this, which model quantities that vary from point to point in three-dimensional space. There are two types of such functions. There are **scalar point functions**, which model scalar quantities like the temperature at a point in a body, and **vector point functions**, which model vector quantities like the velocity of the flow at a point in a liquid. We can express this more formally using the terminology of Chapter 1 of *Modern Engineering Mathematics*. For each scalar point function f we have a

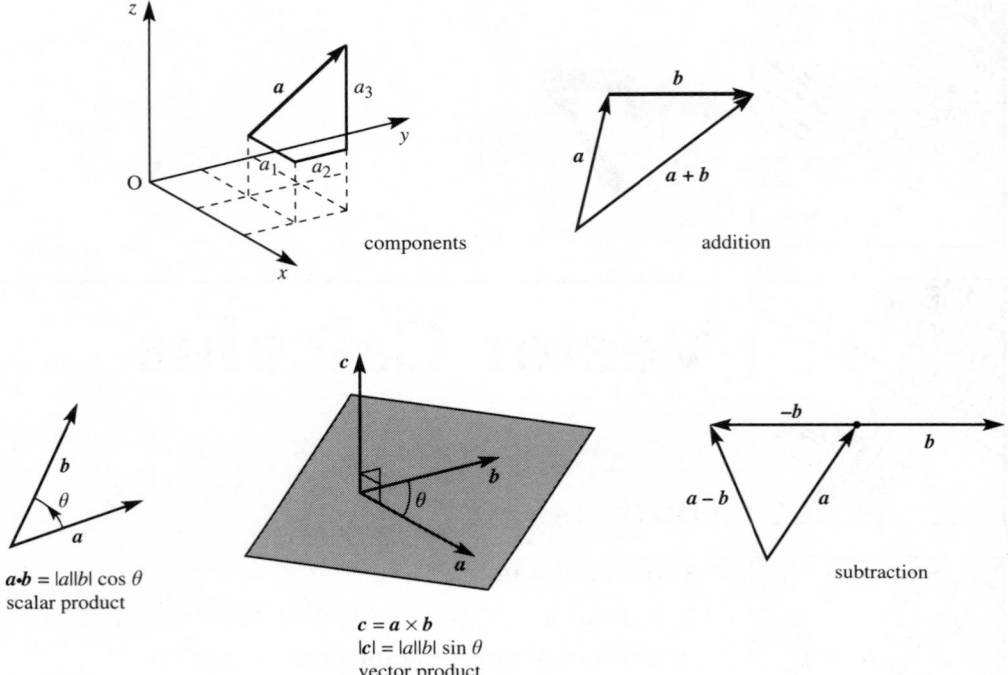

Figure 7.1 Elementary vector algebra.

rule, $u = f(r)$, which assigns to each point with coordinate r in the **domain** of the function a unique real number u. For vector point functions the rule $v = F(r)$ assigns to each r a unique vector v in the range of the function. Vector calculus was designed to measure the variation of such functions with respect to the space variable r. That development made use of the ideas about vectors (components, addition, subtraction, scalar and vector products) described in Chapter 3 of *Modern Engineering Mathematics* and summarized here in Figure 7.1.

The recent development of computer packages for the modelling of engineering problems involving vector quantities has relieved designers of much tedious analysis and computation. To be able to use those packages effectively, however, designers need a good understanding of the mathematical tools they bring to their tasks. It is on that basic understanding that this chapter focuses.

7.1.1   Basic concepts

We can picture a scalar point function $f(r)$ by means of its level surfaces $f(r) = $ constant. For example, the level surfaces of $f(r) = 2x + 2y - z$ are planes

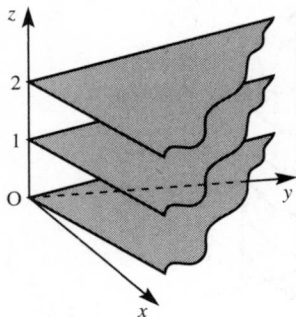

Figure 7.2 Level surfaces of $f(r) = (2, 2, -1) \cdot r = 2x + 2y - z$.

parallel to the plane $z = 2x + 2y$, as shown in Figure 7.2. On the level surface the function value does not change, so the rate of change of the function will be zero along any line drawn on the level surface. An alternative name for a scalar point function is **scalar field**. This is in contrast to the vector point function (or **vector field**). We picture a vector field by its field (or flow) lines. A field line is a curve in space represented by the position vector $r(t)$ such that at each point of the curve its tangent is parallel to the vector field. Thus the field lines of $F(r)$ are given by the differential equation

$$\frac{dr}{dt} = F(r), \qquad \text{where } r(t_0) = r_0$$

and r_0 is the point on the line corresponding to $t = t_0$. This vector equation represents the three simultaneous ordinary differential equations

$$\frac{dx}{dt} = P(x, y, z)$$

$$\frac{dy}{dt} = Q(x, y, z)$$

$$\frac{dz}{dt} = R(x, y, z)$$

where $F = (P, Q, R)$.

Modern computer algebra packages make it easier to draw both the level surfaces of scalar functions and the field lines of vector functions, but to underline the basic ideas we shall consider two simple examples.

EXAMPLE 7.1   Sketch

(a) the level surfaces of the scalar point function $f(r) = z e^{-xy}$;

(b) the field lines of the vector point function $F(r) = (y, -x, 1)$.

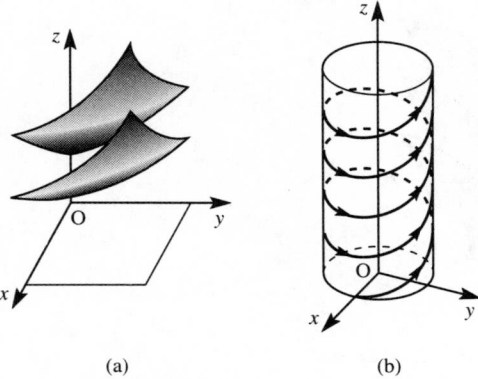

(a)   (b)

Figure 7.3 (a) Level surfaces of $f(r) = z\,e^{-xy}$ (b) Field lines of $F(r) = (y, -x, 1)$.

Solution (a) Consider the level surface given by $f(r) = c$, where c is a number. Then $ze^{-xy} = c$ and so $z = ce^{xy}$. For c, x and y all positive we can easily sketch part of the surface as shown in Figure 7.3(a), from which we can deduce the appearance of the whole family of level surfaces.

(b) For the function $F(r) = (y, -x, 1)$ the field lines are given by

$$\frac{dr}{dt} = (y, -x, 1)$$

that is, by the simultaneous differential equations

$$\frac{dx}{dt} = y$$

$$\frac{dy}{dt} = -x$$

$$\frac{dz}{dt} = 1$$

The general solution of these simultaneous equations is

$$x(t) = A\cos t + B\sin t$$

$$y(t) = B\cos t - A\sin t$$

$$z(t) = t + C$$

where A, B and C are arbitrary constants. Considering, in particular, the field line that passes through $(1, 0, 0)$, we determine the parametric equation

$$(x(t), y(t), z(t)) = (\cos t, -\sin t, t)$$

This represents a circular helix as shown in Figure 7.3(b), from which we can deduce the appearance of the whole family of flow lines.

To investigate the properties of scalar and vector fields further we need to use the calculus of several variables developed in Chapter 9 of *Modern Engineering Mathematics*. Here we shall briefly review the basic ideas and definitions.

Given a function $f(x)$ of a single variable x, we measure its rate of change (or gradient) by its derivative with respect to x. This is

$$\frac{\mathrm{d}f}{\mathrm{d}x} = f'(x) = \lim_{\Delta x \to 0} \frac{f(x + \Delta x) - f(x)}{\Delta x}$$

However, a function $f(x, y, z)$ of three independent variables x, y and z does not have a unique rate of change. The value of the latter depends on the direction in which it is measured. The rate of change of the function $f(x, y, z)$ in the x direction is given by its **partial derivative** with respect to x, namely

$$\frac{\partial f}{\partial x} = \lim_{\Delta x \to 0} \frac{f(x + \Delta x, y, z) - f(x, y, z)}{\Delta x}$$

This measures the rate of change of $f(x, y, z)$ with respect to x when y and z are held constant. We can calculate such partial derivatives by differentiating $f(x, y, z)$ with respect to x, treating y and z as constants. Similarly,

$$\frac{\partial f}{\partial y} = \lim_{\Delta y \to 0} \frac{f(x, y + \Delta y, z) - f(x, y, z)}{\Delta y}$$

and

$$\frac{\partial f}{\partial z} = \lim_{\Delta z \to 0} \frac{f(x, y, z + \Delta z) - f(x, y, z)}{\Delta z}$$

define the partial derivatives of $f(x, y, z)$ with respect to y and z respectively.

For conciseness we sometimes use a suffix notation to denote partial derivatives, for example writing f_x for $\partial f / \partial x$. The rules for partial differentiation are essentially the same as for ordinary differentiation, but it must always be remembered which variables are being held constant.

Higher-order partial derivatives may be defined in a similar manner, with, for example,

$$\frac{\partial^2 f}{\partial x^2} = \frac{\partial}{\partial x}\left(\frac{\partial f}{\partial x}\right) = f_{xx}$$

$$\frac{\partial^2 f}{\partial y \, \partial x} = \frac{\partial}{\partial y}\left(\frac{\partial f}{\partial x}\right) = f_{xy}$$

$$\frac{\partial^3 f}{\partial z \, \partial y \, \partial x} = \frac{\partial}{\partial z}\left(\frac{\partial^2 f}{\partial y \, \partial x}\right) = f_{xyz}$$

EXAMPLE 7.2 Find the first partial derivatives of the functions $f(x, y, z)$ with formula (a) $x + 2y + z^3$, (b) $x^2(y + 2z)$ and (c) $(x + y)/(z^3 + x)$.

Solution   (a) $f(x, y, z) = x + 2y + z^3$. To obtain f_x, we differentiate $f(x, y, z)$ with respect to x, keeping y and z constant. Thus $f_x = 1$, since the derivative of a constant $(2y + z^3)$ with respect to x is zero. Similarly, $f_y = 2$ and $f_z = 3z^2$.

(b) $f(x, y, z) = x^2(y + 2z)$. Here we use the same idea: when we differentiate with respect to one variable, we treat the other two as constants. Thus

$$\frac{\partial}{\partial x}[x^2(y + 2z)] = (y + 2z)\frac{\partial}{\partial x}(x^2)$$

$$= 2x(y + 2z)$$

$$\frac{\partial}{\partial y}[x^2(y + 2z)] = x^2\frac{\partial}{\partial y}(y + 2z)$$

$$= x^2(1)$$

$$= x^2$$

$$\frac{\partial}{\partial z}[x^2(y + 2z)] = x^2\frac{\partial}{\partial z}(y + 2z)$$

$$= x^2(2)$$

$$= 2x^2$$

(c) $f(x, y, z) = (x + y)/(z^3 + x)$. Here we use the same idea, together with basic rules from ordinary differentiation:

$$\frac{\partial f}{\partial x} = \frac{(1)(z^3 + x) - (x + y)(1)}{(z^3 + x)^2} \qquad \text{(quotient rule)}$$

$$= \frac{z^3 - y}{(z^3 + x)^2}$$

$$\frac{\partial f}{\partial y} = \frac{1}{z^3 + x}$$

$$\frac{\partial f}{\partial z} = \frac{-3z^2(x + y)}{(z^3 + x)^2} \qquad \text{(chain rule)}$$

In Example 7.2 we used the **chain** (or **composite-function**) **rule** of ordinary differentiation

$$\frac{\mathrm{d}f}{\mathrm{d}x} = \frac{\mathrm{d}f}{\mathrm{d}u}\frac{\mathrm{d}u}{\mathrm{d}x}$$

to obtain the partial derivative $\partial f/\partial z$. The multivariable calculus form of the chain rule is a little more complicated. If the variables u, v and w are defined in terms of x, y and z then the partial derivative of $f(u, v, w)$ with respect to x is

$$\frac{\partial f}{\partial x} = \frac{\partial f}{\partial u}\frac{\partial u}{\partial x} + \frac{\partial f}{\partial v}\frac{\partial v}{\partial x} + \frac{\partial f}{\partial w}\frac{\partial w}{\partial x}$$

with similar expressions for $\partial f/\partial y$ and $\partial f/\partial z$.

EXAMPLE 7.3 A scalar point function $f(\mathbf{r})$ can be expressed in terms of rectangular cartesian coordinates (x, y, z) or in terms of spherical polar coordinates (r, θ, ϕ), where

$$x = r\sin\theta\cos\phi, \qquad y = r\sin\theta\sin\phi, \qquad z = r\cos\theta$$

as shown in Figure 7.4. Find $\partial f/\partial x$ in terms of the partial derivatives of the function with respect to r, θ and ϕ.

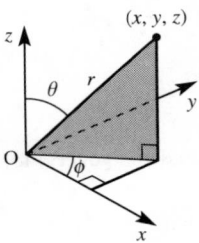

Figure 7.4 Spherical polar coordinates.

Solution Using the chain rule, we have

$$\frac{\partial f}{\partial x} = \frac{\partial f}{\partial r}\frac{\partial r}{\partial x} + \frac{\partial f}{\partial \theta}\frac{\partial \theta}{\partial x} + \frac{\partial f}{\partial \phi}\frac{\partial \phi}{\partial x}$$

From Figure 7.4, $r^2 = x^2 + y^2 + z^2$, $\tan\phi = y/x$ and $\tan\theta = (x^2 + y^2)^{1/2}/z$, so that

$$\frac{\partial r}{\partial x} = \frac{x}{r} = \sin\theta\cos\phi$$

$$\frac{\partial \phi}{\partial x} = \frac{\partial}{\partial x}\left(\tan^{-1}\frac{y}{x}\right) = -\frac{y}{x^2 + y^2} = -\frac{\sin\phi}{r\sin\theta}$$

$$\frac{\partial \theta}{\partial x} = \frac{\partial}{\partial x}\left\{\tan^{-1}\left[\frac{(x^2 + y^2)^{1/2}}{z}\right]\right\} = \frac{xz}{(x^2 + y^2 + z^2)(x^2 + y^2)^{1/2}}$$

$$= \frac{\cos\phi\cos\theta}{r}$$

Thus

$$\frac{\partial f}{\partial x} = \sin\theta\cos\phi\,\frac{\partial f}{\partial r} - \frac{\sin\phi}{r\sin\theta}\frac{\partial f}{\partial \phi} + \frac{\cos\phi\cos\theta}{r}\frac{\partial f}{\partial \theta}$$

7.1.2   Exercises

1 Sketch the contours (in two dimensions) of the scalar functions

(a) $f(x, y) = \ln(x^2 + y^2 - 1)$

(b) $f(x, y) = \tan^{-1}[y/(1 + x)]$

2 Sketch the flow lines (in two dimensions) of the vector functions

(a) $\boldsymbol{F}(x, y) = y\boldsymbol{i} + (6x^2 - 4x)\boldsymbol{j}$

(b) $\boldsymbol{F}(x, y) = y\boldsymbol{i} + (\frac{1}{6}x^3 - x)\boldsymbol{j}$

where $\boldsymbol{i}$ and $\boldsymbol{j}$ are unit vectors in the direction of the x and y axes respectively.

3 Sketch the level surfaces of the functions

(a) $f(\boldsymbol{r}) = z - xy$

(b) $f(\boldsymbol{r}) = z - e^{-xy}$

4 Sketch the field lines of the functions

(a) $\boldsymbol{F}(\boldsymbol{r}) = (xy, y^2 + 1, z)$

(b) $\boldsymbol{F}(\boldsymbol{r}) = (yz, zx, xy)$

5 Find all the first and second partial derivatives of the functions

(a) $f(\boldsymbol{r}) = xyz - x^2 + y - z$

(b) $f(\boldsymbol{r}) = x^2yz^3$

(c) $f(\boldsymbol{r}) = z \tan^{-1}(y/x)$

6 Find df/dt, where

(a) $f(\boldsymbol{r}) = x^2 + y^2 - z$, and $x = t^3 - 1$, $y = 2t$, $z = 1/(t - 1)$

(b) $f(\boldsymbol{r}) = xyz$, and $x = e^{-t} \sin t$, $y = e^{-t} \cos t$, $z = t$

7 Find $\partial f/\partial y$ and $\partial f/\partial z$ in terms of the partial derivatives of f with respect to spherical polar coordinates (r, θ, ϕ) (see Example 7.3).

8 Show that if $u(\boldsymbol{r}) = f(r)$, where $r^2 = x^2 + y^2 + z^2$, as usual, and

$$\frac{\partial^2 u}{\partial x^2} + \frac{\partial^2 u}{\partial y^2} + \frac{\partial^2 u}{\partial z^2} = 0$$

then

$$\frac{d^2 f}{dr^2} + \frac{2}{r}\frac{df}{dr} = 0$$

Hence find the general form for $f(r)$.

9 Show that

$$V(x, y, z) = \frac{1}{z}\exp\left(-\frac{x^2 + y^2}{4z}\right)$$

satisfies the differential equation

$$\frac{\partial^2 V}{\partial x^2} + \frac{\partial^2 V}{\partial y^2} = \frac{\partial V}{\partial z}$$

10 Verify that $V(x, y, z) = \sin 3x \cos 4y \cosh 5z$ satisfies the differential equation

$$\frac{\partial^2 V}{\partial x^2} + \frac{\partial^2 V}{\partial y^2} + \frac{\partial^2 V}{\partial z^2} = 0$$

7.2   Derivatives of a scalar point function

In many practical problems it is necessary to measure the rate of change of a scalar point function. For example, in heat transfer problems we need to know the rate of change of temperature from point to point, because that determines the rate at which heat flows. Similarly, if we are investigating the electric field due to static charges, we need to know the variation of the electric potential from point to point. To determine such information, the ideas of calculus were extended to vector quantities. The first development of this was the concept of the gradient of a scalar point function.

7.2.1   The gradient of a scalar point function

We described in Section 7.1.1 how the gradient of a scalar field depended on the direction along which its rate of change was measured. We now explore this idea further. Consider the rate of change of the function $f(\mathbf{r})$ at the point (x, y, z) in the direction of the unit vector (l, m, n). To find this, we need to evaluate the limit

$$\lim_{\Delta r \to 0} \frac{f(\mathbf{r} + \Delta \mathbf{r}) - f(\mathbf{r})}{\Delta r}$$

where $\Delta \mathbf{r}$ is in the direction of (l, m, n). In terms of coordinates, this means

$$\mathbf{r} + \Delta \mathbf{r} = \mathbf{r} + \Delta r(l, m, n)$$
$$= (x + \Delta x, y + \Delta y, z + \Delta z)$$

so that

$$\Delta x = l\,\Delta r, \qquad \Delta y = m\,\Delta r, \qquad \Delta z = n\,\Delta r$$

Thus we have to consider the limit

$$\lim_{\Delta r \to 0} \frac{f(x + l\,\Delta r, y + m\,\Delta r, z + n\,\Delta r) - f(x, y, z)}{\Delta r}$$

We can rewrite this as

$$\lim_{\Delta r \to 0} \left[\frac{f(x + l\,\Delta r, y + m\,\Delta r, z + n\,\Delta r) - f(x, y + m\,\Delta r, z + n\,\Delta r)}{l\,\Delta r} \right] l$$

$$+ \lim_{\Delta r \to 0} \left[\frac{f(x, y + m\,\Delta r, z + n\,\Delta r) - f(x, y, z + n\,\Delta r)}{m\,\Delta r} \right] m$$

$$+ \lim_{\Delta r \to 0} \left[\frac{f(x, y, z + n\,\Delta r) - f(x, y, z)}{n\,\Delta r} \right] n$$

Evaluating the limits, remembering that $\Delta x = l\,\Delta r$ and so on, we find that the rate of change of $f(\mathbf{r})$ in the direction of the unit vector (l, m, n) is

$$\frac{\partial f}{\partial x} l + \frac{\partial f}{\partial y} m + \frac{\partial f}{\partial z} n = \left(\frac{\partial f}{\partial x}, \frac{\partial f}{\partial y}, \frac{\partial f}{\partial z} \right) \cdot (l, m, n)$$

The vector

$$\left(\frac{\partial f}{\partial x}, \frac{\partial f}{\partial y}, \frac{\partial f}{\partial z} \right)$$

is called the **gradient** of the scalar point function $f(x, y, z)$, and is denoted by grad f or by ∇f, where ∇ is the vector operator

$$\nabla = \mathbf{i} \frac{\partial}{\partial x} + \mathbf{j} \frac{\partial}{\partial y} + \mathbf{k} \frac{\partial}{\partial z}$$

where $\mathbf{i}$, $\mathbf{j}$ and $\mathbf{k}$ are the usual triad of unit vectors.

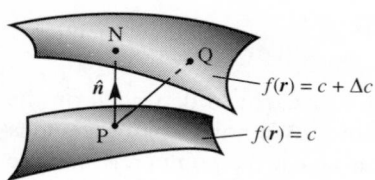

Figure 7.5 Adjacent level surfaces of $f(\mathbf{r})$.

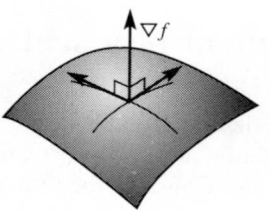

Figure 7.6 grad f acts normally to the surface $f(\mathbf{r}) = c$.

The symbol ∇ is called 'del' or sometimes 'nabla'. Then

$$\text{grad } f = \nabla f = \frac{\partial f}{\partial x}\mathbf{i} + \frac{\partial f}{\partial y}\mathbf{j} + \frac{\partial f}{\partial z}\mathbf{k} \equiv \left(\frac{\partial f}{\partial x}, \frac{\partial f}{\partial y}, \frac{\partial f}{\partial z}\right) \tag{7.1}$$

Thus we can calculate the rate of change of $f(x, y, z)$ along any direction we please. If $\hat{\mathbf{u}}$ is the unit vector in that direction then

$$(\text{grad } f) \cdot \hat{\mathbf{u}}$$

gives the required **directional derivative**, that is, the rate of change of $f(x, y, z)$ in the direction of $\hat{\mathbf{u}}$. Remembering that $\mathbf{a} \cdot \mathbf{b} = |a|\,|b| \cos\theta$, where θ is the angle between the two vectors, it follows that the rate of change of $f(x, y, z)$ is zero along directions perpendicular to grad f and is maximum along the direction parallel to grad f. Furthermore, grad f acts along the normal direction to the level surface of $f(x, y, z)$. We can see this by considering the level surfaces of the function corresponding to c and $c + \Delta c$, as shown in Figure 7.5. In going from P on the surface $f(\mathbf{r}) = c$ to any point Q on $f(\mathbf{r}) = c + \Delta c$, the increase in f is the same whatever point Q is chosen, but the distance PQ will be smallest, and hence the rate of change of $f(x, y, z)$ greatest, when Q lies on the normal $\hat{\mathbf{n}}$ to the surface at P. Thus grad f at P is in the direction of the outward normal $\hat{\mathbf{n}}$ to the surface $f(\mathbf{r}) = u$, and represents in magnitude and direction the greatest rate of increase of $f(x, y, z)$ with distance (Figure 7.6). It is frequently written as

$$\text{grad } f = \frac{\partial f}{\partial n}\hat{\mathbf{n}}$$

where $\partial f/\partial n$ is referred to as the normal derivative to the surface $f(\mathbf{r}) = c$.

EXAMPLE 7.4 Find grad f for $f(\mathbf{r}) = 3x^2 + 2y^2 + z^2$ at the point $(1, 2, 3)$. Hence calculate

(a) the directional derivative of $f(\mathbf{r})$ at $(1, 2, 3)$ in the direction of the unit vector $\frac{1}{3}(2, 2, 1)$;

(b) the maximum rate of change of the function at $(1, 2, 3)$ and its direction.

Solution Since $\partial f/\partial x = 6x$, $\partial f/\partial y = 4y$ and $\partial f/\partial z = 2z$, we have from (7.1) that

$$\text{grad } f = \nabla f = 6x\mathbf{i} + 4y\mathbf{j} + 2z\mathbf{k}$$

At the point $(1, 2, 3)$

$$\text{grad } f = 6i + 8j + 6k$$

Thus the directional derivative of $f(r)$ at $(1, 2, 3)$ in the direction of the unit vector $(\frac{2}{3}, \frac{2}{3}, \frac{1}{3})$ is

$$(6i + 8j + 6k) \cdot (\tfrac{2}{3}i + \tfrac{2}{3}j + \tfrac{1}{3}k) = \tfrac{34}{3}$$

The maximum rate of change of $f(r)$ at $(1, 2, 3)$ occurs along the direction parallel to grad f at $(1, 2, 3)$, that is, parallel to $(6, 8, 6)$. The unit vector in that direction is $(3, 4, 3)/\sqrt{34}$ and the maximum rate of change of $f(r)$ is $2\sqrt{34}$.

If a surface in three dimensions is specified by the equation $f(x, y, z) = c$, or equivalently $f(r) = c$, then grad f is a vector perpendicular to that surface. This enables us to calculate the normal vector at any point on the surface, and consequently to find the equation of the tangent plane at that point.

EXAMPLE 7.5   A paraboloid of revolution has equation $2z = x^2 + y^2$. Find the unit normal vector to the surface at the point $(1, 3, 5)$. Hence obtain the equation of the normal and the tangent plane to the surface at that point.

Solution   A vector normal to the surface $2z = x^2 + y^2$ is given by

$$\text{grad}\,(x^2 + y^2 - 2z) = 2xi + 2yj - 2k$$

At the point $(1, 3, 5)$ the vector has the value $2i + 6j - 2k$. Thus the normal unit vector at the point $(1, 3, 5)$ is $(i + 3j - k)/\sqrt{11}$. The equation of the line through $(1, 3, 5)$ in the direction of this normal is

$$\frac{x - 1}{1} = \frac{y - 3}{3} = \frac{z - 5}{-1}$$

and the equation of the tangent plane is

$$(1)(x - 1) + (3)(y - 3) + (-1)(z - 5) = 0$$

which simplifies to $x + 3y - z = 5$ (see Figure 7.7).

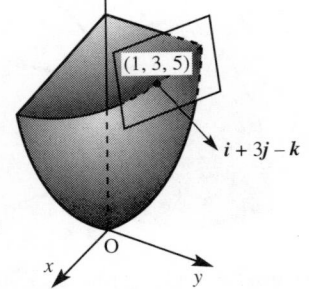

Figure 7.7 Tangent plane at $(1, 3, 5)$ to the paraboloid $2z = x^2 + y^2$.

The concept of the gradient of a scalar field occurs in many applications. The simplest, perhaps, is when $f(\mathbf{r})$ represents the potential in an electric field due to static charges. Then the electric force is in the direction of the greatest decrease of the potential. Its magnitude is equal to that rate of decrease, so that the force is given by $-\operatorname{grad} f$.

7.2.2 Exercises

11 Find grad f for $f(\mathbf{r}) = x^2yz^2$ at the point $(1, 2, 3)$. Hence calculate

(a) the directional derivative of $f(\mathbf{r})$ at $(1, 2, 3)$ in the direction of the vector $(-2, 3, -6)$;

(b) the maximum rate of change of the function at $(1, 2, 3)$ and its direction.

12 Find ∇f where $f(\mathbf{r})$ is

(a) $x^2 + y^2 - z$

(b) $z \tan^{-1}(y/x)$

(c) $e^{-x-y+z}/\sqrt{(x^3 + y^2)}$

(d) $xyz \sin\{\pi(x + y + z)\}$

13 Find the directional derivative of $f(\mathbf{r}) = x^2 + y^2 - z$ at the point $(1, 1, 2)$ in the direction of the vector $(4, 4, -2)$.

14 Find a unit normal to the surface $xy^2 - 3xz = -5$ at the point $(1, -2, 3)$.

15 If $\mathbf{r}$ is the usual position vector $\mathbf{r} = x\mathbf{i} + y\mathbf{j} + z\mathbf{k}$, with $|\mathbf{r}| = r$, evaluate

(a) ∇r \qquad (b) $\nabla\left(\dfrac{1}{r}\right)$

16 If $\nabla\phi = (2xy + z^2)\mathbf{i} + (x^2 + z)\mathbf{j} + (y + 2xz)\mathbf{k}$, find a possible value for ϕ.

17 Given the scalar function of position

$$\phi(x, y, z) = x^2y - 3xyz + z^3$$

find the value of grad ϕ at the point $(3, 1, 2)$. Also find the directional derivative of ϕ at this point in

the direction of the vector $(3, -2, 6)$, that is, in the direction $3\mathbf{i} - 2\mathbf{j} + 6\mathbf{k}$.

18 Find the angle between the surfaces $x^2 + y^2 + z^2 = 9$ and $z = x^2 + y^2 - 3$ at the point $(2, -1, 2)$.

19 Find the equations of the tangent plane and normal line to the surfaces

(a) $x^2 + 2y^2 + 3z^2 = 6$ at $(1, 1, 1)$

(b) $2x^2 + y^2 - z^2 = -3$ at $(1, 2, 3)$

(c) $x^2 + y^2 - z = 1$ at $(1, 2, 4)$.

20 (Spherical polar coordinates) When a function $f(\mathbf{r})$ is specified in polar coordinates, it is usual to express grad f in terms of the partial derivatives of f with respect to r, θ and ϕ and the unit vectors $\mathbf{u}_r$, $\mathbf{u}_\theta$ and $\mathbf{u}_\phi$ in the directions of increasing r, θ and ϕ as shown in Figure 7.8. Working from first principles, show that

$$\nabla f = \operatorname{grad} f = \frac{\partial f}{\partial r}\mathbf{u}_r + \frac{1}{r}\frac{\partial f}{\partial \theta}\mathbf{u}_\theta + \frac{1}{r\sin\theta}\frac{\partial f}{\partial \phi}\mathbf{u}_\phi$$

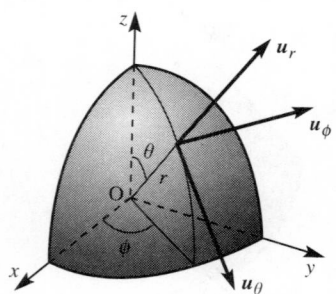

Figure 7.8 Unit vectors associated with spherical polar coordinates.

7.3 | Derivatives of a vector point function

When we come to consider the rate of change of a vector point function $F(r)$, we see that there are two ways of combining the vector operator ∇ with the vector F. Thus we have two cases to consider, namely

$$\nabla \cdot F \quad \text{and} \quad \nabla \times F$$

that is, the scalar product and vector product respectively. Both of these 'derivatives' have physical meanings, as we shall discover in the following sections. Roughly, if we picture a vector field as a fluid flow then at every point in the flow we need to measure the rate at which the field is flowing away from that point and also the amount of spin possessed by the particles of the fluid at that point. The two 'derivatives' given formally above provide these measures.

7.3.1 | Divergence of a vector field

Consider the steady motion of a fluid in a region R such that a particle of fluid instantaneously at the point r with coordinates (x, y, z) has a velocity $v(r)$ that is independent of time. To measure the flow away from this point in the fluid, we surround the point by an 'elementary' cuboid of side $(2\Delta x) \times (2\Delta y) \times (2\Delta z)$, as shown in Figure 7.9, and calculate the average flow out of the cuboid per unit volume.

The flow out of the cuboid is the sum of the flows across each of its six faces. Representing the velocity of the fluid at (x, y, z) by v, the flow out of the face ABCD is given approximately by

$$i \cdot v(x + \Delta x, y, z) \quad (4\Delta y\, \Delta z)$$

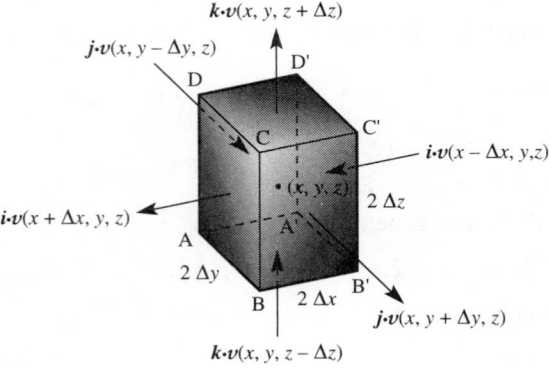

Figure 7.9 Flow out of a cuboid.

The flow out of the face $A'B'C'D'$ is given approximately by

$$-i \cdot v(x - \Delta x, y, z) \quad (4\,\Delta y\,\Delta z)$$

There are similar expressions for the remaining four faces of the cuboid, so that the total flow out of the latter is

$$i \cdot [v(x + \Delta x, y, z) - v(x - \Delta x, y, z)] \quad (4\,\Delta y\,\Delta z)$$
$$+ j \cdot [v(x, y + \Delta y, z) - v(x, y - \Delta y, z)] \quad (4\,\Delta x\,\Delta z)$$
$$+ k \cdot [v(x, y, z + \Delta z) - v(x, y, z - \Delta z)] \quad (4\,\Delta x\,\Delta y)$$

Dividing by the volume $8\,\Delta x\,\Delta y\,\Delta z$, and proceeding to the limit as $\Delta x, \Delta y, \Delta z \to 0$, we see that the flow away from the point (x, y, z) per unit time is given by

$$i \cdot \frac{\partial v}{\partial x} + j \cdot \frac{\partial v}{\partial y} + k \cdot \frac{\partial v}{\partial z}$$

This may be rewritten as

$$\left(i\frac{\partial}{\partial x} + j\frac{\partial}{\partial y} + k\frac{\partial}{\partial z} \right) \cdot v$$

or simply as $\mathbf{V} \cdot v$. Thus we see that the flow away from this point is given by the scalar product of the vector operator $\mathbf{V}$ with the velocity vector v. This is called the **divergence** of the vector v, and is written as div v. In terms of components,

$$\text{div } v = \left(i\frac{\partial}{\partial x} + j\frac{\partial}{\partial y} + k\frac{\partial}{\partial z} \right) \cdot (iv_1 + jv_2 + kv_3)$$

$$= \frac{\partial v_1}{\partial x} + \frac{\partial v_2}{\partial y} + \frac{\partial v_3}{\partial z} \tag{7.2}$$

When v is specified in this way, it is easy to compute its divergence. Note that the divergence of a vector field is a scalar quantity.

EXAMPLE 7.6 Find the divergence of the vector $v = (2x - y^2, 3z + x^2, 4y - z^2)$ at the point $(1, 2, 3)$.

Solution Here $v_1 = 2x - y^2$, $v_2 = 3z + x^2$ and $v_3 = 4y - z^2$, so that

$$\frac{\partial v_1}{\partial x} = 2, \qquad \frac{\partial v_2}{\partial y} = 0, \qquad \frac{\partial v_3}{\partial z} = -2z$$

Thus from (7.2), at a general point (x, y, z),

$$\text{div } v = \mathbf{V} \cdot v = 2 - 2z$$

so that at the point $(1, 2, 3)$

$$\mathbf{V} \cdot v = -4$$

A more general way of defining the divergence of a vector field $F(r)$ at the point r is to enclose the point in an elementary volume ΔV and find the flow or flux out of ΔV per unit volume. Thus

$$\text{div } F = \nabla \cdot F$$

$$= \lim_{\Delta V \to 0} \frac{\text{flow out of } \Delta V}{\Delta V}$$

A non-zero divergence at a point in a fluid measures the rate, per unit volume, at which the fluid is flowing away from or towards that point. That implies that either the density of the fluid is changing at the point or there is a source or sink of fluid there. In the case of a non-material vector field, for example in heat transfer, a non-zero divergence indicates a point of generation or absorption. When the divergence is everywhere zero, the flow entering any element of the space is exactly balanced by the outflow. This implies that the lines of flow of the field $F(r)$ where div $F = 0$ must either form closed curves or finish at boundaries or extend to infinity. Vectors satisfying this condition are sometimes termed **solenoidal**.

7.3.2   Exercises

21 Find div v where

(a) $v(r) = 3x^2 y i + z j + x^2 k$

(b) $v(r) = (3x + y)i + (2z + x)j + (z - 2y)k$

22 If $F = (2xy^2 + z^2)i + (3x^2 z^2 - y^2 z^3)j + (yz^2 - xz^3)k$, calculate div f at the point $(-1, 2, 3)$.

23 Find $\nabla(a \cdot r)$, $(a \cdot \nabla)r$ and $a(\nabla \cdot r)$, where a is a constant vector and, as usual, r is the position vector $r = (x, y, z)$.

24 The vector v is defined by $v = rr^{-1}$, where $r = (x, y, z)$ and $r = |r|$. Show that

$$\nabla(\nabla \cdot v) \equiv \text{grad div } v = -\frac{2}{r^3} r$$

25 Find the value of the constant λ such that the vector field defined by

$$F = (2x^2 y^2 + z^2)i + (3xy^3 - x^2 z)j + (\lambda xy^2 z + xy)k$$

is solenoidal.

26 (Spherical polar coordinates) Using the notation introduced in Exercise 20, show, working from first principles, that

$$\nabla \cdot v = \text{div } v = \frac{1}{r^2} \frac{\partial}{\partial r}(r^2 v_r) + \frac{1}{r \sin \theta} \frac{\partial}{\partial \theta}(v_\theta \sin \theta)$$

$$+ \frac{1}{r \sin \theta} \frac{\partial}{\partial \phi}(v_\phi)$$

where $v = v_r u_r + v_\theta u_\theta + v_\phi u_\phi$.

27 A force field F, defined by the inverse square law, is given by

$$F = r/r^3$$

Show that $\nabla \cdot F = 0$.

7.3.3   Curl of a vector field

It is clear from observations (for example by watching the movements of marked corks on water) that many fluid flows involve rotational motion of the fluid particles. Complete determination of this motion requires knowledge of the axis of rotation,

Figure 7.10 Flow
around a rectangle.

the rate of rotation and its sense (clockwise or anticlockwise). The measure of rotation is thus a vector quantity, which we shall find by calculating its x, y and z components separately. Consider the vector field $v(r)$. To find the flow around an axis in the x direction at the point r, we take an elementary rectangle surrounding r perpendicular to the x direction, as shown in Figure 7.10.

To measure the circulation around the point r about an axis parallel to the x direction, we calculate the flow around the elementary rectangle ABCD and divide by its area, giving

$$[v_2(x, y^*, z - \Delta z)(2\,\Delta y) + v_3(x, y + \Delta y, z^*)(2\,\Delta z)$$
$$- v_2(x, \tilde{y}, z + \Delta z)(2\,\Delta y) - v_3(x, y - \Delta y, \tilde{z})(2\,\Delta z)]/(4\,\Delta y\,\Delta z)$$

where $y^*, \tilde{y} \in (y - \Delta y, y + \Delta y)$, $z^*, \tilde{z} \in (z - \Delta z, z + \Delta z)$ and $v = v_1 i + v_2 j + v_3 k$. Rearranging, we obtain

$$- [v_2(x, \tilde{y}, z + \Delta z) - v_2(x, y^*, z - \Delta z)]/(2\,\Delta z)$$
$$+ [v_3(x, y + \Delta y, z^*) - v_3(x, y - \Delta y, \tilde{z})]/(2\,\Delta y)$$

Proceeding to the limit as $\Delta y\,\Delta z \to 0$, we obtain the x component of this vector as

$$\frac{\partial v_3}{\partial y} - \frac{\partial v_2}{\partial z}$$

By similar arguments, we obtain the y and z components as

$$\frac{\partial v_1}{\partial z} - \frac{\partial v_3}{\partial x}, \qquad \frac{\partial v_2}{\partial x} - \frac{\partial v_1}{\partial y}$$

respectively.

The vector measuring the rotation about a point in the fluid is called the **curl** of v:

$$\text{curl } v = \left(\frac{\partial v_3}{\partial y} - \frac{\partial v_2}{\partial z}\right) i + \left(\frac{\partial v_1}{\partial z} - \frac{\partial v_3}{\partial x}\right) j + \left(\frac{\partial v_2}{\partial x} - \frac{\partial v_1}{\partial y}\right) k$$

$$= \left(\frac{\partial v_3}{\partial y} - \frac{\partial v_2}{\partial z}, \frac{\partial v_1}{\partial z} - \frac{\partial v_3}{\partial x}, \frac{\partial v_2}{\partial x} - \frac{\partial v_1}{\partial y}\right) \qquad (7.3)$$

It may be written formally as

$$\text{curl } v = \begin{vmatrix} i & j & k \\ \dfrac{\partial}{\partial x} & \dfrac{\partial}{\partial y} & \dfrac{\partial}{\partial z} \\ v_1 & v_2 & v_3 \end{vmatrix} \qquad (7.4)$$

or more compactly as

$$\text{curl } v = \nabla \times v$$

EXAMPLE 7.7   Find the curl of the vector $v = (2x - y^2, 3z + x^2, 4y - z^2)$ at the point $(1, 2, 3)$.

Solution   Here $v_1 = 2x - y^2$, $v_2 = 3z + x^2$, $v_3 = 4y - z^2$, so that

$$\text{curl } v = \begin{vmatrix} i & j & k \\ \dfrac{\partial}{\partial x} & \dfrac{\partial}{\partial y} & \dfrac{\partial}{\partial z} \\ 2x - y^2 & 3z + x^2 & 4y - z^2 \end{vmatrix}$$

$$= i\left[\frac{\partial}{\partial y}(4y - z^2) - \frac{\partial}{\partial z}(3z + x^2) \right]$$

$$- j\left[\frac{\partial}{\partial x}(4y - z^2) - \frac{\partial}{\partial z}(2x - y^2) \right]$$

$$+ k\left[\frac{\partial}{\partial x}(3z + x^2) - \frac{\partial}{\partial y}(2x - y^2) \right]$$

$$= i(4 - 3) - j(0 - 0) + k(2x + 2y)$$

$$= i + 2(x + y)k$$

Thus, at the point $(1, 2, 3)$, $\nabla \times v = (1, 0, 6)$.

Figure 7.11
Circulation around
the element ΔS.

More generally, the component of the curl of a vector field $F(r)$ in the direction of the unit vector $\hat{n}$ at a point L is found by enclosing L by an elementary area ΔS that is perpendicular to $\hat{n}$, as in Figure 7.11, and calculating the flow around ΔS per unit area. Thus

$$(\text{curl } F) \cdot \hat{n} = \lim_{\Delta S \to 0} \frac{\text{flow round } \Delta S}{\Delta S}$$

Another way of visualizing the meaning of the curl of a vector is to consider the motion of a rigid body. We can describe such motion by specifying the angular velocity ω of the body about an axis OA, where O is a fixed point in the body together with the translational (linear) velocity v of O itself. Then at any point P in the body the velocity u is given by

$$u = v + \omega \times r$$

as shown in Figure 7.12. Here v and ω are independent of (x, y, z). Thus

$$\text{curl } u = \text{curl } v + \text{curl}(\omega \times r)$$

$$= 0 + \text{curl}(\omega \times r)$$

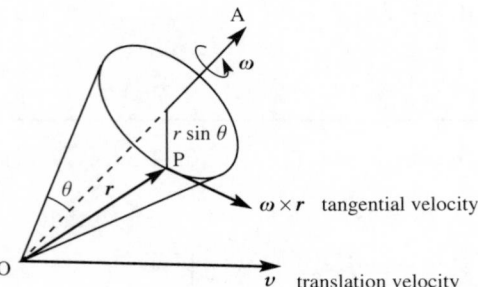

Figure 7.12 Rotation
of a rigid body.

The vector $\boldsymbol{\omega} \times \boldsymbol{r}$ is given by

$$\boldsymbol{\omega} \times \boldsymbol{r} = (\omega_1, \omega_2, \omega_3) \times (x, y, z)$$

$$= (\omega_2 z - \omega_3 y)\boldsymbol{i} + (\omega_3 x - \omega_1 z)\boldsymbol{j} + (\omega_1 y - \omega_2 x)\boldsymbol{k}$$

and

$$\text{curl}\,(\boldsymbol{\omega} \times \boldsymbol{r}) = \begin{vmatrix} \boldsymbol{i} & \boldsymbol{j} & \boldsymbol{k} \\ \dfrac{\partial}{\partial x} & \dfrac{\partial}{\partial y} & \dfrac{\partial}{\partial z} \\ \omega_2 z - \omega_3 y & \omega_3 x - \omega_1 z & \omega_1 y - \omega_2 x \end{vmatrix}$$

$$= 2\omega_1 \boldsymbol{i} + 2\omega_2 \boldsymbol{j} + 2\omega_3 \boldsymbol{k}$$

$$= 2\boldsymbol{\omega}$$

Thus

$$\text{curl}\,\boldsymbol{u} = 2\boldsymbol{\omega}$$

that is,

$$\boldsymbol{\omega} = \tfrac{1}{2}\,\text{curl}\,\boldsymbol{u}$$

Hence when any rigid body is in motion, the curl of its linear velocity at any point is twice its angular velocity in magnitude and has the same direction.

Applying this result to the motion of a fluid, we can see by regarding particles of the fluid as miniature bodies that when the curl of the velocity is zero there is no rotation of the particle, and the motion is said to be **curl-free** or **irrotational**. When the curl is non-zero, the motion is **rotational**.

7.3.4 Exercises

28 Find $\boldsymbol{u} = \text{curl}\,\boldsymbol{v}$ when $\boldsymbol{v} = (3xz^2, -yz, x + 2z)$.

29 A vector field is defined by $\boldsymbol{v} = (yz, xz, xy)$. Show that curl $\boldsymbol{v} = 0$.

30 Show that if $\boldsymbol{v} = (2x + yz, 2y + zx, 2z + xy)$ then curl $\boldsymbol{v} = 0$, and find $f(\boldsymbol{r})$ such that $\boldsymbol{v} = \text{grad}\, f$.

31 By evaluating each term separately, verify the identity

$$\mathbf{\nabla} \times (f\mathbf{v}) = f(\mathbf{\nabla} \times \mathbf{v}) + (\mathbf{\nabla}f) \times \mathbf{v}$$

for $f(\mathbf{r}) = x^3 - y$ and $\mathbf{v}(\mathbf{r}) = (z, 0, -x)$.

32 Find constants a, b and c such that the vector field defined by

$$\mathbf{F} = (4xy + az^3)\mathbf{i} + (bx^2 + 3z)\mathbf{j} + (6xz^2 + cy)\mathbf{k}$$

is irrotational. With these values of a, b and c, determine a scalar function $\phi(x, y, z)$ such that $\mathbf{F} = \mathbf{\nabla}\phi$.

33 If $\mathbf{v} = -y\mathbf{i} + x\mathbf{j} + xyz\mathbf{k}$ is the velocity vector of a fluid, find the local value of the angular velocity at the point $(1, 3, 2)$.

34 If the velocity of a fluid at the point (x, y, z) is given by

$$\mathbf{v} = (ax + by)\mathbf{i} + (cx + dy)\mathbf{j}$$

find the conditions on the constants a, b, c and d in order that

$$\text{div }\mathbf{v} = 0, \qquad \text{curl }\mathbf{v} = 0$$

Verify that in this case

$$\mathbf{v} = \tfrac{1}{2}\,\text{grad}\,(ax^2 + 2bxy - ay^2)$$

35 (Spherical polar coordinates) Using the notation introduced in Exercise 20, show that

$$\mathbf{\nabla} \times \mathbf{v} = \text{curl }\mathbf{v}$$

$$= \frac{1}{r^2 \sin\theta} \begin{vmatrix} \mathbf{u}_r & r\mathbf{u}_\theta & r\sin\theta\,\mathbf{u}_\phi \\ \dfrac{\partial}{\partial r} & \dfrac{\partial}{\partial \theta} & \dfrac{\partial}{\partial \phi} \\ v_r & rv_\theta & r\sin\theta\,v_\phi \end{vmatrix}$$

7.3.5 Further properties of the vector operator $\mathbf{\nabla}$

So far we have used the vector operator in three ways:

$$\mathbf{\nabla}f = \text{grad}\,f = \frac{\partial f}{\partial x}\mathbf{i} + \frac{\partial f}{\partial y}\mathbf{j} + \frac{\partial f}{\partial z}\mathbf{k}, \qquad f(\mathbf{r}) \text{ a scalar field}$$

$$\mathbf{\nabla}\cdot\mathbf{F} = \text{div}\,\mathbf{F} = \frac{\partial f_1}{\partial x} + \frac{\partial f_2}{\partial y} + \frac{\partial f_3}{\partial z}, \qquad \mathbf{F}(\mathbf{r}) \text{ a vector field}$$

$$\mathbf{\nabla}\times\mathbf{F} = \text{curl}\,\mathbf{F}$$

$$= \left(\frac{\partial f_3}{\partial y} - \frac{\partial f_2}{\partial z}\right)\mathbf{i} + \left(\frac{\partial f_1}{\partial z} - \frac{\partial f_3}{\partial x}\right)\mathbf{j} + \left(\frac{\partial f_2}{\partial x} - \frac{\partial f_1}{\partial y}\right)\mathbf{k} \qquad \mathbf{F}(\mathbf{r}) \text{ a vector field}$$

A further application is in determining the directional derivative of a vector field:

$$\mathbf{a}\cdot\mathbf{\nabla}\mathbf{F} = \left(a_1\frac{\partial}{\partial x} + a_2\frac{\partial}{\partial y} + a_3\frac{\partial}{\partial z}\right)\mathbf{F}$$

$$= \left(a_1\frac{\partial f_1}{\partial x} + a_2\frac{\partial f_1}{\partial y} + a_3\frac{\partial f_1}{\partial z}\right)\mathbf{i} + \left(a_1\frac{\partial f_2}{\partial x} + a_2\frac{\partial f_2}{\partial y} + a_3\frac{\partial f_2}{\partial z}\right)\mathbf{j}$$

$$+ \left(a_1\frac{\partial f_3}{\partial x} + a_2\frac{\partial f_3}{\partial y} + a_3\frac{\partial f_3}{\partial z}\right)\mathbf{k}$$

The ordinary rules of differentiation carry over to this vector differential operator, but they have to be applied with care, using the rules of vector algebra. For non-orthogonal coordinate systems a specialist textbook should be consulted. Thus for scalar fields $f(r)$, $g(r)$ and vector fields $u(r)$, $v(r)$ we have

$$\mathbf{V}[f(g(r))] = \frac{df}{dg}\mathbf{V}g \tag{7.5a}$$

$$\mathbf{V}[f(r)g(r)] = g(r)\mathbf{V}f(r) + f(r)\mathbf{V}g(r) \tag{7.5b}$$

$$\mathbf{V}[u(r) \cdot v(r)] = v \times (\mathbf{V} \times u) + u \times (\mathbf{V} \times v) + (v \cdot \mathbf{V})u + (u \cdot \mathbf{V})v \tag{7.5c}$$

$$\mathbf{V} \cdot [f(r)u(r)] = u \cdot \mathbf{V}f + f\mathbf{V} \cdot u \tag{7.5d}$$

$$\mathbf{V} \times [f(r)u(r)] = (\mathbf{V}f) \times u + f\mathbf{V} \times u \tag{7.5e}$$

$$\mathbf{V} \cdot [u(r) \times v(r)] = v \cdot (\mathbf{V} \times u) - u \cdot (\mathbf{V} \times v) \tag{7.5f}$$

$$\mathbf{V} \times [u(r) \times v(r)] = (v \cdot \mathbf{V})u - v(\mathbf{V} \cdot u) - (u \cdot \mathbf{V})v + u(\mathbf{V} \cdot v) \tag{7.5g}$$

Higher-order derivatives can also be formed, giving the following:

$$\text{div}[\text{grad} f(r)] = \mathbf{V} \cdot \mathbf{V}f = \frac{\partial^2 f}{\partial x^2} + \frac{\partial^2 f}{\partial y^2} + \frac{\partial^2 f}{\partial z^2} = \nabla^2 f \tag{7.6}$$

where ∇^2 is called the **Laplacian operator** (sometimes denoted by $\triangle$);

$$\text{curl}[\text{grad} f(r)] = \mathbf{V} \times \mathbf{V}f(r) \equiv 0 \tag{7.7}$$

since

$$\mathbf{V} \times \mathbf{V}f = \left(\frac{\partial^2 f}{\partial y\,\partial z} - \frac{\partial^2 f}{\partial z\,\partial y}\right)i + \left(\frac{\partial^2 f}{\partial z\,\partial x} - \frac{\partial^2 f}{\partial x\,\partial z}\right)j + \left(\frac{\partial^2 f}{\partial x\,\partial y} - \frac{\partial^2 f}{\partial y\,\partial x}\right)k$$

$$= 0$$

when all second-order derivatives of $f(r)$ are continuous;

$$\text{div}[\text{curl} v(r)] = \mathbf{V} \cdot (\mathbf{V} \times v) \equiv 0 \tag{7.8}$$

since

$$\frac{\partial}{\partial x}\left(\frac{\partial v_3}{\partial y} - \frac{\partial v_2}{\partial z}\right) + \frac{\partial}{\partial y}\left(\frac{\partial v_1}{\partial z} - \frac{\partial v_3}{\partial x}\right) + \frac{\partial}{\partial z}\left(\frac{\partial v_2}{\partial x} - \frac{\partial v_1}{\partial y}\right) = 0$$

$$\text{grad}(\text{div} v) = \mathbf{V}(\mathbf{V} \cdot v) = \left(i\frac{\partial}{\partial x} + j\frac{\partial}{\partial y} + k\frac{\partial}{\partial z}\right)\left(\frac{\partial v_1}{\partial x} + \frac{\partial v_2}{\partial y} + \frac{\partial v_3}{\partial z}\right) \tag{7.9}$$

$$\nabla^2 v = \left(\frac{\partial^2}{\partial x^2} + \frac{\partial^2}{\partial y^2} + \frac{\partial^2}{\partial z^2}\right)(v_1 i + v_2 j + v_3 k) \tag{7.10}$$

$$\text{curl}[\text{curl} v(r)] = \mathbf{V} \times (\mathbf{V} \times v) = \mathbf{V}(\mathbf{V} \cdot v) - \nabla^2 v \tag{7.11}$$

EXAMPLE 7.8 Verify that $\mathbf{V} \times (\mathbf{V} \times v) = \mathbf{V}(\mathbf{V} \cdot v) - \mathbf{V}^2 v$ for the vector field $v = (3xz^2, -yz, x + 2z)$.

Solution

$$\mathbf{V} \times v = \begin{vmatrix} i & j & k \\ \dfrac{\partial}{\partial x} & \dfrac{\partial}{\partial y} & \dfrac{\partial}{\partial z} \\ 3xz^2 & -yz & x+2z \end{vmatrix} = (y, 6xz - 1, 0)$$

$$\mathbf{V} \times (\mathbf{V} \times v) = \begin{vmatrix} i & j & k \\ \dfrac{\partial}{\partial x} & \dfrac{\partial}{\partial y} & \dfrac{\partial}{\partial z} \\ y & 6xz - 1 & 0 \end{vmatrix} = (-6x, 0, 6z - 1)$$

$$\mathbf{V} \cdot v = \frac{\partial}{\partial x}(3xz^2) + \frac{\partial}{\partial y}(-yz) + \frac{\partial}{\partial z}(x + 2z)$$

$$= 3z^2 - z + 2$$

$$\mathbf{V}(\mathbf{V} \cdot v) = (0, 0, 6z - 1)$$

$$\mathbf{V}^2 v = (\mathbf{V}^2(3xz^2), \mathbf{V}^2(-yz), \mathbf{V}^2(x + 2z))$$

$$= (6x, 0, 0)$$

Thus

$$\mathbf{V}(\mathbf{V} \cdot v) - \mathbf{V}^2 v = (-6x, 0, 6z - 1)$$

$$= \mathbf{V} \times (\mathbf{V} \times v)$$

Similar verifications for other identities are suggested in Exercises 7.3.6.

EXAMPLE 7.9 Maxwell's equations in free space may be written, in Gaussian units, as

$$\text{div } H = 0, \qquad \text{div } E = 0$$

$$\mathbf{V} \times H = \frac{1}{c} \frac{\partial E}{\partial t}, \qquad \mathbf{V} \times E = -\frac{1}{c} \frac{\partial H}{\partial t}$$

where c is the velocity of light (assumed constant). Show that these equations are satisfied by

$$H = \frac{1}{c} \frac{\partial}{\partial t} \text{grad } \phi \times k, \qquad E = -k \frac{1}{c^2} \frac{\partial^2 \phi}{\partial t^2} + \frac{\partial}{\partial z} \text{grad } \phi$$

where ϕ satisfies

$$\nabla^2 \phi = \frac{1}{c^2} \frac{\partial^2 \phi}{\partial t^2}$$

and k is a unit vector along the z axis.

Solution   (a) $H = \dfrac{1}{c} \dfrac{\partial}{\partial t} \operatorname{grad} \phi \times k$

gives

$$\operatorname{div} H = \frac{1}{c} \frac{\partial}{\partial t} \operatorname{div}(\operatorname{grad}\phi \times k)$$

$$= \frac{1}{c} \frac{\partial}{\partial t} [k \cdot \operatorname{curl}(\operatorname{grad}\phi) - (\operatorname{grad}\phi) \cdot \operatorname{curl} k], \qquad \text{from (7.5f)}$$

By (7.6), $\operatorname{curl}(\operatorname{grad}\phi) = 0$, and since k is a constant vector, $\operatorname{curl} k = 0$, so that

$$\operatorname{div} H = 0$$

(b) $E = -\dfrac{k}{c^2} \dfrac{\partial^2 \phi}{\partial t^2} + \dfrac{\partial}{\partial z} \operatorname{grad} \phi$

gives

$$\operatorname{div} E = -\frac{1}{c^2} \operatorname{div}\left(k \frac{\partial^2 \phi}{\partial t^2}\right) + \frac{\partial}{\partial z} \operatorname{div} \operatorname{grad} \phi$$

$$= -\frac{1}{c^2} \frac{\partial}{\partial z}\left(\frac{\partial^2 \phi}{\partial t^2}\right) + \frac{\partial}{\partial z}(\nabla^2 \phi), \qquad \text{by (7.6)}$$

$$= \frac{\partial}{\partial z}\left(\nabla^2 \phi - \frac{1}{c^2} \frac{\partial^2 \phi}{\partial t^2}\right)$$

and since $\nabla^2 \phi = (1/c^2)\partial^2 \phi/\partial t^2$, we have

$$\operatorname{div} E = 0$$

(c) $\operatorname{curl} H = \dfrac{1}{c} \dfrac{\partial}{\partial t} \operatorname{curl}(\operatorname{grad} \phi \times k)$

$$= \frac{1}{c} \frac{\partial}{\partial t} [(k \cdot \nabla) \operatorname{grad} \phi$$

$$- k(\operatorname{div} \operatorname{grad} \phi) - (\operatorname{grad}\phi \cdot \nabla)k + \operatorname{grad}\phi(\nabla \cdot k)], \qquad \text{from (7.5g)}$$

$$= \frac{1}{c} \frac{\partial}{\partial t}\left(\frac{\partial}{\partial z} \operatorname{grad} \phi - k \nabla^2 \phi\right), \qquad \text{since } k \text{ is a constant vector}$$

$$= \frac{1}{c} \frac{\partial E}{\partial t}$$

(d) $\text{curl } E = -\dfrac{1}{c^2}\text{curl}\left(k\dfrac{\partial^2\phi}{\partial t^2}\right) + \dfrac{\partial}{\partial z}\text{curl grad }\phi$

$$= -\frac{1}{c^2}\begin{vmatrix} i & j & k \\[4pt] \dfrac{\partial}{\partial x} & \dfrac{\partial}{\partial y} & \dfrac{\partial}{\partial z} \\[8pt] 0 & 0 & \dfrac{\partial^2\phi}{\partial t^2} \end{vmatrix}, \qquad \text{since curl grad }\phi = 0 \text{ by (7.7)}$$

$$= -\frac{1}{c^2}\left(i\frac{\partial^3\phi}{\partial y\,\partial t^2} - j\frac{\partial^3\phi}{\partial x\,\partial t^2}\right)$$

Also,

$$\frac{\partial H}{\partial t} = \frac{1}{c}\frac{\partial^2}{\partial t^2}\text{grad }\phi \times k$$

$$= \frac{1}{c}\frac{\partial^2}{\partial t^2}(\text{grad }\phi \times k), \qquad \text{since } k \text{ is a constant vector}$$

$$= \frac{1}{c}\frac{\partial^2}{\partial t^2}\left[\left(\frac{\partial\phi}{\partial x}i + \frac{\partial\phi}{\partial y}j + \frac{\partial\phi}{\partial z}k\right) \times k\right]$$

$$= \frac{1}{c}\frac{\partial^2}{\partial t^2}\left(i\frac{\partial\phi}{\partial y} - j\frac{\partial\phi}{\partial x}\right)$$

$$= \frac{1}{c}\left(i\frac{\partial^3\phi}{\partial y\,\partial t^2} - j\frac{\partial^3\phi}{\partial x\,\partial t^2}\right)$$

so that we have

$$\nabla \times E = -\frac{1}{c}\frac{\partial H}{\partial t}$$

7.3.6   Exercises

36 Show that if g is a function of $r = (x, y, z)$ then

$$\text{grad } g = \frac{1}{r}\frac{dg}{dr}r$$

Deduce that if u is a vector field then

$$\text{div}\,[(u \times r)g] = (r \cdot \text{curl } u)g$$

37 For $\phi(x, y, z) = x^2y^2z^3$ and
$F(x, y, z) = x^2yi + xy^2zj - yz^2k$ determine

(a) $\nabla^2\phi$ (b) grad div F (c) curl curl F

38 Show that if a is a constant vector and r is the position vector $r = (x, y, z)$ then

$$\text{div}\,\{\text{grad}\,[(r \cdot r)(r \cdot a)]\} = 10(r \cdot a)$$

39 Verify the identity

$$\nabla^2v = \text{grad div } v - \text{curl curl } v$$

for the vector field $v = x^2y(xi + yj + zk)$.

40 Verify, by calculating each term separately, the identities

$$\operatorname{div}(u \times v) = v \cdot \operatorname{curl} u - u \cdot \operatorname{curl} v$$
$$\operatorname{curl}(u \times v) = u \operatorname{div} v - v \operatorname{div} u + (v \cdot \nabla)u - (u \cdot \nabla)v$$

when $u = xyj + xzk$ and $v = xyi + yzk$.

41 If r is the usual position vector $r = (x, y, z)$, show that

(a) $\operatorname{div} \operatorname{grad} \left(\dfrac{1}{r} \right) = 0$

(b) $\operatorname{curl} \left[k \times \operatorname{grad} \left(\dfrac{1}{r} \right) \right] + \operatorname{grad} \left[k \cdot \operatorname{grad} \left(\dfrac{1}{r} \right) \right] = 0$

42 If A is a constant vector and r is the position vector $r = (x, y, z)$, show that

(a) $\operatorname{grad} \left(\dfrac{A \cdot r}{r^3} \right) = \dfrac{A}{r^3} - 3 \dfrac{(A \cdot r)}{r^5} r$

(b) $\operatorname{curl} \left(\dfrac{A \times r}{r^3} \right) = \dfrac{2A}{r^3} + \dfrac{3}{r^5}(A \times r) \times r$

43 If r is the position vector $r = (x, y, z)$, and a and b are constant vectors, show that

(a) $\nabla \times r = 0$

(b) $(a \cdot \nabla)r = a$

(c) $\nabla \times [(a \cdot r)b - (b \cdot r)a] = 2(a \times b)$

(d) $\nabla \cdot [(a \cdot r)b - (b \cdot r)a] = 0$

44 By evaluating $\nabla \cdot (\nabla f)$, show that the Laplacian in spherical polar coordinates (see Exercise 20) is given by

$$\nabla^2 f = \frac{1}{r^2} \frac{\partial}{\partial r} \left(r^2 \frac{\partial f}{\partial r} \right) + \frac{1}{r^2 \sin^2 \theta} \frac{\partial^2 f}{\partial \phi^2}$$
$$+ \frac{1}{r^2 \sin \theta} \frac{\partial}{\partial \theta} \left(\sin \theta \frac{\partial f}{\partial \theta} \right)$$

45 Show that Maxwell's equations in free space, namely

$$\operatorname{div} H = 0, \qquad \operatorname{div} E = 0$$
$$\nabla \times H = \frac{1}{c} \frac{\partial E}{\partial t}, \qquad \nabla \times E = -\frac{1}{c} \frac{\partial H}{\partial t}$$

are satisfied by

$$H = \frac{1}{c} \operatorname{curl} \frac{\partial Z}{\partial t}$$
$$E = \operatorname{curl} \operatorname{curl} Z$$

where the Hertzian vector Z satisfies

$$\nabla^2 Z = \frac{1}{c} \frac{\partial^2 Z}{\partial t^2}$$

7.4 Topics in integration

In the previous sections we saw how the idea of the differentiation of a function of a single variable is generalized to include scalar and vector point functions. We now turn to the inverse process of integration. This was discussed in Chapters 7–9 of *Modern Engineering Mathematics*. The fundamental idea of an integral is that of summing all the constituent parts that make a whole. More formally, we define the integral of a function $f(x)$ by

$$\int_a^b f(x)\, dx = \lim_{\substack{n \to \infty \\ \text{all} \, \Delta x_i \to 0}} \sum_{i=1}^n f(\tilde{x}_i)\, \Delta x_i$$

where $a = x_0 < x_1 < x_2 < \ldots < x_{n-1} < x_n = b$, $\Delta x_i = x_i - x_{i-1}$ and $x_{i-1} \leqslant \tilde{x}_i \leqslant x_i$. Geometrically, we can interpret this integral as the area between the graph $y = f(x)$, the x axis and the lines $x = a$ and $x = b$, as illustrated in Figure 7.13.

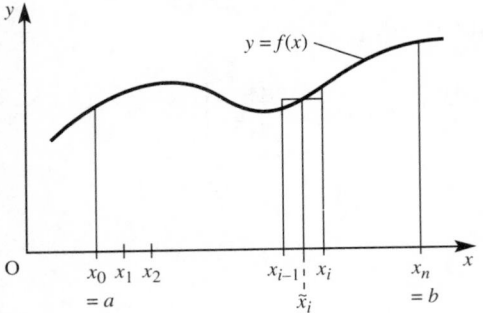

Figure 7.13 Definite integral as an area.

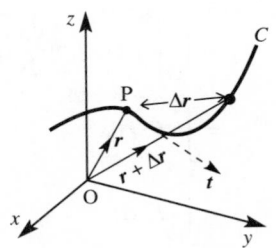

Figure 7.14 Element of arclength.

7.4.1   Line integrals

Consider the integral

$$\int_b^a f(x, y)\,dx, \qquad \text{where } y = g(x)$$

This can be evaluated in the usual way by first substituting for y in terms of x in the integrand and then performing the integration

$$\int_a^b f(x, g(x))\,dx$$

Clearly the value of the integral will, in general, depend on the function $y = g(x)$. It may be interpreted as evaluating the integral $\int_a^b f(x, y)\,dx$ along the curve $y = g(x)$. Note, however, that the integral is *not* in this case the area under the curve. This type of integral is called a **line integral**. There are many different types of such integrals, as described in detail in Section 9.5.1 of *Modern Engineering Mathematics*. In many practical problems line integrals involving vectors occur. Let $P(\boldsymbol{r})$ be a point on a curve C in three dimensions, and let $\boldsymbol{t}$ be the unit tangent vector at P in the sense of the integration (that is, in the sense of increasing arclength s), as indicated in Figure 7.14. Then $\boldsymbol{t}\,ds$ is the vector element of arc at P, and

$$\boldsymbol{t}\,ds = \left[\frac{dx}{ds}\boldsymbol{i} + \frac{dy}{ds}\boldsymbol{j} + \frac{dz}{ds}\boldsymbol{k}\right]ds$$

$$= dx\,\boldsymbol{i} + dy\,\boldsymbol{j} + dz\,\boldsymbol{k}$$

$$= d\boldsymbol{r}$$

If $f_1(x, y, z)$, $f_2(x, y, z)$ and $f_3(x, y, z)$ are the scalar components of a vector field $\boldsymbol{F}(\boldsymbol{r})$ then

$$\int_C [f_1(x, y, z)\,dx + f_2(x, y, z)\,dy + f_3(x, y, z)\,dz]$$

$$= \int_C \left[f_1(x, y, z)\frac{dx}{ds}\,ds + f_2(x, y, z)\frac{dy}{ds}\,ds + f_3(x, y, z)\frac{dz}{ds}\,ds \right]$$

$$= \int_C \boldsymbol{F} \cdot \boldsymbol{t}\,ds$$

$$= \int_C \boldsymbol{F} \cdot d\boldsymbol{r}$$

Thus, given a vector field $\boldsymbol{F}(\boldsymbol{r})$, we can evaluate line integrals of the form $\int_C \boldsymbol{F} \cdot d\boldsymbol{r}$. In order to make it clear that we are integrating along a curve, the line integral is sometimes written as $\int_C \boldsymbol{F} \cdot d\boldsymbol{s}$, where $d\boldsymbol{s} = d\boldsymbol{r}$ (some authors use $d\boldsymbol{l}$ instead of $d\boldsymbol{s}$ in order to avoid confusion with $d\boldsymbol{S}$, the element of surface area). In a similar manner we can evaluate line integrals of the form $\int_C \boldsymbol{F} \times d\boldsymbol{r}$.

EXAMPLE 7.10   Calculate (a) $\int_C \boldsymbol{F} \cdot d\boldsymbol{r}$ and (b) $\int_C \boldsymbol{F} \times d\boldsymbol{r}$, where C is the part of the spiral $\boldsymbol{r} = (a\cos\theta, a\sin\theta, a\theta)$ corresponding to $0 \leqslant \theta \leqslant \frac{1}{2}\pi$, and $\boldsymbol{F} = r^2\boldsymbol{i}$.

Solution   The curve C is illustrated in Figure 7.15.

(a) Since $\boldsymbol{r} = a\cos\theta\,\boldsymbol{i} + a\sin\theta\,\boldsymbol{j} + a\theta\boldsymbol{k}$,

$$d\boldsymbol{r} = -a\sin\theta\,d\theta\boldsymbol{i} + a\cos\theta\,d\theta\boldsymbol{j} + a\,d\theta\boldsymbol{k}$$

so that

$$\boldsymbol{F} \cdot d\boldsymbol{r} = r^2\boldsymbol{i} \cdot (-a\sin\theta\,d\theta\boldsymbol{i} + a\cos\theta\,d\theta\boldsymbol{j} + a\,d\theta\boldsymbol{k})$$

$$= -ar^2\sin\theta\,d\theta$$

$$= -a^3(\cos^2\theta + \sin^2\theta + \theta^2)\sin\theta\,d\theta = -a^3(1 + \theta^2)\sin\theta\,d\theta$$

Figure 7.15 The spiral $\boldsymbol{r} = (a\cos\theta, a\sin\theta, a\theta)$.

since $r = |\boldsymbol{r}| = \sqrt{(a^2\cos^2\theta + a^2\sin^2\theta + a^2\theta^2)}$. Thus,

$$\int_C \boldsymbol{F} \cdot d\boldsymbol{r} = -a^3 \int_0^{\pi/2} (1 + \theta^2)\sin\theta\,d\theta$$

$$= -a^3[\cos\theta + 2\theta\sin\theta - \theta^2\cos\theta]_0^{\pi/2}, \text{ using integration by parts}$$

$$= -a^3(\pi - 1)$$

(b) $\boldsymbol{F} \times d\boldsymbol{r} = \begin{vmatrix} \boldsymbol{i} & \boldsymbol{j} & \boldsymbol{k} \\ r^2 & 0 & 0 \\ -a\sin\theta\,d\theta & a\cos\theta\,d\theta & a\,d\theta \end{vmatrix}$

$$= -ar^2\,d\theta\boldsymbol{j} + ar^2\cos\theta\,d\theta\boldsymbol{k}$$

$$= -a^3(1 + \theta^2)\,d\theta\boldsymbol{j} + a^3(1 + \theta^2)\cos\theta\,d\theta\boldsymbol{k}$$

so that

$$\int_C F \times dr = -ja^3 \int_0^{\pi/2} (1 + \theta^2) \, d\theta + ka^3 \int_0^{\pi/2} (1 + \theta^2) \cos \theta \, d\theta$$

$$= -\frac{\pi a^3}{24}(12 + \pi^2)j + \frac{a^3}{4}(\pi^2 - 4)k$$

The work done as the point of application of a force F moves along a given path C as illustrated in Figure 7.16 can be expressed as a line integral. The work done as the point of application moves from P(r) to P'($r + \delta r$), where $\overrightarrow{PP'} = dr$, is $dW = |dr| \, |F| \cos \theta = F \cdot dr$. Hence the total work done as P goes from A to B is

$$W = \int_C F \cdot dr$$

Figure 7.16 Work done by a force F.

In general, W depends on the path chosen. If, however, $F(r)$ is such that $F(r) \cdot dr$ is an exact differential, say $-dU$, then $W = \int_C -dU = U_A - U_B$, which depends only on A and B and is the same for all paths C joining A and B. Such a force is a **conservative** force, and $U(r)$ is its potential energy, with $F(r) = -\text{grad } U$. Forces that do not have this property are said to be **dissipative** or **non-conservative**.

Similarly, if $v(r)$ represents the velocity field of a fluid then $\oint_C v \cdot dr$ is the flow around the closed curve C in unit time. This is sometimes termed the **net circulation integral** of v. If $\oint_C v \cdot dr = 0$ then the fluid is curl-free or irrotational, and in this case v has a potential function $\phi(r)$ such that $v = -\text{grad } \phi$.

7.4.2   Exercises

46 Evaluate $\int y \, ds$ along the parabola $y = 2\sqrt{x}$ from A($3, 2\sqrt{3}$) to B($24, 4\sqrt{6}$).

47 Evaluate $\int_A^B [2xy \, dx + (x^2 - y^2) \, dy]$ along the arc of the circle $x^2 + y^2 = 1$ in the first quadrant from A($1, 0$) to B($0, 1$).

48 Evaluate the integral $\int_C V \cdot dr$, where $V = (2yz + 3x^2, y^2 + 4xz, 2z^2 + 6xy)$, and C is the curve with parametric equations $x = t^3, y = t^2, z = t$ joining the points $(0, 0, 0)$ and $(1, 1, 1)$.

49 If $A = (2y + 3)i + xzj + (yz - x)k$, evaluate $\int_C A \cdot dr$ along the following paths C:

(a) $x = 2t^2, y = t, z = t^3$ from $t = 0$ to $t = 1$;

(b) the straight lines from $(0, 0, 0)$ to $(0, 0, 1)$, then to $(0, 1, 1)$ and then to $(2, 1, 1)$;

(c) the straight line joining $(0, 0, 0)$ to $(2, 1, 1)$

50 Prove that $F = (y^2 \cos x + z^3)i + (2y \sin x - 4)j + (3xz^2 + z)k$ is a conservative force field. Hence find the work done in moving an object in this field from $(0, 1, -1)$ to $(\pi/2, -1, 2)$.

51 Find the work done in moving a particle in the force field $F = 3x^2i + (2xz - y)j + zk$ along

(a) the curve defined by $x^2 = 4y, 3x^3 = 8z$ from $x = 0$ to $x = 2$;

(b) the straight line from $(0, 0, 0)$ to $(2, 1, 3)$.

Does this mean that F is a conservative force? Give reasons for your answer.

52 Prove that the vector field $F = (3x^2 - y, 2yz^2 - x, 2y^2z)$ is conservative, but not solenoidal. Hence evaluate the scalar line integral $\int_C F \cdot dr$ along any curve C joining the point $(0, 0, 0)$ to the point $(1, 2, 3)$.

53 If $F = xy\mathbf{i} - z\mathbf{j} + x^2\mathbf{k}$ and C is the curve $x = t^2$, $y = 2t, z = t^3$ from $t = 0$ to $t = 1$, evaluate the vector line integral $\int_C F \times d\mathbf{r}$.

54 If $A = (3x + y, -x, y - z)$ and $B = (2, -3, 1)$ evaluate the line integral $\oint_C (A \times B) \times d\mathbf{r}$ around the circle in the (x, y) plane having centre at the origin and radius 2, traversed in the positive direction.

7.4.3 Double integrals

In this section we review the introduction to double integrals given in Section 9.5.3 of *Modern Engineering Mathematics*. In the introduction to Section 7.4 we defined the definite integral of a function $f(x)$ of one variable by the limit

$$\int_a^b f(x)\,dx = \lim_{\substack{n \to \infty \\ \text{all } \Delta x_i \to 0}} \sum_{i=1}^n f(\tilde{x}_i)\,\Delta x_i$$

where $a = x_0 < x_1 < x_2 < \ldots < x_n = b$, $\Delta x_i = x_i - x_{i-1}$ and $x_{i-1} \leqslant \tilde{x}_i \leqslant x_i$. This integral is the area between the curve $y = f(x)$ and the x axis and between $x = a$ and $x = b$, as shown in Figure 7.17.

Now consider $z = f(x, y)$ and a region R of the (x, y) plane, as shown in Figure 7.17. Define the integral of $f(x, y)$ over the region R by the limit

$$\iint_R f(x, y)\,dA = \lim_{\substack{n \to \infty \\ \text{all } \Delta A_i \to 0}} \sum_{i=1}^n f(\tilde{x}_i, \tilde{y}_i)\,\Delta A_i$$

where ΔA_i $(i = 1, \ldots, n)$ is a partition of R into n elements of area ΔA_i and $(\tilde{x}_i, \tilde{y}_i)$ is a point in ΔA_i. Now $z = f(x, y)$ represents a surface, and so $f(\tilde{x}_i, \tilde{y}_i)\,\Delta A_i = \tilde{z}_i\,\Delta A_i$ is the volume between $z = 0$ and $z = \tilde{z}_i$ on the base ΔA_i. The integral $\iint_R f(x, y)\,dA$ is the limit of the sum of all such volumes, and so it is the volume under the surface $z = f(x, y)$ above the region R.

The partition of R into elementary areas can be achieved using grid lines parallel to the x and y axes as shown in Figure 7.18. Then $\Delta A_i = \Delta x_i\,\Delta y_i$, and we can write

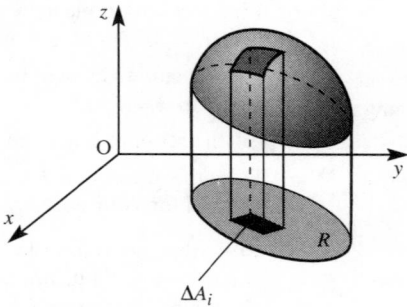

Figure 7.17 Volume as an integral.

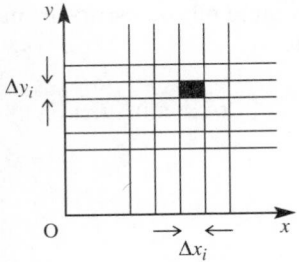

Figure 7.18 A possible grid for the partition of R.

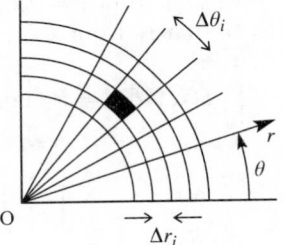

Figure 7.19 Another possible grid for the partition of R.

$$\iint\limits_R f(x, y)\, \mathrm{d}A = \iint\limits_R f(x, y)\, \mathrm{d}x\, \mathrm{d}y = \lim_{n \to \infty} \sum_{i=1}^{n} f(\tilde{x}_i, \tilde{y}_i)\, \Delta x_i\, \Delta y_i$$

Other partitions may be chosen, for example a polar grid as in Figure 7.19. Then the element of area is $(r\,\Delta\theta_i)\Delta r_i = \Delta A_i$ and

$$\iint\limits_R f(x, y)\, \mathrm{d}A = \iint\limits_R f(r\cos\theta, r\sin\theta)\, r\, \mathrm{d}r\, \mathrm{d}\theta \tag{7.12}$$

The expression for ΔA is more complicated when the grid lines do not intersect at right angles; we shall discuss this case in Section 7.4.5.

We can evaluate integrals of the type $\iint_R f(x, y)\,\mathrm{d}x\,\mathrm{d}y$ as repeated single integrals in x and y. Consequently, they are usually called **double integrals**.

Consider the region R shown in Figure 7.20, with boundary ACBD. Let the curve ACB be given by $y = g_1(x)$ and the curve ADB by $y = g_2(x)$. Then we can evaluate $\iint_R f(x, y)\,\mathrm{d}x\,\mathrm{d}y$ by summing for y first over the Δy_i, holding x constant

(a)

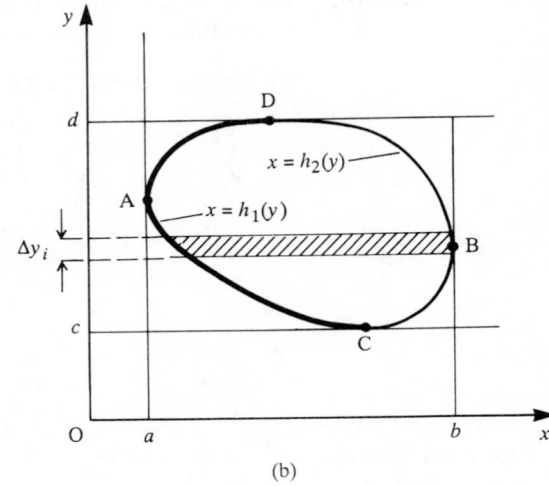

(b)

Figure 7.20 The region R.

$(x = \tilde{x}_i$, say), from $y = g_1(x_i)$ to $y = g_2(x_i)$, and then summing all such strips from A to B, that is, from $x = a$ to $x = b$. Thus we may write

$$\iint\limits_R f(x, y)\,\mathrm{d}A = \lim_{\substack{n \to \infty \\ \text{all } \Delta y_j, \Delta x_i \to 0}} \sum_{i=1}^{n_2} \left[\sum_{j=1}^{n_1} f(\tilde{x}_i, y_j)\,\Delta y_j \right] \Delta x_i \qquad (n = \min(n_1, n_2))$$

$$= \int_a^b \left[\int_{y=g_1(x)}^{y=g_2(x)} f(x, y)\,\mathrm{d}y \right] \mathrm{d}x$$

Here the integral inside the brackets is evaluated first, integrating with respect to y, keeping the value of x fixed, and then the result of this integration is integrated with respect to x.

Alternatively, we can sum for x first and then y. If the curve CAD is represented by $x = h_1(y)$ and the curve CBD by $x = h_2(y)$, we can write the integral as

$$\iint\limits_R f(x, y)\,\mathrm{d}A = \lim_{\substack{n \to \infty \\ \text{all } \Delta y_j, \Delta x_i \to 0}} \sum_{j=1}^{n_1} \left[\sum_{i=1}^{n_2} f(x_i, \tilde{y}_j)\,\Delta x_i \right] \Delta y_j \qquad (n = \min(n_1, n_2))$$

$$= \int_c^d \left[\int_{x=h_1(y)}^{x=h_2(y)} f(x, y)\,\mathrm{d}x \right] \mathrm{d}y$$

If the double integral exists then these two results are equal, and in going from one to the other we have changed the order of integration. Notice that the limits of integration are also changed in the process. Often, when evaluating an integral analytically, it is easier to perform the evaluation one way rather than the other.

EXAMPLE 7.11   Evaluate $\iint_R (x^2 + y^2)\,\mathrm{d}A$ over the triangle with vertices at $(0, 0)$, $(2, 0)$ and $(1, 1)$.

Solution   The domain of integration is shown in Figure 7.21(a). The triangle is bounded by the lines $y = 0$, $y = x$ and $y = 2 - x$.

(a) Integrating with respect to x first, as indicated in Figure 7.21(b), gives

$$\iint\limits_R (x^2 + y^2)\,\mathrm{d}A = \int_0^1 \int_{x=y}^{x=2-y} (x^2 + y^2)\,\mathrm{d}x\,\mathrm{d}y$$

$$= \int_0^1 \left[\tfrac{1}{3}x^3 + y^2 x \right]_{x=y}^{x=2-y} \mathrm{d}y$$

Figure 7.21 Domain of integration for Example 7.11.

(a)   (b)   (c)

$$= \int_0^1 [\tfrac{8}{3} - 4y + 4y^2 - \tfrac{8}{3}y^3]\,dy$$

$$= \tfrac{8}{3} - 2 + \tfrac{4}{3} - \tfrac{2}{3} = \tfrac{4}{3}$$

(b) Integrating with respect to y first, as indicated in Figure 7.21(c), gives

$$\iint_R (x^2 + y^2)\,dA = \int_0^1 \int_{y=0}^{y=x} (x^2 + y^2)\,dy\,dx + \int_1^2 \int_{y=0}^{y=2-x} (x^2 + y^2)\,dy\,dx$$

Note that because the upper boundary of the region R has different equations for it along different parts, the integral has to be split up into convenient subintegrals. Evaluating the integrals we have

$$\int_0^1 \int_{y=0}^{y=x} (x^2 + y^2)\,dy\,dx = \int_0^1 [x^2 y + \tfrac{1}{3}y^3]_{y=0}^{y=x}\,dx$$

$$= \int_0^1 \tfrac{4}{3}x^3\,dx = \tfrac{1}{3}$$

$$\int_1^2 \int_{y=0}^{y=2-x} (x^2 + y^2)\,dy\,dx = \int_1^2 [x^2 y + \tfrac{1}{3}y^3]_{y=0}^{y=2-x}\,dx$$

$$= \int_1^2 (\tfrac{8}{3} - 4x + 4x^2 - \tfrac{4}{3}x^3)\,dx$$

$$= 1$$

Thus

$$\iint_R (x^2 + y^2)\,dA = \tfrac{1}{3} + 1 = \tfrac{4}{3}, \qquad \text{as before}$$

Clearly, in this example it is easier to integrate with respect to x first.

EXAMPLE 7.12   Evaluate $\iint_R (x + 2y)^{-1/2}\,dA$ over the region $x - 2y \leqslant 1$ and $x \geqslant y^2 + 1$.

Solution   The bounding curves intersect where $2y + 1 = y^2 + 1$, which gives $y = 0$ (with $x = 1$) and $y = 2$ (with $x = 5$). The region R is shown in Figure 7.22. In this

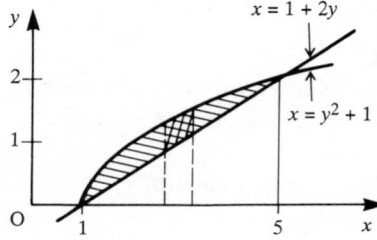

Figure 7.22 Domain of integration for Example 7.12.

example we choose to take x first because the formula for the boundary is easier to deal with: $x = y^2 + 1$ rather than $y = (x - 1)^{1/2}$. Thus we obtain

$$\iint\limits_R (x + 2y)^{-1/2}\, dA = \int_0^2 \int_{y^2+1}^{2y+1} (x + 2y)^{-1/2}\, dx\, dy$$

$$= \int_0^2 [2(x + 2y)^{1/2}]_{x=y^2+1}^{x=2y+1}\, dy$$

$$= \int_0^2 [2(4y + 1)^{1/2} - 2(y + 1)]\, dy$$

$$= [\tfrac{1}{3}(4y + 1)^{3/2} - y^2 - 2y]_0^2 = \tfrac{2}{3}$$

As indicated earlier, the evaluation of integrals over a domain R is not restricted to the use of rectangular cartesian coordinates (x, y). Example 7.13 shows how polar coordinates can be used in some cases to simplify the analytical process.

EXAMPLE 7.13   Evaluate $\iint_R x^2 y\, dA$, where R is the region $x^2 + y^2 \leqslant 1$.

Solution   The fact that the domain of integration is a circle suggests that polar coordinates are a natural choice for the integration process. Then, from (7.12), $x = r \cos \theta$, $y = r \sin \theta$ and $dA = r\, d\theta\, dr$, and the integral becomes

$$\iint\limits_R x^2 y\, dA = \int_{r=0}^1 \int_{\theta=0}^{2\pi} r^2 \cos^2 \theta\, r \sin \theta\, r\, d\theta\, dr$$

$$= \int_{r=0}^1 \int_{\theta=0}^{2\pi} r^4 \cos^2 \theta \sin \theta\, d\theta\, dr$$

Note that in this example the integration is such that we can separate the variables r and θ and write

$$\iint\limits_R x^2 y\, dA = \int_{r=0}^1 r^4 \int_{\theta=0}^{2\pi} \cos^2 \theta \sin \theta\, d\theta\, dr$$

Furthermore, since the limits of integration with respect to θ do not involve r, we can write

$$\iint\limits_R x^2 y\, dA = \int_{r=0}^1 r^4\, dr \int_{\theta=0}^{2\pi} \cos^2 \theta \sin \theta\, d\theta$$

and the double integral in this case reduces to a product of integrals. Thus we obtain

$$\iint\limits_{R} x^2 y \, dA = [\tfrac{1}{5} r^5]_0^1 [-\tfrac{1}{3} \cos^2 \theta]_0^{2\pi}$$

$$= \tfrac{1}{5} \times 0$$

$$= 0$$

7.4.4   Exercises

55 Sketch the domain of integration and evaluate

(a) $\displaystyle\int_1^2 dx \int_x^{2x} \frac{dy}{x^2 + y^2}$

(b) $\displaystyle\int_0^1 dx \int_0^{1-x} (x^2 + y^2) \, dy$

(c) $\displaystyle\int_0^1 dx \int_{\sqrt{(x-x^2)}}^{\sqrt{(1-x^2)}} \frac{1}{\sqrt{(1-x^2-y^2)}} \, dy$

56 Evaluate $\iint \sin\tfrac{1}{2}\pi(x+y) \, dx \, dy$ over the triangle whose vertices are $(0,0)$, $(2,1)$, $(1,2)$.

57 Sketch the domains of integration of the double integrals

(a) $\displaystyle\int_0^1 dx \int_x^1 \frac{xy \, dy}{\sqrt{(1+y^4)}}$

(b) $\displaystyle\int_0^{\pi/2} dy \int_0^y (\cos 2y)\sqrt{(1-k^2 \sin^2 x)} \, dx$

Change the order of integration, and hence evaluate the integrals.

58 Evaluate

$$\int_0^1 dy \int_{\sqrt{y}}^1 \frac{dx}{\sqrt{[y(1+x^2)]}}$$

59 Sketch the domain of integration of the double integral

$$\int_0^1 \int_0^{\sqrt{(x-x^2)}} \frac{x}{\sqrt{(x^2+y^2)}} \, dy \, dx$$

Express the integral in polar coordinates, and hence show that its value is $\tfrac{1}{3}$.

60 Sketch the domain of integration of the double integral

$$\int_0^1 dx \int_0^{\sqrt{(1-x^2)}} \frac{x+y}{\sqrt{(x^2+y^2)}} \, dy$$

and evaluate the integral.

61 Evaluate

$$\iint \frac{x+y}{x^2+y^2+a^2} \, dx \, dy$$

over the portion of the first quadrant lying inside the circle $x^2 + y^2 = a^2$.

62 By using polar coordinates, evaluate the double integral

$$\iint \frac{x^2-y^2}{x^2+y^2} \, dx \, dy$$

over the region in the first quadrant bounded by the arc of the parabola $y^2 = 4(1-x)$ and the coordinate axes.

63 By transforming to polar coordinates, show that the double integral

$$\iint \frac{(x^2+y^2)^2}{(xy)^2} \, dx \, dy$$

taken over the area common to the two circles $x^2 + y^2 = ax$ and $x^2 + y^2 = by$ is ab.

7.4.5   Green's theorem in a plane

This theorem shows the relationship between line integrals and double integrals,

Figure 7.23 Green's theorem.

and will also provide a justification for the general change of variables in a double integral.

Consider a simple closed curve, C, enclosing the region A as shown in Figure 7.23. If $P(x, y)$ and $Q(x, y)$ are continuous functions with continuous partial derivatives then

$$\oint_C (P\,dx + Q\,dy) = \iint_A \left(\frac{\partial Q}{\partial x} - \frac{\partial P}{\partial y}\right) dx\,dy \tag{7.13}$$

where C is traversed in the positive sense (that is, so that the bounded area is always on the left). This result is called **Green's theorem** in a plane.

The proof of this result is straightforward. Consider the first term on the right-hand side. Then, with reference to Figure 7.23,

$$\iint_R \frac{\partial Q}{\partial x}\,dx\,dy = \int_c^d \left[\int_{g_1(y)}^{g_2(y)} \frac{\partial Q}{\partial x}\,dx\right] dy$$

$$= \int_c^d \left[Q(g_2(y), y) - Q(g_1(y), y)\right] dy$$

$$= \int_{LMN} Q(x, y)\,dy - \int_{LKN} Q(x, y)\,dy$$

$$= \int_{LMNKL} Q(x, y)\,dy = \oint_C Q(x, y)\,dy$$

Similarly,

$$-\iint_A \frac{\partial P}{\partial y}\,dx\,dy = \oint_C P(x, y)\,dx$$

and hence

$$\iint_A \left(\frac{\partial Q}{\partial x} - \frac{\partial P}{\partial y}\right) dx\,dy = \oint_C \left[P(x, y)\,dx + Q(x, y)\,dy\right]$$

An elementary application is shown in Example 7.14.

EXAMPLE 7.14 Evaluate $\oint[2x(x + y)\,dx + (x^2 + xy + y^2)\,dy]$ around the square with vertices at $(0,0)$, $(1,0)$, $(1,1)$ and $(0,1)$ illustrated in Figure 7.24.

Solution Here $P(x, y) = 2x(x + y)$ and $Q(x, y) = x^2 + xy + y^2$, so that $\partial P/\partial y = 2x$, $\partial Q/\partial x = 2x + y$ and $\partial Q/\partial x - \partial P/\partial y = y$. Thus the line integral transforms into an easy double integral

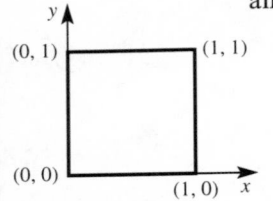

$$\oint_C [2x(x + y)\,dx + (x^2 + xy + y^2)\,dy] = \iint_A y\,dx\,dy$$

$$= \int_0^1 \int_0^1 y\,dx\,dy = \int_0^1 y\,dy \int_0^1 dx$$

$$= \tfrac{1}{2}$$

Figure 7.24 Path of integration for Example 7.14.

It follows immediately from Green's theorem (7.13) that the area A enclosed by the closed curve C is given by

$$A = \oint_C x\,dy \equiv \iint_A 1\,dx\,dy$$

$$= -\oint_C y\,dx \equiv \iint_A 1\,dx\,dy$$

$$= \tfrac{1}{2}\oint_C (-y\,dx + x\,dy)$$

Suppose that under a transformation of coordinates $x = x(u, v)$ and $y = y(u, v)$, the curve becomes C', enclosing an area A'. Then

$$A' = \oint_{C'} u\,dv \equiv \iint_{A'} du\,dv$$

$$= \oint_C u\left(\frac{\partial v}{\partial x}\,dx + \frac{\partial v}{\partial y}\,dy\right)$$

$$= \iint_A \left[\frac{\partial}{\partial x}\left(u\frac{\partial v}{\partial y}\right) - \frac{\partial}{\partial y}\left(u\frac{\partial v}{\partial x}\right)\right] dx\,dy$$

$$= \iint_A \left(\frac{\partial u}{\partial x}\frac{\partial v}{\partial y} - \frac{\partial u}{\partial y}\frac{\partial v}{\partial x}\right) dx\,dy$$

This implies that the element of area $du\,dv$ is equivalent to the element

$$\left|\left(\frac{\partial u}{\partial x}\frac{\partial v}{\partial y}-\frac{\partial u}{\partial y}\frac{\partial v}{\partial x}\right)\right|dx\,dy$$

Here the modulus sign is introduced to preserve the orientation of the curve under the mapping. Similarly, we may prove that

$$dx\,dy=\left|\frac{\partial(x,y)}{\partial(u,v)}\right|du\,dv \tag{7.14}$$

where $\partial(x,y)/\partial(u,v)$ is the **Jacobian**

$$\frac{\partial x}{\partial u}\frac{\partial y}{\partial v}-\frac{\partial x}{\partial v}\frac{\partial y}{\partial x}=J(x,y)$$

This enables us to make a general change of coordinates in a double integral:

$$\iint_{A}f(x,y)\,dx\,dy=\iint_{A'}f(x(u,v),y(u,v))|J|\,du\,dv \tag{7.15}$$

where A' is the region in the (u,v) plane corresponding to A in the (x,y) plane. Note that the above discussion confirms the result

$$\frac{\partial(u,v)}{\partial(x,y)}=\left[\frac{\partial(x,y)}{\partial(u,v)}\right]^{-1}$$

discussed in Section 9.2.5 of *Modern Engineering Mathematics*. Using (7.15), the result (7.12) when using polar coordinates is readily confirmed.

EXAMPLE 7.15   Evaluate $\iint xy\,dx\,dy$ over the region in $x\geqslant0$, $y\geqslant0$ bounded by $y=x^2+4$, $y=x^2$, $y=6-x^2$ and $y=12-x^2$.

Solution   The domain of integration is shown in Figure 7.25(a). The bounding curves can be rewritten as $y-x^2=4$, $y-x^2=0$, $y+x^2=6$ and $y+x^2=12$, so that a

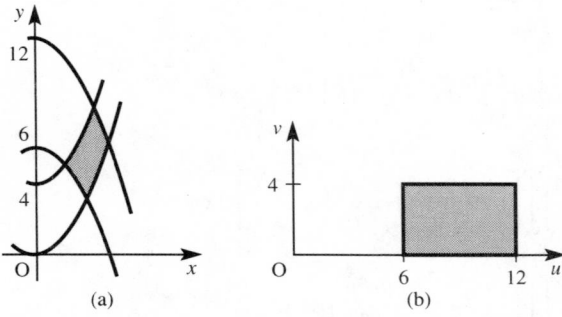

Figure 7.25 Domains of integration for Example 7.15: (a) in the (x,y) plane; (b) in the (u,v) plane.

natural change of coordinates is to set

$$u = y + x^2, \qquad v = y - x^2$$

Under this transformation, the region of integration becomes the rectangle $6 \leqslant u \leqslant 12$, $0 \leqslant v \leqslant 4$, as shown in Figure 7.25(b). Thus since

$$J(x, y) = \frac{\partial(x, y)}{\partial(u, v)} = \left[\frac{\partial(u, v)}{\partial(x, y)} \right]^{-1} = \frac{1}{4x}$$

the integral simplifies to

$$\iint_A xy \, dx \, dy = \iint_{A'} xy \frac{1}{4x} \, du \, dv$$

Hence

$$\iint_A xy \, dx \, dy = \tfrac{1}{4} \iint_{A'} y \, du \, dv$$

$$= \tfrac{1}{8} \iint_{A'} (u + v) \, du \, dv, \qquad \text{since } y = (u + v)/2$$

$$= \tfrac{1}{8} \int_0^4 dv \int_6^{12} (u + v) \, du$$

$$= 33$$

We remark in passing that Green's theorem in a plane may be generalized to three dimensions. Note that the result (7.13) may be written as

$$\oint_C (P, Q, 0) \cdot dr = \iint_A \operatorname{curl} \left[(P, Q, 0) \right] \cdot k \, dx \, dy$$

For a general surface S with bounding curve C as shown in Figure 7.26 this identity becomes

$$\oint_C F(r) \cdot dr = \iint_S \operatorname{curl} F(r) \cdot dS$$

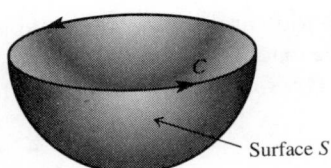

Figure 7.26 Three-dimensional generalization of Green's theorem.

where $d\mathbf{S} = \hat{\mathbf{n}}\,dS$ is the vector element of surface area and $\hat{\mathbf{n}}$ is a unit vector along the normal. This generalization is called Stokes' theorem, and will be discussed in Section 7.4.12 after we have formally introduced the concept of a surface integral.

7.4.6 Exercises

64 Evaluate the line integral

$$\oint_C [\sin y \, dx + (x - \cos y)\,dy]$$

taken in the anticlockwise sense, where C is the perimeter of the triangle formed by the lines

$$y = \tfrac{1}{2}\pi x, \qquad y = \tfrac{1}{2}\pi, \qquad x = 0$$

Verify your answer using Green's theorem in a plane.

65 Use Green's theorem in a plane to evaluate

$$\oint_C [(xy^2 - y)\,dx + (x + y^2)\,dy]$$

as a double integral, where C is the triangle with vertices at $(0,0)$, $(2,0)$ and $(2,2)$ and is traversed in the anticlockwise direction.

66 Evaluate the line integral

$$I = \oint_C (xy\,dx + x\,dy)$$

where C is the closed curve consisting of $y = x^2$ from $x = 0$ to $x = 1$ and $y = \sqrt{x}$ from $x = 1$ to $x = 0$. Confirm your answer by applying Green's

theorem in the plane and evaluating I as a double integral.

67 Use Green's theorem in a plane to evaluate the line integral

$$\oint_C [(e^x - 3y^2)\,dx + (e^y + 4x^2)\,dy]$$

where C is the circle $x^2 + y^2 = 4$. (*Hint*: use polar coordinates to evaluate the double integral.)

68 Evaluate

$$\int_0^a dx \int_x^{2a-x} \frac{y - x}{4a^2 + (y + x)^2}\,dy$$

using the transformation of coordinates $u = x + y$, $v = x - y$.

69 Using the transformation

$$x + y = u, \qquad \frac{y}{x} = v$$

show that

$$\int_0^1 dy \int_y^{2-y} \frac{x + y}{x^2}\,e^{x+y}\,dx$$

$$= \int_0^2 du \int_0^1 e^v\,dv = e^2 - 1$$

7.4.7 Surface integrals

The extensions of the idea of an integral to line and double integrals are not the only generalizations that can be made. We can also extend the idea to integration over a general surface S. Two types of such integrals occur:

(a) $$\iint_S f(x, y, z)\,dS$$

(b) $\displaystyle\iint_S F(r) \cdot \hat{n}\, dS = \iint_S F(r) \cdot dS$

In case (a) we have a scalar field $f(r)$ and in case (b) a vector field $F(r)$. Note that $dS = \hat{n}\, dS$ is the vector element of area, where $\hat{n}$ is the unit vector outward drawn normal to the element dS.

In general, the surface S can be described in terms of two parameters, u and v say, so that on S

$$r = r(u, v) = (x(u,v), y(u,v), z(u,v))$$

The surface S can be specified by a scalar point function $C(r) = c$, where c is a constant. Curves may be drawn on that surface, and in particular if we fix the value of one of the two parameters u and v then we obtain two families of curves. On one, $C_u(r(u, v_0))$, the value of u varies while v is fixed, and on the other, $C_v(r(u_0, v))$, the value of v varies while u is fixed, as shown in Figure 7.27. Then as indicated in Figure 7.27, the vector element of area dS is given by

$$dS = \frac{\partial r}{\partial u}\, du \times \frac{\partial r}{\partial v}\, dv$$

$$= \frac{\partial r}{\partial u} \times \frac{\partial r}{\partial v}\, du\, dv$$

$$= \left(\frac{\partial x}{\partial u}, \frac{\partial y}{\partial u}, \frac{\partial z}{\partial u}\right) \times \left(\frac{\partial x}{\partial v}, \frac{\partial y}{\partial v}, \frac{\partial z}{\partial v}\right) du\, dv$$

$$= (J_1 i + J_2 j + J_3 k)\, du\, dv$$

where

$$J_1 = \frac{\partial y}{\partial u}\frac{\partial z}{\partial v} - \frac{\partial y}{\partial v}\frac{\partial z}{\partial u}$$

$$J_2 = \frac{\partial z}{\partial u}\frac{\partial x}{\partial v} - \frac{\partial z}{\partial v}\frac{\partial x}{\partial u}$$

$$J_3 = \frac{\partial x}{\partial u}\frac{\partial y}{\partial v} - \frac{\partial x}{\partial v}\frac{\partial y}{\partial u}$$

(7.16)

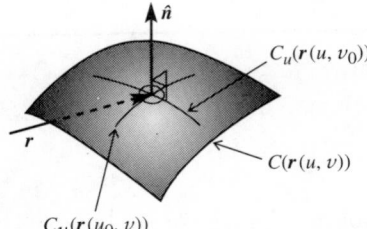

Figure 7.27
Parametric curves on a surface.

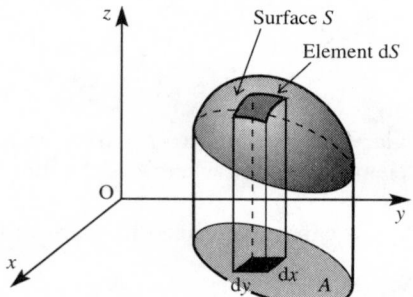

Figure 7.28 A surface
described by
$z = z(x, y)$.

Hence

$$\iint_S F(r) \cdot dS = \iint_A (PJ_1 + QJ_2 + RJ_3)\, du\, dv$$

$$\iint_S f(x, y, z)\, dS = \iint_A f(u, v)\sqrt{(J_1^2 + J_2^2 + J_3^2)}\, du\, dv$$

where $F(r) = (P, Q, R)$ and A is the region of the (u, v) plane corresponding to S. Here, of course, the terms in the integrands have to be expressed in terms of u and v.

In particular, u and v can be chosen as any two of x, y and z. For example, if $z = z(x, y)$ describes a surface as in Figure 7.28 then

$$r = (x, y, z(x, y))$$

with x and y as independent variables. This gives

$$J_1 = -\frac{\partial z}{\partial x}, \qquad J_2 = -\frac{\partial z}{\partial y}, \qquad J_3 = 1$$

and

$$\iint_S F(r) \cdot dS = \iint_A \left(-P\frac{\partial z}{\partial x} - Q\frac{\partial z}{\partial y} + R\right) dx\, dy \qquad \text{(7.17a)}$$

$$\iint_S f(x, y, z)\, dS = \iint_A f(x, y, z(x, y)) \sqrt{\left[1 + \left(\frac{\partial z}{\partial x}\right)^2 + \left(\frac{\partial z}{\partial y}\right)^2\right]} dx\, dy \qquad \text{(7.17b)}$$

EXAMPLE 7.16   Evaluate the surface integral

$$\iint_S (x + y + z)\, dS$$

where S is the portion of the sphere $x^2 + y^2 + z^2 = 1$ that lies in the first quadrant.

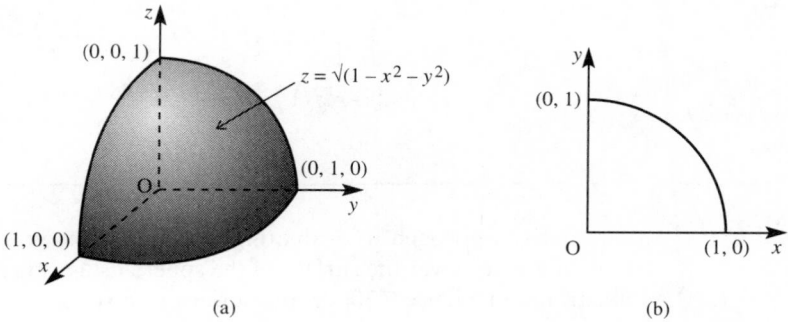

Figure 7.29 (a) Surface S for Example 7.16. (b) Quadrant of a circle in the (x, y) plane.

Solution   The surface S is illustrated in Figure 7.29(a). Taking

$$z = \sqrt{(1 - x^2 - y^2)}$$

we have

$$\frac{\partial z}{\partial x} = \frac{-x}{\sqrt{(1 - x^2 - y^2)}}, \qquad \frac{\partial z}{\partial y} = \frac{-y}{\sqrt{(1 - x^2 - y^2)}}$$

giving

$$\sqrt{\left[1 + \left(\frac{\partial z}{\partial x}\right)^2 + \left(\frac{\partial z}{\partial y}\right)^2\right]} = \sqrt{\left[\frac{x^2 + y^2 + (1 - x^2 - y^2)}{(1 - x^2 - y^2)}\right]} = \frac{1}{\sqrt{(1 - x^2 - y^2)}}$$

Using (7.17) then gives

$$\iint\limits_{S} (x + y + z)\,dS = \iint\limits_{A} [x + y + \sqrt{(1 - x^2 - y^2)}]\frac{1}{\sqrt{(1 - x^2 - y^2)}}\,dx\,dy$$

where A is the quadrant of a circle in the (x, y) plane illustrated in Figure 7.29(b).
Transforming to polar coordinates

$$x = r\cos\theta, \qquad y = r\sin\theta, \qquad dx\,dy = r\,dr\,d\theta$$

gives

$$\iint\limits_{S} (x + y + z)\,dS = \int_0^{\pi/2} \int_0^1 \left[\frac{r(\sin\theta + \cos\theta)}{\sqrt{(1 - r^2)}} + 1\right] r\,dr\,d\theta$$

$$= \int_0^1 \left[\frac{r^2(-\cos\theta + \sin\theta)}{\sqrt{(1 - r^2)}} + r\right]_0^{\pi/2} dr$$

$$= \int_0^1 \left[\frac{2r^2}{\sqrt{(1 - r^2)}} + \tfrac{1}{2}r\pi\right] dr$$

$$= \int_0^1 \left[-2\sqrt{(1 - r^2)} + \frac{2}{\sqrt{(1 - r^2)}} + \tfrac{1}{2} r\pi \right] dr$$

$$= [-r\sqrt{(1 - r^2)} - \sin^{-1} r + 2\sin^{-1} r + \tfrac{1}{4} r^2 \pi]_0^1$$

$$= \tfrac{3}{4}\pi$$

An alternative approach to evaluating the surface integral in Example 7.16 is to evaluate it directly over the surface of the sphere using spherical polar coordinates. As illustrated in Figure 7.30, on the surface of a sphere of radius a we have

$$x = a\sin\theta\cos\phi, \qquad y = a\sin\theta\sin\phi$$

$$z = a\cos\theta, \qquad \mathrm{d}S = \sin\theta\,\mathrm{d}\theta\,\mathrm{d}\phi$$

In the sphere of Example 7.16 the radius $a = 1$, so that

$$\iint_S (x + y + z)\,\mathrm{d}S = \int_0^{\pi/2} \int_0^{\pi/2} (\sin\theta\cos\phi + \sin\theta\sin\phi + \cos\theta)\sin\theta\,\mathrm{d}\theta\,\mathrm{d}\phi$$

$$= \int_0^{\pi/2} [\tfrac{1}{4}\pi\cos\phi + \tfrac{1}{4}\pi\sin\phi + \tfrac{1}{2}]\,\mathrm{d}\phi = \tfrac{3}{4}\pi$$

In a similar manner, when evaluating surface integrals over the surface of a cylinder of radius a, we have, as illustrated in Figure 7.31,

$$x = a\cos\phi, \qquad y = a\sin\phi, \qquad z = z, \qquad \mathrm{d}S = a\,\mathrm{d}z\,\mathrm{d}\phi$$

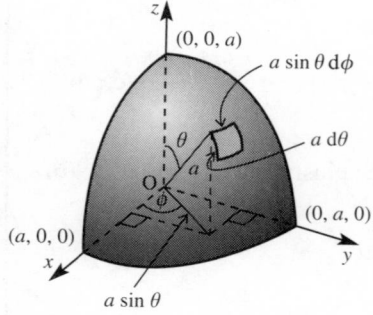

Figure 7.30 Surface element in spherical polar coordinates.

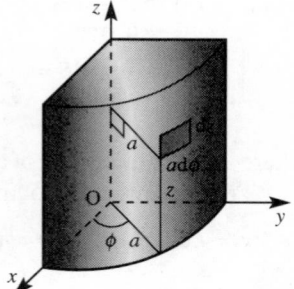

Figure 7.31 Surface element in cylindrical polar coordinates.

EXAMPLE 7.17 Find the surface area of the torus shown in Figure 7.32(a) formed by rotating a circle of radius b about an axis distance a from its centre.

Solution From Figure 7.32(b), the position vector r of a point on the surface is given by

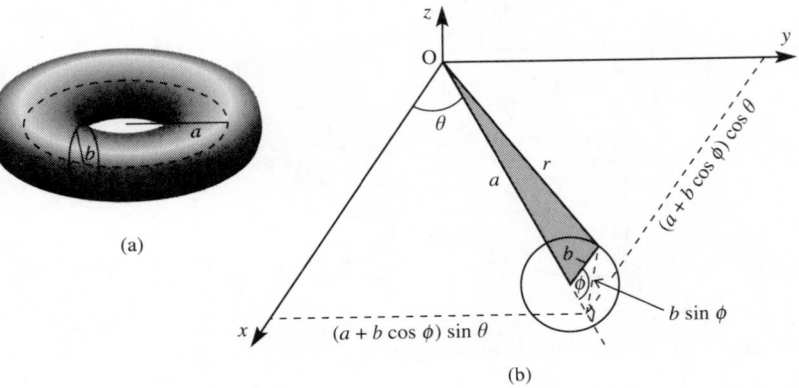

Figure 7.32
(a) Torus of Example
7.17. (b) Position
vector of a point on
the surface of the
torus.

$$r = (a + b\cos\phi)\cos\theta\,i + (a + b\cos\phi)\sin\theta\,j + b\sin\phi\,k$$

(Notice that θ and ϕ are not the angles used for spherical polar coordinates.) Thus using 7.16,

$$J_1 = (a + b\cos\phi)\cos\theta\,(b\cos\phi) - (-b\sin\phi\sin\theta)(0)$$

$$J_2 = (0)(-b\sin\phi\cos\theta) - (b\cos\phi)(a + b\cos\phi)(-\sin\theta)$$

$$J_3 = -(a + b\cos\phi)\sin\theta(-b\sin\phi\sin\theta) - (-b\sin\phi\cos\theta)(a + b\cos\phi)\cos\theta$$

Simplifying, we obtain

$$J_1 = b(a + b\cos\phi)\cos\theta\cos\phi$$

$$J_2 = b(a + b\cos\phi)\sin\theta\sin\phi$$

$$J_3 = b(a + b\cos\phi)\sin\phi$$

and the surface area is given by

$$S = \int_0^{2\pi}\int_0^{2\pi}\sqrt{(J_1^2 + J_2^2 + J_3^2)}\,d\theta\,d\phi$$

$$= \int_0^{2\pi}\int_0^{2\pi} b(a + \cos\phi)\,d\theta\,d\phi$$

$$= 4\pi^2 ab$$

Thus the surface area of the torus is the product of the circumferences of the two circles that generate it.

EXAMPLE 7.18   Evaluate $\iint_S V \cdot dS$, where $V = zi + xj - 3y^2zk$ and S is the surface of the cylinder $x^2 + y^2 = 16$ in the first octant between $z = 0$ and $z = 5$.

Solution   The surface S is illustrated in Figure 7.33. From Section 7.2.1, the outward normal to the surface is in the direction of the vector

$$n = \text{grad}\,(x^2 + y^2 - 16) = 2xi + 2yj$$

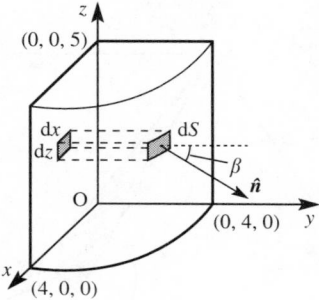

Figure 7.33 Surface S for Example 7.18.

so that the unit outward normal $\hat{\boldsymbol{n}}$ is given by

$$\hat{\boldsymbol{n}} = \frac{2x\boldsymbol{i} + 2y\boldsymbol{j}}{2\sqrt{(x^2 + y^2)}}$$

Since on the surface $x^2 + y^2 = 16$,

$$\hat{\boldsymbol{n}} = \tfrac{1}{4}(x\boldsymbol{i} + y\boldsymbol{j})$$

giving

$$\mathrm{d}\boldsymbol{S} = \mathrm{d}S\,\hat{\boldsymbol{n}} = \tfrac{1}{4}\mathrm{d}S\,(x\boldsymbol{i} + y\boldsymbol{j})$$

Projecting the element of surface $\mathrm{d}S$ onto the (x, z) plane as illustrated in Figure 7.33, the area $\mathrm{d}x\,\mathrm{d}z$ of the projected element is given by

$$\mathrm{d}x\,\mathrm{d}z = \mathrm{d}S\cos\beta$$

where β is the angle between the normal $\hat{\boldsymbol{n}}$ to the surface element and the normal $\boldsymbol{j}$ to the (x, z) plane. Thus

$$\mathrm{d}x\,\mathrm{d}z = \mathrm{d}S\,|\hat{\boldsymbol{n}} \cdot \boldsymbol{j}|$$
$$= \tfrac{1}{4}\mathrm{d}S\,|(x\boldsymbol{i} + y\boldsymbol{j}) \cdot \boldsymbol{j}| = \tfrac{1}{4}\mathrm{d}S\,y$$

giving

$$\mathrm{d}S = \frac{4}{y}\mathrm{d}x\,\mathrm{d}z$$

Also,

$$\boldsymbol{V} \cdot \mathrm{d}\boldsymbol{S} = \boldsymbol{V} \cdot \hat{\boldsymbol{n}}\,\mathrm{d}S$$

$$= (z\boldsymbol{i} + x\boldsymbol{j} - 3y^2 z\boldsymbol{k}) \cdot (x\boldsymbol{i} + y\boldsymbol{j})\frac{4}{y}\mathrm{d}x\,\mathrm{d}z$$

$$= 4\frac{xz + xy}{y}\mathrm{d}x\,\mathrm{d}z$$

so that

$$\iint_S V \cdot dS = 4 \iint_A \frac{xz + xy}{y} \, dx \, dz$$

where A is the rectangular region in the (x, z) plane bounded by $0 \leqslant x \leqslant 4$, $0 \leqslant z \leqslant 5$. Noting that the integrand is still evaluated on the surface, we can write $y = \sqrt{(16 - x^2)}$, so that

$$\iint_S V \cdot dS = 4 \int_0^4 \int_0^5 \left[x + \frac{xz}{\sqrt{(16 - x^2)}} \right] dz \, dx$$

$$= 4 \int_0^4 \left[xz + \frac{xz^2}{2\sqrt{(16 - x^2)}} \right]_0^5 dx$$

$$= 4 \int_0^4 \left[5x + \frac{25x}{2\sqrt{(16 - x^2)}} \right] dx$$

$$= 4 [\tfrac{5}{2}x^2 - \tfrac{25}{2}\sqrt{(16 - x^2)}]_0^4$$

$$= 360$$

An alternative approach in this case is to evaluate $\frac{1}{4}\iint_S (xz + xy) \, dS$ directly over the surface using cylindrical polar coordinates. This is left as Exercise 77 below.

7.4.8   Exercises

70 Evaluate the area of the surface $z = 2 - x^2 - y^2$ lying above the (x, y) plane. (*Hint*: Use polar coordinates to evaluate the double integral.)

71 Evaluate

(a) $\iint_S (x^2 + y^2) \, dS$, where S is the surface area of the plane $2x + y + 2z = 6$ cut off by the planes $z = 0$, $z = 2$, $y = 0$, $y = 3$;

(b) $\iint_S z \, dS$, where S is the surface area of the hemisphere $x^2 + y^2 + z^2 = 1$ ($z > 0$) cut off by the cylinder $x^2 - x + y^2 = 0$.

72 Evaluate $\iint_S v \cdot dS$, where

(a) $v = (xy, -x^2, x + z)$ and S is the part of the plane $2x + 2y + z = 6$ included in the first octant;

(b) $v = (3y, 2x^2, z^3)$ and S is the surface of the cylinder $x^2 + y^2 = 1$, $0 < z < 1$.

73 Show that $\iint_S z^2 \, dS = \frac{1}{2}\pi$, where S is the surface of the sphere $x^2 + y^2 + z^2 = 1$, $z \geqslant 0$.

74 Evaluate the surface integral $\iint_S U(x, y, z) \, dS$, where S is the surface of the paraboloid $z = 2 - (x^2 + y^2)$ above the (x, y) plane and $U(x, y, z)$ is given by

(a) 1   (b) $x^2 + y^2$ (c) z

Give a physical interpretation in each case.

75 Determine the surface area of the plane $2x + y + 2z = 16$ cut off by $x = 0$, $y = 0$ and $x^2 + y^2 = 64$.

76 Show that the area of that portion of the surface of the paraboloid $x^2 + y^2 = 4z$ included between the planes $z = 1$ and $z = 3$ is $\frac{16}{3}\pi(4 - \sqrt{2})$.

77 Evaluate the surface integral in Example 7.18 using cylindrical polar coordinates.

78 If $F = yi + (x - 2xz)j - xyk$, evaluate the surface integral $\iint_S (\text{curl } F) \cdot dS$, where S is the surface of the sphere $x^2 + y^2 + z^2 = a^2$, $z \geqslant 0$.

7.4.9 Volume integrals

In Section 7.4.7 we defined the integral of a function over a curved surface in three dimensions. This idea can be extended to define the integral of a function of three variables through a region T of three-dimensional space by the limit

$$\iiint_T f(x, y, z)\, dV = \lim_{\substack{n \to \infty \\ \text{all } \Delta V_i \to 0}} \sum_{i=1}^{n} f(\tilde{x}_i, \tilde{y}_i, \tilde{z}_i)\, \Delta V_i$$

where ΔV_i $(i = 1, \ldots, n)$ is a partition of T into n elements of volume, and $(\tilde{x}_i, \tilde{y}_i, \tilde{z}_i)$ is a point in ΔV_i as illustrated in Figure 7.34.

In terms of rectangular cartesian coordinates the triple integral can, as illustrated in Figure 7.35, be written as

$$\iiint_T f(x, y, z)\, dV = \int_a^b dx \int_{g_1(x)}^{g_2(x)} dy \int_{h_1(x,y)}^{h_2(x,y)} f(x, y, z)\, dz \qquad \textbf{(7.18)}$$

Note that there are six different orders in which the integration in (7.18) can be carried out.

As we saw for double integrals in (7.14), the expression for the element of volume $dV = dx\, dy\, dz$ under the transformation $x = x(u, v, w)$, $y = y(u, v, w)$, $z = z(u, v, w)$ may be obtained using the Jacobian

$$J = \frac{\partial(x, y, z)}{\partial(u, v, w)} = \begin{vmatrix} \dfrac{\partial x}{\partial u} & \dfrac{\partial y}{\partial u} & \dfrac{\partial z}{\partial u} \\[2mm] \dfrac{\partial x}{\partial v} & \dfrac{\partial y}{\partial v} & \dfrac{\partial z}{\partial v} \\[2mm] \dfrac{\partial x}{\partial w} & \dfrac{\partial y}{\partial w} & \dfrac{\partial z}{\partial w} \end{vmatrix}$$

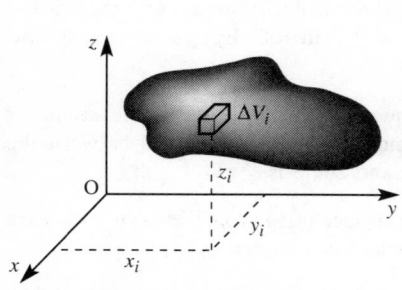

Figure 7.34 Partition of region T into volume elements ΔV_i.

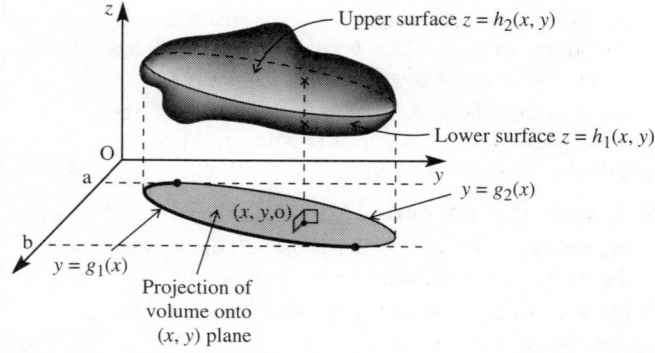

Figure 7.35 The volume integral in terms of rectangular cartesian coordinates.

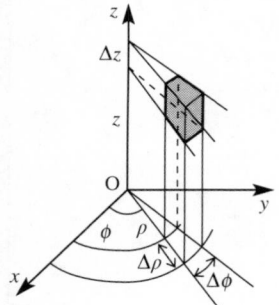

Figure 7.36 Volume element in cylindrical polar coordinates.

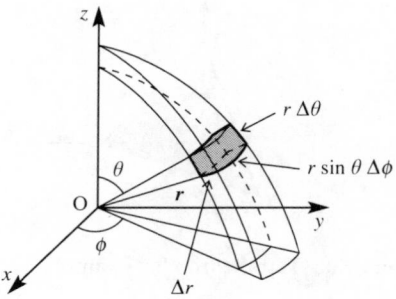

Figure 7.37 Volume element in spherical polar coordinates.

as

$$dV = dx\,dy\,dz = |J|\,du\,dv\,dw \tag{7.19}$$

For example, in the case of cylindrical polar coordinates

$$x = \rho \cos\phi, \qquad y = \rho \sin\phi, \qquad z = z$$

$$J = \rho \begin{vmatrix} \cos\phi & \sin\phi & 0 \\ -\sin\phi & \cos\phi & 0 \\ 0 & 0 & 1 \end{vmatrix} = \rho$$

so that

$$dV = \rho\,d\rho\,d\phi\,dz \tag{7.20}$$

a result illustrated in Figure 7.36.

Similarly, for spherical polar coordinates (r, θ, ϕ)

$$x = r\sin\theta\cos\phi, \qquad y = r\sin\theta\sin\phi, \qquad z = r\cos\theta$$

$$J = \begin{vmatrix} \sin\theta\cos\phi & \sin\theta\sin\phi & \cos\theta \\ r\cos\theta\cos\phi & r\cos\theta\sin\phi & -r\sin\theta \\ -r\sin\theta\sin\phi & r\sin\theta\cos\phi & 0 \end{vmatrix} = r^2\sin\theta$$

so that

$$dV = r^2 \sin\theta\,dr\,d\theta\,d\phi \tag{7.21}$$

a result illustrated in Figure 7.37.

EXAMPLE 7.19   Find the volume and the coordinates of the centroid of the tetrahedron defined by $x \geqslant 0$, $y \geqslant 0$, $z \geqslant 0$ and $x + y + z \leqslant 1$.

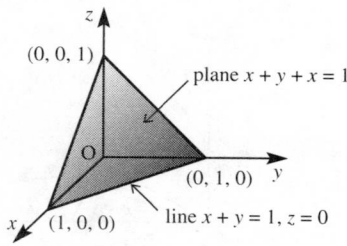

Figure 7.38 Tetrahedron for Example 7.19.

Solution   The tetrahedron is shown in Figure 7.38. Its volume is

$$V = \iiint\limits_{\text{tetrahedron}} dx\,dy\,dz = \int_0^1 dx \int_0^{1-x} dy \int_0^{1-x-y} dz$$

$$= \int_0^1 dx \int_0^{1-x} (1 - x - y)\,dy$$

$$= \int_0^1 \tfrac{1}{2}(1 - x)^2\,dx$$

$$= \tfrac{1}{6}$$

Let the coordinates of the centroid be $(\bar{x}, \bar{y}, \bar{z})$; then

$$\bar{x}V = \iiint\limits_{\text{tetrahedron}} x\,dV = \iiint\limits_{\text{tetrahedron}} x\,dx\,dy\,dz$$

$$= \int_0^1 dx \int_0^{1-x} dy \int_0^{1-x-y} x\,dz$$

$$= \int_0^1 \tfrac{1}{2}x(1 - x)^2\,dx$$

$$= \tfrac{1}{24}$$

Hence $\bar{x} = \tfrac{1}{4}$, and by symmetry $\bar{y} = \bar{z} = \tfrac{1}{4}$.

EXAMPLE 7.20   Find the moment of inertia of a uniform sphere of mass M and radius a about a diameter.

Solution   A sphere of radius a has volume $\tfrac{4}{3}\pi a^3$, so that its density is $3M/4\pi a^3$. Then the moment of inertia of the sphere about the z axis is

$$I = \frac{3M}{4\pi a^3} \iiint\limits_{\text{sphere}} (x^2 + y^2)\,dx\,dy\,dz$$

In this example it is natural to use spherical polar coordinates, so that

$$I = \frac{3M}{4\pi a^3} \iiint_{\text{sphere}} (r^2 \sin^2 \theta) r^2 \sin \theta \, dr \, d\theta \, d\phi$$

$$= \frac{3M}{4\pi a^3} \int_0^a r^4 \, dr \int_0^\pi \sin^3 \theta \, d\theta \int_0^{2\pi} d\phi$$

$$= \frac{3M}{4\pi a^3} (\tfrac{1}{5}a^5)(\tfrac{4}{3})(2\pi)$$

$$= \tfrac{2}{5} M a^2$$

7.4.10   Exercises

79 Evaluate the triple integrals

(a) $\displaystyle \int_0^1 dx \int_0^2 dy \int_1^3 x^2 y z \, dz$

(b) $\displaystyle \int_0^2 \int_1^3 \int_2^4 xyz^2 \, dz \, dy \, dx$

80 Show that

$$\int_{-1}^1 dz \int_0^2 dx \int_{x-z}^{x+z} (x + y + z) \, dy = 0$$

81 Evaluate $\iiint \sin(x + y + z) \, dx \, dy \, dz$ over the portion of the positive octant cut off by the plane $x + y + z = \pi$.

82 Evaluate $\iiint_V xyz \, dx \, dy \, dz$, where V is the region bounded by the planes $x = 0$, $y = 0$, $z = 0$ and $x + y + z = 1$.

83 Sketch the region contained between the parabolic cylinders $y = x^2$ and $x = y^2$ and the planes $z = 0$ and $x + y + z = 2$. Show that the volume of the region may be expressed as the triple integral

$$\int_0^1 \int_{x^2}^{\sqrt{x}} \int_0^{2-x-y} dz \, dy \, dx$$

and evaluate it.

84 Use spherical polar coordinates to evaluate

$$\iiint_V x(x^2 + y^2 + z^2) \, dx \, dy \, dz$$

where V is the region in the first octant lying within the sphere $x^2 + y^2 + z^2 = 1$.

85 Evaluate $\iiint x^2 y^2 z^2 (x + y + z) \, dx \, dy \, dz$ throughout the region defined by $x + y + z \leqslant 1$, $x \geqslant 0$, $y \geqslant 0$, $z \geqslant 0$.

86 Show that if $x + y + z = u$, $y + z = uv$ and $z = uvw$ then

$$\frac{\partial(x, y, z)}{\partial(u, v, w)} = u^2 v$$

Hence evaluate the triple integral

$$\iiint_V \exp\left[-(x + y + z)^3\right] dx \, dy \, dz$$

where V is the volume of the tetrahedron bounded by the planes $x = 0$, $y = 0$, $z = 0$ and $x + y + z = 1$.

87 Evaluate $\iiint_V yz \, dx \, dy \, dz$ taken throughout the prism with sides parallel to the z axis, whose base is the triangle with vertices at $(0, 0, 0)$, $(1, 0, 0)$, $(0, 1, 0)$ and whose top is the triangle with vertices at $(0, 0, 2)$, $(1, 0, 1)$, $(0, 1, 1)$. Find also the position of the centroid of this prism.

88 Evaluate $\iiint z \, dx \, dy \, dz$ throughout the region defined by $x^2 + y^2 \leqslant z^2$, $x^2 + y^2 + z^2 \leqslant 1$, $z > 0$.

89 Using spherical polar coordinates, evaluate $\iiint x \, dx \, dy \, dz$ throughout the positive octant of the sphere $x^2 + y^2 + z^2 = a^2$.

7.4.11 Gauss's divergence theorem

Figure 7.39 Closed volume V with surface S.

In the same way that Green's theorem relates surface and line integrals, Gauss's theorem relates surface and volume integrals.

Consider the closed volume V with surface area S shown in Figure 7.39. The surface integral $\iint_S F \cdot dS$ may be interpreted as the flow of a liquid with velocity field $F(r)$ out of the volume V. In Section 7.3.1 we saw that the divergence of F could be expressed as

$$\operatorname{div} F = \nabla \cdot F = \lim_{\Delta V \to 0} \frac{\text{flow out of } \Delta V}{\Delta V}$$

In terms of differentials, this may be written

$$\operatorname{div} F \, dV = \text{flow out of } dV$$

Consider now a partition of the volume V given by ΔV_i ($i = 1, \dots, n$). Then the total flow out of V is the sum of the flows out of each ΔV_i. That is,

$$\iint_S F \cdot dS = \lim_{n \to \infty} \sum_{i=1}^{n} (\text{flow out of } \Delta V_i)$$

$$= \lim_{n \to \infty} \sum_{i=1}^{n} (\operatorname{div} F \, \Delta V_i)$$

giving

$$\iint_S F \cdot dS = \iiint_V \operatorname{div} F \, dV \tag{7.22}$$

This result is known as the **divergence theorem** or **Gauss's theorem**. It enables us to convert surface integrals into volume integrals, and often simplifies their evaluation.

EXAMPLE 7.21   A vector field $F(r)$ is given by

$$F(r) = x^3 y \boldsymbol{i} + x^2 y^2 \boldsymbol{j} + x^2 y z \boldsymbol{k}$$

Find $\iint_S F \cdot dS$, where S is the surface of the region in the first octant for which $x + y + z \leqslant 1$.

Solution   We begin by sketching the region V enclosed by S, as shown in Figure 7.40. It is clear that evaluating the surface integral directly will be rather clumsy, involving four separate integrals (one over each of the four surfaces). It is simpler in this case to transform it into a volume integral using the divergence theorem (7.22):

$$\iint_S F \cdot dS = \iiint_V \operatorname{div} F \, dV$$

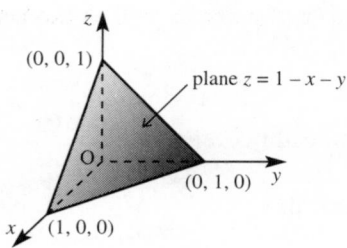

Figure 7.40 Region V and surface S for Example 7.21.

Here

$$\operatorname{div} \boldsymbol{F} = 3x^2y + 2x^2y + x^2y$$

and we obtain

$$\iint\limits_{S} \boldsymbol{F} \cdot d\boldsymbol{S} = \int_0^1 dx \int_0^{1-x} dy \int_0^{1-x-y} 6x^2 y \, dz$$

$$= 6\int_0^1 x^2 \, dx \int_0^{1-x} y \, dy \int_0^{1-x-y} dz$$

$$= 6\int_0^1 x^2 \, dx \int_0^{1-x} [(1-x)y - y^2] \, dy$$

$$= \int_0^1 x^2 (1-x)^3 \, dx = \tfrac{1}{60}$$

EXAMPLE 7.22   Verify the divergence theorem

$$\iint\limits_{S} \boldsymbol{F} \cdot d\boldsymbol{S} = \iiint\limits_{V} \operatorname{div} \boldsymbol{F} \, dV$$

when $\boldsymbol{F} = 2xz\boldsymbol{i} + yz\boldsymbol{j} + z^2\boldsymbol{k}$ and V is the volume enclosed by the upper hemisphere $x^2 + y^2 + z^2 = a^2$, $z \geqslant 0$.

Solution   The volume V and surface S of the hemisphere are illustrated in Figure 7.41. Note that since the theorem relates to a closed volume, the surface S consists

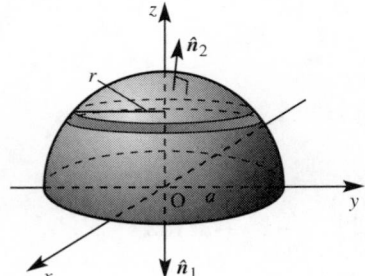

Figure 7.41
Hemisphere for
Example 7.22.

of the flat circular base in the (x, y) plane as well as the hemispherical surface. In this case

$$\text{div } \boldsymbol{F} = 2z + z + 2z = 5z$$

so that the volume integral is readily evaluated as

$$\iiint\limits_V 5z \, dx \, dy \, dz = \int_0^a 5z\pi r^2 \, dz$$

$$= \int_0^a 5\pi z(a^2 - z^2) \, dz$$

$$= \tfrac{5}{4}\pi a^4$$

Considering the surface integral

$$\iint\limits_S \boldsymbol{F} \cdot d\boldsymbol{S} = \iint\limits_{\text{circular base}} \boldsymbol{F} \cdot \hat{\boldsymbol{n}}_1 \, dS + \iint\limits_{\text{hemisphere}} \boldsymbol{F} \cdot \hat{\boldsymbol{n}}_2 \, dS$$

The unit normal to the base is clearly $\hat{\boldsymbol{n}}_1 = -\boldsymbol{k}$, so

$$\boldsymbol{F} \cdot \hat{\boldsymbol{n}}_1 = -z^2$$

giving

$$\iint\limits_{\text{circular base}} \boldsymbol{F} \cdot \hat{\boldsymbol{n}}_1 \, dS = 0$$

since $z = 0$ on this surface.

The hemispherical surface is given by

$$f(x, y, z) = x^2 + y^2 + z^2 - a^2 = 0$$

so the outward unit normal $\hat{\boldsymbol{n}}_2$ is

$$\hat{\boldsymbol{n}}_2 = \frac{\boldsymbol{\nabla}f}{|\boldsymbol{\nabla}f|} = \frac{2x\boldsymbol{i} + 2y\boldsymbol{j} + 2z\boldsymbol{k}}{2\sqrt{(x^2 + y^2 + z^2)}}$$

Since $x^2 + y^2 + z^2 = a^2$ on the surface,

$$\hat{\boldsymbol{n}}_2 = \frac{x}{a}\boldsymbol{i} + \frac{y}{a}\boldsymbol{j} + \frac{z}{a}\boldsymbol{k}$$

giving

$$\boldsymbol{F} \cdot \hat{\boldsymbol{n}}_2 = \frac{2x^2 z}{a} + \frac{y^2 z}{a} + \frac{z^3}{a}$$

Hence

$$\iint\limits_{\text{hemisphere}} \boldsymbol{F} \cdot \hat{\boldsymbol{n}}_2 \, dS = \iint\limits_{\text{hemisphere}} \frac{z}{a}(x^2 + a^2) \, dS$$

since $x^2 + y^2 + z^2 = a^2$ on the surface. Transforming to spherical polar coordinates,

$$x = a \sin \theta \cos \phi, \qquad z = a \cos \theta, \qquad dS = a^2 \sin \theta \, d\theta \, d\phi$$

and the surface integral becomes

$$\iint_{\text{hemisphere}} \boldsymbol{F} \cdot \hat{\boldsymbol{n}}_2 \, dS = a^4 \int_0^{2\pi} \int_0^{\pi/2} (\sin \theta \cos \theta + \sin^3 \theta \cos \theta \cos^2 \phi) \, d\theta \, d\phi$$

$$= a^4 \int_0^{2\pi} \left[\tfrac{1}{2} \sin^2 \theta + \tfrac{1}{4} \sin^4 \theta \cos^2 \phi \right]_0^{\pi/2} d\phi$$

$$= a^4 \int_0^{2\pi} \left[\tfrac{1}{2} + \tfrac{1}{4} \cos^2 \phi \right] d\phi$$

$$= \tfrac{5}{4} \pi a^4$$

thus confirming that

$$\iint_S \boldsymbol{F} \cdot d\boldsymbol{S} = \iiint_V \operatorname{div} \boldsymbol{F} \, dV$$

7.4.12 Stokes' theorem

Stokes' theorem is the generalization of Green's theorem, and relates line integrals in three dimensions with surface integrals. At the end of Section 7.3.3 we saw that the curl of the vector $\boldsymbol{F}$ could be expressed in the form

$$\operatorname{curl} \boldsymbol{F} \cdot \hat{\boldsymbol{n}} = \lim_{\Delta S \to 0} \frac{\text{flow round } \Delta S}{\Delta S}$$

In terms of differentials, this becomes

$$\operatorname{curl} \boldsymbol{F} \cdot d\boldsymbol{S} = \text{flow round } d\boldsymbol{S}$$

Consider the surface S shown in Figure 7.42, bounded by the curve C. Then the line integral $\oint_C \boldsymbol{F} \cdot d\boldsymbol{r}$ can be interpreted as the total flow of a fluid with velocity field $\boldsymbol{F}$ around the curve C. Partitioning the surface S into elements $\Delta S_i \, (i = 1, \ldots, n)$, we can write

$$\oint_C \boldsymbol{F} \cdot d\boldsymbol{r} = \lim_{n \to \infty} \sum_{i=1}^{n} (\text{flow round } \Delta S_i)$$

$$= \lim_{n \to \infty} \sum_{i=1}^{n} (\operatorname{curl} \boldsymbol{F} \cdot \Delta \boldsymbol{S}_i)$$

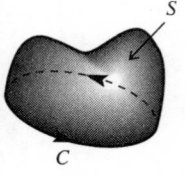

Figure 7.42 Surface S bounded by curve C.

so that

$$\oint_C \mathbf{F} \cdot \mathrm{d}\mathbf{r} = \iint_S (\mathrm{curl}\,\mathbf{F}) \cdot \mathrm{d}\mathbf{S} \qquad (7.23)$$

This result is known as **Stokes' theorem**. It provides a condition for a line integral to be independent of its path of integration. For, if the integral $\int_A^B \mathbf{F} \cdot \mathrm{d}\mathbf{r}$ is independent of the path of integration then

$$\int_{C_1} \mathbf{F} \cdot \mathrm{d}\mathbf{r} = \int_{C_2} \mathbf{F} \cdot \mathrm{d}\mathbf{r}$$

where C_1 and C_2 are two different paths joining A and B as shown in Figure 7.43. Since

$$\int_{C_1} \mathbf{F} \cdot \mathrm{d}\mathbf{r} = - \int_{-C_2} \mathbf{F} \cdot \mathrm{d}\mathbf{r}$$

where $-C_2$ is the path C_2 traversed in the opposite direction, we have

$$\int_{C_1} \mathbf{F} \cdot \mathrm{d}\mathbf{r} + \int_{-C_2} \mathbf{F} \cdot \mathrm{d}\mathbf{r} = 0$$

That is,

$$\oint_C \mathbf{F} \cdot \mathrm{d}\mathbf{r} = 0$$

where C is the combined, closed curve formed from C_1 and $-C_2$. Stokes' theorem implies that if $\oint_C \mathbf{F} \cdot \mathrm{d}\mathbf{r} = 0$ then

$$\iint_S (\mathrm{curl}\,\mathbf{F}) \cdot \mathrm{d}\mathbf{S} = 0$$

for any surface S bounded by C. Since this is true for all surfaces bounded by C, we deduce that the integrand must be zero, that is, curl $\mathbf{F} = \mathbf{0}$. Writing $\mathbf{F} = (F_1, F_2, F_3)$, we then have that

$$\mathbf{F} \cdot \mathrm{d}\mathbf{r} = F_1\,\mathrm{d}x + F_2\,\mathrm{d}y + F_3\,\mathrm{d}z$$

is an exact differential if curl $\mathbf{F} = \mathbf{0}$, that is, if

$$\frac{\partial F_1}{\partial z} = \frac{\partial F_3}{\partial x}, \qquad \frac{\partial F_1}{\partial y} = \frac{\partial F_2}{\partial x}, \qquad \frac{\partial F_2}{\partial z} = \frac{\partial F_3}{\partial y}$$

Thus there is a function $f(x, y, z) = f(\mathbf{r})$ such that

$$F_1 = \frac{\partial f}{\partial x}, \qquad F_2 = \frac{\partial f}{\partial y}, \qquad F_3 = \frac{\partial f}{\partial z},$$

that is, such that $\mathbf{F}(\mathbf{r}) = \mathrm{grad}\,f$.

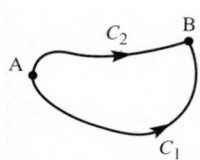

Figure 7.43 Two paths, C_1 and C_2, joining points A and B.

When $F(r)$ represents a field of force, the field is said to be **conservative** (since it conserves rather than dissipates energy). When $F(r)$ represents a velocity field for a fluid, the field is said to be curl-free or **irrotational**.

EXAMPLE 7.23   Verify Stokes' theorem for $F = (2x - y)i - yz^2j - y^2zk$, where S is the upper half of the sphere $x^2 + y^2 + z^2 = 1$ and C is its boundary.

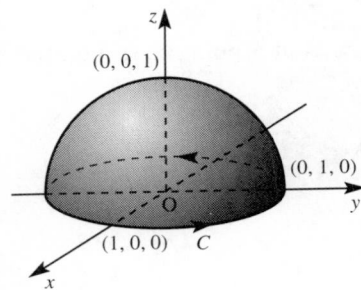

Figure 7.44 Hemispherical surface and boundary for Example 7.23.

Solution   The surface and boundary involved are illustrated in Figure 7.44. We are required to show that

$$\oint_C F \cdot dr = \iint_S \text{curl } F \cdot dS$$

Since C is a circle of unit radius in the (x, y) plane, to evaluate $\oint_C F \cdot dr$, we take

$$x = \cos \phi, \qquad y = \sin \phi$$

so that

$$r = \cos \phi\, i + \sin \phi\, j$$

giving

$$dr = -\sin \phi\, d\phi\, i + \cos \phi\, d\phi\, j$$

Also, on the boundary C, $z = 0$, so that

$$F = (2x - y)i = (2 \cos \phi - \sin \phi)i$$

Thus

$$\oint_C F \cdot dr = \int_0^{2\pi} (2 \cos \phi - \sin \phi)i \cdot (-\sin \phi\, i + \cos \phi\, j)\, d\phi$$

$$= \int_0^{2\pi} (-2 \sin \phi \cos \phi + \sin^2 \phi)\, d\phi$$

$$= \int_0^{2\pi} [-\sin 2\phi + \tfrac{1}{2}(1 + \cos 2\phi)] \, d\phi$$

$$= \pi$$

$$\text{curl } F = \begin{vmatrix} i & j & k \\ \dfrac{\partial}{\partial x} & \dfrac{\partial}{\partial y} & \dfrac{\partial}{\partial z} \\ 2x - y & -yz^2 & -y^2z \end{vmatrix} = k$$

The unit outward drawn normal at a point (x, y, z) on the hemisphere is given by $(x\boldsymbol{i} + y\boldsymbol{j} + z\boldsymbol{k})$, since $x^2 + y^2 + z^2 = 1$. Thus

$$\iint_S \text{curl } \boldsymbol{F} \cdot d\boldsymbol{S} = \iint_S \boldsymbol{k} \cdot (x\boldsymbol{i} + y\boldsymbol{j} + z\boldsymbol{k}) \, dS$$

$$= \iint_S z \, dS$$

$$= \int_0^{2\pi} \int_0^{\pi/2} \cos \theta \sin \theta \, d\theta \, d\phi$$

$$= 2\pi [\tfrac{1}{2} \sin^2 \theta]_0^{\pi/2} = \pi$$

Hence $\oint_C \boldsymbol{F} \cdot d\boldsymbol{r} = \iint_S (\text{curl } \boldsymbol{F}) \cdot d\boldsymbol{S}$, and Stokes' theorem is verified.

7.4.13 Exercises

90 Evaluate $\iint_S \boldsymbol{F} \cdot d\boldsymbol{S}$, where $\boldsymbol{F} = (4xz, -y^2, yz)$ and S is the surface of the cube bounded by the planes $x = 0$, $x = 1$, $y = 0$, $y = 1$, $z = 0$ and $z = 1$.

91 Use the divergence theorem to evaluate the surface integral $\iint_S \boldsymbol{F} \cdot d\boldsymbol{S}$, where $\boldsymbol{F} = xz\boldsymbol{i} + yz\boldsymbol{j} + z^2\boldsymbol{k}$ and S is the closed surface of the hemisphere $x^2 + y^2 + z^2 = 4$, $z > 0$. (Note that you are not required to verify the theorem.)

92 Verify the divergence theorem

$$\iint_S \boldsymbol{F} \cdot d\boldsymbol{S} = \iiint_V \text{div } \boldsymbol{F} \, dV$$

for $\boldsymbol{F} = 4x\boldsymbol{i} - 2y^2\boldsymbol{j} + z^2\boldsymbol{k}$ over the region bounded by $x^2 + y^2 = 4$, $z = 0$ and $z = 3$.

93 Prove that

$$\iiint_V (\text{grad } \phi) \cdot (\text{curl } \boldsymbol{F}) \, dV = \iint_S (\boldsymbol{F} \times \text{grad } \phi) \cdot d\boldsymbol{S}$$

94 Verify the divergence theorem for $\boldsymbol{F} = (xy + y^2)\boldsymbol{i} + x^2 y\boldsymbol{j}$ and the volume V in the first octant bounded by $x = 0$, $y = 0$, $z = 0$, $z = 1$ and $x^2 + y^2 = 4$.

95 Use Stokes' theorem to show that the value of the line integral $\int_A^B \boldsymbol{F} \cdot d\boldsymbol{r}$ for

$$\boldsymbol{F} = (36xz + 6y \cos x, 3 + 6 \sin x + z \sin y,$$
$$18x^2 - \cos y)$$

is independent of the path joining the points A and B.

96 Use Stokes' theorem to evaluate the line integral

$\oint_C A \cdot dr$, where $A = -y i + x j$ and C is the boundary of the ellipse $x^2/a^2 + y^2/b^2 = 1$, $z = 0$.

97 Verify Stokes' theorem by evaluating both sides of

$$\iint_S (\text{curl } F) \cdot dS = \oint_C F \cdot dr$$

where $F = (2x - y)i - yz^2 j - y^2 z k$ and S is the curved surface of the hemisphere $x^2 + y^2 + z^2 = 16$, $z \geq 0$.

98 By applying Stokes' theorem to the function $a f(r)$,

where a is a constant, deduce that

$$\iint_S (n \times \text{grad} f) \, dS = \int_C f(r) \, dr$$

Verify this result for the function $f(r) = 3xy^2$ and the rectangle in the plane $z = 0$ bounded by the lines $x = 0$, $x = 1$, $y = 0$ and $y = 2$.

99 Verify Stokes' theorem for $F = (2y + z, x - z, y - x)$ for the part of $x^2 + y^2 + z^2 = 1$ lying in the positive octant.

7.5   Engineering application: heat transfer

In modelling heat transfer problems we make use of three experimental laws.

(1) Heat flows from hot regions to cold regions of a body.

(2) The rate at which heat flows through a plane section drawn in a body is proportional to its area and to the temperature gradient normal to the section.

(3) The quantity of heat in a body is proportional to its mass and to its temperature.

In the simplest case we consider heat transfer in a medium for which the constants of proportionality in the above laws are independent of direction. Such a medium is called **thermally isentropic**. For any arbitrary region within such a medium we can obtain an equation that models such heat flows. The total amount $Q(t)$ of heat within the region V is

$$Q(t) = \iiint_V c\rho u(r, t) \, dV$$

where c is the specific heat of the medium, ρ is the density and $u(r, t)$ is the temperature at the point r at time t. Heat flows out of the region through its bounding surface S. The experimental laws (1) and (2) above imply that the rate at which heat flows across an element ΔS of that surface is $-k\nabla u \cdot \Delta S$, where k is the thermal conductivity of the medium. (The minus sign indicates that heat flows from hot regions to cold.) Thus the rate at which heat flows across the whole surface of the region is given by

$$\iint_S (-k\nabla u) \cdot dS = -k \iint_S \nabla u \cdot dS$$

Using Gauss's theorem, we deduce that the rate at which heat flows out of the region is

$$-k \iiint\limits_{V} \nabla^2 u \, dV$$

If there are no sources or sinks of heat within the region, this must equal the rate at which the region loses heat, $-dQ/dt$. Therefore

$$-\frac{d}{dt}\left[\iiint\limits_{V} c\rho u(\mathbf{r}, t)\, dV\right] = -k \iiint\limits_{V} \nabla^2 u \, dV$$

Since

$$\frac{d}{dt}\iiint\limits_{V} u(\mathbf{r}, t)\, dV = \iiint\limits_{V} \frac{\partial u}{\partial t}\, dV$$

this implies that

$$\iiint\limits_{V} \left(k\nabla^2 u - c\rho \frac{\partial u}{\partial t}\right) dV = 0$$

This models the situation for any arbitrarily chosen region V. The arbitrariness in the choice of V implies that the value of the integral is independent of V and that the integrand is equal to zero. Thus

$$\nabla^2 u = \frac{c\rho}{k}\frac{\partial u}{\partial t}$$

The quantity k/cp is termed the **thermal diffusivity** of the medium and is usually denoted by the Greek letter kappa, κ. The differential equation models heat flow within a medium. Its solution depends on the initial temperature distribution $u(\mathbf{r}, 0)$ and on the conditions pertaining at the boundary of the region. Methods for solving this equation are discussed in Chapter 8. This differential equation also occurs as a model for water percolation through a dam, for neutron transport in reactors and in charge transfer within charge-coupled devices. We shall now proceed to obtain its solution in a very special case.

EXAMPLE 7.24   A large slab of material has an initial temperature distribution such that one half is at $-u_0$ and the other at $+u_0$. Obtain a mathematical model for this situation and solve it, stating explicitly the assumptions that are made.

Solution   When a problem is stated in such vague terms, it is difficult to know what approximations and simplifications may be reasonably made. Since we are dealing with heat transfer, we know that for an isentropic medium the temperature distribution satisfies the equation

$$\nabla^2 u = \frac{1}{\kappa}\frac{\partial u}{\partial t}$$

Figure 7.45 Region for Example 7.24.

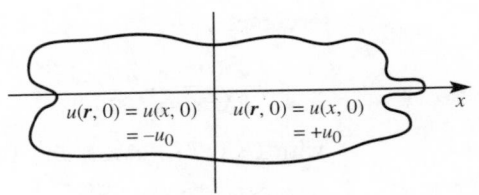

Figure 7.46 Coordinate system for Example 7.24.

throughout the medium. We know that the region we are studying is divided so that at $t = 0$ the temperature in one part is $-u_0$ while that in the other is $+u_0$, as illustrated in Figure 7.45. We can deduce from this figure that the subsequent temperature at a point in the medium depends only on the perpendicular distance of the point from the dividing plane. We choose a coordinate system so that its origin lies on the dividing plane and the x axis is perpendicular to it, as shown in Figure 7.46. Then the differential equation simplifies, since $u(r, t)$ is independent of y and z, and we have

$$\frac{\partial^2 u}{\partial x^2} = \frac{1}{\kappa} \frac{\partial u}{\partial t}$$

with

$$u(x, 0) = \begin{cases} -u_0 & (x < 0) \\ +u_0 & (x \geqslant 0) \end{cases}$$

Thinking about the physical problem also provides us with some further information. The heat flows from the cold region to the hot until (eventually) the temperature is uniform throughout the medium. In this case that terminal temperature is zero, since initially half the medium is at temperature $+u_0$ and the other half at $-u_0$. So we know that $u(x, t) \to 0$ as $t \to \infty$. We also deduce from the initial temperature distribution that $-u_0 \leqslant u(x, t) \leqslant u_0$ for all x and t, since there are no extra sources or sinks of heat in the medium. Summarizing, we have

$$\frac{\partial^2 u}{\partial x^2} = \frac{1}{\kappa} \frac{\partial u}{\partial t} \quad (-\infty < x < \infty, t \geqslant 0)$$

with

$$u(x, 0) = \begin{cases} -u_0 & (x < 0) \\ +u_0 & (x \geqslant 0) \end{cases}$$

$u(x, t)$ bounded for all x

$u(x, t) \to 0$ as $t \to \infty$

There are many approaches to solving this problem (see Chapter 8). One is to investigate the effect of changing the scale of the independent variables x and t. Setting $x = \lambda X$ and $t = \mu T$, where λ and μ are positive constants, the problem becomes

$$\mu \frac{\partial^2 U}{\partial X^2} = \frac{\lambda^2}{\kappa} \frac{\partial U}{\partial T}$$

with $U(X, T) = u(x, t)$ and $U(X, 0) = u_0 \operatorname{sgn} X$. Choosing $\mu = \lambda^2$, we see that

$$\frac{\partial^2 U}{\partial X^2} = \frac{1}{\kappa} \frac{\partial U}{\partial T}, \quad \text{with} \quad U(X, 0) = u_0 \operatorname{sgn} X$$

which implies that the solution $u(x, t)$ of the original equation is also a solution of the scaled equation. Thus

$$u(x, t) = u(\lambda x, \lambda^2 t)$$

which suggests that we should look for a solution expressed in terms of a new variable s that is proportional to the ratio of x to $\sqrt{t}$. Setting $s = ax/\sqrt{t}$, we seek a solution as a function of s:

$$u(x, t) = u_0 f(s)$$

This reduces the partial differential equation for u to an ordinary differential equation for f, since

$$\frac{\partial u}{\partial x} = \frac{au_0}{\sqrt{t}} \frac{df}{ds}, \quad \frac{\partial^2 u}{\partial x^2} = \frac{a^2 u_0}{t} \frac{d^2 f}{ds^2}, \quad \frac{\partial u}{\partial t} = -\frac{1}{2} \frac{axu_0}{t\sqrt{t}} \frac{df}{ds}$$

Thus the differential equation is transformed into

$$\frac{a^2}{t} \frac{d^2 f}{ds^2} = -\frac{ax}{2\kappa t \sqrt{t}} \frac{df}{ds}$$

giving

$$a^2 \frac{d^2 f}{ds^2} = -\frac{s}{2\kappa} \frac{df}{ds}$$

Choosing the constant a such that $a^2 = 1/(4\kappa)$ reduces this to the equation

$$\frac{d^2 f}{ds^2} = -2s \frac{df}{ds}$$

The initial condition is transformed into two conditions, since for $x < 0, s \to -\infty$ as $t \to 0$ and for $x > 0, s \to +\infty$ as $t \to 0$. So we have

$$f(s) \to 1 \quad \text{as} \quad s \to \infty$$

$$f(s) \to -1 \quad \text{as} \quad s \to -\infty$$

Integrating the differential equation once gives

$$\frac{df}{ds} = Ae^{-s^2}, \quad \text{where } A \text{ is a constant}$$

and integrating a second time gives

$$f(s) = B + A \int e^{-s^2} ds$$

The integral occurring here is one that frequently arises in heat transfer problems, and is given a special name. We define the **error function**, erf(x), by the integral

$$\text{erf}(x) = \frac{2}{\sqrt{\pi}} \int_0^x e^{-z^2} dz$$

Its name derives from the fact that it is associated with the normal distribution, which is a common model for the distribution of experimental errors. This is a well-tabulated function, and has the property that erf$(x) \to 1$ as $x \to \infty$.

Writing the solution obtained above in terms of the error function, we have

$$f(s) = A \text{ erf}(s) + B$$

Letting $s \to \infty$ and $s \to -\infty$ gives two equations for A and B:

$$1 = A + B$$
$$-1 = -A + B$$

from which we deduce $A = 1$ and $B = 0$. Thus

$$f(s) = \text{erf}(s)$$

so that

$$u(x,t) = u_0 \text{ erf}\left(\frac{x}{2\sqrt{t}}\right)$$

$$= \frac{2u_0}{\sqrt{\pi}} \int_0^{x/2\sqrt{t}} e^{-z^2} dz$$

7.6 Review exercises (1–20)

1 Show that $u(x,y) = x^n f(t)$, $t = y/x$, satisfies the differential equations

(a) $x\frac{\partial u}{\partial x} + y\frac{\partial u}{\partial y} = nu$

(b) $x^2\frac{\partial^2 u}{\partial x^2} + 2xy\frac{\partial^2 u}{\partial x \partial y} + y^2\frac{\partial^2 u}{\partial y^2} = n(n-1)u$

Verify these results for the function $u(x,y) = x^4 + y^4 + 16x^2y^2$.

2 Find the values of the numbers a and b such that the change of variables $u = x + ay$, $v = x + by$

transforms the differential equation

$$9\frac{\partial^2 f}{\partial x^2} - 9\frac{\partial^2 f}{\partial x \partial y} + 2\frac{\partial^2 f}{\partial y^2} = 0$$

into

$$\frac{\partial^2 f}{\partial u \partial v} = 0$$

Hence deduce that the general solution of the equation is given by

$$u(x,y) = f(x + 3y) + g(x + \tfrac{3}{2}y)$$

where f and g are arbitrary functions.

Find the solution of the differential equation that satisfies the conditions

$$u(x, 0) = \sin x, \quad \frac{\partial u(x, 0)}{\partial y} = 3 \cos x$$

3 A differential $P(x, y, z)\,dx + Q(x, y, z)\,dy + R(x, y, z)\,dz$ is exact if there is a function $f(x, y, z)$ such that

$$P(x, y, z)\,dx + Q(x, y, z)\,dy + R(x, y, z)\,dz$$
$$= \nabla f \cdot (dx, dy, dz)$$

Show that this implies $\nabla \times (P, Q, R) = 0$. Deduce that curl grad $f = 0$.

4 Find grad f, plot some level curves $f = $ constant and indicate grad f by arrows at some points on the level curves for $f(\boldsymbol{r})$ given by

(a) xy (b) $x/(x^2 + y^2)$

5 Show that if $\boldsymbol{\omega}$ is a constant vector then

(a) grad $(\boldsymbol{\omega} \cdot \boldsymbol{r}) = \boldsymbol{\omega}$

(b) curl $(\boldsymbol{\omega} \times \boldsymbol{r}) = 2\boldsymbol{\omega}$

6 (a) Prove that if $f(\boldsymbol{r})$ is a scalar point function then

curl grad $f = 0$

(b) Prove that if $\boldsymbol{v} = \text{grad}\,[zf(\boldsymbol{r})] + \alpha f(\boldsymbol{r})\boldsymbol{k}$ and $\nabla^2 f = 0$, where α is a constant and f is a scalar point function, then

$$\text{div } \boldsymbol{v} = (2 + \alpha)\frac{\partial f}{\partial z}, \quad \nabla^2 \boldsymbol{v} = \text{grad}\left(2\frac{\partial f}{\partial z}\right)$$

7 Show that if $\boldsymbol{F} = (x^2 - y^2 + x)\boldsymbol{i} - (2xy + y)\boldsymbol{j}$, then curl $\boldsymbol{F} = 0$, and find $f(\boldsymbol{r})$ such that $\boldsymbol{F} = \text{grad } f$. Verify that

$$\int_{(1,2)}^{(2,1)} \boldsymbol{F} \cdot d\boldsymbol{r} = [f(\boldsymbol{r})]_{(1,2)}^{(2,1)}$$

8 A force $\boldsymbol{F}$ acts on a particle that is moving in two dimensions along the semicircle $x = 1 - \cos\theta$, $y = \sin\theta$ $(0 \leqslant \theta \leqslant \pi)$. Find the work done when

(a) $\boldsymbol{F} = \sqrt{(x^2 + y^2)}\boldsymbol{i}$ (b) $\boldsymbol{F} = \sqrt{(x^2 + y^2)}\hat{\boldsymbol{n}}$

$\hat{\boldsymbol{n}}$ being the unit vector tangential to the path.

9 A force $\boldsymbol{F} = (xy, -y, 1)$ acts on a particle as it moves along the straight line from $(0, 0, 0)$ to $(1, 1, 1)$. Calculate the work done.

10 The force $\boldsymbol{F}$ per unit length of a conducting wire carrying a current I in a magnetic field $\boldsymbol{B}$ is $\boldsymbol{F} = I \times \boldsymbol{B}$. Find the force acting on a circuit whose shape is given by $x = \sin\theta$, $y = \cos\theta$, $z = \sin\frac{1}{2}\theta$,

when current I flows in it and when it lies in a magnetic field $\boldsymbol{B} = x\boldsymbol{i} - y\boldsymbol{j} + \boldsymbol{k}$.

11 The velocity $\boldsymbol{v}$ at the point (x, y) in a two-dimensional fluid flow is given by $\boldsymbol{v} = (y\boldsymbol{i} - x\boldsymbol{j})/(x^2 + y^2)$. Find the net circulation around the square $x = \pm 1$, $y = \pm 1$.

12 A metal plate has its boundary defined by $x = 0$, $y = x^2/c$ and $y = c$. The density at the point (x, y) is kxy (per unit area). Find the moment of inertia of the plate about an axis through $(0, 0)$ and perpendicular to the plate.

13 A right circular cone of height h and base radius a is cut into two pieces along a plane parallel to and distance c from the axis of the cone. Find the volume of the smaller piece.

14 The axes of two circular cylinders of radius a intersect at right angles. Show that the volume common to both cylinders may be expressed as the triple integral

$$8 \int_0^a dy \int_0^{\sqrt{(a^2 - y^2)}} dx \int_0^{\sqrt{(a^2 - y^2)}} dz$$

and hence evaluate it.

15 The elastic energy of a volume V of material is $q^2 V/2EI$, where q is its stress and E and I are constants. Find the elastic energy of a cylindrical volume of radius r and length l in which the stress varies directly as the distance from its axis, being zero at the axis and q_0 at the outer surface.

16 The velocity of a fluid at the point (x, y, z) has components $(3x^2 y, xy^2, 0)$. Find the flow rate out of the triangular prism bounded by $z = 0$, $z = 1$, $x = 0$, $y = 0$ and $x + y = 1$.

17 An electrostatic field has components $(2xy, -y^2, x + y)$ at the point (x, y, z). Find the total flux out of the sphere $x^2 + y^2 + z^2 = a^2$.

18 Verify Stokes' theorem

$$\oint_C \boldsymbol{F} \cdot d\boldsymbol{r} = \iint_S (\text{curl } \boldsymbol{F}) \cdot d\boldsymbol{S}$$

where $\boldsymbol{F} = (x^2 + y - 4,\ 3xy,\ 2xz + z^2)$ and S is the surface of the hemisphere $x^2 + y^2 + z^2 = 16$ above the (x, y) plane.

19 Use the divergence theorem to evaluate the surface integral

$$\iint\limits_{S} a \cdot dS$$

where $a = xi + yj - 2zk$ and S is the surface of the sphere $x^2 + y^2 + z^2 = a^2$ *above* the (x, y) plane.

20 Evaluate the volume integral

$$\iiint\limits_{V} xyz \, dV$$

where V denotes the wedge-shaped region bounded in the positive octant by the four planes $x = 0$, $y = 0$, $y = 1 - x$ and $z = 2 - x$.

8

Partial Differential Equations

CONTENTS

8.1 Introduction

In *Modern Engineering Mathematics* we considered the role of ordinary differential equations in engineering, and their methods of solution. However, many physical processes fundamental to science and engineering are governed by **partial differential equations**, that is, equations involving partial derivatives. The most familiar of these processes are heat conduction and wave propagation. To describe such phenomena, we make assumptions about gradients (for instance the Fourier law that heat flow is proportional to temperature gradient) and we write down balance equations; partial differential equations are thus produced in a natural way. Unless the situation is very simple, there will be many independent variables, for example a time variable t and a space variable x, and the differential equations *must* involve partial derivatives.

The application of partial differential equations is much wider than the simple situations already mentioned. Maxwell's equations (see Example 7.9) comprise a set of partial differential equations that form the basis of electromagnetic theory, and are fundamental to electrical engineers and physicists. The equations of fluid flow are partial differential equations, and are widely used in aeronautical engineering, acoustics, the study of groundwater flows in civil engineering, the development of most fluid handling devices used in mechanical engineering and in investigating flame and combustion processes in chemical engineering. Quantum mechanics is yet another theory governed by a partial differential equation, the Schrödinger equation, which forms the basis of much of physics, chemistry and electronic engineering. Stress analysis is important in large areas of civil and mechanical engineering, and again requires a complicated set of partial differential equations. This is by no means an exhaustive list, but it does illustrate the importance of partial differential equations and their solution.

One of the major difficulties with partial differential equations is that it is extremely difficult to illustrate their solutions geometrically, in contrast to single-variable problems, where a simple curve can be used. For instance, the temperature in a room, particularly if it is time-varying, is not at all easy to draw or visualize, but such information is of crucial importance to a heating engineer. A second basic problem with partial differential equations is that it is intrinsically more difficult to solve them or even to decide whether a solution exists. Boundaries play a very significant role, and we shall see that a problem can have a solution for one set of boundary conditions but not for another.

The solution of partial differential equations has been greatly eased by the use of computers, which have allowed the rapid numerical solution of problems that would otherwise have been intractable. Such methods have generally been integrated into this chapter, since they are now one of the standard techniques available. However, the finite-element method is considered separately, since it is more complicated, and requires a lot of careful thought and work (the section dealing with it can be omitted on a first reading). The finite-element method originated in stress analysis in civil engineering work, but has now spread into most areas where complicated boundaries are encountered.

There are three basic types of equation that appear in most areas of science and engineering, and it is essential to understand their solutions before any progress can be made on more complicated sets of equations, nonlinear equations or equations with variable coefficients.

8.2   General discussion

The three basic types of equation are referred to as the **wave equation**, the **heat-conduction** or **diffusion equation** and the **Laplace equation**. In this section we briefly discuss the formulation of these three basic forms, and then consider each in more detail in later sections.

8.2.1   Wave equation

$$\frac{1}{c^2}\frac{\partial^2 u}{\partial t^2} = \frac{\partial^2 u}{\partial x^2} + \frac{\partial^2 u}{\partial y^2} + \frac{\partial^2 u}{\partial z^2} = \nabla^2 u \tag{8.1}$$

Many phenomena that involve propagation of a signal require the wave equation (8.1) to be solved in the appropriate number of space dimensions. Perhaps the simplest, in one space dimension, is the vibration of a taut string stretched to a uniform tension T between two fixed points as illustrated in Figure 8.1(a), where u is the displacement, x is measured along the equilibrium position of the string and t is time. Applying Newton's law of motion to an element Δs of the string (Figure 8.1b), for motion in the u direction, we have

net force in u direction = mass element $\times$ acceleration in u direction

that is,

$$T\sin(\psi + \Delta\psi) - T\sin\psi = \rho\Delta s\frac{\partial^2 u}{\partial t^2} \tag{8.2}$$

where ρ is the mass per unit of length of the string. Neglecting terms quadratic in

Figure 8.1 Displacement of an element of a taut string.

small quantities and using the Taylor series expansions

$$\cos \Delta\psi = 1 + O(\Delta\psi^2) \simeq 1, \quad \sin \Delta\psi = \Delta\psi + O(\Delta\psi^3) \simeq \Delta\psi$$

and the expression

$$\Delta s = \sqrt{\left[1 + \left(\frac{\partial u}{\partial x}\right)^2\right]} \Delta x \simeq \Delta x$$

for the arclength, (8.2) becomes

$$T \sin \psi + T \cos \psi \, \Delta\psi - T \sin \psi = \rho \, \Delta x \frac{\partial^2 u}{\partial t^2}$$

or

$$T \cos \psi \frac{\Delta\psi}{\Delta x} = \rho \, \Delta x \frac{\partial^2 u}{\partial t^2}$$

which in the limit as $\Delta x \rightarrow 0$ becomes

$$T \cos \psi \frac{\partial \psi}{\partial x} = \rho \frac{\partial^2 u}{\partial t^2} \tag{8.3}$$

Again assuming that ψ itself is small for small oscillations of the string, we have $\cos \psi \simeq 1$, and the gradient of the string

$$\frac{\partial u}{\partial x} = \tan \psi \simeq \psi$$

and hence from (8.3) we obtain

$$T \frac{\partial^2 u}{\partial x^2} = \rho \frac{\partial^2 u}{\partial t^2}$$

Thus the displacement of the string satisfies the one-dimensional wave equation

$$\frac{1}{c^2} \frac{\partial^2 u}{\partial t^2} = \frac{\partial^2 u}{\partial x^2} \tag{8.4}$$

and the propagation of the disturbance in the string is given by a solution of this equation where $c^2 = T/\rho$.

By considering the theory of small displacements of a compressible fluid, sound waves can likewise be shown to propagate according to (8.1). The one-dimensional form (8.4) will model the propagation of sound in an organ pipe, while the spherically symmetric version of (8.1) will give a solution for waves emanating from an explosion. Because it is known that most wave phenomena satisfy the wave equation, it is reasonable, from a physical standpoint, that the propagation of electromagnetic waves will also satisfy (8.1). A careful analysis of Maxwell's equations in free space is required to show this result (see Example 7.9). We could give further examples of physical phenomena that have (8.1) as a basic equation, but we have described enough here to establish its importance and the need to look at methods of solution. An aspect of the wave equation that is not often discussed is its bad behaviour. Any discontinuities in a variable or its derivatives will, according to the wave equation, propagate with time. An obvious physical manifestation of this is a shock wave. When an aircraft breaks the sound barrier, a shock is produced and the sonic boom can be heard many miles away. How the shock is produced is a complicated nonlinear effect, but once it has been produced it propagates according to the wave equation.

EXAMPLE 8.1 Show that

$$u = u_0 \sin\left(\frac{\pi x}{L}\right) \cos\left(\frac{\pi c t}{L}\right)$$

satisfies the one-dimensional wave equation and the conditions

(a) a given initial displacement $u(x,0) = u_0 \sin(\pi x/L)$, and
(b) zero initial velocity, $\partial u(x,0)/\partial t = 0$.

Solution Clearly the condition (a) is satisfied by inspection. If we now partially differentiate u with respect to t,

$$\frac{\partial u}{\partial t} = -\frac{u_0 \pi c}{L} \sin\left(\frac{\pi x}{L}\right) \sin\left(\frac{\pi c t}{L}\right)$$

so that at $t = 0$ we have $\partial u/\partial t = 0$ and (b) is satisfied.

It remains to show that (8.4) is also satisfied. Using the standard subscript notation for partial derivatives,

$$u_{xx} = \frac{\partial^2 u}{\partial x^2} = -\frac{u_0 \pi^2}{L^2} \sin\left(\frac{\pi x}{L}\right) \cos\left(\frac{\pi c t}{L}\right)$$

$$u_{tt} = \frac{\partial^2 u}{\partial t^2} = -\frac{u_0 \pi^2 c^2}{L^2} \sin\left(\frac{\pi x}{L}\right) \cos\left(\frac{\pi c t}{L}\right)$$

so that the equation is indeed satisfied.

This solution corresponds physically to the fundamental mode of vibration of a taut string plucked at its centre.

EXAMPLE 8.2 Verify that the function

$$u = a \exp\left[-\left(\frac{x}{h} - \frac{ct}{h}\right)^2\right]$$

satisfies the wave equation (8.4). Sketch the graphs of the solution u against x at $t = 0$, $t = 2h/c$ and $t = 4h/c$.

Solution Evaluate the partial derivatives as

$$u_x = \frac{-2a(x - ct)}{h^2} \exp\left[-\left(\frac{x}{h} - \frac{ct}{h}\right)^2\right]$$

$$u_t = \frac{2ac(x - ct)}{h^2}\exp\left[-\left(\frac{x}{h} - \frac{ct}{h}\right)^2\right]$$

and

$$u_{xx} = \frac{-2a}{h^2}\exp\left[-\left(\frac{x}{h} - \frac{ct}{h}\right)^2\right] + \frac{4a(x - ct)^2}{h^4}\exp\left[-\left(\frac{x}{h} - \frac{ct}{h}\right)^2\right]$$

$$u_{tt} = \frac{-2ac^2}{h^2}\exp\left[-\left(\frac{x}{h} - \frac{ct}{h}\right)^2\right] + \frac{4a(x - ct)^2c^2}{h^4}\exp\left[-\left(\frac{x}{h} - \frac{ct}{h}\right)^2\right]$$

Clearly (8.4) is satisfied by these second derivatives.

The curves of u against x are plotted in Figure 8.2, and show a wave initially centred at the origin moving with a constant speed c to the right.

Figure 8.2 Propagating wave in Example 8.2.

8.2.2 Heat-conduction or diffusion equation

$$\frac{1}{\kappa}\frac{\partial u}{\partial t} = \nabla^2 u \tag{8.5}$$

This equation arises most commonly when heat is transferred from a hot area to a cold one by conduction, when the temperature satisfies (8.5).

Let us investigate the heat flow along a thin bar. The bar is assumed to have a uniform cross-sectional area and an insulated outer surface through which no heat is lost. It is also assumed that, at any cross-section $x = $ constant, the temperature $T(x, t)$ is uniform. Consider an element of the bar from x to $x + \Delta x$, where x is measured along the length of the bar, as illustrated in Figure 8.3. An amount of heat $Q(x, t)$ per unit time per unit area enters the left-hand face and an amount $Q(x + \Delta x, t)$ leaves the right-hand face of the element. The net increase

Figure 8.3 Heat flow
in an element.

per unit cross-sectional area in unit time is

$$Q(x,t) - Q(x + \Delta x, t)$$

If c is the specific heat of the bar and ρ is its density then the amount of heat in the element is $c\rho T \Delta x$. The net increase in heat in the element in unit time is

$$c\rho \frac{\partial T}{\partial t} \Delta x$$

and is equated to the net amount entering. Thus

$$c\rho \frac{\partial T}{\partial t} \Delta x = Q(x,t) - Q(x + \Delta x, t)$$

which in the limit as $\Delta x \rightarrow 0$ gives

$$c\rho \frac{\partial T}{\partial t} = -\frac{\partial Q}{\partial x} \tag{8.6}$$

The Fourier law for the conduction of heat states that the heat transferred across unit area is proportional to the temperature gradient. Thus

$$Q = -k \frac{\partial T}{\partial x}$$

where k is the thermal conductivity and the minus sign takes into account the fact that heat flows from hot to cold. Substitution for Q in (8.6) gives the **one-dimensional heat equation**

$$\frac{\partial T}{\partial t} = \kappa \frac{\partial^2 T}{\partial x^2} \tag{8.7}$$

where $\kappa = k/c\rho$ is called the **thermal diffusivity**.

The equations describing more complicated phenomena, such as the time-dependent electromagnetic equations or the equations of fluid mechanics, have the same basic structure as (8.5), but with additional terms or with coupling to other equations of the same type. We certainly need to know how to solve (8.5) before even contemplating solving these more complex versions.

An essential feature of the heat-conduction equation is that, given a long enough time, the temperature will eventually settle down to a steady state. Thus the final solution is independent of time, and hence will satisfy $\partial u/\partial t = 0$ or $\nabla^2 u = 0$. The transient behaviour tells how this solution is approached from its given starting value. Physically it is reasonable that any initial temperature, however complicated, will move to a smooth final solution, and we should not expect the severe difficulties with discontinuities that occur with the wave equation. Exactly how initial discontinuities are treated in a numerical solution, however, can affect the accuracy in the early development of the solution.

EXAMPLE 8.3 Show that

$$T = T_\infty + (T_m - T_\infty)e^{-U(x - Ut)/\kappa} \quad (x \geqslant Ut)$$

satisfies the one-dimensional heat-conduction equation (8.7), together with the boundary conditions $T \to T_\infty$ as $x \to \infty$ and $T = T_m$ at $x = Ut$.

Solution The second term vanishes as $x \to \infty$, for any fixed t, and hence $T \to T_\infty$. When $x = Ut$, the exponential term is unity, so the T_∞s cancel and $T = T_m$. Hence the two boundary conditions are satisfied. Checking both sides of the heat-conduction equation (8.7),

$$\frac{1}{\kappa}\frac{\partial T}{\partial t} = \frac{1}{\kappa}(T_m - T_\infty)\frac{U^2}{\kappa}e^{-U(x - Ut)/\kappa}$$

$$\frac{\partial^2 T}{\partial x^2} = (T_m - T_\infty)\frac{U^2}{\kappa^2}e^{-U(x - Ut)/\kappa}$$

which are obviously equal, so that the equation is satisfied.

The example models a block of material being melted at a temperature T_m, with the melting boundary having constant speed U, and with a steady temperature T_∞ at great distances. An application of this model would be a heat shield on a re-entry capsule ablated by frictional heating.

EXAMPLE 8.4 Show that the function

$$T = \frac{1}{\sqrt{t}}\exp\left(-\frac{x^2}{4\kappa t}\right)$$

satisfies the one-dimensional heat-conduction equation (8.7). Plot T against x for various times t, and comment.

Solution We first calculate the partial derivatives

$$\frac{\partial T}{\partial t} = -\frac{1}{2}\frac{1}{t^{3/2}}\exp\left(\frac{-x^2}{4\kappa t}\right) + \frac{1}{\sqrt{t}}\frac{-x^2}{4\kappa}\frac{-1}{t^2}\exp\left(\frac{-x^2}{4\kappa t}\right)$$

$$\frac{\partial T}{\partial x} = \frac{1}{\sqrt{t}}\frac{-2x}{4\kappa t}\exp\left(\frac{-x^2}{4\kappa t}\right)$$

and

$$\frac{\partial^2 T}{\partial x^2} = \frac{-1}{2\kappa t^{3/2}}\exp\left(\frac{-x^2}{4\kappa t}\right) + \frac{-x}{2\kappa t^{3/2}}\frac{-2x}{4\kappa t}\exp\left(\frac{-x^2}{4\kappa t}\right)$$

Figure 8.4 Solution of the heat-conduction equation starting from an initial spike in Example 8.4.

It is easily checked that (8.7) is satisfied except at the time $t = 0$, where T is not properly defined. The graph of reduced temperature $T/\sqrt{(4\kappa)}$ against distance x at various times $t = L^2/4\kappa$ can be seen in Figure 8.4. Physically, the problem corresponds to a very hot weld being applied instantaneously to the bar. The initial temperature 'spike' at $x = 0$ is seen to spread out as time progresses, and, as expected from the physical interpretation, T tends to zero for all x as the time becomes large.

8.2.3   Laplace equation

$$\nabla^2 u = 0 \tag{8.8}$$

The simplest physical interpretation of this equation has already been mentioned, namely as the steady-state heat equation. So, for example, the two-dimensional Laplace equation

$$\frac{\partial^2 T}{\partial x^2} + \frac{\partial^2 T}{\partial y^2} = 0$$

could represent the steady-state distribution of temperature over a thin rectangular plate in the (x, y) plane.

Heat transfer is well understood intuitively, and good guesses at steady-state solutions can usually be made. Perhaps less commonly understood is the case of the electrostatic potential in a uniform dielectric, which also satisfies the Laplace equation. Working out the electrical behaviour of a capacitor that is charged in a certain manner simply implies solving (8.8) subject to appropriate boundary conditions. Possibly the least obvious, but extremely important, application of the

Laplace equation is in inviscid, irrotational fluid mechanics. To a large extent, subsonic aerodynamics is based on (8.8) as an approximate model. The lift and drag on an aerofoil in a fluid stream can be evaluated accurately from suitable solutions of this equation. It is only close to the aerofoil that viscous and rotational effects become important.

The Laplace equation is a 'smoother' in the sense that it irons out peaks and troughs. Physically, the steady-state heat-conduction context tells us that if a particular point has a higher temperature than neighbouring points then heat will flow from hot to cold until the 'hot spot' is eliminated. Thus there are no interior points at which the solution u of (8.8) is smaller or larger than all of its neighbours. This result can be confirmed mathematically, and establishes that smooth solutions are obtained.

EXAMPLE 8.5 Show that the function

$$\psi = Uy\left(1 - \frac{a^2}{x^2 + y^2}\right)$$

satisfies the Laplace equation, and sketch the curves $\psi = $ constant.

Solution First calculate the partial derivatives:

$$\psi_x = \frac{2xyUa^2}{(x^2 + y^2)^2}$$

$$\psi_y = U - \frac{Ua^2}{x^2 + y^2} + \frac{2y^2Ua^2}{(x^2 + y^2)^2}$$

$$\psi_{xx} = \frac{2yUa^2}{(x^2 + y^2)^2} - \frac{8x^2yUa^2}{(x^2 + y^2)^3}$$

$$\psi_{yy} = \frac{2yUa^2}{(x^2 + y^2)^2} + \frac{4yUa^2}{(x^2 + y^2)^2} - \frac{8y^3Ua^2}{(x^2 + y^2)^3}$$

Substituting into (8.8) gives

$$\nabla^2\psi = \frac{8yUa^2}{(x^2 + y^2)^2} - \frac{8y(x^2 + y^2)Ua^2}{(x^2 + y^2)^3}$$

$$= 0$$

and hence the Laplace equation is satisfied.

Secondly, to sketch the contours, we note that $\psi = 0$ on $y = 0$ and on the circle $x^2 + y^2 = a^2$. On keeping $y = y_0$ and letting $x \to \pm\infty$, the second term vanishes, so the curves tend to $\psi = Uy_0$. Figure 8.5 shows the solution, which corresponds physically to the flow of an inviscid, irrotational fluid past a cylinder placed in a uniform stream.

Figure 8.5 Streamlines for flow past a cylinder of radius 1, from the Laplace equation in Example 8.5.

8.2.4   Other and related equations

We discussed in Section 8.1 applications in science and engineering. Many such applications are governed by equations that are closely related to the three basic equations discussed above. For example, consider the equations of slow, steady, viscous flow in two dimensions, which take the form

$$
\left.
\begin{aligned}
\frac{\partial p}{\partial x} &= \frac{1}{\mathscr{R}}\nabla^2 u, \qquad \frac{\partial p}{\partial y} = \frac{1}{\mathscr{R}}\nabla^2 v \\
\frac{\partial u}{\partial x} &+ \frac{\partial v}{\partial y} = 0,
\end{aligned}
\right\}
\tag{8.9}
$$

where u, v and p are the non-dimensional velocities and pressure, and $\mathscr{R}$ is the Reynolds number. The system has a familiar look about it, and indeed a little simple manipulation gives $\nabla^2 p = 0$, so that the pressure satisfies the Laplace equation. If p can be calculated then $\partial p/\partial x$ and $\partial p/\partial y$ are known, so we have equations of the form

$$
\nabla^2 u = f(x, y)
\tag{8.10}
$$

This equation is called the **Poisson equation**, and is clearly closely related to the Laplace equation. It can be interpreted physically as steady heat conduction with heat sources in the region. A careful study of the solution of the Laplace equation is required before either (8.10) or (8.9) can be attacked.

  If there is good knowledge about the time behaviour of the wave or diffusion equation then we can often obtain important information from them without solving the full equations. For instance, if we put a periodic time dependence $u = e^{j\alpha t}v(x, y, z)$ into (8.1), or if we put an exponentially decaying solution $u = e^{-\beta t}v(x, y, z)$ into (8.5) then the variable v, in both cases, satisfies an equation of the form

$$\nabla^2 v + \lambda v = 0 \qquad (8.11)$$

Equation (8.11) is called the **Helmholtz equation**, and plays an important role in the solution of eigenvalue problems. It is perhaps of relevance that the best studied eigenvalue equation, the **Schrödinger equation**, is almost the same, namely

$$\frac{h^2}{8\pi^2 m} \nabla^2 u - V(x, y, z)u + Eu = 0$$

It is a bit more complicated than (8.11), but it forms the basis of quantum mechanics, on which whole industries are built.

The three classical partial differential equations discussed above are all of second order. First-order equations are rarely of much interest in applications in science and engineering. There is, however, a well developed theory that is much more comprehensive than for second order. One example will give an idea of the power of the theory, but it is left to specialist books to describe the detail.

EXAMPLE 8.6   Find a general solution to the equation

$$\frac{\partial u}{\partial t} + x \frac{\partial u}{\partial x} - y \frac{\partial u}{\partial y} = 0$$

and show that u is constant on the curves $xy = $ constant.

Solution   The theory of first-order equations indicates that we should look at solutions of the ordinary differential equations

$$\frac{\mathrm{d}t}{1} = \frac{\mathrm{d}x}{x} = \frac{\mathrm{d}y}{-y} = \frac{\mathrm{d}u}{0}$$

which are easily computed as $u = C$, $x = Ae^t$ and $y = Be^{-t}$, where A, B and C are arbitrary constants. Any function of these three constants is a solution of the original equations. Thus we seek solutions of the form

$$u = f(xe^{-t}, ye^t)$$

Writing $X = xe^{-t}$ and $Y = ye^t$ and using the chain rule gives

$$\frac{\partial u}{\partial t} = \frac{\partial f}{\partial X} \frac{\partial X}{\partial t} + \frac{\partial f}{\partial Y} \frac{\partial Y}{\partial t} = -xe^{-t}f_X + ye^t f_Y$$

and similarly

$$\frac{\partial u}{\partial x} = e^{-t}f_X, \qquad \frac{\partial u}{\partial y} = e^t f_Y$$

Substituting into the original equation, it is seen that it is satisfied identically for any f.

By rearranging the variables of the function f, it can be written as

$$u = g(t, xy)$$

Taking $Y = xy$ and putting this form into the equation gives

$$0 = u_t + xu_x - yu_y = g_t + xyg_Y - yxg_Y$$

and hence $g_t = 0$. Thus g is independent of t explicitly, and u is only a function of the combination xy. If $xy = $ constant then u is fixed on this curve.

A physical interpretation of this result can be given as follows. If an impurity with concentration u is being transported by a fluid with velocity given by $\mathbf{v} = (x, -y)$ then, for the case when diffusion can be neglected, the impurity concentration satisfies the equation of the problem. Essentially the solution tells us that the impurities are transported along the hyperbolas $xy = $ constant.

So far, all of the equations that we have considered are *linear*, since they have not included any quadratic (or higher) terms in u or its derivatives. As soon as we move from linear to *nonlinear* problems, a whole new crop of theoretical and computational difficulties arises. Very few such equations can be solved analytically, and devising computational schemes is not easy. Even worse, mathematicians cannot always tell whether or not a solution even exists. An act of faith is usually made by scientists and engineers that their problem is modelled correctly and therefore there must be a mathematical solution reflecting the physics. Often the faith is well founded, but modelling is an imperfect art and there are many things that can go wrong. It may be thought that nonlinear problems do not occur in practice, but this is certainly not the case. For some phenomena, like the behaviour of thermionic valves or avalanche semiconductors or pulsed lasers, it is the nonlinearity that produces the desired effects. Other situations arise where the nonlinearity of the system may or may not be important. For instance, the full steady two-dimensional fluid equations are

$$\left.\begin{aligned} u\frac{\partial u}{\partial x} + v\frac{\partial u}{\partial y} &= -\frac{\partial p}{\partial x} + \frac{1}{\mathscr{R}}\nabla^2 u \\ u\frac{\partial v}{\partial x} + v\frac{\partial v}{\partial y} &= -\frac{\partial p}{\partial y} + \frac{1}{\mathscr{R}}\nabla^2 v \\ \frac{\partial u}{\partial x} + \frac{\partial v}{\partial y} &= 0 \end{aligned}\right\} \tag{8.12}$$

where u, v, p and $\mathscr{R}$ are defined as for (8.9). These equations are *nonlinear* because of the presence of quadratic terms such as $u\,\partial u/\partial x$. It can be seen that (8.12) reduce to (8.9) for slow flow when quadratic terms are neglected. While (8.9) would be applicable to the flow of molten glass, we would need the full equations (8.12) to look at flow close to an aerofoil. Indeed, as $\mathscr{R}$ becomes large, the flow becomes turbulent, that is, unstable, and the applicability of these equations comes into question.

8.2.5 Exercises

1 Find the possible values of a and b in the expression

$$u = \cos at \sin bx$$

such that it satisfies the wave equation

$$\frac{1}{c^2}\frac{\partial^2 u}{\partial t^2} = \frac{\partial^2 u}{\partial x^2}$$

2 Taking

$$u = f(x + \alpha t)$$

where f is any function, find the values of α that will ensure that u satisfies the wave equation

$$\frac{1}{c^2}\frac{\partial^2 u}{\partial t^2} = \frac{\partial^2 u}{\partial x^2}$$

3 Find all the possible solutions of the heat-conduction equation

$$\frac{1}{\kappa}\frac{\partial u}{\partial t} = \frac{\partial^2 u}{\partial x^2}$$

of the form

$$u(x, t) = e^{at} V(x)$$

4 Find the values of the constant n for which

$$V = r^n(3\cos^2\theta - 1)$$

satisfies the Laplace equation (in spherical polar coordinates and independent of ϕ)

$$\frac{\partial}{\partial r}\left(r^2\frac{\partial V}{\partial r}\right) + \frac{1}{\sin\theta}\frac{\partial}{\partial\theta}\left(\sin\theta\frac{\partial V}{\partial\theta}\right) = 0$$

for all values of the variables r and θ.

5 The transmission-line equations represent the flow of current along a long, leaky wire such as a transatlantic cable. The equations take the form

$$-\frac{\partial I}{\partial x} = gv + c\frac{\partial v}{\partial t}$$

$$-\frac{\partial v}{\partial x} = rI + L\frac{\partial I}{\partial t}$$

where g, c, r and L are constants and I and v are the current and voltage respectively.

(a) Show that when $r = g = 0$, the equations reduce to the wave equation.

(b) Show that when $L = 0$, the equations reduce to a heat-conduction equation with a forcing term.

Write $W = ve^{gt/c}$ to reduce to the normal form of the equation.

(c) Put $a = \frac{1}{2}(r/L + g/c)$ and then $w = ve^{at}$. Show that when $rc = gL$, w satisfies the wave equation.

6 If $V = x^3 + axy^2$, where a is a constant, show that

$$x\frac{\partial V}{\partial x} + y\frac{\partial V}{\partial y} = 3V$$

Find the value of a if V is to satisfy the equation

$$\frac{\partial^2 V}{\partial x^2} + \frac{\partial^2 V}{\partial y^2} = 0$$

Taking this value of a, show that if $u = r^3 V$, where $r^2 = x^2 + y^2$, then

$$\frac{\partial^2 u}{\partial x^2} + \frac{\partial^2 u}{\partial y^2} = 27rV$$

7 Show that $u = e^{-kt}\cos mx\cos nt$ is a solution of the equation

$$c^2\frac{\partial^2 u}{\partial x^2} = \frac{\partial^2 u}{\partial t^2} + 2k\frac{\partial u}{\partial t}$$

provided that the constants k, m, n and c are related by the equation $n^2 + k^2 = c^2 m^2$.

8 The **telegraph equation** has the form

$$\frac{\partial^2\phi}{\partial x^2} = \frac{1}{c^2}\frac{\partial^2\phi}{\partial t^2} + k\frac{\partial\phi}{\partial t}$$

where c^2 is the speed of light and k is usually small. Given that $\Phi(x, t)$ is a solution of the wave equation

$$\frac{\partial^2\Phi}{\partial x^2} = \frac{1}{c^2}\frac{\partial^2\Phi}{\partial t^2}$$

show that $\phi(x, t) = \Phi(x, t)e^{-kt/2}$ is a solution of the telegraph equation, if terms of order k^2 can be neglected.

9 For a lossless transmission line of uniform inductance L and capacitance C per unit length, the voltage v and current i satisfy the equations

$$\frac{\partial v}{\partial x} = -L\frac{\partial i}{\partial t}, \qquad \frac{\partial i}{\partial x} = -C\frac{\partial v}{\partial t}$$

Eliminate i from these two equations and show that v satisfies the partial differential equation

$$\frac{\partial^2 v}{\partial x^2} = LC\frac{\partial^2 v}{\partial t^2}$$

Show that

$$v = E_0 \sin \omega t \cos (\omega \sqrt{(LC)}x)$$

satisfies this one-dimensional wave equation and the conditions

(a) $v = 0$ for all $x \geqslant 0$ when $t = 0$,

(b) $v = E_0 \sin \omega t$ when $x = 0$ for all $t > 0$, and

(c) $v = 0$ when $x = \pi/(2\omega\sqrt{(LC)})$ for all $t > 0$.

10 Show that if f is a function of x only then

$$u = f(x) \sin (ay + b)$$

where a and b are constants, is a solution of the partial differential equation

$$\frac{\partial^2 u}{\partial y^2} = \frac{\partial^2 u}{\partial x^2} - 2a \frac{\partial u}{\partial x}$$

provided that $f(x)$ satisfies the ordinary differential equation

$$\frac{d^2 f}{dx^2} - 2a \frac{df}{dx} + a^2 f = 0$$

Hence show that

$$u = (A + Bx)e^{ax} \sin (ay + b)$$

where A and B are arbitrary constants, is a solution of the partial differential equation.

8.3   Solution of the wave equation

In this section we consider methods of solving the wave equation introduced in Section 8.2.1.

8.3.1   d'Alembert solution and characteristics

A classical solution of the one-dimensional wave equation

$$\frac{1}{c^2} \frac{\partial^2 u}{\partial t^2} = \frac{\partial^2 u}{\partial x^2} \qquad (8.4)$$

is obtained by changing the axes to reduce the equation to a particularly simple form. Let

$$r = x + ct, \qquad s = x - ct$$

Then, using the chain rule procedure for transformation of coordinates (see Section 7.1.1),

$$u_{xx} = u_{rr} + 2u_{rs} + u_{ss}$$

$$u_{tt} = c^2 (u_{rr} - 2u_{rs} + u_{ss})$$

so that the wave equation (8.4) becomes

$$4c^2 u_{rs} = 0$$

This equation can now be integrated once with respect to s to give

$$u_r = \frac{\partial u}{\partial r} = \theta(r)$$

where θ is an arbitrary function of r. Now, integrating with respect to r, we obtain

$$u = f(r) + g(s)$$

which, on substituting for r and s, gives the solution of the wave equation (8.4) as

$$u = f(x + ct) + g(x - ct) \tag{8.13}$$

where f and g are *arbitrary functions* and f is just the integral of the arbitrary function θ.

The boundary conditions must give just enough information to evaluate f and g, which are functions of the *single* variables $r = x + ct$ and $s = x - ct$ respectively.

In Example 8.2 we have already seen a simple example of a wave of this type. We first deduced that a function of $x - ct$ satisfied the wave equation, and then showed in Figure 8.2 that it represented a wave travelling in the x direction with velocity c. The analysis given above shows a generalized version of the same problem. In Example 8.7 we attempt the more difficult task of fitting initial conditions to the solution.

EXAMPLE 8.7 Solve the wave equation (8.4) subject to the conditions

(a) zero initial velocity, $\partial u(x, 0)/\partial t = 0$ for all x, and

(b) an initial displacement given by

$$u(x, 0) = F(x) = \begin{cases} 1 - x & (0 \leqslant x \leqslant 1) \\ 1 + x & (-1 \leqslant x \leqslant 0) \\ 0 & \text{otherwise} \end{cases}$$

Solution This example corresponds physically to an infinite string initially at rest, and displaced as in Figure 8.6, which is then released.

From (8.13) we have a solution of the wave equation as

$$u = f(x + ct) + g(x - ct)$$

We now fit the given boundary data. Condition (a) gives

$$0 = cf'(x) - cg'(x) \quad \text{for all } x$$

so that

$$f(x) - g(x) = K = \text{an arbitrary constant}$$

and thus

$$u = f(x + ct) + f(x - ct) - K$$

Similarly, condition (b) gives

$$F(x) = 2f(x) - K$$

so that

$$u = \tfrac{1}{2}F(x + ct) + \tfrac{1}{2}F(x - ct) \tag{8.14}$$

We now have the solution to the equation in terms of the function F defined in condition (b). (Note that the same is true for any function F.)

The solution is plotted in Figure 8.7 as u against x for given times. It may be observed from this example that we have two **travelling waves**, one propagating to the right and one to the left. The initial shape is propagated exactly, except for a factor of two, and the shape discontinuities are not smoothed out, as noted in Section 8.2.1.

Figure 8.6 Initial displacement in Example 8.7.

Figure 8.7 Solution to Example 8.7, showing two waves propagating in the $+x$ and $-x$ directions with velocity c.

The analysis in Example 8.7 can be extended to solve the wave equation subject to the general conditions

(a) an initial velocity, $\partial u(x, 0)/\partial t = G(x)$, and

(b) an initial displacement, $u(x, 0) = F(x)$ for all x.

Condition (a) gives

$$G(x) = c[f'(x) - g'(x)]$$

so that

$$c[f(x) - g(x)] = \int_0^x G(x)\,dx + K$$

Condition (b) gives

$$f(x) + g(x) = F(x)$$

and we can solve for $f(x)$ and $g(x)$ as

$$f(x) = \tfrac{1}{2}F(x) + \frac{1}{2c}\int_0^x G(x)\,dx + \tfrac{1}{2}K$$

$$g(x) = \tfrac{1}{2}F(x) - \frac{1}{2c}\int_0^x G(x)\,dx - \tfrac{1}{2}K$$

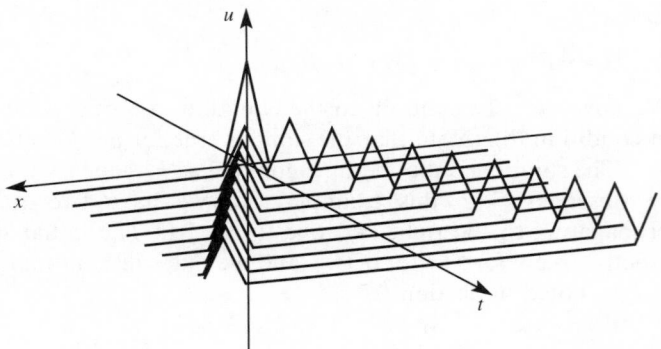

Figure 8.8 Solution to Example 8.7 in (x, t, u) space.

The solution thus becomes

$$u = \tfrac{1}{2}[F(x + ct) + F(x - ct)] + \frac{1}{2c} \int_{x-ct}^{x+ct} G(z)\,dz \qquad \text{(8.15)}$$

which is commonly called the **d'Alembert solution**. As in Examples 8.2 and 8.7, it gives rise to waves propagating in the $+x$ and $-x$ directions.

As mentioned in Section 8.1, a major difficulty is to illustrate the solution of a partial differential equation in a simple way. Figure 8.7 is a 'snapshot' at a particular time t, and if we wish to look at the solution over all (x, t) then we have to draw u as a function of the two variables x and t. With some difficulty, we can draw the solution to Example 8.7 in a three-dimensional diagram as in Figure 8.8, but for any higher-dimensional problem such a diagram is clearly impossible. The 'snapshot' in Figure 8.7 corresponds to a plane slice parallel to the (u, x) plane.

The idea of using an (x, t) plane is a very useful one for the wave equation, since the solution

$$u = f(x + ct) + g(x - ct)$$

gives a representation by **characteristics**. If we plot the lines $x + ct = $ constant and $x - ct = $ constant as in Figure 8.9 then we see that the line AP has equation

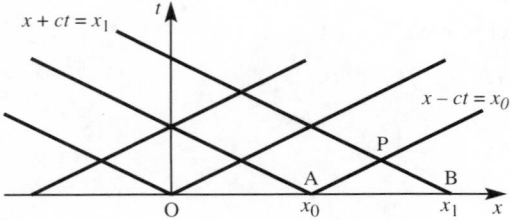

Figure 8.9 Characteristics $x + ct = $ constant and $x - ct = $ constant.

$x - ct = x_0$ and the line BP has equation $x + ct = x_1$. Thus

on the whole of AP $\quad g(x - ct) = g(x_0)$

on the whole of BP $\quad f(x + ct) = f(x_1)$

Thus g takes a constant value on AP and f takes a constant value on BP. If we can calculate f and g on the initial line $t = 0$ then we know the value of u at P, namely

$$u(\text{P}) = f(x_1) + g(x_0) \qquad \qquad \text{(8.16)}$$

Since P is an arbitrary point, the solution at any point would be known. The essential problem is to calculate $f(x)$ and $g(x)$ on the line $t = 0$.

Typical conditions on $t = 0$ are

(a) $u(x, 0) = F(x)$, and

(b) $\partial u(x, 0)/\partial t = G(x)$,

which specify the initial position and velocity of the system. Now

$$c\frac{\partial u}{\partial x} + \frac{\partial u}{\partial t} = cf'(x + ct) + cg'(x - ct) + cf'(x + ct) - cg'(x - ct)$$

$$= 2cf'(x + ct)$$

and similarly

$$c\frac{\partial u}{\partial x} - \frac{\partial u}{\partial t} = 2cg'(x - ct)$$

On $t = 0$ we know that $\partial u/\partial x = F'(x)$ and $\partial u/\partial t = G(x)$, so we can deduce that

$$cF'(x) + G(x) = 2cf'(x)$$

$$cF'(x) - G(x) = 2cg'(x)$$

Since F and G are given, we can compute

$$f'(x) = \tfrac{1}{2}[F'(x) + G(x)/c]$$

$$g'(x) = \tfrac{1}{2}[F'(x) - G(x)/c]$$

and hence $f(x)$ and $g(x)$ can be computed by straightforward integration.

This method is essentially the same as the d'Alembert method, but it concentrates on calculating $f(x)$ and $g(x)$ on the initial line and then constructing the solution at P by the characteristics AP and BP. The method gives great insight into the behaviour of the solution of such equations, but it is not an easy technique to use in practice. Perhaps the best that can be obtained from characteristics is an idea of how the solution depends on the initial data. In Figure 8.10 the characteristics emanating from the initial line are drawn. To evaluate the solution at P, we must have information on the section of the initial line AB, and the rest of the initial line is irrelevant to the solution at P. This is called the **domain of dependence**. The section of the initial line AB has a **domain of influence** determined

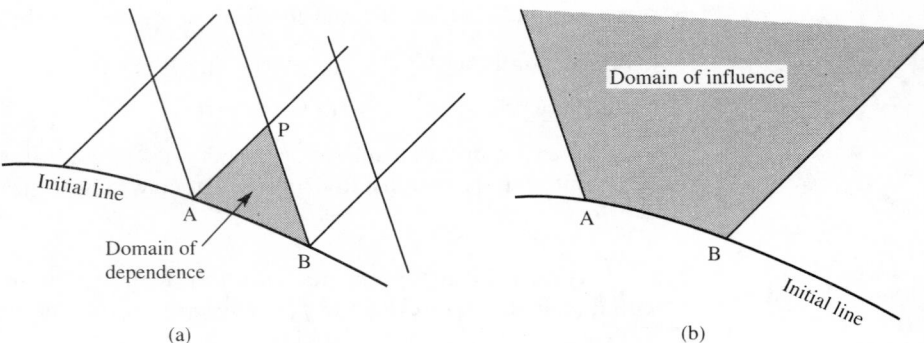

Figure 8.10 Characteristics showing (a) the domain of dependence and (b) the domain of influence.

by the characteristics through the points A and B. The data on AB cannot influence the solution outside the shaded region in Figure 8.10(b).

EXAMPLE 8.8   Use characteristics to compute the solution of the one-dimensional wave equation (8.4), with speed $c = 1$, given the initial conditions that, for all x and $t = 0$, (a) $u = \exp(-|x|)$ and (b) $\partial u/\partial t = 0$.

Solution   Physically, this problem corresponds to an infinite string released from rest with the initial shape given by condition (a).

We know that the solution takes the form

$$u = f(x + t) + g(x - t)$$

and from the general analysis we have

$$G(x) = 0, \qquad F(x) = \exp(-|x|)$$

giving

$$f'(x) = \tfrac{1}{2}F'(x), \qquad g'(x) = \tfrac{1}{2}F'(x)$$

Hence we can integrate to give $f(x)$ and $g(x)$ on $t = 0$ as

$$f(x) = \tfrac{1}{2}\exp(-|x|), \qquad g(x) = \tfrac{1}{2}\exp(-|x|)$$

We choose to compute u at the next time step $t = 0.5$. Looking at Figure 8.11, we see that the characteristics meet on the line $t = 0.5$ in the (x, t) plane. Taking a few typical points, and according to (8.16),

$$u(0, 0.5) = f(0.5 + 0) \ + g(0 - 0.5) \ = 0.3033 + 0.3033 = 0.6066$$

$$u(0.5, 0.5) = f(0.5 + 0.5) + g(0.5 - 0.5) = 0.1839 + 0.5 \quad = 0.6839$$

$$u(1, 0.5) = f(1 + 0.5) \ + g(1 - 0.5) \ = 0.1116 + 0.3033 = 0.4149$$

In a similar manner, all the points on the line $t = 0.5$ can be computed. On the line $t = 1$, that is, the next time step, the characteristics are traced back to the initial line and then computed from the appropriate combination of $f(x)$ and $g(x)$. Figure 8.12 is the table of values obtained in the interval $-3 < x < 3$ for a few time steps, and the results are plotted in Figure 8.13. The two waves move to $+\infty$ and to $-\infty$, as expected.

Figure 8.11
Characteristic
solution of
Example 8.8.

x	$f(x)$	$g(x)$	$u(x, 0)$	$u(x, 0.5)$	$u(x, 1)$	$u(x, 1.5)$	$u(x, 2)$
-3.0000	0.0249	0.0249	0.0498	0.0561	0.0768	0.1171	0.1873
-2.5000	0.0410	0.0410	0.0821	0.0926	0.1267	0.1931	0.3088
-2.0000	0.0677	0.0677	0.1353	0.1526	0.2088	0.3184	0.5092
-1.5000	0.1116	0.1116	0.2231	0.2516	0.3443	0.5249	0.3184
-1.0000	0.1839	0.1839	0.3679	0.4148	0.5677	0.3443	0.2088
-0.5000	0.3033	0.3033	0.6065	0.6839	0.4148	0.2516	0.1526
0.0000	0.5000	0.5000	1.0000	0.6065	0.3679	0.2231	0.1353
0.5000	0.3033	0.3033	0.6065	0.6839	0.4148	0.2516	0.1526
1.0000	0.1839	0.1839	0.3679	0.4148	0.5677	0.3443	0.2088
1.5000	0.1116	0.1116	0.2231	0.2516	0.3443	0.5249	0.3184
2.0000	0.0677	0.0677	0.1353	0.1526	0.2088	0.3184	0.5092
2.5000	0.0410	0.0410	0.0821	0.0926	0.1267	0.1931	0.3088
3.0000	0.0249	0.0249	0.0498	0.0561	0.0768	0.1171	0.1873

Figure 8.12
Computed data for
Example 8.8.

Figure 8.13 Plot of
the data from
Figure 8.12.

The idea of characteristics can be applied to more general classes of second-order partial differential equations. Example 8.9 illustrates a case of a constant-coefficient equation.

EXAMPLE 8.9   Find the characteristics of the equation

$$0 = u_{xx} + 2u_{xt} + 2\alpha u_{tt}$$

Study the case when $\alpha = \frac{3}{8}$ and the solution satisfies the boundary conditions

(a) $\partial u(x,0)/\partial t = 0$ for $x \geqslant 0$

(b) $u(x,0) = F(x) = \begin{cases} 1 & (0 < x < 1) \\ 0 & (x \geqslant 1) \end{cases}$

(c) $u(0,t) = 0$ for all t.

(d) $\partial u(0,t)/\partial x = 0$ for all t

Solution   Since the coefficients of the equation are constants, we know that the characteristics are straight lines, so we look for solutions of the form

$$u = u(x + at)$$

Putting $z = x + at$ and writing $u' = du/dz$ and so on, we obtain

$$0 = u_{xx} + 2u_{xt} + 2\alpha u_{tt} = (1 + 2a + 2a^2\alpha)u''$$

Hence for a solution we require

$$1 + 2a + 2a^2\alpha = 0$$

or

$$a = \frac{-1 \pm \sqrt{(1 - 2\alpha)}}{2\alpha}$$

If $\alpha > \frac{1}{2}$ then the two values of a (a_1 and a_2 say) are complex, and the characteristics $x + a_1 t = $ constant and $x + a_2 t = $ constant do not make sense in the real plane.

If $\alpha = \frac{1}{2}$ then both roots give $a = 1$, and we only have a single characteristic $x + t = $ constant, which is not useful for further computation.

For the case $\alpha < \frac{1}{2}$, we find two real values for a and two sets of characteristics.

It is precisely for this reason that characteristics serve no useful purpose for the heat-conduction or Laplace equations. A further discussion can be found in Section 8.7 after the formal classification of equations has been completed.

Take the case $\alpha = \frac{3}{8}$; then we obtain $a_1 = -2$ and $a_2 = -\frac{2}{3}$, so the solution has the form

$$u = f(x - 2t) + g(x - \tfrac{2}{3}t)$$

where f and g are arbitrary functions and the characteristics are the straight lines $x - 2t = $ constant and $x - \frac{2}{3}t = $ constant.

The boundary conditions given in the problem are a little more complicated than in the d'Alembert solution. Conditions (a) and (b) give

$$0 = \frac{\partial u(x,0)}{\partial t} = -2f'(x) - \tfrac{2}{3}g'(x) \left.\right\}$$
$$F(x) = u(x,0) = f(x) + g(x) \qquad\qquad (x \geqslant 0)$$

Taking $f(0) = g(0) = 0$, we can integrate the first of these expressions and then solve for $f(x)$ and $g(x)$ on the line $t = 0$ as

$$f(x) = -\tfrac{1}{2}F(x), \quad g(x) = \tfrac{3}{2}F(x) \quad (x \geqslant 0)$$

Conditions (c) and (d) say that $u(0,t) = 0$, and $\partial u(0,t)/\partial x = 0$. Thus on the line $x = 0$ we deduce

$$f(z) = g(z) = 0 \quad (z < 0)$$

We can now construct the solution by characteristics. Figure 8.14 illustrates this solution. Because $f(x)$ and $g(x)$ are constant along the respective characteristics, we deduce $u(A) = 0$, $u(B) = -\tfrac{1}{2}$, $u(C) = 1$, $u(D) = 0$, $u(E) = \tfrac{3}{2}$, $u(F) = 0$ at typical points in the six regions that divide up the first quadrant of the (x,t) plane.

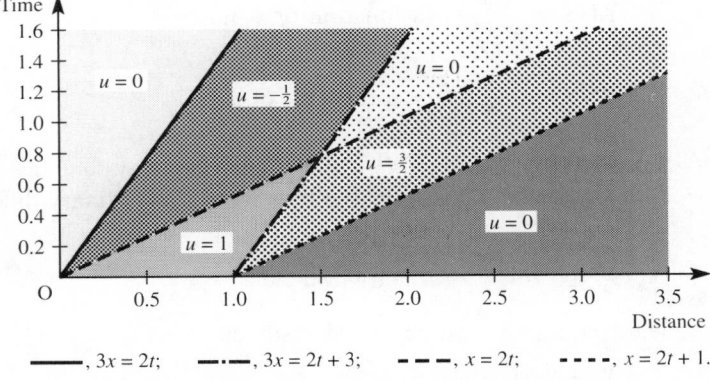

Figure 8.14
Characteristic solution of Example 8.9. The solution u takes the constant values shown in the six regions of the first quadrant.

——— , $3x = 2t$;　—·—· , $3x = 2t + 3$;　– – – , $x = 2t$;　- - - - , $x = 2t + 1$.

For non-constant-coefficient equations the characteristics are not usually straight lines, which causes computational difficulties. In particular, there are some fundamental problems when characteristics of the same family intersect. The solution loses its uniqueness, and 'shocks' can be generated. The classical wave equation (8.4) will propagate these shocks, but it requires 'curved characteristics' to generate them.

8.3.2　Separated solutions

A method of considerable importance is the **method of separation of variables**. The basis of the method is to attempt to look for solutions $u(x,y)$ of a partial differential equation as a product of functions of single variables

$$u(x, y) = X(x)Y(y)$$

The advantage of this approach is that it is sometimes possible to find X and Y as solutions of *ordinary* differential equations. These are very much easier to solve than partial differential equations, and it may be possible to build up solutions of the full equation in terms of the solutions for X and Y. A simple example illustrates the general strategy. Suppose that we wish to solve

$$\frac{\partial u}{\partial x} + \frac{\partial u}{\partial y} = 0$$

Then we should write $u = X(x)Y(y)$ and substitute

$$Y\frac{dX}{dx} + X\frac{dY}{dy} = 0, \quad \text{or} \quad \frac{1}{X}\frac{dX}{dx} = -\frac{1}{Y}\frac{dY}{dy}$$

Note that the partial differentials become ordinary differentials, since the functions are just functions of a single variable. Now

$$\text{LHS} = \frac{1}{X}\frac{dX}{dx} = \text{a function of } x \text{ only}$$

$$\text{RHS} = -\frac{1}{Y}\frac{dY}{dy} = \text{a function of } y \text{ only}$$

Since LHS = RHS for *all* x and y, the only way that this can be achieved is for each side to be a *constant*. We thus have two ordinary differential equations

$$\frac{1}{X}\frac{dX}{dx} = \lambda, \qquad -\frac{1}{Y}\frac{dY}{dy} = \lambda$$

These equations can be solved easily as

$$X = Be^{\lambda x}, \qquad Y = Ce^{-\lambda y}$$

and thus the solution of the original partial differential equation is

$$u(x, y) = X(x)Y(y) = Ae^{\lambda(x-y)}$$

where $A = BC$. The constants A and λ are arbitrary. The crucial question is whether the boundary conditions imposed by the problem can be satisfied by a sum of solutions of this type.

The method of separation of variables can be a very powerful technique, and we shall see it used on all three of the basic partial differential equations. It should be noted, however, that all equations do not have separated solutions, and even when they can be obtained it is not always possible to satisfy the boundary conditions with such solutions.

In the case of the heat-conduction equation and the wave equation, the form of one of the functions in the separated solution is dictated by the physics of the problem. We shall see that the separation technique becomes a little simpler when such physical arguments are used. However, for the Laplace equation there is no help from the physics, so the method just described needs to be applied.

In most wave equation problems we are looking for either a travelling-wave solution as in Section 8.3.1 or for periodic solutions, as a result of plucking a violin string for instance. It therefore seems natural to look for specific solutions that have periodicity built into them. These will not be general solutions, but they will be seen to be useful for a whole class of problems. The essential mathematical simplicity of the method comes from only having to solve ordinary differential equations.

The above argument suggests that we seek solutions of the wave equation

$$\frac{1}{c^2}\frac{\partial^2 u}{\partial t^2} = \frac{\partial^2 u}{\partial x^2} \tag{8.4}$$

of the form either

$$u = \sin(c\lambda t)v(x) \tag{8.17a}$$

or

$$u = \cos(c\lambda t)v(x) \tag{8.17b}$$

both of which when substituted into (8.4) give the ordinary differential equation

$$\frac{\mathrm{d}^2 v}{\mathrm{d}x^2} = -\lambda^2 v$$

This is a simple-harmonic equation with solutions $v = \sin \lambda x$ or $v = \cos \lambda x$. We can thus build up a general solution of (8.4) from linear multiples of the four basic solutions

$$u_1 = \cos \lambda ct \sin \lambda x \tag{8.18a}$$

$$u_2 = \cos \lambda ct \cos \lambda x \tag{8.18b}$$

$$u_3 = \sin \lambda ct \sin \lambda x \tag{8.18c}$$

$$u_4 = \sin \lambda ct \cos \lambda x \tag{8.18d}$$

and try to satisfy the boundary conditions using appropriate linear combinations of solutions of this type. We saw an example of such a solution in Example 8.1.

EXAMPLE 8.10 Solve the wave equation (8.4) for the vibration of a string stretched between the points $x = 0$ and $x = l$ and subject to the boundary conditions

(a) $u(0, t) = 0$ $(t \geqslant 0)$ (fixed at the end $x = 0$);

(b) $u(l, t) = 0$ $(t \geqslant 0)$ (fixed at the end $x = l$);

(c) $\partial u(x, 0)/\partial t = 0$ $(0 \leqslant x \leqslant l)$ (with zero initial velocity);

(d) $u(x, 0) = \begin{cases} x & (0 \leqslant x \leqslant \frac{1}{2}l) \\ l - x & (\frac{1}{2}l \leqslant x \leqslant l) \end{cases}$ (given initial displacement).

Solution Clearly, we are solving the problem of a stretched string, held at its ends $x = 0$ and $x = l$, plucked at its midpoint, and released from rest.

By inspection, we see that the solutions (8.18b, d) cannot satisfy condition (a). We see that condition (b) is satisfied by the solutions (8.18a, c), provided that

$$\sin \lambda l = 0, \quad \text{or} \quad \lambda l = n\pi \quad (n = 1, 2, 3, \ldots)$$

It may be noted that only specific values of λ in (8.18) give permissible solutions. Thus the string can only vibrate with given frequencies, $nc/2l$. The solution (8.18) appropriate to this problem takes the form either

$$u = \cos\left(\frac{nc\pi t}{l}\right) \sin\left(\frac{n\pi x}{l}\right) \tag{8.19a}$$

or

$$u = \sin\left(\frac{nc\pi t}{l}\right) \sin\left(\frac{n\pi x}{l}\right) \tag{8.19b}$$

$(n = 1, 2, 3, \ldots)$. To satisfy condition (c) for all x, we must choose the solution (8.19a) and omit (8.19b). Clearly, it is not possible to satisfy the initial condition (d) with (8.19a). However, because the wave equation is linear, any *sum* of such solutions is also a solution. Thus we build up a solution

$$u = \sum_{n=1}^{\infty} b_n \cos\left(\frac{nc\pi t}{l}\right) \sin\left(\frac{n\pi x}{l}\right) \tag{8.20}$$

The condition (d) for $u(x, 0)$ simply gives

$$\sum_{n=1}^{\infty} b_n \sin\left(\frac{n\pi x}{l}\right) = f(x) = \begin{cases} x & (0 \leqslant x \leqslant \tfrac{1}{2}l) \\ l - x & (\tfrac{1}{2}l \leqslant x \leqslant l) \end{cases}$$

and thus to determine b_n we must find the Fourier sine series expansion of the function $f(x)$ over the finite interval $0 \leqslant x \leqslant l$. We have from (4.33) that

$$b_n = \frac{2}{l} \int_0^l f(x) \sin\left(\frac{n\pi x}{l}\right) dx$$

$$= \frac{2}{l} \int_0^{l/2} x \sin\left(\frac{n\pi x}{l}\right) dx + \frac{2}{l} \int_{l/2}^l (l - x) \sin\left(\frac{n\pi x}{l}\right) dx$$

$$= \frac{4l}{\pi^2 n^2} \sin\left(\tfrac{1}{2} n\pi\right) \quad (n = 1, 2, 3, \ldots)$$

The complete solution of the wave equation in this case is therefore

$$u(x, t) = \frac{4l}{\pi^2} \sum_{n=1}^{\infty} \frac{1}{n^2} \sin\left(\tfrac{1}{2} n\pi\right) \cos\left(\frac{nc\pi t}{l}\right) \sin\left(\frac{n\pi x}{l}\right) \tag{8.21}$$

or

$$u(x, t) = \frac{4l}{\pi^2} \left[\cos\left(\frac{c\pi t}{l}\right) \sin\left(\frac{\pi x}{l}\right) - \tfrac{1}{9} \cos\left(\frac{3c\pi t}{l}\right) \sin\left(\frac{3\pi x}{l}\right) \right.$$

$$\left. + \tfrac{1}{25} \cos\left(\frac{5c\pi t}{l}\right) \sin\left(\frac{5\pi x}{l}\right) + \ldots \right]$$

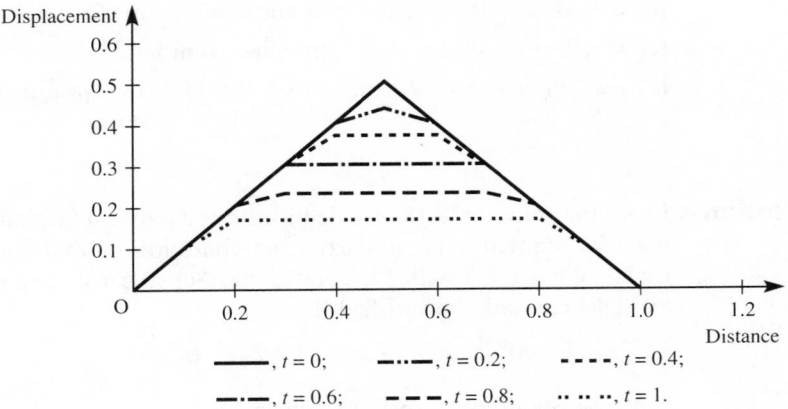

Displacement

0.6
0.5
0.4
0.3
0.2
0.1

O   0.2   0.4   0.6   0.8   1.0   1.2
Distance

——, $t = 0$;   —··—, $t = 0.2$;   - - - -, $t = 0.4$;
—·—, $t = 0.6$;   – – –, $t = 0.8$;   ·· ·· ··, $t = 1$.

Figure 8.15 Solution of Example 8.10 with $c = \frac{1}{3}$ and $l = 1$.

The complete solution to Example 8.10 gives some very useful information. We see that all the even 'harmonics' have disappeared from the solution and the amplitudes of the harmonics decrease like $1/n^2$. A beautiful theory of musical instruments can be built up from such solutions. We see that for different instruments different harmonics are important and have different amplitudes. It is this that gives an instrument its characteristic sound.

A sensible question that we can ask is whether we can use the sum of the series in (8.21) to plot u. In Chapter 4 we saw that, at discontinuities in particular, Fourier series can be very slow to converge, so that, although (8.21) is a complete solution, does it provide us with any useful information? In the present case there is no particular problem, but the general comment should be noted. The solution (8.21) is plotted in Figure 8.15 with $l = 1$ and $c = \frac{1}{3}$. We note that even with 10 terms $u(0.5, 0) = 0.4899$ instead of the correct value 0.5, so there is a 2% error in the calculated value. Perhaps the most pertinent comment that we can make is that a good number of terms in the series are required to obtain a solution, and exact solutions may not be as useful as we might expect.

Separated solutions depend on judicious use of the known solutions (8.18) of the wave equation to fit the boundary conditions. Although it is not always possible to solve any particular problem using separated solutions, the idea is sufficiently straightforward that it is always worth a try. The extension to other equations and coordinate systems is possible, and some of these will be discussed in Sections 8.4 and 8.5.

EXAMPLE 8.11   Solve the wave equation (8.4) for vibrations in an organ pipe subject to the boundary conditions

(a) $u(0, t) = 0$ $(t \geqslant 0)$ (the end $x = 0$ is closed);

(b) $\partial u(l, t)/\partial x = 0$ $(t \geqslant 0)$ (the end $x = l$ is open);

(c) $u(x, 0) = 0$ $(0 \leqslant x \leqslant l)$ (the pipe is initially undisturbed);

(d) $\partial u(x, 0)/\partial t = v = \text{constant}$ $(0 \leqslant x \leqslant l)$ (the pipe is given an initial uniform blow).

Solution   From the solution (8.18), we deduce from condition (a) that solutions (8.18b, d) must be omitted, and similarly from condition (c) that solution (8.18a) is not useful. We are left with the solution (8.18c) to satisfy the boundary condition (b). This can only be satisfied if

$$\cos \lambda l = 0, \qquad \text{or} \qquad \lambda l = (n + \tfrac{1}{2})\pi \quad (n = 0, 1, 2, \ldots)$$

Thus we obtain solutions of the form

$$u = b_n \sin\left[\frac{(n + \tfrac{1}{2})\pi c t}{l}\right] \sin\left[\frac{(n + \tfrac{1}{2})\pi x}{l}\right] \quad (n = 0, 1, 2, \ldots)$$

giving a general solution

$$u = \sum_{n=0}^{\infty} b_n \sin\left[\frac{(n + \tfrac{1}{2})\pi c t}{l}\right] \sin\left[\frac{(n + \tfrac{1}{2})\pi x}{l}\right]$$

The condition (d) gives

$$v = \sum_{n=0}^{\infty} b_n \frac{(n + \tfrac{1}{2})\pi c}{l} \sin\left[\frac{(n + \tfrac{1}{2})\pi x}{l}\right]$$

which, on using (4.33) to obtain the coefficients of the Fourier sine series expansion of the constant v over the finite interval $0 \leqslant x \leqslant l$, gives

$$b_n = \frac{2v}{(n + \tfrac{1}{2})\pi} \frac{l}{(n + \tfrac{1}{2})\pi c} = \frac{8lv}{\pi^2 c} \frac{1}{(2n + 1)^2}$$

Our complete solution of the wave equation is therefore

$$u = \frac{8lv}{\pi^2 c} \sum_{n=0}^{\infty} \frac{1}{(2n + 1)^2} \sin\left[(n + \tfrac{1}{2})\pi \frac{ct}{l}\right] \sin\left[(n + \tfrac{1}{2})\pi \frac{x}{l}\right]$$

or,

$$u = \frac{8lv}{\pi^2 c}\left[\sin\left(\frac{\pi c t}{2l}\right)\sin\left(\frac{\pi x}{2l}\right) + \tfrac{1}{9}\sin\left(\frac{3\pi c t}{2l}\right)\sin\left(\frac{3\pi x}{2l}\right)\right.$$
$$\left. + \tfrac{1}{25}\sin\left(\frac{5\pi c t}{2l}\right)\sin\left(\frac{5\pi x}{2l}\right) + \cdots\right]$$

It would be instructive to compute this solution and compare it with Figure 8.15, which corresponds to the solution of Example 8.10.

8.3.3   Laplace transform solution

For linear problems that are time-varying from 0 to ∞, as in the case of the wave equation, Laplace transforms provide a formal method of solution. The only difficulty is whether the final inversion can be performed.

First we obtain the Laplace transforms of the partial derivatives

$$\frac{\partial u}{\partial x}, \quad \frac{\partial u}{\partial t}, \quad \frac{\partial^2 u}{\partial x^2}, \quad \frac{\partial^2 u}{\partial t^2}$$

of the function $u(x, t)$, $t \geqslant 0$. Using the same procedure as that used to obtain the Laplace transform of standard derivatives in Section 2.3.1, we have the following.

(a) $\displaystyle \mathscr{L}\left\{\frac{\partial u}{\partial x}\right\} = \int_0^\infty e^{-st} \frac{\partial u}{\partial x} \, dt = \frac{d}{dx} \int_0^\infty e^{-st} u(x, t) \, dt$

using Leibniz' rule (see *Modern Engineering Mathematics*) for differentiation under an integral sign. Noting that

$$\mathscr{L}\{u(x, t)\} = U(x, s) = \int_0^\infty e^{-st} u(x, t) \, dt$$

we have

$$\mathscr{L}\left\{\frac{\partial u}{\partial x}\right\} = \frac{d}{dx} U(x, s) \tag{8.22}$$

(b) Writing $y(x, t) = \partial u / \partial x$, repeated application of the result (8.22) gives

$$\mathscr{L}\left\{\frac{\partial y}{\partial x}\right\} = \frac{d}{dx} \mathscr{L}\{y(x, t)\} = \frac{d}{dx}\left(\frac{d}{dx} U(x, s)\right)$$

so that

$$\mathscr{L}\left\{\frac{\partial^2 u}{\partial x^2}\right\} = \frac{d^2 U(x, s)}{dx^2} \tag{8.23}$$

(c) $\displaystyle \mathscr{L}\left\{\frac{\partial u}{\partial t}\right\} = \int_0^\infty e^{-st} \frac{\partial u}{\partial t} \, dt$

$$= [e^{-st} u(x, t)]_0^\infty + s \int_0^\infty e^{-st} u(x, t) \, dt$$

$$= [0 - u(x, 0)] + sU(x, s)$$

so that

$$\mathscr{L}\left\{\frac{\partial u}{\partial t}\right\} = sU(x, s) - u(x, 0) \tag{8.24}$$

where we have assumed that $u(x, t)$ is of exponential order.

(d) Writing $v(x, t) = \partial u/\partial t$, repeated application of (8.24) gives

$$\mathcal{L}\left\{\frac{\partial v}{\partial t}\right\} = sV(x, s) - v(x, 0)$$

$$= s[sU(x, s) - u(x, 0)] - v(x, 0)$$

so that

$$\mathcal{L}\left\{\frac{\partial^2 u}{\partial t^2}\right\} = s^2 U(x, s) - su(x, 0) - u_t(x, 0) \tag{8.25}$$

where $u_t(x, 0)$ denotes the value of $\partial u/\partial t$ at $t = 0$.

Let us now return to consider the wave equation (8.4)

$$c^2 \frac{\partial^2 u}{\partial x^2} = \frac{\partial^2 u}{\partial t^2}$$

subject to the boundary conditions $u(x, 0) = f(x)$ and $\partial u(x, 0)/\partial t = g(x)$. Taking Laplace transform on both sides of (8.4) and using the results (8.23) and (8.25) gives

$$c^2 \frac{d^2 U(x, s)}{dx^2} = s^2 U(x, s) - g(x) - sf(x) \tag{8.26}$$

The problem has thus been reduced to an ordinary differential equation in $U(x, s)$ of a straightforward type. It can be solved for given conditions at the ends of the x range, and the solution can then be inverted to give $u(x, t)$.

EXAMPLE 8.12 Solve the wave equation (8.4) for a semi-infinite string by Laplace transforms, given that

(a) $u(x, 0) = 0$ $(x \geqslant 0)$ (string initially undisturbed);
(b) $\partial u(x, 0)/\partial t = xe^{-x/a}$ $(x \geqslant 0)$ (string given an initial velocity);
(c) $u(0, t) = 0$ $(t \geqslant 0)$ (string held at $x = 0$);
(d) $u(x, t) \rightarrow 0$ as $x \rightarrow \infty$ for $t \geqslant 0$ (string held at infinity).

Solution Using conditions (a) and (b) and substituting for $f(x)$ and $g(x)$ in the result (8.26), the transformed equation in this case is

$$c^2 \frac{d^2}{dx^2} U(x, s) = s^2 U(x, s) - xe^{-x/a}$$

By seeking a particular integral of the form

$$U = \alpha xe^{-x/a} + \beta e^{-x/a}$$

we obtain a solution of the differential equation as

$$U(x, s) = Ae^{sx/c} + Be^{-sx/c} - \frac{e^{-x/a}}{c^2/a^2 - s^2}\left[x + \frac{2c^2/a}{c^2/a^2 - s^2}\right]$$

where A and B are arbitrary constants.

Transforming the given boundary conditions (c) and (d), we have $U(0, s) = 0$ and $U(x, s) \rightarrow 0$ as $x \rightarrow \infty$, which can be used to determine A and B. From the second condition $A = 0$, and the first condition then gives

$$B = \frac{2c^2/a}{(c^2/a^2 - s^2)^2}$$

so that the solution becomes

$$U(x, s) = \frac{2c^2/a}{(c^2/a^2 - s^2)^2}e^{-sx/c} - \frac{e^{-x/a}}{(c^2/a^2 - s^2)}\left[x + \frac{2c^2/a}{(c^2/a^2 - s^2)}\right]$$

Fortunately in this case these transforms can be inverted from tables of Laplace transforms.

Using the second shift theorem (2.45) together with the Laplace transform pairs

$$\mathcal{L}\{\sinh \omega t\} = \frac{\omega}{s^2 - \omega^2}, \qquad \mathcal{L}\{\cosh \omega t\} = \frac{s}{s^2 - \omega^2}$$

$$\mathcal{L}\left\{\frac{\omega t \cosh \omega t - \sinh \omega t}{2\omega^3}\right\} = \frac{1}{(s^2 - \omega^2)^2}$$

we obtain the solution as

$$u = \frac{a}{c}\left[(ct - x)\cosh\left(\frac{ct - x}{a}\right)H(ct - x) - cte^{-x/a}\cosh\left(\frac{ct}{a}\right)\right]$$

$$+ \frac{a}{c}\left[e^{-x/a}(x + a)\sinh\left(\frac{ct}{a}\right) - a\sinh\left(\frac{ct - x}{a}\right)H(ct - x)\right]$$

where $H(t)$ is the Heaviside step function defined in Section 2.5.1.

8.3.4   Exercises

11 The spherically symmetric version of the wave equation (8.4) takes the form

$$\frac{1}{c^2}\frac{\partial^2 u}{\partial t^2} = \frac{\partial^2 u}{\partial r^2} + \frac{2}{r}\frac{\partial u}{\partial r}$$

Show, by putting $v = ru$, that it has a solution

$$ru = f(ct - r) + g(ct + r)$$

Interpret the terms as spherical waves.

12 Using the trigonometric identity

$$\sin A \cos B = \tfrac{1}{2}\sin(A - B) + \tfrac{1}{2}\sin(A + B)$$

rewrite the solution (8.21) to Example 8.10 as a progressive wave.

13 Find the solutions to the wave equation (8.4) subject to the boundary conditions

(a) $\partial u(x, 0)/\partial t = 0$ for all x

(b) $u = \begin{cases} 1 - x & (0 \leqslant x \leqslant 1) \\ 1 + x & (-1 \leqslant x \leqslant 0) \\ 0 & (|x| \geqslant 1) \end{cases}$ at $t = 0$

using (i) d'Alembert's method and (ii) the Laplace transform method. Compare with Example 8.7.

14 Compute the characteristics of the equation

$$3u_{xx} + 6u_{xy} + u_{yy} = 0$$

15 Use characteristics to compute the solution of the wave equation (8.4), with speed $c = 1$, given the initial conditions that for all x and $t = 0$

(a) $u = 0$ (b) $\partial u / \partial t = \exp(-|x|)$

Use a time step of 0.5 to compute (on a spreadsheet or other package) the first four steps over the range $-3 < x < 3$.

16 Using the separated solution approach of Section 8.3.2, obtain a series solution of the wave equation

$$\frac{\partial^2 u}{\partial x^2} = \frac{1}{c^2} \frac{\partial^2 u}{\partial t^2}$$

subject to the boundary conditions

(a) $u(0, t) = 0$ $(t > 0)$

(b) $\partial u(x, 0)/\partial t = 0$ $(0 < x < \pi)$

(c) $u(\pi, t) = 0$ $(t > 0)$

(d) $u(x, 0) = \pi x - x^2$ $(0 < x < \pi)$

17 The end at $x = 0$ of an infinitely long string, initially at rest along the x axis, undergoes a periodic displacement $a \sin \omega t$, for $t > 0$, transverse to the x axis. The displacement $u(x, t)$ of any point on the string at any time is given by the solution of the wave equation

$$\frac{\partial^2 u}{\partial t^2} = c^2 \frac{\partial^2 u}{\partial x^2} \quad (x > 0, t > 0)$$

subject to the boundary conditions

(a) $u(x, 0) = 0$ $(x > 0)$

(b) $\partial u(x, 0)/\partial t = 0$ $(x > 0)$

(c) $u(0, t) = a \sin \omega t$ $(t > 0)$

(d) $|u(x, t)| < L$, L constant

where the last condition specifies that the displacement is bounded.

Using the Laplace transform method, show that the displacement is given by

$$u(x, t) = a \sin \left[\omega \left(t - \frac{x}{c} \right) \right] H \left(t - \frac{x}{c} \right)$$

where $H(t)$ is the Heaviside step function.

Plot a graph of $u(x, t)$, and discuss.

18 The function $u(r, t)$ satisfies the partial differential equation

$$\frac{\partial^2 u}{\partial r^2} + \frac{2}{r} \frac{\partial u}{\partial r} = \frac{1}{c^2} \frac{\partial^2 u}{\partial t^2}$$

where c is a positive constant. Show that this equation has a solution of the form

$$u = \frac{g(r)}{r} \cos \omega t$$

where ω is a constant and g satisfies

$$\frac{d^2 g}{dr^2} + \frac{\omega^2 g}{c^2} = 0$$

Show that, if u satisfies the conditions

$$u(a, t) = \beta \cos \omega t$$

$$u(b, t) = 0$$

then the solution is

$$u(r, t) = \frac{\beta a \cos \omega t}{r} \frac{\sin [\omega(b - r)/c]}{\sin [\omega(b - a)/c]}$$

19 Find the solution to the wave equation

$$c^2 \frac{\partial^2 u}{\partial x^2} = \frac{\partial^2 u}{\partial t^2}$$

that satisfies the conditions

(a) $u(x, 0) = 0$ for all x

(b) $\partial u(x, 0)/\partial t = a \cos \omega x$ for all x

8.3.5 Numerical solution

For all but the simplest problems, we have to find a numerical solution. In Section 8.3.1 we saw that characteristics give a possible numerical way of working by

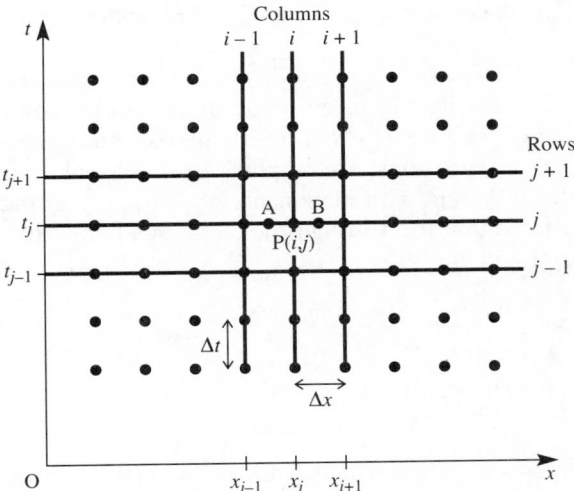

Figure 8.16 Mesh points for a numerical solution of the wave equation.

extending the solution away from the initial line. While this method is possible, it is difficult to program except for the simplest problems, where other methods would be preferred anyway. In particular, when characteristics are curved it becomes difficult to keep track of the solution front. However, calculus methods suffer because they cannot cope with discontinuities, so that, should these occur, the methods described in this section will tend to 'smear out' the shocks. Characteristics provide one of the few methods that will trap the shocks when we use the fact that the latter are propagated along the characteristics.

In Sections 10.6 and 11.5 of *Modern Engineering Mathematics* the numerical solution of ordinary differential equations was studied in some detail. The basis of the methods was to construct approximations to differentials in terms of values of the required function at discrete points. The commonest approximation was discussed in Section 7.4.1 of *Modern Engineering Mathematics*, namely the 'chord approximation'

$$\frac{\mathrm{d}f(a)}{\mathrm{d}x} \simeq \frac{f(a + h) - f(a - h)}{2h}$$

and for the second derivative

$$\frac{\mathrm{d}^2 f(a)}{\mathrm{d}x^2} \simeq \frac{f(a + h) - 2f(a) + f(a - h)}{h^2}$$

The justification of these approximations and the computation of the errors involved depend on the Taylor expansions of the functions. In partial differentiation the approximations are the same except that there is a partial derivative in both x and t for the function $u(x, t)$.

Figure 8.16 illustrates a mesh of points, or **nodes**, with spacing Δx in the x direction and Δt in the t direction. Each node is specified by a pair of integers

(i, j), so that the coordinates of the nodal points take the form

$$x_i = a + i\,\Delta x, \qquad t_j = b + j\,\Delta t$$

and a and b specify the origin chosen. The mesh points or nodes lie on the intersection of the **rows** ($j = $ constant) and **columns** ($i = $ constant).

The approximations are applied to a typical point P, with discretized coordinates (i, j), and with increments $\Delta x = x_{i+1} - x_i$ and $\Delta t = t_{j+1} - t_j$, which are taken to be uniform through the mesh. We know that at the points A and B we can approximate

$$\left(\frac{\partial u}{\partial x}\right)_A \simeq \frac{u(i, j) - u(i - 1, j)}{\Delta x}$$

$$\left(\frac{\partial u}{\partial x}\right)_B \simeq \frac{u(i + 1, j) - u(i, j)}{\Delta x}$$

so that the second derivative at P has the numerical form

$$\frac{\partial^2 u}{\partial x^2} = \frac{(\partial u/\partial x)_B - (\partial u/\partial x)_A}{\Delta x}$$

$$= \frac{u(i + 1, j) - 2u(i, j) + u(i - 1, j)}{\Delta x^2}$$

Similarly,

$$\frac{\partial^2 u}{\partial t^2} = \frac{u(i, j + 1) - 2u(i, j) + u(i, j - 1)}{\Delta t^2}$$

Thus the wave equation $\partial^2 u/\partial t^2 = c^2\,\partial^2 u/\partial x^2$ becomes

$$\frac{u(i, j + 1) - 2u(i, j) + u(i, j - 1)}{\Delta t^2} = c^2 \frac{u(i + 1, j) - 2u(i, j) + u(i - 1, j)}{\Delta x^2}$$

which can be rearranged as

$$u(i, j + 1) = 2u(i, j) - u(i, j - 1) + \lambda^2 [u(i + 1, j) - 2u(i, j) + u(i - 1, j)]$$

$$(8.27)$$

where

$$\lambda = c\,\Delta t/\Delta x$$

Equation (8.27) is a **finite-difference representation** of the wave equation, and provided that u is known on rows $j - 1$ and j then $u(i, j + 1)$ can be computed on row $j + 1$ from (8.27) and thus the solution continued. On the zeroth row the boundary conditions $u(x, 0) = f(x)$ and $\partial u(x, 0)/\partial t = g(x)$ are known, so that $f_i = u(i, 0)$ and $g_i = \partial u(i, 0)/\partial t$ are also known at each node on this row, and these are used to start the process off. From Figure 8.17, we see that

$$g_i = \frac{\partial u}{\partial t} = \frac{u(i, 1) - u(i, -1)}{2\,\Delta t}$$

$$(8.28)$$

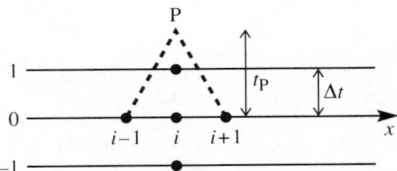

Figure 8.17 The first rows of mesh points in the numerical solution of the wave equation.

Now (8.27) with $j = 0$ becomes

$$u(i, 1) = 2u(i, 0) - u(i, -1) + \lambda^2[u(i + 1, 0) - 2u(i, 0) + u(i - 1, 0)]$$

Since $u(i, 0) = f_i$ and $u(i, -1) = u(i, 1) - 2\Delta t\, g_i$, (8.27) now takes the form

$$u(i, 1) = (1 - \lambda^2)f_i + \tfrac{1}{2}\lambda^2(f_{i+1} + f_{i-1}) + \Delta t\, g_i \qquad \textbf{(8.29)}$$

Thus the basic strategy is to compute row zero from $u(i, 0) = f_i$, evaluate row one from (8.29), and then march forward for general row j by (8.27).

EXAMPLE 8.13   Solve the wave equation $\partial^2 u/\partial t^2 = c^2\,\partial^2 u/\partial x^2$ for a semi-infinite string, given the initial conditions

(a) $u(x, 0) = x\exp[-5(x-1)^2]$ $(x \geqslant 0)$ (string given an initial displacement);

(b) $\partial u(x, 0)/\partial t = 0$ $(x \geqslant 0)$ (string at rest initially);

(c) $u(0, t) = 0$ $(t \geqslant 0)$ (string held at the point $x = 0$).

Solution   Since $g_i = 0$ in (8.29), only the one parameter λ needs to be specified. Figure 8.18 shows the solution of u over eight time steps with $\lambda = 0.5$. It can be seen that the solution splits into two waves, one moving in the $+x$ direction and the other in the $-x$ direction. At a given time $t = 0.8/c$, the u values are presented in the table shown in Figure 8.19 for various values of λ. We see that for $\lambda < 1$

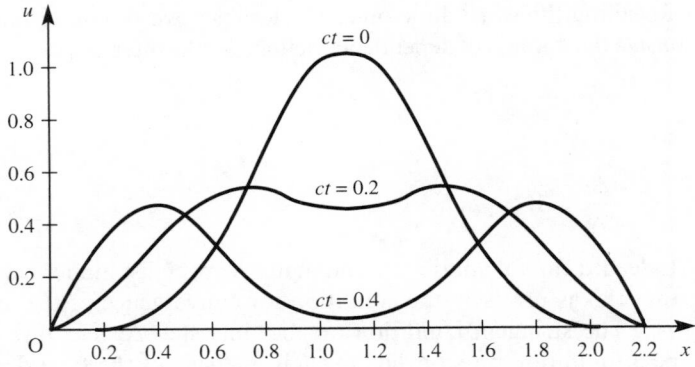

Figure 8.18 Solution of Example 8.13 with $\Delta x = 0.2$, $\lambda = 0.5$ for successive values of ct.

x	0	0.2	0.4	0.6	0.8	1.0
$u(\lambda = 0.25)$	0	0.3451	0.4674	0.3368	0.1353	0.0236
$u(\lambda = 0.5)$	0	0.3487	0.4665	0.3318	0.1340	0.0272
$u(\lambda = 1)$	0	0.3652	0.4582	0.3105	0.1322	0.0408
$u(\lambda = 2)$	0	0.1078	0.3571	0.6334	0.5742	0.2749

Figure 8.19 Table of values of u for a numerical solution of Example 8.13 with $\Delta x = 0.2$ and $ct = 0.8$.

the solution is reasonably consistent, and we have errors of a few per cent. However, for $\lambda = 2$ the solution looks very suspect. A further two time steps gives, at $ct = 1.6$, the solution

x	0	0.2	0.4	0.6	0.8	1
$u(\lambda = 2)$	0	-3.12	21.75	-10.25	-34.70	32.72

Clearly the solution has gone wild!

Looking back to Figure 8.17, we can attempt an explanation for the apparent divergence of the solution in Example 8.13. The characteristics through the points $(x_{i-1}, 0)$ and $(x_{i+1}, 0)$ are

$$x_{i-1} = x - ct$$
$$x_{i+1} = x + ct$$

which can be solved to give, at the point P,

$$x_P = \tfrac{1}{2}(x_{i+1} + x_{i-1})$$
$$ct_P = \tfrac{1}{2}(x_{i+1} - x_{i-1}) = \Delta x$$

Recalling the work done on characteristics, we should require the new point to be *inside* the domain of dependence defined by the interval (x_{i-1}, x_{i+1}). Hence we require

$$t_P \geqslant \Delta t$$

so

$$\frac{c\,\Delta t}{\Delta x} \leqslant 1 \tag{8.30}$$

Indeed, a careful analysis, found in many specialist numerical analysis books, shows that this is precisely the condition for convergence of the method.

The stringent condition on the time step Δt has always been considered to be a limitation on so-called **explicit methods** of the type described here, but such methods have the great merit of being very simple to program. As computers get faster, the very short time step is becoming less of a problem, and vector or array processors allow nodes to be dealt with simultaneously, thus making such methods even more competitive.

There are, however, clear advantages in the stability of calculations if an **implicit method** is used. In Figure 8.16 the approximation to u_{xx} may be formed by the average of the approximations from rows $j + 1$ and $j - 1$. Thus

$$[u(i, j + 1) - 2u(i, j) + u(i, j - 1)]/c^2\, \Delta t^2$$

$$= \tfrac{1}{2}[u(i + 1, j + 1) - 2u(i, j + 1) + u(i - 1, j + 1)$$

$$+ u(i + 1, j - 1) - 2u(i, j - 1) + u(i - 1, j - 1)]/\Delta x^2$$

Assuming that u is known on rows j and $j - 1$, we can rearrange the equation into the convenient form

$$-\lambda^2 u(i + 1, j + 1) + 2(1 + \lambda^2)u(i, j + 1) - \lambda^2 u(i - 1, j + 1)$$

$$= 4u(i, j) + \lambda^2 u(i + 1, j - 1) - 2(1 + \lambda^2)u(i, j - 1) + \lambda^2 u(i - 1, j - 1) \quad \textbf{(8.31)}$$

The right-hand side of (8.31) is known, since it depends only on rows j and $j - 1$. The unknowns on row $j + 1$ appear on the left-hand side. The equations must now be solved simultaneously using the Thomas algorithm for a tridiagonal matrix (described in Section 4.5.2 of *Modern Engineering Mathematics*). This algorithm is very rapid and requires little storage. It can be shown that the method will proceed satisfactorily for any λ, so that the time step is unrestricted. The evaluation of rows 0 and 1 is the same as for the explicit method, so this can reduce the accuracy, and clearly the algorithm needs a finite x region to allow the matrix inversion.

EXAMPLE 8.14   Solve the wave equation $\partial^2 u/\partial t^2 = c^2\, \partial^2 u/\partial x^2$ by an implicit method given

(a) $u(0, t) = 0 \quad (t \geqslant 0)$ (fixed at $x = 0$);

(b) $u(1, t) = 0 \quad (t \geqslant 0)$ (fixed at $x = 1$);

(c) $\partial u(x, 0)/\partial t = 0 \quad (0 \leqslant x \leqslant 1)$ (zero initial velocity);

(d) $u(x, 0) = \begin{cases} 1 & (x = \tfrac{1}{4}) \\ 0 & \text{otherwise} \end{cases}$ (displaced at the one point $x = \tfrac{1}{4}$).

Compare the solutions at a fixed time for various λ.

Solution   Here we have a wave equation solved for a string stretched between two points and displaced at a single point.

The numerical solution shows the expected behaviour of a wave splitting into two waves, one moving in the $-x$ direction and the other in the $+x$ direction. The waves are reflected from the ends, and eventually give a complicated wave shape.

The computations were performed with $\Delta x = 0.125$ and various λ or Δt, with $\lambda = c\Delta t/\Delta x$. The values of u are given at the same time, $T = \Delta x/c$, for various λ:

x	0	0.125	0.25	0.375	0.5	0.625	0.75	0.875	1
$u(\lambda = 0.2)$	0	0.3394	0.2432	0.3412	0.0352	0.0019	0.0001	0	0
$u(\lambda = 0.1)$	0	0.3479	0.2297	0.3493	0.0344	0.0014	0	0	0
$u(\lambda = 0.05)$	0	0.3506	0.2254	0.3519	0.0341	0.0013	0	0	0
$u(\lambda = 0.025)$	0	0.3514	0.2243	0.3526	0.0340	0.0014	0	0	0

Although the method converges for all λ, the accuracy still requires a small λ (or time step), but the value $\lambda = 0.05$ certainly gives an accuracy of less than 1%. It may be noted that at the chosen value of T the wave has split but has not progressed far enough to be reflected from the end $x = 1$.

The methods described in this section all extend to higher dimensions, and some to nonlinear problems. The work involved is correspondingly greater of course.

8.3.6   Exercises

20 Use an explicit method to solve the wave equation $\partial^2 u/\partial t^2 = c^2\, \partial^2 u/\partial x^2$ for the boundary conditions

(a) $u(0, t) = 0 \quad (t \geq 0)$

(b) $u(1, t) = 0 \quad (t \geq 0)$

(c) $u(x, 0) = 0 \quad (0 \leq x \leq 1)$

(d) $\dfrac{\partial u(x, 0)}{\partial t} = \begin{cases} x & (0 \leq x \leq \frac{1}{2}) \\ 1 - x & (\frac{1}{2} \leq x \leq 1) \end{cases}$

Use $\Delta x = \Delta t = \frac{1}{4}$ and study the behaviour for a variety of values of λ for the first three time steps. Compare your result with the implicit version in (8.31).

21 An oscillator is started at the end of a tube, and oscillations propagate according to the wave equation. The displacement $u(x, t)$ satisfies

$$\frac{\partial^2 u}{\partial x^2} = \frac{1}{c^2}\frac{\partial^2 u}{\partial t^2}$$

in $0 < x < l$, for $t > 0$, with the boundary conditions

(a) $u(0, t) = a \sin \omega t, \quad u(l, t) = 0 \quad (t > 0)$

(b) $u(x, 0) = \dfrac{\partial u(x, 0)}{\partial t} = 0 \quad (0 \leq x \leq l)$

where c, a and ω are real positive constants. Show

that the solution of the partial differential equation is

$$u(x, t) = \frac{a \sin \omega t \sin\left[\omega(l - x)/c\right]}{\sin(\omega l/c)}$$

$$+ \sum_{n=1}^{\infty} \frac{2la c\omega}{\omega^2 l^2 - n^2\pi^2 c^2} \sin\left(\frac{n\pi x}{l}\right)\sin\left(\frac{n\pi ct}{l}\right)$$

provided that $\omega l/\pi c$ is not an integer.

Compare this solution with one computed using the explicit numerical method. Use $l = 1$, $c = 1$, $\omega = \frac{1}{2}\pi$, $\Delta x = 0.2$ and $\Delta t = 0.02$ to evaluate $u(x, 0.06)$.

22 Solve the equation

$$c^2 \frac{\partial^2 u}{\partial x^2} + 2 = \frac{\partial^2 u}{\partial t^2}$$

numerically, subject to the conditions

$$u = x(1 - x), \quad \frac{\partial u}{\partial t} = 0 \quad \text{for all } x \text{ at } t = 0$$

Use

(a) an explicit method with $\Delta x = \Delta t = 0.2$ and $\lambda = 0.5$;

(b) an implicit method with $\Delta x = \Delta t = 0.2$ and $\lambda = 0.5$.

23 Solve the equation

$$c^2 \frac{\partial^2 u}{\partial x^2} + 2 = \frac{\partial^2 u}{\partial t^2}$$

numerically, subject to the conditions

$$u = x(1-x), \quad \frac{\partial u}{\partial t} = 0 \quad (0 < x < 1) \quad \text{at } t = 0$$

$$u = 0 \quad (x = 0, 1) \quad \text{for } t > 0$$

Use

(a) an explicit method with $\Delta x = \Delta t = 0.2$ and $\lambda = 0.5$;

(b) an implicit method with $\Delta x = \Delta t = 0.2$ and $\lambda = 0.5$.

Compare your solution with that in Exercise 22.

8.4 Solution of the heat-conduction/diffusion equation

In this section we consider methods for solving the heat-conduction/diffusion equation introduced in Section 8.2.2.

8.4.1 Separation method

It was with the aim of solving heat-conduction problems that Fourier (c. 1800) first used the idea of separation of variables. As indicated in Section 4.1, many mathematicians at the time argued about the validity of his approach, while he continued to solve many practical problems.

In Section 8.2.2 we noted that the heat-conduction equation

$$\frac{1}{\kappa} \frac{\partial u}{\partial t} = \nabla^2 u \tag{8.5}$$

has a steady-state solution U satisfying

$$\nabla^2 U = 0$$

and appropriate boundary conditions. One useful way to write the general solution is

$$u = U + v$$

where v also satisfies (8.5) and the boundary conditions for $u - U$. Certainly the heat-conduction interpretation supports this idea, and we base our strategy on first finding U and then determining the transient v that takes the solution from its initial to its final state. We note that $v \to 0$ as $t \to \infty$, so that $u \to U$, and an obvious method is to try an exponential decay to zero. Thus, in the one-dimensional form of the heat-conduction equation

$$\frac{1}{\kappa}\frac{\partial v}{\partial t} = \frac{\partial^2 v}{\partial x^2} \tag{8.32}$$

we seek a separated solution of the special type discussed in Section 8.3.2, where the physics indicates a solution

$$v = e^{-\alpha t}w(x)$$

which on substitution gives

$$-\frac{\alpha}{\kappa}w = \frac{d^2w}{dx^2}$$

Letting $\alpha/\kappa = \lambda^2$, we can solve this simple-harmonic equation to give

$$w = A\sin\lambda x + B\cos\lambda x$$

and hence

$$v = e^{-\alpha t}(A\sin\lambda x + B\cos\lambda x) \tag{8.33}$$

Taking the hint from Section 8.3.2, we expect in general to take sums of terms like (8.33) to satisfy all the boundary conditions. Thus we build up a solution

$$v = \sum_{n=1}^{\infty} e^{-\alpha t}(A_n\sin\lambda x + B_n\cos\lambda x) \tag{8.34}$$

EXAMPLE 8.15 Solve the heat-conduction equation $\partial T/\partial t = \kappa\,\partial^2 T/\partial x^2$ subject to the boundary conditions

(a) $T = 0$ at $x = 0$ and for all $t > 0$ (held at zero temperature);

(b) $\partial T/\partial x = 0$ at $x = l$ and for all $t > 0$ (no heat loss from this end);

(c) $T = T_0\sin(3\pi x/2l)$ at $t = 0$ and for $0 \leqslant x \leqslant l$ (given initial temperature profile).

Solution We first note that as $t \to \infty$ the solution will be $T = 0$, so the steady-state solution is zero, and so from (8.31) and (8.33) we consider a solution of the form

$$T = e^{-\alpha t}(A\sin\lambda x + B\cos\lambda x) \tag{8.35}$$

In order to satisfy the boundary condition (a), it is clear that it is not possible to include the cosine term, so $B = 0$. To satisfy the condition (b) then requires

$$\frac{\partial T}{\partial x} = Ae^{-\alpha t}\lambda\cos\lambda x = 0 \quad (x = l)$$

so that

$$\cos\lambda l = 0, \quad \text{or} \quad \lambda l = (n + \tfrac{1}{2})\pi \quad (n = 0, 1, 2, 3, \ldots)$$

leading to the solution

$$T = Ae^{-\alpha t}\sin\left[(n + \tfrac{1}{2})\pi\frac{x}{l}\right]$$

We now compare the T from condition (c) with the solution just obtained at time $t = 0$, giving

$$Ae^{-0}\sin\left[(n + \tfrac{1}{2})\pi\frac{x}{l}\right] = T_0\sin\left(\frac{3\pi x}{2l}\right)$$

The unknown parameters can now be identified as $n = 1$ and $A = T_0$, and hence the final solution is

$$T = T_0\exp\left(-\frac{9\kappa\pi^2 t}{4l^2}\right)\sin\left(\frac{3\pi x}{2l}\right)$$

EXAMPLE 8.16   Solve the heat-conduction equation $\partial u/\partial t = \kappa\,\partial^2 u/\partial t^2$ subject to the boundary conditions

(a) $u(0, t) = 0$ $(t \geqslant 0)$ (zero temperature at the end $x = 0$);

(b) $u(l, t) = 0$ $(t \geqslant 0)$ (zero temperature at the end $x = l$);

(c) $u(x, 0) = u_0(\tfrac{1}{2} - x/l)$ $(0 < x < l)$ (a given initial temperature profile).

Solution   We are solving the problem of heat conduction in a bar that is held at zero temperature at its ends and with a given initial temperature profile.

It is clear that the final solution as $t \to \infty$ is $u = 0$, so that $U = 0$ is the steady-state solution, and hence from (8.33) we seek a solution of the form

$$u = e^{-\alpha t}(A\sin\lambda x + B\cos\lambda x)$$

subject to the given boundary conditions. The first of these conditions (a) gives $B = 0$, while the second condition (b) gives

$$\sin\lambda l = 0, \qquad \text{or} \qquad \lambda l = n\pi \quad (n = 1, 2, \ldots)$$

Recalling that $\lambda^2 = \alpha/\kappa$, we find solutions of the form

$$u = Ae^{-\kappa n^2\pi^2 t/l^2}\sin\left(\frac{n\pi x}{l}\right) \quad (n = 1, 2, \ldots)$$

Clearly we cannot satisfy (c) from a single solution, so, as indicated in (8.34), we revert to the sum

$$u = \sum_{n=1}^{\infty} A_n e^{-\kappa n^2\pi^2 t/l^2}\sin\left(\frac{n\pi x}{l}\right) \tag{8.36}$$

which is also a solution.

Using the boundary condition (c), we then have

$$u_0(\tfrac{1}{2} - x/l) = \sum_{n=1}^{\infty} A_n\sin\left(\frac{n\pi x}{l}\right)$$

and hence, by (4.33),

$$\tfrac{1}{2}lA_n = u_0 \int_0^l \left(\tfrac{1}{2} - \frac{x}{l}\right) \sin\left(\frac{n\pi x}{l}\right) dx = \begin{cases} 0 & \text{(odd } n) \\ u_0 l/n\pi & \text{(even } n) \end{cases}$$

Note again that we have used a periodic extension of the given function to obtain a Fourier sine series valid over the interval $0 \leqslant x \leqslant l$. Outside the interval $0 \leqslant x \leqslant l$ we have no physical interest in the solution. Substituting back into (8.36) gives as a final solution

$$u = \frac{u_0}{\pi} \sum_{m=1}^{\infty} \frac{1}{m} e^{-4\kappa m^2 \pi^2 t/l^2} \sin\left(\frac{2m\pi x}{l}\right) \tag{8.37}$$

or, in an expanded form,

$$u = \frac{u_0}{\pi}\left[e^{-4\kappa\pi^2 t/l^2} \sin\left(\frac{2\pi x}{l}\right) + \tfrac{1}{2} e^{-16\kappa\pi^2 t/l^2} \sin\left(\frac{4\pi x}{l}\right) + \tfrac{1}{3} e^{-36\kappa\pi^2 t/l} \sin\left(\frac{6\pi x}{l}\right) \right.$$

$$\left. + \ldots \right]$$

In Figure 8.20, u/u_0 is plotted against x/l at successive times $T = t(4\kappa\pi^2/l^2) = 0, 0.5, 1, 1.5$.

Taking successive terms in the series for the values $T = t(4\kappa\pi^2/l^2) = 0.5$ and $x/l = 0.2$, we get

	1 term	2 terms	3 terms	4 terms
u/u_0	0.1836	0.1963	0.1956	0.1953

and we see that three terms of this series would probably be sufficient to give three-figure accuracy. In all such problems some numerical experimentation is

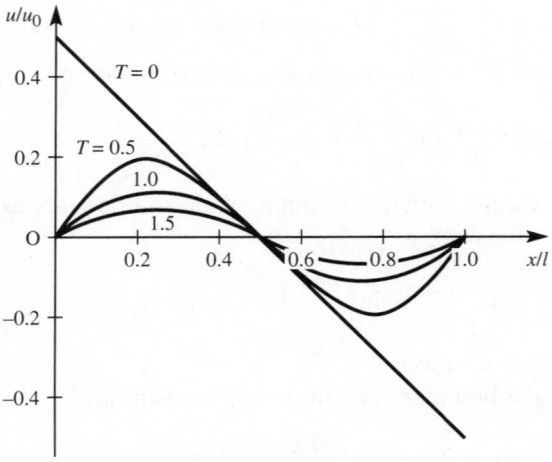

Figure 8.20 Solution of Example 8.16 with $T = t(4\kappa\pi^2/l^2)$.

required to determine how many terms are required. For small t and x we should expect to need a large number of terms, since the temperature at the end switches from $\frac{1}{2}u_0$ to 0 at time $t = 0$. It is well known, as we saw in Chapter 4, that discontinuities cause convergence difficulties for Fourier series.

It may be noted in Example 8.16 that the initial discontinuity is smoothed out, as we expected from the physical ideas that we outlined in Section 8.2.2.

EXAMPLE 8.17   Solve the heat-conduction equation $\partial u/\partial t = \kappa\, \partial^2 u/\partial x^2$ in a bar subject to the boundary conditions

(a) $u(0, t) = 0$ $(t \geqslant 0)$ (the end $x = 0$ is held at zero temperature);

(b) $u(1, t) = 1$ $(t \geqslant 0)$ (the end $x = 1$ is at temperature 1);

(c) $u(x, 0) = x(2 - x)$ $(0 \leqslant x \leqslant 1)$ (the initial temperature profile is given).

Solution   First it is clear that the final steady-state solution is $U = x$, since this satisfies (a) and (b) and also $\nabla^2 U = 0$. Secondly, $u = U + v$, where v satisfies (8.32), but now the boundary conditions on v are

(a') $v(0, t) = 0$

(b') $v(1, t) = 0$

(c') $v(x, 0) = x(2 - x) - x = x - x^2$

The appropriate solutions in (8.33) can now be selected; the condition (a') gives $B = 0$, while the condition (b'), $v(1, t) = 0$, gives

$$\sin \lambda = 0, \quad \text{or} \quad \lambda = n\pi \quad (n = 1, 2, \ldots)$$

From (8.34) we then have

$$v = \sum_{n=1}^{\infty} a_n e^{-\kappa n^2 \pi^2 t} \sin n\pi x$$

and condition (c') gives

$$x - x^2 = \sum_{n=1}^{\infty} a_n \sin n\pi x$$

Determining the Fourier coefficient using (4.33),

$$\tfrac{1}{2} a_n = \int_0^1 (x - x^2) \sin n\pi x \, dx = \begin{cases} 4/n^3 \pi^3 & \text{(odd } n) \\ 0 & \text{(even } n) \end{cases}$$

Thus the complete solution is

$$u = x + \frac{8}{\pi^3} \sum_{n=1}^{\infty} \frac{1}{(2n - 1)^3} e^{-\kappa(2n-1)^2 \pi^2 t} \sin (2n - 1)\pi x$$

or, in expanded form,

$$u = x + \frac{8}{\pi^3}[e^{-\kappa\pi^2 t}\sin\pi x + \tfrac{1}{27}e^{-9\kappa\pi^2 t}\sin 3\pi x$$

$$+ \tfrac{1}{125}e^{-25\kappa\pi^2 t}\sin 5\pi x + \ldots]$$

8.4.2   Laplace transform method

As we saw for the wave equation in Section 8.3.3, Laplace transforms provide an alternative method of solution for the heat-conduction equation. The method has the merit of dealing with the boundary conditions easily, but it suffers from the usual difficulty of performing the final inversion. The following example serves to illustrate these points.

EXAMPLE 8.18   Using the Laplace transform method, solve the heat-conduction equation

$$\frac{\partial u}{\partial t} = \kappa\frac{\partial^2 u}{\partial x^2} \quad (x > 0, t > 0)$$

given that $u(x, t)$ remains bounded and satisfies the boundary conditions

(a) $u(x, 0) = 0 \quad (x > 0)$

(b) $u(a, t) = T\delta(t)$

Solution   This problem models a semi-infinite insulated bar, coincident with the positive x axis, that is initially at zero temperature and is subjected to an instantaneous heat source (a spot weld) of strength T at the point $x = a > 0$.

Using (8.23) and (8.24) and taking Laplace transforms gives

$$sU(x, s) - u(x, 0) = \kappa\frac{d^2 U(x, s)}{dx^2}$$

which, on using condition (a), leads to the ordinary differential equation

$$\frac{d^2 U}{dx^2} - \frac{s}{\kappa}U = 0$$

This is readily solved to give

$$U(x, s) = Ae^{\sqrt{(s/\kappa)}x} + Be^{-\sqrt{(s/\kappa)}x}$$

Since the temperature of the bar remains bounded, A must be zero, so that

$$U(x, s) = Be^{-\sqrt{(s/\kappa)}x}$$

Condition (b) then gives

$$U(a, s) = \mathcal{L}\{T\delta(t)\} = T = Be^{-\sqrt{(s/\kappa)}a}$$

so that

$$B = Te^{\sqrt{(s/\kappa)}a}$$

giving

$$U(x, s) = Te^{-(x-a)\sqrt{(s/\kappa)}}$$

To find the solution $u(x, t)$, we must invert the Laplace transform. However, in this case, the methods discussed in Chapter 2 do not suffice, and it is necessary to resort to the use of the complex inversion integral, which is dealt with in specialist texts on Laplace transforms (see also Chapter 5, Review exercise 7). Alternatively, we can turn to the extensive tables that exist of Laplace transform pairs, to find that

$$\mathcal{L}^{-1}\{e^{-b\sqrt{s}}\} = \frac{b}{2\sqrt{\pi}} t^{-3/2} e^{-b^2/4t}$$

We can then carry out the required inversion to give the solution

$$u(x, t) = \frac{T(x-a)}{2\sqrt{(\pi\kappa)}} t^{-3/2} e^{-(x-a)^2/4\kappa t} \quad (t > 0)$$

It should be noted that the solution of Example 8.18 is not variable and could not be obtained from the methods of Section 8.4.1.

8.4.3   Exercises

24 Use separation of variables to obtain a solution to the heat-conduction equation $\partial u/\partial t = \kappa \, \partial^2 u/\partial x^2$, given

(a) $\partial u(0, t)/\partial x = 0 \quad (t \geqslant 0)$

(b) $u(l, t) = 0 \quad (t \geqslant 0)$

(c) $u(x, 0) = u_0(\frac{1}{2} - x/l) \quad (0 \leqslant x \leqslant l)$

Compare the solution with that obtained in Example 8.16.

25 The spherically symmetric form of the heat-conduction equation is

$$u_{rr} + \frac{2}{r} u_r = \frac{1}{\kappa} u_t$$

By putting $ru = v$, show that v satisfies the standard one-dimensional heat-conduction equation. What can we expect of a solution as $r \to \infty$?

26 Show that the equation

$$\theta_t = \kappa\theta_{xx} - h(\theta - \theta_0)$$

can be reduced to the standard heat-conduction equation by writing $u = e^{ht}(\theta - \theta_0)$. How do you interpret the term $h(\theta - \theta_0)$?

27 The voltage v at a time t at a distance x along an electric cable of length L with capacitance and resistance only, satisfies

$$\frac{\partial^2 v}{\partial x^2} = \frac{1}{\kappa}\frac{\partial v}{\partial t}$$

Verify that a form of the solution appropriate to the conditions that $v = v_0$ when $x = 0$, and $v = 0$ when $x = L$, for all values of t, is given by

$$v = v_0\left(1 - \frac{x}{L}\right) + \sum_{n=1}^{\infty} c_n\exp\left(\frac{-\kappa n^2\pi^2 t}{L^2}\right)\sin\left(n\pi\frac{x}{L}\right)$$

where v_0 and the c_n are constants.

Show that if, in addition, $v = 0$ when $t = 0$ for $0 < x < L$,

$$c_n = -\frac{2v_0}{n\pi}$$

28 Find the solution to the equation

$$\frac{\partial u}{\partial t} = \kappa \frac{\partial^2 u}{\partial x^2}$$

satisfying the conditions

(a) $\partial u/\partial x = 0$ at $x = 0$ for all t

(b) $u = 0$ at $x = 1$ for all t

(c) $u = a \cos(\pi x) \cos(\tfrac{1}{2}\pi x)$ for $0 \leqslant x \leqslant 1$ when $t = 0$

29 A uniform bar of length l has its ends maintained at a temperature of $0\,°C$. Initially, the temperature at any point between the ends of the bar is $10\,°C$, and, after a time t, the temperature $u(x, t)$ at a distance x from one end of the bar satisfies the one-dimensional heat-conduction equation

$$\frac{\partial^2 u}{\partial x^2} = \frac{1}{\kappa}\frac{\partial u}{\partial t} \quad (x > 0)$$

Write down boundary conditions for the bar and show that the solution corresponding to these conditions is

$$u(x, t) = \frac{20}{\pi} \sum_{n=1}^{\infty} \frac{1}{n}(1 - \cos n\pi)\exp\left(\frac{-\kappa n^2 \pi^2 t}{l^2}\right)$$
$$\times \sin\left(\frac{\pi n x}{l}\right)$$

30 The function $\phi(x, t)$ satisfies the equation

$$\frac{\partial \phi}{\partial t} = a\frac{\partial^2 \phi}{\partial x^2} + b \quad (-h < x < h, t > 0)$$

with the boundary conditions

(a) $\phi(-h, t) = \phi(h, t) = 0 \quad (t > 0)$

(b) $\phi(x, 0) = 0 \quad (-h < x < h)$

where a, b and h are positive real constants. Show that the Laplace transform of the solution $\phi(x, t)$ is

$$\frac{b}{s^2}\left\{1 - \frac{\cosh\left[(s/a)^{1/2}x\right]}{\cosh\left[(s/a)^{1/2}h\right]}\right\}$$

8.4.4 Numerical solutions

As for the wave equation, except for the most straightforward problems, we must resort to numerical solutions of the heat-conduction equation. Even when analytical solutions are known, they are not always easy to evaluate because of convergence difficulties near to singularities. They are, of course, crucial in testing the accuracy and efficiency of numerical methods.

We can write the heat-conduction equation

$$\frac{1}{\kappa}\frac{\partial u}{\partial t} = \frac{\partial^2 u}{\partial x^2} \tag{8.38}$$

in the usual *finite-difference* form, using the notation of Figure 8.21.

Figure 8.21 Mesh for marching forward the solution of the heat-conduction equation (8.38).

We assume that we know the solution up to time step j and we wish to calculate the solution at time step $j + 1$. In Section 8.3.5 we showed how to approximate the second derivative as

$$\frac{\partial^2 u}{\partial x^2} = \frac{u(i + 1, j) - 2u(i, j) + u(i - 1, j)}{\Delta x^2}$$

To obtain the time derivative, we use the approximation between rows j and $j + 1$:

$$\frac{\partial u}{\partial t} = \frac{u(i, j + 1) - u(i, j)}{\Delta t}$$

Putting these into (8.38) gives

$$\frac{u(i, j + 1) - u(i, j)}{\kappa \, \Delta t} = \frac{u(i - 1, j) - 2u(i, j) + u(i + 1, j)}{\Delta x^2}$$

or, on rearranging,

$$u(i, j + 1) = \lambda u(i - 1, j) + (1 - 2\lambda)u(i, j) + \lambda u(i + 1, j) \qquad \textbf{(8.39)}$$

where $\lambda = \kappa \, \Delta t / \Delta x^2$. Equation (8.39) gives a finite-difference representation of (8.38), and provided that all the values are known on row j, we can then compute u on row $j + 1$ from the simple **explicit formula** (8.39).

EXAMPLE 8.19   Solve the heat-conduction equation (8.38) subject to the boundary conditions

(a) $\partial u(0, t)/\partial x = 0$ $(t \geqslant 0)$ (no heat flow through the end $x = 0$);

(b) $u(1, t) = 1$ $(t \geqslant 0)$ (unit temperature held at $x = 1$);

(c) $u(x, 0) = x^2$ $(0 \leqslant x \leqslant 1)$ (a given initial temperature distribution).

Solution   To fit the condition (a) most easily, we allow the first mesh space to straddle the t axis as illustrated in Figure 8.22, where six intervals are used in the x direction. The mesh implies that $\Delta x = 1/6.5 = 0.1538$; condition (a) gives $u(0, j) = u(1, j)$ while condition (b) gives $u(7, j) = 1$.

The following table gives values for u at the three times $t = 0$, $0.2 \, \Delta x^2/\kappa$ and $20 \, \Delta x^2/\kappa$, calculated with $\lambda = 0.2$. These results are then compared at

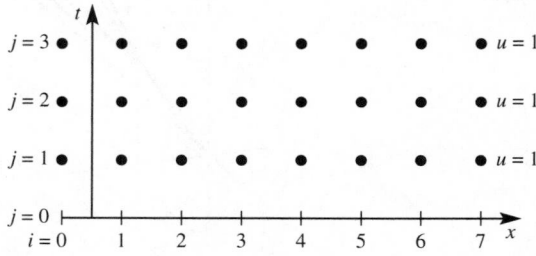

Figure 8.22   Mesh for Example 8.19; $u(7, j) = 1$ and $u(0, j) = u(1, j)$ for all j; $\Delta x = 1/6.5 = 0.1538$.

$t = 20\,\Delta x^2/\kappa$, computed with λ taken to be 0.5. It may be noted that there are errors in the third significant figure between the two cases.

i		0	1	2	3	4	5	6	7
$\lambda = 0.2$	$\begin{cases} j = 0 \\ j = 1 \\ j = 100 \end{cases}$	0.0059	0.0059	0.0533	0.1479	0.2899	0.4793	0.7160	1
		0.0154	0.0154	0.0627	0.1574	0.2994	0.4888	0.7255	1
		0.6817	0.6817	0.7002	0.7362	0.7874	0.8510	0.9233	1
$\lambda = 0.5$	$j = 40$	0.6850	0.6850	0.7033	0.7389	0.7896	0.8526	0.9241	1

For $\lambda = 0.54$ we can obtain a solution that compares with the solution given, but for $\lambda = 0.6$ the solution diverges wildly. Figure 8.23 shows a plot of

Figure 8.23
Numerical solution of Example 8.19 at time $t = 20\,\Delta x^2/x$, for two values of λ.

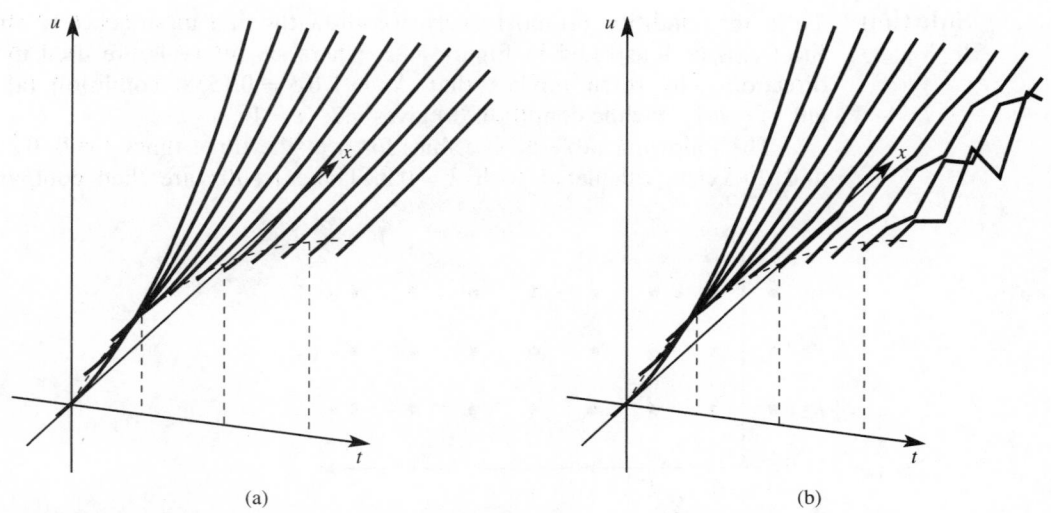

(a)   (b)

Figure 8.24 Plots of u against x and t from the solution of Example 8.19 with (a) $\lambda = 0.2$; (b) $\lambda = 0.55$.

the solution near the critical value of λ at a fixed time $t = 20\,\Delta x^2/\kappa$. As in the table, the solutions are accurate to about 1% for small λ, but when λ gets much above 0.5, oscillations creep in and the solution is meaningless. In Figure 8.24 a further graph illustrates the development of the solution in the two cases $\lambda = 0.2$ and $\lambda = 0.55$. One solution progresses smoothly as time advances, while the other produces oscillations that will eventually lead to divergence.

Comparing Example 8.19 with the numerical solution of the wave equation undertaken in Example 8.13, we observe similar behaviour for the explicit scheme, namely that the method will only converge for small enough time steps or λ. From (8.39) it may be noted that the middle term changes sign at $\lambda = 0.5$, and above this value we might anticipate difficulties. Indeed, some straightforward numerical analysis shows that convergence is certain for $\lambda < 0.5$. It is sufficient here to note that λ must not be too large.

To avoid the limitation on λ, we can again look at an **implicit** formulation of the numerical equations. Returning to Figure 8.21, the idea is to approximate the x derivative by an average of row j and row $j + 1$:

$$u(i, j + 1) - u(i, j) = \lambda\{(1 - \alpha)[u(i - 1, j) - 2u(i, j) + u(i + 1, j)]$$
$$+ \alpha[u(i - 1, j + 1) - 2u(i, j + 1) + u(i + 1, j + 1)]\}$$

where $0 \leqslant \alpha \leqslant 1$ is an averaging parameter. The case $\alpha = 0$ corresponds to the explicit formulation (8.39), while $\alpha = \frac{1}{2}$ is the best known implicit formulation, and constitutes the **Crank–Nicolson method**. With $\alpha = \frac{1}{2}$, we have

$$-\lambda u(i - 1, j + 1) + 2(1 + \lambda)u(i, j + 1) - \lambda u(i + 1, j + 1)$$
$$= \lambda u(i - 1, j) + 2(1 - \lambda)u(i, j) + \lambda u(i + 1, j) \tag{8.40}$$

We know the solution on row j, so the right-hand side of (8.40) is known, and the unknowns on row $(j + 1)$ have to be solved for simultaneously.

Fortunately the system is tridiagonal, so the very rapid Thomas algorithm can be used. The method performs extremely well: it converges for all λ, and is the best known approach to heat conduction equations. The programming is harder than for the explicit case, but it is usually worth the extra effort. The basic algorithm is given in Figure 8.25.

[read λ and final time]
[set up $u(i, 0)$ on the initial line]
[set up end conditions $u(0, j)$, $u(N, j)$]
repeat
　　　[Use Thomas algorithm on (8.40) to evaluate $u(i, j + 1)$ for each i]
until [final time is reached]
[write out results]

Figure 8.25 An outline pseudocode algorithm for the Crank–Nicolson method.

EXAMPLE 8.20   Solve the heat-conduction equation (8.38) using the implicit formulation (8.40) for the boundary conditions

(a) $u(0, t) = 0$ $(t \geqslant 0)$ (the end $x = 0$ is kept at zero temperature);

(b) $u(1, t) = 1$ $(t \geqslant 0)$ (the end $x = 0$ is kept at unit temperature);

(c) $u(x, 0) = 0$ $(0 \leqslant x \leqslant 1)$ (initially the bar has zero temperature).

Solution   Here a bar is initially at zero temperature. At one end the temperature is raised to the value 1 and kept at that value.

The results of the calculation are presented in Figure 8.26. At time step 0 the temperature distribution is discontinuous. The successive time steps 1, 10, 100 are shown, and the final distribution $u = x$ is labelled ∞.

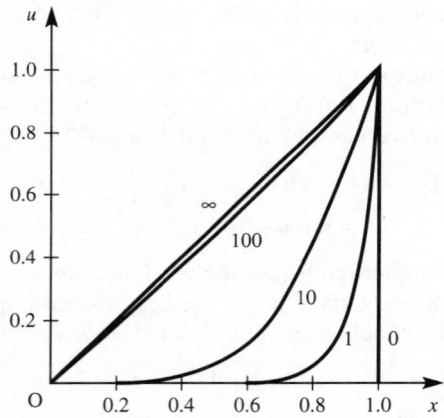

Figure 8.26 Solution of Example 8.20 with $\Delta x = 0.1$, $\lambda = 0.3$ using the Crank–Nicolson scheme.

8.4.5 Exercises

31 Derive the usual explicit finite-difference representation of the equation

$$\frac{\partial u}{\partial t} = \frac{\partial^2 u}{\partial x^2}$$

Using this scheme with $\Delta t = 0.02$ and $\Delta x = 0.2$, determine an approximate solution of the equation at $t = 0.06$, given that

$u = x^2$ when $t = 0$ $(0 \leqslant x \leqslant 1)$

$u = 0$ when $x = 0$ $(t > 0)$

$u = 1$ when $x = 1$ $(t > 0)$

32 Use both explicit and implicit numerical formulations to obtain solutions of the heat-conduction equation subject to the boundary conditions

(a) $u(0, t) = 0$ $(t \geqslant 0)$

(b) $u(1, t) = e^{-t}$ $(t \geqslant 0)$

(c) $u(x, 0) = 0$ $(0 \leqslant x < 1)$

Compare the two results for $t = 1$.

33 Given that u satisfies the equation

$$\frac{\partial u}{\partial t} = \frac{\partial^2 u}{\partial x^2}$$

and is subject to the boundary conditions

$$\frac{\partial u}{\partial x} = 1 \quad (x = 0, t > 0)$$

$$u = 0 \quad (x = 1, t > 0)$$

$$u = x(1 - x) \quad (t = 0, 0 \leqslant x \leqslant 1)$$

derive a set of algebraic equations from the implicit formulation in Section 8.4.4 using $\Delta x = 0.2$ and $\Delta t = 0.02$. Use the Thomas algorithm to find the solution at $t = 0.02$.

8.5   Solution of the Laplace equation

In this section we consider methods of solving the Laplace equation introduced in Section 8.2.3.

8.5.1   Separated solutions

It is much less obvious how to construct separated solutions for the Laplace equation, since there is less physical feel for the behaviour except that the solution will be smooth. We shall therefore work more formally, as in Section 8.3.2, and seek a solution of the Laplace equation

$$\frac{\partial^2 u}{\partial x^2} + \frac{\partial^2 u}{\partial y^2} = 0 \tag{8.41}$$

in the form

$$u = X(x)Y(y)$$

which gives on substitution

$$Y \frac{d^2 X}{dx^2} + X \frac{d^2 Y}{dy^2} = 0$$

or

$$\frac{d^2 X}{dx^2} \bigg/ X = - \frac{d^2 Y}{dy^2} \bigg/ Y = \lambda \tag{8.42}$$

Now $(d^2 X/dx^2)/X$ is a function of x only and $-(d^2 Y/dy^2)/Y$ is a function of y only. Since they must be equal for *all* x and y, both sides of (8.42) must be a constant, λ . We therefore obtain two equations of simple-harmonic type

$$\frac{d^2 X}{dx^2} = \lambda X, \qquad \frac{d^2 Y}{dy^2} = -\lambda Y$$

The type of solution depends on the sign of λ, and we have a variety of possible solutions:

$$\lambda = -\mu^2 < 0: \qquad u = (A \sin \mu x + B \cos \mu x)(C e^{\mu y} + D e^{-\mu y}) \qquad (8.43a)$$

$$\lambda = \mu^2 > 0: \qquad u = (A e^{\mu x} + B e^{-\mu x})(C \sin \mu y + D \cos \mu y) \qquad (8.43b)$$

$$\lambda = 0: \qquad u = (Ax + B)(Cy + D) \qquad (8.43c)$$

where A, B, C and D are arbitrary constants. Using the definitions of the hyperbolic functions, it is sometimes more convenient to express the solution (8.43a) as

$$u = (A \sin \mu x + B \cos \mu x)(C \cosh \mu y + D \sinh \mu y) \qquad (8.43d)$$

and (8.43b) as

$$u = (A \sinh \mu x + B \cosh \mu x)(C \sin \mu y + D \cos \mu y) \qquad (8.43e)$$

The actual form of the solution depends on the problem in hand, as illustrated in the following examples.

EXAMPLE 8.21   Use the separated solutions (8.43) of the Laplace equation to find the solution to (8.41) satisfying the boundary conditions

$$u(x, 0) = 0 \quad (0 < x < 2)$$
$$u(x, 1) = 0 \quad (0 < x < 2)$$
$$u(0, y) = 0 \quad (0 < y < 1)$$
$$u(2, y) = a \sin 2\pi y \quad (0 < y < 1)$$

Solution   To satisfy the first two conditions, we need to choose the separated solutions that include the $\sin \mu y$ terms. Thus we take solution (8.43b)

$$u = (A e^{\mu x} + B e^{-\mu x})(C \sin \mu y + D \cos \mu y)$$

The first boundary condition gives

$$(A e^{\mu x} + B e^{-\mu x})D = 0 \quad (0 < x < 2)$$

so that $D = 0$. Thus

$$u = (A' e^{\mu x} + B' e^{-\mu x}) \sin \mu y$$

where $A' = AC$ and $B' = BC$. The second boundary condition then gives

$$(A' e^{\mu x} + B' e^{-\mu x}) \sin \mu = 0 \quad (0 < x < 2)$$

so that $\sin \mu = 0$, or $\mu = n\pi$ with n as integer. Thus

$$u = (A' e^{n\pi x} + B' e^{-n\pi x}) \sin n\pi y$$

From the third boundary condition,

$$(A' + B') \sin n\pi y = 0 \quad (0 < y < 1)$$

so that $B' = -A'$, giving

$$u = A'(e^{n\pi x} - e^{-n\pi x})\sin n\pi y$$

$$= 2A' \sinh n\pi x \sin n\pi y$$

The final boundary condition then gives

$$2A' \sinh 2n\pi \sin n\pi y = a \sin 2\pi y \quad (0 < y < 1)$$

We must therefore choose $n = 2$, and $a = 2A' \sinh 2n\pi = 2A' \sinh 4\pi$, or $2A' = a/\sinh 4\pi$. The solution is therefore

$$u = a \sin 2\pi y \frac{\sinh 2\pi x}{\sinh 4\pi}$$

EXAMPLE 8.22 Solve the Laplace equation (8.41) for steady heat conduction in the semi-infinite region $0 \leqslant y \leqslant 1$, $x \geqslant 0$ and subject to the boundary conditions

(a) $u(x, 0) = 0 \quad (x \geqslant 0)$

(b) $u(x, 1) = 0 \quad (x \geqslant 0)$ } (temperature kept at zero on two sides and at infinity);

(c) $u(x, y) \to 0 \quad$ as $x \to \infty$

(d) $u(0, y) = 1 \quad (0 \leqslant y \leqslant 1)$ (unit temperature on the fourth side).

Solution Clearly from condition (c) we need a solution that is exponential in x, so we take (8.43b):

$$u = (Ae^{\mu x} + Be^{-\mu x})(C \sin \mu y + D \cos \mu y)$$

and since the solution must tend to zero as $x \to \infty$, we have $A = 0$, giving

$$u = e^{-\mu x}(C' \sin \mu y + D' \cos \mu y)$$

where $C' = BC$ and $D' = BD$. Condition (a) then gives $D' = 0$, and (b) gives $\sin \mu = 0$, or $\mu = n\pi$ $(n = 1, 2, \ldots)$, so the solution becomes $u = C'e^{-n\pi x} \sin n\pi y$ $(n = 1, 2, \ldots)$. Because of the linearity of the Laplace equation, we sum over n to obtain the more general solution

$$u = \sum_{n=1}^{\infty} C'_n e^{-n\pi x} \sin n\pi y$$

Condition (d) then gives, as before, a classic Fourier series problem

$$1 = \sum_{n=1}^{\infty} C'_n \sin n\pi y \quad (0 \leqslant y \leqslant 1)$$

so that, using (4.33),

$$C' = 2 \int_0^1 \sin n\pi y \, dy = \begin{cases} 4/n\pi & \text{(odd } n) \\ 0 & \text{(even } n) \end{cases}$$

The complete solution is therefore

$$u = \frac{4}{\pi} \sum_{n=1}^{\infty} \frac{1}{2n-1} e^{-(2n-1)\pi x} \sin(2n-1)\pi y$$

or, in expanded form,

$$u = \frac{4}{\pi}(e^{-\pi x}\sin \pi y + \tfrac{1}{3}e^{-3\pi x}\sin 3\pi y + \tfrac{1}{5}e^{-5\pi x}\sin 5\pi y + \ldots)$$

In Figure 8.27 the solution $u(x,t)$ is plotted in the (x,y) plane. Because of the discontinuity at $x = 0$, for $x = 0.05$ thirty terms of the series were required to compute u to four-figure accuracy, while for $x = 1$, one or two terms were quite sufficient.

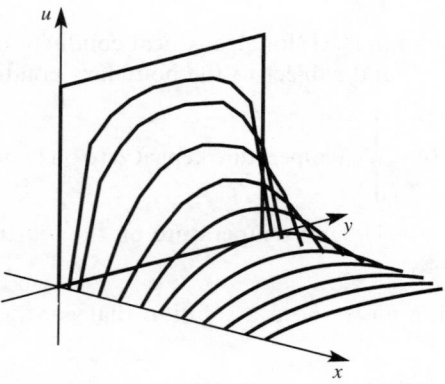

Figure 8.27 Solution of the Laplace equation in Example 8.22.

It is clear from Example 8.22 that the solutions (8.43) can only be used for rectangular regions. For various cylindrical and spherically symmetric regions separated solutions can be constructed, but they need more complicated Bessel and Legendre functions. There is great merit in calculating exact solutions where we can, since they give significant insight. However, with modern computing techniques it is certainly not necessarily quicker than a straight numerical solution.

EXAMPLE 8.23   Solve the Laplace equation (8.41) in the region $0 \leqslant x \leqslant 1$, $0 \leqslant y \leqslant 2$ with the conditions

(a) $u(x,0) = x$ $(0 \leqslant x \leqslant 1)$

(b) $u(x,2) = 0$ $(0 \leqslant x \leqslant 1)$

(c) $u(0,y) = 0$ $(0 \leqslant y \leqslant 2)$

(d) $\partial u(1,y)/\partial x = 0$ $(0 \leqslant y \leqslant 2)$

Figure 8.28 Region and boundary conditions for Example 8.23.

Solution   The steady heat-conduction interpretation of this problem, looking at Figure 8.28, gives a zero temperature on ABC, an insulated boundary on CD and a linear temperature on AD.

Of the solutions (8.43), we require zeros on AB and zero derivative on CD, so we might expect to use trigonometric solutions in the x direction and exponential (or equivalently sinh and cosh) solutions in the y direction. We therefore take a solution of the form (8.43d):

$$u = (A \sin \mu x + B \cos \mu x)(C \cosh \mu y + D \sinh \mu y)$$

From condition (c), we must take $B = 0$, giving

$$u = (C' \cosh \mu y + D' \sinh \mu y) \sin \mu x$$

where $C' = AC$ and $D' = AD$. Condition (d) then gives $\cos \mu = 0$ or

$$\mu = (n + \tfrac{1}{2})\pi \quad (n = 0, 1, 2, \ldots)$$

so the solution becomes

$$u = [C' \cosh (n + \tfrac{1}{2})\pi y + D' \sinh (n + \tfrac{1}{2})\pi y] \sin (n + \tfrac{1}{2})\pi x \quad (n = 0, 1, 2, \ldots)$$

$$\textbf{(8.44)}$$

To satisfy condition (b), it is best to rewrite (8.44) in the equivalent form

$$u = \sin [(n + \tfrac{1}{2})\pi x]\{E \cosh [(n + \tfrac{1}{2})\pi(2 - y)]$$
$$+ F \sinh [(n + \tfrac{1}{2})\pi(2 - y)]\} \quad (n = 0, 1, 2, \ldots)$$

We see that (b) now implies $E = 0$, so that our basic solution, summed over all n, is

$$u = \sum_{n=0}^{\infty} F_n \sin [(n + \tfrac{1}{2})\pi x] \sinh [(n + \tfrac{1}{2})\pi(2 - y)]$$

The final condition (a) then gives the standard Fourier series problem

$$x = \sum_{n=0}^{\infty} F_n \sinh [(2n + 1)\pi] \sin [(n + \tfrac{1}{2})\pi x]$$

so that, using (4.33),

$$\tfrac{1}{2}F_n \sinh(2n+1)\pi = \int_0^1 x \sin\left[(n+\tfrac{1}{2})\pi x\right] dx$$

$$= \frac{\sin(n+\tfrac{1}{2})\pi}{\pi^2(n+\tfrac{1}{2})^2}$$

The solution in expanded form is therefore

$$u = \frac{8}{\pi^2}\left[\sin\tfrac{1}{2}\pi x \frac{\sinh\tfrac{1}{2}\pi(2-y)}{\sinh\pi} - \frac{\sin\tfrac{3}{2}\pi x \sinh\tfrac{3}{2}\pi(2-y)}{9\sinh 3\pi}\right.$$

$$\left. + \sin\tfrac{5}{2}\pi x \frac{\sinh\tfrac{5}{2}\pi(2-y)}{25\sinh 5\pi} + \cdots\right]$$

Curiously, Laplace transform solutions are not natural for the Laplace equation, since there is no obvious semi-infinite parameter. Even in cases like Example 8.22, where we have a semi-infinite region, the Laplace transform in x requires information that is not available.

Another technique for solution of the Laplace equation involves complex variables. It is a method that was very widely used in aerodynamics and in electrostatic problems. Since the advent of modern computers, with highly efficient Laplace solvers, the method has fallen somewhat into disuse. It was the cornerstone of all early flight calculations and, for those interested in either the historical context or in the beautiful mathematical theory, the study of complex-variable solutions is essential.

EXAMPLE 8.24   If $f(z) = \phi(x,y) + j\psi(x,y)$ is a complex function of the complex variable $z = x + jy$, verify that ϕ and ψ satisfy the Laplace equation for the case $f(z) = z^2$. Sketch the contours of $\phi = $ constant and $\psi = $ constant.

Solution   Now

$$f(z) = z^2 = (x^2 - y^2) + j2xy$$

and thus

$$\phi = x^2 - y^2, \qquad \psi = 2xy$$

It is trivial to differentiate these functions, and both clearly satisfy the Laplace equation:

$$\nabla^2\phi = 0, \quad \nabla^2\psi = 0$$

The contours of ϕ and ψ are plotted in Figure 8.29. They are both hyperbolas, which intersect at right angles. The usual interpretation of these solutions is as irrotational inviscid fluid flow into a corner.

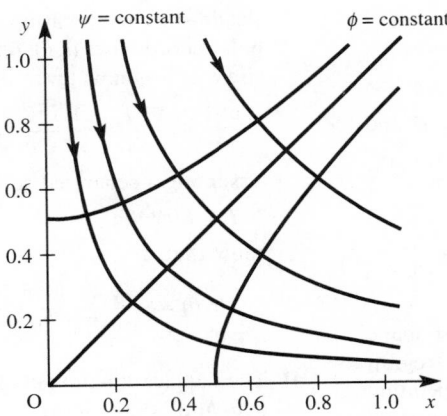

Figure 8.29 Complex-variable solution to the Laplace equation in Example 8.24, showing the streamlines of flow into a corner.

8.5.2 Exercises

34 Solve the Laplace equation $\partial^2 u/\partial x^2 + \partial^2 u/\partial y^2 = 0$ in the region $0 < x < 1$, $0 < y < 1$ subject to the boundary conditions $u(0, y) = 0$, $u(x, 0) = 0$, $u(1, y) = 1$, $u(x, 1) = 1$ by separation methods.

35 (Hadamard example) Show that the Laplace equation

$$\partial^2 u/\partial x^2 + \partial^2 u/\partial y^2 = 0$$

with $u(0, y) = 0$, $u_x(0, y) = (1/n) \sin ny$ $(n > 0)$ has the solution

$$u(x, y) = \frac{1}{n^2} \sinh nx \sin ny$$

Compare this solution, for large n, with the solution to the 'neighbouring' problem, when $u(0, y) = 0$, $u_x(0, y) = 0$, and the solution $u(x, y) = 0$.

36 Show that

$$u(r, \theta) = Br^n \sin n\theta$$

satisfies the Laplace equation in polar coordinates,

$$u_{rr} + \frac{1}{r}u_r + \frac{1}{r^2}u_{\theta\theta} = 0$$

A circular plate given by $0 \leqslant r \leqslant 1$, $-\pi \leqslant \theta \leqslant \pi$ has a portion of its rim $r = 1$, $0 < \theta < \pi$ kept at $50\,°C$ and a portion $r = 1$, $-\pi < \theta < 0$ kept at $-50\,°C$.

Show that the steady-state temperature u (in $°C$) at (r, θ) is given by

$$u(r, \theta) = \sum_{n=1}^{\infty} B_n r^n \sin n\theta$$

where

$$B_n = \begin{cases} 0 & (\text{even } n) \\ \dfrac{200}{n\pi} & (\text{odd } n) \end{cases}$$

37 Verify that

$$u = \frac{-2y}{x^2 + y^2 + 2x + 1}, \qquad v = \frac{x^2 + y^2 - 1}{x^2 + y^2 + 2x + 1}$$

both satisfy the Laplace equation, and sketch the curves $u = \text{constant}$ and $v = \text{constant}$. Show that

$$u + jv = \frac{j(z - 1)}{z + 1}$$

where $z = x + jy$.

38 A long bar of square cross-section $0 \leqslant x \leqslant a$, $0 \leqslant y \leqslant a$ has the faces $x = 0$, $x = a$ and $y = 0$ maintained at zero temperature, and the face $y = a$ at a control temperature u_0. Under steady-state conditions the temperature $u(x, y)$ at a point in a cross-section satisfies the Laplace equation

$$\frac{\partial^2 u}{\partial x^2} + \frac{\partial^2 u}{\partial y^2} = 0$$

Write down the boundary conditions for $u(x, y)$, and hence show that $u(x, y)$ is given by

$$u(x, y) = \frac{4u_0}{\pi} \sum_{n=0}^{\infty} \frac{\text{cosech}\,(2n + 1)\pi}{2n + 1}$$

$$\sinh\left[(2n + 1)\frac{\pi y}{a}\right] \sin\left[(2n + 1)\frac{\pi x}{a}\right]$$

39 Heat is flowing steadily in a metal plate whose shape is an infinite rectangle occupying the region $-a < x < a, y > 0$ of the (x, y) plane. The temperature at the point (x, y) is denoted by $u(x, y)$. The sides $x = \pm a$ are insulated, the temperature approaches zero as $y \to \infty$, while the side $y = 0$ is maintained at a fixed temperature $-T$ for $-a < x < 0$ and T for $0 < x < a$. It is known that $u(x, y)$ satisfies the Laplace equation

$$\frac{\partial^2 u}{\partial x^2} + \frac{\partial^2 u}{\partial y^2} = 0$$

and the boundary conditions

(a) $u \to 0$ as $y \to \infty$ for all x in $-a < x < a$

(b) $\partial u/\partial x = 0$ when $x = \pm a$

(c) $u(x, 0) = \begin{cases} -T & (-a < x < 0) \\ T & (0 < x < a) \end{cases}$

Using the method of separation, obtain the solution $u(x, y)$ in the form

$$u(x, y) = \frac{4T}{\pi} \sum_{n=0}^{\infty} \frac{1}{2n + 1} \exp\left[-(n + \tfrac{1}{2})\frac{\pi y}{a}\right]$$

$$\sin\left[(n + \tfrac{1}{2})\frac{\pi x}{a}\right]$$

40 A thin semicircular plate of radius a has its bounding diameter kept at zero temperature and its curved boundary at a constant temperature T_0. The

steady-state temperature $T(r, \theta)$ at a point having polar coordinates (r, θ), referred to the centre of the circle as origin, is given by the Laplace equation

$$\frac{\partial^2 T}{\partial r^2} + \frac{1}{r}\frac{\partial T}{\partial r} + \frac{1}{r^2}\frac{\partial^2 T}{\partial \theta^2} = 0$$

Assuming a separated solution of the form

$$T = R(r)\Theta(\theta)$$

show that

$$T(r, \theta) = \frac{4T_0}{\pi} \sum_{n=0}^{\infty} \frac{(r/a)^{2n+1}}{2n + 1} \sin(2n + 1)\theta$$

41 The Laplace equation in spherical polar coordinates (r, θ, ϕ) takes the form

$$\frac{\partial}{\partial r}\left(r^2 \frac{\partial V}{\partial r}\right) + \frac{1}{\sin\theta}\frac{\partial}{\partial \theta}\left(\sin\theta \frac{\partial V}{\partial \theta}\right)$$

$$+ \frac{1}{\sin^2\theta}\frac{\partial^2 V}{\partial \phi^2} = 0$$

If V is only a function of r and θ, and V takes the form

$$V = R(r)y(x), \qquad \text{where} \quad x = \cos\theta$$

show that

$$\frac{d}{dr}\left(r^2 \frac{dR}{dr}\right) = k(k + 1)R$$

$$(1 - x^2)\frac{d^2 y}{dx^2} - 2x\frac{dy}{dx} + k(k + 1)y = 0$$

where k is a constant.

The function V satisfies the Laplace equation in the region $a \leqslant r \leqslant b$. On $r = a$, $V = 0$ and on $r = b$, $V = \alpha \sin^2\theta$, where α is a constant. Given that solutions for y are

$$y = \begin{cases} 1 & (k = 0) \\ x & (k = 1) \\ \tfrac{1}{2}(3x^2 - 1) & (k = 2) \end{cases}$$

find V throughout the region.

8.5.3 Numerical solution

Of the three classical partial differential equations, the Laplace equation proves to be the most difficult to solve. The other two have a natural time variable in them, and it is possible, with a little care, to march forward either by a simple

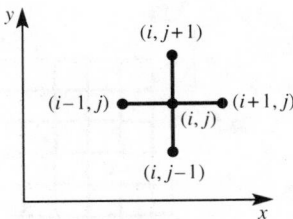

Figure 8.30 Five-point computational module for the Laplace equation.

explicit method or by an implicit procedure. In the case of the Laplace equation, information is given around the whole of the boundary of the solution region, so the field variables at *all* mesh points must be solved simultaneously. This in turn leads to a solution by matrix inversion discussed in Chapter 4 of *Modern Engineering Mathematics*.

The usual numerical approximation for the partial derivatives, discussed in Section 8.3.5, are employed, so that the equation

$$\frac{\partial^2 u}{\partial x^2} + \frac{\partial^2 u}{\partial y^2} = 0 \tag{8.45}$$

at a typical point, illustrated in Figure 8.30, becomes

$$\frac{u(i+1, j) - 2u(i, j) + u(i-1, j)}{\Delta x^2} + \frac{u(i, j+1) - 2u(i, j) + u(i, j-1)}{\Delta y^2} = 0$$

For the case $\Delta x = \Delta y$ rearranging gives

$$4u(i, j) = u(i+1, j) + u(i-1, j) + u(i, j+1) + u(i, j-1) \tag{8.46}$$

In the typical five-point module (8.46) the increments Δx and Δy are taken to be the same and it is noted that the middle value $u(i, j)$ is the average of its four neighbours. This corresponds to the absence of 'hot spots'. We now examine how (8.46) can be implemented.

EXAMPLE 8.25   Solve the Laplace equation (8.45) in the square region $0 \leqslant x \leqslant 1$, $0 \leqslant y \leqslant 1$ with the boundary conditions

(a) $u = 0$ on $x = 0$

(b) $u = 1$ on $x = 1$

(c) $u = 0$ on $y = 0$

(d) $u = 0$ on $y = 1$

Solution   For a first solution we take the simplest mesh, illustrated in Figure 8.31(a), which contains only four interior points labelled u_1, u_2, u_3 and u_4. The four equations obtained from (8.46) are

(a)　　　　　　　　　　　　　　　　(b)

Figure 8.31 Meshes for the solution of the Laplace equation in Example 8.25: (a) a simple mesh containing 4 interior points; (b) a larger mesh with 49 interior points.

$$4u_1 = 0 + 0 + u_2 + u_4$$

$$4u_2 = 0 + 1 + u_3 + u_1$$

$$4u_3 = 1 + 0 + u_4 + u_2$$

$$4u_4 = 0 + 0 + u_1 + u_3$$

which in turn can be written in matrix form as

$$
\begin{bmatrix}
4 & -1 & 0 & -1 \\
-1 & 4 & -1 & 0 \\
0 & -1 & 4 & -1 \\
-1 & 0 & -1 & 4
\end{bmatrix}
\begin{bmatrix}
u_1 \\ u_2 \\ u_3 \\ u_4
\end{bmatrix}
=
\begin{bmatrix}
0 \\ 1 \\ 1 \\ 0
\end{bmatrix}
$$

This has the solution $u_1 = 0.125$, $u_2 = 0.375$, $u_3 = 0.375$, $u_4 = 0.125$. A larger mesh obtained by dividing the sides up into eight equal parts is indicated in Figure 8.31(b). The equations now take the form

$$4u(1, 1) = u(2, 1) + 0 \qquad + u(1, 2) + 0$$

$$4u(2, 1) = u(3, 1) + u(1, 1) + u(2, 2) + 0$$

$$\vdots \qquad\qquad \vdots$$

$$4u(7, 1) = 1 \qquad + u(6, 1) + u(7, 2) + 0$$

$$4u(1, 2) = u(2, 2) + 0 \qquad + u(1, 3) + u(1, 1)$$

$$4u(2, 2) = u(3, 2) + u(1, 2) + u(2, 3) + u(2, 1)$$

$$\vdots \qquad\qquad \vdots$$

$$4u(7, 2) = 1 \qquad + u(6, 2) + u(7, 3) + u(7, 1)$$

$$\vdots \qquad\qquad \vdots$$

We thus generate 49 linear equations in 49 unknowns, which can be solved by any convenient matrix inverter. The matrices take the block form

$$
A = \begin{bmatrix}
4 & -1 & 0 & 0 & 0 & 0 & 0 \\
-1 & 4 & -1 & 0 & 0 & 0 & 0 \\
0 & -1 & 4 & -1 & 0 & 0 & 0 \\
0 & 0 & -1 & 4 & -1 & 0 & 0 \\
0 & 0 & 0 & -1 & 4 & -1 & 0 \\
0 & 0 & 0 & 0 & -1 & 4 & -1 \\
0 & 0 & 0 & 0 & 0 & -1 & 4
\end{bmatrix}
$$

$$
B = \begin{bmatrix}
-1 & 0 & 0 & 0 & 0 & 0 & 0 \\
0 & -1 & 0 & 0 & 0 & 0 & 0 \\
0 & 0 & -1 & 0 & 0 & 0 & 0 \\
0 & 0 & 0 & -1 & 0 & 0 & 0 \\
0 & 0 & 0 & 0 & -1 & 0 & 0 \\
0 & 0 & 0 & 0 & 0 & -1 & 0 \\
0 & 0 & 0 & 0 & 0 & 0 & -1
\end{bmatrix}
$$

$$
C = \begin{bmatrix}
0 \\ 0 \\ 0 \\ 0 \\ 0 \\ 0 \\ 1
\end{bmatrix},
\qquad
U_k = \begin{bmatrix}
u(1, k) \\ u(2, k) \\ \vdots \\ u(7, k)
\end{bmatrix}
$$

so that the equations become

$$
\begin{bmatrix}
A & B & 0 & 0 & 0 & 0 & 0 \\
B & A & B & 0 & 0 & 0 & 0 \\
0 & B & A & B & 0 & 0 & 0 \\
0 & 0 & B & A & B & 0 & 0 \\
0 & 0 & 0 & B & A & B & 0 \\
0 & 0 & 0 & 0 & B & A & B \\
0 & 0 & 0 & 0 & 0 & B & A
\end{bmatrix}
\begin{bmatrix}
U_1 \\ U_2 \\ U_3 \\ U_4 \\ U_5 \\ U_6 \\ U_7
\end{bmatrix}
=
\begin{bmatrix}
C \\ C \\ C \\ C \\ C \\ C \\ C
\end{bmatrix}
\tag{8.47}
$$

The matrix equation (8.47) can be solved by an elimination technique or an iterative method like **successive over-relaxation** (SOR). As indicated in Section 4.5.4 of *Modern Engineering Mathematics*, SOR is the simplest to program, and elimination techniques are best performed by a package from a computer library. For the current problem we present the solution in Figure 8.32, where the cases $\Delta x = \frac{1}{8}$ and $\Delta x = \frac{1}{4}$ are both shown. It may be seen from this example that the accuracy of the solution is quite tolerable when the cases $\Delta x = \frac{1}{4}$ and $\Delta x = \frac{1}{8}$ are compared. Note the averaging behaviour of the Laplace equation and observe that the discontinuity in the corner does not spread into the solution. The corner nodes are never used in the numerical calculation, so the discontinuity is avoided.

j values

	0	1	2	3	4	5	6	7	8
8	0	0	0	0	0	0	0	0	1
7	0	0.017	0.038	0.064	0.103	0.164	0.269	0.483	1
6	0	0.032	0.069	0.117	0.184	0.282	0.431	0.661	1
5	0	0.042	0.089	0.150	0.233	0.350	0.512	0.731	1
4	0	0.045	0.096	0.162	0.250	0.371	0.556	0.749	1
			(0.098)		(0.250)		(0.527)		
3									
2	0		(0.071)		(0.188)		(0.429)		1
1									
0	0		0		0		0		1
	0	1	2	3	4	5	6	7	8	*i* values

Figure 8.32 The solution of Example 8.25. The solution is symmetric about the line $j = 4$; the solution with $\Delta x = 0.125$ is given in the upper half and the solution with $\Delta x = 0.25$ is shown in parentheses in the lower half.

Because of its simplicity, SOR is an attractive method for solving Laplace-type problems. Equations (8.46) are rewritten with an iteration superscript as

$$u^{n+1}(i, j) = u^n(i, j) + \tfrac{1}{4}w[u^n(i + 1, j) + u^n(i - 1, j) + u^n(i, j + 1)$$
$$+ u^n(i, j - 1) - 4u^n(i, j)] \tag{8.48}$$

and w is a relaxation factor, discussed in Chapter 4 of *Modern Engineering Mathematics*.

Knowing all the $u(i, j)$ at iteration n, we can use (8.48) to evaluate $u(i, j)$ at iteration $n + 1$. Normally the $u(i, j)$ are over-written in the computer as they are computed, so that some of the ns in the right-hand side of (8.48) become $(n + 1)$s. The order of evaluation of the is and js in (8.48) is critical, but the most obvious methods by rows or columns prove to be satisfactory.

A great deal is known about the optimum relaxation factor w. It is closely related to the value of the maximum eigenvalue of the matrix associated with the problem. For square regions with unit side and with u given on the boundary and equal mesh spacing it can be shown that $w = 2/(1 + \sin \Delta x)$ is the best value. For other problems this is usually used as a starting guess, but numerical experimentation is required to determine an optimum or near-optimum value.

Figure 8.33 Fictitious nodes, $i = -1$, introduced outside the boundary.

We have only considered u to be given on the boundary, and it is essential to know how to deal with derivative boundary conditions, since these are very common. Let us consider a typical example:

$$\frac{\partial u}{\partial x} = g(y) \quad \text{on } x = 0$$

We then insert a fictitious line of nodes, as shown in Figure 8.33. Approximately, the boundary condition gives

$$u(1, j) - u(-1, j) = g(y_j)2\,\Delta x$$

so that

$$u(-1, j) = u(1, j) - 2\,\Delta x\, g(y_j) \tag{8.49}$$

Equations (8.46) or (8.48) are now solved for $i = 0$ as well as $i > 0$, but at the end of a sweep $u(-1, j)$ will be updated via (8.49).

EXAMPLE 8.26   Solve the Laplace equation (8.45), for steady heat conduction, in the unit square, given that

(a) $\partial u/\partial x = 1$ on $x = 0$ (steady heat supply along this boundary);
(b) $u = y^2$ on $x = 1$⎫
(c) $u = 0$ on $y = 0$⎬ (temperature given on three sides).
(d) $u = x$ on $y = 1$⎭

Solution   The region is illustrated in Figure 8.34, with mesh spacing $\Delta x = \Delta y = \frac{1}{4}$.

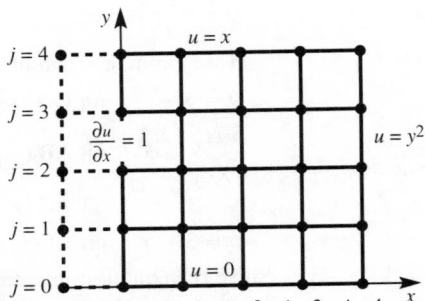

Figure 8.34 The mesh used in Example 8.26.

Equation (8.49) just gives $u(-1, j) = u(1, j) - \frac{1}{2}$ for each j. From (8.46), we can write the equations as

$$4u(0, 1) = u(-1, 1) + u(1, 1) + 0 + u(0, 2) = -\frac{1}{2} + 2u(1, 1) + u(0, 2)$$

$$4u(1, 1) = u(0, 1) + u(2, 1) + 0 + u(1, 2)$$

$$4u(2, 1) = u(1, 1) + u(3, 1) + 0 + u(2, 2)$$

and so on, and hence obtain 12 equations in 12 unknowns. These can be solved by any convenient method to give a solution as shown in Figure 8.35.

$j = 4$	0.0000	0.2500	0.5000	0.7500	1.0000
$j = 3$	−0.1190	0.1114	0.3067	0.4644	0.5625
$j = 2$	−0.1987	0.0077	0.1511	0.2384	0.2500
$j = 1$	−0.1912	−0.0330	0.0516	0.0881	0.0625
$j = 0$	0.0000	0.0000	0.0000	0.0000	0.0000
	$i = 0$	$i = 1$	$i = 2$	$i = 3$	$i = 4$

Figure 8.35 Data from the solution of Example 8.26 using a step length 0.25 in each direction.

8.5.4 Exercises

42 Use the five-point difference approximation in (8.46) to solve

$$\frac{\partial^2 u}{\partial x^2} + \frac{\partial^2 u}{\partial y^2} = 0 \quad (0 \leqslant x \leqslant 1, 0 \leqslant y \leqslant 1)$$

where $u(x, 0) = u(0, y) = 0$, $u(x, 1) = x$, $u(1, y) = y(2 - y)$. Find the approximations for $u(\frac{1}{2}, \frac{1}{2})$ for grid sizes $\Delta x = \Delta y = \frac{1}{2}$ and $\Delta x = \Delta y = \frac{1}{4}$.

43 Use a mesh $\Delta x = \Delta y = \frac{1}{2}$ to solve

$$\frac{\partial^2 u}{\partial x^2} + \frac{\partial^2 u}{\partial y^2} = 0 \quad (0 < x < 1, 0 < y < 1)$$

satisfying $u(0, y) = 0$, $\partial u(x, 0)/\partial y = 0$, $u(1, y) = 1$, $\partial u/\partial y + u = 0$ on $y = 1$.

44 A numerical solution is to be determined for the loading of a uniform plate, where the displacement w satisfies the equation

$$\frac{\partial^2 w}{\partial x^2} + \frac{\partial^2 w}{\partial y^2} + 20 = 0$$

and a square mesh of side h is used. Show that, at

an interior point 0 with neighbours 1, 2, 3 and 4, the approximation to the equation is

$$4w_0 = w_1 + w_2 + w_3 + w_4 + 20h^2$$

The plate is in the shape of a trapezium whose vertices can be represented by the points $(0, 0)$, $(5, 0)$, $(2, 3)$ and $(0, 3)$. The plate is held on its edges so that on the boundary $w = 0$. Compute the solution for w at the five interior points if h is taken as 1.

45 The function $\phi(x, y)$ satisfies the equation

$$\frac{\partial^2 \phi}{\partial x^2} + \frac{\partial^2 \phi}{\partial y^2} = x$$

and the boundary conditions (see Figure 8.36)

$$\phi = 3 - y^2 \quad \text{on OA } (x = 0, 0 \leqslant y \leqslant 1)$$

$$\frac{\partial \phi}{\partial y} = -\phi \quad \text{on AB } (y = 1, 0 < x < 1)$$

$$\phi = 1 \quad \text{on BC } (x = 1, 0 \leqslant y \leqslant 1)$$

$$\phi = 3 - x \quad \text{on CO } (y = 0, 0 < x < 1)$$

Solve the equation numerically, using a mesh of (a) $h = \frac{1}{2}$ in each direction, (b) $h = \frac{1}{4}$ in each direction.

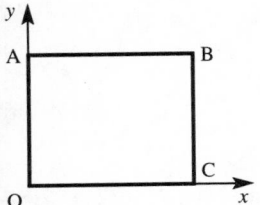

Figure 8.36 Region for Exercise 45.

46 The function $\phi(x, y)$ satisfies the Laplace equation

$$\frac{\partial^2 \phi}{\partial x^2} + \frac{\partial^2 \phi}{\partial y^2} = 0$$

inside the region shown in Figure 8.37. The function ϕ takes the value $\phi = 9x^2$ at all points on the boundary. Making full use of symmetry, formulate a set of finite-difference equations to solve for the

nodal values of ϕ on a square grid of side $h = \frac{1}{3}$. Solve for ϕ at the nodal points.

Figure 8.37 Region for Exercise 46.

8.6 Finite elements

In Section 8.5.3 we sought numerical solutions of the Laplace equation, but we noted that only simple geometries could be handled using finite differences. The region described in Exercise 44 is about as difficult as can be treated easily. To adapt methods to awkward regions is not easy, so alternative strategies have been sought. Great advances took place in the 1960s, when civil engineers pioneered the method of finite elements. To solve plate bending problems, they solved the appropriate equations for small patches and then 'stitched' the latter together to form an overall solution. The job is not an easy one, and requires a large amount of arithmetic. It was only when large, fast computers became available that the method was viable. This method is now very widely used, and forms the basis of most calculations in stress analysis and, recently, for many fluid flows. It is very adaptable and physically satisfying, but is very difficult to program. This is in contrast to finite differences, which are reasonably easy. In general the advice to anyone employing this technique is to use a finite element 'package', available in most computer libraries, and not to write one's own program. It is important, however, to understand the basis of the method. We shall illustrate this method for a simple situation, but refer to specialist books for details and extensions: for example see P. E. Lewis and J. P. Ward *The Finite Element Method* (Addison-Wesley, Reading, MA, 1991).

We consider solutions to the Poisson equation

$$\frac{\partial^2 u}{\partial x^2} + \frac{\partial^2 u}{\partial y^2} = \rho(x, y) \qquad\qquad (8.50)$$

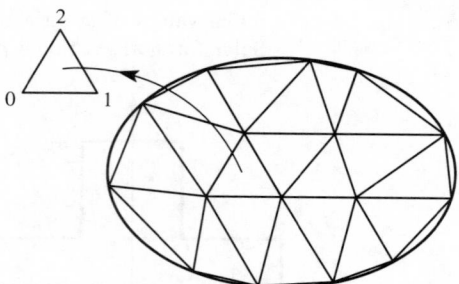

Figure 8.38 Triangular finite-element mesh, with the local numbering of a typical element.

in a region R with u given on the boundary of R. The region R is divided up into a triangular mesh as in Figure 8.38. We aim to calculate the value of u at the nodal points of the mesh, but with the function suitably interpolated in each triangle. The simplest situation is obtained if, in a typical triangle, u is approximated as a linear function

$$u = ax + by + c \tag{8.51}$$

taking the values u_0, u_1 and u_2 at the corners. This function can be written explicitly in terms of the functions

$$L_0 = \begin{vmatrix} x & y & 1 \\ x_1 & y_1 & 1 \\ x_2 & y_2 & 1 \end{vmatrix} \Big/ \begin{vmatrix} x_0 & y_0 & 1 \\ x_1 & y_1 & 1 \\ x_2 & y_2 & 1 \end{vmatrix}$$

$$L_1 = \begin{vmatrix} x & y & 1 \\ x_2 & y_2 & 1 \\ x_0 & y_0 & 1 \end{vmatrix} \Big/ \begin{vmatrix} x_1 & y_1 & 1 \\ x_2 & y_2 & 1 \\ x_0 & y_0 & 1 \end{vmatrix} \tag{8.52}$$

$$L_2 = \begin{vmatrix} x & y & 1 \\ x_0 & y_0 & 1 \\ x_1 & y_1 & 1 \end{vmatrix} \Big/ \begin{vmatrix} x_2 & y_2 & 1 \\ x_0 & y_0 & 1 \\ x_1 & y_1 & 1 \end{vmatrix}$$

each of which is taken to be zero outside the triangle with vertices (x_0, y_0), (x_1, y_1) and (x_2, y_2). The denominators are just $2A$, where A is the area of the triangle. The function L_0, illustrated in Figure 8.39(a), takes the values 1 at (x_0, y_0), 0 at (x_1, y_1) and (x_2, y_2); it is linear in the triangle and is taken to be zero elsewhere. The functions L_1 and L_2 behave similarly. The field variable u in the element, denoted by u^e, can now be written as

$$u^e(x, y) = u_0 L_0 + u_1 L_1 + u_2 L_2 \tag{8.53}$$

The situation is illustrated in Figure 8.39(b). Note that $u^e(x, y)$ is a linear function in x and y, $u^e(x_0, y_0) = u_0$, $u^e(x_1, y_1) = u_1$ and $u^e(x_2, y_2) = u_2$, and hence gives an explicit form for the function in (8.51) that has the correct values at the nodes.

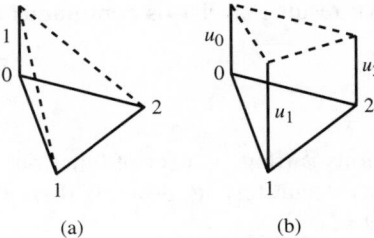

(a)   (b)

Figure 8.39 (a) The function L_0. (b) u approximated as a linear function in the element.

EXAMPLE 8.27   Find the linear function that has the values u_0 at $(0,0)$, u_1 at $(1,1)$ and u_2 at $(\frac{1}{2}, 1)$.

Solution   From (8.52), the functions L_0, L_1 and L_2 are given by

$$L_0 = \begin{vmatrix} x & y & 1 \\ 1 & 1 & 1 \\ \frac{1}{2} & 1 & 1 \end{vmatrix} \bigg/ \begin{vmatrix} 0 & 0 & 1 \\ 1 & 1 & 1 \\ \frac{1}{2} & 1 & 1 \end{vmatrix} = (\tfrac{1}{2} - \tfrac{1}{2}y)/\tfrac{1}{2} = 1 - y$$

$$L_1 = \begin{vmatrix} x & y & 1 \\ \frac{1}{2} & 1 & 1 \\ 0 & 0 & 1 \end{vmatrix} \bigg/ \frac{1}{2} = 2x - y$$

$$L_2 = \begin{vmatrix} x & y & 1 \\ 0 & 0 & 1 \\ 1 & 1 & 1 \end{vmatrix} \bigg/ \frac{1}{2} = 2y - 2x$$

Thus, from (8.53), the required linear function is

$$u = (1 - y)u_0 + (2x - y)u_1 + 2(y - x)u_2$$

or

$$u = x(2u_1 - 2u_2) + y(-u_0 - u_1 + 2u_2) + u_0$$

We build up the solution of (8.50) as the sum over all the elements of the functions constructed to be linear in an element and zero outside the element. Thus

$$u = \sum u^e$$

To be of use, this function must satisfy (8.50) in some approximate sense. The function cannot be differentiated across the element boundaries, since it has discontinuous behaviour. We therefore have to satisfy the equation in an integrated or **'weak'** form.

We use the well-known result that if V is continuous and

$$\iint\limits_R V\phi\,dx\,dy = 0 \qquad (8.54)$$

for a complete set of functions ϕ (that is, a set of functions that will approximate any continuous function as accurately as desired) then $V \equiv 0$ in R. Using the residual of (8.50) in (8.54) gives

$$0 = \iint\limits_R \left(\frac{\partial^2 u}{\partial x^2} + \frac{\partial^2 u}{\partial y^2} - \rho\right)\phi\,dx\,dy$$

$$= \iint\limits_R \left[\frac{\partial}{\partial x}\left(\phi\frac{\partial u}{\partial x}\right) + \frac{\partial}{\partial y}\left(\phi\frac{\partial u}{\partial y}\right) - \frac{\partial u}{\partial x}\frac{\partial \phi}{\partial x} - \frac{\partial u}{\partial y}\frac{\partial \phi}{\partial y} - \rho\phi\right]dx\,dy$$

$$= -\iint\limits_R (u_x\phi_x + u_y\phi_y + \rho\phi)\,dx\,dy - \int_C (\phi u_y\,dx - \phi u_x\,dy)$$

where the final integral is obtained over the boundary C of R using Green's theorem

$$\iint\limits_R \left(\frac{\partial N}{\partial x} - \frac{\partial M}{\partial y}\right)dx\,dy = \int_C (M\,dx + N\,dy)$$

described in Section 7.4.5.

Choosing ϕ to be zero on the boundary C, we have an integrated form for (8.50) as

$$0 = \iint\limits_R (u_x\phi_x + u_y\phi_y + \rho\phi)\,dx\,dy \qquad (8.55)$$

It is this integrated or 'weak' form of (8.50) that we shall satisfy. We are therefore satisfying the equation in a global sense over the whole region. In comparison, finite-difference approximations are local to the mesh point. Clearly, we cannot use (8.55) with a complete set of functions ϕ, since there must be infinitely many of them. The best that can be done is to use N test functions ϕ_n ($n = 1,\ldots,N$) when there are N interior nodes. There will then be N equations for the N unknowns u_n ($n = 1,\ldots,N$) at the node points. As $N \to \infty$, the functions ϕ_n must form a complete set, and then the weak form of (8.55) will be satisfied identically rather than approximately. The most popular set of functions ϕ_i is that due to Galerkin, who used the pyramid functions illustrated in Figure 8.40. At a typical point 0 with neighbours $1, 2, 3, \ldots, m$ we have

$$\phi = \left\{\begin{array}{ll} 1 & \text{at node } 0 \\ 0 & \text{at nodes } 1, 2, \ldots, m \\ \text{identically zero outside the neighbouring triangles} \end{array}\right\} \begin{array}{l} \text{and piecewise-linear in each} \\ \text{of the neighbouring triangles} \end{array} \qquad (8.56)$$

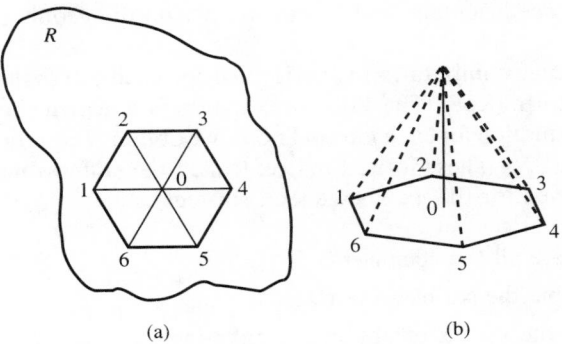

Figure 8.40 (a) A typical node and its neighbours in the region R. (b) The pyramid function used at the typical node.

If there are N nodes in the mesh then these are N pyramid functions of the type (8.56). We substitute each of these functions in turn into (8.55) to satisfy the weak form of our original Poisson equation. Taking a typical node, we see that ϕ is piecewise-linear in the neighbouring triangles. For a typical such triangle 012, ϕ is just the linear function L_0 defined earlier. We substitute $\phi = L_0$ into the right-hand side of (8.55) and use the fact that

$$u = u_0 L_0 + u_1 L_1 + u_2 L_2$$

to obtain the contribution from this particular triangle as

$$I_e = \iint_{\triangle_{012}} \left[\left(u_0 \frac{\partial L_0}{\partial x} + u_1 \frac{\partial L_1}{\partial x} + u_2 \frac{\partial L_2}{\partial x} \right) \frac{\partial L_0}{\partial x} \right.$$

$$\left. + \left(u_0 \frac{\partial L_0}{\partial y} + u_1 \frac{\partial L_1}{\partial y} + u_2 \frac{\partial L_2}{\partial y} \right) \frac{\partial L_0}{\partial y} + \rho_e L_0 \right] dx\, dy$$

where ρ_e is taken to be constant in the triangle. Since L_i $(i = 0, 1, 2)$ are linear, $\partial L_i/\partial x$ and $\partial L_i/\partial y$ are constants, and hence the integrals can be performed explicitly, giving

$$I_e = u_0 [(y_1 - y_2)^2 + (x_1 - x_2)^2] + u_1 [(y_2 - y_0)(y_1 - y_2) + (x_2 - x_0)(x_1 - x_2)]$$

$$+ u_2 [(y_0 - y_1)(y_1 - y_2) + (x_0 - x_1)(x_1 - x_2)] + \tfrac{2}{3} A \rho_e$$

From (8.55) with ϕ chosen as (8.56), we obtain for the point 0 the sum of such terms over neighbouring elements:

$$\sum_e I_e = 0$$

This is just an equation of the form

$$\sum_{i=0}^{m} a_i u_i + b = 0$$

where the coefficients a_i and b depend only on the geometry and *not* on the field variables.

A similar computation is performed for each internal node, with ϕ taken to be of the form (8.56). The Poisson equation is linear in the u_i, and since there is one such equation for each internal node, we obtain N equations in the N unknowns u_i ($i = 1, \ldots, N$). These form a matrix (called the **stiffness matrix**) equation, which can be solved for the u_i. The general strategy is

(i)   calculate all the coefficients;

(ii) assemble the stiffness matrix;

(iii) invert the matrix to obtain the unknowns u_i ($i = 1, 2, 3, \ldots, N$);

(iv) calculate any required data from the solution.

EXAMPLE 8.28 Solve the Laplace equation $\partial^2 u/\partial x^2 + \partial^2 u/\partial y^2 = 0$ in the region shown in Figure 8.41, subject to the boundary conditions indicated.

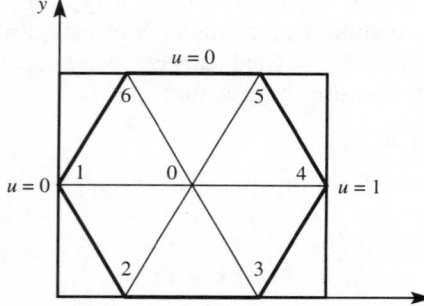

Figure 8.41 Mesh for the finite element solution to Example 8.28.

Solution Here we have a simple rectangular region with $\rho = 0$, and which is the same problem as Example 8.25.

$\triangle 012$	gives a contribution	$0.3125u_0 - 0.1875u_1 - 0.1250u_2$
$\triangle 023$	„	$0.2500u_0 - 0.1250u_2 - 0.1250u_3$
$\triangle 034$	„	$0.3125u_0 - 0.1250u_3 - 0.1875u_4$
$\triangle 045$	„	$0.2500u_0 - 0.1875u_4 - 0.1250u_5$
$\triangle 056$	„	$0.2500u_0 - 0.1250u_5 - 0.1250u_6$
$\triangle 061$	„	$0.3125u_0 - 0.1250u_6 - 0.1875u_1$

Adding all these contributions for the point 0, which is the only unspecified point, gives

$$0 = 1.75u_0 - 0.365u_1 - 0.25u_2 - 0.25u_3 - 0.365u_4 - 0.25u_5 - 0.25u_6$$

so that, knowing $u_1 = u_2 = u_3 = u_5 = u_6 = 0$ and $u_4 = 1$, we obtain $u_0 = 0.2086$. Comparing with Example 8.25, we see that our result is not particularly accurate, which is not surprising, since the mesh chosen here is particularly crude.

It is clear from Example 8.28 that the contributions from each triangle need considerable computational effort and the finite-element method is unsuitable for hand computations.

EXAMPLE 8.29   Solve the Laplace equation in the region shown in Figure 8.42 with the given boundary conditions.

Figure 8.42 The boundary conditions for the solution of Example 8.29.

Solution   It should be noted that we have included derivative boundary conditions in this problem. To derive (8.55), we eliminated the boundary integral since $\phi = 0$ on C. In this case $\phi \neq 0$, but $u_y = 0$ on the top and bottom portions and $u_x = 0$ on the left- and right-hand sides, so the line integral is still zero. To calculate

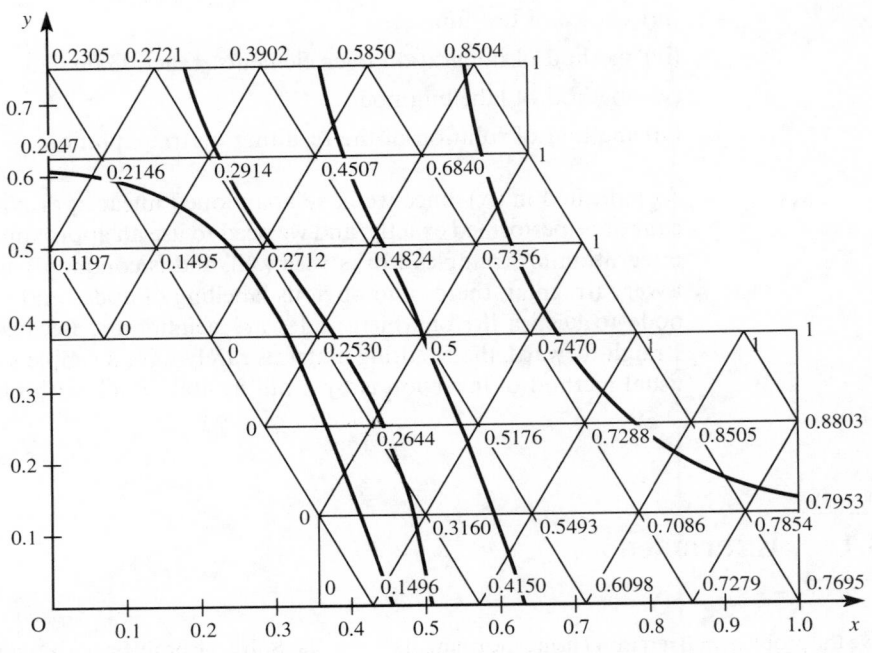

Figure 8.43 The solution of Example 8.29; the nodal values are given and the streamlines drawn.

the equation for u on these boundaries, fictitious triangles can be added outside the region, and the derivative boundary condition used to extend the solution to the points outside the physical region. This procedure is not necessary, since the weak formulation will satisfy the derivative boundary conditions at least approximately. However, it can improve accuracy and speed up iterative solution methods.

The example chosen is such that the triangles are all equilateral triangles, so the coefficients are relatively easy to compute and, because of the uniformity, there is a sensible ordering to the elements. The solutions at the 33 unknown points are shown in Figure 8.43, and the streamlines in the figure illustrate the 'flow' through the configuration.

In this section no more than the 'flavour' of the finite-element method has been given. The intimate connection with computers makes it difficult to do more than show the complications that occur and give an outline of how they are dealt with.

For many problems a linear approximation is not good enough, for example, in stress analysis for finite deformations, when high derivatives are required. Also, there is no good reason why a triangle is chosen rather than a quadrilateral. There are several choices that must be made at the start of the calculation:

(i)   division of the region into triangles, quadrilaterals, ...;

(ii) level of approximation, linear, quadratics, cubics, ...;

(iii) choice of test function;

(iv) method of integration over elements: exact, Gaussian, ...;

(v)   method of labelling nodes;

(vi) method of solution of the resulting matrix equation.

As indicated in (iv), once we have abandoned linear approximations, the integrals cannot be performed exactly, and we need to use an approximate method. Gaussian integration for triangles works very well, and is commonly used. When the region is very irregular, there is no obvious labelling of nodes and it is necessary for each node to keep a list of which nodes are neighbours. Because the labelling is not straightforward, the resulting matrices rarely have a simple structure, and the most usual method of inversion is by a full frontal attack with Gaussian elimination.

8.6.1   Exercises

47 Solve the problem in Exercise 44 using the triangular finite-element mesh shown in Figure 8.44.

48 Solve the problem in Exercise 46 using the triangular finite-element mesh shown in Figure 8.45.

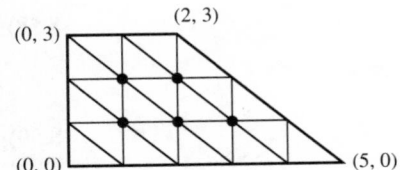

Figure 8.44 Finite-element mesh for Exercise 47.

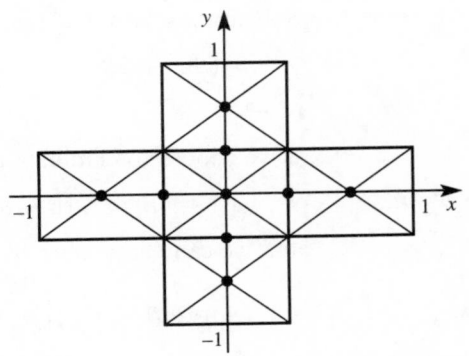

Figure 8.45 Finite-element mesh for Exercise 48.

8.7 General considerations

There are properties of a general nature that can be deduced without reference to any particular partial differential equation. The formal classification of second-order equations and their intimate connection with the appropriateness of boundary conditions will be considered in this section. The much more difficult problems of the existence and uniqueness is left to specialist texts.

8.7.1 Formal classification

In the preceding sections we have discussed in general terms the three classic partial differential equations. We shall now show that second-order equations can be reduced to one of these three types.

Consider the general form of a second-order equation:

$$Au_{xx} + 2Bu_{xy} + Cu_{yy} + Du_x + Eu_y + F = 0 \qquad (8.57)$$

where $A, B, C, \ldots$ are constants. If we make a change of variable

$$r = ax + y, \qquad s = x + by$$

then the chain rule gives

$$u_{xx} = a^2 u_{rr} + 2a u_{rs} + u_{ss}$$

$$u_{xy} = a u_{rr} + (1 + ab) u_{rs} + b u_{ss}$$

$$u_{yy} = u_{rr} + 2b u_{rs} + b^2 u_{ss}$$

Substituting into (8.57) gives

$$u_{rr}(Aa^2 + 2Ba + C) + 2u_{rs}(aA + B + abB + bC) + u_{ss}(A + 2Bb + b^2C)$$
$$+ (aD + E)u_r + (D + Eb)u_s + F = 0$$

If we choose to eliminate the u_{rs} term then we must put

$$a(A + bB) = -(B + bC) \tag{8.58}$$

and we can eliminate a by substitution to obtain

$$(A + 2bB + b^2C)\left[u_{ss} + \frac{AC - B^2}{(A + Bb)^2} u_{rr} \right] + \ldots = 0 \tag{8.59}$$

We can see immediately that the behaviour of (8.59) depends critically on the sign of $AC - B^2$ and this leads to the following classification.

Case 1: $AC - B^2 > 0$, elliptic equations

On putting $(AC - B^2)/(A + Bb)^2 = \lambda^2$, (8.59) becomes

$$\alpha(u_{ss} + \lambda^2 u_{rr}) + \ldots = 0$$

and on further putting $q = r/\lambda$,

$$u_{ss} + u_{qq} + \ldots = 0$$

The second-order terms are just the same as the Laplace operator. Equations such as (8.57) with $AC - B^2 > 0$ are called **elliptic equations**.

Case 2: $AC - B^2 = 0$, parabolic equations

In this case (8.59) simply becomes

$$u_{ss} + \ldots = 0$$

with only one second-order term surviving. The equation is almost identical to the heat conduction equation. Equations such as (8.57) with $AC - B^2 = 0$ are called **parabolic equations**.

Case 3: $AC - B^2 < 0$, hyperbolic equations

On putting $(AC - B^2)/(A + Bb)^2 = -\mu^2$, (8.59) becomes

$$\alpha(u_{ss} - \mu^2 u_{rr}) + \ldots = 0$$

and on further putting $t = r/\mu$,

$$u_{ss} - u_{tt} + \ldots = 0$$

which we can identify with the terms of the wave equation. Equations such as (8.57) with $AC - B^2 < 0$ are called **hyperbolic equations**.

Thus we see that simply by changing axes and adjusting length scales, the general equation (8.57) is reduced to one of the three standard types. We therefore have strong reasons for studying the three classical equations very closely. An example illustrates the process.

EXAMPLE 8.30   Discuss the behaviour of the equation

$$u_{xx} + 2u_{xy} + 2\alpha u_{yy} = 0$$

for various values of the constant α.

Solution   In the notation of (8.57), $A = 1$, $B = 1$ and $C = 2\alpha$, so from (8.58)

$$a = -\frac{1 + 2\alpha b}{1 + b}$$

and the change of variables $r = ax + y$, $s = x + by$ gives

$$u_{ss} + \frac{2\alpha - 1}{(1 + b)^2} u_{rr} = 0$$

Thus if $\alpha > \frac{1}{2}$ and $q = r(1 + b)/\sqrt{(2\alpha - 1)}$, we have the elliptic equation

$$u_{ss} + u_{qq} = 0$$

If $\alpha = \frac{1}{2}$, we have the parabolic equation

$$u_{ss} = 0$$

If $\alpha < \frac{1}{2}$ and $t = r(1 + b)/\sqrt{(1 - 2\alpha)}$, we have the hyperbolic equation

$$u_{ss} - u_{tt} = 0$$

In (8.57) the assumption was that $A, B, C, \ldots$ were constants. Certainly for many problems this is not the case, and $A, B, \ldots$ are functions of x and y, and possibly u also. Therefore the analysis described does not hold globally for variable-coefficient equations. However, we can follow the same analysis at each point of the region under consideration. If the equation at *every* point is of one type, say elliptic, then we call the equation elliptic. There are good physical problems where its type can change. One of the best known examples is for transonic flow, where the equation is of the form

$$\left(1 - \frac{u^2}{c^2}\right)\psi_{xx} - \frac{2uv}{c^2}\psi_{xy} + \left(1 - \frac{v^2}{c^2}\right)\psi_{yy} + f(\psi) = 0$$

where u and v are the velocity components and c is a constant. We calculate

$$AC - B^2 = \left(1 - \frac{u^2}{c^2}\right)\left(1 - \frac{v^2}{c^2}\right) - \left(\frac{uv}{c^2}\right)^2$$

$$= 1 - \frac{u^2 + v^2}{c^2} = 1 - \frac{q^2}{c^2}$$

If we put $q/c = M$, the Mach number, then for $M > 1$ the flow is hyperbolic and supersonic, while for $M < 1$ it is elliptic and subsonic. It is easy to appreciate that transonic flows are very difficult to compute, since different boundary conditions and techniques are required on the subsonic and supersonic sides.

8.7.2   Boundary conditions

In the preceding sections we chose natural boundary conditions for the three classical partial differential equations. We can formalize these ideas a bit further and look at appropriate boundary conditions and the consequences of choosing inappropriate conditions. We shall confine ourselves to two-variable situations, but it is possible to extend the theory to problems with more variables.

Suppose that we are trying to obtain the solution $u(x, y)$ to a partial differential equation in a region R with boundary C. The commonest boundary conditions involve u or the normal derivative $\partial u/\partial n$ on C. The normal derivative (which is discussed in Section 7.2.1) at a point P on C is the rate of change of u with respect to the variable n along the line that is normal to C at P. The three conditions that are found to occur most regularly are

Cauchy conditions

u and $\dfrac{\partial u}{\partial n}$ given on C

Dirichlet conditions

u given on C

Neumann conditions

$\dfrac{\partial u}{\partial n}$ given on C

It is common for different conditions to apply to different parts of the boundary C. A boundary is said to be **closed** if conditions are specified on the whole of it, or **open** if conditions are only specified on part of it. The boundary can of course include infinity; conditions at infinity are specified if the boundary is closed or unspecified if it is open.

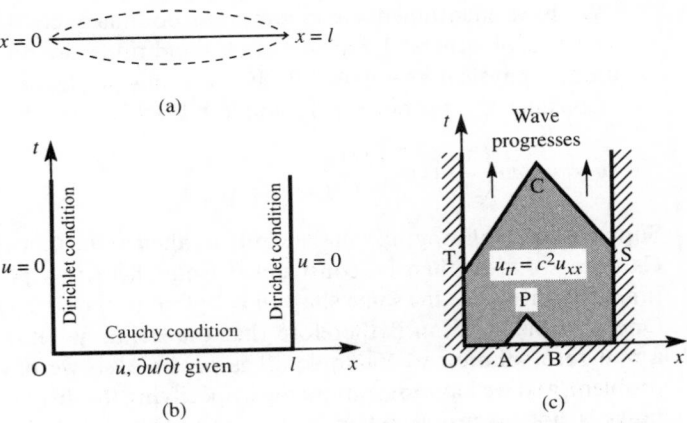

Figure 8.46 (a) A vibrating string fixed at its ends $x = 0$ and $x = l$. (b) The corresponding region and boundary conditions in the (x, t) plane. (c) Wave moving forward with time.

The natural conditions for the *wave equation* are Cauchy conditions on an open boundary. The d'Alembert solution (8.15) in the (x, t) plane in Section 8.3.1 corresponds to u and $\partial u/\partial t$ given on the open boundary, $t = 0$. Physically these conditions correspond to a given displacement and velocity at time $t = 0$. However the vibrations of a finite string, say a violin string, will be given by mixed conditions (Figure 8.46a). On the initial line $0 \leqslant x \leqslant l, t = 0$ (Figure 8.46b) Cauchy conditions will hold, with both u and $\partial u/\partial t$ given. The ends of the string are held fixed, so we have Dirichlet conditions $u = 0$ on $x = 0$, $t \geqslant 0$ and $u = 0$ on $x = l$, $t \geqslant 0$.

Figure 8.46 is typical of the hyperbolic-type equations in the two variables x and t that arise in wave propagation problems. For the second-order system

$$Au_{xx} + 2Bu_{xy} + Cu_{yy} = 0$$

the characteristics are defined by

$$\frac{\mathrm{d}y}{\mathrm{d}x} = \frac{B \pm \sqrt{(B^2 - AC)}}{A} \tag{8.60}$$

For a hyperbolic equation, $B^2 - AC > 0$, so there are two chracteristics, which for constant A, B and C are straight lines. Each of the characteristics carries one piece of information from the boundary into the solution region. This is illustrated in Figure 8.46(c), where the solution at P is completely determined from the information on AB. The pair of characteristics then allows us to push the solution further into the region using the characteristics TC and SC. It is clear that Cauchy or initial data is required on the line $x = 0$ and that a hyperbolic equation will be an initial-value-type problem.

There is no reason why the boundaries cannot be at infinity – an extremely long string can sensibly be modelled in this way. Care at such infinite boundaries must be taken, since the modelling of what happens there is not always obvious; certainly it requires thought.

We have mentioned the commonest boundary conditions, but it is possible to conceive of others. However, such conditions do not always give a unique solution; a physical example will illustrate this point.

Consider the problem in Example 8.1, which has the solution

$$u = u_0 \sin\left(\frac{\pi x}{L}\right) \cos\left(\frac{\pi c t}{L}\right)$$

Suppose that a photograph of the string is taken at the times $t = L/2c$ and $t = 3L/2c$. Can the solution then be constructed from these two photographs? At the two times the string has the same shape $u = 0$; that is, the string is in its resting position. One possible solution is therefore that the string has not moved. We know that a non-zero solution to Example 8.1 is possible, so we have two solutions to our problem, and we have lost uniqueness. Specifying the displacement at two successive times is not a sensible set of boundary conditions. Although we have stated an extreme case for clarity, the same problem is there for any T, and non-unique solutions can occur if incorrect boundary conditions are imposed.

The *boundary conditions* for the heat-conduction equation (8.7) for the one-dimensional case are given by specifying u or the normal derivative $\partial u/\partial n$ on a curve C in the (x, t) plane, that is, *Dirichlet* or *Neumann conditions* respectively. Because there is only one time derivative in (8.7), we need only specify one function at $t = 0$ (say), rather than two as in the wave equation. In the simplest one-dimensional problem, at time $t = 0$ the temperature in a bar is given, $u(x, 0) = f(x)$, and at the ends some temperature condition is satisfied for all time. Typical conditions might be $u(0, t) = 0$, so that the end $x = 0$ is kept at zero temperature, and $\partial u(L, t)/\partial x = 0$, which implies no heat loss from the end $x = L$. The situation is illustrated in Figure 8.47. It is clear that, no matter what the starting temperature $f(x)$ is, the solution must tend to $u = 0$ as the final solution.

In the case of a parabolic equation we have $B^2 - AC = 0$, so the characteristics in (8.60) coalesce. Imagine that there are two characteristics very close together.

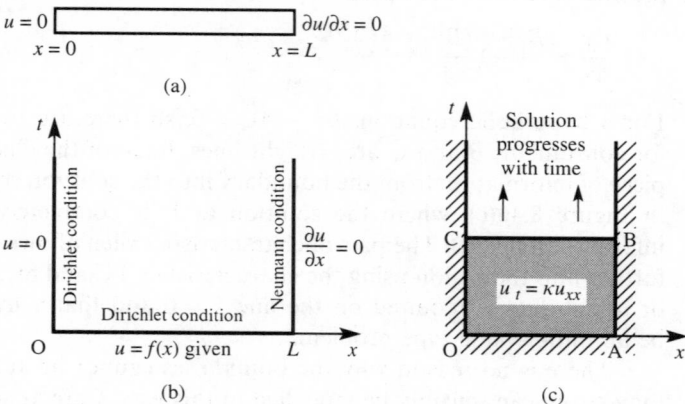

Figure 8.47 (a) A heated bar with a temperature $u = 0$ at $x = 0$ and insulated, $\partial u/\partial x = 0$, at $x = L$. (b) The corresponding region and boundary conditions in the (x, t) plane. (c) Solution can be computed at successive times.

Then the information on the boundaries will propagate a long way, since the two lines will meet 'close to infinity'. We should therefore expect that information on the initial line would propagate forward in time, and because there is only one characteristic that one piece of information on the boundary curve would be sufficient. Figure 8.47(c) illustrates the situation, with the solution on CB being determined by a single boundary condition on each of CO, OA and AB.

Again, as with the wave equation, there is no reason why the bar cannot be of infinite length, at least in a mathematical idealization, so that the initial curve C can include infinite parts. The conditions at infinity are usually quite clear and cause little difficulty.

An interesting feature is that it is very difficult to integrate the heat-conduction equation backwards in time. Suppose we are given a temperature distribution at time $t = T$ and seek the initial distribution at $t = 0$ that produces such a distribution of temperature at $t = T$. If there is an exact solution then the problem can be solved, but it is unstable in the sense that small changes at $t = T$ can lead to huge changes at $t = 0$. This phenomenon, in particular, leads to almost insuperable difficulties when a numerical solution is sought, since errors are inherent in any numerical method. Such a situation applies, for instance, when a space capsule is required to have a specified temperature distribution on reaching its final orbit. The designer wants to know an initial temperature distribution that will achieve this end.

The boundary conditions most relevant to the Laplace equation are *Dirichlet* or *Neumann conditions*. These specify respectively u or the normal derivative $\partial u/\partial n$ on a closed physical boundary. One condition around the whole boundary, which may include an infinite part, is sufficient for this equation. Typically, on a rectangular plate as shown in Figure 8.48, the temperature is maintained at 1 on CD, at 0 on AB and AD, and there is no heat loss from CB.

Figure 8.48 is typical of an elliptic equation where we have conditions on a closed boundary. In (8.60) we have the condition that $B^2 - AC < 0$, so the characteristics associated with the solution do not make sense in the real plane. There is no 'time' in elliptic problems; such problems are concerned with steady-state behaviour and not propagation with time. We are dealing with a fundamentally different situation from the hyperbolic and parabolic cases. The interpretation of the idea of characteristics is unclear physically, and does not prove to be a useful direction to explore, although advanced theoretical treatments do use the concept.

Figure 8.48 Typical boundary conditions for the Laplace equation in a rectangular plate.

Data	Boundary	$\nabla^2 u = u_{tt}$ Hyperbolic	$\nabla^2 u = 0$ Elliptic	$\nabla^2 u = u_t$ Parabolic
Dirichlet or Neumann	Open	Insufficient data	Insufficient data	Unique, stable solution for $t > 0$
	Closed	Not unique	Unique, stable (to an arbitrary constant in the Neumann case)	Overspecified
Cauchy	Open	Unique, stable	Solution may exist, but is unstable	Overspecified
	Closed	Overspecified	Overspecified	Overspecified

Figure 8.49 Appropriateness of boundary conditions to the three classical partial differential equations (adapted from P. M. Morse and H. Feshbach, *Methods of Theoretical Physics*, Volume I. McGraw-Hill, New York, 1953).

It is possible to solve the Laplace equation with other boundary conditions, for instance Cauchy conditions u and $\partial u/\partial x$ on the y axis. However, an example due to Hadamard (see Exercise 35) shows that the solution is unstable in the sense that small changes in the boundary conditions cause large changes in the solution. This type of problem is not well posed, and should not occur in a physical situation; however, mistakes are made and this type of behaviour should be carefully noted.

Figure 8.49 gives in tabular form a summary of the appropriate boundary conditions for these problems.

8.7.3 Exercises

49 Determine the type of each of the following partial differential equations, and reduce them to the standard form by change of axes:

(a) $u_{xx} + 2u_{xy} + u_{yy} = 0$

(b) $u_{xx} + 2u_{xy} + 5u_{yy} + 3u_x + u = 0$

(c) $3u_{xx} - 5u_{xy} - 2u_{yy} = 0$

50 Find the general solution of the equation Exercise 49(c).

51 Establish the nature of the Tricomi equation

$$yu_{xx} + u_{yy} = 0$$

in the regions (a) $y > 0$, (b) $y = 0$ and (c) $y < 0$. Use

(8.60) to determine the characteristics of the equation where they are real.

52 Determine the nature of the equation

$$2q\frac{\partial^2 v}{\partial p^2} + 4p\frac{\partial^2 v}{\partial p\,\partial q} + 2q\frac{\partial^2 v}{\partial q^2} + 2\frac{\partial v}{\partial q} = 0$$

Show that if $p = \frac{1}{2}(x^2 - y^2)$ and $q = \frac{1}{2}(x^2 + y^2)$, the equation reduces to the Laplace equation in x and y.

53 Show that the equation

$$x^2\frac{\partial^2 u}{\partial x^2} - y^2\frac{\partial^2 u}{\partial y^2} = 0$$

is hyperbolic. Sketch the domain of dependence and range of influence from the characteristics.

8.8 Engineering application: wave propagation under a moving load

A wide range of practical problems can be studied under the general heading of moving loads. Cable cars that carry passengers, buckets that remove spoil to waste tips, and cable cranes are very obvious examples, while electric train pantographs on overhead wires are perhaps less obvious. Extending the problem to beams opens up a whole range of new problems, such as trains going over bridges, gantry cranes and the like. An excellent general discussion and wide range of applications is given by L. Fryba, *Vibration of Solids and Structures under Moving Loads* (Noordhoff, Groningen, 1973), and *Initial Value Problems, Fourier Series, Overhead Wires, Partial Differential Equations of Applied Mathematics, Open University Mathematics Unit* M321, 5, 6 and 7 (Milton Keynes, 1974) treats pantographs on overhead wires.

A straightforward linearized theory of a cable tightly stretched between fixed supports provides important information about the behaviour of such systems. Certainly, if such a theory could not be solved then more complicated problems involving large deformations, slack cables or beams would be beyond reach. The basic assumptions are

(a) the deflections from the horizontal are small compared with the length of the cable;

(b) deflections due to the weight of the cable itself are neglected;

(c) the horizontal tension in the cable is so large compared with the perturbations caused by the load that it may be regarded as constant.

Figure 8.50 shows the situation under study and the coordinate system used.

Because the problem is one of small deflections, the basic equation is the wave equation with a forcing term from the moving load:

$$-c^2 \frac{\partial^2 z}{\partial x^2} + \frac{\partial^2 z}{\partial t^2} = p(x, t)$$

Since the two ends are fixed, we have

$$z(0, t) = z(l, t) = 0 \quad (t \geqslant 0) \tag{8.61}$$

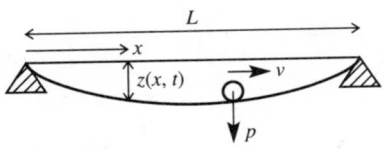

Figure 8.50 Moving load across a taut wire.

A trolley is assumed to start at $x = 0$, with the cable initially at rest; that is

$$z(x, 0) = \frac{\partial}{\partial t} z(x, 0) = 0 \quad (0 \leqslant x \leqslant l) \tag{8.62}$$

It remains to specify the forcing function $p(x, t)$ due to the moving load. We use the simplest assumption of the delta function and step function, as defined in Section 2.5, namely

$$-c^2 \frac{\partial^2 z}{\partial x^2} + \frac{\partial^2 z}{\partial t^2} = P\delta\left(t - \frac{x}{v}\right)[1 - H(x - l)] \tag{8.63}$$

The delta function models the impulse of the trolley at time t at distance x, while the step function switches off the forcing function when the trolley reaches the end $x = l$.

There are several ways of solving this equation, but here the Laplace transform method will be used. Taking the transform of (8.63) using (8.23) and (8.25) together with the initial condition (8.62), we obtain the ordinary differential equation

$$-c^2 Z'' + s^2 Z = Pe^{-sx/v}[1 - H(x - l)]$$

Since we have no interest in the case $x > l$, the final bracket can be omitted, since it is just 1 if $x < l$ and 0 if $x > l$. It is now straightforward to solve this equation as

$$Z = Ae^{sx/c} + Be^{-sx/c} + \frac{Pe^{-sx/v}}{s^2(1 - c^2/v^2)}$$

Before evaluating A and B, it is clear that the speed $v = c$ causes problems, since the third term is then infinite, and the solution is not valid for this case. The solution is going to depend on whether the trolley speed is subcritical $v < c$ or supercritical $v > c$.

Equation (8.61) gives $Z(0, s) = Z(l, s) = 0$ for the boundary conditions, so that A and B can now be evaluated from

$$0 = A + B + \frac{P}{s^2(1 - c^2/v^2)}$$

$$0 = Ae^{sl/c} + Be^{-sl/c} + \frac{Pe^{-sl/v}}{s^2(1 - c^2/v^2)}$$

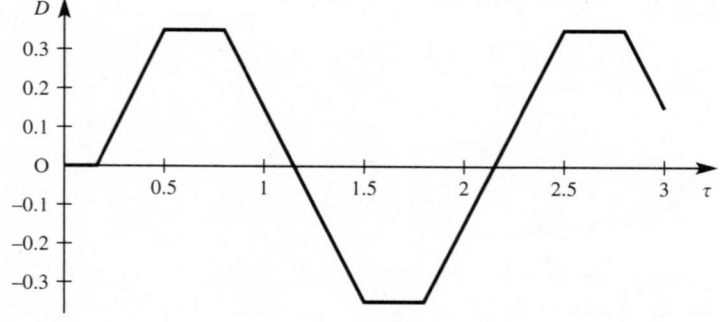

Figure 8.51 Solution of the moving-load problem for $x = \frac{1}{2}l$ and $\lambda = 0.3$; the supercritical case.

Some straightforward algebra gives A and B, and hence Z, as

$$Z = \frac{P}{s^2(1 - c^2/v^2)} \left\{ e^{-sx/v} - e^{-sl/v} \frac{\sinh(sx/c)}{\sinh(sl/c)} + \frac{\sinh[s(x-l)/c]}{\sinh(sl/c)} \right\}$$

It is easy to check that the two boundary conditions at $x = 0$ and $x = l$ are satisfied. As with all transform solutions, the main question is whether the inversion can be performed. Fortunately the three terms can be found in tables of transforms, to give

$$\frac{z}{P} \left(1 - \frac{c^2}{v^2}\right) = \left(t - \frac{x}{v}\right) H\left(t - \frac{x}{v}\right)$$

$$- H\left(t - \frac{l}{v}\right) \left\{ \frac{x}{l} \left(t - \frac{l}{v}\right) + \frac{2l}{c\pi^2} \sum_{n=1}^{\infty} \frac{(-1)^n}{n^2} \sin\frac{n\pi x}{l} \sin\left[\left(\frac{n\pi c}{l}\right)\left(t - \frac{l}{v}\right)\right] \right\}$$

$$+ \left\{ \left(\frac{x-l}{l}\right) t + \frac{2l}{c\pi^2} \sum_{n=1}^{\infty} \frac{(-1)^n}{n^2} \sin\left[\frac{n\pi(x-l)}{l}\right] \sin\left[\frac{n\pi ct}{l}\right] \right\}$$

$$(8.64)$$

The three terms can be identified immediately. The first is the displacement caused by the trolley moving with speed v and hitting the value x after a time $t = x/v$; the second term only appears for $t > l/v$, and gives the reflected wave from $x = l$; while the third term is the wave caused by the trolley disturbance propagating in the cable with wave speed c.

To look a little more closely at the solution (8.64), we shall consider the case $x = \frac{1}{2}l$. Thus the motion of the midpoint will be considered as a function of time. Plotting such waves is easier in non-dimensional form, so we first rewrite (8.64) in terms of

$$D = \frac{cz}{Pl} \left(1 - \frac{c^2}{v^2}\right), \qquad \tau = \frac{ct}{l}, \qquad \lambda = \frac{c}{v}$$

so that D is the non-dimensional displacement, τ is the non-dimensional time, with $\tau = 1$ corresponding to the time for the wave to propagate the length of the cable, and λ is the ratio of wave speed to trolley speed. The second step is then to take $x = \frac{1}{2}l$ to give

$$D = (\tau - \tfrac{1}{2}\lambda) H(\tau - \tfrac{1}{2}\lambda)$$

$$- H(\tau - \lambda) \left\{ \tfrac{1}{2}(\tau - \lambda) - \frac{2}{\pi^2} [\sin\pi(\tau - \lambda) - \tfrac{1}{9}\sin 3\pi(\tau - \lambda) \right.$$

$$\left. + \tfrac{1}{25}\sin 5\pi(\tau - \lambda) \ldots] \right\} - \tfrac{1}{2}\tau + \frac{2}{\pi^2}(\sin\pi\tau - \tfrac{1}{9}\sin 3\pi\tau + \tfrac{1}{25}\sin 5\pi\tau \ldots)$$

In Figure 8.51 the supercritical case, $\lambda = 0.3$, is displayed. It may be noted that the three terms 'switch on' at times $\tau = 0.15$, $\tau = 0.8$ and $\tau = 0.5$ respectively,

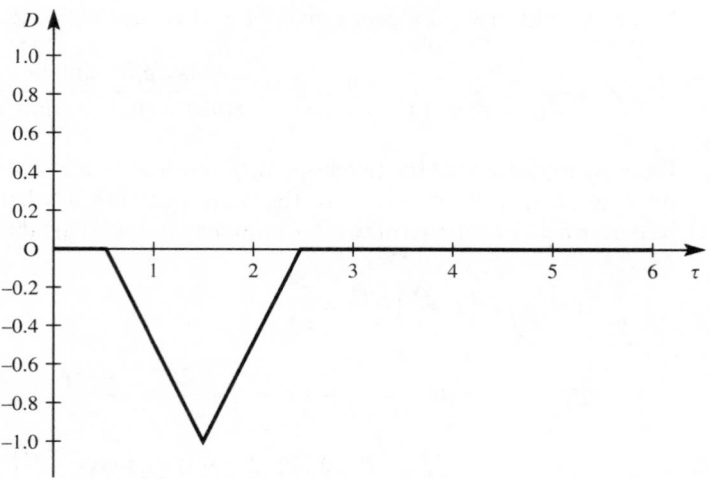

Figure 8.52 Solution of the moving-load problem for $x = \frac{1}{2}l$ and $\lambda = 3$; the subcritical case.

corresponding physically to the trolley hitting, the reflected wave arriving and the initial wave arriving. The motion is subsequently periodic, as indicated in the figure.

Similarly, the subcritical case $\lambda = 3$ is shown in Figure 8.52. Here the switches are at $\tau = 1.5$, 3.5 and 0.5 respectively for the three terms, with the same interpretation as above. Because of the very odd choice of parameter λ, only one pulse is seen at the centre point, with the terms subsequently cancelling.

While the model illustrates many of the obvious properties of wave propagation, it clearly has its limitations. The discontinuous behaviour in the gradient of the displacement looks unrealistic, and the absence of damping means that oscillations once started continue for ever. It is clear that more subtle modelling of the phenomenon is required to make the solutions realistic, but the general behaviour of the solution would still be followed.

8.9 Engineering application: blood flow model

A problem of considerable interest is how to deal with the flow of a fluid through a tube with distensible walls and hence variable cross-section. An obvious application is to the flow of blood in a blood vessel. The full Navier–Stokes equations for viscous flow are difficult to solve and the distensible wall, where boundary conditions are not clear, makes for an impossible problem. An alternative, simpler and more heuristic approach is possible and some useful solutions can be deduced. The work is based on a paper by A. Singer (*Bulletin of Mathematical*

Biophysics **31** (1969) 453–70), where more details can be found about the practical application to blood flows.

The assumptions required to set up the model are as follows:

(1) the flow is one-dimensional;
(2) the flow is incompressible and laminar;
(3) the flow is slow, so that all quadratic terms can be neglected;
(4) the resistance to flow is assumed to be proportional to the velocity;
(5) there is a leakage through the walls that is proportional to the pressure;
(6) the cross-sectional area S is a function of the pressure only.

We take the situation illustrated in Figure 8.53, and we denote the pressure by p, the velocity by v, the time by t and the axial distance along the tube by x. The first equation that we derive is a continuity equation, which states that in a time Δt the fluid that comes into the element must leave the element:

$$(S_{t+\Delta t} - S_t)\,\Delta x = -(vS)_{x+\Delta x}\,\Delta t + (vS)_x\,\Delta t - gpS\,\Delta x\,\Delta t$$

$$\underbrace{\hphantom{(S_{t+\Delta t})}}_{\substack{\text{volume}\\\text{after}}} \quad \underbrace{\hphantom{S_t}}_{\substack{\text{volume}\\\text{before}}} \quad \underbrace{\hphantom{(vS)_{x+\Delta x}}}_{\substack{\text{volume out of}\\\text{right-hand end}}} \quad \underbrace{\hphantom{(vS)_x}}_{\substack{\text{volume into}\\\text{left-hand end}}} \quad \underbrace{\hphantom{gpS}}_{\text{leakage}}$$

The proportionality constant g is the leakage per unit volume of tube per unit time. The equation can be rewritten as

$$\frac{S_{t+\Delta t} - S_t}{\Delta t} + \frac{(vS)_{x+\Delta x} - (vS)_x}{\Delta x} + gpS = 0$$

or

$$\frac{\partial S}{\partial t} + \frac{\partial}{\partial x}(vS) + gpS = 0 \tag{8.65}$$

A second equation is required to evaluate v, and this comes from Newton's law that the force is proportional to the rate of change of momentum. The force in the x direction acting on the element in Figure 8.53 is

$$\text{force} = (pS)_x - (pS)_{x+\Delta x} - vrS\,\Delta x$$

$$\qquad\quad \underbrace{\hphantom{(pS)_x}}_{\substack{\text{pressure force}\\\text{on left-hand end}}} \underbrace{\hphantom{(pS)_{x+\Delta x}}}_{\substack{\text{pressure force}\\\text{on right-hand end}}} \underbrace{\hphantom{vrS}}_{\text{resistance}}$$

where r is the resistance per unit length per unit cross-section per unit time, and is the proportionality constant in assumption (4). The change in the momentum

Figure 8.53 An element of the flexible tube in the blood flow problem.

in time Δt is more difficult to compute because of the convection due to the moving fluid. However, these effects only involve second-order terms, and hence can be omitted by assumption (3). The calculation is straightforward under this assumption, so that

$$\Delta M = \text{change in momentum} = \rho(v_{t+\Delta t})S\,\Delta x - \rho(v_t)S\,\Delta x$$

momentum before   momentum after

where ρ is the density of the fluid. Thus

$$\frac{\partial M}{\partial t} = \rho S \frac{\partial v}{\partial t}\Delta x$$

Putting the force equal to the rate of change of momentum, we obtain, on taking the limit as $\Delta x \to 0$,

$$\rho S \frac{\partial v}{\partial t} = -\frac{\partial(pS)}{\partial x} - vrS \tag{8.66}$$

Now assumption (6) gives $S = S(p)$, so that

$$\frac{1}{S}\frac{\partial S}{\partial x} = \frac{1}{S}\frac{dS}{dp}\frac{\partial p}{\partial x}$$

$$\frac{1}{S}\frac{\partial S}{\partial t} = \frac{1}{S}\frac{dS}{dp}\frac{\partial p}{\partial t}$$

We define $c = (1/S)\,dS/dp$ as the **distensibility** of the tube, that is, the change in S per unit area per unit change in p. Equations (8.65) and (8.66) become

$$cp_t + v_x + cp_x v + gp = 0$$

$$\rho v_t + p_x + cp_x p + rv = 0$$

and since the term vp_x and pp_x can be neglected by assumption (3), we arrive at our final equations

$$\left.\begin{array}{l} cp_t + v_x + gp = 0 \\ \rho v_t + p_x + rv = 0 \end{array}\right\} \tag{8.67}$$

These are the linearized flow equations, and are identical with the **transmission line** equations describing the flow of electricity down a long, leaky wire such as a transatlantic cable (see Exercise 5).

We can now look at special cases that will prove to be very informative about the various terms in the equation.

Case (i): $c = \text{constant}, r = g = 0$

This case corresponds to constant distensibility, which in turn gives $S = A\,e^{cp}$, since S must satisfy $c = (1/S)\,dS/dp$. Thus we have made a specific assumption about how S depends on p. The $r = g = 0$ implies the absence of resistance and leakage.

Eliminating p between the two equations in (8.67) gives

$$v_{xx} = (c\rho)v_{tt}$$

which is just the wave equation. We know that any pulse will propagate perfectly with a velocity $u = 1/\sqrt{(c\rho)}$. The assumption in the problem is that the tube is one-dimensional and has no branches. Clearly a heart pulse will propagate to the nearest branch, but there will then be reflection and a complicated behaviour near the branch. In long arteries like the femoral artery the theory can be checked for its validity.

Case (ii): S = constant

Here we are considering a rigid tube where the cross-sectional area does not vary, and hence $c = 0$. Eliminating p between the two equations in (8.67) gives

$$\rho v_t - \frac{1}{g}v_{xx} + rv = 0$$

Substituting $v = Ve^{-rt/\rho}$, we have

$$\rho\left(V_t - \frac{rV}{\rho}\right) - \frac{V_{xx}}{g} + rV = 0$$

so that

$$V_t = \frac{1}{\rho g}V_{xx}$$

which is just the diffusion equation. The solution for this rigid-tube case is therefore a damped, diffusion solution. Typically, if we start with a delta-function pulse at the origin then it can be checked that the solution is

$$v = A\frac{e^{-rt/\rho}}{t^{1/2}}e^{-\rho gx^2/4t}$$

where A is a constant. This solution is plotted in Figure 8.54, and shows the rapid

Figure 8.54
Development of the solution to the blood flow problem from a delta function for successive times t_1, t_2 and t_3.

8.54

damping. Such a pulse would be most unlikely to propagate far enough for blood to reach the whole of the system.

The two cases considered are extremes, but, just from the analysis performed, some conclusions can be drawn. If there is no distensibility then pulses will not propagate but will just diffuse through the system. We conclude that to move blood through the system with a series of pulses is not possible with rigid blood vessels, and we need flexible walls. Certainly for older people with hardening of the arteries, a major problem is to pump blood round the whole system, and this fact is confirmed by the mathematics.

The actual situation is somewhere between the two cases cited, but there are no simple solutions for such cases except for the 'balanced line' case when $cr = g\rho$ (see Exercise 5 and Review exercise 21). Singer solves the equations numerically for data appropriate to a dog aorta, and compares his results with experiment. Although the agreement is good, there are problems, since there appears to be a residual pressure after each pulse. The overall pressure would therefore build up to levels that are clearly not acceptable.

8.10   Review exercises (1–22)

1 A uniform string is stretched along the x axis and its ends fixed at the points $x = 0$ and $x = a$. The string at the point $x = b$ $(0 < b < a)$ is drawn aside through a small displacement ε perpendicular to the x axis, and released from rest at time $t = 0$. By solving the one-dimensional wave equation, show that at any subsequent time t the transverse displacement y is given by

$$y = \frac{2\varepsilon a^2}{\pi^2 b(a-b)} \sum_{n=1}^{\infty} \frac{1}{n^2} \sin\left(\frac{n\pi b}{a}\right) \sin\left(\frac{n\pi x}{a}\right)$$
$$\times \cos\left(\frac{n\pi ct}{a}\right)$$

where c is the transverse wave velocity in the string.

2 The function $\phi(x, t)$ satisfies the wave equation

$$\frac{\partial^2 \phi}{\partial x^2} = \frac{\partial^2 \phi}{\partial t^2} \quad (t > 0, 0 \leqslant x \leqslant l)$$

and the conditions

$$\phi(x, 0) = x^2 \quad (0 \leqslant x \leqslant l)$$
$$\frac{\partial \phi}{\partial t}(x, 0) = 0 \quad (0 \leqslant x \leqslant l)$$
$$\phi(0, t) = 0 \quad (t > 0)$$

$$\frac{\partial \phi}{\partial x}(l, t) = 2l \quad (t > 0)$$

Show that the Laplace transform of the solution is

$$\frac{2}{s^3} + \frac{x^2}{s} - \frac{2}{s^3} \frac{\cosh s(x-l)}{\cosh sl}$$

Using tables of Laplace transforms, deduce that the solution of the wave equation is

$$2xl - \frac{32l^2}{\pi^3} \sum_{n=0}^{\infty} \frac{(-1)^n}{(2n+1)^3} \cos\left[\frac{(2n+1)(x-l)\pi}{2l}\right]$$
$$\times \cos\left[\frac{(2n+1)\pi t}{2l}\right]$$

3 The damped vibrations of a stretched string are governed by the equation

$$\frac{1}{c^2}\frac{\partial^2 y}{\partial t^2} + \frac{1}{c^2\tau}\frac{\partial y}{\partial t} = \frac{\partial^2 y}{\partial x^2} \tag{8.68}$$

where $y(x, t)$ is the transverse deflection, t is the time, x is the position coordinate along the string, and c and τ are positive constants. A taut elastic string, $0 \leqslant t \leqslant l$, is fixed at its end points so that $y(0) = y(l) = 0$. Show that separation of variable solutions of (8.68) satisfying these boundary conditions are of the form

$$y_n(x, t) = T_n(t) \sin \left(\frac{n\pi x}{l} \right) \quad (n = 1, 2, \ldots)$$

where

$$\frac{1}{c^2} \frac{d^2 T_n}{dt^2} + \frac{1}{c^2 \tau} \frac{dT_n}{dt} + \frac{n^2 \pi^2 T_n}{l^2} = 0$$

Show that if the parameters c, τ and l are such that $2\pi c\tau > l$, the solutions for T_n are all of the form

$$T_n(t) = e^{-t/2\tau}(a_n \cos \omega_n t + b_n \sin \omega_n t)$$

where

$$\omega_n = \frac{n\pi c}{l} \left(1 - \frac{l^2}{4\pi^2 n^2 c^2 \tau^2} \right)^{1/2}$$

and a_n and b_n are constants.

Hence find the general solution of (8.68) satisfying the given boundary conditions.

Given the initial conditions $y(x, 0) = 4 \sin (3\pi x/l)$ and $(\partial y/\partial t)_{t=0} = 0$, find $y(x, t)$.

4 A thin uniform beam OA of length l is clamped horizontally at both ends. For small transverse vibrations of the beam the displacement $u(x, t)$ at time t at a distance x from O satisfies the equation

$$\frac{\partial^4 u}{\partial x^4} + \frac{1}{a^2} \frac{\partial^2 u}{\partial t^2} = 0$$

where a is a constant. The restriction that the beam is clamped horizontally gives the boundary conditions

$$u = 0, \quad \frac{\partial u}{\partial x} = 0 \quad (x = 0, l)$$

Show that for periodic solutions of the type

$$u(x, t) = V(x) \sin (\omega t + \varepsilon)$$

where ω and ε are constants, to exist, V must satisfy an equation of the form

$$\frac{d^4 V}{dx^4} = \alpha^4 V \qquad (8.69)$$

where $\alpha^4 = (\omega/a)^2$, and the boundary conditions

$$V(0) = V'(0) = V(l) = V'(l) = 0$$

Verify that

$$V = A \cosh \alpha x + B \cos \alpha x + C \sinh \alpha x + D \sin \alpha x$$

where A, B, C and D are constants, satisfies (8.69), and show that this function satisfies the boundary conditions provided that

$$B = -A, \quad D = -C$$

and α is a root of

$$\cos \alpha l \cosh \alpha l = 1$$

5 In a uniform bar of length l the temperature $\theta(x, t)$ at a distance x from one end satisfies the equation

$$\frac{\partial^2 \theta}{\partial x^2} = a^2 \frac{\partial \theta}{\partial t}$$

where a is a constant. The end $x = l$ is kept at zero temperature and the other end $x = 0$ is perfectly insulated, so that

$$\theta(l, t) = 0, \quad \frac{\partial \theta}{\partial x}(0, t) = 0 \quad (t > 0)$$

Using the method of separation of variables, show that if initially the temperature in the bar is $\theta(x, 0) = f(x)$ then subsequently the temperature is

$$\theta(x, t) = \sum_{n=0}^{\infty} A_{2n+1} \cos \left[\frac{(2n + 1)\pi x}{2l} \right]$$

$$\exp \left[-\frac{(2n + 1)^2 \pi^2 t}{4a^2 l^2} \right]$$

where

$$A_{2n+1} = \frac{2}{l} \int_0^l f(x) \cos \left[\frac{(2n + 1)\pi x}{2l} \right] dx$$

Given $\theta(x, 0) = \theta_0(l - x)$, where θ_0 is a constant, determine the subsequent temperature in the bar.

6 Prove that if $z = x/\sqrt{t}$ and $\phi(x, t) = f(z)$ satisfies the heat-conduction equation

$$\kappa \frac{\partial^2 \phi}{\partial x^2} = \frac{\partial \phi}{\partial t} \qquad (8.70)$$

then $f(z)$ must be of the form

$$f(z) = A \operatorname{erf} \left(\frac{z}{2\sqrt{\kappa}} \right) + B,$$

where A and B are constants and the **error function** is defined as

$$\operatorname{erf}(\xi) = \frac{2}{\sqrt{\pi}} \int_0^\xi e^{-u^2} du$$

A heat-conducting solid occupies the semi-infinite region $x \geqslant 0$. At time $t = 0$ the temperature everywhere in the solid has the value T_0. The temperature at the surface, $x = 0$, is suddenly raised, at $t = 0$, to the constant value $T_0 + \phi_0$ and is then maintained at this temperature. Assuming that the temperature field in the solid has the form

$$T = \phi(x, t) + T_0$$

where ϕ satisfies (8.70) in $x > 0$, find the solution of this problem.

7 Use the explicit method and the Crank–Nicolson formula to solve the heat-conduction equation

$$\frac{\partial^2 \phi}{\partial x^2} = \frac{\partial \phi}{\partial t}$$

given that ϕ satisfies the conditions

$$\phi = 1 \quad (0 \leqslant x \leqslant 1, t = 0)$$

$$\frac{\partial \phi}{\partial x} = \begin{cases} \phi & (x = 0) \\ -\phi & (x = 1) \end{cases} \quad (t \geqslant 0)$$

Compute $\phi(x, t)$ at $x = 0, 0.2, 0.4, 0.6, 0.8, 1$ when $t = 0.004$ and $t = 0.008$.

8 An infinitely long bar of square cross-section has faces $x = 0$, $x = a$, $y = 0$, $y = a$. The bar is made of heat-conducting material, and under steady-state conditions the temperature T satisfies the Laplace equation

$$\frac{\partial^2 T}{\partial x^2} + \frac{\partial^2 T}{\partial y^2} = 0$$

All the faces except $y = 0$ are kept at zero temperature, while the temperature in the face $y = 0$ is given by $T(x, 0) = x(a - x)$. Show that the temperature distribution in the bar is

$$\frac{8a^2}{\pi^3} \sum_{r=0}^{\infty} \frac{\sin\left[(2r + 1)\pi x/a\right] \sinh\left[(2r + 1)\pi(a - y)/a\right]}{(2r + 1)^3 \sinh(2r + 1)\pi}$$

9 (Harder) The function ϕ satisfies the Poisson equation

$$\frac{\partial^2 \phi}{\partial x^2} + \frac{\partial^2 \phi}{\partial y^2} = xy^2$$

inside the area bounded by the parabola $y^2 = x$ and the line $x = 2$. The function ϕ is given at all points on the boundary as $\phi = 1$. By using a square grid of side $\frac{1}{2}$ and making full use of symmetry, formulate a set of finite-difference equations for the unknown values ϕ, and solve.

10 A semi-infinite region of incompressible fluid of density ρ and viscosity μ is bounded by a plane wall in the plane $z = 0$ and extends throughout the region $z \geqslant 0$. The wall executes oscillations in its own plane so that its velocity at time t is $U \cos \omega t$. No pressure gradients or body forces are operative. It can be shown that the velocity of the liquid satisfies the equation

$$\frac{\partial u}{\partial t} = v \frac{\partial^2 u}{\partial z^2}$$

where $v = \mu/\rho$. Establish that an appropriate solution

of the equation is

$$u = U e^{-\alpha z} \cos(\omega t - \alpha z)$$

where $\alpha = \sqrt{(\omega/2v)}$.

11 Determine the value of the constant k so that

$$U = t^k e^{-r^2/4t}$$

satisfies the partial differential equation

$$\frac{1}{r^2} \frac{\partial}{\partial r}\left(r^2 \frac{\partial U}{\partial r}\right) = \frac{\partial U}{\partial t}$$

Sketch the solution for successive values of t.

12 The function $z(x, y)$ satisfies

$$\frac{\partial z}{\partial x} + \frac{\partial z}{\partial y} = 0$$

with the boundary conditions

$$z = 2x \quad \text{when } y = -x \quad (x > 0)$$

Find the unique solution for z and the region in which this solution holds.

13 The function $\phi(x, y)$ satisfies the Laplace equation

$$\frac{\partial^2 \phi}{\partial x^2} + \frac{\partial^2 \phi}{\partial y^2} = 0$$

in the region $0 < x < \pi$, $0 < y < \infty$, and also the boundary conditions

$$\phi \to 0 \quad \text{as } y \to \infty$$

$$\phi(0, y) = \phi(\pi, y) = 0$$

Show that an appropriate separation of variables solution is

$$\phi = \sum_{n=1}^{\infty} c_n \sin(nx) e^{-ny}$$

Show that if further

$$\phi(x, 0) = x(\pi - x)$$

then $c_{2m} = 0$ while the odd coefficients are given by

$$c_{2m+1} = \frac{8}{\pi(2m + 1)^3}$$

14 The boundary-value problem associated with the torsion of a prism of rectangular cross-section $-a \leqslant x \leqslant a$, $-b \leqslant y \leqslant b$ entails the solution of

$$\frac{\partial^2 \chi}{\partial x^2} + \frac{\partial^2 \chi}{\partial y^2} = -2$$

subject to $\chi = 0$ on the boundary. Show that the differential equation and the boundary conditions on $x = \pm a$ are satisfied by a solution of the form

$$\chi = a^2 - x^2 + \sum_{n=0}^{m} A_{2n+1} \cosh\left[\frac{(2n+1)\pi y}{2a}\right]$$
$$\cos\left[\frac{(2n+1)\pi x}{2a}\right]$$

From the condition $\chi = 0$ on the boundaries $y = \pm b$, evaluate the coefficients A_{2n+1}.

15 When $0 < x < 1$ and $t > 0$ the function $u(x, t)$ satisfies the wave equation

$$\frac{\partial^2 u}{\partial x^2} = \frac{\partial^2 u}{\partial t^2}$$

and is also subject to the following boundary conditions:

(a) $u(0, t) = u(1, t) = 0$ for all $t > 0$

(b) $\dfrac{\partial u}{\partial t}(x, 0) = 0 \quad (0 < x < 1)$

(c) $u(x, 0) = 1 - x \quad (0 < x < 1)$

Use the separation method to find the solution for $u(x, t)$ that is valid for $0 < x < 1$ and $t > 0$.

16 A viscous fluid occupies the region above the horizontal plane $z = 0$, and is set into motion by the movement of this plane with velocity $U(t)$ in the x direction. The velocity of the fluid is of the form $(u(z, t), 0, 0)$, where $u(z, t)$ satisfies

$$\rho \frac{\partial u}{\partial t} = \mu \frac{\partial^2 u}{\partial z^2}$$

with ρ being the density and μ the viscosity of the fluid. State the boundary condition on $u(z, t)$.

For the case when $U(t) = u_0 \cos \omega t$, where u_0 and ω are constants, show that if $u(z, t) = \text{Re}[f(z) e^{j\omega t}]$ then

$$f''(z) - 2jK^2 f(z) = 0$$

where $K^2 = \rho\omega/2\mu$. Hence, using the fact that $(1 + j)^2 = 2j$, obtain the solution for $u(z, t)$.

17 The excess porewater pressure $u(z, t)$ in an infinite layer of clay satisfies the diffusion equation

$$\frac{\partial u}{\partial t} = c \frac{\partial^2 u}{\partial z^2} \quad (t > 0, \, 0 < z < h)$$

where t is the time in minutes, z is the vertical height in metres from the base of the clay layer and c is the coefficient of consolidation. There is complete drainage at the top and bottom of the clay layer, which is of thickness h. The distribution of excess porewater pressure $u(z, t)$ is A at $t = 0$ where A is a constant. Show that

$$u(z, t) = \frac{4A}{\pi} \sum_{n=0}^{\infty} \frac{\sin[(2n+1)\pi z/h]}{2n+1} e^{-c\pi^2(2n+1)^2 t/h^2}$$

18 By seeking a separated solution of the form $\phi = X(x)T(t)$, find a solution to the telegraph equation

$$\frac{\partial^2 \phi}{\partial x^2} = \frac{1}{c^2}\left(\frac{\partial^2 \phi}{\partial t^2} + K\frac{\partial \phi}{\partial t}\right)$$

satisfying the conditions

(a) $\phi = A \cos px$ for all values of x and for $t = 0$ for the case when $c^2 p^2 > \frac{1}{4}K^2$;

(b) $\phi = A$ and $\partial\phi/\partial t = -\frac{1}{2}AK$ for $x = 0$ and $t = 0$.

19 For the two-dimensional flow of an incompressible fluid the continuity equation may be expressed as

$$\frac{\partial}{\partial r}(rv_r) + \frac{\partial v_\theta}{\partial \theta} = 0$$

where r and θ are polar coordinates in a plane parallel to the flow, and v_r and v_θ are the respective velocity components. Show that there exists a stream function ψ such that

$$v_r = \frac{1}{r}\frac{\partial \psi}{\partial \theta}$$

$$v_\theta = -\frac{\partial \psi}{\partial r}$$

satisfy the continuity equation.

Take

$$\psi = Ur\sin\theta - \frac{Ua^2}{r}\sin\theta$$

and interpret the solution physically.

20 (An extended problem) Section 8.8 looked at wave propagation caused by moving loads on cables. For loads on beams a similar analysis models such problems as trains going over bridges or loads moving on gantry cranes. Use a similar analysis for the beam equation

$$a^2 \frac{\partial^4 u}{\partial x^4} + \frac{\partial^2 u}{\partial t^2} = p(x, t)$$

21 (An extended problem) In the blood flow model in Section 8.9 consider the following cases:

(a) $S = $ constant, $g = 0$ for a pulsating flow
$$v = v_0 e^{j\omega t} \quad \text{at } x = 0 \text{ for all } t$$

(b) $S = $ constant, $r = 0$ for a pulsating flow
$$v = v_0 e^{j\omega t} \quad \text{at } x = 0 \text{ for all } t$$

(c) the balanced-line case when $g\rho = rc$. Show that $v = e^{-gt/c}U$ gives

$$\frac{\partial^2 U}{\partial t^2} = \frac{1}{c\rho}\frac{\partial^2 U}{\partial x^2}$$

Solve the equation and interpret your solution.

22 (An extended problem) Fluid flows steadily in the two-dimensional channel shown in Figure 8.55. The

Figure 8.55 An element of the channel in Review exercise 22.

temperature $\theta = \theta(x, t)$ depends only on the distance x along the channel and the time t. The fluid flows at a constant rate so that an amount L crosses any given section in unit time. The specific heat of the fluid is a constant c, and the heat H in a length δx with cross-section S is therefore

$$H = c(S\,\delta x)\theta$$

Heat is transferred through the walls of the channel, AB and DC, at a rate proportional to the temperature difference between the inside and outside. Heat conduction in the x direction is neglected. Show that the heat balance in the element ABCD leads to the equation

$$cS\frac{\partial\theta}{\partial t} = -Lc\frac{\partial\theta}{\partial x} + k_1(\theta'' - \theta) + k_2(\theta' - \theta)$$

This type of analysis can now be applied to the long heat exchanger illustrated in Figure 8.56. The configuration is considered to be two-dimensional and symmetric with respect to the x axis; in the inner region the flow is to the right, while in the outer regions it is to the left. The regions are separated by metal walls in which similar assumptions

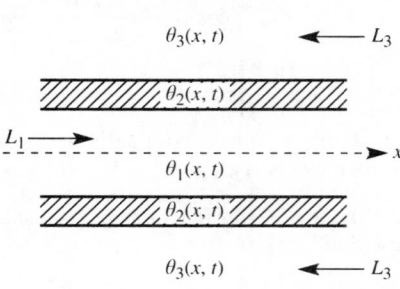

Figure 8.56 Heat-exchanger configuration in Review exercise 22.

to the above are made, except of course there is no fluid flow.

Set up the equations of the system in the form

$$c_1 S_1 \frac{\partial\theta_1}{\partial t} = -L_1 c_1 \frac{\partial\theta_1}{\partial x} + 2k_1(\theta_2 - \theta_1)$$

$$c_2 S_2 \frac{\partial\theta_2}{\partial t} = -k_1(\theta_1 - \theta_2) + k_2(\theta_3 - \theta_2)$$

$$c_3 S_3 \frac{\partial\theta_3}{\partial t} = L_3 c_3 \frac{\partial\theta_3}{\partial x} + k_2(\theta_2 - \theta_3)$$

where the assumption is made that there is no heat flow through the outside lagged walls. Solve the steady-state equations and fit the arbitrary constants to the conditions that at the inlet ($x = 0$) the fluid enters the inner region at a given temperature $\theta_1 = T_1$, while at the outlet ($x \to \infty$) the fluid in the outer regions enters at a given temperature $\theta_3 = T_3$. Find flow rates that ensure that this situation is possible, and discuss the implications of any results obtained.

Discuss the assumptions made in setting up this problem, the limitations imposed by the assumptions, possible applications of this type of analysis, and extensions of the work, for example a time-dependent solution.

9

Optimization

CONTENTS

9.1 Introduction

The need to get the 'best' out of a system is a very strong motivation in much of engineering. A typical problem may be to obtain the maximum amount of product or to minimize the cost of a process or to find a configuration that gives maximum strength. Sometimes what is 'best' is easy to define, but frequently the problem is not so clear cut, and a lot of thought is required to reach an appropriate function to optimize. In most cases there are very severe and natural constraints operating: the problem may be one of maximizing the amount of product, subject to the supply of materials; or it may be minimizing the cost of production, with constraints due to safety standards. Indeed, much of modern optimization is concerned with constraints and how to deal with them.

We have seen in Chapter 9 of *Modern Engineering Mathematics* how to obtain the maximum and minimum of a function of many variables. However, the methods described there founder very quickly because it becomes impossible to solve the resulting equations analytically. A simple one-dimensional example soon shows that a numerical solution is required.

EXAMPLE 9.1   Find the positive x value that maximizes the function

$$y = \frac{\tanh x}{1 + x}$$

Solution   Equating the derivative to zero gives

$$\frac{\mathrm{d}y}{\mathrm{d}x} = 0 = \frac{(1 + x)\operatorname{sech}^2 x - \tanh x}{(1 + x)^2}$$

so that we need to solve

$$1 + x = \tfrac{1}{2}\sinh 2x$$

which has no simple positive solutions that can be obtained analytically.

To solve such problems, a set of numerical algorithms was developed during the 1960s as fast computers became available to perform the large amounts of arithmetic required. These algorithms will be described in Section 9.4. Perhaps the main stimulus for this development came from the space industries, where small percentage savings, achieved by doing some mathematics, could save vast amounts of money. The ideas were quickly taken up by 'expensive' areas of engineering, such as the chemical and steel industries and aircraft production.

The idea of dealing with constraints is not new: Lagrange developed the theory of **equality**-constrained optimization around the 1800s. However, it was not until the 1940s that **inequality** constraints were studied with any seriousness. The use of Lagrange multipliers for equality constraints was also introduced in Chapter 9 of *Modern Engineering Mathematics*, and will be looked at again in more detail in Section 9.3 below. The only work on inequality constraints will be for linear programming problems in Section 9.2. Where inequality constraints are nonlinear, the problems become very difficult to deal with, and are the province of specialist books on optimization. Linear programming, however, is much more straightforward, and the basic simplex algorithm has been spectacularly successful – so successful in fact that many workers try to force their problems to be linear when they are clearly not. The computer scientist's maxim GIGO ('garbage in, garbage out') is very applicable to people who try to fit the problem to the mathematics rather than the mathematics to the problem!

Before considering detailed methods of solution of optimization problems, we shall look at a few examples. Let us first revisit an extended form of the milk carton problem considered in Example 8.4 (and illustrated in Figure 8.9) of *Modern Engineering Mathematics*.

EXAMPLE 9.2   A milk carton is designed from a sheet of waxed cardboard as illustrated in Figure 9.1, where a 5 mm overlap has been allowed.

It is to contain 2 pints of milk, and we require the minimum surface area for the carton.

Figure 9.1 Waxed cardboard milk container opened up, with measurements in millimetres and with a 5 mm overlap.

Solution   The only difference between this example and Example 8.4 of *Modern Engineering Mathematics* is that we no longer insist on a square cross-section. The total area in square millimetres is

$$A = (2b + 2w + 5)(h + b + 10)$$

and the volume of the two-pint container is

$$\text{volume} = hbw = 1\,136\,000 \text{ mm}^3$$

We first note that a constraint, the volume, occurs naturally in the problem. Because of its simplicity, we can eliminate w from the constraint to give

$$A = (h + b + 10)\left(\frac{2\,272\,000}{hb} + 2b + 5\right)$$

Following the standard minimization procedure (Chapter 9 of *Modern Engineering Mathematics*), and equating partial derivatives to zero gives

$$\frac{\partial A}{\partial h} = \frac{2\,272\,000}{hb} + 2b + 5 - (h + b + 10)\frac{2\,272\,000}{h^2b} = 0$$

$$\frac{\partial A}{\partial b} = \frac{2\,272\,000}{hb} + 2b + 5 - (h + b + 10)\left(\frac{-2\,272\,000}{hb^2} + 2\right) = 0$$

We therefore have two highly nonlinear equations in the two unknowns h and b, which cannot be solved without resorting to numerical techniques. We shall return to this problem later in Examples 9.11 and 9.17 to see how a practical solution can be obtained.

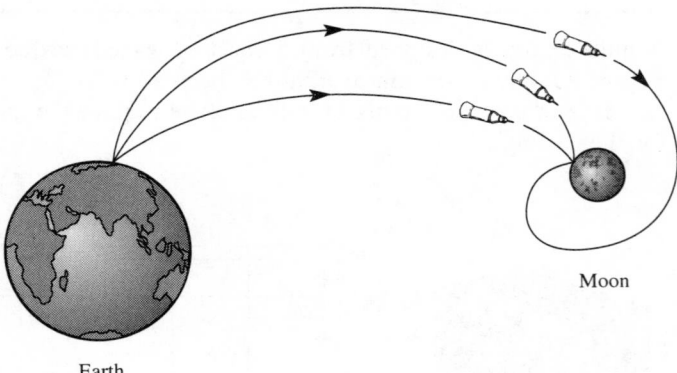

Figure 9.2 The moonshot problem.

Most practical optimization problems come from very expensive projects where savings of a few per cent can be very significant. Laying natural gas or water pipe networks are typical examples. Without considering the expense of installing compressors, the problem is to minimize the capital cost. This cost is directly related to the weight of the pipe, subject to constraints imposed by pressure-drop limitations, which in turn depend on the pipe diameter in a nonlinear way. Adding the compressors imposes further costs and constraints.

Heat exchangers provide an example of a system where we try to remove heat. We design the flow rates, the pipe sizes and pipe spacing to maximize the heat transferred. A related heating problem might be the design of an industrial furnace. It is required that the energy consumption be minimized subject to constraints on the heat flow and the maintenance of various temperatures.

A final example, the moonshot problem, illustrates a large-scale, very complicated problem that stimulated much of the recent developments in optimization (see Figure 9.2). Which path from a point on the Earth to a point on the Moon should be chosen to minimize the weight of fuel carried by a rocket? The complicated relation between the weight of fuel, the mechanical equations of the rocket and the path must be established before it is possible to proceed to obtain the optimum. The numerous constraints on the strengths of materials, the maximum tolerable acceleration etc. add to the difficulty of the problem.

In the problems discussed we have assumed that an optimum exists at a point, and we have asked for the mathematical conditions that must hold. The other way round is much more difficult. Given that the appropriate conditions hold, does an optimum exist, and if so what type of optimum is it? For many simple finite-dimensional problems these conditions are known, but may not be very simple to apply. To serve as a reminder, the condition $f'(0) = 0$ is a necessary condition for a maximum to exist for the differentiable function $f(x)$ at $x = 0$. It is not sufficient, however, as can be seen from the three functions $f_1(x) = x^2$, $f_2(x) = x^3$ and $f_3(x) = -x^2$, which have respectively a minimum, a point of inflection and a maximum at the origin. In many dimensions the difficulties are similar, but much more complicated.

9.2 Linear programming (LP)

9.2.1 Introduction

In Section 9.1 it was indicated that constraints are very important in most applications. When all functions are linear, there is an extremely efficient algorithm, developed by Danzig in the 1940s, which will be described for the **linear programming (LP)** problem.

We shall start by posing a particular problem and looking at a simple graphical solution.

EXAMPLE 9.3   A manufacturing company makes two circuit boards R1 and R2, constructed as follows:

   R1 comprises 3 resistors, 1 capacitor, 2 transistors and 2 inductances;

   R2 comprises 4 resistors, 2 capacitors and 3 transistors.

The available stocks for a day's production are 2400 resistors, 900 capacitors, 1600 transistors and 1200 inductances. It is required to calculate how many R1 and how many R2 the company should produce daily in order to maximize its overall profits, knowing that it can make a profit on an R1 circuit of 5p and on an R2 circuit of 9p.

Solution   If the company produces daily x of type R1 and y of type R2 then its stock limitations give

$$3x + 4y \leqslant 2400 \tag{9.1a}$$

$$x + 2y \leqslant 900 \tag{9.1b}$$

$$2x + 3y \leqslant 1600 \tag{9.1c}$$

$$2x \qquad \leqslant 1200 \tag{9.1d}$$

$$x \geqslant 0, \qquad y \geqslant 0$$

and it makes a profit z given by

$$z = 5x + 9y \tag{9.2}$$

These inequalities are plotted on a diagram as in Figure 9.3(a). The shaded region defines the area for which *all* the inequalities are satisfied, and is called the **feasible region**. The lines of constant profit $z = $ constant, defined by (9.2),

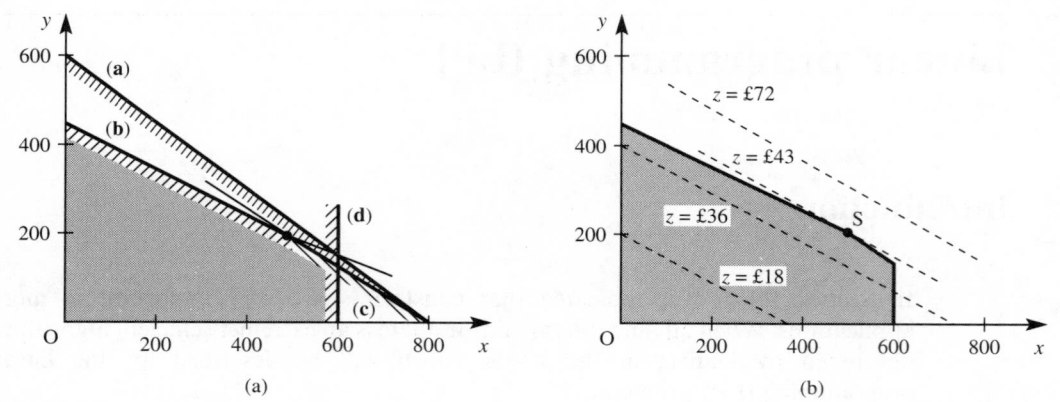

Figure 9.3 (a) Feasible region for the circuit board manufacture problem. (b) Lines of constant z show that S $(500, 200)$ gives the optimum.

are plotted as 'dashed' lines in Figure 9.3(b). It is clear from the geometry that the largest possible value of z that intersects the feasible region is at S with $x = 500$, $y = 200$, and this gives the optimal solution. At this point we can analyse the usage of the stocks as in Figure 9.4 and note that a profit of £43 has been made.

	Available	Used	Left over
Resistors	2400	2300	100
Capacitors	900	900	0
Transistors	1600	1600	0
Inductances	1200	1000	200

Figure 9.4 Table of stock usage.

Example 9.3 has encapsulated much of the LP method, and we shall try to extract the maximum amount of information from this example. The graphical method will only work if the problem has two variables, so we need to consider how to translate the geometry into an algebraic form that will work with any number of variables. Although we shall concentrate in this chapter on small problems in order to illustrate the methods, in practical problems there can be hundreds of variables and constraints. Large problems bring further difficulties that will not be considered here; for instance, how a large amount of information can be input into a computer accurately or how large data sets are handled in the computer.

From Figure 9.3 it can be seen that the solutions must be at a 'corner' of the feasible region, other than in the exceptional case when the profit line $z = $ constant is parallel to one of the constraints. This follows through into many-dimensional problems, so that it is *only necessary to inspect the corners of the feasible region.*

The **simplex method**, described in Section 9.2.3, uses this fact and selects a starting corner, chooses the neighbouring corner that increases z the most, and then repeats the process until no improvement is possible. The method writes the equations into a standard form; it then automates the choice of corner and finally reprocesses the equations back to the standard form again.

Once a solution has been obtained, it may be observed from Figures 9.3 and 9.4 that the **binding constraints** (b) and (c) intersect at S and are satisfied identically, so that all the stocks are used, while the **non-binding constraints** (a) and (d) leave some stock unused. It can also be seen from Figure 9.3 that the constraint (a) is redundant since it does not intersect the feasible region. These might appear obvious comments, but they prove to be useful and relevant observations when a sensitivity analysis is performed. Such an analysis asks whether or not the solution changes as the stocks vary or the costs vary, or the coefficients are changed. In practice, parameters vary over a period, and we wish to know whether a new calculation must be performed or whether the solution that we have already can be used.

There are a whole series of special cases that we must consider:

(a) Does a feasible region exist? If the system is modelled correctly, a feasible region always exists for a sensible problem; but if an error is made then it is easy to eliminate the region completely. For instance, in (9.1d) putting -1200 instead of 1200 would give an empty region, and this must be detected by any program.

(b) Is the solution degenerate? If the profit lines $z = $ constant are parallel to any one of the final binding constraints then any feasible part of the constraint gives a solution.

(c) Can we get unbounded regions and solutions? Again it is very easy to construct problems where the regions are unbounded and finite solutions may or may not exist. Just maximizing (9.2) subject only to the single constraint (9.1d) provides an unbounded region. Interpreting this situation, the only constraint that we have is on the inductances. If this were true, we could make infinitely many circuits of type R2 and make an infinite profit!

9.2.2　Simplex algorithm: an example

We now need to convert the ideas of Section 9.2.1 into a useful algebraic algorithm. There is a whole array of technical terms that are used in LP, and they will be introduced as we reconsider Example 9.3 to develop the solution method. The first step is to introduce **slack variables** r, s, t and u into (9.1) to make the inequality constraints into equality constraints.

If we are given x and y in the feasible region, the variables r, s, t and u provide a measure of how much 'slack' is available before all the corresponding resource is used up, so

$$3x + 4y + r \qquad\qquad = 2400 \qquad\qquad\text{(9.3a)}$$

$$x + 2y \quad + s \qquad\quad = 900 \qquad\qquad\text{(9.3b)}$$

$$2x + 3y \qquad\quad + t \qquad = 1600 \qquad\qquad\text{(9.3c)}$$

$$2x \qquad\qquad\qquad + u = 1200 \qquad\qquad\text{(9.3d)}$$

where x, y, r, s, t and u are now all greater than or equal to zero. We now have more variables than equations, and this enables us to construct a **feasible basic solution** by inspection:

$$\underbrace{x = y = 0;}_{\substack{\text{non-basic}\\\text{variables}}} \qquad \underbrace{r = 2400, \quad s = 900, \quad t = 1600, \quad u = 1200}_{\text{basic variables}}$$

with 4 **basic variables** (the same number as constraints, which are non-zero) and 2 **non-basic variables** (the remainder of the variables, which are zero).

The algebraic equivalent of moving to a neighbouring corner is to increase one of the non-basic variables from zero to its largest possible value. From the profit function given in (9.2), we have

$$z = 5x + 9y$$

Currently z has the value zero, and it seems sensible to change y, since the coefficient of y is larger; this will increase z the most. So keep $x = 0$ in (9.3) and increase y to its maximum value in each case: either

(a) change y to 600 and reduce r to zero, or

(b) change y to 450 and reduce s to zero, or

(c) change y to $533\frac{1}{3}$ and reduce t to zero, or

(d) note that there is no effect on changing y.

Choose option (b), since increasing y above 450 will make s negative, which would then violate the condition that all variables must be positive. Interchange s and y between the set of basic and non-basic variables and rewrite in the same form as (9.3). This is achieved by solving for y from (b) and substituting to give

$$x - 2s + r \qquad\qquad = 600 \qquad\qquad\text{(9.4a)}$$

$$\tfrac{1}{2}x + \tfrac{1}{2}s \quad + y \qquad\quad = 450 \qquad\qquad\text{(9.4b)}$$

$$\tfrac{1}{2}x - \tfrac{3}{2}s \qquad\quad + t \qquad = 250 \qquad\qquad\text{(9.4c)}$$

$$2x \qquad\qquad\qquad + u = 1200 \qquad\qquad\text{(9.4d)}$$

and, from (9.2),

$$z = 4050 + \tfrac{1}{2}x - \tfrac{9}{2}s \qquad\qquad\text{(9.4e)}$$

The problem is now reduced to exactly the same form as (9.3), and the same procedure can be applied. The non-basic variables are $x = s = 0$, and the basic variables are $r = 600$, $y = 450$, $t = 250$ and $u = 1200$, and z has increased its value from 0 to 4050.

Now only x can be increased, since increasing the other non-basic variable, s, would decrease z. Increasing x to 500 in (9.4c) and reducing t to 0 is the best that can be done. Using (9.4c) to write $x = 3s - 2t + 500$, we now eliminate x from the other equations to give

$$s - 2t + r \qquad\qquad = 100 \tag{9.5a}$$

$$2s - t \quad + y \qquad = 200 \tag{9.5b}$$

$$-3s + 2t \qquad + x \quad = 500 \tag{9.5c}$$

$$6s - 4t \qquad\quad + u = 200 \tag{9.5d}$$

and

$$z = 4300 - 3s - t \tag{9.5e}$$

We now have the final solution, since increasing s or t can only decrease z. Thus we have $x = 500$, $y = 200$, which is in agreement with the previous graphical solution, the maximum profit is $z = 4300$ as before, and the amounts left over in Figure 9.4 are just the 100 and 200 appearing on the right-hand sides of (9.5a, d).

We have just described the essentials of the **simplex algorithm**, although the method of working may have appeared a little haphazard. It can be tidied up and formalized by writing the whole system in **tableau form**. Equations (9.3) are written with the basic variables in the left-hand column, the coefficients in the equations placed in the appropriate array element and the objective function z placed in the first row with minus signs inserted.

		Non-basic variables		Basic variables				
		x	y	r	s	t	u	Solution
Objective function z		-5	-9	0	0	0	0	0
Basic variables	r	3	4	1	0	0	0	2400
	s	1	2	0	1	0	0	900
	t	2	3	0	0	1	0	1600
	u	2	0	0	0	0	1	1200

The current solution can easily be read from the tableau. The basic variables in the left-hand column are equal to the values in the solution column, so $r = 2400$, $s = 900, t = 1000$ and $u = 1200$. The remaining non-basic variables are zero, namely $x = y = 0$. The profit z is read similarly as the entry in the solution column, namely $z = 0$. The negative signs in the z row ensure that z remains positive in the subsequent manipulation. It should be noted that a 4×4 unit matrix (shown shaded above) occurs in the tableau in the basic variable columns, with zeros occurring above in the z row. This standard display is always the starting place for the simplex method, with the only possible complication being that the columns of the unit matrix might be shuffled around. The algorithm can now be performed in a series of steps:

Step 1

Choose the most negative entry in the z row and mark that column (the y column in this case).

Step 2

Evaluate the ratios of the solution column and the *positive* entries in the y column, choose the smallest of these and mark that row (the s row in this case).

	x	y	r	s	t	u	Solution	
z	-5	-9	0	0	0	0	0	Ratios
r	3	4	1	0	0	0	2400	$2400/4 = 600$
s	1	②	0	1	0	0	900	$900/2 = 450$
t	2	3	0	0	1	0	1600	$1600/3 = 533\frac{1}{3}$
u	2	0	0	0	0	1	1200	—

Step 3

Change the marked basic variable in the left-hand column to the marked non-basic variable in the top row (in this case s changes to y in the left-hand column).

Step 4

Make the pivot (the element in the position where the marked row and column cross) 1 by dividing through. In this case we divide the row elements by 2. These series of steps lead to the tableau

	x	y	r	s	t	u	Solution
z	-5	-9	0	0	0	0	0
r	3	4	1	0	0	0	2400
y	$\frac{1}{2}$	1	0	$\frac{1}{2}$	0	0	450
t	2	2	0	0	1	0	1600
u	2	0	0	0	0	1	1200

Step 5

Clear the y column by subtracting an appropriate multiple of the y row (this is just Gaussian elimination); for example (z row) $+ 9 \times$ (y row), (r row) $- 4 \times$ (y row) and so on. This leads to the tableau

	x	y	r	s	t	u	Solution
z	$-\frac{1}{2}$	0	0	$\frac{9}{2}$	0	0	4050
r	1	0	1	-2	0	0	600
y	$\frac{1}{2}$	1	0	$\frac{1}{2}$	0	0	450
t	$\frac{1}{2}$	0	0	$-\frac{3}{2}$	1	0	250
u	2	0	0	0	0	1	1200

This tableau can now easily be recognized as (9.4). It may be noted that the unit matrix appears in the tableau again, with the columns permuted, and the z row has zero entries in the basic variable columns.

The tableau is in exactly the standard form, and is ready for reapplication of the five given steps. *Steps 1 and 2* give the tableau

	x	y	r	s	t	u	Solution	Ratios
z	$-\frac{1}{2}$	0	0	$\frac{9}{2}$	0	0	4050	
r	1	0	1	-2	0	0	600	600
y	$\frac{1}{2}$	1	0	$\frac{1}{2}$	0	0	450	900
t	$\frac{1}{2}$	0	0	$-\frac{3}{2}$	1	0	250	500
u	2	0	0	0	0	1	1200	600

Steps 3, 4 and 5 then produce a final tableau

	x	y	r	s	t	u	Solution
z	0	0	0	3	1	0	4300
r	0	0	1	1	-2	0	100
y	0	1	0	2	-1	0	200
x	1	0	0	-3	2	0	500
u	0	0	0	6	-4	1	200

All the entries in the z row are now positive, so the optimum is achieved. The solution is read from the tableau directly; the left-hand column equals the right-hand column, giving $z = 4300$, $r = 100$, $y = 200$, $x = 500$ and $u = 200$, which is in agreement with the solution obtained in Example 9.3.

9.2.3   Simplex algorithm: general theory

We can now generalize the problem to the standard form of finding the **maximum** of the objective function

$$z = c_1 x_1 + c_2 x_2 + \ldots + c_n x_n$$

subject to the constraints

$$\left.\begin{array}{l} a_{11} x_1 + a_{12} x_2 + \ldots + a_{1n} x_n \leqslant b_1 \\ a_{21} x_1 + a_{22} x_2 + \ldots + a_{2n} x_n \leqslant b_2 \\ \quad\vdots \qquad\quad \vdots \qquad\qquad \vdots \qquad \vdots \\ a_{m1} x_1 + a_{m2} x_2 + \ldots + a_{mn} x_n \leqslant b_m \end{array}\right\}$$

(9.6)

by the **simplex algorithm**, where the $b_1, b_2, \ldots, b_m$ are all positive. By introducing the slack variables $x_{n+1}, \ldots, x_{n+m} \geqslant 0$ we convert (9.6) into the **standard tableau**

	x_1	x_2	...	x_n	x_{n+1}	x_{n+2}	...	x_{n+m}	Solution
z	$-c_1$	$-c_2$	...	$-c_n$	0	0	...	0	0
x_{n+1}	a_{11}	a_{12}	...	a_{1n}	1	0	...	0	b_1
x_{n+2}	a_{21}	a_{22}	...	a_{2n}	0	1	...	0	b_2
$\vdots$	$\vdots$	$\vdots$		$\vdots$	$\vdots$	$\vdots$		$\vdots$	$\vdots$
x_{n+m}	a_{m1}	a_{m2}	...	a_{mn}	0	0	...	1	b_m

Any subsequent tableau takes this general form, with an $m \times m$ unit matrix in the basic variables columns. As noted in the previous example, the basic variables change, so the left-hand column will have m entries, which can be any of the variables, $x_1, \ldots, x_{m+n}$, and the unit-matrix columns are usually not in the above neat form but are permuted.

The five basic steps in the algorithm follow quite generally:

Step 1

Choose the most negative value in the z row, say $-c_i$.   (Identify column i)
If all the entries are positive then the maximum has
been achieved.

Step 2

Evaluate $b_1/a_{1i}, b_2/a_{2i}, \ldots, b_m/a_{mi}$ for all *positive* a_{ki}.   (Identify row j)
Select the minimum of these numbers, say b_j/a_{ji}.

Step 3

Replace x_{n+j} by x_i in the basic variables in the   (Change the basis)
left-hand column.

Step 4

In row j replace a_{jk} by a_{jk}/a_{ji} for $k = 1, \ldots, n+m+1$.   (Make pivot = 1)
(Note that the first row and the final column are
treated as part of the tableau for computation purposes,
$-c_p = a_{0p}$, $b_q = a_{q(n+m+1)}$.)

Step 5

In all other rows, $l \neq j$, replace a_{lk} by $a_{lk} - a_{li}a_{jk}$ for (Gaussian elimination) all $k = 1, \ldots, m + n + 1$ and for each row $l = 0, \ldots, m$ ($l \neq j$).

The algorithm is then repeated until at Step 1 the maximum is achieved. The method provides an extremely efficient way of searching through the corners of the feasible region. To inspect all corners would require the computation of $\binom{m+n}{m}$ points, while the simplex algorithm reduces this very considerably, often down to something of the order of $m + n$.

Several checks should be made at the completion of each cycle, since it may be possible to identify an exceptional case. Perhaps the most complicated of the exceptions is when one of the $b_i = 0$ during the calculation, implying that one of the basic variables is zero. This can be a temporary effect, in which case the problem goes away at the next iteration, or it may be permanent, and that basic variable is indeed zero in the optimal solution. The best that may be said, other than going into sophisticated techniques found in specialist books on LP, is that problems are possible and the computation should be watched carefully. The solution can get into a cycle that cannot be broken.

A second exception that should be noted carefully occurs when one of the $c_i = 0$ for a *non-basic* variable in the optimal tableau. The normal simplex algorithm can then change the solution without changing the z row by selecting this i column at Step 1. Because $c_i = 0$, Step 5 is never used on the z row at all. This case corresponds to a degenerate solution with many **alternative solutions** to the problem, and geometrically the profit function is parallel to one of the constraints.

The third exception occurs at Step 2 when all the $a_{1i}, a_{2i}, \ldots, a_{mi}$ in the optimal column are zero or negative and it becomes impossible to identify a row to continue the method. The region in this case is **unbounded**, and a careful look at the original problem is required to decide whether this is reasonable, since it may still be possible to get a solution to such a problem.

EXAMPLE 9.4 Find the maximum of

$$z = 5x_1 + 4x_2 + 6x_3$$

subject to

$$4x_1 + x_2 + x_3 \leqslant 19$$
$$3x_1 + 4x_2 + 6x_3 \leqslant 30$$
$$2x_1 + 4x_2 + x_3 \leqslant 25$$
$$x_1 + x_2 + 2x_3 \leqslant 15$$
$$x_1, x_2, x_3 \geqslant 0$$

Solution The example cannot be solved graphically, since it has three variables, but is in a correct form for the simplex algorithm. The initial tableau gives the solution $x_4 = 19$, $x_5 = 30$, $x_6 = 25$, $x_7 = 15$ and non-basic variables $x_1, = x_2 = x_3 = 0$.

	x_1	x_2	x_3	x_4	x_5	x_6	x_7	Solution	
z	-5	-4	-6	0	0	0	0	0	Ratios
x_4	4	1	1	1	0	0	0	19	$19/1 = 19$
x_5	3	4	⑥	0	1	0	0	30	$30/6 = 5$
x_6	2	4	1	0	0	1	0	25	$25/1 = 25$
x_7	1	1	2	0	0	0	1	15	$15/2 = 7.5$

In the initial tableau the pivot is identified, and x_5 is removed from the basic variable column and replaced by x_3. The pivot is made equal to unity by dividing the x_3 row by 6. The other entries in the x_3 column are then made zero by the Gaussian elimination in Step 5. This gives the tableau

	x_1	x_2	x_3	x_4	x_5	x_6	x_7	Solution	
z	-2	0	0	0	1	0	0	30	Ratios
x_4	$\frac{7}{2}$	$\frac{1}{3}$	0	1	$-\frac{1}{6}$	0	0	14	4
x_3	$\frac{1}{2}$	$\frac{2}{3}$	1	0	$\frac{1}{6}$	0	0	5	10
x_6	$\frac{3}{2}$	$\frac{10}{3}$	0	0	$-\frac{1}{6}$	1	0	20	13.3
x_7	0	$-\frac{1}{3}$	0	0	$-\frac{1}{3}$	0	1	5	—

The process is then repeated and the pivot is again found, x_4 is replaced by x_1 in the first column, and the next tableau is constructed by following the remaining steps of the simplex algorithm, giving the tableau

	x_1	x_2	x_3	x_4	x_5	x_6	x_7	Solution
z	0	$\frac{4}{21}$	0	$\frac{4}{7}$	$\frac{19}{21}$	0	0	38
x_1	1	$\frac{2}{21}$	0	$\frac{2}{7}$	$-\frac{1}{21}$	0	0	4
x_3	0	$\frac{13}{21}$	1	$-\frac{1}{7}$	$\frac{4}{21}$	0	0	3
x_6	0	$\frac{67}{21}$	0	$-\frac{3}{7}$	$-\frac{2}{21}$	1	0	14
x_7	0	$-\frac{1}{3}$	0	0	$-\frac{1}{3}$	0	1	5

Thus the solution is now optimal, and gives $x_1 = 4$, $x_2 = 0$, $x_3 = 3$, and $z = 38$ as the maximum value. Note that the first two constraints are binding, that is satisfied exactly, while the other two are not. This can easily be deduced by looking at the slack variables. We have $x_4 = x_5 = 0$, corresponding to the first two constraints, and $x_6 \neq 0$, $x_7 \neq 0$ for the last two constraints.

EXAMPLE 9.5   A firm has two plants, P1 and P2, that can produce a particular chemical. The product is made from three constituents, A, B and C. In a given period there are 36 000 litres of A, 30 000 litres of B and 12 000 litres of C available. Plant P1 requires the constituents A, B, C to be mixed in the ratio 4:2:1 respectively, and the manufacturer makes a profit of £1.50 per litre of product; plant P2 requires the ratio 3:3:1, and gives a profit of £1 per litre of product.

Determine how production should be allocated to each plant to maximize the profits, and how much of A, B and C remain.

There is a major breakdown in the supply of chemical C, so that only 8000 litres are available in the given period. How should production be changed to maximize the profits, how much has profit been reduced, and how much of A, B and C remain?

Solution   For each 1000 litres produced in plant P1, $\frac{4}{7} \times 1000$ will be constituent A, $\frac{2}{7} \times 1000$ will be B and $\frac{1}{7} \times 1000$ will be C. For each 1000 litres produced in plant P2, $\frac{3}{7} \times 1000$ will be constituent A, $\frac{3}{7} \times 1000$ will be B and $\frac{1}{7} \times 1000$ will be C. Thus, taking the three constituents in turn and letting x_1 and x_2 represent respectively the amount (in 1000 litre units) produced in plants P1 and P2, we obtain

$$\tfrac{4}{7}x_1 + \tfrac{3}{7}x_2 \leqslant 36$$

$$\tfrac{2}{7}x_1 + \tfrac{3}{7}x_2 \leqslant 30$$

$$\tfrac{1}{7}x_1 + \tfrac{1}{7}x_2 \leqslant 12$$

$$x_1,\ x_2 \geqslant 0$$

or

$$4x_1 + 3x_2 \leqslant 252$$

$$2x_1 + 3x_2 \leqslant 210$$

$$x_1 + x_2 \leqslant 84$$

and the profit

$$z = 1.5x_1 + x_2$$

We can immediately construct the initial tableau

	x_1	x_2	x_3	x_4	x_5	Solution	
z	−1.5	−1	0	0	0	0	Ratios
x_3	④	3	1	0	0	252	63
x_4	2	3	0	1	0	210	105
x_5	1	1	0	0	1	84	84

The pivot has been found, and hence we introduce x_1 into the basis and construct the next tableau following the steps of the simplex algorithm:

	x_1	x_2	x_3	x_4	x_5	Solution
z	0	$\frac{1}{8}$	$\frac{3}{8}$	0	0	94.5
x_1	1	$\frac{3}{4}$	$\frac{1}{4}$	0	0	63
x_4	0	$\frac{3}{2}$	$-\frac{1}{2}$	1	0	84
x_5	0	$\frac{1}{4}$	$-\frac{1}{4}$	0	1	21

The z row is all positive, and hence we can immediately read off the solution (multiply by 1000 to re-establish proper costs)

$$x_1 = 63\,000, \qquad x_2 = 0, \qquad z = £94\,500$$

and only plant P1 is utilized. Since $x_3 = 0$, there are zero litres of A remaining; $x_4 = 84$, so that we have $(84/7) \times 1000 = 12\,000$ litres of B remaining; and $x_5 = 21$, so that $(21/7) \times 1000 = 3000$ litres of C remain.

After the breakdown, the 12 000 litres of C are reduced to 8000 litres, so that the first tableau becomes

	x_1	x_2	x_3	x_4	x_5	Solution	
z	-1.5	-1	0	0	0	0	Ratios
x_3	4	3	1	0	0	252	63
x_4	2	3	0	1	0	210	105
x_5	①	1	0	0	1	56	56

We note that we have a different pivot, and hence we expect a different solution. The next tableau is derived in the usual way, giving

	x_1	x_2	x_3	x_4	x_5	Solution
z	0	0.5	0	0	1.5	84
x_3	0	-1	1	0	-4	28
x_4	0	1	0	1	-2	98
x_1	1	1	0	0	1	56

The tableau is again optimal, so

$$x_1 = 56\,000, \qquad x_2 = 0, \qquad z = £84\,000$$

The profit is thus reduced by £10 500 by the breakdown, but still only plant P1 is used. The remaining amounts of A, B and C can be checked to be 4000, 14 000 and zero litres respectively.

Since this problem has only two variables, it would be instructive to check these results using the graphical method.

EXAMPLE 9.6   Find the maximum of

$$z = 4x_1 + 2x_2 + 4x_3$$

subject to

$$3x_1 + x_2 + 2x_3 \leqslant 320$$
$$x_1 + x_2 + x_3 \leqslant 100$$
$$2x_1 + x_2 + 2x_3 \leqslant 200$$

Solution

	x_1	x_2	x_3	x_4	x_5	x_6	Solution	
z	-4	-2	-4	0	0	0	0	Ratios
x_4	3	1	2	1	0	0	320	160
x_5	1	1	①	0	1	0	100	100
x_6	2	1	2	0	0	1	200	100

Note that in the above tableau there is some arbitrariness in the choices in both Steps 1 and 2. In Step 1 the column is chosen arbitrarily between the x_1 and x_3 columns. From the ratios, the x_5 row is selected from the x_5 and x_6 rows at Step 2, which both have equal ratios. Steps 3–5 are then followed to give the tableau

	x_1	x_2	x_3	x_4	x_5	x_6	Solution
z	0	2	0	0	4	0	400
x_4	1	-1	0	1	-2	0	120
x_3	①	1	1	0	1	0	100
x_6	0	-1	0	0	-2	1	0

Although this is the optimal solution with $x_1 = x_2 = 0$, $x_3 = 100$ and $z = 400$, we have $c_1 = 0$ in the z row. Since x_1 is a non-basic variable, there is degeneracy. If we follow through the algorithm, choosing the first column at Step 1, we obtain an equally optimal solution in the following tableau. Replace x_3 by x_1 in the basic variables, and subtract the x_1 row from the x_4 row:

	x_1	x_2	x_3	x_4	x_5	x_6	Solution
z	0	2	0	0	4	0	400
x_4	0	-2	-1	1	-3	0	20
x_1	1	1	1	0	1	0	100
x_6	0	-1	0	0	-2	1	0

> This solution gives $x_1 = 100$, $x_2 = x_3 = 0$ and $z = 400$ once more. It can easily be deduced that $x_1 = 100(1 - \alpha)$, $x_2 = 0$, $x_3 = 100\alpha$ is an optimal solution for any $0 \leqslant \alpha \leqslant 1$ with $z = 400$. We could have observed this fact geometrically, since z is just a multiple of the left-hand side of the last constraint.

9.2.4   Exercises

1 Use the graphical method to find the maximum value of

$$f = 4x + 5y$$

subject to

$$3x + 7y \leqslant 10$$
$$2x + y \leqslant 3$$
$$x, y \geqslant 0$$

2 Find $x_1, x_2, x_3, x_4 \geqslant 0$ that maximize

$$f = 6x_1 + x_2 + 2x_3 + 4x_4$$

subject to

$$2x_1 + x_2 \qquad\quad + x_4 \leqslant 3$$
$$x_1 \qquad + x_3 + x_4 \leqslant 4$$
$$x_1 + x_2 + 3x_3 + 2x_4 \leqslant 10$$

3 A manufacturer produces two types of cupboard, which are constructed from chipboard and oak veneer that both come in standard widths. The first type requires 4 m of chipboard and 5 m of oak veneer, takes 5 h of labour to produce and gives a profit of £24 per unit. The second type requires 5 m of chipboard and 2 m of oak veneer, takes 3 h of labour to produce and gives a £12 profit per unit.

On a weekly basis there are 400 m of chipboard available, 200 m of oak veneer and a maximum of 250 h of labour. Write this problem in a linear programming form. Use the simplex method to determine how many cupboards of each type should be made to maximize profits. How much profit is made? Which of the scarce resources remain unused? Show that the amount of oak veneer available can be reduced to 175 m without affecting the basis. What is the new solution, and by how much is the profit reduced?

4 A factory manufactures nails and screws. The profit yield is 2p per kg nails and 3p per kg screws. Three

units of labour are required to manufacture 1 kg nails and 6 units to make 1 kg screws. Twenty-four units of labour are available. Two units of raw material are needed to make 1 kg nails and 1 unit for 1 kg screws. Determine the manufacturing policy that yields maximum profit from 10 units of raw material.

5 A manufacturer makes two types of cylinder, CYL1 and CYL2. Three materials, M1, M2 and M3, are required for the manufacture of each cylinder. The following information is provided:

	Quantities of materials required		
	M1	M2	M3
CYL1	1	1	2
CYL2	5	2	1

Quantities of materials available		
M1	M2	M3
45	21	24

£4 profit is made on one CYL1 and £3 profit on one CYL2. How many of each cylinder should the manufacturer make in order to maximize profit?

6 Find the optimal solution of the following LP problem: maximize

$$z = \lambda x_1 + 20x_2$$

subject to

$$x_1 + 2x_2 \leqslant 20$$
$$3x_1 + x_2 \leqslant 25$$
$$x_1, x_2 \geqslant 0$$

where λ is a positive parameter representing variable profitability. Use both the simplex method and the graphical method, and interpret the results geometrically.

7 Use the simplex method to solve the following problem: maximize

$$2x_1 + x_2 + 4x_3 + x_4$$

subject to

$$2x_1 \quad + x_3 \quad \leqslant 3$$
$$x_1 \quad + 3x_3 + x_4 \leqslant 4$$
$$4x_2 + x_3 + x_4 \leqslant 3$$
$$x_1, x_2, x_3, x_4 \geqslant 0$$

8 The Yorkshire Clothing Company makes two styles of jacket, the 'York' and the 'Wetherby'. The York requires 3 m of cloth and 3 h of labour, and makes a profit of £25. The Wetherby needs 4 m of cloth and 2 h of labour, and makes a profit of £30. The Yorkshire has 400 m of cloth available and 300 h of labour available each week. Advise the company on the number of each style it should produce in order to maximize profits.

The company is prepared to buy more cloth to increase its profits, but it will not employ any more labour. Under this revised policy, is there a strategy that will increase its profits?

9 A publisher has three books available for printing, B1, B2 and B3. The books require varying amounts of paper, and the total paper supplies are limited:

	B1	B2	B3	Total units available
Units of paper required per 1000 copies	3	2	1	60
Profit per 1000 copies	£900	£800	£300	

Books B1 and B2 are similar in content, and the total combined market for these two books is estimated to be at most 15 000 copies. Determine how many copies of each book should be printed to maximize the overall profit.

10 Euroflight is considering the purchase of new aircraft. Long-range aircraft cost £4 million each, medium-range £2 million each and short-range £1 million each, and Euroflight has £60 million to invest. The estimated profit from each type of aircraft is £0.4 million, £0.3 million and £0.15 million respectively. The company has trained pilots for at most a total 25 aircraft. Maintenance facilities are limited to a maximum of the equivalent of 30 short-range aircraft. Long-range aircraft need twice as much maintenance as short-range ones, and medium-range 1.5 times as much. Set this up as a linear programming problem, and solve it. Aircraft can only be bought in integer numbers, so estimate how many of each type should be bought.

9.2.5 Two-phase method

The previous section only dealt with '$\leqslant$' constraints and did not consider '$\geqslant$' constraints. These prove to be much more troublesome, since there is no obvious initial feasible solution, and Phase 1 of the **two-phase method** is solely concerned with getting such a solution. Once this has been obtained, we then move to Phase 2. This is the standard simplex method, starting from the solution just obtained from Phase 1. A simple example will illustrate the problems involved and the basic ideas of the two-phase method.

EXAMPLE 9.7 Find the maximum of

$$z = x + y$$

subject to

$$-x + 2y \leqslant 6$$

$$x \qquad \leqslant 4$$

$$2x + y \geqslant 4$$

$$x, \ y \geqslant 0$$

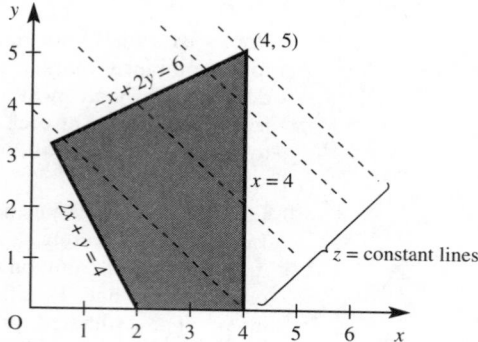

Figure 9.5 The feasible region.

Solution   The region defined by the constraints is shown in Figure 9.5. It is clear from the figure that the origin is *not* in the feasible region and that $x = 4$, $y = 5$ gives the optimal solution. We have already appreciated that the graphical method is only useful for two-dimensional problems, and we must explore how the simplex method copes with this problem.

Add in the positive variables r, s and t to give

$$-x + 2y + r \qquad\qquad = 6$$

$$x \qquad\quad + s \qquad = 4$$

$$2x + y \qquad\quad - t = 4$$

The r and s are the usual slack variables. Because we must substract t to take away the surplus, t is called a **surplus variable**. The obvious solution $x = y = 0$, $r = 6$, $s = 4$, $t = -4$ does *not* satisfy the condition that all variables be positive. The algebra is saying that the origin is not in the feasible region. Because the simplex method works so well, the last equation is forced into standard form by adding in yet another variable, u, called an **artificial variable**, to give

$$2x + y - t + u = 4$$

Now we have a feasible solution $x = y = t = 0$, $r = 6$, $s = 4$, $u = 4$, but not to the problem we originally stated. As the term 'artificial variable' implies, we wish to get rid of u and then reduce the problem back to our original one at a feasible corner. The variable u can be eliminated by forcing it to zero and this can be done by entering **Phase 1** with a new cost function

$$z' = -u$$

We see that if we can maximize z' then this is at $u = 0$, and our Phase 1 will be complete. The simplex tableau for Phase 1 then takes the form

— artificial variable

change to 0.

	x	y	r	s	t	u	Solution
z	-1	-1	0	0	0	0	0
z'	0	0	0	0	0	1	0
r	-1	2	1	0	0	0	6
s	1	0	0	1	0	0	4
u	2	1	0	0	-1	1	4

where z has been included for the elimination but does *not* enter the optimization: only the z' is considered in Phase 1. It may be observed that the tableau is not of standard form, since u is a basic variable and the (z', u) entry is non-zero. This must be remedied by subtracting the u row from the z' row to give the standard-form tableau

	x	y	r	s	t	u	Solution
z	-1	-1	0	0	0	0	0
z'	-2	-1	0	0	1	0	-4
r	-1	2	1	0	0	0	6
s	1	0	0	1	0	0	4
u	$②$	1	0	0	-1	1	4

Manipulation using the usual simplex algorithm gives the tableau

	x	y	r	s	t	u	Solution
z	0	$-\frac{1}{2}$	0	0	$-\frac{1}{2}$	$\frac{1}{2}$	2
z'	0	0	0	0	0	1	0
r	0	$\frac{5}{2}$	1	0	$-\frac{1}{2}$	$\frac{1}{2}$	8
s	0	$-\frac{1}{2}$	0	1	$\frac{1}{2}$	$-\frac{1}{2}$	2
x	1	$\frac{1}{2}$	0	0	$-\frac{1}{2}$	$\frac{1}{2}$	2

At this stage $z' = 0$ and $u = 0$, so that we have driven u out of the problem, and the z' row and u column can now be deleted. The Phase 1 solution gives $x = 2, y = 0$, which can be observed to be a corner of the feasible region in Figure 9.5.

We now enter **Phase 2**, with the z' row and u column deleted, and perform the usual sequence of steps. The initial tableau is

	x	y	r	s	t	Solution
z	0	$-\frac{1}{2}$	0	0	$-\frac{1}{2}$	2
r	0	$\left(\frac{5}{2}\right)$	1	0	$-\frac{1}{2}$	8
s	0	$-\frac{1}{2}$	0	1	$\frac{1}{2}$	2
x	1	$\frac{1}{2}$	0	0	$-\frac{1}{2}$	2

Two further cycles are required, leading sequentially to the following two tableaux:

	x	y	r	s	t	Solution
z	0	0	$\frac{1}{5}$	0	$-\frac{3}{5}$	$\frac{18}{5}$
y	0	1	$\frac{2}{5}$	0	$-\frac{1}{5}$	$\frac{16}{5}$
s	0	0	$\frac{1}{5}$	1	$\left(\frac{2}{5}\right)$	$\frac{18}{5}$
x	1	0	$-\frac{1}{5}$	0	$-\frac{2}{5}$	$\frac{2}{5}$

	x	y	r	s	t	Solution
z	0	0	$\frac{1}{2}$	$\frac{3}{2}$	0	9
y	0	1	$\frac{1}{2}$	$\frac{1}{2}$	0	5
t	0	0	$\frac{1}{2}$	$\frac{5}{2}$	1	9
x	1	0	0	1	0	4

We now have an optimum solution, since all the z row entries are non-negative with $x = 4$, $y = 5$ and objective function $z = 9$ in agreement with the graphical solution.

The general **two-phase strategy** is then as follows:

Phase 1

(a) Introduce slack and surplus variables.

(b) Introduce artificial variables alongside the surplus variables, say $x_p, \ldots, x_q$.

(c) Write the artificial cost function

$$z' = -x_p - x_{p+1} \ldots - x_q$$

(d) Subtract rows $x_p, x_{p+1}, \ldots, x_q$ from the cost function z' to ensure there are zeros in the entries in the z' row corresponding to the basic variables.

(e) Use the standard simplex method to maximize z' (keeping the z row as an extra row) until $z' = 0$ and

$$x_p = x_{p+1} = \ldots = x_q = 0$$

Phase 2

(a) Eliminate the z' row and artificial columns $x_p, \ldots, x_q$.

(b) Use the standard simplex method to maximize the objective function z.

There are other approaches to obtaining an initial feasible basic solution, but Phase 1 of the two-phase method gives an efficient way of obtaining a starting point. Geometrically, it uses the simplex method to search the non-feasible vertices until it is driven to a vertex in the feasible region.

EXAMPLE 9.8   Use the two-phase method to solve the following LP problem: maximize

$$z = 4x_1 + \tfrac{1}{2}x_2 + x_3$$

subject to

$$x_1 + 2x_2 + 3x_3 \geqslant 2$$
$$2x_1 + x_2 + x_3 \leqslant 5$$
$$x_1, x_2, x_3 \geqslant 0$$

Solution

Phase 1   Introduce a surplus variable x_4 and a corresponding artificial variable x_5 into the first inequality. A slack variable x_6 is required for the second inequality. The artificial cost is just

$$z' = -x_5$$

and we can construct the initial tableau

	x_1	x_2	x_3	x_4	x_5	x_6	Solution
z	-4	$-\tfrac{1}{2}$	-1	0	0	0	0
z'	0	0	0	0	1	0	0
x_5	1	2	3	-1	1	0	2
x_6	2	1	1	0	0	1	5

We subtract the x_5 row from the z' row to eliminate the 1 from the (z', x_5) element, giving the tableau

	x_1	x_2	x_3	x_4	x_5	x_6	Solution
z	-4	$-\frac{1}{2}$	-1	0	0	0	0
z'	-1	-2	-3	1	0	0	-2
x_5	1	2	$③$	-1	1	0	2
x_6	2	1	1	0	0	1	5

We now apply the steps of the simplex algorithm to give the tableau

	x_1	x_2	x_3	x_4	x_5	x_6	Solution
z	$\frac{11}{3}$	$\frac{1}{6}$	0	$-\frac{1}{3}$	$\frac{1}{3}$	0	$\frac{2}{3}$
z'	0	0	0	0	1	0	0
x_3	$\frac{1}{3}$	$\frac{2}{3}$	1	$-\frac{1}{3}$	$\frac{1}{3}$	0	$\frac{2}{3}$
x_6	$\frac{5}{3}$	$\frac{1}{3}$	0	$\frac{1}{3}$	$-\frac{1}{3}$	1	$\frac{13}{3}$

Since $z' = 0$ and the artificial variable x_5 has been driven into the non-basic variables, phase 1 ends.

Phase 2   The z' row and the x_5 column are now deleted, and the following sequence of tableaux constructed following the rules of the simplex algorithm:

	x_1	x_2	x_3	x_4	x_6	Solution
z	$\frac{11}{3}$	$\frac{1}{6}$	0	$-\frac{1}{3}$	0	$\frac{2}{3}$
x_3	$①\atop\frac{1}{3}$	$\frac{2}{3}$	1	$-\frac{1}{3}$	0	$\frac{2}{3}$
x_6	$\frac{5}{3}$	$\frac{1}{3}$	0	$\frac{1}{3}$	1	$\frac{13}{3}$

	x_1	x_2	x_3	x_4	x_6	Solution
z	0	$\frac{15}{2}$	11	-4	0	8
x_1	1	2	3	-1	0	2
x_6	0	-3	-5	$②$	1	1

	x_1	x_2	x_3	x_4	x_6	Solution
z	0	$\frac{3}{2}$	1	0	2	10
x_1	1	$\frac{1}{2}$	$\frac{1}{2}$	0	$\frac{1}{2}$	$\frac{5}{2}$
x_4	0	$-\frac{3}{2}$	$-\frac{5}{2}$	1	$\frac{1}{2}$	$\frac{1}{2}$

The solution is now optimal, with $x_1 = \frac{5}{2}$, $x_2 = x_3 = 0$ and $z = 10$. Note that the first inequality is not binding, since $x_4 \neq 0$, while the second inequality is binding.

EXAMPLE 9.9   Three ores, A, B and C, are blended to form 100 kg of alloy; the percentage contents and the costs are as follows:

Ore	A	B	C
Iron	70	60	0
Lead	20	10	40
Copper	10	30	60
Cost ($£\,kg^{-1}$)	3000	2000	1000

The alloy must contain at least 20% iron, at least 25% lead but less than 48% copper. Find the blend of ores that minimizes the cost of the alloy.

Solution   Let x_1, x_2 and x_3 be the weights (kg) of ores A, B and C respectively in the 100 kg of alloy. The constraints give

$$\text{iron} \quad 0.7x_1 + 0.6x_2 \qquad\qquad \geqslant 20$$
$$\text{lead} \quad 0.2x_1 + 0.1x_2 + 0.4x_3 \geqslant 25$$
$$\text{copper} \quad 0.1x_1 + 0.3x_2 + 0.6x_3 \leqslant 48$$

and to make the 100 kg of alloy,

$$x_1 + x_2 + x_3 = 100$$

The cost is

$$3000x_1 + 2000x_2 + 1000x_3$$

which is to be *minimized*.

To reduce the problem to standard form, we change the problem to a *maximization* of

$$z = -3000x_1 - 2000x_2 - 1000x_3$$

For the inequality constraints we use surplus variables x_4 and x_5 and a slack variable x_6. We require two artificial variables x_7 and x_8 alongside the surplus variables. Thus the inequalities become

$$0.7x_1 + 0.6x_2 \qquad\quad - x_4 \qquad\quad + x_7 \qquad = 20$$
$$0.2x_1 + 0.1x_2 + 0.4x_3 \qquad - x_5 \qquad\quad + x_8 = 25$$
$$0.1x_1 + 0.3x_2 + 0.6x_3 \qquad\qquad + x_6 \qquad\quad = 48$$

To deal with the equality constraint, we introduce a further artificial variable x_9:

$$x_1 + x_2 + x_3 + x_9 = 100$$

We must drive x_9 to zero, to ensure that the equality holds, so it is essential to put x_9 into the artificial cost function. (Note that this is the standard way of dealing with an equality constraint.) We first enter *Phase 1*. Steps (a)–(c) of

Phase 1 of the two-phase method give the initial tableau

	x_1	x_2	x_3	x_4	x_5	x_6	x_7	x_8	x_9	Solution
z	3000	2000	1000	0	0	0	0	0	0	0
z'	0	0	0	0	0	0	1	1	1	0
x_7	0.7	0.6	0	-1	0	0	1	0	0	20
x_8	0.2	0.1	0.4	0	-1	0	0	1	0	25
x_6	0.1	0.3	0.6	0	0	1	0	0	0	48
x_9	1	1	1	0	0	0	0	0	1	100

It is necessary to remove the 1s from the z' row in the basic variable columns x_7, x_8 and x_9. Following (d) of the general strategy, we replace the z' row by $(z'$ row$) - (x_7$ row$) - (x_8$ row$) - (x_9$ row$)$ to give the tableau

	x_1	x_2	x_3	x_4	x_5	x_6	x_7	x_8	x_9	Solution
z	3000	2000	1000	0	0	0	0	0	0	0
z'	-1.9	-1.7	-1.4	1	1	0	0	0	0	-145
x_7	0.7	0.6	0	-1	0	0	1	0	0	20
x_8	0.2	0.1	0.4	0	-1	0	0	1	0	25
x_6	0.1	0.3	0.6	0	0	1	0	0	0	48
x_9	1	1	1	0	0	0	0	0	1	100

Several tableaux need to be completed to drive z' to zero and complete Phase 1, with the final tableau being

	x_1	x_2	x_3	x_4	x_5	x_6	x_7	x_8	x_9	Solution
z	0	-2000	0	0	$-10\,000$	0	0	10000	-1000	$-250\,000$
z'	0	0	0	0	0	0	1	1	1	0
x_1	1	1.5	0	0	5	0	0	-5	2	75
x_3	0	-0.5	1	0	-5	0	0	5	-1	25
x_6	0	0.45	0	0	2.5	1	0	-2.5	0.4	25.5
x_4	0	0.45	0	1	3.5	0	-1	-3.5	1.4	32.5

Removing the artificial variables and the z' row gives the tableau

	x_1	x_2	x_3	x_4	x_5	x_6	Solution
z	0	-2000	0	0	$-10\,000$	0	$-250\,000$
x_1	1	1.5	0	0	5	0	75
x_3	0	-0.5	1	0	-5	0	25
x_6	0	0.45	0	0	2.5	1	25.5
x_4	0	0.45	0	1	3.5	0	32.5

The algorithm is now ready for *Phase 2*, since a sensible feasible basic solution is available. The standard procedure leads, after many cycles, to the final tableau

	x_1	x_2	x_3	x_4	x_5	x_6	Solution
z	333.3	0	0	0	0	3333.3	$-140\,000$
x_4	0.3	0	0	1	0	-2	4
x_3	-0.67	0	1	0	0	3.33	60
x_2	1.67	1	0	0	0	-3.33	40
x_5	-0.3	0	0	0	1	1	3

and the solution can be read off as

$$x_1 = 0, \qquad x_2 = 40, \qquad x_3 = 60$$

with the cost minimized at £140 000. (Note that the cost in the tableau is negative, since the original problem is a minimization problem.) It may be noted that $x_6 = 0$, so the copper constraint is binding while the iron constraint gives 4% more than the required minimum and the lead constraint gives 3% more than the required minimum.

9.2.6   Exercises

11 Use the simplex method to find positive values of x_1 and x_2 that minimize

$$f = 10x_1 + x_2$$

subject to

$$4x_1 + x_2 \leqslant 32$$
$$2x_1 + x_2 \geqslant 12$$
$$2x_1 - x_2 \leqslant 4$$
$$-2x_1 + x_2 \leqslant 8$$

Sketch the points obtained by the simplex method on a graph, indicating how the points progress through Phases 1 and 2 to the solution.

12 Solve the following LP problem: minimize

$$2x_1 + 7x_2 + 4x_3 + 5x_4$$

subject to

$$x_1 - x_3 - x_4 \geqslant 0$$
$$x_2 + x_3 \geqslant 2$$
$$x_1, \, x_2, \, x_3, \, x_4 \geqslant 0$$

13 A trucking company requires antifreeze that contains at least 50% of pure glycol and at least 5% of anticorrosive additive. The company can buy three products, A, B and C, whose constituents and costs are as follows:

	A	B	C
% glycol	65	25	80
% additive	10	3	0
Cost (£/litre)	1.8	0.9	1.5

What blend will provide the required antifreeze solution at minimum cost? What is the cost of 100 litres of solution?

14 A builder is constructing three different styles of house on an estate, and is deciding which styles to erect in the next phase of building. There are 40 plots of equal size, and the different styles require 1, 2 and 2 plots respectively. The builder anticipates shortages of two materials, and estimates the requirements and supplies (in appropriate units) to be as follows:

	Requirements			Total supply
	Style 1	Style 2	Style 3	
Facing stone	1	2	5	58
Weather boarding	3	2	1	72

The local authority insists that there be at least 5 more houses of style 2 than style 1. If the profits on the houses are £1000, £1500 and £2500 for styles 1, 2 and 3 respectively, find how many of each style the builder should construct to maximize the total profit.

15 The Footsie company produces boots and shoes. If no boots are made, the company can produce a maximum of 250 pairs of shoes in a day. Each pair of boots takes twice as long to make as each pair of shoes. The maximum daily sales of boots and shoes are 200, but 25 pairs of boots must be produced to satisfy an important customer. The profits per pair of boots and shoes are £8 and £5 respectively. Determine the daily production plan to maximize profits. Use the two-phase method to obtain the solution, and verify your result with a graphical solution.

16 In Exercise 9 there is an additional union agreement that at least 50 000 books must be printed. Does the solution change? If so, calculate the new optimum strategy.

17 A manufacturer produces three types of carpeting, C1, C2 and C3. Two of the raw materials, M1 and M2, are in short supply. The following table gives the supplies of M1 and M2 available (in 1000s of kg), the quantities of M1 and M2 required for each $1000 \, m^2$ of carpet, and the profits made from each type of carpet (in £1000s per $1000 \, m^2$):

	Quantities required		Profit
	M1	M2	
C1	1	1	2
C2	1	1	3
C3	1	0	0
Quantities available	5	4	

Carpet of type C3 is non-profit-making, but is included in the range in order to enable the company to satisfy its customers. The company has policies that require that, if x_1, x_2 and x_3 1000s of m^2 of C1, C2 and C3 respectively are made then

$$x_1 \geqslant 1$$

and

$$x_1 - x_2 + x_3 \geqslant 2$$

How much carpet of each type should the company manufacture in order to satisfy the constraints and maximize profits?

Lagrange multipliers

9.3.1 Equality constraints

In Section 9.2 we looked at the situation where all the functions were linear. As soon as functions become nonlinear, the problems become very much more difficult.

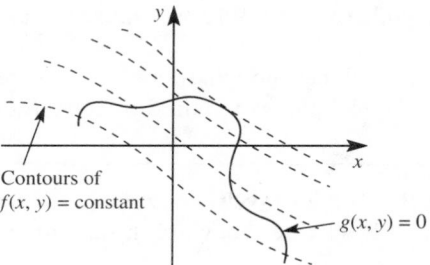

Figure 9.6 Lagrange multiplier problem.

This is generally the case in most of mathematics, and is certainly true in optimization problems.

In Section 9.4.4 of *Modern Engineering Mathematics* it was shown how to use Lagrange multipliers to solve the problem of the optimization of a nonlinear function of many variables subject to **equality constraints**. For the general problem it was shown that the necessary conditions for the extremum of

$$f(x_1, x_2, \ldots, x_n)$$

subject to

$$g_i(x_1, x_2, \ldots, x_n) = 0 \quad (i = 1, 2, \ldots, m \, (m < n))$$

are

$$\frac{\partial f}{\partial x_k} + \lambda_1 \frac{\partial g_1}{\partial x_k} + \lambda_2 \frac{\partial g_2}{\partial x_k} + \ldots + \lambda_m \frac{\partial g_m}{\partial x_k} = 0 \quad (k = 1, 2, \ldots, n) \tag{9.7}$$

where $\lambda_1, \lambda_2, \ldots, \lambda_m$ are the **Lagrange multipliers**. These n equations must be solved together with the m constraints $g_i = 0$. Thus there are $n + m$ equations in the $n + m$ unknowns $x_1, x_2, \ldots, x_n$ and $\lambda_1, \lambda_2, \ldots, \lambda_m$.

For a two-variable problem of finding the extremum of

$$f(x, y) \quad \text{subject to the single constraint} \quad g(x, y) = 0$$

the problem is illustrated geometrically in Figure 9.6. We are looking for the maximum, say, of the function $f(x, y)$, but *only* considering those points in the plane that lie on the curve $g(x, y) = 0$. The mathematical conditions look much simpler of course, as

$$\left. \begin{array}{l} f_x + \lambda g_x = 0 \\ f_y + \lambda g_y = 0 \\ g = 0 \end{array} \right\} \tag{9.8}$$

There are two comments that should be noted. First, the method fails if $g_x = g_y = 0$ at the solution point. Such points are called **singular points**: fortunately they are rare, but their existence should be noted. Secondly, sufficient conditions for a maximum, a minimum or a saddle point can be derived, but they are difficult to apply and not very useful. Example 9.12 will illustrate an intuitive approach to sufficiency.

A few examples should be enough to remind the reader of the problems involved and to show the techniques required to solve the equations.

EXAMPLE 9.10

Fermat stated in 1661 that 'Light travels along the shortest path'. Find the path that joins the eye to an object when they are in separate media (Figure 9.7).

Figure 9.7 Fermat's shortest-path problem.

Solution

The velocities of light in the two media are v and V. The time of transit of light is given by the geometry as

$$T = \frac{a}{v\cos\alpha} + \frac{b}{V\cos\beta}$$

and is then subject to the geometrical constraint that

$$L = a\tan\alpha + b\tan\beta$$

Applying (9.8),

$$0 = \frac{\partial T}{\partial\alpha} + \lambda\frac{\partial g}{\partial\alpha} = \frac{a}{v}\sec\alpha\tan\alpha + \lambda a\sec^2\alpha$$

$$0 = \frac{\partial T}{\partial\beta} + \lambda\frac{\partial g}{\partial\beta} = \frac{b}{V}\sec\beta\tan\beta + \lambda b\sec^2\beta$$

These give as the only solution

$$\sin\alpha = -\lambda v, \qquad \sin\beta = -\lambda V$$

or

$$\frac{\sin\alpha}{\sin\beta} = \frac{v}{V} = \mu$$

which is known as **Snell's law**.

In Example 9.10, to obtain Snell's law, the solution of the equation was quite straightforward, but this is rarely so easy. Frequently it is technically the most difficult task, and it is easy to miss solutions. We return to the 'milk carton' problem discussed earlier to illustrate the point.

EXAMPLE 9.11   Find the minimum area of the milk carton problem stated in Example 9.2 and illustrated in Figure 9.1.

Solution   Taking measurements in millimetres, the basic mathematical problem is to minimize

$$A = (2b + 2w + 5)(h + b + 10)$$

subject to

$$hbw = 1\,136\,000$$

Applying the Lagrange multiplier equations (9.7), we obtain

$$0 = (2b + 2w + 5) \qquad\qquad\qquad + \lambda bw$$

$$0 = (2b + 2w + 5) + 2(h + b + 10) + \lambda hw$$

$$0 = \qquad\qquad\qquad 2(h + b + 10) + \lambda hb$$

giving four equations in the four unknowns h, b, w and λ. If we eliminate λ and w from these equations, we are left with the same equations that we derived in Example 9.2, which have no simple analytical solutions.

The only way to proceed further with Example 9.11 is by a numerical solution. Thus, even with simple problems such as this one, we need a numerical algorithm, and in most realistic problems in science and engineering we encounter similar severe computational difficulties. It is often a problem even to write down the function or the constraints explicitly. Such functions frequently emerge as numbers from a complicated computer program. It is therefore essential to look for efficient numerical algorithms to optimize such functions. This will be the substance of Section 9.4.

A final example shows the situation where there are more than two variables involved. An indication will be given of the difficulties of *proving* that the point obtained is a maximum.

EXAMPLE 9.12   A hopper is to be made from a cylindrical portion connected to a conical portion as indicated in Figure 9.8. It is required to find the maximum volume subject to a given surface area.

Figure 9.8 Hopper.

Solution We can compute the volume of the hopper as

$$V = \pi R^2 L + \tfrac{1}{3}\pi R^3 \tan\alpha$$

and find its maximum subject to the surface area being given as

$$A = 2\pi RL + \pi R^2 \sec\alpha$$

Applying (9.7) with the appropriate variables, we obtain

$$0 = \frac{\partial V}{\partial R} + \lambda\frac{\partial g}{\partial R} = 2\pi RL + \pi R^2 \tan\alpha + \lambda(2\pi L + 2\pi R \sec\alpha)$$

$$0 = \frac{\partial V}{\partial L} + \lambda\frac{\partial g}{\partial L} = \pi R^2 + \lambda 2\pi R$$

$$0 = \frac{\partial V}{\partial \alpha} + \lambda\frac{\partial g}{\partial \alpha} = \tfrac{1}{3}\pi R^3 \sec^2\alpha + \lambda\pi R^2 \sec\alpha\tan\alpha$$

First, λ can be easily evaluated as $\lambda = -\tfrac{1}{2}R$. The last of the above three equations becomes

$$\pi R^2 \sec^2\alpha\left(\tfrac{1}{3}R + \lambda\sin\alpha\right) = 0$$

and hence $\sin\alpha = \tfrac{2}{3}$. Since $0 \leqslant \alpha \leqslant \tfrac{1}{2}\pi$, we have $\alpha = 0.730$ rad or $41.8°$. A little further algebraic manipulation between the constraints and the above equations gives $R^2 = A/\pi\sqrt{5}$, so that $R = 0.377A^{1/2}$ and $V = 0.126A^{3/2}$.

Normally it would be assumed that this is a maximum for the volume on intuitive or geometrical grounds. To prove this rigorously, we take small variations around the suspected maximum and show that the volume is larger than all its neighbours. For simplicity let $R^2 = (A/\pi\sqrt{5})(1 + \delta)$, $\sec\alpha = (3/\sqrt{5})(1 + \varepsilon)$, evaluate L from the constraint $g = 0$ and then calculate V to *second order* in ε and δ by Taylor's theorem. Some careful algebra gives

$$V = \frac{A^{3/2}}{3\pi^{1/2}5^{1/4}}\left(1 - \tfrac{1}{8}\delta^2 - \tfrac{9}{16}\varepsilon^2\right)$$

This shows that for any non-zero values of ε and δ we obtain a smaller volume, and hence we have proved that we have found a maximum.

It should be reiterated that the major problem lies in solving the Lagrange multiplier equations and not in writing them down. This is typical, and supports the need for good numerical algorithms to solve such problems; they only have to be marginally more difficult than Example 9.12 to become impossible to manipulate analytically.

9.3.2   Inequality constraints

Although we do not intend to consider them in any detail here, for reference we shall state the basic extension of (9.7) to the case of **inequality constraints**. Kuhn and Tucker proved the following result in the 1940s.

To maximize the function

$$f(x_1, \ldots, x_n)$$

subject to

$$g_1(x_1, \ldots, x_n) \leqslant 0 \quad (i = 1, \ldots, m)$$

the equivalent conditions to (9.7) are

$$\frac{\partial f}{\partial x_k} - \lambda_1 \frac{\partial g_1}{\partial x_k} - \cdots - \lambda_m \frac{\partial g_m}{\partial x_k} = 0 \quad (k = 1, \ldots, n)$$

$$\left. \begin{array}{c} \lambda_i g_i = 0 \\ \lambda_i \geqslant 0 \\ g_i \leqslant 0 \end{array} \right\} \quad (i = 1, \ldots, m)$$

The equation $\lambda_i g_i = 0$ gives two alternative conclusions for each constraint, either

(a) $g_i = 0$, in which case the constraint is 'active' and the corresponding $\lambda_i > 0$, or

(b) $\lambda_i = 0$ and $g_i < 0$, so that the optimum is away from this constraint and the Lagrange multiplier is not necessary.

Implementation of the Kuhn–Tucker result is not very easy, even though in principle it looks straightforward. There are so many cases to check that it becomes very susceptible to error.

9.3.3   Exercises

18 Find the optimum of $f = xy^2z$ subject to $x + 2y + 3z = 6$ using a Lagrange multiplier method.

19 Show that the stationary points of $f = x^2 + y^2 + z^2$ subject to $x + y - z = 0$ and $yz + 2zx - 2xy = 1$ are given by the solution of the equations

$$0 = 2x + \lambda + (2z - 2y)\mu$$

$$0 = 2y + \lambda + (z - 2x)\mu$$

$$0 = 2z - \lambda + (y + 2x)\mu$$

Add the last of these two equations, and show that

either $\mu = -2$ or $y + z = 0$. Hence deduce the stationary points.

20 A rectangular box without a lid is to be made. It is required to maximize the volume for a given surface area. Find the dimensions of the box when the total surface area is A.

21 Find the shortest distance from the origin to the ellipse

$$\frac{x^2}{a^2} + \frac{y^2}{b^2} = 1 \quad (a < b)$$

22 Determine the lengths of the sides of a rectangle with maximum area that can be inscribed within the ellipse

$$\frac{x^2}{a^2} + \frac{y^2}{b^2} = 1$$

23 (Harder) The lowest frequency of vibration, α, of an elastic plate can be computed by minimizing

$$I[\omega] = \iint\limits_{R} (\nabla^2 \omega)^2 \, dx \, dy$$

subject to

$$\iint\limits_{R} \omega^2 \, dx \, dy = 1$$

over all functions $\omega(x, y)$, where R is the region of the plate in the (x, y) plane. If R is the square region $|x| \leqslant 1$, $|y| \leqslant 1$ and the plate is clamped at its edges,

use the approximation

$$\omega = A \cos^2 \tfrac{1}{2}\pi x \cos^2 \tfrac{1}{2}\pi y$$

to show that $I[\omega_{\min}] = \alpha^2 = \tfrac{8}{9}\pi^4$.

Use the improved approximation

$$\omega = \cos^2 \tfrac{1}{2}\pi x \cos^2 \tfrac{1}{2}\pi y \, (A + B\cos \tfrac{1}{2}\pi x \cos \tfrac{1}{2}\pi y)$$

to get a better estimate of α.

(*Note*: $\int_{-1}^{1} \cos^{2n} \tfrac{1}{2}\pi z \, dz = (2n)!/(n!)^2 \, 2^{2n-1}$ for non-negative integers n. Preferably use an algebraic symbolic manipulator, for example MAPLE, to evaluate the differentials and integrals.)

24 Use the Kuhn–Tucker criteria to find the minimum of

$$2x_1^2 + x_2^2 + 2x_1 x_2$$

subject to

$$x_1 - x_2 \leqslant \alpha$$

where α is a parameter. Find the critical value of α at which the nature of the solution changes. Sketch the situation geometrically to illustrate the change.

9.4 Hill climbing

9.4.1 Single-variable search

Most practical problems give calculations that cannot be performed explicitly, and need a numerical technique. Typical cases are those in Examples 9.1 and 9.11, where the final equations cannot be solved analytically and we need to resort to numerical methods. This is not an uncommon situation, and **hill climbing methods** were devised, mainly in the 1960s, to cope with just such problems.

In many engineering problems the functions that we are trying to optimize cannot be written down explicitly. Take for example a vibrational problem where the frequencies of vibration are calculated from an eigenvalue problem. These frequencies will depend on the parameters of the physical system, and it may be necessary to make the largest frequency as low as possible. To illustrate this idea, suppose that the eigenvalues come from the equation

$$\begin{vmatrix} a - \lambda & -1 & 0 \\ -1 & -\lambda & -1 \\ 0 & -1 & a^2 - \lambda \end{vmatrix} = 0$$

where there is just one parameter a. In this case the mathematical problem is to find $\min_{a}(\lambda_{max})$. We note that there is no explicit formula for λ_{max} as a simple function of a, and our function is the result of a solution of the determinantal equation. For some values of a the function can be calculated easily, $\lambda_{max}(-1) = \sqrt{3}$, $\lambda_{max}(0) = \sqrt{2}$ and $\lambda_{max}(1) = 2$, but any other value requires a considerable amount of work. Calculating the derivative of the function with respect to a is too difficult even to contemplate.

In the determinant example we have a function of a single variable, but in most problems there are many variables. One of the commonest methods of attack is to obtain the maximum or minimum as a *sequence* of single-variable searches. We choose a direction and search in this direction until we have found the optimum of the function in the chosen direction. We then select a new direction and repeat the process. For this to be a successful method, we need to be able to perform single-variable searches very efficiently. This section therefore deals with single-variable problems, and only then in Section 9.4.3 are multivariable techniques discussed. In deciding on a strategy for solution, one crucial point is whether derivatives can or cannot be calculated. In the eigenvalue problem, calculation of the derivative is difficult, and would probably not be attempted. If the derivative can be obtained, however, more information is available, and any numerical method can be speeded up considerably. With the increase in sophistication of computers, this is becoming a less important consideration, since a good numerical approximation to the derivative is usually quite satisfactory.

The basic problem is to determine the maximum of a function $y = f(x)$ that is difficult to evaluate and for which the derivative may or may not be available. The task is performed in two stages: in Stage 1 we bracket the maximum by obtaining x_1 and x_2 such that $x_1 \leqslant x_{max} \leqslant x_2$ as described in Figures 9.9 and 9.10, and in Stage 2 we devise a method that iterates to the maximum to any desired accuracy, as in Figures 9.11 and 9.12.

A **bracket** is most quickly achieved by starting at a given point, taking a step in the increasing direction and proceeding in this direction, doubling the step length at each step until the bracket is obtained (Figure 9.9). The basic idea is summarized in Figure 9.10, which gives a pseudocode procedure for this technique. It is written as a 'stand-alone' segment, but it would normally be incorporated in a more general program. It is assumed that sensible values for a and h have been chosen, but in a working program great care has to be taken. A great deal of effort is required to cope with inappropriate choices and to prevent the program aborting.

Figure 9.9 Bracketing procedure.

(a) {Derivative not known}
    read (keyb, a, h, n)
    it ← 0
    old val ← f(a)
    a ← a + h; val ← f(a)
    repeat
        old old val ← old val; old val ← val
        it ← it + 1; h ← 2*h; a ← a + h
        val ← f(a)
    until (((val < old val) and (old old val < old val)) or (it > n))
    if it > n then write (vdu, no max)
        else write (vdu, 'bracket given by', a − 3h, a)
    end if

(b) {Derivative known} read (keyb, a, h, n)
    it ← 0; deriv ← fdash(a); a ← a + h
    if fdash(a) < 0 then stop else
        repeat
            it ← it + 1
            deriv ← fdash(a)
            h = 2*h; a ← a + h
        until (deriv < 0) or (it > n)
        if (it > n) then write(vdu, 'no max')
        else write (vdu, 'bracket given by', a − 3h/2, a − h).
        endif
    endif

Figure 9.10 Pseudocode for obtaining a bracket for the maximum of $f(x)$. Function segments for $f(a)$ and $fdash(a)$ are declared elsewhere.

The algorithm works very efficiently provided that appropriate safeguards are included, but it is not foolproof. The maximum number of steps chosen, n, is usually 10, and the initial value of h is small compared with the overall dimension of the problem under consideration.

EXAMPLE 9.13   Find a bracket for the first maximum of $f(x) = x \sin x$ using the algorithm in Figure 9.10.

Solution   Choose $a = 0$ and $h = 0.01$; the algorithm then gives

a	0	0.01	0.02	0.04	0.08	0.16	0.32	0.64	1.28	2.56	5.12
f	0	0.000	0.000	0.002	0.006	0.025	0.101	0.382	1.226	1.406	−4.701
f'	0	0.020	0.040	0.080	0.160	0.317	0.618	1.111	1.325	−1.590	—

If the derivative is *not* used then the bracket is $1.28 \leqslant x \leqslant 5.12$.
If the derivative is used then the bracket is $1.28 \leqslant x \leqslant 2.56$.

```
read (keyb, x₁, x₂, x₃, f₁, f₂, f₃, eps)
repeat
    {compute xstar from (9.10)}
    fstar ← f(xstar)
    if fstar > f₂
        then
            if xstar < x₂ then x₃ ← x₂ else x₁ ← x₂
            endif
            x₂ ← xstar
        else
            if xstar < x₂ then x₁ ← xstar else x₃ ← xstar
            endif
    endif
until (abs(x₂ − xstar) < eps)
write (vdu, 'best value', 'x =', xstar, 'f =', fstar)
```

(a)

(b)

Figure 9.11 (a) Pseudocode for the quadratic approximation algorithm; the function segment for $f(x)$ is declared elsewhere.   (b) Diagrams corresponding to the four cases considered in the program.

Stage 2 of the calculation is to use the bracket just obtained and then iterate to an accurate maximum. A simple and efficient approach is to use a **polynomial approximation** to estimate the maximum and then choose the 'best' points to repeat the calculation. The method was discussed briefly in Exercise 5 in Section 8.2.2 of *Modern Engineering Mathematics*.

If it is assumed that *no derivative* is available then a bracket is known from the algorithm of Figure 9.10, so that x_1, x_2, x_3 and the corresponding f_1, f_2, f_3, with $f_1 < f_2$ and $f_3 < f_2$, are given. The *quadratic polynomial* through these points can be written down immediately: it is just the **Lagrange interpolation formula** that was discussed in Section 1.5.1 of *Modern Engineering Mathematics*. It can easily be checked that the quadratic which passes through the required points is given by

$$f \simeq F = \frac{(x - x_1)(x - x_2)}{(x_3 - x_1)(x_3 - x_2)} f_3 + \frac{(x - x_2)(x - x_3)}{(x_1 - x_2)(x_1 - x_3)} f_1$$

$$+ \frac{(x - x_3)(x - x_1)}{(x_2 - x_3)(x_2 - x_1)} f_2 \tag{9.9}$$

Then $F' = 0$ at the point x^*, which is given, after a little algebra, by

$$x^* = \frac{(x_2^2 - x_3^2) f_1 + (x_3^2 - x_1^2) f_2 + (x_1^2 - x_2^2) f_3}{2[(x_2 - x_3) f_1 + (x_3 - x_1) f_2 + (x_1 - x_2) f_3]} \tag{9.10}$$

A pseudocode procedure for the algorithm that uses this new x^* and f^* is given in Figure 9.11, where the *best* three values are chosen for the next iteration.

The method works exceptionally well, but again it is not totally foolproof, and remedial checks need to be put into a working program. The stopping criterion used in the program is based on the difference between the x values. This is not always necessarily the best one to use. The criterion is very problem-dependent, and requires thought and numerical experimentation.

```
read (keyb, x₁, x₂, f₁, f₂, fdash₁, fdash₂, eps)
   repeat at
      {evaluate a,b,c from (9.11)}
      {calculate xstar from 9.12)}
      fstar ← f(xstar); fdashstar ← fdash(xstar)
   if fdashstar > 0        then x₁ ← xstar; f₁ ← fstar;
      fdash₁ ← fdashstar else x₂ ← xstar; f₂ ← fstar;
      fdash₂ ← fdashstar
   endif
   until (abs(f dashstar) < eps)
write (vdu, 'max at', xstar; 'f =', fstar)
```

(a)

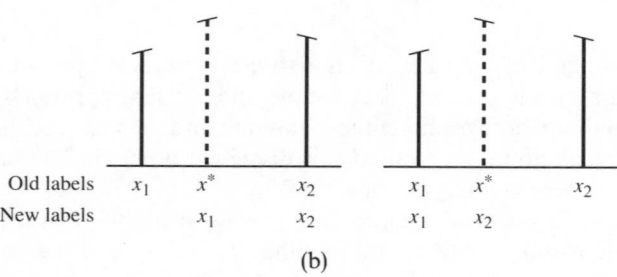

(b)

Figure 9.12 (a) Pseudocode for the cubic approximation algorithm for the maximum of $f(x)$; the function segments $f(x)$ and *fdash*(x) are declared elsewhere. (b) Diagrams corresponding to the two cases considered in the program.

EXAMPLE 9.14   Find the first maximum of $f(x) = x \sin x$ given the values from Example 9.13, namely $x_1 = 1.28$, $x_2 = 2.56$, $x_3 = 5.12$, $f_1 = 1.226$, $f_2 = 1.406$ and $f_3 = -4.701$.

Solution   From (9.10), $x^* = 2.03$ and $f^* = 1.820$, so for the next iteration choose

$$x_1 = 1.28, \qquad x_2 = 2.03, \qquad x_3 = 2.56$$
$$f_1 = 1.226, \qquad f_2 = 1.820, \qquad f_3 = 1.406$$

From (9.10), $x^* = 1.98$ and $f^* = 1.816$, so for the next iteration choose

$$x_1 = 1.98, \qquad x_2 = 2.03, \qquad x_3 = 2.56$$
$$f_1 = 1.816, \qquad f_2 = 1.820, \qquad f_3 = 1.406$$

From (9.10), $x^* = 2.027$ and $f^* = 1.820$, so the method has almost converged.

When the *derivative* is available, a better approximating polynomial than (9.9) can be used, since $x_1, f_1, f_1' (> 0), x_2, f_2$ and $f'_2 (< 0)$ are known from the bracketing algorithm, and this data can be fitted to a *cubic polynomial*

$$f \simeq F = ax^3 + bx^2 + cx + d$$
$$F' = 3ax^2 + 2bx + c$$

In this case fitting the values just gives the matrix equation

$$\begin{bmatrix} f_1 \\ f_2 \\ f_1' \\ f_2' \end{bmatrix} = \begin{bmatrix} x_1^3 & x_1^2 & x_1 & 1 \\ x_2^3 & x_2^2 & x_2 & 1 \\ 3x_1^2 & 2x_1 & 1 & 0 \\ 3x_2^2 & 2x_2 & 1 & 0 \end{bmatrix} \begin{bmatrix} a \\ b \\ c \\ d \end{bmatrix} \tag{9.11}$$

and the maximum of F is given by $F' = 0$, so that

$$x^* = \frac{-b \pm (b^2 - 3ac)^{1/2}}{3a} \tag{9.12}$$

and the negative sign is chosen (the positive sign for a minimum problem) to ensure that $x_1 < x^* < x_2$.

A simple algorithm uses these results to choose the appropriate bracket for the next iteration. The algorithm is illustrated in Figure 9.12, and is an efficient iterative way of evaluating the maximum. Unfortunately it is very easy to make errors in a hand computation, and many people prefer the quadratic algorithm for this purpose. On a computer, however, the cubic approximation method is almost universally used.

EXAMPLE 9.15   Find the first maximum of $f(x) = x \sin x$ given the bracket values from Example 9.13, namely $x_1 = 1.28$, $f_1 = 1.226$, $f_1' = 1.325$, and $x_2 = 2.56$, $f_2 = 1.406$, $f_2' = -1.590$.

Solution   Solving (9.11) gives $a = -0.3328$, $b = 0.7783$ and $c = 0.9683$, and hence, from (9.12),

$$x^* = 2.036, \qquad f^* = 1.820, \qquad f^{*\prime} = -0.0184$$

Thus x_2, f_2 and f_2' are replaced by x^*, f^* and $f^{*\prime}$, and x_1, f_1 and f_1' are retained. Equation (9.11) is now recomputed and solved to give

$$a = -0.4635, \qquad b = 1.417, \qquad c = -0.0242$$

Hence, from (9.12),

$$x^* = 2.030, \qquad f^* = 1.820, \qquad f^{*\prime} = -0.0021$$

Further iterations may be performed to get an even more accurate value. Comparison with Example 9.14 shows that both the quadratic and cubic algorithms work well for this function.

9.4.2   Exercises

25 (a) Find a bracket for the minimum of the function $f(x) = x + 1/x^2$. Start at $x = 0.1$ and $h = 0.2$.

(b) Use two cycles of the quadratic approximation to obtain an estimate of the minimum.

(c) Use one cycle of the cubic approximation to obtain an estimate of the minimum.

26 The function

$$f = \frac{\sin x}{1 + x^2}$$

has been computed as follows:

x	-0.5	0	1	3
f	-0.3825	0	0.4207	0.0141
f'	0.3952	1	-0.1506	-0.1075

Compare the brackets, obtained from the bracketing procedure, to be used in calculating the maximum of the function: (a) without using the derivatives, and (b) using the derivatives. Use these brackets to perform one iteration of each of the quadratic and the cubic algorithms. Compare the values obtained from the two calculations.

27 Starting with the bracket $1 < x < 3$, determine an approximation to the maximum of the function

$$f(x) = x(e^{-x} - e^{-2x})$$

(a) using two iterations of the quadratic algorithm, and

(b) using two iterations of the cubic algorithm.

28 (Harder) Use the quadratic algorithm to obtain an estimate of the value of x that gives the minimum value to the largest root of the eigenvalue equation (that is, $\min_x [\lambda_{\max}(x)]$)

$$\begin{vmatrix} x - \lambda & -1 & 0 \\ -1 & -\lambda & -1 \\ 0 & -1 & x^2 - \lambda \end{vmatrix} = 0$$

Use the bracket given by $x = 1$ and $x = -1$.

29 Show that if $x_1 = x_2 - h$ and $x_3 = x_2 + h$ then

(9.10) reduces to

$$x^* = x_2 + \tfrac{1}{2}h\frac{f_1 - f_3}{f_1 - 2f_2 + f_3}$$

(*Note*: This provides a better hand computation method than the Lagrange interpolation approach. The best x value is chosen and h is replaced by $\tfrac{1}{2}h$ after each step.) Show that this formula is a numerical form of the Newton–Raphson method applied to the equation $f'(x) = 0$.

9.4.3 Simple multivariable searches

As indicated in Section 9.4.1, many multivariable search methods use a sequence of single-variable searches to achieve a maximum. The fundamental question is how to choose a sensible direction in which to search for the top of the hill with a very limited amount of local information. The problem can be visualized when no derivatives are available as sitting in a dense fog and trying to get to the top of the hill with only an altimeter available. If derivatives are available then the fog has lifted a little, and we can now see a few feet around, so that at least we can see which is the uphill direction. The criteria for choosing a direction are (a) an easy choice of direction and (b) one that gives an efficient climbing method. This is not a simple task, and although the methods described in this section are rarely used nowadays, they do provide the basis for more advanced methods. Modern methods are difficult to program, not because the basic method is difficult but because of the vast amount of remedial action that must be taken to prevent the program failing when something goes wrong. The general advice here is to understand the basic idea behind the method and then to implement it using a program from a reliable software library such as NAG (distributed by Numerical Algorithms Group Ltd of Oxford, UK).

Perhaps the most obvious method of choosing a search direction is to use the locally steepest direction. For the function $f(x_1, x_2, \ldots, x_n)$ this is known to be in the gradient direction $\boldsymbol{G} = \operatorname{grad} f = [\partial f/\partial x_1 \quad \partial f/\partial x_2 \quad \ldots \quad \partial f/\partial x_n]$. If the derivatives are not available then in current practice they are evaluated numerically.

The gradient direction can be easily proved to give the maximum change. From a given point $(a_1, \ldots, a_n)$, we proceed in the direction $(h_1, h_2, \ldots, h_n)$ with given step length h so that $h_1^2 + h_2^2 + \ldots + h_n^2 = h^2$. We then require

$$\max F = f(a_1 + h_1, \ldots, a_n + h_n) - f(a_1, \ldots, a_n)$$

subject to the constraint

$$h_1^2 + \ldots + h_n^2 = h^2$$

The problem is one of Lagrange multipliers, so

$$0 = \frac{\partial F}{\partial h_i} - \lambda 2 h_i = \frac{\partial f}{\partial h_i} - 2\lambda h_i \quad (i = 1, \ldots, n)$$

Thus

$$\frac{\partial f}{\partial h_i} = \frac{\partial f}{\partial x_i} = 2\lambda h_i \quad (i = 1, \ldots, n)$$

read (keyb, a₁,..., aₙ)
   repeat
      {evaluate f(**a**) and $G_1 = \partial f/\partial x_1, G_2 = \partial f/\partial x_2, \ldots$}
      {maximize g(t) in (9.13) by the cubic algorithm
         to give a new point $\mathbf{a} \leftarrow \mathbf{a} + t_{max}\mathbf{G}$}
   until {**G** = 0}

Figure 9.13 Steepest-ascent algorithm.

and hence

$$[h_1, h_2, \ldots, h_n] \quad \text{is proportional to} \quad \left[\frac{\partial f}{\partial x_1}, \ldots, \frac{\partial f}{\partial x_n} \right] = \mathbf{G}$$

The method of **steepest ascent** (or **steepest descent**, for minima) then proceeds from the point **a** by choosing the gradient direction **G** (or −**G** for minima) for a search direction. We therefore need to find

$$\max_{t} \{g(t) = f(a_1 + tG_1, a_2 + tG_2, \ldots, a_n + tG_n)\} \tag{9.13}$$

Since (9.13) is a function of a single variable t, the methods of Section 9.4.1 are appropriate, and we should expect the cubic algorithm to be used in the optimization. Once the best available point in the search direction has been found, $\mathbf{a} + t_{max}\mathbf{G}$, the new gradient direction is computed and the whole process is repeated. The algorithm is fairly straightforward, and is summarized in Figure 9.13.

The steepest-ascent (or descent) method has the great advantage of being simple and secure, but it has the disadvantage of being very slow, particularly near to the optimum. It is rarely used nowadays, but does form the basis of the hill climbing methods described in Section 9.4.5.

EXAMPLE 9.16 Find the maximum of the function

$$f(x_1, x_2) = -(x_1 - 1)^4 - (x_1 - x_2)^2$$

by the steepest-ascent method, starting at the point $(0, 0)$.

Solution It is clear that $(1, 1)$ gives the maximum, but this example is used to illustrate the basic method. The gradient is easily calculated from the partial derivatives

$$\frac{\partial f}{\partial x_1} = -4(x_1 - 1)^3 - 2(x_1 - x_2), \qquad \frac{\partial f}{\partial x_2} = 2(x_1 - x_2)$$

Cycle 1: At the point $(0, 0)$, $f = -1$, $\mathbf{G} = [4 \quad 0]$, the search direction is $x_1 = 4t$, $x_2 = 0$, and we require

$$\max_{t} \{g(t) = -(4t - 1)^4 - 16t^2\}$$

This can be calculated as $t_{max} = 0.102\,56$, so that we can start Cycle 2.

Cycle 2: Here $x = (0.410\,25, 0)$, $f = -0.259$ and $G = [0 \quad 0.8205]$. The next search is in the direction $x_1 = 0.410\,25$, $x_2 = 0.8205t$, and we require

$$\max_t \{g(t) = -0.1210 - (0.410\,25 - 0.8205t)^2\}$$

This has the obvious solution $t_{max} = \frac{1}{2}$, so that we can move to Cycle 3.

Cycle 3: Here $x = (0.410\,25, 0.410\,25)$, $f = -0.1210$, and $G = [0.8205 \quad 0]$.

The calculation can be continued until $G = 0$ to the required accuracy.

There are one or two points to note from this calculation. The function value is steadily increasing, which is a good feature of the method, but after the first few iterations the method progresses in a large number of very small steps. The successive search directions are parallel to the axes, and hence are perpendicular to each other. This perpendicularity is just a restatement of the known result that the gradient vector is perpendicular to the contours (see Section 7.2.1). In Example 9.16 the function $g(t)$ is written down explicitly for clarity. In practice on a computer this would not be done, since once the search direction has been established, x_1 and x_2 are known functions of t only, and by the chain rule we have

$$\frac{dg}{dt} = \frac{\partial f}{\partial x_1}\frac{dx_1}{dt} + \frac{\partial f}{\partial x_2}\frac{dx_2}{dt} = \frac{\partial f}{\partial x_1}G_1 + \frac{\partial f}{\partial x_2}G_2$$

Since x_1 and x_2 are known, both $\partial f/\partial x_1$ and $\partial f/\partial x_2$ can be calculated, and $G = [G_1 \quad G_2]$ is the known search direction; therefore dg/dt is computed without explicitly writing down the function g.

The major criticism of the steepest-ascent method is that it is slow to converge, and so the question arises as to how it can be speeded up. It is well known that Newton–Raphson methods (see Section 8.5.5 of *Modern Engineering Mathematics*) converge very rapidly, so the same basic idea is tried for these problems. It is convenient to employ matrix notation, and indeed most multidimensional optimization methods are written in matrix form. This gives a compact notation, and arrays appear naturally in computer languages.

Taylor's theorem (see Section 9.4 of *Modern Engineering Mathematics*) can be written in matrix form to second order as

$$f(a_1 + h_1, \ldots, a_n + h_n) \simeq f(a_1, \ldots, a_n) + h^T G + \tfrac{1}{2}h^T Jh \tag{9.14}$$

where

$$h = \begin{bmatrix} h_1 \\ \vdots \\ h_n \end{bmatrix}, \quad G = \begin{bmatrix} \dfrac{\partial f}{\partial x_1} \\ \vdots \\ \dfrac{\partial f}{\partial x_n} \end{bmatrix}, \quad J = \begin{bmatrix} \dfrac{\partial^2 f}{\partial x_1^2} & \cdots & \dfrac{\partial^2 f}{\partial x_1\,\partial x_n} \\ \vdots & & \vdots \\ \dfrac{\partial^2 f}{\partial x_n\,\partial x_1} & \cdots & \dfrac{\partial^2 f}{\partial x_n^2} \end{bmatrix}$$

The form (9.14) can be verified by multiplying out the matrices and comparing with the standard form of Taylor's theorem. The vector G is just the gradient vector and J is an $n \times n$ symmetric matrix of second derivatives called the **Hessian matrix**.

The **Newton method** takes (9.14) as an approximation to f, finds the maximum (or minimum) of the quadratic approximation, and uses this best value to start the cycle again.

The optimum of (9.14) is given by $\partial f/\partial h_i = 0$ $(i = 1, 2, \ldots, n)$. The first of these conditions gives

$$0 = \frac{\partial f}{\partial h_1} = [1 \quad 0 \quad 0 \quad \ldots \quad 0]G + \tfrac{1}{2}[1 \quad 0 \quad \ldots \quad 0]Jh + \tfrac{1}{2}h^{\mathrm{T}}J\begin{bmatrix}1\\0\\0\\\vdots\\0\end{bmatrix} \qquad (9.15)$$

Noting that, since J is symmetric, for any vectors a and b we have

$$a^{\mathrm{T}}Jb = (a^{\mathrm{T}}Jb)^{\mathrm{T}} = b^{\mathrm{T}}Ja$$

and hence (9.15) can be written as

$$0 = [1 \quad 0 \quad 0 \quad \ldots \quad 0](G + Jh)$$

Similarly for the other components we obtain

$$0 = [0 \quad 1 \quad 0 \quad \ldots \quad 0](G + Jh)$$
$$\vdots \qquad\qquad \vdots$$
$$0 = [0 \quad 0 \quad 0 \quad \ldots \quad 1](G + Jh)$$

The only way to satisfy this set of equations is to have

$$G + Jh = 0$$

and hence

$$h = -J^{-1}G$$

The basic algorithm is now very straightforward, as indicated in Figure 9.14.

repeat
{a_i known, calculate G_i, J_i}
{evaluate $a_{i+1} = a_i - J_i^{-1}G_i$}
until {sufficient accuracy}

Figure 9.14 Newton algorithm.

When Newton's algorithm of Figure 9.14 converges, it does so very rapidly and satisfies our request for a fast method. Unfortunately it is very unreliable, particularly for higher-dimensional problems, unless the starting value is close to the maximum. The reason for this is fairly clear. The analysis given only uses the necessary condition for a maximum, but it would apply equally well to a minimum or saddle point. In multidimensional problems saddle points are abundant, and the usual failure of the Newton method is that it proceeds towards a distant saddle point and then diverges.

EXAMPLE 9.17   Use Newton's method to find the maximum of

$$A = (h + b + 10)\left(\frac{2\,272\,000}{hb} + 2b + 5\right)$$

Solution   Here we have returned to the 'milk carton' problem of Example 9.2. We can calculate

$$\frac{\partial A}{\partial h} = \left(\frac{2\,272\,000}{hb} + 2b + 5\right) - (h + b + 10)\frac{2\,272\,000}{h^2 b}$$

$$\frac{\partial A}{\partial b} = \left(\frac{2\,272\,000}{hb} + 2b + 5\right) + (h + b + 10)\left(-\frac{2\,272\,000}{hb^2} + 2\right)$$

$$\frac{\partial^2 A}{\partial h^2} = 2(b + 10)\frac{2\,272\,000}{h^3 b}$$

$$\frac{\partial^2 A}{\partial b\,\partial h} = 2 + \frac{10 \times 2\,272\,000}{h^2 b^2}$$

$$\frac{\partial^2 A}{\partial b^2} = 4 + \frac{2 \times 2\,272\,000(h + 10)}{hb^3}$$

Iteration 1

$$a = \begin{bmatrix} 100 \\ 100 \end{bmatrix}, \quad G = \begin{bmatrix} -44.92 \\ 375.1 \end{bmatrix}, \quad J = \begin{bmatrix} 4.998 & 2.227 \\ 2.227 & 8.998 \end{bmatrix}$$

$$a_{\text{new}} = \begin{bmatrix} 100 \\ 100 \end{bmatrix} - \begin{bmatrix} 0.2249 & -0.0557 \\ -0.0557 & 0.1249 \end{bmatrix}\begin{bmatrix} -44.92 \\ 375.1 \end{bmatrix} = \begin{bmatrix} 131 \\ 50.6 \end{bmatrix}$$

Iteration 2

$$a = \begin{bmatrix} 131 \\ 50.6 \end{bmatrix}, \quad G = \begin{bmatrix} -52.3 \\ -465.7 \end{bmatrix}, \quad J = \begin{bmatrix} 2.421 & 2.517 \\ 2.517 & 41.75 \end{bmatrix}$$

$$a_{\text{new}} = \begin{bmatrix} 131 \\ 50.6 \end{bmatrix} - \begin{bmatrix} -0.4407 & -0.0266 \\ -0.0266 & 0.0255 \end{bmatrix}\begin{bmatrix} -52.3 \\ 465.7 \end{bmatrix} = \begin{bmatrix} 141.7 \\ 61.1 \end{bmatrix}$$

Iteration 3

$$a = \begin{bmatrix} 141.7 \\ 61.1 \end{bmatrix}, \qquad G = \begin{bmatrix} -4.493 \\ -98.76 \end{bmatrix}, \qquad J = \begin{bmatrix} -1.858 & -2.303 \\ 2.303 & 25.33 \end{bmatrix}$$

$$a_{\text{new}} = \begin{bmatrix} 141.7 \\ 61.1 \end{bmatrix} - \begin{bmatrix} 0.6067 & -0.0552 \\ -0.0552 & 0.0445 \end{bmatrix} \begin{bmatrix} -4.493 \\ -98.76 \end{bmatrix} = \begin{bmatrix} 139 \\ 65.2 \end{bmatrix}$$

The iterations converge very rapidly; $h = 139, b = 65$ is not far from the solution, and gives $A = 827\,\text{cm}^2$.

9.4.4 Exercises

30 Follow the first two complete cycles in the steepest-descent algorithm for finding the minimum of the function

$$f(x_1, x_2) = x^{\text{T}} \begin{bmatrix} 1 \\ 0 \end{bmatrix} + \tfrac{1}{2} x^{\text{T}} \begin{bmatrix} 1 & -1 \\ -1 & 2 \end{bmatrix} x$$

starting at $a = \begin{bmatrix} 1 \\ 1 \end{bmatrix}$.

31 Show that the function

$$f(x, y) = 2(x + y)^2 + (x - y)^2 + 3x + 2y$$

has a minimum at the point $(-\tfrac{7}{16}, -\tfrac{3}{16})$.
Starting at the point $(0, 0)$, use one iteration of

the steepest-descent algorithm to determine an approximation to the minimum point. Show that one iteration of Newton's method yields the minimum point from *any* starting point.

32 Use one complete cycle of the steepest-ascent method to find the maximum of the function

$$f(x, y, z) = -(x - y + z)^2 - (2x + z - 2)^2 - z^4$$

starting from $(2, 2, 2)$.

33 Minimize the function

$$f(x, y, z) = (x - y + z)^2 + (2x + z - 2)^2 + z^4$$

by Newton's method. Complete one cycle of the iteration, starting at $(2, 2, 2)$.

9.4.5 Advanced multivariable searches

To overcome the problems of evaluating second derivatives, which are rarely available, and of the unreliability of the Newton method, but to use its speed of convergence, several methods were produced in the early 1960s. Two have survived and are now the methods currently available in most program libraries. **Conjugate-gradient methods** give one approach, but these will not be described here. We shall look at a method due to Davidon, commonly called **DFP** (after Davidon, Fletcher and Powell, who developed the method) or **quasi-Newton methods**. There is a whole class of such methods, but only one will be studied.

The basic idea of the DFP method is to look for the *minimum* of the function $f(x_1, \ldots, x_n)$ with gradient $G = [\partial f / \partial x_1 \quad \partial f / \partial x_2 \quad \ldots \quad \partial f / \partial x_n]^{\text{T}}$ by iterating with a matrix H_i, which will be updated at each iteration, so that

read {initial values $\mathbf{x}_0, \mathbf{H}_0 = \mathbf{I}$}
    {calculate the gradient $\mathbf{G}_0$ and f_0}
repeat
    {Find $\min_{\lambda} f(\mathbf{x}_i - \lambda \mathbf{H}_i \mathbf{G}_i)$, by the cubic algorithm}
    {Put $\mathbf{x}_{i+1} = \mathbf{x}_i - \lambda_{\min} \mathbf{H}_i \mathbf{G}_i$}
    {Calculate f_{i+1}, $\mathbf{G}_{i+1}$ and hence $\mathbf{h}_i = \mathbf{x}_{i+1} - \mathbf{x}_i$
       and $\mathbf{y}_i = \mathbf{G}_{i+1} - \mathbf{G}_i$}
    {Update $\mathbf{H}_i$ to $\mathbf{H}_{i+1}$ by (9.19)}
until {sufficient accuracy}

Figure 9.15 DFP algorithm for the minimum of $f(x_1, x_2, \ldots, x_n)$.

$$a_{i+1} = a_i - \lambda H_i G_i \tag{9.16}$$

The reliable but slow steepest-descent method chooses $H_i = I$, the unit matrix, and $\lambda = \lambda_{\min}$, while the less reliable but fast Newton method chooses $H_i = J_i^{-1}$ and $\lambda = 1$. Thus the idea is to compute a sequence of H_i so that $H_0 = I$ and $H_i \to J^{-1}$ as the minimum is approached. The basic analysis required to implement this scheme is quite difficult and beyond the scope of this book, so only the briefest of outlines will be given. For a quadratic function

$$f = c + x_i^T G + \tfrac{1}{2} x_i^T J x_i$$

at two successive points the gradient is given by

$$G_i = G + J x_i$$

$$G_{i+1} = G + J x_{i+1}$$

so, subtracting,

$$G_{i+1} - G_i = J(x_{i+1} - x_i)$$

Writing $h_i = x_{i+1} - x_i$ and $y_i = G_{i+1} - G_i$ and working on the assumption that $H_i J = I$ since we require $H_i \to J^{-1}$, we obtain

$$H_i y_i = H_i J h_i = h_i \tag{9.17}$$

It is found to be impossible to satisfy (9.17) unless an exact solution is known, so the next best thing is to satisfy (9.17) one step behind as

$$H_{i+1} y_i = h_i \tag{9.18}$$

There is a whole class of matrices that satisfy the key equation (9.18) but only the original Davidon matrix (and still one of the best) is quoted here, namely

$$H_{i+1} = H_i - \frac{H_i y_i y_i^T H_i}{y_i^T H_i y_i} + \frac{h_i h_i^T}{h_i^T y_i} \tag{9.19}$$

It can be shown that for a quadratic function this sequence of Hs produces J^{-1} in n iterations, where n is the dimension of the problem. The basic algorithm is described in Figure 9.15 for the minimum of a general function $f(x_1, \ldots, x_n)$ with gradient $G = [\partial f/\partial x_1 \quad \cdots \quad \partial f/\partial x_n]^T$.

This method was a major breakthrough in the early 1960s, and is still one of the best and most reliable available. Proofs of convergence and computational experience are available in advanced texts on optimization. To repeat a word of warning: these programs are very long and tedious to write because of the large amount of checking and remedial work that has to be inserted to prevent the program stopping. Such programs are available in software libraries, and these should be used.

EXAMPLE 9.18   Use the DFP method to find the minimum of

$$f(x, y) = (x - y - 1)^4 + (2x + y - 5)^2$$

starting at $(0, 0)$.

Solution   Note that only the first derivatives

$$G = \begin{bmatrix} 4(x - y - 1)^3 + 4(2x + y - 5) \\ -4(x - y - 1)^3 + 2(2x + y - 5) \end{bmatrix}$$

are required in this method.

Iteration 1

$$a_0 = \begin{bmatrix} 0 \\ 0 \end{bmatrix}, \qquad G_0 = \begin{bmatrix} -24 \\ -6 \end{bmatrix}, \qquad H_0 = \begin{bmatrix} 1 & 0 \\ 0 & 1 \end{bmatrix}, \quad f_0 = 26$$

and we search in the direction

$$a = \begin{bmatrix} 0 \\ 0 \end{bmatrix} - \lambda \begin{bmatrix} 1 & 0 \\ 0 & 1 \end{bmatrix} \begin{bmatrix} -24 \\ -6 \end{bmatrix} = \begin{bmatrix} 24\lambda \\ 6\lambda \end{bmatrix}$$

for a minimum of f, that is, we search for

$$\min_{\lambda} \{(18\lambda - 1)^4 + (54\lambda - 5)^2\}$$

The cubic algorithm gives $\lambda_{\min} = 0.089\,72$, so

$$a_1 = \begin{bmatrix} 2.153 \\ 0.538 \end{bmatrix}, \qquad G_1 = \begin{bmatrix} 0.306 \\ -1.241 \end{bmatrix}$$

$$h_0 = \begin{bmatrix} 2.153 \\ 0.538 \end{bmatrix}, \qquad y_0 = \begin{bmatrix} 24.31 \\ 4.76 \end{bmatrix}$$

Thus

$$H_1 = \begin{bmatrix} 1 & 0 \\ 0 & 1 \end{bmatrix} - \frac{1}{613.4} \begin{bmatrix} 24.31 \\ 4.76 \end{bmatrix} [24.31 \quad 4.76] + \frac{1}{54.89} \begin{bmatrix} 2.153 \\ 0.538 \end{bmatrix} [2.153 \quad 0.538]$$

$$= \begin{bmatrix} 0.1214 & -0.1675 \\ -0.1675 & 0.9684 \end{bmatrix}$$

Iteration 2

$$a_1 = \begin{bmatrix} 2.153 \\ 0.538 \end{bmatrix}, \quad G_1 = \begin{bmatrix} 0.306 \\ -1.241 \end{bmatrix}, \quad H_1 = \begin{bmatrix} 0.1214 & -0.1675 \\ -0.1675 & 0.9684 \end{bmatrix}, \quad f_1 = 0.167$$

We now search in the direction

$$a = \begin{bmatrix} 2.153 \\ 0.538 \end{bmatrix} - \lambda \begin{bmatrix} 0.1214 & -0.1675 \\ -0.1675 & 0.9684 \end{bmatrix} \begin{bmatrix} 0.306 \\ -1.241 \end{bmatrix} = \begin{bmatrix} 2.153 - 0.2449\lambda \\ 0.538 + 1.2525\lambda \end{bmatrix}$$

and the cubic algorithm gives $\lambda_{min} = 0.272$. We can now compute the next point and its gradient as

$$a_2 = \begin{bmatrix} 2.086 \\ 0.879 \end{bmatrix}, \qquad G_2 = \begin{bmatrix} 0.2427 \\ 0.0678 \end{bmatrix}$$

and then calculate the vectors

$$h_1 = \begin{bmatrix} -0.0666 \\ 0.3407 \end{bmatrix}, \qquad y_1 = \begin{bmatrix} -0.0636 \\ 1.3083 \end{bmatrix}, \qquad H_1 y_1 = \begin{bmatrix} -0.2269 \\ 1.2776 \end{bmatrix}$$

The new Davidon matrix is calculated from (9.19) as

$$H_2 = \begin{bmatrix} 0.1007 & -0.0460 \\ -0.0460 & 0.2582 \end{bmatrix}$$

Iteration 3

$$a_2 = \begin{bmatrix} 2.086 \\ 0.879 \end{bmatrix}, \quad G_2 = \begin{bmatrix} 0.2427 \\ 0.0678 \end{bmatrix}, \quad H_2 = \begin{bmatrix} 0.1007 & -0.0460 \\ -0.0460 & 0.2582 \end{bmatrix}, \quad f = 0.0044$$

The iterations continue until convergence at $x = 2$ and $y = 1$.

To compare the three methods considered above, we apply them to the same function

$$f(x, y) = 100(y^2 - x)^2 + (1 - x)^2$$

By plotting the contours of the function as in Figure 9.16 and superimposing the paths followed by the three methods, we can compare their performance. We start from $(-0.6, 1)$. The Newton and DFP methods converge to 5 figures of accuracy in 6 and 18 iterations respectively, while the steepest-descent method has not converged in 40 iterations. The following table gives some indication of the way the methods progress for this example:

Iteration	5	10	15	20
Newton	(1, 0.998)	Converged		
DFP	(0.012, 1.026)	(0.791, 0.608)	(0.992, 0.982)	Converged
Steepest-descent	(−0.788, 0.632)	(−0.768, 0.587)	—	(−0.718, 0.513)

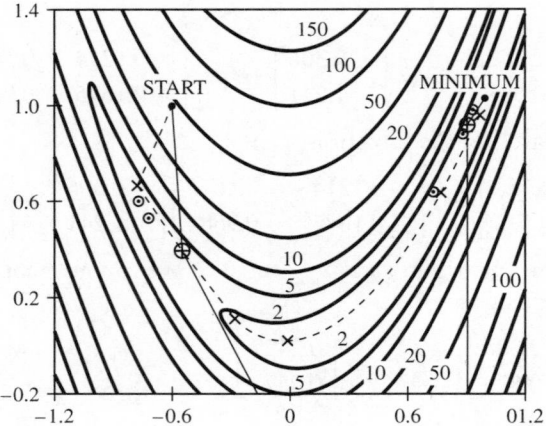

Figure 9.16 Minimum of the function $f = 100(y^2 - x)^2 + (1 - x)^2$: $\oplus$————$\oplus$, Newton's method at iterations 1, 2 (off diagram), 3, 6; $\times$————$\times$, DFP method at iterations 1, 2, 5, 10, 15; $\odot$......$\odot$, Steepest descent at iterations 10, 20, 21, 30, 40.

A major development since the 1970s has been in devising modifications that avoid the line searches. It was found that the latter were very time-consuming, so there was great pressure to avoid them. The searches were replaced by a single step in the search direction and, provided that the function value is reduced by a sufficient amount, this is accepted for recalculation of **H**. To be efficient, the method requires a variant of the DFP updating, and it needs more care when failures occur; it is, however, one of the most competitive methods available.

The early development of numerical optimization algorithms led to very distinct methods for cases when derivatives were or were not available. As computers developed in speed, this difference became less necessary, since derivatives could be calculated very rapidly by a numerical method. The only difference between the two cases in modern programs is that the quadratic or cubic algorithms are used for the line searches in the two cases. A DFP-type algorithm or a conjugate-gradient method (mentioned earlier) is then used to iterate to the minimum.

Adapting methods to deal with constraints is of intense interest in practice, and has been a major thrust in the subject. For fully nonlinear problems with nonlinear constraints the practical difficulties are very severe, and the production of efficient, robust programs is at a premium. If the constraints are all linear then the problem is easier, and methods of projection onto 'active' constraints reduce it to an unconstrained problem of the type discussed in this section. When the function and the constraints are all linear we have the linear programming problem of Section 9.2.

9.4.6   Exercises

34 Minimize the following functions by the DFP method, completing two cycles:

(a) $f(x, y) = (x - y)^2 + 4(x - 1)^2$, starting at $(2, 2)$;

(b) $f(x, y, z) = (x - y + z)^2 + (2x + z - 2)^2 + z^4$, starting at $(0, 0, 0)$.

35 Show that the updating formula

$$H_{i+1} = H_i + \frac{(h_i - H_i y_i)(h_i - H_i y_i)^T}{(h_i - H_i y_i)^T y_i}$$

satisfies (9.18). Follow the DFP method through for two cycles, but using this update for H, on the functions

(a) $x^2 + 2y^2$, starting at $(1, 2)$;

(b) $x^2 + y^2 + 2z^4$, starting at $(1, 2, 3)$.

36 Show that the update formula (with suffixes suppressed)

$$H' = H + vp^T - Huq^T$$

satisfies the basic quasi-Newton equation (9.18)

$$H'u = v$$

where p and q are vectors satisfying

$$p^Tu = 1, \qquad q^Tu = 1$$

but are otherwise arbitrary.

By making a suitable choice of α, β and α', β' in the expressions

$$p = \alpha v + \beta Hu$$

$$q = \alpha'v + \beta'Hu$$

show that the Davidon formula (9.19) and the formula in Exercise 35 can be obtained.

9.5   Engineering application: chemical processing plant

A chemical processing plant consists of a main processing unit and two recovery units. Chemicals A and B are fed into the plant, and produce a maximum output of $100\,t\,day^{-1}$ of material C. The effluent stream is rich in chemical B, which can be recovered from the primary and secondary recovery units. The total recovered, when at full throughput, is $10\,t\,day^{-1}$ of pure B, and it is fed back into the incoming stream of chemical B. The process is illustrated in Figure 9.17; the numbers in

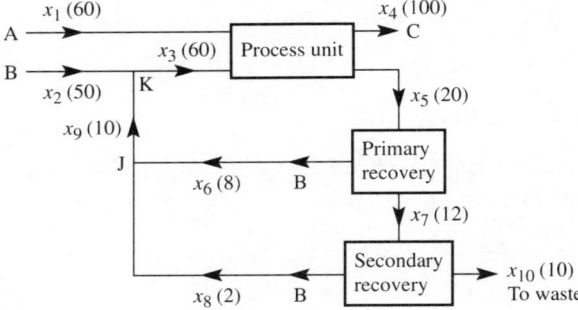

Figure 9.17 Schematic diagram of a chemical processing plant. The numbers in parentheses give the maximum flow.

parentheses indicate the maximum flow (in $t\,day^{-1}$) that can be sent down the pipes, and the x_i indicate the actual flow (in $t\,day^{-1}$).

The chemistry of the process implies that the chemicals must be mixed in given ratios. For the present system it is found that

$$x_1:x_3 = 1:1, \quad x_1:x_4 = 3:5, \quad x_1:x_5 = 3:1, \quad x_5:x_7 = 5:3$$

$$x_5:x_6 = 5:2, \quad x_7:x_8 = 6:1 \quad x_7:x_{10} = 6:5$$

must be maintained for any flow through the system. Chemical A costs $£100\,t^{-1}$, chemical B costs $£120\,t^{-1}$ and chemical C sells for $£220\,t^{-1}$. The running costs are as follows:

	Variable costs	Fixed costs
Process unit	$£70\,t^{-1}$ of product	$£500\,day^{-1}$
Primary recovery	$£30\,t^{-1}$ of input	$£200\,day^{-1}$
Secondary recovery	$£40\,t^{-1}$ of input	$£100\,day^{-1}$
Disposal of waste	$£30\,t^{-1}$	
Indirect cost		$£400\,day^{-1}$

It is required to find the most profitable operating policy that can be achieved.

The profit can be written down for a day's production as

$$z = -(\text{fixed costs}) + (\text{profit from sale of C}) - (\text{costs of chemicals A and B})$$

$$- (\text{process unit costs}) - (\text{primary unit costs}) - (\text{secondary unit costs})$$

$$- (\text{waste product costs})$$

$$= -1200 + (220x_4) - (100x_1 + 120x_2)$$

$$- (70x_4) - (30x_5) - (40x_7)$$

$$- 13x_{10}$$

$$z = -1200 - 10x_1 - 120x_2 + 150x_4$$

$$- 30x_5 - 40x_7 - 30x_{10}$$

The constraints on the flow, given by the maximum throughput, are

$$x_1 \leqslant 60, \quad x_2 \leqslant 50, \quad x_3 \leqslant 60, \quad x_4 \leqslant 100, \quad x_5 \leqslant 20, \quad x_6 \leqslant 8, \quad x_7 \leqslant 12,$$

$$x_8 \leqslant 2, \quad x_9 \leqslant 10, \quad x_{10} \leqslant 10$$

The constraints on the chemistry given by the fixed ratios can be written in a convenient form as

$$x_1 - x_3 = 0, \quad 5x_1 - 3x_4 = 0, \quad x_1 - 3x_5 = 0$$

$$3x_5 - 5x_7 = 0, \quad 2x_5 - 5x_6 = 0$$

$$x_7 - 6x_8 = 0, \quad 5x_7 - 6x_{10} = 0$$

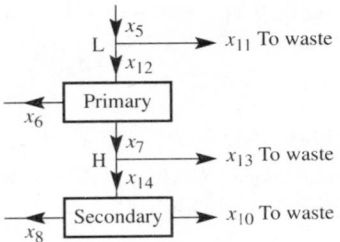

Figure 9.18 Modification to the chemical processing plant.

Finally, at the junctions J and K, continuity (what flows in equals what flows out) gives

$$x_6 + x_8 - x_9 = 0, \qquad x_2 + x_9 - x_3 = 0$$

The problem thus has 10 variables, 10 inequality constraints and 9 equality constraints. The choice is whether to use the equality constraints to eliminate some of the variables or just to treat the 19 constraints directly by LP. The equations are sufficiently simple to solve for the variables as

$$x_2 = \tfrac{5}{6}x_1, \qquad x_3 = x_1, \qquad x_4 = \tfrac{5}{3}x_1, \qquad x_5 = \tfrac{1}{3}x_1,$$

$$x_6 = \tfrac{2}{15}x_1, \qquad x_7 = \tfrac{1}{5}x_1, \qquad x_8 = \tfrac{1}{30}x_1, \qquad x_9 = \tfrac{2}{15}x_1$$

$$x_{10} = \tfrac{1}{6}x_1, \qquad z = 27x_1 - 1200$$

Thus x_1 must be as large as possible, that is, at the value 60, giving a maximum of £420 day^{-1}. We must check that all the constraints are satisfied, and indeed this is the case. It is easily seen that each variable reaches its maximum possible value indicated in Figure 9.17.

However, as soon as we look at variations on the problem, since it becomes less clear whether to eliminate or just to use LP directly on the equations given. For instance a very sensible question is whether it is worth using the primary or secondary recovery units. We can consider this question by allowing a portion to go to waste (at the same cost given previously), as indicated in Figure 9.18.

We add to the previous continuity equations similar equations for the junctions L and H:

$$x_5 - x_{11} - x_{12} = 0$$

$$x_7 - x_{13} - x_{14} = 0$$

The inputs to the primary and secondary units are now x_{12} and x_{14}, so we need to modify the fixed ratio chemical constraint as follows:

replace	$3x_5 - 5x_7 = 0$	by	$3x_{12} - 5x_7 = 0$	
replace	$2x_5 - 5x_6 = 0$	by	$2x_{12} - 5x_6 = 0$	
replace	$x_7 - 6x_8 = 0$	by	$x_{14} - 6x_8 = 0$	
replace	$5x_7 - 6x_{10} = 0$	by	$5x_{14} - 6x_{10} = 0$	

In the cost function x_5 is replaced by x_{12}, and x_7 by x_{14}, and the additional waste costs $(-30x_{11} - 30x_{13})$ must be added:

$$z = -1200 + 150x_4 - 100x_1 - 120x_2$$
$$- 30x_{12} - 30x_{11} - 40x_{14} - 30x_{13} - 30x_{10}$$

We now have three free variables, so we shall certainly need an LP approach. An LP package was used to obtain the solution

$x_1 = 57.69,$	$x_2 = 50,$	$x_3 = 57.69,$	$x_4 = 96.15$
$x_5 = 19.23,$	$x_6 = 7.69,$	$x_7 = 11.54,$	$x_8 = 0$
$x_9 = 7.69,$	$x_{10} = 0,$	$x_{11} = 0,$	$x_{12} = 19.23$
$x_{13} = 11.54,$	$x_{14} = 0$		

and the profit is £530.77 day^{-1}. It can be seen that $x_{11} = 0$, so nothing is sent to waste before the primary recovery unit; but $x_{14} = 0$, so that all the material from the primary to the secondary goes to waste, and the secondary unit is bypassed. The effect of this strategy is to increase the profit by about 20%.

There are many other variations that can be considered for this model. For instance, pumps often go wrong, so it is important to investigate what happens if the maximum flows are reduced or even cut completely. Once the basic program has been set up, such variations are quite straightforward to implement.

9.6 Engineering application: heating fin

A heating fin is of the shape indicated in Figure 9.19, where the wall temperature is T_1, the ambient temperature is T_0 and within the fin the value $T = T(x)$ is

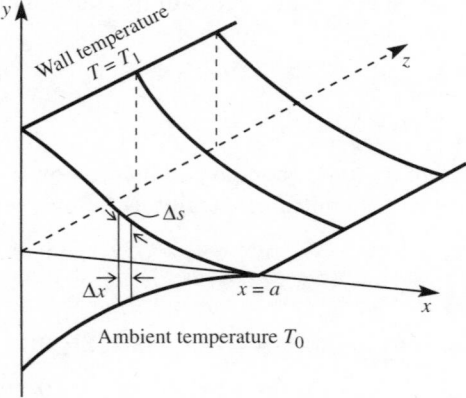

Figure 9.19 Heating fin.

assumed to depend only on x and to be independent of y and z. Heat is transferred by conduction along the fin, which has thermal conductivity k, and heat is transferred to the outside according to Newton's law of cooling, with surface heat-transfer coefficient h. Considering an area of the fin of unit width in the z direction and height $2y$, the heat transferred by conduction in the x direction is $k2y \, dT/dx$. The net transfer through the element illustrated is $(d/dx)(k2y \, dT/dx)$. The total heat lost through a surface element of unit width in the z direction and length $\Delta s = [1 + (dy/dx)^2]^{1/2} \, \Delta x$ along the surface is $h(T - T_0)\Delta s$. Since there are two surfaces, we can write the heat-transfer equation as

$$2\frac{d}{dx}\left[ky\frac{d}{dx}(T - T_0)\right] = 2h(T - T_0)\left[1 + \left(\frac{dy}{dx}\right)^2\right]^{1/2}$$

Provided that dy/dx is not too large, $(dy/dx)^2$ can be neglected, giving

$$\frac{d}{dx}\left[y\frac{d}{dx}(T - T_0)\right] = \frac{h}{k}(T - T_0) \tag{9.20}$$

The mass of the fin is given, so that its cross-sectional area is known, and hence

$$\int_0^a y \, dx = \tfrac{1}{2}A \tag{9.21}$$

Finally, we wish to maximize the heat transfer, so we require the maximum of

$$I = 2h \int_0^a (T - T_0) \, dx \tag{9.22}$$

over all possible functions $y(x)$.

The problem involves choosing a function $y(x)$ that satisfies (9.21) and then solving (9.20) for $T - T_0$. This is then substituted into (9.22) and the integral evaluated. Out of all possible such functions y, we choose the one that maximizes I. The scheme outlined is extremely difficult and belongs to a class called **variational problems**. An alternative approximate method must be sought. The *assumption* made is that the temperature falls linearly with x as

$$T - T_0 = (T_1 - T_0)(1 - \alpha x)$$

We also assume that $y = 0$ at $x = a$. We thus have two free parameters, α and a, which we can use to give an approximate solution. Given $T - T_0$, y can be computed from (9.20) as

$$y = \frac{h}{k\alpha}(a - \tfrac{1}{2}\alpha a^2 - x + \tfrac{1}{2}\alpha x^2)$$

It can be seen that our basic assumption implies that y is quadratic in x. To satisfy the area constraint (9.21), a simple integral is performed to give

$$\tfrac{1}{2}A = \frac{h}{k\alpha}a^2(\tfrac{1}{2} - \tfrac{1}{3}\alpha a)$$

which gives a relation between α and a. The function I is now integrated as

$$I = 2h(T_1 - T_0) \int_0^a (1 - \alpha x)\,dx$$

or

$$\frac{I}{2h(T_1 - T_0)} = a - \tfrac{1}{2}\alpha a^2$$

Thus the very difficult problem has been reduced to a Lagrange multiplier problem of maximizing

$$f = a - \tfrac{1}{2}\alpha a^2$$

subject to

$$g = 0 = \frac{a^2}{2\alpha} - \tfrac{1}{3}a^3 - S^3 \qquad (9.23)$$

where $S^3 = kA/2h$. The Lagrange multiplier analysis gives the equations

$$\frac{\partial(f - \lambda g)}{\partial a} = 1 - \alpha a - \lambda\left(\frac{a}{\alpha} - a^2\right) = 0$$

$$\frac{\partial(f - \lambda g)}{\partial \alpha} = -\tfrac{1}{2}a^2 + \lambda\frac{a^2}{2\alpha^2} = 0$$

Hence

$$\lambda = \alpha^2$$

$$1 - 2\alpha a + \alpha^2 a^2 = 0$$

so that $a\alpha = 1$. Substituting back into the constraint (9.23) gives

$$S^3 = \tfrac{1}{6}a^3, \qquad \text{or} \qquad a = \left(\frac{3kA}{h}\right)^{1/3}$$

and therefore

$$T - T_0 = (T_1 - T_0)\left(1 - \frac{x}{a}\right)$$

so that

$$\frac{y}{a} = \frac{ha}{2k}\left(1 - \frac{x}{a}\right)^2$$

Thus, given the physical parameters k, h and A, the 'best' shape can be derived. This model shows how a very difficult mathematical problem in optimization can be reduced to a much more straightforward one by an appropriate choice of test functions for $T - T_0$.

9.7 Review exercises (1–20)

1 Use the simplex method to find the maximum of the function

$$F = 12x_1 + 8x_2$$

subject to the constraints

$$x_1 + x_2 \leqslant 350$$
$$2x_1 + x_2 \leqslant 600$$
$$x_1 + 3x_2 \leqslant 900$$
$$x_1, x_2 \geqslant 0$$

Check your results with a graphical solution.

2 A motor manufacturer makes a 'standard', a 'super' and a 'deluxe' version of a particular model of car. It is found that each week two of the materials are in limited supply: that of chromium trim being limited to 1600 m per week and that of soundproofing material to 1500 m² per week. The quantity of each of these materials required by a car of each type is as follows:

	Standard	Super	Deluxe
Chromium trim (m)	10	20	30
Soundproofing (m²)	10	15	20

All other materials are in unlimited supply.

The manufacturer knows that any number of standard models can be sold, but it is estimated that the combined market for the super and deluxe versions is limited to 50 models per week. In addition there is a contractual obligation to supply a total of 70 cars (of any type) each week.

The profits on a standard, super and deluxe model are £100, £300 and £400 respectively. Assuming that the facilities to manufacture any number of cars are available, how many of each model should be made to maximize the weekly profit, and what is that profit?

3 A manufacturer makes three types of sailboard and is trying to decide how many of each to make in a given week. There are 400 h of labour available, and the three types of sailboard require respectively 10, 20 and 30 h of labour to construct. A shortage of fibreglass and of resin coating is anticipated. The

quantities required by each type of sailboard are as follows:

	Type 1	Type 2	Type 3	Total supplies
Fibreglass (kg)	5	10	25	290
Resin coating (litres)	3	2	1	72

If the profits on types 1, 2 and 3 are £10, £15 and £25 respectively, how many of each type should the manufacturer make to maximize profit?

4 A poor student lives on bread and cheese. The bread contains 1000 calories and 25 g protein in each kilogram, and the cheese has 2000 calories and 100 g per kg. To maintain a good diet, the student requires at least 3000 calories and 100 g of protein per day. Bread costs 60p per kg and cheese 180p per kg. Find the minimum cost of bread and cheese needed per day to maintain the diet.

5 Use Lagrange multipliers to find the maximum and minimum distances from the origin to the point P lying on the curve

$$x^2 - xy + y^2 = 1$$

6 A solid body of volume V and surface area S is formed by joining together two cubes of different sizes so that every point on one side of the smaller cube is in contact with the larger cube. If $S = 7\,\text{m}^2$, find the maximum and/or minimum values of V for which both cubes have non-zero volumes.

7 Find the maximum distance from the point $(1, 0, 0)$ to the surface represented by

$$2x + y^2 + z = 8$$

8 Find the local extrema of the function

$$F(x, y, z) = x + 2y + 3z$$

subject to the constraint

$$x^2 + y^2 + z^2 = 14$$

Obtain also the *global* maximum and minimum values of F in the region

$$x \geqslant 0, \quad y \geqslant 0, \quad z \geqslant 0, \quad x^2 + y^2 + z^2 \leqslant 14$$

9 A cylindrical can of radius R (cm) and height H (cm) is to be made with volume $1000\,\text{cm}^3$. The cost of making the can is proportional to

(amount of metal) $\times$ (machine factor)

where the amount of metal is proportional to the surface area of the can (including the two ends) and the machine factor is given by $1 + [1 - (H/4R)]^2$ and reflects the difficulty of machining the can. Show that the cost is

$$2\left(\frac{1000}{R} + \pi R^2\right)\left[1 + \left(1 - \frac{1000}{4\pi R^3}\right)^2\right]$$

Find a bracket for R and use the quadratic algorithm to estimate the radius that minimizes the cost.

10 Use the quadratic approximation method to obtain a first estimate of the minimum of the function

$$f(x) = 1 - t + t^2$$

where t is the non-negative root of

$$t^2 + tx - (1 - x^2) = 0$$

Start with the interval $0 \leqslant x \leqslant 1$ and note that for $x = 0.5$, $t = 0.6514$ and $f = 0.7729$.

11 Use (a) the steepest-descent method, (b) the Newton method and (c) the DFP method to find the position of the minimum of the function

$$f(x, y) = (x - y)^2 + \tfrac{1}{16}(x + y + 1)^4$$

starting at $(0, 0)$. Perform two cycles of each method, and compare your results.

12 A method called **Partan** uses the notation $D^{(i)}$ for the gradient of f evaluated at $x = x^{(i)}$. The iteration scheme for evaluating the minimum of f using Partan is

$$x^{(2)} = x^{(1)} - \mu_1 D^{(1)}$$

$$\left.\begin{array}{l} z^{(i)} = x^{(i)} - \mu_i D^{(i)} \\ x^{(i+1)} = z^{(i)} + \lambda_i(z^{(i)} - x^{(i-1)}) \end{array}\right\} \quad (i = 2, 3, \ldots)$$

where μ_i and λ_i are chosen by optimum line searches. Sketch the progress of this method up to the point $x^{(4)}$ for a scalar function of two variables $f(x_1, x_2)$.

Illustrate the use of Partan and the method of steepest descent on the quadratic function

$$f = (x_1 - x_2)^2 + (x_1 - 1)^2$$

starting at $(0, 0)$.

13 The Newton method described in Section 9.4.3 often fails to converge. One way of overcoming this problem is to restrict the step length at each iteration. Given that $x = a + h$, this can be implemented by constraining h to have length L, where

$$h^\mathsf{T} h = L^2$$

Use a Lagrange multiplier λ to show that the result gives

$$x_{\text{new}} = x_{\text{old}} - (J + \lambda I)^{-1} G$$

The algorithm is then implemented by successively using $\lambda = 0, 1, 10, 100, \ldots$ until a reduction in the function f is obtained.

Starting at $x = [1 \quad 1]^\mathsf{T}$, perform one complete step of the modified algorithm on the function

$$f = x^2 + y^2 - x^2 y$$

14 It is required to use a Newton method to minimize a function F that is a sum of squares

$$F(x_1, x_2, \ldots, x_n) = f_1^2(x_1, \ldots, x_n) + \ldots$$
$$+ f_m^2(x_1, \ldots, x_n)$$

where the derivatives of $f_1, f_2, \ldots, f_m$ are available. In matrix notation we define

$$x = \begin{bmatrix} x_1 \\ \vdots \\ x_n \end{bmatrix}, \quad a = \begin{bmatrix} a_1 \\ \vdots \\ a_n \end{bmatrix}, \quad f = \begin{bmatrix} f_1 \\ \vdots \\ f_m \end{bmatrix}$$

and the matrix of derivatives as

$$J = \begin{bmatrix} \dfrac{\partial f_1}{\partial x_1} & \cdots & \dfrac{\partial f_1}{\partial x_n} \\ \vdots & & \vdots \\ \dfrac{\partial f_m}{\partial x_1} & \cdots & \dfrac{\partial f_m}{\partial x_n} \end{bmatrix}$$

The functions $f_1, \ldots, f_m$ are replaced by their linear approximation about the point $x = a$, derived from Taylor's theorem. Show that the minimum of F is obtained at

$$x = a - (J^\mathsf{T} J)^{-1} J^\mathsf{T} f$$

where all the terms on the right-hand side are evaluated at $x = a$.

Construct an algorithm to iterate to the minimum based on this idea.

Use the method on the functions

(a) $F = (x - y)^2 + \tfrac{1}{16}(x + y + 1)^4$, starting at $x = 0$, $y = 0$;

(b) $F = \left(\dfrac{1}{x+y}\right)^2 + \left(\dfrac{x}{1+2x+y}\right)^2$, starting at $x = 1$, $y = 1$.

15 It is known from experience that a curve of the form

$$y = 1/(a+bx)$$

should give a good fit to experimental data in the form of a set of points

$$(x_i, y_i) \quad (i = 1, 2, \ldots, p)$$

It is required to calculate a and b by a best least-squares fit, and thus to minimize

$$F(a, b) = \sum_{i=1}^{p}\left(y_i - \frac{1}{a+bx_i}\right)^2$$

Use the least-squares algorithm described in Review exercise 14 to fit the function to the data points

$$(0, 1) \quad (1, 0.6) \quad (2, 0.3) \quad (3, 0.2)$$

16 A quadratic function $f(x_1, x_2, \ldots, x_n)$ with a unique minimum is given in matrix form as

$$f = c + \boldsymbol{b}^{\mathrm{T}}\boldsymbol{x} + \tfrac{1}{2}\boldsymbol{x}^{\mathrm{T}}\boldsymbol{A}\boldsymbol{x}$$

Show that a search in the direction

$$\boldsymbol{x} = \boldsymbol{a} + \lambda\boldsymbol{d}$$

produces the minimum at

$$\lambda_{\min} = \frac{-(\boldsymbol{b} + \boldsymbol{A}\boldsymbol{a})^{\mathrm{T}}\boldsymbol{d}}{\boldsymbol{d}^{\mathrm{T}}\boldsymbol{A}\boldsymbol{d}}$$

17 Complete two complete cycles of the steepest-descent algorithm for the function

$$f(x, y) = (1 - x)^2 + (x - y)^2$$

starting at $x = 0$, $y = 0$. Use Review exercise 16 for the minimization in the search directions.

Show that the minimum is obtained in a single iteration of the Newton method.

18 (Harder) It is required to solve the differential equation

$$yy'' - y'^2 + y' = 0$$

with the boundary conditions $y(0) = 1$ and $y(1) = 3$, by a shooting method. The equation is solved for the initial conditions

$$y(0) = 1, \qquad y'(0) = \alpha$$

by any suitable method (for example by a Runge–Kutta method). With this solution, calculate

$$F(\alpha) = y(1)$$

and then try to drive F to the value 3 by minimization of

$$[F(\alpha) - 3]^2$$

In this example illustrate the method by using the exact solution

$$y = (1 + b)\,\mathrm{e}^{x/b} - b$$

for the forward integration.

19 (An extended problem) In the chemical processing plant model in Section 9.5 consider the profits when

(a) the primary pump is faulty and the constraint $x_5 \leqslant 12$ is imposed;

(b) the waste pump between primary and secondary fails so that $x_{13} = 0$ (see Figure 9.18).

20 (An extended problem) Extend the heating fin analysis in Section 9.6, using a higher approximation to the temperature:

$$T - T_0 = (T_1 - T_0)(1 - \alpha x - \beta x^2)$$

Compare the shape of the fin with that given in the text, and compute the heat transferred in each case.

10

Applied Probability and Statistics

CONTENTS

10.1 Introduction

Applications of probability and statistics in engineering are very far-reaching. Data from experiments have to be analysed and conclusions drawn, decisions have to be made, production and distribution have to be organized and monitored, and quality has to be controlled. In all of these activities probability and statistics have at least a supporting role to play, and sometimes a central one.

The distinction between applied probability and statistics is blurred, but essentially it is this: **applied probability** is about mathematical modelling of a situation that involves random uncertainty, whereas **statistics** is the business of handling data and drawing conclusions, and can be regarded as a branch of applied probability. Most of this chapter is about statistics, but Section 10.10 on queueing theory is applied probability.

When applying statistical methods to a practical problem, the most visible activity is the processing of data, using either a hand calculator or, increasingly often, a computer statistical package. Either way, a formula or standard procedure from a textbook is being applied to the data. The relative ease and obviousness of this activity sometimes leads to a false sense that there is nothing more to it. On the contrary, the handling of the data (by whatever means) is quite superficial compared with the essential task of trying to understand both the problem at hand and the assumptions upon which the various statistical procedures are based. If the wrong procedure is chosen, a wrong conclusion may be drawn.

It is, unfortunately, all too easy to use a formula while overlooking its theoretical basis, which largely determines its applicability. It is true that there are some statistical methods that continue to work reliably even where the assumptions upon which they are based do not hold (such methods are called **robust**), but it is unwise to rely too heavily upon this and even worse to be unaware of the assumptions at all.

The conclusions of a statistical analysis are often expressed in a qualified way such as 'We can be 95% sure that ...'. At first this seems vague and inadequate. Perhaps a decision has to be made, but the statistical conclusion is not expressed simply as 'yes' or 'no'. A statistical analysis is rather like a legal case in which the witness is required to tell 'the whole truth and nothing but the truth'. In the present context 'the whole truth' means that the statistician must glean as much information from the data as is possible until nothing but pure randomness remains. 'Nothing but the truth' means that the statistician must not state the conclusion with any greater degree of certainty or confidence than is justified by the analysis. In fact there is a practical compromise between truth and precision that will be explained in Section 10.3.3. The result of all this is that the decision-maker is aided by the analysis but not pre-empted by it.

In this chapter we shall first review the basic theory of probability and then cover some applications that are beneficial in engineering and many other fields: the statistics of means, proportions and correlation, linear regression and goodness-of-fit testing, queueing theory and quality control.

10.2 Review of basic probability theory

This section contains an overview of the basic theory used in the remainder of this chapter. No attempt is made to explain or justify the ideas or results: a full account can be found in Chapter 13 of *Modern Engineering Mathematics* or elsewhere. For the same reason there are no examples or exercises. In the process of reviewing the basic theory, this section also establishes the pattern of notation used throughout the chapter, which follows standard conventions as far as possible. No reader should embark on this chapter without having a fairly thorough understanding of the material in this section.

10.2.1 The rules of probability

We associate a probability $P(A)$ with an **event** A, which in general is a subset of a **sample space** S. The usual set-theoretic operations apply to the events (subsets) in S, and there are corresponding rules that must be satisfied by the probabilities.

Complement rule

$$P(S - A) = 1 - P(A)$$

The **complement** of an event A is often written as $\bar{A}$.

Addition rule

$$P(A \cup B) = P(A) + P(B) - P(A \cap B)$$

For **disjoint** events, $A \cap B = \varnothing$, and the addition rule takes the simple form

$$P(A \cup B) = P(A) + P(B)$$

Product rule

$$P(A \cap B) = P(A)P(B \mid A)$$

This is actually the definition of the **conditional probability** $P(B \mid A)$ of B given A. If A and B are **independent** then the product rule takes the simple form

$$P(A \cap B) = P(A)P(B)$$

10.2.2 Random variables

A **random variable** has a sample space of possible numerical values together with a **distribution** of probabilities. Random variables can be either **discrete** or **continuous**.

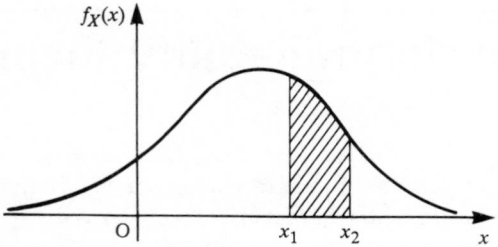

Figure 10.1 Probability of interval from density function.

For a discrete random variable (X, say) the possible values can be written as a list $\{v_1, v_2, v_3, \ldots\}$ with corresponding probabilities $P(X = v_1)$, $P(X = v_2)$, $P(X = v_3), \ldots$. The **mean** of X is then defined as

$$\mu_X = \sum_k v_k P(X = v_k)$$

(sum over all possible values), and is a measure of the central location of the distribution. The **variance** of X is defined as

$$\mathrm{Var}\,(X) = \sigma_X^2 = \sum_k (v_k - \mu_X)^2 P(X = v_k)$$

and is a measure of dispersion of the distribution about the mean. The symbols μ and σ^2 are conventional for these quantities. In general, the **expected value** of a function $h(X)$ of X is defined as

$$E\{h(X)\} = \sum_k h(v_k) P(X = v_k)$$

of which the mean and variance are special cases. The **standard deviation** σ_X is the square root of the variance.

For a **continuous** random variable (X, say), there is a **probability density function** $f_X(x)$ and a **cumulative distribution function** $F_X(x)$. The cumulative distribution function is defined as

$$F_X(x) = P(X \leqslant x)$$

and is the indefinite integral of the density function:

$$F_X(x) = \int_{-\infty}^{x} f_X(t)\, dt$$

These functions determine the probabilities of events for the random variable. The probability that the variable X takes a value within the real interval (x_1, x_2) is the area under the density function over that interval, or equivalently the difference in values of the distribution function at its ends:

$$P(x_1 < X < x_2) = \int_{x_1}^{x_2} f_X(t)\, dt = F_X(x_2) - F_X(x_1)$$

(see Figure 10.1). Note that the events $x_1 < X < x_2$, $x_1 \leqslant X < x_2$, $x_1 < X \leqslant x_2$

and $x_1 \leqslant X \leqslant x_2$ are all equivalent in probability terms for a continuous random variable X because the probability of X being exactly equal to either x_1 or x_2 is zero. The mean and variance of X, and the expected value of a function $h(X)$, are defined in terms of the density function by

$$\mu_X = \int_{-\infty}^{\infty} x f_X(x) \, dx$$

$$\text{Var}(X) = \sigma_X^2 = \int_{-\infty}^{\infty} (x - \mu_X)^2 f_X(x) \, dx$$

$$E\{h(X)\} = \int_{-\infty}^{\infty} h(x) f_X(x) \, dx$$

These definitions assume that the random variable is defined for values of x from $-\infty$ to ∞. If the random variable is defined in general for values in some real interval, say (a, b), then the domain of integration can be restricted to that interval, or alternatively the density function can be defined to be zero outside that interval.

Just as events can be independent (and then obey a simple product rule of probabilities), so can random variables be independent. We shall consider this in more detail in Section 10.4. Means and variances of random variables (whether discrete or continuous) have the following important properties (X and Y are random variables, and c is an arbitrary constant):

$$E(cX) = cE(X) = c\mu_X$$

$$\text{Var}(cX) = c^2 \text{Var}(X) = c^2 \sigma_X^2$$

$$E(X + c) = E(X) + c = \mu_X + c$$

$$\text{Var}(X + c) = \text{Var}(X) = \sigma_X^2$$

$$E(X + Y) = E(X) + E(Y) = \mu_X + \mu_Y$$

(this applies whether or not X and Y are independent),

$$\text{Var}(X + Y) = \text{Var}(X) + \text{Var}(Y) = \sigma_X^2 + \sigma_Y^2$$

(this applies only when X and Y are independent).

It is also useful to note that $\text{Var}(X) = E(X^2) - [E(X)]^2$.

10.2.3   The Bernoulli, binomial and Poisson distributions

The simplest example of a discrete distribution is the **Bernoulli distribution**. This has just two values: $X = 1$ with probability p and $X = 0$ with probability $1 - p$, from which the mean and variance are p and $p(1 - p)$ respectively.

The binomial and Poisson distributions are families of discrete distributions whose probabilities are generated by formulae, and which arise in many real situations. The **binomial distribution** governs the number (X, say) of 'successes' in n independent 'trials', with a probability p of 'success' at each trial:

$$P(X = k) = \binom{n}{k} p^k (1 - p)^{n-k}$$

where the range of possible values (k) is $\{0, 1, 2, \ldots, n\}$. The binomial distribution can be thought of as the sum of n independent Bernoulli random variables. This distribution (more properly, *family* of distributions) has two **parameters**, n and p. In terms of these parameters, the mean and variance are

$$\mu_X = np$$
$$\sigma_X^2 = np(1 - p)$$

The **Poisson distribution** is defined as

$$P(X = k) = \frac{\lambda^k e^{-\lambda}}{k!}$$

where the range of possible values (k) is the set of non-negative integers $\{0, 1, 2, \ldots\}$. This has mean and variance both equal to the single parameter λ (see Section 10.7.1), and, by setting $\lambda = np$, provides a useful approximation to the binomial distribution that works when n is large and p is small (see Section 10.7.2). As a guide, the approximation can be used when $n \geqslant 25$ and $p \leqslant 0.1$. The Poisson distribution has many other uses, as will be seen in Section 10.10.

10.2.4   The normal distribution

This is a family of continuous distributions with probability density function given by

$$f_X(x) = \frac{1}{\sigma_X \sqrt{(2\pi)}} \exp\left[-\frac{1}{2}\left(\frac{x - \mu_X}{\sigma_X}\right)^2 \right]$$

for $-\infty < x < +\infty$, where the parameters μ_X and σ_X are the mean and standard deviation of the distribution. It is conventional to denote the fact that a random variable X has a normal distribution by

$$X \sim N(\mu_X, \sigma_X^2)$$

The **standard normal distribution** is a special case with zero mean and unit variance, often denoted by Z:

$$Z \sim N(0, 1)$$

Tables of the standard normal cumulative distribution function

$$\Phi(z) = P(Z \leqslant z) = \frac{1}{\sqrt{(2\pi)}} \int_{-\infty}^{z} e^{-t^2/2} \, dt$$

z	.00	.01	.02	.03	.04	.05	.06	.07	.08	.09
.0	.5000	.5040	.5080	.5120	.5160	.5199	.5239	.5279	.5319	.5359
.1	.5398	.5438	.5478	.5517	.5557	.5596	.5636	.5675	.5714	.5753
.2	.5793	.5832	.5871	.5910	.5948	.5987	.6026	.6064	.6103	.6141
.3	.6179	.6217	.6255	.6293	.6331	.6368	.6406	.6443	.6480	.6517
.4	.6554	.6591	.6628	.6664	.6700	.6736	.6772	.6808	.6844	.6879
.5	.6915	.6950	.6985	.7019	.7054	.7088	.7123	.7157	.7190	.7224
.6	.7257	.7291	.7324	.7357	.7389	.7422	.7454	.7486	.7517	.7549
.7	.7580	.7611	.7642	.7673	.7704	.7734	.7764	.7794	.7823	.7852
.8	.7881	.7910	.7939	.7967	.7995	.8023	.8051	.8078	.8106	.8133
.9	.8159	.8186	.8212	.8238	.8264	.8289	.8315	.8340	.8365	.8389
1.0	.8413	.8438	.8461	.8485	.8508	.8531	.8554	.8577	.8599	.8621
1.1	.8643	.8665	.8686	.8708	.8729	.8749	.8770	.8790	.8810	.8830
1.2	.8849	.8869	.8888	.8907	.8925	.8944	.8962	.8980	.8997	.9015
1.3	.9032	.9049	.9066	.9082	.9099	.9115	.9131	.9147	.9162	.9177
1.4	.9192	.9207	.9222	.9236	.9251	.9265	.9279	.9292	.9306	.9319
1.5	.9332	.9345	.9357	.9370	.9382	.9394	.9406	.9418	.9429	.9441
1.6	.9452	.9463	.9474	.9484	.9495	.9505	.9515	.9525	.9535	.9545
1.7	.9554	.9564	.9573	.9582	.9591	.9599	.9608	.9616	.9625	.9633
1.8	.9641	.9649	.9656	.9664	.9671	.9678	.9686	.9693	.9699	.9706
1.9	.9713	.9719	.9726	.9732	.9738	.9744	.9750	.9756	.9761	.9767
2.0	.9772	.9778	.9783	.9788	.9793	.9798	.9803	.9808	.9812	.9817
2.1	.9821	.9826	.9830	.9834	.9838	.9842	.9846	.9850	.9854	.9857
2.2	.9861	.9864	.9868	.9871	.9875	.9878	.9881	.9884	.9887	.9890
2.3	.9893	.9896	.9898	.9901	.9904	.9906	.9909	.9911	.9913	.9916
2.4	.9918	.9920	.9922	.9925	.9927	.9929	.9931	.9932	.9934	.9936
2.5	.9938	.9940	.9941	.9943	.9945	.9946	.9948	.9949	.9951	.9952
2.6	.9953	.9955	.9956	.9957	.9959	.9960	.9961	.9962	.9963	.9964
2.7	.9965	.9966	.9967	.9968	.9969	.9970	.9971	.9972	.9973	.9974
2.8	.9974	.9975	.9976	.9977	.9977	.9978	.9979	.9979	.9980	.9981
2.9	.9981	.9982	.9982	.9983	.9984	.9984	.9985	.9985	.9986	.9986
3.0	.9987	.9987	.9987	.9988	.9988	.9989	.9989	.9989	.9990	.9990
3.1	.9990	.9991	.9991	.9991	.9992	.9992	.9992	.9992	.9993	.9993
3.2	.9993	.9993	.9994	.9994	.9994	.9994	.9994	.9995	.9995	.9995
3.3	.9995	.9995	.9995	.9996	.9996	.9996	.9996	.9996	.9996	.9997
3.4	.9997	.9997	.9997	.9997	.9997	.9997	.9997	.9997	.9997	.9998

z	1.282	1.645	1.960	2.326	2.576	3.090	3.291	3.891	4.417
$\Phi(z)$	.90	.95	.975	.99	.995	.999	.9995	.999 95	.999 995
$2[1 - \Phi(z)]$	.20	.10	.05	.02	.01	.002	.001	.000 1	.000 01

Figure 10.2 Table of the standard normal cumulative distribution function $\Phi(z)$.

are widely available (see for example Figure 10.2). These tables can be used for probability calculations involving arbitrary normal random variables. For example, if $X \sim N(\mu_X, \sigma_X^2)$ then

$$P(X \leqslant a) = P\left(\frac{X - \mu_X}{\sigma_X} \leqslant \frac{a - \mu_X}{\sigma_X}\right) = \Phi\left(\frac{a - \mu_X}{\sigma_X}\right)$$

The key result for applications of the normal distribution is the **central limit theorem**: if $\{X_1, X_2, \ldots, X_n\}$ are independent and identically distributed random variables (the distribution being arbitrary), each with mean μ_X and variance σ_X^2, and if

$$W_n = \frac{X_1 + \cdots + X_n}{n}, \qquad Z_n = \frac{X_1 + \cdots + X_n - n\mu_X}{\sigma_X\sqrt{n}}$$

then, as $n \to \infty$, the distributions of W_n and Z_n tend to $W_n \sim N(\mu_X, \sigma_X^2/n)$ and $Z_n \sim N(0, 1)$ respectively. Loosely speaking, the sum of independent identically distributed random variables tends to a normal distribution.

This theorem is proved in Section 10.7.3, and is the key to many statistical processes, some of which are described in Section 10.3. One corollary is that the normal distribution can be used to approximate the binomial distribution when n is sufficiently large: if X is binomial with parameters n and p then the approximating distribution (by equating the means and variances) is $Y \sim N(np, np(1 - p))$. This is explained (together with the important **continuity correction**) in Section 13.5.5 of *Modern Engineering Mathematics*, and the approximation is used as follows:

$$P(X \leqslant k) \simeq \Phi\left(\frac{k + 0.5 - np}{\sqrt{[np(1 - p)]}}\right)$$

$$P(X = k) \simeq \Phi\left(\frac{k + 0.5 - np}{\sqrt{[np(1 - p)]}}\right) - \Phi\left(\frac{k - 0.5 - np}{\sqrt{[np(1 - p)]}}\right)$$

As a guide, the approximation can be used when $n \geqslant 25$ and $0.1 \leqslant p \leqslant 0.9$.

10.2.5 Sample measures

It is conventional to denote a random variable by an upper-case letter (X, say), and an actual observed value of it by the corresponding lower-case letter (x, say). An observed value x will be one of the set of possible values (sample space) for the random variable, which for a discrete random variable may be written as a list of the form $\{v_1, v_2, v_3, \ldots\}$. It is possible to observe a random variable many times (say n times) and obtain a series of values. In this case we assume that the random variable X refers to a **population** (whose characteristics may be unknown), and the series of random variables $\{X_1, X_2, \ldots, X_n\}$ as a **sample**. Each X_i is assumed to have the characteristics of the population, so they all have the same distribution. The actual series of values $\{x_1, x_2, \ldots, x_n\}$ consists of data upon which we can work, but it is useful to define certain sample measures in terms of the random variables $\{X_1, X_2, \ldots, X_n\}$ in order to interpret the data. Principal among these measures are the **sample average** and **sample variance**, defined as

$$\bar{X} = \frac{1}{n}\sum_{i=1}^n X_i, \quad S_X^2 = \frac{1}{n}\sum_{i=1}^n (X_i - \bar{X})^2$$

respectively, and it is useful to note that the sample variance is the average of the squares minus the square of the average:

$$S_X^2 = \overline{X^2} - (\overline{X})^2$$

We shall also need the following alternative definition of sample variance in Section 10.3.5:

$$S_{X,n-1}^2 = \frac{1}{n-1} \sum_{i=1}^{n} (X_i - \overline{X})^2$$

We can use the properties of means and variances (summarized in Section 10.2.2) to find the mean and variance of the sample average as follows:

$$E(\overline{X}) = \frac{1}{n} E(X_1 + \cdots + X_n) = \frac{1}{n}[E(X_1) + \cdots + E(X_n)]$$

$$= \frac{n\mu_X}{n} = \mu_X$$

$$\text{Var}(\overline{X}) = \frac{1}{n^2} \text{Var}(X_1 + \cdots + X_n) = \frac{1}{n^2}[\text{Var}(X_1) + \cdots + \text{Var}(X_n)]$$

$$= \frac{n\sigma_X^2}{n^2} = \frac{\sigma_X^2}{n}$$

Here we are assuming that the population mean and variance are μ_X and σ_X^2 respectively (which may be unknown values in practice), and that the observations of the random variables X_i are *independent*, a very important requirement in statistics.

10.3 Estimating parameters

10.3.1 Interval estimates and hypothesis tests

The first step in statistics is to take some data from an experiment and make inferences about the values of certain parameters. Such parameters could be the mean and variance of a population, or the correlation between two variables for a population. The data are never sufficient to determine the values exactly, but two kinds of inferences can be made:

(a) a range of values can be quoted, within which it is believed with high probability that the population parameter value lies, or

(b) a decision can be made as to whether or not the data are compatible with a particular value of the parameter.

The first of these is called **interval estimation**, and provides an assessment of the value that is rather more honest than merely quoting a single number derived from the sample data, which may be more or less uncertain depending upon the sample size. The second approach is called **hypothesis testing** and allows a value of particular interest to be assessed. These two approaches are usually covered in separate chapters in introductory textbooks on statistics, but they are closely related and are often used in conjunction with each other. Tests of simple hypotheses about parameter values will therefore be covered here within the context of interval estimation.

10.3.2 Distribution of the sample average

Suppose that a clearly identified population has a numerical characteristic with an unknown mean value, such as the mean lifetime for a kind of electronic component or the mean salary for a job category. A natural way to estimate this unknown mean is to take a sample from the population, measure the appropriate characteristic, and find the average value. If the sample size is n and the measured values are $\{x_1, x_2, \ldots, x_n\}$ then the average value

$$\bar{x} = \frac{1}{n} \sum_{i=1}^{n} x_i$$

is a reasonable estimate of the population mean μ_X provided that the sample is *representative* and *independent*, and the size n is sufficiently large.

We can be more precise about how useful this estimate is if we treat the sample average as a random variable. Now we have a sample $\{X_1, X_2, \ldots, X_n\}$ with average

$$\bar{X} = \frac{1}{n} \sum_{i=1}^{n} X_i$$

and the mean and variance of $\bar{X}$ are given by

$$E(\bar{X}) = \mu_X, \qquad \mathrm{Var}(\bar{X}) = \frac{\sigma_X^2}{n}$$

(see Section 10.2.5). This shows that the expected value of the average is indeed equal to the population mean, and that the variance is smaller for larger samples. However, we can go further. The central limit theorem (Section 10.2.4) tells us that sums of identical random variables tend to have a normal distribution regardless of the distribution of the variables themselves. The only requirement is that a sufficient number of variables contribute to the sum (the actual number required depends very much on the shape of the underlying distribution). The sample average is a sum of random variables, and therefore has (approximately) a normal distribution for a sufficiently large sample:

$$\bar{X} \sim N(\mu_X, \sigma_X^2/n)$$

This allows us to use a general method of inference concerning means instead of a separate method for each underlying distribution – even if this were known, which is usually not the case. In practice, a sample size of 25 or more is usually sufficient for the normal approximation.

EXAMPLE 10.1   For all children taking an examination, the mean mark was 60%, with a standard deviation of 8%. A particular class of 30 children achieved an average of 63%. Is this unusual?

Solution   The average of 63% is higher than the mean, but not by very much. We do not know the true distribution of marks, but the sample average has (approximately) a normal distribution. We can test the idea that this particular class result is a fluke by reducing the sample average to a standard normal in the manner described in Section 10.2.4 and checking its value against the table of the cumulative distribution function $\Phi(z)$ (Figure 10.2):

$$P(\bar{X} \geqslant 63) = P\left(\frac{\bar{X} - 60}{8/\sqrt{30}} \geqslant \frac{63 - 60}{8/\sqrt{30}}\right) = 1 - \Phi(2.054) = 0.020$$

It is unlikely (one chance in 50) that an average as high as this could occur by chance, assuming that the ability of the class is typical. Figure 10.3 illustrates that the result is towards the tail of the distribution. It therefore seems that this class is unusually successful.

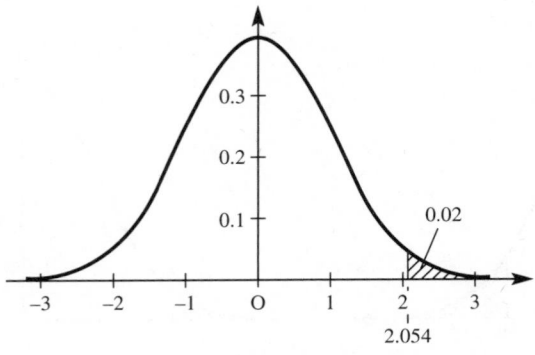

Figure 10.3 Normal density function for Example 10.1.

10.3.3   Confidence interval for the mean

A useful notation will be introduced here. For the standard normal distribution, define z_α to be the point on the z axis for which the area under the density function to its right is equal to α:

$$P(Z > z_\alpha) = \alpha$$

or equivalently

$$\Phi(z_\alpha) = 1 - \alpha$$

(see Figure 10.4a). From the standard normal table we have $z_{0.05} = 1.645$ and $z_{0.025} = 1.96$. By symmetry

$$P(-z_{\alpha/2} < Z < z_{\alpha/2}) = 1 - \alpha$$

(see Figure 10.4b). Assuming normality of the sample average, we have

$$P\left(-z_{\alpha/2} < \frac{\bar{X} - \mu_X}{\sigma_X/\sqrt{n}} < z_{\alpha/2}\right) = 1 - \alpha$$

which, after multiplying through the inequality by $\sigma_X/\sqrt{n}$ and changing the sign, gives

$$P\left(-z_{\alpha/2}\frac{\sigma_X}{\sqrt{n}} < \mu_X - \bar{X} < z_{\alpha/2}\frac{\sigma_X}{\sqrt{n}}\right) = 1 - \alpha$$

so that

$$P\left(\bar{X} - z_{\alpha/2}\frac{\sigma_X}{\sqrt{n}} < \mu_X < \bar{X} + z_{\alpha/2}\frac{\sigma_X}{\sqrt{n}}\right) = 1 - \alpha$$

Assume for now that the standard deviation of X is known (it is actually very rare for σ_X to be known when μ_X is unknown, but we shall discuss this case first for simplicity and later consider the more general situation where both μ_X and σ_X are

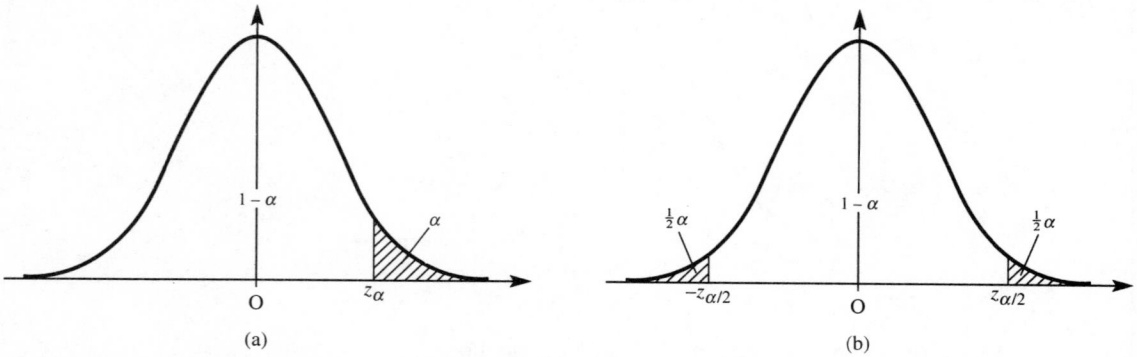

(a)   (b)

Figure 10.4 Normal density functions with (a) z_α and (b) $z_{\alpha/2}$.

unknown). The interval defined by $(\bar{X} \pm z_{\alpha/2}\sigma_X/\sqrt{n})$ is called a **100(1 − α)% confidence interval for the mean**, with variance known. If a value for α is specified, the upper and lower limits of this interval can be calculated from the sample average. The probability is $1 - \alpha$ that the true mean lies between them.

EXAMPLE 10.2   The temperature (in degrees Celsius) at ten points chosen at random in a large building is measured, giving the following list of readings:

$$\{18°, 16.5°, 17.5°, 18°, 19.5°, 16.5°, 18°, 17°, 19°, 17.5°\}$$

The standard deviation of temperature through the building is known from past experience to be 1°C. Find a 90% confidence interval for the mean temperature in the building.

Solution   The average of the ten readings is 17.75 °C, and, using $z_{0.05} = 1.645$, the 90% confidence interval is

$$(17.75 \pm 1.645(1/\sqrt{10})) = (17.1, 18.3)$$

The confidence interval is used to indicate the degree of uncertainty in the sample average. The simplicity of the calculation is deceptive because the idea is very important and easily misunderstood. It is not the mean that is random but rather the interval that would enclose it $100(1 - \alpha)\%$ of the times the experiment is performed. It is tempting to think of the interval as fixed by the experiment and the mean as a random variable that has a probability $1 - \alpha$ of lying within it, but this is not correct.

Typical values of α are $0.1, 0.05$ and 0.01, giving 90%, 95% and 99% confidence intervals respectively. The value chosen is a compromise between truth and precision, as illustrated in Figure 10.5. A statement saying that the mean lies within the interval $(-\infty, \infty)$ is 100% true (certain to be the case), but totally uninformative because of its total imprecision. None of the possible values is ruled out. On the other hand, saying that the mean equals the exact value given by the sample average is maximally precise, but again of limited value because the statement is false – or rather the probability of its truth is zero. A statement quoting a finite

Figure 10.5 Confidence intervals: (a) infinite interval; (b) finite interval; (c) point value.

interval for the mean has a probability of being true, chosen to be quite high, and at the same time it rules out most of the possible values and therefore is highly informative. The higher the probability of truth, the lower the informativeness, and vice versa.

The width of the interval also depends on the sample size. A larger experiment yields a more precise result. If figures for the confidence $1 - \alpha$ and precision (width of the interval) are specified in advance then the sample size can be chosen sufficiently large to satisfy these requirements. In some experimental situations (for example destructive testing) there are incentives to keep sample sizes as small as possible. The experimenter must weigh up these conflicting objectives and design the experiment accordingly.

EXAMPLE 10.3   A machine fills cartons of liquid; the mean fill is adjustable but the dial on the gauge is not very accurate. The standard deviation of the quantity of fill is 6 ml. A sample of 30 cartons gave a measured average content of 570 ml. Find 90% and 95% confidence intervals for the mean.

Solution   Using $\alpha = 0.05$ and $z_{0.025} = 1.96$, the 95% confidence interval is

$$(570 \pm 1.960(6/\sqrt{30})) = (567.8, 572.1)$$

Likewise, using $\alpha = 0.1$ and $z_{0.05} = 1.645$, the 90% confidence interval is

$$(570 \pm 1.645(6/\sqrt{30})) = (568.2, 571.8)$$

As expected, the 95% interval is slightly wider.

10.3.4   Testing simple hypotheses

As explained in Section 10.3.1, the testing of hypotheses about parameter values is complementary to the estimation process involving an interval. A 'simple' hypothesis is one that specifies a particular value for the parameter, as opposed to an interval, and it is this type that we shall consider. The following remarks apply generally to parameter hypothesis testing, but will be directed in particular to hypotheses concerning means.

There are two kinds of errors that can occur when testing hypotheses:

(a) a true hypothesis can be rejected (this is usually referred to as a **type I error**), or

(b) a false hypothesis can be accepted (this is usually called a **type II error**).

In reality, all hypotheses that prescribe particular values for parameters are false, but they may be approximately true and rejection may be the result of an

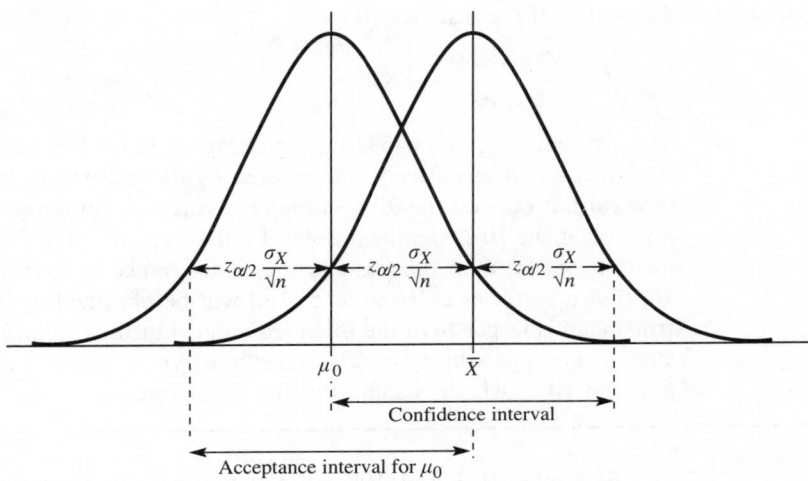

Figure 10.6 Confidence interval and hypothesis test.

experimental fluke. This is the sense in which a type I error can occur. Any hypothesis will be rejected if the sample size is large enough. Acceptance really means that there is insufficient evidence to reject the hypothesis, but this is not an entirely negative view because if the hypothesis has survived the test then it has some degree of dependability.

Normally a simple hypothesis is tested by evaluating a **test statistic**, a quantity that depends upon the sample and leads to rejection of the hypothesized parameter value if its magnitude exceeds a certain threshold. If the hypothesized mean is μ_0 then the test statistic for the mean is

$$Z = \frac{\bar{X} - \mu_0}{\sigma_X / \sqrt{n}}$$

with the hypothesis 'rejected at significance level α' if $|Z| > z_{\alpha/2}$.

The **significance level** can be regarded as the probability of false rejection, an error of type I. If the hypothesis is true then Z has a standard normal distribution and the probability that it will exceed $z_{\alpha/2}$ in magnitude is α. If Z does exceed this value then either the hypothesis is wrong or else a rare event has occurred. It is easy to show that the test statistic lies on this threshold (for significance level α) exactly when the hypothesized value lies at one or other extreme of the $100(1 - \alpha)\%$ confidence interval (see Figure 10.6). An alternative way to test the hypothesis is therefore to see whether or not the value lies within the confidence interval.

EXAMPLE 10.4   For the situation described in Example 10.3 test the hypothesis that the mean fill of liquid is 568 ml (one imperial pint).

Solution   The value of the test statistic is

$$Z = \frac{570 - 568}{6/\sqrt{30}} = 1.83$$

This exceeds $z_{0.05} = 1.645$ (10% significance), but is less than $z_{0.025} = 1.96$ (5% significance). Alternatively, the quoted figure lies within the 95% confidence interval but outside the 90% confidence interval. Either way, the hypothesis is rejected at the 10% significance level but accepted at the 5% level. If the actual mean is 568 ml then there is less than one chance in 10 (but more than one in 20) that a result as extreme as 570 ml will be obtained. It looks as though the true mean is larger than the intended value, but the evidence is not particularly strong. The probability of false rejection (type I error) is somewhere between 5% and 10%, which is small but not negligible.

Examples 10.3 and 10.4 set the pattern for the interpretation and use of confidence intervals. We shall now see how to apply these ideas more generally.

10.3.5   Other confidence intervals and tests concerning means

Mean when variance is unknown

With the basic ideas of interval estimation and hypothesis testing established, it is relatively easy to cover other cases. The first and most obvious is to remove the assumption that the variance is known. If the sample size is large then there is essentially no problem, because the sample standard deviation $S_{X,n-1}$ can be used in place of σ_X in the confidence interval, where

$$S_{X,n-1}^2 = \frac{1}{n-1} \sum_{i=1}^{n} (X_i - \bar{X})^2$$

This definition was introduced in Section 10.2.5. Note that the sum is divided by $n-1$ rather than n. For a large sample this makes little difference, but for a small sample this form must be used because the 't distribution' requires it.

Suppose that the sample size is small, say less than 25. Using $S_{X,n-1}$ in place of σ_X adds an extra uncertainty because this estimate is itself subject to error. Furthermore, the central limit theorem cannot be relied upon to ensure that the sample average has a normal distribution. We have to assume that the data themselves are normal. In this situation the random variable

$$T_n = \frac{\bar{X} - \mu_X}{S_{X,n-1}/\sqrt{n}}$$

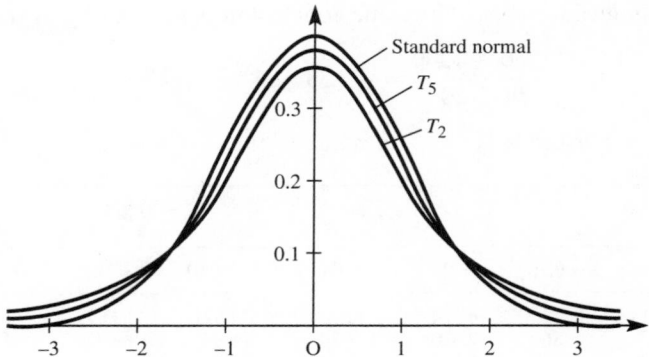

Figure 10.7 Density functions of T_n and Z.

has a *t* **distribution** with parameter $n - 1$. This distribution resembles the normal distribution, as can be seen in Figure 10.7, which shows the density functions of T_2 and T_5 together with that of the standard normal distribution. In fact T_n tends to the standard normal distribution as $n \to \infty$. The parameter of the t distribution (whose value here is one less than the size of the sample) is usually called the **number of degrees of freedom**.

Defining $t_{\alpha,n-1}$ by

$$P(T_n > t_{\alpha,n-1}) = \alpha$$

(by analogy with z_α), we can derive a $100(1 - \alpha)\%$ confidence interval for the mean by the method used in Section 10.3.3:

$$\left(\bar{X} \pm t_{\alpha/2,n-1} \frac{S_{X,n-1}}{\sqrt{n}} \right)$$

This takes explicit account of the uncertainty caused by the use of $S_{X,n-1}$ in place of σ_X. Values of $t_{\alpha,n-1}$ for typical values of α can be read directly from the table of the t distribution, an example of which is shown in Figure 10.8. To obtain a test statistic for an assumed mean μ_0, simply replace μ_X by μ_0 in the definition of T_n.

EXAMPLE 10.5   The measured lifetimes of a sample of 20 electronic components gave an average of 1250 h, with a sample standard deviation of 96 h. Assuming that the lifetime has a normal distribution, find a 95% confidence interval for the mean lifetime of the population, and test the hypothesis that the mean is 1300 h.

Solution   The appropriate figure from the t table is $t_{0.025,19} = 2.093$, so the 95% confidence interval is

$$(1250 \pm 2.093(96)/\sqrt{20}) = (1205, 1295)$$

The claim that the mean lifetime is 1300 h is therefore rejected at the 5%

significance level. The same conclusion is reached by evaluating

$$T_n = \frac{1250 - 1300}{96/\sqrt{20}} = -2.33$$

which exceeds $t_{0.025, 19}$ in magnitude.

n	$\alpha = 0.10$	$\alpha = 0.05$	$\alpha = 0.025$	$\alpha = 0.01$	$\alpha = 0.005$	n
1	3.078	6.314	12.706	31.821	63.657	1
2	1.886	2.920	4.303	6.965	9.925	2
3	1.638	2.353	3.182	4.541	5.841	3
4	1.533	2.132	2.776	3.747	4.604	4
5	1.476	2.015	2.571	3.365	4.032	5
6	1.440	1.943	2.447	3.143	3.707	6
7	1.415	1.895	2.365	2.998	3.499	7
8	1.397	1.860	2.306	2.896	3.355	8
9	1.383	1.833	2.262	2.821	3.250	9
10	1.372	1.812	2.228	2.764	3.169	10
11	1.363	1.796	2.201	2.718	3.106	11
12	1.356	1.782	2.179	2.681	3.055	12
13	1.350	1.771	2.160	2.650	3.012	13
14	1.345	1.761	2.145	2.624	2.977	14
15	1.341	1.753	2.131	2.602	2.947	15
16	1.337	1.746	2.120	2.583	2.921	16
17	1.333	1.740	2.110	2.567	2.898	17
18	1.330	1.734	2.101	2.552	2.878	18
19	1.328	1.729	2.093	2.539	2.861	19
20	1.325	1.725	2.086	2.528	2.845	20
21	1.323	1.721	2.080	2.518	2.831	21
22	1.321	1.717	2.074	2.508	2.819	22
23	1.319	1.714	2.069	2.500	2.807	23
24	1.318	1.711	2.064	2.492	2.797	24
25	1.316	1.708	2.060	2.485	2.787	25
26	1.315	1.706	2.056	2.479	2.779	26
27	1.314	1.703	2.052	2.473	2.771	27
28	1.313	1.701	2.048	2.467	2.763	28
29	1.311	1.699	2.045	2.462	2.756	29
∞	1.282	1.645	1.960	2.326	2.576	∞

Figure 10.8 Table of the t distribution $t_{\alpha, n}$. (Based on Table 12 of *Biometrika Tables for Statisticians*, Vol. 1. Cambridge University Press, 1954. By permission of the *Biometrika* trustees.)

Difference between means

Now suppose that we have not just a single sample but two samples from different populations, and that we wish to compare the separate means. Assume also that the variances of the two populations are equal but unknown (the most common situation). Then it can be shown that the $100(1 - \alpha)\%$ confidence interval for the difference $\mu_1 - \mu_2$ between the means is

$$\left(\bar{X}_1 - \bar{X}_2 \pm t_{\alpha/2,n} S_p \sqrt{\left(\frac{1}{n_1} + \frac{1}{n_2} \right)} \right)$$

where $\bar{X}_1$ and $\bar{X}_2$ are the respective sample averages, n_1 and n_2 are the respective sample sizes, S_1^2 and S_2^2 are the respective sample variances (using the '$n - 1$' form as above),

$$S_p^2 = \frac{(n_1 - 1)S_1^2 + (n_2 - 1)S_2^2}{n_1 + n_2 - 2}$$

is a pooled estimate of the unknown variance, and

$$n = n_1 + n_2 - 2$$

is the parameter for the t table. The corresponding test statistic for an assumed difference $d_0 = \mu_1 - \mu_2$ is

$$T_n = \frac{\bar{X}_1 - \bar{X}_2 - d_0}{S_p\sqrt{(1/n_1 + 1/n_2)}}$$

For small samples the populations have to be normal, but for larger samples this is not required and the t-table figure can be replaced by $z_{\alpha/2}$.

EXAMPLE 10.6 Two kinds of a new plastic material are to be compared for strength. From tensile strength measurements of 10 similar pieces of each type, the sample averages and standard deviations were as follows:

$$\bar{X}_1 = 78.3, \quad S_1 = 5.6, \quad \bar{X}_2 = 84.2, \quad S_2 = 6.3$$

Compare the mean strengths, assuming normal data.

Solution The pooled estimate of the standard deviation is 5.960, the t table gives $t_{0.025,18} = 2.101$, and the 95% confidence interval for the difference between means is

$$(78.3 - 84.2 \pm 2.101(5.96)/\sqrt{5}) = (-11.5, -0.3)$$

The difference is significant at the 5% level because zero does not lie within the interval. Also, assuming zero difference gives

$$T_n = \frac{78.3 - 84.2}{5.96/\sqrt{5}} = -2.21$$

which confirms the 5% significance.

It is also possible to set up confidence intervals and tests for the variance σ_X^2, or for comparing two variances for different populations. The process of testing means and variances within and between several populations is called **analysis of variance**. This has many applications, and is well covered in statistics textbooks.

10.3.6   Interval and test for proportion

The ideas of interval estimation do not just apply to means. If probability is interpreted as a long-term proportion (which is one of the common interpretations) then measuring a sample proportion is a way of estimating a probability. The binomial distribution (Section 10.2.3) points the way. We count the number of 'successes', say X, in n 'trials', and estimate the probability p of success at each trial, or the long-term proportion, by the sample proportion

$$\hat{p} = \frac{X}{n}$$

(it is common in statistics to place the 'hat' symbol $\hat{}$ over a parameter to denote an estimate of that parameter). This only provides a point estimate. To obtain a confidence interval, we can exploit the normal approximation to the binomial (Section 10.2.4)

$$X \sim N(np, np(1 - p))$$

approximately, for large n. Dividing by n preserves normality, so

$$\hat{p} \sim N\left(p, \frac{p(1 - p)}{n}\right)$$

Following the argument in Section 10.3.3, we have

$$P\left(p - z_{\alpha/2}\sqrt{\left[\frac{p(1 - p)}{n}\right]} < \hat{p} < p + z_{\alpha/2}\sqrt{\left[\frac{p(1 - p)}{n}\right]}\right) = 1 - \alpha$$

and, after rearranging the inequality,

$$P\left(\hat{p} - z_{\alpha/2}\sqrt{\left[\frac{p(1 - p)}{n}\right]} < p < \hat{p} + z_{\alpha/2}\sqrt{\left[\frac{p(1 - p)}{n}\right]}\right) = 1 - \alpha$$

Because p is unknown, we have to make a further approximation by replacing p by $\hat{p}$ inside the square root, to give an approximate $100(1 - \alpha)\%$ confidence interval for p:

$$\left(\hat{p} \pm z_{\alpha/2}\sqrt{\left[\frac{\hat{p}(1 - \hat{p})}{n}\right]}\right)$$

The corresponding test statistic for an assumed proportion p_0 is

$$Z = \frac{X - np_0}{\sqrt{[np_0(1 - p_0)]}}$$

with $\pm z_{\alpha/2}$ as the rejection points for significance level α.

EXAMPLE 10.7   In an opinion poll conducted with a sample of 1000 people chosen at random, 30% said that they support a certain political party. Find a 95% confidence interval for the actual proportion of the population who support this party.

Solution   The required confidence interval is obtained directly as

$$\left(0.3 \pm 1.96 \sqrt{\left[\frac{(0.3)(0.7)}{1000}\right]}\right) = (0.27, 0.33)$$

A variation of about 3% either way is therefore to be expected when conducting opinion polls with sample sizes of this order, which is fairly typical, and this figure is often quoted in the news media as an indication of maximum likely error.

A similar argument that also exploits the fact that the difference between two independent normal random variables is also normal leads to the following $100(1 - \alpha)\%$ confidence interval for the difference between two proportions, when $\hat{p}_1$ and $\hat{p}_2$ are the respective sample proportions:

$$\left(\hat{p}_1 - \hat{p}_2 \pm z_{\alpha/2} \sqrt{\left[\frac{\hat{p}_1(1 - \hat{p}_1)}{n_1} + \frac{\hat{p}_2(1 - \hat{p}_2)}{n_2}\right]}\right)$$

Again it is assumed that n_1 and n_2 are reasonably large. The test statistic for equality of proportions is

$$Z = \frac{\hat{p}_1 - \hat{p}_2}{\sqrt{[\hat{p}(1 - \hat{p})(1/n_1 + 1/n_2)]}}$$

where $\hat{p} = (X_1 + X_2)/(n_1 + n_2)$ is a pooled estimate of the proportion.

EXAMPLE 10.8   One hundred samples of an alloy are tested for resistance to fatigue. Half have been prepared using a new process and the other half by a standard process. Of those prepared by the new process, 35 exhibit good fatigue resistance, whereas only 25 of those prepared in the standard way show the same performance. Is the new process better than the standard one?

Solution   The proportions of good samples are 0.7 for the new process and 0.5 for the standard one, so a 95% confidence interval for the difference between the true proportions is

$$\left(0.7 - 0.5 \pm 1.96 \sqrt{\left[\frac{(0.7)(0.3)}{50} + \frac{(0.5)(0.5)}{50}\right]}\right) = (0.01, 0.39)$$

The pooled estimate of proportion is

$$\hat{p} = (35 + 25)/(50 + 50) = 0.6$$

so that

$$Z = \frac{0.7 - 0.5}{\sqrt{[(0.6)(0.4)/25]}} = 2.04.$$

Both approaches show that the difference is significant at the 5% level. However, it is only just so: if one more sample for the new process had been less fatigue-resistant, the difference would not have been significant at this level. This suggests that the new process is effective – but, despite the apparently large difference in success rates, the evidence is not very strong.

This method only applies to independent sample proportions. It would not be legitimate to apply it, for instance, to a more elaborate version of the opinion poll (Example 10.7) in which respondents can choose between two (or more) political parties or else support neither. Support for one party usually precludes support for another, so the proportions of those interviewed who support the two parties are not independent. More elaborate confidence intervals, based on the multinomial distribution, can handle such situations. This shows how important it is to understand the assumptions upon which statistical methods are based. It would be very easy to look up 'difference between proportions' in an index and apply an inappropriate formula.

10.3.7   Exercises

1 An electrical firm manufactures light bulbs whose lifetime is approximately normally distributed with a standard deviation of 50 h.

(a) If a sample of 30 bulbs has an average life of 780 h, find a 95% confidence interval for the mean lifetime of the population.

(b) How large a sample is needed if we wish to be 95% confident that our sample average will be within 10 h of the population mean?

2 Quantities of a trace impurity in 12 specimens of a new material are measured (in parts per million) as follows:

8.8, 7.1, 7.9, 10.2, 8.9, 7.7, 10.6, 9.4, 9.2, 7.5, 9.0, 8.4

Find a 95% confidence interval for the population mean, assuming that the distribution is normal.

3 A sample of 30 pieces of a semiconductor material gave an average resistivity of $73.2\,\text{m}\Omega\,\text{m}$, with a

sample standard deviation of $5.4\,\text{m}\Omega\,\text{m}$. Obtain a 95% confidence interval for the resistivity of the material, and test the hypothesis that this is $75\,\text{m}\Omega\,\text{m}$.

4 The mean weight loss of 16 grinding balls after a certain length of time in mill slurry is 3.42 g, with a standard deviation of 0.68 g. Construct a 99% confidence interval for the true mean weight loss of such grinding balls under the stated conditions.

5 While performing a certain task under simulated weightlessness, the pulse rate of 32 astronaut trainees increased on the average by 26.4 beats per minute, with a standard deviation of 4.28 beats per minute. Construct a 95% confidence interval for the true average increase in the pulse rate of astronaut trainees performing the given task.

6 The quality of a liquid being used in an etching process is monitored automatically by measuring the attenuation of a certain wavelength of light passing through it. The criterion is that when the

attenuation reaches 58%, the liquid is declared as 'spent'. Ten samples of the liquid are used until they are judged as 'spent' by the experts. The light attenuation is then measured, and gives an average result of 56%, with a standard deviation of 3%. Is the criterion satisfactory?

7 A fleet car company has to decide between two brands A and B of tyre for its cars. An experiment is conducted using 12 of each brand, run until they wear out. The sample averages and standard deviations of running distance (in km) are respectively 36 300 and 5000 for A, and 39 100 and 6100 for B. Obtain a 95% confidence interval for the difference in means, assuming the distributions to be normal, and test the hypothesis that brand B tyres outrun brand A tyres.

8 A manufacturer claims that the lifetime of a particular electronic component is unaffected by temperature variations within the range 0–60 °C. Two samples of these components were tested, and their measured lifetimes (in hours) recorded as follows:

  0 °C: 7250, 6970, 7370, 7910, 6790, 6850, 7280, 7830

  60 °C: 7030, 7270, 6510, 6700, 7350, 6770, 6220, 7230

Assuming that the lifetimes have a normal distribution, find 90% and 95% confidence intervals for the difference between the mean lifetimes at the two temperatures, and hence test the manufacturer's claim at the 5% and 10% significance levels.

9 Suppose that out of 540 drivers tested at random, 38 were found to have consumed more than the legal limit of alcohol. Find 90% and 95% confidence intervals for the true proportion of drivers who were over the limit during the time of the tests. Are the results compatible with the hypothesis that this proportion is less than 5%?

10 It is known that approximately one-quarter of all houses in a certain area have inadequate loft insulation. How many houses should be inspected if the difference between the estimated and true proportions having inadequate loft insulation is not to exceed 0.05, with probability 90%? If in fact 200 houses are inspected, and 55 of them have inadequate loft insulation, find a 90% confidence interval for the true proportion.

11 A drug-manufacturer claims that the proportion of patients exhibiting side-effects to their new anti-arthritis drug is at least 8% lower than for the standard brand X. In a controlled experiment 31 out of 100 patients receiving the new drug exhibited side-effects, as did 74 out of 150 patients receiving brand X. Test the manufacturer's claim using 90% and 95% confidence intervals.

12 Suppose that 10 years ago 500 people were working in a factory, and 180 of them were exposed to a material which is now suspected as being carcinogenic. Of those 180, 30 have since developed cancer, whereas 32 of the other workers (who were not exposed) have also since developed cancer. Obtain a 95% confidence interval for the difference between the proportions with cancer among those exposed and not exposed, and assess whether the material should be considered carcinogenic, on this evidence.

10.4 Joint distributions and correlation

Just as it is possible for events to be dependent upon one another in that information to the effect that one has occurred changes the probability of the other, so it is possible for random variables to be associated in value. In this section we show how the degree of dependence between two random variables can be defined and measured.

10.4.1   Joint and marginal distributions

The idea that two variables, each of which is random, can be associated in some way might seem mysterious at first, but can be clarified with some familiar examples. For instance, if one chooses a person at random and measures his or her height and weight, each measurement is a random variable – but we know that taller people also tend to be heavier than shorter people, so the outcomes will be related. On the other hand, a person's birthday and telephone number are not likely to be related in any way. In general, we need a measure of the simultaneous distribution of two random variables.

For two discrete random variables X and Y with possible values $\{u_1, \ldots, u_m\}$ and $\{v_1, \ldots, v_n\}$ respectively, the **joint distribution** of X and Y is the set of all joint probabilities of the form

$$P(X = u_k \cap Y = v_j) \quad (k = 1, \ldots, m; j = 1, \ldots, n)$$

The joint distribution contains all relevant information about the random variables separately, as well as their joint behaviour. To obtain the distribution of one variable, we sum over the possible values of the other:

$$P(X = u_k) = \sum_{j=1}^{n} P(X = u_k \cap Y = v_j) \quad (k = 1, \ldots, m)$$

$$P(Y = v_j) = \sum_{k=1}^{m} P(X = u_k \cap Y = v_j) \quad (j = 1, \ldots, n)$$

The distributions obtained in this way are called **marginal distributions** of X and Y.

EXAMPLE 10.9   Two textbooks are selected at random from a shelf containing three statistics texts, two mathematics texts and three engineering texts. Denoting the number of books selected in each subject by S, M and E respectively, find (a) the joint distribution of S and M, and (b) the marginal distributions of S, M and E.

Solution   (a) The joint distribution (shown in Figure 10.9) is built up element by element using the addition and product rules of probability as follows:

$$P(S = M = 0) = P(E = 2) = (\tfrac{3}{8})(\tfrac{2}{7}) = \tfrac{3}{28}$$

that is, the probability that the first book is an engineering text (three chances out of eight) times the probability that the second book is also (two remaining chances out of seven). Continuing,

$$P(S = 0 \cap M = 1) = P(M = 1 \cap E = 1)$$

$$= (\tfrac{2}{8})(\tfrac{3}{7}) + (\tfrac{3}{8})(\tfrac{2}{7}) = \tfrac{3}{14}$$

that is, the probability that the first book is a mathematics text and the second

	M			
S	0	1	2	Total
0	$\dfrac{3}{28}$	$\dfrac{3}{14}$	$\dfrac{1}{28}$	$\dfrac{5}{14}$
1	$\dfrac{9}{28}$	$\dfrac{3}{14}$		$\dfrac{15}{28}$
2	$\dfrac{3}{28}$			$\dfrac{3}{28}$
Total	$\dfrac{15}{28}$	$\dfrac{3}{7}$	$\dfrac{1}{28}$	1

Figure 10.9 Joint distribution for Example 10.9.

an engineering text, plus the (equal) probability of the books being the other way round. The other probabilities are derived similarly.

(b) The marginal distributions of S and M are just the row and column totals as shown in Figure 10.9. The marginal distribution of E can also be derived from the table:

$$P(E = 2) = P(S = M = 0) = \tfrac{3}{28}$$

$$P(E = 1) = P(S = 1 \cap M = 0) + P(S = 0 \cap M = 1) = \tfrac{15}{28}$$

$$P(E = 0) = P(S = 2) + P(S = 1 \cap M = 1) + P(M = 2) = \tfrac{5}{14}$$

This is the same as the marginal distribution of S, which is not surprising, because there are the same numbers of engineering and statistics books on the shelf.

In order to apply these ideas of joint and marginal distributions to continuous random variables, we need to build on the interpretation of the probability density function. The **joint density function** of two continuous random variables X and Y, denoted by $f_{X,Y}(x, y)$, is such that

$$P(x_1 < X < x_2 \quad \text{and} \quad y_1 < Y < y_2) = \int_{x_1}^{x_2} \int_{y_1}^{y_2} f_{X,Y}(x, y)\, dy\, dx$$

for all intervals (x_1, x_2) and (y_1, y_2). This involves a double integral over the two variables x and y. This is necessary because the joint density function must indicate the relative likelihood of every combination of values of X and Y, just as the joint distribution does for discrete random variables. The joint density function is transformed into a probability by integrating over an interval for both variables. The double integral here can be regarded as a pair of single-variable integrations, with the outer variable (x) held constant during the integration with respect to the inner variable (y). In fact the same answer is obtained if the integration is performed the other way around.

The **marginal density functions** for X and Y are obtained from the joint density function in a manner analogous to the discrete case: by integrating over all values of the unwanted variable:

$$f_X(x) = \int_{-\infty}^{\infty} f_{X,Y}(x, y)\,dy \quad (-\infty < x < \infty)$$

$$f_Y(y) = \int_{-\infty}^{\infty} f_{X,Y}(x, y)\,dx \quad (-\infty < y < \infty)$$

EXAMPLE 10.10 The joint density function of random variables X and Y is

$$f_{X,Y}(x, y) = \begin{cases} 1 & (0 \leqslant x \leqslant 1, \ cx \leqslant y \leqslant cx + 1) \\ 0 & \text{otherwise} \end{cases}$$

where c is a constant such that $0 \leqslant c \leqslant 1$ (which means that $f_{X,Y}(x, y)$ is unity over the trapezoidal area shown in Figure 10.10 and zero elsewhere). Find the marginal distributions of X and Y. Also find the probability that neither X nor Y exceeds one-half, assuming $c = 1$.

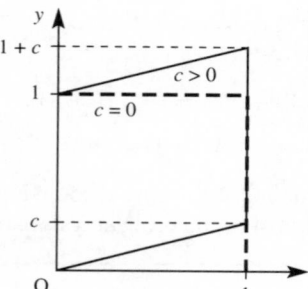

Figure 10.10 Density function for Example 10.10.

Solution To find the marginal distribution of X, we integrate with respect to y:

$$f_X(x) = \begin{cases} \displaystyle\int_{cx}^{cx+1} dy = 1 & (0 \leqslant x \leqslant 1) \\ \\ 0 & \text{otherwise} \end{cases}$$

The marginal distribution for Y is rather more complicated. Integrating with respect to x and assuming that $0 < c \leqslant 1$,

$$f_Y(y) = \begin{cases} 1 - \dfrac{1}{c}(y - 1) & (1 \leqslant y \leqslant 1 + c) \\ 1 & (c \leqslant y \leqslant 1) \\ \dfrac{y}{c} & (0 \leqslant y \leqslant c) \end{cases}$$

(Exercise 15). When $c = 0$, the marginal distribution for Y is the same as that for X. Finally, when $c = 1$,

$$P(X \leqslant \tfrac{1}{2} \quad \text{and} \quad Y \leqslant \tfrac{1}{2}) = \int_0^{1/2} \int_x^{1/2} 1 \, dy \, dx$$

$$= \int_0^{1/2} (\tfrac{1}{2} - x) \, dx = \tfrac{1}{8}$$

Here the inner integral (with respect to y) is performed with x treated as constant, and the resulting function of x is integrated to give the answer.

The definitions of joint and marginal distributions can be extended to any number of random variables.

10.4.2 Independence

The idea of independence of events can be extended to random variables to give us the important case in which no information is shared between them. This is important in experiments where essentially the same quantity is measured repeatedly, either within a single experiment involving repetition or between different experiments. As mentioned before, independence within a sample is one of the properties that qualifies the sample for analysis and conclusion.

Two random variables X and Y are called **independent** if their joint distribution factorizes into the product of their marginal distributions:

$$P(X = u_k \cap Y = v_j) = P(X = u_k)P(Y = v_j) \quad \text{in the discrete case}$$

$$f_{X,Y}(x, y) = f_X(x)f_Y(y) \qquad\qquad\qquad \text{in the continuous case}$$

For example, the random variables X and Y in Example 10.10 are independent if and only if $c = 0$.

EXAMPLE 10.11 The assembly of a complex piece of equipment can be divided into two stages. The times (in hours) required for the two stages are random variables (X and Y, say) with density functions e^{-x} and $2e^{-2y}$ respectively. Assuming that the stage assembly times are independent, find the probability that the assembly will be completed within four hours.

Solution The assumption of independence implies that

$$f_{X,Y}(x, y) = f_X(x)f_Y(y) = 2 e^{-(x + 2y)}$$

If the time for the first stage is x, the total time will not exceed four hours if

$$Y < 4 - x$$

so the required value is

$$P(X + Y < 4) = \int_0^4 \int_0^{4-x} f_{X,Y}(x, y) \, dy \, dx = \int_0^4 \int_0^{4-x} 2 e^{-(x+2y)} \, dy \, dx$$

$$= \int_0^4 (e^{-x} - e^{-(8-x)}) \, dx = 0.964$$

Where random variables are dependent upon one another, it is possible to express this dependence by defining a **conditional distribution** analogous to conditional probability, in terms of the joint distribution (or density function) and the marginal distributions. Instead of pursuing this idea here, we shall consider a numerical measure of dependence that can be estimated from sample data.

10.4.3   Covariance and correlation

The use of mean and variance for a random variable is motivated partly by the difficulty in determining the full probability distribution in many practical cases. The joint distribution of two variables presents even greater difficulties. Since we already have numerical measures of location and dispersion for the variables individually, it seems reasonable to define a measure of association of the two variables that is independent of their separate means and variances so that the new measure provides essentially new information about the variables.

There are four objectives that it seems reasonable for such a measure to satisfy. Its value should

(a) be zero for independent variables,

(b) be non-zero for dependent variables,

(c) indicate the degree of dependence in some well-defined sense, detached from the individual means and variances,

(d) be easy to estimate from sample data.

It is actually rather difficult to satisfy all of these, but the most popular measure of association gets most of the way.

The **covariance** of random variables X and Y, denoted by $\mathrm{Cov}\,(X, Y)$, is defined as

$$\mathrm{Cov}\,(X, Y) = E\{(X - \mu_X)(Y - \mu_Y)\}$$

$$= \begin{cases} \displaystyle\sum_{k=1}^{m} \sum_{j=1}^{n} (u_k - \mu_X)(v_j - \mu_Y)P(X = u_k \cap Y = v_j) \\ \displaystyle\int_{-\infty}^{\infty} \int_{-\infty}^{\infty} (x - \mu_X)(y - \mu_Y)f_{X,Y}(x, y) \, dx \, dy \end{cases}$$

for discrete and continuous variables respectively. The **correlation** $\rho_{X,Y}$ is the covariance divided by the product of the standard deviations:

$$\rho_{X,Y} = \frac{\text{Cov}(X, Y)}{\sigma_X \sigma_Y}$$

If whenever the random variable X is larger than its mean the random variable Y also tends to be larger than its mean then the product $(X - \mu_X)(Y - \mu_Y)$ will tend to be positive. The same will be true if both variables tend to be smaller than their means simultaneously. The covariance is then positive. A negative covariance implies that the variables tend to move in opposite directions with respect to their means. Both covariance and correlation therefore measure association relative to the mean values of the variables. It turns out that correlation measures association relative to the standard deviations as well.

It should be noted that the variance of a random variable X is the same as the covariance with itself:

$$\text{Var}(X) = \text{Cov}(X, X)$$

Also, by expanding the product within the integral or sum in the definition of covariance, it is easy to show that an alternative expression is

$$\text{Cov}(X, Y) = E(XY) - E(X)E(Y)$$

Although the sign of the covariance indicates the direction of the dependence, its magnitude depends not only on the degree of dependence but also upon the variances of the random variables, so it fails to satisfy the objective (c). In contrast, the correlation is limited in range

$$-1 \leqslant \rho_{X,Y} \leqslant +1$$

and it adopts the limiting values of this range only when the random variables are linearly related:

$$\rho_{X,Y} = \pm 1 \quad \text{if and only if there exist } a, b \text{ such that } Y = aX + b$$

(this is proved in most textbooks on probability theory). The magnitude of the correlation indicates the degree of linear relationship, so that objective (c) is satisfied.

EXAMPLE 10.12 Find the correlation of the random variables S and M in Example 10.9.

Solution The joint and marginal distributions of S and M are shown in Figure 10.9. First we find the expected values of S and S^2 from the marginal distribution, and hence the variance and standard deviation:

$$E(S) = \tfrac{15}{28} + (2)(\tfrac{3}{28}) = \tfrac{21}{28}, \qquad E(S^2) = \tfrac{15}{28} + (4)(\tfrac{3}{28}) = \tfrac{27}{28}$$

$$\text{Var}(S) = \tfrac{27}{28} - (\tfrac{21}{28})^2$$

from which

$$\sigma_S = \tfrac{3}{28}\sqrt{35}$$

Next we do the same for M:

$$E(M) = \tfrac{3}{7} + (2)(\tfrac{1}{28}) = \tfrac{1}{2}, \qquad E(M^2) = \tfrac{3}{7} + (4)(\tfrac{1}{28}) = \tfrac{4}{7}$$

$$\text{Var}(M) = \tfrac{4}{7} - \tfrac{1}{4} = \tfrac{9}{28}$$

from which

$$\sigma_M = \tfrac{3}{2}\sqrt{\tfrac{1}{7}}$$

All products of S and M are zero except when both are equal to one, so the expected value of the product is

$$E(SM) = \tfrac{3}{14}$$

The correlation now follows easily:

$$\rho_{S,M} = \frac{E(SM) - E(S)E(M)}{\sigma_S \sigma_M} = \frac{\tfrac{3}{14} - (\tfrac{21}{28})(\tfrac{1}{2})}{(\tfrac{3}{28}\sqrt{35})(\tfrac{3}{2}\sqrt{\tfrac{1}{7}})} = -\frac{1}{\sqrt{5}}$$

The correlation is negative because if there are more statistics books in the selection then there will tend to be fewer mathematics books, and vice versa.

EXAMPLE 10.13 Find the correlation of the random variables X and Y in Example 10.10.

Solution Proceeding as in Example 10.12, we have for X

$$E(X) = \int_0^1 x \, dx = \tfrac{1}{2}$$

$$E(X^2) = \int_0^1 x^2 \, dx = \tfrac{1}{3}$$

so that $\text{Var}(X) = E(X^2) - [E(X)]^2 = \tfrac{1}{12}$. Also, for Y

$$E(Y) = \int_0^c \frac{y^2}{c} \, dy + \int_c^1 y \, dy + \int_1^{1+c} y \left[1 - \frac{1}{c}(y-1) \right] dy$$

$$= \tfrac{1}{2}(1 + c) \qquad \text{after simplification}$$

$$E(Y^2) = \int_0^c \frac{y^3}{c} \, dy + \int_c^1 y^2 \, dy + \int_1^{1+c} y^2 \left[1 - \frac{1}{c}(y-1) \right] dy$$

$$= \tfrac{1}{3}(1 + c^2) + \tfrac{1}{2}c \qquad \text{after simplification}$$

so that $\text{Var}(Y) = E(Y^2) - [E(Y)]^2 = \tfrac{1}{12}(1 + c^2)$. For the expected value of the product we have

$$E(XY) = \int_0^1 \int_{cx}^{cx+1} xy \, dy \, dx = \frac{1}{2} \int_0^1 x(1 + 2cx) \, dx$$

$$= \tfrac{1}{4} + \tfrac{1}{3}c$$

Finally, the correlation between X and Y is

$$\rho_{X,Y} = \frac{E(XY) - E(X)E(Y)}{\sqrt{[\text{Var}(X)\,\text{Var}(Y)]}} = \frac{\frac{1}{4} + \frac{1}{3}c - \frac{1}{4}(1 + c)}{\frac{1}{12}\sqrt{(1 + c^2)}}$$

$$= \frac{c}{\sqrt{(1 + c^2)}}$$

Note that in fact the result of Example 10.13 holds for any value of c, and not just for the range $0 \leqslant c \leqslant 1$ assumed in Example 10.10. As the value of c increases (positive or negative), the correlation increases also, but its magnitude never exceeds one. It is also clear that if X and Y are independent then $c = 0$ and the correlation is zero. Refer to Figure 10.10 for a geometrical interpretation. When $c = 0$, the sample space is a square within which all points are equally likely, so there is no association between the variables. As c increases (positive or negative), the sample space becomes more elongated as the variables become more tightly coupled to one another.

The general relationship between independence and correlation is expressed as follows: if the random variables X and Y are independent then their correlation is zero. This is easily shown as follows for continuous random variables (or by a similar argument for discrete random variables). First we have

$$f_{X,Y}(x, y) = f_X(x)f_Y(y)$$

and then

$$\int_{-\infty}^{\infty} \int_{-\infty}^{\infty} (x - \mu_X)(y - \mu_Y)f_X(x)f_Y(y)\,\mathrm{d}x\,\mathrm{d}y$$

$$= \int_{-\infty}^{\infty} (x - \mu_X)f_X(x)\,\mathrm{d}x \int_{-\infty}^{\infty} (y - \mu_Y)f_Y(y)\,\mathrm{d}y$$

$$= (\mu_X - \mu_X)(\mu_Y - \mu_Y) = 0$$

Unfortunately, the converse does not hold: zero correlation does not imply independence. In general, correlation is a measure of linear dependence, and may be zero or very small for variables that are dependent in a *nonlinear* way (see Exercise 14). Objective (a) is satisfied, therefore, but not objective (b) in general.

Another problem with correlation is that a non-zero value does not imply the presence of a causal relationship between the variables or the phenomena that they measure. Correlation can be 'spurious', deriving from some third variable that may be unrecognized at the time. For example, among the economic statistics that are gathered together from many countries and published, there are figures for the number of telephones per head of population, birth rate, and the gross domestic product per capita (GDP). It turns out that there is a large negative correlation between number of telephones per head and the birth rate, but no-one would suggest that telephones have any direct application in birth control. The GDP is a measure of wealth, and there is a large positive correlation between this and the number of telephones per head, and a large negative correlation between

GDP and birth rate, both for quite genuine reasons. The correlation between telephones and birth rate is therefore spurious, and a more sophisticated measure called the **partial correlation** can be used to eliminate the third variable (provided that it is recognized and measured).

We have considered all the objectives except (d); that this is satisfied is shown in Section 10.4.4.

10.4.4 Sample correlation

There are two kinds of situations where we take samples of values of two random variables X and Y. First we might be interested in the same property for two different populations. Perhaps there is evidence that the mean values are different, so we take samples of each and compare them. This situation was discussed in Section 10.3.5. The second kind involves two different properties for the same population. It is to this situation that correlation applies. We take a single sample from the population and measure the pair of random variables (X_i, Y_i) for each $i = 1, \ldots, n$.

For a sample $\{(X_1, Y_1), \ldots, (X_n, Y_n)\}$ the **sample correlation coefficient** is defined as

$$r_{X,Y} = \frac{\dfrac{1}{n} \sum_{i=1}^{n} [(X_i - \bar{X})(Y_i - \bar{Y})]}{S_X S_Y}$$

Like the true correlation, the sample correlation is limited in value to the range $[-1, 1]$ and $r_{X,Y} = \pm 1$ when (and only when) all of the points lie along a line. Figure 10.11 contains four typical **scatter diagrams** of samples plotted on the (x, y) plane, with an indication of the correlation for each one. The range of behaviour is shown from independence (a) through imperfect correlation (b) and (c) to a perfect linear relationship (d).

By expanding the product within the outer bracket in the numerator, it is

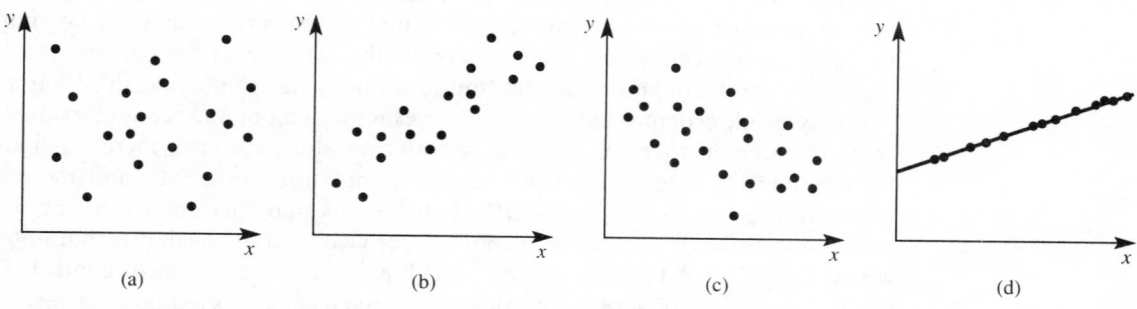

Figure 10.11 Scatter plots for two random variables: (a) $\rho_{X,Y} = 0$; (b) $\rho_{X,Y} > 0$; (c) $\rho_{X,Y} < 0$; (d) $\rho_{X,Y} = 1$.

```
{   Program to compute sample correlation.
x(k) and y(k) are the arrays of data,
n is the sample size,
xbar and ybar are the sample averages,
sx and sy are the sample standard deviations,
rxy is the sample correlation,
Mx, My, Qx, Qy, Qxy hold running totals.   }


Mx ← 0; My ← 0
Qx ← 0; Qy ← 0
Qxy ← 0
for k is 1 to n do
    diffx ← x(k) − Mx
    diffy ← y(k) − My
    Mx ← ((k − 1) * Mx + x(k))/k
    My ← ((k − 1) * My + y(k))/k
    Qx ← Qx + (1 − 1/k) * diffx * diffx
    Qy ← Qy + (1 − 1/k) * diffy * diffy
    Qxy ← Qxy + (1 − 1/k) * diffx * diffy
endfor
xbar ← Mx; ybar ← My
sx ← sqr(Qx/n); sy ← sqr(Qy/n)
rxy ← Qxy/(n * sx * sy)
```

Figure 10.12 Pseudocode listing for sample correlation.

easy to show that an alternative expression is

$$r_{X,Y} = \frac{\overline{XY} - (\bar{X})(\bar{Y})}{S_X S_Y}$$

which is useful for hand calculation. For computer calculation the best method involves the successive sums of products:

$$Q_{XY,k} = \sum_{i=1}^{k} (X_i - M_{X,k})(Y_i - M_{Y,k})$$

where

$$M_{X,k} = \frac{1}{k} \sum_{i=1}^{k} X_i, \qquad M_{Y,k} = \frac{1}{k} \sum_{i=1}^{k} Y_i$$

and then $r_{X,Y} = Q_{XY,n}/nS_X S_Y$. The pseudocode listing in Figure 10.12 exploits the recurrence relation

$$Q_{XY,k} = Q_{XY,k-1} + \left(1 - \frac{1}{k}\right)(X_k - M_{X,k-1})(Y_k - M_{Y,k-1})$$

which allows for a single pass through the data with no loss of accuracy.

EXAMPLE 10.14 A material used in the construction industry contains an impurity suspected of having an adverse effect upon the material's performance in resisting long-term operational stresses. Percentages of impurity and performance indexes for 22 specimens of this material are as follows:

% Impurity X_i	4.4	5.5	4.2	3.0	4.5	4.9	4.6	5.0	4.7	5.1	4.4
Performance Y_i	12	14	18	35	23	29	16	12	18	21	27

% Impurity X_i	4.1	4.9	4.7	5.0	4.6	3.6	4.9	5.1	4.8	5.2	5.2
Performance Y_i	13	19	22	20	16	27	21	13	18	17	11

Find the sample correlation coefficient.

Solution The following quantities are easily obtained from the data:

$$\bar{X} = 4.6545, \quad S_X = 0.550\,81, \quad \bar{Y} = 19.1818 \quad S_Y = 6.0350, \quad \overline{XY} = 87.3591$$

(Note that it is advisable to record these results to several significant digits in order to avoid losing precision when calculating the difference within the numerator of $r_{X,Y}$.) The sample correlation is then $r_{X,Y} = -0.58$, the negative value suggesting that the impurity has an adverse affect upon performance. It remains to be seen whether this is statistically significant.

10.4.5   Interval and test for correlation

Correlation is more difficult to deal with than mean and proportion, but for normal random variables X and Y with a true correlation $\rho_{X,Y}$ the sample statistic

$$Z = \frac{\sqrt{(n-3)}}{2}\ln\left[\frac{(1+r_{X,Y})(1-\rho_{X,Y})}{(1-r_{X,Y})(1+\rho_{X,Y})}\right]$$

is approximately standard normal for large n. This can be used directly as a test statistic for an assumed value of $\rho_{X,Y}$. Alternatively, an approximate $100(1-\alpha)\%$ confidence interval for $\rho_{X,Y}$ can be derived:

$$\left(\frac{1+r-c(1-r)}{1+r+c(1-r)}, \frac{1+r-(1-r)/c}{1+r+(1-r)/c}\right)$$

where

$$c = \exp\left[\frac{2z_{\alpha/2}}{\sqrt{(n-3)}}\right]$$

(the subscripts X and Y have been dropped from $r_{X,Y}$ in this formula).

EXAMPLE 10.15 For the data in Example 10.14 find 95% and 99% confidence intervals for the true correlation between percentage of impurity and performance index, and test the hypothesis that these are independent.

Solution The sample correlation (from the 22 specimens) was found in Example 10.14 to be -0.58. For the 95% confidence interval the constant $c = 2.458$ and the interval itself is $(-0.80, -0.21)$. Similarly, the 99% confidence interval is $(-0.85, -0.07)$. Assuming $\rho_{XY} = 0$, the value of the test statistic is $Z = -2.89$, which exceeds $z_{0.005} = 2.576$ in magnitude. Either way, we can be more than 99% confident that the impurity has an adverse effect upon performance.

10.4.6   Rank correlation

As has been previously emphasized the correlation only works as a measure of dependence if

(1) n is reasonably large,

(2) X and Y are *numerical* characteristics,

(3) the dependence is *linear*, and

(4) X and Y each have a *normal* distribution.

There is an alternative form of sample correlation, which has greater applicability, requiring only that

(1) n is reasonably large,

(2) X and Y are *rankable* characteristics, and

(3) the dependence is *monotonic* (that is, always in the same direction, which may be forward or inverse, but not necessarily linear).

The variables X and Y can have any distribution. For a set of data $X_1, \ldots, X_n$, a **rank** of 1 is assigned to the smallest value, 2 to the next-smallest and so on up to a rank of n assigned to the largest. This applies wherever the values are distinct. Tied values are given the mean of the ranks they would receive if slightly different. The following is an example:

X_i	8	3	5	8	1	9	6	5	3	5	7	2
Rank	10.5	3.5	6	10.5	1	12	8	6	3.5	6	9	2

The **Spearman rank correlation coefficient** r_S for data $(X_1, Y_1, \ldots, (X_n, Y_n)$ is the correlation of the ranks of X_i and Y_i, where the data $X_1, \ldots, X_n$ and $Y_1, \ldots, Y_n$ are ranked separately. If the number of tied values is small compared with n then

$$r_S \simeq 1 - \frac{6}{n(n^2 - 1)} \sum_{i=1}^{n} d_i^2$$

where d_i is the difference between the rank of X_i and that of Y_i. The value of r_S always lies in the interval $[-1, 1]$, and adopts its extreme values only when the rankings precisely match (forwards or in reverse).

To test for dependence, special tables must be used for small samples ($n < 20$), but for larger samples the test statistic

$$Z = r_S \sqrt{(n-1)}$$

is approximately standard normal.

EXAMPLE 10.16 Find and test the rank correlation for the data in Example 10.14.

Solution The data with their ranks are as follows:

X_i	4.4	5.5	4.2	3.0	4.5	4.9	4.6	5.0	4.7	5.1	4.4
Rank	5.5	22	4	1	7	14	8.5	16.5	10.5	18.5	5.5

Y_i	12	14	18	35	23	29	16	12	18	21	27
Rank	2.5	6	11	22	18	21	7.5	2.5	11	15.5	19.5

X_i	4.1	4.9	4.7	5.0	4.6	3.6	4.9	5.1	4.8	5.2	5.2
Rank	3	14	10.5	16.5	8.5	2	14	18.5	12	20.5	20.5

Y_i	13	19	22	20	16	27	21	13	18	17	11
Rank	4.5	13	17	14	7.5	19.5	15.5	4.5	11	9	1

From this, the rank correlation is $r_S = -0.361$, and $Z = -1.66$, which exceeds $z_{0.05} = 1.645$ and is therefore just significant at the 10% level. If the approximate formula is used, the sum of squares of differences is 2398, so

$$r_S \simeq 1 - \frac{(6)(2398)}{(22)(483)} = -0.354$$

and $Z = -1.62$, which is just short of significance.

These results show that the rank correlation is a more conservative test than the sample correlation $r_{X,Y}$, in that a larger sample tends to be needed before the hypothesis of independence is rejected. A price has to be paid for the wider applicability of the method.

10.4.7 Exercises

13 Suppose that the random variables X and Y have the following joint distribution:

		X	
Y	1	2	3
1	0	0.17	0.08
2	0.20	0.11	0
3	0.14	0.25	0.05

Find (a) the marginal distributions of X and Y, (b) $P(Y = 3 \,|\, X = 2)$, and (c) the mean, variance and correlation coefficient of X and Y.

14 Consider the random variable X with density function

$$f_X(x) = \begin{cases} 1 & (-\tfrac{1}{2} < x < \tfrac{1}{2}) \\ 0 & \text{otherwise} \end{cases}$$

Show that the covariance of X and X^2 is zero. (This shows that zero covariance does not imply independence, because obviously X^2 is dependent on X.)

15 The joint density function of random variables X and Y is

$$f_{X,Y}(x, y) = \begin{cases} 1 & (0 \leqslant x \leqslant 1; \, cx \leqslant y \leqslant cx + 1) \\ 0 & \text{otherwise} \end{cases}$$

where c is a constant such that $0 \leqslant c \leqslant 1$. Find the marginal density function for Y (see Example 10.10).

16 Let the random variables X and Y have joint density function given by

$$f_{X,Y}(x, y) = \begin{cases} c(1 - y) & (0 \leqslant x \leqslant y \leqslant 1) \\ 0 & \text{otherwise} \end{cases}$$

Find (a) the value of the constant c, (b) $P(x < \tfrac{3}{4}, y > \tfrac{1}{2})$, and (c) the marginal density functions for X and Y.

17 Let the random variables X and Y represent the lifetimes (in hundreds of hours) of two types of components used in an electronic system. The joint density function is given by

$$f_{X,Y}(x, y) = \begin{cases} \tfrac{1}{8}x e^{-(x+y)/2} & (x > 0, y > 0) \\ 0 & \text{otherwise} \end{cases}$$

Find (a) the probability that two components (one of each type) will each last longer than 100 h, and (b) the probability that a component of the second type (Y) will have a lifetime in excess of 200 h.

18 The ball and socket of a joint are separately moulded and then assembled together. The diameter of the ball is a random variable X between 29.8 and 30.3 mm, all values being equally likely. The internal diameter of the socket is a random variable Y between 30.1 and 30.6 mm, again with all values equally likely. The condition for an acceptable fit is that $0 \leqslant Y - X \leqslant 0.6$ mm. Find the probability of this condition being satisfied, assuming that the random variables are independent.

19 The following are the measured heights and weights of eight people:

Height (cm)	182.8	162.5	175.2	185.4	170.1	167.6	177.8	172.7
Weight (kg)	86.1	58.3	83.0	92.4	60.2	69.3	83.6	72.7

Find the sample correlation coefficient.

20 The number of minutes it took 10 mechanics to assemble a piece of machinery in the morning (X) and in the late afternoon (Y) were measured, with the following results:

X	11.1	10.3	12.0	15.1	13.7	18.5	17.3	14.2	14.8	15.3
Y	10.9	14.2	13.8	21.5	13.2	21.1	16.4	19.3	17.4	19.0

Find the sample correlation coefficient.

21 If the sample correlation between resistance and failure time for 30 overloaded resistors is 0.7, find a 95% confidence interval for the true correlation.

22 Find a 95% confidence interval for correlation between height and weight using the data in Exercise 19.

23 Marks obtained by 20 students taking examinations in mathematics and computer studies were as follows:

Math.	45 77 43 64 58 64 58 54 71 45 57 52 67 57 54 54
	61 58 55 42
Comp.	64 67 47 75 42 65 58 42 70 44 44 67 49 70 51 58
	37 60 42 36

Find the sample correlation coefficient and the 90% and 95% confidence intervals. Hence test the hypothesis that the two marks are independent at the 5% and 10% significance levels. Also find and test the rank correlation.

10.5   Regression

A procedure that is very familiar to engineers is that of drawing a good straight line through a set of points on a graph. When calibrating a measuring instrument, for example, known inputs are applied, the readings are noted and plotted, a straight line is drawn as close to the points as possible (there are bound to be small errors, so they will not all lie on the line), and the graph is then used to interpret the readings for unknown inputs. It is possible to draw the line by eye, but there is a better way, which involves calculating the slope and intercept of the line from the data. The given line then minimizes the total squared error for the data points. This procedure (which for historical reasons is called **regression**) can be applied in general to pairs of random variables.

Computer packages are very often used to carry out the regression calculations and display the results. This is of special value when the data tend to follow a curve and various nonlinear models are tried and compared (see Section 10.5.4).

10.5.1   The method of least squares

The correlation was introduced in Section 10.4.3 as a way of measuring the dependence between random variables. Subsequently, we have seen how the correlation can be estimated and the dependence tested using sample data. We can take the idea of correlation between variables (say X and Y) a stage further by assuming that the sample pairs $\{(X_1, Y_1), \ldots, (X_n, Y_n)\}$ satisfy a linear relationship of the form

$$Y_i = a + bX_i + E_i \quad (i = 1, \ldots, n)$$

where a and b are unknown coefficients and the random variables E_i have zero mean and represent residual errors. This assumption is prompted by the scatter diagrams in Figure 10.11, which illustrate how the points may be concentrated around a line. Figure 10.13 shows a typical scatter diagram again, this time with the line drawn in. If we can estimate the coefficients a and b so as to give the best fit, we shall be able to predict the value of Y when the value of X is known.

The least-squares approach is to choose estimates $\hat{a}$ and $\hat{b}$ to minimize the sum of squares of the values E_i:

$$Q = \sum_{i=1}^{n} E_i^2 = \sum_{i=1}^{n} [Y_i - (\hat{a} + \hat{b}X_i)]^2$$

Equating to zero the partial derivatives of this sum with respect to the two coefficients gives a pair of equations that determine the minimum:

Figure 10.13 Scatter plot with regression line (Example 10.17).

$$\frac{\partial Q}{\partial \hat{a}} = 0 = -2 \sum_{i=1}^{n} [Y_i - (\hat{a} + \hat{b}X_i)]$$

$$\frac{\partial Q}{\partial \hat{b}} = 0 = -2 \sum_{i=1}^{n} X_i [Y_i - (\hat{a} + \hat{b}X_i)]$$

These can be rewritten as

$$n\hat{a} + (\Sigma_i X_i)\hat{b} = (\Sigma_i Y_i)$$

$$(\Sigma_i X_i)\hat{a} + (\Sigma_i X_i^2)\hat{b} = (\Sigma_i X_i Y_i)$$

(where $\Sigma_i = \Sigma_{i=1}^{n}$) from which the solution is

$$\hat{b} = \frac{S_{XY}}{S_X^2}, \quad \hat{a} = \bar{Y} - \hat{b}\bar{X}$$

where

$$\bar{X} = \frac{1}{n}\Sigma_i X_i, \qquad \bar{Y} = \frac{1}{n}\Sigma_i Y_i$$

and

$$S_{XY} = \frac{1}{n}\Sigma_i (X_i - \bar{X})(Y_i - \bar{Y}) = \overline{XY} - (\bar{X})(\bar{Y})$$

$$S_X^2 = \frac{1}{n}\Sigma_i (X_i - \bar{X})^2 = \overline{X^2} - (\bar{X})^2$$

$$S_Y^2 = \frac{1}{n}\Sigma_i (Y_i - \bar{Y})^2 = \overline{Y^2} - (\bar{Y})^2$$

are the sample variances and covariance.

This process of fitting a straight line through a set of data of the form $\{(X_1, Y_1), \ldots, (X_n, Y_n)\}$ is called **linear regression**, and the coefficients are called **regression coefficients**.

EXAMPLE 10.17 A strain gauge has been bonded to a steel beam, and is being calibrated. The resistance of the strain gauge is converted into a voltage appearing on a meter. Known forces (X, in kN) are applied and voltmeter measurements (Y, in V) are as follows:

X	1	2	3	4	5	6	7	8	9	10	11	12	13	14
Y	4.4	4.9	6.4	7.3	8.8	10.3	11.7	13.2	14.8	15.3	16.5	17.2	18.9	19.3

Fit a regression line through the data and estimate the tension in the beam when the meter reading is 13.8 V.

Solution The following quantities are calculated from the data:

$$\bar{X} = 7.5, \quad S_X = 4.031\,13, \quad \bar{Y} = 12.0714, \quad S_Y = 4.950\,68, \quad \overline{XY} = 110.421$$

(When using a hand calculator to solve linear regression problems, it is advisable to work to at least five or six significant digits during intermediate calculations, because the subtraction in the numerator of $\hat{b}$ often results in the loss of some leading digits.) From these results, $\hat{b} = 1.22$ and $\hat{a} = 2.89$ (Figure 10.13). The estimated value of tension for a reading of $Y = 13.8$ V is given by

$$13.8 = 2.89 + 1.22X$$

from which $X = 8.9$ kN.

Figure 10.14 shows a pseudocode listing for linear regression. The program is very similar to that in Figure 10.12 for the sample correlation, and the link between these will be explained in Section 10.5.3. In addition to the regression coefficients $\hat{a}$ and $\hat{b}$, an estimate of the residual standard deviation is returned, which is explained below.

10.5.2   Normal residuals

The process of fitting a straight line through the data by minimizing the sum of squares of the errors does not involve any statistics as such. However, we often need to test whether the slope of the regression line is significantly different from zero, because this will reveal whether there is any dependence between the random variables. For this purpose we must make the assumption that the errors E_i, called the **residuals**, have a normal distribution:

$$E_i \sim N(0, \sigma_E^2)$$

The unknown variance σ_E^2 can be estimated by defining

```
{   Program to compute linear regression coefficients.
x(k) and y(k) are the arrays of data,
n is the sample size,
xbar and ybar are the sample averages,
sx and sy are the sample standard deviations,
bhat is the regression slope result,
ahat is the regression intercept result,
se is the residual standard deviation,
Mx, My, Qx, Qy, Qxy hold running totals.   }

Mx ← 0; My ← 0
Qx ← 0; Qy ← 0
Qxy ← 0
for k is 1 to n do
    diffx ← x(k) − Mx
    diffy ← y(k) − My
    Mx ← ((k − 1) * Mx + x(k))/k
    My ← ((k − 1) * My + y(k))/k
    Qx ← Qx + (1 − 1/k) * diffx * diffx
    Qy ← Qy + (1 − 1/k) * diffy * diffy
    Qxy ← Qxy + (1 − 1/k) * diffx * diffy
endfor
xbar ← Mx; ybar ← My
sx ← sqr(Qx/n); sy ← sqr(Qy/n)
bhat ← Qxy/(n * sx * sx)
ahat ← ybar − bhat * xbar
se ← sqr(sy * sy − bhat * bhat * sx * sx)
```

Figure 10.14 Pseudocode listing for linear regression.

$$S_E^2 = \frac{1}{n} \sum_{i=1}^{n} E_i^2 = \frac{1}{n} \sum_{i=1}^{n} [Y_i - (\hat{a} + \hat{b}X_i)]^2$$

Using the earlier result that $\hat{a} = \bar{Y} - \hat{b}\bar{X}$ gives a more convenient form:

$$S_E^2 = \frac{1}{n}\Sigma_i[(Y_i - \bar{Y}) - \hat{b}(X_i - \bar{X})]^2$$

$$= \frac{1}{n}\Sigma_i[(Y_i - \bar{Y})^2 - 2\hat{b}(X_i - \bar{X})(Y_i - \bar{Y}) + \hat{b}^2(X_i - \bar{X})^2]$$

$$= S_Y^2 - 2\hat{b}S_{XY} + \hat{b}^2 S_X^2$$

$$= S_Y^2 - \hat{b}^2 S_X^2$$

This result is used in the pseudocode listing (Figure 10.14).

Various confidence intervals are derived in more advanced texts covering linear regression. Here the most useful results will simply be quoted. The

$100(1 - \alpha)\%$ confidence interval for the regression slope b is given by

$$\left(b \pm t_{\alpha/2, n-2} \frac{S_E}{S_X \sqrt{(n-2)}} \right)$$

It is often useful to have an estimate of the mean value of Y for a given value of X, say $X = x$. The point estimate is $\hat{a} + \hat{b}x$, and the $100(1 - \alpha)\%$ confidence interval for this is

$$\left(\hat{a} + \hat{b}x \pm t_{\alpha/2, n-2} S_E \sqrt{\left[\frac{1 + (x - \bar{X})^2 / S_X^2}{n - 2} \right]} \right)$$

EXAMPLE 10.18   Estimate the residual standard deviation and find a 95% confidence interval for the regression slope for the data in Example 10.17. Also test the hypothesis that the tension in the beam is 10 kN when a voltmeter reading of 15 V is obtained.

Solution   Using the results obtained in Example 10.17, the residual standard deviation is

$$S_E = 0.418$$

and, using $t_{0.025, 12} = 2.179$, the 95% confidence interval for b is

$$\left(1.22 \pm 2.179 \frac{0.418}{(4.031)\sqrt{12}} \right) = (1.16, 1.29)$$

Obviously the regression slope is significant – but this is not in doubt. To test the hypothesis that the tension is 10 kN, we can use the 95% confidence interval for the corresponding voltage, which is

$$\left(2.89 + 1.22(10) \pm 2.179(0.418) \sqrt{\left[\frac{1 + (10 - 7.5)^2/(4.031)^2}{12} \right]} \right)$$

$$= (14.8, 15.4)$$

The measured value of 15 V lies within this interval, so the hypothesis is accepted at the 5% level. A better way to approach this would be to reverse the regression (use force as the Y variable and voltage as the X variable), so that a confidence interval for the tension in the beam for a given voltage could be obtained and the assumed value tested. For the present data this gives $(9.6, 10.1)$ at 95%, so again the hypothesis is accepted (Exercise 25).

10.5.3   Regression and correlation

Both regression and correlation are statistical methods for measuring the linear dependence of one random variable upon another, so it is not surprising that there is a connection between them. From the definition of the sample correlation $r_{X,Y}$ (Section 10.4.4) and the result for the regression slope $\hat{b}$, it follows immediately that

$$r_{X,Y} = \frac{S_{XY}}{S_X S_Y} = \frac{\hat{b} S_X}{S_Y}$$

Another expression for the residual variance is then

$$S_E^2 = S_Y^2 - \left(\frac{S_Y r_{X,Y}}{S_X}\right)^2 S_X^2$$
$$= S_Y^2 (1 - r_{X,Y}^2)$$

This result has an important interpretation. S_Y^2 is the total variation in the Y values, and S_E^2 is the residual variation after the regression line has been identified, so $r_{X,Y}^2$ is the proportion of the total variation in the Y values that is accounted for by the regression on X: informally, it represents how closely the points are clustered about the line. This is a measure of goodness of fit that is especially useful when the dependence between X and Y is nonlinear and different models are to be compared.

10.5.4 Nonlinear regression

Sometimes the dependence between two random variables is nonlinear, and this shows clearly in the scatter plot; see for instance Figure 10.15. Fitting a straight line through the data would hardly be appropriate. Instead, various models of the dependence can be assumed and tested. In each case the value of $r_{X,Y}^2$ indicates the success of the model in capturing the dependence. One form of nonlinear regression model involves a quadratic or higher-degree polynomial:

$$Y_i = a_0 + a_1 X_i + a_2 X_i^2 + E_i \quad (i = 1, \dots, n)$$

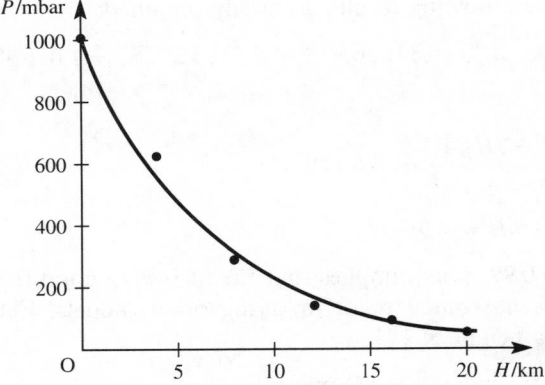

Figure 10.15 Nonlinear regression (Example 10.19).

The three coefficients a_0, a_1 and a_2 can be identified by a multivariate regression method that is beyond the scope of this text. A simpler approach is to try models of the form

$$Y_i = aX_i^b F_i \quad (i = 1, \ldots, n)$$

or

$$Y_i = F_i \exp(a + bX_i) \quad (i = 1, \ldots, n)$$

where each F_i is a residual multiplicative error. On taking logarithms, these models reduce to the standard linear form:

$$\ln Y_i = \ln a + b \ln X_i + E_i \quad (i = 1, \ldots, n)$$

or

$$\ln Y_i = a + bX_i + E_i \quad (i = 1, \ldots, n)$$

which can be solved by the usual method.

EXAMPLE 10.19 The following data for atmospheric pressure (P, in mbar) at various heights (H, in km) have been obtained:

Height H	0	4	8	12	16	20
Pressure P	1012	621	286	141	104	54

The relationship between height and pressure is believed to be of the form

$$P = e^{a + bH}$$

where a and b are constants. Fit and assess a model of this form and predict the atmospheric pressure at a height of 14 km.

Solution Taking logarithms and setting $Y = \ln P$ gives

$$Y_i = a + bH_i + E_i$$

for which the following results are easily obtained:

$$\bar{H} = 10, \quad S_H = 6.831\,30, \quad \bar{Y} = 5.431\,52, \quad S_Y = 1.016\,38, \quad \overline{HY} = 47.4081$$

Hence

$$\hat{b} = \frac{\overline{HY} - (\bar{H})(\bar{Y})}{S_H^2} = -0.148$$

$$\hat{a} = \bar{Y} - \hat{b}\bar{H} = 6.91$$

Also, $r_{H,Y}^2 = 0.99$, which implies that the fit is very good (Figure 10.15). In this case there is not much point in trying other models. Finally, the predicted pressure at a height of 14 km is

$$P = e^{6.91 - 0.148(14)} = 126\,\text{mbar}$$

10.5.5 Exercises

24 Measured deflections (in mm) of a structure under a load (in kg) were recorded as follows:

Load X	1	2	3	4	5	6	7	8	9	10	11	12
Deflection Y	16	35	45	74	86	96	106	124	134	156	164	182

Draw a scatter plot of the data. Find the linear regression coefficients and predict the deflection for a load of 15 kg.

25 Using the data in Example 10.17, carry out a regression of force against voltage, and obtain a 95% confidence interval for the tension in the beam when the voltmeter reads 15 V, as described in Example 10.18.

26 Weekly advertising expenditures X_i and sales Y_i for a company are as follows (in units of £100):

X_i	40	20	25	20	30	50	40	20	50	40	25	50
Y_i	385	400	395	365	475	440	490	420	560	525	480	510

(a) Fit a regression line and predict the sales for an advertising expenditure of £6000.

(b) Estimate the residual standard deviation and find a 95% confidence interval for the regression slope. Hence test the hypothesis that the sales do not depend upon advertising expenditure.

(c) Find a 95% confidence interval for the mean sales when advertising expenditure is £6000.

27 A machine that can be run at different speeds produces articles, of which a certain number are defective. The number of defective items produced per hour depends upon machine speed (in rev s^{-1}) as indicated in the following experimental run:

Speed	8	9	10	11	12	13	14	15
Defectives per hour	7	12	13	13	13	16	14	18

Find the regression line for number of defectives against speed, and a 90% confidence interval for the mean number of defectives per hour when the speed is 14 rev s^{-1}.

28 Sometimes it is required that the regression line passes through the origin, in which case the only regression coefficient is the slope of the line. Use the least-squares procedure to show that the estimate of the slope is then

$$\hat{b} = (\Sigma_i X_i Y_i)/\Sigma_i X_i^2$$

29 A series of measurements of voltage across and current through a resistor produced the following results:

Voltage (V)	1	2	3	4	5	6	7	8	9	10	11	12
Current (mA)	6	18	27	30	42	48	58	69	74	81	94	99

Estimate the resistance, using the result of the previous exercise.

30 The pressure P of a gas corresponding to various volumes V was recorded as follows:

V (cm³)	50	60	70	90	100
P (kg cm^{-2})	64.7	51.3	40.5	25.9	7.8

The ideal gas law is given by the equation

$$PV^\lambda = C$$

where λ and C are constants. By taking logarithms and using the least-squares method, estimate λ and C from the data and predict P when $V = 80 \text{ cm}^3$.

31 The following data show the unit costs of producing certain electronic components and the number of units produced:

Lot size X_i	50	100	250	500	1000	2000	5000
Unit cost Y_i	108	65	21	13	4	2.2	1

Fit a model of the form $Y = aX^b$ and predict the unit cost for a lot size of 300.

10.6   Goodness-of-fit tests

The common classes of distributions, especially the binomial, Poisson and normal distributions, which often govern the data in experimental contexts, are used as the basis for statistical methods of estimation and testing. A question that naturally arises is whether or not a given set of data actually follows an assumed distribution. If it does then the statistical methods can be used with confidence. If not then some alternative should be considered. The general procedure used for testing this can also be used to test for dependence between two variables.

10.6.1   Chi-square distribution and test

No set of data will follow an assumed distribution exactly, but there is a general method for testing a distribution as a statistical hypothesis. If the hypothesis is accepted then it is reasonable to use the distribution as an approximation to reality.

First the data must be partitioned into classes. If the data consist of observations from a discrete distribution then they will be in classes already, but it may be appropriate to combine some classes if the numbers of observations are small. For each class the number of observations that would be expected to occur under the assumed distribution can be worked out. The following quantity acts as a test statistic for comparing the observed and expected class numbers:

$$\chi^2 = \sum_{k=1}^{m} \frac{(f_k - e_k)^2}{e_k}$$

where f_k is the number of observations in the kth class, e_k is the expected number in the kth class and m is the number of classes. Clearly, χ^2 is a non-negative quantity whose magnitude indicates the extent of the discrepancy between the histogram of data and the assumed distribution. For small samples the histogram is erratic

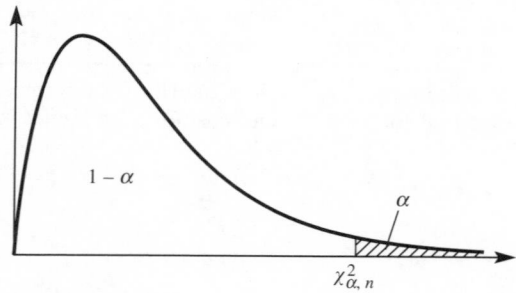

Figure 10.16 The chi-square distribution with $\chi^2_{\alpha,n}$.

and the comparison invalid, but for large samples the histogram should approximate the true distribution. It can be shown that for a large sample the random variable χ^2 has a **'chi-square' distribution**. This class of distributions is widely used in statistics, and a typical chi-square probability density function is shown in Figure 10.16. We are interested in particular in the value of $\chi^2_{\alpha,n}$ to the right of which the area under the density function curve is α, where n is the (single) parameter of the distribution. These values are extensively tabulated; a typical table is shown in Figure 10.17.

The hypothesis of the assumed distribution is rejected if

$$\chi^2 > \chi^2_{\alpha,m-t-1}$$

where α is the significance level and t is the number of independent parameters estimated from the data and used for computing the e_k values. The significance level is the probability of false rejection, as discussed in Section 10.3.4. The only

n	$\alpha = 0.05$	$\alpha = 0.025$	$\alpha = 0.01$	$\alpha = 0.005$	n
1	3.841	5.024	6.635	7.879	1
2	5.991	7.378	9.210	10.597	2
3	7.815	9.348	11.345	12.838	3
4	9.488	11.143	13.277	14.860	4
5	11.070	12.832	15.086	16.750	5
6	12.592	14.449	16.812	18.548	6
7	14.067	16.013	18.475	20.278	7
8	15.507	17.535	20.090	21.955	8
9	16.919	19.023	21.666	23.589	9
10	18.307	20.483	23.209	25.188	10
11	19.675	21.920	24.725	26.757	11
12	21.026	23.337	26.217	28.300	12
13	22.362	24.736	27.688	29.819	13
14	23.685	26.119	29.141	31.319	14
15	24.996	27.488	30.578	32.801	15
16	26.296	28.845	32.000	34.267	16
17	27.587	30.191	33.409	35.718	17
18	28.869	31.526	34.805	37.156	18
19	30.144	32.852	36.191	38.582	19
20	31.410	34.170	37.566	39.997	20
21	32.671	35.479	38.932	41.401	21
22	33.924	36.781	40.289	42.796	22
23	35.172	38.076	41.638	44.181	23
24	36.415	39.364	42.980	45.558	24
25	37.652	40.646	44.314	46.928	25
26	38.885	41.923	45.642	48.290	26
27	40.113	43.194	46.963	49.645	27
28	41.337	44.461	48.278	50.993	28
29	42.557	45.722	49.588	52.336	29
30	43.773	46.979	50.892	53.672	30

Figure 10.17 Table of the chi-square distribution $\chi^2_{\alpha,n}$.

difference is that there is now no estimation procedure underlying the hypothesis test, which must stand alone. Sometimes the hypothesis is deliberately vague, for example a parameter value may be left unspecified. If the data themselves are used to fix parameter values in the assumed distribution before testing then the test must be strengthened to allow for this in the form of a correction t in the chi-square parameter.

A useful rule of thumb when using this test is that there should be at most a small number (one or two) of classes with an expected number of observations less than five. If necessary, classes in the tails of the distribution can be merged.

EXAMPLE 10.20   A die is tossed 600 times, and the numbers of occurrences of the numbers one to six are recorded respectively as 89, 113, 98, 104, 117 and 79. Is the die fair or biased?

Solution   The expected values are $e_k = 100$ for all k, and the test value is $\chi^2 = 10.4$. This is less than $\chi^2_{0.05,5} = 11.07$, so we should expect results as erratic as this at least once in 20 similar experiments. The die may well be biased, but the data are insufficient to justify this conclusion.

EXAMPLE 10.21   The numbers of trucks arriving per hour at a warehouse are counted for each of 500 h. Counts of zero up to eight arrivals are recorded on respectively 52, 151, 130, 102, 45, 12, 5, 1 and 2 occasions. Test the hypothesis that the numbers of arrivals have a Poisson distribution, and estimate how often there will be nine or more arrivals in one hour.

Solution   The hypothesis stipulates a Poisson distribution, but without specifying the parameter λ. Since the mean of the Poisson distribution is λ and the average number of arrivals per hour is 2.02 from the data, it is reasonable to assume that $\lambda = 2$. The columns in the table in Figure 10.18 show the observed counts f_k, the Poisson probabilities p_k, the expected counts $e_k = 500p_k$ and the individual χ^2 values for each class. The last two classes have been combined because the numbers are so small. One parameter has been estimated from the data, so the total χ^2 value is compared with $\chi^2_{0.05,6} = 12.59$. The Poisson hypothesis is

Trucks	f_k	p_k	e_k	χ^2
0	52	0.1353	67.7	3.63
1	151	0.2707	135.3	1.81
2	130	0.2707	135.3	0.21
3	102	0.1804	90.2	1.54
4	45	0.0902	45.1	0.00
5	12	0.0361	18.0	2.02
6	5	0.0120	6.0	0.17
7	3	0.0046	2.3	0.24
Totals	500	1.0	500	9.62

Figure 10.18 Chi-square calculation for Example 10.21.

accepted, and on that basis the probability of nine or more trucks arriving in one hour is

$$P(9 \text{ or more}) = 1 - \sum_{k=0}^{8} \frac{2^k e^{-2}}{k!} = 0.000\,237$$

This will occur roughly once in every 4200 h of operation.

Because so many statistical methods assume normal data, it is important to have a test for normality, and the chi-square method can be used (Exercise 36 and Section 10.8.4).

10.6.2   Contingency tables

In Section 10.4.3 the correlation was introduced as a measure of dependence between two random variables. The sample correlation (Section 10.4.4) provides an estimate from data. This measure only applies to numerical random variables, and then only works for linear dependence (Exercise 14). The rank correlation (Section 10.4.6) has more general applicability, but still requires that the data be classified in order of rank. The chi-square testing procedure can be adapted to provide at least an indicator of dependence that has the widest applicability of all.

Suppose that each item in a sample of size n can be separately classified as one of $A_1, \ldots, A_r$ by one criterion, and as one of $B_1, \ldots, B_c$ by another, (these may be numerical values, but not necessarily). The number f_{ij} of items in the sample that are classified as 'A_i and B_j' can be counted for each $i = 1, \ldots, r$ and $j = 1, \ldots, c$. The table of these numbers (with r rows and c columns) is called a **contingency table** (Figure 10.19). The question is whether the two criteria are independent. If not then some combinations of A_i and B_j will occur significantly more often (and others less often) than would be expected under the assumption of independence. We first have to work out how many would be expected under an assumption of independence.

Class	B_1	$\cdots$	B_c	Total
A_1	f_{11}	$\cdots$	f_{1c}	f_{1+}
.	.	.	.	.
.	.	.	.	.
.	.	.	.	.
A_r	f_{r1}	$\cdots$	f_{rc}	f_{r+}
Total	f_{+1}	$\cdots$	f_{+c}	n

Figure 10.19 Contingency table.

Let the row and column totals be denoted by

$$f_{i+} = \sum_{j=1}^{c} f_{ij} \quad (i = 1, \ldots, r)$$

$$f_{+j} = \sum_{i=1}^{r} f_{ij} \quad (j = 1, \ldots, c)$$

If the criteria are independent then the joint probability for each combination can be expressed as the product of the separate marginal probabilities:

$$P(A_i \cap B_j) = P(A_i)P(B_j)$$

The chi-square procedure will be used to see how well the data fit this assumption. To test it, we can estimate the marginal probabilities from the row and column totals,

$$P(A_i) \simeq \frac{f_{i+}}{n}, \qquad P(B_j) \simeq \frac{f_{+j}}{n}$$

and multiply the product of these by n to obtain the expected number e_{ij} for each combination:

$$e_{ij} = n \frac{f_{i+}}{n} \frac{f_{+j}}{n} = \frac{f_{i+}f_{+j}}{n}$$

The chi-square goodness-of-fit statistic follows from the actual and expected numbers (f_{ij} and e_{ij}) as a sum over all the rows and columns:

$$\chi^2 = \sum_{i=1}^{r} \sum_{j=1}^{c} \frac{(f_{ij} - e_{ij})^2}{e_{ij}}$$

If the value of this is large then the hypothesis of independence is rejected, because the actual and expected counts differ by more than can be attributed to chance. As explained in Section 10.6.1, the largeness is judged with respect to $\chi^2_{\alpha,m-t-1}$ from the chi-square table. The number of classes, m, is the number of rows times the number of columns, rc. The number of independent parameters estimated from the data, t, is the number of independent marginal probabilities $P(A_i)$ and $P(B_j)$:

$$t = (r - 1) + (c - 1)$$

The number is not $r + c$, because the row and column totals must equal one, so when all but one are specified, the last is determined. Finally,

$$m - t - 1 = rc - (r + c - 2) - 1 = (r - 1)(c - 1)$$

The hypothesis of independence is therefore rejected (at significance level α) if

$$\chi^2 > \chi^2_{\alpha,(r-1)(c-1)}$$

EXAMPLE 10.22 An accident inspector makes spot checks on working practices during visits to industrial sites chosen at random. At one large construction site the numbers of accidents occurring per week were counted for a period of three years, and

	Number of accidents				
	0	1	2	3	Total
Visit Residual	**20** (13.38) 2.96	**3** (7.08) −1.99	**1** (2.46) −1.07	**0** (1.08) −1.16	24
No visit Residual	**67** (73.62) −2.96	**43** (38.92) 1.99	**15** (13.54) 1.07	**7** (5.92) 1.16	132
Total	87	46	16	7	156

Figure 10.20 Contingency table for Example 10.22.

each week was also classified as to whether or not the inspector had visited the site during the previous week. The results are shown in bold print in Figure 10.20. Do visits by the inspector tend to reduce the number of accidents, at least in the short term?

Solution   The respective row and column totals are shown in Figure 10.20, together with the expected numbers e_{ij} in parentheses in each cell. For example, the top left cell has observed number 20, row total 24, column total 87, $n = 156$, and hence the expected number

$$e_{11} = (24)(87)/156 = 13.38$$

The chi-square sum is

$$\chi^2 = \frac{(20 - 13.38)^2}{13.38} + \cdots + \frac{(7 - 5.92)^2}{5.92} = 8.94$$

With two rows, four columns and a significance level of 5%, the appropriate number from the chi-square table is $\chi^2_{0.05,3} = 7.815$. The calculated value exceeds this, and by comparing the observed and expected numbers in the table, it seems clear that the visits by the inspector do tend to reduce the number of accidents. This is not, however, significant at the 2.5% level.

A significant chi-square value does not by itself reveal what part or parts of the table are responsible for the lack of independence. A procedure that is often helpful in this respect is to work out the **adjusted residual** for each cell, defined as

$$d_{ij} = \frac{f_{ij} - e_{ij}}{\sqrt{[e_{ij}(1 - f_{i+}/n)(1 - f_{+j}/n)]}}$$

Under the assumption of independence, these are approximately standard normal, so a significant value for a cell suggests that that cell is partly responsible for the dependence overall. The adjusted residuals for the contingency table in Example 10.22 are shown in Figure 10.20, and support the conclusion that visits by the inspector tend to reduce the number of accidents.

For a useful survey of procedures for analysing contingency tables see B. S. Everitt, *The Analysis of Contingency Tables*, 2nd edn (Chapman & Hall, London, 1992).

10.6.3 Exercises

32 The number of books borrowed from a library that is open five days a week is as follows: Monday 153, Tuesday 108, Wednesday 120, Thursday 114, Friday 145. Test (at 5% significance) whether the number of books borrowed depends on the day of the week.

33 A new process for manufacturing light fibres is being tested. Out of 50 samples, 32 contained no flaws, 12 contained one flaw and 6 contained two flaws. Test the hypothesis that the number of flaws per sample has a Poisson distribution.

34 In an early experiment on the emission of α-particles from a radioactive source, Rutherford obtained the following data on counts of particles during constant time intervals:

Number of particles	0	1	2	3	4	5	6	7	8	9	10	>10
Number of intervals	57	203	383	525	532	408	273	139	45	27	10	6

Test the hypothesis that the number of particles emitted during an interval has a Poisson distribution.

35 A quality control engineer takes daily samples of four television sets coming off an assembly line. In a total of 200 working days he found that on 110 days no sets required adjustments, on 73 days one set requires adjustments, on 16 days two sets and on 1 day three sets. Use these results to test the hypothesis that 10% of sets coming off the assembly line required adjustments, at 5% and 1% significance levels. Also test this using the confidence interval for proportion (Section 10.3.6), using the total number of sets requiring adjustments.

36 Two samples of 100 data have been grouped into classes as shown in Figure 10.21. The sample average and standard deviation in each case were 10.0 and 2.0 respectively.

(a) Draw the histogram for each sample.

(b) Test each sample for normality using the measured parameters.

Class	Sample 1	Sample 2
<6.5	4	3
6.5– 7.5	6	6
7.5– 8.5	16	16
8.5– 9.5	16	13
9.5–10.5	17	26
10.5–11.5	20	7
11.5–12.5	12	19
12.5–13.5	6	5
>13.5	3	5

Figure 10.21 Data classification for Exercise 36.

37 Shipments of electronic devices have been received by a firm from three sources: A, B and C. Each device is classified as either perfect, intermediate (imperfect but acceptable), or unacceptable. From source A 89 were perfect, 23 intermediate and 12 unacceptable. Corresponding figures for source B were 62, 12 and 8 respectively, and for source C 119, 30 and 21 respectively. Is there any significant difference in quality between the devices received from the three sources?

38 Cars produced at a factory are chosen at random for a thorough inspection. The number inspected and the number of those that were found to be unsuitable for shipment were counted monthly for one year as follows:

Month	Jan.	Feb.	Mar.	Apr.	May	Jun.
Inspected	450	550	550	400	600	450
Defective	8	14	6	3	7	8

Month	Jul.	Aug.	Sep.	Oct.	Nov.	Dec.
Inspected	450	200	450	600	600	550
Defective	16	5	12	6	15	9

Is there a significant variation in quality through the year?

10.7   Moment generating functions

This section is more difficult than the rest of this chapter, and can be treated as optional during a first reading. It contains the proofs of theoretical results, such as the central limit theorem, that are of great importance, as seen earlier in this chapter. The technique introduced here is the moment generating function, which is a useful tool for finding means and variances of random variables as well as for proving these essential results. The moment generating function also bears a striking resemblance to the Laplace transform considered in Chapter 2.

10.7.1   Definition and simple applications

The **moment generating function** of a random variable X is defined as

$$M_X(t) = E(e^{tX}) = \begin{cases} \displaystyle\sum_{k=1}^{m} e^{tv_k} P(X = v_k) & \text{in the discrete case} \\ \displaystyle\int_{-\infty}^{\infty} e^{tx} f_X(x)\,dx & \text{in the continuous case} \end{cases}$$

where t is a real variable. This is an example of the expected value of a function $h(X)$ of the random variable X (Section 10.2.2). The moment generating function does not always exist, or it may exist only for certain values of t. In cases where it fails to exist there is an alternative (called the **characteristic function**) which always exists and has similar properties. When the moment generating function does exist, it is unique in the sense that no two distinct distributions can have the same moment generating function.

To see how the moment generating function earns its name, the first step is to differentiate it with respect to t and then let t tend to zero:

$$\frac{d}{dt} M_X(t)\big|_{t=0} = E(X\,e^{tX})\big|_{t=0}$$

$$= E(X) = \mu_X$$

Thus the first derivative gives the mean. Differentiating again gives

$$\frac{d^2}{dt^2} M_X(t)\big|_{t=0} = E(X^2\,e^{tX})\big|_{t=0} = E(X^2)$$

From this result we obtain the variance (from Section 10.2.2)

$$\text{Var}(X) = E(X^2) - [E(X)]^2$$

We can summarize these results as follows. If a random variable X has mean μ_X, variance σ_X^2 and moment generating function $M_X(t)$ defined for t in some neighbourhood of zero then

$$\mu_X = M_X^{(1)}(0), \qquad \sigma_X^2 = M_X^{(2)}(0) - [M_X^{(1)}(0)]^2$$

where the superscript in parentheses denotes the order of the derivative. Furthermore,

$$E(X^k) = M_X^{(k)}(0) \quad (k = 1, 2, \ldots)$$

EXAMPLE 10.23 Show that the mean and variance of the Poisson distribution with parameter λ are both equal to λ (Section 10.2.3).

Solution If X has a Poisson distribution then

$$P(X = k) = \frac{\lambda^k e^{-\lambda}}{k!} \quad (k = 0, 1, 2, \ldots)$$

and the moment generating function is

$$M_X(t) = \sum_{k=0}^{\infty} e^{kt} \frac{\lambda^k e^{-\lambda}}{k!}$$

$$= e^{-\lambda} \sum_{k=0}^{\infty} \frac{(\lambda e^t)^k}{k!} = \exp\left[\lambda(e^t - 1)\right]$$

Differentiating this with respect to t gives

$$M_X^{(1)}(t) = \lambda e^t \exp\left[\lambda(e^t - 1)\right]$$

$$M_X^{(2)}(t) = (\lambda^2 e^{2t} + \lambda e^t)\exp[\lambda(e^t - 1)]$$

from which

$$\mu_X = M_X^{(1)}(0) = \lambda$$

$$\sigma_X^2 = M_X^{(2)}(0) - \mu_X^2 = \lambda$$

as expected.

EXAMPLE 10.24 Show that the mean and standard deviation of the exponential distribution

$$f_X(x) = \begin{cases} \lambda e^{-\lambda x} & (x \geqslant 0) \\ 0 & (x < 0) \end{cases}$$

are both equal to $1/\lambda$ (Section 10.10.2).

Solution The moment generating function is

$$M_X(t) = \int_0^{\infty} \lambda e^{-(\lambda - t)x} \, dx = \frac{\lambda}{\lambda - t}$$

Note that the integral only exists for $t < \lambda$, but we can differentiate it and set $t = 0$ for any positive value of λ:

$$M_X^{(1)}(0) = \lambda^{-1} = \mu_X$$
$$M_X^{(2)}(0) = 2\lambda^{-2}$$

from which $\sigma_X^2 = \lambda^{-2}$.

10.7.2   The Poisson approximation to the binomial

In addition to its utility for finding means and variances, the moment generating function is a very useful theoretical tool. In this section and the next we shall use it to prove two of the most important results in probability theory, but first we need the following general property of moment generating functions.

Suppose that X and Y are independent random variables with moment generating functions $M_X(t)$ and $M_Y(t)$. Then the moment generating function of their sum is given by

$$M_{X+Y}(t) = M_X(t)M_Y(t)$$

To prove this, we shall assume that X and Y are continuous random variables with a joint density function $f_{X,Y}(x, y)$; however, the proof is essentially the same if either or both are discrete. By definition,

$$M_{X+Y}(t) = E[e^{t(X+Y)}] = \int_{-\infty}^{\infty} \int_{-\infty}^{\infty} e^{t(x+y)} f_{X,Y}(x, y)\, dx\, dy$$

Both factors of the integrand themselves factorize (noting the independence of X and Y) to give

$$M_{X+Y}(t) = \int_{-\infty}^{\infty} \int_{-\infty}^{\infty} [e^{tx} f_X(x)][e^{ty} f_Y(y)]\, dx\, dy$$

The two integrals can now be separated, and the result follows:

$$M_{X+Y}(t) = \int_{-\infty}^{\infty} e^{tx} f_X(x)\, dx \int_{-\infty}^{\infty} e^{ty} f_Y(y)\, dy$$
$$= M_X(x)M_Y(y)$$

It follows that if $\{X_1, \ldots, X_n\}$ are independent and identically distributed random variables, each with moment generating function $M_X(t)$, and if $Z = X_1 + \cdots + X_n$, then

$$M_Z(t) = [M_X(t)]^n$$

We now proceed to the main result. If the random variable Y has a binomial distribution with parameters n and p and the random variable X has a Poisson distribution with parameter $\lambda = np$ then as $n \to \infty$ and $p \to 0$, the distribution of X tends to that of Y.

First let the random variable B have a Bernoulli distribution with parameter p (Section 10.2.3). The moment generating function of B is then

$$M_B(t) = e^t p + (1 - p) = 1 + p(e^t - 1)$$

Since the binomial random variable Y is the sum of n copies of B, it follows that the moment generating function of the binomial distribution is

$$M_Y(t) = [1 + p(e^t - 1)]^n$$

It can be proved that for any real z

$$\lim_{n \to \infty} \left(1 + \frac{z}{n}\right)^n = e^z$$

Now let $z = np(e^t - 1)$ and assume that $\lambda = np$:

$$M_Y(t) = \left(1 + \frac{z}{n}\right)^n \simeq e^z = \exp[\lambda(e^t - 1)] = M_X(t)$$

(the moment generating function for the Poisson distribution was derived in Example 10.23). The uniqueness of the moment generating function implies that the distributions of X and Y must be similar, provided that n is sufficiently large. It is also required that $p \to 0$ as $n \to \infty$, so that z does not grow without bound.

This approximation has many applications; see for example Section 10.9.2.

10.7.3 Proof of the central limit theorem

This theorem is of vital importance in statistics because it tells us that the sample average for a sample of at least moderate size tends to have a normal distribution even when the data themselves do not. The result (Section 10.2.4) is here restated and proved using the moment generating function.

THEOREM 10.1 **The central limit theorem**

If $\{X_1, \ldots, X_n\}$ are independent and identically distributed random variables, each with mean μ_X and variance σ_X^2, and if

$$Z_n = \frac{X_1 + \cdots + X_n - n\mu_X}{\sigma_X \sqrt{n}}$$

then the distribution of Z_n tends to the standard normal distribution as $n \to \infty$.

Proof First let the random variables Y_i be defined by

$$Y_i = \frac{X_i - \mu_X}{\sigma_X \sqrt{n}} \quad (i = 1, \ldots, n)$$

so that

$$E(Y_i) = 0,$$

$$E(Y_i^2) = \frac{1}{n}$$

$$E(Y_i^3) = \frac{c}{n\sqrt{n}}, \qquad \text{where } c \text{ is a constant}$$

Expanding the moment generating function $M_Y(t)$ for each Y_i as a Maclaurin series (to four terms – see Chapter 8 of *Modern Engineering Mathematics* for more information on Maclaurin series) gives

$$M_Y(t) \simeq M_Y(0) + M_Y^{(1)}(0)t + M_Y^{(2)}(0)\frac{t^2}{2!} + M_Y^{(3)}(0)\frac{t^3}{3!}$$

By the results in Section 10.7.1, the coefficients of this series can be replaced by the successive moments $E(Y_i^k)$:

$$M_Y(t) \simeq E(1) + E(Y_i)t + E(Y_i^2)\frac{t^2}{2!} + E(Y_i^3)\frac{t^3}{3!}$$

$$\simeq 1 + \frac{t^2}{2n} + \frac{ct^3}{6n\sqrt{n}}$$

Now Z_n is the sum of the variables Y_i,

$$Z_n = \sum_{i=1}^{n} Y_i$$

so the moment generating function of Z_n is the nth power of that of Y_i:

$$M_{Z_n}(t) = [M_Y(t)]^n$$

Retaining only the first two terms of a binomial expansion of this gives

$$M_{Z_n}(t) = \left(1 + \frac{t}{2n}\right)^n + n\left(1 + \frac{t^2}{2n}\right)^{n-1}\left(\frac{ct^3}{6n\sqrt{n}}\right) + \cdots$$

$$\rightarrow e^{t^2/2} \quad \text{as } n \rightarrow \infty$$

because all terms except the first will tend to zero.

It only remains to show that this is the moment generating function for the standard normal distribution; see Exercise 43. □

10.7.4   Exercises

39 A continuous random variable X has density function

$$f_X(x) = \begin{cases} cxe^{-2x} & (x > 0) \\ 0 & (x \leqslant 0) \end{cases}$$

Find the value of the constant c. Derive the moment generating function, and hence find the mean and variance of X.

40 Prove that if $X_1, \ldots, X_n$ are independent Poisson random variables with parameters $\lambda_1, \ldots, \lambda_n$ then their sum

$$Y = X_1 + \cdots + X_n$$

is also Poisson, with parameter $\lambda = \lambda_1 + \cdots + \lambda_n$.

41 A factory contains 30 machines each with breakdown probability 0.01 in any one hour and 40 machines each with breakdown probability 0.005 in any one hour. Use the result of Exercise 40, together with the Poisson approximation to the binomial, to find the probability that a total of three or more machine breakdowns will occur in any one hour.

42 A manufacturer has agreed to dispatch small servomechanisms in cartons of 100 to a distributor. The distributor requires that 90% of cartons contain at most one defective servomechanism. Assuming the Poisson approximation to the binomial, obtain an equation for the Poisson parameter λ such that the distributor's requirements are just satisfied. Solve for λ by one of the standard methods for nonlinear equations (approximate solution 0.5), and hence find the required proportion of manufactured servomechanisms that must be satisfactory.

43 Show that the moment generating function of the standard normal distribution is $e^{t^2/2}$. (*Hint*: Complete the square in the exponential.)

10.8   Engineering application: analysis of engine performance data

10.8.1   Introduction

Statistical methods are often used in conjunction with each other. So far in this chapter the examples and exercises have almost always been designed to illustrate the various topics one at a time. This section contains an example of a more extended problem to which several topics are relevant, and correspondingly there are several stages to the analysis.

The background to the problem is this. Suppose that the fuel consumption of a car engine is tested by measuring the time that the engine runs at constant speed on a litre of standard fuel. Two prototype engines, A and B, are being compared for fuel consumption. For each engine a series of tests is performed in various ambient temperatures, which are also recorded. Figure 10.22 contains the data. There are 30 observations each for the four random variables concerned:

A, running time in minutes for engine A;

T, ambient temperature in degrees Celsius for engine A;

B, running time in minutes for engine B;

U, ambient temperature in degrees Celsius for engine B.

The histograms for the running times are compared in Figure 10.23(a) and those

Engine A				Engine B			
A	T	A	T	B	U	B	U
27.7	24	24.1	7	24.9	13	24.3	17
24.3	25	23.1	14	21.4	19	24.5	16
23.7	18	23.4	16	24.1	18	26.1	18
22.1	15	23.1	9	27.5	19	27.7	14
21.8	19	24.1	14	27.5	21	24.3	19
24.7	16	28.6	23	25.7	17	26.1	5
23.4	17	20.2	14	24.9	17	24.0	17
21.6	14	25.7	18	23.3	19	24.9	18
24.5	18	24.6	18	22.5	21	26.7	23
26.1	20	24.0	12	28.5	12	27.3	28
24.8	15	24.9	18	25.9	17	23.9	18
23.7	15	21.9	20	26.9	13	23.1	10
25.0	22	25.1	16	27.7	17	25.5	25
26.9	18	25.7	16	25.4	23	24.9	22
23.7	19	23.5	11	25.3	30	25.9	16

Figure 10.22 Data for engine case study.

for the temperatures in Figure 10.23(b). The overall profile of temperatures is very similar for the two series of tests, differing only in the number of unusually high or low figures encountered. The profiles of running times appear to differ rather

Figure 10.23 Histograms of engine data: (a) running times; (b) temperatures.

more markedly. It is clear that displaying the data in this way is useful, but some analysis will have to be done in order to determine whether the differences are significant.

When planning the analysis, it is as well to consider the questions to which most interest attaches. Do the mean running times for the two engines differ? Does the running time depend on temperature? If so, and if there is a difference in the temperatures for the test series on engines A and B, can this account for any apparent difference in fuel consumption? More particularly, are the data normal? This has a bearing on the methods used, and hence on the conclusions drawn.

10.8.2   Difference in mean running times and temperatures

The sample averages and both versions of standard deviation for the data in Figure 10.22 are as follows:

$$\bar{A} \quad = 24.20, \quad \bar{T} \quad = 16.70, \quad \bar{B} \quad = 25.36, \quad \bar{U} \quad = 18.07$$

$$S_A \quad = 1.761, \quad S_T \quad = 4.001, \quad S_B \quad = 1.657, \quad S_U \quad = 4.932$$

$$S_{A,n-1} = 1.791, \quad S_{T,n-1} = 4.070, \quad S_{B,n-1} = 1.685, \quad S_{U,n-1} = 5.017$$

The average running time for engine B is slightly higher than for engine A. The sample standard deviations are very similar, so we can assume that the true standard deviations are equal and use the method for comparing means discussed in Section 10.3.5. The pooled estimate of the variance is

$$S_p^2 = \frac{(n-1)(S_{A,n-1}^2 + S_{B,n-1}^2)}{2(n-1)} = \frac{3.208 + 2.839}{2} = 3.023$$

and the relevant value from the t-table is $t_{0.025,58} = 1.960$. In fact the sample is large enough for the value for the normal distribution to be taken. The 95% confidence interval for the difference $\mu_B - \mu_A$ is

$$(\bar{B} - \bar{A} \pm 1.96 S_p/\sqrt{15}) = (0.28, 2.04)$$

Even the 99% confidence interval $(0.12, 2.20)$ does not contain the zero point, so we can be almost certain that the difference in mean running times is significant.

Following the same procedure for the temperatures gives the 95% confidence interval for the difference $\mu_U - \mu_T$ to be $(-0.94, 3.68)$. Superficially, this is not significant – and even if the running times do depend on temperature, the similarity of the two test series in this respect enables this factor to be discounted. If so, the fuel performance for engine B is superior to that for engine A. However, if the temperature sensitivity were very high then even a difference in the average too small to give a significant result by this method could create a misleading difference in the fuel consumption figures. This possibility needs to be examined.

10.8.3 Dependence of running time on temperature

The simplest way to test for dependence is to correlate times and temperatures for each engine. To compute the sample correlations, we need the following additional results from the data:

$$\overline{AT} = 407.28, \quad \overline{BU} = 457.87$$

The sample correlations (Section 10.4.4) of A and T and of B and U are then

$$r_{A,T} = \frac{\overline{AT} - (\overline{A})(\overline{T})}{S_A S_T} = 0.445, \qquad r_{B,U} = \frac{\overline{BU} - (\overline{B})(\overline{U})}{S_B S_U} = -0.030$$

and the respective 95% confidence intervals (Section 10.4.5) are

$$(0.10, 0.69), \qquad (-0.39, 0.34)$$

This is a quite definitive result: the running time for engine A depends positively upon the ambient temperature, but that for engine B does not. The confidence intervals are based on the assumption that all the variables A, T, B and U are normal. The histograms have this character, and a test for normality will be covered later.

Linear regression also reveals the dependence of running time on temperature. Here we assume that the variables are related by a linear model as follows:

$$\left. \begin{array}{l} A_i = c_A + d_A T_i + E_i \\ B_i = c_B + d_B U_i + F_i \end{array} \right\} \quad (i = 1, \ldots, n)$$

where c_A, d_A, c_B and d_B are constants, and the random variables E_i and F_i represent residual errors. Using the results of the least-squares analysis in Section 10.5.1, for engine A we have

$$\hat{d}_A = \frac{\overline{AT} - (\overline{A})(\overline{T})}{S_T^2} = 0.196, \qquad \hat{c}_A = \overline{A} - \hat{d}_A \overline{T} = 20.9$$

Likewise, for engine B

$$\hat{d}_B = -0.010, \qquad \hat{c}_B = 25.5$$

Figure 10.24 contains scatter plots of the data with these regression lines drawn. The points are well scattered about the lines. The residual variances, using the results in Section 10.5.2 and 10.5.3, are

$$S_E^2 = S_A^2 - \hat{d}_A^2 S_T^2 = S_A^2 (1 - r_{A,T}^2) = 2.49$$

$$S_F^2 = 2.74$$

As explained in Section 10.5.3, the respective values of r^2 indicate the extent to which the variation in running times is due to the dependence on temperature. For engine B there is virtually no such dependence. For engine A we have

Figure 10.24 Regression of running time against temperature: (a) engine A; (b) engine B.

$r_{A,T}^2 = 0.198$, so nearly 20% of the variation in running times is accounted for in this way.

If we assume that the residuals E_i and F_i are normal, we can obtain confidence intervals for the regression slopes. The appropriate value from the t table is $t_{\alpha/2,n-2} = t_{0.025,28} = 2.048$, so the 95% confidence interval for d_A is

$$\left(d_A \pm 2.048 \frac{S_E}{S_T\sqrt{28}} \right) = (0.04, 0.35)$$

The significance shown here confirms that found for the correlation. The 95% confidence interval for d_B is $(-0.14, 0.12)$.

We now return to the main question. We know that the average running time for engine A was significantly lower than that for engine B. However, we also know that the running time for engine A depends on temperature, and that the average temperature during the test series for engine A was somewhat lower than for engine B. Could this account for the difference?

A simple way to test this is to look at the average values. The difference in average temperatures is $(18.07 - 16.70) = 1.37$ and the regression slope d_A is estimated to be 0.196, so that a deficit in the average running time of $(1.37)(0.196) \simeq 0.27\,\text{min}$ is predicted on this basis. This cannot account for the actual difference of 1.16 min, and does not even bring the zero point within the 95% confidence interval for the difference in means $\mu_B - \mu_A$.

To examine this more carefully, we can try using the regression slopes to correct all running times to the same temperature. Choosing the average temperature for the series B for this purpose, we can let

$$\left. \begin{array}{l} X_i = A_i + \hat{d}_A(\bar{U} - T_i) \\ Y_i = B_i + \hat{d}_B(\bar{U} - U_i) \end{array} \right\} \quad (i = 1, \dots, n)$$

The 95% confidence interval for the difference between mean running times,

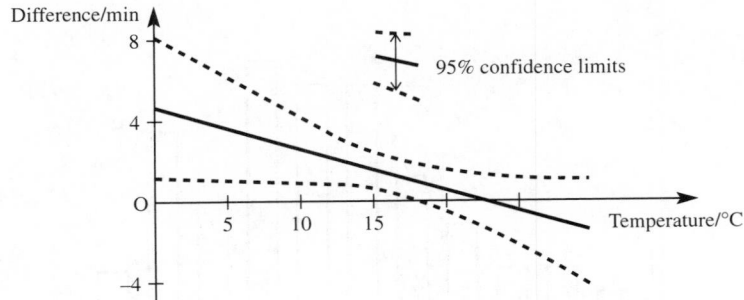

Figure 10.25 Predicted difference in mean running times.

$\mu_Y - \mu_X$, at this temperature is then $(0.06, 1.72)$, using the method in Section 10.3.5. The problem with this is that the estimates of d_A and d_B themselves have rather wide confidence intervals, and it is not satisfactory to adopt a point value to apply the temperature correction.

We need a more direct way to obtain the confidence interval for the difference between mean running times at any particular temperature. This is possible using a more general theory of linear regression, formulated using matrix algebra, which allows for any number of regression coefficients instead of just two; see for example G. A. F. Seber, *Linear Regression Analysis* (Wiley, New York, 1977). Applied to the present problem, estimates of the regression slopes d_A and d_B and intercepts c_A and c_B are obtained simultaneously, with the same values as before, and it now becomes possible to obtain a confidence interval for any linear combination of these four unknowns. In particular, the confidence interval for the difference between mean running times at any temperature t is based on the linear combination

$$(c_B + d_B t) - (c_A + d_A t)$$

Space precludes coverage of the analysis here, but the results can be seen in Figure 10.25. At any temperature below 22.4 °C engine B is predicted to have the advantage over engine A (this temperature being the point at which the regression lines cross). At any temperature below 18.1 °C the 95% confidence interval for the difference is entirely positive, and we should say that engine B has a significant advantage. This is the best comparison of the engines that is possible using the data presented.

10.8.4   Test for normality

The confidence interval statistics are all based on the assumption of normality of the data. Although the sample sizes are reasonably large, so that the central limit theorem can be relied upon to weaken this requirement, it is worth applying a test for normality to see whether there is any clear evidence to the contrary. Here the regression residuals E_i and F_i will be tested using the method described in Section 10.6.1.

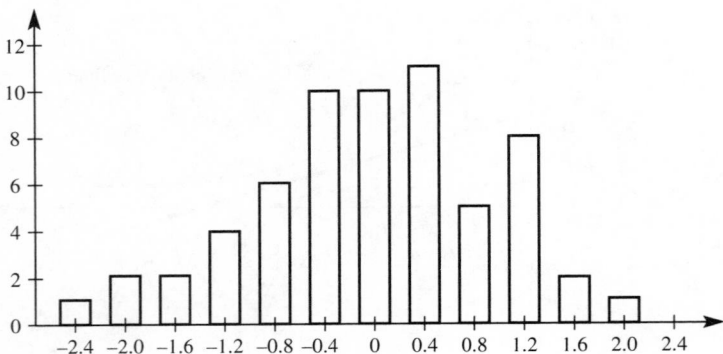

Figure 10.26 Histogram of residuals.

Figure 10.26 shows the histogram of all 60 'standardized' residuals. The residuals have zero mean in any case, and are standardized by dividing by the standard deviation so that they can be compared with a standard normal distribution. It is convenient to use intervals of width 0.4, and the comparison is developed in Figure 10.27.

The normal probabilities for each interval are obtained from the standard normal table of the cumulative distribution function $\Phi(z)$, Figure 10.2, taking successive differences:

$$P(z_1 < Z < z_2) = \Phi(z_2) - \Phi(z_1)$$

These probabilities are multiplied by 60 to obtain the expected number in each interval, and the difference between the observed and expected number for each interval is squared and then divided by the expected number to give the contribution to the total chi-square:

$$\chi^2 = \sum_{k=1}^{m} \frac{(f_k - e_k)^2}{e_k} = 4.81$$

Interval	Observed (f_k)	Probability	Expected (e_k)	Chi-square
$(-\infty, -1.4)$	5	0.0808	4.848	0.005
$(-1.4, -1.0)$	4	0.0779	4.674	0.097
$(-1.0, -0.6)$	6	0.1156	6.936	0.126
$(-0.6, -0.2)$	10	0.1464	8.784	0.168
$(-0.2, +0.2)$	8	0.1586	9.516	0.242
$(+0.2, +0.6)$	11	0.1464	8.784	0.559
$(+0.6, +1.0)$	5	0.1156	6.936	0.540
$(+1.0, +1.4)$	8	0.0779	4.674	2.367
$(+1.4, +\infty)$	3	0.0808	4.848	0.704
Totals	60	1.0	60	4.809

Figure 10.27 Table of the test for normality.

This is small compared with $\chi^2_{0.05,8} = 15.507$, so the hypothesis of normality is accepted.

It is unwise when applying this test in general to have many classes with expected numbers less than five, so the intervals in the tails of the histogram have been merged.

10.8.5   Conclusions

All the questions posed in Section 10.8.1 have now been answered. Engine B has an average running time that is significantly higher than that for engine A, showing that it has the advantage in fuel consumption. However, this statement requires qualification. The running time for engine A depends upon ambient temperature. The temperature difference between the two test series was not significant, and does not account for the difference in average running times. However, engine B will only maintain its fuel advantage up to a certain point. This point has been estimated, but cannot be identified very precisely because of considerable residual scatter in the data. There are many potential sources of this scatter, such as errors in measuring out the fuel, or variations in the quantity and consistency of the engine oil. The scatter has a normal distribution, which justifies the statistics behind the conclusions reached.

10.9   Engineering application: statistical quality control

10.9.1   Introduction

Every manufacturer recognizes the importance of quality, and every manufacturing process involves some variation in the quality of its output, however that is to be measured. Experience shows that tolerating a lack of quality tends to be more costly in the end than promoting a quality approach. It follows that quality control is a major and increasing concern, and methods of statistical quality control are more important than ever. The domain of these methods now extends to the construction and service industries as well as to manufacturing – wherever there is a process that can be monitored in quantitative terms.

Traditionally, quality control involved the accumulation of batches of manufactured items, the testing of samples extracted from these batches, and the acceptance or rejection (with appropriate rectifying action) of these batches depending upon the outcome. The essential problem with this is that it is too late within the process: it is impossible to inspect or test quality into a product. More recently the main concern has been to design the quality into the product or service and to monitor the process to ensure that the standard is maintained, in order to prevent any deficiency. Assurance can then be formally given to the customer that proper procedures are in place.

Control charts play an important role in the implementation of quality. The idea of these is introduced in Section 13.6 in *Modern Engineering Mathematics*, where Shewhart charts for counts of defectives are described. In order for this section to be as self-contained as possible, some of that material is repeated here. This section then covers more powerful control charts and extends the scope of what they monitor.

First note that there are two main alternative measures of quality: **attribute** and **variable**. In attribute measure, regular samples from the process are inspected and for each sample the number that fail according to some criterion is plotted on a chart. In variable measure, regular samples are again taken, but this time the sample average for some numerical measure (such as dimension or lifetime) is plotted.

10.9.2   Shewhart attribute control charts

Figure 10.28 is an example of a Shewhart control chart: a plot of the count of 'defectives' (the number in the sample failing according to some chosen criterion) against sample number. It is assumed that a small (specified) proportion of 'defective' items in the process is permitted. Also shown on the chart are two limits on the count of defectives, corresponding to probabilities of one in 40 and one in 1000 of a sample count falling outside if the process is 'in control', that is, conforming to the specification. These are called **warning** and **action limits** respectively, and are denoted by c_W and c_A.

Any sample point falling outside the action limit would normally result in the process being suspended and the problem corrected. Roughly one in 40 sample

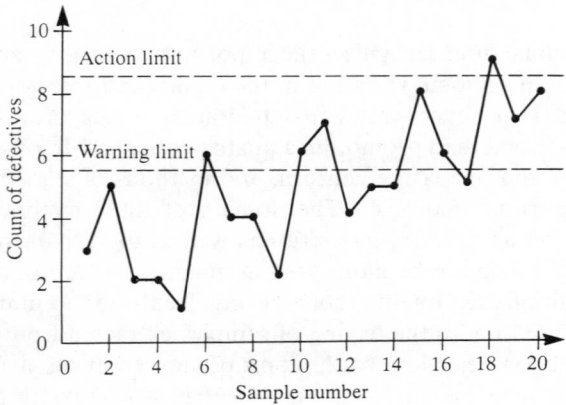

Figure 10.28 Attribute control chart for Example 10.25.

points will fall outside the warning limit purely by chance, but if this occurs repeatedly or if there is a clear trend upwards in the counts of defectives then action may well be taken before the action limit itself is crossed.

To obtain the warning and action limits, we use the Poisson approximation to the binomial. If the acceptable proportion of defective items is p, usually small, and the sample size is n then for a process in control the defective count C, say, will be a binomial random variable with parameters n and p. Provided that n is not too small, the Poisson approximation can be used (Section 10.7.2):

$$P(C \geqslant c) \simeq \sum_{k=c}^{\infty} \frac{(np)^k \, e^{-np}}{k!}$$

Equating this to $\frac{1}{40}$ and then to $\frac{1}{1000}$ gives equations that can be solved for the warning limit c_W and the action limit c_A respectively, in terms of the product np. This is the basis for the table shown in Figure 10.29, which enables c_W and c_A to be read directly from the value of np.

c_W or c_A	np for c_W	np for c_A
1.5	<0.44	<0.13
2.5	0.44– 0.87	0.13– 0.32
3.5	0.87– 1.38	0.32– 0.60
4.5	1.38– 1.94	0.60– 0.94
5.5	1.94– 2.53	0.94– 1.33
6.5	2.53– 3.16	1.33– 1.77
7.5	3.16– 3.81	1.77– 2.23
8.5	3.81– 4.48	2.23– 2.73
9.5	4.48– 5.17	2.73– 3.25
10.5	5.17– 5.87	3.25– 3.79
11.5	5.87– 6.59	3.79– 4.35
12.5	6.59– 7.31	4.35– 4.93
13.5	7.31– 8.05	4.93– 5.52
14.5	8.05– 8.80	5.52– 6.12
15.5	8.80– 9.55	6.12– 6.74
16.5	9.55–10.31	6.74– 7.37
17.5	10.31–11.08	7.37– 8.01
18.5	11.08–11.85	8.01– 8.66
19.5	11.85–12.63	8.66– 9.31
20.5	12.63–13.42	9.31– 9.98
21.5	13.42–14.21	9.98–10.65
22.5	14.21–15.00	10.65–11.33
23.5	15.00–15.80	11.33–12.02
24.5	15.80–16.61	12.02–12.71
25.5	16.61–17.41	12.71–13.41
26.5	17.41–18.23	13.41–14.11
27.5	18.23–19.04	14.11–14.82
28.5	19.04–19.86	14.82–15.53
29.5	19.86–20.68	15.53–16.25
30.5		16.25–16.98
31.5		16.98–17.70
32.5		17.70–18.44
33.5		18.44–19.17
34.5		19.17–19.91
35.5		19.91–20.66

Figure 10.29 Shewhart attribute control limits: n is sample size, p is probability of defect, c_W is warning limit and c_A is action limit.

EXAMPLE 10.25 Regular samples of 50 are taken from a process making electronic components, for which an acceptable proportion of defectives is 5%. Successive counts of defectives in each sample are as follows:

Sample	1	2	3	4	5	6	7	8	9	10	11	12	13	14	15	16	17	18	19	20
Count	3	5	2	2	1	6	4	4	2	6	7	4	5	5	8	6	5	9	7	8

At what point would the decision be taken to stop and correct the process?

Solution The control chart is shown in Figure 10.28. From $np = 2.5$ and Figure 10.29 we have the warning limit $c_W = 5.5$ and the action limit $c_A = 8.5$. The half-integer values are to avoid ambiguity when the count lies on a limit. There are warnings at samples 6, 10, 11, 15 and 16 before the action limit is crossed at sample 18. Strictly, the decision should be taken at that point, but the probability of two consecutive warnings is less than one in 1600 by the product rule of probabilities, which would justify taking action after sample 11.

An alternative practice (especially popular in the USA) is to dispense with the warning limit and to set the action limit (called the **upper control limit, UCL**) at three standard deviations above the mean. Because the count of defectives is binomial with mean np and variance $np(1 - p)$, this means that

$$UCL = np + 3\sqrt{[np(1 - p)]}$$

EXAMPLE 10.26 Find the UCL and apply it to the data in Example 10.25.

Solution From $n = 50$ and $p = 0.05$ we infer that UCL = 7.1, which is between the warning limit c_W and the action limit c_A in Example 10.25. The decision to correct the process would be taken after the 15th sample, the first to exceed the UCL.

10.9.3 Shewhart variable control charts

Suppose now that the appropriate assessment of quality involves measurement on a continuous scale rather than success or failure under some criterion. This arises whenever some dimension of the output is critical for applications. Again we take samples, but this time we measure this critical dimension and average the results. The Shewhart chart for this variable measure is a plot of successive sample averages against sample number.

The warning and action limits c_W and c_A on a Shewhart chart are those points for which the probabilities of a false alarm (where the result exceeds the limit even though the process is in control) are one in 40 and one in 1000 respectively. For variable measure the critical quantity can be either too high or too low, so the sample average must be tested in each direction with the stated probability of exceedance for each limit. It follows that the limits are determined by

$$P(\bar{X} > \mu_X + c_W) = P(\bar{X} < \mu_X - c_W) = \tfrac{1}{40}$$
$$P(\bar{X} > \mu_X + c_A) = P(\bar{X} < \mu_X - c_A) = \tfrac{1}{1000}$$

where $\bar{X}$ is the sample average and μ_X the design mean.

Provided that the sample size n is not too small, the central limit theorem allows the sample average to be assumed normal (Section 10.3.2),

$$\bar{X} \sim N(\mu_X, \sigma_X^2/n)$$

and the normal distribution table (Figure 10.2) then gives

$$c_W = \frac{1.96\sigma_X}{\sqrt{n}}, \qquad c_A = \frac{3.09\sigma_X}{\sqrt{n}}$$

EXAMPLE 10.27 Measurements of sulphur dioxide concentration (in $\mu g\,m^{-3}$) in the air are taken daily at five locations, and successive average readings are as follows:

> 64.2, 56.9, 57.7, 67.9, 61.7, 59.7, 55.6, 63.7
> 58.3, 66.4, 67.2, 65.2, 63.1, 67.6, 64.1, 66.7

It is suspected that the mean increased during that time. Assuming normal data with a long-term mean of 60.0 and standard deviation of 8.0, investigate whether an increase occurred.

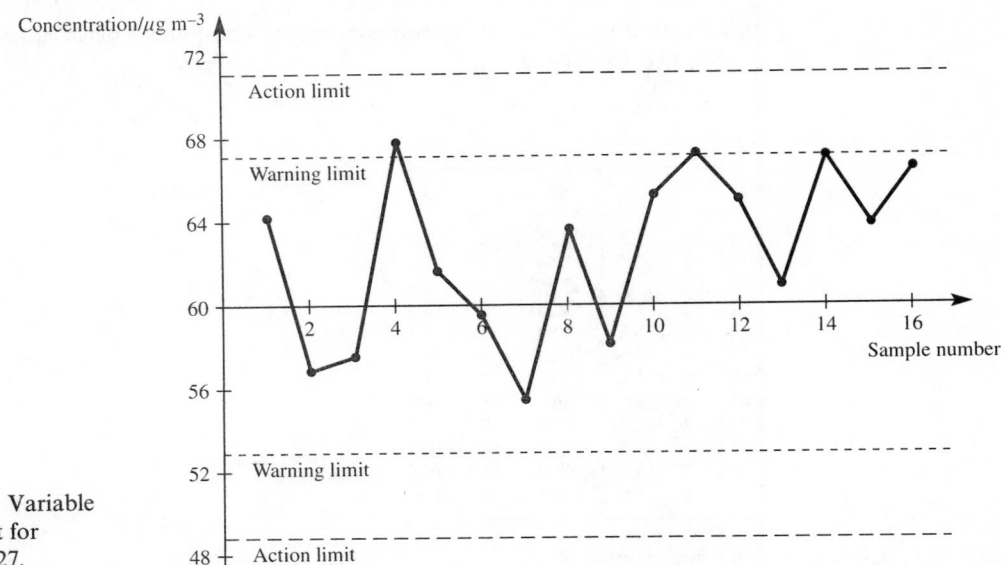

Figure 10.30 Variable control chart for Example 10.27.

Solution From $n = 5$ and $\sigma_X = 8$ we have $c_W = 7.0$ and $c_A = 11.1$ (Figure 10.30). The warning limit is 67.0, which is exceeded by sample numbers 4, 11 and 14. The action limit is 71.1, which is not exceeded. The readings are suspiciously high – but not sufficiently so for the conclusion to be justified.

As discussed in Section 10.9.2, the practice in the USA is somewhat different: there are no warning limits, only action limits at three standard deviations on either side of the mean. For a variable chart this allows a deviation from the mean of at most $3\sigma_X/\sqrt{n}$, which is very close to the action limit usually used in the UK.

10.9.4 Cusum control charts

The main concern in designing a control chart is to achieve the best compromise between speedy detection of a fault on the one hand and avoidance of a proliferation of false alarms on the other. If the chart is too sensitive, it will lead to a large number of unnecessary shutdowns. The Shewhart charts, on the other hand, are rather conservative in that they are slow to indicate a slight but genuine shift in performance away from the design level. This derives from the fact that each sample point is judged independently and may well lie inside the action limits, whereas the cumulative evidence over several samples might justify an earlier decision. Rather informal methods involving repeated warnings and trends are used, but it is preferable to employ a more powerful control chart. The **cumulative sum (cusum)** chart achieves this, and is easily implemented on a small computer.

Suppose that we have a sequence $\{Y_1, Y_2, \ldots\}$ of observations, which may be either counts of defectives or sample averages. From this a new sequence $\{S_0, S_1, \ldots\}$ is obtained by setting

$$S_0 = 0,$$

np	r	h	np	r	h
0.22	1	1.5	2.35	4	4.5
0.39	1	2.5	2.60	4	5.5
0.51	2	1.5	2.95	5	4.5
0.62	1	4.5	3.24	5	5.5
0.69	1	5.5	3.89	6	5.5
0.79	2	2.5	4.16	6	6.5
0.86	3	1.5	5.32	7	8.5
1.05	2	3.5	6.07	8	8.5
1.21	3	2.5	7.04	9	9.5
1.52	3	3.5	8.01	10	10.5
1.96	3	5.5	9.00	11	11.5
2.16	5	2.5	10.00	12	12.5

Figure 10.31 Cusum attribute chart control data.

$$S_m = \max\{0, S_{m-1} + Y_m - r\} \quad (m = 1, 2, \dots)$$

where r is a constant 'reference value'. This gives a cumulative sum of values of $Y_m - r$, which is reset to zero whenever it goes negative. The out-of-control decision is made when

$$S_m > h$$

where h is a constant 'decision interval'. This will detect an increasing mean; a separate but similar procedure can be used to detect a decreasing mean. Values of r and h for both attribute and variable types of control can be obtained from tables such as those in J. Murdoch, *Control Charts* (Macmillan, London, 1979), from which the attribute table in Figure 10.31 has been extracted. For variable measure (with process design mean μ_X and standard deviation σ_X) the following are often used:

$$r = \mu_X + \frac{\sigma_X}{2\sqrt{n}}, \qquad h = 5\frac{\sigma_X}{\sqrt{n}}$$

EXAMPLE 10.28   Regular samples of 50 are taken from a process making electronic components, for which an acceptable proportion of defectives is 5%. Successive counts of defectives in each sample are as follows:

Sample	1	2	3	4	5	6	7	8	9	10	11	12	13	14	15	16	17	18	19	20
Count	3	5	2	2	1	6	4	4	2	6	7	4	5	5	8	6	5	9	7	8

At what point would the decision be taken to stop and correct the process?

Solution   The acceptable proportion of defectives is $p = 0.05$ and the regular sample size is $n = 50$. From the table in Figure 10.31, with $np = 2.5$ the nearest figures for reference value and decision interval are $r = 4$ and $h = 5.5$. The following shows the cusum S_m below each count of defectives Y_m, and the cusum is also plotted in Figure 10.32:

Figure 10.32 Cusum control chart for Example 10.28.

Count	3	5	2	2	1	6	4	4	2	6	7	4	5	5	8	6	5	9	7	8
Cusum	0	1	0	0	0	2	2	2	0	2	5	5	6	7	11	13	14	19	22	26

For example,

$$S_{13} = S_{12} + Y_{13} - r = 5 + 5 - 4 = 6$$

and because this exceeds $h = 5.5$, the decision to take action would be made after the 13th sample. This result can be compared with that of a Shewhart chart applied to the same data (Example 10.25), which suggests that action should be taken after 18 samples.

EXAMPLE 10.29 Construct a cusum chart for the sulphur dioxide data in Example 10.27.

Solution From $\mu_X = 60$, $\sigma_X = 8$ and $n = 5$ we have

$$r = 60 + \frac{8}{2\sqrt{5}} = 61.8, \qquad h = 5\frac{8}{\sqrt{5}} = 17.9$$

The following table shows the sample average $\bar{X}_m$ and cusum S_m for $1 \leqslant m \leqslant 16$, and the cusum is also plotted in Figure 10.33:

Average	64.2	56.9	57.7	67.9	61.7	59.7	55.6	63.7
Cusum	2.4	0	0	6.1	6.0	3.9	0	1.9
Average	58.3	66.4	67.2	65.2	63.1	67.6	64.1	66.7
Cusum	0	4.6	10.0	13.4	14.7	20.5	22.8	27.7

Figure 10.33 Cusum control chart for Example 10.29.

Because $S_{14} = 20.5$ exceeds $h = 17.9$, this chart suggests that the SO_2 concentration did increase during the experiment, a stronger result than that obtained from the Shewhart chart in Example 10.27.

It can be shown that the cusum method will usually detect an out-of-control condition (involving a slight process shift) much sooner than the strict Shewhart method, but with essentially the same risk of a false alarm. For instance, the cusum method leads to a decision after 13 samples in Example 10.28 compared with 18 samples in Example 10.25 for the same data. The measure used to compare the two methods is the **average run length (ARL)**, which is the mean number of samples required to detect an increase in proportion of defectives (or process average) to some specified level. It has been shown that the ARL for the Shewhart chart can be up to four times that for the cusum chart (J. Murdoch, *Control Charts*, Macmillan, London, 1979).

10.9.5   Moving-average control charts

The cusum chart shows that the way to avoid the relative insensitivity of the Shewhart chart is to allow the evidence of a shift in performance to accumulate over several samples. There are also **moving-average control charts**, which are based upon a weighted sum of a number of observations. The best of these, which is very similar to the cusum chart in operation, is the **geometric moving-average (GMA) chart**. This will be described here for variable measure, but it also works for attribute measure (Exercise 52).

Suppose that the successive sample averages are $\bar{X}_1, \bar{X}_2, \ldots,$ each from a sample of size n. Also suppose that the design mean and variance are μ_X and σ_X^2. Then the GMA is the new sequence given by

$$S_0 = \mu_X$$
$$S_m = r\bar{X}_m + (1 - r)S_{m-1} \quad (m = 1, 2, \ldots)$$

where $0 < r \leqslant 1$ is a constant. The statistical properties of this sequence are simpler than for the cusum sequence. First, by successively substituting for S_{m-1}, S_{m-2} and so on, we can express S_m directly in terms of the sample averages:

$$S_m = r \sum_{i=0}^{m-1} [(1 - r)^i \bar{X}_{m-i}] + (1 - r)^m \mu_X$$

Then, using the summation formula

$$\sum_{i=0}^{m-1} x^i = \frac{1 - x^m}{1 - x} \quad (|x| < 1)$$

it is easy to show (Exercise 53) that the mean and variance of S_m are

$$\mu_{S_m} = E(S_m) = \mu_X$$

$$\sigma_{S_m}^2 = \mathrm{Var}\,(S_m) = \frac{r}{2-r}[1-(1-r)^{2m}]\frac{\sigma_X^2}{n}$$

After the first few samples the variance of S_m tends to a constant value:

$$\sigma_{S_m}^2 \to \left(\frac{r}{2-r}\right)\frac{\sigma_X^2}{n} \quad \text{as } m \to \infty$$

If US practice is followed then the upper and lower control limits can be set at $(\mu_X \pm 3\sigma_{S_m})$. If UK practice is followed then, from the approximate normality of the sample averages and the fact that sums of normal random variables are also normal, it follows that S_m is approximately normal, so the warning and action limits can be set at $(\mu_X \pm 1.96\sigma_{S_m})$ and $(\mu_X \pm 3.09\sigma_{S_m})$ respectively (although the warning limits now have less significance).

It remains to choose a value for r. If we set $r = 1$, the whole approach reduces to the standard Shewhart charts. Small values of r (say around 0.2) lead to early recognition of small shifts of process mean, but if r is too small, a large shift may remain undetected for some time.

EXAMPLE 10.30 Construct GMA charts for the sulphur dioxide data in Example 10.27, using $r = 0.2$ and $r = 0.4$.

Solution The control charts can be seen in Figure 10.34. Clearly the warning and action limits converge fairly quickly to constant values, so little is lost by using those values in practice. The warning limit is exceeded from sample 11 for both values of r. The action limit is exceeded from sample 14 for $r = 0.2$ (as for the cusum chart in Example 10.29) and at sample 16 for $r = 0.4$.

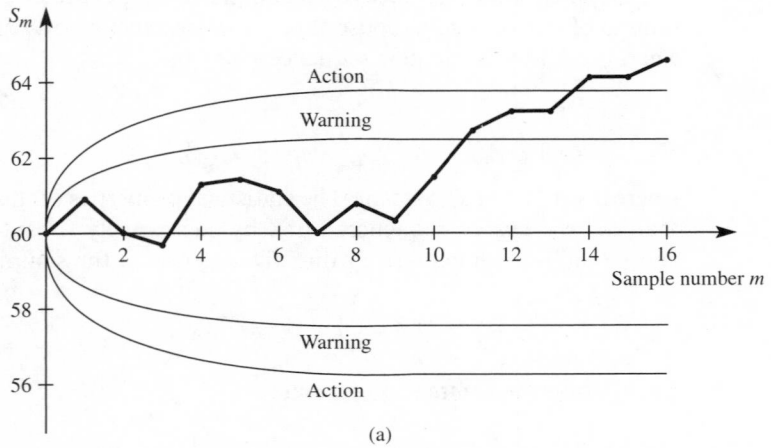

Figure 10.34 Moving-average control chart for Example 10.30: (a) $r = 0.2$; (b) $r = 0.4$.

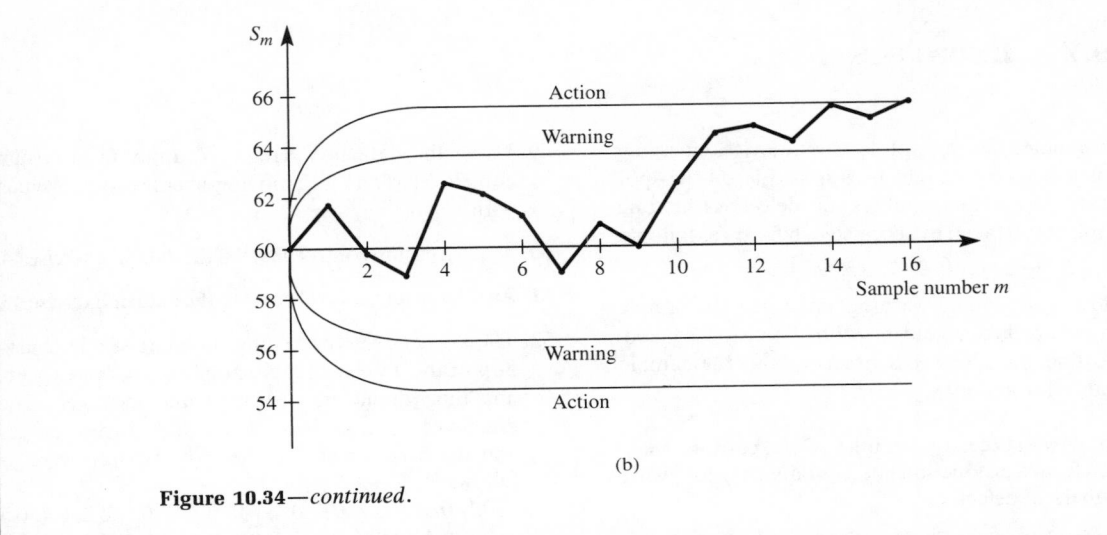

(b)

Figure 10.34—*continued*.

10.9.6   Range charts

The **sample range** is defined as the difference between the largest and smallest values in the sample. The range has two functions in quality control where the quality is of the variable rather than the attribute type. First, if the data are normal then the range (R, say) provides an estimate $\hat{\sigma}$ of the standard deviation σ by

$$\hat{\sigma} = R/d$$

where d is a constant that depends upon the sample size n as follows:

n	2	3	4	5	6	7	8	9	10	11	12
d	1.128	1.693	2.059	2.326	2.534	2.704	2.847	2.970	3.078	3.173	3.258

It is clearly quicker to evaluate this than the sample standard deviation S, and for the small samples typically used in quality control the estimate is almost as good.

The other reason why the range is important is because the quality of production can vary in dispersion as well as (or instead of) in mean. Control charts for the range R are more commonly used than charts for the sample standard deviation S when monitoring variability within the manufacturing process, and all three types of chart discussed above (Shewhart, cusum and moving-average) can be applied to the range. **Range charts** (or **R charts**) are designed using tables that can be found in specialized books on quality control, for example D. C. Montgomery, *Introduction to Statistical Quality Control*, 2nd edn (Wiley, New York, 1991).

10.9.7 Exercises

44 It is intended that 90% of electronic devices emerging from a machine should pass a simple on-the-spot quality test. The numbers of defectives among samples of 50 taken by successive shifts are as follows:

> 5, 8, 11, 5, 6, 4, 9, 7, 12, 9, 10, 14

Find the action and warning limits, and the sample number at which an out-of-control decision is taken. Also find the UCL (US practice) and the sample number for action.

45 Thirty-two successive samples of 100 castings each, taken from a production line, contained the following numbers of defectives

> 3, 3, 5, 3, 5, 0, 3, 1, 3, 5, 4, 2, 4, 3, 5, 4
> 3, 4, 5, 6, 5, 6, 4, 4, 7, 5, 4, 8, 5, 6, 6, 7

If the proportion that are defective is to be maintained at 0.02, use the Shewhart method (both UK and US standards) to indicate whether this proportion is being maintained, and if not then give the number of samples after which action should be taken.

46 A bottling plant is supposed to fill bottles with 568 ml (one imperial pint) of liquid. The standard deviation of the quantity of fill is 3 ml. Regular samples of 10 bottles are taken and their contents measured. After subtracting 568 from the sample averages, the results are as follows:

> −0.2, 1.3, 2.1, 0.3, −0.8, 1.7, 1.3, 0.6, 2.5, 1.4, 1.6, 3.0

Using a Shewhart control chart, determine whether the mean fill requires readjustment.

47 Average reverse-current readings (in nA) for samples of 10 transistors taken at half-hour intervals are as follows:

> 12.8, 11.2, 13.4, 12.1, 13.6, 13.9, 12.3, 12.9, 13.8, 13.1
> 12.9, 14.0, 13.7, 13.4, 14.2, 13.1, 14.0, 14.0, 15.1, 14.3

The standard deviation is 3 nA. At what point, if any, does the Shewhart control method indicate that the reverse current has increased from its design value of 12 nA?

48 Using the data in Exercise 46, apply (a) a cusum control chart and (b) a moving-average control chart with $r = 0.3$.

49 Using the data in Exercise 47, apply (a) a cusum control chart and (b) a moving-average control chart with $r = 0.3$.

50 Apply a cusum control chart to the data in Exercise 44.

51 Apply a cusum control chart to the data in Exercise 45.

52 The diameters of the castings in Exercise 45 are also important. Twelve of each sample of 100 were taken, and their diameters measured and averaged. The differences (in mm) between the successive averages and the design mean diameter of 125 mm were as follows:

> 0.1, 0.3, −0.2, 0.4, 0.1, 0.0, 0.2, −0.1, 0.2, 0.4, 0.5
> 0.1, 0.4, 0.6, 0.3, 0.4, 0.3, 0.6, 0.5, 0.4, 0.2, 0.3
> 0.5, 0.7, 0.3, 0.1, 0.6, 0.5, 0.6, 0.7, 0.4, 0.5

Use (a) Shewhart, (b) cusum and (c) moving-average (with $r = 0.2$) control methods to test for an increase in actual mean diameter, assuming a standard deviation of 1 mm.

53 Prove that the mean and variance of the geometric moving-average S_m defined in Section 10.9.5 for variable measure are given by

$$E(S_m) = \mu_X$$
$$\sigma_{S_m}^2 = \text{Var}(S_m) = \frac{r}{2-r}[1 - (1-r)^{2m}]\frac{\sigma_X^2}{n}$$

54 Suppose that the moving-average control chart is to be applied to the counts of defectives in attribute quality control. Find the mean and variance of S_m in terms of the sample size n, the design proportion of defectives p and the coefficient r. Following US practice, set the upper control limit at three standard deviations above the mean, and apply the method to the data in Example 10.28, using $r = 0.2$.

55 The design diameter of a moulded plastic component is 6.00 cm, with a standard deviation of 0.2 cm. The following data consist of successive averages of samples of 10 components:

> 6.04, 6.12, 5.99, 6.02, 6.04, 6.11, 5.97, 6.06, 6.05, 6.06
> 6.17, 6.03, 6.13, 6.05, 6.17, 5.97, 6.07, 6.14, 6.03, 5.99
> 6.10, 6.01, 5.96, 6.12, 6.02, 6.20, 6.11, 5.98, 6.02, 6.12

After how many samples do the Shewhart, cusum and moving-average (with $r = 0.2$) control methods indicate that action is needed?

10.10   Poisson processes and the theory of queues

Probability theory is often applied to the analysis and simulation of systems, and this can be a valuable aid to design and control. This section, which is therefore applied probability rather than statistics, will illustrate how this progresses from an initial mathematical model through the analysis stage to a simulation.

10.10.1   Typical queueing problems

Queues are everywhere: in banks and ticket offices, at airports and seaports, traffic intersections and hospitals, and in computer and communication networks. Somebody has to decide on the level of service facilities. The problem, in essence, is that it is costly to keep customers waiting for a long time, but it is also costly to provide enough service facilities so that no customer ever has to wait at all. Queues of trucks, aeroplanes or ships may be costly because of the space they occupy or the lost earnings during the idle time. Queues of people may be costly because of lost productivity or because people will often go elsewhere in preference to joining a long queue. Queues of jobs or packets in computer networks are costly in loss of time-efficiency. Service facilities are costly in capital, staffing and maintenance. Probabilistic modelling, often combined with simulation, allows performance evaluation for queues and networks, which can be of great value in preparing the ground for design decisions.

The mathematical model of a simple queueing system is based on the situation shown in Figure 10.35. **Customers** join the queue at random times that are independent of each other – the **inter-arrival time** (between successive arrivals) is a random variable. When a **service channel** is free, the next customer to be served is selected from the queue in a manner determined by the **service discipline**. After being served the customer departs from the queueing system. The **service time** for each customer is another random variable. The distributions of inter-arrival time and service time are usually assumed to take one of a number of standard patterns.

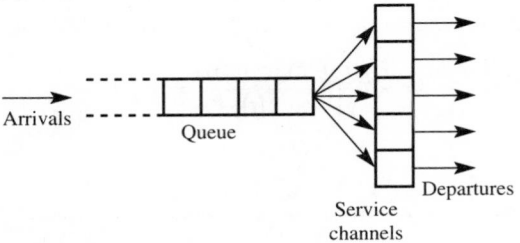

Figure 10.35 A typical queueing system.

The commonest assumption about service discipline is that the next customer to be served is the one who has been queueing the longest time (first in, first out).

The queueing system may be regarded from either a static or a dynamic viewpoint. Dynamically, the system might start from an initial state of emptiness and build up with varying rates of arrivals and varying numbers of service channels depending upon queue length. This is hard to deal with mathematically, but can be treated by computer simulation. Useful information about queues can, however, be obtained from the static viewpoint, in which the rate at which arrivals occur is constant, as is the number of service channels, and the system is assumed to have been in operation sufficiently long to have reached a steady state. At any time the queue length will be a random variable, but the distribution of queue length is then independent of time.

We need to find the distributions of queue length and of waiting time for the customer, and how these vary with the number of service channels. Costs can be worked out from these results.

10.10.2   Poisson processes

Consider the arrivals process for a queueing system. We shall assume that the customers join the queue at random times that are independent of each other. Other assumptions about the pattern of arrivals would give different results, but this is the most common one. We can therefore think of the arrivals as a stream of events occurring at random along a time axis, as depicted in Figure 10.36. The inter-arrival time T, say, will be a continuous random variable with probability density function $f_T(t)$ and cumulative distribution function $F_T(t)$.

One way to formulate the assumption of independent random arrivals is to assert that at any moment the distribution of the time until the next arrival is independent of the time elapsed since the previous arrival (because arrivals are 'blind' to each other). This is known as the **memoryless property**, and can be expressed as

$$P(T \leqslant t + h \mid T > t) = P(T \leqslant h) \quad (t, h \geqslant 0)$$

where t denotes the actual time since the previous arrival and h denotes a possible time until the next arrival. Using the definition of conditional probability (Section 10.2.1), we can write this in terms of the distribution function $F_T(t)$ as

$$\frac{P(t < T \leqslant t + h)}{1 - P(T \leqslant t)} = \frac{F_T(t + h) - F_T(t)}{1 - F_T(t)} = F_T(h)$$

Time

Figure 10.36 Random events (×) on a time axis.

Rearranging at the second equality and then dividing through by h gives

$$\frac{1}{h}[F_T(t + h) - F_T(t)] = \frac{F_T(h)}{h}[1 - F_T(t)]$$

Letting $h \to 0$, we obtain a first-order linear differential equation for $F_T(t)$:

$$\frac{d}{dt}F_T(t) = \lambda[1 - F_T(t)]$$

where

$$\lambda = \lim_{h \to 0} \frac{F_T(h)}{h}$$

With the initial condition $F_T(0) = 0$ (because inter-event times must be positive), the solution is

$$F_T(t) = 1 - e^{-\lambda t} \quad (t \geqslant 0)$$

and hence the probability density function is

$$f_T(t) = \frac{d}{dt}F_T(t) = \lambda e^{-\lambda t} \quad (t \geqslant 0)$$

This is the density function of an **exponential distribution with parameter** λ, and it follows that the mean time between arrivals is $1/\lambda$ (see Section 10.7.1). The parameter λ is the **rate of arrivals** (number per unit time).

EXAMPLE 10.31   A factory contains 30 machines of a particular type, each of which breaks down every 100 operating hours on average. It is suspected that the breakdowns are not independent. The operating time intervals between 10 consecutive breakdowns (of any machine) are measured and the shortest such interval is only six minutes. Does this lend support to the suspicion of non-independent breakdowns?

Solution   Collectively, the machines break down at the rate of 30/100 or 0.3 per hour. If the breakdowns are independent then the interval between successive breakdowns will have an exponential distribution with parameter 0.3. The probability that such an interval will exceed six minutes is

$$P(\text{interval} > 0.1) = \int_{0.1}^{\infty} 0.3\, e^{-0.3t}\, dt = e^{-0.3(0.1)} = 0.9704$$

and the probability that all nine intervals (between 10 breakdowns) will exceed this time is $(0.9704)^9 = 0.763$. Hence the probability that the shortest interval will be six minutes or less is one minus this, or 0.237. This is quite likely to have happened by chance, so it does not support the suspicion of non-independent intervals.

The assumption of independent random arrivals therefore leads to a particular distribution of inter-arrival time, parametrized by the rate of arrivals. Two further conclusions also emerge. First, the number of arrivals that occur during a fixed interval of length H has a Poisson distribution with parameter λH:

$$P(k \text{ arrivals during interval of length } H) = \frac{(\lambda H)^k e^{-\lambda H}}{k!} \quad (k = 0, 1, 2, \ldots)$$

This will not be proved here, but is easily seen to be consistent with an exponential distribution of inter-arrival time T because

$$F_T(t) = P(T \leqslant t) = 1 - P(T > t)$$

$$= 1 - P \text{ (no event during interval of length } t)$$

$$= 1 - e^{-\lambda t}$$

using the Poisson distribution. Because of this distribution, events conforming to these assumptions are known as a **Poisson process**.

The other conclusion is that the probability that an arrival occurs during a short interval of length h is equal to $\lambda h + O(h^2)$, regardless of the history of the process. Suppose that a time t has elapsed since the previous arrival, and consider a short interval of length h starting from that point:

$$P(\text{arrival during } (t, t + h)) = P(T \leqslant t + h \mid T > t)$$

$$= F_T(h)$$

$$= 1 - e^{-\lambda h}$$

$$= \lambda h + O(h^2)$$

using the memoryless property and the expansion of $e^{\lambda h}$ to first order. Furthermore, the probability of more than one arrival during a short interval of length h is $O(h^2)$.

EXAMPLE 10.32 A computer receives on average 60 batch jobs per day. They arrive at a constant rate throughout the day and independently of each other. Find the probability that more than four jobs will arrive in any one hour.

Solution The assumptions for a Poisson process hold, so the number of jobs arriving in one hour is a Poisson random variable with parameter $\lambda H = 60/24$. Hence

$$P(\text{more than four jobs}) = 1 - P(0 \text{ or } 1 \text{ or } 2 \text{ or } 3 \text{ or } 4 \text{ jobs})$$

$$= 1 - e^{-\lambda H}\left[1 + \lambda H + \frac{(\lambda H)^2}{2!} + \frac{(\lambda H)^3}{3!} + \frac{(\lambda H)^4}{4!}\right]$$

$$= 0.109$$

10.10.3   Single service channel queue

Consider a queueing system with a Poisson arrival process with mean rate λ per unit time, and a single service channel. The behaviour of the queueing system depends not only on the arrival process but also upon the distribution of service times. A common assumption here is that the service time distribution (like that of inter-arrival time) is exponential. Thus the probability density function of service time S is

$$f_S(s) = \mu e^{-\mu s} \quad (s \geqslant 0)$$

Unlike the inter-arrival time distribution in Section 10.10.2, this is not based on an assumption of independence or the memoryless property, but simply on the fact that in many queueing situations most customers are served quickly but a few take a lot longer, and the form of the distribution conforms with this fact. This assumption is therefore on much weaker ground than that for the arrival time distribution. The parameter μ is the mean number of customers served in unit time (with no idle periods), and the mean service time is $1/\mu$. With this service distribution, the probability that a customer in the service channel will have departed after a short time h is equal to $\mu h + O(h^2)$, independent of the time already spent in the service channel.

Distribution of the number of customers in the system

We can now derive the distribution of the number of customers in the queueing system. Considering the system as a whole (queue plus service channel), the number of customers in the system at time t is a random variable. Let $p_n(t)$ be the distribution of this random variable:

$$p_n(t) = P(n \text{ customers in the system at time } t) \quad (n = 0, 1, 2, \ldots)$$

Consider the time $t + h$, where h is small. The probability of more than one arrival or more than one departure during this time is $O(h^2)$, and will be ignored. There are four ways in which there can be n (assumed greater than zero) customers in the system at that time:

(1) there are n in the system at t, and no arrival or departure by $t + h$; the probability of this is given by

$$p_n(t)(1 - \lambda h)(1 - \mu h) + O(h^2) = p_n(t)(1 - \lambda h - \mu h) + O(h^2)$$

(2) there are n in the system at t, and one arrival and one departure by $t + h$; the probability is given by

$$p_n(t)(\lambda h)(\mu h) + O(h^2) = O(h^2)$$

(3) there are $n - 1$ in the system at t, and one arrival but no departure by $t + h$; the probability is given by

$$p_{n-1}(t)(\lambda h)(1 - \mu h) + O(h^2) = p_{n-1}(t)(\lambda h) + O(h^2)$$

(4) there are $n + 1$ in the system at t, and no arrivals but one departure by $t + h$; the probability is given by

$$p_{n+1}(t)(1 - \lambda h)(\mu h) + O(h^2) = p_{n+1}(t)(\mu h) + O(h^2)$$

Summing the probabilities of these mutually exclusive events gives the probability of n customers in the system at time $t + h$ as

$$p_n(t + h) = p_n(t)(1 - \lambda h - \mu h) + p_{n-1}(t)(\lambda h) + p_{n+1}(t)(\mu h) + O(h^2)$$
$$(n = 1, 2, \ldots) \qquad \textbf{(10.1)}$$

Similarly, there are two ways in which the system can be empty ($n = 0$) at time $t + h$: empty at t and no arrival before $t + h$, or one customer at t who departs before $t + h$. This gives

$$p_0(t + h) = p_0(t)(1 - \lambda h) + p_1(t)(\mu h) + O(h^2) \qquad \textbf{(10.2)}$$

Rearranging Equations (10.1) and (10.2) and taking the limit as $h \to 0$, we obtain

$$\frac{d}{dt} p_n(t) = \lim_{h \to 0} \frac{1}{h} [p_n(t + h) - p_n(t)]$$
$$= -(\lambda + \mu)p_n(t) + \lambda p_{n-1}(t) + \mu p_{n+1}(t) \quad (n = 1, 2, \ldots)$$
$$\frac{d}{dt} p_0(t) = -\lambda p_0(t) + \mu p_1(t)$$

This is a rather complex set of recursive differential equations for the probabilities $p_n(t)$. If we assume that the arrival and service parameters λ and μ are constant and that the system has been in operation for a long time then the distribution will not depend upon t; the derivatives therefore vanish, and we are left with the following algebraic equations for the *steady-state* distribution p_n:

$$0 = -(\lambda + \mu)p_n + \lambda p_{n-1} + \mu p_{n+1} \quad (n = 1, 2, \ldots)$$
$$0 = -\lambda p_0 + \mu p_1$$

Defining the ratio of arrival and service parameters λ and μ as $\rho = \lambda/\mu$ and dividing through by μ, we have

$$p_{n+1} = (1 + \rho)p_n - \rho p_{n-1} \quad (n = 1, 2, \ldots)$$
$$p_1 = \rho p_0$$

To solve these, we first assume that $p_n = \rho^n p_0$. Clearly this works for $n = 0$ and $n = 1$. Substituting,

$$p_{n+1} = (1 + \rho)\rho^n p_0 - \rho\rho^{n-1}p_0 = \rho^{n+1}p_0$$

Figure 10.37 Geometric distribution (with $\rho = 0.75$).

so the assumed form holds for $n + 1$, and therefore for all n by induction. It remains only to identify p_0 from the fact that the distribution must sum to unity over $n = 0, 1, 2, \ldots$:

$$1 = p_0 \sum_{n=0}^{\infty} \rho^n = \frac{p_0}{1 - \rho}$$

Hence $p_0 = 1 - \rho$ and

$$p_n = (1 - \rho)\rho^n \quad (n = 0, 1, 2, \ldots)$$

This is known as the **geometric distribution**, and is a discrete version of the exponential distribution (Figure 10.37). Note that this result requires that $\rho < 1$, or equivalently $\lambda < \mu$. If this condition fails to hold, the arrival rate swamps the capacity of the service channel, the queue gets longer and longer, and no steady-state condition exists.

Queue length and waiting time

The queue length distribution now follows easily:

$$P(\text{queue empty}) = p_0 + p_1$$

$$= 1 - \rho^2$$

$$P(n \text{ in queue}) = P(n + 1 \text{ in system})$$

$$= (1 - \rho)\rho^{n+1} \quad (n = 1, 2, \ldots)$$

Denoting the mean numbers of customers in the system and in the queue by N_S

and N_Q respectively,

$$N_S = \sum_{n=0}^{\infty} np_n = \frac{\rho}{1 - \rho}, \qquad N_Q = \sum_{n=1}^{\infty} (n - 1)p_n = \frac{\rho^2}{1 - \rho}$$

(Exercise 58). Since in the steady state the mean time between departures must equal the mean time between arrivals $(1/\lambda)$, it is plausible that the mean total time in the system for each customer, W_S say, is given by

W_S = mean number in system × mean time between departures

$$= \frac{\rho/\lambda}{1 - \rho} = \frac{1}{\mu - \lambda}$$

The mean waiting time in the queue, W_Q say, is then

W_Q = mean time in system − mean service time

$$= W_S - \frac{1}{\mu} = \frac{\rho}{\mu - \lambda}$$

These results for W_S and W_Q can be derived more formally from the respective waiting time distributions. For example, the distribution of total time in the system can be shown to be exponential with parameter $\mu - \lambda$, and the waiting time in the queue can be expressed as

$$P(\text{waiting time in queue} \geq t) = \rho e^{-(\mu - \lambda)t} \quad (t > 0)$$

EXAMPLE 10.33 If customers in a shop arrive at a single check-out point at the rate of 30 per hour and if the service times have an exponential distribution, what mean service time will ensure that 80% of customers do not have to wait more than five minutes in the queue and what will be the mean queue length?

Solution With $\lambda = 0.5$ and $t = 5$, the queue waiting time gives

$$0.2 = \rho e^{-(\mu - \lambda)t}$$

that is,

$$0.2\mu = 0.5 e^{2.5 - 5\mu}$$

This is a nonlinear equation for μ, which may be solved by standard methods to give $\mu = 0.743$. The mean service time is therefore $1/\mu$ or $1.35 \, \text{min}$, and the mean queue length is

$$N_Q = \frac{\rho^2}{1 - \rho} = 1.39, \qquad \text{using } \rho = \frac{\lambda}{\mu} = 0.673$$

EXAMPLE 10.34 Handling equipment is to be installed at an unloading bay in a factory. An average of 20 trucks arrive during each 10 h working day, and these must be unloaded. The following three schemes are being considered:

Scheme	Fixed cost/ £ per day	Operating cost/ £ per hour	Mean handling rate/ trucks per hour
A	90	45	3
B	190	50	4
C	450	60	6

Truck waiting time is costed at £30 per hour. Assuming an exponential distribution of truck unloading time, find the best scheme.

Solution Viewing this as a queueing problem, we have

$$\lambda = \text{arrival rate per hour} = 2.0$$

$$\mu = \text{unloading rate per hour}$$

$$\text{mean waiting time for each truck} = 1/(\mu - \lambda)$$

Hence the mean delay cost per truck is

$$\frac{30}{\mu - 2}$$

and the mean delay cost per day is

$$\frac{20 \times 30}{\mu - 2}$$

The proportion of time that the equipment is running is equal to the probability that the system is not empty (the **utilization**), which is

$$1 - p_0 = \frac{\lambda}{\mu} = \rho$$

Hence the mean operating cost per day is 10ρ times operating cost per hour. The total cost per day (in £) is the sum of the fixed, operating and delay costs, as follows:

Scheme	μ	ρ	Fixed	Operating	Delay	Total
A	3	0.6667	90	300	600	990
B	4	0.5	190	250	300	740
C	6	0.3333	450	200	150	800

Hence scheme B minimizes the total cost.

10.10.4 Queues with multiple service channels

For the case where there are c service channels, all with an exponential service time distribution with parameter μ, a line of argument similar to that in Section 10.10.3 can be found in many textbooks on queueing theory. In particular, it can be shown that the distribution p_n of the number of customers in the system is

$$
p_n = \begin{cases} \dfrac{\rho^n}{n!} p_0 & (0 \leqslant n \leqslant c) \\ \dfrac{\rho^n}{c^{n-c} c!} p_0 & (n > c) \end{cases}
$$

where $\rho = \lambda/\mu$ and

$$
p_0 = \left[\sum_{n=0}^{c-1} \frac{\rho^n}{n!} + \frac{\rho^c}{(c-1)!(c-\rho)} \right]^{-1}
$$

The mean numbers in the queue and in the system are

$$
N_Q = \frac{\rho^{c+1}}{(c-1)!(c-\rho)^2} p_0, \qquad N_s = N_Q + \rho
$$

and the mean waiting times in the queue and in the system are

$$
W_Q = \frac{N_Q}{\lambda}, \qquad W_s = W_Q + \frac{1}{\mu}
$$

EXAMPLE 10.35 For the unloading bay problem in Example 10.34 a fourth option would be to install two sets of equipment under scheme A (there is space available to do this). The fixed costs would then double but the operating costs per bay would be the same. Evaluate this possibility.

Solution With two bays under scheme A, we have $\lambda = 2$, $\mu = 3$ and $c = 2$, so that $\rho = \frac{2}{3}$, and the probability that the system is empty at any time is

$$
p_0 = \left(1 + \rho + \frac{\rho^2}{2-\rho} \right)^{-1} = \frac{1}{2}
$$

The probabilities of one truck (one bay occupied) and of two or more trucks (both bays occupied) are then

$$
P_1 = \rho p_0 = \frac{1}{3}
$$

P(two or more trucks) $= 1 - \frac{1}{2} - \frac{1}{3} = \frac{1}{6}$

The total operating cost per day is the operating cost for when one or other bay is working (£45 per hour) plus that for when both bays are working (£90 per hour), which is

$$10[\tfrac{1}{3}(45) + \tfrac{1}{6}(90)] = 300$$

The mean number in the queue is

$$\frac{\rho^3}{(2 - \rho)^2} p_0 = 0.08333$$

so that the mean total time in the system for each truck is

$$\tfrac{1}{2}(0.08333) + \tfrac{1}{3} = 0.375$$

Multiplying by the cost per hour and the number of trucks gives the delay cost per day:

$$20(30)(0.375) = 225$$

The total cost per day of this scheme is therefore

$$2(90) + 300 + 225 = £705$$

This is less than the £740 under scheme B, the best of the single-bay options.

10.10.5 Queueing system simulation

The assumption that the service time distribution is exponential, which underlies the results in Sections 10.10.3 and 10.10.4, is often unrealistic. It is known that it leads to predicted waiting times that tend to be pessimistic, as a result of which costs based on these predictions are often overestimated. Theoretical results for other service distributions exist (see for example E. Page, *Queuing Theory in OR.* Butterworth, London, 1972), but it is often instructive to simulate a queueing system and find the various answers numerically. It is then easy to vary the arrival and service distributions, and the transient (non-steady-state) behaviour of the system also reveals itself.

Figure 10.38 shows a pseudocode listing of a single-channel queueing system simulation, which is easily modified to cope with multiple channels. Each event consists of either an arrival or a departure. The variables next_arrival and next_departure are used to represent the time to the next arrival and the time to the next departure respectively, and the type of the next event is determined by whichever is the smaller. New arrival and departure times are returned by the functions arrival_time and departure_time, which generate values from appropriate exponential distributions. The distribution of the number of customers in the system is built up as an array, normalized at the end of the simulation, from which the mean and other results can be obtained.

What is typically found from such a simulation (with Poisson arrivals and an

```
{   Procedure to simulate a single-channel queueing system.
time is the running time elapsed,
limit is the simulation length,
number is the number of items in the system,
maximum is the maximum number allowed in the system,
system[i] is the distribution (array) of times with i in the
    system, assumed initialized to zero,
mean is the mean number in the system,
infinity contains a very large number,
arrival_rate is the arrival distribution parameter,
service_rate is the service distribution parameter,
next_arrival is the time to the next arrival,
next_departure is the time to the next departure,
rnd( ) is a function assumed to return a uniform random (0,1)
    number.
The simulation starts with the system empty,
limit, maximum, arrival_rate and service_rate must be set.    }


time ← 0
next_arrival ← arrival_time(arrival_rate)
next_departure ← infinity
number ← 0
repeat
   if next_arrival < next_departure then
      time ← time + next_arrival
      system[number] ← system[number] + next_arrival
      arrival( )
   else
      time ← time + next_departure
      system[number] ← system[number] + next_departure
      departure( )
   endif
until time > limit
mean ← 0
for i is 0 to maximum do
   system[i] ← system[i]/time
   mean ← mean + i * system[i]
endfor
********************
procedure arrival( )
{   procedure to handle an arrival,
changes the values of next_arrival, next_departure, and number    }
   if number = 0 then
      next_departure ← departure_time(service_rate)
   else
      next_departure ← next_departure − next_arrival
   endif
   number ← number + 1
   if number = maximum then
      next_arrival ← infinity
```

```
        else
            next_arrival ← arrival_time(arrival_rate)
        endif
    endprocedure
********************
    procedure departure()
    {   procedure to handle a departure,
    changes the values of next_arrival, next_departure, and number   }
        if number = maximum then
            next_arrival ← arrival_time(arrival_rate)
        else
            next_arrival ← next_arrival − next_departure
        endif
        number ← number − 1
        if number = 0 then
            next_departure ← infinity
        else
            next_departure ← departure_time(service_rate)
        endif
    endprocedure
********************
    function arrival_time(arrival_rate)
    {   function to generate a new arrival time   }
        U ← rnd()
        return( − (log(U))/arrival_rate)
    endfunction
    function departure_time(service_rate)
    {   function to generate a new departure time   }
        U ← rnd()
        return( − (log/U))/service_rate)
    endfunction
```

Figure 10.38 Pseudocode listing for queueing system simulation.

exponential service distribution) is that there is good agreement with the predicted results as long as $\rho = \lambda/\mu$ is small, but the results become more erratic as $\rho \to 1$. It takes a very long time for the distribution to reach its steady-state form when the value of ρ is close to unity. In that situation the theoretical steady-state results may be of limited value.

10.10.6   Exercises

56 A sea area has on average 15 gales annually, evenly distributed throughout the year. Assuming that the gales occur independently, find the probability that more than two gales will occur in any one month.

57 Suppose that the average number of telephone calls arriving at a switchboard is 30 per hour, and that they arrive independently. What is the probability that no calls will arrive in a three-minute period?

What is the probability that more than five calls will arrive in a five-minute period?

58 Show that for a single-channel queue with Poisson arrivals and exponential service time distribution the mean numbers of customers in the system and in the queue are

$$N_S = \frac{\rho}{1 - \rho}, \qquad N_Q = \frac{\rho^2}{1 - \rho}$$

where ρ is the ratio of arrival and service rates. (*Hint*: Differentiate the equation

$$\sum_{n=0}^{\infty} \rho^n = \frac{1}{1 - \rho}$$

with respect to ρ.)

59 Patients arrive at the casualty department of a hospital at random, with a mean arrival rate of three per hour. The department is served by one doctor, who spends on average 15 minutes with each patient, actual consulting times being exponentially distributed. Find

(a) the proportion of time that the doctor is idle;

(b) the mean number of patients waiting to see the doctor;

(c) the probability of there being more than three patients waiting;

(d) the mean waiting time for patients;

(e) the probability of a patient having to wait longer than one hour.

60 A small company operates a cleaning and re-catering service for passenger aircraft at an international airport. Aircraft arrive requiring this service at a mean rate of λ per hour, and arrive independently of each other. They are serviced one at a time, with an exponential distribution of service time. The cost for each aircraft on the ground is put at c_1 per hour, and the cost of servicing the planes at a rate μ is $c_2 \mu$ per hour. Prove that the service rate that minimizes the total cost per hour is

$$\mu = \lambda + \sqrt{\left(\frac{c_1 \lambda}{c_2} \right)}$$

61 The machines in a factory break down in a Poisson pattern at an average rate of three per hour during the eight-hour working day. The company has two service options, each involving an exponential service time distribution. Option A would cost £20 per hour, and the mean repair time would be 15 min. Option B would cost £40 per hour, with a mean repair time of 12 min. If machine idle time is costed at £60 per hour, which option should be adopted?

62 Ships arrive independently at a port at a mean rate of one every three hours. The time a ship occupies a berth for unloading and loading has an exponential distribution with a mean of 12 hours. If the mean delay to ships waiting for berths is to be kept below six hours, how many berths should there be at the port?

63 In a self-service store the arrival process is Poisson, with on average one customer arriving every 30 s. A single cashier can serve customers every 48 s on average, with an exponential distribution of service time. The store managers wish to minimize the mean waiting time for customers. To do this, they can either double the service rate by providing an additional server to pack the customer's goods (at a single cash desk) or else provide a second cash desk. Which option is preferable?

10.11 Bayes' theorem and its applications

To end this chapter, we return to the foundations of probability and inference. The definition of conditional probability is fundamental to the subject, and from it there follows the theorem of Bayes, which has far-reaching implications.

10.11.1 Derivation and simple examples

The definition in Section 10.2.1 of the conditional probability of an event B given that another event A occurs can be rewritten as

$$P(A \cap B) = P(B \mid A)P(A)$$

If A and B are interchanged then this becomes

$$P(A \cap B) = P(A \mid B)P(B)$$

The left-hand sides are equal, so we can equate the right-hand sides and rearrange, giving

$$P(A \mid B) = \frac{P(B \mid A)P(A)}{P(B)}$$

Now suppose that B is known to have occurred, and that this can only happen if one of the mutually exclusive events

$$\{A_1, \ldots, A_n\}, \qquad A_i \cap A_j = \varnothing \quad (i \neq j)$$

has also occurred, but which one is not known. The relevance of the various events A_i to the occurrence of B is expressed by the conditional probabilities $P(B \mid A_i)$. Suppose that the probabilities $P(A_i)$ are also known. The examples below will show that this is a common situation, and we should like to work out the conditional probabilities

$$P(A_i \mid B) = \frac{P(B \mid A_i)P(A_i)}{P(B)}$$

To find the denominator, we sum from 1 to n:

$$\sum_{i=1}^{n} P(A_i \mid B) = 1 = \frac{1}{P(B)} \sum_{i=1}^{n} P(B \mid A_i)P(A_i)$$

The sum is equal to 1 by virtue of the assumption that B could not have occurred without one of the A_i occurring. We therefore obtain a formula for $P(B)$:

$$P(B) = \sum_{i=1}^{n} P(B \mid A_i)P(A_i)$$

which is sometimes called the **rule of total probability**. Hence we have the following theorem.

THEOREM 10.2   Bayes' theorem

If $\{A_1, \ldots, A_n\}$ are mutually exclusive events, one of which must occur given that another event B occurs, then

$$P(A_i \mid B) = \frac{P(B \mid A_i)P(A_i)}{\displaystyle\sum_{j=1}^{n} P(B \mid A_j)P(A_j)} \quad (i = 1, \ldots, n) \qquad \square$$

EXAMPLE 10.36 Three machines produce similar car parts. Machine A produces 40% of the total output, and machines B and C produce 25% and 35% respectively. The proportions of the output from each machine that do not conform to the specification are 10% for A, 5% for B and 1% for C. What proportion of those parts that do not conform to the specification are produced by machine A?

Solution Let D represent the event that a particular part is defective. Then, by the rule of total probability, the overall proportion of defective parts is

$$P(D) = P(D \mid A)P(A) + P(D \mid B)P(B) + P(D \mid C)P(C)$$

$$= (0.1)(0.4) + (0.05)(0.25) + (0.01)(0.35) = 0.056$$

Using Bayes' theorem,

$$P(A \mid D) = \frac{P(D \mid A)P(A)}{P(D)} = \frac{(0.1)(0.4)}{0.056} = 0.714$$

so that machine A produces 71.4% of the defective parts.

EXAMPLE 10.37 Suppose that 0.1% of the people in a certain area have a disease D and that a mass screening test is used to detect cases. The test gives either a positive or a negative result for each person. Ideally, the test would always give a positive result for a person who has D, and would never do so for a person who has not. In practice the test gives a positive result with probability 99.9% for a person who has D, and with probability 0.2% for a person who has not. What is the probability that a person for whom the test is positive actually has the disease?

Solution Let T represent the event that the test gives a positive result. Then the proportion of positives is

$$P(T) = P(T \mid D)P(D) + P(T \mid \bar{D})P(\bar{D})$$

$$= (0.999)(0.001) + (0.002)(0.999) \simeq 0.003$$

and the desired result is

$$P(D \mid T) = \frac{P(T \mid D)P(D)}{P(T)} = \frac{(0.999)(0.001)}{0.003} = \tfrac{1}{3}$$

Despite the high basic reliability of the test, only one-third of those people receiving a positive result actually have the disease. This is because of the low incidence of the disease in the population, which means that a positive result is twice as likely to be a false alarm as it is to be correct.

In connection with Example 10.37, it might be wondered why the reliability of the test was quoted in the problem in terms of

$P(\text{positive result} \mid \text{disease})$ and $P(\text{positive result} \mid \text{no disease})$

instead of the seemingly more useful

$P(\text{disease} \mid \text{positive result})$ and $P(\text{disease} \mid \text{negative result})$

The reason is that the latter figures are contaminated, in a sense, by the incidence of the disease in the population. The figures quoted for reliability are intrinsic to the test, and may be used anywhere the disease occurs, regardless of the level of incidence.

10.11.2   Applications in probabilistic inference

The scope for applications of Bayes' theorem can be widened considerably if we assume that the calculus of probability can be applied not just to events as subsets of a sample space but also to more general statements about the world. Events are essentially statements about facts that may be true on some occasions and false on others. Scientific theories and hypotheses are much deeper statements, which have great explanatory and predictive power, and which are not so much true or false as gaining or lacking in evidence. One way to assess the extent to which some evidence E supports a hypothesis H is in terms of the conditional probability $P(H \mid E)$. The relative frequency interpretation of probability does not normally apply in this situation, so a subjective interpretation is adopted. The quantity $P(H \mid E)$ is regarded as a **degree of belief** in hypothesis H on the basis of evidence E. In an attempt to render the theory as objective as possible, the rules of probability are strictly applied, and an inference mechanism based on Bayes' theorem is employed.

Suppose that there are in fact two competing hypotheses H_1 and H_2. Let X represent all background information and evidence relevant to the two hypotheses. The probabilities $P(H_1 \mid X)$ and $P(H_1 \mid X \cap E)$ are called the **prior** and **posterior probabilities** of H_1, where E is a new piece of evidence. Similarly, there are prior and posterior probabilities of H_2. Applying Bayes' theorem to both H_1 and H_2 and cancelling the common denominator $P(E)$ gives

$$\frac{P(H_1 \mid X \cap E)}{P(H_2 \mid X \cap E)} = \frac{P(E \mid H_1 \cap X)}{P(E \mid H_2 \cap X)} \frac{P(H_1 \mid X)}{P(H_2 \mid X)}$$

The left-hand side and the second factor on the right-hand side are called the **posterior odds** and **prior odds** respectively, favouring H_1 over H_2. The first factor on the right-hand side is called the **likelihood ratio**, and it measures how much more likely it is that the evidence event E would occur if the hypothesis H_1 were true than if H_2 were true. The new evidence E therefore 'updates' the odds, and the process can be repeated as often as desired, provided that the likelihood ratios can be calculated.

EXAMPLE 10.38 From experience it is known that when a particular type of single-board microcomputer fails, this is twice as likely to be caused by a short on the serial interface (H_1) as by a faulty memory circuit (H_2). The standard diagnostic test is to measure the voltage at a certain point on the board, and from experience it is also known that a drop in voltage there occurs nine times out of ten when the memory circuit is faulty but only once in six occasions of an interface short. How does the observed drop in voltage (E) affect the assessment of the cause of failure?

Solution The prior odds are two to one in favour of H_1, and the likelihood ratio is $(1/6)/(9/10)$, so the posterior odds are given by

$$\frac{P(H_1 \mid E)}{P(H_2 \mid E)} = (\tfrac{10}{54})(2) = 0.370$$

The evidence turns the odds around to about 2.7 to one in favour of H_2.

EXAMPLE 10.39 An oil company is prospecting for oil in a certain area, and is conducting a series of seismic experiments. It is known from past experience that if oil is present in the rock strata below then there is on average one chance in three that a characteristic pattern will appear on the trace recorded by the seismic detector after a test. If oil is absent then the pattern can still appear, but is less likely, appearing only once in four tests on average. After 150 tests in the area the pattern has been seen on 48 occasions. Assuming prior odds of 3:1 against the presence of oil, find the updated odds. Also find the 90% confidence interval for the true probability of the pattern appearing after a test, and hence consider whether oil is present or not.

Solution Let H_1 and H_2 represent the hypotheses that oil is present and that it is absent respectively. There were effectively 150 pieces of evidence gathered, and the odds need to be multiplied by the likelihood ratio for each. Each time the pattern is present the likelihood ratio is

$$\frac{P(\text{pattern} \mid H_1)}{P(\text{pattern} \mid H_2)} = \tfrac{1}{3}/\tfrac{1}{4} = \tfrac{4}{3}$$

and each time it is absent the likelihood ratio is

$$\frac{P(\text{no pattern} \mid H_1)}{P(\text{no pattern} \mid H_2)} = \tfrac{2}{3}/\tfrac{3}{4} = \tfrac{8}{9}$$

The updated odds, letting E represent the total evidence, become

$$\frac{P(H_1 \mid E)}{P(H_2 \mid E)} = (\tfrac{4}{3})^{48}(\tfrac{8}{9})^{102}(\tfrac{1}{3}) = 2.01$$

The odds that there is oil present are therefore raised to 2:1 in favour.

Confidence intervals for proportions were covered in Section 10.3.6. The proportion of tests for which the pattern was observed is 48/150 or 0.32, so the 90% confidence interval for the probability of appearance is

$$\left(0.32 \pm 1.645 \sqrt{\left[\frac{(0.32)(0.68)}{150}\right]}\right) = (0.26, 0.38)$$

The hypothesis that oil is absent is not compatible with this, because the pattern should then appear with probability 0.25, whereas the hypothesis that oil is present is fully compatible.

For the problem in Example 10.38 it is conceivable that there could be enough repetitions for the relative frequency interpretation to be placed on the probabilities of the two hypotheses. In contrast, in Example 10.39 the probability of the presence or absence of oil is not well suited to a frequency interpretation, but the subjective interpretation is available.

Example 10.39 also provides a contrast between the 'Bayesian' and 'classical' inference approaches. The classical confidence interval appears to lead to a definite result: H_1 is true and H_2 is false. This definiteness is misleading, because it is possible (although not likely) that the opposite is the case, but the evidence supports one hypothesis more than the other. The Bayesian approach has the merit of indicating this relative support quantitatively.

One area where Bayesian inference is very important is in decision support and expert systems. In classical decision theory Bayesian inference is used to update the probabilities of various possible outcomes of a decision, as further information becomes available. This allows an entire programme of decisions and their consequences to be planned (see D. V. Lindley, *Making Decisions*, 2nd edn. Wiley, London, 1985). Expert systems often involve a process of reasoning from evidence to hypothesis with a Bayesian treatment of uncertainty (see for example R. Forsyth, ed., *Expert Systems, Principles and Case Studies*. Chapman & Hall, London, 1984).

10.11.3   Exercises

64 An explosion at a construction site could have occurred as a result of (a) static electricity, (b) malfunctioning of equipment, (c) carelessness or (d) sabotage. It is estimated that such an explosion would occur with probability 0.25 as a result of (a), 0.20 as a result of (b), 0.40 as a result of (c) and 0.75 as a result of (d). It is also judged that the prior probabilities of the four causes of the explosion are (a) 0.20, (b) 0.40, (c) 0.25, (d) 0.15. Find the posterior probabilities and hence the most likely cause of the explosion.

65 Three marksmen (A, B and C) fire at a target. Their success rates at hitting the target are 60% for A, 50% for B and 40% for C. If each marksman fires one shot at the target and two bullets hit it, then which is more probable: that C hit the target, or did not?

66 An accident has occurred on a busy highway between city A, of 100 000 people, and city B, of 200 000 people. It is known only that the victim is from one of the two cities and that his name is Smith.

A check of the records reveals that 10% of city A's population is named Smith and 5% of city B's population has that name. The police want to know where to start looking for relatives of the victim. What is the probability that the victim is from city A?

67 In a certain community, 8% of all adults over 50 have diabetes. If a health service in this community correctly diagnoses 95% of all persons with diabetes as having the disease, and incorrectly diagnoses 2% of all persons without diabetes as having the disease, find the probabilities that

(a) the community health service will diagnose an adult over 50 as having diabetes,

(b) a person over 50 diagnosed by the health service as having diabetes actually has the disease.

68 A stockbroker correctly identifies a stock as being a good one 60% of the time and correctly identifies a stock as being a bad one 80% of the time. A stock has a 50% chance of being good. Find the probability that a stock is good if

(a) the stockbroker identifies it as good,

(b) k out of n stockbrokers of equal ability independently identify it as good.

69 On a communications channel, one of three sequences of letters can be transmitted: AAAA, BBBB and CCCC, where the prior probabilities of the sequences are 0.3, 0.4 and 0.3 respectively. It is known from the noise in the channel that the probability of correct reception of a transmitted letter is 0.6, and the probability of incorrect reception of the other two letters is 0.2 for each. It is assumed that the letters are distorted independently of each other. Find the most probable transmitted sequence if ABCA is received.

70 The number of accidents per day occurring at a road junction was recorded over a period of 100 days. There were no accidents on 84 days, one accident on 12 days, and two accidents on four days. One hypothesis is that the number of accidents per day has a Poisson distribution with parameter λ (unspecified), and another is that the distribution is binomial with parameters $n = 3$ and p (unspecified). Use the average number of accidents per day to identify the unspecified parameters and compare the hypotheses assuming that the binomial is initially thought to be twice as likely as the Poisson.

71 The following **multinomial distribution** is a generalization of the binomial distribution. Suppose that there are k distinct possible outcomes of an experiment, with probabilities $p_1, \ldots, p_k$, and that the experiment is repeated n times. The probability of obtaining a number n_1 of occurrences of the first possible outcome, n_2 of the second, and so on up to n_k of the kth is

$$P(n_1, \ldots, n_k) = \frac{n!}{n_1! \cdots n_k!}(p_1)^{n_1} \cdots (p_k)^{n_k}$$

Suppose now that there are two competing hypotheses H_1 and H_2. H_1 asserts that the probabilities are $p_1, \ldots, p_k$ as above, and H_2 asserts that they are $q_1, \ldots, q_k$. Prove that the logarithm of the likelihood ratio is

$$\ln\left[\frac{P(n_1, \ldots, n_k \mid H_1)}{P(n_1, \ldots, n_k \mid H_2)}\right] = \sum_{i=1}^{k} n_i \ln\left(\frac{p_i}{q_i}\right)$$

72 According to the design specification, of the components produced by a machine, 92% should have no defect, 5% should have defect A alone, 2% should have defect B alone and 1% should have both defects. Call this hypothesis H_1. The user suspects that the machine is producing more components (say a proportion p_B) with defect B alone, and also more components (say a proportion p_{AB}) with both defects, but is satisfied that 5% have defect A alone. Call this hypothesis H_2. Of a sample of 1000 components, 912 had no defects, 45 had A alone, 27 had B alone and 16 had both. Using the multinomial distribution (as in Exercise 71), maximize $\ln P(912, 45, 27, 16 \mid H_2)$ with respect to p_B and p_{AB}, and find the posterior odds assuming prior odds of 5:1 in favour of H_1.

73 It is suggested that higher-priced cars are assembled with greater care than lower-priced cars. To investigate this, a large luxury model A and a compact hatchback B were compared for defects when they arrived at the dealer's showroom. All cars were manufactured by the same company. The numbers of defects for several of each model were recorded:

    A: $\{5, 4, 3, 5, 3, 4\}$
    B: $\{8, 6, 8, 9, 5\}$

The number of defects in each car can be assumed to be governed by a Poisson distribution with parameter λ. Compare the hypothesis H_1 that $\lambda_A \neq \lambda_B$ with H_2 that $\lambda_A = \lambda_B = \lambda$, using the average numbers of defects to identify the λ values and assuming no initial preference between the hypotheses.

10.12 Review exercises (1–8)

1 The amplitude d of vibration of a damped pendulum is expected to diminish by

$$d = d_0 e^{-\lambda t}$$

Successive amplitudes are measured from a trace as follows:

t	1.01 2.04 3.12 4.09 5.22 6.30 7.35 8.39 9.44 10.50
d	2.46 1.75 1.26 0.94 0.90 0.79 0.52 0.49 0.31 0.21

Find a 95% confidence interval for the damping coefficient λ.

2 Successive masses of 1 kg were hung from a wire, and the position of a mark at its lower end was measured as follows:

Load/kg	0	1	2	3	4	5	6	7
Position/cm	6.12	6.20	6.26	6.32	6.37	6.44	6.50	6.57

It is expected that the extension Y is related to the force X by

$$Y = LX/EA$$

where $L = 101.4$ cm is the length, $A = 1.62 \times 10^{-5}$ cm^2 is the area and E is the Young's modulus of the material. Find a 95% confidence interval for the Young's modulus.

3 The table in Figure 10.39 gives the intervals, in hours, between arrivals of cargo ships at a port during a period of six weeks. It is helpful to the port authorities to know whether the times of arrival are random or whether they show any regularity. Fit an exponential distribution to the data and test for goodness-of-fit.

4 When large amounts of data are processed, there is a danger of transcription errors occurring (for example a decimal point in the wrong place), which could bias the results. One way to avoid this is to test for **outliers** in the data. Suppose that $X_1, \ldots, X_n$ are independent exponential random variables, each with a common parameter λ. Let the random variable Y be the largest of these divided by the sum:

$$Y = X_{max} \Big/ \sum_i X_i$$

It can be shown (V. Barnett and T. Lewis, *Outliers in Statistical Data*. Wiley, Chichester, 1978) that the distribution function of Y is given by

$$F_Y(y) = \sum_{k=0}^{[1/y]} (-1)^k \binom{n}{k}(1 - ky)^{n-1} \quad \left(\frac{1}{n} \leqslant y \leqslant 1\right)$$

where $[1/y]$ denotes the integer part of $1/y$. For the data in the Review exercise 3 (Figure 10.39) test the largest value to see whether it is reasonable to expect such a value if the data truly have an exponential distribution. Find 95% confidence intervals for the mean inter-arrival time with this value respectively included and excluded from the data.

5 A surgeon has to decide whether or not to perform an operation on a patient suspected of suffering from a rare disease. If the patient has the disease, he has a 50:50 chance of recovering after the operation but only a one in 20 chance of survival if the operation is not performed. On the other hand, there is a one in five chance that a patient who has not got the disease would die as a result of the operation. How will the decision depend upon the surgeon's assessment of the probability p that the patient has the disease? (*Hint*: Use $P(B \mid A) = P(B \mid A \cap C)P(C) + P(B \mid A \cap \bar{C})P(\bar{C})$, where A and C are independent.)

6 A factory contains 200 machines, each of which becomes misaligned on average every 200 h of

6.8	2.1	1.0	28.1	5.8	19.7	2.9	16.3	10.7	25.3	12.5	1.6	3.0	9.9	15.9
21.3	9.1	6.9	5.6	2.0	2.2	10.2	6.5	6.8	42.5	2.9	7.3	3.1	2.6	1.0
3.8	14.7	3.8	13.9	2.9	4.1	22.7	5.8	7.6	6.4	11.3	51.6	15.6	2.6	7.6
1.2	0.7	1.9	1.8	0.7	0.4	72.0	10.7	8.3	15.1	3.6	6.0	0.1	3.1	12.9
2.2	17.6	3.6	2.4	3.2	0.4	4.4	17.1	7.1	10.1	18.8	3.4	0.2	4.9	12.9
1.8	22.4	11.6	4.2	18.0	3.0	16.2	6.8	3.7	13.6	15.7	0.7	2.7	18.8	29.8
4.9	6.8	10.7	0.9	2.4	3.8	9.0	8.8	4.8	0.3	4.6	4.9	6.1	33.0	6.5

Figure 10.39 Time interval data for Review exercise 3.

operation, the misalignments occurring at random and independently of each other and of other machines. To detect the misalignments, a quality control chart will be followed for each machine, based on one sample of output per machine per hour. Two options have been worked out: option A would cost £1 per hour per machine, whereas option B would cost £1.50 per hour per machine. The control charts differ in their average run lengths (ARL) to a signal of action required. Option A (Shewhart) has an ARL of 20 for a misaligned machine, but will also generate false alarms with an ARL of 1000 for a well-adjusted machine. Option B (cusum) has an ARL of four for a misaligned machine and an ARL of 750 for a well-adjusted machine.

When a control chart signals action required, the machine will be shut down and will join a queue of machines awaiting servicing. A single server will operate, with a mean service time of 30 min and standard deviation of 15 min, regardless of whether the machine was actually misaligned. This is all that is known of the service time distribution, but use can be made of the **Pollaczek–Khintchine formula**, which applies to single-channel queues with arbitrary service distributions:

$$N_\text{s} = \rho + \frac{(\lambda \sigma_\text{s})^2 + \rho^2}{2(1 - \rho)}$$

(the notation is as in Section 10.10.3, with σ_s the standard deviation of service time).

During the time that a machine is in the queue and being serviced, its lost production is costed at £200 per hour. In addition, if the machine is found to have been misaligned then its output for the previous several hours (given on average by the ARL) must be examined and if necessary rectified, at a cost of £10 per production hour.

Find the total cost per hour for each option, and hence decide which control scheme should be implemented.

7 A transmission channel for binary data connects a source to a receiver. The source emits a 0 with probability α and a 1 with probability $1 - \alpha$, each symbol independent of every other. The noise in the channel causes some bits to be interpreted incorrectly. The probability that a bit will be inverted is p (whether a 0 or a 1, the channel is 'symmetric').

(a) Using Bayes' theorem, express the four probabilities that the source symbol is a 0 or a 1 given that the received symbol is a 0 or a 1.

(b) If p is small and the receiver chooses to deliver whichever source symbol is the more likely given the received symbol, find the conditions on α such that the source symbol is assumed to be the same as the received symbol.

8 If discrete random variables X and Y can take possible values $\{u_1, \ldots, u_m\}$ and $\{v_1, \ldots, v_n\}$ respectively, with joint distribution $P(u_k, v_j)$ (see Section 10.4.1), the **mutual information** between X and Y is defined as

$$I(X; Y) = \sum_{k=1}^{m} \sum_{j=1}^{n} P(u_k, v_j) \log_2 \frac{P(u_k, v_j)}{P(X = u_k)P(Y = v_j)}$$

Show that for the binary symmetric transmission channel referred to in Review exercise 7, if X is the source symbol, Y the received symbol and $\alpha = \frac{1}{2}$ then

$$I(X; Y) = 1 + p \log_2 p + (1 - p) \log_2 (1 - p)$$

The interpretation of this quantity is that it measures (in 'bits') the average amount of information received for each bit of data transmitted. Show that $I(X; Y) = 0$ when $p = \frac{1}{2}$ and that $I(X; Y) \to 1$ as $p \to 0$ and as $p \to 1$. Interpret this result.

Answers to Exercises

CHAPTER 1

Exercises

1 (a) $y = \frac{5}{2}x + \frac{13}{4}$
   (b) $y = \frac{1}{4}x + \frac{3}{4}$

2 $z = 2, \frac{1}{2}\pi$

3 $u = 6v$

6 Semi-infinite strip $v > 0$, $|u| < 1$

7 (a) $u = v\sqrt{3} - 4$
   (b) $v = -u\sqrt{3}$
   (c) $(u + 1)^2 + (v - \sqrt{3})^2 = 4$
   (d) $u^2 + v^2 = 8$

8 (a) $\alpha = \frac{1}{5}(-2 + j)$, $\beta = \frac{3}{5}(1 + 2j)$
   (b) $u + 2v < 3$
   (c) $(u - 1)^2 + (v - 2)^2 < 4$
   (d) $\frac{3}{10}(1 + 3j)$

9 Interior of circle, centre $(0, -1/2c)$, radius $1/2c$; half-plane $v < 0$; region outside the circle, centre $(0, -1/2c)$, radius $1/2c$)

10 Circle, centre $(\frac{1}{2}, -\frac{2}{3})$, radius $\frac{7}{6}$

11 $\mathrm{Re}\,(w) = 1/2a$, half-plane $\mathrm{Re}\,(w) > 1/2a$

12 $w = \dfrac{z + 1}{jz - j}$,
$\mathrm{Re}\,(z) = \mathrm{const}\,(k)$ to circles
$$u^2 + \left(v - \frac{k}{1 - k}\right)^2 = \frac{1}{(1 - k)^2} \text{ plus } v = -1(k = 1)$$
$\mathrm{Im}\,(z) = \mathrm{const}\,(l)$ to circles $\left(u + \dfrac{1}{l}\right)^2 + (v + 1)^2 = \dfrac{1}{l^2}$
plus $u = 0$ $(l = 0)$

13 (a) $1 + j$, 1, ∞
   (b) $|w| > \sqrt{2}$
   (c) $v = 0$, $(u - 1)^2 + v^2 = 1$
   (d) $\pm 2^{1/4}\,e^{j\pi/8}$

14 Segment of the imaginary axis from $(0, 1)$ to $(0, -1)$

15 (a) Upper segment of the circle, centre $(\frac{2}{3}, -\frac{2}{3})$, radius $\frac{1}{3}\sqrt{5}$, cut off by the line $u - 3v = 1$

16 Circle, centre $(\frac{5}{3}, 0)$, radius $\frac{4}{3}$

17 $z_0 = j$, $\theta_0 = \pi$

18 $|w + \frac{1}{2}j| < 2$, $|w| < 2$

19 $w = e^{j\theta_0}\dfrac{z - z_0}{z_0^* z - 1}$, where θ_0 is any real number

20 Region enclosed between the inverted parabola $v = 2 - (u^2/8)$ and the real axis

21 $u = 0$, $2mu = (1 - m^2)v$

23 $u = x + \dfrac{x}{x^2 + y^2}$, $v = y - \dfrac{y}{x^2 + y^2}$; $v = 0$; ellipses, $u^2 + v^2 = r^2$ and $x^2 + y^2 = r^2$

24 (a) $e^z(z + 1)$ (b) $4\cos 4z$ (d) $-2\sin 2z$

25 $a = -1$, $b = 1$
$w = z^2 + jz^2$, $dw/dz = 2(1 + j)z$

26 $v = 2y + x^2 - y^2$

27 $e^x(x\sin y + y\cos y)$, $z\,e^z$

28 $\cos x \sinh y$, $\sin z$

29 (a) $x^4 - 6x^2y^2 + y^4 = \beta$
   (b) $2e^{-x}\sin y + x^2 - y^2 = \beta$

30 (a) $(x^2 - y^2)\cos 2x - 2xy\sin 2y$
     $+ j[2xy\cos 2x + (x^2 - y^2)\sin 2y]$
   (b) $\sin 2x \cosh 2y + j\cos 2x \sinh 2y$

31 $u = \cos^{-1}$
    $\{2y^2\{x^2 + y^2 - 1 + \sqrt{[(x^2 + y^2 - 1)^2 + 4y^2]}\}\}$
   $v = \sinh^{-1}$
    $\sqrt{\{\frac{1}{2}(x^2 + y^2 - 1) + \frac{1}{2}\sqrt{[(x^2 + y^2 - 1)^2 + 4y^2]}\}}$

33 (a) 0 (b) $3, 4$ (c) $2, -1 + j\sqrt{3}, -1 - j\sqrt{3}$

34 $z = \pm j$

35 (a) region outside unit circle
(b) $1 \leqslant u^2 + v^2 < e^2$, $0 \leqslant v \leqslant u \tan 1$
(c) outside unit circle, u and v of opposite sign

36

$x = k \rightarrow$ hyperbola
$y = k \rightarrow$ ellipse

37 $4a$, ellipse centred at origin, since axes are $\dfrac{b}{a^2+b^2}$

and $\dfrac{b}{|b^2-a^2|}$

38 (a) $j + z - jz^2 - z^3 + jz^4 + \dots$
(b) $\dfrac{1}{z} + \dfrac{j}{z^2} - \dfrac{1}{z^3} - \dfrac{j}{z^4} + \dfrac{1}{z^5} + \dots$
(c) $1 - (z-1-j) + (z-1-j)^2 - (z-1-j)^3 + \dots$

39 (a) $1 - 2z^2 + 3z^4 - 4z^6 + \dots$
(b) $1 - 3z^2 + 6z^4 - 10z^6 + \dots$

40 (a) $\frac{1}{2} - \frac{1}{4}(z-1) + \frac{1}{8}(z-1)^2 - \frac{1}{16}(z-1)^3$; 2
(b) $\frac{1}{4} - \frac{1}{16}(z-2j)^2 + \frac{1}{128}(z-2j)^4 - \frac{1}{256}(z-2j)^6$; 2
(c) $-\frac{1}{2}j + \frac{1}{2}(1+j)(z-1-j) + \frac{3}{4}(z-1-j)^2 + \frac{1}{2}(j-1)(z-1-j)^3$; $\sqrt{2}$

41 $1 - z + z^3 + \dots$

42 $1, 1, \sqrt{5}$; f is singular at $z = j$

43 $z + \frac{1}{3}z^2 + \frac{2}{15}z^5 + \dots$; $\frac{1}{2}\pi$

44 (a) $-\dfrac{1}{z} - 2 - 3z - 4z^2 - \dots$ $(0 < |z| < 1)$
(b) $\dfrac{1}{(z-1)^2} - \dfrac{1}{z-1} + 1 - (z-1) + (z-1)^2 - \dots$ $(0 < |z-1| < 1)$

45 (a) $\dots + \dfrac{1}{5!z^3} - \dfrac{1}{3!z} + z$
(b) $z - \dfrac{1}{3!z} + \dfrac{1}{5!z^3} - \dots$
(c) $a^2 \sin\dfrac{1}{a} + zf'(a) + \dots$

46 (a) $-\frac{1}{2}z - \frac{3}{4}z^2 - \frac{7}{8}z^3 - \frac{15}{16}z^4 - \dots$
(b) $\dots + \dfrac{1}{z^2} + \dfrac{1}{z} + 1 + \frac{1}{2} + \frac{1}{8}z^3 + \dots$
(c) $-\dfrac{1}{z} - \dfrac{3}{z^2} - \dfrac{7}{z^3} - \dfrac{15}{z^4} - \dots$
(d) $-\dfrac{1}{z-1} - \dfrac{2}{(z-1)^2} - \dfrac{2}{(z-1)^3} - \dots$
(e) $1 - \dfrac{2}{z-2} - (z-2) + (z-2)^2 - (z-2)^3 + (z-2)^4) - \dots$

47 (a) $z = 0$, double pole
(b) $z = j$, simple pole; $z = -j$, double pole
(c) $z = \pm 1$, $\pm j$, simple poles
(d) $z = jn\pi$ (n an integer), simple poles
(e) $z = \pm j\pi$, simple poles
(f) $z = 1$, essential singularity
(g) Simple zero at $z = 1$ and simple poles at $z = \pm j$
(h) Simple zero at $z = -j$, simple pole at $z = 3$ and a pole of order 3 at $z = -2$
(i) Simple poles at $z = 2+j$, $2-j$ and a pole of order 2 at $z = 0$

48 (a) $\dfrac{z}{2!} - \dfrac{z^3}{4!} + \dfrac{z^5}{5!} - \dots$ (removable singularity)
(b) $\dfrac{1}{z^3} + \dfrac{1}{z} + \dfrac{z}{2!} + \dfrac{z^3}{3!} + \dfrac{z^5}{4!} + \dfrac{z^7}{5!} + \dots$ (pole of order 3)
(c) $\dfrac{1}{2} - \dfrac{1}{2!z^3} + \dfrac{1}{4!z^5} - \dots$ (essential singularity)
(d) $z^2 - z^6 + \dfrac{z^{10}}{2!} - \dfrac{z^{14}}{3!} + \dots$ (analytic point)

50 (a) Simple poles at $z = -1, 2$; residues $\frac{1}{3}, \frac{5}{3}$
(b) Simple pole at $z = 1$, double pole at $z = 0$; residues $-1, 1$
(c) Simple poles at $z = 1, 3j, -3j$; residues $\frac{1}{2}$, $\frac{5}{12}(3-j)$, $\frac{5}{12}(3+j)$
(d) Simple poles at $z = 0, 2j, -2j$; residues $\frac{1}{4}$, $-\frac{3}{8}+\frac{3}{4}j$, $-\frac{3}{8}-\frac{3}{4}j$
(e) Pole of order 5 at $z = 1$, residue 19
(f) Pole of order 2 at $z = 1$, residue 4
(g) Simple pole at $z = -3$, double pole at $z = 1$; residues $-\frac{1}{8}, \frac{1}{8}$
(h) Simple poles at $z = 0, -2, -1$; residues $\frac{3}{2}, -\frac{5}{2}, 1$

51 (a) 1 (simple pole)
(b) $-\frac{1}{12}(3+j\sqrt{3})\sin\left[\frac{1}{2}(1+j\sqrt{3})\right]$ (simple pole)
(c) $\frac{1}{4}(1+j)\sqrt{2}$ (simple pole)
(d) $-\pi$ (simple pole)   (e) $-j\frac{1}{4}$ (double pole)

52 (a) $-\frac{1}{2}$ (triple pole) (b) $-\frac{14}{25}$ (double pole)
(c) $e^{n\pi}$ (double pole)

53 $-\frac{44}{3} - j\frac{8}{3}$, all cases

54 0, all cases

56 0, $2\pi j$

57 $\frac{2}{5}\pi j$, $2\pi j$

58 $\frac{4}{17}\pi(9 + j2)$, 0

59 (a) $-\frac{3}{8}\pi j$ (b) 0

60 (a) 0 (b) $2\pi j$

61 (a) $-\frac{4}{9}\pi j$ (b) $\frac{14}{9}\pi j$

62 $z = j, -\frac{3}{10}j; z = -j, \frac{3}{10}j; z = j\sqrt{6}, \frac{2}{15}j\sqrt{6}; z = -j\sqrt{6},$
$-\frac{2}{15}j\sqrt{6}$
All integrals are zero

63 (a) 0 (b) 0

64 (a) πj, $6\pi j$
(b) 0, $\frac{2}{25}\pi(1 - j)$
(c) 0, $\frac{19}{108}\pi j$, $-\frac{19}{108}\pi j$
(d) $0 - \frac{1}{162}\pi j$, $-\frac{3}{2}\pi j$

65 (a) $2\pi/\sqrt{3}$ (b) $\frac{1}{2}\pi$ (c) $\frac{5}{288}\pi$ (d) $\frac{1}{12}\pi$ (e) $\frac{8}{3}\pi$
(f) $\frac{7}{50}\pi$ (g) π (h) $2\pi/\sqrt{2}$ (i) $\frac{1}{2}\pi$ (j) $\pi(1 - 3\sqrt{5})$

66 $2axV_0/(x^2 + y^2)$

67 (a) (0,0), (0,1), (0,7), (7,0)
(b) $v = 0$ (c) $u = 0$

68 $H(x, y) = 2y - y^2 + x^2$;
$W = 2z - jz^2$

70 (a) (0,0), (1,0), (-1,0)
(b) $u = 0$ (c) $v = 0$

1.9 Review exercises

1 (a) 3j (b) 7 + j4 (c) 1 (d) j2

2 $y = 2x$ gives $3u + v = 3, u + 2v = 3$ and $3v - u = 1$
respectively
$x + y = 1$ gives $v = 1, v - u = 3$ and $u = 1$ respectively

3 (a) $\alpha = -\frac{1}{5}(3 + j4), \beta = 3 + j$
(b) $13 < 3u + 4v$
(c) $|w - 3 - j| = 1$
(d) $\frac{5}{4}(1 + j)$

4 (a) $u^2 + v^2 + u - v = 0$
(b) $u = 3v$
(c) $u^2 + v^2 + u - 2v = 0$
(d) $4(u^2 + v^2) = u$

5 Left hand — Right hand

$$x = k \rightarrow \left(u - \frac{2k - 1}{2k - 2}\right) + v^2 = \frac{1}{(2k - 2)^2}$$

$$y = 1 \rightarrow (u - 1)^2 + \left(v + \frac{1}{l}\right)^2 = \frac{1}{l^2}$$

Find points: $e^{\pi j/4}$, $e^{5\pi j/4}$

6 Fixed points $z = 1, -1, j, -j$
$r = 1 \Rightarrow u = 0$

7 $u = x^3 - 3xy^2, v = 3x^2y - y^3$

8 $(z \sin z) v = y \sin x \cosh y + x \cos x \sinh y$

9 $w = 1/z$

10 Ellipse is given by $\dfrac{x^2}{(R + a^2/4k)^2} + \dfrac{y^2}{(R - a^2/4k)^2} = 1$

11 $1 - z^3 + z^6 - z^9 + z^{12} - \cdots;$
$1 - 2z^3 + 3z^6 - 4z^9 + \cdots$

12 (a) $1 - 2z + 2z^2 - 2z^3$; 1
(b) $\frac{1}{2} - \frac{1}{2}(z - 1) + \frac{1}{6}(z - 1)^3 - \frac{1}{24}(z - 1)^4$; $\sqrt{2}$
(c) $\frac{1}{2}(1 + j) - \frac{1}{2}j(z - j) - \frac{1}{8}(1 + j)(z - j)^2 - \frac{1}{6}(z - j)^3$;
$\sqrt{2}$

13 1, 1, 1, $\frac{1}{2}\sqrt{5}$, $2\sqrt{2}$ respectively

14 (a) $\dfrac{1}{z} - z + z^3 - z^5 + \cdots \quad (0 < |z| < 1)$
(b) $\frac{1}{2} - (z - 1) + \frac{3}{2}(z - 1)^2 + \cdots \quad (|z - 1| < 1)$

15 (a) Taylor series
(b) and (c) are essential singularities, the principal
parts are infinite

16 (a) $\frac{1}{2}(e^{2x} \cos 2y - 1) + j\frac{1}{2}e^{2x} \sin 2y$
(b) $\cos 2x \cosh 2y - j \sin 2x \sinh 2y$
(c)
$$\frac{x \sin x \cosh y + y \cos x \sinh y + j(x \cos x \sinh - y \sin x \cosh y)}{x^2 + y^2}$$
(d) $\dfrac{\tan x(1 - \tanh^2 y) + j \tanh y(1 + \tan^2 x)}{1 + \tan^2 x \tanh^2 y}$

17 (a) Conformal
(b) j, $-1 - j$
(c) ± 0.465, $\pm j0.465$

18

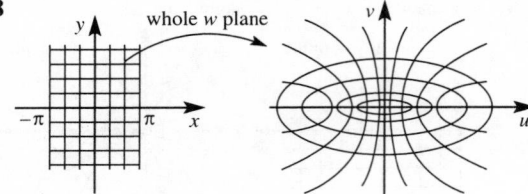

whole w plane

$x = k \rightarrow$ hyperbolas, $\dfrac{u^2}{\cos^2 k} - \dfrac{y^2}{\sin^2 k} = 1$

$y = 1 \rightarrow$ ellipses, $\dfrac{u^2}{\cosh^2 l} + \dfrac{v^2}{\sinh^2 l} = 1$

19 (a) Simple pole at $z = 0$
(b) Double poles at $z = 2, 2e^{2\pi j/3}, 2e^{4\pi j/3}$
(c) Simple poles at $z = \pm 1, \pm j$
(d) Simple poles at $z = \frac{1}{2}(2n + 1)\pi j$
    $(n = 0, \pm 1, \pm 2, \ldots)$
(e) No singularities in finite plane (entire)
(f) Simple poles at $z = 1/n\pi$ $(n = \pm 1, \pm 2, \ldots)$
(g) Essential (non-isolated) singularity at $z = 0$

20 (a) $2e^{-2}$ (b) $\frac{1}{2}$ (c) $\frac{1}{2}$ (d) 0

21 Zeros: $\pm 1, -\frac{3}{2} \pm \frac{1}{2}j\sqrt{11}$
Poles: $0, e^{\pi j/4}, e^{3\pi j/4}, e^{5\pi j/4}, e^{7\pi j/4}$

Residues (respectively) $5, \dfrac{9 + 3\sqrt{2}}{4} - \dfrac{7}{4}j, \dfrac{9 - 3\sqrt{2}}{4} + \dfrac{7j}{4}$,

$\dfrac{9 - 3\sqrt{2}}{4} - \dfrac{7j}{4}, \dfrac{9 + 3\sqrt{2}}{4} + \dfrac{7j}{4}$

22 $-202 - 322j$

23 (a) $-\frac{2}{5}\pi j$ (b) 0   (c) (i) 0, (ii) $-2\pi j$ (d) 0, 0

(e) $-\pi$ (f) $j\dfrac{\pi}{6}, -\dfrac{4\pi}{3}j$

24 (a) $\frac{7}{50}\pi$ (b) $\frac{1}{8}\pi\sqrt{2}$ (c) $\frac{1}{4}\pi$ (d) $\frac{1}{6}\pi$

CHAPTER 2

Exercises

1
(a) $\dfrac{s}{s^2 - 4}$, $\mathrm{Re}\,(s) > 2$ (b) $\dfrac{2}{s^3}$, $\mathrm{Re}\,(s) > 0$

(c) $\dfrac{3s + 1}{s^2}$, $\mathrm{Re}\,(s) > 0$ (d) $\dfrac{1}{(s + 1)^2}$, $\mathrm{Re}\,(s) > -1$

2 (a) 5   (b) -3 (c) 0   (d) 3   (e) 2
(f) 0   (g) 0   (h) 0   (i) 2   (j) 3

3 (a) $\dfrac{5s - 3}{s^2}$, $\mathrm{Re}\,(s) > 0$ (b) $\dfrac{42}{s^4} - \dfrac{6}{s^2 + 9}$, $\mathrm{Re}\,(s) > 0$

(c) $\dfrac{3s - 2}{s^2} + \dfrac{4s}{s^2 + 4}$, $\mathrm{Re}\,(s) > 0$

(d) $\dfrac{s}{s^2 - 9}$, $\mathrm{Re}\,(s) > 3$

(e) $\dfrac{2}{s^2 - 4}$, $\mathrm{Re}\,(s) > 2$

(f) $\dfrac{5}{s + 2} + \dfrac{3}{s} - \dfrac{2s}{s^2 + 4}$, $\mathrm{Re}\,(s) > 0$

(g) $\dfrac{4}{(s + 2)^2}$, $\mathrm{Re}\,(s) > -2$

(h) $\dfrac{4}{s^2 + 6s + 13}$, $\mathrm{Re}\,(s) > -3$

(i) $\dfrac{2}{(s + 4)^3}$, $\mathrm{Re}\,(s) > -4$

(j) $\dfrac{36 - 6s + 4s^2 - 2s^3}{s^4}$, $\mathrm{Re}\,(s) > 0$

(k) $\dfrac{2s + 15}{s^2 + 9}$, $\mathrm{Re}\,(s) > 0$ (l) $\dfrac{s^2 - 4}{(s^2 + 4)^2}$, $\mathrm{Re}\,(s) > 0$

(m) $\dfrac{18s^2 - 54}{(s^2 + 9)^3}$, $\mathrm{Re}\,(s) > 0$

(n) $\dfrac{2}{s^3} - \dfrac{3s}{s^2 + 16}$, $\mathrm{Re}\,(s) > 0$

(o) $\dfrac{2}{(s + 2)^3} + \dfrac{s + 1}{s^2 + 2s + 5} + \dfrac{3}{s}$, $\mathrm{Re}\,(s) > 0$

4 (a) $\frac{1}{4}(e^{-3t} - e^{-7t})$ (b) $-e^{-t} + 2e^{3t}$
(c) $\frac{4}{9} - \frac{1}{3}t - \frac{4}{9}e^{-3t}$ (d) $2\cos 2t + 3\sin 2t$
(e) $\frac{1}{64}(4t - \sin 4t)$ (f) $e^{-2t}(\cos t + 6\sin t)$
(g) $\frac{1}{8}(1 - e^{-2t}\cos 2t + 3e^{-2t}\sin 2t)$
(h) $e^t - e^{-t} + 2te^{-t}$
(i) $e^{-t}(\cos 2t + 3\sin 2t)$ (j) $\frac{1}{2}e^t - 3e^{2t} + \frac{11}{2}e^{3t}$
(k) $-2e^{-3t} + 2\cos(\sqrt{2}\,t) - \sqrt{\frac{1}{2}}\sin(\sqrt{2}\,t)$
(l) $\frac{1}{5}e^t - \frac{1}{5}e^{-t}(\cos t - 3\sin t)$
(m) $e^{-t}(\cos 2t - \sin 2t)$ (n) $\frac{1}{2}e^{2t} - 2e^{3t} + \frac{3}{2}e^{-4t}$
(o) $-e^t + \frac{3}{2}e^{2t} - \frac{1}{2}e^{-2t}$ (p) $4 - \frac{9}{2}\cos t + \frac{1}{2}\cos 3t$
(q) $9e^{-2t} - e^{-3t/2}[7\cos(\frac{1}{2}\sqrt{3}\,t) - \sqrt{3}\sin(\frac{1}{2}\sqrt{3}\,t)]$
(r) $\frac{1}{9}e^{-t} - \frac{1}{10}e^{-2t} - \frac{1}{90}e^{-t}(\cos 3t + 3\sin 3t)$

5 (a) $x(t) = e^{-2t} + e^{-3t}$
(b) $x(t) = \frac{35}{78}e^{4t/3} - \frac{3}{26}(\cos 2t + \frac{2}{3}\sin 2t)$
(c) $x(t) = \frac{1}{5}(1 - e^{-t}\cos 2t - \frac{1}{2}e^{-t}\sin 2t)$
(d) $y(t) = \frac{1}{25}(12e^{-t} + 30te^{-t} - 12\cos 2t + 16\sin 2t)$
(e) $x(t) = -\frac{7}{5}e^t + \frac{4}{3}e^{2t} + \frac{1}{15}e^{-4t}$
(f) $x(t) = e^{-2t}(\cos t + \sin t + 3)$
(g) $x(t) = \frac{13}{12}e^t - \frac{1}{3}e^{-2t} + \frac{1}{4}e^{-t}(\cos 2t - 3\sin 2t)$
(h) $y(t) = -\frac{2}{3} + t + \frac{2}{3}e^{-t}[\cos(\sqrt{2}\,t) + \sqrt{\frac{1}{2}}\sin(\sqrt{2}\,t)]$

(i) $x(t) = (\frac{1}{8} + \frac{3}{4}t)e^{-2t} + \frac{1}{2}t^2 e^{-2t} + \frac{3}{8} - \frac{1}{2}t + \frac{1}{4}t^2$

(j) $x(t) = \frac{1}{5} - \frac{1}{5}e^{-2t/3}(\cos\frac{1}{3}t + 2\sin\frac{1}{3}t)$

(k) $x(t) = te^{-4t} - \frac{1}{2}\cos 4t$

(l) $y(t) = e^{-t} + 2te^{-2t/3}$

(m) $x(t) = \frac{5}{4} + \frac{1}{2}t - e^t + \frac{5}{12}e^{2t} - \frac{2}{3}e^{-t}$

(n) $x(t) = \frac{9}{20}e^{-t} - \frac{7}{16}\cos t + \frac{25}{16}\sin t - \frac{1}{80}\cos 3t$
    $\quad - \frac{3}{80}\sin 3t$

6 (a) $x(t) = \frac{1}{4}(\frac{15}{4}e^{3t} - \frac{11}{4}e^t - e^{-2t})$, $y(t) = \frac{1}{8}(3e^{3t} - e^t)$

(b) $x(t) = 5\sin t + 5\cos t - e^t - e^{2t} - 3$
    $\quad y(t) = 2e^t - 5\sin t + e^{2t} - 3$

(c) $x(t) = 3\sin t - 2\cos t + e^{-2t}$
    $\quad y(t) = -\frac{7}{2}\sin t + \frac{9}{2}\cos t - \frac{1}{2}e^{-3t}$

(d) $x(t) = \frac{3}{2}e^{t/3} - \frac{1}{2}e^t$, $y(t) = -1 + \frac{1}{2}e^t + \frac{3}{2}e^{t/3}$

(e) $x(t) = 2e^t + \sin t - 2\cos t$
    $\quad y(t) = \cos t - 2\sin t - 2e^t$

(f) $x(t) = -3 + e^t + 3e^{-t/3}$
    $\quad y(t) = t - 1 - \frac{1}{2}e^t + \frac{3}{2}e^{-t/3}$

(g) $x(t) = 2t - e^t + e^{-2t}$, $y(t) = t - \frac{7}{2} + 3e^t + \frac{1}{2}e^{-2t}$

(h) $x(t) = 3\cos t + \cos(\sqrt{3}t)$
    $\quad y(t) = 3\cos t - \cos(\sqrt{3}t)$

(i) $x(t) = \cos(\sqrt{\frac{3}{10}}t) + \frac{3}{4}\cos(\sqrt{6}t)$
    $\quad y(t) = \frac{5}{4}\cos(\sqrt{\frac{3}{10}}t) - \frac{1}{4}\cos(\sqrt{6}t)$

(j) $x(t) = \frac{1}{3}e^t + \frac{2}{3}\cos 2t + \frac{1}{3}\sin 2t$
    $\quad y(t) = \frac{2}{3}e^t - \frac{2}{3}\cos 2t - \frac{1}{3}\sin 2t$

7 $I_1(s) = \dfrac{E_1(50+s)s}{(s^2+10^4)(s+100)^2}$

$I_2(s) = \dfrac{Es^2}{(s^2+10^4)(s+100)^2}$

$i_2(t) = E(-\frac{1}{200}e^{-100t} + \frac{1}{2}te^{-100t} + \frac{1}{200}\cos 100t)$

9 $i_1(t) = 20\sqrt{\frac{1}{7}}e^{-t/2}\sin(\frac{1}{2}\sqrt{7}t)$

10 $x_1(t) = -\frac{3}{2}\cos(\sqrt{3}t) - \frac{1}{2}\cos(\sqrt{13}t)$
     $x_2(t) = -\frac{1}{2}\cos(\sqrt{3}t) + \frac{3}{2}\cos(\sqrt{13}t)$, 3, $\sqrt{13}$

13 $f(t) = tH(t) - tH(t-1)$

14 (a) $f(t) = 3t^2 - [3(t-4)^2 + 22(t-4) + 43]H(t-4)$
        $\quad - [2(t-6) + 4]H(t-6)$
        $F(s) = \dfrac{6}{s^3} - \left(\dfrac{6}{s^3} + \dfrac{22}{s^2} + \dfrac{43}{s}\right)e^{-4s} - \left(\dfrac{2}{s^3} + \dfrac{4}{s}\right)e^{-6s}$

(b) $f(t) = t - 2(t-1)H(t-1) + (t-2)H(t-2)$
    $F(s) = \dfrac{1}{s^2} - \dfrac{2}{s^2}e^{-s} + \dfrac{1}{s^2}e^{-2s}$

15 (a) $\frac{1}{6}(t-5)^3 e^{2(t-5)}H(t-5)$

(b) $\frac{3}{2}[e^{-(t-2)} - e^{-3(t-2)}]H(t-2)$

(c) $[t - \cos(t-1) - \sin(t-1)]H(t-1)$

(d) $\sqrt{\frac{1}{3}}e^{-(t-\pi)/2}\{\sqrt{3}\cos[\frac{1}{2}\sqrt{3}(t-\pi)]$
    $\quad + \sin[\frac{1}{2}\sqrt{3}(t-\pi)]\}H(t-\pi)$

(e) $H(t - \frac{4}{5}\pi)\cos 5t$

(f) $[t - \cos(t-1) - \sin(t-1)]H(t-1)$

16 $x(t) = e^{-t} + (t-1)[1 - H(t-1)]$

17 $x(t) = 2e^{-t/2}\cos(\frac{1}{2}\sqrt{3}t) + t - 1 - 2H(t-1)$
     $\{t - 2 + e^{-(t-1)/2}\{\cos[\frac{1}{2}\sqrt{3}(t-1)]$
     $\quad - \sqrt{\frac{1}{3}}\sin[\frac{1}{2}\sqrt{3}(t-1)]\}\}$
     $\quad + H(t-2)\{t - 3 + e^{-(t-2)/2}$
     $\quad \{\cos[\frac{1}{2}\sqrt{3}(t-2)] - \sqrt{\frac{1}{3}}\sin[\frac{1}{2}\sqrt{3}(t-2)]\}\}$

18 $x(t) = e^{-t} + \frac{1}{10}(\sin t - 3\cos t + 4e^\pi e^{-2t}$
     $\quad - 5e^{\pi/2}e^{-t})H(t - \frac{1}{2}\pi)$

19 $f(t) = 3 + 2(t-4)H(t-4)$
     $F(s) = \dfrac{3}{s} + \dfrac{2}{s^2}e^{-4s}$
     $x(t) = 3 - 2\cos t + 2[t - 4 - \sin(t-4)]H(t-4)$

20 $\theta_0(t) = \frac{3}{10}(1 - e^{-3t}\cos t - 3e^{-3t}\sin t)$
     $\quad - \frac{3}{10}[1 - e^{3a}e^{-3t}\cos(t-a)$
     $\quad - 3e^{3a}e^{-3t}\sin(t-a)]H(t-a)$

21 $\theta_0(t) = \frac{1}{32}(3 - 2t - 3e^{-4t} - 10te^{-4t})$
     $\quad + \frac{1}{32}[2t - 3 + (2t-1)e^{-4(t-1)}]H(t-1)$

23 $\dfrac{3 - 3e^{-2s} - 6se^{-4s}}{s^2(1 - e^{-4s})}$

24 $\dfrac{K}{s^2} - \dfrac{KT}{s}\dfrac{e^{-sT}}{1 - e^{-sT}}$

25 (a) $2\delta(t) + 9e^{-2t} - 19e^{-3t}$

(b) $\delta(t) - \frac{5}{2}\sin 2t$

(c) $\delta(t) - e^{-t}(2\cos 2t + \frac{1}{2}\sin 2t)$

26 (a) $x(t) = (\frac{1}{6} - \frac{2}{3}e^{-3t} + \frac{1}{2}e^{-4t})$
        $\quad + (e^{-3(t-2)} - e^{-4(t-2)})H(t-2)$

(b) $x(t) = \frac{1}{2}e^{6\pi}e^{-3t}H(t-2\pi)\sin 2t$

(c) $x(t) = 5e^{-3t} - 4e^{-4t}$
    $\quad + (e^{-3(t-3)} - e^{-4(t-3)})H(t-3)$

27 (a) $f'(t) = g'(t) - 43\delta(t-4) - 4\delta(t-6)$

$g'(t) = \begin{cases} 6t & (0 \leqslant t < 4) \\ 2 & (4 \leqslant t < 6) \\ 0 & (t \geqslant 6) \end{cases}$

(b) $g'(t) = \begin{cases} 1 & (0 \leqslant t < 1) \\ -1 & (1 \leqslant t < 2) \\ 0 & (t \geqslant 2) \end{cases}$

(c) $f'(t) = g'(t) + 5\delta(t) - 6\delta(t-2) - 15\delta(t-4)$

$g'(t) = \begin{cases} 2 & (0 \leqslant t < 2) \\ -3 & (2 \leqslant t < 4) \\ 2t - 1 & (t \geqslant 4) \end{cases}$

28 $x(t) = -\frac{10}{9}e^{-5t} + \frac{10}{9}e^{-2t} - \frac{4}{3}te^{-2t}$

30 $q(t) = \frac{E}{Ln}e^{-\mu t}\sin nt$, $n^2 = \frac{1}{LC} - \frac{R^2}{4L^2}$, $\mu = \frac{R}{2L}$

$i(t) = \frac{E}{Ln}e^{-\mu t}(n\cos nt - \mu\sin nt)$

31 $y(x) = \frac{1}{48EI}[2Mx^4/l + 8W(x - \frac{1}{2}l)^3 H(x - \frac{1}{2}l)$
$\quad - 4(M + W)x^3 + (2M + 3W)l^2 x]$

32 $y(x) = \dfrac{w(x_2^2 - x_1^2)x^2}{4EI} - \dfrac{w(x_2 - x_1)x^3}{6EI}$

$\quad + \dfrac{w}{24EI}[(x - x_1)^4 H(x - x_1)$
$\quad\quad - (x - x_2)^4 H(x - x_2)]$

$y_{max} = wl^4/8EI$

33 $y(x) = \frac{W}{EI}[\frac{1}{6}x^3 - \frac{1}{6}(x - b)^3 H(x - b) - \frac{1}{2}bx^2]$

$\quad = \begin{cases} -\dfrac{Wx^2}{6EI}(3b - x) & (0 < x \leqslant b) \\[2mm] -\dfrac{Wb^2}{6EI}(3x - b) & (b < x \leqslant l) \end{cases}$

34 (a) $\dfrac{3s + 2}{s^2 + 2s + 5}$

(b) $s^2 + 2s + 5 = 0$, order 2

(c) Poles $-1 \pm j2$; zero $-\frac{2}{3}$

35 $\dfrac{s^2 + 5s + 6}{s^3 + 5s^2 + 17s + 13}$, $s^3 + 5s^2 + 17s + 13 = 0$

order 3, zeros $-3, -2$, poles $-1, -2 \pm j3$

36 (a) Marginally stable   (b) Unstable   (c) Stable
(d) Stable   (e) Unstable

37 (a) Unstable   (b) Stable   (c) Marginally stable
(d) Stable   (e) Stable

40 $K > \frac{2}{3}$

41 (a) $3e^{-7t} - 3e^{-8t}$ (b) $\frac{1}{3}e^{-4t}\sin 3t$
(c) $\frac{2}{3}(e^{4t} - e^{-2t})$ (d) $\frac{1}{3}e^{2t}\sin 3t$

42 $\dfrac{s + 8}{(s + 1)(s + 2)(s + 4)}$

47 $\frac{2}{7}, \frac{4}{5}$

49 (a) $\frac{1}{54}[2 - e^{-3t}(9t^2 + 6t + 2)]$
(b) $\frac{1}{125}[e^{-3t}(5t + 2) + e^{2t}(5t - 2)]$
(c) $\frac{1}{16}(4t - 1 + e^{-4t})$

51 $e^{-3t} - e^{-4t}$

$x(t) = \frac{1}{12}A[1 - 4e^{-3t} + 3e^{-4t} - (1 - 4e^{-3(t-T)}$
$\quad + 3e^{-4(t-T)})H(t - T)]$

52 $e^{-2t}\sin t$, $\frac{1}{5}[1 - e^{-2t}(\cos t + 2\sin t)]$

2.8 Review exercises

1 (a) $x(t) = \cos t + \sin t - e^{-2t}(\cos t + 3\sin t)$
(b) $x(t) = -3 + \frac{13}{7}e^t + \frac{15}{7}e^{-2t/5}$

2 (a) $e^{-t} - \frac{1}{2}e^{-2t} - \frac{1}{2}e^{-t}(\cos t + \sin t)$
(b) $i(t) = 2e^{-t} - 2e^{-2t}$
$\quad\quad + V[e^{-t} - \frac{1}{2}e^{-2t} - \frac{1}{2}e^{-t}(\cos t + \sin t)]$

3 $x(t) = -t + 5\sin t - 2\sin 2t$,
$y(t) = 1 - 2\cos t + \cos 2t$

4 $\frac{1}{5}(\cos t + 2\sin t)$
$e^{-t}[(x_0 - \frac{1}{5})\cos t + (x_1 + x_0 - \frac{3}{5})\sin t]$
$\sqrt{\frac{1}{5}}$, $63.4°$ lag

6 (a) (i) $\dfrac{s\cos\phi - \omega\sin\phi}{s^2 + \omega^2}$

(ii) $\dfrac{s\sin\phi + \omega(\cos\phi + \sin\phi)}{s^2 + 2\omega s + \omega^2}$

(b) $\frac{1}{20}(\cos 2t + 2\sin 2t) + \frac{1}{20}e^{-2t}(39\cos 2t + 47\sin 2t)$

7 (a) $e^{-2t}(\cos 3t - 2\sin 3t)$
(b) $y(t) = 2 + 2\sin t - 5e^{-2t}$

8 $x(t) = e^{-8t} + \sin t$, $y(t) = e^{-8t} - \cos t$

9 $q(t) = \frac{1}{500}(5e^{-100t} - 2e^{-200t})$
$\quad - \frac{1}{500}(3\cos 100t - \sin 100t)$,
current leads by approximately $18.5°$

10 $x(t) = \frac{29}{20}e^{-t} + \frac{445}{1212}e^{-t/5} + \frac{1}{3}e^{-2t}$
$\quad - \frac{1}{505}(76\cos 2t - 48\sin 2t)$

11 (a) $\theta = \frac{1}{100}(4e^{-4t} + 10te^{-4t} - 4\cos 2t + 3\sin 2t)$
(b) $i_1 = \frac{1}{7}(e^{4t} + 6e^{-3t})$, $i_2 = \frac{1}{7}(e^{-3t} - e^{4t})$

12 $i = \dfrac{E}{R}[1 - e^{-nt}(\cos nt - \sin nt)]$

13 $i_1 = \dfrac{E(4 - 3e^{-Rt/L} - e^{-3Rt/L})}{6R}$, $i_2 \to E/3R$

14 $x_1(t) = \frac{1}{3}[\sin t - 2\sin 2t + \sqrt{3}\sin(\sqrt{3}t)]$
$x_2(t) = \frac{1}{3}[\sin t + \sin 2t - \sqrt{3}\sin(\sqrt{3}t)]$

15 (a) (i) $e^{-t}(\cos 3t + \sin 3t)$ (ii) $e^t - e^{2t} + 2te^t$
(b) $y(t) = \frac{1}{2}e^{-t}(8 + 12t + t^3)$

16 (a) $\frac{5}{2}e^{7t}\sin 2t$

(b) $\dfrac{n^2 i}{Ks(s^2 + 2Ks + n^2)}$, $\theta(t) = \dfrac{i}{K}(1 - e^{-Kt}) - it\,e^{-Kt}$

17 (a) (ii) $e^{-(t-\alpha)}[\cos 2(t - \alpha) - \tfrac{1}{2}\sin 2(t - \alpha)]H(t - \alpha)$

   (b) $y(t) = \tfrac{1}{10}[e^{-t}(\cos 2t - \tfrac{1}{2}\sin 2t) + 2\sin t - \cos t]$
$\qquad + \tfrac{1}{10}[e^{-(t-\pi)}(\cos 2t - \tfrac{1}{2}\sin 2t) + \cos t$
$\qquad - 2\sin t]H(t - \pi)$

18 $i(t) = \tfrac{1}{250}[e^{-40t} - 2H(1 - \tfrac{1}{2}T)e^{-40(t - T/2)}$
$\qquad + 2H(t - T)e^{-40(t - T)}$
$\qquad - 2H(t - \tfrac{3}{2}T)e^{-40(t - 3T/2)} + \dots]$

  Yes, since time constant is large compared with T

19 $e^{-t}\sin t$, $\tfrac{1}{2}[1 - e^{-t}(\cos t + \sin t)]$

20 $EI\dfrac{d^4 y}{dx^4} = 12 + 12H(x - 4) - R\delta(x - 4)$,

$\qquad y(0) = y'(0) = y(4) = y^{(2)}(5) = y^{(3)}(0) = 0$

$\qquad y(x) =$
$\begin{cases} \tfrac{1}{2}x^4 - 4.25x^3 + 9x^2 & (0 \leqslant x \leqslant 4) \\ \tfrac{1}{2}x^4 - 4.25x^3 + 9x^2 + \tfrac{1}{2}(x - 4)^4 - 7.75(x - 4)^3 \end{cases}$
$\hfill (4 \leqslant x \leqslant 5)$

$\qquad 25.5\,\text{kN},\ 18\,\text{kN m}$

21 (a) $f(t) = H(t - 1) - H(t - 2)$
$\qquad x(t) = H(t - 1)(1 - e^{-(t-1)})$
$\qquad - H(t - 2)(1 - e^{-(t-2)})$

   (b) 0, E/R

23 (a) $t - 2 + (t + 2)e^{-t}$
   (b) $y = t + 2 - 2e^t + 2t\,e^t$, $y(t) = \tfrac{1}{2}t^2 + y_1$

24 $y = \tfrac{2}{9}Wl\,x^2 - \tfrac{10}{81}Wx^3 - \dfrac{W(x - l)^3}{6EI}H(x - l)$

$\qquad EI\dfrac{d^4 y}{dx^4} = W\delta(x - l) + w[H(x) - H(x - l)]$

25 (a) $x(t) =$
$\tfrac{1}{6}\{1 + e^{3(t-a)/2}[\sqrt{3}\sin(\tfrac{1}{2}\sqrt{3}\,t) - \cos(\tfrac{1}{2}\sqrt{3}\,t)]H(t - a)\}$

26 (a) No   (b) $\dfrac{1}{s^2 + 2s + (K - 3)}$ (d) $K > 3$

27 (a) 4 (b) $\tfrac{1}{10}$

28 (a) $\dfrac{K}{s^2 + (1 + K_1)s + 1}$
   (c) $K = 12.5$, $K_1 = 0.178$
   (d) $0.65\,\text{s}$, $2.48\,\text{s}$, $1.86\,\text{s}$

29 (a) $K_2 = M_2\omega^2$

30 (b) Unstable   (c) $\beta = 2.5 \times 10^{-5}$, $92\,\text{dB}$
   (d) $-8\,\text{dB}$, $24°$
   (e) $K = 10^6$, $\tau_1 = 10^{-6}$, $\tau_2 = 10^{-7}$, $\tau_3 = 4 \times 10^{-8}$
   (f) $s^3 + 36 \times 10^6 s^2 + 285 \times 10^{12} s$
$\qquad + 25 \times 10^{18}(1 + 10^7 \beta) = 0$

CHAPTER 3

Exercises

1 (a) $\dfrac{4}{4z + 1}$, $|z| > \tfrac{1}{4}$ (b) $\dfrac{z}{z - 3}$, $|z| > 3$

   (c) $\dfrac{z}{z + 2}$, $|z| > 2$ (d) $\dfrac{-z}{z - 2}$, $|z| > 2$

   (e) $3\dfrac{z}{(z - 1)^2}$, $|z| > 1$

2 $e^{-2\omega kT} \leftrightarrow \dfrac{z}{z - e^{-2\omega T}}$

4 $\dfrac{1}{z^3}\dfrac{2z}{2z - 1} = \dfrac{2}{z^2(2z - 1)}$

5 (a) $\dfrac{5z}{5z + 1}$ (b) $\dfrac{z}{z + 1}$

6 $\dfrac{2z}{2z - 1}$, $\dfrac{2z}{(2z - 1)^2}$

8 (a) $\{e^{-4kT}\} \leftrightarrow \dfrac{z}{z - e^{-4T}}$

   (b) $\{\sin kT\} \leftrightarrow \dfrac{z\sin T}{z^2 - 2z\cos T + 1}$

   (c) $\{\cos 2kT\} \leftrightarrow \dfrac{z(z - \cos 2T)}{z^2 - 2z\cos 2T + 1}$

11 (a) 1 (b) $(-1)^k$ (c) $(\tfrac{1}{2})^k$ (d) $\tfrac{1}{3}(-\tfrac{1}{3})^k$
   (e) j^k (f) $(-j\sqrt{2})^k$ (g) 0 $(k = 0)$, 1 $(k > 0)$
   (h) 1 $(k = 0)$, $(-1)^{k+1}$ $(k > 0)$

12 (a) $\tfrac{1}{3}[1 - (-2)^k]$ (b) $\tfrac{1}{7}[3^k - (-\tfrac{1}{2})^k]$
   (c) $\tfrac{1}{3} + \tfrac{1}{6}(-\tfrac{1}{2})^k$ (d) $\tfrac{2}{3}(\tfrac{1}{2})^k + \tfrac{2}{3}(-1)^{k+1}$
   (e) $\sin\tfrac{1}{2}k\pi$ (f) $2^k\sin\tfrac{1}{6}k\pi$
   (g) $\tfrac{5}{2}k + \tfrac{1}{4}(1 - 3^k)$ (h) $k + 2\sqrt{\tfrac{1}{3}}\cos(\tfrac{1}{3}k - \tfrac{3}{2}\pi)$

13 (a) $\{0, 1, 0, 0, 0, 0, 0, 2\}$ (b) $\{1, 0, 3, 0, 0, 0, 0, 0, 0, -2\}$
   (c) $\{0, 5, 0, 1, 3\}$ (d) $\{0, 0, 1, 1\} + \{(-\tfrac{1}{3})^k\}$
   (e) 1 $(k = 0)$, $\tfrac{5}{2}$ $(k = 1)$ $\tfrac{5}{4}$ $(k = 2)$ $-\tfrac{1}{8}(-\tfrac{1}{2})^{k-3}$ $(k \geqslant 3)$
   (f) $\begin{cases} 0 & (k = 0) \\ 3 - 2k + 2^{k-1} & (k \geqslant 1) \end{cases}$
   (g) $\begin{cases} 0 & (k = 0) \\ 2 - 2^{k-1} & (k \geqslant 1) \end{cases}$

14 $y_{k+2} + \tfrac{1}{2}y_{k+1} = x_k$, $y_{k+2} + \tfrac{1}{4}y_{k+1} - \tfrac{1}{5}y_k = x_k$

15 (a) $y_k = k$ (b) $y_k = \tfrac{3}{10}(9^k) + \tfrac{17}{10}(-1)^k$
   (c) $2^{k-1}\sin\tfrac{1}{2}k\pi$ (d) $2(-\tfrac{1}{2})^k + 3^k$

16 (a) $y_k = \tfrac{2}{5}(-\tfrac{1}{2})^k - \tfrac{9}{10}(\tfrac{1}{3})^k + \tfrac{1}{2}$
   (b) $y_k = \tfrac{7}{2}(3^k) - 6(2^k) + \tfrac{5}{2}$

(c) $y_n = \frac{2}{5}(3^n) - \frac{2}{3}(2^n) + \frac{4}{15}(\frac{1}{2})^n$

(d) $y_n - 2(3^{n-1})\sin\frac{1}{6}n\pi + 1$

(e) $y_n = \frac{18}{5}(-\frac{1}{2})^n - \frac{8}{5}(-2)^n - 2n - 1$

(f) $y_n = -\frac{1}{2}[2^n + (-2)^n] + 1 - n$

17 (b) 7, £4841

18 $y_k = 2^k - \frac{1}{2}(3^k) + \frac{1}{2}$

19 As $k \to \infty$, $I_k \to 2G$ as a damped oscillation

21 (a) $\dfrac{1}{z^2 - 3z + 2}$ (b) $\dfrac{z-1}{z^2 - 3z + 1}$

(c) $\dfrac{z+1}{z^3 - z^2 + 2z + 1}$

22

23 (a) $\frac{1}{2}\{(-\frac{1}{4})^k - (-\frac{1}{2})^k\}$

(b) $2(3^k)\sin\frac{1}{6}(k+1)\pi$

(c) $\frac{2}{3}(0.4)^k + \frac{1}{3}(-0.2)^k$

(d) $4^{k+1} + 2^k$

24 $\begin{cases} 0 & (k=0) \\ 2^{k-1} - 1 & (k \geqslant 1) \end{cases}$
$\begin{cases} 0 & (k=0) \\ 2^{k-1} & (k \geqslant 1) \end{cases}$

25 (a), (b) and (c) are stable; (d) is unstable; (e) is marginally stable

26 $2 - (\frac{1}{2})^k$

27 $y_n = -4(\frac{1}{2})^n + 2(\frac{1}{3})^n + 2(\frac{2}{3})^n$

29 q form:
$(Aq^2 + Bq + C)y_k = \Delta^2(q^2 + 2q + 1)u_k$
δ form:
$[A\Delta^2\delta^2 + (2\Delta A + \Delta B)\delta + (A + B + C)]y_k$
$= \Delta^2(4 + 4\Delta\delta + \Delta^2\delta^2)u_k$
$A = 2\Delta^2 + 6\Delta + 4$
$B = 4\Delta^2 - 8$
$C = 2\Delta^2 - 6\Delta + 4$

30 $\dfrac{1}{s^3 + 2s^2 + 2s + 1}$
$[(\Delta^3 + 4\Delta^2 + 8\Delta + 8)\delta^3 + (6\Delta^2 + 16\Delta + 16)\delta^2$
$+ (12\Delta + 16)\delta + 8]y_k = (2 + T\delta)^3 u_k$

32 $\dfrac{12(z^2 - z)}{(12 + 5\Delta)z^2 + (8\Delta - 12)z - \Delta}$

$\dfrac{12\gamma(1 + \Delta\gamma)}{\Delta(12 + 5\Delta)\gamma^2 + (8\Delta - 12)\gamma + 12}$

3.10 Review exercises

4 $3 + 2k$

5 $\frac{1}{6} + \frac{1}{3}(-2)^k - \frac{1}{2}(-1)^k$

7 $\dfrac{2z}{(z-e)^{3T}} - \dfrac{z}{z - e^{-2T}}$

8 (a) $\left\{\dfrac{1}{a-b}(a^n - b^n)\right\}$

(b) (i) $3^{k-1}k$ (ii) $2\sqrt{\frac{1}{3}}\sin\frac{1}{3}k\pi$

9 $\frac{3}{2} - \frac{1}{2}(-1)^k - 2^k$

10 $(-1)^k$

13 $\frac{1}{2}A[2 - 2(\frac{1}{2})^k - k(\frac{1}{2})^{k-1}]$

CHAPTER 4

Exercises

1 (a) $f(t) = -\frac{1}{4}\pi - \dfrac{2}{\pi}\displaystyle\sum_{n=1}^{\infty}\dfrac{\cos(2n-1)t}{(2n-1)^2}$
$+ \displaystyle\sum_{n=1}^{\infty}\left[\dfrac{3\sin(2n-1)t}{2n-1} - \dfrac{\sin 2nt}{2n}\right]$

(b) $f(t) = \frac{1}{4}\pi + \dfrac{2}{\pi}\displaystyle\sum_{n=1}^{\infty}\dfrac{\cos(2n-1)t}{(2n-1)^2} - \displaystyle\sum_{n=1}^{\infty}\dfrac{\sin nt}{n}$

(c) $f(t) = \dfrac{2}{\pi}\displaystyle\sum_{n=1}^{\infty}\dfrac{\sin nt}{n}$

(d) $f(t) = \dfrac{2}{\pi} + \dfrac{4}{\pi}\displaystyle\sum_{n=1}^{\infty}\dfrac{(-1)^{n+1}\cos 2nt}{4n^2 - 1}$

(e) $f(t) = \dfrac{2}{\pi} + \dfrac{4}{\pi}\displaystyle\sum_{n=1}^{\infty}\dfrac{(-1)^{n+1}\cos nt}{4n^2 - 1}$

(f) $f(t) = \frac{1}{2}\pi - \dfrac{4}{\pi}\displaystyle\sum_{n=1}^{\infty}\dfrac{\cos(2n-1)t}{(2n-1)^2}$

(g) $f(t) = -\dfrac{4}{\pi}\displaystyle\sum_{n=1}^{\infty}\dfrac{\cos(2n-1)t}{(2n-1)^2} - \displaystyle\sum_{n=1}^{\infty}\dfrac{\sin 2nt}{n}$

(h) $f(t) = \left(\frac{1}{2}\pi + \dfrac{1}{\pi}\sinh\pi\right)$
$+ \dfrac{2}{\pi}\displaystyle\sum_{n=1}^{\infty}\left[\dfrac{(-1)^n - 1}{n^2} + \dfrac{(-1)^n\sinh\pi}{n^2 + 1}\right]\cos nt$
$- \dfrac{2}{\pi}\displaystyle\sum_{n=1}^{\infty}\dfrac{(-1)}{n^2 + 1}\sinh\pi\sin nt$

2 $f(t) = \frac{1}{3}\pi^2 + 4\sum_{n=1}^{\infty}\frac{\cos nt}{n^2}$

Taking $t = \pi$ gives the required result.

3 $q(t) = E\left[\frac{1}{2} - 4\sum_{n=1}^{\infty}\frac{\cos(2n-1)t}{(2n-1)^2}\right]$

4 $f(t) = \frac{5}{\pi} + \frac{5}{2}\sin t - \frac{10}{\pi}\sum_{n=1}^{\infty}\frac{\cos 2nt}{4n^2-1}$

5 Taking $t = 0$ and $t = \pi$ gives the required answers.

6 $f(t) = \frac{1}{4}\pi - \frac{2}{\pi}\sum_{n=1}^{\infty}\frac{\cos(4n-2)t}{(2n-1)^2}$

Taking $t = 0$ gives the required series.

7 $f(t) = \frac{3}{2} + \frac{4}{\pi^2}\sum_{n=1}^{\infty}\frac{\cos(2n-1)t}{(2n-1)^2}$

Replacing t by $t - \frac{1}{2}\pi$ gives the following sine series of odd harmonics:

$f(t - \frac{1}{2}\pi) - \frac{3}{2} = -\frac{4}{\pi^2}\sum_{n=1}^{\infty}\frac{(-1)^n\sin(2n-1)t}{(2n-1)^2}$

8 $f(t) = \frac{2l}{\pi}\sum_{n=1}^{\infty}\frac{(-1)^{n+1}}{n}\sin\frac{n\pi t}{l}$

9 $f(t) = \frac{2K}{\pi}\sum_{n=1}^{\infty}\frac{1}{n}\sin\frac{n\pi t}{l}$

10 $f(t) = \frac{3}{2} + \frac{6}{\pi}\sum_{n=1}^{\infty}\frac{1}{(2n-1)}\frac{\sin(2n-1)\pi t}{5}$

11 $v(t) = \frac{A}{\pi}\left(1 + \frac{1}{2}\pi\sin\omega t - 2\sum_{n=1}^{\infty}\frac{\cos 2n\omega t}{4n^2-1}\right)$

12 $f(t) = \frac{1}{3}T^2 + \frac{4T^2}{\pi^2}\sum_{n=1}^{\infty}\frac{(-1)^n}{n^2}\cos\frac{n\pi t}{T}$

13 $e(t) = \frac{E}{2}\left(1 - \frac{2}{\pi}\sum_{n=1}^{\infty}\frac{1}{n}\sin\frac{2\pi nt}{T}\right)$

15 $f(t) = -\frac{8}{\pi^2}\sum_{n=1}^{\infty}\frac{1}{(2n-1)^2}\cos(2n-1)\pi t$

16 (a) $f(t) = \frac{2}{3} - \frac{1}{\pi^2}\sum_{n=1}^{\infty}\frac{1}{n^2}\cos 2n\pi t + \frac{1}{\pi}\sum_{n=1}^{\infty}\frac{1}{n}\sin 2n\pi t$

(b) $f(t) = \frac{1}{\pi}\sum_{n=1}^{\infty}\frac{1}{n}\sin 2n\pi t$
$+ \frac{2}{\pi}\sum_{n=1}^{\infty}\left[\frac{1}{2n-1} + \frac{4}{\pi^2(2n-1)^3}\right]$
$\times \sin(2n-1)\pi$

(c) $f(t) = \frac{2}{3} + \frac{4}{\pi^2}\sum_{n=1}^{\infty}\frac{(-1)^{n+1}}{n^2}\cos n\pi t$

17 $f(t) = \frac{1}{6}\pi^2 - \sum_{n=1}^{\infty}\frac{1}{n^2}\cos 2nt$

$f(t) = \frac{8}{\pi}\sum_{n=1}^{\infty}\frac{1}{(2n-1)^3}\sin(2n-1)t$

18 $f(x) = \frac{8a}{\pi^2}\sum_{n=1}^{\infty}\frac{(-1)^n}{(2n-1)^2}\sin\frac{(2n-1)\pi x}{l}$

19 $f(x) = \frac{2l}{\pi^2}\sum_{n=1}^{\infty}\frac{(-1)^{n+1}}{(2n-1)^2}\sin\frac{2(2n-1)\pi x}{l}$

20 $f(t) = \frac{1}{2}\sin t + \frac{4}{\pi}\sum_{n=1}^{\infty}\frac{n(-1)^{n+1}}{4n^2-1}\sin 2nt$

21 $f(x) = -\frac{1}{2}A - \frac{4A}{\pi^2}\sum_{n=1}^{\infty}\frac{1}{(2n-1)^2}\cos\frac{(2n-1)\pi x}{l}$

22 $T(x) = \frac{8KL^2}{\pi^3}\sum_{n=1}^{\infty}\frac{1}{(2n-1)^3}\sin\frac{(2n-1)\pi t}{L}$

23 $f(t) = \frac{1}{\pi}\sum_{n=1}^{\infty}\frac{1}{4n^2-1}\sin 2n\pi t$
$- \frac{2}{\pi}\sum_{n=1}^{\infty}\frac{1}{2n-1}\sin(2n-1)\pi t$

26 (c) $1 + 4\sum_{n=1}^{\infty}\frac{(-1)^{n+1}}{n}\sin nt$

29 (a) $\frac{1}{6}\pi^2 + \sum_{n=1}^{\infty}\frac{2}{n^2}(-1)^n\cos nt$
$+ \sum_{n=1}^{\infty}\frac{1}{\pi}\left[-\frac{\pi^2}{n}(-1)^n + \frac{2}{n^3}(-1)^n\right.$
$\left. - \frac{2}{n^3}\right]\sin nt$

(b) $a_n = 0$
$b_n = \frac{4}{n\pi}(\cos n\pi - \cos\frac{1}{2}n\pi)$
$+ 2\left(\frac{3\pi}{4n^2}\sin\frac{1}{2}n\pi - \frac{\pi^2}{8n}\cos\frac{1}{2}n\pi\right.$
$+ \frac{3}{n^3}\cos\frac{1}{2}n\pi - \frac{6}{\pi n^4}\sin\frac{1}{2}n\pi\right),$
$\frac{1}{\pi}[(\frac{3}{2}\pi^2 - 16)\sin t + \frac{1}{8}(32 + \pi^3 - 6\pi)\sin 2t$
$- \frac{1}{3}(\frac{32}{9} + \frac{1}{2}\pi^2)\sin 3t + \dots]$

(c) $-\frac{4}{\pi^2}\sum_{n=1}^{\infty}\frac{\cos(2n-1)\pi t}{(2n-1)^2} + \frac{2}{\pi}\sum_{n=1}^{\infty}\frac{\sin(2n-1)t}{(2n-1)}$

(d) $\frac{1}{4} + \frac{2}{\pi^2}\sum_{n=1}^{\infty}\frac{1}{(2n-1)^2}\cos 2(2n-1)\pi t$

30 $e(t) = 5 + \frac{20}{\pi}\sum_{n=1}^{\infty}\frac{1}{2n-1}\sin(2n-1)100\pi t$
$i_{ss}(t) \simeq 0.008\cos(100\pi t - 1.96)$
$+ 0.005\cos(300\pi t - 0.33)$

31 $f(t) = \dfrac{400}{\pi} \displaystyle\sum_{n=1}^{\infty} \dfrac{1}{2n-1} \sin(2n-1)t$

$x_{ss}(t) \simeq 0.14 \sin(\pi t - 0.1) + 0.379 \sin(3\pi t - 2.415)$
$\qquad + 0.017 \sin(5\pi t - 2.415)$

32 $f(t) = \dfrac{50}{\pi} \displaystyle\sum_{n=1}^{\infty} \dfrac{(-1)^{n+1}}{n} \sin 2\pi nt$

$x_{ss}(t) \simeq 0.022 \sin(2\pi t - 3.13) - 0.0026 \sin(4\pi t - 3.14)$

33 $e(t) = \dfrac{100}{\pi} + 50 \sin 50\pi t - \dfrac{200}{\pi} \displaystyle\sum_{n=1}^{\infty} \dfrac{\cos 100\pi nt}{4n^2 - 1}$

$i_{ss}(t) \simeq 0.86 \cos(50\pi t + 2.66) - 0.01 \sin(100\pi t + 2.3)$

35 $f(t) = \dfrac{1}{2} + \displaystyle\sum_{n=-\infty}^{\infty} \dfrac{j}{2n\pi} [(-1)^n - 1] e^{jn\pi t/2}$

36 (a) $\dfrac{3}{4}\pi + \displaystyle\sum_{\substack{n=-\infty \\ n \neq 0}}^{\infty} \dfrac{1}{2\pi} \left\{ \dfrac{j\pi}{n} - \dfrac{1}{n^2}[1 + (-1)^n] \right\} e^{jnt}$

(b) $\displaystyle\sum_{n=-\infty}^{\infty} \dfrac{a}{2\pi(n^2 - 1)} [(-1)^n + 1] e^{jn\omega t}$

(c) $\dfrac{3}{2} + \displaystyle\sum_{\substack{n=-\infty \\ n \neq 0}}^{\infty} \dfrac{j}{2\pi n} [1 - (-1)^n] e^{jnt}$

(d) $\dfrac{2}{\pi} + \displaystyle\sum_{\substack{n=-\infty \\ n \neq 0}}^{\infty} \dfrac{1}{1 - n^2} [1 + (-1)^n] e^{jnt}$

38 (b) (i) 17.74, (ii) 17.95   (c) 18.14; (i) 2.20%, (ii) 1.05%

39 (a) $c_0 = 15, \; c_n = \dfrac{30}{jn\pi}(1 - e^{-jn\pi/2})$

$15, \dfrac{30}{\pi}(1-j), -\dfrac{30}{\pi}j, -\dfrac{10}{\pi}(1+j), 0, \dfrac{6}{\pi}(1-j)$

(b) 15 W, 24.32 W, 12.16 W, 2.70 W, 0.97 W
(c) 60 W
(d) 91.9%

40 0.19, 0.10, 0.0675

41 (c) $c_0 = 0, c_1 = \dfrac{3}{2}, c_2 = 0, c_3 = -\dfrac{7}{8}$

42 (c) $c_0 = \dfrac{1}{4}, c_1 = \dfrac{1}{2}, c_2 = \dfrac{5}{16}, c_3 = 0$

46 (b) $c_1 = 0, c_2 = \sqrt{(2\pi)}, c_3 = 0$, MSE $= 0$

4.9 Review exercises

1 $f(t) = \dfrac{1}{6}\pi^2 + \displaystyle\sum_{n=1}^{\infty} \dfrac{2}{n^2}(-1)^n \cos nt$

$\qquad + \displaystyle\sum_{n=1}^{\infty} \left[\dfrac{\pi}{2n-1} - \dfrac{4}{\pi(2n-1)^3} \right] \sin(2n-1)t$

$\qquad - \displaystyle\sum_{n=1}^{\infty} \dfrac{\pi}{2n} \sin 2nt$

Taking $T = \pi$ gives the required sum

2 $f(t) = \dfrac{1}{9}\pi + \dfrac{2}{\pi} \displaystyle\sum_{n=1}^{\infty} \left\{ \cos\dfrac{1}{3}n\pi - \dfrac{1}{3}[2 + (-1)^n] \right\} \cos nt$

$\dfrac{2}{9}\pi$

3 (a) $f(t) = \dfrac{2T}{\pi^2} \displaystyle\sum_{n=1}^{\infty} \dfrac{(-1)^{n+1}}{(2n-1)^2} \sin\dfrac{2(2n-1)\pi t}{T}$

(b) $-\dfrac{1}{4}T$; (c) Taking $t = \dfrac{1}{4}T$ gives $S = \dfrac{1}{8}\pi^2$

5 $f(t) = \dfrac{4}{\pi} \displaystyle\sum_{n=1}^{\infty} \dfrac{(-1)^n \sin(2n-1)t}{(2n-1)^2}$

8 $f(x) = \dfrac{4}{\pi} \displaystyle\sum_{n=1}^{\infty} \dfrac{(-1)^{n+1}}{(2n-1)^2} \sin(2n-1)x$

$f(x) = \dfrac{1}{4}\pi - \dfrac{2}{\pi} \displaystyle\sum_{n=1}^{\infty} \dfrac{\cos 2(2n-1)x}{(2n-1)^2}$

10 (a) $f(t) = \displaystyle\sum_{n=1}^{\infty} \dfrac{2}{n} \sin nt$

(b) $f(t) = \dfrac{1}{2}\pi + \dfrac{4}{\pi} \displaystyle\sum_{n=1}^{\infty} \dfrac{1}{(2n-1)^2} \cos(2n-1)t$

13 (b) $f(t) = \dfrac{1}{2}\pi - \dfrac{4}{\pi} \displaystyle\sum_{n=1}^{\infty} \dfrac{1}{(2n-1)^2} \cos(2n-1)t$

$g(t) = \dfrac{4}{\pi} \displaystyle\sum_{n=1}^{\infty} \dfrac{1}{2n-1} \sin(2n-1)t$

15 (a) $v(t) = \dfrac{10}{\pi} + 5 \sin\dfrac{2\pi t}{T}$

$\qquad - \dfrac{10}{\pi} \displaystyle\sum_{n=2}^{\infty} \dfrac{1 + \cos n\pi}{n^2 - 1} \cos\dfrac{2n\pi t}{T}$

(b) 2.5 W, 9.01%

16 $g(t) = \dfrac{4}{\pi} \displaystyle\sum_{n=1}^{\infty} \dfrac{1}{2n-1} \sin(2n-1)t$

$f(t) = 1 + g(t)$

18 (b) $\dfrac{\sin \omega t - \omega \cos \omega t}{1 + \omega^2}$

$\dfrac{4}{\pi} \displaystyle\sum_{n=1}^{\infty} \dfrac{\sin \alpha t - \alpha \cos \alpha t}{(2n-1)(1 + \alpha^2)}$

$\alpha = (4n - 2)\pi/T$

19 (c) $T_0 = 1, T_1 = x_1, T_2 = 2x^2 - 1, T_3 = 4x^3 - 3x$

(d) $\dfrac{1}{16}T_5 - \dfrac{7}{8}T_4 + \dfrac{33}{16}T_3 - \dfrac{5}{2}T_2 + \dfrac{95}{5}T_1 - \dfrac{79}{8}T_0$

(e) $\dfrac{33}{4}x^3 - 5x^2 + \dfrac{91}{16}x - \dfrac{59}{8}, \dfrac{11}{16}, t = -1$

CHAPTER 5

Exercises

1 $\dfrac{2a}{a^2 - \omega^2}$

2 $4j\omega \operatorname{sinc}^2 \dfrac{\omega t}{2}$

3 $AT\operatorname{sinc}^2 \dfrac{\omega t}{2}$

4 $8k \operatorname{sinc} 2\omega, \ 2k \operatorname{sinc} \omega, \ 2k(4 \operatorname{sinc} 2\omega - \operatorname{sinc} \omega)$

5 $4 \operatorname{sinc} \omega - 4 \operatorname{sinc} 2\omega$

7 $\dfrac{\omega_0}{(a + j\omega)^2 + \omega_0^2}$

10 $F_s = \dfrac{x}{x^2 + a^2}, \quad F_c = \dfrac{a}{x^2 + a^2}$

12 $\dfrac{1}{(1 - \omega^2) + 3j\omega}$

13 $4 \operatorname{sinc} 2\omega - 2 \operatorname{sinc} \omega$

14 $\frac{1}{2}T[\operatorname{sinc} \frac{1}{2}(\omega_0 - \omega)T + \operatorname{sinc} \frac{1}{2}(\omega_0 + \omega)T]$

15 $\frac{1}{2}Te^{-j\omega}[e^{j\omega_0 T/2} \operatorname{sinc} \frac{1}{2}(\omega - \omega_0)T$
$\qquad\qquad + e^{-j\omega_0 T/2} \operatorname{sinc} \frac{1}{2}(\omega + \omega_0)T]$

16 $j[\operatorname{sinc}(\omega + \omega_0) - \operatorname{sinc}(\omega - \omega_0)]$

18 $4AT \cos \omega \tau \operatorname{sinc} \omega T$

19 High pass filter

20 $\pi e^{-a|\omega|}$

21 $T[\operatorname{sinc}(\omega - \omega_0)T + \operatorname{sinc}(\omega + \omega_0)T]$

26 $\frac{1}{2}\pi j[\delta(\omega + \omega_0) - \delta(\omega - \omega_0)] + \dfrac{\omega_0}{\omega_0^2 - \omega^2}$

28 $\{2, 0, 2, 0\}$

29 $\{2, 0, 2, 0\}$

5.9 Review exercises

1 $\dfrac{\sin \omega}{\omega^2} - \dfrac{\cos 2\omega}{\omega}$

2 $-\dfrac{\pi j}{\omega} \operatorname{sinc} 2\omega$

7 (a) $\dfrac{1}{a - b}(e^{at} - e^{bt})H(t)$

(b) (i) $t e^{2t}H(t)$ (ii) $(t - 1 + e^{-t})H(t)$

8 (a) $-\sin \omega_0(t + \frac{1}{4}\pi)$

(b) $\cos \omega_0 t$

(c) $j e^{j\omega_0 t}$

(d) $-j e^{-j\omega_0 t}$

17 (a) $\dfrac{a + 2\pi s}{a^2 + 4\pi^2 s^2}$ (b) $\dfrac{1}{2\pi s}(\sin 2\pi s T - \cos 2\pi s T + 1)$

CHAPTER 6

Exercises

1 (a) $\lambda^3 - 12\lambda^2 + 40\lambda - 35 = 0$

(b) $\lambda^4 - 4\lambda^3 + 2\lambda^2 + 5\lambda + 2 = 0$

2 (a) $2, 0; [1 \ \ 1]^T, [1 \ \ -1]^T$

(b) $4, -1; [2 \ \ 3]^T, [1 \ \ -1]^T$

(c) $9, 3, -3; [-1 \ \ 2 \ \ 2]^T, [2 \ \ 2 \ \ 1]^T,$
$[2 \ \ 1 \ \ -2]^T$

(d) $3, 2, 1; [2 \ \ 2 \ \ 1]^T, [1 \ \ 1 \ \ 0]^T, [0 \ \ -2 \ \ 1]^T$

(e) $14, 7, -7; [2 \ \ 6 \ \ 3]^T, [6 \ \ -3 \ \ 2]^T,$
$[3 \ \ 2 \ \ -6]^T$

(f) $2, 1, -1; [-1 \ \ 1 \ \ 1]^T, [1 \ \ 0 \ \ -1]^T,$
$[1 \ \ 2 \ \ -7]^T$

(g) $5, 3, 1; [2 \ \ 3 \ \ -1]^T, [1 \ \ -1 \ \ 0]^T, [0 \ \ -1 \ \ 1]^T$

(h) $4, 3, 1; [2 \ \ -1 \ \ -1]^T, [2 \ \ -1 \ \ 0]^T,$
$[4 \ \ 1 \ \ -2]^T$

3 (a) $5, [1 \ \ 1 \ \ 1]^T; 1$ (repeated) with two linearly
independent eigenvectors, e.g. $[0 \ \ 1 \ \ 2]^T,$
$[1 \ \ 0 \ \ -1]^T$

(b) $-1, [8 \ \ 1 \ \ 3]^T; 2$ (repeated) with one linearly
independent eigenvector, e.g. $[1 \ \ -1 \ \ 0]^T$

(c) $1, [4 \ \ 1 \ \ -3]^T; 2$ (repeated) with one linearly
independent engenvector, e.g. $[3 \ \ 1 \ \ -2]^T$

(d) $2, [2 \ \ 1 \ \ 2]^T; 1$ (repeated) with two linearly
independent eigenvectors, e.g. $[0 \ \ 2 \ \ -1]^T,$
$[2 \ \ 0 \ \ 3]^T$

4 $1, [-3 \ \ 1 \ \ 1]^T$

5 $2,$ e.g. $[1 \ \ 0 \ \ 1]^T, [0 \ \ 1 \ \ 1]^T$

8 $-6, 3, 2; [2 \ \ 1 \ \ 1]^T, [-1 \ \ 1 \ \ 1]^T, [0 \ \ 1 \ \ -1]^T$

9 $[1 \ \ -1 \ \ 0]^T$

10 $8.59, [0.61 \ \ 0.71 \ \ 0.35]^T$

11 (a) $3.62, [0.62 \ \ 1 \ \ 1]^T$

(b) $7, [0.25 \ \ 0.5 \ \ 1]^T$

(c) $3.62, [-0.62 \ \ 1 \ \ -1 \ \ 0.62]^T$

12 $\lambda_1 = 6; \lambda_2 = 3, e_2 = [1 \ \ 1 \ \ -1]^T; \lambda_3 = 2,$
$e_3 = [1 \ \ -1 \ \ 0]^T$

14 $10.132, 4.491, 0.373$

15 (b) 0.59

16 $5, 2, -1; [-1 \ \ 5 \ \ 3]^T, [0 \ \ 2 \ \ 1]^T, [1 \ \ 0 \ \ 0]^T$

17 $6, 3, 1; [1 \ \ 2 \ \ 0]^T, [0 \ \ 0 \ \ 1]^T, [2 \ \ -1 \ \ 0]^T$

18 $18, 9, -9; [2 \ \ 1 \ \ 2]^T, [1 \ \ 2 \ \ -2]^T, [-2 \ \ 2 \ \ 1]^T$

19 $2, 1, -1; [1 \ \ 3 \ \ 1]^T, [3 \ \ 2 \ \ 1]^T, [1 \ \ 0 \ \ 1]^T$

20 $-9, 6, 3; [1 \ \ 2 \ \ -2]^T, [2 \ \ 1 \ \ 2]^T, [-2 \ \ 2 \ \ 1]^T$

$L = \frac{1}{3}M$, M modal matrix

21 $[0 \ \ 0 \ \ 1]^T$, $\begin{bmatrix} 2 & 2 & 0 \\ 2 & 5 & 0 \\ 0 & 0 & 3 \end{bmatrix}$

22 $J = \begin{bmatrix} 1 & 1 & 0 \\ 0 & 1 & 1 \\ 0 & 0 & 1 \end{bmatrix}$

23 $\lambda = -2$: $[0 \ \ 1 \ \ 1 \ \ 0]^T$, $[1 \ \ 0 \ \ 0 \ \ 1]^T$
$\lambda = 4$: $[0 \ \ 1 \ \ -1 \ \ 0]^T$, $[6 \ \ -1 \ \ 0 \ \ -6]^T$

$J = \begin{bmatrix} -2 & 0 & 0 & 0 \\ 0 & -2 & 0 & 0 \\ 0 & 0 & 4 & 1 \\ 0 & 0 & 0 & 4 \end{bmatrix}$

24 (a) Positive-definite
(b) Positive-semidefinite
(c) Indefinite

25 $2a > 1$, $2b^2 < 6a - 3$

26 Positive-semidefinite, eigenvalues 3, 3, 0

27 $k > 2$; when $k = 2$ Q is positive-semidefinite

28 -3

29 $\lambda > 5$

31 (a) $\begin{bmatrix} 3 & 4 \\ 2 & 3 \end{bmatrix}$ (b) $\begin{bmatrix} 7 & 10 \\ 5 & 7 \end{bmatrix}$ (c) $\begin{bmatrix} 17 & 24 \\ 12 & 17 \end{bmatrix}$

32 (a) $\frac{1}{3}\begin{bmatrix} 2 & -1 \\ -1 & 2 \end{bmatrix}$ (b) $\frac{1}{11}\begin{bmatrix} -2 & 5 & -1 \\ -1 & -3 & 5 \\ 7 & -1 & -2 \end{bmatrix}$

33 $\begin{bmatrix} 47\,231 & 47\,342 & 47\,270 \\ 47\,342 & 47\,195 & 47\,306 \\ 47\,270 & 47\,306 & 47\,267 \end{bmatrix}$

34 (a) $\begin{bmatrix} e^t & 0 \\ t\,e^t & e^t \end{bmatrix}$ (b) $\begin{bmatrix} e^t & 0 \\ e^{2t} - e^t & e^{2t} \end{bmatrix}$

36 (a) $\begin{bmatrix} 2t & 2 \\ -1 & 2t-1 \end{bmatrix}$ (b) $\begin{bmatrix} \frac{10}{3} & 0 \\ \frac{7}{2} & \frac{23}{6} \end{bmatrix}$

37 $\begin{bmatrix} t^4 + 2t^2 + t - 4 & t^3 - t^2 + t - 1 \\ 5t^2 + 5 & 5t - 5 \end{bmatrix}$

38 (a) $\dot{x} = \begin{bmatrix} 0 & 1 & 0 \\ 0 & 0 & 1 \\ -4 & -5 & -4 \end{bmatrix}x + \begin{bmatrix} 0 \\ 0 \\ 1 \end{bmatrix}u$,
$y = [1 \ \ 0 \ \ 0]x$

(b) $\dot{x} = \begin{bmatrix} 0 & 1 & 0 & 0 \\ 0 & 0 & 1 & 0 \\ 0 & 0 & 0 & 1 \\ 0 & -4 & -2 & 0 \end{bmatrix}x + \begin{bmatrix} 0 \\ 0 \\ 0 \\ 5 \end{bmatrix}u$,
$y = [1 \ \ 0 \ \ 0 \ \ 0]x$

39 (a) $\dot{x} = \begin{bmatrix} 0 & 1 & 0 \\ 0 & 0 & 1 \\ -7 & -5 & -6 \end{bmatrix}x + \begin{bmatrix} 0 \\ 0 \\ 1 \end{bmatrix}u$,
$y = [5 \ \ 3 \ \ 1]x$

(b) $\dot{x} = \begin{bmatrix} 0 & 1 & 0 \\ 0 & 0 & 1 \\ 0 & -3 & -4 \end{bmatrix}x + \begin{bmatrix} 0 \\ 0 \\ 1 \end{bmatrix}u$,
$y = [2 \ \ 3 \ \ 1]x$

40 $\dot{x} = \begin{bmatrix} -R_1/L_1 & -R_1/L_1 & -1/L_1 \\ -R_1/L_1 & -(R_1 + R_2)/L_2 & -1/L_2 \\ 1/C & 1/C & 1/C \end{bmatrix}x$
$+ \begin{bmatrix} 1/L_1 \\ 1/L_2 \\ 0 \end{bmatrix}u$, $y = [0 \ \ R_2 \ \ 0]x$

41 A possible model is
$\dot{x} = \begin{bmatrix} B(M_1 + M)/MM_1 & 1 & 0 & 0 \\ -(K_1 M + KM_1 + KM)/MM_1 & 0 & 1 & 0 \\ -K_1 B/MM_1 & 0 & 0 & 1 \\ -K_1 K/MM_1 & 0 & 0 & 0 \end{bmatrix}x$
$+ \begin{bmatrix} 0 \\ 0 \\ K_1 B/MM_1 \\ K_1 K_2/MM_1 \end{bmatrix}u$, $y = [1 \ \ 0 \ \ 0 \ \ 0]x$

42 $\begin{bmatrix} \dot{x}_1 \\ x_2 \end{bmatrix} = -\begin{bmatrix} \dfrac{(R_1 + R_2 + R_4)}{\alpha C_1} & \dfrac{R_1}{\alpha C_1} \\ \dfrac{R}{\alpha C_2} & -\dfrac{R_1 + R_3}{\alpha C_2} \end{bmatrix}\begin{bmatrix} x_1 \\ x_2 \end{bmatrix}$

$\qquad + \begin{bmatrix} \dfrac{R_2 + R_4}{\alpha C_1} \\ \dfrac{R_3}{\alpha C_2} \end{bmatrix} u$

$\begin{bmatrix} y_1 \\ y_2 \end{bmatrix} = \begin{bmatrix} \dfrac{R_1}{\alpha} & -\dfrac{R_1 + R_3}{\alpha} \\ -\dfrac{R_3}{\alpha}(R_1 + R_2 + R_4) & \dfrac{R_1 R_3}{\alpha} \end{bmatrix}$

$\qquad + \begin{bmatrix} \dfrac{R_3}{\alpha} \\ \dfrac{R_3}{\alpha}(R_4 + R_2) \end{bmatrix} u,$

$\qquad \alpha = R_1 R_3 + (R_1 + R_3)(R_2 + R_4)$
$\qquad -2.6 \times 10^2, \; -1.2 \times 10^2$

44 $\begin{bmatrix} e^t & 0 \\ t\,e^t & e^t \end{bmatrix}$

45 $\begin{bmatrix} e^{-t}(1 + t) & t\,e^{-t} \\ -t\,e^{-t} & e^{-t}(1 - t) \end{bmatrix}, \quad y = e^{-t}(1 + 2t)$

46 $[e^t \quad e^t(t + 1)]^T$

47 $x_1 = 2 - 4e^{-2t} + 3e^{-3t}, \; x_2 = 8e^{-2t} - 15e^{-3t}$

48 $x_1 = 4t\,e^{-2t} + e^{-2t} - e^{-t}, x_2 = 3e^{-t} - 2e^{-2t} - 4t\,e^{-t}$

49 $x(t) = \begin{bmatrix} -5 + \tfrac{8}{3}e^{-t} + \tfrac{10}{3}e^{5t} \\ 3 - \tfrac{8}{3}e^{-t} + \tfrac{5}{3}e^{5t} \end{bmatrix}$

50 Same as Exercise 49

51 $x_1 = x_2 = 2e^{-2t} - e^{-3t}$

52 $\tfrac{15}{4} - \tfrac{5}{2}t + \tfrac{5}{4}e^{-2t} - 6e^{-t}$

53 $x(t) = \begin{bmatrix} 4t\,e^{-t} + e^{-2t} \\ -4t\,e^{-t} - 2e^{-2t} + 2e^{-t} \end{bmatrix}$

54 $x(t) = e^t[3 \quad 2]^T - e^{-3t}[1 \quad -2]^T$

55 $x(t) = \tfrac{1}{5}\begin{bmatrix} 14e^{-t} - 4e^{-2t} \\ 7e^{-t} + 8e^{-2t} \end{bmatrix}$

56 $x(t) = e^{-2t}\{(\cos 2t - \sin 2t)[2 \quad 1]^T$
$\qquad - (\cos 2t + \sin 2t)[0 \quad 1]^T\}$

57 $\dot{z} = \begin{bmatrix} 2 & 0 & 0 \\ 0 & 1 & 0 \\ 0 & 0 & -1 \end{bmatrix} z + \begin{bmatrix} \tfrac{1}{3} \\ 0 \\ -\tfrac{4}{3} \end{bmatrix} u,$

$\qquad y = [1 \quad -4 \quad -2]z$

58 $\alpha_0 = \tfrac{1}{2}, \; \alpha_1 = -\tfrac{1}{2}, \; \alpha_2 = \tfrac{1}{2}$

59 $6, 1, [4 \quad 1]^T, [1 \quad -1]^T$
$\qquad x_1 = 4e^{6t} - 3e^t, \; x_2 = e^{6t} + 3e^t$

60 Same as Exercise 50

61 $\dot{z} = \begin{bmatrix} -1 & 0 & 0 \\ 0 & -2 & 0 \\ 0 & 0 & -3 \end{bmatrix} z + \begin{bmatrix} 121 \\ \tfrac{335}{2} \\ \tfrac{99}{2} \end{bmatrix} u, \quad y = [1 \quad 1 \quad 1]z$

The system is stable, controllable and observable

62 $\dot{z} = \begin{bmatrix} 0 & 0 & 0 \\ 0 & -1 & 0 \\ 0 & 0 & -5 \end{bmatrix} z + \begin{bmatrix} \tfrac{1}{5} \\ -\tfrac{1}{4} \\ \tfrac{1}{20} \end{bmatrix} u,$

$\qquad y = [5 \quad \tfrac{23}{10} \quad \tfrac{3}{10}]z$

The system is marginally stable, controllable and observable

63 (a) $\dfrac{2^k}{4}\begin{bmatrix} 2 & 1 \\ 4 & 2 \end{bmatrix} + \dfrac{(-2)^k}{4}\begin{bmatrix} 2 & -1 \\ -4 & 2 \end{bmatrix}$

(b) $\dfrac{(-4)^k}{2}\begin{bmatrix} 1 & -1 \\ -1 & 1 \end{bmatrix} + 2^{k-1}\begin{bmatrix} 1 & 1 \\ 1 & 1 \end{bmatrix}$

(c) $(-1)^k\begin{bmatrix} 1 & -k \\ 0 & 1 \end{bmatrix}$

64 $x(k) = 5^k(\cos k\theta + \sin k\theta), \; y(k) = 5^k(2\cos k\theta),$
$\qquad \cos \theta = -\tfrac{3}{5}$

65 $x(k) = \begin{bmatrix} \tfrac{25}{18} - \tfrac{17}{6}(-0.2)^k + \tfrac{22}{9}(-0.8)^k \\ \tfrac{7}{18} - (3.4/6)(-0.2)^k - (17.6/9)(-0.8)^k \end{bmatrix}$

66 $y(k) = \dfrac{1}{\sqrt{5}}\left[\left(\dfrac{1 + \sqrt{5}}{2}\right)^k - \left(\dfrac{1 - \sqrt{5}}{2}\right)^k\right]$

67 $u(t) = [-\tfrac{33}{2} \quad -\tfrac{17}{2}]x(t) + u_{\text{ext}}$

68 $u(t) = [-\tfrac{99}{4} \quad -\tfrac{35}{4}]x(t) + u_{\text{ext}}$

69 $u(t) = [-\tfrac{35}{6} \quad -\tfrac{31}{6}]x(t) + u_{\text{ext}}$
$\qquad u(t) = [-31 \quad -11]x(t) + u_{\text{ext}}$

71 $M = \begin{bmatrix} 2 & -2 \\ 1 & -1 \end{bmatrix}$, rank 1, $M = \begin{bmatrix} 0 & 1 \\ 1 & \tfrac{1}{2} \end{bmatrix}$, rank 2

6.11 Review exercises

1 (a) $5, 2, -1; [11 \quad 5 \quad 3]^T, [8 \quad 2 \quad 1]^T, [1 \quad 0 \quad 0]^T$

(b) $3, 2, 1; [1 \quad 2 \quad 1]^T, [2 \quad 1 \quad 0]^T, [1 \quad 0 \quad -1]^T$

(c) $3, 1, 0; [1 \quad -2 \quad 1]^T, [0 \quad 1 \quad -1]^T, [1 \quad 1 \quad 1]^T$

2 $6, 3, 1; [1 \quad 1 \quad 1]^T, [1 \quad 1 \quad -2]^T, [1 \quad -1 \quad 0]^T$

3 $b = 1, c = 2; \lambda = 2, 4, 1;$
$[1 \quad -2 \quad -1]^T, [1 \quad 1 \quad -1]^T$

4 5.4

5 (a) $4.56; [0.72 \quad 0.84 \quad 1]^T$

(b) 1.75

(c) (i) 1.19 (ii) 1.75

6 $[0 \quad -1 \quad 1]^T$

7 $3, 2, 1; [2 \quad 1 \quad 1]^T, [3 \quad 2 \quad 1]^T, [4 \quad 3 \quad 2]^T$

8 $[\frac{1}{3} \quad -\frac{2}{3} \quad -\frac{2}{3}]^T, [\frac{2}{3} \quad \frac{2}{3} \quad -\frac{1}{3}]^T, [\frac{2}{3} \quad -\frac{1}{3} \quad \frac{2}{3}]^T$

9 $6, -4, -2, 0; [1 \quad -3 \quad 3 \quad -1]^T, [0 \quad 1 \quad -2 \quad 1]^T,$
$[0 \quad 0 \quad 1 \quad -1]^T, [0 \quad 0 \quad 0 \quad 1]^T;$
$C - C e^{-6t} + 3 C e^{-4t} - 3 C e^{-2t}$

10 (a) (i) $\begin{bmatrix} -29 & 0 \\ -32 & 3 \end{bmatrix}$ (ii) $\begin{bmatrix} 2^k & 0 \\ 2^k - 1 & 1 \end{bmatrix}$

(b) $\begin{bmatrix} 1 & \frac{1}{2}(1 - e^{-2t}) \\ 0 & e^{-2t} \end{bmatrix}$

11 $e_1 = [1 \quad 0 \quad 0]^T, e_2^* = [\frac{3}{8} \quad \frac{1}{2} \quad 0]^T, e_3^* = [0 \quad 0 \quad \frac{1}{8}]^T$

12 $2, 2 \pm \sqrt{2}; 1:0:-1, 1:-\sqrt{2}:1, 1:\sqrt{2}:1$

13 (a) Positive-semidefinite

(b) Positive-definite

(c) Indefinite

(d) Negative-semidefinite

(e) Negative-definite

14 $1; 3, [1 \quad 1 \quad 0]^T; -1, [0 \quad -1 \quad 1]^T$

15 (c) $4e^{-2t} - 3e^{-3t}, y(t) = 1 \ (t \geq 0)$

16 $[1 \quad 3 \quad 1]^T, [3 \quad 2 \quad 1]^T, [1 \quad 0 \quad 1]^T$

$x(k) = \begin{bmatrix} \frac{1}{6}(-1)^k - \frac{1}{2}(2^k) + \frac{3}{2} \\ 1 - 2^k \\ \frac{1}{6}(-1)^k - \frac{1}{3}(2^k) + \frac{1}{2} \end{bmatrix}$

17 $\Lambda = \begin{bmatrix} 2 & 0 & 0 \\ 0 & 1 & 0 \\ 0 & 0 & -1 \end{bmatrix}, b_1 = [\frac{1}{3} \quad 0 \quad -\frac{4}{3}]^T,$

$c = [1 \quad -4 \quad -2]^T$

The system is uncontrollable but observable; it is stable

18 $x(t) = \begin{bmatrix} e^{-t} \cos t \\ 1 - e^{-t}(\cos t - \sin t) \end{bmatrix}$

$H(s) = \dfrac{s + 2}{(s + 1)^2 + 1}$

$e^{-t}(\cos t + \sin t)$

19 $D(z) = \dfrac{z + 3}{z^2 + 4z - 5}$ (i) $M_c = \begin{bmatrix} 1 & -3 \\ 0 & -2 \end{bmatrix}$

(ii) $M_c^{-1} = \begin{bmatrix} 1 & -\frac{3}{2} \\ 0 & -\frac{1}{2} \end{bmatrix}$ (iii) $v^T = [0 \quad -\frac{1}{2}]$

(iv) $T = \begin{bmatrix} 0 & -\frac{1}{2} \\ 1 & \frac{1}{2} \end{bmatrix}$ (v) $T^{-1} = \begin{bmatrix} 1 & 1 \\ -2 & 0 \end{bmatrix}$

$\alpha = -5, \beta = 4$

20 (a) $6, [3 \quad 2 \quad 1]^T; 3, [1 \quad -1 \quad 0]^T, [\frac{1}{3} \quad \frac{1}{3} \quad \frac{1}{3}]^T$

(c) $\dfrac{1}{3} \begin{bmatrix} (-3 + 3t) e^{3t} + 3e^{6t} \\ (1 + 3t) e^{3t} + 2e^{6t} \\ -e^{3t} + e^{6t} \end{bmatrix}$

21 $1, -1, -2; [1 \quad 0 \quad -1]^T, [1 \quad -1 \quad 0]^T, [0 \quad 0 \quad 1]^T$
$u(t) = -6\{x_1(t) + x_2(t)\}$

22 $x_1 = \frac{5}{3} \cos t + 2 \sin t - \frac{2}{3} \cos 2t$
$x_2 = \frac{5}{3} \cos t + 2 \sin t + \frac{1}{3} \cos 2t$

CHAPTER 7

Exercises

1 (a) Circles centre $(0, 0)$, $x^2 + y^2 = 1 + e^C$

(b) Straight lines through $(-1, 0)$, $y = (x + 1) \tan C$

2 (a) Family of curves $y^2 = 4x^2(x - 1) + C$

(b) Family of curves $y^2 = \frac{1}{12}x^2(x^2 - 12) + C$

3 (a) $z - xy = C$

(b) $xy = \ln(C + z)$

4 (a) $(A \cos(t + B), \tan(t + B), Ce^t)$, curves on hyperbolic cylinders

(b) Curves defined by the intersections of mutually orthogonal hyperbolic cylinders, $x^2 - y^2 = c$, $x^2 - z^2 = k$

5 (a) $f_x = yz - 2x, f_y = xz + 1, f_z = xy - 1,$
$f_{xx} = -2, f_{xy} = z, f_{xz} = y, f_{yy} = 0, f_{yz} = x, f_{zz} = 0$

(b) $f_x = 2xyz^3, f_y = x^2z^3, f_z = 3x^2yz^2, f_{xx} = 2yz^3,$
$f_{xy} = 2xz^3, f_{xz} = 6xyz^2, f_{yy} = 0, f_{yz} = 3x^2z^2,$
$f_{zz} = 6x^2y$

(c) $f_x = -z/(x^2 + y^2), f_y = zx/(x^2 + y^2),$
$f_z = \tan^{-1}(y/x), f_{xx} = 2xz/(x^2 + y^2)^2,$
$f_{xy} = 2yz/(x^2 + y^2)^2, f_{xz} = -1/(x^2 + y^2), f_{zz} = 0,$
$f_{yy} = -2xyz/(x^2 + y^2)^2, f_{yz} = x/(x^2 + y^2)$

6 (a) $2t(3t^6 - 6t^5 + 3t^4 - 3t^3 + 4t^2 + 3t + 4)/(t - 1)^2$

(b) $te^{-2t}(\cos 2t - \sin 2t) + \frac{1}{2}e^{-2t} \sin 2t$

7 $\dfrac{\partial f}{\partial y} = \dfrac{\partial f}{\partial r}\sin\theta\sin\phi + \dfrac{\partial f}{\partial\theta}\dfrac{\sin\phi\cos\theta}{r} + \dfrac{\partial f}{\partial\phi}\dfrac{\cos\phi}{r\sin\theta}$

$\dfrac{\partial f}{\partial z} = \dfrac{\partial f}{\partial r}\cos\theta - \dfrac{\partial f}{\partial\theta}\dfrac{\sin\theta}{r}$

8 $A/r + B$

11 (a) $\frac{117}{7}$
(b) $39,\ \frac{1}{13}(12, 3, 4)$

12 (a) $(2x, 2y, -1)$
(b) $(-yz/(x^2 + y^2),\ xz/(x^2 + y^2),\ \tan^{-1}(y/x))$
(c) $\dfrac{e^{-x-y+z}}{(x^3 + y^2)^{3/2}}$
$(-x^3 - y^2 - \frac{3}{2}x^2,\ -x^3 - y^2 - y,\ x^3 + y^2)$
(d) $(yz\sin\pi(x + y + z) + \pi xyz\cos\pi(x + y + z),$
$\ \ xy\sin\pi(x + y + z) + \pi xyz\cos\pi(x + y + z),$
$\ \ xz\sin\pi(x + y + z) + \pi xyz\cos\pi(x + y + z))$

13 3

14 $(5\boldsymbol{i} + 4\boldsymbol{j} + 3\boldsymbol{k})/\sqrt{50}$

15 (a) $\boldsymbol{r}/r$ (b) $-\boldsymbol{r}/r^3$

16 $\phi = x^2 y + z^2 x + zy$

17 $-9\boldsymbol{j} + 3\boldsymbol{k},\ \frac{36}{7}$

18 $54° 25'$

19 (a) $x + 2y + 3z = 6,\ x - 1 = \frac{1}{2}(y - 1) = \frac{1}{3}(z - 1)$
(b) $2x + 2y - 3z = -3,$
$\ \ \frac{1}{2}(x - 1) = \frac{1}{2}(y - 2) = \frac{1}{3}(3 - z)$
(c) $2x + 4y - z = 6,\ \frac{1}{2}(x - 1) = \frac{1}{4}(y - 2) = 4 - z$

21 (a) $6xy$ (b) 4

22 -61

23 $a,\ a,\ 3a$

25 -13

28 $(y, 6xz - 1, 0)$

30 $x^2 + y^2 + z^2 + xyz$

32 $a = 2, b = 2, c = 3; \phi = 2x^2 y + 2z^3 x + 3zy + \text{const}$

33 $2\sqrt{11}\ \text{rad s}^{-1}$

34 $d = -a,\ c = b$

37 (a) $2y^2 z^3 + 2x^2 z^3 + 6x^2 y^2 z$
(b) $2y(1 + z)\boldsymbol{i} + 2(x + xz - z)\boldsymbol{j} + 2y(x - 1)\boldsymbol{k}$
(c) $2yz\boldsymbol{i} + 2(x - z)\boldsymbol{j} + 2yx\boldsymbol{k}$

46 156

47 0

48 $\frac{61}{12}$

49 (a) $\frac{288}{35}$ (b) 10   (c) 8

50 $15 + 4\pi$

51 (a) 16   (b) 16   (c) No

52 35

53 $-\frac{9}{10}\boldsymbol{i} - \frac{2}{3}\boldsymbol{j} + \frac{7}{5}\boldsymbol{k}$

54 $4\pi(7\boldsymbol{i} + 3\boldsymbol{j})$

55 (a) $(\ln 2)\tan^{-1}(\frac{1}{3})$ (b) $\frac{1}{6}$ (c) $\frac{1}{2}\pi - 1$

56 $-4/3\pi^2$

57 (a) $\frac{1}{4}(\sqrt{2} - 1)$
(b) $[(1 - k^2)^{3/2} - 1]/3k^2$

58 $2(\sqrt{2} - 1)$

60 1

61 $2a(1 - \frac{1}{4}\pi)$

62 $\frac{1}{3}(6\pi - 20)$

64 $\frac{1}{4}\pi + 2/\pi - 1$

65 0

66 $\frac{11}{60}$

67 0

68 $\frac{1}{2}a(1 - \frac{1}{4}\pi)$

70 $\frac{13}{3}\pi$

71 (a) $\frac{183}{4}$ (b) $\frac{1}{4}\pi$

72 (a) $\frac{27}{4}$ (b) 0

74 (a) $\frac{13}{3}\pi$ (b) $\frac{149}{30}\pi$ (c) $\frac{37}{10}\pi$

75 24π

77 90

78 0

79 (a) $\frac{8}{3}$ (b) $\frac{448}{3}$

81 $\frac{1}{2}\pi^2 - 2$

82 $\frac{1}{90}$

83 $\frac{11}{30}$

84 $\frac{1}{24}\pi$

85 $\frac{13}{60}$

86 $(1 - e^{-1})/6$

87 $\frac{2}{15};\ (\frac{5}{16}, \frac{5}{16}, \frac{11}{16})$

88 $\frac{1}{8}\pi$

89 $\frac{1}{16}\pi a^4$

90 $\frac{3}{2}$

91 12π

92 84π

96 $2\pi ab$

97 16π

7.6 Review exercises

2 $\sin(x + 3y)$

7 $\frac{1}{3}x^3 - y^2x + \frac{1}{2}x^2 + \frac{1}{2}y^2 + C$

8 (a) $\frac{8}{3}$ (b) 8

9 $\frac{5}{6}$

10 $-\frac{4}{3}j$

11 0

12 $\frac{13}{80}kc^6$

13 $\frac{2}{3}ha^2\left[\frac{1}{2}\pi - \sin^{-1}\left(\frac{c}{a}\right)\right] - \frac{1}{3}hcl - \frac{hc^3}{3a}\tanh^{-1}\left(\frac{l}{a}\right),$
$l = \sqrt{(a^2 - c^2)}$

14 $\frac{16}{3}a^3$

15 $\pi q_0^2 r^2 l/4EI$

16 $\frac{1}{3}$

17 0

19 0

20 $\frac{13}{240}$

CHAPTER 8

Exercises

1 $a^2 = b^2c^2$

2 $\alpha = \pm c$

3 For $\alpha = 0$:
$V = A + Bx$
For $\alpha > 0$:
$V = A\sinh at + B\cosh at$, where $a^2 = \alpha/\kappa$
or $Ce^{at} + De^{-at}$
For $\alpha < 0$:
$V = A\cos bt + B\sin bt$, where $b^2 = -\alpha/\kappa$

4 $n = -3, 2$

5 (a) $I_{xx} = (Lc)I_{tt}$
(b) $v_{xx} = (rg)v + (rc)v_{tt}$ and $W_{xx} = (rc)W_{tt}$
(c) $w_{xx} = (Lc)w_{tt}$

6 $a = -3$

12 $u = \dfrac{2l}{\pi^2}\left\{\left[\sin\dfrac{\pi(x-ct)}{l} - \dfrac{1}{9}\sin\dfrac{3\pi(x-ct)}{l}\right.\right.$
$\left. + \dfrac{1}{25}\sin\dfrac{5\pi(x-ct)}{l} + \dots\right]$
$+ \left[\sin\dfrac{\pi(x+ct)}{l} - \dfrac{1}{9}\sin\dfrac{3\pi(x+ct)}{l}\right.$
$\left.\left. + \dfrac{1}{25}\sin\dfrac{5\pi(x+ct)}{l} + \dots\right]\right\}$

13 $u = \frac{1}{2}F(x - ct) + \frac{1}{2}F(x + ct)$, where
$$F(z) = \begin{cases} 1 - z & (0 \leqslant z \leqslant 1) \\ 1 + z & (-1 \leqslant z \leqslant 0) \\ 0 & (|z| \geqslant 1) \end{cases}$$

14 $x + (-3 - \sqrt{6})y = $ constant
and
$x + (-3 + \sqrt{6})y = $ constant

15

x	$f(x)$	$u(x,0)$	$u(x,0.5)$	$u(x,1)$	$u(x,1.5)$	$u(x,2)$
−3.0	0.024893	0	0.025943	0.058509	0.106010	0.180570
−2.5	0.041042	0	0.042774	0.096466	0.174781	0.297710
−2.0	0.067667	0	0.070522	0.159046	0.288166	0.490842
−1.5	0.111565	0	0.116272	0.262222	0.475106	0.681635
−1.0	0.183939	0	0.191700	0.432332	0.655692	0.791166
−0.5	0.303265	0	0.316060	0.585169	0.748392	0.847392
0	0.5	0	0.393469	0.632120	0.776869	0.864664
0.5	0.696734	0	0.316060	0.585169	0.748392	0.847392
1.0	0.816060	0	0.191700	0.432332	0.655692	0.791166
1.5	0.888434	0	0.116272	0.262222	0.475106	0.681635
2.0	0.932332	0	0.070522	0.159046	0.288166	0.490842
2.5	0.958957	0	0.042774	0.096466	0.174781	0.297710
3.0	0.975106	0	0.025943	0.058509	0.106010	0.180570

16 $u = \dfrac{8}{\pi}\displaystyle\sum_{n=1}^{\infty}\dfrac{1}{(2n-1)^3}\sin(2n-1)x\cos(2n-1)ct$

19 $u = \dfrac{a}{\omega c}\sin\omega ct\cos\omega x$

20 Explicit with $\lambda = 0.5$

x	$t = 0$	$t = 0.25$	$t = 0.5$	$t = 1$	$t = 1.5$
0	0	0	0	0	0
0.25	0	0.0625	0.125	0.179687	0.210937
0.50	0	0.125	0.21875	0.265625	0.269531
0.75	0	0.0625	0.125	0.179687	0.210937
1.00	0	0	0	0	0

Implicit with $\lambda = 0.25$

x	$t=0$	$t=0.25$	$t=0.5$	$t=1$
0	0	0	0	0
0.25	0	0.0625	0.12245	0.17407
0.50	0	0.125	0.22449	0.2815
0.75	0	0.0625	0.12245	0.17407
1.00	0	0	0	0

21 Explicit

x	$t=0$	$t=0.02$	$t=0.04$	$t=0.06$	$t=0.08$
0	0	0.031410	0.062790	0.094108	0.125333
0.2	0	0	0.000314	0.001249	0.003101
0.4	0	0	0	0.000003	0.000018
0.6	0	0	0	0	0.000000
0.8	0	0	0	0	0
1.0	0	0	0	0	0

22 Explicit

x	$t=0$	$t=0.2$	$t=0.4$	$t=0.6$
0	0	0.03	0.12	0.27
0.2	0.16	0.19	0.28	0.43
0.4	0.24	0.27	0.36	0.51
0.6	0.24	0.27	0.36	0.51
0.8	0.16	0.19	0.28	0.43
1.0	0	0.03	0.12	0.27

23 Explicit

x	$t=0$	$t=0.2$	$t=0.4$	$t=0.6$
0	0	0	0	0
0.2	0.16	0.19	0.2725	0.38875
0.4	0.24	0.27	0.36	0.508125
0.6	0.24	0.27	0.36	0.508125
0.8	0.16	0.19	0.2725	0.38875
1.0	0	0	0	0

24 $u = \sum_{n=0}^{\infty} a_n \exp\left[\dfrac{-\kappa(n+\frac{1}{2})^2\pi^2 t}{l^2}\right] \cos\left[(n+\tfrac{1}{2})\dfrac{\pi x}{l}\right]$

where

$$a_n = u_0\left[\dfrac{8}{(2n+1)^2\pi^2} - \dfrac{2(-1)^n}{(2n+1)\pi}\right]$$

26 The term represents heat loss at a rate proportional

to the excess temperature over θ_0.

28 $u = \frac{1}{2}a\left[\exp(-\frac{9}{4}\kappa\pi^2 t)\cos\frac{3}{2}\pi x + \exp(-\frac{1}{4}\kappa\pi^2 t)\cos\frac{1}{2}\pi x\right]$

29 $u(0,t) = u(l,t) = 0$ for all t
$u(x,0) = 10$ for $0 < x < l$

31

x	$t=0$	$t=0.02$	$t=0.04$	$t=0.06$	$t=0.08$	$t=0.1$
0	0	0	0	0	0	0
0.2	0.04	0.08	0.1	0.12	0.135	0.1475
0.4	0.16	0.2	0.24	0.27	0.295	0.315
0.6	0.36	0.4	0.44	0.47	0.495	0.515
0.8	0.64	0.68	0.7	0.72	0.735	0.7475
1.0	1	1	1	1	1	1

32 At $t=1$ with $\lambda = 0.4$ and $\Delta t = 0.05$
Explicit

x	0	0.2	0.4	0.6	0.8	1.0
u	0	0.1094	0.2104	0.2939	0.3497	0.3679

Implicit

x	0	0.2	0.4	0.6	0.8	1.0
u	0	0.1056	0.2045	0.2883	0.3465	0.3679

33

$$A = \begin{bmatrix} 1 & 0 & -1 & 0 & 0 & 0 \\ -0.5 & 3 & -0.5 & 0 & 0 & 0 \\ 0 & -0.5 & 3 & -0.5 & 0 & 0 \\ 0 & 0 & -0.5 & 3 & -0.5 & 0 \\ 0 & 0 & 0 & -0.5 & 3 & -0.5 \\ 0 & 0 & 0 & 0 & -0.5 & 3 \end{bmatrix}$$

$$b = \begin{bmatrix} -0.4 \\ -0.04 \\ 0.28 \\ 0.44 \\ 0.44 \\ 0.28 \end{bmatrix} \quad Au = b \text{ gives} \quad u = \begin{bmatrix} -0.27996 \\ -0.03999 \\ 0.120036 \\ 0.200202 \\ 0.201178 \\ 0.126863 \end{bmatrix}$$

34 $u = x + \dfrac{2}{\pi}\sum_{n=1}^{\infty} \dfrac{\sin n\pi x}{n \sinh n\pi}$
$\times \{\sinh n\pi y + (-1)^n \sinh n\pi(1-y)\}$

37 $v = $ const gives circles with centre $\left(\dfrac{-v}{v-1}, 0\right)$ and radius $1/|v-1|$

$u = $ const gives circles with centre $\left(1, \dfrac{-1}{u}\right)$ and radius $1/|u|$

38 Boundary conditions are $u(0, y) = u(a, y) = 0$, $0 \leqslant y < a$; and $u(x, 0) = 0$, $0 \leqslant x \leqslant a$, $u(x, a) = u_0$, $0 < x < a$

41 $V = \dfrac{2\alpha}{3} \dfrac{\left(1 - \dfrac{a}{r}\right)}{\left(1 - \dfrac{a}{b}\right)} - \dfrac{\alpha}{3}(2 - 3\sin^2\theta) \dfrac{\left(r^2 - \dfrac{a^5}{r^3}\right)}{\left(b^2 - \dfrac{a^5}{b^3}\right)}$

42 For $\Delta x = \Delta y = 0.5$ $u(0.5, 0.5) = 0.3125$
For $\Delta x = \Delta y = 0.25$ $u(0.5, 0.5) = 0.3047$

43 $u(0.5, 0) = 0.4839$, $u(0.5, 0.5) = 0.4677$, $u(0.5, 1) = 0.3871$

44 $u(1, 1) = 10.674$, $u(2, 1) = 12.360$, $u(3, 1) = 8.090$, $u(1, 2) = 10.337$, $u(2, 2) = 10.674$

45 $h = 1/2$ gives $\phi(0.5, 0.5) = 1.8611$ and $\phi(0.5, 1) = 1.3194$
For $h = 1/4$ ϕ is given in the table

y					
1	2	1.6015666	1.2867647	1.0565216	1
0.75	2.4375	1.9679551	1.5818015	1.2572287	1
0.5	2.75	2.2665772	1.8465073	1.4374669	1
0.25	2.9375	2.5174715	2.1314338	1.6930064	1
0.0	3	2.75	2.5	2.25	1
x	0	0.25	0.5	0.75	1

46 $\phi(0, 0) = 1.5909$, $\phi(0, \tfrac{1}{3}) = 2.0909$, $\phi(0, \tfrac{2}{3}) = 4.7727$, $\phi(\tfrac{1}{3}, 0) = 1.0909$, $\phi(\tfrac{2}{3}, 0) = 0.7727$ and other values can be obtained by symmetry.

49 Parabolic; $r = x - y$ and $s = x + y$ gives $u_{ss} = 0$
Elliptic; $r = -3x + y$ and $s = x + y$ gives $8(u_{ss} + u_{rr}) - 9u_r + 3u_s + u = 0$
Hyperbolic; $r = 9x + y$ and $s = x + y$ gives $49u_{rr} - u_{ss} = 0$

50 $u = f(2x + y) + g(x - 3y)$

51 (a) elliptic; (b) parabolic; (c) hyperbolic
For $y < 0$ characteristics are $(-y)^{3/2} \pm \tfrac{3}{2}x = $ constant

52 $p > q$ or $p < -q$ then hyperbolic; $p = q$ then parabolic; $-q < p < q$ then elliptic

8.10 Review exercises

3 $y = 4e^{-t/2\tau} \sin\left(3\pi \dfrac{x}{l}\right)\left(\cos \omega_3 t + \dfrac{1}{2\omega_3 \tau} \sin \omega_3 t\right)$
where $\omega_3 = 3\pi\dfrac{c}{l}\left(1 - \dfrac{l^2}{36\pi^2 c^2 \tau^2}\right)^{1/2}$

5 $A_{2n+1} = 8\theta_0 l/\pi^2(2n+1)^2$

6 $T = T_0 + \phi_0[1 - \mathrm{erf}(x/2\sqrt{(\kappa t)})]$

7 Explicit

x	$t = 0$	$t = 0.004$	$t = 0.008$
0	1	1	0.96
0.2	1	1	1
0.4	1	1	1
0.6	1	1	1
0.8	1	1	1
1.0	1	1	0.96

Implicit

x	$t = 0$	$t = 0.004$	$t = 0.008$
0	1	0.9103	0.8357
0.2	1	0.9959	0.9851
0.4	1	0.9998	0.9989
0.6	1	0.9998	0.9989
0.8	1	0.9959	0.9851
1.0	1	0.9103	0.8357

9

	$x = 0$	$x = 0.5$	$x = 1$	$x = 1.5$
$y = 1$			1	0.928 592 5
$y = 0.5$		0.987 574 3	0.956 962 1	0.937 999 5
$y = 0$	1	0.984 980 8	0.964 774 6	0.960 193 4

11 $k = -\tfrac{3}{2}$

12 $z = x - y$, valid in the region $x \geqslant y$

14 $A_{2n+1} = \dfrac{32a^2(-1)^{n+1}}{\pi^3(2n+1)^3 \cosh\left[\dfrac{(2n+1)\pi b}{2a}\right]}$

15 $u(x, t) = \dfrac{2}{\pi} \displaystyle\sum_{n=1}^{\infty} \dfrac{1}{n} \sin n\pi x \cos n\pi t$

16 Boundary conditions: $u(0, t) = U(t)$ and $u(z, t) \to 0$ as $z \to \infty$.
Solution: $u(z, t) = u_0 e^{-kz} \cos(\omega t - kz)$
(Compare the solution method with Review exercise 8.10.)

18 $\phi = A \cos(px) e^{-Kt/2} \cos \omega t$, where $\omega^2 = c^2 p^2 - \frac{1}{4} K^2$

19 On $r = a$, $v_r = 0$, so there is no flow through the cylinder $r = a$. As $r \to \infty$, $v_r \to U \cos \theta$ and $v_\theta \to -U \sin \theta$, so the flow is steady at infinity and parallel to the x axis.

CHAPTER 9

Exercises

1 $x = 1$, $y = 1$, $f = 9$

2 $x_1 = 1.5$, $x_2 = 0$, $x_3 = 2.5$, $x_4 = 0$, $f = 14$

3 Original problem:
20 of type 1, 50 of type 2, profit = £1080, 70 m chipboard remain
Revised problem:

5 of type 1, 75 of type 2, profit = £1020, 5 m chipboard remain

4 4 kg nails, 2 kg screws, profit 14 p

5 9 of CYL1, 6 of CYL2 and profit £54

6 For $\lambda \geqslant 60$: $x_1 = \frac{25}{3}$, $x_2 = 0$, $z = \frac{25}{3}\lambda$
For $60 \geqslant \lambda \geqslant 10$: $x_1 = 6$, $x_2 = 7$, $z = 140 + 6\lambda$
For $\lambda \leqslant 10$: $x_1 = 0$, $x_2 = 10$, $z = 200$

7 $x_1 = 1$, $x_2 = 0.5$, $x_3 = 1$, $x_4 = 0$, $f = 6.5$

8 LP solution gives $x_1 = 66.67$, $x_2 = 50$, $f = £3166.67$. Profit is improved if more cloth is bought; for example, if the amount of cloth is increased to 410 m then $x_1 = 63.33$, $x_2 = 55$ and $f = £3233.33$.

9 B1, 0; B2, 15 000; B3, 30 000; profit £21 000

10 Long range 15, medium range 0, short range 0, estimated profit £6 million

11 $x_1 = 1$, $x_2 = 10$, $f = 20$

12 $x_1 = 2$, $x_2 = 0$, $x_3 = 2$, $x_4 = 0$, $f = 12$

13 36.63% of A, 44.55% of B, 18.81% of C, profit per 100 litres £134.26

14 6 of style 1, 11 of style 2, 6 of style 3, total profit £37 500

15 Boots 50, shoes 150, profit £1150

16 B1, 0; B2, 10 000; B3, 40 000; profit is down to £20 000

17 $x_1 = 2500 \, \text{m}^2$, $x_2 = 1500 \, \text{m}^2$, $x_3 = 1000 \, \text{m}^2$, profit £9500

18 Several possible optima: $(0, 3, 0)$; $(0, 0, 2)$; $(6, 0, 0)$; $(\frac{3}{2}, \frac{3}{2}, \frac{1}{2})$; $(6 - 3t, 0, t)$ for any t

19 $(0, 1, 1)$; $(0, -1, -1)$; $(2, -1, 1)/\sqrt{7}$; $-(2, -1, 1)/\sqrt{7}$

20 For given surface area S, $b = c = 2a$, where $a^2 = \frac{1}{12}S$ and $V = 4a^3$

21 $x = \pm a$ and $y = 0$

22 $x = a\sqrt{2}$, $y = b\sqrt{2}$, area $= 8ab$

23 $A = 1.33$, $B = 0.2$, $I = 130$

24 For $\alpha \geqslant 0$ minimum at $(0, 0)$; for $\alpha < 0$ minimum at $(-2\alpha, 3\alpha)$

25 (a) Bracket (without using derivatives) $0.7 < x < 3.1$
(b) Iteration 1:

a	0.7	$f(a)$	2.7408
b	1.9	$f(b)$	2.17
c	3.1	$f(c)$	3.2041

Iteration 2:

a	0.7	$f(a)$	2.7408
b	1.7253	$f(b)$	2.0612
c	1.9	$f(c)$	2.17

gives $b = 1.5127$ and $f(b) = 1.9497$
(c)

	Iteration 1		Iteration 2	
x	0.7	3.1	0.7	1.5129
$f(x)$	2.7408	3.2041	2.708	1.9498
$f'(x)$	-4.8309	0.9329	-4.8309	0.4224

gives $x = 1.1684$ and $f = 1.9009$

26 (a) Iteration 1:

a	0	f(a)	0
b	1	f(b)	0.420 74
c	3	f(c)	0.014 11

Iteration 2:

a	0	f(a)	0
b	1	f(b)	0.420 74
c	1.5113	f(c)	0.303 96

gives $x = 0.989\,79$ and $f = 0.422\,24$
(b)

	Iteration 1		Iteration 2	
x	0	1	0	0.8667
$f(x)$	0	0.4207	0	0.4352
$f'(x)$	1	−0.1506	1	−0.0612

gives $x = 0.8242$, $f = 0.4371$, $f' = -0.0247$

27 (a) Iteration 1:

a	1	f(a)	0.232 54
b	1.6667	f(b)	0.255 33
c	3	f(c)	0.141 93

Iteration 2:

a	1	f(a)	0.232 54
b	1.6200	f(b)	0.257 15
c	1.6667	f(c)	0.255 33

gives $x = 1.4784$ and $f = 0.260\,22$
(b) Iteration 1:

x	1	3
$f(x)$	0.232 54	0.141 93
$f'(x)$	0.101 32	−0.059 30

Iteration 2:

x	1	1.507 7
$f(x)$	0.232 54	0.259 90
$f'(x)$	0.101 32	−0.013 68

gives $x = 1.446\,2$, $f = 0.260\,35$, $f' = -0.000\,14$

28 $x = 1$, $\lambda_{max} = 2$; $x = 0$, $\lambda_{max} = 1.414\,21$; $x = -1$, $\lambda_{max} = 1.732\,05$. One application of the quadratic algorithm gives $x = -0.148\,26$ and $\lambda_{max} = 1.3854$.

30 Iteration 1:
$$a = \begin{bmatrix} 1 \\ 1 \end{bmatrix}, \quad f = \tfrac{3}{2}, \quad \nabla f = \begin{bmatrix} 1 \\ 1 \end{bmatrix}$$
Iteration 2:
$$a = \begin{bmatrix} -1 \\ -1 \end{bmatrix}, \quad f = -\tfrac{1}{2}, \quad \nabla f = \begin{bmatrix} 1 \\ -1 \end{bmatrix}$$
Iteration 3:
$$a = \begin{bmatrix} -\tfrac{5}{4} \\ -\tfrac{3}{4} \end{bmatrix}, \quad f = -\tfrac{27}{32}, \quad \nabla f = \begin{bmatrix} \tfrac{1}{2} \\ -\tfrac{1}{4} \end{bmatrix}$$

31 Steepest descent gives the point $(-0.382, -0.255)$ and $f = 0.828$

32 $(-0.754, 0.598, 0.218)$ and $f = -0.9284$

33 $(0.333, 1.667, 1.333)$ and $f = 3.161$

34 (a) After step 1
$$a = \begin{bmatrix} 1.2 \\ 2 \end{bmatrix}, \quad f = 0.8, \quad g = \begin{bmatrix} 0 \\ 1.6 \end{bmatrix}$$
$$H = \begin{bmatrix} 0.1385 & 0.1923 \\ 0.1923 & 0.9615 \end{bmatrix}$$
After step 2 the exact solution $x = 1$, $y = 1$ is obtained
(b) After cycle 1
$$a_1 = \begin{bmatrix} 0.768 \\ 0 \\ 0.384 \end{bmatrix}, \quad f = 1.355, \quad g_1 = \begin{bmatrix} 1.984 \\ -2.304 \\ 4.835 \end{bmatrix}$$
$$H_1 = \begin{bmatrix} 0.509 & 0.126 & -0.455 \\ 0.126 & 0.971 & 0.111 \\ -0.455 & 0.111 & 0.587 \end{bmatrix}$$
After cycle 2
$$a_2 = \begin{bmatrix} 0.615 \\ 0.177 \\ 0.012 \end{bmatrix}, \quad f = 0.776, \quad g_2 = \begin{bmatrix} -2.132 \\ -0.899 \\ 3.337 \end{bmatrix}$$
$$H_2 = \begin{bmatrix} 0.171 & 0.302 & -0.086 \\ 0.302 & 0.886 & -0.116 \\ -0.086 & -0.116 & 0.377 \end{bmatrix}$$

35 (a) After cycle 1

$$a = \begin{bmatrix} 0.485 \\ -0.061 \end{bmatrix}, \quad f = 0.239, \quad g = \begin{bmatrix} 0.970 \\ -0.242 \end{bmatrix}$$

$$H = \begin{bmatrix} 0.995 & -0.062 \\ -0.062 & 0.258 \end{bmatrix}$$

After cycle 2 the minimum at $x = 0$, $y = 0$ is obtained

(b) After cycle 1

$$a_1 = \begin{bmatrix} 0.970 \\ 1.940 \\ -0.218 \end{bmatrix}, \quad f = 4.711, \quad g_1 = \begin{bmatrix} 1.940 \\ 3.881 \\ -0.083 \end{bmatrix}$$

$$H_1 = \begin{bmatrix} 1 & 0 & -0.0001 \\ 0 & 1 & -0.0003 \\ -0.0001 & -0.0003 & 0.0149 \end{bmatrix}$$

After cycle 2

$$a_2 = \begin{bmatrix} 0 \\ 0 \\ -0.2171 \end{bmatrix}, \quad f = 0.004,$$

$$g_2 = \begin{bmatrix} 0 \\ 0 \\ -0.0819 \end{bmatrix}$$

$$H_2 = \begin{bmatrix} 0.7 & -0.6 & 0.0003 \\ -0.6 & -0.2 & 0.0005 \\ 0.0003 & 0.0005 & 0.0149 \end{bmatrix}$$

Note that there is considerable rounding error in the calculation of H_2.

9.7 Review exercises

1 $x_1 = 250$, $x_2 = 100$, $F = 3800$

2 Standard 20, super 10, deluxe 40, profit £21 000

3 $x_1 = 22$, $x_2 = 0$, $x_3 = 6$, profit £370

4 2 kg bread and 0.5 kg cheese, cost 210 p

5 Maximum at $(1, 1)$ and $(-1, -1)$, with distance $= \sqrt{2}$ Minimum at $(\sqrt{\tfrac{1}{3}}, \sqrt{\tfrac{1}{3}})$ and $-(\sqrt{\tfrac{1}{3}}, \sqrt{\tfrac{1}{3}})$, with distance $= \sqrt{\tfrac{2}{3}}$

6 Sides are $3\sqrt{\tfrac{1}{10}}$ and $2\sqrt{\tfrac{1}{10}}$

7 $(\tfrac{17}{5}, 0, \tfrac{6}{5})$, with distance 2.638

8 $(1, 2, 3)$ with $F = 14$, and $(-1, -2, -3)$ with $F = -14$. These also give the global maximum and minimum.

9 Bracket:

R	3.5	5.5	9.5
Cost	1124	704	1418

Quadratic algorithm gives $R = 6.121$ and cost $= 802$, so $R = 5.5$ still gives the best result.

10 Quadratic algorithm always gives $x = 0.5$ for any intermediate value. However, taking

x	t	f
0.4	0.7381	0.8067
0.5	0.6514	0.7729
1.0	0	1

gives $x = 0.578$, $t = 0.577$, $f = 0.756$

11 Both steepest-descent and DFP give convergence at the first minimization to the exact solution $x = -0.5$, $y = -0.5$, $f = 0$. The Newton method gives

$$a_1 = \begin{bmatrix} -0.1667 \\ -0.1667 \end{bmatrix}, \quad f = 0.0123$$

$$a_2 = \begin{bmatrix} -0.2778 \\ -0.2778 \end{bmatrix}, \quad f = 0.002\,44$$

12 Partan

$$x_1 = \begin{bmatrix} 0 \\ 0 \end{bmatrix}, \quad f = 1$$

$$x_2 = \begin{bmatrix} 0.5 \\ 0 \end{bmatrix}, \quad f = 0.5$$

$$z_2 = \begin{bmatrix} 0.5 \\ 0.5 \end{bmatrix}, \quad f = 0.25$$

$$x_3 = \begin{bmatrix} 1 \\ 1 \end{bmatrix}, \quad f = 0$$

Steepest-descent

$$x_1 = \begin{bmatrix} 0 \\ 0 \end{bmatrix}, \quad f = 1$$

$$x_2 = \begin{bmatrix} 0.5 \\ 0 \end{bmatrix}, \quad f = 0.5$$

$$x_3 = \begin{bmatrix} 0.5 \\ 0.5 \end{bmatrix}, \quad f = 0.25$$

$$x_4 = \begin{bmatrix} 0.75 \\ 0.5 \end{bmatrix}, \quad f = 0.125$$

13 Start values:

$$\boldsymbol{a}_0 = \begin{bmatrix} 1 \\ 1 \end{bmatrix}, \qquad f = 1$$

$\lambda = 0$:

$$\boldsymbol{a}_1 = \begin{bmatrix} 1.5 \\ 1 \end{bmatrix}, \qquad f = 1 \qquad \text{(no improvement)}$$

$\lambda = 1$:

$$\boldsymbol{a}_1 = \begin{bmatrix} 0.5 \\ 0 \end{bmatrix}, \qquad f = 0.25 \quad \text{(ready for next iteration)}$$

14 (a)

$$\boldsymbol{a}_0 = \begin{bmatrix} 0 \\ 0 \end{bmatrix}, \qquad F = 0.0625$$

$$\boldsymbol{a}_1 = \begin{bmatrix} -0.25 \\ -0.25 \end{bmatrix}, \qquad F = 0.0039$$

$$\boldsymbol{a}_2 = \begin{bmatrix} -0.375 \\ -0.375 \end{bmatrix}, \qquad F = 0.0002$$

(b)

$$\boldsymbol{a}_0 = \begin{bmatrix} 1 \\ 1 \end{bmatrix}, \qquad F = 0.3125$$

$$\boldsymbol{a}_1 = \begin{bmatrix} 0.333 \\ 3.667 \end{bmatrix}, \qquad F = 0.125$$

15

$$\boldsymbol{a}_0 = \begin{bmatrix} 1 \\ 0 \end{bmatrix}, \qquad F = 1.29$$

$$\boldsymbol{a}_1 = \begin{bmatrix} 1.07 \\ 0.27 \end{bmatrix}, \qquad F = 0.239$$

17

$$\boldsymbol{a}_0 = \begin{bmatrix} 0 \\ 0 \end{bmatrix}, \qquad f = 1$$

$$\boldsymbol{a}_1 = \begin{bmatrix} 0.5 \\ 0 \end{bmatrix}, \qquad f = 0.5$$

$$\boldsymbol{a}_2 = \begin{bmatrix} 0.5 \\ 0.5 \end{bmatrix}, \qquad F = 0.25$$

18 Bracket gives

α	$[F(\alpha) - 3]^2$
1.4	0.0776
1.5	0.0029
1.6	0.0369

Quadratic algorithm gives $\alpha^* = 1.518$ and $f = 9 \times 10^{-5}$

CHAPTER 10

Exercises

1 (a) $(762, 798)$ (b) 97

2 $(8.05, 9.40)$

3 $(71.2, 75.2)$, accept

4 $(2.92, 3.92)$

5 $(24.9, 27.9)$

6 95% confidence interval $(53.9, 58.1)$, criterion satisfactory

7 $(-1900, 7500)$, reject

8 90% : $(34, 758)$, 95% : $(-45, 837)$, reject at 10% but accept at 5%

9 90% : $(0.052, 0.089)$, 95% : $(0.049, 0.092)$, reject at 10% but accept at 5%. Test statistic leads to rejection at both 10% and 5% levels, and is more accurate

10 203, $(0.223, 0.327)$

11 90% : $(-0.28, -0.08)$, 95% : $(-0.30, -0.06)$, accept at 10% but reject at 5%

12 $(0.003, 0.130)$, carcinogenic

13 (a) X: $(0.34, 0.53, 0.13)$, Y: $(0.25, 0.31, 0.44)$
(b) 0.472, (c) $E(X) = 1.79$, $\text{Var}(X) = 0.426$, $E(Y) = 2.19$, $\text{Var}(Y) = 0.654$, $\rho_{X,Y} = -0.246$

16 (a) 6,   (b) 0.484,   (c) $f_X(x) = 6(\frac{1}{2} - x + \frac{1}{2}x^2)$, $f_Y(y) = 6(1 - y)y$

17 (a) 0.552, (b) 0.368

18 0.84

19 0.934

20 0.732

21 $(0.45, 0.85)$

22 $(0.67, 0.99)$

23 0.444, 90% : $(0.08, 0.70)$, 95% : $(0.00, 0.74)$, just significant at 5%, rank correlation 0.401, significant at 10%

24 $a = 6.318$, $b = 14.64$, $y = 226$

26 (a) $a = 343.7$, $b = 3.221$, $y = 537$; (b) $(0.46, 5.98)$, reject; (c) $(459, 615)$

27 $a = 0.107$, $b = 1.143$, $(14.4, 17.8)$

29 120Ω

30 $\lambda = 2.66$, $C = 2.69 \times 10^6$, $P = 22.9$

31 $a = 7533$, $b = -1.059$, $y = 17.9$

32 $\chi^2 = 12.3$, significant at 5%

33 $\chi^2 = 1.35$, accept Poisson

34 $\chi^2 = 12.97$, accept Poisson

35 $\chi^2 = 11.30$, significant at 5% but not at 1%, for proportion 95% : $(0.111, 0.159)$, 99% : $(0.104, 0.166)$, significant at 1%

37 $\chi^2 = 1.30$, not significant

38 $\chi^2 = 20.54$, significant at 5%

39 $c = 4$, $M_X(t) = 4/(t-2)^2$, $E(X) = 1$, $\text{Var}(X) = \frac{1}{2}$

41 0.014

42 0.995

44 Warning 9.5, action 13.5, sample 12, UCL $= 11.4$, sample 9

45 UK sample 28, US sample 25

46 Action 2.93, sample 12

47 Action 14.9, sample 19 but repeated warnings

48 (a) sample 9, (b) sample 9

49 (a) sample 10, (b) sample 12

50 sample 10

51 sample 16

52 (a) Repeated warnings, (b) sample 15, (c) sample 14

54 sample 11

55 Shewhart, sample 26; cusum, sample 13; moving-average, sample 11

56 0.132

57 0.223, 0.042

59 (a) $\frac{1}{4}$, (b) $2\frac{1}{4}$, (c) 0.237, (d) 45 min, (e) 0.276

61 Mean costs per hour: A, £200; B, £130

62 6

63 Second cash desk

64 Sabotage

65 $P(C \mid \text{two hits}) = 0.526$

66 $\frac{1}{2}$

67 (a) 0.0944, (b) 0.81

68 (a) $\frac{3}{4}$, (b) $[1 + (\frac{1}{3})^k 2^{n-k}]^{-1}$

69 AAAA

70 1.28:1 in favour of Poisson

72 2.8:1 in favour of H_2

73 12.8:1 in favour of H_1

10.12 Review exercises

1 $(0.202, 0.266)$

2 $(96.1 \times 10^6, 104.9 \times 10^6)$

3 $\chi^2 = 3.35$ (using class intervals of length 5, with a single class for all values greater than 30), accept exponential

4 Outlier 72 significant at 5%, outlier included $(7.36, 11.48)$; excluded $(7.11, 10.53)$

5 Operate if $p > \frac{4}{13}$

6 Cost per hour: A, £632.5; B, £603.4

7 (a) $P(\text{input } 0 \mid \text{output } 0) = \dfrac{\bar{p}\alpha}{\bar{p}\alpha + p\bar{\alpha}}$ etc.

   (b) $p < \alpha < 1 - p$

Index

Emboldened terms indicate where an entry has been defined in the text